UNIVERSITY CASEBOOK SERIES®

REAL ESTATE TRANSACTIONS

CASES AND MATERIALS ON LAND TRANSFER, DEVELOPMENT AND FINANCE

SIXTH EDITION

by

GERALD KORNGOLD
Professor of Law
New York Law School
and Visiting Fellow
Lincoln Institute of Land Policy

PAUL GOLDSTEIN
Lillick Professor of Law
Stanford University

FOUNDATION
PRESS

University Casebook Series is a trademark registered in the U.S. Patent and Trademark Office.

© 1980, 1985, 1988, 1993, 1997, 2002 FOUNDATION PRESS
© 2009 By THOMSON REUTERS/FOUNDATION PRESS
© 2015 LEG, Inc. d/b/a West Academic
     444 Cedar Street, Suite 700
     St. Paul, MN 55101
     1-877-888-1330

Printed in the United States of America

ISBN: 978-1-60930-220-7

Mat #41337345

To David,
Ethan, Ellie, Gabriel and Benjamin,
Margaret and Matt,
and, especially, Alice

G.K.

To Jan

P.G.

PREFACE

American real estate practice over the past thirty-five years has been marked by significant changes. The U.S. mortgage finance crisis beginning in 2008 and its aftermath triggered the largest upheaval in residential and commercial mortgage loans since the Great Depression, and its effect on business and legal structures continues to evolve. What began as a cataclysm in the secondary market for American home mortgages became a global financial crisis because many lenders held secondary market securities or had issued "credit default swaps" that effectively made them insurers of the securities. When the value of the securities dropped, the closely tied financial system was on the brink.

The 2008 financial crisis was emblematic of one of the key changes in U.S. real estate transactions over recent decades--a move in many areas towards nationalization and uniformity in what is technically an area of the law within the purview of state regulation. For example, the growth of title insurance has increased the security and efficiency of real estate transactions and contributed to the evolution of a national market for real estate finance. Because title policies are backed by large, resourceful institutions and generally follow nationally uniform standards, title insurance has drawn major institutional lenders and sophisticated financing schemes into every corner of the country. The federal government, the secondary mortgage market, and securitization of mortgage debt have played an increasingly important role in nationalizing and systematizing real estate finance; form mortgage documents promulgated and required by national lenders and insurers are increasingly replacing local finance documents. Enhanced federal and state environmental regulation influences virtually every real estate sale, exposing the parties to potentially devastating liability; public sector incentives as well as private commitment have led to green building initiatives across the country. The civil rights and consumer movements have also left their mark, principally on residential real estate sales. Globalization has increasingly affected American real estate transactions, as U.S. companies expand abroad and U.S. real estate debt is held by non-U.S. entities and individuals. Technology and new service providers across the country have brought competition and commoditization of aspects of work, resulting in changes in how lawyers represent clients in transactions.

The 2008 mortgage crisis was triggered by a combination of various factors: the value of residential mortgage-backed securities in the secondary market crashed, due to speculative lending practices, an unmanaged subprime market, and the bursting of the bubble of an overheated property market. The secondary market essentially collapsed and as of today has only partially rebounded. Federal agencies are still grappling with implementing rules to prevent risky lending behavior and defining permitted credit default swaps for the future. Various agencies have recently settled actions with lenders packaged and sold misleading mortgage-backed securities, with more likely to come. Fannie Mae and Freddie Mac, quasi-governmental agencies that insured home mortgages and facilitated the secondary market, were placed into conservatorship by the federal government because of looming liabilities; their future has not yet been resolved. The story of the secondary market continues to evolve.

As the mortgage crisis spread into a larger financial crisis, borrowers defaulted on home mortgages when they lost their jobs. Often the values of their homes sank below the amounts they still owed on their loans. This led to widespread foreclosures. The foreclosures spawned significant litigation attempting to unwind assignments of mortgages from secondary market transactions and to determine whether the party bringing foreclosure truly had standing under centuries old doctrines. There was a spate of lender misbehavior in some of the foreclosure activities as well, triggering equitable relief and consumer law actions. Federal and state legislation was passed to assist troubled borrowers, including loan modification programs. While the number of foreclosure actions has decreased as of this writing, troubled borrowers remain and the residential real estate markets in many areas remain well below their 2008 levels. This too is a real estate story that continues to unfold.

Some of the recent changes in real estate transactions, such as the spread of title insurance, have taken work away from lawyers. Other changes, because they implicate a wide and complex range of legal issues, have magnified and complicated the real estate lawyer's role. It is no longer sufficient to know the law on title conveyancing and mortgages. The real estate lawyer today must also grasp at least the basics of federal income taxation, personal property security, environmental regulation, bankruptcy, and products liability law. After the 2008 financial crash, the real estate lawyer will also need to understand federal and state lending and consumer credit regulation and ongoing changes in that law. The attorney must also have a feel for the informal legal culture created by the many nongovernmental institutions and individuals involved in real estate transactions—brokers, title companies, surveyors, appraisers, lenders and their various trade associations.

And yet, despite the rise and effect of new forces, real estate practice still requires a firm grounding in fundamental concepts such as real estate contracts, mortgages and foreclosure, title systems, and brokerage. These are the vocabulary and the grammar of the sophisticated real estate lawyer. New judicial decisions, legislation, business practices, and transaction structures that respond to emerging economic and social demands are built on this foundation. For example, court opinions and legislative debate on the proper response to the post-2008 foreclosure crisis almost always have been framed within the context of applying or changing longstanding doctrines in order to achieve a desired result; alternative financing vehicles designed by lenders have been based on past precedent and practices.

The essential role of the real estate lawyer has also not altered over the years. This book continues to frame issues from the perspective of a lawyer assembling a successful transaction and not simply litigating a deal gone bad. The task of the transactional lawyer requires great sophistication, wisdom, and at times subtlety. All parties in a deal want it to close, and according to the economists each should be in a better position if it does. Each party, however, wants to obtain as great of an advantage as possible. The skilled transactional lawyer will advance the client's interest but also will ensure that the interests of all parties are aligned (or else the transaction ultimately will fail), the parties don't walk away from the deal, and the long term relationship between the parties remains intact.

This book, therefore, encompasses emerging, as well as traditional, fields of real estate law. Part One covers the basic elements of real estate transactions, using the residential transaction and as-built commercial transaction as a vehicle for exposing the fundamentals of the role of the attorney, brokers, real estate contracts and conveyancing, title assurance, and secured financing. Part Two covers commercial real estate transactions, exploring contemporary innovations in financing and leasing techniques and examining current issues related to distressed properties, environmental regulation and green buildings, globalization of real estate transactions, and the development and operation of shopping centers. Part Three presents all tax materials, including residential and commercial issues.

Although real estate transactions have become increasingly subject to nationalizing influences, real estate law remains in many respects the creature of local rules. As a consequence, one message should be emphasized here: no real estate lawyer can safely ignore applicable state law when counseling on any transaction, large or small.

Real estate law is a happy blend of practical insight and academic perspective, a mix that we have tried to convey in the pages that follow. Colleagues in practice and in academe have provided helpful comments for the preparation of various editions of this book. We are particularly grateful to Todd Davis and Jonathan Adler for their help with the environmental law materials, Edward Hurtuk, Charles Daroff and Zachary Paris for their insights on new developments in real estate law, Andy Morriss for his ideas on many subjects, Leon Gabinet for his comments on the tax materials, and Hiram Chodosh and Erik Jensen for insights on globalization issues. We also appreciate Kevin McMunigal's and Bob Lawry's comments on professional responsibility issues, Morris Shanker's comments on bankruptcy, and Bill Warren's ideas on shopping centers. Last but not least, Jim Hagy has been a generous and terrific source of wisdom on real estate law, lawyering, and pedagogy.

Many law teachers who used various editions of this casebook have been generous with their suggestions. For their thoughtful comments, we are indebted to Professors Steven B. Baslaw, J. Wendell Bayles, Roger Bernhardt, Zareh H. Beylerian, William M. Blackburn, Michael Braunstein, Pamela W. Bray, John D. Briggs II, D. Barlow Burke, Jr., K.C. Collette, John W. Fisher II, Robert L. Flores, Ken Harmon, Theodore B. Hertel, Jr., John F. Hicks, Alex Johnson, John W. Larson, Carl H. Lisman, Ward F. McDonald, George K. Miller, Thomas Mitchell, C. Robert Morris, Phillip J. Nexon, Lindsay F. Nielsen, John R. Nolon, Georgette Chapman Poindexter, Patrick A. Randolph, Jr.,

Robert S. Rollinger, Peter W. Salsich, Jr., M. John Schubert, John M. Tyson, G. Graham Waite, Robert Weiler and Alan M. Weinberger.

A Note on Style. Most of the cases and other materials appearing in these pages have been edited. The deletion of sentences and paragraphs is indicated by ellipses; the deletion of citations is not indicated. Most footnotes have been excised. The remaining footnotes retain their original numbering. Authors' footnotes are lettered.

G.K.
P.G.

New York, New York
Stanford, California
September, 2014

SUMMARY OF CONTENTS

TABLE OF CONTENTS

PART TWO. ELEMENTS OF THE COMMERCIAL
REAL ESTATE TRANSACTION

TABLE OF CASES

The principal cases are in bold type.

UNIVERSITY CASEBOOK SERIES®

REAL ESTATE TRANSACTIONS

CASES AND MATERIALS ON LAND TRANSFER, DEVELOPMENT AND FINANCE

SIXTH EDITION

PART ONE

Basic Elements of the Real Estate Transaction

1

CHAPTER I

ARRANGING THE DEAL

A. AN INTRODUCTION TO THE CONVEYANCING INDUSTRY

While it is possible to generalize about the process, cast of characters, and documents involved in a "typical" U.S. residential real estate purchase and sale, an important caveat must be kept in mind: not only does state law govern these transactions but also local customs within each jurisdiction play an important role in how these deals are structured and memorialized and who comprises the cast of characters. Despite these jurisdictional differences it is possible, however, to describe a "typical" American residential real estate transaction. The arrangement described below applies as well in most respects to the sale of a basic, as-built commercial property.

Finding a Counterparty: Brokers

An owner of a home seeking to sell the property ("seller") but lacking the contacts and skill to market the house will engage a broker to represent the seller and to assist in the sale. The seller and the broker ("listing broker") will execute one of a variety of brokerage agreements. These agreements differ most fundamentally on the question of what actions the broker must accomplish in order to collect a commission, with some providing that the listing broker gets paid even if another broker brings in the customer. Ideally the seller had retained a lawyer to review the brokerage agreement before signing and to counsel the client about the different types of arrangements, but most often this is not the case. The law provides that the listing broker must act as the seller's fiduciary, owing a duty of care and loyalty.

At the same time, a person seeking to purchase a house (the "buyer") will be working with a broker (the "selling broker") to help the buyer find a home, typically without any agreement between them. The selling broker introduces the buyer to seller's house. Despite the mistaken belief by most buyers, the selling broker is not the agent of the buyer but rather the seller's subagent, owing fiduciary duty to the seller and not the buyer.

Forming the Deal: The Contract of Sale

After discussions, the seller and buyer will come to general agreement on key terms, such a price, date of possession, inclusion of personal property, and the like. It is at this point, where practice differs across the United States. In a number of states, in almost all situations the brokers would present a contract of sale which the parties would execute and which would bind them to transfer the property according to the agreement's terms. In other jurisdictions, though, almost always the brokers would not present an agreement and lawyers for the seller and buyer would enter the picture and negotiate the terms of a contract which the parties would then sign. In some states, both methods are used. The variation in practice is due to custom, threats of unauthorized practice of law litigation against brokers, the parties' sophistication and appetite for risk, the temperature of the market and whether there is pressure to quickly lock up the house with a binding agreement, the value of the house and complexity of the issues, and other factors.

A real estate transaction contemplates multiple stages: the execution of the contract of sale; followed by an interim or executory period (between thirty to ninety days usually, depending on custom and need); and then closing where the parties exchange performance, most notably the payment of the price and the passing of title via a deed. The statute of frauds requires that both the contract and the deed be in writing, adequately describe the property, and signed by the seller. Typically, a deposit (often ten percent of the sales price) is paid upon the signing of the contract and held in escrow by one of the parties' attorneys, the title insurance company, or some other third party.

The contract of the sale (called a purchase and sale, agreement of sale, offer to purchase, and various other names in different places) drives the rest of the transaction and thus is the essential document in the deal. The contract of sale includes various implied obligations of the seller with respect to the property, such as the implied warranty of marketable title that requires the seller to deliver title free of liens and claims that a reasonable buyer would find objectionable; sets, through default rules, certain expectations of the buyer and seller, such as which party bears the risk of sudden destruction of the property during the executory period; and may create express warranties on the parties or conditions on closing, such as releasing the buyer if the buyer is unable to obtain a mortgage to finance the purchase. A well-drawn contract might provide for remedies for both the buyer and seller in the event that the other side breaches, such as retention of the deposit by the seller, rather than leaving the parties to common law contract remedies. If the contract does not provide for a certain right or protection, such as conditioning the buyer's obligation to close on the obtaining of financing, then the buyer is stuck with that suboptimal deal. Those who argue that only lawyers should negotiate contracts of sale may believe that lawyers can best anticipate and obtain necessary protections, free from the broker's potential conflicting interest of getting a signed contract in order to earn a commission.

The Interim Period: Financing, Title, and Other Issues

The interim period between the contract of sale and closing serves several functions. It allows the buyer to obtain mortgage financing to purchase the property; permits the buyer to have the title searched to determine if there are outstanding claims that would breach the seller's implied warranty of marketability; and lets the parties fulfill any other conditions necessary to closing, such as an express undertaking by the seller to formalize an existing sewer easement that serves the property as the buyer would want to ensure the permanence of such an arrangement.

The buyer will apply to a lender for a loan to enable the purchase of the property. (While the loan is typically referred to as a "mortgage" by both lawyers and laypersons alike, a mortgage transaction really involves two documents—a note, which is the promise to repay the loan at a certain interest rate on a certain schedule, and the "mortgage"—or deed of trust in some states—which is the document granting the lender a security interest in the property and which allows the lender to have the property sold in satisfaction of the debt if the borrower fails to make payments.) Up until some thirty years ago, home borrowers typically obtained their loans from local banks, often savings and loan institutions. Today, a wide variety of lenders originate residential loans, such as mortgage brokers, mortgage companies, and local and regional banks, among others. Moreover, while in the past originators often held the mortgages during their term, currently they usually sell the mortgages into the secondary market as described below.

Many borrowers today "pre-qualify" for a loan, by having a lender examine their income, employment history, and related data even before the buyer begins the house search. But even with a pre-qualified buyer, the lender must perform further analysis once the buyer finds the property before issuing a commitment to make a loan. This analysis will primarily focus on the value of the property and whether it is able to support the amount of the loan that it will secure. Assuming that the lender is satisfied with the buyer's financial position, the security of the property, and the terms of the loan, the lender will issue a mortgage commitment to the buyer promising to the buyer to fund the loan at a set interest rate and terms. The commitment will expire within a limited period of time, so this creates pressure on the parties to close expeditiously.

During the interim period, the quality of the title will be investigated by a company that performs such searches, usually called an abstracting company. There will be several impetuses for this inquiry: the seller is obligated by implication to deliver a marketable title at closing and may be required by contract to provide documentation of this good title; the buyer's lender may require the buyer to provide evidence of clear title since the lender does not wish to rely on security with defective title; and the buyer may want independent corroboration of the quality of title.

Moreover, today it is quite likely that the lender will insist upon the buyer's delivery of a title insurance policy insuring the validity of the lender's mortgage as a condition of the loan. Additionally, a buyer today will usually purchase a title insurance policy insuring the buyer's good title to the property, in order to secure the investment. Title insurance differs from actuarial-based insurance that calculates the likelihood of an occurrence of an event among a pool and charges enough premiums to build a reserve to pay the claims to those few individuals in the pool who predictably suffer a loss. Rather, a title insurance company searches the title of the property it proposes to insure and provides a report to the insured listing the existing title defects against the property. The company then in essence guarantees its work by stating that the insured owns the property in fee simple subject only to the matters the company listed and promises that it will pay for any loss suffered by the insured if the title company missed any defect in the record. There are sometimes disputes as to whether a particular exception claimed by the title company truly is a cloud on the title, such as a long dormant right of way extinguished by adverse possession. Lawyers of the buyer, seller, and title company play an important role in negotiating whether certain purported defects really are concerns and should be stricken from the title insurance policy so that the buyer and lender receive "clean" policies.

Exchanging Performance: The Closing

If either the buyer or seller is unable to render performance as required by the contract of sale, in the absence of a controlling contractual provision, the non-defaulting party will have a cause of action for remedies that may include specific performance of the contract or damages for the loss of bargain due to non-performance. If both parties, however, have complied with their conditions and obligations, the deal will proceed to closing where the parties will render ultimate performance to each other. There are two basic types of closing procedures, with different states and regions without a state following one or the other as a matter of custom. Some places have an "around the table closing" where all parties gather together in a single room, render performance to each other, and when each is satisfied they adjourn and walk away. The other major method is the "escrow closing," where the parties agree on a certain person or entity (such as a title company or lending institution) to serve as escrow agent, the parties send their performance to the escrow agent, and then once the escrow agent has collected all of the necessary performances the agent will release them to the relevant party. Escrows serve as the agents of both parties and operate pursuant to instructions agreed to by them. The escrow mechanism may be more convenient by obviating the need to get together. Around the table closings, though, may allow the parties and their lawyers to work out last minute problems on the spot and avoid postponements.

At closing, the seller will deliver a written and signed deed, which will be recorded, to the buyer. The deed will serve to convey title, vesting in the buyer a fee simple absolute estate. Moreover, the deed will supplant the contract of sale, especially with respect to the seller's promise as to the quality of title. The buyer may refuse to accept the deed because of breach of the contract's implied warranty of marketable title, but once the buyer accepts the deed the buyer's title protection, if any, will be determined by the seller's deed. A general warranty deed protects against all title defects in existence at time of closing, a special warranty deed covers only those defects that the grantor created, and a quitclaim deed gives no title protection. The contract of sale determines the type of deed to be delivered, and in the absence of a provision gap filler rules, such as custom, will apply.

In exchange for the deed, the buyer will pay the remaining price to the seller. When the buyer is taking a loan for the acquisition, the lender actually will provide the funds on the buyer's behalf. In exchange for these funds, the buyer will execute the note and mortgage at closing, with the mortgage recorded against the property. At closing the title insurance company will issue a Loan Policy to the lender and an Owner's Policy to the buyer, insuring the validity of their interests in the newly acquired property. Finally, the parties will do adjustments, reimbursing each other as appropriate for prepaid or underpaid local and state taxes and user fees. With that, the deal is done. The buyer has obtained title to the house, and the seller has been paid.

The Secondary Market: Uniform Practices

Many originators of residential mortgages sell their loans to other lenders, creating a secondary mortgage market. In the height of the secondary market in the 1990s and the early 2000s, local originators such as mortgage brokers sold their loans to local banks which sold them up a chain that included regional banks and national banks and ultimately to investment banks. Each seller of a loan assigned the note and mortgage to the buyer. The buying bank paid the selling entity the outstanding amount of the loan (plus a fee for generating the loan), allowing the local entities to get back its capital and lend it again to local markets in need of capital.

The investment banks then issued securities, typically bonds, representing the right to receive certain payments under the mortgages (usually slicing the right to receive portions of the income and principal payments into various "tranches.") These bonds were purchased by other banks and investors such as insurance companies, pension funds, and hedge funds. As described in Part I, Chapter 5, the system came crashing down in 2008 when mortgages within the bond bundles began defaulting.

While the volume of securitization of residential mortgages has substantially decreased since 2008 due to increased regulation, lender behavior, and market resistance, sale of residential mortgages in the secondary market continues. The secondary market has demanded uniformity of notes and mortgages in order to reduce transaction costs in the purchase and sale of residential loans. Form documents promulgated by federal actors, such as Fannie Mae and Freddie Mac, have become the gold standard for residential transactions and are only rarely deviated from.

Conclusion

The purchase and sale of a house or simple commercial property requires a substantial process, documentation, and players. While millions of dollars of securities can be bought and sold with an email, telephone call, or click of a mouse, the law requires extensive formalities for the transfer of a fifty thousand dollar house. Why this is the case is unclear. Does this complexity merely reflect the historical importance of real property in the Anglo-American legal tradition, where Blackacre was once the quintessential source of wealth, political power, and social prestige? Should the current land transaction system be rationalized to be less expensive and more efficient? Is the detailed process and due diligence still worth the cost because the family home remains the major economic asset of so many American families? The answers to these and related questions are replete with empirical issues and normative choices. We bring these questions to you for your consideration now and for your reconsideration during and after your study of these course materials.

United States Department of Housing and Urban Development, A Study of Closing Costs for FHA Mortgages

viii–xiii (2008).

This study presents findings on how much FHA borrowers pay in closing costs when they buy a house, how much these costs vary, and factors to which the variation is related. The analysis uses data from a national sample of 7,560 FHA-insured, 30-year fixed-rate home purchase loans closed in May and June of 2001. Data were collected on how much borrowers paid for lender or broker services, title services, and real estate agent's services, and linked to information on borrower and loan characteristics, including loan amounts, interest rates, credit history, income, borrowers' race and ethnicity, and the racial composition and educational attainment in the borrower's neighborhood. The analysis focuses in turn on fees paid to lenders and mortgage brokers, to title companies, and to real estate agents.

Findings from this study shed new light on important questions about the competitiveness and transparency of the home purchase and financing process. There is a growing awareness that many consumers struggle to understand the costs associated with the purchase of a home, especially when mortgages have numerous and complex terms. The Real Estate Settlement Procedures Act (RESPA), passed in 1975 was intended to assure competition in the mortgage market and to make it easier for borrowers to shop for mortgage loans by mandating good disclosures. The Department of Housing and Urban Development (HUD) is responsible for writing the regulations for and enforcing RESPA, but has, until this study, lacked any data with which it might assess its effectiveness. In addition, as the role of mortgage brokers in home lending has grown, their compensation has become controversial, because they may be paid both by borrowers (in upfront fees) and by lenders (in payments called yield-spread premiums which depend on the interest rate on the loan). This study builds on past research to explore variations in these charges and the extent to which they affect the total closing costs paid by homebuyers.

Lenders and Mortgage Brokers

Total loan charges paid to the mortgage lender and/or broker are substantial, averaging just under $3,400 on loans with an average initial principal balance of $105,000. The average fees for brokered loans ($4000) are higher than the average for direct lender loans ($3,150). Upfront cash charges paid by the borrower average $1,400 for direct lender loans and $1,600 for brokered loans. In addition, depending on the interest rate on a loan, the lender may deliver at closing an amount that exceeds the actual loan principal. This additional cash—called a yield-spread premium (YSP) may be kept by the mortgage broker, used to pay some of the borrower's closing costs, or simply credited to the borrower. Direct lenders and mortgage brokers operate in the same capital market and receive comparable benefit from higher interest rates. This benefit is not reported on the HUD-1 and is therefore estimated for this study. On brokered loans reported YSPs average $2,400, while *estimated* YSPs for direct loans average $1,800.

Loan fees vary widely. One would expect these fees to vary and to depend on factors related to lenders' costs and risks, such as the loan amount, property value, the borrower's credit score, and on relevant features of the state regulatory environment. However, after controlling for these legitimate cost factors, total loan fees still vary significantly based on characteristics of the lender, the borrower, education levels and racial composition in the borrower's neighborhood, and the state where the home sale occurs. Specifically,

- Loans made by mortgage brokers are approximately $300 to $425 more expensive than those made by direct lenders, other loan characteristics being equal. Depositories (banks, thrifts, and credit unions) are the lowest cost originator, followed by large mortgage banks. The smaller mortgage banks have terms closer to those of mortgage brokers than to large mortgage banks and depositories.

- African-American borrowers pay an additional $415 for their loans after accounting for other borrower differences and Latino borrowers pay an additional $365, on average.

- On average, borrowers who completed college are charged $1100 *less* than borrowers who did not go to college at all, other things equal. Education is measured as the fraction of adults in the borrower's census tract with a college degree. Comparing two hypothetical borrowers with the same loan amount, same income, same credit score, but one buying a house in a neighborhood where all adults have a college education, and the other in a neighborhood where no adult has a college education, the borrower buying into the more educated neighborhood on average pays $1,100 *less* than a borrower who buys in a neighborhood where no adult has a college education, other things being equal.

- Finally, after controlling for relevant factors, the most expensive States—Nevada, Michigan, and Utah—are more than $2,500 per loan more costly than the least expensive State, Alaska.

Total loan costs are higher when yield-spread premiums, discount points, and seller contributions to closing costs are present. In a market where all participants understand the terms of sale and both buyers and sellers are numerous, prices should not depend on the mode of payment. For example, the price of a basket of groceries is unrelated to whether the shopper pays with cash, a credit card, or a check, or whether the seller must make change. In principle, the mortgage market could be equally transparent and competitive. If it were, the data would reveal a clear trade-off between the upfront cash borrowers pay and the interest rates on their loans, where more up-front cash yields a lower rate and vice versa. The present value difference in payments at the higher interest rate should equal the reduction in up-front cash. Borrowers whose loans have a yield-spread premium (reflecting a higher interest rate) should pay less in up-front cash. Borrowers who pay points to reduce their interest rate should have a lower present value of payments approximately equal to the cash points paid. And if the seller contributes to the buyer's closing costs, the total closing costs should be unaffected.

The data reveal a market that is not even close to this ideal. How far the market is from the ideal varies by type of lender, but no type is close. Yield-spread premiums, discount points, and seller contributions to closing costs are all sources of complexity in a mortgage loan. Borrowers end up with more expensive loans when the terms are more complex:

- Borrowers on average save only $20 in up-front cash for each $100 they pay in yield-spread premium, for a net loss (or extra cost) of $80. Those who borrow through mortgage brokers see a benefit of only $7 per $100, for a net loss of $93, while those who borrow from large mortgage banks see a net loss of $71 on average, with depositories and smaller mortgage banks in between.

- The terms for "discount points" are on average similar, but more diverse among types of originators. Overall, borrowers see a benefit of only $20 for each $100 of points paid, for a net loss of $80. Those who borrow through mortgage brokers see no benefit at all from paying points, either in lower interest rates or in lower fees with other names. Customers of depositories see benefits of roughly $65 per $100 of points paid (for a net loss of $35), while terms from other direct lenders lie between these.

- When sellers contribute to closing costs one would expect borrowers to save $100 themselves for each $100 contributed by the seller. On average, however, borrowers pay $50 less themselves for each $100 that sellers contribute to their closing costs. Again, terms differ by type of lender. For each $100 the seller contributes, borrowers see a benefit of roughly $70 from depositories and large mortgage banks, but closer to $40 when dealing with brokers.

"No-cost" loans cost less. Borrowers who want to avoid up-front cash fees for loan origination can do so with so-called "no-cost" loans. Borrowers who go for no-cost loans simplify their mortgage shopping because they can compare loans on the basis of just the interest rate, liberating themselves from the difficult rate/cash trade-off. Of course, such loans are not really "no-cost;" in principle, they should have higher interest rates than loans on which borrowers pay up-front cash fees and indeed, they do. But all things considered, borrowers with "no-cost" loans effectively pay $1,200 less for loan origination services than borrowers who pay some lender/broker fees in cash.

The "no-cost" loans also reveal a market that looks more competitive in other important ways: Among these loans, there is little relation between the level of education in a borrower's neighborhood and how much the borrower is charged, and almost no relation to the borrower's race or racial characteristics of the borrower's neighborhood.

The lower prices and absence of relationships between price and either education or race among the no-cost loans suggests that the complexity introduced by loan terms that involve a combination of cash and interest rate, with variations in yield-spread premiums, points, and even seller contributions makes it more difficult for consumers to figure out their total costs and contributes to higher prices and higher fees for lenders and brokers.

Lenders appear to make lower-priced offers to borrowers they expect to be familiar with market terms. Even on FHA-insured loans, lenders suffer some loss when a loan defaults. However, loan approval rates are only slightly related to loan and borrower characteristics known to be related to the likelihood of default. In fact, lenders appear to raise prices rather than reject less promising loans. Nonetheless, differences in default rates are not the source of the large differences seen in pricing. In particular, after accounting for other differences (notably loan amount and credit scores), defaults are unrelated to education levels in the borrower's neighborhood, but total loan prices are substantially lower for borrowers in neighborhoods with high educational attainment than for those in neighborhoods with low education levels (again, neighborhood educational attainment serves as a proxy here for borrowers' education level, which is not observed directly).

Lenders and brokers are professionals and always know what competitive loan terms are. It appears that they also have views regarding what their customers know. Lenders make lower-priced offers to borrowers in high-education neighborhoods, evidently expecting them to be familiar with competitive market terms, and these offers are accepted with high frequency (only two percent of lender's offers are on average rejected in neighborhoods where all adults have a college education). In neighborhoods where borrowers may not be so familiar with prevailing competitive terms, or may be willing to accept worse terms to avoid another application. Lenders make higher-priced offers, and some are accepted. Lenders have higher walk-away rates in these neighborhoods (on average 23 percent in neighborhoods where no adults have a college education), but the profit on the loans that are made appears to more than make up for the cost of processing applications approved but not accepted.

Price discrimination of this type does not arise in competitive markets where shoppers are well informed. Even a consumer who is willing to pay a high price (such as a minority borrower who is especially averse to loan rejection) should be able to easily find and get the competitive price in a competitive market. For price discrimination to be possible, there must be some friction—some inhibition to competition such as high transactions costs or search costs or some limitation on information that makes it difficult for one side of the market (borrowers) to see all available prices. The findings reported here suggest that loan complexity itself creates such friction and that improved consumer disclosures could help many borrowers obtain better terms.

Title Services

In addition to loan fees, homebuyers pay substantial amounts at closing for title services. As with lender/broker fees, title fees vary widely in ways that suggest that markets are not fully transparent or competitive, and that many consumers may be paying more than necessary for these services.

Fees for title services vary widely, are related to education and race, and are highest when other closing costs are also high. Total fees paid for title services average $1,200 per loan. Even after controlling for factors that one would expect to contribute to higher fees, considerable unexplained variation remains:

- Borrowers in African-American neighborhoods pay on average an additional $120 for title services and those in Latino census tracts pay an additional $110, as compared to borrowers residing in neighborhoods with no minorities. How much more minorities pay rises with the concentration of minorities in their neighborhoods. As with lender/broker fees, the differential charges related to education are large: on average borrowers from neighborhoods where all adults have a college degree pay $200 less than those from neighborhoods where none do, other things equal.

- Differences in average title charges (taking loan and borrower characteristics into account) from the lowest-cost state—North Carolina—to the highest cost states—New York, Texas, California, and New Jersey—is more than $1000. The type of title insurance regulation adopted by states explains only a small fraction of this variation.

- Title charges are higher when fees paid to lenders, brokers, and real estate agents are also high, again controlling for all relevant loan and borrower characteristics. In other words, the same borrowers are being charged above-average fees for multiple components of their closing costs.

Real Estate Agents Services

Real estate agents do not uniformly charge six percent of house value. Among transactions involving a real estate agent, almost half (47 percent) had real estate agent fees below six percent of house value, 29 percent were exactly six percent, and 24 percent were above six percent. One percent had fees above eight percent. In general, real estate agent's fees are related to both house values and to down payment amounts; for two houses of the same value, the real estate agent's fees are lower when the buyer has a smaller down payment. In addition, the real estate agents' fees rise with the fraction of adults in a neighborhood who have a college education. And real estate fees are on average $55 lower in Latino neighborhoods, other things equal. However, no other relations to individual or neighborhood race are present in the fees of real estate agents.

NOTES

1. *The Cost of Conveyancing Services.* Many professionals and specialists participate in residential sales. Among the more evident are brokers, lawyers, loan officers, appraisers, title assurance personnel, surveyors, house inspectors and escrow agents. Other participants stay in the background. There are, for example, the many brokers who may have shown a house with no success, and the many bureaucrats who administer the recording system. As the HUD study indicates, these participants seek to be paid and add to the cost of the transaction. Professor Quintin Johnstone has suggested that the costs could be lower:

> It is at least arguable that some land transfer service prices charged consumers are higher than they should be. Real estate brokers' commissions and lawyers' fees are both vulnerable to this criticism; and title insurance rates, despite the modest profitability record of title insurance underwriting, could be reduced somewhat with more intense competition. Further, it has been claimed that title insurance rates fail adequately to reflect variations in risk and title evaluation costs among different categories of insureds. Title insurers also have been faulted for price discrimination, charging different prices for substantially the same service. . . . Increased efficiencies at any other point in the transfer servicing process, if savings were passed back to consumers, could also have an effect in cutting or holding down prices.

Land Transfers: Process and Processors, 22 Val.U.L.Rev. 493, 535–36 (1988).

For additional overviews of a basic real estate transaction, see Payne, A Typical House Purchase Transaction in the United States, 30 The Conveyancer 194 (1966); Upham, An Introduction to the Principles of Private Land Ownership, Transfer, and Control in the United States in Sanchez Jordan & Gambaro (eds.), Land Law In Comparative Perspective, pp. 37–53 (2002). For further discussion of the cost of conveyancing, see Wachter, Residential Real Estate Brokerage: Rate Uniformity and Moral Hazard, 10 Res.L. & Econ. 189 (1987); Goldberg & Horwood, The Costs of Buying and Selling Houses: Some Canadian Evidence, 10 Res.L. & Econ. 143, 144 (1987). See also Stephen, Love, Gillanders & Paterson, Testing for Price Discrimination in the Market for Conveyancing Services, 12 Int'l Rev.L. & Econ. 397 (1992).

2. *RESPA.* The Real Estate Settlement Procedures Act, 12 U.S.C.A. § 2601 *et seq.,* enacted in 1974 and substantially amended a year later, sought to lower conveyancing costs by increasing the price information available to residential buyers. The Act requires lenders to give residential mortgage borrowers an itemized estimate of projected closing costs and a HUD-prepared booklet describing the nature and purpose of each closing cost and the choices available to consumers "in selecting persons to provide necessary services incident to a real estate settlement." 12 U.S.C.A. §§ 2603, 2604(b)(4). The Act also introduced incentives to modernize "local recordkeeping of land title information" and rules reducing "the amounts home buyers are required to place in escrow accounts established to insure the payment of real estate taxes and insurance."

RESPA also focuses on the financial aspects of conveyancing. It outlaws covert economic arrangements between conveyancing firms—"No person shall give and no person shall accept any fee, kickback, or thing of value pursuant to any agreement or understanding, oral or otherwise, that business incident to or a part of a real estate settlement service involving a federally related mortgage loan shall be referred to any person." 12 U.S.C.A. §§ 2601(b), (3), (4); 2607(a). The kickback provision is limited, however. In Freeman v. Quicken Loans, Inc., 132 S.Ct. 2034 (2012), the Supreme Court unanimously held that an allegedly unearned fee charged by a lender (i.e., a fee paid by the borrower to receive a lower rate that did not actually result in such a discount) but not shared with another party was outside of the purview of the Act since there was not "portion, split, or percentage" of a charge. Moreover, many courts have held that RESPA cannot be used for broad challenges of lender fees as "excessive." See, e.g., Martinez v. Wells Fargo Home Mortgage, Inc., 598 F.3d 549 (9th Cir. 2010) (denying plaintiffs' claim that $800 underwriting fee was unearned or an invalid overcharge under the Act); Cavendish, American's Largest Appellate Court Speaks: RESPA Not A Price Control Scheme, 127 Banking L.J. 318 (2010).

Congress in 1990 amended RESPA to add two new objects of disclosure: escrow accounts and the transfer of mortgage servicing arrangements. 12 U.S.C.A. §§ 2605, 2609.

The problem with reform efforts like those embodied in RESPA is that they only scratch the surface. It seems idle to hope that one of RESPA's key objects—more and better information for consumers—will lower settlement costs. Buyers and sellers defer, and probably will continue to defer, to advice from real estate specialists—brokers, lawyers and mortgage lenders. Because time is so often essential in residential transactions, buyers are not likely to jeopardize a deal by taking the time to shop and compare settlement prices. Also, the buyer or seller who *does* take the time to comparison shop will find substantial uniformity in the prices quoted by title companies, brokers and others providing closing services. Rate regulation of title insurers and the absence of any real price competition among brokers make price disclosure at best a futile gesture in the direction of reducing costs.

For a detailed chronicle of events surrounding passage of RESPA, see D.B. Burke, Jr., American Conveyancing Patterns 133–199 (1978). See generally, P. Barron, Federal Regulation of Real Estate and Mortgage Lending (3d ed. 1992); Hirschler, RESPA Revised and Revisited, 11 U.Rich.L.Rev. 571 (1977); Field, RESPA in a Nutshell, 11 Real Prop., Probate & Trust J. 447 (1976); Jaworski, RESPA at the Millennium: a Y2K Problem or a Problem Solved?, 55 Bus. Law. 1349 (2000); Stoppello, Federal Regulation of Home Mortgage Settlement Costs: RESPA and its Alternatives, 63 Minn.L.Rev. 367 (1979); Wallace, "Explicit Pricing," Fraud, and Consumer Information: The Reform of RESPA, 12 Rutgers L.J. 183 (1981); Note, The Rise and Fall of Consumer Protection under RESPA, 68 U.M.K.C.L. Rev. 331 (1999); Kolar, Zalenski & Cubita, RESPA: The Changing Landscape, 58 Bus. Law. 1259 (2003); Mahaffey, A Product of Compromise: Or why Non-Pecuniary Damages Should Not Be Recoverable Under Section 2605 of the Real Estate Settlement Procedures Act, 28 U. Dayton L.Rev. 1 (2002).

B. LAWYERS

American Bar Association, Model Rules of Professional Conduct (2014)*

Rule 1.7: Conflict of Interest: Current Clients

(a) Except as provided in paragraph (b), a lawyer shall not represent a client if the representation involves a concurrent conflict of interest. A concurrent conflict of interest exists if:

(1) the representation of one client will be directly adverse to another client; or

(2) there is a significant risk that the representation of one or more clients will be materially limited by the lawyer's responsibilities to another client, a former client or a third person or by a personal interest of the lawyer.

(b) Notwithstanding the existence of a concurrent conflict of interest under paragraph (a), a lawyer may represent a client if:

(1) the lawyer reasonably believes that the lawyer will be able to provide competent and diligent representation to each affected client;

(2) the representation is not prohibited by law;

(3) the representation does not involve the assertion of a claim by one client against another client represented by the lawyer in the same litigation or other proceeding before a tribunal; and

(4) each affected client gives informed consent, confirmed in writing.

American Bar Association, Code of Professional Responsibility (1975).*

CANON 5ᵃ

A Lawyer Should Exercise Independent Professional Judgment on Behalf of a Client

ETHICAL CONSIDERATIONS

Interests of Multiple Clients

EC 5–14 Maintaining the independence of professional judgment required of a lawyer precludes his acceptance or continuation of employment that will adversely affect his judgment on behalf of or dilute his loyalty to a client. This problem arises whenever a lawyer is asked to represent two or more clients who may have differing interests, whether such interests be conflicting, inconsistent, diverse, or otherwise discordant.

EC 5–15 If a lawyer is requested to undertake or to continue representation of multiple clients having potentially differing interests, he must weigh carefully the possibility that his judgment may be impaired or his loyalty divided if he accepts or continues the employment. He should resolve all doubts against the propriety of the representation. A lawyer should never represent in litigation multiple clients with differing interests; and there are few situations in which he would be justified in representing in litigation multiple clients with potentially differing interests. If a lawyer accepted such employment and the interests did become actually differing, he would have to withdraw from employment with likelihood of resulting hardship on the clients; and for this reason it is preferable that he refuse the employment initially. On the other hand, there are many instances in which a lawyer may properly serve multiple clients having potentially differing interests in matters not involving litigation. If the interests vary only slightly, it is generally likely that the lawyer will not be subjected to an adverse influence and that he can retain his independent judgment on behalf of each client; and if the interests become differing, withdrawal is less likely to have a disruptive effect upon the causes of his clients.

EC 5–16 In those instances in which a lawyer is justified in representing two or more clients having differing interests, it is nevertheless essential that each client be given the opportunity to

---

ᵃ "The Canons are statements of axiomatic norms, expressing in general terms the standards of professional conduct expected of lawyers in their relationships with the public, with the legal system, and with the legal profession. They embody the general concepts from which the Ethical Considerations and the Disciplinary Rules are derived.

"The Ethical Considerations are aspirational in character and represent the objectives toward which every member of the profession should strive. They constitute a body of principles upon which the lawyer can rely for guidance in many specific situations.

"The Disciplinary Rules, unlike the Ethical Considerations, are mandatory in character. The Disciplinary Rules state the minimum level of conduct below which no lawyer can fall without being subject to disciplinary action."

evaluate his need for representation free of any potential conflict and to obtain other counsel if he so desires. Thus before a lawyer may represent multiple clients, he should explain fully to each client the implications of the common representation and should accept or continue employment only if the clients consent. If there are present other circumstances that might cause any of the multiple clients to question the undivided loyalty of the lawyer, he should also advise all of the clients of those circumstances.

DISCIPLINARY RULES

DR 5–105 Refusing to Accept or Continue Employment If the Interests of Another Client May Impair the Independent Professional Judgment of the Lawyer.

(A) A lawyer shall decline proffered employment if the exercise of his independent professional judgment in behalf of a client will be or is likely to be adversely affected by the acceptance of the proffered employment, or if it would be likely to involve him in representing differing interests, except to the extent permitted under DR 5–105(C).

(B) A lawyer shall not continue multiple employment if the exercise of his independent professional judgment in behalf of a client will be or is likely to be adversely affected by his representation of another client, or if it would be likely to involve him in representing differing interests, except to the extent permitted under DR 5–105(C).

(C) In the situations covered by DR 5–105(A) and (B), a lawyer may represent multiple clients if it is obvious that he can adequately represent the interest of each and if each consents to the representation after full disclosure of the possible effect of such representation on the exercise of his independent professional judgment on behalf of each.

(D) If a lawyer is required to decline employment or to withdraw from employment under a Disciplinary Rule, no partner, or associate, or any other lawyer affiliated with him or his firm, may accept or continue such employment.

In re Lanza

Supreme Court of New Jersey, 1974.
65 N.J. 347, 322 A.2d 445.

PER CURIAM.

The Bergen County Ethics Committee filed a presentment with this Court against respondent, Guy J. Lanza, who has been a practicing member of the bar of this State since 1954.

The Committee specifically found that respondent's conduct violated DR 5–105. This Disciplinary Rule forbids an attorney to represent adverse interests, except under certain very carefully circumscribed conditions.

In April or May of 1971, Elizabeth F. Greene consulted respondent with respect to the sale of her residence property in Palisades Park, New Jersey. Mr. Lanza agreed to act for her. In due course a contract, apparently prepared by a broker, was signed by Mrs. Greene as seller as well as by the prospective purchasers, James and Joan Connolly. The execution and delivery of the contract took place in Mr. Lanza's office, although he seems to have played little or no part in the negotiation of its terms. By this time he had agreed with the Connollys that he would represent them, as well as Mrs. Greene, in completing the transaction. The testimony is conflicting as to whether or not Mrs. Greene had been told of this dual representation at the time she signed the contract. Mr. Lanza says that she had been told, but according to her recollection she only learned of this at a later date from Mrs. Connolly. In any event it is quite clear that respondent agreed to act for the purchasers before discussing the question of such additional representation with Mrs. Greene.

The contract as originally drawn provided for a closing date in late July, 1971. At Mrs. Greene's request this date was postponed to September 1. A short time later, circumstances having again changed, Mrs. Greene found that she would now prefer the original date. This proved satisfactory to the purchasers but Mr. Connolly told Mrs. Greene that at this earlier date he would not have in hand funds sufficient to make up the full purchase price of $36,000. Of this sum he would lack $1,000. He suggested, however, that the parties might close title upon the earlier date if Mrs. Greene would accept, as part of the purchase price, a check for $1,000 postdated approximately 30 days. Mrs. Greene was personally agreeable to this. She consulted respondent who advised her that he saw no reason why she should not follow this course.

The closing accordingly took place late in July and in accordance with the foregoing arrangement, Mrs. Greene received, as part of the purchase price, Mr. Connolly's check in the sum of $1,000 dated August 31, 1971. Shortly after this latter date she deposited the check for collection and it was returned because of insufficient funds. When questioned, Mr. Connolly said that after he and his wife had taken possession of the property they discovered a serious water condition in the cellar. He added that Mrs. Greene had made an explicit representation that the cellar was at all times dry. For this reason he refused to make good the check, saying that it would cost him $1,000 to rectify the condition in the cellar. Mrs. Greene denied that she had ever made any representation whatsoever. She immediately got in touch with respondent who did nothing effective on her behalf. She then retained other counsel and has subsequently initiated legal proceedings against the Connollys.

We find respondent's conduct to have been unprofessional in two respects. In the first place, the way in which he undertook the dual representation failed to meet the standards imposed upon an attorney who elects to follow such a course. In the second place, after the latent conflict of interests of the two clients had become acute, he nevertheless continued to represent both parties. At that point, rather than going forward with the matter as he did, he should have withdrawn altogether.

Mr. Lanza first undertook to act for the seller, Mrs. Greene. This immediately placed upon him an obligation to represent her with undivided fidelity. Despite this obligation, he later agreed, without prior consultation with Mrs. Greene, to represent Mr. and Mrs. Connolly, whose interest in the matter was of course potentially adverse to that of his client. He should not have undertaken to represent the purchasers until he had initially conferred with Mrs. Greene. He should have first explained to her all the facts and indicated in specific detail all the areas of potential conflict that foreseeably might arise. He should also have made her aware that if indeed any of these contingencies should thereafter eventuate and not prove susceptible of ready solution in a manner fair and agreeable to all concerned, it would then become his professional duty immediately to cease acting for all parties. Only after such a conference with his client, and following her informed consent, would he have been at liberty to consider representing the purchasers. They, too, were entitled to the same explanation as is set forth above, as well as being told of respondent's existing attorney-client relationship with the seller.

The second instance of misconduct arose after respondent learned that the purchasers would not be able to pay the full purchase price in cash at the time of closing title. At that point adequate representation of the seller required that her attorney first strongly insist on her behalf that cash be forthcoming. Failing this, and if the seller persisted in her wish to close upon the earlier date, her attorney should have vigorously urged the execution and delivery to her of a mortgage from the purchasers in the amount of $1,000, or of other adequate security, in order to protect her interest pending receipt of the full cash payment. We think it fair to assume that had respondent not found himself in a position of conflicting loyalties, his representation of the seller would have taken some such course. Had the purchasers persisted in their unwillingness to pay the full amount in cash at the time of closing and had they also refused to execute and deliver a mortgage or other security, respondent should have immediately withdrawn from the matter, advising both parties to secure independent counsel of their respective choosing. At that point in time it would have clearly been impossible for any single attorney adequately and fairly to represent both sides.

This case serves to emphasize the pitfalls that await an attorney representing both buyer and seller in a real estate transaction. The Advisory Committee on Professional Ethics, in its Opinion 243, 95 N.J.L.J. 1145 (1972) has ruled that in all circumstances it is unethical for the same attorney to represent buyer and seller in negotiating the terms of a contract of sale. Here the respondent did not enter into these negotiations so he does not come under the ban of this rule. Canon 6 declared, however, that "[i]t is unprofessional to represent conflicting interests, except by express consent of all concerned given after a full disclosure of the facts." DR 5–105 is at least as strict in the requirements it lays down and in subparagraph (C) carries forward the injunction quoted above by prohibiting multiple representation unless "each [party] consents to the representation after full disclosure of the facts and of the possible effect of such representation on the exercise of his [the attorney's] independent professional judgment on behalf of each."

The extent of the necessary disclosure is what is important. As Opinion 243, supra, makes clear, this is a question that must be conscientiously resolved by each attorney in the light of the particular facts and circumstances that a given case presents. It is utterly insufficient simply to advise a client that he, the attorney, foresees no conflict of interest and then to ask the client whether the latter will consent to the multiple representation. This is no more than an empty form of words. A client cannot foresee and cannot be expected to foresee the great variety of potential areas of disagreement that may arise in a real estate transaction of this sort. The attorney is or should be familiar with at least the more common of these and they should be stated and laid before the client at some length and with considerable specificity. Of course all eventualities cannot be foreseen, but a great many can. Here respondent was representing Mrs. Greene, a seller of property. Generally a seller who has entered into a mutually binding contract of sale is principally interested in securing the full purchase price to which he or she is entitled. As counsel experienced in this field of practice well know, to allow a purchaser to take possession of the premises in question before the entire consideration has been received, either in the form of cash or purchase money mortgage, will often prove contrary to the seller's best interests. So it was here.

For the reasons set forth above, we deem respondent's conduct to merit censure. He is hereby reprimanded.

For reprimand: CHIEF JUSTICE HUGHES and JUSTICES JACOBS, HALL, MOUNTAIN, SULLIVAN, PASHMAN and CLIFFORD-7.

Opposed: None.

PASHMAN, J. (concurring).

It is virtually impossible for one attorney in any manner and under any circumstances to faithfully and with undivided allegiance represent both a buyer and seller. This concurrence, therefore, stands for the position of the majority and further holds that dual representation in a buyer-seller situation should be totally forbidden. The reasons for this seem to me fairly obvious. In this type of transaction, it is most certainly in the public interest to safeguard and protect both parties from any abuses, whether they be ill-advised or inadvertent. The potential conflict in home buying or selling may never come to fruition. However, when it does surface, both sides explode in anger and accusations. The attorney will then withdraw, leaving the situation no better than when it occurred and, for that matter, probably a bit worse. This is not fair to either party.

It is my contention that neither buyer nor seller can ever possibly fully appreciate all the complexities involved. That is precisely the reason why full disclosure and informed consent are illusory. What most people typically do is rely upon the representation of their attorney when he reassures them that everything will be properly handled. However, the attorney is, unfortunately, not a clairvoyant who can foresee problem areas, although he realizes that there is certainly the potential for genuine conflict. Even where his motives are of the highest, as they usually are, and in good faith believes that he can effect a meeting of the minds, he really is not sure. Because of that dangerous uncertainty, I believe attorneys would, generally, welcome this prohibition against potential conflict.

Numerous situations like the present instance require affirmative legal action and demand an attorney's undivided loyalty. If two separate attorneys were individually retained, both parties would be sure that they were receiving the best possible legal attention. If and when a conflict developed, they would be duly represented, instead of deserted. The inconvenience in retaining separate attorneys is minimal when weighed against the dangers involved, and the cost differential in the final analysis would be inconsequential.

NOTES

1. *The Lawyer's Role in Residential Transactions.* According to a pamphlet published by the American Bar Association's Special Committee on Residential Real Estate Transactions, there is plenty for each party's lawyer to do. Seller's lawyer should oversee negotiations to modify the broker's form of listing agreement. "The objections to form contracts are that they may be inappropriate to the particular transaction, badly drawn initially or incorrectly filled in. Any seller signing such a contract should have it approved by the seller's attorney before signing." Residential Real Estate Transactions: The Lawyer's Proper Role—Services—Compensation 3 (1978).

In preliminary negotiations between buyer and seller, "a great deal of trouble can be avoided if both the buyer and the seller consult their own lawyers during the course of the negotiations." For example, "they should consider such problems as the mode of paying the purchase price and the tax consequences resulting therefrom, the status of various articles as fixtures or personal property, the time set for occupancy and the effect of loss by casualty pending the closing." pp. 4–5. The contract of sale must be drafted, with careful attention paid to the financing contingency. And, since standard forms will typically be used, "any insertion should be carefully checked by the buyer's and seller's attorneys."

The buyer's lawyer "should inform the buyer of the limitations, if any, which impair the title." p. 6. One lawyer may have to obtain and record affidavits to cure defective title. Lawyers for the other parties would then review the affidavits for sufficiency. The deed and mortgage or deed of trust must be prepared, and the buyer advised "as to the tax and other effects of the manner in which title is taken." p. 7. Finally, one of the lawyers should draft a closing statement and, "as a part of the closing, arrangements must be made for insurance, taxes, and other incidents of ownership. Instruments must be recorded and a final check of title made." p. 8.

Real estate lawyers also play an important role as transactional lawyers in shaping the law. According to Professor Daniel Bogart:

> Transactional lawyers—not just litigators, legislators, and judges—make law. To some, this may seem a novel thought. The regimen of law school study, and the manner in which the law, courtrooms, lawyers, and judges are portrayed in the media, sometimes distort our view of how 'the law' is created, renewed, and destroyed. Even lawyers are subject to these misperceptions. Lawyers, too, often envision the law as resulting solely from enactments of legislatures, or from courtroom battles where two or more sides argue their positions and a judge renders an opinion. Those of us who have practiced 'telephone law' know the fallacy of this view, however. We also 'make' law. We make law when we convince our opponents to concede a point where the case law underlying the negotiation is unclear and unresolved. And when enough similarly situated attorneys arguing on behalf of their clients about a contractual provision convince some

adequate number of opponents, also similarly situated, that the 'law' is on their side, at some point negotiations cease and custom or practice takes over. This transactional law is conveyed in its own unique way, across jurisdictional boundaries, as one lawyer incorporates the innovation of another in his or her own contracts and documents.

Bogart, Games Lawyers Play: Waivers of the Automatic Stay in Bankruptcy and the Single Asset Loan Workout, 43 U.C.L.A.L. Rev. 1117, 1118 (1996).

Professor Caryl Yzenbaard has asserted that lawyers play an essential role in residential real estate transactions:

> The purchase and sale of the family home is probably the greatest investment made by the average family. Notwithstanding that fact, most buyers and sellers enter into the initial stages of the transaction without the benefit of their own legal counsel, and may continue without such representation throughout the transactions. This lack of adequate representation is particularly acute during the time of negotiating and drafting the contract of sale, the instrument which is the crucial document in the transaction. In fact, the role of the lawyer in the negotiation and preparation of the contract of sale has been severely limited and questioned during the past decade. Courts tend to reflect the general popular sentiment that the expertise of a lawyer is not needed at this "initial" stage.

> The author of this Article adopts the position that lawyers are crucial in the residential real estate transaction, particularly during the negotiation and drafting of the contract of sale.

Drafting the Residential Contract of Sale, 9 Wm. Mitchell L. Rev. 37, 37–39 (1983).

Professor Michael Braunstein, however, offers a different view. He asserts that lawyers have become marginalized in residential real estate transactions and that, in almost all states, non-lawyers negotiate contracts of sale. Moreover, Professor Braunstein concludes that the traditional assertions about the benefits of lawyer involvement are "vague, trivial, or implausible." Braunstein, Structural Change and Inter-Professional Competitive Advantage: An Example Drawn from Residential Real Estate Conveyancing, 62 Mo. L. Rev. 241 (1997).

2. *Multiple Representation: Costs and Benefits.* The ideal world envisioned by the ABA pamphlet, in which each party is individually represented by counsel, is not commonly realized in practice. The parties may perceive the residential sale to be sufficiently complex, and their investment sufficiently large, to warrant one lawyer, but not large enough to warrant two. And they may also suspect that the price of two lawyers will be more than twice the price of one. Time must be spent, and bills rendered, for the resolution of conflicts or potential conflicts that a single lawyer would probably glide over.

What would happen if lawyers followed the rule proposed in Justice Pashman's *Lanza* concurrence, allowing attorneys to represent no more than one party to a residential sale? Is it likely that each party would secure individual counsel? Is it likely that some or all parties would go without any legal advice at all? Is Pashman saying that no representation is preferable to representation shared with a potential adversary?

In Baldasarre v. Butler, 132 N.J. 278, 625 A.2d 458 (1993), the sellers' attorney also represented the buyers in a commercial real estate transaction, with both parties consenting to the dual representation after full disclosure. The transaction was complex, involving the sale of forty acres of undeveloped land with complicated contingencies about financing and subdivision approval. After the deal closed, the sellers brought an action against the attorney and the buyers alleging fraud. The sellers claimed that after the contract was signed (but before closing) the attorney represented the buyers in making a contract to resell the property to a third party and that the attorney committed fraud by refusing to disclose the existence of the resale contract when the sellers asked about it. Even though the attorney settled with sellers before oral argument, the court declared:

> This case graphically demonstrates the conflicts that arise when an attorney, even with both clients' consent, undertakes the representation of the buyer and the seller in a complex commercial real estate transaction. The disastrous consequences of [the attorney's] dual representation convinces us that a new bright-line rule prohibiting dual representation is necessary in commercial real estate transactions where large sums of money are at stake, where contracts contain complex contingencies, or where options are numerous. The potential for conflict in that type of complex real estate transaction is too great to permit even consensual dual representation of buyer and seller. Therefore, we hold that an attorney may not represent both the buyer and the seller in a complex commercial real estate transaction even if both give their informed consent.

132 N.J. at 295–296, 625 A.2d at 467. In light of the parties' settlement of the case, this statement is dictum. It may be important, however, as an indication of the court's position in future disciplinary actions against attorneys. Is *Lanza* still good law in light of the court's statement in *Baldasarre*?

3. *Multiple Representation: The Duty to Disclose.* What amount of disclosure would *Lanza* require for informed consent? If you were the lawyer in that transaction, what would you have disclosed to Mrs. Greene and the Connollys? Would you have anticipated the specific problem that subsequently arose? Would you have felt comfortable referring to the problem in general terms—"Disagreements may arise between you about how payment is to be made"—or still more generally—"Disagreements may arise with respect to the details of closing"? Form of payment is one of the more easily disclosed areas of dispute in residential sales. How would you have explained the harder, more intricate questions that arise in determining whether seller's title is marketable?

Buyers who are financing their purchase through an institutional lender sometimes agree to be represented by the lender's lawyer. Is the lawyer in this situation under a duty to describe important provisions of the loan instrument to the buyer-borrower? Say the note restricts the borrower's statutory right to redeem or waives the protection of antideficiency rules. Must the lender's lawyer disclose the effect of these clauses, the lender's relative willingness to delete them, and the willingness of competing lenders to exclude these clauses?

How would, and should, the New Jersey Supreme Court have decided *Lanza* under Rule 1.7 of the Model Rules of Professional Conduct? For an extensive analysis of the multiple representation issue under both the Code and Model Rules, see Comment, Conflicts of Interest in Real Estate Transactions: Dual Representation—Lawyers Stretching the Rules, 6 W. New Eng. L.Rev. 73 (1983).

On the conflict issue, see Bassett, Three's A Crowd: A Proposal to Abolish Joint Representation, 32 Rutgers L.J. 387 (2001); Zacharias, Waiving Conflicts of Interest, 108 Yale L.J. 407 (1998); Note, One For All Is Worth Two in the Bush: Mixing Metaphors Creates Lawyer Conflict of Interest Problems in Residential Real Estate Transactions, 56 U.Cinn. L.Rev. 639 (1987).

4. *Malpractice.* The American Bar Association Standing Committee on Lawyers Professional Liability in 2012 issued a Profile of Malpractice Cases: 2008–2011. The Study indicated that the highest number of malpractice claims (20.3%) during the period was filed in connection with residential and commercial real estate matters. This surpassed claims against personal injury lawyers. For all areas of law, complaints included failure to know/properly apply the law (13.6%), procrastination in performance (9.7%), and lost file/document (7/1%). See Scott, Recent ABA Study Suggests Emerging New Trends in Legal Malpractice, The View, vol. 28, no. 4, Oct. 2012, https://www.mlmins.com/TheView/October%202012 %20The%20View.pdf.

Malpractice liability may also arise out of the joint representation of clients with conflicting interests, such as buyer and seller, landlord and tenant, or mortgagor and mortgagee, or acting as an escrow agent or real estate broker in addition to representing one or more of the clients to a transaction. Blumberg, Avoiding Malpractice in Real Estate Law Practice, 2 Calif.Real Prop. J. 1 (Summer 1984). Thus, lawyer liability for money damages might be found in a scenario such as *Lanza.* See generally Meyer v. Maus, 626 N.W.2d 281 (N.D.2001).

To prevail in a malpractice action, the victim must show that the attorney failed to exercise the degree of care and skill commonly possessed by an ordinary member of the legal community and that the negligence was the proximate cause of the injury. See Logalbo v. Plishkin, Rubano & Baum, 163 A.D.2d 511, 514, 558 N.Y.S.2d 185, 188 (1990), appeal dismissed, 77 N.Y.2d 940, 569 N.Y.S.2d 613, 572 N.E.2d 54 (1991) (oral notice of cancellation of contract of sale by buyers' attorney was legal malpractice as a matter of law when contract expressly required written notice of cancellation within a specified period of time; "[t]he state of the law on the exercise of an option to cancel a real estate contract requiring that written notice be given within a specified time is clearly defined and firmly imbedded in our jurisprudence so as to be beyond doubt or debate").

An unrepresented party to a real estate transaction will sometimes pursue a malpractice action against an attorney for one of the other parties. The traditional rule has barred liability in the absence of privity. See, e.g., Noth v. Wynn, 59 Ohio App.3d 65, 571 N.E.2d 446 (1988) (lender's attorney did not owe duty to buyers to disclose restriction on purchased property).

However, many courts allow recovery if the injured party was a third party beneficiary of the attorney-client relationship. See Crossland Savings FSB v. Rockwood Insurance Co., 700 F.Supp. 1274 (S.D.N.Y.1988) (issuer of surety bonds may take advantage of opinion letter addressed to borrower where it was understood that surety was also to benefit from the letter). Some courts go further, permitting recovery by individuals who the lawyer knew relied upon his work. See, e.g., Collins v. Binkley, 750 S.W.2d 737 (Tenn.1988) (seller's attorney liable to buyer for approving deed that failed to contain language required for recordation). Is such expanded attorney liability appropriate? Will it encourage or discourage parties from retaining their own counsel? What effect will such liability have on the cost of legal services? Which parties to the transaction will ultimately bear the increased costs due to expanded liability of the attorney?

5. *Unauthorized Practice.* Various data indicate that many residential home purchasers are not represented by lawyers. According to a study of 132 home purchasers in Columbus, Ohio, less than half the buyers retained their own lawyers and a quarter of that number first met the lawyer at or shortly before closing. Braunstein & Genn, Odd Man Out: Preliminary Findings Concerning the Diminishing Role of Lawyers in the Home-Buying Process, 52 Ohio St.L.J. 469 (1991). Lawyers interviewed for the study indicated that the use of title insurance rather than title opinions accounted for the decline in lawyer representation of buyers. Would buyers be better off if they had lawyers? The study's preliminary results indicated no: purchasers currently using lawyers are no better informed, satisfied, or likely to avoid disputes than purchasers not retaining lawyers. Id. at 471–472.

A 1978 American Bar Foundation study found that in the estimated annual 5.5 million residential purchases, there was only a 40% probability that the purchaser will consult a lawyer. "When a lawyer is not contacted the most frequently mentioned sources of advice and help are real estate brokers, financial institutions and title companies." Curran, Survey of the Public's Legal Needs, 64 A.B.A. J. 848, 850 (1978). For a more recent survey, finding that lawyer involvement varies by location, see Moore, Lawyers and the Residential Real Estate Transaction, 26 Real Est. L.J. 351 (1998). Because residential transactions are pervaded by legal issues and heavily papered with legal instruments, the work performed by these nonlawyers unavoidably borders on the practice of law. This has led to criticism and legal actions claiming unauthorized practice of law.

Brokers have been a main target of unauthorized practice charges, chiefly in connection with their preparation of sales contracts. Charges of unauthorized practice are also lodged against title companies, largely from their involvement in closings—preparing deeds and title reports and obtaining affidavits to clear title. For background on unauthorized practice, see Onys Rentz, Note: Laying Down the Law: Bringing Down the Legal Cartel in Real Estate Settlement Services and Beyond, 40 Ga.L.Rev. 293 (2005); Goudey, Too Many Hands in the Cookie Jar: The Unauthorized Practice of Law By Real Estate Brokers, 75 Or. L. Rev. 889 (1996); Marks, The Lawyers and the Realtors: Arizona's Experience, 49 A.B.A. J. 139 (1963); Riggs, Unauthorized Practice and the Public Interest: Arizona's Recent Constitutional Amendment, 37 So.Cal.L.Rev. 1 (1964); Note, 19 De Paul L.Rev. 319 (1969).

The New Jersey Supreme Court ruled on a "long-simmering" unauthorized practice dispute between realtors and title company officers on one side and lawyers on the other. In re Opinion No. 26 of the Committee on Unauthorized Practice of Law, 139 N.J. 323, 654 A.2d 1344 (1995). An earlier decision had prohibited brokers from drafting contracts of sale generally; however, it allowed them to prepare residential sale contracts if the first page of the contract conspicuously displayed a clause permitting attorney review and, based on that attorney's review, cancellation by either party within three days of execution. New Jersey State Bar Ass'n v. New Jersey Ass'n of Realtor Boards, 93 N.J. 470, 461 A.2d 1112 (1983). In re Opinion No. 26 built on this earlier decision, holding that residential sellers and buyers could proceed without counsel so long as the broker specifically disclosed the broker's conflicting interest with the seller and buyer and warned of potential dangers of not using an attorney.

The court determined that a broker could participate in a closing where only one party, or neither, had been represented by counsel and could order abstracts, title binders, and title policies. Also, title companies can clear minor title objections without attorney involvement. The court noted that while many activities of brokers and title officers constitute practice of law, the public interest did not require a finding that they constituted the *unauthorized* practice of law. The court stated:

> We believe that parties to the sale of a family home, both seller and buyer, would be better served if each were represented by counsel from the beginning to the end of the transaction, from contract signing through closing. We are persuaded, however, that they should continue to have the right to choose not to be represented. . . . While the risks of non-representation are many and serious, the record contains little proof of actual damage to either buyer or seller. . . . [T]he record demonstrates what is obvious, that sellers and buyers without counsel save counsel fees. We believe, given this record, that the parties must continue to have the right to decide whether those savings are worth the risks of not having lawyers to advise them in what is almost always the most important transaction they will ever undertake. We realize this conclusion means that throughout the transaction, sellers and buyers may not have the benefit of their own counsel but will look to brokers and title officers, often with conflicting interests, for practical guidance and advice.

139 N.J. at 327–328, 654 A.2d at 1346.

Did the court strike an appropriate balance between consumer protection and the free play of the market?

In 1996, the Alaska Legislature granted broad powers to brokers to prepare real property contracts "and other documents related to real property if the documents are prepared by the person in the course of the person's work as a licensed real estate broker." Alaska Stat. § 08.88.405. Who benefits from such legislation? Contrast this with the Georgia Supreme Court's In re UPL Advisory Opinion 2003–2, 277 Ga. 472, 588 S.E.2d 741 (2003), holding that only attorneys can prepare deeds and requiring attorney participating in virtually all closings and with Toledo Bar Ass'n v. Chelsea Title Agency, 100 Ohio St.3d 356, 800 N.E.2d 29

(2003), holding that preparation of a deed by a title agency was unauthorized practice of law.

Lenders may also find themselves accused of unauthorized practice. See, e.g., King v. First Capital Financial Services Corp., 215 Ill.2d 1, 293 Ill.Dec. 657, 828 N.E.2d 1155 (2005) (the pro se exception to unauthorized practice applied to preparation of loan documents for a fee by mortgage lenders' employees).

6. *What Constitutes Unauthorized Practice?* The real question, of course, is what constitutes the practice of law? The general principle, followed everywhere, is that, aside from court appearances and preparation of pleadings, law practice consists of giving advice or drafting instruments affecting legal rights. More specific tests vary from state to state.

The "Incidental" Test. A nonlawyer may perform some legal tasks if they are minor and only incidental to the main service being offered. For example, the principal job of brokers is to bring buyers and sellers together; their incidental job is to keep them together. Because the contract of sale serves that collateral purpose, some states allow brokers to fill in the blanks in sales contracts. The obvious problem with this test is that it is totally unrelated to the client's need for expert and independent legal advice.

The "Simple-Complex" Test. Nonlawyers may perform simple legal tasks; only lawyers may perform complex ones. See, e.g., Dressel v. Ameribank, 468 Mich. 557, 664 N.W.2d 151 (2003). The problem with this test is that, while there certainly are complex legal tasks, it is hard to find a simple one. Advising a husband and wife to take title as joint tenants might appear to be a simple matter. In fact it is quite complex, implicating their motives, income, family plans and estate plans.

The "Personal Representation" Test. While a nonlawyer may not give legal advice to others, he may perform legal services for himself. The problem in applying this test arises when the services take the form of an opinion that is then justifiably relied on by a third party. For example, a title company's title examination and report serve as more than the basis for the company's decision to insure title. It will unavoidably affect the buyer's decision to proceed with the purchase on the assumption that title is in fact clear.

Threading the Needing. Real Estate Bar Ass'n for Mass., Inc. v. Nat'l Real Estate Information Services, 495 Mass. 512, 946 N.E.2d 665 (2011), illustrates the difficulties in characterizing an action as practice of law. The case, with a vivid history through the state and federal courts, involved a claim by state real estate bar that a national mortgage settlement services company was engaged in unauthorized practice of law. The court stated that it must evaluate the facts of each particular service and activity under the rubric of "conveyancing" to determine if there was a violation. The court concluded that on the facts, title examination, preparation of abstracts, preparation of HUD closing statements, review of documents to determine that they were signed, and recording executed documents were not the practice of law; opining on marketable title, providing title certifications, and preparation of deeds ("directly affect significant legal rights and obligations") were practice of law. This decision mooted an earlier federal district court opinion in the litigation that had found for the servicing company and that had noted "the public interest would be best served by preserving competition in the markets for real estate conveyancing and title insurance services." 609 F.Supp.2d 135, 147 (2009), vacated by 608 F.3d 110 (1st Cir. 2010).

See generally, Payne, Title Insurance and the Unauthorized Practice of Law Controversy, 53 Minn.L.Rev. 423 (1969).

7. *Anticompetitive   Practices   Among   Lawyers.*   Longstanding anticompetitive practices of the bar have doubtless increased the cost of residential closings. Some of these practices have recently come under attack. In Goldfarb v. Virginia State Bar, 421 U.S. 773, 95 S.Ct. 2004, 44 L.Ed.2d 572 (1975), the Court ruled that a minimum fee schedule for lawyers' title examinations, published by the Fairfax County Bar Association and enforced by the Virginia State Bar, violated section 1 of the Sherman Act. The Goldfarbs, after contracting to buy a house in Fairfax County, sought to obtain a title insurance policy. Under the state bar's unauthorized practice rules, only a lawyer could perform the title examination necessary for a title insurance policy to issue. The first lawyer contacted by the Goldfarbs quoted them precisely the fee suggested by the Fairfax County Bar Association schedule—1% of the contract price. The Goldfarbs then tried but failed to find a lawyer to examine title for a lower fee. Of the nineteen lawyers who replied to the Goldfarbs' letters requesting fee information, "none indicated that he would charge less than the rate fixed by the schedule; several stated that they knew of no attorney who would do so." Id. 421 U.S. at 776, 95 S.Ct. at 2007.

The Supreme Court found that "respondents' activities constitute a classic illustration of price fixing," and rejected the bar association's multifaceted defense that the fee schedule was merely advisory; that its effect on interstate commerce was only incidental and remote; that, as a learned profession, law was not "trade or commerce" subject to antitrust regulation; and that, as state action, bar-enforced fee schedules were immune from antitrust regulation. Id. 421 U.S. at 783, 95 S.Ct. at 2011. The court ruled that the fee schedule was not advisory because it "was enforced through the prospective professional discipline from the State Bar, and the desire of attorneys to comply with announced professional norms." Id. 421 U.S. at 781, 95 S.Ct. at 2010. The national scope of real estate finance, and lenders' universal requirement that title be examined, sufficiently implicated fee structures in interstate commerce. The court answered the "learned profession" defense by noting that "the examination of a land title is a service; the exchange of such a service for money is 'commerce' in the most common usage of that word." Id. 421 U.S. at 787–88, 95 S.Ct. at 2013–14. The Court's answer to the state action defense was that the state bar "has voluntarily joined in what is essentially a private anticompetitive activity." Id. 421 U.S. at 792, 95 S.Ct. at 2016.

Arrangements between lawyers and other conveyancing professionals and institutions have also been attacked. See, e.g., Blair & Jernigan, "Sweetheart" Arrangements Between Lenders and Their Title Lawyers— Are They Really? 37 Wash. & Lee L.Rev. 343 (1980); Roussel, Pera & Rosenberg, Bar-Related Title Insurance Companies: An Antitrust Analysis, 24 Vill.L.Rev. 639 (1979); Marcotte, Kickbacks to Lawyers Rapped, A.B.A.J., Nov. 1, 1986, p. 30. Problems may also arise when an attorney attempts to fill the role of other conveyancing professionals. See, e.g., Mortland, Attorneys As Real Estate Brokers: Ethical Considerations, 25 Real Prop. Probate & Trust J. 755 (1991).

It remains to be seen whether bar practices will prevail against antitrust attacks on yet another front: state bar rules on unauthorized practice that effectively define the scope of the bar's monopoly. A former head of the Justice Department's Antitrust Division has challenged statements of principles and treaties between the organized bar and other professional associations: "As a general rule, two competitors may not agree with each other to allocate markets, or bids, or even functions. . . . At the least, this traditional antitrust principle raises some questions about the legal effect of such 'statements of principles.' " 63 A.B.A. J. 299 (1977). See Virginia State Bar v. Surety Title Ins. Agency, Inc., 571 F.2d 205 (4th Cir.1978).

C. BROKERS

Beth E. Nagalski, Note, Ending the Uniformity of Residential Real Estate Brokerage Services: Analyzing the National Association of Realtors' Multiple Listing Service Under the Sherman Act
73 Brooklyn Law Review 771, 776–789 (2008).

A. The Real Estate Agent's Role in the Residential Real Estate Transaction

   1.   The Traditional Brokerage Model

In the traditional model for conducting a residential real estate transaction (also known as "full service brokerage"), the seller contracts with a broker to list his or her property for sale. The broker markets the property and helps the seller negotiate the deal. This broker is called the "listing agent." The listing broker's contract with the seller will usually be an "exclusive right to sell listing." In an exclusive listing agreement, the seller agrees not to seek the services of another broker, which limits his or her dealings with buyers to only the one listing agent. Agency law governs the relationship between agents and their clients. Therefore, a real estate agent owes a fiduciary duty to his or her client, including the duties of loyalty and good faith.

Generally, the seller's agreement with the listing broker requires the broker to list the seller's property on the MLS. All brokers with MLS access are then welcome to show the property to potential purchasers. The agents who show the property to buyers-called "selling brokers" or "cooperating brokers"—are traditionally considered a mandatory sub-agent of the seller. Therefore, under the traditional model, the broker who interacts with the buyer, showing them properties, is actually an agent of the seller. Accordingly, it is to the seller that the agent owes a fiduciary duty. The listing broker and the selling broker then split the commission, which the listing broker sets, and the buyer usually pays.

. . .

   2.   New Brokerage Models

Consumer demand and changing technology have resulted in the development of new service models for real estate brokerage. The growing dominance of the Internet in society has increased public access to information and created pressure for the broker's role in the real estate transaction to change. As a result, new brokers sometimes "unbundle" brokerage services by allowing clients to pick and choose the specific services traditionally included in full-service brokerage that they want. Clients can then pay a lower commission rate based on which services they use. This a la carte model caters to consumers of varying sophistication levels who desire different levels of service and do not necessarily require all of the services of a traditional real estate broker. These brokers might provide very limited services, such as simply listing their clients' property for sale on the MLS for a flat fee. Although a seller using a flat-fee listing broker will probably still need to offer the selling broker a commission to bring in a buyer, the seller could still save almost fifty percent over what he or she would need to pay under the traditional model.

Another new type of broker is the exclusive buyer's agent. As a result of rising consumer awareness regarding the problem of dual agency, these agents are becoming more popular. More homebuying guides and other mainstream media outlets are recommending that buyers consider using a broker exclusive to their side of the transaction. These agents market themselves as trustworthy alternatives to the traditional real estate agent who genuinely work for their clients' best interests. Exclusive buyers' agents do not accept any listings, ensuring that they will avoid the inevitable conflict of interest that arises when a buyer client wants to buy the house of a selling client.

A third new type of agent acts solely as a "lead generator" for other agents. These lead generators assess the needs of a given customer and match them with an appropriate agency. The referred agencies then give part of their commissions to the "lead generator." The "lead generator" then passes part of this commission on to the consumer as a rebate. Thus, the consumer is ultimately paying less in commission than under the traditional model.

These new brokerage models continue to develop and grow in popularity, enhancing consumer choice. As a result, consumers are able to pay less for brokerage services that are better tailored to their needs.

B.   Competition in the Residential Real Estate Industry

The Consumer Federation of America recently called the residential real estate industry "the last remaining unregulated cartel functioning in America." This statement is just one small part of a resurgence of debate over the anticompetitive conditions in the residential real estate industry. Discussion of the problem, however, is not a new phenomenon. In fact, the last half century has seen much similar debate, flush with both private and government litigation challenging various anticompetitive practices in the industry. Several features of the real estate market that have troubled commentators remain today: broker commission rates have remained steadily high over time; the traditional model for brokerage remains dominant even in a climate of alternative models for brokerage arguably more attractive to consumers; and control of the MLS, an indispensable tool of the trade, remains largely in the hands of one trade association.

Even as housing prices have changed over time and technological advances have arguably made the broker's job easier, commission rates in the industry have remained remarkably steady at around five to six percent. Such stable commission rates have led analysts to question whether there is some kind of "informal collusion" keeping commission rates at this level. In fact, the traditional model does give a direct economic incentive to the listing and the selling broker to cooperate in maintaining a high commission rate because they will split the commission when the deal closes. Even worse, the traditional model allows one broker to represent both sides of the transaction. A dual agent clearly has an incentive to maintain the high commission rate because she will retain the entire fee. Alternative brokerage models, on the other hand, offer consumers the opportunity to choose limited services for discount rates.

Some commentators, however, argue that the dominance of the traditional model for brokerage suppresses the growth of alternative brokerage models. These commentators note that the "commonality of the structure [for brokerage services] and its persistence over time suggest the possibility that alternative models have not had a fair chance to compete." Since the traditional brokerage method allows little opportunity for the consumer to negotiate the broker's commission rate, alternative brokers have complained that consumers do not even know that they can shop around for different service packages and rates. Additionally, discrimination against alternative brokers by traditionalist brokers may contribute to the limited growth of these types of brokers. Traditional brokers do not want the industry to be infiltrated by brokers offering lower prices. Therefore, traditionalists have an economic incentive to deal only with other traditionalists who work for the same standard commission rate.

Analysts speculate that a truly competitive residential real estate industry would feature lower commission rates and "a greater range and variety of services [offered] at varying prices." Therefore, expansion and growth of the new alternative models for real estate brokerage should be encouraged.

C. The NAR Actively Stifles the Development of Alternative Models of Real Estate Brokerage

Rather than encouraging development of new brokerage models, the NAR and its local affiliates rigorously support the traditional model for real estate brokerage. The NAR aggressively lobbies for legislation that ensures the dominance of the traditional model for brokerage. In fact, the general counsel of the NAR has made it clear that this is the NAR's agenda, stating recently that "Realtor associations have the right to lobby for legislative and regulatory action that they support-even if the effect of such action would be anticompetitive."

The NAR receives a vast amount of funding to pursue its lobbying activities through annual membership dues collected from its 1.3 million members. Membership dues generate around $100 million annually. In its 2005 annual report, the NAR stated that it used fifteen percent of membership dues for "public policy." Therefore, by forcing all real estate agents wishing to access the MLS to pay membership dues to the NAR, all real estate agents are in effect contributing money to be used in part to lobby against competitive changes in the industry. This is especially problematic for alternative brokers, who would probably prefer not to contribute to a fund that will be used in part to advocate for policies adverse to their interests.

The NAR and traditional brokers, however, have a great incentive to continue to advocate for adherence to the status quo in brokerage because any break in uniformity is likely to result in lower commission rates. Additionally, the NAR clearly has strong incentives to require membership in the NAR in order for a broker to obtain MLS access-millions of dollars to use in forwarding its traditionalist agenda and the power to control who uses the MLS and on what terms.

NOTES

1. *Structure of the Residential Brokerage Industry.* An extensive, nationwide study by staff members of the Federal Trade Commission indicates that approximately 80% of home sales were negotiated through a broker. Of all homes sold through brokers, about 90% were listed with a local multiple listing service. "Our investigation indicates that while there is some variation in commission rates contracted for and paid in every local community surveyed, commission rates in all markets do tend to be roughly uniform from sale to sale." A 1979 survey revealed that "85 percent of the sellers surveyed alleged they were quoted a commission rate either of 6 or 7 percent by the broker whom they used, and ultimately 78 percent paid either 6 or 7 percent." Staff Report by the Los Angeles Regional Office of the FTC, The Residential Real Estate Brokerage Industry, 15, 19 (December 1983). See Owen, Kickbacks, Specialization, Price Fixing, and Efficiency in Residential Real Estate Markets, 29 Stan. L. Rev. 931 (1977).

The Staff Report also sought to solve the puzzle of relatively uniform prices in a highly atomized industry. Interdependency among brokers, facilitated by the multiple listing service, appeared to be the cause. In the typical multiple listing service, a broker who has obtained an exclusive listing from a seller submits the listing to the service. At this point, every other member of the service is free to try to sell the property by procuring a buyer. The commission from such "cooperative" sales is divided between the listing and the cooperating broker. "Many observers believe that most firms, and especially small firms and new entrants, are dependent upon the MLS and cooperative sales and cannot take any risks that might lessen the cooperation they will receive."

Specifically, while "brokers might attract many listings by advertising low commission fees, those brokers might encounter problems in cooperatively selling their listings. Cooperating brokers usually are compensated by the listing broker's splitting his or her commission with the cooperating brokers. 'Discount' or 'alternative' brokers may offer potential cooperating brokers substantially less compensation than that provided by 'traditional' brokers. For this reason (and also because a cooperating traditional broker who charges the higher prevailing commission rate will be a competitor of the listing discount broker for future listings) many traditional brokers are alleged to quite understandably steer potential buyers to homes listed by brokers charging the prevailing commission rate and offering the prevailing split." As a result, price competition may become "a potentially unsuccessful competitive strategy and it is our belief that is the most important factor explaining the general uniformity of commission rates in most local markets." Staff Report 17–19.

A recent study indicated some elasticity in the commission price, although the study was limited to closings of 30 year fixed rate FHA insured mortgages averaging $105,000 in principal amount. Department of Housing and Urban Development, A Study of Closing Costs for FHA Mortgages (2008). The study, conducted by Susan E. Woodward, examined a national sample of 7,560 loans closed in May and June of 2001. She concluded that "real estate agents do not uniformly charge six percent of house value." Id. at xiii. Of the transactions that involved agents, 47% had fees below 6%, 29% were at 6%, and 25% were above 6%.

2. *Licensing.* All fifty states license real estate brokers and salespeople through laws covering practically every activity performed for a fee in connection with a real estate transaction. (Lawyers, when performing legal work, are typically exempted.) Applicants are tested on subjects ranging from reading, writing and arithmetic to applicable real property law and the practical aspects of deeds, mortgages, contracts and agency. In a few states they are tested on ethics and the basic principles of land economics and appraising. Some states require relevant work experience and some require that the applicant successfully complete a real estate course approved by the state.

Licenses may be revoked for such delicts as fraud, deceptive advertising, untrustworthiness or incompetence (N.Y.Real Prop.Law § 441–c(1)(a)); acting for more than one party without the knowledge or consent of all, or commingling funds (Cal.Bus. & Prof.Code § 10176(d), (e)); acting in the dual capacity of broker and undisclosed principal, charging an undisclosed commission for a principal, or not giving a copy of the purchase and sale agreement to buyer and seller (Mass.Gen.Laws Ann. ch. 112, § 87AAA(b), (f), (i)).

3. *Real Estate Boards and Associations.* Most brokers belong to local, state and national groups that lobby actively on their behalf, oversee their professional conduct and provide or support marketing facilities. The main locus of day-to-day activities is the local real estate board, a voluntary association offering market and industry information to its members. Local boards belonging to the National Association of Realtors, the largest national organization of real estate professionals, enforce the Association's Code of Ethics through grievance and hearing committees. Membership in a local board may also be a prerequisite to participation in a multiple listing service.

4. *Trends in the Brokerage Industry.* Brokerage firms, traditionally small and independent, have recently begun to expand nationwide through branches, referral networks and franchise operations. The growth of brokerage chains has been more than geographic. The giants have also expanded their services to include home finance, insurance, and escrow and other closing services. Some small independents have responded by forming cooperative networks in which a relocating seller is referred by her hometown broker to a cooperating broker in the locale to which she is moving. Other local brokers have joined national franchising operations, receiving in return for payment of an initial fee and percentage of gross revenues, the benefits of advertising, name recognition, training, and office management expertise.

Computer technology has doubtless spurred these developments, fostering nationwide listing networks through which a potential buyer, sitting at a terminal in an office on one side of the country, can summon up all current listings in a locale on the other side of the country. The same computer-communications technologies have also helped to nationalize and shorten the otherwise local and protracted search for financing. Several computer-based networks now give brokers continuously updated lists of mortgage lenders and itemize the availability and terms of their loans. Some networks will evaluate the borrower's creditworthiness, process the loan documents and even commit the funds.

5. *Antitrust Violations.* Broker groups have employed price fixing and exclusionary practices to restrict competition in the conveyancing industry. Mandatory commission schedules were the earliest form of price fixing. In United States v. National Ass'n of Real Estate Boards, 339 U.S. 485, 70 S.Ct. 711, 94 L.Ed. 1007 (1950), the United States Supreme Court held that these schedules violated section 3 of the Sherman Act. Local boards subsequently confined themselves to recommending "fair and reasonable" rates. These recommendations came under Justice Department attack in a flurry of actions brought in the early 1970's. See, for example, United States v. Prince George's County Bd. of Realtors, Inc., 1971 Trade Cas. ¶ 73,393, 1970 WL 546 (D.Md.1970); United States v. Long Island Bd. of Realtors, Inc., 1972 Trade Cas. ¶ 74,068, 1972 WL 584 (E.D.N.Y.1972). As a result, real estate boards entirely dropped recommended rate schedules.

Exclusionary practices arise mainly in connection with access to multiple listing service facilities and have been attacked from three quarters: federal antitrust law, state antitrust statutes and common law doctrine. See generally, Trombetta, The MLS Access Issue: A Rule of Reason Analysis, 11 Seton Hall L.Rev. 396 (1981); Erxleben, In Search of Price and Service Competition in Residential Real Estate Brokerage: Breaking the Cartel, 56 Wash.L.Rev. 179 (1981); Austin, Real Estate Boards and Multiple Listing Systems as Restraints of Trade, 70 Colum.L.Rev. 1325 (1970).

Federal antitrust actions were for many years hobbled by the belief that the local nature of broker activities insulated them from federal jurisdiction. Ultimately, however, the Supreme Court took a different view, holding 8–0 that to "establish the jurisdictional element of a Sherman Act violation it would be sufficient for petitioners to demonstrate a substantial effect on interstate commerce generated by respondents' brokerage activity." McLain v. Real Estate Board of New Orleans, Inc., 444 U.S. 232, 242, 100 S.Ct. 502, 509, 511, 62 L.Ed.2d 441, 451, 453 (1980). See Stoppello, Sherman Act Extends to Activities of Real Estate Brokers: Federal Regulation of Brokers May Be on the Way, 9 Real Estate L.J. 151 (1980); Mann, The Applicability of Antitrust Law to Activities of Real Estate Boards: Before and After *McLain,* 18 Hous.L.Rev. 317 (1981).

The United States Department of Justice brought a suit in 2005 claiming various anti-competitive practices by the National Association of Realtors. U.S. v. National Ass'n of Realtors, 2006 WL 3434263 (N.D.Ill.2006). Under a settlement in 2008, the NAR was required to allow Internet-based and other discount brokers access to the MLS. NAR rules had limited dissemination of these listings to traditional means and through traditional, full-service brokers. Prohibitions against referrals to

Internet-based brokerages were also prohibited. The settlement is available at 2008 WL 2850402 (N.D.Ill.2008).

See Freeman v. San Diego Ass'n of Realtors, 322 F.3d 1133 (9th Cir.), cert. denied, 540 U.S. 940 (2003) (fixed fees for MLS support services violated the Sherman Act). For a survey of several other areas in which broker practices are subject to antitrust attack, see Jennings, Real Estate Transactions: More Antitrust Litigation is on its Way, 10 Real Est.L.J. 52 (1981); Epley & Parsons, Real Estate Transactions and the Sherman Act: How to Approach an Antitrust Suit, 5 Real Est.L.J. 3 (1976).

6. *Brokers and Housing Discrimination.* As gatekeepers to their communities, real estate brokers contributed to racially discriminatory patterns of home ownership. Probably the most notorious practice was blockbusting, in which brokers stimulated sales by representing to fearful home owners that the racial composition of their neighborhood was about to change and real estate values about to plummet. State and local governments have enacted criminal and civil prohibitions against blockbusting. The practice has also been outlawed by Title VIII of the Civil Rights Act of 1968. Title VIII provides in part that it shall be unlawful "For profit, to induce or attempt to induce any person to sell or rent any dwelling by representations regarding the entry or prospective entry into the neighborhood of a person or persons of a particular race, color, religion, sex, handicap, familial status or national origin." 42 U.S.C.A. § 3604(e). Is it possible that by prohibiting brokers from encouraging sales in the face of racial change, section 3604(e) may inadvertently spur brokers to *discourage* sales to minority group members, directly contravening the overriding purposes of Title VIII?

Title VIII of the 1968 Civil Rights Act has also been interpreted to prohibit racial steering, another discriminatory practice, in which the broker directs white buyers to white neighborhoods, and minority buyers to minority or mixed neighborhoods. Some support has also been found in the 1866 Civil Rights Act, 42 U.S.C.A. § 1982. See Zuch v. Hussey, 394 F.Supp. 1028 (E.D.Mich.1975). As late as 1950, the National Association of Realtors (then called the National Association of Real Estate Boards) expressly encouraged racial steering. The Association's Code of Ethics, Article 34, provided that "A realtor should never be instrumental in introducing into a neighborhood . . . members of any race or nationality, or any individual whose presence would be clearly detrimental to property values in that neighborhood." Today the Association endorses the principle that brokers "have the responsibility to offer equal service to all clients and prospects without regard to race." National Association of Realtors, Realtors' Guide to Practice Equal Opportunity in Housing 5 (1973).

Apart from general statutory sanctions, a broker who participates in racially discriminatory practices may lose her license. In a small number of states, licensing statutes specifically make discriminatory practices a ground for suspension or revocation. Other states discipline brokers on more general and traditional grounds. In New York, the Secretary of State has disciplined brokers on the ground that discriminatory practices constitute "untrustworthy" behavior. See, for example, Kamper v. Department of State, 22 N.Y.2d 690, 291 N.Y.S.2d 804, 238 N.E.2d 914 (1968). By contrast, Wisconsin's Supreme Court has held discrimination not to constitute "incompetency," "improper dealing," or "untrustworthiness" as those terms are used in the state's license revocation statute. Ford v.

Wisconsin Real Estate Examining Board, 48 Wis.2d 91, 179 N.W.2d 786 (1970). See generally, Suspension or Revocation of Real Estate Broker's License on Ground of Discrimination, 42 ALR3d 1099 (1972).

For a detailed, but somewhat dated, description of broker practices, see R. Helper, Racial Policies and Practices of Real Estate Brokers (1969). On blockbusting, see Note, Blockbusting, 59 Geo.L.J. 170 (1970). On steering, see Note, Racial Steering: The Real Estate Broker and Title VIII, 85 Yale L.J. 808 (1976).

7. *Bibliographic Note.* For an excellent treatise covering the field generally, see D.B. Burke, Jr., Law of Real Estate Brokers (3d ed. 2008).

1.   SELLER'S AND BUYER'S LIABILITY TO BROKER

Business Consulting Services, Inc. v. Wicks

Supreme Court of Iowa, 2005.
703 N.W.2d 427.

PER CURIAM.

Leroy Wicks, as seller, and Hawkeye Business Brokers Company (Hawkeye), as broker, entered into a listing contract for the sale of Wicks' business. When Wicks refused to pay a commission as demanded by Hawkeye, Hawkeye sued and obtained a judgment against Wicks. We reverse and remand.

I.   Facts and Prior Proceedings.

Hawkeye is a company, called a "business broker," that provides brokerage services to buyers and sellers of businesses, similar to the services of a real estate broker. Wicks is a Des Moines businessman who owned a security business called Homeguard Security, providing antitheft and antiburglary security services for homes and businesses.

The contract relationship between Wicks and Hawkeye began when Joy Jones—one of Hawkeye's brokers—learned that Wicks was interested in selling Homeguard. Ironically, Jones acquired this information from the person who ultimately purchased the business— David Gutfreund. Gutfreund had previously been the general manager for Per Mar Security Company, a company that worked closely with Homeguard by providing monitoring services for alarm calls triggered by Homeguard's alarms. Gutfreund left Per Mar in December of 2001. After Gutfreund left Per Mar, he contacted Jones and told her that he was interested in locating a business, that Homeguard was for sale, and that he was interested in purchasing a business "like" Homeguard. Gutfreund did not feel he could purchase Homeguard, however, because his attorney had advised him that doing so might create a conflict of interest with Per Mar because of Gutfreund's former employment at Per Mar.

After she learned that Wicks was selling Homeguard, Jones contacted Wicks and offered to assist him with the sale. On January 24, 2002, Wicks and Jones (on behalf of Hawkeye) signed a listing agreement, which was to run until March 24, 2002. The listing contract was nonexclusive, but if Jones produced a ready, willing, and able buyer during the listing period, Wicks would pay Hawkeye a ten percent commission.

Additionally, the agreement contained an "extension clause" that provided:

> Seller agrees to pay the full commission set forth in this Agreement to the Broker in the event the property described herein is within one year after the termination of this Agreement, sold, traded or otherwise conveyed to *anyone referred to Seller by the Broker* or with whom Seller had negotiations during the term of this Agreement.

(Emphasis added.)

Generally speaking, an extension clause is intended to afford a measure of protection to a broker against an unscrupulous and fraudulent attempt on the part of a property owner to secure the advantage of the broker's services and yet avoid paying him a commission through the device of delaying sale of the listed property to a purchaser interested therein by the broker until after the expiration of the listing agreement. On the other hand, and in somewhat the same manner as such an extension clause provides protection to a broker, the imposition of a fixed and definite limitation upon the interval of time in which the broker has the authority—and particularly where he has the exclusive authority—to deal with the designated property, safeguards the owner from claims by the broker for a commission upon any sale of the property consummated after the expiration of such time limit regardless of whether or not such sale resulted from the broker's efforts.

J.R. Kemper, Annotation, Construction of Provision in Real-Estate Broker's Listing Contract that Broker Shall Receive Commission on Sale After Expiration of Listing Period to One With Whom Broker has "Negotiated" During Listing Period, 51 A.L.R.3d 1149, 1175 (1973) [hereinafter Kemper, Extension Clauses].

The listing contract also had a clause, handwritten, stating that "Seller will not accept less than $600,000." The business sold for less than that, and Wicks raises this as a second issue on his appeal—that Hawkeye did not meet the terms of the contract. There is some doubt as to whether Wicks preserved error on this issue, but in any event, we need not address it because we resolve Wicks' appeal on another ground.

The district court made no finding with respect to any negotiations instituted by the broker, and it does not appear the business was actually "shown" by the broker to the buyer. In fact, except for the broker's revelation to the buyer that the business was for sale—a fact the buyer already knew—the broker did virtually nothing to bring the sale to fruition. The broker testified that she encouraged two potential buyers, including Gutfreund, to bid on the property. Also, she spent approximately forty-five minutes meeting with Wicks and corresponded with him in connection with "confidentiality agreements." She could not recall whether she had advertised the business.

Pursuant to the terms of the extension agreement, Hawkeye sent a letter to Wicks reminding him of the terms of the extension agreement under which Wicks would be liable for a commission on any sale to a buyer referred by the broker. The letter listed Gutfreund as one of six parties to whom Jones claimed to have "shown," and therefore referred, the property. Hawkeye informed Wicks that a sale to any of the six parties would result in liability for the commission.

II. Standard of Review.

When reviewing the judgment of a district court in a nonjury law case, our review is for correction of errors at law. The trial court's findings have the effect of a special verdict and are binding if supported by substantial evidence. Evidence is substantial when a reasonable mind would accept it as adequate to reach a conclusion. Hansen v. Seabee Corp., 688 N.W.2d 234, 237–38 (Iowa 2004).

III. Analysis.

In Wicks' first argument, he contends the district court erred in ruling for Hawkeye because it did not establish that Hawkeye was the "efficient procuring cause" of the sale. Under common law, a broker is entitled to a commission, even if the sale occurs after the termination of the brokerage agreement, if the broker is the "efficient procuring cause" of the sale. McCulloch Inv. Co. v. Spencer, 246 Iowa 433, 437–38, 67 N.W.2d 924, 927 (1955); Kellogg v. Rhodes, 231 Iowa 1340, 1344–45, 4 N.W.2d 412, 415 (1942); see Mellos v. Silverman, 367 So.2d 1369, 1371 n. 1 (Ala.1979) ("Procuring cause refers to a cause originating with a series of events which without break in their continuity result in procuring a purchaser ready, willing and able to buy on the owner's terms.").

> Under the "procuring cause rule," a party may be entitled to a commission on a sale made after the termination of a contract if that party procured the sale through its activities prior to the termination, but such rule applies only if the contract does not expressly provide when a commission will be paid.

12 Am.Jur.2d Brokers § 270, at 918 (1997).

The "efficient procuring cause" doctrine only applies if the contract between the parties is silent on the issue of a sale after the expiration of the original listing period. In other words, it is the default rule. See id. It is said that

> the courts have . . . made it clear that the parties to a listing contract are free to frame their agreement in whatever terms they may see fit—provided that such terms are neither unlawful nor contrary to public policy—and that in so doing they may make a broker's right to compensation depend upon the happening of a designated event, or upon the fulfillment of a particular set of circumstances, rather than upon the procurement of a purchaser.

> Such, in essence, is the position which has been taken by a number of courts which have held . . . that where an extension clause in a listing contract provides for payment of a commission to a broker upon a sale of the listed property, after the expiration of such agreement, to a party with whom, during the term thereof, the broker had negotiated (or had otherwise dealt, as required by the particular language of the clause), the broker is not required, in order to be entitled to a

commission, to show that he was the "procuring cause" of such sale. . . .

Kemper, Extension Clauses, 51 A.L.R.3d at 1168; see Mellos, 367 So.2d at 1371 ("Under the language typically employed in extension clauses, it is not necessary that the actions of the brokers be the 'procuring' cause of the sale. . . ."); accord Galbraith v. Johnston, 92 Ariz. 77, 373 P.2d 587, 589 (1962); Leonard v. Fallas, 51 Cal.2d 649, 335 P.2d 665, 668 (1959); Restatement (Second) of Agency § 448 cmt. b, at 356 (1958). We agree with this general rule and hold that, because the listing agreement between Hawkeye and Wicks contained an extension clause, its terms are controlling on the "referral" issue, and Hawkeye need not prove it was the efficient procuring cause.

The question remains whether Hawkeye complied with the terms of the agreement. That turns on whether Hawkeye's "referral" of Gutfreund without any proof of a causal connection with the ultimate sale was sufficient to comply with the terms of the agreement. We decide this issue as one of law, setting aside a very legitimate question of fact raised by Wicks, i.e., whether Hawkeye actually "referred" Gutfreund to Wicks in view of the fact that Gutfreund was the one who first broached the subject of his desire to purchase a security company and specifically mentioned to Hawkeye that Homeguard was for sale.

"Refer" is not defined in the contract, and the contract does not set out the conditions under which the broker will be considered to have referred the buyer to the seller. Hawkeye does not claim a causal relationship between its referral of Gutfreund and the ultimate sale, arguing that it was not necessary under the parties' contract to show any more than the fact that a sale was ultimately made to a buyer referred to Wicks by Hawkeye.

We believe that words such as "referred," "solicit," or similar words[1] necessarily incorporate an unexpressed, but inferentially essential, requirement that a broker do more than merely refer or point a potential buyer to a seller. If such a requirement is not read into such words, they are too general to have any real meaning. Authorities illustrating this point are discussed later.

In contrast to vague words such as "referred," extension clauses providing commissions for sales to buyers "procured" by a broker have been held to be enforceable. See Moore v. Prindable, 815 S.W.2d 25, 27–28 (Mo.Ct.App.1991). This is understandable because words such as "procured," in contrast to a word such as "referred," are well-defined terms in real estate sales law. Similarly, an extension agreement allowing a commission for sales to a broker if the property is "contracted by or through the broker" has been held to be enforceable. See Ira E. Berry, Inc. v. Sloan, 662 S.W.2d 922, 924 (Mo.Ct.App.1983); see also Kemper, Extension Clauses, 51 A.L.R.3d at 1181 ("[P]erhaps the one most frequently employed is the word 'negotiate,' or some form thereof, such as 'negotiated with' or 'had negotiations with.' ").

In Chapman Co. v. Western Nebraska Broadcasting Co., 213 Neb. 322, 329 N.W.2d 107 (1983), an extension clause provided for a

---

[1]   See, e.g., Korstad v. Hoffman, 221 Cal.App.2d Supp. 805, 35 Cal.Rptr. 61, 62 (1963) (clause applied to party to whom broker "introduced" the property; "introduction" of property without connection to sale held insufficient).

commission to be paid for a sale to anyone "solicited" by the broker. The broker mailed announcements of the proposed sale to 323 potential purchasers. One of the recipients of the mailed notice eventually purchased the business but the broker had no part in negotiations or the ultimate closing of the sale. Chapman, 329 N.W.2d at 109. The court agreed that the broker had in fact "solicited" the buyer, but that was not enough because

> the broker must show some minimal causal connection between the efforts of the broker and the ultimate sale before the broker may receive the compensation.

Id. at 111. The court noted that the requirement for a causal connection was the clear majority rule. Id. Another source, discussing cases from several jurisdictions, notes:

> [I]n order for a broker to be entitled to a commission, under and in accordance with an extension clause, he must ordinarily be able to establish at least some causal connection between his actions and efforts in regard or relation to the listed property and the ultimate purchaser thereof, and with the sale eventually made to such purchaser.

Kemper, Extension Clauses, 51 A.L.R.3d at 1156.

We adopt the majority rule and hold that a broker seeking to recover under an extension clause must establish some causal connection between the broker's efforts and the eventual sale. This might include negotiations between the parties or actual assistance in the closing of the sale. In this case, Hawkeye has not shown it was involved in any negotiations or the closing of the sale. As the Nebraska court said in Chapman, a rule that would allow recovery for merely soliciting a buyer without requiring a causal connection with the sale would burden the owner's right to dispose of his property. 329 N.W.2d at 111. We agree, and we also believe it would be poor public policy to reward brokers who, through such mailings or other forms of mass communication, would receive a substantial commission without diligent effort toward the conclusion of a sale. While the broker in this case did not mass mail to prospects, but rather, limited her contacts to six possible buyers, the point remains that "referring," as the broker did in this case, without more, is insufficient. As the court observed in Patterson v. Blair, 123 Utah 216, 257 P.2d 944 (1953),

> although the clause with which we are concerned is perfectly valid and to be invoked for the broker's protection in a proper case, it surely was not intended to benefit a real estate man who has done nothing, by conferring upon him a "windfall" commission because he casually or inadvertently mentioned the listing to someone who thereafter happened to purchase it in the normal course of affairs and quite independent of the broker's activities. If so, he might well content himself with letting everyone possible know of a listing in the hope that some such eventuality would inure to his benefit, instead of really working on selling the property.

Patterson, 257 P.2d at 946.

The plaintiff has failed to establish a causal connection between its referral of the buyer and the ultimate sale. We therefore reverse the judgment of the district court and remand for dismissal of the plaintiff's petition.

REVERSED AND REMANDED.

Tristram's Landing, Inc. v. Wait

Supreme Judicial Court of Massachusetts, 1975.
367 Mass. 622, 327 N.E.2d 727.

TAURO, CHIEF JUSTICE.

This is an action in contract seeking to recover a brokerage commission alleged to be due to the plaintiffs from the defendant. The case was heard by a judge, sitting without a jury, on a stipulation of facts. The judge found for the plaintiffs in the full amount of the commission. The defendant filed exceptions to that finding and appealed.

The facts briefly are these: The plaintiffs are real estate brokers doing business in Nantucket. The defendant owned real estate on the island which she desired to sell. In the past, the plaintiffs acted as brokers for the defendant when she rented the same premises.

The plaintiffs heard that the defendant's property was for sale, and in the spring of 1972 the plaintiff Van der Wolk telephoned the defendant and asked for authority to show it. The defendant agreed that the plaintiffs could act as brokers, although not as exclusive brokers, and told them that the price for the property was $110,000. During this conversation there was no mention of a commission. The defendant knew that the normal brokerage commission in Nantucket was five per cent of the sale price.

In the early months of 1973, Van der Wolk located a prospective buyer, Louise L. Cashman (Cashman), who indicated that she was interested in purchasing the defendant's property. Her written offer of $100,000, dated April 29, was conveyed to the defendant. Shortly thereafter, the defendant's husband and attorney wrote to the plaintiffs that "a counter-offer of $105,000 with an October 1st closing" should be made to Cashman. Within a few weeks, the counter offer was orally accepted, and a purchase and sale agreement was drawn up by Van der Wolk.

The agreement was executed by Cashman and was returned to the plaintiffs with a check for $10,500, representing a ten per cent down payment. The agreement was then presented by the plaintiffs to the defendant, who signed it after reviewing it with her attorney. The down payment check was thereafter turned over to the defendant.

The purchase and sale agreement signed by the parties called for an October 1, 1973, closing date. On September 22, the defendant signed a fifteen day extension of the closing date, which was communicated to Cashman by the plaintiffs. Cashman did not sign the extension. On October 1, 1973, the defendant appeared at the registry of deeds with a deed to the property. Cashman did not appear for the closing and thereafter refused to go through with the purchase. No formal action has been taken by the defendant to enforce the agreement or to recover damages for its breach, although the defendant has retained the down payment.

Van der Wolk presented the defendant with a bill for commission in the amount of $5,250, five per cent of the agreed sales price. The defendant, through her attorney, refused to pay, stating that "[t]here has been no sale and consequently the 5% commission has not been earned." The plaintiffs then brought this action to recover the commission.

In the course of dealings between the plaintiffs and the defendant there was no mention of commission. The only reference to commission is found in the purchase and sale agreement signed by Cashman and the defendant, which reads as follows: "It is understood that a broker's commission of five (5) per cent on the said sale is to be paid to . . . [the broker] by the said seller." The plaintiffs contend that, having produced a buyer who was ready, willing and able to purchase the property, and who was in fact accepted by the seller, they are entitled to their full commission. The defendant argues that no commission was earned because the sale was not consummated. We agree with the defendant, and reverse the finding by the judge below.

1.   The general rule regarding whether a broker is entitled to a commission from one attempting to sell real estate is that, absent special circumstances, the broker "is entitled to a commission if he produces a customer ready, able, and willing to buy upon the terms and for the price given the broker by the owner." Gaynor v. Laverdure, 362 Mass. 828, 291 N.E.2d 617 (1973), quoting Henderson & Beal, Inc. v. Glen, 329 Mass. 748, 751, 110 N.E.2d 373 (1953). In the past, this rule has been construed to mean that once a customer is produced by the broker and accepted by the seller, the commission is earned, whether or not the sale is actually consummated. Furthermore, execution of a purchase and sale agreement is usually seen as conclusive evidence of the seller's acceptance of the buyer.

Despite these well established and often cited rules, we have held that "[t]he owner is not helpless" to protect himself from these consequences. "He may, by appropriate language in his dealings with the broker, limit his liability for payment of a commission to the situation where not only is the broker obligated to find a customer ready, willing and able to purchase on the owner's terms and for his price, but also it is provided that no commission is to become due until the customer actually takes a conveyance and pays therefor." Gaynor v. Laverdure, supra, at 835, 291 N.E.2d at 622.

In the application of these rules to the instant case, we believe that the broker here is not entitled to a commission. We cannot construe the purchase and sale agreement as an unconditional acceptance by the seller of the buyer, as the agreement itself contained conditional language. The purchase and sale agreement provided that the commission was to be paid "on the said sale," and we construe this language as requiring that the said sale be consummated before the commission is earned.

In two of the more recent cases where we were faced with this issue, we declined to follow the developing trends in this area, holding that the cases presented were inappropriate for that purpose. See LeDonne v. Slade, 355 Mass. 490, 492, 245 N.E.2d 434 (1969); Gaynor v. Laverdure, 362 Mass. 828, 291 N.E.2d 617. We believe, however, that it is both appropriate and necessary at this time to clarify the law, and we now join the growing minority of States who have adopted the rule of Ellsworth Dobbs, Inc. v. Johnson, 50 N.J. 528, 236 A.2d 843 (1967).[6]

In the *Ellsworth* case, the New Jersey court faced the task of clarifying the law regarding the legal relationships between sellers and brokers in real estate transactions. In order to formulate a just and proper rule, the court examined the realities of such transactions. The court noted that "ordinarily when an owner of property lists it with a broker for sale, his expectation is that the money for the payment of commission will come out of the proceeds of the sale." Id. at 547, 236 A.2d at 852. It quoted with approval from the opinion of Lord Justice Denning, in Dennis Reed, Ltd. v. Goody, [1950] 2 K.B. 277, 284–285, where he stated: "When a house owner puts his house into the hands of an estate agent, the ordinary understanding is that the agent is only to receive a commission if he succeeds in effecting a sale. . . . The common understanding of men is . . . that the agent's commission is payable out of the purchase price. . . . The house-owner wants to find a man who will actually buy his house and pay for it. He does not want a man who will only make an offer or sign a contract. He wants a purchaser 'able to purchase and able to complete as well.'" Id. at 549, 236 A.2d at 853.

The court went on to say that the principle binding "the seller to pay commission if he signs a contract of sale with the broker's customer, regardless of the customer's financial ability, puts the burden on the wrong shoulders. Since the broker's duty to the owner is to produce a prospective buyer who is financially able to pay the purchase price and take title, a right in the owner to assume such capacity when the broker presents his purchaser ought to be recognized." Id. at 548, 236 A.2d at 853. Reason and justice dictate that it should be the broker who bears the burden of producing a purchaser who is not only ready, willing and able at the time of the negotiations, but who also consummates the sale at the time of closing.

Thus, we adopt the following rules: "When a broker is engaged by an owner of property to find a purchaser for it, the broker earns his commission when (a) he produces a purchaser ready, willing and able to buy on the terms fixed by the owner, (b) the purchaser enters into a binding contract with the owner to do so, and (c) the purchaser completes the transaction by closing the title in accordance with the provisions of the contract. If the contract is not consummated because of lack of financial ability of the buyer to perform or because of any other default of his . . . there is no right to commission against the seller. On the other hand, if the failure of completion of the contract results from the wrongful act or interference of the seller, the broker's claim is valid and must be paid." Id. at 551, 236 A.2d at 855.

Accordingly, we hold that a real estate broker, under a brokerage agreement hereafter made, is entitled to a commission from the seller

---

[6]   Both Kansas and Oregon have adopted the *Ellsworth* rule in its entirety. See Winkelman v. Allen, 214 Kansas 22, 519 P.2d 1377 (1974); Brown v. Grimm, 258 Or. 55, 59–61, 481 P.2d 63 (1971). Additionally, Vermont, Connecticut and Idaho have cited the case with approval. See also Potter v. Ridge Realty Corp., 28 Conn.Supp. 304, 311, 259 A.2d 758 (1969); Rogers v. Hendrix, 92 Idaho 141, 438 P.2d 653 (1968); Staab v. Messier, 128 Vt. 380, 384, 264 A.2d 790 (1970). Other States and the District of Columbia also have similar, but more limited, rules which were adopted prior to the *Ellsworth* case. See generally Gaynor v. Laverdure, 362 Mass. 828 n. 2, 291 N.E.2d 617 (1973).

only if the requirements stated above are met. This rule provides necessary protection for the seller and places the burden with the broker, where it belongs. In view of the waiver of the counts in quantum meruit, we do not now consider the extent to which the broker may be entitled to share in a forfeited deposit or other benefit received by the seller as a result of the broker's efforts.

We recognize that this rule could be easily circumvented by language to the contrary in purchase and sale agreements or in agreements between sellers and brokers. In many States a signed writing is required for an agreement to pay a commission to a real estate broker. See Restatement 2d: Contracts, 418, 420 (Tent. drafts Nos. 1–7, 1973). Such a requirement may be worthy of legislative consideration, but we do not think we should establish such a requirement by judicial decision. Informal agreements fairly made between people of equal skill and understanding serve a useful purpose. But many sellers, unlike brokers, are involved in real estate transactions infrequently, perhaps only once in a lifetime, and are thus unfamiliar with their legal rights. In such cases agreements by the seller to pay a commission even though the purchaser defaults are to be scrutinized carefully. If not fairly made, such agreements may be unconscionable or against public policy.

Exceptions sustained.

Judgment for the defendant.

NOTES

1. *Forms of Listing Agreement.* There are four basic types of listing agreement: exclusive right to sell; exclusive agency; open; and net. The exclusive right to sell listing is the most favorable to the listing broker, giving him the right to a commission if the property is sold by anyone, even the owner, during the term of the listing agreement. An exclusive agency listing entitles the broker to a commission if he or any other broker sells the property, but not if the property is sold through the efforts of the owner. In an open or nonexclusive listing, the seller agrees to pay a commission only if the broker is the first to procure a buyer; if the property is sold through the efforts of the seller or anyone else, the broker has no claim. In a net listing, the seller agrees to accept a specified price for the property and the broker receives any amount paid over that price.

2. *Interpreting the Listing Agreement.* Sellers typically list their homes through form agreements drafted by broker associations. As a result, disputes over the seller's duties to the broker turn principally on contract interpretation and on judicial estimates of relative bargaining power. Four interpretational questions recur.

One question concerns the type of listing agreement broker and seller made. If the agreement is ambiguous, a court will generally construe it against the broker on the grounds of superior bargaining position and responsibility for selecting the form of listing agreement. For example, in Lockhart v. Holiday Homes of St. John, Inc., 678 F.2d 1176 (3d Cir.1982), the form agreement specified an "Exclusive Right to Sell Basis," but also provided that the commission would be payable only upon the broker's procurement of a ready, willing and able buyer. The court seized on this ambiguity to hold that an exclusive right to sell agreement had not been created. As a general rule an open listing will be found unless exclusivity is clearly indicated. Similarly, where there is doubt, an agreement will be held to create an exclusive agency, rather than an exclusive right to sell, listing. See Bourgoin v. Fortier, 310 A.2d 618 (Me.1973).

Second, when has a "sale" occurred, perfecting the broker's right to a commission under an exclusive right to sell listing? An exchange of property usually constitutes a sale for these purposes. See Donlon v. Babin, 44 So.2d 134 (La.App.1950). But what if the house is taken by eminent domain while the listing agreement is in effect? See, e.g., Lundstrom, Inc. v. Nikkei Concerns, Inc., 52 Wash.App. 250, 758 P.2d 561 (1988) (no commission awarded). If the house is leased, not sold, during the term of the listing agreement? Leased with an option to purchase that is later exercised? Taken off the market? Listing agreements sometimes provide that seller's withdrawal of the property from the market during the listing period is equivalent to a sale, entitling the broker to a commission based on the listing price. While the provision might seem unfair to the seller who withdraws because she cannot get an offer close to her listing price, it has been upheld against charges that it is a penalty. See Blank v. Borden, 11 Cal.3d 963, 115 Cal.Rptr. 31, 524 P.2d 127 (1974).

The third question, which arises in open listing agreements, is whether one broker rather than another was the "procuring cause" of the sale and thus entitled to the commission. There are few reasoned rules on the point, but colorful metaphors abound. See, for example, Vincent v. Weber, 13 Ohio Misc. 280, 232 N.E.2d 671, 42 O.O.2d 347, 351 (1965) (the broker must establish that she was the primary, proximate and procuring cause, not merely the one who "planted the seed from which the harvest was reaped"); Gilmer v. Fauteux, 168 Vt. 636, 638, 723 A.2d 1150, 1152 (1998) (the broker must "show that his efforts dominated the transaction").

Fourth, the broker must produce a buyer who is "ready, willing and able" to purchase the property under the terms of the listing agreement. Typically, the agreement will set out the acceptable price, financing, closing date, and other terms with specificity. The seller may ultimately agree to take less advantageous terms and, if so, the seller will be liable for the commission. See, e.g., East Kendall Investments, Inc. v. Bankers Real Estate Partners, 742 So.2d 302 (Fla.App.1999) (commission due when seller accepted lower price); Blackstone v. Thalman, 949 S.W.2d 470 (Tex.App.1997) (no commission payable since broker did not find buyer meeting exact terms of listing agreement, and buyer and seller never agreed to a sale on modified terms). What is necessary to show that the buyer is financially "able"? That she has the cash on hand, an adequate credit rating to obtain a mortgage, a mortgage commitment in hand, etc.? As of what time must the buyer be ready, willing, and able? Who should bear the burden in showing this, the buyer or the seller? See D. Barlow Burke, The Law of Real Estate Brokers, § 5.02 (3d ed. 2012)

See also Levmore, Commissions and Conflicts in Agency Arrangements: Lawyers, Real Estate Brokers, Underwriters, and Other Agents' Rewards, 36 J.L. & Econ. 503 (1993); Black, Client Liability to Real Estate Brokers: From Contract to Punitive Damages, 25 Real Est. L.J. 78 (1996).

3.   *Ellworth Dobbs.* Ellsworth Dobbs, Inc. v. Johnson, 50 N.J. 528, 236 A.2d 843 (1967), relied on in Tristram's Landing, Inc. v. Wait, is a modern landmark, adjusting legal rules to customary broker and seller expectations about when the broker's commission becomes due. The court recognized that the seller's reasonable expectation is that the commission will be paid out of the sale proceeds, and that this expectation is reinforced by the common broker practice of not requesting the commission until the closing. *Ellsworth Dobbs'* interpretational presumption—no closing, no commission—has since been followed by some courts that have considered the issue, e.g., Blumfield Agency v. Little Belt, Inc., 666 P.2d 1164 (Mont. 1983); Setser v. Commonwealth, Inc., 256 Or. 11,470 P.2d 142 (1970). *Ellsworth Dobbs* and *Tristram's Landing* remain clear minority positions, however, with most recent decisions following the traditional rule of awarding a commission on the procurement of a ready, willing, and able buyer even if the deal does not close. See, e.g., Margaret H. Wayne Trust v. Lipsky, 123 Idaho 253, 846 P.2d 904 (Idaho 1993); Glassberg v. Washawsky, 266 Ill. App.3d 585, 638 N.E.2d 749 (1994); Coldwell Banker Village Green Realty v. Pillsworth, 818 N.Y.S.2d 868 (App. Div. 2006).

Ellsworth Dobbs announced a second. The rule is one of contract illegality rather than interpretation. According to the court, whenever "there is substantial inequality of bargaining power" between broker and seller, a clause entitling the broker to a commission on the contract signing is "so contrary to the common understanding of men, and also so contrary to fairness, as to require a court to condemn it as unconscionable." 50 N.J. at 555, 236 A.2d at 857. In Currier v. Kosinski, 24 Mass. App. Ct. 106, 108, 506 N.E.2d 895, 897 (1987), the court held that a clause in the brokerage agreement stating that commission would be earned upon producing a customer ready, willing, and able to buy on the terms of the agreement was not enforceable. The court noted that "[a] seeler not practiced in the subtleties of real estate sales is not, by this language, sufficiently put on notice that he may incur liability for a broker's commission even though he does not enter into a purchase and sale agreement or, if he does, even though the buyer defaults."

4. *Ellsworth Dobbs and Tristram's Landing Applied.* Like many other pioneering decisions, *Ellsworth Dobbs* and *Tristram's Landing* are short on implementing details. Consider, for example, a sales contract requiring buyer to pay 10% down on closing, and requiring seller to take back a note and mortgage under which buyer will pay the remainder of the purchase price over ten years (a not uncommon form of purchase money financing). At what point does the broker become entitled to a commission: At closing? Or ten years hence, after all financing risk is past? What if a ten-year installment land contract is used as the financing device?

Ellsworth Dobbs and *Tristram's Landing* do not completely relieve seller from liability for the commission on an aborted sale. Instead, they allocate liability according to fault. If it was the seller's fault that the sale did not go through, the seller remains liable for the commission. If it was the buyer's fault, seller has no liability. Who should bear the risk when, through the fault of no one, the sale fails to close? In Hecht v. Meller, 23 N.Y.2d 301, 296 N.Y.S.2d 561, 244 N.E.2d 77 (1968), broker was awarded her commission even though the property had been substantially destroyed by fire before the closing and the contract of sale had been rescinded. The court rested its decision on the traditional view that a broker's right to a commission attaches when she procures a ready, willing, and able buyer.

Would a court following *Ellsworth Dobbs* and *Tristram's Landing* reach a different result?

On the issue, see Bernhardt & Whitman, When Is A Commission Due?, 27 Probate & Prop. 30 (Jan./Feb. 2013).

5. *Does a Broker Have Any Rights Against a Buyer?* Because their contract is with the seller, residential brokers have in the past had few routes to recovery against buyers who have maneuvered them out of their commissions or prevented the deal from closing. Third party beneficiary theory, tortious interference with contractual relations and the emerging tort of unlawful interference with prospective economic advantage have been the main grounds for relief.

In Harris v. Perl, 41 N.J. 455, 464, 197 A.2d 359, 364 (1964), plaintiff broker had shown a house to defendant buyer. During negotiations between buyer and seller, seller conveyed the property to a bank to satisfy an earlier obligation to the bank that had been secured by the property. Learning of the transfer, and that the bank had not engaged a broker to sell the house, buyer purchased the property directly from the bank. Broker sued buyer for her lost commission and won, the court observing that she was "not a meddlesome interloper," and that when buyer "accepted plaintiff's services, it was with the obligation which all decent men would recognize, that they would not line their purse with the money value of those services. . . . [T]he law protects not only contracts but also the reasonable expectations of economic gain." Before your sympathy for the broker leads you to the same conclusion, remember that Article 6 of the Realtor's Code of Ethics recommends that brokers "urge the exclusive listing of property," and that under a typical exclusive listing the seller's transfer to the bank would have constituted a "sale" entitling the broker to a commission from the seller.

Even though tort actions traditionally lay against only outrageous buyer shenanigans, the broker was nonetheless well protected. Broker actions against less culpable buyers were unnecessary, for the seller was in any event liable for the commission at the moment broker presented a ready, willing, and able buyer. But with more recent decisions, like *Ellsworth Dobbs* and *Tristram's Landing,* brokers, to recover, must look to the defaulting buyer, whether the default was willful or not. *Ellsworth Dobbs* sought to protect the broker in these situations by enlarging the occasions for buyer liability: "when a prospective buyer solicits a broker to find or to show him property which he might be interested in buying, and the broker finds property satisfactory to him which the owner agrees to sell at the price offered, and the buyer knows the broker will earn a commission for the sale from the owner, the law will imply a promise on the part of the buyer to complete the transaction with the owner." 50 N.J. at 559, 236 A.2d at 859.

At least one state has followed *Ellsworth Dobbs'* implied promise theory and two have rejected it. Compare Donnellan v. Rocks, 22 Cal.App.3d 925, 99 Cal.Rptr. 692 (1972), with Rich v. Emerson-Dumont Distributing Corp., 55 Mich.App. 142, 222 N.W.2d 65 (1974); Professional Realty Corp. v. Bender, 216 Va. 737, 222 S.E.2d 810 (1976). *Ellsworth Dobbs* itself was limited by the New Jersey Supreme Court in Rothman Realty Corp. v. Bereck, 73 N.J. 590, 376 A.2d 902 (1977). Buyers there suffered a sudden stock market reversal making it impossible for them to come up with the cash needed to close the purchase of a house. The court recognized that buyers' "implied promise to the broker to complete the transaction did not encompass a failure to close where they had acted in good faith, and the inability to consummate the deal . . . was due to a circumstance beyond their control." 73 N.J. at 604, 376 A.2d at 909. The court distinguished *Ellsworth Dobbs* on the ground that the buyer there was engaged in a commercial enterprise; the "bargaining power and expertise of such buyers are far superior to those of the average home purchaser." 73 N.J. at 602, 376 A.2d at 908.

Does the expansion of tort theory, as in *Harris,* and of implied contract theory, as in *Ellsworth Dobbs,* point to an emerging fiduciary tie between broker and buyer? Would such a tie necessarily dilute the broker's fiduciary duties to the seller?

2.   BROKER'S DUTIES TO SELLER AND TO BUYER

National Association of Realtors, Code of Ethics and Standards of Practice (2014)*

Article 1

When representing a buyer, seller, landlord, tenant, or other client as an agent, REALTORS® pledge themselves to protect and promote the interests of their client. This obligation to the client is primary, but it does not relieve REALTORS® of their obligation to treat all parties honestly. When serving a buyer, seller, landlord, tenant or other party in a non-agency capacity, REALTORS® remain obligated to treat all parties honestly.

Joseph M. Grohman, A Reassessment of the Selling Real Estate Broker's Agency Relationship with the Purchaser

61 St. John's Law Review 560, 560–563, 584–588 (1987).

I.   INTRODUCTION

Real property sellers have traditionally utilized real estate brokerage services to sell their properties. Typically, the seller and broker enter into a listing agreement which expressly authorizes the broker to act as the seller's exclusive agent in selling the specified property. This broker is commonly referred to as a listing broker. One of the listing broker's responsibilities is to inform others of the seller's desire to convey the property. The listing broker often accomplishes this by registering the property with a multiple listing service ("MLS"). This service aids the listing broker in informing other MLS members of the pertinent facts regarding the property and the sale. As a result, access to the MLS is one of the most important services a broker could offer to a client. Usually, when a cooperating MLS member, working with a potential purchaser, prepares to make an offer on the listed property, the cooperating or selling broker is deemed a subagent of the listing broker. Generally, subagents are in a fiduciary relationship with their

---

*   Article 1 is one of the seventeen basic principles of the Code of Ethics and Standards of Practice of the NATIONAL ASSOCIATION OF REALTORS®. To review the Code and Standards in its entirety go to Realtor.com.

principals. As a result, they owe their principal—the seller—the same duties as those which an agent owes the principal.

Without expressly agreeing to retain a broker as their agent, purchasers may also utilize a broker's services to locate property which they may opt to purchase. The real estate broker, in many cases, is the purchaser's sole source of expertise and material information regarding real property purchases. Often, this broker is not the same as the seller's listing broker. First, the broker will attempt to interest the purchaser in property listed with his office. If successful, he will not have to share the sales commission with an outside broker. If unsuccessful, the broker will try to interest the purchaser in property listed with the MLS. If successful in this attempt, the broker will be referred to as the "selling" or "cooperating" broker for that property even though another broker's office had originally listed it. As a result, the brokers will share the commission. Once the buyer has located a property in which he is interested, the selling broker normally aids the buyer in determining the terms of his offer and then assists the buyer in presenting the offer to the seller, usually through the listing broker.

A clear distinction exists between the listing broker and the selling broker. It is the seller of real property who usually initiates the relationship with the listing broker. It is the purchaser who typically initiates the relationship with the selling broker. For some time, federal courts, state courts, professional real estate organizations, sellers, and purchasers have questioned the status of the selling broker's relationship and his duties to the real estate purchaser. Absent a specific contractual relationship, case law generally concludes and authors opine that the selling broker is the seller's subagent and not the purchaser's agent. Therefore, he has little, if any, fiduciary obligation to the purchaser. The real estate broker's primary obligation to the purchaser is to deal honestly and fairly with him. This obligation, rather than emanating from an agency relationship, arises, at least partially, from the position of public trust which brokers occupy, and is supported by their virtual monopoly in real estate sales. As a result, the purchaser, without an attorney, is the least protected and most vulnerable party in a real estate transaction. . . .

IV. AVAILABLE ALTERNATIVES

A.   *Mandatory Duty to Disclose Subagency to Purchaser*

One of the reactions to the assertion that the current system misleads the real property purchaser is to proffer the idea that the selling broker must advise the purchaser that he will be acting solely as the seller's agent. Such a proposition would prove fruitless for two reasons.

First, brokers are reluctant to disclose such information to purchasers. Psychologically, it is to the broker's and seller's advantage to get the buyer committed in writing as soon as possible. Advising the purchaser in advance that neither broker represents him most likely would encourage him to seek alternative representation and delay the process. This is the antithesis of the sales concept. It is unlikely that many brokers would encourage such activity. Disclosures probably would be infrequent. This presumption follows from the brokers' past failures in being open with purchasers and sellers where it appears that such openness in disclosure would be contrary to the brokers' best interests. For example, brokers have failed to disclose to real estate participants how negotiable real estate commissions might be. Also, they have failed to advise the parties about each participant's role in the real estate transaction. Consequently, the purchaser is virtually unaware that the person upon whom he is relying may actually have interests adverse to his. So, too, brokers frequently fail to show prospective purchasers homes listed with other brokers who discount their commissions. There is little reason, therefore, to believe that brokers would be any more informative in disclosing their subagency relationship than they are presently in disclosing other information.

Second, a mere revelation that a subagency relationship exists still fails to provide the purchaser with what he needs. It is necessary to recognize that an agency relationship exists and this will provide the purchaser with the same advocacy and protection that the seller receives.

B. Dual Agency

Another response to the problem is to propose the dual agency theory whereby the selling broker would be the agent for both the seller and the buyer. Again, this theory is unlikely to provide adequate protection for purchasers.

First, in all but the most basic transactions, there are conflicts inherent in a dual agency. The dual agent owes both principals the same degree of care and duty as if he represented each alone. He must, as to both, act loyally, act in good faith and fairly, and openly and fully disclose all relevant facts known to him or which he should have discovered in carrying out his duties. In many real estate dealings this is an impossibility because of the contrasting motivations of the seller and purchaser, and the selling broker's duty to disclose to each. Likewise, he would have to disclose to the purchaser the seller's need for sale proceeds.

Moreover, where there are conflicts between the two principals, the dual agent must obtain the consent of each principal before embarking on the dual agency. The basic principle underlying this requirement is "to prevent the agent from putting himself in a position in which to be honest must be a strain on him, and to elevate him to a position where he cannot be tempted to betray his principal." Defining the selling agent as a dual agent in a transaction that is fraught with inherent conflicts, places a strain on him to be honest and enhances the difficulty of not betraying his principal, even though he may betray the principal negligently. The broker's falling prey to such temptation has resulted in courts referring to it without citation.

Unfortunately, because of the nature of agency relationships, one can infer such a relationship in many transactions solely from the parties' actions. Therefore, the agent may have acted already without obtaining the necessary consents. Doing so gives each principal who did not have prior knowledge of the dual representation the right to void the agency and the transaction. As a result, a broker acting in this fashion may have already breached his fiduciary obligations and lost his right to a commission by the time he attempts to obtain each party's consent. It is important to note that the primary exception to the general dual agency rule is where the broker acts as a middleman.

A third problem with the dual agency theory is that the dual agent must withdraw from representing the principals when a conflict between the two arises because he is unable to represent adequately each principal's interests. By the selling dual agent's withdrawal from the agency, the purchaser loses the affirmative representation he sought and expected. The seller, on the other hand, may still have the listing broker acting as his agent. Therefore, such a theory fails to remedy the inequities inherent in the current system.

C. Purchaser's Agent

Another way to deal with the question is to recognize that elements already exist in the typical relationship between a purchaser and a selling broker which make the selling broker the purchaser's agent. As a result, the purchaser has the agent that he needs and that both he and the seller already expect him to have. The purchaser's agent would be better able to serve the purchaser without fear of conflicts of interest or fear of losing his right to reimbursement for failure to obtain the necessary consents for dual agency. The agent would no longer be faced with the problem of trying to determine what to disclose and when to withdraw when conflicts arise in dual agencies. The purchaser then has an agent who will assist him in determining the best price at which he can obtain the property, in determining the most favorable terms under which the seller is willing to convey, in deciding what inspections to have, and, generally, in taking all usual steps inherent in the prudent purchase of real property.

In recognizing and applying agency principles to the selling broker-purchaser relationship, the law would balance inequities inherent in the existing system. Presently, the seller knows the most about his property. The broker is expert in comparing the property in question with similar properties and in discovering material information about the property for sale. The typical purchaser not only does not have the seller's information about his home, but, also, is without the broker's general expertise. Presumably, the purchaser represented by a broker should fare better in negotiations for the purchase of property.

Daubman v. CBS Real Estate Co.

Supreme Court of Nebraska, 1998.
254 Neb. 904, 580 N.W.2d 552.

CAPORALE, JUSTICE.

I. STATEMENT OF CASE

Claiming that defendant-appellant CBS Real Estate Co. and its agent, defendant-appellant Arlene Engelbert, breached their fiduciary duties, plaintiffs-appellees, Allen E. Daubman and his wife, Renee A. Daubman, sought the return of the real estate sales commission they paid. Following a bench trial, the district court entered judgment in favor of the Daubmans. CBS and Engelbert appealed to the Nebraska Court of Appeals, claiming that the district court had erred in (1) finding that they breached their fiduciary duties, (2) failing to find that the Daubmans ratified and otherwise acquiesced in their actions, (3) finding that the Daubmans sustained damages, and (4) awarding prejudgment interest. Concluding that the evidence failed to support the district court's judgment, the Court of Appeals vacated the judgment and remanded the cause with directions to dismiss. See Daubman v. CBS Real Estate Co., 6 Neb.App. 390, 573 N.W.2d 802 (1998). The Daubmans thereupon successfully petitioned for further review, claiming, in summary, that the Court of Appeals erroneously set aside the district court's factual findings. For the reasons hereinafter set forth, we reverse, and remand with direction.

II. SCOPE OF REVIEW

This action is one for assumpsit for money had and received, an action which may be brought where a party has received money which in equity and good conscience should be repaid to another. Kramer v. Kramer, 252 Neb. 526, 567 N.W.2d 100 (1997); Wrede v. Exchange Bank of Gibbon, 247 Neb. 907, 531 N.W.2d 523 (1995). In such a circumstance, the law implies a promise on the part of the person who received the money to reimburse the payor in order to prevent unjust enrichment. *Kramer*, supra; *Wrede*, supra. The action, although falling under the common-law class of assumpsit, is really in the nature of a bill in equity and lies wherever the party should by equity and natural principles of justice refund the money. Boman v. Olson, 158 Neb. 636, 64 N.W.2d 310 (1954). Although founded on equitable principles, an action in assumpsit for money had and received is an action at law. *Kramer*, supra; *Wrede*, supra.

The judgment and factual findings of the trial court in an action at law tried to the court without a jury have the effect of a verdict and will not be set aside unless clearly wrong. In re Estate of Wagner, 253 Neb. 498, 571 N.W.2d 76 (1997). In reviewing an action at law, an appellate court reviews the evidence in the light most favorable to the prevailing party. *Id.* However, regarding questions of law, an appellate court is obligated to reach a conclusion independent of determinations reached by the lower courts. State v. Hill, 254 Neb. 460, 577 N.W.2d 259 (1998).

III. FACTS

As the Daubmans were considering building a new home, they wished to explore the amount for which they could sell their current home. To that end, they contacted Engelbert, a real estate saleswoman working through CBS. Engelbert met with the Daubmans, and the Daubmans asked her to prepare a competitive market analysis on the property to determine its market value. Engelbert prepared the analysis and forwarded the results to the Daubmans.

Engelbert informed the Daubmans that she was working with Thomas and Brenda Pedersen, who were looking for a residence similar in features and price to the Daubman property. According to Allen Daubman, Engelbert also stated that the Pedersens "had been pre-approved for credit in an amount more than necessary to purchase [the] home." Engelbert also stated, according to Allen Daubman, that the Pedersens had sufficient financial ability to purchase the home and that financing would not be a problem; that the Pedersens were preapproved with a particular lender for a $180,000 loan. Engelbert contradicted Allen Daubman, testifying that she did not state that the Pedersens had been preapproved for a particular amount of credit. Rather,

Engelbert claims that she told the Daubmans not that the Pedersens were preapproved but that they were "qualified buyers, that [she] had been working with them, that . . . they had a savings plan, they had been paying off their debts, and they had the cash to close." Engelbert admitted telling the Daubmans that the Pedersens were capable of buying the home.

Engelbert offered to show the property to the Pedersens if the Daubmans signed a "one-party listing agreement" with CBS granting it an exclusive right to sell the property to the Pedersens only. The next day, the Daubmans signed the one-party listing agreement. Pursuant to this agreement, the Daubmans agreed to give CBS the sole and exclusive right to sell the property for $139,950 "cash or as terms agreed" to the Pedersens only, and to pay CBS a cash commission of 7 percent of the gross sales price. At the time the agreement was signed, the Daubmans notified Engelbert that they might be interested in leasing back the property or moving into an apartment, since they were contemplating building a new home, which would not be completed before the sale of their current property closed.

Engelbert showed the property to the Pedersens that same day, and later that day the Pedersens requested that Engelbert prepare an offer. Engelbert prepared an offer, which provided that the Pedersens would purchase the property for $132,000 and rent the property back to the Daubmans for a period of time. That evening, Engelbert presented the offer to the Daubmans.

Allen Daubman testified that upon receiving the offer, he told Engelbert that he was not interested, that he was very disappointed, and that he no longer wished to pursue the matter with the Pedersens. He further explained to Engelbert that he was concerned about the Pedersens' ability to obtain financing, based on the fact that their offer provided for a 95–percent loan. According to Allen Daubman, Engelbert was insistent on working something out and stated that the Pedersens' credit was "squeaky-clean." Engelbert denies using the term "squeaky-clean."

The Daubmans' plan to build a new home would require several financial obligations, including renting an apartment. Thus, if the Pedersens could not obtain a loan, the Daubmans could face the situation of not having their house sold but having to pay rent on an apartment and payments on a construction loan. To offset their risk, the Daubmans suggested to Engelbert that the Pedersens make a $5,000 nonrefundable earnest deposit. According to Allen Daubman, Engelbert recommended very strongly against such a proposal, saying that it was unnecessary, and reiterated that the Pedersens were financially strong, asserting that "they had been saving money in anticipation of buying a house; that they had cleaned up their bills; and that financing, again, should not be any problem whatsoever."

The following day, Allen Daubman prepared and faxed a counteroffer to CBS, specifying a purchase price of $139,900; an earnest deposit of $2,000; approval of financing in 30 days; closing within 30 days; and possession to be given the Pedersens at closing, all contingent upon the Pedersens being able to obtain financing of 95 percent of the purchase price at 8.5 percent for 30 years. The counteroffer would also allow the Daubmans to continue listing and showing the property for purposes of obtaining backup offers in the event the Pedersens were unable to obtain financing.

The next day, the Pedersens requested that CBS prepare another offer. The new offer provided that they would purchase the property for $139,900 with an earnest deposit of $2,000, conditional on their obtaining a conventional loan secured by a mortgage or deed of trust on the property in the sum of $132,900. The offer further provided that the Pedersens were to apply for financing within 5 business days of its acceptance and that if financing was not approved within 30 days of acceptance of the offer, the offer would be null and void, and the earnest deposit would be returned to the Pedersens. The offer further provided that if processing of the Pedersens' loan application was not completed within 30 days, the time limit would be automatically extended until the lending agency either approved or rejected the application. The transaction was to be closed on July 29, 1992, by an escrow agent and possession given to the Pedersens on July 30. The Daubmans accepted the offer on June 12, 1992, on the condition that the possession date be subject to the availability of a mover acceptable to them. The Pedersens accepted this condition.

The Pedersens met with Residential Mortgage Services on June 15, 1992, to apply for a loan, with Engelbert in attendance. At the appointment, Engelbert did not learn of any information that would jeopardize the Pedersens' loan application, and after the appointment, she communicated the information she learned to Allen Daubman. On June 25, the Daubmans entered into an agreement for the construction of a new home. On July 9, Residential Mortgage Services notified Engelbert that it probably would not be able to make a loan to the Pedersens and recommended that the loan application be moved to another lender.

After learning of the probable denial by Residential Mortgage Services, Engelbert contacted Capital Financial Services to determine whether it could approve a loan to the Pedersens on the terms contained in their purchase agreement. On July 10, 1992, Capital Financial Services informed Engelbert that it could probably make the loan and asked her to have the loan file transferred to it. On the same day, the loan file was moved from Residential Mortgage Services to Capital Financial Services, and the Pedersens made an appointment to meet with a Capital Financial Services representative on July 13. Engelbert testified that she personally gave the loan file to the representative.

After moving the loan file, Engelbert informed the Daubmans on July 10, 1992, of the transfer, that the chances for loan approval were good, and that she would know more on July 13. According to Allen Daubman, Engelbert told him on July 10 that she assisted the Pedersens in making a separate second loan application with a different lender on July 9. The Daubmans had not authorized CBS or Engelbert to seek alternative financing on behalf of the Pedersens in the event the first financial institution turned them down. Allen Daubman asked Engelbert why she moved the Pedersens over to a second lender without first calling him, and stated that the purchase agreement was now null and void because the Pedersens had not made the second loan application within the 5-day period. Engelbert told Allen Daubman that he was wrong and that

> as long as any loan application is pending, not just the first one, but any loan application is pending, when the 30–day time period under the purchase agreement hits, that I had no choice but to wait until whatever loan application was pending is either approved or rejected by that particular lender.

Allen Daubman was concerned that if he insisted the purchase agreement was void, he could face possible legal actions by the Pedersens and CBS. Engelbert testified that she now realized that Allen Daubman's interpretation of the purchase agreement was correct and that the rejection from Residential Mortgage Services rendered the purchase agreement null and void.

The Pedersens applied for a loan to Capital Financial Services on July 13, 1992. Also on that day, Allen Daubman requested that Engelbert ask the Pedersens if they would delay the closing and possession until the end of August. The Pedersens rejected this request. Allen Daubman then asked Engelbert to contact the Pedersens and ask them if they would agree to make the $2,000 deposit nonrefundable so that the Daubmans could sign a 6-month apartment lease at the Washington Heights apartment complex. The Pedersens rejected this request as well.

Engelbert and Allen Daubman met with a representative of Capital Financial Services on July 16, 1992, to discuss the Pedersens' loan prospects. On July 17, Allen Daubman faxed a letter to Engelbert informing her that in order to perform according to the purchase agreement and vacate the property at the end of July, the Daubmans needed to sign a 6-month apartment lease. However, because the Pedersens' loan had not yet been approved, the Daubmans were unwilling to sign the apartment lease. Thus, Allen Daubman suggested that the parties enter into an amendment whereby the Pedersens would make the $2,000 deposit nonrefundable and the Pedersens would be given an additional 2 weeks to obtain loan approval. According to Allen Daubman, before even discussing the proposal with the Pedersens, Engelbert told him that the proposed amendment would not be acceptable to the Pedersens. Engelbert denies that she prematurely told Allen Daubman that the Pedersens would deny the amendment. On July 18, the Pedersens rejected the amendment.

The Daubmans had located an apartment in the Washington Heights apartment complex, and the complex operator was willing to lease to them on a 6-month basis. The operator told the Daubmans that they eventually needed to sign the lease, but was not pressing them to do so. The Daubmans were trying to delay the signing as long as possible. When the Pedersens told Engelbert that they would not agree to the Daubmans' amendment, Brenda Pedersen also informed Engelbert that she had called the complex operator to check on the availability of apartments there. After speaking with the Pedersens, Engelbert called the complex operator to find out whether any apartments were available for lease, notwithstanding that the Daubmans had not authorized her to do so. According to Engelbert, "because Mrs. Pedersen had called, [the operator] was starting to put two and two together and asked me if it was about the Daubmans. And

I said yes." Engelbert then called the Daubmans on July 18, 1992, and informed them of the Pedersens' rejection of the amendment. Shortly after talking to Engelbert about the proposed amendment, the complex operator called the Daubmans and insisted that they sign the lease no later than the evening of July 27.

Shortly after the "apartment incident," Allen Daubman contacted a senior vice president of CBS, indicated that he no longer wished to work with Engelbert, and requested that another salesperson handle the matter. According to Allen Daubman, he also told the vice president during this conversation that he did not think it was appropriate that CBS receive a commission. The vice president denied that Daubman indicated at this time that he did not want to pay a commission.

Engelbert learned on July 21, 1992, from the vice president that Allen Daubman did not want her calling him. Engelbert called Capital Financial Services on July 20, 21, 22, and 23 and visited their office on July 24 to find out the status of the Pedersens' loan. She learned that Capital Financial Services had received mortgage approval that day and would be receiving formal loan approval on July 27. Engelbert prepared and faxed a letter to Allen Daubman that afternoon explaining this. On July 27, Engelbert learned that the Pedersens received formal loan approval and called Allen Daubman the same day to communicate this news to him.

On July 27, 1992, the Daubmans entered into a 6-month apartment lease. On July 30, Allen Daubman informed CBS that he did not want the escrow agent to pay CBS a commission and sent a letter to the escrow agent demanding that no moneys be withheld by it and paid to CBS for its services. The escrow agent informed Allen Daubman that it could not close the sale unless either the Daubmans agreed to allow it to deduct the commission or CBS agreed to forfeit its commission. Neither the Daubmans nor CBS would so agree. CBS' vice president told Allen Daubman that the commission had to be paid out of the closing, despite the fact that neither the listing agreement nor the purchase agreement so provided.

An employee of the escrow agent testified that in the event of a commission dispute, either the parties have to resolve the problem or the real estate agent has to give authorization to close without withholding the commission. According to this witness, "I can't go on what a seller is telling me until I get authorization from the [real estate] company to not charge a commission or whatever."

On July 31, 1992, Allen Daubman faxed an agreement to the CBS vice president informing him that the Daubmans would allow the sale to be closed and the commission to be paid out of the proceeds of the sale of the house if CBS agreed that such payment would be without prejudice to any claim the Daubmans might have over whether the commission was payable under the circumstances. The vice president agreed, and Allen Daubman then instructed the escrow agent to close the sale.

CBS received a commission of $9,793 on August 3, 1992, and the parties stipulated that the Daubmans had suffered no damages, special or general. Finding that Engelbert and, through her, CBS had breached the fiduciary duties they owed the Daubmans, the district court awarded the Daubmans the amount of the commission, together with prejudgment interest from and after July 31, 1992, and costs.

IV. ANALYSIS

1. PETITION FOR FURTHER REVIEW

We begin our analysis by focusing on the issues raised by the Daubmans' petition for further review. In considering whether the evidence supports the district court's finding that Engelbert and CBS breached their fiduciary duties to the Daubmans and whether such breach justifies a forfeiture of their commission, we recall that generally, an agent is required to act solely for the benefit of the principal in all matters connected with the agency and adhere faithfully to the instructions of the principal. Fletcher v. Mathew, 233 Neb. 853, 448 N.W.2d 576 (1989); Walker Land & Cattle Co. v. Daub, 223 Neb. 343, 389 N.W.2d 560 (1986); Allied Securities, Inc. v. Clocker, 185 Neb. 524, 176 N.W.2d 914 (1970). An agent and principal are in a fiduciary relationship such that the agent has an obligation to refrain from doing any harmful act to the principal. *Fletcher*, supra; Grone v. Lincoln Mut. Life Ins. Co., 230 Neb. 144, 430 N.W.2d 507 (1988).

More specifically, a real estate agent owes the principal a fiduciary duty to use reasonable care, skill, and diligence in performing her or his obligations and to act honestly and in good faith. Barta v. Kindschuh, 246 Neb. 208, 518 N.W.2d 98 (1994). The rule requiring an agent to act with utmost good faith toward the principal places the agent under a legal obligation to make a full, fair, and prompt disclosure to the principal of all facts within the agent's knowledge which are or may be material to the matter in connection with which the agent is employed, which might affect the principal's rights and interests or influence the principal's action in relation to the subject matter of the employment, or which in any way pertain to the discharge of the agency which the agent has undertaken. Brezina v. Hill, 202 Neb. 773, 277 N.W.2d 224 (1979). In a number of instances, we have held that a real estate agent's breach of duty prevented the collection of a commission. E.g., Elson v. Pool, 235 Neb. 469, 455 N.W.2d 783 (1990) (agent forged principal's signature); Firmature v. Brannon, 223 Neb. 123, 388 N.W.2d 119 (1986) (agent denigrated property); *Brezina*, supra (to protect buyer, agent signed and filed purchase agreement in violation of selling principal's wishes); Vogt v. Town & Country Realty of Lincoln, Inc., 194 Neb. 308, 231 N.W.2d 496 (1975) (agent had undisclosed interest in purchase); *Allied Securities, Inc.*, supra (agent had undisclosed interest in purchase); Schepers v. Lautenschlager, 173 Neb. 107, 112 N.W.2d 767 (1962) (agent had undisclosed interest in purchase and failed to inform principal of prospective purchaser willing to pay more than sale price); Pearlman v. Snitzer, 112 Neb. 135, 198 N.W. 879 (1924) (agent failed to declare he already had buyer at price above which agent was to recover commission); Campbell v. Baxter, 41 Neb. 729, 60 N.W. 90 (1894) (agent received commission from both buyer and seller); Jansen v. Williams, 36 Neb. 869, 55 N.W. 279 (1893) (agent interfered with principal's right of direct sale).

The district court based its legal conclusion that Engelbert placed her interests and those of the Pedersens above those of the Daubmans upon the following specific findings of fact:

[E]very effort was made by . . . Engelbert to consummate sale of the premises with the Pedersens only. When the Pedersens' financial condition was shown to be precarious . . . Engelbert took several steps to keep the transaction alive for the Pedersens, and, more to the point, even when events became detrimental to the [Daubmans]. As the series of events became more convoluted and the [Daubmans] made arrangements to enter into a six-month lease of an apartment during construction of their new home . . . Engelbert on her own initiative contacted their lessor to ascertain for herself whether the Daubmans could continue to lease the property if there was a delay in the closing of the sale of [the] Daubmans' home. This "end run" is the most glaring example of the extent to which . . . Engelbert put her own interests and the interests of the Pedersens ahead of the [Daubmans']. More damaging was the fact that closing of the sale of the Daubman home was contingent upon payment of Engelbert's and CBS' commission.

Since the listing agreement restricted Engelbert to selling only to the Pedersens, the fact that that was her sole effort could not have constituted a breach of her duty to the Daubmans. Moreover, while Engelbert and CBS refused to voluntarily forfeit their commission, it was the escrow agent that refused to close the transaction unless either the commission was voluntarily forfeited by Engelbert and CBS or the Daubmans allowed it to be paid. Thus, neither does this occurrence support the district court's legal conclusion.

However, Engelbert's effort with regard to the Pedersens' loan applications is another matter. Because it was not until July 13, 1992, that the Pedersens met with Capital Financial Services and because Engelbert took the position that the Daubmans had no choice but to wait and see whether Capital Financial Services approved or rejected the Pedersens' loan application, the Daubmans faced a considerable time problem. The purchase agreement provided that the Pedersens would take possession on July 30. Thus, the Daubmans would need to rent an apartment in order to vacate by that date. Residential Mortgage Services took 24 days on the Pedersens' loan application, and there was no way of telling exactly how long Capital Financial Services would take to either approve or reject the Pedersens' application. Moreover, as part of her effort to complete the sale no matter what the effect on the Daubmans, Engelbert, without the Daubmans' knowledge, contacted the operator of the apartment complex to check on the availability of apartments and confirmed to the operator that her inquiry concerned the Daubmans, with the result that the Daubmans were pressured into executing a lease by July 27. Although Engelbert was authorized to sell only to the Pedersens, she should not have continued to push the sale when the situation began to look detrimental to the interests of the Daubmans.

In addition, it must be remembered that although Engelbert claimed she stated only that the Pedersens were prequalified, Allen Daubman testified that Engelbert erroneously told them that the Pedersens had been preapproved with a particular lender for a $180,000 loan, enough to buy their home. While the district court made no specific finding with regard to this issue, the rule that in a bench trial, the trial court's entry of judgment in favor of a party warrants the conclusion that the trial court found in that party's favor on all issuable facts requires that we conclude the district court resolved this issue in favor of the Daubmans. See, Peterson v. Kellner, 245 Neb. 515, 513 N.W.2d 517 (1994); Burgess v. Curly Olney's, Inc., 198 Neb. 153, 251 N.W.2d 888 (1977). (This rule is not made inapplicable merely because in addition to a general finding, the trial court also mentioned certain matters specifically. *Burgess*, supra.)

The district court's factual findings with regard to Engelbert's treatment of the Pedersens' loan applications, her contact with the apartment complex operator, and her representation as to the preapproval of the Pedersens for a loan support the district court's legal conclusion that Engelbert and, through her, CBS put their interests in completing the sale, and thereby collecting the commission, and the interests of the Pedersens in acquiring the property ahead of the Daubmans' interests in selling the property in a manner and under a time schedule which least inconvenienced them. All of Engelbert's actions taken together support the district court's legal conclusion that she and, through her, CBS materially breached the duties they, as agents, owed their principals, the Daubmans.

2. CLAIMS ON APPEAL

Having so determined, we turn our attention to the errors on appeal claimed by CBS and Engelbert.

(a) Breach of Duties

The claim that the district court erred in concluding that CBS and Engelbert breached their fiduciary duties has been resolved in considering the Daubmans' petition for further review and requires no further analysis.

(b) Acceptance of Actions

Next, CBS and Engelbert argue that the Daubmans ratified or otherwise acquiesced in their actions. On the other hand, the Daubmans contend that they timely disavowed CBS' and Engelbert's actions. However, ratification and acquiescence are concepts involved in determining whether an agent's actions may bind the principal or whether the agent is liable to the principal for damages resulting from an alleged breach of duty. CBS and Engelbert point out that "[t]he effect of acquiescence or ratification by the principal is that the agent is released from liability to the principal for its losses." Brief for appellants at 32. See Barta v. Kindschuh, 246 Neb. 208, 518 N.W.2d 98 (1994). However, this theory has no application in the instant case, and the district court did not err in failing to find that the Daubmans ratified or acquiesced in the actions of CBS and Engelbert.

(c) Damages

Next, CBS and Engelbert allege that the district court erred in finding that the Daubmans sustained damages, as the parties stipulated otherwise. However, the issue of damages is not relevant when determining whether an agent's breach of duty results in a loss of commission.

A commission for services cannot be collected by the agent if the agent has willfully disregarded, in a material respect, an obligation which the law devolves upon the agent by reason of the agency. Elson v. Pool, 235 Neb. 469, 455 N.W.2d 783 (1990); Walker Land & Cattle Co. v. Daub, 223 Neb. 343, 389 N.W.2d 560 (1986); Vogt v. Town & Country Realty of Lincoln, Inc., 194 Neb. 308, 231 N.W.2d 496 (1975). A principal whose agent has violated her or his duties may properly refuse to pay compensation. *Walker Land & Cattle Co.*, supra; Allied Securities, Inc. v. Clocker, 185 Neb. 524, 176 N.W.2d 914 (1970); Restatement (Second) of Agency § 399 (1958).

. . .

V. JUDGMENT

For the foregoing reasons, we reverse the judgment of the Court of Appeals and remand the cause thereto with the direction that it affirm the judgment of the district court, modified in accordance with this opinion.

REVERSED AND REMANDED WITH DIRECTION.

WRIGHT, J., not participating.

Hoffman v. Connall

Supreme Court of Washington, 1987.
108 Wash.2d 69, 736 P.2d 242.

ANDERSEN, JUSTICE.

FACTS OF CASE

At issue in this case is whether a real estate broker[1] is liable for innocently misrepresenting a material fact about real estate to a buyer.

In January 1983, Bryan G. and Connie J. Connall, hereinafter referred to as the sellers, signed a listing agreement with Cardinal Realty, Inc. and Charles Huggins, an associate broker with Cardinal Realty. The sellers wanted to sell 5 acres of land north of Spokane. A few days after signing the listing agreement, one of the sellers showed the property to the Cardinal broker. The seller pointed to a stake or piece of pipe as the southeast corner of the property, and the broker saw that the stake lined up with an old fence line to apparently form the east boundary. The sellers had built a new fence approximately 6 inside the old fence line and a corral and horse shed stood just inside the new fence. The seller insisted that his corral was inside the property line.

The seller then showed the broker a wooden stake, which he said marked the southwest corner of the property. The broker saw that the stake was in line with a row of poplar trees that evidently formed the west boundary. To the north of the trees was a pole that apparently was near the northwest corner. The seller could not find the stake marking the northwest corner of the property, and the two men felt they were close to but could not exactly locate the northeast boundary.

The broker later stated that the seller "was very emphatic about what he bought and where he built", and never gave the broker any indication that the boundaries he pointed out were incorrect. The seller

---

[1]   As have the parties, we use the term "broker" herein to include real estate agents and salespeople.

told the broker that the property had been surveyed before he and his wife bought it. The broker did not verify that statement.

James and Verna Hoffman, the buyers herein, read about the property in the newspaper. The property's improvements—corral, cattle chute, barn and shed—were important to the buyers because they owned a horse and wanted to get involved with 4–H horse activities. They called the broker and visited the property with him. He pointed out the fence as the east boundary, and the pole as the northwest boundary. He gave an approximate indication of the northeast corner but could not find the marker for the southwest corner. The broker later testified that in telling the buyers about the property, "there was no doubt in my mind of where the proper property line was". The broker did not recommend that the buyers obtain a survey.

The buyers bought the property on February 28, 1983. In May 1983 a neighbor told them that a recent survey showed that their east fence encroached upon his property. The buyers had their own survey done and discovered that their east-side improvements encroached upon their neighbor's property by 18 to 21 feet. The encroachment consisted of the fence built by the sellers and part of the corral, cattle run and horse shed. The buyers discovered it would cost almost $6,000 to move the improvements onto their own property.

On September 18, 1984, the buyers brought an action for damages against the sellers and the broker, alleging that they misrepresented the true boundary lines. Following a bench trial, the trial court found as a fact that there was nothing to give the broker or the sellers notice that anything was wrong with the property lines. The court concluded that the broker did not breach the standard of care of a reasonably prudent real estate broker, and that the sellers were not liable since they were unaware of any problem with the boundaries as represented. A judgment of dismissal was thereupon entered against the buyers.

The Court of Appeals reversed, holding that an owner of realty who innocently misrepresents its boundaries is liable to the purchaser. The court then extended liability for innocent misrepresentation to an owner's real estate agent and, in the alternative, held that the broker breached his duty to take reasonable steps to avoid disseminating false information to buyers. The seller did not appeal the Court of Appeals decision. Thus, the question of the *owner's* liability is not before this court. The broker and the real estate company sought review of the Court of Appeals decision and we granted review pursuant to RAP 13.4(b).

Two principal issues are presented.

ISSUES

ISSUE ONE. Should a real estate broker be held liable for innocently misrepresenting a material fact to a buyer of real property?

ISSUE TWO. Was the broker negligent in failing to verify the sellers' statements concerning the property's boundaries?

DECISION

ISSUE ONE.

CONCLUSION. A real estate broker is held to a standard of reasonable care and is liable for making "negligent", though not "innocent", misrepresentations concerning boundaries to a buyer.

The Restatement (Second) of Torts defines the tort of innocent misrepresentation as follows:

Misrepresentation in Sale, Rental or Exchange Transaction

(1) One who, in a sale, rental or exchange transaction with another, makes a misrepresentation of a material fact for the purpose of inducing the other to act or to refrain from acting in reliance upon it, is subject to liability to the other for pecuniary loss caused to him by his justifiable reliance upon the misrepresentation, even though it is not made fraudulently or negligently.

Restatement (Second) of Torts § 552C(1) (1977).

The Restatement, however, leaves open the question of whether such a cause of action lies against real estate brokers. While the Court of Appeals in *Hoffman* was the first Washington court to apply § 552C to brokers, prior established Washington case law recognizes a cause of action against *owners* who innocently misrepresent the boundaries of their property to a purchaser. Owners are liable for such misrepresentations because they are presumed to know the character and attributes of the land which they convey.

We recognize that some jurisdictions have agreed with the viewpoint of the Court of Appeals in this case and have held real estate brokers liable for making innocent misrepresentations on which buyers justifiably rely.[7] Courts that so hold do so because of their belief that the innocent buyer's reliance tips the balance of equity in favor of the buyer's protection. The courts justify placing the loss on the innocent broker on the basis that the broker is in a better position to determine the truth of his or her representations.

This approach has been criticized for imposing a standard of strict liability for all misrepresentations that a broker might make or communicate, however innocent, in a real estate transaction.[9] Another commentator observes the obvious—that there is a problem with subjecting brokers to liability for innocent misrepresentations without imposing a corresponding duty of inspection for defects, and that without such a duty, a broker may be tempted to provide less information to a buyer, fearing that his or her chances of exposure to liability for innocent misrepresentations will multiply with the quantity of information provided.

At the other end of the spectrum from liability for innocent misrepresentation is the view that a real estate broker is an agent of the seller, not of the buyer, and is protected from liability under agency law. Thus, an agent would be permitted to repeat misinformation from

---

[7] Note, Realtor Liability for Innocent Misrepresentation and Undiscovered Defects: Balancing the Equities Between Broker and Buyer, 20 Val.U.L.Rev. 255, 260 (1986).

[9] Fossey & Roston, The Broker's Liability in a Real Estate Transaction: Bad News and Good News for Defense Attorneys, 12 U.C.L.A.—Alaska L.Rev. 37, 40 (1982–1983) * * *

his principal without fear of liability unless the agent knows or has reason to know of its falsity. This principle has been upheld by approximately half the jurisdictions that have addressed the issue of broker liability for innocent misrepresentations. The Supreme Court of Vermont recently reaffirmed this rule, holding that "[r]eal estate brokers and agents are marketing agents, not structural engineers or contractors. They have no duty to verify independently representations made by a seller unless they are aware of facts that 'tend to indicate that such representation[s are] false.' "[14]

A recent decision of our Court of Appeals declared a middle ground that we find persuasive. At issue in Tennant v. Lawton, 26 Wash.App.701, 615 P.2d 1305 (1980) was a broker's liability for misrepresenting that a parcel of land could support a sewage system and thus was "buildable". The *Tennant* court echoed the Vermont court in holding that a broker is negligent if he or she repeats material representations made by the seller and knows, or reasonably should know, of their falsity. The court went on, however, to hold that a broker has a limited duty toward a purchaser of real property.

> The underlying rationale of [a broker's] duty to a buyer who is not his client is that he is a professional who is in a unique position to verify critical information given him by the seller. His duty is to take reasonable steps to avoid disseminating to the buyer false information. The broker is required to employ a reasonable degree of effort and professional expertise to confirm or refute information from the seller which he knows, or should know, is pivotal to the transaction from the buyer's perspective.

(Citations omitted.) *Tennant*, at 706, 615 P.2d 1305; *see also* McRae v. Bolstad, 32 Wash.App.173, 646 P.2d 771 (1982); *aff'd*, 101 Wash.2d 161, 676 P.2d 496 (1984).

We perceive no persuasive reason to hold real estate brokers to a higher standard of care than other professionals must satisfy. We have held that lawyers must demonstrate " 'that degree of care, skill, diligence and knowledge commonly possessed and exercised by a reasonable, careful and prudent lawyer in the practice of law in this jurisdiction.' " Chiropractors and other drugless healers owe their patients a duty to exercise reasonable care in diagnosing and treating them. RCW 7.70.040(1) requires physicians and surgeons to adhere to a standard of reasonable prudence.

Of relevance in this connection is RCW 18.85.230(5), which provides that a real estate license may be suspended or revoked if the holder is found guilty of

> *[k]nowingly committing*, or being a party to, any material fraud, misrepresentation, concealment, conspiracy, collusion, trick, scheme or device whereby any other person lawfully relies upon the word, representation or conduct of the licensee;
> . . .

---

[14] Provost v. Miller, 144 Vt. 67, 69–70, 473 A.2d 1162 (1984), quoting Lyons v. Christ Episcopal Church, 71 Ill.App.3d 257, 259–60, 27 Ill.Dec. 559, 561, 389 N.E.2d 623, 625 (1979).

(Italics ours.) Under this statute, a broker is only guilty of *knowingly committing* a misrepresentation. Consistent with this reading is one that would similarly find liability only when a broker is a *knowing party* to a misrepresentation.

Absent a legislative directive to the contrary, we do not consider it appropriate to impose liability on a real estate broker without a similar requirement of knowledge. Knowledge, or any reasonable notice, that the boundaries pointed out by the seller were incorrect is absent in this case, as the trial court found in its findings of fact. The following findings by the trial court are illustrative:

> There was no evidence on the property which suggested to [the broker] he should investigate the boundary lines further.

> There was nothing in the surrounding circumstances that would have put [the broker] . . . on notice that there may have been something wrong with the property lines.

This broker was thus not the guarantor of the seller's representations. If the buyers had wanted full protection against potential defects or misrepresentations, they could have purchased appropriate title insurance. . . .

While a broker must be alert to potential misrepresentations made by a seller, we decline to hold that a broker must guarantee every statement made by the seller. Nor, however, can a broker relay false information to a buyer without fear of liability. The trial court did not err in concluding as follows:

> A real estate broker must take reasonable steps to avoid disseminating false information to buyers. The broker is required to make reasonable efforts and use his [or her] professional expertise to confirm or refute information from a seller which he [or she] knows is pivotal to the buyer.

A real estate broker must exercise the degree of care that a reasonably prudent broker would use under all of the circumstances.

In short, a real estate broker must act as a professional, and will be held to a standard of reasonable care. If a broker willfully or negligently conveys false information about real estate to a buyer, the broker is liable therefor. We decline, however, to turn this professional into a guarantor. Real estate agents and brokers are not liable for innocently and nonnegligently conveying a seller's misrepresentations to a buyer.

ISSUE TWO.

CONCLUSION. The broker did not breach the standard of care of a reasonably prudent broker.

In *Tennant*, the court found that the real estate broker failed to exercise due care to verify the "critical contingency" of an approved septic tank site on the property. When the broker asked the owner for evidence of an approved percolation site evaluation for the property, the owner produced two applications for perc hole permits and asked the broker to see if they had expired. The broker reported that the applications had expired and promised to renew them. The applications stated on their face that they were for adjoining 2½–acre parcels rather than the 6–acre parcel at issue. The broker neglected to read them, to renew them, or even to check on the site evaluation, even though the buyers had made an approved septic tank site an express condition of their offer. While the broker in *Tennant* acted without malice or fraudulent intent,

> she failed to take the simple steps within her area of expertise and responsibility which would have disclosed the absence of any health district approved site on the subject property. This failure constituted negligence as a matter of law which resulted in damages to the Tennants.

Tennant, at 707–08, 615 P.2d 1305.

In the present case, the improvements on the property were important to the buyers because they wanted to raise and ride horses. The broker saw markers for some of the boundaries when he walked the property with the seller, but could not locate all of the boundaries with certainty. Trees and other physical features on the land supported the sellers' representations regarding the boundaries, however, and the broker testified that the seller assured him that the improvements were inside the property line. The trial court accepted this testimony, as it was entitled to do as the fact finder in a bench trial, and expressly found that "there was absolutely nothing, I think, that would have put [the broker] . . . on notice that there may have been something wrong with the property line that imposed a duty to . . . do anything further than [he] did do in this case."

The trial court is sustainable in its view that, contrary to the broker in *Tennant,* the broker in this case had no notice that anything was wrong with the boundaries as represented by the sellers. While hindsight suggests that the broker would have done well to check on the alleged survey, there was no testimony that such a check was the prevailing practice in the real estate business. Moreover, natural and man-made boundaries reinforced the sellers' representations concerning the legal boundaries. Accordingly, the trial court did not err in finding and concluding that the broker in this case was not negligent.

Our resolution of these issues disposes of the other issues raised. The Court of Appeals decision overturning the trial court's decision on the broker's liability is incorrect.

Reversed.

PEARSON, C.J., and UTTER, BRACHTENBACH, CALLOW, DURHAM, JJ., and CUNNINGHAM, J. Pro Tem., concur.

DORE, JUSTICE (dissenting).

Contrary to the majority, I believe that a broker should be liable for any material misrepresentation he or she makes which induces buyers to act to their detriment. Furthermore, even applying the majority's far more lax standard of care, I would find the broker liable in this case. Therefore, I dissent.

LIABILITY FOR "INNOCENT" MISREPRESENTATIONS

Brokers possess more knowledge than buyers about the attributes of the property to be sold, and innocent buyers should be able to rely on representations made by the broker. I would follow the increasing trend of state courts to impose liability on real estate brokers for any kind of misrepresentation. . . .

In this case, both the majority and I conclude that the broker made a material misrepresentation which induced the Hoffmans to purchase the land, and that as a result, the Hoffmans incurred significant damages. The broker represented the property line to be located some 20 feet from where it actually was; consequently the corral, cattle run and horse shed all had to be moved so as not to encroach on their neighbor's land. Even if the majority is correct and this misrepresentation was innocently, and not negligently, made—a conclusion I dispute—I would still hold the broker liable. Between innocent purchasers, who may justifiably rely on the broker's knowledge and expertise, and a broker, who is in a far better position to check the accuracy of any purported boundary lines, I believe the broker should be liable for any misrepresentation as to the boundary's location. Equity demands such a result.

THE TENNANT APPROACH

The majority cites Tennant v. Lawton, 26 Wash.App.701, 615 P.2d 1305 (1980) for the proposition that the rule of law should be "that the broker is liable because of material representations of the principal if he repeats them and knows, or reasonably should know, of their falsity." *Tennant*, at 706, 615 P.2d 1305. While I note in passing that this decision is in conflict with our earlier decision in Lawson v. Vernon, [38 Wash. 422, 80 P. 559 (1905),] I believe that even following the rule set forth in *Tennant*, the broker in this case should still be liable.

The broker in this case testified that Mr. Connall was emphatic about the boundary of his property and that an earlier survey had indicated that his property ended just to the east of where he built his fence. Report of Proceedings, at 167–68. Nevertheless, an expert witness testified that any such survey would be a public record, and that no survey had been made of this property. Report of Proceedings, at 25. While under the standard of care propounded by the majority, a reasonably prudent broker would not be required to verify the accuracy of Connall's comments by a detailed investigation of the survey that Connall believed had been completed, the broker should at least verify the existence of the survey. This he did not do, and this failure, even under the majority's standard of care, was a breach of the duty "to take reasonable steps to avoid disseminating to the buyer false information." *Tennant*, at 706, 615 P.2d 1305. Thus, even under the majority's more lax standard of care, the broker was negligent, and therefore, liable for the damages to the Hoffmans.

GOODLOE, J., concurs.

NOTES

1. *Daubman v. CBS Real Estate*. What did Englebert do wrong? How were the Daubmans injured by Englebert's actions? Would other sellers have objected to Englebert's efforts? How do her actions compare to the behavior described in the court's parentheticals which it cites in section IV.1. of the opinion? Was the type of listing agreement signed by the parties in *Daubman* relevant in assessing the broker's liability? Does the "fiduciary" label/model make sense in the real estate agent context? See Real Estate Brokers Are Not "Fiduciaries": A Call for Developing A New Legal Framework, 40 Real Estate L.J. 376 (2011)

The usual remedy for breach of fiduciary duty is to deprive the broker of the entire sales commission, ostensibly as a penalty to deter serious breaches of trust. Would it make more sense in borderline cases like *Daubman* to limit the seller to damages suffered from the breach? Compare Cogan v. Kidder, Mathews & Segner, Inc., 97 Wash.2d 658, 648 P.2d 875 (1982), in which the broker's failure to inform the seller that, acting as a dual agent, it also represented the buyer, was held to bar the broker from recovering the agreed-upon $19,000 commission, even though the nondisclosure caused the seller at most $660 damages.

2.   *Self-Dealing.* The rules on broker self-dealing are fairly clear. A broker cannot, without the seller's informed consent, purchase the property himself, split a commission, or take a rebate from buyer or buyer's broker. See, e.g., Kirkruff v. Wisegarver, 297 Ill.App.3d 826, 231 Ill.Dec. 852, 697 N.E.2d 406 (1998); but see Dubbs v. Stribling & Assocs., 96 N.Y.2d 337, 728 N.Y.S.2d 413, 752 N.E.2d 850 (2001) (finding no breach since broker did not buy next door property that client had sought until after agency relationship had ended). Litigation frequently centers on the broker's duty of disclosure when he has some pre-existing business or family relationship with the buyer. The general rule is to require full disclosure, even if the broker does not stand to profit from the relationship, and even if disclosure would not alter the seller's decision to list or sell. See, e.g., Thompson v. Hoagland, 100 N.J.Super. 478, 242 A.2d 642 (App.Div.1968).

But the conflict between the broker's and the client's interests may be more subtle than a blatant case of self-dealing. Consider the abstract from a paper by Steven D. Levitt and Chad Syverson:

> Agents are often better informed than the clients who hire them and may exploit this informational advantage. Real-estate agents, who know much more about the housing market than the typical homeowner, are one example. Because real estate agents receive only a small share of the incremental profit when a house sells for a higher value, there is an incentive for them to convince their clients to sell their houses too cheaply and too quickly. We test these predictions by comparing home sales in which real estate agents are hired by others to sell a home to instances in which a real estate agent sells his or her own home. In the former case, the agent has distorted incentives; in the latter case, the agent wants to pursue the first-best. Consistent with the theory, we find homes owned by real estate agents sell for about 3.7 percent more than other houses and stay on the market about 9.5 days longer, even after controlling for a wide range of housing characteristics. Situations in which the agent's informational advantage is larger lead to even greater distortions.

Levitt & Syverson, Market Distortions When Agents Are Better Informed: The Value of Information in Real Estate, National Bureau of Economic Research, Working Paper No. 11053 (Jan. 2005), http://www.nber.org/papers/w11053. See also Nanda & Pancak, Real Estate Brokers' Duties to Their Clients: Why Some States Mandate Minimum Service Requirements, 12 Cityscape 105 (2010).

3.   *Broker as "Middleman."* The broker who functions only as an intermediary—bringing the parties together, but without discretion to negotiate terms or perform other services—can act for both the buyer and seller without being held to a fiduciary duty to either. According to one landmark case, "If A. is employed by B. to find him a purchaser for his house upon terms and conditions to be determined by B. when he meets the purchaser, I can see nothing improper or inconsistent with any duty he owes B. for A. to accept an employment from C. to find one who will sell his house to C. upon terms which they may agree upon when they meet." Knauss v. Gottfried Krueger Brewing Co., 142 N.Y. 70, 75, 36 N.E. 867, 868 (1894). See also Wardley Corp. v. Welsh, 962 P.2d 86 (Utah App.1998). Was a middleman defense available under the facts of *Daubman?*

4. *Cooperating Brokers and Misled Buyers.* As Professor Grohman's article indicates, traditional doctrine which holds a selling broker to be the subagent of the listing broker, owing a fiduciary duty only to the seller, contradicts the expectations of typical buyers and sellers. According to the F.T.C. Staff Report described at page 32 above, "where two brokers were involved, 74 percent of the sellers and 71 percent of the buyers believed the cooperating broker (the broker working directly with the buyer) was, in some sense, 'representing' the buyer." Staff Report, page 22.

The rule treating the selling broker as the listing broker's subagent was affirmed in Stortroen v. Beneficial Finance Co. of Colorado, 736 P.2d 391 (Colo.1987). The court there rejected seller's claim that the selling broker was buyer's agent, and held that a notice of acceptance of the sales contract given by buyer to the broker bound the seller. The court stated that a contrary rule would open the door to finding that the broker was the dual agent of both parties, with the complications that such arrangements create. Moreover, the court ruled that the buyer could lose rights against the seller based on the broker's misrepresentations if the broker was no longer considered to be the seller's agent. The facts of the case were unusual in that it was the seller, not the buyer, who sought to treat the selling broker as the buyer's agent.

A few courts have rejected the general rule. The Alabama Supreme Court took this innovative approach in Cashion v. Ahmadi, 345 So.2d 268 (Ala.1977), where the buyer, on discovering a periodic water problem in the basement, abandoned the house and sued the seller and the two real estate firms that had brokered the transaction, claiming that all had known of the defect. Affirming the lower court judgment for the seller and the listing broker on strict *caveat emptor* grounds, the court reversed the judgment for the cooperating broker, holding that, as to him, a jury could find an agency relationship with the buyer and, consequently, a duty to disclose knowledge of the defect. Among the facts to be considered on remand were whether the broker's statements indicated a belief that he was primarily representing buyer or seller. For a thoughtful comment on *Cashion,* see Payne, Broker's Liability for Nondisclosure of Known Defects in Sale Property—Caveat Emptor Still Applies, 6 Real Est. L.J. 341 (1978).

In addition to the alternatives suggested in the Grohman excerpt, some states have passed legislation or implemented regulations requiring brokers to submit a disclosure statement to the parties indicating whether the broker will function as the agent of buyer or seller. See, e.g., N.Y. Real Prop. Law § 443. Cashion v. Ahmadi was pre-empted by a similar statute. Ala. Code §§ 34–27–80 through –88. Will such disclosure be adequate to protect buyers?

For an excellent and comprehensive treatment of the subject, see Brown, Grohman, and Valcarcel, Real Estate Brokerage: Recent Changes in Relationships and a Proposed Cure, 29 Creighton L. Rev. 25 (1995). See generally, Wilson, Nonagent Brokerage: Real Estate Agents Missing in Action, 52 Okla. L. Rev. 85 (1999); Wolf & Jennings, Seller/Broker Liability In Multiple Listing Service Real Estate Sales: A Case For Uniform Disclosure, 20 Real Est.L.J. 22 (1991).

5. *Does Buyer Have Any Rights Against a Broker?* Courts generally hold that, whether or not there is a Multiple Listing Service arrangement, the listing broker owes no fiduciary duty to the buyer. See, e.g., Richard Brown Auction & Real Estate, Inc. v. Brown, 583 So.2d 1313 (Ala.1991) (no duty to disclose title defects); Andrie v. Chrystal-Anderson & Associates Realtors, Inc., 187 Mich.App. 333, 466 N.W.2d 393 (1991), appeal denied, 439 Mich. 903, 478 N.W.2d 652 (1991) (no duty to convey buyer's offer to seller). Many of the cases where the buyer seeks to hold the broker liable involve defects in the property.

Despite the general rule, courts have found liability by the listing broker to the buyer on various theories. One approach is to find that an agency relationship did exist between the broker and the buyer, creating a fiduciary relationship. See, e.g., Lewis v. Long & Foster Real Estate, Inc., 85 Md.App. 754, 584 A.2d 1325, cert. denied, 323 Md. 34, 591 A.2d 250 (1991) (question for jury whether agency relationship arose between buyer and broker).

Even where the broker is not found to be the buyer's agent, the broker may become liable to buyer under other theories. Under fraud doctrine, a broker will be liable to a buyer for concealment of material information, see, e.g., Roberts v. Estate of Barbagallo, 366 Pa.Super. 559, 531 A.2d 1125 (1987) (presence of hazardous urea formaldehyde foam insulation concealed by broker), or failure to disclose known information materially affecting the property which could not be discovered with ordinary diligence, see, e.g., Gray v. Boyle Investment Co., 803 S.W.2d 678 (Tenn.App.1990) (failure to disclose that property was undergoing foreclosure and only notice was published in trade papers which buyer is not expected to read). Legislation in California requires brokers involved in residential sales to "conduct a reasonably competent and diligent visual inspection" and to disclose to the buyer facts uncovered by the investigation which materially affect the "value or desirability of the property." Cal.Civ. Code § 2079(a). Under this rule, brokers have been held liable for failure to disclose that to buyer that existing liens against the property were so significant that the seller would not be able to perform unless the lender agreed to a short sale of the buyer placed significant sums in escrow to clear the title. Holmes v. Summer, 188 Cal.App.4th 1510, 116 Cal.Rptr.3d 419 (2010). Ariz. Admin. Code 124–28–1101(A) requires seller's broker to "deal fairly with all parties to a transaction," which is a more limited duty than the full disclosure owed to the seller. The broker, however, will be liable to the buyer for failure to disclose known defects. See Aranki v. RKP Investments, Inc., 194 Ariz. 206, 979 P.2d 534 (App.1999).

Other theories are available to the buyer who is unable to meet the requirements of common law fraud. One theory is to impose a constructive trust for buyer's benefit on any gains from broker self-dealing. See, for example, Harper v. Adametz, 142 Conn. 218, 113 A.2d 136 (1955). Another is to imply a private right of action for damages against a broker violating the disclosure and self-dealing provisions of the state broker licensing statute. See Sawyer Realty Group, Inc. v. Jarvis Corp., 89 Ill.2d 379, 59 Ill.Dec. 905, 432 N.E.2d 849 (1982). At least one court has found the broker liable to buyers under "a general duty not to negligently cause them harm." Gerard v. Peterson, 448 N.W.2d 699, 702 (Iowa App.1989) (broker responded to buyers' question by stating that a mortgage contingency clause was not necessary in sales contract). After a deal has collapsed, a buyer may recover any earnest money held by the broker. See, e.g., Mader v. James, 546 P.2d 190 (Wyo.1976).

Additionally, where the broker serves as the agent of both buyer and seller, the broker will be liable to the buyer for failure to disclose defects. See, e.g., Assilzadeh v. California Fed. Bank, 82 Cal.App.4th 399, 98 Cal.Rptr.2d 176 (2000) (broker fulfilled obligation by disclosing existence of construction defect lawsuit).

Hoffman v. Connall addresses the difficult problem of innocent misrepresentations by the broker. While courts agree that a knowing misrepresentation subjects a broker to liability, they differ on innocent misrepresentations. Did the *Hoffman* court strike the right balance? Will buyer be adequately compensated? Will such misrepresentations be more or less likely to occur if a court were to choose a different rule? How does the court view the role of the broker in a real estate transaction?

In addition to the articles cited in *Hoffman*, see generally Brown & Thurlow, Buyers Beware: Statutes Shield Real Estate Brokers and Sellers Who Do Not Disclose That Properties are Psychologically Tainted, 49 Okla. L. Rev. 625 (1996); Fain, An Overview of Real Estate Agent or Broker Liability, 23 Real Est.L.J. 257 (1995); Larson, To Disclose or Not to Disclose: The Dilemma of Homeowners and Real Estate Brokers Under Wisconsin's "Megan's Law," 81 Marq. L. Rev. 1161 (1998); Note, Potential Liability for Misrepresentations in Residential Real Estate Transactions: Let the Broker Beware, 16 Ford.Urb.L.J. 127 (1988).

6.   *Expanding Broker Liability: Personal Injuries.* Hopkins v. Fox & Lazo Realtors, 132 N.J. 426, 625 A.2d 1110 (1993), broke new ground on the question of broker liability. The court held that a real estate broker holding an open house was liable for injuries suffered by a potential customer due to a dangerous condition in a tile floor that caused her to fall. The court ruled that implicit in the broker's invitation to buyers is a responsibility for their safety when visiting the house, and a duty to warn of any dangers known to, or reasonably discoverable, by the broker:

> We thus determine that a broker is under a duty to conduct a reasonable broker's inspection when such an inspection would comport with the customary standards governing the responsibilities and functions of real-estate brokers with respect to open-house tours. . . . That inspection would impose on the broker to warn of any such discoverable physical features or conditions of the property that pose a hazard or danger to such visitors.

132 N.J. at 444–445, 625 A.2d at 1118–1119. The court also held that the more comprehensive duty of the property owner does not supersede the limited responsibility of the broker.

Does this decision properly allocate risk among customers, brokers, and owners?

7.   *Net Listing Agreements.* Net listing agreements, in which the seller authorizes sale at a specified price, allowing the broker to retain as commission the difference between that price and the price at which the property is in fact sold, harbor serious potential for broker abuse. They have been regulated accordingly. A rule promulgated by New York's Secretary of State, 19 NYCRR 175.19 (1962), flatly prohibits net listing agreements, presumably to "prevent overreaching and unfair dealing." Express Realty Co. v. Zinn, 39 Misc.2d 733, 735, 241 N.Y.S.2d 954, 956 (Nassau Cty.Dist.Ct.1963).

In states where they are permitted, net listing agreements inevitably complicate the already thorny conceptual issues raised by broker self-dealing. On the one hand, if the broker buys the land for herself, it can be argued that there has been no self-dealing because the broker is only capturing the land's surplus value, which she would have received in any event had the land been sold to an unrelated person. On the other hand, it is difficult to rest liability on the fact that the broker lured the seller into a net listing agreement: no fiduciary duties can precede the listing agreement because, until the agreement is made, no principal-agent relationship exists between the seller and the broker. Judicial efforts to escape this conundrum have not been entirely successful. Compare Allen v. Dailey, 92 Cal.App. 308, 268 P. 404 (1928), with Loughlin v. Idora Realty Co., 259 Cal.App.2d 619, 66 Cal.Rptr. 747 (1st Dist.1968).

CHAPTER II

PERFORMING THE CONTRACT

A. RISK OF LOSS

Brush Grocery Kart, Inc. v. Sure Fine Market, Inc.

Supreme Court of Colorado, en banc, 2002.
47 P.3d 680.

JUSTICE COATS delivered the Opinion of the Court.

Brush Grocery Kart, Inc. sought review of the court of appeals' judgment affirming the district court's determination of Brush's obligation on an option contract to purchase a building from Sure Fine Market, Inc. *Brush Grocery Kart v. Sure Fine Market*, 30 P.3d 810 (Colo. App. 2001). The district court found that Brush was not entitled to a price abatement for damages caused by a hail storm that occurred during litigation between the parties over the purchase price of the property. The court of appeals affirmed on the grounds that equitable title to the property vested in Brush when it exercised its option to purchase, whether or not it also had a right of possession, and therefore Brush bore the risk of any casualty loss after that time. Because we hold that Brush was entitled to specific performance of the contract with an abatement of the purchase price reflecting the casualty loss, the judgment of the court of appeals is reversed.

I. FACTUAL AND PROCEDURAL HISTORY

In October 1992 Brush Grocery Kart, Inc. and Sure Fine Market, Inc. entered into a five-year "Lease with Renewal Provisions and Option to Purchase" for real property, including a building to be operated by Brush as a grocery store. Under the contract's purchase option provision, any time during the last six months of the lease, Brush could elect to purchase the property at a price equal to the average of the appraisals of an expert designated by each party.

Shortly before expiration of the lease, Brush notified Sure Fine of its desire to purchase the property and begin the process of determining a sale price. Although each party offered an appraisal, the parties were unable to agree on a final price by the time the lease expired. Brush then vacated the premises, returned all keys to Sure Fine, and advised Sure Fine that it would discontinue its casualty insurance covering the property during the lease. Brush also filed suit, alleging that Sure Fine failed to negotiate the price term in good faith and asking for the appointment of a special master to determine the purchase price. Sure Fine agreed to the appointment of a special master and counterclaimed, alleging that Brush negotiated the price term in bad faith and was therefore the breaching party.

During litigation over the price term, the property was substantially damaged during a hail storm. With neither party carrying casualty insurance, each asserted that the other was liable for the damage. The issue was added to the litigation at a stipulated amount of

73

$60,000. The court appointed a special master pursuant to C.R.C.P. 53 and accepted his appraised value of $375,000. The court then found that under the doctrine of equitable conversion, Brush was the equitable owner of the property and bore the risk of loss. It therefore declined to abate the purchase price or award damages to Brush for the loss.

Brush appealed the loss allocation, and the court of appeals affirmed on similar grounds. It considered the prior holdings of this court acknowledging the doctrine of equitable conversion and found that in *Wiley v. Lininger*, 119 Colo. 497, 204 P.2d 1083 (1949), that doctrine was applied to allocate the risk of casualty loss occurring during the executory period of a contract for the purchase of real property. Relying heavily on language from the opinion purporting to adopt the "majority rule," the court of appeals found that our characterization of the rule as placing the risk of casualty loss on a vendee who "is in possession," *id.* at 502, 204 P.2d at 1086, reflected merely the facts of that case rather than any intent to limit the rule to vendees who are actually in possession. Noting that allocation of the risk of loss in circumstances where the vendee is not in possession had not previously been addressed by an appellate court in this jurisdiction, the court of appeals went on to conclude that a "bright line rule" allocating the risk of loss to the vendee, without regard to possession, would best inform the parties of their rights and obligations under a contract for the sale of land.

Brush petitioned for a writ of certiorari to determine the proper allocation of the risk of loss and the appropriate remedy under these circumstances.

. . .

III. THE RISK OF CASUALTY LOSS IN THE ABSENCE OF STATUTORY AUTHORITY

In the absence of statutory authority, the rights, powers, duties, and liabilities arising out of a contract for the sale of land have frequently been derived by reference to the theory of equitable conversion. *People v. Alexander*, 663 P.2d 1024, 1030 n.6 (Colo. 1983) (quoting III *American Law of Property* § 11.22, at 62–63 (A. Casner ed. 1974)). This theory or doctrine, which has been described as a legal fiction, *see Chain O'Mines v. Williamson*, 101 Colo. 231, 234, 72 P.2d 265, 266 (1937), is based on equitable principles that permit the vendee to be considered the equitable owner of the land and debtor for the purchase money and the vendor to be regarded as a secured creditor. *Alexander*, 663 P.2d at 1030 n.6. The changes in rights and liabilities that occur upon the making of the contract result from the equitable right to specific performance. *Id.* Even with regard to third parties, the theory has been relied on to determine, for example, the devolution, upon death, of the rights and liabilities of each party with respect to the land, *see Chain O'Mines*, 101 Colo. at 234–35, 72 P.2d at 266, and to ascertain the powers of creditors of each party to reach the land in payment of their claims. *Alexander*, 663 P.2d at 1030 n.6.

The assignment of the risk of casualty loss in the executory period of contracts for the sale of real property varies greatly throughout the jurisdictions of this country. What appears to yet be a slim majority of states, *see* Randy R. Koenders, Annotation, *Risk of Loss by Casualty*

Pending Contract for Conveyance of Real Property—Modern Cases, 85 A.L.R.4th 233 (2001), places the risk of loss on the vendee from the moment of contracting, on the rationale that once an equitable conversion takes place, the vendee must be treated as owner for all purposes. *See Skelly Oil v. Ashmore*, 365 S.W.2d 582, 588 (Mo. 1963) (criticizing this approach). Once the vendee becomes the equitable owner, he therefore becomes responsible for the condition of the property, despite not having a present right of occupancy or control. In sharp contrast, a handful of other states reject the allocation of casualty loss risk as a consequence of the theory of equitable conversion and follow the equally rigid "Massachusetts Rule," under which the seller continues to bear the risk until actual transfer of the title, absent an express agreement to the contrary. *See, e.g., Skelley Oil*, 365 S.W.2d at 588–89. A substantial and growing number of jurisdictions, however, base the legal consequences of no-fault casualty loss on the right to possession of the property at the time the loss occurs. *Koenders*, 85 A.L.R. 233 *supra*, §§ 6, 7. This view has found expression in the Uniform Vendor and Purchaser Risk Act,[2] and while a number of states have adopted some variation of the Uniform Act, others have arrived at a similar position through the interpretations of their courts. *See, e.g., Lucenti v. Cayuga Apartments*, 48 N.Y.2d 530; 399 N.E.2d 918, 923–24; 423 N.Y.S.2d 886 (N.Y. 1979); *see also Koenders*, 85 A.L.R.4th 233 *supra*, §§ 6, 7.

This court has applied the theory of equitable conversion in limited circumstances affecting title, *see Konecny v. von Gunten*, 151 Colo. 376, 379 P.2d 158 (1963) (finding vendors incapable of unilaterally changing their tenancy in common to joint tenancy during the executory period of the contract because their interest had been equitably converted into a mere security interest and the vendee's interest into realty), and refused to apply it in some circumstances, *see Chain O'Mines*, 101 Colo. 231, 72 P.2d 265 (holding that even if the doctrine applies to option contracts, no conversion would take place until the option were exercised by the party having the right of election). It has also characterized the theory as affording significant protections to purchasers of realty in Colorado. *See Dwyer v. Dist. Court*, 188 Colo. 41, 532 P.2d 725 (1975) (finding personal jurisdiction over out-of-state vendee in part because of the protections afforded vendees of land in this jurisdiction during the executory period of the contract). It has

---

[2]   Under the Uniform Vendor and Purchaser Risk Act § 1, 14 U.L.A. 471 (1968) ("Risk of Loss"):

> Any contract hereafter made in this State for the purchase and sale of realty shall be interpreted as including an agreement that the parties shall have the following rights and duties, unless the contract expressly provides otherwise:

(a) If, when neither the legal title nor the possession of the subject matter of the contract has been transferred, all or a material part thereof is destroyed without fault of the purchaser or is taken by eminent domain, the vendor cannot enforce the contract, and the purchaser is entitled to recover any portion of the price that he has paid;

(b) If, when either the legal title or the possession of the subject matter of the contract has been transferred, all or any part thereof is destroyed without fault of the vendor or is taken by eminent domain, the purchaser is not thereby relieved from a duty to pay the price, nor is he entitled to recover any portion thereof that he has paid.

never before, however, expressly relied on the theory of equitable conversion alone as allocating the risk of casualty loss to a vendee.

In *Wiley v. Lininger*, 119 Colo. 497, 204 P.2d 1083, where fire destroyed improvements on land occupied by the vendee during the multi-year executory period of an installment land contract, we held, according to the generally accepted rule, that neither the buyer nor the seller, each of whom had an insurable interest in the property, had an obligation to insure the property for the benefit of the other. *Id.* at 502, 204 P.2d at 1085–86. We also adopted a rule, which we characterized as "the majority rule," that "the vendee under a contract for the sale of land, being regarded as the equitable owner, assumes the risk of destruction of or injury to the property *where he is in possession*, and the destruction or loss is not proximately caused by the negligence of the vendor." *Id.* (emphasis added). The vendee in possession was therefore not relieved of his obligation to continue making payments according to the terms of the contract, despite material loss by fire to some of the improvements on the property.

Largely because we included a citation, preceded by the introductory signal, "see," to an A.L.R. annotation, describing a "majority rule" without reference to possession, *see* 101 A.L.R. 1241 (superceded by *Koenders*, 85 A.L.R.4th 233 *supra*), the court of appeals found our characterization of the rule, as imposing the risk on vendees who are in possession, to be uncontrolling. While it may have been unnecessary to determine more than the obligations of a vendee in possession in that case, rather than limit the holding to that situation, this court pointedly announced a broader rule. The rule expressly articulated by this court limited the transfer of the risk of loss to vendees who are already in possession. Had this not been the court's deliberate intention, there would have been no need to mention possession at all because a rule governing all vendees would necessarily include vendees in possession. Whether or not a majority of jurisdictions would actually limit the transfer of risk in precisely the same way, the rule as clearly stated and adopted by this court was supported by strong policy and theoretical considerations at the time, and those considerations apply equally today.

Those jurisdictions that indiscriminately include the risk of casualty loss among the incidents or "attributes" of equitable ownership do so largely in reliance on ancient authority or by considering it necessary for consistent application of the theory of equitable conversion. *See Skelley Oil*, 365 S.W.2d at 592 (Stockman, J. dissenting) (quoting 4 Williston, *Contracts*, § 929, at 2607: "Only the hoary age and frequent repetition of the maxim prevents a general recognition of its absurdity."); *see also Paine v. Meller*, (1801) 6 Ves. Jr. 349, 31 Eng. Reprint 1088. Under virtually any accepted understanding of the theory, however, equitable conversion is not viewed as entitling the purchaser to every significant right of ownership, and particularly not the right of possession. As a matter of both logic and equity, the obligation to maintain property in its physical condition follows the right to have actual possession and control rather than a legal right to force conveyance of the property through specific performance at some future date. *See* 17 Samuel Williston, *A Treatise On the Law of Contracts* § 50:46, at 457–58 (Richard A. Lord ed., 4th ed. 1990) ("It is wiser to have the party in possession of the property care for it at his peril, rather than at the peril of another.").

The equitable conversion theory is literally stood on its head by imposing on a vendee, solely because of his right to specific performance, the risk that the vendor will be unable to specifically perform when the time comes because of an accidental casualty loss. It is counterintuitive, at the very least, that merely contracting for the sale of real property should not only relieve the vendor of his responsibility to maintain the property until execution but also impose a duty on the vendee to perform despite the intervention of a material, no-fault casualty loss preventing him from ever receiving the benefit of his bargain. Such an extension of the theory of equitable conversion to casualty loss has never been recognized by this jurisdiction, and it is neither necessary nor justified solely for the sake of consistency.

By contrast, there is substantial justification, both as a matter of law and policy, for not relieving a vendee who is entitled to possession before transfer of title, like the vendee in *Wiley*, of his duty to pay the full contract price, notwithstanding an accidental loss. In addition to having control over the property and being entitled to the benefits of its use, an equitable owner who also has the right of possession has already acquired virtually all of the rights of ownership and almost invariably will have already paid at least some portion of the contract price to exercise those rights. By expressly including in the contract for sale the right of possession, which otherwise generally accompanies transfer of title, *see, e.g.*, § 38–30–120, 10 C.R.S. (2001) ("Conveyance carries right of possession"), the vendor has for all practical purposes already transferred the property as promised, and the parties have in effect expressed their joint intention that the vendee pay the purchase price as promised. Williston, *supra*, § 50:46 at 454–55.

In *Wiley*, rather than adopting a rule to the effect that a vendee assumes the risk of casualty loss as an incident of equitable ownership, our holding stands for virtually the opposite proposition. Despite being the equitable owner, the vendee in that case was prohibited from rescinding only because he was already rightfully in possession at the time of the loss. While *Wiley* could be read to have merely resolved the situation under an installment contract for the sale of land that gave the vendee a right of immediate possession, the rule we adopted foreshadowed the resolution of this case as well. In the absence of a right of possession, a vendee of real property that suffers a material casualty loss during the executory period of the contract, through no fault of his own, must be permitted to rescind and recover any payments he had already made. *Cf.* Uniform Vendor and Purchaser Risk Act § 1.

Furthermore, where a vendee is entitled to rescind as a result of casualty loss, the vendee should generally also be entitled to partial specific performance of the contract with an abatement in the purchase price reflecting the loss. Where the damage is ascertainable, permitting partial specific performance with a price abatement allows courts as nearly as possible to fulfill the expectations of the parties expressed in the contract, while leaving each in a position that is equitable relative to the other. *Lucenti*, 399 N.E.2d at 923–24 (applying common law rule allowing partial specific enforcement with price abatement for casualty loss in order to effectuate substance of parties agreement). Partial specific performance with a price abatement has long been recognized in this jurisdiction as an alternative to rescission in the analogous situation in which a vendor of real property is unable to convey marketable title to all of the land described in the contract. *See Murdock v. Pope*, 156 Colo. 7, 396 P.2d 841 (1964) (collecting cases into the nineteenth century); *cf.* § 38–30–167.

Here, Brush was clearly not in possession of the property as the equitable owner. Even if the doctrine of equitable conversion applies to the option contract between Brush and Sure Fine and could be said to have converted Brush's interest to an equitable ownership of the property at the time Brush exercised its option to purchase, *see Chain O'Mines*, 101 Colo. at 235, 72 P.2d at 266, neither party considered the contract for sale to entitle Brush to possession. Brush was, in fact, not in possession of the property, and the record indicates that Sure Fine considered itself to hold the right of use and occupancy and gave notice that it would consider Brush a holdover tenant if it continued to occupy the premises other than by continuing to lease the property. The casualty loss was ascertainable and in fact stipulated by the parties, and neither party challenged the district court's enforcement of the contract except with regard to its allocation of the casualty loss. Both the court of appeals and the district court therefore erred in finding that the doctrine of equitable conversion required Brush to bear the loss caused by hail damage.

IV. CONCLUSION

Where Brush was not an equitable owner in possession at the time of the casualty loss, it was entitled to rescind its contract with Sure Fine. At least under the circumstances of this case, where Brush chose to go forward with the contract under a stipulation as to loss from the hail damage, it was also entitled to specific performance with an abatement of the purchase price equal to the casualty loss. The judgment of the court of appeals is therefore reversed and the case is remanded for further proceedings consistent with this opinion.

NOTES

1. *Risk of Loss.* Brush Grocery Kart, Inc. v. Sure Fine Market, Inc. explored three factors shaping the contemporary land sale contract: conditions, remedies and risk of loss. The factors are interrelated. For example, courts are reluctant to order specific performance of heavily conditioned contracts. And, as the number and flexibility of conditions increase, and the buyer's chances of getting specific performance decrease, the argument for equitable conversion also diminishes and, with it, the argument that buyer should bear the risk of loss from unexpected destruction.

Brush Grocery also touched on a fourth factor shaping the land sale contract: the statute of frauds. The statute of frauds is closely connected to the other three factors. For example, if a contract only barely complies with the statute of frauds and is not complete in all material respects, courts will often refuse to specifically enforce it. Thus, in Phillips v. Johnson, 266 Or. 544, 514 P.2d 1337 (1973), the Oregon Supreme Court upheld the trial court's specific enforcement of an earnest money receipt even though questions existed concerning the accuracy with which the instrument described the parcel to be conveyed and whether the instrument was anything more than an "agreement to agree." The court held, however, that the terms by which seller agreed to finance the purchase were too ambiguous to be specifically enforced. The court further held that since the instrument gave buyer an election to purchase outright for cash, the contract could be enforced on the condition that buyer made this election.

For excellent practical overviews of the elements of a residential land sale contract, see Yzenbaard, Drafting the Residential Contract of Sale, 9 Wm. Mitchell L.Rev. 37 (1983); Scheid, Buying Blackacre: Form Contracts and Prudent Provisions, 23 John Marshall L.Rev. 15 (1989).

2. *Allocation of Risk of Loss.* Equitable conversion, though it has suffered substantial inroads, continues to represent the majority rule in the United States for allocating risk of loss from destruction during the executory period. The rule may have made some practical sense under early, agrarian conditions when land, not buildings, was presumed to be the real object of any sale. Fortuitous destruction of the improvements would not excuse the buyer from performance for he would still get what he bargained for.

There is a growing trend in the United States today to replace the rule of equitable conversion with a rule that allocates risk of loss to the party— whether seller or buyer—who is in possession at the time the premises are destroyed. The technical rationale for this newer, minority rule is almost as formalistic as the rationale for the majority rule: "the purchaser in possession is substantial owner of the property and should bear the burdens of ownership, while the purchaser out of possession is not substantial owner." 3 American Law of Property § 11.30 (A.J. Casner, ed. 1952). The better reason for the minority rule is that the party in possession is best placed to guard against the hazards of destruction, to insure the premises, and to conserve any evidence bearing on destruction.

The most striking aspect of both the majority and minority rules is that there should be any need for them at all. They are rules of implication, not rules of law, and can be easily altered by contract terms expressly allocating the risk of loss. ("Buyer shall not be obligated to perform if, during the executory period and before Buyer takes possession, the premises are substantially or entirely destroyed by natural causes or if, during the executory period, and without regard to whether Buyer is in possession, the premises are substantially or entirely taken by eminent domain.") Since buyer and seller can shift the risk of loss in their contract, and can insure against the risk, the question to consider in devising a rule today is whether, in the usual case, buyer or seller is better placed to raise risk of loss as a bargaining point and to obtain casualty coverage. Why do you suppose residential buyers and sellers, and their lawyers and brokers, are so reluctant to address and resolve the question of executory period losses? Even if the issue is raised, will the drafted language be adequate to express the parties' intent? See Bryant v. Willison Real Estate Co., 177 W.Va. 120, 350 S.E.2d 748 (1986) (clause stating that "the owner is responsible for said property until the Deed has been delivered to said purchaser" placed risk on seller despite "as is" clause and provision requiring the buyer to insure). See generally, McDowell, Insurable Interest in Property Revisited, 17 Cap.U.L.Rev. 165 (1988).

Courts have applied equitable conversion to allocate rights and obligations between sellers and buyers other than those respecting risk of casualty loss. As indicated in *Brush Grocery*, the doctrine derives from the equitable principle that, upon signing the contract, the buyer acquires a realty interest, leaving the seller with only a personal property interest (i.e., a claim to the unpaid purchase price) secured by the legal title that seller retains in the land. If the buyer and the seller die after executing a contract of sale for Blackacre, each leaving a will that provides for separate disposition of their respective real and personal property, the devisee of the buyer's real property would be entitled to Blackacre (with the purchase price to be paid out of the estate's general funds, as with other debts) and the legatee of the seller's personal property would take the claim to the unpaid purchase price. See 3 A.J. Casner (ed.), Amer. Law of Prop. §§ 11.26–11.27 (1952); Coe v. Hays, 105 Md.App. 778, 661 A.2d 220 (1995) (title to property was marketable, so that equitable conversion occurred, making proceeds of sale personal property that passed to seller's legatee).

For background on equitable conversion and allocation of risk of loss during the executory interval, see Flores, A Comparison of the Rules and Rationales for Allocating Risks Arising in Realty Sales Using Executory Sale Contracts and Escrows, 59 Mo.L.Rev. 307 (1994); Dunham, Vendor's Obligation as to Fitness of Land for a Particular Purpose, 37 Minn.L.Rev. 108 (1953); Hume, Real Estate Contracts and the Doctrine of Equitable Conversion in Washington: Dispelling the Ashford Cloud, 7 U. Puget Sound L.Rev. 233 (1984); Note, Equitable Conversion and its Effect on Risk of Loss in Executory Contracts for the Sale of Real Property, 22 Drake L.Rev. 626 (1973); Lewis & Reeves, How the Doctrine of Equitable Conversion Affects Land Sale Contract Forfeitures, 3 Real Est.L.J. 249 (1975).

3. *U.V.P.R.A.* The Uniform Vendors and Purchasers Risk Act, referenced in *Brush Grocery*, alters the traditional rule by shifting the risk of loss from destruction or condemnation from seller to buyer only if the buyer has taken possession or title. If the reason behind assigning the risk of loss to the buyer in possession is that he is best placed to guard against hazards, to insure, and to conserve evidence bearing on destruction, does it not follow that seller should bear the risk of loss when *she* is in possession, even though the buyer has title? Or is the reasoning that, having taken possession or title, the buyer is too far committed to the transaction to be allowed to back out because of fortuitous destruction? Can the U.V.P.R.A. rule be easily applied? Had "possession" passed in *Brush Grocery?* Had it reverted? See also Caulfield v. Improved Risk Mutuals, Inc., 66 N.Y.2d 793, 497 N.Y.S.2d 903, 488 N.E.2d 833 (1985) (risk of loss passed when deed was placed in escrow).

The brain child of Professor Samuel Williston, the U.V.P.R.A. was promulgated by the National Conference of Commissioners on Uniform State Laws in 1935. At last count, the Act has been adopted in thirteen states: California (Civ.Code § 1662); Hawaii (Rev.Stat. § 508–1); Illinois (I.L.C.S. §§ 65/1–65/3); Michigan (Comp.Laws Ann. §§ 565.701–565.703); Nevada (Nev.Rev.Stats. 113.030–113.050); New Mexico (N.M. Stat. § 47–1A–2); New York (Gen.Oblig.Law § 5–1311); North Carolina (Gen.Stat. §§ 39–36 through 39–39); Oklahoma (Stat.Ann. tit. 16 §§ 201–203); Oregon (Rev.Stat. §§ 93.290–93.300); South Dakota (Comp.Laws Ann. §§ 43–26–5 through 43–26–8); Texas (VTCA Property Code § 5.007); Wisconsin (Stat.Ann. § 706.12).

With three exceptions, these statutes almost literally track the language of the original Act. The Illinois version differs in one detail—assigning special consequence to passage of title through escrow. The New York Act makes two changes. It expressly provides that its terms are not intended to deprive the seller or buyer of any right to recover damages against the other for breach of contract occurring prior to the destruction or condemnation. Second, it provides that if buyer has taken neither possession nor title, and an "immaterial part" is destroyed or taken, neither seller nor buyer "is thereby deprived of the right to enforce the contract; but there shall be, to the extent of the destruction or taking, an abatement of the purchase price." Eminent domain takings are not covered by the North Carolina version of the statute.

4. *U.L.T.A.* The Uniform Land Transactions Act, approved in 1975 by the National Conference of Commissioners on Uniform State Laws, represents a comprehensive effort to harmonize, simplify and modernize state law governing land transactions. The U.L.T.A. regulates contract conditions, remedies and formalities (Article 2) and secured transactions (Article 3). The U.L.T.A. is frankly modeled on the Uniform Commercial Code. However, the U.L.T.A. has not had the enthusiastic reception enjoyed by the U.C.C. No jurisdiction has adopted the U.L.T.A. Recognizing the difficulties with the statute, in 1985 the National Conference of Commissioners on Uniform State Laws promulgated a new statute, the Uniform Land Security Interest Act, which is essentially Article 3 of U.L.T.A. The recent emphasis of the National Conference has been on the adoption of the U.L.S.I.A. rather than the U.L.T.A. Nevertheless, the U.L.T.A. has had some influence on the courts. See, e.g., Kuhn v. Spatial Design, Inc., at page 140. For a discussion of the fate of the U.L.T.A., see Symposium, Whatever Happened to the Uniform Land Transactions Act?, 20 Nova L.Rev. 1017–1185 (1996), with articles by Ronald Benton Brown, Richard B. Amandes, Marion W. Benfield, Jr., Gerald Korngold, Peter B. Maggs, Barbara Taylor Mattis, Patrick A. Randolph, Jr., and James Charles Smith. For an analysis of some of the problems of the U.L.T.A., see Bruce, Mortgage Law Reform Under the Uniform Land Transactions Act, 64 Geo.L.J. 1245 (1976). On the U.L.S.I.A., see Note 5 at Page 349.

U.L.T.A. § 2–406, dealing with destruction of premises, modifies the approach taken by the U.V.P.R.A. Section 2–406(c)(2) adopts the Illinois rule on sales closed through escrow, and section 2–406(b)(2)(i) incorporates the New York approach to abatement of purchase price for nonmaterial diminutions in value.

5. *Allocation of Insurance Proceeds Between Buyer and Seller.* American courts, which have widely followed the English rule of equitable conversion for allocating risk of loss during the executory interval, have not followed the English position on a related question: Who is entitled to the proceeds paid on the seller's insurance policy? The English rule, formulated in Rayner v. Preston, 18 Ch.Div. 1 (1881), is that the seller is entitled to retain the proceeds free of any claim by the buyer. American courts generally hold that the buyer is entitled to the insurance proceeds, chiefly to avoid giving the seller a windfall (the full purchase price plus the full insurance proceeds). See, for example, Hillard v. Franklin, 41 S.W.3d 106 (Tenn.App.2000). Moreover, the proceeds have been held transferrable to the buyer despite a prohibition in the insurance contract against assignment. See, e.g., Smith v. Buege, 182 W.Va. 204, 387 S.E.2d 109

(1989). It would appear to follow under the American approach that if a state adopts the minority rule on risk of loss, and as a consequence allocates that risk to seller rather than to buyer, the seller will be entitled to retain the insurance proceeds. See generally, West Bend Mutual Insurance Co. v. Salemi, 158 Ill.App.3d 241, 110 Ill.Dec. 608, 511 N.E.2d 785 (1987) (allowing seller to proceed against buyer's insurer where buyer agreed to insure for seller's benefit).

The English rule rests on the perception that the insurance policy is strictly a personal contract between the seller and her insurer, and that its benefits do not pass with the land into the buyer's hands. American courts justify their position on three closely connected grounds: that the insurance proceeds are held by the seller in trust for the purchaser; that since, under equitable conversion, the buyer is the equitable owner of the land, he should also be considered the equitable owner of the insurance proceeds which stand in place of the land; and that since insurance is customarily considered to be for the benefit of the property rather than the person insured, the proceeds should go with the land. 3 American Law of Property § 11.31 (A.J. Casner, ed. 1952).

B. STATUTE OF FRAUDS

Hahne v. Burr

Supreme Court of South Dakota, 2005.
705 N.W.2d 867.

ZINTER, JUSTICE.

A dispute arose between Bill Hahne and Clarence Burr concerning an oral agreement for the sale of land. Hahne sued for specific performance of the agreement. The trial court denied relief, entering summary judgment against Hahne because of the statute of frauds. Hahne appeals the statute of frauds determination, and Burr appeals (by notice of review) the trial court's refusal to grant Rule 11 sanctions. We affirm the trial court on all issues.

Facts and Procedural History

On February 23, 2000, Hahne and Steve Schneider (lessees) entered into a three-year lease of real property with Burr (lessor). At the end of the lease, Hahne and Burr discussed a possible sale of the land. Although there is a dispute about the content of those discussions and who initiated them, there is no dispute that the parties discussed a sale to Hahne. Although money was subsequently exchanged, some closing documents were drawn, and further conversations occurred concerning the sale, Burr ultimately declined to sell the property, and this suit was commenced.

Under Hahne's version of the facts, by December 2002, Burr and Hahne orally agreed to all aspects of the sale, including the price. Later that month, the parties realized that a sale could not be completed before January 1, 2003, and therefore, Hahne agreed to pay further rent for the period of time between the first of the year and the eventual closing.

In early January 2003, purportedly upon Burr's request, Hahne retained attorney Andrew Aberle to prepare closing documents. Hahne asserts that Aberle talked to Burr and that all of the terms of the agreement were verified. Aberle also prepared letters, a deed, and a certificate of value, which he sent to Burr to close the sale. Hahne also tendered a $15,000 check, which he contends was partially for rent and partially for a down payment on the land.[1] Hahne finally asserts that, during this period of time, he did not purchase or lease other land needed in his farming operation because of his reliance on the agreement.

However, in February 2003, Burr's grandson, allegedly acting as Burr's agent, sent Hahne an e-mail informing him that Burr had decided not to sell the property. Hahne sued Burr for specific performance of the alleged agreement. The trial court granted summary judgment in favor of Burr based upon the statute of frauds. The trial court denied Burr's request for sanctions and attorney's fees. Hahne appeals the following issues:

(1) Whether there were sufficient writings regarding the sale of real estate to satisfy the statute of frauds;

(2) Whether the trial court erred in granting summary judgment on the issues of partial performance and estoppel.

. . .

Analysis and Decision

In reviewing summary judgment, "we decide only whether genuine issues of material fact exist and whether the law was correctly applied. If any legal basis exists to support the trial court's ruling, we will affirm." Schulte v. Progressive N. Ins. Co., 2005 SD 75, ¶ 5, 699 N.W.2d 437, 438 (citations omitted). All reasonable inferences "must be viewed in favor of the non-moving party." Northstream Invs., Inc. v. 1804 Country Store Co., 2005 SD 61, ¶ 11, 697 N.W.2d 762, 765 (citation omitted). Furthermore, "[t]he burden is on the moving party to clearly show an absence of any genuine issue of material fact and an entitlement to judgment as a matter of law." Id. (citations omitted).

Sufficiency of Writings to Bind Burr

Under the statute of frauds, a contract for the sale of land must be in writing to be enforceable. Jacobson v. Gulbransen, 2001 SD 33, ¶ 15, 623 N.W.2d 84, 88. The statute, SDCL 53–8–2, provides in relevant part:

The following contracts are not enforceable by action unless the contract or some memorandum thereof is in writing and subscribed by the party to be charged or his agent, as authorized in writing:

. . .

---

[1]   Hahne wrote two checks, both containing a memo restriction indicating the check was either for the lease or the down payment. Burr rejected the first check because it was not made out to the attorney's trust account. The second check was rejected because of the memo restriction; more specifically, Burr did not want the act of endorsing the check to constitute an admission that the check was for a down payment.

(3) An agreement for sale of real estate or an interest therein, or lease of the same, for a period longer than one year. However, this does not abridge the power of any court to compel specific performance of any agreement for sale of real estate in case of part performance thereof. . . .

We have stated that "[t]he role of the statute of frauds is evidentiary in nature, and serves to remove uncertainty by requiring 'written evidence of an enforceable obligation.' " Harriman v. United Dominion Indus., Inc., 2005 SD 18, ¶ 15, 693 N.W.2d 44, 48 (citations omitted).

Although there is a significant dispute whether there was an agreement, for purposes of summary judgment we assume there was an oral agreement to sell the real estate. With respect to the sufficiency of writings, Hahne contends that his attorney, Aberle, personally verified all of the terms of the contract with Burr. Hahne also points out that Aberle drafted a letter forwarding a deed and certificate of value attempting to close the transaction. Hahne finally relies upon an e-mail sent by Burr's alleged agent reflecting an awareness that a sale was pending.

However, Aberle's conversations are not writings, and Hahne did not produce any writing signed by Burr (or his agent) *confirming* an agreement to the sale of the land. This is significant because an agreement for the sale of real property is not enforceable unless the document is "subscribed by the party to be charged." SDCL 53–8–2; Wiggins v. Shewmake, 374 N.W.2d 111, 114 (S.D.1985). Here, Aberle was not the agent of the party to be charged, and the e-mail, even if signed by Burr's agent, did not confirm an agreement. On the contrary, the e-mail expressly disavowed Burr's intent to sell the property. Therefore, the trial court correctly determined that these conversations and writings by others were not sufficient to satisfy the statute of frauds.

Statute of Frauds Exceptions—
Partial Performance and Estoppel

Even if there is no agreement in writing, SDCL 53–8–2(3) allows a "court to compel specific performance of any agreement for sale of real estate in case of part performance. . . ." SDCL 53–8–2(3). Estoppel may also justify specific performance.

An oral promise to convey real property is enforceable by specific performance where the grantee *has partially performed* or *has acted in reliance upon the promise* of the grantor in such manner that it would invoke a fraud or prejudice against the grantee not to grant specific performance thereon.

Durkee v. Van Well, 2002 SD 150, & 21, 654 N.W.2d 807, 815 (citations omitted).

Partial Performance

Hahne asserts that a number of actions constituted partial performance. He first relies on his "down payment." We initially note that there is a dispute whether the $15,000 Hahne paid to Burr was a down payment on the sale or whether it was a lease payment for 2003.[2] However, even assuming that it was a down payment, this Court has long held that "payment of the whole or a part of the purchase price is not sufficient in itself to take a case out of the operation of the statute of frauds." Boekelheide v. Snyder, 71 S.D. 470, 473, 26 N.W.2d 74, 75 (1947). See also Ells v. Ells, 245 N.W.2d 498, 500 (1976) (stating that payment of a portion of the purchase price is "an act that has long been held insufficient to take a contract out of the . . . statute of frauds") (citation omitted). Therefore, the trial court correctly concluded that the payment, in and of itself, "would not constitute partial payment or partial performance of the purchase price."

Hahne recognizes this rule and, therefore, contends that his possession of the land must also be considered. This Court has indicated "that the most important acts to constitute sufficient part performance are actual possession and permanent improvements made on the land." Williams v. Denham, 83 S.D. 518, 523, 162 N.W.2d 285, 288 (1968) (citation omitted). However, in this case Hahne's possession of the land is irrelevant because he was in continued possession after expiration of a written lease. See Skjoldal v. Myren, 86 S.D. 111, 119, 191 N.W.2d 809, 813 (1971) (concluding that where an option to purchase property had expired, but the lessee retained possession and farmed the land on a crop share basis, partial performance had not been established); Shaw v. George, 82 S.D. 62, 66, 141 N.W.2d 405, 407 (1966) (stating that where one party was in possession under an existing lease, the continued possession could not be regarded as an act of partial performance). Furthermore, there is no evidence Hahne made permanent improvements to the property. Therefore, we agree with the trial court that Hahne's possession of the land was not "sufficient to constitute partial performance because . . . [h]e was . . . there under a written lease and [thus,] he was a holdover tenant."

Hahne next contends that he partially performed because he incurred attorney and title policy fees in an attempt to close the transaction. However, in order for an act by the plaintiff "to be sufficient to constitute part performance, it 'must be unequivocally referable to the contract.'" Morton v. Lanier, 311 Mont. 301, 55 P.3d 380, 385 (2002) (citations omitted). What conduct constitutes partial performance will depend on the facts of each case. Nelson v. Elway, 908 P.2d 102, 119 (Colo.1995); Veum v. Sheeran, 95 Minn. 315, 104 N.W. 135, 137 (1905). And, whether those acts are sufficient to constitute partial performance is a matter of law to be decided by the court. Simons v. Simons, 134 Idaho 824, 11 P.3d 20, 23 (2000).

Here, the trial court concluded that Hahne hired the attorney to take care of Hahne's personal interests, and therefore, the retention of the attorney was not partial performance of the *terms and conditions of the contract*. The trial court correctly noted:

> I think the partial performance has to relate to the terms and conditions of the agreement. I think the fact that Bill Hahne went out and hired an attorney was not any allegation even by Bill Hahne that that was part of the terms and conditions of

---

[2]   Fifteen thousand dollars was the annual lease payment required under the parties' lease. There is no dispute that the $15,000 was ultimately used for the lease payment in 2003.

the agreement. . . . [H]e hired Andy Aberle for his own personal needs to take care of the legal matters. So I don't believe that hiring Andy Aberle would constitute partial performance of the terms and conditions of the contract.

Finally, with respect to the title policy, the trial court noted that according to a letter from Aberle to Burr, it was unknown who was to pay this fee. Based upon this uncontested evidence, the trial court found that there was no agreement concerning who was to pay for the title policy. We agree. A review of Aberle's letter reflects that he was only asking Burr how he wanted to approach the payment of the title policy. This did not reflect an agreement as to who would pay. Furthermore, as we noted in Williams, 83 S.D. at 523, 162 N.W.2d at 288, neither ordering abstracts (which is analogous to the procurement of a title policy) nor drawing up a contract constitutes partial performance.

For all the foregoing reasons, the trial court correctly determined that the partial performance exception to the statute of frauds was not applicable.

Estoppel

Hahne contends that Burr should be estopped from denying that a contract existed between the parties. Hahne relies on equitable estoppel and promissory estoppel. There are four elements of equitable estoppel:

1.   False representations or concealment of material facts must exist; . . .

2.   The party to whom it was made must have been without knowledge of the real facts; . . .

3.   The representations or concealment must have been made with the intention that it should be acted upon; and

4.   The party to whom it was made must have relied thereon to his prejudice or injury.

Cleveland v. Tinaglia, 1998 SD 91, ¶ 38, 582 N.W.2d 720, 727 (citations omitted).

"[P]romissory estoppel may be invoked where a promisee alters his position to his detriment in the reasonable belief that a promise would be performed." Canyon Lake Park, LLC v. Loftus Dental, P.C., 2005 SD 82, ¶ 38, 700 N.W.2d 729, 739 (citing Garrett v. BankWest, Inc., 459 N.W.2d 833, 848 (S.D.1990)). The three elements of promissory estoppel are:

1) the detriment suffered in reliance must be substantial in an economic sense; 2) the loss to the promisee must have been foreseeable by the promisor; and 3) the promisee must have acted reasonably in justifiable reliance on the promise made.

Id. Estoppel is not applicable if any of these elements are lacking or have not been proven by clear and convincing evidence. Century 21 Associated Realty v. Hoffman, 503 N.W.2d 861, 866 (S.D.1993) (citations omitted).

Assuming that a promise or false representation was made, these two forms of estoppel have a common element. Hahne was required to prove that he detrimentally relied on the promise or false representation. Hahne contends that he established this element because he did not look for other land in reliance on the agreement. Hahne also argues that he had previously reduced the size of his cattle herd and that by securing Burr's land, he would have been able to expand his herd again. However, Hahne has failed to direct us to any evidence to support these arguments. Moreover, a letter from Hahne's lawyer to the title company indicates that Steven, Todd, and Kelly Landis, not Hahne, were actually purchasing the property from Burr. The title policy also indicated that the Landises were to become the insureds under an "owner's" policy. Because the evidence referenced on appeal indicates that Hahne was not ultimately purchasing the land, he failed to establish detrimental reliance on any promise or representation.

. . .

Affirmed.

GILBERTSON, CHIEF JUSTICE, and SABERS, KONENKAMP, and MEIERHENRY, JUSTICES, concur.

NOTES

1. *Statute of Frauds.* Most American statutes of frauds are closely patterned after the original English Statute of Frauds, 29 Car. II c. 3 (1677), and require both that land sale contracts be in writing and signed by the parties and that deeds conveying an interest in land be in writing and signed by the grantor. Should the writing requirement for contracts be applied less stringently than the writing requirement for deeds? Deeds form links in a parcel's chain of title that must be relied upon to identify the parcel and its owner decades, and even centuries, later, when all witnesses to the transaction have disappeared and a prospective buyer is seeking to determine whether his seller has good title. Sales contracts, by contrast, have short lives—typically 45 or 60 days at most—and are rarely recorded. Once the executory period expires, they are not relied on by anyone for any purpose. Cf. McFadden, Oral Transfers of Land in Illinois, 1988 U.Ill.L.Rev. 667 (arguing for recognition of oral conveyances and maintaining that recording laws could adequately protect third parties).

Some American jurisdictions have abandoned the statute of frauds. See, e.g., N.J.S.A. 25:1–13, effective in 1996, permits oral agreements for the sale of land to be enforced if they can be shown by clear and convincing evidence. See, e.g., McBarron v. Kipling Woods L.L.C., 365 N.J.Super. 114, 838 A.2d 490 (2004).

2. *Signed Writing.* While the placing of a formal signature meets the statute of frauds, other types of "signing" may be sufficient. In Hessenthaler v. Farzin, 388 Pa.Super. 37, 564 A.2d 990 (1989), the sellers sent a mailgram accepting a sales contract which had been executed by the purchasers. The court permitted the purchasers to specifically enforce the contract even though there was no signature by the sellers. The court held that no particular form of a signature is required as long as there is reliable indication that the person intended to authenticate the writing. See also George W. Watkins Family v. Messenger, 115 Idaho 386, 766 P.2d 1267 (App.1988), affirmed, 118 Idaho 537, 797 P.2d 1385 (1990) (initials were adequate under the statute).

The increased use of facsimile machines has raised issues under the statute of frauds. Parma Tile Mosaic & Marble Co. v. Estate of Short, 87 N.Y.2d 524, 640 N.Y.S.2d 477, 663 N.E.2d 633 (1996), addressed the question of whether a fax machine's automatic imprinting of the sender's name and address at the top of each page satisfied the subscription requirement. The printed nature of the name on the fax was not in itself a problem since, under New York law, any written or printed "signature" affixed with the actual or apparent intent to authenticate a writing will satisfy the statute. The court found, however, that there was no intent to authenticate the document in question. It rejected the argument that programming the machine with the sender's name sufficed and ruled that the programming did not have the statute of frauds in view for any particular document. See generally Piccoli, Executing Real Estate Contracts by Fax, 9 Probate & Prop. 15 (May/June 1995); Bordman, Telefacsimile Documents: A Survey of Uses in the Legal Setting, 36 Wayne L.Rev. 1361 (1990).

The courts have given mixed reception at best to attempt to show signing by email. In Vista Developers Corp. v. VFP Realty LLC, 17 Misc.3d 914, 847 N.Y.S.2d 416 (2007), the court held that email exchanges between the buyer and seller could not constitute a "signed writing" under the New York's statute of frauds. The court found that a legislative amendment permitting emails to create binding agreements did not apply to real estate contracts since "the purpose of the statute of frauds is to remove uncertainty." But see Rosenfeld v. Zerneck, 4 Misc.3d 193, 776 N.Y.S.2d 458 (2004) (dictum finding emails to be sufficient); Stevens v. Publicis, S.A., 50 A.D.3d 253, 854 N.Y.S.2d 690 (2008) (email sufficient for statute of frauds in employment agreement). What was the *Hahne* court's view on whether email could be binding?

3.   *Adequacy of Description.* Some courts treat contract descriptions far more liberally than deed descriptions, holding that a land sale contract will be enforced if it identifies the land to be conveyed to the exclusion of all other parcels. So long as the description offers some clue or key to identifying the land, parol evidence will be admitted to complete the identification. Thus, in Stachnik v. Winkel, 50 Mich.App. 316, 213 N.W.2d 434 (1973), reversed on other grounds, 394 Mich. 375, 230 N.W.2d 529 (1975), the court held that a contract for "your [seller's] property located in Glen Arbor Twp. Lee Lanau Co. situated on Wheeler Rd.," was sufficiently definite to comply with the statute of frauds. External evidence showed that this was the only property that the sellers owned in Lee Lanau County.

At the other extreme, a few courts insist that the contract description contain all of the detail required for deeds. Martin v. Seigel, 35 Wash.2d 223, 212 P.2d 107 (1949), represents this more stringent, minority position. The Washington Supreme Court there refused specific performance even though the contract identified the parcel by street address, city, county and state, and even though parol evidence further provided the parcel's lot and block numbers. The court subsequently extended the same harsh requirement to real estate brokers, holding that the statute of frauds barred a broker from recovering his commission under a listing agreement that described the property as the "O.H. Faulstich Farm, Route 1, Snohomish, Snohomish County, Wash." Heim v. Faulstich, 70 Wash.2d 688, 424 P.2d 1012 (1967). The court partially recanted its rigid view when it overruled *Heim* in House v. Erwin, 83 Wash.2d 898, 524 P.2d 911 (1974). The holding was, however, expressly limited to descriptions in listing agreements and did not overrule the standard as applied to contracts of sale.

4.   *Part Performance.* Do you agree with the court in *Hahne* on the part performance issue? What type of acts were claimed? What would a buyer have to show, and could a tenant ever meet that burden? See 3 American Law of Property § 11.7 (A.J. Casner ed. 1952); Braunstein, Remedy, Reason, and the Statute of Frauds: A Critical Economic Analysis, 1989 Utah L.Rev. 383 (arguing that exceptions to statute are applied not because they provide satisfactory evidence of an agreement but because adherence to the statute in such cases would sanction economically wasteful behavior).

5.   *Lawyer's Duty.* In The Florida Bar v. Belleville, 591 So.2d 170 (Fla.1991), Belleville was retained as counsel for Bloch who had entered into an agreement to purchase an apartment building from Cowan. Cowan was eighty-three years old, with a third grade education, although he had substantial experience selling real estate when he was younger. Although Bloch and Cowan had negotiated only for the sale of the building, the documents stated that Cowan was selling both the building and his house. Belleville drafted the sales documents to include a legal description of Cowan's house. Cowan signed the documents without realizing that the house was included, and no one at closing explained that to him. Moreover, in exchange for the properties Cowan only received a note, not a mortgage. When Cowan received the documents after closing, he realized that they differed from the terms to which he thought he agreed. A disciplinary action was brought against Belleville.

The Supreme Court reversed the referee's finding of no discipline and suspended the attorney for thirty days:

> When faced with this factual scenario, we believe an attorney is under an ethical obligation to do two things. First, the attorney must explain to the unrepresented opposing party the fact that the attorney is representing an adverse interest. Second, the attorney must explain the material terms of the documents that the attorney has drafted for the clients so that the opposing party fully understands their actual effect. When the transaction is as onesided as that in the present case, counsel preparing the documents is under an ethical duty to make sure that an unrepresented party understands the possible detrimental effect of the transaction and the fact that the attorney's loyalty lies with the client alone.

Id. at 172.

Is this a proper result? How should this scenario be treated under Model Rules of Professional Conduct R. 4.3?

> In dealing on behalf of a client with a person who is not represented by counsel, a lawyer shall not state or imply that the lawyer is disinterested. When the lawyer knows or reasonably should know that the unrepresented person misunderstands the lawyer's role in the matter, the lawyer shall make reasonable efforts to correct the misunderstanding.

6.   *Electronic Transactions and Signatures.* President Clinton signed the Electronic Signatures in Global and National Commerce Act (the Act) into law in 2000. 15 U.S.C.A. § 7001 et seq. Section 7001 of the Act provides:

> Notwithstanding any statute, regulation, or other rule of law . . . with respect to any transaction in or affecting interstate or foreign commerce—
>
> **(1)** a signature, contract, or other record relating to such transaction may not be denied legal effect, validity, or enforceability solely because it is in electronic form; and
>
> **(2)** a contract relating to such transaction may not be denied legal effect, validity, or enforceability solely because an electronic signature or electronic record was used in its formation.

The sale, lease, exchange or other disposition of an interest in land are defined as "transactions" covered by the Act. 15 U.S.C.A. § 7006(13)(B).

A real estate contract thus can be valid even though it is in electronic form, and an "electronic signature" will be valid if it is a "symbol . . . attached to or logically associated with a contract or other record and executed or adopted by a person with the intent to sign the record." 15 U.S.C.A. § 7006(5). As Professor Patrick A. Randolph, Jr. suggests:

> So, for instance, if you sent me an e-mail that said: 'I'll buy your property at 450 W. Meyer in Chicago for $50,000,' and I typed at the top of this message 'OK' and hit 'return,' it is quite likely that we would have a binding real estate contract. All you would have to show is that the typing of the word 'OK' indicated my intent to express agreement. The fact that I did not type out my name would not matter, because I 'attached' an 'electronic symbol' (i.e., the word 'OK') to a contract.

Randolph, Has E-sign Murdered the Statute of Frauds?, 15 Probate & Prop. 23, 24 (No. 4, July/August 2001). Professor Randolph cautions that parties may unintentionally bind themselves in such e-mail scenarios and that the Act also increases the risk of forgery. Does the statute of frauds still have meaning in e-transactions? Will the Act lead to an erosion of the statute in paper transactions? For other discussion of the Act, see Doversberger, Conveyancing at the Crossroads: The Transition to E-Conveyancing Applications in the U.S. and Abroad, 20 Ind. Int'l & Comp. L.Rev. 281 (2010); Note, E-Sign: Will the New Law Increase Internet Security Allowing Online Mortgage Lending to Become Routine? 5 N.C. Banking Inst. 523 (2001).

States can supersede the Act by adopting the Uniform Electronic Transactions Act (UETA), 7A Unif. Laws Ann. 21 (Supp. 2001), which was promulgated by the National Conference of Commissioners of Uniform State Laws in 1999, or by adopting legislation that is consistent with the Act and does not favor one technology over others. 15 U.S.C.A. § 7002. See Gardella, E-Commerce in Real Estate Transactions, 15 Probate & Prop. 45 (No. 4, July/August 2001). Forty-six states and the District of Columbia have adopted UETA. The federal Act includes much of the substance of UETA and, it has been suggested, was designed to advance the goals of UETA on a national scale. See Jones & Winn, The Future Is . . . E-commerce Gets A Boost With E-Sign (Two Takes), 10 Bus. Law Today 8–9 (No. 4, March/April 2001).

C. CONTRACT CONDITIONS

The typical land sale contract contains several conditions, some express, others implied, that must be met or waived for the sale to close. Conditions are essentially substitutes for information—information about the home finance market, the condition of title and of the premises and local government regulations. Conditions postpone contract performance to a point when that information can be obtained—through a lender's response to the loan application, a title report, a housing inspection, an environmental audit, and a land use review.

One persistent question is whether the prescribed conditions leave so many terms open that no enforceable contract has been formed. Failure to specify the financing terms, the condition of the premises and the land use restrictions that will be acceptable to the buyer may void the contract for indefiniteness under the applicable statute of frauds. See Anand v. Marple, 167 Ill.App.3d 918, 118 Ill.Dec. 826, 522 N.E.2d 281 (1988) (inadequately completed printed form was not proper contract). And, even if the statute's requirements are met, the conditional contract may be held too indefinite to support a specific performance decree for buyer or seller. Since conditions will characteristically be phrased in general terms, and their fulfillment left to the exclusive control of one of the parties, there is the added question of illusoriness or mutuality of obligation. Generally, the problem is small, for the concept of good faith goes far toward preventing reneging parties from using a financing, title or other condition as an excuse for nonperformance. In such cases, the court will examine the motives of the party relying on the condition. See Greer Properties, Inc. v. LaSalle National Bank, 874 F.2d 457 (7th Cir.1989) (court had to determine whether contract was canceled because of condition permitting seller to terminate if cost of removal of environmental contamination was "economically impracticable" or because seller could now obtain a higher price from another buyer).

The converse problem arises when the conditions have been drafted with excessive detail. A financing clause that specifies the acceptable interest rate to two decimal places and also itemizes points, loan fees, prepayment penalties, term and amortization will inevitably be hard to meet in every respect, giving the buyer considerable opportunity to renege for reasons totally unrelated to financing. Should good faith be required of the parties when the contract condition is overly narrow rather than overly broad? For a thoughtful review of these issues, see Note, Contingency Financing Clauses in Real Estate Sales Contracts in Georgia, 8 Ga.L.Rev. 186 (1973).

1. FINANCING

Homler v. Malas

Court of Appeals of Georgia, 1997.
229 Ga.App. 390, 494 S.E.2d 18.

McMURRAY, PRESIDING JUDGE.

Plaintiffs Robert Homler and Barbara Homler filed this breach of contract action against defendant Mohannad Malas. The complaint alleges that defendant Malas agreed to buy and plaintiffs agreed to sell a single family residence, that the agreement was conditioned on defendant obtaining a loan to finance the purchase, and that defendant breached the agreement by failing to diligently pursue in good faith his applications for a loan. The plaintiffs seek damages for the alleged breach of contract, and also expenses of litigation pursuant to OCGA § 13–6–11 and disbursement of $25,000 earnest money paid by defendant and held by the real estate agent who effected the sale, defendant Harry Norman Realtors. Defendant Malas answered denying plaintiffs' claims, and via counterclaim and cross-claim against defendant Harry Norman Realtors sought return of the earnest money. The defendant broker, Harry Norman Realtors, interpleaded the earnest money into the registry of the trial court and sought attorney fees for having to interplead.

Defendant Malas moved for summary judgment on the ground that the contract sought to be enforced is too vague and indefinite to be enforced in that the terms of the loan to be obtained by defendant under the terms of the financing contingency are not sufficiently identified. Summary judgment was granted in favor of defendant Malas both as to plaintiffs' claims and as to defendant's counterclaim seeking return of the earnest money. Attorney fees of $807.50 were awarded to defendant Harry Norman Realtors and the balance of the earnest money was ordered disbursed to defendant. Plaintiffs appeal. *Held*:

The document executed by the parties was created using a pre-printed contract. The form included a number of blank spaces for insertion of various information. With regard to the loan contingency provisions there were blank spaces for certain terms of the loan to be obtained by the buyer. Blank spaces were completed to indicate that the agreement was conditioned on the buyer "obtaining" a loan in the principal amount of 80 percent of the purchase price to be paid in monthly installments over a term of no less than 30 years. (Although not germane to our decision of the case, we note that the pre-printed contingency clause had been altered by striking a portion of a provision that the agreement was conditioned on buyer's "ability to obtain" a loan as described and substituting the word "obtaining.") Two spaces where interest rates could have been provided, as well as a third space where a monthly payment amount could have been provided and from which an interest rate could be calculated, were left blank.

The appellate courts of Georgia have consistently held that such a contract is too vague and indefinite to be enforced since the failure to specify at what rate the buyer is to obtain a mortgage loan causes a failure of a condition precedent to the enforceability of the contract.

Bonner v. Jordan, 218 Ga. 129, 126 S.E.2d 613; Morgan v. Hemphill, 214 Ga. 555, 105 S.E.2d 580; Scott v. Lewis, 112 Ga.App. 195, 144 S.E.2d 460; Scarborough v. Novak, 92 Ga.App. 488, 88 S.E.2d 800; Williams v. Gottlieb, 90 Ga.App. 438(1), 83 S.E.2d 245. While plaintiffs assert that there was no need to specify the interest rate of the loan to be obtained by defendant Malas because third-party financing, such as contemplated in the loan contingency executed by the parties, invokes a less stringent requirement to state the specific terms of the anticipated loan, the absence of any authority approving of the omission of such an essential loan term as the interest rate must be noted. Plaintiffs cite Walker v. Anderson, 131 Ga.App. 596, 206 S.E.2d 833, in which the interest rate was not omitted but incorporated by reference to the "prevailing interest rate" and this Court held that a loan contingency anticipating a third-party loan was enforceable under this less stringent standard even though it did not state a payment schedule for the loan such as would be necessary in the case of a deferred-payment-to seller clause. It must be noted that variations in the payment schedule would be a matter between the lender and the buyer which would not affect a buyer's obligations to a seller. In contrast, the interest rate is an essential term necessary to enable the courts to enforce the contract between buyer and seller.

Contrary to plaintiffs' assertion, Barto v. Hicks, 124 Ga.App. 472, 474, 184 S.E.2d 188, like Walker v. Anderson, 131 Ga.App. 596, 206 S.E.2d 833, supra, is not a case in which there is a failure to specify the interest rate of the anticipated loan. Instead, the interest rate in *Barto* was specified by reference to the readily ascertainable "current prevailing rate." There is nothing in the document at issue in the present case which amounts to a reference to any source from which an interest rate for the loan which defendant Malas was to seek may be determined.

Butts v. Atlanta Fed. Sav., etc., Assn., 152 Ga.App. 40, 262 S.E.2d 230, involves issues which arise when a person signs a writing containing blanks which are then filled in by the other party. In the case sub judice, the blanks which could have provided an interest rate for the loan to be obtained by defendant Malas were never filled in so this authority has no relevance to the facts of the case sub judice.

Plaintiffs argue at some length that Hawk v. Daugherty, 148 Ga.App. 371, 251 S.E.2d 390 involves facts similar to those in the case sub judice. Yet, that case may be easily distinguished on the facts in that it did not involve a loan contingency, that is, "the statement as to the loan . . . does not involve the purchaser's obligation as to the seller." *Id.* at 372, 251 S.E.2d 390.

Plaintiffs cite Tipton v. Harden, 128 Ga.App. 517, 197 S.E.2d 746 as a case in which "the financing contingency did not specify an interest rate, yet the contract was held to be valid and enforceable." While some reference is made in that opinion to a contention before the lower court concerning the enforceability of the contract, that issue is not discussed in the holding of the opinion. Under these circumstances, the cited case provides no support to plaintiff's position.

Finally, the plaintiffs' reliance upon Brack v. Brownlee, 246 Ga. 818, 273 S.E.2d 390 is misplaced. As noted in Denton v. Hogge, 208 Ga.App. 734(2), 431 S.E.2d 728, the issue of mutuality of obligation discussed in *Brack* is a separate matter from the defense of vagueness and indefiniteness involved in the case sub judice.

The superior court did not err in granting summary judgment in favor of defendant Malas on plaintiffs' claims. It follows that the grant of summary judgment in favor of defendant Malas on his counterclaim seeking the return of the earnest money was proper. Denton v. Hogge, 208 Ga.App. 734(2), 431 S.E.2d 728, supra. Plaintiffs have expressly withdrawn their third enumeration of error seeking reversal of the award of attorney fees to defendant Harry Norman Realtors.

Judgment affirmed.

BEASLEY and SMITH, JJ., concur.

NOTES

1. *Indefiniteness, Illusoriness, and the Financing Condition.* Judicial treatment of the financing condition exemplifies current attitudes toward contract indefiniteness and illusoriness generally. Increasingly, indefiniteness is being resolved in terms of reasonableness, and illusoriness in terms of good faith. Courts will fill in incomplete financing clauses by looking to the circumstances surrounding the contract, including the prevailing money market conditions, to infer the parties' original intent. See, for example, Hunt v. Shamblin, 179 W.Va. 663, 371 S.E.2d 591 (1988). Could the court have saved the contract from indefiniteness in Homler v. Malas? Courts also hold that a contract will be saved from illusoriness by the implied requirement that the buyer diligently seek financing on the terms specified. See, e.g., Liuzza v. Panzer, 333 So.2d 689 (La.App.1976) (no good faith when buyer attempted to get loan from only one institution even though other sources were available); see Grossman v. Melinda Lowell, Attorney at Law, P.A., 703 F.Supp. 282 (S.D.N.Y.1989) (language requiring "best efforts" to secure loan imposed an obligation to make more than a good faith effort).

It is not always easy to keep the two questions, indefiniteness and illusoriness, separate. Note that the two grounds are strategically different. Failure of a condition after good faith efforts excuses only the buyer, while indefiniteness allows both buyer and seller to get out of the contract— although a buyer may be able to cure indefiniteness simply by obtaining financing. See, e.g., Highlands Plaza, Inc. v. Viking Investment Corp., 2 Wash.App. 192, 467 P.2d 378 (1970).

A well drafted contingency clause should prescribe the timing and type of notice that must be given in order to terminate the contract under the contingency clause. Compare Logalbo v. Plishkin, Rubano & Baum, discussed at page 24 above (strictly construing notice provisions), with Armstrong, Gibbons v. Southridge Investment Assocs., 589 A.2d 836 (R.I.1991) (deviating from the usual rule of closely reading terms of a contingency clause and allowing oral notice to be adequate). See generally, Note, The Mortgage Contingency Clause: A Trap for the Residential Real Estate Purchaser Using a Mortgage Broker, 17 Cardozo L.Rev. 299 (1995).

2. *Sufficiency of Terms.* Consider the contingency clause from a contract discussed in Williams v. Ubaldo, 670 A.2d 913, n. 1 (Me.1996):

FINANCING: This contract is subject to an approved conventional mortgage of 80% of the purchase price at an interest rate not to exceed current % and amortized over a period of not less than 30 years. The Seller(s) agrees to pay no more than 0 points, and the Purchaser(s) agrees to pay no more than current points, if required by the lender on the above mortgage.

a.   This contract is subject to a written statement from the lender, within seven (7) days of the Effective Date, that the Purchaser(s) has made application. Loan approval shall be obtained within sixty (60) days of the Effective Date of this contract.

b.   The Purchaser(s) is under a good-faith obligation to seek and accept financing on the above-described terms. The Purchaser(s) acknowledges that a breach of this good-faith obligation to seek and accept financing on the above-described terms . . . will be a breach of this contract.

c.   If either of these conditions is not met within said time periods, the Seller(s) may declare this contract null and void, and the earnest money shall be returned to the purchaser.

Does this clause address the concerns raised by *Homler*? Does it cover the important points that should be addressed in a finance contingency clause? How would you improve it?

3.   *Financing as a Substitute for Other Conditions.* If the financing condition in a land sale contract specifies not only the terms of an acceptable mortgage loan but also the particular institution that is to make the loan, will the buyer be excused if that institution rejects the loan application, but some other institutional lender agrees to make the loan on the terms specified? What if no institutional lender will make the loan, but the seller agrees to finance the transaction herself?

In Kovarik v. Vesely, 3 Wis.2d 573, 575, 89 N.W.2d 279, 281 (1958), the court rejected buyers' argument that, because their contract specified Fort Atkinson Savings & Loan, good faith did not require them to accept financing from the seller. 3 Wis.2d at 583, 89 N.W.2d at 285. Was *Kovarik* correctly decided? Why should a buyer care about the source of his funds? Justice Fairchild, dissenting, offered two possible reasons: "the buyer will feel more confident of his own judgment of the price he is to pay if a lending institution is willing to make a loan" and "the buyer would rather have the matter, in the event of default, in the hands of an established lending institution than in the hands of an individual who might be less able, if not less willing, to adjust matters reasonably." 3 Wis.2d at 585, 89 N.W.2d at 286. For a case reaching a result opposite to *Kovarik*, see Gardner v. Padro, 164 Ill.App.3d 449, 115 Ill.Dec. 445, 517 N.E.2d 1131 (1987).

Is it fair or efficient to let buyers use the financing condition, and the lender's appraisal, to test their own judgment on the worth of the property, giving them an excuse to get out of the contract if financing is refused because the appraisal comes in at less than the contract price? For valuable insights into the appraisal process and its implications for lender liability, see Malloy, Lender Liability for Negligent Real Estate Appraisals, 1984 U.Ill.L.Rev. 53. Is it fair or efficient to let buyers use the financing condition, and the lender's examination of title, to save the buyer the expense of ordering a title report himself? To allow the financing condition to serve as a substitute for the marketable title condition?

2. MARKETABLE TITLE

Caselli v. Messina

Supreme Court of New York, Appellate Term, 1990.
148 Misc.2d 671, 567 N.Y.S.2d 972, aff'd, 193 A.D.2d 775, 598 N.Y.S.2d 265 (1993).

Before MONTELEONE, J.P., and PIZZUTO and SANTUCCI, JJ.

Appeal by plaintiffs and cross-appeal by defendants from an order of the Civil Court, Kings County (Diamond, J.) filed on January 11, 1990 which denied the motion by defendants for summary judgment and dismissal of the complaint and which denied the cross motion of the plaintiffs for summary judgment.

Order modified with $10 costs to defendants, motion for summary judgment in favor of the defendants granted and complaint dismissed and, as so modified, order affirmed.

Plaintiffs entered into a contract to purchase the house of the defendants Messina and pursuant to the contract, a downpayment was deposited with the defendant Ajello. The contract provided that it was to be sold subject to "Covenants, restrictions, reservations * * * of record * * * provided same are not violated by present structure or the present use of premises" and the parties added to said clause the phrase "or render title unmarketable." Another clause of the contract provided that "Sellers shall give and purchasers shall accept such title as any New York City title company will be willing to approve and insure in accordance with their standard form of title policy, subject only to the matters provided for in this contract." After receipt of the title report, plaintiffs notified the defendants that the title was unmarketable due to the restrictions and covenants of record and demanded the return of their downpayment. When the demand was refused, this suit was commenced.

The language of this contract, does not call for an unqualified or unlimited title policy. It calls for a standard policy, "subject only to the matters provided for in this contract." This would include that first clause mentioned above in which the property was sold subject to these covenants and restrictions of record *provided that the present structure did not violate them and provided that title was not rendered unmarketable.*

In Laba v. Carey, 29 N.Y.2d 302, 307–309, 327 N.Y.S.2d 613, 277 N.E.2d 641, rearg. denied 30 N.Y.2d 694, 332 N.Y.S.2d 1025, 283 N.E.2d 432, the contract of sale contained somewhat similar provisions, covenants and restrictions but did not have the additional phrase "or render title unmarketable." The Court of Appeals noted that the policy issued by the title company would only have to comply with the provisions of the contract of sale and that "The contract before us addressed itself to the existence of easements and [restrictions] * * * of record. The title company, disclosing the existence of a telephone easement and 'Waiver of Legal Grades' restrictive covenant, excluded these items from coverage, except insofar as to say that they had not been violated. In so insuring, it was assuming responsibility for no less than that which respondents had expressly agreed to accept. The exceptions were matters specifically contemplated by the contract . . ." The court went on to state:

> "Accordingly, where a purchaser agrees to take title subject to easements and restrictive covenants of record which are not violated, this is the precise kind of title that the seller is obligated to tender and we are not persuaded that, *absent an expression of a contrary intent in the contract*, that obligation is broadened by the existence of the usual 'insurance' clause in a form contract. . . . A conclusion that the seller would nevertheless be required to furnish title, insurable without exception, would not only render nugatory the 'subject to' clause, but would give every purchaser dissatisfied with his bargain a way of avoiding his contractual responsibilities. Surely, this was not contemplated in the contract before us." (Emphasis added)

In *Laba*, as in the case at bar, neither the easements nor the restrictive covenants were violated by the present use and the contract was *silent* as to any special use intended by the plaintiffs for the property.

The essential issue in this case is whether the mere existence of covenants and restrictions of record renders the title unmarketable. An understanding of what renders title unmarketable can be found in the case of Regan v. Lanze, 40 N.Y.2d 475, 481–482, 387 N.Y.S.2d 79, 354 N.E.2d 818, wherein the Court stated:

> "The disposition of this case turns on the marketability of defendants' title. A marketable title has been defined as one that may freely be made the subject of resale (Trimboli v. Kinkel, 226 NY 147–152 [123 N.E. 205]; see 62 NY Jur, Vendor and Purchaser, § 48; 3 Warren's Weed New York Real Property, Marketability of Title, § 2.01). It is one which can be readily sold or mortgaged to a person of reasonable prudence, the test of the marketability of title being whether there is an objection thereto such as would interfere with a sale or with the market value of the property (Brokaw v. Duffy, 165 NY 391, 399 [59 N.E. 196]; Heller v. Cohen, 154 NY 299, 306 [48 N.E. 527]; Vought v. Williams, 120 NY 253, 257 [24 N.E. 195]; Schwartz, Real Estate Manual, p. 581). The law assures to a buyer a title free from reasonable doubt, but not from every doubt [citing authority], and the mere possibility or suspicion of a defect, which according to ordinary experience has no probable basis, does not demonstrate an unmarketable title * * *.

> To be sure, a purchaser is entitled to a marketable title unless the parties stipulate otherwise in the contract (Laba v. Carey, 29 NY2d 302, 311 [327 N.Y.S.2d 613, 277 N.E.2d 641]). Except for extraordinary instances in which it is very clear that the purchaser can suffer no harm from a defect or incumbrance, he will not be compelled to take title when there is a defect in the record title which can be cured only by a resort to parol evidence or when there is an apparent incumbrance which can be removed or defeated only by such evidence * * *."

(*See also,* Voorheesville Rod & Gun Club v. Tompkins County, 158 A.D.2d 789, 551 N.Y.S.2d 382; DeJong v. Mandelbaum, 122 A.D.2d 772, 774, 505 N.Y.S.2d 659; Weiss v. Cord Helmer Realty Corp., 140 N.Y.S.2d 95, 98–99; 62 NY Jur., Vendor and Purchaser, § 48).

In applying these rules to the facts of the case at bar, it is readily apparent that the contract was silent as to any special use that plaintiffs may have had in mind for the property. It is also conceded that the present use of the property did not violate said covenants and restrictions of record. It is therefore concluded that no reasonable person, in the absence of contractual provision calling for a special use of the property, would be denied reasonable enjoyment of the property for his "intended and announced purposes" (DeJong v. Mandelbaum, *supra*). The mere existence of covenants and restrictions of record which did not affect the present use of the property as set forth in the contract between the parties herein provided purchasers with what they had contracted for. Since they were in default under the terms of the contract of sale, they were not entitled to the return of their downpayment.

MONTELEONE, J.P., and SANTUCCI, J., concur.

PIZZUTO, J., dissents in a separate memorandum.

PIZZUTO, Justice, dissents and votes to modify the order of the Court below by granting plaintiffs' motion for summary judgment in the following memorandum.

The majority did not give proper weight to the significance of the fact that added to and made a part of the typed Paragraph 1 of the Rider, which provided that the premises was sold subject to: "(b) covenants, restrictions, reservations, utilities, easements and agreements, of record, insofar as the same may now be in force or effect, provided same are not violated by the present structure or the present use of premises . . .", there was an inked insertion, "*or* render title unmarketable" (emphasis supplied).

Both the NYBTU standard form of contract and the two-page typed rider contained handwritten modifications made at the contract signing, obviously due to the negotiations of the attorneys as to the terms of the contract prior to the execution thereof by the parties.

The issue then becomes whether or not exceptions listed in the report of the Chicago Title Insurance Company concerning a declaration contained in Liber 6150 at Page 569 and Liber 6150 at Page 573 as well as an easement in Liber 6131 at Page 276 and Liber 6104 at Page 65 render title unmarketable. Clearly, the purchasers' attorney modified the aforementioned quoted subject clause by the addition of the words in the disjunctive "*or* render title unmarketable" (emphasis supplied). Those words must be given some meaning in determining under what circumstances, the purchasers were obligated to take title.

The declaration contained in Liber 6150 at Page 573 was a covenant restricting the use of the land, not mentioned anywhere in the contract. The restrictive covenant provided that no building may be erected other than private dwellings, limited the use to two-families, limited the carrying-on of a trade or business at the premises, prescribed minimum setbacks and portions of the land on which no building was to be erected, prohibited the carrying-on of noxious or offensive trades, and prohibited anything being done thereon which may become an annoyance to the neighborhood.

The covenant and restrictions further provided that they shall run with the land and provided that in the event an owner violates or attempts to violate any of the covenants, any other person owning any real estate described in said restrictions may bring an action against the violator seeking an injunction or damages.

These covenants (although not violated by the existing structure or use thereof) prescribed minimum setbacks, restricted the type of building and structure that could be placed on the land and the type of activities that could be carried out on the land. Such restrictions render title unmarketable. (*See,* Golden Development Corp. v. Weyant, et al., 269 App.Div. 1039, 58 N.Y.S.2d 687 [setback restriction]; Rosenberg v. Centre Davis Corp., 15 A.D.2d 506, 222 N.Y.S.2d 391 [restrictive covenants permitting construction or maintenance of one-family house only].) In Antin v. O'Shea, 270 App.Div. 1046, 63 N.Y.S.2d 97, cited in Rosenberg v. Centre Davis Corp., *supra*, the contract provided in part that the property was sold "subject to covenants and restrictions contained in former recorded deeds affecting said premises, *provided they do not render title unmarketable.*" (Emphasis supplied.) A former deed contained a covenant "that there shall not be erected upon any portion of said premises any building for the sale of intoxicating drinks or garden for the sale of ale or beer." The appellate court held that title was unmarketable and granted the purchaser's motion for summary judgment for foreclosure of its lien and recovery of the down payments and expenses.

In Laba v. Carey, 29 N.Y.2d 302, 327 N.Y.S.2d 613, 277 N.E.2d 641, cited and relied upon by the majority, although it contained similar provisions as to title insurance, did not contain similar provisions as to marketability of title.

The pertinent provisions contained in the NYBTU form of contract in the *Laba* case were as follows. It provided that the seller shall give and the purchaser shall accept a title such as any reputable title company would accept and insure. The contract also expressly provided that the sale and conveyance was subject to:

"4.   Covenants, restrictions, utility agreements easements of record if any, now in force, provided same are not now violated.

5.   Any set of facts an accurate survey may show provided same does not render title unmarketable."

The court there held that the purchaser received exactly what he had bargained for in the contract. The purchaser was not entitled to an unconditional title policy without exception since he agreed to take title subject to the covenants, restrictions, utility agreements and easements of record provided that they were not violated, which they were not. There was no additional proviso in the *Laba* case, as there is in this case, to wit: "or render title unmarketable." The only proviso made with reference to marketable title had to do with facts that might be shown on a survey.

The instant case is obviously distinguishable. The purchaser in this case has not been offered that which he had bargained and negotiated for.

In conclusion, to adopt the construction suggested by the majority would do violence to the specific intent of the parties at the time that contract was executed. The majority proposal, that a provision added to the contract is superfluous is contrary to the basic principles of contract law (*see*, 22 NY Jur 2d, Contracts, § 221).

NOTES

1. *What is Marketable Title?* The excerpt from Regan v. Lanze, quoted in Caselli v. Messina, typifies the standard, circular formula for determining whether a seller's title is marketable. One variant of the formula is the rule that a marketable title is one "which at all times and under all circumstances, may be forced upon an unwilling purchaser," Pyrke v. Waddingham, 10 Hare 1, 68 Eng.Rep. 813 (Chancery 1852). Another is that a marketable title is one that can be held quietly without fear of litigation to determine its validity. Stack v. Hickey, 151 Wis. 347, 138 N.W. 1011 (1912).

What is the effect on the buyer's marketable title protection of language making the conveyance subject to covenants, restrictions and reservations of record, such as appeared in Laba v. Carey, discussed in *Caselli* ? Does such a clause favor the buyer or seller? How did the parties in *Caselli* modify the language and to what effect? As developed in the following notes, the majority opinion in *Caselli* departs from the general rule that holds that the mere existence of a covenant or condition automatically makes title unmarketable. See M. Friedman, Contracts and Conveyances of Real Property 600–615 (5th ed.1991).

No condition has produced more litigation or confusion than marketable title. The main reason for the confusion is that courts have tried to apply a single formula to a diverse array of questions and have failed to observe important functional distinctions. The principal relevant distinction is between claims of unmarketability based on defects in the record chain of title and those based on encumbrances. Another important distinction is between those encumbrances that will be apparent to a buyer viewing the land and those that will not. It is also important to distinguish between three overlapping concepts—marketable title, insurable title and record title. The notes that follow examine these distinctions.

2. *Chain of Title Defects.* Chain of title defects affect ownership. They may arise from a fraudulent transfer, an irregularity in the conduct of a mortgage foreclosure, tax sale or probate proceeding, or a technical error or omission in a prior conveyance, such as a misspelling in the name of a party, a misdescription of the parcel or the absence of a proper acknowledgement. They may also result from future interests such as possibilities of reverter and rights of entry.

The standard marketability formula of Regan v. Lanze should properly be applied only to chain of title defects. Every state has remedial statutes exclusively aimed at curing chain of title defects and making title freely transferable. Curative acts, statutes of limitations, marketable title acts and recording acts dictate which title defects impair title and which, with the passage of time, have been cured. While these statutes are not specifically concerned with the resolution of contract disputes over marketable title, they do provide an independent and objective basis for determining the sort of title that a seller may be allowed to force upon a buyer and, by implication, the sort of title that the buyer may be allowed to force on some future buyer. A title with a defect that has been cured by passage of the statutory period, or by the occurrence of the statutorily-prescribed events, is not only good in some abstract sense. It is also marketable in the sense that, as a matter of public policy, the legislature has determined that a buyer should, in acquiring this title, feel confident that he can later sell it without fear that it will then be held unmarketable. For an example of the title clearance system at work in the context of a contract dispute over marketable title, see Tesdell v. Hanes, 248 Iowa 742, 82 N.W.2d 119 (1957).

3. *Encumbrances.* Encumbrances reduce the value of land in ways that fall short of breaks in the chain of title. Mainly they take the form of third party claims to money, possession or use affecting the land. Mechanics liens, mortgage liens and judgment liens are typical money claims. Claims of lessees or tenants in common typify possessory encumbrances. And easements, servitudes and party wall agreements are typical encumbrances affecting land use.

No system of independent, objective benchmarks exists for resolving marketable title disputes over encumbrances. Whether, and to what extent, a servitude, right of way easement or encroachment impairs a parcel's value will vary from time to time and from parcel to parcel. As a result, the correct resolution between one buyer and seller may not be the correct resolution as between another two or, more important, as between the present buyer and some future buyer from him. In the context of encumbrances, the standard formula, that a marketable title is one that may freely be made the subject of resale, is simply conclusional.

Properly conceived, the effect of encumbrances on marketability boils down to a single question: who, as between buyer and seller, has best access to the information that will avoid loss? The answer may turn on whether the encumbrance is visible from an inspection of the parcel.

Invisible Encumbrances. Encumbrances imposing use restrictions are completely within the knowledge of the seller at the time she enters into the contract of sale. She presumably knows of the record restrictions existing at the time she purchased, for she should have obtained an abstract of title or title insurance policy at that time. Any subsequent encumbrances would have been the consequence of her own acts.

Buyer is best placed to know about the uses that he plans to make of the property. If the buyer negotiates for the contract to provide that he will take title subject to all restrictions of record except any that prohibit his intended use, the burden should be on seller to provide title free of the specified restrictions or suffer rescission. Probably the same result should follow if there is no specific contract provision on the point, but buyer has told seller of his intended use, or the intended use can easily be inferred from the circumstances—such as buying a residence for residential purposes. Buyer should lose in this context only when he has done nothing to inform the seller of his intended use and his use is unexpected in the circumstances—as, for example, commercial use of a lot in a residential neighborhood.

Visible Encumbrances. Encumbrances in the form of easements or encroachments require a different allocation of responsibility. If an easement or encroachment is visible from a view of the land, rather than just from the paper record, it probably should not excuse buyer performance because it presumably formed an element of the buyer's expectations, and of buyer's and seller's negotiations on price. Courts have as a general rule followed this approach only in the case of public roads running through the property, and have rested their decisions on one of several theories: custom, buyer knowledge, implied waiver, the private benefit to the property afforded by the public road, the road's public importance, and the minimal nature of the interference.

Courts divide, however, on the effect of other physical intrusions, such as private rights of way and irrigation ditches, with the majority leaning toward the position that they are encumbrances excusing performance. Compare Waters v. North Carolina Phosphate Corp., 310 N.C. 438, 312 S.E.2d 428 (1984) (because easement for 100–foot wide right of way, lined with large towers and five power transmission lines, would have materially interfered with buyer's intended use, buyer was excused from performing), with Alcan Aluminum Corp. v. Carlsberg Financial Corp., 689 F.2d 815 (9th Cir.1982) (buyer conclusively presumed to have intended to take property subject to a utility easement where, although easement did not appear in title report, high tension lines were visible from several points on the property).

4. *Access.* Does the lack of access to the property from a public road create an unmarketable title defect or merely affect the value of the property that buyer will receive? Compare Sinks v. Karleskint, 130 Ill.App.3d 527, 85 Ill.Dec. 807, 474 N.E.2d 767 (1985) (distinguishing "merchantability" of title from market value and holding that lack of access does not breach seller's obligation) with Myerberg, Sawyer & Rue, P.A. v. Agee, 51 Md.App. 711, 446 A.2d 69 (1982) (lack of access breached marketability obligation; pending litigation to establish easement by necessity did not adequately free title from doubt). On the question of access, is there unequal availability of information to buyer and seller so that the law should place a burden on seller to address the problem? Or is the availability of access simply a market calculation, such as good property location, that all parties are expected to make and which the law will not normally adjust?

5. *Marketable Title, Record Title and Insurable Title Compared.* Marketable title can be compared to two other forms of title conditions sometimes obtained by buyers as an alternative, or in addition, to marketable title. *Record title* is title, typically in fee simple absolute, that can be proved by reference to the record alone and without resort to collateral proceedings such as quiet title actions brought to establish seller's title by adverse possession. Perfect record title does not necessarily constitute perfect title. A title that, from the record, appears to be perfect may in fact be entirely invalid because of fraud, nondelivery or a wild deed somewhere in the chain of title. *Insurable title* is title that a title insurance company is willing to insure as valid. Insurable title need not be good record title. For example, a title insurer may decide that, because seller's adverse possession appears to be uncontrovertible, it will insure seller's title to the adversely claimed land even though seller has no record title to it. Also, as indicated in Casseli v. Messina, insurable title may not be marketable title, for the title policy may except defects or encumbrances that make the title unmarketable.

6. *Drafting Exercise.* Assume that you represent the Buyer negotiating a contract of sale. In light of *Caselli*, draft a title clause that would protect your client but that you could get the Seller's attorney to find acceptable. How would you draft a title clause if you had a copy of the title report that the Seller received when the Seller purchased the property ten years before?

3. OTHER PROBLEM AREAS

a. ZONING

Dover Pool & Racquet Club, Inc. v. Brooking

Supreme Judicial Court of Massachusetts, 1975.
366 Mass. 629, 322 N.E.2d 168.

BRAUCHER, JUSTICE.

On January 31, 1972, the parties entered into a written contract for the sale of real estate in Dover and Medfield. A few days earlier, unknown to them, the planning board of Medfield had published a notice of a public hearing on a proposed amendment to the zoning by-law. The proposed amendment would newly require a special permit for the use of the premises contemplated by both the vendor and the purchaser, and under G.L. c. 40A, § 11, the amendment if adopted would have effect retroactive to the date of publication. The purchaser sought rescission of the contract and return of its deposit. A judge of the Superior Court decreed rescission and return because of a mutual mistake of fact, and we affirm.

The case was referred to a master, whose report was confirmed except for its conclusions. We summarize the master's findings. The Brookings owned about fifty acres of land, nine acres in Medfield and the rest in Dover, used as a single family residence. The buildings were in Dover, and the only established access was through the Medfield portion. During negotiations with the purchaser (the Club) the Brookings were informed that the Club intended to use the property for a nonprofit tennis and swim club.

Both the Dover and the Medfield zoning by-laws permitted use of the premises as of right for a "club when not conducted for profit and not containing more than five sleeping rooms." The parties discussed the zoning by-law of Dover. The Brookings asked their broker about zoning, and he replied that everything would be all right under the existing Dover and Medfield by-laws. The vice-president of the Club who signed the agreement checked both the Dover and the Medfield zoning by-laws.

The agreement, signed on January 31, 1972, provides for conveyance of "a good and clear record and marketable title thereto, free from encumbrances, except (a) Provisions of existing building and zoning laws. . . ." The planning board of Medfield on January 27 and February 3, 1972, published notice of a public hearing on February 14, 1972, on proposed amendments to the Medfield zoning by-law, including a requirement of a special permit for use of the Medfield portion of the premises as a "non-profit country, hunting, fishing, tennis or golf club without liquor license." Neither of the parties was aware of the notice, but the Club's board of directors became aware of it about ten days before the agreed closing date of March 1, 1972. The parties met on the closing date, and the Brookings were prepared to deliver a deed, but the Club refused to proceed with the purchase. The proposed zoning amendment was adopted at the Medfield town meeting on March 21, 1972, and approved by the Attorney General in July, 1972.

In general, building and zoning laws in existence at the time a land contract is signed are not treated as encumbrances, and the purchaser has no recourse against the vendor by virtue of restrictions imposed by such laws on the use of the property purchased.

Moreover, changes in such laws after the contract is signed have commonly been held to be part of the risk assumed by the purchaser. In some such cases, however, specific performance at the suit of the vendor has been denied, particularly where both parties knew of the contemplated use later prohibited.

In the present case the agreement itself makes it explicit that "existing building and zoning laws" are not included in the vendor's obligation to convey "free from encumbrances." The Club argues, by contrasting the quoted exception with other exceptions, that the building and zoning laws excepted are those "existing" on the date of the agreement, but we think it is clear that the reference is to laws "existing" on the date of the deed. In other words, the purchaser bore the risk of zoning laws in effect on the date of closing.

We have upheld a decree of rescission of a sale of land by reason of misrepresentations of the zoning situation by the vendors, and in doing so assumed that there would be no liability for bare nondisclosure. In other States rescission has been decreed on the basis of mutual mistake of fact in circumstances like those before us. We have long recognized that land contracts may be rescinded for mutual mistake. But we seem not to have been called on to pass upon a mistake as to zoning.

The Medfield zoning amendment was not an "existing" zoning law at the time of the closing. It was not an encumbrance and it was not within the exception in the agreement. Yet under G.L. c. 40A, § 11,[a] the notice published four days before the agreement was signed had a material impact on the purchaser's intended use of the premises. After the notice was published, the issuance of a building permit or the beginning of work on a building or structure would not protect the purchaser if the steps required for the adoption of the proposed amendment were taken in their usual sequence without unnecessary or unreasonable delay. Meanwhile, no special permit could be issued under the proposed amendment before it was enacted. The agreement provides "that time is of the essence of this agreement," and the record does not indicate any willingness by the vendor to extend the time for closing until after the town meeting which was to act on the proposed amendment. Under Harrison v. Building Inspector of Braintree, 350 Mass. 559, 561, 215 N.E.2d 773 (1966), use of the only established access to the premises might be barred if no special permit were obtained.

---

[a]   Now codified at Mass.Gen.Laws Ann. ch. 40A, § 6.

Thus at the time the contract was made both parties made the assumption that the zoning by-laws interposed no obstacle to the use of the premises for a nonprofit tennis and swim club. That assumption was mistaken, and we think it was a basic assumption on which the contract was made. It could not yet be said that the purchaser's principal purpose had been frustrated. But a right of vital importance to the purchaser did not exist, and as a result of the mistake enforcement of the contract would be materially more onerous to the purchaser than it would have been had the facts been as the parties believed them to be. The contract was therefore voidable by the purchaser unless it bore the risk of the mistake. The agreement does not provide for that risk, and the case is not one of conscious ignorance or deliberate risk-taking on the purchaser's part. Nor do we think there is any common understanding that purchasers take the risk of the unusual predicament in which the purchaser found itself. We therefore agree with the judge's conclusion that the contract was voidable for mutual mistake of fact.

Decree affirmed with costs of appeal.

b.   QUANTITY

Cedar Lane Ranch, Inc. v. Lundberg

Supreme Court of Montana, 1999.
297 Mont. 145, 991 P.2d 440.

JUSTICE WILLIAM E. HUNT, SR., delivered the Opinion of the Court.

Cedar Lane Ranch, Inc. (Cedar Lane Ranch), brought an action to quiet title to the following parcel of disputed property lying in Granite County:

> All of that portion of the Northeast Quarter of the Northeast Quarter (NE 1/4 NE 1/4) of Section 26, Township 10 North, Range 13 West, M.P.M., Granite County, Montana lying West of Montana Highway 1 running between Drummond and Anaconda, Montana.

Carl Nelson Ranch Company (Carl Nelson Ranch) appeals from the order of the Third Judicial District Court, Granite County, granting summary judgment to Cedar Lane Ranch and quieting title to the disputed property. We affirm.

Prior to 1994, both the Cedar Lane Ranch and the Carl Nelson Ranch believed that only seven of the forty acres in the NE 1/4 NE 1/4 of Section 26 were located on the west side of Montana Highway 1 and owned by the Cedar Lane Ranch; both ranches also believed that the remaining thirty-three acres in the NE 1/4 NE 1/4 of Section 26 were located east of the highway and owned by the Carl Nelson Ranch. However, pursuant to a right-of-way survey performed by the Montana Department of Highways of 1994, it was discovered that "more than seven acres and as many as thirteen acres" of the NE 1/4 NE 1/4 of Section 26 may in fact be located on the west side of Montana Highway 1. The disputed property in this quiet title action is that portion of the NE 1/4 NE 1/4 of Section 26 in *excess* of seven acres lying west of Montana Highway 1.

In its quiet title action, Cedar Lane Ranch named as defendants Wilford and Heber Lundberg, title holders of record to the disputed property and predecessors in interest to the Cedar Lane Ranch, and Carl Nelson and the Carl Nelson Ranch. Although the Lundbergs were served notice by publication, they failed to appear and default judgment was entered against them. However, Carl Nelson Ranch appeared at the quiet title action and, based upon the results of the 1994 highway survey, asserted a counterclaim to an indeterminate six acres in the disputed property. Cedar Lane Ranch subsequently moved for summary judgment on the complaint and the counterclaim, and its motion was granted by the District Court.

Issues

There are essentially two issues on appeal, restated as follows:

(1.) Did the District Court err in concluding that the disputed property was transferred in gross and, therefore, that the actual acreage of the conveyance was immaterial?

(2.) Did the District Court err in alternatively concluding that summary judgment was proper because Cedar Lane Ranch holds title to the disputed property by adverse possession?

Factual and Procedural Background

In 1892, Albert Tinklepaugh (Tinklepaugh), the common predecessor in interest, obtained a patent to the lands that today comprise both the Cedar Lane Ranch and the Carl Nelson Ranch. Since the time of Tinklepaughs first conveyance, a common boundary existed between the two ranches in the form of a country road that is today Montana Highway 1; the Cedar Lane Ranch lies to the west of the highway, and the Carl Nelson Ranch to the east.

In 1902, Tinklepaugh deeded a parcel of land to James McGowan, a predecessor in interest to the Cedar Lane Ranch. This parcel of land was bounded by a county road (now Montana Highway 1) to the east, and was bounded by section lines to the north, south, and west. By deed, Tinklepaugh described the conveyed land as follows: "About seven acres of land off of the west side of the N.E. 1/4 N.E. 1/4 of Sec. 26 Township 10 N. Range 13 West. Said piece of land being west of the of the foot of the hill, where county road now runs." This parcel has never been severed by sale or otherwise from the holdings of the Cedar Lane Ranch, and has been fenced-in and continuously "ranched" since the 1950s.

In 1916, Tinklepaugh conveyed his land on the *east side* of the county road to Carl Nelson, purportedly including all of Tinklepaugh's remaining ownership in the NE 1/4 NE 1/4 of Section 26. The deed described this conveyance as follows:

> The Northwest quarter (NW 1/4) of Section Twenty-five (25), the *North-east quarter (NE 1/4) of the North-east quarter (NE 1/4) of Section Twenty-six (26) except that portion of approximately seven (7) acres off of the west side, all lying on the west side of the public highway,* and about seven (7) acres of land off of the east side of the South-east quarter (SE 1/4) of the South-east quarter (SE 1/4) of Section Twenty-three (23) all in Township Ten (10) North, Range Thirteen (13) West of

Montana, Meridian, Montana, containing Two Hundred Acres, more or less. [Emphasis added.]

In 1944, McGowans heirs sold what is today the entire Cedar Lane Ranch, including the disputed property, to the Lundbergs. Although the disputed property has never been severed from the holdings of the Cedar Lane Ranch, the legal description of the disputed property was inadvertently omitted from the chain of title beginning in 1950. In 1950, the Lundbergs contracted with Woodrow and Billie Wallace to sell the land that today comprises the Cedar Lane Ranch; the legal description of the disputed property was omitted from that agreement. The contract was paid in 1958, at which time the Lundbergs conveyed the ranch by warranty deed to the Wallaces; that deed also omitted the legal description of the disputed property. In 1972, the Wallaces conveyed the land by warranty deed to the Cedar Lane Ranch, again omitting the legal description of the disputed property. These oversights were not discovered until the 1994 highway survey indicated the acreage discrepancies in Tinklepaughs transfers.

In 1964, Carl Nelson deeded his land to the Carl Nelson Ranch. The legal description in the warranty deed purported to convey the following parcel: "Section 26: NE 1/4 NE 1/4 except that portion of approximately 7 acres off of west side, all lying on the west side of the public highway."

The District Court quieted title to the disputed acreage in the Cedar Lane Ranch. In quieting title, the court ruled that: (1) the Carl Nelson Ranch did not possess any title interest in the disputed property since the parcel west of the highway had been transferred to the Cedar Lane Ranch "in gross" and, therefore, that the parties had assumed any risk of an acreage variance; and that (2) even if the Carl Nelson Ranch had a title interest in the disputed property, the Cedar Lane Ranch had obtained title to that parcel through adverse possession.

Discussion

(1.) Did the District Court err in concluding that the disputed property was transferred in gross and, therefore, that the actual acreage of the conveyance was immaterial?

We review a district court's entry of summary judgment *de novo*. Motarie v. Northern Mont. Joint Refuse Disposal Dist. (1995), 274 Mont. 239, 242, 907 P.2d 154, 156; Mead v. M.S.B., Inc. (1994), 264 Mont. 465, 470, 872 P.2d 782, 785. When we review a district court's award of summary judgment, we apply the same analysis as the district court based upon Rule 56, M.R.Civ.P. *See* Bruner v. Yellowstone County (1995), 272 Mont. 261, 264, 900 P.2d 901. 903.

In its order, the District Court reasoned as follows:

Whether the size of the parcel is 7 acres or 13 acres is not important as to the outcome of this case. When Mr. Tinklepaugh conveyed what is now the disputed parcel he stated "about 7 acres" after identifying the area by boundaries, being the foot of the hill and the county road.

"A contract of sale by the acre is one wherein a specified quantity is material. Under such a contract the purchaser does not take the risk of any deficiency and the vendor does not take the risk of any excess. The contract of sale by the tract or in gross is one wherein boundaries are specified, but quantity is not specified, or if specified, the existence of the exact quantity specified is not material; each party takes the risk of the actual quantity varying to some extent from what he [or she] expects it to be." Parcel v. Myers, 214 Mont. 225, [228], 697 P.2d[, 94] (1985) [(*quoting* 77 Am.Jur.2d *Vendor and Purchaser* § 90)].

Mr. Tinklepaugh conveyed the property in gross after identifying the boundaries. The exact quantity is not material as each party takes the risk of the actual quantity varying.

Carl Nelson Ranch disputes the District Court's conclusion that "[a]n inaccurate estimation of the size of the parcel is not a genuine issue of material fact." The court's conclusion was premised on the fact that Tinklepaugh had conveyed what is now the disputed property "after identifying the area by boundaries, being the foot of the hill and the county road." In opposition to Cedar Lane Ranch's motion for summary judgment, Carl Nelson Ranch introduced two affidavits indicating that both ranches had believed, prior to the 1994 highway survey, that the Cedar Lane Ranch owned only seven acres of the NE 1/4 NE 1/4 of Section 26. Carl Nelson Ranch thus contends that genuine issues of material fact exist as to the size of the disputed property.

In response, Cedar Lane Ranch argues that the liberal use of "words of estimation" in the relevant conveyances strongly suggest that the transfers were in gross, and that, pursuant to *Parcel* and pertinent rules of construction, the District Court properly concluded that the amount of acreage at issue is immaterial because of the consistent references to fixed, permanent boundaries in the conveyances. We agree.

"Generally when land is sold in gross, a variation in acreage from what the parties had contemplated is not grounds for rescission or other relief." Hardin v. Hill (1967), 149 Mont. 68, 74, 423 P.2d 309, 312. Although words of estimation alone do not necessarily create a sale in gross, Cedar Lane Ranch avers that where, as here, words of estimation in a deed are combined with a negotiated lump sum sale price and an absence of any reference to a price per acre, a sale in gross may be created. *See* Turner v. Ferrin (1988), 232 Mont. 146, 151, 757 P.2d 335, 338.

In *Turner*, the purchasers sued for rescission based on an "acreage shortfall" which was discovered by a subsequent survey of the property. *See Turner*, 232 Mont. at 147–49, 757 P.2d at 336–37. Based on evidence showing that the purchasers had paid a lump sum purchase price of $230,000 for the property without any deed reference to a price per acre, that the purchasers had been personally shown the property boundaries prior to the sale, and that the deed had provided for a conveyance of "93.76 acres, more or less," the district court held that the sale had been in gross. *See Turner*, 232 Mont. at 148–51, 757 P.2d at 336–38. Therefore, the district court denied rescission to the purchasers. In affirming, this Court concluded:

> Although we do not hold that the use of the language "more or less" alone creates a "sale in gross," we do hold that it is sufficient, combined with the observation of the property by

the [purchasers], the sale price as a negotiated lump sum, and the lack of a statement of price per acre, to create a "sale in gross."

Turner, 232 Mont. at 151, 757 P.2d at 338.

According to Cedar Lane Ranch, the requirements for a sale in gross have been met: although it is impossible to determine from the record whether either McGowan or Carl Nelson personally observed the properties prior to the 1902 or 1916 conveyances, both Tinklepaugh deeds use words of estimation to describe the size of the property conveyed, contain a lump sum purchase price, and exclude any reference to a price per acre.

Carl Nelson Ranch argues, however, that under a plain language construction of the 1902 and 1916 deeds, Tinklepaugh clearly conveyed only seven acres to the Cedar Lane Ranch and the remaining thirty-three acres of the NE 1/4 NE 1/4 of Section 26 to the Carl Nelson Ranch. In making this claim, Carl Nelson Ranch suggests that the plain meaning of "about" is the same as "approximately," which is defined in part as "nearly exact, accurate, complete or perfect." Webster's II New College Dictionary, 3, 56 (2d ed. 1995).

We determine that the plain meaning of the words "about" and "approximately" utilized respectively in the 1902 and 1916 deeds is the same as the more commonly used phrase "more or less." As this Court explained in *Turner*:

> "The use of the words 'more or less' excludes the assumption of an exact number of acres and makes it clear that the precise dimensions of the property are not of the essence of the contract, the parties either not knowing themselves the exact number of acres in the land, or purposely not intending to state it."

Turner, 232 Mont. at 151, 757 P.2d at 338 (quoting 1 A.L.R.2d at 47–48). Furthermore, courts have construed similar words and phrases with like meaning: "The same interpretation that is given to the term 'more or less' has also been given to other terms of similar connotation, such as 'about,' 'by estimation,' 'approximately,' 'supposed to contain,' 'in the aggregate,' and 'nearly.'" C.T. Drechsler, Annotation, *Relief by Way of Rescission or Adjustment of Purchase Price for Mutual Mistake as to Quantity of Land, Where the Sale is in Gross*, 1 A.L.R.2d § 18, at 49–50 (1948) (footnotes omitted); *accord* 77 Am.Jur.2d *Vendor and Purchaser* § 110, at 201 (1997).

An unambiguous deed must, to the extent possible, be interpreted according to its language as written. Ferriter v. Bartmess (1997), 281 Mont. 100, 103, 931 P.2d 709, 711 (citing §§ 70–1–513 and 28–3–401, MCA). This Court will "neither put words into a deed which are not there, nor put a construction on words directly contrary to their obvious meaning." McReynolds v. McReynolds (1966), 147 Mont. 476, 480, 414 P.2d 531, 533.

We hold that the plain meaning of the words "about" and "approximately" indicates that the parties did not intend to convey a precise number of acres by the 1902 and 1916 deeds. The specification of acreage quantities in the deeds, being qualified by words of estimation or approximation, renders the acreage quantities merely descriptive rather than material to the agreement. In other words, the stated acreage quantities are not of the essence of the contract, thus indicating a sale in gross. *See Turner*, 232 Mont. at 151, 757 P.2d at 338 (quoting 1 A.L.R.2d at 47–48); 77 Am.Jur.2d *Vendor and Purchaser* § 110, at 200 (1997).

The original 1902 Tinklepaugh deed specifically described certain boundaries, the "foot of the hill" and the "county road," and only estimated the quantity of acres affected by the conveyance at "[a]bout 7." The record indicates that the consideration for the 1902 conveyance was another piece of land, with an estimated value of $100, which was apparently exchanged for the disputed property. There being no indication in the record that this consideration was based upon the relative acreage of the two parcels exchanged, we conclude that the 1902 transfer was for a lump sum which, in conjunction with the use of "*about*" as a term of acreage estimation in the deed, created a sale in gross. We further conclude that the 1916 deed's specific reference to the same boundaries as the 1902 deed combined with a lump sum purchase price of $10,000 and the use of words of estimation (excluding "*approximately* seven" acres west of the highway from the total conveyance of "Two Hundred Acres, *more or less*") also created a bulk real estate transaction.

Having held that the intent of the 1902 and 1916 deeds, when read together, was to transfer Tinklepaugh's ownership in the NE 1/4 NE 1/4 of Section 26 in gross, it is clear that the parties assumed the risk that the actual acreage transferred would vary from that stated in the deeds. The general rule is that:

> "[O]n a sale of land by its legal description, or other specific description by which its boundaries are made certain, for a sum in gross, the *boundaries will control in case of a discrepancy as to quantity*, and . . . such a sale in gross affords no remedy to the grantor or the grantee for an excess or deficiency unless such excess is so great as to raise a presumption of fraud." [Emphasis added.]

Parcel, 214 Mont. at 228, 697 P.2d at 94 (quoting Carrel v. Lux (1966), 101 Ariz. 430, 420 P.2d 564, 572). We hold that the description of the disputed property in the 1902 deed as "being west of the foot of the hill, where county road now runs," and in the 1916 deed as "lying on the west side of the public highway" controls over any discrepancy in acreage quantities stated in the two deeds.

As mentioned earlier, the disputed property lies to the west of Montana Highway 1, and is bordered on the three other sides by section lines. The record makes it clear that what is now Montana Highway 1 has long served as a "common boundary" between the two ranches dividing their respective holdings in the NE 1/4 NE 1/4 of Section 26, with the Cedar Lane Ranch fencing the land to the west of the highway and the Carl Nelson Ranch fencing the land to the east. Carl Nelson Ranch also claims that it has a valid deed to the disputed property by virtue of the 1964 conveyances, which, in conjunction with the omission of the description of the disputed property from Cedar Lane Ranch's chain of title beginning in 1950, shows that Cedar Lane Ranch does not have a valid deed to the disputed property. However, we agree with the District Court that Carl Nelson Ranch cannot "claim the disputed parcel under color of title because their deed of 1964 excludes the area in dispute" lying west of Montana Highway 1. Indeed, the 1964 deed does not purport to convey any land west of the highway, nor does it identify the Carl Nelson Ranch as the owner of the disputed property. This Court notes that Carl Nelson Ranch does not offer any suggestion, based on the relevant conveyances, as to how to identify which six acres west of the highway in the NE 1/4 NE 1/4 of Section 26 it lays claim to without either inserting what was omitted or omitting was inserted in the deeds. Section 1–4–101, MCA.

The District Court properly found that the acreage discrepancies in the relevant conveyances did not raise a genuine issue of material fact precluding summary judgment, since the grantor's consistent description of the property boundaries controls over the inconsistent acreage estimates in the conveyances. See *Parcel*, 214 Mont. at 228, 697 P.2d at 94. This Court need not reach the second issue on appeal.

Affirmed.

JAMES C. NELSON, JIM REGNIER, KARLA M. GRAY, and W. WILLIAM LEAPHART, JJ., concur.

CHIEF JUSTICE J.A. TURNAGE did not participate.

JUSTICE TERRY N. TRIEWEILER dissenting.

I dissent from the majority's conclusion that the property at issue in this case was transferred in gross and that the actual acreage conveyed was immaterial.

In Parcel v. Myers (1984), 214 Mont. 225, 697 P.2d 92, we approved the following distinction between sale by the acre and sale in gross:

> The legal authority is unequivocal on this subject. 77 Am.Jur.2d, Vendor and Purchaser, § 90 provides:
>
> "A contract of sale by the acre is one wherein a specified quantity is material. Under such a contract the purchaser does not take the risk of any deficiency and the vendor does not take the risk of any excess. *The contract of sale by the tract or in gross is one wherein boundaries are specified, but quantity is not specified.* Or if specified, the existence of the exact quantity specified is not material; each party takes the risk of the actual quantity varying to some extent from what he expects it to be."
>
> We adopt the rationale of the Arizona Supreme Court which, citing the above legal authority, held:
>
> . . .
>
> "Therein, the rule was stated that on a sale of land by its legal description or other specific description by which its boundaries are made certain, for a sum in gross, the boundaries will control in case of a discrepancy as to quantity, and that such a sale in gross affords no remedy to the grantor or the grantee for an excess or deficiency unless such excess is so great as to raise the presumption of fraud." Carrel v. Lux (1966), 101 Ariz. 430, 420 P.2d 564, 572.

Parcel, 214 Mont. at 228, 697 P.2d at 94 (emphasis added).

The majority's conclusion that the sale at issue was a sale in gross is based on its conclusion that: "The original 1902 Tinklepaugh deed specifically described certain boundaries." However, I disagree.

The original 1902 grant conveyed "about (7) seven acres of land *off of the west side* of the Northeast quarter (NE 1/4) of the Northeast quarter (NE 1/4) of Section Twenty-six (26), Township Ten (10) North, Range Thirteen (13) West. Said piece of land being west of the foot of the hill, where the county road now runs." In other words, the only reference to a boundary for the transferred land is that it lay on the west side of the county road. There was no description of the north, south, or east boundary of the portion conveyed. However, there was reference to the approximate size of the property transferred. It was described as "about seven (7) acres." Although words of approximation such as "about" leave some room for variation from the number of acres specified, they don't permit a construction which would nearly double the number of acres specified.

Because the contract of sale in 1902 does not specify the boundaries of the property transferred and because the specific quantity was specified, the transfer in this case could not be in gross as we defend that term in *Parcel*. For these reasons, I would reverse the District Court's conclusion that the actual acreage of the conveyance was immaterial and dissent from that portion of the majority's opinion which holds otherwise.

. . .

c.   ATTORNEY APPROVAL

Moran v. Erk

Court of Appeals of New York, 2008.
11 N.Y.3d 452, 901 N.E.2d 187.

READ, J.

On December 13, 1995, defendants Mehmet and Susan Erk signed a real estate contract to purchase the home of plaintiffs James J. and Kathleen D. Moran, a 5,000-square-foot ranch-style house located in Clarence, New York. The contract, which was executed by the Morans on December 22, 1995, provided for a purchase price of $505,000, and contained a rider with an "attorney approval contingency" stating as follows:

> "This Contract is contingent upon approval by attorneys for Seller and Purchaser by the third business day following each party's attorney's receipt of a copy of the fully executed Contract (the "Approval Period"). . . . If either party's attorney disapproves this Contract before the end of the Approval Period, it is void and the entire deposit shall be returned."

Both the contract and the rider were form documents copyrighted and approved by the Greater Buffalo Association of Realtors, Inc. and the Bar Association of Erie County.*

---

* The form contract, which is available electronically on the Bar Association's website (see http://www.eriebar.org/pdfs/Contract. pdf [last accessed November 17, 2008]), contains the

After signing the contract, the Erks developed qualms about purchasing the Morans' house. They discussed their misgivings with each other and with friends and family, and ultimately decided to buy a different residence. As a result, they instructed their attorney to disapprove the contract, and she did so on December 28, 1995, which was within the three-day period for invoking the attorney approval contingency.

The Morans—who had moved out of their Clarence residence in September 1995—kept the house on the market until it was eventually sold for $385,000 in late 1998. Shortly thereafter, they sued the Erks in Supreme Court, alleging breach of contract. They sought to recover as damages the difference between the contract price of $505,000 and the eventual sale price of $385,000, as well as "carrying costs" for marketing the Clarence property for almost three years beyond the date of the 1995 contract with the Erks.

After a bench trial, Supreme Court found in the Morans' favor, and entered a judgment against the Erks for $234,065.75, which represented the difference between the contract price and the eventual sale price, plus statutory interest. Citing McKenna v. Case (123 A.D.2d 517 [4th Dept 1986]) and Ulrich v. Daly (225 A.D.2d 229 [3d Dept 1996]), Supreme Court opined that "[i]t is well settled law that where a Buyer acts in bad faith by instructing his attorney to disapprove a real estate contract, the condition that the contract be approved by an attorney is deemed waived and a contract is formed." Likewise relying on McKenna, the Appellate Division affirmed in a short memorandum opinion. We subsequently granted the Erks' motion for leave to appeal, and now reverse.

Attorney approval contingencies are routinely included in real estate contracts in upstate New York (see e.g. Dorothy H. Ferguson, Subject to the Approval of My Attorney Clauses, 35 N.Y. Real Prop LJ 35 [Spr/Sum 2007]; Alice M. Noble-Allgire, Attorney Approval Clauses in Residential Real Estate Contracts—Is Half a Loaf Better than None? 48 U. Kan. L. Rev. 339, 342 [2000]). Requiring a real estate contract to be "subject to" or "contingent upon" the approval of attorneys for both contracting parties ensures that real estate brokers avoid the unauthorized practice of law (see Matter of Duncan & Hill Realty v. Department of State of State of N.Y., 62 A.D.2d 690, 701 [4th Dept 1978], lv denied 45 N.Y.2d 709 and 45 N.Y.2d 821 [1978]; 1996 Ops Atty Gen No. 96–F11), and allows both contracting parties to have agents representing their respective legal interests (see generally Real Property Law § 443 et seq.; Rivkin v. Century 21 Teran Realty LLC, 10 NY3d 344, 352–56 [2008] [discussing brokers' agency relationships and duties in real estate transactions, and emphasizing that, absent express disclosure to the contrary, a real estate broker does not represent the

---

subject attorney approval contingency as paragraph "ATC1" (see id. at 9). A boldface header to paragraph ATC1 provides:

    "**ATTORNEY APPROVAL CONTINGENCY. CAUTION:** *The deletion or modification of Paragraph ATC1(A) or Paragraph ATC1(B), unless such modification extends the Attorney Approval Period or Addendum Approval Period, shall result in the automatic withdrawal of any bar association approval of this form*" (id. at 9 [all emphases in original]).

interests of both parties to a transaction]). Where a real estate contract states that it is "subject to" or "contingent upon" the approval of each party's attorney, this language means what is says: no vested rights are created by the contract prior to the expiration of the contingency period (see Black's Law Dictionary 828 [8th ed 2004], contingent interest ["An interest that the holder may enjoy only upon the occurrence of a condition precedent"] [emphasis added]).

Here, as previously noted, the contract between the Erks and the Morans explicitly stated that "[t]his Contract is *contingent upon approval by attorneys for Seller and Purchaser* by the third business day following each party's attorney's receipt of a copy of the fully executed Contract," and further provided that "[i]f either party's attorney disapproves this contract before the end of the Approval Period, *it is void*" (emphases added). The Morans argue that the contract nonetheless created an implied limitation upon an attorney's discretion to approve or disapprove the contract. We do not ordinarily read implied limitations into unambiguously worded contractual provisions designed to protect contracting parties. The Morans, however, contend—and the lower courts apparently agreed—that the implied covenant of good faith and fair dealing implicitly limits an attorney's ability to approve or disapprove a real estate contract pursuant to an attorney approval contingency. This argument misconstrues the implied covenant of good faith and fair dealing under New York law.

The implied covenant of good faith and fair dealing between parties to a contract embraces a pledge that "neither party shall do anything which will have the effect of destroying or injuring the right of the other party to receive the fruits of the contract" (511 W. 232nd Owners Corp. v. Jennifer Realty Co., 98 N.Y.2d 144, 153 [2002], quoting Dalton v. Educational Testing Serv., 87 N.Y.2d 384, 389 [1995] [additional citation omitted]). Yet the plain language of the contract in this case makes clear that any "fruits" of the contract were contingent on attorney approval, as any reasonable person in the Morans' position should have understood (see 511 W. 232nd Owners Corp., 98 N.Y.2d at 153 [implied covenant of good faith and fair dealing encompasses "promises which a reasonable person in the position of the promisee would be justified in understanding were included"] [citations omitted]).

Further, considerations of clarity, predictability, and professional responsibility weigh against reading an implied limitation into the attorney approval contingency. Clarity and predictability are particularly important in the interpretation of contracts (see Maxton Bldrs. v. Lo Galbo, 68 N.Y.2d 373, 381 [1986] ["when contractual rights are at issue, where it can be reasonably be assumed that settled rules are necessary and necessarily relied upon, stability and adherence to precedent are generally more important than a better or even a 'correct' rule of law"] [quotation marks and citation omitted]), and "[t]his is perhaps true in real property more than any other area of the law" (Holy Props. v. Cole Prods., 87 N.Y.2d 130, 134 [1995] [citation omitted]). But the bad faith rule advocated by the Morans, which derives from the McKenna decision, advances none of those objectives.

In McKenna, a short memorandum opinion, the Appellate Division held that an attorney's disapproval pursuant to an attorney approval contingency "would terminate plaintiff's rights under the contract, unless said disapproval is occasioned by bad faith" (123 A.D.2d 517, 517 [internal citations omitted; emphasis added]). The court further stated,

> "[w]hile the issue of 'bad faith' usually raises a question of fact precluding summary judgment, the uncontradicted proof demonstrates conclusively that defendant acted in bad faith by instructing his attorney to disapprove the contract. Defendant, by interfering and preventing his attorney from considering the contract, acted in bad faith and, therefore, the condition that the contract be approved by seller's attorney must be deemed waived and the contract formed" (id. [citations omitted]).

Reading a bad faith exception into an attorney approval contingency would create—as the McKenna court itself recognized—a regime where "question[s] of fact precluding summary judgment" would "usually [be] raise[d]" by a disappointed would-be seller or buyer *any time* an attorney disapproved a real estate contract pursuant to an attorney approval contingency. In an area of law where clarity and predictability are particularly important, "this novel notion would be entirely dependent on the subjective equitable variations of different Judges and courts instead of the objective, reliable, predictable and relatively definitive rules" of plain-text contractual language (Ely-Cruikshank Co. v. Bank of Montreal, 81 N.Y.2d 399, 403 [1993]).

The circumstances of this case illustrate the chanciness inherent in a bad faith rule. The Erks' attorney disapproved the contract for the sale of the Morans' Clarence house in late 1995. The Erks soon bought a house in a different community, and continued on with their lives, relying on their attorney's disapproval of a contract that declared that such disapproval rendered it "void." Some three years after their last contact with the Morans, the Erks were served with the complaint in this breach-of-contract lawsuit. Now—10 years after their attorney disapproved the contract within a three-day disapproval period—the Erks are fighting a six-figure judgment for putatively breaching an unwritten covenant because of something Mrs. Erk may have said or neglected to say in a single conversation with her attorney.

Indeed, any inquiry into whether a particular attorney disapproval was motivated by bad faith will likely require factual examination of communications between the disapproving attorney and that attorney's client (see e.g. McKenna, 123 A.D.2d at 517 ["defendant acted in bad faith *by instructing his attorney to disapprove the contract*"] [emphasis added]; Moran v. Erk, 45 AD3d 1329, 1329 [2007] ["the evidence supports the court's determination that defendants acted in bad faith *by instructing their attorney to disapprove the contract*"] [emphasis added]). That is, the disapproving attorney will be subpoenaed to testify about communications the disclosure of which might be detrimental to that attorney's client-a direct conflict with an attorney's duty to preserve a client's confidences and secrets (see 22 NYCRR 1200.19[a] [defining "secret" as "information gained in the professional relationship that the client has requested be held inviolate or the disclosure of which would be embarrassing or would be likely to be detrimental to the client"]). This is precisely what occurred here, where the lower courts' findings of bad faith were expressly grounded in the deposition testimony of the Erks' attorney. Moreover, the threat to attorney-client confidentiality under a bad faith regime could harm the attorney-client relationship itself in the context of real estate transactions. A diligent attorney, cognizant of the risk of being subpoenaed to testify as to the basis for a disapproval, would face a perverse incentive to avoid candid communications with his or her client regarding a transaction in which the attorney is supposed to represent the client's legal interest.

All these potential problems vanish when an attorney approval contingency is interpreted according to its plain meaning, as our sister state of New Jersey has long done (see New Jersey State Bar Assoc. v. New Jersey Association of Realtor Bds., 452 A.2d 1323 [Superior Ct 1982] [approving "broad construction" of attorney approval clause "enabling an attorney to disapprove a contract or lease for any reason or reasons which would not be subject to review"], modified on other grounds and affd 461 A.2d 1112 [NJ 1983]). We therefore hold that where a real estate contract contains an attorney approval contingency providing that the contract is "subject to" or "contingent upon" attorney approval within a specified time period and no further limitations on approval appear in the contract's language, an attorney for either party may timely disapprove the contract for any reason or for no stated reason. Since no explicit limitations were placed on the attorney approval contingency in the contract in this case, the Erks' attorney's timely disapproval was valid, and the contract is void by its express terms.

Accordingly, the order of the Appellate Division should be reversed, with costs, and the complaint dismissed.

* * *

Order reversed, with costs, and complaint dismissed.

CHIEF JUDGE KAYE and JUDGES CIPARICK, GRAFFEO, SMITH, PIGOTT and JONES concur.

NOTES

1. *Land Use Controls Enacted Before Contract Signing.* In deciding whether to treat compliance with zoning and other public land use controls as a condition to be implied into land sale contracts, courts almost uniformly reject the superficial analogy to private land use controls such as easements, covenants and servitudes. *Dover Pool* accurately states the general rule that ordinances enacted prior to the contract "are not treated as encumbrances, and the purchaser has no recourse against the vendor by virtue of restrictions imposed by such laws on the use of the property purchased." The rule apparently stems from the position that contracts are subject to laws in force at the time of their formation. See Josefowicz v. Porter, 32 N.J.Super. 585, 108 A.2d 865 (App.Div.1954).

Courts have been cautious to rescind for mutual mistake where the adverse land use controls existed at the time the contract was signed. In Rosique v. Windley Cove, Ltd., 542 So.2d 1014 (Fla.App.1989), the contract of sale contemplated that zoning would permit 25 units per acre. Before closing, however, the buyer learned of uncertainties concerning the zoning but nonetheless elected to proceed. The court denied rescission of the contract when buyer ultimately learned that only 15 units per acre were permitted. The buyer's predicament in the case seemed to be "one of conscious ignorance or deliberate risk-taking on the purchaser's part," in the words of *Dover Pool*. On the other hand, the court in Britton v. Parkin, 176 Mich.App. 395, 438 N.W.2d 919 (1989), ordered the sales contract rescinded since both seller and buyer mistakenly believed that the property was zoned for commercial uses. The court held that a clause making the contract subject to building and use restrictions did not put the risk of zoning on the buyer since seller represented in the listing agreement, advertisements, and drawings that the property was zoned commercial.

Land Use Controls Enacted After Contract Signing. Courts divide on whether land use ordinances enacted *during* the executory period should be treated similarly. A few cases excuse buyer performance. See, e.g., Clay v. Landreth, 187 Va. 169, 45 S.E.2d 875 (1948). Most courts, however, hold that the buyer should bear the risk of changes in the law. Some of these courts rest their position on the ground that the situation does not materially differ from cases in which the law was enacted prior to the contract. Others follow the example of equitable conversion, perceiving "no cogent argument for treating losses resulting from zoning changes occurring between the execution of the Agreement of Sale and settlement differently from casualty and other kinds of loss occurring between those periods." DiDonato v. Reliance Standard Life Insurance Co., 433 Pa. 221, 225, 249 A.2d 327, 330 (1969). The court there observed that, as in the casualty context, the parties could have shifted the burden of loss by contract. One court declined to cancel a transaction for frustration of purpose where the county government imposed wetlands regulation limiting development for commercial purposes after the contract was signed. Because the buyer did not condition the deal on the successful development of the land, he implicitly assumed the risk that unforeseen circumstances would frustrate his planned use. Felt v. McCarthy, 130 Wash.2d 203, 922 P.2d 90 (1996).

Say that, after buyer and seller sign a contract for the sale of a house, the local zoning ordinance is amended. The house would violate the new minimum lot size requirements but for a provision in the ordinance permitting prior nonconforming structures. However, under the ordinance, if the structure is ever destroyed, only a smaller, conforming structure can be built on the parcel. The house is destroyed by fire during the executory period. Who should bear the risk of which loss? Will the answer differ depending on whether equitable conversion or the U.V.P.R.A. applies? Compare Goldfarb v. Dietz, 8 Wash.App. 464, 506 P.2d 1322 (1973).

Land Use Controls Violated Before Contract Signing. Courts also split on the effect of land use control violations existing at the time the contract of sale is signed. One line of authority treats these violations like encumbrances, placing the burden on seller. For example, in Lohmeyer v. Bower, 170 Kan. 442, 227 P.2d 102 (1951), buyers were granted rescission when, after signing the contract, they discovered that the house violated not only deed restrictions but also a local zoning ordinance. Focusing on the ordinance, the court observed that it is not "the existence of protective restrictions, as shown by the record, that constitutes the encumbrances alleged by the appellants; but rather it is the presently existing violation of one of these restrictions that constitutes such encumbrance, in and of itself." 170 Kan. at 454, 227 P.2d at 111 (citing Hebb v. Severson, 32

Wash.2d 159, 172, 201 P.2d 156, 162 (1948)). For the opposing view, that existing violations do not excuse buyer performance, see Gnash v. Saari, 44 Wash.2d 312, 267 P.2d 674 (1954).

For further discussion, see Garrrison & Reitzel, Zoning Restrictions and Marketability of Title, 35 Real Est. L.J. 257 (2006); Lefcoe, How Buyers and Sellers of Development Land Deal with Regulation Risk, 32 Real Prop. Probate & Tr. J. 301 (1997).

2. *Drafting Exercise.* Turn back the clock to the time that the contract of sale was being negotiated in *Dover Pool*, before the events and the case occurred. You represent Buyer at that time. Buyer wants to be able to develop and operate a swimming and tennis club on the property and is concerned about whether zoning will permit this. Your task: draft a clause that you will propose to Seller to be inserted in the contract of sale that will address Buyer's concerns. Note: this can be done in a sentence or two.

3. *Defective Descriptions.* Cedar Lane Ranch v. Lundberg correctly states the general rules to be applied when the seller owns less, or more, than the land described in the contract. Was the court correct, however, to characterize the sale as in gross? Note that there was a discrepancy of almost double the amount of acres. Would the use of the phrase "more or less" after the number of acres affect the result? See Marcus v. Bathon, 72 Md.App. 475, 531 A.2d 690 (1987), cert. denied, 313 Md. 612, 547 A.2d 189 (1988). Does an in gross presumption—what you see is what you get—make sense for the farmer or rancher who counts her profits by the number of acres that can be planted or left for grazing, or for the developer who thinks in terms of salable lots or rentable square feet? Or does it make sense only in the residential context, where the buyer's view of the property is sufficient to tell him whether it will suit his needs? The court may have been saying that if precise acreage really meant so much to the Hardins, they should have ordered a survey before going into possession.

Mistaken descriptions occur because it is hard to express the parties' actual expectations and perceptions in terms that coincide with the correct legal description. A homebuyer is in no position to rely on the technically phrased legal description. Rather, he relies on what he sees, visually locating the boundaries by any available physical evidence—hedges, fences, driveways, streets. Although these physical boundaries may not correspond with the property's legal description, devices exist to bridge the gap between legal description and natural expectation. The legal description may refer to monuments such as stone walls or iron pins from which the buyer can approximate the parcel's boundaries. If the area has been mapped and platted, the buyer may be able to identify the parcel with the aid of a lot map. A professionally performed survey offers even more accuracy, locating not only the parcel's boundaries, but also any easements or encroachments that may lie on it.

A contract of sale may also describe the personal property included in the sale of the realty. Generally, a sale of personal property will not be implied as part of the land sale. In Wilkin v. 1st Source Bank, 548 N.E.2d 170 (Ind.App.1990), the personal representative of Olga Mestrovic, the widow of the noted sculptor, Ivan Mestrovic, entered a contract of sale for the decedent's home. After closing, the buyers complained that the premises were left cluttered with personal property. The personal representative and the buyers agreed that the buyers could clean the premises themselves and retain any personal property that they desired rather than having the personal representative hire a cleaning service. The buyers found and claimed eight paintings and one plaster sculpture, all by Ivan Mestrovic. The court found that the parties shared a mutual mistake as to the nature of the property on the premises, not believing it to be works of art but rather "stuff" or "junk." Thus, there was no meeting of the minds and no agreement to sell or dispose of the works.

4. *Attorney Approval Clauses.* Did the court in Moran v. Erk reach the right conclusion? The ostensible purpose of attorney approval clauses is "to give the parties to a contract, who may not be sophisticated in matters relating to real estate and/or contracts, a chance to have their attorneys scrutinize the offer before final acceptance." Olympic Restaurant Corp. v. Bank of Wheaton, 251 Ill.App.3d 594, 601, 190 Ill.Dec. 874, 879, 622 N.E.2d 904 (1993). What other purposes might such a clause serve?

See generally M. Friedman, Contracts and Conveyances of Real Property § 1.3 (5th ed.1991); Blyth, What You Should Know About "Subject to the Approval of My Attorney" Clauses, 12 Prac. Real Est.Law. 81 (May 1996); Noble-Allgire, Attorney Approval Clauses in Residential Real Estate Contracts—Is Half a Loaf Better Than None?, 48 U.Kan.L.Rev. 339 (2000); Annot., Construction and Effect of Clause in Real Estate Contract Making Contract Contingent Upon Approval By Attorney for Either Party, 15 A.L.R.4th 760 (1982).

5. *Is Time of the Essence?* If on the date set for closing seller fails to tender a deed, or buyer fails to tender the purchase price, is the other party discharged from the obligation to perform? The answer will turn on whether the action is in law or in equity. When a legal remedy is sought, performance on the closing date will be considered essential unless the contract discloses a contrary intent. In actions for an equitable remedy, time is not of the essence unless the contract or surrounding circumstances indicate that it should be. See, e.g., Pines Plaza Ltd. Partnership v. Berkley Trace, LLC, 431 Md. 652, 66 A.3d 720 (2013) (failure to meet closing deadline was not basis for forfeiture of $200,000 deposit); see CDC Nassau Associates v. Fatoullah, 163 A.D.2d 227, 558 N.Y.S.2d 946 (1990), appeal denied, 77 N.Y.2d 802, 566 N.Y.S.2d 587, 567 N.E.2d 981 (1991) (use of phrase "time being of the essence" in connection with exercise of purchase option but not in the immediately following sentence specifying closing date, together with the circumstances, permitted specific performance at a later date). These rules apply not only to closing dates, but also to other deadlines specified in the contract such as the deadline for obtaining a financing commitment. See Kakalik v. Bernardo, 184 Conn. 386, 439 A.2d 1016 (1981). Moreover, a "time of the essence" clause can be waived, not only expressly but by implication, such as when the party entitled to enforce the provision continues to work toward a closing rather than declaring a breach. See, e.g., Galdjie v. Darwish, 113 Cal.App.4th 1331, 7 Cal.Rptr.3d 178 (2003).

6. *When One Closing Is Conditioned on Another.* Conditions are sometimes more complex than timeliness of performance, marketability of title and availability of financing. For example, when the closing of one sale is conditioned on the closing of another, and the second sale is conditioned on yet a third, the conditions can recur like the receding images in multiple mirrors. The results are no less elusive or tantalizing.

In Mann v. Addicott Hills Corp., 238 Va. 262, 384 S.E.2d 81 (1989), the sales contract for a home under construction included a clause, inserted at the buyers' request, allowing them to terminate their obligation to perform if they could not find a buyer for their home during the ninety day period after the framing of the new house began. The clause also required the buyers to list their home with a realtor and to provide evidence of the listing within 15 days after the framing started. Although framing began, the purchasers refused to list their home since they believed that the developer could not provide a delivery date for the new house and they did not want to sell their current home and not have a place in which to live. The seller terminated the contract citing the failure to list the current house and executed a contract of sale with another party. The buyers sought specific performance of their contract with the seller claiming a right to unilaterally waive the contingency. The court rejected the claim, finding that the contingency was also "critical" to the seller since its construction loan required it to meet sales quotas and the inability of buyers to sell their home would make closing on the new house less certain. The court concluded that the breach of such a material provision prevented the purchasers from obtaining specific relief.

Was the court's reading of the clause correct? Would a more typical seller have an interest in terminating a contract if the buyer's home is not sold? Should the fact that the house was not completed for ten months after the framing began have been relevant? Could a better clause have been drafted to account for the fact that the house was being constructed?

Complex conditions more frequently arise in commercial transactions, where purchases of land for development purposes must be carefully conditioned on the completion of arrangements for construction and permanent financing and receipt of all the government approvals necessary for the projected development. Sellers, concerned with illusoriness and with the possibility that their land will be tied up for the duration of the government approval process, sometimes insist on an option rather than a contract of sale.

7. *Whose Condition Is It?* Contracts will often be imprecise in reflecting the parties' intentions and needs as to who may exercise a condition. Dale Mortgage Bankers Corp. v. 877 Stewart Avenue Associates, 133 A.D.2d 65, 518 N.Y.S.2d 411 (1987), appeal denied, 70 N.Y.2d 612, 523 N.Y.S.2d 496, 518 N.E.2d 7 (1987), held that the buyer could not unilaterally waive a financing condition and proceed on an all cash basis. The court strictly applied the contingency clause which stated that either party could void the sale if the purchaser could not obtain financing. Did the court correctly decide the issue? Was the seller only asserting the cancellation right in order to renegotiate the contract or find a better price? Or was the seller just trying to avoid the delay of waiting until closing to find out that the buyer would not be able to perform?

8. *Role of the Lawyer.* In Schafer v. Barrier Island Station, Inc., 946 F.2d 1075 (4th Cir.1991), plaintiffs alleged that when they purchased three condominium units from defendant, defendant had agreed to repurchase the units on prescribed conditions. The only evidence of this agreement was one version signed by plaintiffs, a different version signed by defendant, and a letter from defendant's attorney to plaintiffs stating that defendant had agreed to the version signed by the plaintiffs. The court held that the attorney's letter was inadequate to bind defendant:

> The attorney-client relationship, by custom, however, does not imply that an attorney has authority to act as principal and resolve matters of substance.... [W]hen a client retains an attorney to represent the client in a transaction, the attorney has implied authority to negotiate the terms of an agreement or operative papers to their final form. But custom of the relationship does not imply an authority for the attorney to execute the documents on behalf of the client.

Id. at 1079.

The court acknowledged that representations by the principal to third persons may give an attorney apparent authority, but found that none of the defendant's conduct or statements to the plaintiffs indicated greater authority than is customary in the attorney-client relationship.

D. THE CALCULUS OF REMEDIES

A buyer whose seller has breached their land sale contract has four possible remedies. He can obtain a decree of specific performance ordering seller to convey title to him in return for payment of the purchase price. He can obtain damages measured by the difference between the parcel's market value at the date of breach and the contract price, together with any incidental expenses and losses incurred. He can rescind and recover any deposit made. Finally—although this remedy is not much used—the buyer has a lien (called a "vendee's lien") on seller's legal title, securing the seller's obligation to refund the buyer's deposit in the event the seller breaches. The lien can be foreclosed and the land sold to satisfy this obligation if the seller fails to refund the deposit.

A seller whose buyer has breached also has four remedies, closely paralleling the remedies available to buyer. The seller can obtain a decree of specific performance requiring buyer to pay the purchase price in return for the seller's conveyance of title. The seller can obtain damages measured by the difference between the contract price and the parcel's market value at the date of breach, together with incidental expenses and losses. She can in most jurisdictions rescind and retain any deposits made by the buyer on account. Finally, seller has a lien (called a "vendor's lien") on buyer's equitable title, securing the buyer's obligation to pay the purchase price. If buyer fails to perform, the lien can be foreclosed and the land sold to satisfy the buyer's obligation.

1. SPECIFIC PERFORMANCE

a. BUYER'S RIGHT TO SPECIFIC PERFORMANCE

American Law Institute, Restatement of the Law of Contracts—Second*

Section 360, comment e (1981).

Contracts for the sale of land. Contracts for the sale of land have traditionally been accorded a special place in the law of specific performance. A specific tract of land has long been regarded as unique

---

and impossible of duplication by the use of any amount of money. Furthermore, the value of land is to some extent speculative. Damages have therefore been regarded as inadequate to enforce a duty to transfer an interest in land, even if it is less than a fee simple. Under this traditional view, the fact that the buyer has made a contract for the resale of the land to a third person does not deprive him of the right to specific performance. If he cannot convey the land to his purchaser, he will be held for damages for breach of the resale contract, and it is argued that these damages cannot be accurately determined without litigation. Granting him specific performance enables him to perform his own duty and to avoid litigation and damages.

Kelley v. Leucadia

Supreme Court of Utah, 1992.
846 P.2d 1238.

STEWART, JUSTICE:

This case presents the issue of whether a buyer of real estate can obtain specific performance of a standard Utah Earnest Money Sales Agreement against a defaulting seller.

First Security Bank (FSB) agreed to sell real property to William R. Kelley pursuant to a standard Earnest Money Sales Agreement.[1] FSB could not provide marketable and insurable title because of a boundary dispute. Kelley filed an action for a declaratory judgment and for specific performance of the agreement. The trial court entered an order directing FSB to convey the property to Kelley.

The court of appeals reversed the trial court, holding in an unpublished opinion that the terms of the standard Earnest Money Sales Agreement preclude a buyer from obtaining specific performance against a breaching seller. The court held that when a seller fails to provide a marketable and insurable title, the standard agreement limits the buyer to one of two remedies: (1) enforcement of the agreement, but only after the buyer tenders full payment of the contract price; or (2) rescission of the contract with a refund of the earnest money. We granted certiorari because of the potential effect of that ruling on real estate transactions using the standard Utah Earnest Money Sales Agreement.

On March 2, 1987, Kelley and FSB executed an earnest money sales agreement by which FSB agreed to sell residential property in Park City, Utah, to Kelley. Kelley paid $10,000 in earnest money to FSB and began liquidating some of his assets to obtain the balance due. The closing was set for April 20, 1987.

The agreement, written on a standard form, included the following general provisions: (1) The seller would furnish good and marketable title, subject to encumbrances and exceptions provided in the contract, "evidenced by a current policy of title insurance"; (2) if title insurance was unobtainable due to title defects, the buyer could elect to waive the defects or to terminate the agreement and have the earnest money refunded; and (3) time was of the essence. The seller added a

---

[1]   On appeal, Leucadia has been substituted for FSB as defendant.

handwritten provision stating that the property was sold " 'as is,' without warranty. Title conveyed by special warranty deed."

FSB acquired the property by quitclaim deed from the former owners, who had defaulted on loans secured by the property. The property, consisting of approximately thirteen acres, included a residence, a stream, and a spring. The stream fed a trout pond located in front of the house and provided irrigation water for the property.

After execution of the agreement, a survey revealed that FSB's quitclaim deed contained an erroneous property description, which misplaced a boundary line by 15.22 feet, thereby excluding the stream and spring. In an attempt to cure the defect, FSB asked the adjoining property owners, the Armstrongs, to convey the disputed property. The Armstrongs refused and cut off the water to the pond, causing it to dry up.

On April 22, 1987, two days after the specified closing date, FSB and Kelley agreed to extend the date to June 1, 1987, so that FSB could clear up the boundary problem. Thereafter, the parties agreed to extend the closing date to July 1, 1987, and then to August 31, 1987.

In July 1987, FSB filed a complaint against the Armstrongs to quiet title to the disputed portion of the property and to recover damages caused by vandalism. FSB informed Kelley that he need not retain an attorney because the bank would handle the litigation.

On September 4, 1987, four days after the last agreed upon closing date, FSB's attorney sent a letter to Kelley, demanding that he close the transaction by September 15, 1987. The letter stated that FSB would consider the agreement terminated if the closing were not consummated by the 15th and that FSB was ready and able to sell the property " 'as is' without warranty in accordance with the terms of the earnest money agreement." FSB also stated that it would not proceed with the Armstrong litigation and that it had only pursued the lawsuit because it was interested in closing the deal with Kelley and not because it had a legal obligation to deliver clear title. FSB offered to assign its rights in the Armstrong litigation to Kelley and recommended that Kelley obtain counsel. FSB also offered to refund Kelley's earnest money should he choose to "walk away from the deal."

Kelley, who was then living in Massachusetts, did not receive the letter until September 8, 1987. He immediately replied by telegram to FSB, stating that he would not abandon the deal. Kelley then retained counsel, who contacted FSB and requested copies of all documents relating to the boundary litigation. Kelley's counsel asked for a thirty-day extension of the closing date so that Kelley could evaluate the litigation and its effect on the value of the property. FSB agreed to extend the closing date only one week, to September 22, but stated that it would cooperate fully with respect to the litigation. Kelley's attorney, however, did not receive the necessary documents from FSB's attorney until October 15, 1987. Nevertheless, on September 22, 1987, Kelley's attorney wrote to FSB and tendered Kelley's performance. The letter stated that Kelley was ready, willing, and able to close and that the necessary funds had been transferred to Williamsburg Savings Bank in Salt Lake City to be paid at closing. The letter also stated that the "tender is conditioned only upon First Security honoring its obligations pursuant to the earnest money sales agreement and delivering the property free from those defects which it has undertaken to cure." On the same day, Kelley filed a complaint against FSB for a declaratory judgment, damages for breach of contract, and specific performance. Kelley's funds were subsequently deposited with the Summit County clerk.

On September 24, 1987, FSB executed a release of Kelley's $10,000 earnest money deposit, but Kelley refused to accept it. The next day, Leucadia Financial Corporation formally offered to purchase the property from FSB, and on November 2, 1987, Leucadia and FSB entered into an earnest money sales agreement. Leucadia purchased the property on November 25, 1987.

FSB moved to dismiss Kelley's complaint on the grounds that Kelley's tender was defective and specific performance was not a remedy available under the agreement. Kelley countered with a motion for partial summary judgment, asserting that he was entitled to specific performance and an abatement in the purchase price. The court denied FSB's motion to dismiss and granted Kelley's motion for partial summary judgment, ruling that Kelley was entitled to specific performance. The court reserved for trial Kelley's claim for damages and an abatement in the purchase price. Kelley and FSB subsequently settled the abatement and damages issues, and the trial court entered a decree of specific performance directing FSB to convey the undisputed portion of the property by special warranty deed and the disputed portion by quitclaim deed.

The parties stipulated to substitute Leucadia for FSB and Leucadia appealed to this Court. Pursuant to *Rule 42 of the Utah Rules of Appellate Procedure*, we transferred the case to the court of appeals. The court of appeals held that Kelley was not entitled to the equitable remedy of specific performance because Kelley's remedies were limited by paragraphs G and H of the agreement. Given that ruling, the court of appeals did not decide whether Kelley's tender was legally sufficient.

I. A BUYER'S RIGHT TO SPECIFIC PERFORMANCE UNDER THE STANDARD EARNEST MONEY SALES AGREEMENT

The terms of the standard Earnest Money Sales Agreement have been approved by the Utah Real Estate Commission and the Attorney General. With some exceptions not relevant here, real estate agents may fill out only those forms approved by the Utah Real Estate Commission and the Attorney General. *Utah Code Ann. § 61–2–20* (1989). According to the Utah Association of Realtors, which appeared as amicus curiae, the standard form Earnest Money Sales Agreement is used in the majority of real estate transactions conducted by its members.

Paragraphs G and H, which deal with title inspection and title insurance, were construed by the court of appeals to provide a buyer's exclusive remedies against a breaching seller. *Kelley v. Leucadia Financial Corp.*, No. 880534–CA, slip op. at 3 (Utah Ct. App. Jan. 5, 1990). Paragraph G provides that if there are defects in the title that the seller does not cure, the buyer may declare the agreement null and have all monies returned. The last sentence of paragraph G states:

> If said defect(s) is not curable through an escrow agreement at closing, this Agreement shall be null and void at the option of the Buyer, and all monies received herewith shall be returned to the respective parties.

The court of appeals held that because Kelley had not declared the agreement null and void under paragraph G, his remedies were limited to those stated in paragraph H.

Paragraph H deals with title insurance and confers on the buyer a right to nonjudicial rescission if the agreed-upon title insurance is not provided. Paragraph H provides:

> If title insurance is elected, Seller authorizes the Listing Brokerage to order a preliminary commitment for a standard form ALTA policy of title insurance to be issued by such title insurance company as Seller shall designate. Title policy to be issued shall contain no exceptions other than those provided for in said standard form, and the encumbrances or defects excepted under the final contract of sale. *If title cannot be made so insurable through an escrow agreement at closing, the earnest money shall, unless Buyer elects to waive such defects or encumbrances, be refunded to Buyer, and this Agreement shall thereupon be terminated.*

(Emphasis added.) The court of appeals held that paragraph H allows a buyer either to (1) waive the title defect and pay the full purchase price or (2) rescind the agreement and receive a refund of his earnest money. Under that construction, Kelley's refusal to waive the title defects caused the agreement to terminate by its own terms.

Leucadia argues that Kelley is limited to the remedies set forth in paragraphs G and H. That position is untenable. Paragraphs G and H do not purport to be exclusive remedies, nor do they in any way limit the traditional common law or equitable remedies available to a buyer. Rather, these provisions are designed to give buyers the right to walk away from the contract and obtain a refund of their earnest money without having to obtain judicial redress. Thus, the remedies set out in paragraphs G and H are for the sole benefit of the buyer.

A seller is not entitled to take advantage of a provision intended to benefit the buyer alone. *E.g., Ace Realty, Inc. v. Looney, 531 P.2d 1377, 1380 (Okla. 1975). Ace Realty* construed a provision of an earnest money sales agreement similar to paragraph H. The court stated, "The contractual provision that title is to be good and merchantable or the contract will be void and the earnest money returned is for the benefit of the purchaser, rather than the seller." *Id.* The court then held that a seller could not avoid its contractual obligations under a provision clearly for the benefit of the buyer. *Id. at 1381.* Similarly, the court in *Reed v. Wadsworth, 553 P.2d 1024, 1034 (Wyo. 1976),* held that the sellers of real property could not terminate an earnest money agreement under a provision permitting the buyers to demand a refund of their earnest money when the sellers had breached the contract. Accordingly, paragraphs G and H give the buyer the absolute right to rescind the agreement if the seller defaults, but they do not confer on a defaulting seller the right to compel the buyer to either terminate the agreement or pay full value notwithstanding the seller's defective performance.

Moreover, to construe paragraphs G and H as barring a buyer's right to specific performance would allow a seller to breach the contract without consequence, since the buyer's only remedy would be to rescind the agreement. Not only would a seller have no motivation to clear title, but the cost of clearing title would be shifted to a buyer determined to purchase the property. Thus, Leucadia's construction would place buyers in a disadvantageous position relative to sellers and deny them traditional remedies, such as specific performance. The evenhanded protection that a uniform contract form ought to give both parties would become, in effect, illusory.

Leucadia's position that paragraphs G and H provide exclusive remedies is also inconsistent with paragraph N, which makes clear that those provisions were not intended to be a buyer's sole remedy. Paragraph N deals generally with the remedies available in the event of a default by either the buyer or the seller. It states:

> In the event of default by Buyer, Seller may elect to either retain the earnest money as liquidated damages or to institute suit to enforce any rights of Seller. In the event of default by Seller, or if this sale fails to close because of the nonsatisfaction of any express condition or contingency to which the sale is subject pursuant to this Agreement (other than by virtue of any default by Buyer), the earnest money deposit shall be returned to Buyer. *Both parties agree that should either party default in any of the covenants or agreements herein contained, the defaulting party shall pay all costs and expenses, including a reasonable attorney's fee, which may arise or accrue from enforcing or terminating this Agreement, or in pursuing any remedy provided hereunder or by applicable law,* whether such remedy is pursued by filing suit or otherwise.

(Emphasis added.) Paragraph N clearly contemplates that both buyers and sellers may pursue "any remedy provided hereunder or by applicable law." The language "any remedy . . . under applicable law" means all applicable statutory, common law, and equitable remedies. Specific performance with an abatement in the purchase price has long been recognized as an appropriate remedy when a seller refuses to convey. *Castagno v. Church, 552 P.2d 1282, 1284 (Utah 1975).*

Buyers and sellers are, of course, at liberty to modify a standard agreement and negotiate terms that limit or expand the remedies of one or both parties. There is no evidence here, however, to suggest that the parties intended to limit Kelley's remedies to preclude specific performance.

II. TENDER

We now turn to the issue of whether Kelley made a timely and unconditional tender of his performance to FSB. The trial court found that Kelley made an unconditional tender. The court of appeals, however, did not address the issue because it held that paragraphs G and H controlled Kelley's remedies. The parties have briefed this issue, and we address it in the interest of judicial expediency.

To obtain a decree for specific performance against a defaulting party, the aggrieved party must make an unconditional tender of the performance required by the agreement. *Century 21 All Western Real Estate & Inv., Inc. v. Webb, 645 P.2d 52, 56 (Utah 1982); see also Baxter v. Camelot Properties, Inc., 622 P.2d 808, 811 (Utah 1981); Zion's Properties, Inc. v. Holt, 538 P.2d 1319, 1322 (Utah 1975).* Neither party to an agreement "can be said to be in default (and thus susceptible to a judgment for damages or a decree for specific performance) until the other party has tendered his own performance." *Century 21, 645 P.2d at 56.* In other words, "a party must make a tender of his own agreed performance in order to put the other party in default." *Id.; see also Fischer v. Johnson, 525 P.2d 45, 46–47 (Utah 1974).*

The tender cannot impose on the other party a new condition or requirement not already imposed by the contract. *Century 21, 645 P.2d at 56; accord* 5A Arthur L. Corbin, *Corbin on Contracts* § 1233 (1964) [hereinafter "Corbin"]. If the law were otherwise, one could use a tender to compel the other party to comply with new contractual terms. Accordingly, a tender, as a general rule, must be unconditional. A tender that contains an improper condition or requirement disqualifies a party from obtaining a decree of specific performance. *Baxter, 622 P.2d at 811; Century 21, 645 P.2d at 56.* A party to a bilateral contract may, however, properly condition a tender on the other's performance, since such a condition does not impose a requirement beyond that already contained in the contract. 5A *Corbin* § 1233.

Leucadia argues that Kelley's tender was defective because Kelley's demand for a title free from the boundary defect was a new condition not contained in the agreement. Kelley responds that his demand did not impose a new condition on FSB, but insisted only that FSB do that which it had promised to do in the agreement and had, in fact, undertaken to do by filing the lawsuit against the Armstrongs.

Whether Kelley's demand that FSB cure the title defect constituted a conditional tender depends on whether the agreement already obligated FSB to do so. Paragraph 3 of the agreement states that the seller "agrees to furnish good and marketable title to the property, subject to encumbrances and exceptions noted herein." The primary obligation of a seller under an earnest money sales agreement is to provide marketable title. Marketable title is one that may be "freely made the subject of resale" and that can be sold at a "fair price to a reasonable purchaser or mortgaged to a person of reasonable prudence as security for the loan of money." *77 Am. Jur. 2d Vendor and Purchaser § 131,* at 313–14 (1975). Generally, when a seller agrees to convey marketable title, the seller must undertake to cure defects if it can be done in the exercise of reasonable diligence and within a reasonable time. *See, e.g., Ace Realty, Inc. v. Looney, 531 P.2d 1377, 1380 (Okla. 1975).*

The boundary dispute with the Armstrongs constituted a cloud on the title and adversely affected the value and marketability of the property, a fact FSB admitted in its complaint against the Armstrongs. FSB argued to the trial court that the " 'as is' without warranty" language in the handwritten notation referred to warranties of title and therefore released FSB from any obligation to resolve the boundary dispute. That argument is not valid. In the same notation, FSB agreed to convey the property to Kelley by special warranty deed. A special warranty deed, although not as broad as a general warranty deed, carries with it certain warranties of title. Therefore, the "as is" language did not modify FSB's express promise to convey marketable title.

FSB's own conduct and statements support this conclusion. FSB acknowledged its obligation to provide clear title when it undertook the Armstrong litigation and told Kelley that he need not retain an attorney. For a period of four months, FSB, by its actions and statements, led Kelley to believe that FSB would resolve the boundary problem and deliver clear and marketable title, as it was obligated to do under the contract. Not until its letter of September 4 did FSB disclaim any obligation to do what it had previously acknowledged. It was only then, and for the first time, that FSB stated that it had undertaken the litigation, not because it was obligated to, but because of FSB's interest in closing the deal with Kelley.

In view of FSB's express promise to provide clear and marketable title and its having undertaken litigation to do so, we hold that Kelley's tender did not impose a new condition, but was merely a request that FSB do what it was contractually obligated to do.

III. TIMELINESS

Finally, Leucadia argues that Kelley cannot seek specific performance because time was of the essence and Kelley failed to tender his performance by the closing date. Because the closing date had been extended several times by mutual agreement, Kelley properly tendered his performance on September 22, the last agreed upon closing date. We therefore reject FSB's argument.

The judgment of the court of appeals is reversed, and the trial court's judgment is affirmed.

b. SELLER'S RIGHT TO SPECIFIC PERFORMANCE

American Law Institute, Restatement of the Law of Contracts—Second*

Section 360, comment e (1981).

Contracts for the sale of land. Contracts for the sale of land have traditionally been accorded a special place in the law of specific performance. . . .

[T]he seller who has not yet conveyed is generally granted specific performance on breach by the buyer. Here it is argued that, because the value of land is to some extent speculative, it may be difficult for him to prove with reasonable certainty the difference between the contract price and the market price of the land. Even if he can make this proof, the land may not be immediately convertible into money and he may be deprived of funds with which he could have made other investments. Furthermore, before the seller gets a judgment, the existence of the contract, even if broken by the buyer, operates as a clog on saleability, so that it may be difficult to find a purchaser at a fair price. The fact that specific performance is available to the buyer has sometimes been regarded as of some weight under the now discarded doctrine of

---

"mutuality of remedy" (see Comment *c* to § 363), but this is today of importance only because it enables a court to assure the vendee that he will receive the agreed performance if he is required to pay the price. The fact that legislation may have prohibited imprisonment as a means of enforcing a decree for the payment of money does not affect the seller's right to such a decree. After the seller has transferred the interest in the land to the buyer, however, and all that remains is for the buyer to pay the price, a money judgment for the amount of the price is an adequate remedy for the seller.

Mohrlang v. Draper

Supreme Court of Nebraska, 1985.
219 Neb. 630, 365 N.W.2d 443.

OPINION

Larry Draper appeals a money judgment awarded by the district court for Adams County in an action brought by John R. Mohrlang for specific performance of a contract for the sale of real estate. Mohrlang cross-appeals the district court's denial of specific performance. We reverse and remand with directions.

On June 8, 1981, in a written offer, a "Purchase Agreement" prepared by his realtor, Mohrlang offered to purchase an unimproved tract owned by Draper, a lot in a proposed subdivision to be known as "Draper Subdivision." The purchase agreement specified a purchase price of $14,875, namely, $500 earnest money paid by Mohrlang when he signed the purchase agreement, $2,475 payable at "closing" on January 1, 1982, and the balance of the purchase price, $11,900, payable in monthly installments of $131.14 per month based on a 20-year schedule, with a "balloon" payment in 5 years and interest at the rate of 12 percent per annum on the unpaid purchase price.

The purchase agreement also contained the following provisions: Draper was required to obtain the release of a "right-of-way" easement across the lot and termination of a buried gasline belonging to Kansas-Nebraska Natural Gas Company, Inc., and Draper would bear the cost of relocating the gas company's line and paving a street abutting the lot to be purchased.

On June 9 Draper signed his written acceptance of Mohrlang's offer submitted and contained in the purchase agreement of June 8. Mohrlang hired an architectural firm and embarked upon plans for a solar home requiring the southern exposure available on the Draper lot.

The gas company's line was located in an easement 33 feet wide which diagonally crossed the subject lot for approximately 200 feet. After visiting with personnel of the gas company, Draper, by an estimate of cost prepared by the gas company on July 7, was informed that the cost of relocating the gasline would be $10,050. Continued location of the gasline rendered the lot unusable for the residential construction intended by Mohrlang.

Mohrlang had obtained finances to complete the purchase, but the gasline was not moved and the abutting street was not paved. Although his realtor had numerous contacts with Draper about a closing, Mohrlang was unsuccessful in scheduling a closing notwithstanding

Draper's failure to provide paving on the street adjacent to the subject lot and relocate the gasline. Draper offered, but Mohrlang refused, another lot as a substitute for the agreed lot.

Mohrlang filed a petition on July 29, 1982, and requested specific performance of his agreement with Draper for sale of the lot in question. In his answer Draper alleged that he had attempted to relocate the gasline, but had neither the power nor means to obtain such relocation. Further, Draper alleged that Mohrlang had an adequate remedy at law.

At trial Mohrlang testified that, although other real estate had been investigated, no other lot had the particular features and adaptability found in the Draper lot sought to be purchased by Mohrlang. A representative of the gas company testified that the gasline could have been moved at a cost of $10,050, as indicated in the gas company estimate prepared for Draper. Draper did not present any evidence of his inability preventing performance of the Mohrlang contract and never described any hardship to be suffered if he were required to perform the contract.

The district court found that Mohrlang had offered to perform his contract with Draper; that Mohrlang was "ready, willing and able to perform" such contract; but that "ordering of specific performance of the contract by the Court would work an undue hardship" on Draper. Instead of specific performance, the district court awarded damages to Mohrlang.

As the assignment of error in his appeal, Draper claims the district court "erred in awarding [Mohrlang] monetary damages," because Mohrlang had not mentioned or requested damages in his petition. In his cross-appeal Mohrlang contends that the district court should have granted specific performance of the Mohrlang-Draper contract for the sale of real estate.

Because the questions to be reviewed have arisen from an action in equity for specific performance of a written contract for the sale of real estate, and as with any equity action, we review this matter de novo on the record. See *Litz v. Wilson, 208 Neb. 483, 304 N.W.2d 48 (1981)*. An action for specific performance is governed by the elements, conditions, and incidents which control the administration of all equitable remedies. See *Bauer v. Bauer, 136 Neb. 329, 285 N.W. 565 (1939)*.

When land or any interest therein is the subject matter of a contract, the power of a court of equity to grant specific performance is beyond question. *Russell v. Western Nebraska Rest Home, Inc., 180 Neb. 728, 144 N.W.2d 728 (1966)*. We have held that specific performance should generally be granted as a matter of course or right regarding a contract for the sale of real estate where a valid, binding contract exists which is definite and certain in its terms, mutual in its obligation, free from overreaching fraud and unfairness, and where the remedy at law is inadequate. *Reese v. Hatfield, 201 Neb. 540, 270 N.W.2d 898 (1978)*. Real estate is assumed to possess the characteristic of uniqueness, and, therefore, special value, necessary for availability of specific performance. See *Moser v. Thorp Sales Corp., 256 N.W.2d 900 (Iowa 1977)*. This assumption is based upon the status of land as the favorite and favored subject in England and all countries of Anglo-Saxon origin.

See 81 C.J.S. *Specific Performance* § 76 (1977). In an action for specific performance of a contract to sell real estate, generally, it is no defense that there is other available land as good as or even better than the land which is the subject of the contract to be performed. See *Shreeve v. Greer, 65 Ariz. 35, 173 P.2d 641 (1946)*.

Exoneration from specific performance may be available when specific performance would be inequitable or unjust due to hardship on the one from whom performance is sought. Whether a contract is fair, and, therefore, subject to equitable enforcement, is determined by the circumstances existing when the contract is entered rather than by subsequent events intervening before specific performance is sought. See *Shell Oil Co. v. Kapler, 235 Minn. 292, 50 N.W.2d 707 (1951)*.

Although *Wilson & Co., Inc. v. Fremont Cake & Meal Co., 153 Neb. 160, 43 N.W.2d 657 (1950),* was an action at law for damages due to a breach of contract, the principles stated in *Wilson* regarding excuse for nonperformance—impossibility in a law action vis-a-vis hardship in an equitable action—are applicable in the present case:

> "Inconvenience or the cost of compliance, though they might make compliance a hardship, cannot excuse a party from the performance of an absolute and unqualified undertaking to do a thing that is possible and lawful. Parties sui juris bind themselves by their lawful contracts, and courts cannot alter them because they work a hardship. . . . A contract is not invalid, nor is the obligor therein in any manner discharged from its binding effect, because it turns out to be difficult or burdensome to perform. It has been said that difficulties, even if unforeseen and however great, are no excuse, and that the fact that a contract has become more burdensome in its operation than was anticipated is not ground for its rescission." . . .

> ". . . A contract which is possible of performance when made does not become invalid or unenforceable because conditions afterwards arise which render performance impossible. * * * If a party by his own contract creates a duty or imposes a charge on himself, he must under any and all conditions substantially comply with the undertaking."

Id. at 177, 43 N.W.2d at 666–67.

One form of hardship equitably excusing specific performance of a contract may be a circumstance unforeseeable at entry into the contract. Hardship of such nature, however, cannot be self-inflicted or caused through inexcusable neglect on the part of the person seeking to be excused or exonerated from specific performance. See *Derwell Company v. Apic, Inc., 278 A.2d 338 (Del. Ch. 1971)*. See, also, *Craft Builders, Inc. v. Ellis D. Taylor, Inc., 254 A.2d 233 (Del. 1969)*. Were the rule otherwise, one would derive a benefit from his or her own inexcusable neglect.

Draper entered the contract on June 9 and through the gas company's estimate of July 7 learned about the cost of relocating the gasline. The inescapable inference is that complete information about relocating the gasline was available when Draper entered the contract to sell his lot. The contract expressly required that Draper bear the cost of relocating the gasline, as well as paving the street. Although the exact extent of expense for relocating the gasline was apparently unknown to Draper when he entered the agreement, relocating the gasline was a burden undertaken by Draper when the parties made their contract. Draper's belated realization that his financial burden under the contract was greater than initially anticipated at origination of the agreement does not constitute hardship excusing specific performance of his contract with Mohrlang. An imprudent or bad bargain in and of itself is not an excuse for nonperformance of a contract. See *Dean v. Gregg, 34 Wash. App. 684, 663 P.2d 502 (1983)*. See, also, *Craft Builders, Inc. v. Ellis D. Taylor, Inc., supra*. It was Draper's neglect which increased his burden, not an unforeseeable circumstance.

Because there is no hardship equitably excusing Draper from specific performance of the contract in question, we reverse and set aside the judgment of the district court and remand this matter to the district court with directions to order specific performance of the Mohrlang-Draper contract in accordance with the provisions contained in the written agreement of the parties.

Reversed and remanded with directions.

2.   DAMAGES

a.   BUYER'S DAMAGES

Beard v. S/E Joint Venture

Court of Appeals of Maryland, 1990.
321 Md. 126, 581 A.2d 1275.

RODOWSKY, JUDGE.

This case involves the measure of damages for the breach by vendors of a contract to construct a residence and then to convey the improved realty. The real estate market for the subject property was escalating during the potentially relevant period. Purchasers sought specific performance or damages. Specific performance became unavailable when the vendors rejected the contract in bankruptcy. We shall hold that the purchasers' damages are not limited to certain out-of-pocket losses, as held by the courts below, but that the purchasers may also recover damages for loss of the benefit of their bargain. In computing damages the property may be valued as if improved as promised, and it may be valued as of the date when specific performance became unavailable, in contrast with valuation as of an earlier date when the vendors anticipatorily repudiated the contract.

The purchasers are the petitioners, DeLawrence and Lillian M. Beard (the Beards), who were plaintiffs in the circuit court. The vendors, respondents here and defendants in the circuit court, are Diana C. Etheridge (Etheridge) and Gene Stull (Stull), joint venturers in S/E Joint Venture. Etheridge is a licensed real estate agent and Stull is a home builder. S/E Joint Venture had acquired an unimproved lot in Piney Glen Farms subdivision in the Potomac section of Montgomery County for the purpose of building a home for speculation.

PERFORMING THE CONTRACT **133**

Protracted negotiations between the Beards and S/E Joint Venture led to a contract formed on March 17, 1986, under which S/E Joint Venture would construct a house on the lot and convey the improved premises to the Beards for $785,000. The contract in part provided "that the PURCHASER is purchasing a completed dwelling [and] that the SELLER is not acting as a contractor for the PURCHASER in the construction of the dwelling[.]" The contract recited that "the approximate date of completion of the improvements now scheduled by the SELLER is November 30, 1986." For a period of ninety days the contract was contingent on the sale of two residences, one the then residence of the Beards and the other that of Mrs. Beard's mother, who also was to occupy the home to be built.

Matters did not proceed smoothly. On March 16, 1987, the vendors, through counsel, terminated the contract. The letter declaring the contract terminated invoked a provision under which

> "the SELLER shall have the right to return the PURCHASER'S deposit and to declare this Contract null and void if, in the SELLER'S sole discretion, it determines that . . . performance within 365 days from the date hereof will not be possible."

In May 1987 the Beards filed a two count complaint against respondents. It sought specific performance under count I and, in the alternative, damages for breach of contract in count II.

During the pendency of the action by the Beards, S/E Joint Venture sought the protection of Chapter 11 of the Bankruptcy Act. The Bankruptcy Court on April 8, 1988, ruled that it would approve rejection by S/E Joint Venture of its contract with the Beards. The order of the Bankruptcy Court that effected that ruling was passed on June 17, 1988, the last business day prior to the commencement of the nonjury trial of the subject action in the Circuit Court for Montgomery County.

In a written opinion the circuit judge found, on conflicting evidence, that the vendors had breached the contract by the purported termination of March 16, 1987. The trial judge concluded

> "that it is implicit that before the right of termination can be exercised the defendants must have acted in good faith to try to complete construction of the house within the stated time period; this, in the court's judgment, they did not do."

The circuit court found that Stull "knew some two months after the inception of the contract that he would be unable to meet the time deadline." This was found to be "significant because defendants were aware that the plaintiffs and [Mrs. Beard's mother] had to sell their homes in order to meet their financial commitment[.]" The trial court also found undue delay in the performance of plumbing work, which "had a ripple effect on the subsequent course of construction."

The trial judge did not address the specific performance claim, saying in a footnote: "As to count one Plaintiffs make no argument in their written argument, or otherwise, and the court treats the count as abandoned."

Itemizing claimed damages in their post trial memorandum, the Beards included $100,000 for "loss of bargain." Factually, the $100,000 figure is said to represent the excess of the value of the property, with the home completed in accordance with the contract, as of March 16, 1987, over the contract price. The plaintiffs undertook to prove the value of the property by calling Etheridge as their own witness. Plaintiffs' conclusion that $100,000 represents the difference between market value and contract price requires interpreting Etheridge's testimony. At times she seems to refer to the value of the house which S/E Joint Venture originally planned, and at times to the value of the house called for by the Beards' contract. The circuit court never reached this issue because it disposed of the Beards' contention on legal grounds.

Legally to support their loss of the bargain claim, the plaintiffs relied on Horner v. Beasley, 105 Md. 193, 65 A. 820 (1907). Horner was a purchaser's action against a vendor for breach of a contract to convey, for $1,200, improved realty worth $1,800. The vendor's defense was that title to the property was involved in litigation. Judgment for the plaintiff was reversed because of an error in the admission of evidence of value. This Court, however, approved a jury instruction that if

"the defendant acted in good faith in failing to perform the contract of sale, the plaintiff was entitled to recover only the amount of his deposit with interest and the expense if any incurred in the investigation of the title; but if they found that the defendant did not act in good faith then in addition to the amounts aforesaid the plaintiff could recover the excess, if any, of the market value of the property, at the time of the sale, over the contract price."

Id. at 198, 65 A. at 822.

The Beards, also citing Charles County Broadcasting Co. v. Meares, 270 Md. 321, 311 A.2d 27 (1973), argued that, because the respondents were able to perform, their breach was in "bad faith," so that benefit of the bargain damages should be awarded. The trial court did not accept this contention, explaining that it did "not award any damages for loss of the benefit of the bargain[,] finding no evidence of bad faith in the sense that the termination was activated by malice, fraud or the like."

The circuit court awarded the plaintiffs $124,594 in damages, representing the deposit on the property ($75,000), a deposit for a security system ($2,000), a deposit for telephones and intercoms ($1,000), rental payments for substitute housing ($32,000), mortgage commitment fee ($4,250) and storage costs ($10,344).

All parties appealed to the Court of Special Appeals which, in an unreported opinion, modified the judgment and affirmed it as modified. The intermediate appellate court, approving the trial court's analysis of the loss of bargain claim, reasoned that "[o]nce [the trial judge] found a breach on the Sellers' part but failed to find any evidence of fraud, malice or the like, [the trial judge] could not award damages in accordance with Charles County Broadcasting based on either good faith or bad faith."

We granted certiorari as to the following questions from the Beards' petition.

"1. Whether a seller of real estate who fails to exercise good faith in the performance of the sales contract is liable for the purchasers' loss of bargain?

I

Damages for breach of a contract ordinarily are that sum which would place the plaintiff in as good a position as that in which the plaintiff would have been, had the contract been performed. These expectation interest damages embrace both losses incurred and gains prevented. See Restatement (Second) of Contracts § 347 (1981); Restatement, Contracts § 329 (1932). Here the circuit court undertook to apply an exception to the ordinary rule. The exception traces to *Flureau v. Thornhill*, 2 W. Black. 1078, 96 Eng.Rep. 635 (K.B.1776). In England, and in the diminishing number of American states that recognize *Flureau*, the exception applies only where, due to no fault on the part of the seller, there is an inability to convey good title. In the case at hand respondents' breach had nothing to do with title to the property. Further, under the trial court's findings, the inability timely to deliver a completed house, which motivated the wrongful termination of March 16, 1987, is not a "good faith" failure to perform within the meaning of the *Flureau* exception. In any event, "good faith," per the *Flureau* rule, is not so all inclusive as to embrace any breach which was not "activated by malice, fraud or the like," as the trial judge said. Thus, the trial court applied an erroneous legal standard when it refused to consider benefit of the bargain damages.

In *Flureau*, the plaintiff had purchased at auction a property that paid an advantageous rent in relation to the purchase price. The seller, however, could not produce good title. In the ensuing suit the court's instructions limited the jury to awarding the return of the deposit paid, plus interest; but the jury allowed an additional twenty pounds. A new trial was ordered. The report of the judgment of De Grey, C.J., reads in full:

"I think the verdict wrong in point of law. Upon a contract for a purchase, if the title proves bad, and the vendor is (without fraud) incapable of making a good one, I do not think that the purchaser can be entitled to any damages for the fancied goodness of the bargain, which he supposes he has lost."

Flureau, 2 W. Black. 1078, 96 Eng.Rep. 635. The judgment of Blackstone, J., explained that "[t]hese contracts are merely upon condition, frequently expressed, but always implied, that the vendor has a good title." Id. at 1078–79, 96 Eng.Rep. at 635.

It has been recognized in England that the *Flureau* exception was an "anomalous rule" brought about by the difficulties in that country, as late as 1899 (if not later), "in shewing a good title to real property" and that the exception "ought not be extended to cases in which the reasons on which it is based do not apply." Day v. Singleton, [1899] 2 Ch. 320, 329 (C.A.).[2]

---

[2] The difficulties included the absence of a land register. The deeds evidencing the chain of title were delivered by the solicitor for the vendor to the solicitor for the purchaser. "Neither

Although English courts have struggled over the scope of the *Flureau* exception, the English cases considering *Flureau* have all concerned some aspect of title. See Hopkins v. Grazebrook, 6 B. & C. 31 (K.B.1826) (vendor who knows he has no title, but expects to be able to procure it prior to sale cannot rely on *Flureau* exception); Engell v. Fitch, [1869] L.R. 4 Q.B. 659 (Ex.Ch.) (*Flureau* limitation on damages not available where failure to convey results from vendor's refusal to oust a tenant); Bain v. Fothergill, [1874] L.R. 7 H.L. 158 (1873–74) (overruling Hopkins v. Grazebrook; *Flureau* applies when inability to convey interest in mining royalty results from inability to get permission from lessor); Day v. Singleton, [1899] 2 Ch. 320 (C.A.) (*Flureau* limitation on damages unavailable in sale of leasehold, where vendor fails to use best efforts to obtain lessor's consent to sale); In re Daniel, [1917] 2 Ch. 405 (*Flureau* not applicable where difficulty in conveyance results from inability to obtain partial release of mortgage); Braybrooks v. Whaley, [1919] 1 K.B. 435 (*Flureau* not applicable where failure to convey relates to noncompliance with Emergency Powers Act, rather than title defect).

More recently, *Flureau* has been given a very narrow reading in England. In Malhotra v. Choudhury, [1979] 1 All E.R. 186 (C.A.), a partner in a medical practice, Malhotra, conveyed the medical office to the junior partner, Choudhury, and the latter's wife. The partnership agreement provided that, if Choudhury left the practice, Malhotra would have the option to buy back the property at fair market value. The next year Malhotra gave notice of dissolution of the partnership, exercised the option, and later brought an action for specific performance, which was denied. Two years later Malhotra sought damages. The trial court found that Choudhury could not convey good title because of his wife's refusal to join and, applying *Flureau*, limited the recovery to reliance damages. The Court of Appeal reversed, holding that the *Flureau* rule was an exception to be applied only where the vendor showed best efforts to make a good title. Id. at 199–201. The court reasoned that the origin of the exception virtually required that bad faith be defined as a failure to make best efforts, with no requirement for fraud, and that failure of the vendor to demonstrate good faith precluded the *Flureau* exception. Id.

With respect to this country, Professor Corbin summarizes:

> "A great many courts in the United States have not been inclined to follow the English courts or to differentiate land contracts from other contracts. The rule they adopt is that, if the seller fails to convey the title that he contracted to convey, the buyer has a right to damages measured by the value of the land at the time it should have been conveyed, less the contract price as yet unpaid."

---

possession of the land nor possession of the deeds was a sufficient guarantee of a good title. Deeds might be suppressed intentionally, or as the result of mistake or accident." 15 W. Holdsworth, A History of English Law 173 (A. Goodhart & H. Hanbury ed. 1965) (footnote omitted).

In Donovan v. Bachstadt, 91 N.J. 434, 441, 453 A.2d 160, 164 (1982), the court attributes to Lord Westbury, a mid-nineteenth century Lord Chancellor, the description of a bundle of documents evidencing title as "difficult to read, disgusting to touch, and impossible to understand."

5 A. Corbin, Corbin on Contracts § 1098, at 525 (1964) (footnote omitted). "Some of the courts, however, have recognized the English rule. . . ." Id. at 525–28 (footnote omitted). But even among American courts applying *Flureau*, "[i]f the seller in fact has title and refuses to perform his contract without excuse, the buyer has a right to damages." Id. at 529 (footnote omitted). Other treatises and commentators agree. See 3 American Law of Property § 11.67.a, at 168–69 (1952); J. Calamari & J. Perillo, The Law of Contracts § 14–30 (2d ed. 1977); D. Dobbs, Law of Remedies § 12.8 (1973); M. Friedman, Contracts & Conveyances of Real Property § 12.2(a)2 (4th ed. 1984); 8A G. Thompson, Real Property § 4478, at 451–52 (1963); 11 S. Williston, Law of Contracts § 1399 (Jaeger 3d ed. 1968).

The first mention of *Flureau* in the reports of this Court is in Baltimore Permanent Bldg. & Land Soc'y v. Smith, 54 Md. 187 (1880). The land was Solomon's Island, described in the contract as about "sixty-five acres." The vendor's retained land, however, surveyed at thirty-six acres. In the purchaser's damage action the trial court instructed that return of the deposit plus interest and expenses of title examination could be awarded together with benefit of the bargain damages. This Court reversed and remanded for a new trial. The "different rule" in England under *Flureau* was noted. Id. at 206. This Court traced the rule through commentators and noted that it had been followed in a great number of cases in England. Citing 2 Addison on Contracts § 529, the rule limiting recovery to reliance damages was said to apply where the vendor had " 'reasonable ground for believing that he was the owner of the property, and had the right to sell at the time he agreed to sell, but is prevented by an unexpected defect of title. . . .' " Id. at 207. The opinion by Judge Cooley in Hammond v. Hannin, 21 Mich. 374 (1870), citing many cases in this country applying the English rule, was reviewed. This Court held that the jury should have been instructed that damages were limited to return of the deposit, interest and cost of investigating the title if the jury found

> "that after [the vendor] had entered into said contract, the said defendant discovered that there was a large deficiency in the quantity of land . . . and shall further believe that the non-execution [i.e. non-performance] of said agreement on the part of the defendant, was occasioned simply by its honest inability to make title to about sixty-five acres of land. . . ."

54 Md. at 209 (referring to passage, quoted here, at 193).

Hartsock v. Mort, 76 Md. 281, 25 A. 303 (1892), and Horner v. Beasley, 105 Md. 193, 65 A. 820 (1907), both involving vendor's breaches, recognized that expectation interest damages were appropriate and the *Flureau* exception was not applied. In the former action the vendor refused to accept a take back purchase money mortgage that conformed to the contract. In the latter case the jury apparently rejected the vendor's explanation that the title was in litigation, where the contract price at the time of contracting was about two-thirds of the value. Thereafter this Court did not have occasion again to consider *Flureau* until the 1973 decision in Charles County Broadcasting, 270 Md. 321, 311 A.2d 27, discussed, infra.

The Court of Special Appeals has approved expectation interest damages for the vendor's breach of a contract to build a home and then to convey the improved premises. See Fran Realty, Inc. v. Thomas, 30 Md.App. 362, 354 A.2d 196 (1976) (holding vendor breached by attempted, unilateral rescission based on previously discoverable, subsurface conditions).

Respondents have no basis for invoking the *Flureau* exception because they do not even assert that inability to convey title produced their breach of the contract to convey. Respondents deny, however, that the *Flureau* rule applies so narrowly, and they cite Charles County Broadcasting in support. That case involved breach of a contract to sell the license of an FM radio station, subject to Federal Communication Commission (FCC) approval of the transfer of ownership and of a relocation of the transmitter. The subjects of the sale were the stock of a subsidiary corporation of the seller, certain equipment, goodwill, contracts and insurance policies, and a lease of realty to be assumed by the buyer. See Appellant Charles County Broadcasting Co.'s Record Extract at 62–69. The seller agreed to cooperate fully in obtaining all needed approvals from the FCC, and it is that covenant which the seller breached. The buyer initially sought specific performance, to require the seller to sign a document needed for FCC approval, but, by the time of trial, the buyer elected damages under the prayer for further relief. The trial court awarded benefit of the bargain damages. On appeal the seller challenged that award, advancing a variety of reasons, none of which was that *Flureau* applied. This Court affirmed loss of the bargain damages.

The opinion in *Charles County Broadcasting* opened with a general discussion of specific performance law and of the award of damages in equity. It quoted Hartsock v. Mort, 76 Md. at 288–89, 25 A. 303, in turn quoting Hammond v. Hannin, 21 Mich. at 387, for the rule as to the measure of damages:

> " 'If the vendor acts in bad faith,—as, if having title he refuses to convey, or disables himself from conveying,—the proper measure of damages is the value of the land at the time of the breach; the rule, in such case, being the same in relation to real as to personal property. But, on the other hand, if the contract of sale was made in good faith, and the vendor for any reason is unable to perform it, and is guilty of no fraud, the clear weight of authority is that the vendee is limited in his recovery to the consideration money (paid) and interest, with perhaps in addition, the costs of investigating the title.' "

270 Md. at 326, 311 A.2d at 31. After concluding that there was sufficient evidence of value to support loss of the bargain damages, the Court said that "in breach of a contract to sell, damages are based on value at the time the transfer was to be made, and not on contract price. . . ." 270 Md. at 332, 311 A.2d at 34. *Charles County Broadcasting* concluded by saying: "As we pointed out earlier, loss of bargain damages are available when a vendor acts in bad faith, Hartsock v. Mort, supra, and may be recovered in a specific performance suit under a prayer for general relief. . . ." 270 Md. at 334, 311 A.2d at 35.

Respondents' position necessarily has two steps,(1) that *Charles County Broadcasting* expands *Flureau* beyond problems of title, and (2) that respondents breached the subject contract in good faith. But we do not read *Charles County Broadcasting* to hold that loss of the bargain damages are not recoverable for a good faith breach of contract, other than where the breach results from certain problems involving title to realty. No party in *Charles County Broadcasting* argued that realty was involved there. This Court's quote of the damage rule from Hartsock v. Mort was appropriate. Part of that rule is that damages for breach of a contract to sell personalty are the same as those for a "bad faith" breach of a contract to convey realty.[4]

But, even if respondents were correct in their first step, *Charles County Broadcasting* refutes their second step. If the sellers' refusal to execute a document needed for FCC approval was "bad faith" in *Charles County Broadcasting*, then respondents' termination of the instant contract similarly is "bad faith" under the rule. *Charles County Broadcasting*, as well as all of the other authorities reviewed above, make clear that bad faith is not limited to "malice, fraud or the like." The standard applied by the trial court in the present case is not the law.

Thus, the trial court erred in failing to consider breach of the bargain damages.

II

As of what date should the premises be valued to determine any excess of value over the contract price? . . . As we have seen, the ordinary rule for computing loss of the bargain damages is to value the property at the time of breach. Breach by failure to perform usually occurs when the promised performance is due.

. . .

Where, as here, the purchaser sues for specific performance upon breach of a contract to convey realty, and specific performance becomes unavailable during the pendency of the action, the loss of the bargain damages, awarded in substitution for specific performance, may properly be computed by valuing the property at the time specific performance becomes unavailable. The rule for which petitioners contend is the rule in England and in those states in this country in which the issue appears to have been raised. Respondents have not referred us to any authority to the contrary.

. . .

III

Respondents assert that if benefit of the bargain damages are permitted then the damages which had been awarded by the trial court cannot also be awarded. Benefit of the bargain damages will be the amount by which the value of the premises on the appropriate valuation date exceeds the purchase price. The Beards' down payment on the house forms part of the price and is not represented in loss of the bargain compensation. Payments by way of rental for substitute housing were recognized as proper consequential damages, ancillary to the award of specific performance, in Miller v. Talbott, 239 Md. 382, 391–92, 211 A.2d 741, and are not inconsistent with benefit of the bargain damages.

---

[4] We disapprove of any implication in *Charles County Broadcasting* that the *Flureau* exception is not limited to title problems that result in an inability to convey realty.

The mortgage placement fee and the deposits for electronic systems are out of pocket expenditures by the Beards that apparently are lost, in that the trial court neither treated them as part of the contract price nor as subject to the doctrine of avoidable consequences. On this record they are recoverable. But, those expenditures also represent part of what the cost of the finished home would be in addition to the contract price. The expenditures should be added to the contract price, and that total subtracted from the value, as of the appropriate date, in determining the loss of the bargain.

[Judgment vacated and remanded for further proceedings consistent with this opinion.]

b. SELLER'S DAMAGES

Kuhn v. Spatial Design, Inc.

Superior Court of New Jersey, Appellate Division, 1991.
245 N.J.Super. 378, 585 A.2d 967.

Before JUDGES LONG, R.S. COHEN and STERN.

The opinion of the court was delivered by

R.S. COHEN, J.A.D.

Plaintiffs John and Marlene Kuhn contracted to buy a home from defendant Spatial Design, Inc. The sale was contingent on the Kuhns' obtaining a mortgage to finance the purchase. They applied to Prudential Home Mortgage Company through a mortgage broker, defendant Sterling National Mortgage Company, Inc., with the help of Sterling employees, defendants Ellberger and Wolf. Prudential issued a mortgage commitment but later withdrew it. The Kuhns then sought to void their purchase contract with Spatial Design for failure of the mortgage contingency. When they did not get their deposit back, they started suit. Spatial Design counterclaimed for damages for breach of contract. Judge Patrick J. McGann, Jr., heard the matter and found that the Kuhns had breached. He therefore denied their claim and awarded Spatial Design damages on the counterclaim. We affirm substantially for the reasons expressed in Judge McGann's oral opinion of March 22, 1990, in which he meticulously and thoroughly expressed his findings of fact and conclusions of law. There are two matters, however, on which we feel it would be useful to express our own views.

Judge McGann concluded on compelling evidence that the Kuhns and Sterling's people purposely submitted a mortgage application that presented a materially false picture of the Kuhns' income and assets, because they knew that revealing their true financial situation would not produce the loan they sought. The judge further found that the Kuhns and Sterling were encouraged to submit such an application by Prudential's dependably credulous way of dealing with income and asset information submitted to it.

The Kuhns knew that their application showed that Kuhn was an Air Force colonel, but did not reveal that he had already been approved for retirement; that Mrs. Kuhn had a substantial income from "Plants-R-You," a florist business which existed only in the minds of the Kuhns and Sterling's people; that the fictitious business had assets of $50,000, which did not exist at all; that the $50,000 deposit on the purchase came from savings, when in fact it was borrowed on a second mortgage on the Kuhns' present home, and that the Kuhns had jewelry, antiques, stamps and the like worth $123,000, which Kuhn actually thought would fetch some $47,000.

Kuhn knew that his true current income and assets would not support the mortgage application. He and his wife also knew that Wolf had left some figures blank in the application they signed. Wolf had said they were not going to be "boy scouts" in the matter. Predictably, Sterling's president, Ellberger, who knew what numbers it took to make the application viable, supplied some impressive ones. They showed bank balances of some $240,000 instead of the real $10,000, and total family income of some $218,000 instead of the real $65,000 or even the fictitious $95,000 that earlier appeared. Not surprisingly, Prudential issued a commitment for a $300,000 mortgage for the $515,000 purchase.

All of this was possible because the Kuhns were making a "no documentation" loan application. That meant that Prudential would probably not check to see if the represented facts showing the career Air Force officer's improbably comfortable financial situation were true.[2]

Colonel Kuhn expected the whole business to be ultimately supported by a high-salaried but not-yet-identified private sector job he hoped to find before he retired. The $30,000 in income he thought was going to be attributed to "Plants-R-You" (Ellberger eventually settled on $9400 per month.) was really his Air Force pension. The $65,000 he thought he showed as service income (Ellberger made it $8800 per month.) would be covered by the private sector job he had not yet sought.

When Kuhn put the present home up for sale and looked for a private sector job, he found both the real estate market and the job market unwelcoming. He heard that Spatial Design might have sold the house across the street from their new one for much less than they were paying. He therefore decided to climb down from the shaky limb he was on. He telephoned Prudential and wrote to Sterling, stating that he had decided to retire from the Air Force, and would thus lose some $40,000 in annual income. He inquired innocently if that would affect the mortgage commitment.

Almost simultaneously, Kuhn wrote to the Air Force to withdraw his approved retirement, thus falsifying the sole expressed basis of his communications with Prudential and Sterling. Prudential withdrew its commitment on the basis of the new information. It had retained the right to withdraw "if any material facts appear that have not previously been revealed by [the applicant]." Kuhn then unsuccessfully tried to cancel the purchase contract on the thesis that the mortgage contingency was not satisfied.

The Kuhns sued Spatial Design, which counterclaimed for the deposit and damages. They then sued Sterling, Wolf and Ellberger for indemnification against the counterclaim. Spatial Design crossclaimed

---

[2]   It is impossible to tell from the evidence if Prudential greeted improbable information in "no documentation" applications with a knowing wink, and counted on ever-rising property values to pick up the slack.

against Sterling, Wolf and Ellberger for fraud, tortious interference, conspiracy and negligence.

After a bench trial, Judge McGann found in favor of Spatial Design and against the Kuhns, and assessed damages at almost $100,000, less the retained deposit of $50,000. He denied the Kuhns' indemnification claim and Spatial Design's damage claim against the mortgage brokers.

Spatial Design has not crossappealed from the denial of its damage claim against the mortgage brokers. We therefore do not comment on it.[5] In all respects material to this appeal, however, Judge McGann's findings and conclusions on the conduct of the parties are supported by compelling evidence. We have considered his conclusions that as wrongdoers the Kuhns are not entitled to indemnification, and that whatever limited knowledge the Kuhns' real estate broker Flo Pulda had about the mortgage application was not attributable to Spatial Design. Those conclusions were factually supported and legally sound.

Now, as to damages. The contract price was $515,000, subject to a real estate commission of 5% or $25,750. The house was eventually sold, free of commission, for $434,000. In the interim, there were carrying charges for taxes and interest. There was no reason suggested by the evidence to doubt the reasonableness either of the time it took to resell the house or the sale price obtained.

Damages arose from two different sources. The first was the decreasing value of the house due to general market conditions. The second was the cost of holding the house until it could be resold. The holding costs are not the subject of this appeal. The Kuhns have two arguments, however, about the loss-of-value damages.

The first argument is that the true measure of a seller's damages for breach of contract by a buyer of real estate is the difference between the contract price and the market value at the time of the breach, less credit for any deposit retained by the seller. . . . They point out that if values were steadily declining, as the judge found, they had declined very little in the few months between contract and breach, and certainly much less than at the time of resale, many months later. Thus, the Kuhns argue, it was error to measure Spatial Design's damages by the difference between the two contract prices.

Neither of the cases cited by the Kuhns involved the assessment of damages resulting from a breach in a falling market. In such circumstances, two basic rules must be consulted. One is that contract damages are designed to put the injured party in as good a position as if performance had been rendered as promised. The other, from Hadley v. Baxendale, is that damages should be such as may fairly be considered either arising naturally, *i.e.*, according to the usual course of things, from the breach, or such as may reasonably be supposed to have been in the contemplation of both parties, at the time they contracted, as the probable result of the breach. Donovan v. Bachstadt, 91 N.J. 434, 444–445, 453 A.2d 160 (1982).

---

[5] We do note N.J.S.A. 17:11B–14g, which prohibits material misrepresentations, circumventions and concealments by mortgage brokers, and N.J.S.A. 17:11B–17, which makes willful violations third-degree crimes. We do not say whether these statutes create a cause of action, or whether the disappointed seller would have standing to sue.

In the usual course of things, a $515,000 house cannot be resold the instant a contract buyer breaches, and a reasonable time for resale must therefore be allowed. In addition, it is not uncommon for property values to experience a general fall-off after a period of intense run-up. In a falling market, buyers take longer to find, and they buy at reduced prices.

A rule that restricts damages for breach of a contract to buy real estate to the difference between contract price and value at the time of breach (plus expenses) works fairly only in a static market. A damage rule works fairly in a declining market only if it takes account of slowing sales and falling values. In such cases, where the seller puts the property back on the market and resells, the measure is not contract price less value at the time of breach, but rather the resale price, if it is reasonable as to time, method, manner, place and terms. These are matters for the factfinder, who may or may not conclude from the evidence that what actually occurred after breach by way of resale was reasonable and thus provides an accurate measure of damages. Judge McGann found that it did here, on sufficient credible evidence.

We adopt,[6] for these purposes, the essence of the sellers' damage rules provided for sellers of goods in the Uniform Commercial Code, *N.J.S.A.* 12A:2–706 and 708, and adapted for sellers of real estate in §§ 504–507 of the Uniform Land Transactions Act (ULTA), which New Jersey has not adopted. We adopt these rules because they take account of the effect of changing market conditions in sound ways which New Jersey's reported decisions have not yet taken into account.

Where a buyer of real estate wrongfully rejects, repudiates or materially breaches as to a substantial part of the contract, the seller may resell in a manner that is reasonable as to method, manner, time, place and terms. The defaulting buyer must have reasonable notice of the time after which resale will take place. If the resale is a public sale, the defaulting buyer must have notice of the time and place, and may buy. The seller may then recover the amount by which the unpaid contract price and any incidental and consequential damages exceed the resale price, less expenses avoided because of the buyer's breach. See ULTA § 2–504, 13 *U.L.A.* 552 (1977); *N.J.S.A.* 12A:2–706.

A seller's incidental damages include any reasonable out-of-pocket expenses incurred because of the buyer's breach. A seller's consequential damages include any loss the buyer knew or at the time of contracting had reason to know would result from the buyer's breach and which reasonably could not be avoided by the seller. *See* ULTA § 507, 13 *U.L.A.* 555 (1977).

The case may be different where the seller does not put the property back on the market. In such a case, the measure of the seller's damages is the amount by which the unpaid contract price and any incidental and consequential damages exceed the fair market value of the property at the time of breach, less expenses avoided because of the buyer's breach. See ULTA § 2–505(a), 13 *U.L.A.* 553 (1977) (using the

---

[6] The Kuhn contract did not contain a liquidated damage clause, either forfeiting the deposit on the buyer's breach without proof of damages, or limiting liability of the buyer to the amount of the deposit. We do not intend by this opinion to affect the applicability or enforceability of such provisions.

value at the time set for conveyance instead of at the time of breach); *see also N.J.S.A.* 12A:2–708(1). Without a resale, value at the time of breach is used, even in a declining market, because the choice of any other time would be so speculative. We need not explore application of the exceptions made by ULTA 2–505(b) and *N.J.S.A.* 12A:2–708(2) for situations in which the difference between contract price and fair market value is inadequate to put the seller in as good a position as performance would have.

[Judgment affirmed.]

3. RESCISSION

Mutual rescission doubtless represents the most common resolution of land sale contract breaches, at least in the residential setting. By agreeing on rescission, buyer and seller can avoid the expense, delay and uncertainty of litigation and can, through the seller's return of part or all of the buyer's down payment, reach some rough justice between themselves. Mutual rescission creates problems only in retrospect, when one side tries to avoid the asserted rescission, and a court must determine whether rescission has in fact occurred. (*B* writes to *S*, "this whole deal is really a bad idea;" *S* responds, "I guess you could say so".) And, even if a court can piece together an intent to rescind from ambiguous words and conduct, the question remains how the *status quo ante* is to be restored.

Unilateral rescission can take either of two forms. In *equitable rescission,* sometimes called an action *for* a rescission, the disappointed buyer or seller seeks a judicial decree terminating the contract. In *legal rescission,* sometimes called an action *on* a rescission, the buyer or seller simply declares that the other's conduct constitutes grounds for terminating the contract. Legal rescission contains more than the usual hazards of self-help. Pitfalls surround the requirements that the rescission be effected by notice and that the notice be timely. (What constitutes effective notice? At what point does notice become untimely?) There is also the risk that the asserted misconduct does not in fact constitute grounds for termination. A seller wishing to rescind when her buyer fails to perform on the closing date must consider the possibility that time will be held not of the essence. A buyer who wishes to rescind when his seller contracts to sell the land to someone else must consider the possibility that the subsequent buyer will not qualify as a bona fide purchaser who can defeat the original buyer's claims. An added cost of guessing wrong about the effect of the other side's conduct may be a finding that, by seeking to rescind, the rescinding party anticipatorily repudiated the contract.

4. VENDEE'S AND VENDOR'S LIENS

a. VENDEE'S LIEN

New York Law Revision Commission, Recommendation to the Legislature Relating to the Vendee's Lien on Land to Secure Restitution or Damages
Legis. Document No. 65 (1946).

In Elterman v. Hyman, 192 N.Y. 113 (1908), it was held that where the vendor of land was unable to convey the title required by the contract, the vendee was entitled to a lien upon the land to secure his right to reimbursement for the payments made under the contract, but in Davis v. William Rosenzweig Realty Operating Co., 192 N.Y. 128 (1908), a vendee who sued in equity for rescission of the contract because of the fraud of the vendor was denied a lien on the ground that the lien depended upon the contract and that the vendee had rendered the contract void *ab initio* by securing rescission.

In most states a lien is given regardless of the form of action. The rule adopted in the *Davis* case is not only contrary to the weight of authority in other states, but has been widely criticized by courts and writers. The Commission believes that the premise adopted by the majority of the court, that the lien depends upon the continued existence of the contract, is erroneous, for the lien is simply a remedy created by the courts, and has no connection with the contract except that the vendor's failure to perform his contractual obligations furnished the justification for the application of this remedy. Furthermore, the idea that the contract subsists in an action for breach of contract but does not subsist in an action for rescission is questionable, for whatever the relief sought, the vendee does not contemplate performance of the contract. The distinction drawn by the Court of Appeals between a case like Elterman v. Hyman and a case like Davis v. William Rosenzweig Realty Operating Co. has been found difficult to apply by the courts, with resulting confusion.

The rule making the protection given to the vendee depend on the form of the action, rather than the equities of the case, may frequently result in hardship. Particularly at the present time, when many residential properties of moderate value are changing hands, the vendee may well need the security of the lien because of the vendor's inability to make restitution or respond in damages.

The statute proposed by the Commission, while changing the rule in the *Davis* case, is so drawn as not to preclude the granting of a lien in a proper case in actions based upon failure, invalidity or disaffirmance of an agreement, as well as in actions for or based upon rescission.

The Commission therefore recommends the addition of the following new section 112–h to Article 9 of the Civil Practice Act:

§ 112–h. Vendee's lien not to depend upon form of action. When relief is sought in an action or proceeding or by way of defense or counterclaim, by a vendee under an agreement for the sale or exchange of real property, because of the failure, invalidity, disaffirmance or rescission of such agreement, a vendee's lien upon the property shall not be denied merely because the claim for relief is for rescission, or is based upon the rescission, failure, invalidity or disaffirmance of such agreement.

COLE v. HAYNES, 216 Miss. 485, 62 So.2d 779 (1953), ETHRIDGE, J: Appellee argues, however, that even if he has a duty to refund to appellant the amount of the down-payment, still appellant's right is solely in personam; that appellant must therefore sue appellee in the county of appellee's residence; and that appellant therefore cannot bring a suit in equity in Holmes County where the land is located, seeking to impose an equitable lien on the land. However, established principles of justice and law indicate a different conclusion. 55 Am.Jur., Vendor and Purchaser, § 548, states that the general rule is that a purchaser under an executory contract for the sale and purchase of land is entitled to an equitable lien upon the land for the amount which he has paid upon the purchase price, where the vendor is in default or unable to make a good title. Section 549 says this with reference to the nature and basis of the lien:

"The lien of a purchaser of land under an executory contract for the amount which he has paid is to secure to him the repayment of expenditures made in pursuance of the contract. The exact nature of this lien is not clear. The doctrine has been quite generally applied without any discussion as to the nature of the lien, except, perhaps, the statement in general terms that it was an equitable lien, very similar to that of a vendor for unpaid purchase money. It has been said that the basis of the lien is the well-known fundamental rule that in equity what is agreed to be done is regarded as done, so that from the time that a contract is made for the purchase of real estate, the vendor is, in a sense, a trustee for the purchaser, and the purchaser in a sense is the real owner of the land, so that each, under the ordinary equitable rules, has a lien for his protection. The whole practice in equity with reference to such contracts is clearly on the basis that the parties are under equal equitable obligations to each other. It has also been said that all the reasoning by which the vendor's equitable lien for the purchase money after a conveyance is established is applicable in support of the vendee's lien after full or part payment and before conveyance, and that it is difficult to imagine upon what principle a court of equity could enforce the one and deny the other."

b.   VENDOR'S LIEN

Askren v. 21st Street Inn

United States Court of Appeals for the Seventh Circuit, 1993.
988 F.2d 38.

Before BAUER, CHIEF JUDGE, and POSNER and COFFEY, CIRCUIT JUDGES.

POSNER, CIRCUIT JUDGE.

This is a diversity suit to enforce a vendor's lien. We can simplify the facts. The plaintiff, Askren, owner of a two-acre parcel of land in Indianapolis, made a contract with Cardinal Industries, a hotel chain, to sell the parcel to Cardinal for $250,000. Half of the purchase price was to be paid in cash to Askren at the closing and the other half was to be paid in equal installments, together with interest at 9 percent a year, on the first and second anniversaries of the closing. The agreement was on a printed form, but a clause had been typed in which stated that Askren's "Security [for payment of the balance of the purchase price is] to be a Cardinal . . . promissory note." At the closing, Askren received $125,000 in cash plus a promissory note the terms of which were identical to those specified in the agreement of sale. Cardinal borrowed a considerable sum of money to build a hotel on the parcel it had bought. The loan was secured by a mortgage on the real estate and its improvements. The loan and mortgage were later assigned to the principal defendant in this case, Third Savings and Loan Company. Cardinal went broke and failed to make either of the installment payments that it owed Askren, who brought this suit to foreclose his implied land vendor's lien on the parcel. The district judge granted summary judgment for the savings and loan company on the ground that Askren had waived his lien, and dismissed the suit, precipitating this appeal.

Indiana law, which the parties agree governs the substantive issues in this suit, creates a vendor's lien whenever someone sells real estate and is not paid in full at the time of the closing, that is, at the time the real estate is conveyed. Old First National Bank & Trust Co. v. Scheuman, 214 Ind. 652, 668, 13 N.E.2d 551, 558 (1938); Lincoln National Life Ins. Co. v. Overmyer, 530 N.E.2d 784, 786 (Ind.App.1988); Prell v. Trustees, 179 Ind.App. 642, 386 N.E.2d 1221, 1227 (1979). Whenever title passes before payment is completed, the seller is in effect lending money to the buyer; and Indiana law gives the seller an automatic security interest in the real estate, to secure this loan-gives him, in other words, a purchase-money mortgage. The lien is created by the law, not by the contract of sale, and it need not be recorded in order to be effective. It was not recorded in this case, or mentioned in the contract, which is why we called it an implied lien.

Why the law should create a lien in these circumstances is obscure. The origin of the doctrine of the vendor's land lien is equitable, and in turn Roman; the principle is said to be that "a thing may well be deemed to be unconscientiously obtained, when the consideration is not paid." 3 Story's Equity Jurisprudence § 1626 at p. 263 (W.H. Lyon, Jr., ed., 14th ed. 1918). Well, of course, but the issue comes up only when the vendor is contesting with a third party, such as the mortgagee in this case, rather than with the defaulting vendee. The doctrine arbitrarily advances the vendor over the vendee's other creditors, and complicates real estate financing. It has been abolished in a number of states, but not in Indiana. All this is an aside, however. Although the lien is created by the law, it is created for the seller's benefit, so he can waive it. Old First National Bank & Trust Co. v. Scheuman, supra, 214 Ind. at 668, 13 N.E.2d at 558; Lincoln National Life Ins. Co. v. Overmyer, supra, 530 N.E.2d at 786. The only question we need decide is whether the evidence adequately establishes that Askren did waive his implied land vendor's lien.

The contract of sale states that the security for the buyer's performance, that is, for the completion of payment, is a promissory note by Cardinal Industries: "Security [is] to be" Cardinal's note. If the security was to be the note, it was not to be the land. "As a general rule the taking of other independent security for the purchase money is an implied waiver of the vendor's lien." Old First National Bank & Trust Co. v. Scheuman, supra, 214 Ind. at 668, 13 N.E.2d at 558; cf. Rader v. Dawes, 651 S.W.2d 629, 633 (Mo.App.1983). Askren argues that, so interpreted, the clause about security was illusory, since if Cardinal defaulted he could always sue on the agreement of sale-what would a note add? Well, something. Promissory notes are generally assumed to be easier to sue on than regular contracts, Burrill v. Commissioner, 93 T.C. 643, 662 (1989), though the basis for this belief is obscure, at least in a state such as Indiana which has abolished "confession of judgment" clauses, a device for erasing the promisor's procedural rights. Ind.Code § 34-2-25-1. More important, promissory notes standardly provide for awarding the promisee his attorney's fees and other costs of enforcing the note-though Cardinal's note to Askren did not. Most important, such a note can be negotiated, if the promisee wants his money before it is due, to a holder in due course who will not be subject to the defenses the promisor might have had to a suit by the promisee. UCC § 3-305(b). This feature, not exploited by Askren, be it noted, makes a promissory note almost as good as cash-provided, of course, that the promisor is solvent. The Supreme Court of Indiana did not doubt, in the *Scheuman* case, that a note could be security in lieu of the real estate, though the court held it was not in that case; for one thing it had been given long after the conveyance, apparently to secure a later loan-not the loan implicit in conveying the real estate before it had been completely paid for. Old First National Bank & Trust Co. v. Scheuman, supra, 214 Ind. at 668, 13 N.E.2d at 558.

Askren also points to a clause which states that the sale agreement shall survive, after the conveyance of the property is completed, until all the terms and conditions of the agreement have been performed. The agreement is seven pages of fine print and imposes numerous obligations on the parties. All that the survival clause means is that if any of these obligations have not been met by the closing, they remain enforceable. So, for example, Cardinal's personal obligation to complete paying for the parcel survived the transfer of the parcel from Askren to it. This may seem too obvious a function to assign to the survival clause. That clause, however, may itself be a survival-of the era when the doctrine of "merger," now however greatly curtailed, extinguished all contractual obligations in the sale agreement that were not carried over into the deed. Roger A. Cunningham, William B. Stoebuck, and Dale A. Whitman, The Law of Property § 10.12 at pp. 696–98 (1984).

Askren argues that a property right should not lightly be deemed forfeited. An equal and opposite maxim is that invisible encumbrances should not lightly be deemed subsistent. There is no written evidence of Askren's so-called lien. It is neither in the sale agreement nor anywhere else. Askren did not record the lien until Cardinal declared bankruptcy-he did not until then even know that he *had* a vendor's lien. The principal defendant is an Ohio lender, and Ohio has made implied vendors' liens ineffective against mortgagees, Ohio Rev.Code. § 5301.26, so the lender was hardly likely to spot the invisible lien when it took the assignment of the mortgage. Well, it did business in Indiana, so should have known better. But legal doctrines that confer property rights on people who neither possess the property openly nor have a recorded paper title should be interpreted cautiously in order to facilitate sale and financing transactions, and persons claiming rights under such doctrines should be encouraged to record their claims. United States v. Speers, 382 U.S. 266, 275–76, 86 S.Ct. 411, 416–17, 15 L.Ed.2d 314 (1965); Krauss Bros. Lumber Co. v. Dimon Steamship Corp., 290 U.S. 117, 125, 54 S.Ct. 105, 107–08, 78 L.Ed. 216 (1933); Security Warehousing Co. v. Hand, 143 Fed. 32, 41 (7th Cir.1906), aff'd, 206 U.S. 415, 27 S.Ct. 720, 51 L.Ed. 1117 (1907); Miller v. Wells Fargo Bank Int'l Corp., 540 F.2d 548, 558–59 n. 13 (2d Cir.1976). So the Indiana Supreme Court stated with specific reference to implied vendors' liens more than a century ago. Woody v. Fislar, 55 Ind. 592, 594 (1877). While that court later denied that the implied vendor's lien was "not in favor" in Indiana, Old First National Bank & Trust Co. v. Scheuman, supra, 214 Ind. at 665, 13 N.E.2d at 556, we do not think the court meant to throw all caution to the winds and wrap real estate lending in a fog of uncertainty.

There is no injustice in extinguishing Mr. Askren's lien. His lawyer admitted at oral argument that his client didn't know he was retaining such an interest when he sold the parcel, and no one suggests that Cardinal paid him less in recognition of the valuable interest that he claims to have retained. The savings and loan company that has had to foreclose on the parcel and its improvements had no reason to suppose that the parcel was encumbered by a prior lien. But the equities of the case are neither here nor there. The waiver of the land vendor's implied lien was clear. Askren had no lien to foreclose on, and the judgment dismissing his foreclosure suit is therefore

Affirmed.

NOTES

1. *Remedial Strategies.* The several remedies available to buyer and seller on breach by the other offer considerable opportunity for strategic maneuvering. The requirement that a party seeking specific performance remain ready to perform puts a burden on the buyer, who must arrange with his lender to keep his loan commitment alive, as well as on the seller, who may have intended to move from the house, using the cash from its sale to buy another. Yet, a seller facing a rapidly falling market, or a buyer facing a rapidly rising one, may prefer specific performance, with all its disadvantages, to the prospect that, in the circumstances, damages will not make her whole. And the rule that specific performance will be denied if the contract involves inadequate consideration or is unconscionable or oppressive to the party against whom it is sought to be enforced does not necessarily promise that the plaintiff will do any better in an action for damages at law where his oppressive conduct may turn the jury against him.

Foreclosure on the vendor's lien may offer an attractive alternative to the seller who is unable to tender the marketable title required for specific performance or whose misconduct would disqualify her from specific performance. See Charles v. Scheibel, 128 Misc. 275, 218 N.Y.S. 545 (N.Y.Sup.Ct.1926). Also, by securing the seller's claim for the contract price, the vendor's lien may give the seller a preferred position over the buyer's general creditors. Two possible disadvantages of foreclosing on the vendor's lien are that, as in mortgage foreclosure, deficiency judgments may be prohibited and statutory redemption periods may be required. For the buyer, the vendee's lien provides security for the return of his deposit but typically will not secure his claim for title examination and survey costs and benefit of bargain damages. See Comment, The Vendee's Lien in New York: Its Development, Application and Status, 37 Alb.L.Rev. 470, 482–485 (1973).

The use, or threatened use, of certain remedies may expose a party to liability. In Askari v. R & R Land Company, 179 Cal.App.3d 1101, 225 Cal.Rptr. 285 (1986), a buyer brought an action against the seller and filed a notice of lis pendens. The seller ultimately prevailed. The court ruled that the seller could recover consequential damages for the period from the beginning of the suit until the dissolution of the lis pendens if the seller could show that during that time it attempted to resell the property but the lis pendens made the title unmarketable. (By the way, is this just another way of addressing the general rule described in *Kuhn* which calculates seller's damages as of the date of breach?) Moreover, the court noted in dictum that while the filing of a lis pendens was privileged and could not be the basis of a slander of title suit, an action for malicious prosecution might be possible. Cf. Piep v. Baron, 133 Misc.2d 248, 506 N.Y.S.2d 838 (Civ.Ct.1986) (no abuse of process found where lis pendens was filed in action by buyer to enforce a contract of sale since the buyer's goal of preventing the sale of the property to another did not show an intent to do harm without excuse or justification nor was the filing a perversion of the process). In some situations, a wrongfully intransigent party can be liable for other damages. See, e.g., Schaumberg v. Friedmann, 72 Mass.App.Ct. 52, 888 N.E.2d 963 (2008) (defaulting realty company vendor of condominium unit that wrongfully refused to return buyer's deposit held liable for treble damages—trebling buyer's inspection and appraisal fees—under state unfair trade practices statute).

The attorney also risks sanctions in these cases. For example, in DeWald v. Isola, 180 Mich.App. 129, 446 N.W.2d 620 (1989), appeal after remand, 188 Mich.App. 697, 470 N.W.2d 505 (1991), the attorney who brought an action to enforce a draft sales agreement against a seller was sanctioned for asserting a frivolous claim. The seller had never signed the document and an unauthorized notation on it by the sales agent that seller had agreed to the terms—which seller denied—was inadequate to bind the seller under the statute of frauds. The court reasoned that in light of "basic, longstanding, and unmistakenly evident" reasons in the common and statutory law, and which were brought to the attorney's attention several times, it should have been clear to the attorney that the claim was worthless. 180 Mich.App. at 136, 446 N.W.2d at 623. Would the attorney's behavior in *DeWald* also violate DR 7–102(A)(2) of the Code of Professional Responsibility which states that a lawyer shall not "[k]nowingly advance a claim or defense that is unwarranted under existing law, except that he may advance such claim or defense if it can be supported by good faith argument of an extension, modification, or reversal of existing law?"

The agreement of sale may limit the remedies available to the parties by prescribing or proscribing various remedial alternatives. Are such limitations desirable to the parties? Kelley v. Leucadia indicates that sometimes the limitations may be unclear. Did the court in *Kelley* satisfactorily interpret these provisions? Which party did the standard broker's agreement favor in its limitations of remedy provisions? A contract of sale may also limit access to courts by imposing an arbitration requirement. See, e.g., Johnson v. Siegel, 84 Cal.App.4th 1087, 101 Cal.Rptr.2d 412 (2000) (upholding clause in purchase and sale agreement requiring arbitration of "any" dispute arising from the transaction and finding that it applied to alleged misrepresentation concerning flooding problems).

2. *Specific Performance.* Rationales abound for the rule making specific performance generally available to land sellers as well as to land buyers. Courts and commentators have enthusiastically shored up the rule with new rationales as the old rationales disintegrated. In addition to the three rationales that Pomeroy cites are another three that you may find more plausible. First, land may possess unique *dis*advantages for the seller, such as exposure to liability for dangerous conditions on the land. Second, a buyer's asserted cause of action may make it impossible for the seller to dispose of the property elsewhere so long as the claim is outstanding. And, third, "in the absence of some objective indicator of the land's market price, such as value established by frequent sales or condemnation proceedings of substantially similar land, it is apparent that the vendor may in fact not have an adequate remedy at law." Comment, 48 Temp.L.Q. 847, 851–852 (1975). See Restatement (Second) of Contracts § 360 Comment e (1979).

Courts have always found occasions to refuse specific performance to buyer or seller. Unfairness, inadequate consideration, unconscionability and overreaching are just a few. But courts have only recently confronted the rule of general availability head on. Centex Homes Corp. v. Boag, 128 N.J.Super. 385, 320 A.2d 194 (Ch.Div.1974), typifies the contemporary challenge. Plaintiff, developer of a high-rise condominium, sought specific performance against defendants who had reneged on their contract for the purchase of a condominium unit. Asserting that "the mutuality of remedy concept has been the prop which has supported equitable jurisdiction to grant specific performance in actions by vendors of real estate," and that "mutuality of remedy is not an appropriate basis for granting or denying specific performance," the court concluded that the "disappearance of the mutuality of remedy doctrine from our law dictates the conclusion that specific performance relief should no longer be automatically available to a vendor of real estate, but should be confined to those special instances where a vendor will otherwise suffer an economic injury for which his damage remedy at law will not be adequate, or where other equitable considerations require that the relief be granted." 128 N.J.Super. at 390–393, 320 A.2d at 197–198.

The *Centex* court went on to observe that "the subject matter of the real estate transaction—a condominium apartment unit—has no unique quality but is one of hundreds of virtually identical units being offered by a developer for sale to the public." 128 N.J.Super. at 393, 320 A.2d at 198. In the circumstances, was the observation gratuitous, or does it imply that, in an action by the buyers against the developer, the court would also have withheld specific performance? See Suchan v. Rutherford, 90 Idaho 288, 410 P.2d 434 (1966). Later cases in New Jersey have rejected *Centex*. See, e.g., Pruitt v. Graziano, 215 N.J.Super. 330, 521 A.2d 1313 (App.Div.1987) (contracts for sales of condominiums are specifically enforceable like other real estate contracts irrespective of any proof of uniqueness).

Similarly, at least some courts, have questioned the underlying theory of specific performance for sellers. In Kesler v. Marshall, 792 N.E.2d 893, 897 (Ind.App.2003), the court not only felt that remedies at law were adequate on the facts but also doubted the wisdom of specific performance by sellers in any situation:

> In this case, the trial court concluded that Marshall [seller] was entitled to specific performance. However, none of the court's findings support the conclusion that monetary damages would be insufficient to fully compensate Marshall. Rather, Marshall could have kept Kesler's [buyer's] earnest money and terminated the contract, or resold the property and held Kesler liable for the difference between the actual sale price and the price under the contract. In either case, Marshall would have been fully compensated by damages for Kesler's failure to perform. Further, the traditional rationale underlying the grant of specific performance in real estate transactions, i.e., that each piece of property is unique, does not apply here to the party seeking specific performance, Marshall, because he is not obtaining the property in the transaction, but rather only money. Under these circumstances, the trial court abused its discretion in ordering Kesler to specifically perform the contract.

In awarding a buyer specific performance, a court may exercise its equitable powers to rewrite the underlying contracts. A court, for example, may order specific performance for the buyer with an abatement of the price for defects in the property. See, e.g., Billy Williams Builders & Developers, Inc. v. Hillerich, 446 S.W.2d 280 (Ky.1969) (abatement for construction defects); but see Merritz v. Circelli, 361 Pa. 239, 64 A.2d 796 (1949) (following older rule that abatement is permitted only for defects in title or quantity of land). In usual circumstances, the court might instead increase the obligations of buyer in order to get specific performance. See, e.g., Kessler v. Tortoise Development, Inc., 134 Idaho 264, 1 P.3d 292 (2000) (because of the joint venture relationship between buyer and seller, buyer was required to pay his share of cost overruns before obtaining specific performance).

In what ways do these doctrines reduce the desirability of the specific performance remedy for the buyer? Is the Mohrlang v. Draper court's refusal to allow "equitable considerations" to bar an injunction correct? What effect will *Mohrlang* type decisions have on parties' positions in contract disputes and on the land transactions dynamic?

See Marsh, Sometimes Blackacre Is A Widget: Rethinking Commercial Real Estate Contract Remedies, 88 Neb. L.Rev. 635 (2010); Kirwan, Note, Appraising a Presumption: A Modern Look at the Doctrine of Specific Performance in Real Estate Contracts, 47 Wm. & Mary L.Rev. 697 (2005); Note, To Pay or Convey?: A Theory of Remedies for Breach of Real Estate Contracts, 1995 Ann. Survey Am.L. 319 (criticizing the granting by courts of specific performance instead of damages); Note, Doyle v. Ortega: Is Specific Performance Available for Buyers in An Earnest Money Contract?, 9 B.Y.U.J.Pub.L. 367 (1995) (examining clause limiting buyer's remedies).

3. *Buyer's Damages: The Rule of Flureau v. Thornhill.* Beard v. S/E Joint Venture recognizes past Maryland precedent that limits the buyer's damages for "bad faith" defects in title—consider what types of defects that would encompass. This is based on the English rule of Flureau v. Thornhill. The *Flureau* rule has been justified on three grounds. One, probably the original ground for the decision, is to curb the jury's freedom to award unbounded and speculative damages. A second ground, relied on in subsequent cases, is that land records were in such poor shape that it would be unfair to burden the seller with damages unless she in fact knew that her title was bad. Third is the modern ground that marketable title represents a condition, not a covenant, in the contract of sale and that unmarketability gives rise only to rescission and not to damages for breach of warranty.

Approximately fifteen jurisdictions expressly follow the *Flureau* rule. The rule was incorporated in the original Field Civil Code adopted in California, Montana and South Dakota. North Dakota, a Field Code state, amended the *Flureau* rule in its original code in 1895, and Oklahoma, not a Code state, has adopted a statutory formulation of *Flureau*. Doubtless, many other states, even those explicitly rejecting the *Flureau* rule, effectively adopt its result by construing marketable title as a condition rather than as a covenant.

There is a discernible trend away from the rule of Flureau v. Thornhill and toward adoption of an "American" rule. See, for example, Donovan v. Bachstadt, 91 N.J. 434, 441, 453 A.2d 160, 164 (1982): "There is nothing in [our] statute that prevents the Court from adopting the American rule and awarding loss of the benefit of the bargain damages. We are satisfied that the American rule is preferable. The English principle developed because of the uncertainties of title due to the complexity of the rules governing title to land during the eighteenth and nineteenth centuries. At that time the only evidence of title was contained in deeds which were in a phrase attributed to Lord Westbury, 'difficult to read, disgusting to touch, and impossible to understand.' The reason for the English principle that creates an exception to the law governing damages for breaches of executory contracts for the sale of property is no longer valid, and the exception should be eliminated." Still, recent cases in *Flureau* jurisdictions continue to follow the rule. See, e.g., Grover v. Jacksonville Golfair, Inc., 914 So.2d 995 (2005).

4. *Seller's Damages.* The general rule, measuring seller's damages from the date of buyer's breach rather than from the date of resale, has been criticized for failing to account for the difficulties and delay in reselling land. See Korngold, Seller's Damages from a Defaulting Buyer of Realty: The Influence of the Uniform Land Transactions Act on the Courts, 20 Nova L.Rev. 1069 (1996) (analyzing *Kuhn* and criticizing the traditional rule); Note, Damages: The Illogical Differences in Measuring Breach of Contract Damages When the Contract Involves Land Rather than Goods, 26 Okla.L.Rev. 277 (1973) (suggesting a damage measure analogous to U.C.C. § 2–706). Despite this criticism, *Kuhn* is an atypical decision, and most courts continue to follow the general rule. See M. Friedman, Contracts and Conveyances of Real Property 1031–1037 (5th ed.1991).

Is the date of resale measure necessary in light of the other remedies available to the seller, remedies generally not available to sellers of goods at common law or under the U.C.C.? Supporters of the general rule maintain that the seller who faces a long delay and declining market before resale can be made whole through a decree of specific performance for the contract price. Possibly, just by reminding the buyer of the disadvantages of specific performance to him, the seller will be able to persuade the buyer to settle on a compromise sufficient to make the seller whole. It is also argued that quick resale, even in a declining market, will probably make the seller whole, for the resale price is good, and sometimes *prima facie,* evidence of the land's value at the time of breach, particularly if the sale was made at arm's length and shortly after the breach. See Costello v. Johnson, 265 Minn. 204, 121 N.W.2d 70 (1963). Consequential damages will also help if the seller can introduce evidence that the land's value at the time of breach was depressed by the dissemination of information about the broken contract. Further, the seller can collect for maintenance expenses incurred between breach and resale. See Abrams v. Motter, 3 Cal.App.3d 828, 83 Cal.Rptr. 855 (2d Dist.1970). Finally, in most cases, seller's retention of the buyer's deposit should suffice to make her whole.

The argument against the present damage measure would appear to be strongest when one or another of these alternative remedies is not available to the seller. For example, measuring damages from the time of breach rather than resale might very well be unfair to the seller if she is in a jurisdiction that, following *Centex,* would deny her specific performance. Moreover, consider cases like *Kuhn* where specific performance is available but impracticable. If a buyer does not close because he lacks the funds to do so, what real effect—and strategic leverage—can a specific performance decree have? The court will not imprison the buyer for nonpayment of the price. See Restatement (Second) of Contracts § 360, comment e. If the court orders the sale of the property, with the buyer to pay the difference between the amount raised and the contract price—i.e., the equivalent of holding the buyer to time of resale damages—the seller will be protected. See U.L.T.A. § 2–504, comment 1. If, however, the court instead orders the buyer to either specifically perform or pay damages and the court calculates the damages based on the difference between the contract price and the value at the date of breach, the seller will be left with the loss due to the declining market. See Brett v. Wall, 530 So.2d 797 (Ala.1988) (where trial court ordered buyer either to specifically perform or pay damages equal to the difference between the contract price and value of the property on the date of trial, appellate court reversed and required damages based on date of breach).

5. *Earnest Money.* It is customary on the execution of a land sale contract for buyer to give seller an earnest money deposit securing his performance. The deposit, which commonly ranges from 1% to 10% of the purchase price, may be held by the seller, by the broker or by the escrow agent. The principal question surrounding these deposits is whether the seller may retain the earnest money in the event of the buyer's breach, or must return it in whole or in part.

The rule in most states is that the seller may keep the buyer's deposit even though forfeiture is not expressly prescribed by the contract, and even though the sum exceeds the seller's provable damages. See Uzan v. 845 UN Ltd. Partnership, 778 N.Y.S.2d 171 (Sup.Ct.2004) (forfeiture of $8 million down payment equal to 25% of purchase price for four apartments in The Trump World Tower upheld); see generally M. Friedman, Contracts and Conveyances of Real Property 1043–1060 (5th ed. 1991). The Restatement of Contracts, which in section 357 adopts a general rule that a defaulting buyer can recover the excess of his deposit over the seller's damages, makes an exception for payments of "earnest money, or if the contract provides that it [buyer's part performance] may be retained and it is not so greatly in excess of the defendant's harm that the provision is rejected as imposing a penalty." Restatement of Contracts § 357(2) (1932). Accord Restatement (Second) of Contracts § 374, Comment c (1979).

In a handful of jurisdictions, the seller can keep only so much of the deposit as is necessary to cover her damages. To avoid unjust enrichment, she must return the rest to the buyer. Yet, even in these states, the seller will as a practical matter probably be allowed to retain the entire deposit, for the buyer's burden of proving that the deposit exceeds seller's damages will not be easy to discharge. For an example of the difficulties encountered in discharging this burden see Zirinsky v. Sheehan, 413 F.2d 481 (8th Cir.1969), cert. denied, 396 U.S. 1059, 90 S.Ct. 754, 24 L.Ed.2d 753 (1970).

6. *Liquidated Damages.* Sellers can by contract forestall claims of unjust enrichment by characterizing the deposit obligation as a liquidated damages provision. This might also serve the buyer's interest since treating the deposit as earnest money leaves the seller free to pursue the full range of remedies while treating it as liquidated damages by definition bars the damages route. See also Colonial at Lynnfield, Inc. v. Sloan, 870 F.2d 761 (1st Cir.1989) (liquidated damages of $200,000 on contract price of $3,375,000 were denied when seller resold property for $251,000 more than buyers agreed to pay since actual damages turned out to be easily ascertainable and liquidated damages were grossly disproportionate to the "loss").

Legislation in Washington permits a contract provision limiting seller's remedy to forfeiture of the deposit as long as the amount forfeited does not exceed 5% of the contract price. The statute requires specific language, typeface, and initialing or signing of the clause by the parties. Wash.Rev. Code Ann. § 64.04.005(1).

Liquidated damage clauses have their own requirements. To be upheld, the liquidated sum must be proportioned to the contract price and must represent a reasonable forecast of compensation for the harm caused by the breach. Further, the harm caused by the breach must be of the sort that is difficult to estimate accurately. Compare Johnson v. Carman, 572 P.2d 371 (Utah 1977) (to allow seller to retain $34,596.10 paid by buyer, when seller's actual damages were only $25,650.00, would be "grossly excessive and disproportionate to any possible loss") with Vines v. Orchard Hills, Inc., 181 Conn. 501, 435 A.2d 1022 (1980) ("A liquidated damages clause allowing the seller to retain 10 percent [$7,880] of the contract price as earnest money is presumptively a reasonable allocation of the risks associated with default"). The states are about evenly split between those following a "first look" approach, which considers the reasonableness of the liquidated damages only as of the time of contract formation, and a "second look" approach, which looks at reasonableness at the time of breach in addition to the time of contract formation. See Kelly v. Marx, 428 Mass. 877, 705 N.E.2d 1114 (1999).

7. *Vendor's Lien.* A vendor's lien attaches to the buyer's equitable interest in the property automatically upon execution of the contract. The lien has uses even apart from the strategic advantages described in Note 1 above. As in *Askren*, the seller may assert the vendor's lien to secure any unpaid amount of the purchase price. If the buyer breaches an executory contract of sale, the seller can foreclose the vendor's lien and sell the buyer's

equitable interest to satisfy a judgment on the contract price. The vendor's lien may be particularly important in an installment sale contract (discussed at pages 520–533 below) enabling the seller to foreclose the buyer's interest on default, before completing the contract, much like the foreclosure of a purchase money mortgage. See Milton Friedman, Contracts and Conveyances of Real Property § 12.1(d) (5th ed.1991); Grant Nelson and Dale Whitman, Real Estate Finance Law (5th ed. 2007) § 3.32.

In light of In re Lanza, at page 17 above, should a lawyer ever structure a deal relying on a vendor's lien?

8.   *Drafting Exercise.* In light of the issues raised in Kelley v. Leucadia discussed in Note 1 above and what you have learned about the potential remedies available to the parties, draft clauses limiting (a) buyer's remedies and (b) seller's remedies. In doing so, consider how the two parties would draft the clause differently and what form of clause they might ultimately both find agreeable.

CHAPTER III

CLOSING THE CONTRACT

John H. Kupillas, Jr., Attorney Etiquette at
Residential Real Estate Closings*
62 New York State Bar Journal 44 (No. 4, May 1990).

The closing of a residential real estate transaction is not an adversary proceeding. Despite law school training and experience in other areas of law (most notably litigation) there is no reason to treat the settlement of the purchase of a one or two family dwelling, cooperative apartment or condominium unit, as a cross-examination.

Why then do many attorneys take this hard line adversarial approach? There are several reasons as follows:

1. This is how we are taught. An attorney's job is to look out for the best interests of his client. They only consider their client. Many attorneys translate this into a tough unyielding attitude.

2. In many areas of law it works. This hard-nosed approach can be quite successful in litigation. The reputation of many "bombers" in the field of matrimonial litigation attests to this. The fact is when things have gotten to the litigation stage, being steadfast and visibly tough can mean great gains for your client. The problem in residential real estate areas is that such an attitude can turn a friendly transaction into litigation. Unfortunately to a litigator this seems to be the natural course of events—until the economics of the situation are revealed. In residential real estate cases, clients more often than not are the real losers.

3. Clients like attorneys who are tough. One of the great paradoxes that attorneys face is this: the public's perception of attorneys is terrible and getting worse. People view attorneys as insensitive, money hungry, and unscrupulous. Ironically, this is the very kind of lawyer they want to represent *them*. I believe that one of the reasons attorneys come on this way is because that is what the public wants. Lawyers are not completely at fault for their image and behavior; clients encourage it.

4. Unprepared lawyers can aggravate this situation. The closing of a residential real estate transaction is viewed as routine and easy by many attorneys. This is because the title company and the lender's attorney tend to many of the serious details of insurability of title, accuracy of the legal description, and searches. However, to rely on title companies and bank attorneys will give you a false sense of security. . . . It can be very annoying when an attorney shows up at a closing without ever having taken a look at the title report. This can lead to long delays and very short tempers, as the prepared attorney loses patience with his less diligent colleague.

---

* Reprinted with permission from New York State Bar *Journal* May 1990, Vol. 62, No. 4, published by the New York State Bar Association, One Elk Street, Albany, New York 12207.

5. Little things get blown out of proportion. Of course, clients can often get extremely upset over "little" things. Missing light fixtures, table and chairs as well as other items of personal property can be the source of much conflict. Why? Because the purchase and sale of residential real estate is to a very large degree, an emotional event. Therefore, seemingly insignificant things can set off these emotions. It is our job as attorneys to diffuse this over-reaction by putting things in perspective. An effective attorney in this area (as in most areas) must be a good psychologist. The ability to deal with people in this area is a far greater asset than legal knowledge.

A. THE FORMALITIES OF TRANSFER

McDonald v. Plumb

California Court of Appeal, Second District, 1970.
12 Cal.App.3d 374, 90 Cal.Rptr. 822.

ALLPORT, J.

The record before us discloses without conflict that on February 4, 1960, one Elizabeth Esterline owned certain real property located in Los Angeles County. On June 22, 1960, unknown to her and without consideration, Stanley Scott Singley caused a deed of said property to be recorded, purporting to convey title to Frank N. Debbas. The grantor's signature was forged. The forged signature was falsely acknowledged by Glen E. Plumb, a notary public bonded as such by United States Fidelity and Guaranty Co. in the penal amount of $5,000. Subsequently the property was deeded, without consideration, by Debbas to Singley and thereafter by Singley to Jack W. and Patricia L. McDonald. The latter transaction was for consideration. Following a nonjury trial judgment was entered quieting title of Esterline to said property against any claims of Singley and the McDonalds and granting judgment in favor of McDonalds and against Singley in the sum of $21,063.51, together with costs in the amount of $254.88. The McDonalds were denied relief against Plumb and United States Fidelity and Guaranty Co., his surety. The litigation was dismissed as to Debbas. The McDonalds have appealed from that portion of the judgment denying them recovery against Plumb and United States Fidelity and Guaranty Co.

It is contended on appeal that the trial court erred as a matter of law in finding that the false acknowledgment of the deed from Esterline to Debbas by Plumb was not the efficient or any other cause of the damage suffered by the McDonalds. We agree with this contention.

The specific finding involved was as follows: "That the false acknowledgment by cross-defendant, Glen E. Plumb, upon the purported deed from Elizabeth Esterline to Frank N. Debbas was not the efficient or any other cause of any damage suffered by cross-complainants or either of them."

Simply stated the trial court found that the false notarial acknowledgment on the forged Esterline deed to Debbas was not the efficient or any other cause of the damage suffered by McDonalds since it was not in fact relied upon in the course of the latters' purchase from

Singley and that the McDonalds' damages were solely the proximate result of the fraudulent plans, schemes and acts of Singley against whom they were given judgment.

There appears to be no dispute as to the facts nor as to the sufficiency of evidence to support the judgment. The sole question to be answered is whether or not the trial court erred as a matter of law in finding and concluding that the false notarial acknowledgment was not a proximate cause of the McDonalds' damage.

In order for the McDonalds to prevail in this action they have the burden of establishing first, a duty on the part of defendant Plumb, second, a violation of that duty, third, that such violation was a proximate cause of injury to them, and, fourth, the nature and extent of their damage.

The basis for liability in a case of this type is set forth in Burck v. Buchen, 46 Cal.App.2d 741, at pages 746–747, 116 P.2d 958, as follows: "When taking an acknowledgment, 'the officer should require the acknowledging party to appear in person before him, as he is required to certify that such party "personally appeared." (§ 1189, Civil Code.) If an instrument is acknowledged in violation of this rule, as where it is acknowledged through a telephone, the officer would undoubtedly be liable in damages if it should turn out that it was acknowledged by an imposter.' (1 Cal.Jur. 247.) However, in order 'To render the officer liable for damages, it is, of course, necessary that his act in taking an acknowledgment be the proximate cause of the damage sustained. . . . [A]nd, where the right of action is founded on the negligence of the officer, *that the plaintiff be not guilty of contributory negligence.*' "

In this case the duty was created by statute. (Civ.Code, § 1185.[1])

Respondent concedes a violation of that duty. The violation creates a liability upon the notary's surety. (Gov.Code, § 8214.[2]) It is undisputed that the McDonalds sustained damage in the sum of $21,063.51.

. . . It seems fundamental to us that the requirement of notarial acknowledgment in real estate transactions such as this is calculated to prevent fraud. The failure of the notary in this case to fulfill his duty permitted Singley to defraud the McDonalds. This failure was a basic underlying cause of the loss and, if not the sole proximate cause, at least a proximate cause thereof.

It is argued that other transactions involving this property subsequent to the making of the false acknowledgment broke the chain of causation. We do not agree. We fail to see wherein such can be deemed to have eliminated the false acknowledgment as being at least

---

[1]   Civil Code, section 1185 reads as follows: "The acknowledgment of an instrument must not be taken, unless the officer taking it knows or has satisfactory evidence, on the oath or affirmation of a credible witness, that the person making such acknowledgment is the individual who is described in and who executed the instrument; or, if executed by a corporation, that the person making such acknowledgment is the president or secretary of such corporation, or other person who executed it on its behalf."

[2]   Government Code, section 8214 reads as follows: "For the official misconduct or neglect of a notary public, he and the sureties on his official bond are liable to the persons injured thereby for all the damages sustained."

one of the proximate causes. In Homan v. Wayer, 9 Cal.App. 123 at pp. 127–128, 98 P. 80, at 82, it was said:

"It is apparent, then, that the fact that others have aided in the transaction, and contributed to bringing about the conditions from which the plaintiff's loss arose, does not relieve defendants from liability for the loss of the plaintiff, if the latter relied upon the false certificate when paying out his money. In taking an acknowledgment to a deed a notary's official services are limited. He certifies to the identity of the grantor named in the instrument, but he has no control over the deed to which his certificate is attached. This must be delivered to the grantee by the grantor, or some one on his behalf, in order to become effective. No *official* act of the notary in certifying an acknowledgment to a deed can alone result in injury to anyone. The deed cannot become the means of defrauding anyone until used in some transaction entirely outside of the official duties of the notary. For this reason the statutory right of action is not dependent upon a showing that the acts of others have not contributed to the injury, or defeated by a showing that they have so contributed, if it appear that the party defrauded relied upon the notary's false certificate.

"The terms, 'proximate cause,' 'negligence,' and 'contributory negligence,' as used in appellants' presentation of the case, are somewhat misleading here. No official misconduct or neglect of a notary public in taking or certifying the acknowledgment of a deed could ever be the *sole* proximate cause of loss or injury to any person but we cannot for that reason say no recovery can be had for a loss due to a false certificate of acknowledgment under the provisions of section 801 of the Political Code."

Without citation of authority it is urged by Plumb that the issuance of a policy of title insurance at McDonalds' request indicated a lack of reliance upon the original notarial acknowledgment, thus breaking the chain of causation. This contention is answered to the contrary in Inglewood Park Mausoleum Co. v. Ferguson, . . . 9 Cal.App.2d 217, 49 P.2d 305. While it is true that McDonalds did not rely directly upon the false acknowledgment in the original deed, direct reliance is not required. On the contrary, indirect reliance is sufficient. In relying upon the record title as of the date of sale, the McDonalds were relying upon the chain of title creating such record title, one link of which was the validity of the deed from Esterline to Debbas. We conclude that the trial court erred in finding and concluding that the false acknowledgment by Plumb was not a proximate cause of the injury to the McDonalds. We find to the contrary.

That portion of the judgment appealed from is reversed with directions to the trial court to enter judgment on the cross-complaint in favor of Jack W. McDonald and Patricia L. McDonald and against defendant Glen E. Plumb in the sum of $21,063.51, together with costs, and against United States Fidelity and Guaranty Co., a corporation, in accordance with the terms and conditions of the bond.

SCHWEITZER, ACTING P.J., and COBEY, J., concur.

NOTES

1. *McDonald v. Plumb.* What, if anything, could the McDonalds have done before closing to discover the fraudulent transfer to Debbas? Could their title insurer have discovered it? Plumb's surety? Plumb? Would the McDonalds have been protected by a title insurance policy providing the coverage of the A.L.T.A. Owner's Policy set out in the *Statute, Form, and Problem Supplement?* Of all the individuals and institutions involved in residential real estate transactions, did the court impose liability on those best placed to bear it?

The California legislature subsequently amended Civil Code § 1185, relied on in *McDonald,* to relax the proof of identity on which a notary can legally rely. Stats.1982, c. 197 § 1; Stats.1987, c. 307 § 1; Stats.1988, c. 842 § 1; Stats.1993, c. 1044 § 1. At the time *McDonald* was decided, the notary had to know the signer personally, or at least had to know the witness who swore to the signer's identity. The 1982 amendment provides that the notary can rely on wallet identification such as a California driver's license. Is this amendment likely to increase opportunities for the type of fraud that occurred in *McDonald?* Would it be better to abolish the acknowledgment formality entirely? Consider the following assertion:

> Notary-related dishonesty appears to be on the rise. Many notarizations do not deserve the level of trust and confidence traditionally given to them. Notaries commonly backdate documents and witness signatures for people who do not appear before them personally. In the case of employee-notaries, they tend to do whatever their employers direct them to do, even if shortcuts and misconduct are involved.

> Some of the worst offenders are lawyers who, as notaries, disregard the legal requirements for valid notarization and, as employers, order their employee-notaries to stamp documents in violation of legal standards.

Closen, Why Notaries Get Little Respect, Nat'l L.J., 10/9/95, p. A24. See Closen & Faerber, The Case That There Is A Common Law Duty of Notaries Public to Create and Preserve Detailed Journal Records of Their Official Acts, 42 J. Marshall L.Rev. 231 (2009); Brussack, Reform of American Conveyancing Formality, 32 Hastings L.J. 561 (1981); Van Alstyne, The Notary's Duty of Care for Identifying Document Signers, 32 J. Marshall L. Rev. 1003 (1999); see also Notaries Public—Lost in Cyberspace, Or Key Business Professionals of the Future?, 15 J. Marshall J. Computer & Info. L. 703 (1997); Spyke, Taking Note of Notary Employees: Employer Liability for Employee Misconduct, 50 Me. L. Rev. 23 (1998)

2. *Forgery.* A forged deed is inadequate to pass title. Thus, even innocent purchasers like the McDonalds lose title to owners like Esterline, another innocent party. See R. Natelson, Modern Law of the Deeds to Real Property (1992) 391–396. What reasons support this rule? What effect does the rule have on the marketplace? What burdens does it place on buyers? Suppose the McDonalds had improved the property before Esterline asserted her claim. How should the court account for this added value? See Nunes v. Allstate Inv. Props., 69 So.3d 988 (Fla.App.2011) (wife who had constructive notice of forged deed by her husband could not prevail against bona fide purchaser); Butler v. Hayes, 254 Va. 38, 487 S.E.2d 229 (1997) (refusing to protect improver who knew of the forgery).

3. *The Benefits and Costs of Formal Requirements.* Because land is immovable, and because ownership of land is so often separate from possession, interests in land cannot be transferred physically and must instead be transferred through the ritualistic delivery of documents symbolizing the interests. But documents are easily lost, mishandled or counterfeited. Someone bent on fraud need only go to the county recorder's office, find a recorded deed to a vacant piece of land, forge the grantee's name as grantor on a new deed, hoodwink a notary, record the fraudulent deed, and then dispose of the land to an unwitting buyer. See Reuben, Real Estate Title Forgeries Seen Increasing, 100 Los Angeles Daily J., May 11, 1987, p. 5, col. 1 (reporting one title company's experience that forgery claims rose from 3.8% to 12.9% of total claims between 1970 and 1985); Church, Spotting Title Forgeries, 4 Prac. Real Est. Law. 13 (Sept. 1988) (describing fact patterns which give clues to forgeries).

Conveyancers early hoped that strict compliance with formal requirements would reduce the occasions for fraud and produce unassailable chains of title. Legislatures and courts responded by enacting and rigorously enforcing requirements that a deed had to be formally correct and complete and had to clearly and accurately describe the interest being transferred. And, to avoid fraudulent transfers, the deed also had to be properly acknowledged, delivered, accepted and recorded.

One obvious and oft-lamented cost of these formal requirements is that, by invalidating imperfect transfers, the requirements penalize grantors and grantees who retained inept lawyers or no lawyers at all. But formal requirements have another, possibly more substantial cost. By inducing grantees and grantors to reduce their transactions to writing and to have these writings acknowledged and recorded, the American conveyancing system also encourages future grantees to rely on the paper record as perfectly evidencing the current state of title. Unfortunately, as indicated in *McDonald,* even the most perfect-appearing paper record is sometimes flawed.

See generally, Andersen, Conveyancing Reform: A Great Place to Start, 25 Real Prop. Probate & Trust J. 333 (1990).

1.   DEED ELEMENTS AND CONSTRUCTION

There is a modern trend to simplify the form and content of real property deeds. Many states have enacted short form deed statutes, prescribing language that eliminates most of the customary redundancies and flourishes. Even so, most deeds contain all of the basic elements that have traditionally been employed since the earliest English deeds.

Deeds typically begin with the *premises* of the deed—the names of grantor and grantee; the words of grant; background facts and purposes; consideration; and the legal description of the parcels conveyed. The next portion of the deed, usually beginning with the phrase, "To have and to hold," is the *habendum,* which describes the interest taken by the grantee, any conditions on the grant and any covenants of title (these covenants are sometimes said to comprise the *warranty clause*). The *execution clause* contains the grantor's signature, her seal, and the date of the deed. (In states that require the deed to be witnessed, the signatures of the witnesses would also appear in the execution clause.) Finally, beneath the grantor's signature is the *acknowledgment,* in which a public officer, typically a notary, attests to the execution.

Although several formalities continue to be required for other aspects of the conveyancing process, most states today require few formalities of a deed. The deed must be written. It must name the grantor and grantee and contain express words of grant. And it must describe the parcel conveyed to the exclusion of all other parcels in the world.

What formalities are *not* required for a deed to be effective? Although it was once commonly required that for a deed to be effective it had to be sealed—stamped with the grantor's mark—most states have since eliminated the requirement. And, even in those states that still impose the requirement, it is easily met through use of the written word, "Seal," or through use of the initials "L.S.," (signifying *locus sigilli,* or "the place of the seal"). And only a few states require acknowledgment for a deed to be effective between the parties. Acknowledgment is, however, required for a deed to be legally recorded. Acknowledgment has traditionally conferred two other benefits. It makes the deed admissible into evidence without further proof of execution, and it creates a presumption that the deed is genuine.

Priest v. Ernest W. Ball & Associates, Inc.

Supreme Court of Alabama, 2010.
62 So.3d 1013.

BOLIN, JUSTICE.

This appeal is from a judgment in a declaratory-judgment action seeking an interpretation and declaration of the legal effect of certain language in a deed.

Facts and Procedural History

On November 6, 2008, William Buxton and Judy Buxton filed a complaint for a judgment declaring certain language in a deed conveying real property to them to be a conveyance of the property in fee simple with a right of survivorship. The Buxtons brought the action against the law firm Ernest W. Ball & Associates, Inc. (hereinafter "Ball"), that had prepared the deed. The deed was attached to the complaint and states as follows:

> "KNOW ALL MEN BY THESE PRESENTS, that for and in consideration of the sum of Ten and No/100 Dollars ($10.00) and other good and valuable consideration to the undersigned Grantors, in hand paid by the Grantees herein, the receipt whereof is hereby acknowledged, THOMAS F. LOPPNOW AND WIFE, RONNA L. LOPPNOW, herein referred to as Grantors, do hereby grant, bargain, sell and convey unto WILLIAM BUXTON AND JUDY BUXTON, HUSBAND AND WIFE, herein referred to as Grantees, for and during their life and upon their death, then to their heirs in fee simple, together with every contingent remainder and right of

reversion, the following described real estate hereinafter the 'Premises', situated in MORGAN County, Alabama, to-wit

"[Description of the property]

"THERE ARE EXCEPTED FROM THE WARRANTIES OF THIS DEED ALL EASEMENTS, RESTRICTIONS OF RECORD, AND CURRENT AD VALOREM TAXES.

"AND SAID GRANTORS DO, for themselves and their heirs and assigns, covenant with said Grantees, their heirs and assigns that they are lawfully seized in fee simple of said premises; that it is free from all encumbrances, except as otherwise noted above, that they have a good right to sell and convey the said premises; that they will warrant and defend the same unto the said Grantees, their heirs, executors and assigns forever, against the lawful claims of said Grantors and all persons claiming by and through said Grantors, but not against the claims of any others, except for current ad valorem taxes, restrictions, easements, ways and building setback lines applicable to the above described property, if any, as shown of record in said Probate Office."

Ball answered and asserted several affirmative defenses. On January 7, 2009, the Buxtons filed a motion for a summary judgment. On March 24, 2009, the Buxtons filed a motion to add Blake Horton and Devon Horton[1] as defendants because their interests might be adversely affected by a judgment and to appoint a guardian ad litem to represent any unknown heirs of the Buxtons. On May 1, 2009, the trial court added the Hortons as defendants and appointed Christopher M. Priest as guardian ad litem. On May 18, 2009, Priest filed an answer. On September 28, 2009, Priest filed a response to the Buxtons' summary-judgment motion. On May 25, 2010, Ernest Ball, a principal in Ball, filed an affidavit stating:

"I am an attorney and the owner of the law firm, Ernest W. Ball & Associates, Inc. On May 27, 2003, my firm prepared a deed in which property was purchased by the [Buxtons]. The deed was recorded at Book 2003, Page 3781 in the Probate Office of Morgan County, Alabama on May 29, 2003.

"The deed stated that the property was conveyed to the [Buxtons] 'for and during their life and upon their death, then to their heirs in fee simple, together with every contingent remainder and right of reversion.' (hereinafter 'the Subject Language'). The Subject Language is ambiguous and not very clear so in at least 75 deeds in Morgan County alone, the language has been construed to convey a fee simple interest as evidence of the deed being overwritten."

On May 26, 2010, the trial court entered a summary judgment in favor of the Buxtons, holding, in pertinent part, as follows:

. . .

"Pursuant to Section 35–4–3 of the Code of Alabama, in the present action, the language contained in the deed is

---

[1]   The record does not indicate who Blake Horton and Devon Horton are or the nature of their relationship with the Buxtons.

ambiguous, and, as such, shall be construed as granting a fee simple estate.[' "]

. . .

The trial court made the summary-judgment order final pursuant to Rule 54(b), Ala. R. Civ. P. Priest timely appealed.

. . .

Discussion

Section 35–4–2, Ala.Code 1975, provides: "Every estate in lands is to be taken in fee simple, although the words necessary to create an estate of inheritance are not used, unless it clearly appears that a less estate was intended." The issue before this Court is whether the deed in question clearly establishes that an estate lesser than fee simple, i.e., a life estate, was created, or whether an ambiguity was present such that § 35–4–2 mandates that the Buxtons took a fee-simple estate in the property.

In *Barnett v. Estate of Anderson,* 966 So.2d 915, 918 (Ala.2007), this Court reaffirmed the following principle:

> "Regarding the construction of deeds, it is well settled that a deed is construed most strongly against the grantor. See *Moss v. Williams,* 822 So.2d 392, 396–97 (Ala.2001) ('This Court has long recognized that § 35–4–2 is simply "a statutory affirmance of the general rule that a deed is construed most strongly against the grantor." '). '[G]reater strictness is required in the construction of deeds than of wills.' *Porter v. Henderson,* 203 Ala. 312, 315, 82 So. 668, 671 (1919)."

In construing deeds, this Court stated in *Financial Investment Corp. v. Tukabatchee Area Council, Inc.,* 353 So.2d 1389, 1391 (Ala.1977):

> "It is, of course, a fundamental rule of construction that the real inquiry in construing the terms of a deed is to ascertain the intention of the parties, especially that of the grantor, and if that intention can be ascertained from the entire instrument, resort to arbitrary rules of construction is not required. *Wilkins v. Ferguson,* 294 Ala. 25, 310 So.2d 879 (1975); *Gulf Oil Corp. v. Deese,* 275 Ala. 178, 153 So.2d 614 (1963).

> "The courts, in construing conveyances, must ascertain and give effect to the intention and meaning of the parties, 'to be collected from the entire instrument.' *Brashier v. Burkett,* 350 So.2d 309 (Ala.1977); *Stratford v. Lattimer,* 255 Ala. 201, 50 So.2d 420 (1951).

> ". . . It is, of course, true that where a deed is of doubtful meaning, or where the language of a deed is ambiguous, the intent of the parties to the deed as to what property is conveyed may be ascertained by reference to facts existing when the instrument was made, to which the parties may be presumed to have had reference. *Lietz v. Pfuehler,* 283 Ala. 282, 215 So.2d 723 (1968).

"However, if the language is plain and certain, acts and declarations of the parties cannot be resorted to, to aid construction. *Id.; Hall v. Long,* 199 Ala. 97, 74 So. 56 (1916).

". . . .

"In ascertaining the intention of the parties, the plain and clear meaning of the deed's terms must be given effect, and parties must be legally presumed to have intended what is plainly and clearly set out. *Camp v. Milam,* 291 Ala. 12, 277 So.2d 95 (1973)."

With these rules of construction in mind, we now turn to the deed in the present case and try and ascertain the intent of the grantors from the four corners of the instrument, reconciling all provisions if possible. The granting clause conveys the property to the Buxtons "for and during their life and upon their death, then to their heirs in fee simple, together with every contingent remainder and right of reversion. . . ." The deed next contains a description of the property, and the only other clause is a warranty clause that provides as follows: "[T]hat they will warrant and defend the same unto the said Grantees, their heirs, executors and assigns forever, against the lawful claims of said Grantors. . . ."

The trial court entered a summary judgment in favor of the Buxtons on the ground that the language in the granting clause was ambiguous and that, based on the presumption of § 35–4–2, it did not reserve a life estate in favor of the Buxtons. Applying § 35–4–2, this Court has stated: "The intention to create a lesser estate must clearly appear, for the courts will not construe a grantor's words as conveying a lesser estate if clearly a different meaning can be given them." *Windham v. Henderson,* 658 So.2d 431, 433 (Ala.1995). The trial court's reliance on § 35–4–2 to support the finding of a fee-simple estate is misplaced because the granting clause in the present case contains words that clearly and expressly convey a life estate. The trial court also relied on *Hacker v. Carlisle,* 388 So.2d 947 (Ala.1980), in which this Court held that the language in the deed, when viewed as a whole, coupled with the parties' conduct after the conveyance, indicated that the estate conveyed was in fee simple.

In *Hacker,* Jasper Carlisle executed a deed in 1914 giving real property to his son, John. The deed contained a handwritten clause providing: "It is understood that [John Carlisle] is not to sell above described lands but it is to go to his heirs." 388 So.2d at 949. After John Carlisle died, his heirs sought an interpretation and declaration of the interest conveyed by the deed. The trial court found that Jasper had conveyed a life estate to John with a remainder to John's heirs. This Court reversed the trial court's judgment. It noted that all the clauses except the handwritten clause were consistent with the conveyance of a fee-simple estate. Although the granting clause contained no words of inheritance, the Court looked to the habendum and warranty clauses to find a conveyance in fee simple, both of which contained the words "his heirs and assigns," traditional words of inheritance connoting a fee-simple estate. This Court disagreed with the argument that the handwritten clause diminished the interest conveyed to a life estate with a remainder to the grantee's heirs. This Court recognized that handwritten portions of a deed take precedence over printed language when there is a conflict between the two, but the handwritten clause failed to clearly designate a life estate.

> "The handwritten clause does not limit the grantee's estate to 'for his life' or 'at his death.' The language 'is not to sell above described lands' is certainly no indication of a life estate as such estates are as alienable as fee simple estates. And the language 'but it is to go to his heirs' indicates merely words of limitation or inheritance."

388 So.2d at 951. The language in the handwritten clause did not clearly designate a life estate in derogation of § 35–4–2. Instead, the language was in the nature of a restraint on alienation and, viewed as a whole, appeared to be an attempt to create a fee-tail estate, and fee-tail estates are converted into fee-simple estates under § 35–4–3. This Court also noted that the parties' conduct indicated their intention that the deed conveyed a fee-simple estate.

Hacker does not support the trial court's conclusion that the granting clause was ambiguous. In *Hacker,* this Court discussed deeds in three prior cases, noting that in those deeds the language clearly and expressly defined a life estate with the "telltale language of 'for his life' or 'at his death,'" 388 So.2d at 951, whereas the handwritten language in the deed at issue in *Hacker* did not clearly convey a life estate. Here, the granting clause clearly contains the "telltale language" of a life estate.

We recognize that the warranty clause of the deed contains language that refers to the Buxtons' "heirs, executors, and assigns." There should be no reason to refer to the Buxtons' executors when their interest is a life estate, because there could not arise an occasion where a warranty of title could flow to the executor of the estate of a deceased holder of a life estate, because that estate would necessarily terminate upon the death of the life tenant and there would be no interest for a personal representative to thereafter administer.[2] However, an ambiguity in a warranty clause would not conflict with an unambiguous granting clause because a warranty clause does not convey title. The purpose of the warranty clause is to indemnify the purchaser against loss or injury due to a defect in the title. It is well settled that

> "the granting clause in a deed determines the interest conveyed, and that, unless there be repugnancy, obscurity or ambiguity in that clause, it prevails over introductory statements or recitals in conflict therewith, and over the habendum, too, if that clause is contradictory of or repugnant to it. [citations omitted-eds.] The reason underlying the rule that introductory statements and recitals must yield to the granting clause is that they are non-essential to the validity of the deed, while the granting clause is its very essence. It has been said that the habendum must give way, because the granting clause is necessary to make the deed effective, while the habendum clause is not. [*Ratliffe*] *v. Marrs,* 87 Ky. 26, 7

---

[2] A reference to the Buxtons' heirs would not create an ambiguity as to the life estate because the grantors would be warranting title to the heirs who would receive the property upon the end of the life estate. Similarly, the grantors would also be warranting title to any potential assignees of the grantees' life estates and, hence, no ambiguity.

S.W. 395, 8 S.W. 876 [(1888)]. And by another court it has been said: 'It is a rule in the construction of deeds that of two repugnant clauses therein the first shall prevail against the second; and, according to this rule, the meaning of the premises shall not be changed by the words of the habendum as to irreconcilable differences.' *Chamberlain v. Runkle,* 28 Ind.App. 599, 63 N.E. 486 [(1902)]; [citations omitted—eds.]

In *Porter v. Henderson,* 203 Ala. 312, 317–18, 82 So. 668, 673–74 (1919), the Court cited a federal case explaining why other clauses must yield to the granting clause:

"In *Dickson v. Wildman,* 183 Fed. 398, 403, 105 C.C.A. 618, 623 [(1910)], Judge Shelby said:

" 'If it were conceded that there was repugnancy between the granting clause on the one side and the preliminary recitals and the habendum on the other, and that the conflict was such that the true intent of the grantor could not be ascertained, it is manifest that the court must decide which part of the deed shall prevail. The rule in such case is that the granting clause determines the interest conveyed, and when it is clear and unambiguous, as in the deed in question here, it prevails over introductory recitals in conflict with it, and prevails also over the habendum, if that is in conflict with it. The reason sometimes given for the rule is that a deed founded upon a valuable consideration is to be construed most strongly against the grantor, and, when the conflict is in the habendum, that the grantor in the latter part of the deed will not be permitted to deny or retract the grant previously made. The rule is very old, and it may be that it is founded on an effort to enforce the cardinal rule to ascertain and give effect to the intention. The granting clause is naturally looked to see what it was intended to convey, whereas recitals are often merely introductory, and are not a necessary part of the deed. The granting clause is the very essence of the contract. It is required to transfer title, but the habendum clause is not absolutely necessary to make a deed effective. Where a conflict exists, therefore, in the different parts of a deed, the true intent of the grantor as to what was intended to be conveyed is more likely to be found in the granting clause. The settled rule of construction in Alabama and in many other jurisdictions is that in case of repugnancy between the granting clause and other parts of the deed the former will prevail.' "

Although Section § 35–4–2 provides that every conveyance of real estate conveys all the grantor's estate unless the intent to convey a lesser estate expressly appears or is necessarily implied in the terms used in the granting clause, such an intention to convey a lesser estate appears in the granting clause here and, thus, § 35–4–2 has no field of operation. The only ambiguities are in the warranty clause, and, as discussed, the warranty clause must yield to an unambiguous granting clause.

Conclusion

As we stated, the real inquiry in construing the terms of a deed is the intent of the parties, especially that of the grantor, and if that intent can be ascertained from the instrument, there is no need to resort to arbitrary rules of construction. The intent of the grantor is ascertained from the words used in the four corners of the deed. The intention of the parties will be presumed to accord with the established meaning of the words of settled legal import. "Otherwise, there would be little stability of land titles." *Creswell v. Bank of Greenwood,* 210 S.C. 47, 41 S.E.2d 393 (1947). Accordingly, the judgment of the trial court is reversed, and the cause is remanded for proceedings consistent with this opinion.

REVERSED AND REMANDED.

COBB, C.J., and LYONS, Stuart, AND Murdock, JJ., CONCUR.

NOTE

Courts called on to construe real property deeds typically start from the proposition noted in Priest v. Ernest W. Ball & Associates that "the courts in construing conveyances must ascertain and give effect to the intention of the parties 'to be collected from the entire instrument.' " However, "where the deed is of doubtful meaning . . . the intent . . . as to what property is conveyed may be ascertained by reference to facts existing when the instrument was made."

The challenge in *Priest* was the interpretation of a deed with potentially conflicting granting, habendum, warranty, and recitals. The court examines various constructional canons that have been employed to resolve these conflicts. Do decisions based on these canons truly represent the parties' intent? Is that relevant? For a discussion of these canons, see 3 American Law of Property § 12.90 (A.J. Casner ed. 1952). For illustrative cases, see Lusk v. Broyles, 694 So.2d 4 (Ala.Civ.App.1997); Lucareli v. Lucareli, 237 Wis.2d 487, 614 N.W.2d 60 (App.2000). See generally, Herd, Deed Construction and the "Repugnant to the Grant" Doctrine, 21 Tex.Tech.L.Rev. 635 (1990).

It is the rare deed dispute in which some of these canons cannot be asserted on one side, and some on the other. Would these canons help you in giving a title opinion on an ambiguous deed executed thirty or forty years earlier? Consider whether you would feel more or less comfortable with your opinion knowing that, in addition to these canons of construction, a court interpreting the deed will often look to "all the attendant circumstances as to situation of the parties, relationship, object of the conveyance, person who drew the deed, and all surrounding situations which may throw light on the meaning which the parties attached to ambiguous or inconsistent portions of the instruments. And unless forbidden by some rule of law, the courts will follow the construction given a deed by the parties themselves as shown by their subsequent admissions or conduct." 3 American Law of Property § 12.91 (A.J. Casner ed. 1952).

Is it preferable for a court construing a deed to attempt to discern the actual, subjective intent of the original grantor and grantee, or to refuse to look outside the deed's four corners? Which rule will better promote certainty among title examiners and their clients over the long term?

2. DELIVERY AND ESCROW

a. DELIVERY

A deed will not effectively transfer title to an interest in land unless and until it is delivered. Delivery is a term of art, and means something more than physical transfer of the document. In its ideal form, delivery requires both physical transfer and a present intent by the grantor to transfer an interest in the property to the grantee. Often, though, both elements are not clearly present. Physical transfer alone is insufficient. Thus, if the transferor hands a deed to the transferee, delivery will not occur if the requisite intent is missing (e.g., "I am giving you this deed to hold for safekeeping in the event I later decide to give Blackacre to you"). See Jorgensen v. Crow, 466 N.W.2d 120 (N.D.1991) (where transferee picked up deed at closing but grantors lacked intent to transfer, no delivery occurred). If, however, the intent is clear, courts will often find delivery without physical transfer, through devices such as symbolic, constructive or agency delivery (e.g., "I am presently transferring Blackacre to you, but I will hold the deed for you until you reach 18"). Intent is thus pivotal.

Tension exists between this emphasis on intent, provable by parol, and the aim of the conveyancing system to confine all title matters to the paper record. It is no surprise, then, that presumptions have developed bringing delivery rules into line with the reasonable expectations of title searchers. Thus, although physical transfer does not constitute delivery, it is widely held to create a presumption of delivery. Conversely, failure to transfer the deed creates a presumption of non-delivery. Other facts creating a presumption of delivery are recordation of the deed and the deed's acknowledgment.

In order for a deed to be effectively delivered, the grantee must accept the delivery. In most cases, because the grant will benefit the grantee, acceptance will be presumed. However, courts will not presume acceptance if the conveyance might be disadvantageous to the grantee. And, even if the conveyance will be advantageous, courts will allow the presumption of acceptance to be rebutted by evidence that the grantee did not in fact wish to accept title to the land. See Hood v. Hood, 384 A.2d 706 (Me.1978). Recording is not required for delivery. See Graham v. Lyons, 377 Pa.Super. 4, 546 A.2d 1129 (1988), appeal denied, 522 Pa. 576, 559 A.2d 38 (1989).

Additionally, the grantor must have adequate mental capacity to execute a deed and cannot be subject to undue influence. See In re Conservatorship of Williams, 724 So.2d 1022 (Miss.Ct.App.1998) (capacity); Mulato v. Mulato, 705 So.2d 57 (Fla.App.1997). Deeds obtained by fraud are voidable. See Schiavon v. Arnaudo Bros., 84 Cal.App.4th 374, 100 Cal.Rptr.2d 801 (2000). A person cannot form a true donative intent in such situations.

Wiggill v. Cheney

Supreme Court of Utah, 1979.
597 P.2d 1351.

MAUGHAN, JUSTICE:

This case involves the disposition of certain real property located in Weber County, State of Utah. The judgment before us invalidated a Warranty Deed, because of no valid delivery. We affirm. No costs awarded.

The material facts are undisputed. Specifically, on the 25th day of June, 1958, Lillian W. Cheney signed a deed to certain real property located in the city of Ogden, Utah, wherein the defendant, Flora Cheney, was named grantee. Thereafter Lillian Cheney placed this deed in a sealed envelope and deposited it in a safety deposit box in the names of herself and the plaintiff, Francis E. Wiggill. Following the deposition of the deed, Lillian Cheney advised plaintiff his name was on the safety deposit box and instructed plaintiff that upon her death, he was to go to the bank where he would be granted access to the safety deposit box and its contents. Lillian Cheney further instructed, "in that box is an envelope addressed to all those concerned. All you have to do is give them that envelope and that's all." At all times prior to her death, Lillian Cheney was in possession of a key to the safety deposit box and had sole and complete control over it. Plaintiff was never given the key to the safety deposit box.

Following the death of Lillian Cheney, plaintiff, after gaining access to the safety deposit box, delivered the deed contained therein to Flora Cheney, the named grantee.

The sole issue presented here on appeal is whether or not the acts of plaintiff constitute a delivery of the deed such as will render it enforceable as a valid conveyance.

The rule is well settled that a deed, to be operative as a transfer of the ownership of land, or an interest or estate therein, must be delivered. It was equally settled in this and the vast majority of jurisdictions that a valid delivery of a deed requires it pass beyond the control or domain of the grantor. The requisite relinquishment of control or dominion over the deed may be established, notwithstanding the fact the deed is in possession of the grantor at her death, by proof of facts which tend to show delivery had been made with the intention to pass title and to explain the grantor's subsequent possession. However, in order for a delivery effectively to transfer title, the grantor must part with possession of the deed or the right to retain it.

The evidence presented in the present case establishes Lillian Cheney remained in sole possession and control of the deed in question until her death. Because no actual delivery of the deed occurred prior to the death of the grantor, the subsequent manual delivery of the deed by plaintiff to defendant conveyed no title to the property described therein, or any part thereof, or any of its contents.

CROCKETT, C.J., and HALL, WILKINS and STEWART, JJ., concur.

NOTE

Modern escrow practices, considered in the next section, have virtually eliminated delivery as an issue when land is being transferred for consideration. However, delivery remains an issue in donative transfers like the one involved in *Wiggill* and, as a consequence, raises problems for any buyer whose chain of title has a gift as one of its links.

Say that, upon receiving the deed from Francis Wiggill, Flora Cheney recorded it and then conveyed her interest, for value, to a buyer relying on her apparently good record title. How could the buyer have protected himself against the finding that Flora in fact had no title to convey? Obviously, record title and possession in the seller—the traditional indicia of ownership—are insufficient to assure that the seller has anything to convey. Would a standard policy of title insurance offer sufficient protection? A lawyer's opinion on an abstract of title? The local statute of limitations respecting causes of action for recovery of real property?

Compare Agrelius v. Mohesky, 208 Kan. 790, 494 P.2d 1095 (1972). In 1940, the grantors, husband and wife, executed two deeds, one conveying an 80–acre parcel to their son Clair, and one conveying another 80–acre parcel to their son, Kenneth. Neither deed was recorded during the grantors' lifetimes but, in 1944, the grantors placed the deeds in a safe deposit box leased in their names and in Clair's. Sometime later that year, Clair's father told him of the two deeds and, handing the key to the safe deposit box to Clair, said that this would constitute delivery to him. Many years later, after his parent's death, Clair claimed that "delivery of his own deed was effected when his father handed him the key to the safety deposit box, but that the deed to Kenneth was not delivered at that or any other time." 208 Kan. at 798, 494 P.2d at 1102. The Kansas Supreme Court disagreed on the second point, finding support in the evidence for the lower court's ruling that the grantor's actions "constituted an effective constructive delivery of the deeds, and all the circumstances showed a purpose on the part of the grantors that there should be an immediate vesting of title in Clair and Kenneth, enjoyment only being postponed until the death of the grantors." 208 Kan. at 795, 494 P.2d at 1100.

Delivery has even been found absent any physical transfer, symbolic or otherwise. In Grimmett v. Estate of Beasley, 29 Ark.App. 88, 777 S.W.2d 588 (1989), deeds found in the grantor's possession expressly stating that they were effective on grantor's death were valid to convey the properties to grantor's brother. The court noted that when a deed reserves a life estate to the grantor, as in this case, there is no requirement to transfer the instrument beyond grantor's dominion and control. See Case Note, 44 Ark.L.Rev. 219 (1991).

For an excellent analysis of delivery rules and the issues they raise, see A. Dunham, Modern Real Estate Transactions 355–359 (2d ed. 1958). See also, Note, Compressing Testamentary Intent Into Inter Vivos Delivery: What Makes a Conveyance Effective, 64 Wash.L.Rev. 479 (1989).

In an effort to provide an alternative to the delivery scenario described in *Wiggil*, a Uniform Real Property Transfer on Death Act has been promulgated. Nine states and the District of Columbia have enacted the statute which permits transfer-on-death deeds. This legislation permits a deed to serve as a nonprobate transfer at the time of death, providing certain requirements are met (such as recording). For discussions of "TOD" deeds, see Gary, Transfer-On-Death Deeds: The Nonprobate Revolution Continues, 41 Real Prop. Probate & Tr.J. 529 (2006); Kirtland & Seal, The Significance of the Transfer On Death Deed, 21 Probate & Prop. 42 (No. 4, July/Aug. 2007).

b.   ESCROWS

In areas of the country that follow the custom of having a "round the table" closing, the various parties—buyer, seller, lender, title insurer, brokers, etc.—meet together on the closing date to exchange documents and funds. Such a practice does not require the use of an escrow if all goes well. If, however, issues need to be resolved after the closing, someone may act as an escrow to hold the deed or funds until the outstanding performance is rendered.

In other places the practice is for the buyer and seller to close their contract through escrow, an arrangement under which a third party— the escrow holder—holds the deed from seller and the purchase money from buyer and buyer's lender pending fulfillment of the contract conditions. If all conditions are fulfilled, the escrow holder will on the date set for closing deliver and record the deed and mortgage to buyer and lender respectively, deliver the note to the lender, and deliver the purchase money to the seller. (In these areas, the parties do not typically meet together to close the transactions.) If, however, one or more of the contract conditions is not fulfilled, the escrow holder will return the documents and funds to the appropriate parties. This type of escrow arrangement is used both where the contract of sale provides for a short executory period and where the purchase is being made under a long term installment contract.

Since the escrow holder is generally expected to act mechanically, and not to exercise judgment on any point, well-drafted escrow instructions will contain only objectively verifiable conditions. Thus, instead of the judgmental direction to the escrow holder, "You are to close this escrow upon seller's delivery of marketable title," the instructions might read, "You are to close this escrow when there has been deposited into this escrow an irrevocable commitment by the Union Title Insurance Company to issue to Buyer an A.L.T.A. Owner's Policy, Form B-1970 naming buyer as owner in fee simple absolute of the Property described above, and insuring title in fee simple absolute of said property in the amount of $200,000, subject only to a first lien mortgage held by Surety National Bank, in the amount of $160,000, and to taxes for the fiscal year 1985, which are a lien but not delinquent." See generally, Walker & Eshee, The Safeguards and Dilemmas of Escrows, 16 Real Est.L.J. 45 (1987).

In re Akivis

Supreme Court of New York, 1985.
128 Misc.2d 965, 492 N.Y.S.2d 316.

HERBERT KRAMER, JUSTICE.

An action was started against the sellers of real property for damages arising out of the sale in New York County, which was dismissed for failure to prosecute. A second action was then brought in New York County for similar relief which is still pending. Subsequently, the instant Article 78 proceeding was instituted against the escrowees seeking an accounting and damages for failure of possession in broom-clean condition.[a] In its previous decision Akivis v. Brecher, 125 Misc.2d 582, 480 N.Y.S.2d 412, this court limited relief to a direction to acknowledge, account for possession and to perform their duties as attorneys, if, as and when determined. An answer and additional affidavits have not been filed.

The contract provides:

"6. (A) Seller shall have Sixty (60) days after closing to remove contents from the building and agrees to leave the building 'broom clean.' . . .

(C) To insure seller's removal from premises within aforesaid sixty (60) day period, they will leave sum (sic) of $5000.00 in escrow with Brecher-Yodowitz. If not so removed, commencing with 61st day seller shall pay to purchasers Twelve ($12.00) Dollars per day until they remove from premises."

The petitioner contends *removal* (6[C] contract) is defined in paragraph 6(A) above and further contends that the escrowee is responsible for all incidental and inherent acts of negligence. The respondents contend that the escrow (6[C]) is conditioned solely on physical removal without content removal (broom-clean) condition and further that the escrow agreement does not require prior notice of transfer of the escrow funds to any of the parties.

This court holds that the contract requires construction of Article 6 as an entirety. *Removal* in paragraph 6(C) is not limited to the delivery of the keys or other indicia of possession. It is referable to paragraph (A) which requires the removal of the building contents. Additionally, the contract does not otherwise define removal.

An escrow agent becomes the trustee of both parties after receipt of the funds or instrument in question (Farago v. Burke, 262 N.Y. 229, 186 N.E. 683). An escrowee is required to hold the funds to insure strict compliance with the condition (*Farago v. Burke, supra*; see, also 28 Am.Jur.2d, Escrow, Section 21).

Additionally, absent an agreement to the contrary, the escrowee may not await an agreement of the parties of compliance with the condition and may be surcharged for late release of the escrowed item upon such insistence (Lindley v. Robillard, 208 Misc. 532, 144 N.Y.S.2d 33). An escrowee must make an independent determination of compliance with the condition, except under circumstances where compliance is beyond the escrowee's ability to do so. In that event he may be required to bring an action for a court determination of compliance (*Lindley v. Robillard, supra*; Corpus Juris Secundum, Escrow p. 990 and cases cited therein).

In the case at bar in the answer, the escrowee acknowledged receipt of the fund in his answer and also indicated that he disbursed the fund to the sellers upon receipt of notice of compliance. There is no

---

[a] The escrowee was sellers' attorney, David Brecher, of the law firm Brecher & Yodowitz. Akivis v. Brecher, 125 Misc. 2d 582, 480 N.Y.S.2d 412 (Sup. Ct. 1984).

indication that the attorney made an independent inspection or other valid independent determination of such compliance. This court holds that the attorney is personally responsible for such that an independent inspection would have shown.

If the parties did not physically remove their possession from the premises, the attorney is liable for the lesser of $12.00 a day until removal, or the cost of removal.

In making that determination, the damages chargeable against the escrowee is limited to those necessarily inherent to the removal.

The employer of an independent contractor is liable for damages caused by negligence necessarily inherent in the nature of the work performed (Rupp v. New York City Transit Authority, 15 A.D.2d 800, 224 N.Y.S.2d 1007). The employer of an independent contractor is not responsible for negligence merely incidental to the work performed (Berg v. Parsons, 156 N.Y. 109, 50 N.E. 95, Hexamer v. Webb, 101 N.Y. 377, 4 N.E. 75, Hyman v. Barrat, 224 N.Y. 436, 121 N.E. 271).

This court holds that the liability of an escrowee is akin to that of the employer of an independent contractor. While this court could hold a hearing as to the various factual issues presented, it declines to do so at this time due to the pendency of the New York County action against the sellers. This court would request the trial court in New York County to make a determination of which of the damages was incidental to the work performed and which was inherent therein.[b] The parties may apply either for judgment upon compliance with the request, or a hearing.

NOTES

1. *Escrow Duties.* How could plaintiff in *Akivis* have avoided the difficulties that arose during the escrow? How, if at all, could he have better structured the escrow arrangement at the outset? Consider Turbiville v. Hansen, 233 Mont. 487, 761 P.2d 389 (1988), where the escrow holder's duty under the agreement was, "upon demand," to immediately return the documents to the sellers in the event of a default. The court held that the agreement did not require the escrow agent to determine if the demand for return was justified.

What special responsibilities does a lawyer bear when he or she acts as an escrow agent? Compare *Akivis* with In re Lanza and the rules governing representation of clients with potentially conflicting interests, pages 15 to 29 above. Courts in Connecticut have barred an attorney for one of the parties from serving as escrow. See, for example, Galvanek v. Skibitcky, 55 Conn.App. 254, 738 A.2d 1150 (1999). In 2000, the Connecticut legislature superseded this rule and permitted lawyers to serve as escrows in such situations. Public Act 00–74.

For background on escrow rules see R. Kratovil, Real Estate Law ch. 13 (6th ed. 1974). For an excellent practical overview of closing procedures, see R. Werner, Real Estate Closings (1979).

---

[b] In the New York County action, the buyers alleged that during the removal of the contents, "substantial damage" was done to the building. Akivis v. Sixty Four Reade Corp., 111 A.D.2d 97, 489 N.Y.S.2d 229 (1985).

2. *Escrow Costs.* Practices vary from region to region as to who serves the escrow function—lawyer, broker, lender, title company or independent escrow company. Overall closing costs may vary as a result. The HUD/VA study of closing costs, cited at page 8, above, compared average title costs in the counties of Denver ($137), King (Seattle) ($291) and Los Angeles ($436) and concluded that one reason for Denver's lower charges was that escrow services there were performed by the lender and the broker, who included their charges in the lender's origination fee and the broker's commission. By contrast, in King and Los Angeles Counties, independent escrow agents performed these services, at fees averaging $135 and $148 respectively.

Escrow agents in King and Los Angeles counties performed tasks well beyond the usual shuffling of papers. According to the HUD/VA study, they also initiated title searches, secured earnest money deposits and balance due statements on existing loans, drew up deeds, computed prepaid items to be paid at closing, arranged financing, recorded instruments, disbursed funds to the seller and the broker, and furnished buyer and seller with statements of charges and disbursements made in the escrow. Dept. of Housing and Urban Development and Veteran's Administration, Mortgage Settlement Costs: Report to Sen. Comm. on Banking, Housing and Urban Affairs, 92nd Cong. 2d Sess. 25–28 (Comm.Print 1972). For an informative breakdown of closing procedures, customs and charges in fifteen geographic areas of the United States, see id. at 443–513.

3. *Regulation.* Several states regulate escrow personnel. Texas supervises escrow officers as part of its general regulation of title insurance companies and requires that escrow officers be licensed and bonded and possess "reasonable experience or instruction in the field of title insurance." Tex.Ins.Code Ann. §§ 9.41, 9.43B(2) (Vernon 1981 & Supp.1991). Other states regulate escrow practices rather than personnel. New Jersey, for example, specifically enjoins real estate brokers from commingling escrowed funds with their own money. N.J.Stat.Ann. 45:15–17(*o*) (West 1978 & Supp.1991).

California, where independent escrow agents flourish in the southern part of the state, has enacted a law specifically tailored to their activities, regulating both personnel and practices. The law imposes licensing and bonding requirements and controls the details of escrow practice including the proper form of escrow instructions, receipt and disbursement of escrow funds and advertising. Cal.Fin.Code § 17000 et seq.

For an excellent analysis of escrow misconduct see Flores, A Comparison of the Rules and Rationales for Allocating Risks Arising in Realty Sales Using Executory Sale Contracts and Escrows, 59 Mo.L.Rev. 307 (1994).

4. *Drafting Exercise.* Consider In Re Akivis and turn back the clock to the time the contract of sale was being drafted. You are the attorney being asked to hold the escrow funds. You want to provide service to your client but avoid the type of problems described by the *Akivis* court. Your task: draft a clause that you will propose to the parties to be inserted in the contract of sale that will have you act as escrow but also protect you. Note: This can be done in two or three sentences, and you may want to substitute your clause for existing language in the contract set out in the case.

3. THE DESCRIPTION

To be valid, a deed must adequately describe the property conveyed. The clear trend has been away from punctilio and toward a minimal requirement that the description enable location of the parcel to the exclusion of all others—essentially the standard imposed for land descriptions in contracts. See generally 3 American Law of Property § 12.98 (A.J. Casner ed. 1952).

A deed can employ any one or more of three principal techniques to describe the land conveyed: *metes and bounds,* typically using courses and distances, *reference to government survey,* and *reference to a recorded instrument,* typically a subdivision map. The lawyer counseling a buyer or seller in a real estate transaction should be familiar with all three techniques to assure not only that the proposed deed description complies with the statute of frauds, but also that it is accurate and that the buyer will get precisely the land he thinks he is getting. The introductory excerpts in this section describe these three land description techniques.

**Donald A. Wilson, Reading, Interpreting, and Writing
Land Descriptions, in *Land Surveys: A Guide for Lawyers
and Other Professionals* (Mitchell G. Williams, ed.)***
171–172, 173–175, 186–187 (3d ed. 2012).

One of the most common problems shared by lawyers, surveyors, and others dealing with land records is that of land, or land-related descriptions. There are more deeds and related documents than in almost any other category of concern, and therefore not only more rules and guidelines governing them, but also more potential for confusion, ultimately resulting in more disagreements and more litigation.

When the word "description" is mentioned, one immediately thinks of a deed, and often the two are equated. However, they are not one and the same. Deeds *contain* descriptions, but so do wills and other probate records, especially partitions, grants and patents, purchase and sales agreements, mortgages and foreclosure instruments, eminent domain proceedings, and town line perambulations and maps—the latter especially where dedicated easements are concerned. Generally speaking, the same rules apply to all, equally.

Since deeds and related title documents are a form of contract, basic contract requirements include the identification of the subject matter of the contract. In a deed conveying land, the description of the property to be conveyed must be such as to identify it or afford the means of identification, aided by extrinsic evidence.

II.   Types of Descriptions

Metes and bounds. *Mete* means to measure, while *bounds* means the limits or boundaries of a tract of land. While there have been a number of types of descriptions placed in this category, strictly speaking a *metes-and-bounds* description is one that has a defined point of beginning and travels around the parcel in a clockwise or counterclockwise direction, usually reciting courses, distances, monuments, and abutting parcels as they are encountered, returning to the point of beginning. Generally, an area of the parcel so traversed is recited. The theoretical parcel will contain all of the above elements; however in reality, there is a combination of the foregoing, with information lacking in many instances.

The *metes-and-bounds* description is commonly found in the eastern part of the United States and Canada, termed the "metes-and-bounds states," and is often used in present day. Smaller, irregular parcels lend themselves readily to this type of description, explaining its frequency in certain circumstances within the U.S. Public Land Survey System.

. . .

Lot and range. A number of towns and townships were originally laid out in regular design, usually in rectangles and sometimes in squares or parallelograms, with an occasional triangle. Initial conveyancing, particularly original granting to proprietors, consisted of original lots, or parts thereof. Subsequently, depending on the area and extent of conveyancing, these lots have been further subdivided into regular parts thereof, or into smaller parcels described by metes and bounds. In some areas, descriptions remain in terms of lots or parts thereof.

The complicating factor with this type of description is that the original lotting scheme must be known since each town was lotted independently, and each one is likely to be different from any of the abutting towns. Many are unique in design as there was no set pattern. Design, number, and arrangement of lots were governed by the shape of the town, the terrain, the number of original grantees or proprietors, and the instructions given to the surveyors or the "lot layers." It is therefore essential that one have a copy of the original lotting plan whenever possible. When there is no plan available, one must be reconstructed from available evidence of surrounding descriptions and physical evidence. Occasionally it is necessary to reconstruct an entire town or a large portion thereof in order to determine the scheme.

Towns were often laid out in *divisions,* which was a planned scheme to take advantage of and grant accordingly the quality of the land. There are frequently several divisions in any given town, so any lot number may appear several times, once in each division. There was also common land left in many towns for later granting, compensating for lot deficiencies or for the use of the public. Some of this was granted, or lotted, indiscriminately. The term "pitch" is used for this procedure in some locations.

Plan reference. Some descriptions merely refer to a plan (commonly termed "plat" where a subdivision of land is concerned), which by rule of law makes the plan part of the description. Therefore, the plan must also be consulted in order to determine the location of the parcel as well as the definition of its lines and corners. This is most important since there is usually an abundance of information appearing on the plan that is not included within the deed.

The problem arises with this type of description when the plan is not on public record, or worse, when it cannot be found. Sometimes a lengthy search is necessary to locate such a plan, and because it may give additional information or information contrary to the deed description (e.g., if the description was written incorrectly from the plan), its importance cannot be overemphasized.

This is a very common type of description in modern conveyancing, where there have been numerous subdivisions of land under the various laws and regulations and then descriptions written from those plans. Because extreme care has not been taken in all cases, there is often incomplete information in the deed or conflicting statements between the deed description and that appearing on the plan.

Block and lot. Many of the early municipal surveys and lottings, and some modern subdivisions—particularly larger ones or those with several phases of development—have been designed with lots within blocks, or sections. Great care must be taken when dealing with a lot number since that particular number may apply to several lots, depending on which block or section is concerned.

Some include other forms of description under this category: arpent lotting, lot and range, townsites, and occasionally other variations. The common denominator is that they all require a map, plan, or plat to show the lot and its particulars. Problems arise when such map cannot be found or is lost. In such situations, sometimes a large area, or the entire subdivision, must be reconstructed to determine what is being described.

. . .

Relative importance of conflicting elements. In determining the boundaries of a tract of land, it is not permissible to disregard any of the calls if they can be applied and harmonized in any reasonable manner. In doing so, conflicts may arise within a description such that it is not possible to harmonize all of the calls. However, the courts have agreed upon a classification and gradation of calls in a grant, survey, or entry of land by which their relative importance and weight are to be determined. These rules are not artificial or based on theory but are the results of human experience. They are not binding requirements, or rules of evidence, or merely helpful guidelines in determining which of two conflicting calls should control, but *rules of construction,* that are adaptable to the circumstances of each case. A call that would defeat the intention of the parties will be rejected regardless of the comparative dignity of the conflicting calls, and, where calls of a higher order are made by mistake, the calls of the lower order may control as indicating the intention of the grant.

The rules for the order of conflicting description elements are founded upon the principle that those elements are to control in which error is least likely to occur.

Relative Importance of Conflicting Elements

A.   Natural Monuments

B.   Artificial Monuments

Maps, Plats, and Field Notes

Adjoiners

Metes and Bounds

C.   Courses

Angles

D.   Distances

E.   Area

Marshall v. Soffer

Appellate Court of Connecticut, 2000.
58 Conn.App. 737, 756 A.2d 284.

Before EDWARD Y. O'CONNELL, C.J., and ZARELLA and DUPONT, JS.

DUPONT, J.

This is an appeal from the judgment rendered by the trial court in favor of the plaintiffs, Patrick Marshall and Deborah Marshall, quieting title in them to a parcel of property located on Damascus Road in the town of Branford, and ordering that the defendant, Joseph Soffer, remove a fence and other material placed on the property and restore the area to its prior condition, "insomuch as that is reasonably possible, by the said removal and the removal of any dead brush, limbs or other debris."[2]

The defendant claims that the court should have (1) concluded that the plaintiffs' deed to the parcel was rendered ambiguous because a starting monument of the deed had been lost, (2) applied the doctrine of acquiescence in a boundary and (3) concluded that the defendant acquired title to the property by adverse possession.[3] The issue on appeal is whether the judgment of the court that quieted title in the plaintiffs was reached by a legally correct methodology, supported by the facts in the record. We affirm the judgment of the trial court.

The plaintiffs' complaint sought a determination of the common boundary line between their property and that of the defendant, and to quiet title to the land area that lies between the two disputed boundary lines. The facts that follow were either found by the court or are not in dispute. The plaintiffs' property was originally part of a farm owned by the defendant's family. The property that is now owned by the plaintiffs was carved out of the property comprising the farm, and was first conveyed by Louis Soffer to Jacob Soffer by warranty deed in 1952. The description in that warranty deed, which is the same as the description in the plaintiffs' deed, was plotted by the plaintiffs' surveyor on a map. That map was introduced into evidence as exhibit A. The map is not referenced, however, in any relevant deed and is not recorded. It differs from a 1967 map, which was introduced into evidence as exhibit E. The 1967 map was prepared for the defendant and recorded in the land

---

[2]   While the appeal was pending, the plaintiffs filed a motion in the trial court to terminate the stay of execution of the orders. The court granted the motion as to the removal of the fence only, ordering that it be removed within thirty days.

[3]   The defendant alleged in a special defense that he had acquired title to the disputed land by adverse possession.

records of the town of Branford in 1968 without being referenced to any deed or to any grantor or grantee. The map is not signed and bears the following notation: "Lines as agreed on by Soffer and Huzar."

From 1962 to 1972, the property now owned by the plaintiffs was owned by John Huzar and Anna Huzar. In 1972, John Huzar and Anna Huzar conveyed the property to Andrew Huzar and Edith Huzar. The latter Huzars conveyed the property to the plaintiffs' predecessor in title in 1979. The plaintiffs acquired the property in 1986. The description in the plaintiffs' deed is the same description used in the deeds of each of the predecessors in title. The outline of the property on the 1967 map does not follow the legal description of the warranty deed of the plaintiffs. The property now owned by the defendant was described in a 1957 conveyance, which description excepted the parcel now owned by the plaintiffs. The excepted parcel in that 1957 deed is particularly described, using the same description as is contained in the deed to the plaintiffs. Thus, no deed description in the chain of title of either the plaintiffs or the defendant matches that of the 1967 map.

The court found that there was no recorded boundary line agreement that referred to the 1967 map or to the notation on it, and that the plaintiffs had no notice of that map. The court concluded that (1) there was no evidence to support the defendant's special defense of adverse possession, (2) the 1967 map did not supersede the description in the deeds in the plaintiffs' chain of title, (3) the descriptions in the plaintiffs' deed and the deeds of their predecessors in title are not ambiguous[5] and (4) the boundary as claimed by the defendant has not been established by acquiescence.

The ambiguity claimed by the defendant is that the northwest corner of the property, which is the place of beginning as described in the plaintiffs' deed and in the deeds of their predecessors in title, could not be located on the ground at the time the plaintiffs took title. The defendant also claims that the street line of Damascus Road (formerly Stony Creek Road) was undetermined in 1952 when the plaintiffs' property was first conveyed by Louis Soffer to Jacob Soffer.

The defendant argues that the northwest corner was evidenced by a stone wall but that when exhibit A was prepared, the northwest corner as a starting point had become uncertain because the stone wall had fluctuated in location over the years. The defendant concedes that the words used in the description of the plaintiffs' deed are unambiguous and that the deed is not ambiguous on its face, but claims that the deed contains a latent ambiguity because its starting point eventually became uncertain when compared to the actual land that the deed purported to convey. In other words, it is the defendant's claim that when it is no longer possible to replicate a starting point on the ground to correspond with a deed description that begins with that starting point, the deed becomes ambiguous because it contains references to monuments that no longer exist or that have changed. The defendant agrees, however, that "[t]he physical disappearance of a monument does not terminate its status as a boundary marker, provided that its former location can be ascertained through extrinsic

---

[5]   The court's conclusions that the description in the plaintiffs' deed is not ambiguous and that the 1967 map does not supersede that description or render the deed description ambiguous will be discussed together.

evidence." (Internal quotation marks omitted.) Koennicke v. Maiorano, 43 Conn. App. 1, 12, 682 A.2d 1046 (1996).

The defendant claims that the court made no effort to reconstruct the location of the stone wall as a monument or the location of Damascus Road but, instead, improperly concluded that the deed description as shown on exhibit A controlled the resolution of this case. The defendant claims that the deed description shown on exhibit A is fundamentally flawed because it uses the end of the existing stone wall as the northwest corner and starting point for the deed description.

The court disregarded the 1967 map because it was not indexed in the land records as being in the chain of title of either the plaintiffs or the defendant. The court credited the testimony of the plaintiffs' expert who had prepared exhibit A and concluded that the original description in the deed of Louis Soffer to Jacob Soffer, the same property now owned by the plaintiffs, could be replicated or found on the ground.

The 1967 map was not referenced in any deed, and no deed description after that date in the chain of title of either the plaintiffs or the defendant was amended to reflect any change in the boundaries of land conveyed. We do not agree with the defendant that a map that is not indexed as being in the chain of title of either the plaintiffs or the defendant should alter the plaintiffs' deeded description without actual or constructive notice of the map or without an agreement recorded in the land records.

According to the plaintiffs, the 1967 map is equivalent to an unrecorded instrument because it does not involve their chain of title. Although maps that are part of the deeds to which they refer may be filed in a special index in a town clerk's office, the filing is not sufficient to charge a title holder with notice of the map unless the terms of a relevant recorded deed point to the map. See Kulmacz v. Milas, 108 Conn. 538, 541–42, 144 A. 32 (1928). There is no notice of the contents of a map except if the terms of a recorded deed refer to the map. Powers v. Olson, 252 Conn. 98, 108, 742 A.2d 799 (2000).

In determining the location of a boundary line expressed in a deed, if the description is clear and unambiguous, it governs and the actual intent of the parties is irrelevant. *Koennicke v. Maiorano, supra,* 43 Conn. App at 10, 682 A.2d 1046; see also F. & AK, Inc. v. Sleeper, 161 Conn. 505, 510, 289 A.2d 905 (1971). The deed in the present case begins with the words "at the Northwest corner of land herein at its intersection of land now or formerly of Katherine Link Knapp. . . ." The description does not begin with words relating to a stone wall, and only mentions a stone wall to describe the end of the westerly boundary at Knapp's land the northerly boundary "along said stone wall to the point or place of beginning."[6]

---

[6]   The deed description of the land now owned by the plaintiffs remained the same since 1952 and is as follows: "[A]ll that certain piece or parcel of land beginning at the Northwest corner of land herein at its intersection of land now or formerly of Katherine Link Knapp; thence Easterly along Stony Creek Road, ninety (90) feet; thence Southerly at right angles to Stony Creek Road, along land now or formerly of Louis Soffer, one hundred fifty (150) feet; thence Westerly at a right angle to the last described line along land now or formerly of Louis Soffer to a stone wall separating land herein from land now or formerly of Katherine Link Knapp; thence Northeasterly along said stone wall to the point or place of beginning, bounded: NORTHERLY: BY Stony Creek Road; EASTERLY: by land now or formerly of Louis Soffer;

A latent ambiguity arises from extraneous or collateral facts that make the meaning of a deed uncertain although its language is clear and unambiguous on its face. Heyman Associates No. 1 v. Ins. Co. of Pennsylvania, 231 Conn. 756, 782, 653 A.2d 122 (1995). A latent ambiguity can exist if the distances given in a deed do not "strike land" of a landowner as mentioned in the deed; *F. & AK, Inc. v. Sleeper, supra*, 161 Conn. At 510–11, 289 A.2d 905; or if a discrepancy as to the direction of one of the four borders exists Apostles of the Sacred Heart v. Curott, 187 Conn. 591, 598, 448 A.2d 157 (1982); or if the description is too general, such as one fixing the location of a boundary as "the top of the mountain"; Young Men's Christian Assn. v. Zemel Bros., Inc., 171 Conn. 310, 311, 370 A.2d 937 (1976); or if a deed refers to a map that is ambiguous or unclear. Lake Garda Improvement Assn. v. Battistoni, 160 Conn. 503, 510–11, 280 A.2d 877 (1971). In the event a latent ambiguity is found, the ambiguous language in the grant is ordinarily construed against the grantor and in favor of the grantee, and "the grantee may adopt the boundary most favorable to him." *Id.*, at 514, 280 A.2d 877. In the present case, the court correctly concluded that no such latent ambiguity exists and that the plaintiffs' deed description was not ambiguous.

There is nothing ambiguous about the deed description in the present case. In 1986 when the plaintiffs acquired title, without notice of the 1967 map, they could have followed easily the deed description on the ground. The stone wall runs south to north along property "now or formerly of Katherine Link Knapp." The boundaries are described in terms of the abutting land owners and the road, not a stone wall. Adjacent land may be a monument if the boundary of it is fixed. Staff v. Hawkins, 135 Conn. 316, 319, 64 A.2d 176 (1949).

The court correctly concluded that the plaintiffs' deed was not ambiguous and that the 1967 map did not amend or supersede the deed's description.

The defendant next claims that the plaintiffs or their predecessors in title acquiesced in the boundary as established in the 1967 map. Acquiescence in the use and development of an area by a landowner is defined as a consent to the boundary as claimed by an adjoining owner and can estop the acquiescing landowner from pursuing a claim of ownership. See Del Buono v. Brown Boat Work, Inc., Conn.App. 524, 533, 696 A.2d 1271, cert. denied, 243 Conn. 906, 701 A.2d 328 (1997). The acquiescence must occur under circumstances that indicate an assent to such a use. *Id.*

The defendant introduced applications for building permits to show that a predecessor in title of the plaintiffs had acquiesced in the boundary as depicted on the 1967 map. The court found that the distances shown on the building permits did not conform to the distances described in the plaintiffs' deed or in the 1967 map. Because of the contradicting dimensions, the court discounted the evidence. We conclude that the record does not establish that the plaintiffs or their predecessors in title agreed that the disputed land could be used by the

---

SOUTHERLY: by land now or formerly of Louis Soffer; and WESTERLY: by land now or formerly of Katherine Link Knapp."

defendant or that the boundaries were those of the 1967 map, rather than those in their deed description.

The last claim of the defendant is that he acquired title to the disputed land by adverse possession. The court found that the defendant produced no evidence to support this claim. The court also noted that all of the witnesses indicated that neither the defendant nor his agents or employees ever conducted any activity or business on the disputed land or treated it as the defendant's property. There was evidence, however, that the plaintiffs had treated portions of the area as their own. The defendant claims that some witnesses testified that "the line of occupation" (the disputed area) had been observed by the plaintiffs' predecessors in title, but admitted that the land was overgrown and that there was little evidence of cultivation. The plaintiffs' immediate predecessor in title testified that while he owned the land, he had deposited debris there, but that the defendant and his predecessors had not cultivated, graded or trimmed anything on the land. The defendant paid property tax to the town of Branford on the disputed land, but that is only one relevant factor to be considered in determining whether the defendant acquired the land by adverse possession and does not, by itself, require reversal of the court's judgment. We hold that the court properly concluded that the defendant had not proven by clear and convincing evidence that he had ousted the plaintiffs or their predecessors of exclusive possession for fifteen years by open, visible and adverse acts. See Clark v. Drska, 1 Conn.App. 481, 485, 473 A.2d 325 (1984).

The judgment is affirmed.

In this opinion the other judges concurred.

NOTES

1.   *Ambiguous Descriptions: Validity of the Deed.* Traditionally, for a deed to be valid the instrument had to describe the parcel conveyed to the exclusion of all other parcels in the world. Contemporary courts have relaxed this requirement somewhat by resorting to parol evidence—oral statements, extrinsic writings, the physical condition of the land and improvements—in order to cure omissions or ambiguities within the deed's four corners.

Colman v. Butkovich, 556 P.2d 503, 505 (Utah 1976), typifies the modern trend. In an action to quiet title, the question arose whether a deed description—"All unplatted land in this Block (29 P.C.) and all land West of this Blk. and Pt. Lot 1: Pt. Lot A"—was sufficient. Upholding the deed, the court observed:

> It is not to be questioned that in order to be valid, a deed must contain a sufficiently definite description to identify the property it conveys. . . . The problem lies in ascertaining the intent with which it was executed. It should be resolved, if possible, by looking to the terms of the instrument itself and any reasonable inferences to be drawn therefrom; and if there then remains any uncertainty or ambiguity it can be aided by extrinsic evidence. If from that process the property can be identified with reasonable certainty, the deed is not invalid for uncertainty.

Doubtless the main reason courts are reluctant to invalidate deeds like the one in *Colman* is that the grantor, although she may have been less than clear in describing the parcel conveyed, has been crystal clear in expressing her intention to convey *something* to the grantee; if parol evidence will resolve the ambiguity and make the deed enforceable, it should be admitted.

Which will better serve an efficient conveyancing system: a rule that validates the deed by focusing on buyer's and seller's actual intent, or one that invalidates the deed if that intent has not been expressed clearly in the written instrument? Is the threat of invalidation likely to spur buyers and sellers to draft clear descriptions? For some thoughtful reflections along these lines, see Note, The Use of Extrinsic Evidence to Interpret Real Property Conveyances: A Suggested Limitation, 65 Cal.L.Rev. 897 (1977).

2. *Ambiguous Descriptions: Construction of the Deed.* Parol evidence fades over time and eventually disappears entirely. By contrast, the express language of a deed is indelible and can guide buyer and seller expectations indefinitely. Thus, although results like Marshall v. Soffer may harm original grantees who may have relied on parol evidence, the rule can be justified in terms of the interests of the countless, future buyers and their sellers who will not have access to this parol evidence.

Even where a mutual mistake by the original parties results in an incorrect description, courts will not reform the deed if a bona fide purchaser owns the lot that will be disadvantaged by the reformation. See, e.g., Florida Masters Packing, Inc. v. Craig, 739 So.2d 1288 (Fla.App.1999) (court refused to reform surveyor error that placed boundary 35 feet farther to the north than original grantor and grantee intended); see Buk Lhu v. Dignoti, 431 Mass. 292, 727 N.E.2d 73 (2000). A court will not even consider reformation if the mistake was not mutual. See, e.g., Resort of Indian Spring, Inc. v. Indian Spring Country Club, Inc., 747 So.2d 974 (Fla.App.1999) (no reformation since there was some testimony that original grantee did expect that disputed portion was part of the transfer, even though there was substantial evidence to the contrary).

Moreover, as *Marshall* indicates (but rejects on the facts), the effects on the immediate buyer will frequently be meliorated by adverse possession rules. An owner who invests in mistaken reliance on parol representations will gain title to the land he mistakenly possesses if his possession is not objected to by the true owner for the period prescribed by the statute of limitations. The doctrine of acquiescence, also rejected by the *Marshall* court on the facts, may provide relief in some cases.

3. *Canons of Construction.* The main work of courts dealing with deed descriptions is to interpret ambiguous or conflicting language. Professors Cribbet and Johnson have helpfully distilled ten canons of construction from the cases. J. Cribbet & C. Johnson, Principles of the Law of Property 210–212 (3d ed. 1989). Some of these canons can truly help courts to divine the seller's and buyer's original intent. One canon states that in case of a conflict between the various indicators and measures used in a description, "monuments control distances and courses; courses control distances; and quantity is the least reliable guide of all." The canon presumably corresponds with the expectations of buyer and seller: "most monuments would be difficult to mistake so they are probably identified correctly. A course, 'northerly at a 90° angle' is more certain than a distance 'thence 80 ft.,' since most people cannot measure distances with the naked eye." Distance is also subject to the hazards of uneven terrain.

Another helpful canon is that when "a tract of land is bounded by a monument which has width, such as a highway or a stream, the boundary line extends to the center, provided the grantor owns that far." Again, the canon presumably reflects the parties' original expectations—in this case, that the grantee would receive the grantor's entire interest in the parcel. To mark the boundary at the near edge of the highway or stream would mean that if the highway is later abandoned, or the stream diverted, the grantor would have title to the strip between the edge and the center.

Other canons are, as Professors Cribbet and Johnson acknowledge, simply conclusional, explaining rather than predicting results. Among these are, "extrinsic evidence will be allowed to explain a latent ambiguity but a patent ambiguity must be resolved within the four corners of the deed." (What is patent? What is latent? Consider *Marshall*.) "Useless or contradictory words may be disregarded as mere surplusage." (What is useless? What is contradictory?) And, "particular descriptions control over general descriptions, although a false particular may be disregarded to give effect to a true general description." (Huh?) See also Note, Operation and Construction of Deeds, 6 St. Mary's L.J. 806 (1975).

Some legislatures have codified these canons. See, e.g., Mont. Code Ann. § 70–20–201, applied in Ferriter v. Bartmess, 281 Mont. 100, 931 P.2d 709 (1997).

4. *Surveyor Malpractice.* Surveyor liability for malpractice has expanded over the recent decades. Breach of contract, the traditional ground of recovery for a faulty survey or description, has recently been joined by the tort of negligent misrepresentation. This tort has no privity requirement and thus can give relief to distant purchasers as well as to the buyer or developer who first contracted with the surveyor. Liability is also being extended by the "discovery" rule under which the statute of limitations for negligent misrepresentation does not begin to run until the misrepresentation has been, or should have been, discovered.

Doctrines limiting surveyor liability are, however, still applied. Some courts will blunt the thrust of liability by limiting the amount of damages that can be awarded. In Allan & Leuthold, Inc. v. Terra Investment Co., 271 Or. 335, 532 P.2d 218 (1975), a surveyor whose errors required a corrective survey was held liable for the costs of the resurvey, but not for additional plumbing costs that did not directly result from the errors.

5. *Regulation of Surveyors.* Surveying is a closely regulated profession. A state license is generally required of anyone who performs surveying activities within the state. Applicants must meet stiff training requirements to obtain a surveyor's license. They may be required to have completed a four-year undergraduate course of study, with an emphasis on land surveying, and also to have completed two or more years of training in the field. More extensive field experience can in some states substitute for a full college program. An applicant may also be required to successfully complete an examination testing knowledge of basic math and science as well as applied surveying principles.

Once licensed, the surveyor may be required to comply with rigorous professional standards of practice. A surveyor can lose his or her license, or be otherwise disciplined, for committing fraud, failing to meet administratively established requirements such as following the specified forms for maps, plats, plans or designs, or inability to practice in accordance with the standards of the profession. See, for example, Wyo.Stat. § 33–29–114 et seq.; N.Y.Educ.Law § 7200 et seq.; Cal.Bus. & Prof.Code § 8700 et seq.; S.D.Comp.Laws Ann. § 36–18 et seq.

6. *Bibliographic Note.* For background on property description and surveys see, in addition to the works excerpted above, Hixson, What to Look for When Examining A Survey Map, 18 Prob. & Prop. 54 (Sep./Oct. 2004); J. Grimes, A Treatise on the Law of Surveying and Boundaries (4th ed. 1976); J. Palomar, Patton & Palomar on Land Titles (3d ed. 2002); Keith, Government Land Surveys and Related Problems, 38 Iowa L.Rev. 86 (1952); Boyd & Uelmen, Resurveys and Metes and Bounds Descriptions, 1953 Wis.L.Rev. 657; Miller, Working with Legal Descriptions, 13 Prac. Real Est. Law. 43 (Mar. 1997); DeBole, Verifying Property Descriptions in Deeds, 10 Prac. Real Est.Law. 77 (May 1994).

B. LIABILITIES THAT SURVIVE THE DEED

Under the doctrine of merger, a deed conveying real property supersedes any conflicting terms in the contract of sale and becomes the sole measure of the parties' rights and liabilities as between themselves and others. This means that even if the contract of sale contains an express or implied covenant that seller will deliver marketable title on closing, buyer's acceptance of the deed will bar buyer from an action against seller if title later proves to be unmarketable—except to the extent that the deed itself contains express warranties of title.

In practice, merger doctrine is not nearly so clear-cut, nor buyer's prospects so bleak. First, merger is a rule of construction, not a rule of law, and when the interests of third parties will not be prejudiced, courts will weigh parol evidence in interpreting the deed. Also, just as the deed may specify obligations not mentioned in the contract, so the contract may effectively provide that it, and not the deed, is to control certain obligations. And, although most courts will not imply title covenants into deeds, many courts today will imply covenants respecting fitness of the premises. See generally, Dunham, Merger by Deed—Was it Ever Automatic?, 10 Ga.L.Rev. 419 (1976).

Merger is characteristically a seller's doctrine, employed to repel buyer claims based on pre-closing undertakings. Can—and should— merger also be used as a *buyer* doctrine to support the claim that post-closing warranties supersede less extensive undertakings made in the contract of sale? Consider the next principal case.

Reed v. Hassell

Superior Court of Delaware, 1975.
340 A.2d 157.

CHRISTIE, JUDGE.

By contract dated August 16, 1969, the plaintiffs, Thomas J. Reed and Sally Reed, his wife, agreed to purchase from Andrew Hassell (who died before the transaction was completed) and Loretta Hassell, his wife, Lots 82 and 83, Second Addition, Bay View Park, Baltimore Hundred, Sussex County, Delaware.

The printed contract form used by the parties provided that the title was to be "good and merchantable, free of liens and encumbrances except . . . publicly recorded easements for public utilities and other easements which may be observed by the inspection of the property."

By deed dated February 4, 1970, Loretta Hassell (the surviving seller and the defendant in this action) conveyed the lots to plaintiffs pursuant to the contract using a special warranty deed as required by the contract.

At the time of the contract and at the time of the conveyance, there was an existing road known as Hassell Avenue which (contrary to the information on the recorded plot plan) seriously encroached upon Lot 82 so as to deprive that lot of about 25 percent of its square footage. This encroachment reduced the lot to a relatively small, inconvenient lot which will be difficult to build upon in view of zoning requirements which include set-back and side line restrictions.

By this suit, plaintiffs seek damages on account of the encroachment. There is no evidence that defendant knew that the road constituted an encroachment at the time of settlement and, of course, the plaintiffs were unaware of the encroachment at the time of settlement.

The evidence indicates that the intention of the seller was to convey building lots essentially as they were shown on the plot plan, and the intention of the buyers was to buy such lots because they were of such size and shape as to be suitable for the construction of houses. Although there was an exception in the contract as to easements observable by inspection of the property, it is clear that the agreement would never have been entered into if it had been known that there was a major encroachment which severely limited the usefulness of the lot. Indeed, the seller made an innocent and unknowing representation to the buyers to the effect that she was able to convey such lots essentially as shown on the plot plan. This the seller was unable to do.

At the time of settlement there was heavy and tall growth on the lots which made it impossible to inspect the boundaries of the land or to measure the lots without costly or time-consuming work to cut down portions of the growth. During the two summers after settlement, the plaintiffs personally cleared the land. In October, 1973, the land had been cleared to the extent that a survey could be conducted and then, for the first time, it was discovered by a professional surveyor that the road was so located as to constitute a major encroachment on Lot 82.

Plaintiffs seek damages based upon alleged "misrepresentation, deceit and fraud" and, by informal amendment of the complaint, they, in the alternative, seek damages on account of an alleged breach of the covenant of warranty contained in the deed.

At the hearing, plaintiffs failed to establish a factual basis for recovery on account of "misrepresentation, deceit and fraud" as such, but it was clearly established that the road constituted a breach of the covenant of special warranty of fee simple title free of encumbrances which the law reads into deeds such as the deed issued by the seller to the buyers in this case.

Thus, the question to be resolved by the Court is whether a major encroachment not known to be an encroachment by either the seller or the buyers at the time of settlement gives rise to an action for damages after such encroachment is discovered by the buyers many months after the deed had been accepted by the buyers. Resolution of this issue, in turn, depends in part upon the effect or lack of effect which is given to the provision in the sales contract which excepted from the title guarantees contained in such contract "easements which may be observed by an inspection of the property."

As to this provision of the contract, plaintiffs claim first of all that the encroachment could not be discovered by inspection because of the heavy and tall growth on the land. Plaintiffs' testimony about the growth is supported by a surveyor who indicated that it would have been necessary to cut a portion of the growth in order to make a survey.

The encroaching road itself was, of course, in plain sight and easily accessible. It appears to constitute the access to the lots. What was not readily accessible were the boundaries of the lots, a survey of which would have shown that the road encroached in Lot 82. Had these boundaries been established by survey, it would have been apparent that the existing road cut across Lot 82 so as to deprive it of about 25 percent of its square footage.

I find that, under the circumstances here present, the encroachment was one which may have been observed by an inspection of the property, but I also find that the parties did not intend that the risk of a major encroachment was to be assumed by the buyers under the contract or the deed here involved. The contract did not specify that the only easements excepted from the title guarantees were those discoverable by any easy-to-conduct amateur inspection free of cost, and it is apparent that a meaningful inspection would involve physical labor and the cost of hiring a surveyor. Plaintiffs' election not to go this expense did not render the inspection impossible; rather, plaintiff assumed the risk of easement encroachments not going to the essence of the contract. The contractual provision provided in legal effect that defendant did not guarantee against existing easements which would be revealed by a survey, but it was also clearly implied in the contract that seller owned and was in a position to convey essentially what was shown on the plot plan as Lot 82.

Plaintiffs also contend that, in any event, the contract "merged" with the deed at time of settlement and, at that time, the contract became void as a separate document. Plaintiffs say the effect of this "merger" is that the seller is now held to the terms of the special warranty of title which the law attaches to a deed and seller is deprived of any benefit from the less exacting terms of the contract pursuant to which the special warranty deed was issued.

We come at last to the real crux of the case: Does a savings clause in the real estate sales contract survive the issuance of a special warranty deed so as to protect the grantor from liability for an encumbrance which was unrecognized by the parties but was in fact in basic derogation of the title the deed purported to convey?

The solution to the problem lies in the application of the merger rule under which the law is generally deemed to provide that a deed makes full execution of a contract of sale and constitutes the overriding contract between the parties as to what the seller conveyed to the buyer thereby rendering ineffective or obsolete any inconsistent terms of the prior contract.

This rule is summarized in 26 C.J.S. Deeds § 91 in the following language:

"Accordingly, although the terms of preliminary agreements may vary from those contained in the deed, the deed alone must be looked to for determination of the rights of the parties, in the absence of fraud or mistake, and the rule as to merger has been held to deny operative effect to prior agreements with respect to set-back restrictions, the amount of land to be conveyed, the nature of the title transferred, freedom from encumbrances, permissible use of the property, and reservation of an easement."

Judge Daniel J. Layton confirmed this rule of law in Delaware in the case of Re v. Magness Construction Co., Del.Super., 117 A.2d 78 (1955) when he wrote the following:

"The authorities are uniform in holding that where a Deed is executed and delivered pursuant to a Contract of Sale of Realty, the latter merges with the former and becomes void."

The C.J.S. article goes on to observe, however, that the merger rule is subject to exceptions and *the intent of the parties is controlling,* the question being one of construction (emphasis added).

The difficulty with the merger rule as applied to the case at bar is that it does not appear to have been developed to resolve the type of problem here posed. The merger rule appears to have been developed to resolve issues raised where a seller of real property undertook certain obligations in a contract of sale and then delivered something less than he promised as, for example, when seller delivered a deed not carrying out all the contract promises or a lot with certain encumbrances or containing a lesser acreage than contracted for. So it is that the annotation as to this type of merger is titled "Deed as superseding or merging provisions of antecedent contract *imposing obligations upon the vendor."* 38 A.L.R.2d 1310 (emphasis added). The annotation then goes on to show that, although all jurisdictions considering the matter recognize the merger rule, still there are many special situations where the seller is required to comply with promises made in the sales contract even though a deed has been delivered and accepted. The actual use of the merger rule can often be explained as a way of regarding the delivery and acceptance of the deed as a sort of accord and satisfaction.

It could be argued that this large collection of cases and the learned writings about these cases find little direct application here because, in the case before the Court, the sales contract contained an escape clause as to easements for the benefit of the seller. The cited merger cases deal with situations where the purchaser is seeking to get what he originally bargained for but didn't get because the deed he received failed to carry out the express terms of the contract. The case at bar, on the other hand, deals with a case where the seller is seeking to get by with delivering what she claims the purchaser bargained for (i.e., a lot subject to any existing easements which could be discovered by inspection) even though the deed which the seller delivered to the purchaser appears to go beyond the requirements of the sales contract and purports to convey a title clear of such flaws.

Under the merger rule, a deed is often deemed to supersede promises contained in the sales contract and, if the purchaser accepts the deed as compliance with the sales contract, he cannot seek additional rights he formerly had under the contract unless those additional rights survived the acceptance of the deed because they fell within one of the numerous exceptions to the merger rule. Is the converse true? That is, does an unconditional special warranty deed supersede the lesser undertakings or escape clauses contained in the sales contract so that the seller must make good on the warranties of the deed even though the seller was expressly excused from such undertaking in the sales contract?

I think, under the circumstances here present, the merger rule should be applied and the seller should be held to the warranties contained in the deed because the obvious intent of the parties from the very beginning was that the seller would convey and the buyers would receive the two building lots essentially as shown on the plot plan. The exception as to easements contained in the sales contract is found to have been intended to protect the seller against only such easements as do not go to the essence of the bargain and do not seriously limit the usefulness of the lot. The exception surely was not intended to force buyers to accept a lot with such a serious encroachment therein as to render the lot almost useless for the declared purpose which buyers had in mind when they bought.

In short, I find that plaintiffs have established their right to recover damages because defendant failed to convey a good title to Lot 82 to plaintiffs free and clear of all easements except such discoverable easements as did not destroy or severely limit the intended use of the lot. Such major failure and mistake constituted not only a breach of the terms of the sales contract, but more importantly from a technical legal viewpoint, such failure is contrary to the terms of the special warranty deed delivered by defendant to plaintiffs. The merger rule is deemed to apply here because it serves to carry out the basic intent of the parties. The warranties in the deed are deemed to be binding on the seller under the circumstances.

Arguments were not specifically presented under the theory of mutual mistake of fact, but a similar result might have been reached under that theory.

The evidence on damages appears to be somewhat inconclusive since the parties presented their damage evidence under vastly differing theories as to the correct measure of damages.

Further argument and possibly further evidence will be considered before the Court designates the amount of damages.

NOTES

1. *Collateral Promises.* Under an important limit on the merger doctrine, "collateral" promises—those unrelated to title or possession of the property—are not merged into the deed and so survive closing. Courts generally agree that certain promises are collateral, such as seller's

promise to build or repair the premises and express and implied promises as to quality of the property. M. Friedman, Contracts and Conveyances of Real Property 887–897 (5th ed. 1991). A fairly standard definition states: "If a stipulation makes reference to title, possession, quantity or emblements of land it will generally be considered to inhere to the subject matter of a warranty deed, and shall be considered merged and, thus, not a collateral stipulation." Belstler v. Sheler, 151 Idaho 819, 264 P.3d 926 (2011).

The difficulty is in applying such statements to facts. Compare American National Self Storage, Inc. v. Lopez-Aguiar, 521 So.2d 303 (Fla.App.1988), review denied, 528 So.2d 1182 (Fla.1988) (express warranty that property had water, sewer, and electric service was collateral and survived delivery of the deed) with Toys R Us, Inc. v. Atlanta Economic Development Corporation, 195 Ga.App. 195, 393 S.E.2d 44 (1990), cert. denied (seller's promise in the sales agreement to provide a building pad of certain specifications merged into the deed and was extinguished). How important was the fact that the closing statement in *Toys R Us* expressly stated that all provisions of the sales contract merge into the deed?

In Bickerstaff Real Estate Management, LLC v. Hanners, 292 Ga.App. 554, 665 S.E.2d 705 (2008), the court held that a warranty that the seller had no knowledge of hazardous substances was merged into the deed. Does that fit within the definition of a collateral promise? For an excellent analysis of the merger doctrine, see Teich, A Second Call for Abolition of the Rule of Merger by Deed, 71 U.Det. Mercy L.Rev. 543 (1994).

2. *The Function of Merger Doctrine.* Merger, though rooted in general contract principles, serves a special function in the context of real property transactions, where the needs of future as well as present buyers and sellers must be served. While the immediate buyer and seller can safely look outside the deed to resolve their mutual intent, a future buyer of the land can rely only on the intent expressed within the four corners of a recorded deed.

Courts today generally recognize the importance of this distinction. They will look outside the deed when only the parties to the immediate transaction will be affected by their decision, but will give the deed conclusive effect when the interests of third parties are implicated. For example, merger will be strictly applied against contract covenants respecting title and freedom from encumbrances, and these covenants will not survive the closing unless restated in the deed. This application of the merger rule enhances efficient conveyancing, for all successors in interest to the original buyer will be able to rely exclusively on recorded instruments to determine whether title covenants have been given whose benefits will run to them. See generally, Berger, Merger By Deed—What Provisions of a Contract for the Sale of Land Survive the Closing? 21 Real Est.L.J. 22 (1992); Note, Merger of Land Contract in Deed, 25 Alb.L.Rev. 122 (1961).

In a recent opinion, the Utah Court of Appeals reviewed the policies underlying the merger rule:

The supreme court has described the merger doctrine as 'an admittedly harsh rule of law.' Nevertheless, Utah adheres to the merger doctrine because it 'preserves the integrity of the final document of conveyance and encourages the diligence of the parties.' Parties to real estate transactions have a duty 'to make certain that their agreements have in fact been fully included in the final document.'

Maynard v. Wharton, 912 P.2d 446, 451 (Utah Ct.App.1996).

3. *Fraud.* Merger does not affect seller liability for fraud. Before and after closing, the buyer who meets the strict requirements for proving fraud can obtain rescission and, in some cases, damages. See Ouseley v. Foss, 188 Ga.App. 766, 374 S.E.2d 534 (1988). Liability for fraud is covered at pages 193–204 below.

4. *U.L.T.A.* Section 1–309 of the Uniform Land Transactions Act abolishes the doctrine of merger.

1. FITNESS OF THE PREMISES

Buyers disappointed with the quality of the property which they have purchased have enjoyed some recent, albeit limited, success in attacking the doctrine of caveat emptor. Relief has come under theories of tort (primarily fraud, misrepresentation, and a developing doctrine of nondisclosure) and new notions of implied warranty. Statutes have also come to their aid. Key variables for the courts have been whether the property is residential or commercial and whether it is new or used.

A critical issue of quality is the liability of sellers (and others) for pollutants on the property. Environmental issues are addressed at pages 735–800 below.

a. LIABILITY OF SELLER

i. Tort

Buyers have found some relief under tort law. Remedies have been extended to buyers of new and used, commercial and residential properties. It is well established that an action lies for misrepresentation, provided that the assertion was untrue, fraudulent or material, and was reasonably relied upon by the buyer. E. Farnsworth, Contracts 249–272 (2d ed.1990). See Crawford v. Williams, 258 Ga. 806, 375 S.E.2d 223 (1989) (false statement that well was located on property might form basis for fraudulent misrepresentation action but there was no reasonable reliance since buyers made no effort to ascertain the boundaries of the parcel). Courts have recognized claims for fraudulent concealment by equating a seller's action in concealing a defect to a false assertion. See, e.g., Stemple v. Dobson, 184 W.Va. 317, 400 S.E.2d 561 (1990) (sellers disguised termite damage by installing new timbers stained to match old wood).

Many courts have imposed liability on sellers who failed to disclose the condition of the property. Consider the following cases. *Thacker*, involving the nondisclosure of major problems with the home's foundations, represents the modern rule. *Stambovsky* is from a jurisdiction that had continued to find no liability for nondisclosure.

THACKER v. TYREE, 171 W.Va. 110, 113, 297 S.E.2d 885, 888 (1982), MILLER, Chief Justice: [W]e conclude that where a vendor is aware of defects or conditions which substantially affect the value or habitability of the property and the existence of which are unknown to the purchaser and would not be disclosed by a reasonably diligent inspection, then the vendor has a duty to disclose the same to the purchaser. His failure to disclose will give rise to a cause of action in favor of the purchaser. As earlier stated, we express no view as to the ultimate outcome but merely hold that the plaintiff's case could not be dismissed as a matter of law on summary judgment based on the doctrine of *caveat emptor.*

Stambovsky v. Ackley

Supreme Court, Appellate Division, First Department of New York, 1991.
169 A.D.2d 254, 572 N.Y.S.2d 672.

Before MILONAS, J.P., and ROSS, KASSAL, SMITH and RUBIN, JJ.

RUBIN, JUSTICE.

Plaintiff, to his horror, discovered that the house he had recently contracted to purchase was widely reputed to be possessed by poltergeists, reportedly seen by defendant seller and members of her family on numerous occasions over the last nine years. Plaintiff promptly commenced this action seeking rescission of the contract of sale. Supreme Court reluctantly dismissed the complaint, holding that plaintiff has no remedy at law in this jurisdiction.

The unusual facts of this case, as disclosed by the record, clearly warrant a grant of equitable relief to the buyer who, as a resident of New York City, cannot be expected to have any familiarity with the folklore of the Village of Nyack. Not being a "local," plaintiff could not readily learn that the home he had contracted to purchase is haunted. Whether the source of the spectral apparitions seen by defendant seller are parapsychic or psychogenic, having reported their presence in both a national publication ("Readers' Digest") and the local press (in 1977 and 1982, respectively), defendant is estopped to deny their existence and, as a matter of law, the house is haunted. More to the point, however, no divination is required to conclude that it is defendant's promotional efforts in publicizing her close encounters with these spirits which fostered the home's reputation in the community. In 1989, the house was included in a five-home walking tour of Nyack and described in a November 27th newspaper article as "a riverfront Victorian (with ghost)." The impact of the reputation thus created goes to the very essence of the bargain between the parties, greatly impairing both the value of the property and its potential for resale. The extent of this impairment may be presumed for the purpose of reviewing the disposition of this motion to dismiss the cause of action for rescission (*Harris v. City of New York,* 147 A.D.2d 186, 188–189, 542 N.Y.S.2d 550) and represents merely an issue of fact for resolution at trial.

While I agree with Supreme Court that the real estate broker, as agent for the seller, is under no duty to disclose to a potential buyer the phantasmal reputation of the premises and that, in his pursuit of a legal remedy for fraudulent misrepresentation against the seller, plaintiff hasn't a ghost of a chance, I am nevertheless moved by the spirit of equity to allow the buyer to seek rescission of the contract of sale and recovery of his downpayment. New York law fails to recognize any remedy for damages incurred as a result of the seller's mere silence, applying instead the strict rule of caveat emptor. Therefore, the theoretical basis for granting relief, even under the extraordinary facts of this case, is elusive if not ephemeral.

"Pity me not but lend thy serious hearing to what I shall unfold" (William Shakespeare, Hamlet, Act I, Scene V [Ghost]).

From the perspective of a person in the position of plaintiff herein, a very practical problem arises with respect to the discovery of a paranormal phenomenon: "Who you gonna call?" as the title song to the movie "Ghostbusters" asks. Applying the strict rule of caveat emptor to a contract involving a house possessed by poltergeists conjures up visions of a psychic or medium routinely accompanying the structural engineer and Terminix man on an inspection of every home subject to a contract of sale. It portends that the prudent attorney will establish an escrow account lest the subject of the transaction come back to haunt him and his client—or pray that his malpractice insurance coverage extends to supernatural disasters. In the interest of avoiding such untenable consequences, the notion that a haunting is a condition which can and should be ascertained upon reasonable inspection of the premises is a hobgoblin which should be exorcised from the body of legal precedent and laid quietly to rest.

It has been suggested by a leading authority that the ancient rule which holds that mere non-disclosure does not constitute actionable misrepresentation "finds proper application in cases where the fact undisclosed is patent, or the plaintiff has equal opportunities for obtaining information which he may be expected to utilize, or the defendant has no reason to think that he is acting under any misapprehension" (Prosser, Law of Torts § 106, at 696 [4th ed., 1971]). However, with respect to transactions in real estate, New York adheres to the doctrine of caveat emptor and imposes no duty upon the vendor to disclose any information concerning the premises (*London v. Courduff,* 141 A.D.2d 803, 529 N.Y.S.2d 874) unless there is a confidential or fiduciary relationship between the parties (*Moser v. Spizzirro,* 31 A.D.2d 537, 295 N.Y.S.2d 188, affd., 25 N.Y.2d 941, 305 N.Y.S.2d 153, 252 N.E.2d 632; *IBM Credit Fin. Corp. v. Mazda Motor Mfg. (USA) Corp.,* 152 A.D.2d 451, 542 N.Y.S.2d 649) or some conduct on the part of the seller which constitutes "active concealment" (*see, 17 East 80th Realty Corp. v. 68th Associates,* 173 A.D.2d 245, 569 N.Y.S.2d 647 [dummy ventilation system constructed by seller]; *Haberman v. Greenspan,* 82 Misc.2d 263, 368 N.Y.S.2d 717 [foundation cracks covered by seller]). Normally, some affirmative misrepresentation (e.g., *Tahini Invs., Ltd. v. Bobrowsky,* 99 A.D.2d 489, 470 N.Y.S.2d 431 [industrial waste on land allegedly used only as farm]); *Jansen v. Kelly,* 11 A.D.2d 587, 200 N.Y.S.2d 561 [land containing valuable minerals allegedly acquired for use as campsite] or partial disclosure (*Junius Constr. Corp. v. Cohen,* 257 N.Y. 393, 178 N.E. 672 [existence of third unopened street concealed]; *Noved Realty Corp. v. A.A.P. Co.,* 250 App.Div. 1, 293 N.Y.S. 336 [escrow agreements securing lien concealed]) is required to impose upon the seller a duty to communicate undisclosed conditions affecting the premises (contra, *Young v. Keith,* 112 A.D.2d 625, 492 N.Y.S.2d 489 [defective water and sewer systems concealed]).

Caveat emptor is not so all-encompassing a doctrine of common law as to render every act of non-disclosure immune from redress, whether legal or equitable. "In regard to the necessity of giving information which has not been asked, the rule differs somewhat at law and in equity, and while the law courts would permit no recovery of *damages* against a vendor, because of mere concealment of facts *under certain circumstances,* yet if the vendee refused to complete the contract because of the concealment of a material fact on the part of the other, equity would refuse to compel him so to do, because equity only compels the specific performance of a contract which is fair and open, and in regard to which all material matters known to each have been communicated to the other" (*Rothmiller v. Stein,* 143 N.Y. 581, 591–592, 38 N.E. 718 [emphasis added]). Even as a principle of law, long before exceptions were embodied in statute law (see, e.g., UCC 2–312, 313, 314, 315; 3–417[2][e]), the doctrine was held inapplicable to contagion among animals, adulteration of food, and insolvency of a maker of a promissory note and of a tenant substituted for another under a lease (*see, Rothmiller v. Stein,* supra, at 592–593, 38 N.E. 718 and cases cited therein). Common law is not moribund. *Ex facto jus oritur* (law arises out of facts). Where fairness and common sense dictate that an exception should be created, the evolution of the law should not be stifled by rigid application of a legal maxim.

The doctrine of caveat emptor requires that a buyer act prudently to assess the fitness and value of his purchase and operates to bar the purchaser who fails to exercise due care from seeking the equitable remedy of rescission (*see, e.g., Rodas v. Manitaras,* 159 A.D.2d 341, 552 N.Y.S.2d 618). For the purposes of the instant motion to dismiss the action pursuant to CPLR 3211(a)(7), plaintiff is entitled to every favorable inference which may reasonably be drawn from the pleadings . . . specifically, in this instance, that he met his obligation to conduct an inspection of the premises and a search of available public records with respect to title. It should be apparent, however, that the most meticulous inspection and search would not reveal the presence of poltergeists at the premises or unearth the property's ghoulish reputation in the community. Therefore, there is no sound policy reason to deny plaintiff relief for failing to discover a state of affairs which the most prudent purchaser would not be expected to even contemplate (see, *Da Silva v. Musso,* 53 N.Y.2d 543, 551, 444 N.Y.S.2d 50, 428 N.E.2d 382).

The case law in this jurisdiction dealing with the duty of a vendor of real property to disclose information to the buyer is distinguishable from the matter under review. The most salient distinction is that existing cases invariably deal with the physical condition of the premises (*e.g., London v. Courduff, supra* [use as a landfill]; *Perin v. Mardine Realty Co.,* 5 A.D.2d 685, 168 N.Y.S.2d 647 *affd.* 6 N.Y.2d 920, 190 N.Y.S.2d 995, 161 N.E.2d 210 [sewer line crossing adjoining property without owner's consent]), defects in title (*e.g., Sands v. Kissane,* 282 App.Div. 140, 121 N.Y.S.2d 634 [remainderman]), liens against the property (*e.g., Noved Realty Corp. v. A.A.P. Co., supra*), expenses or income (*e.g., Rodas v. Manitaras, supra* [gross receipts]) and other factors affecting its operation. No case has been brought to this court's attention in which the property value was impaired as the result of the reputation created by information disseminated to the public by the seller (or, for that matter, as a result of possession by poltergeists).

Where a condition which has been created by the seller materially impairs the value of the contract and is peculiarly within the knowledge of the seller or unlikely to be discovered by a prudent purchaser exercising due care with respect to the subject transaction, nondisclosure constitutes a basis for rescission as a matter of equity. Any other outcome places upon the buyer not merely the obligation to exercise care in his purchase but rather to be omniscient with respect to any fact which may affect the bargain. No practical purpose is served by imposing such a burden upon a purchaser. To the contrary, it encourages predatory business practice and offends the principle that equity will suffer no wrong to be without a remedy.

Defendant's contention that the contract of sale, particularly the merger or "as is" clause, bars recovery of the buyer's deposit is unavailing. Even an express disclaimer will not be given effect where the facts are peculiarly within the knowledge of the party invoking it (*Danann Realty Corp. v. Harris,* 5 N.Y.2d 317, 322, 184 N.Y.S.2d 599, 157 N.E.2d 597; *Tahini Invs., Ltd. v. Bobrowsky, supra*). Moreover, a fair reading of the merger clause reveals that it expressly disclaims only representations made with respect to the physical condition of the premises and merely makes general reference to representations concerning "any other matter or things affecting or relating to the aforesaid premises". As broad as this language may be, a reasonable interpretation is that its effect is limited to tangible or physical matters and does not extend to paranormal phenomena. Finally, if the language of the contract is to be construed as broadly as defendant urges to encompass the presence of poltergeists in the house, it cannot be said that she has delivered the premises "vacant" in accordance with her obligation under the provisions of the contract rider.

To the extent New York law may be said to require something more than "mere concealment" to apply even the equitable remedy of rescission, the case of *Junius Construction Corporation v. Cohen,* 257 N.Y. 393, 178 N.E. 672, *supra,* while not precisely on point, provides some guidance. In that case, the seller disclosed that an official map indicated two as yet unopened streets which were planned for construction at the edges of the parcel. What was not disclosed was that the same map indicated a third street which, if opened, would divide the plot in half. The court held that, while the seller was under no duty to mention the planned streets at all, having undertaken to disclose two of them, he was obliged to reveal the third (*see also, Rosenschein v. McNally,* 17 A.D.2d 834, 233 N.Y.S.2d 254).

In the case at bar, defendant seller deliberately fostered the public belief that her home was possessed. Having undertaken to inform the public at large, to whom she has no legal relationship, about the supernatural occurrences on her property, she may be said to owe no less a duty to her contract vendee. It has been remarked that the occasional modern cases which permit a seller to take unfair advantage of a buyer's ignorance so long as he is not actively misled are "singularly unappetizing" (Prosser, Law of Torts § 106, at 696 [4th ed. 1971]). Where, as here, the seller not only takes unfair advantage of the buyer's ignorance but has created and perpetuated a condition about which he is unlikely to even inquire, enforcement of the contract (in whole or in part) is offensive to the court's sense of equity. Application of the remedy of rescission, within the bounds of the narrow exception to the doctrine of caveat emptor set forth herein, is entirely appropriate to relieve the unwitting purchaser from the consequences of a most unnatural bargain.

Accordingly, the judgment of the Supreme Court, New York County (Edward H. Lehner, J.), entered April 9, 1990, which dismissed the complaint pursuant to CPLR 3211(a)(7), should be modified, on the law and the facts and in the exercise of discretion, and the first cause of action seeking rescission of the contract reinstated, without costs.

Judgment, Supreme Court, New York County (Edward H. Lehner, J.), entered on April 9, 1990, modified, on the law and the facts and in the exercise of discretion, and the first cause of action seeking rescission of the contract reinstated, without costs.

All concur except MILONAS, J.P. and SMITH, J., who dissent in an opinion by SMITH, J.

SMITH, JUSTICE (dissenting).

I would affirm the dismissal of the complaint by the motion court.

Plaintiff seeks to rescind his contract to purchase defendant Ackley's residential property and recover his down payment. Plaintiff alleges that Ackley and her real estate broker, defendant Ellis Realty, made material misrepresentations of the property in that they failed to disclose that Ackley believed that the house was haunted by poltergeists. Moreover, Ackley shared this belief with her community and the general public through articles published in *Reader's Digest* (1977) and the local newspaper (1982). In November 1989, approximately two months after the parties entered into the contract of sale but subsequent to the scheduled October 2, 1989 closing, the house was included in a five-house walking tour and again described in the local newspaper as being haunted.

Prior to closing, plaintiff learned of this reputation and unsuccessfully sought to rescind the $650,000 contract of sale and obtain return of his $32,500 down payment without resort to litigation. The plaintiff then commenced this action for that relief and alleged that he would not have entered into the contract had he been so advised and that as a result of the alleged poltergeist activity, the market value and resaleability of the property was greatly diminished. Defendant Ackley has counterclaimed for specific performance.

"It is settled law in New York that the seller of real property is under no duty to speak when the parties deal at arm's length. The mere silence of the seller, without some act or conduct which deceived the purchaser, does not amount to a concealment that is actionable as a fraud. . . . The buyer has the duty to satisfy himself as to the quality of his bargain pursuant to the doctrine of caveat emptor, which in New York State still applies to real estate transactions." *London v. Courduff,* 141 A.D.2d 803, 804, 529 N.Y.S.2d 874, *app. dism'd.,* 73 N.Y.2d 809, 537 N.Y.S.2d 494, 534 N.E.2d 332.

The parties herein were represented by counsel and dealt at arm's length. This is evidenced by the contract of sale which, inter alia, contained various riders and a specific provision that all prior understandings and agreements between the parties were merged into the contract, that the contract completely expressed their full agreement and that neither had relied upon any statement by anyone else not set forth in the contract. There is no allegation that defendants, by some specific act, other than the failure to speak, deceived the plaintiff. Nevertheless, a cause of action may be sufficiently stated where there is a confidential or fiduciary relationship creating a duty to disclose and there was a failure to disclose a material fact, calculated to induce a false belief. *County of Westchester v. Welton Becket Assoc.,* 102 A.D.2d 34, 50–51, 478 N.Y.S.2d 305, aff'd., 66 N.Y.2d 642, 495 N.Y.S.2d 364, 485 N.E.2d 1029. However, plaintiff herein has not alleged and there is no basis for concluding that a confidential or fiduciary relationship existed between these parties to an arm's length transaction such as to give rise to a duty to disclose. In addition, there is no allegation that defendants thwarted plaintiff's efforts to fulfill his responsibilities fixed by the doctrine of caveat emptor. *See London v. Courduff, supra,* 141 A.D.2d at 804, 529 N.Y.S.2d 874.

Finally, if the doctrine of caveat emptor is to be discarded, it should be for a reason more substantive than a poltergeist. The existence of a poltergeist is no more binding upon the defendants than it is upon this court.

Based upon the foregoing, the motion court properly dismissed the complaint.

NOTES

1.   *Theoretical Bases.* Various theories have been offered for imposing an obligation on seller to disclose. First, a key factor in finding liability is the relative access of buyer and seller to pertinent information—what each knew or should have known about the purported defect and what the comparative costs are of discovering the information. As the cases indicate, despite seller's increased duty to disclose, the buyer still has a duty to inquire. The buyer will be presumed to have exercised due diligence in examining the title and premises. Consider what information the buyer in *Stambovsky* could have discovered by reasonable inquiry and what information the seller had available. Is the relative sophistication of the parties relevant? Should a buyer be obligated to use a professional inspector to help discover defects? Should newcomers to the neighborhood be treated differently than long term residents? Should the buyer's inspection be limited to the property under contract?

Others see the disclosure duty as part of a changing moral standard in the marketplace. The court in Ollerman v. O'Rourke Co., 94 Wis.2d 17, 30–34, 288 N.W.2d 95, 101–103 (1980) explained:

> Under the doctrine of caveat emptor no person was required to tell all that he or she knew in a business transaction, for in a free market the diligent should not be deprived of the fruits of superior skill and knowledge lawfully acquired. The business world, and the law reflecting business mores and morals, required the parties to a transaction to use their faculties and exercise ordinary business sense, and not to call on the law to stand *in loco parentis* to protect them in their ordinary dealings with other business people. * * * Over the years society's attitudes toward good faith and fair dealing in business transactions have undergone

significant change, and this change has been reflected in the law. * * * The test Dean Keeton derives from the cases to determine when the rule of nondisclosure should be abandoned that is "whenever justice, equity and fair dealing demand it" [quoting Fraud Concealment and Nondisclosure, 15 Tex. L. Rev. 1, 31 (1936)] presents, as one writer states, "a somewhat nebulous standard, praiseworthy as looking toward more stringent business ethics, but possibly difficult of practical application." Case Note, Silence as Fraudulent Concealment Vendor & Purchaser Duty to Disclose, 36 Wash.L.Rev. 202, 204 (1961).

Commentators have examined the effect of disclosure rules on the efficient operation of the marketplace. See Kronman, Mistake, Disclosure, Information, and the Law of Contracts, 7 J.Leg.Stud. 1 (1978) (arguing that there will be a disincentive to obtain information if one must disclose it without compensation, but maintaining that information acquired without much cost should be disclosed); R. Posner, Economic Analysis of Law 97 (3d ed.1986) (noting that a seller does not invest much in discovering defects about his house and so should disclose them, in contrast to a buyer who will be deterred from gathering information about hidden value of the property if he must disclose it). For an excellent discussion of these positions and an added perspective on the issue see Wonnell, The Structure of a General Theory of Nondisclosure, 41 Case W.Res.L.Rev. 329 (1991) (arguing that efficiency gains result from the merger of a resource and information about it, i.e., when a knowing buyer does not disclose, but not when a seller simply severs the resource and information).

On the issue of disclosure in the sale of realty, see Stern, Temporal Dynamics of Disclosure: The Example of Residential Real Estate Conveyancing, 2005 Utah L.Rev. 57; Orth, Sale of Defective Houses, 6 Green Bag 2d 163 (2003); Powell, The Seller's Duty to Disclose in Sales of Commercial Property, 28 Am.Bus.L.J. 245 (1990); Comment, Risk Allocation and the Sale of Defective Used Housing in Ohio—Should Silence be Golden, 20 Capital U.L.Rev. 215 (1991); see also Comment, Commercial Real Estate Buyer Beware: Sellers May Have the Right to Remain Silent, 70 So. Cal. L. Rev. 1571 (1997).

2. *Extent of Disclosure.* What facts must be disclosed? In *Thacker*, there were "major problems" with the foundation due to water under the footers; after the buyers moved in, the house's walls cracked, part of the basement wall collapsed, and the window sills came loose. *Thacker* limited the disclosure obligation to defects that "substantially affect the value or the habitability of the property." Why limit the rule in this way? Does this reflect a concern that a seller might not remember lesser problems and that all buyers of used housing should reasonably expect some minor defects? Did the court in *Stambovsky* actually think that there were ghosts in the house? If not, why find for buyer?

The facts of Weintraub v. Krobatsch, 64 N.J. 445, 447, 317 A.2d 68, 69 (1974), raise the issues of discoverability and the types of defects that must be disclosed. During the executory period, the buyers entered the unoccupied house at night and when they turned on the lights were "astonished to see roaches literally running in all directions, up the walls, drapes, etc." The court ordered rescission of the contract for seller's failure to disclose. Do you agree?

In Mitchell v. Christensen, 31 P.3d 572 (Utah 2001), the purchaser, several times before closing, inspected a backyard swimming pool included in the house sale. The pool was full of water each time, with no visible signs of a leak. Buyer's house inspector reported no problems with the pool based on a visible inspection of the accessible portions of the pool, but advised the buyer to have a licensed pool company perform a full inspection if she was concerned about the pool's inaccessible operating systems. After closing, a number of leaks in the pool's piping were found. The court held that the buyer was not on notice of a possible defect in the inaccessible portions of the pool system. Thus, buyer was not obligated to have hired a pool inspector to check these areas. Is this decision correct?

3. *Jurisdictional Variations.* The New York rule described in *Stambovsky* and the case itself deviate from the developing rules in the area (as exemplified by *Thacker*) on both extremes. (Beach 104 St. Realty, Inc. v. Kisslev-Mazel Realty, LLC, 76 A.D.3d 661, 906 N.Y.S.2d 614 (2010) ("New York adheres to the doctrine of caveat emptor and imposes no duty on the seller or the seller's agent to disclose any information concerning the premises when the parties deal at arm's length, unless there is some conduct on the part of the seller or the seller's agent which constitutes active concealment."))

New York's general refusal to find liability for nondisclosure of physical problems with the property, the court's unwillingness to find a damages remedy, the limitation of relief to rescission, and the opinion's emphasis that relief was appropriate since the problem had been caused by the seller herself, are pro-seller when compared to other jurisdictions. In 2002 New York enacted the "Property Condition Disclosure Act" that requires the seller to deliver to buyer a detailed disclosure statement about the property before the contract for sale is signed. Real Property Law § 462. Curiously, the remedy provisions for breach of the disclosure obligation render the statute a virtual nullity. If seller fails to deliver the statement, the buyer's only remedy is to receive a $500 credit against the purchase price at closing. § 465(1). Thus sellers can easily "opt out" of the statute. Bishop v. Graziano, 10 Misc.3d 342, 804 N.Y.S.2d 236 (2005).

On the other hand, many states have passed statutes relieving the seller from disclosing that the property was the scene of a homicide, other felony, or suicide, or that the prior occupant had AIDS, or that a registered sexual offender lives in the vicinity, even though such facts, like a "haunting," arguably would affect the market price of the property. See, e.g., Ariz. Rev. Stat. § 32–2156; Cal.Civ. Code § 1710.2 (West Supp.1992) (partially superseding Reed v. King, 145 Cal.App.3d 261, 193 Cal.Rptr. 130 (1983)); Conn.Gen.Stat.Ann. § 20–329cc (West Supp.1992); N.M.Ann.Stat. § 47–13–2 (1992); Or.Rev.Stat. § 93.275 (1991).

On the recovery and calculation of damages, see Wall v. Swilley, 562 So.2d 1252 (Miss.1990) (damages should give the purchaser the benefit of the bargain).

4. *Buyer's Disclosure Obligation.* In evaluating seller's obligation to disclose, consider that courts generally hold that a buyer has no duty to disclose information that she knows concerning the property's value which the seller does not know. See E. Farnsworth, Contracts 255–256 (2d ed.1990); Restatement (Second) Torts § 551 (stating exceptions).

In Zaschak v. Traverse Corp., 123 Mich.App. 126, 333 N.W.2d 191 (1983), the court found that plaintiffs failed to state a factual basis to support their assertion that defendant had a duty to disclose certain information regarding the productivity of their property. The court stated:

> [P]laintiffs, despite numerous amendments, failed to state a factual basis to support the assertion that defendant Robert Faith had a duty to disclose certain alleged information regarding the potential productivity of plaintiffs' property. . . . Plaintiff Robert Zaschak testified by deposition that defendant Faith, in response to questioning regarding the property, told plaintiffs that he was unaware of any oil and gas exploration activity in the area. Because Faith possesses a graduate degree in geology and undoubtedly had information regarding oil and gas exploration in the area of plaintiffs' land, we have little doubt that Faith could have concealed material facts from plaintiff. However, Michigan law dictates that a prospective purchaser is under no duty to disclose facts or possible opportunities within his knowledge which materially affect the value of the property. Furman v. Brown, 227 Mich. 629, 199 N.W. 703 (1924); Stuart v. Dorow, 216 Mich. 591, 185 N.W. 662 (1921), see also Williams v. Spurr, 24 Mich. 335 (1872) (no duty by purchaser to disclose the extent and value of iron deposits on the property). Michigan courts have not yet recognized a duty on the part of a vendee to disclose facts relevant to the value of the real estate in question even when specifically asked. We decline to promulgate such a duty on the facts of this case. Although plaintiffs claim that they would not have sold the mineral rights absent Faith's alleged concealment of facts, the record discloses that plaintiffs received what was then the accepted value for the rights, $200 per acre. Moreover, rather than obtain an independent appraisal of the property's mineral potential, plaintiffs relied upon [defendant] Francisco, with whom they have previously settled, who assured them that $200 per acre was the going rate for mineral rights.

Id. at 129–130, 333 N.W.2d at 192–193.

While courts generally agree with *Zaschak* that there is no obligation on buyer to disclose, (see, e.g., Nussbaum v. Weeks, 214 Cal.App.3d 1589, 263 Cal.Rptr. 360 (1989) (buyer who was general manager of water district did not disclose to seller that property was subject to a new water policy which would make it more valuable); Noss v. Abrams, 787 S.W.2d 834 (Mo.App.1990)), some courts do not permit a buyer to conceal information about which she is directly asked. 3 Amer. Law of Property 56–59 (A.J. Casner, ed., 1952).

Were defendant's actions in *Zaschak* ethical? What role does access to information play in the decision? What type of activity does the court's rule reward and what disincentives would be created with a contrary rule?

5. *Statutory Provisions.* Some state legislation mandates disclosure by sellers. See, e.g., Cal.Civil Code § 1102 et seq. (Supp. 1991) (providing specific form of disclosure statement and providing damages remedy); Vanderwier v. Baker, 937 N.E.2d 396 (Ind. App. 2010) (finding seller liable for violation of disclosure obligation under Ind. Code 32–21–5–7). See

Washburn, Residential Real Estate Condition Disclosure Legislation, 44 DePaul L.Rev. 381 (1995); Pancak, Miceli, and Sirmans, Residential Disclosure Laws: The Further Demise of Caveat Emptor, 24 Real Est.L.J. 291 (1996); Note, Ohio's Homeowner Disclosure Law, 45 Case W.Res.L.Rev. 1149 (1995). For an excellent critique of the disclosure legislation, see Weinberger, Let the Buyer Be Well Informed?—Doubting the Demise of Caveat Emptor, 55 Md.L.Rev. 387, 415 (1996) (arguing that disclosure statutes "constitute a brake on the erosion of the doctrine of caveat emptor"); Moore & Smolen, Real Estate Disclosure Forms and Information Transfer, 28 Real Est. L.J. 319 (2000); Lefcoe, Property Condition Disclosure Forms: How the Real Estate Industry Eased the Transition from *Caveat Emptor* to "Seller Tell All," 39 Real Prop. Probate & Tr.J. 193 (2004).

The Interstate Land Sales Full Disclosure Act, 15 U.S.C.A. § 1701 et seq. offers other disclosure requirements. For a comprehensive analysis of the Act, see Malloy, The Interstate Land Sales Full Disclosure Act: Its Requirements, Consequences, and Implications for Persons Participating in Real Estate Development, 24 B.C.L.Rev. 1187 (1983); see also Jaworski, RESPA 1998: The Long and Winding Road, 54 Bus. Law 1357 (1999); Note, An Implied Cause of Action under the Real Estate Settlement Procedures Act, 95 Mich. L. Rev. 1381 (1997).

6.   *Effect of "As Is" Clauses.* Real estate contracts often state that the transfer is made "as is." Most courts find that an "as is" clause will not bar recovery based on fraud. See, e.g., *Weintraub*, discussed above in note 2; Van Der Stok v. Van Voorhees, 151 N.H. 679, 866 A.2d 972 (2005) (misrepresentation concerning potential use of the land); Stemple v. Dobson, 184 W.Va. 317, 400 S.E.2d 561 (1990) (permitting recovery for undisclosed structural damage due to termites). This apparently follows the theory that the fraud tainted the bargaining process concerning the condition of the property so that there could be no meaningful assent by the buyer to the clause. See Ritchey v. Pinnell, 324 S.W.3d 815 (Tex.App.2010) ("as is" clause limited contract action for defects in house with purchaser to rely own inspection, but did not bar fraud claim for false statement on disclosure form that electrical work was done with permits and subject to code requirements). Other courts minimize the applicability of "as is" clauses by holding that they do not limit seller's obligation to disclose *patent* defects, but only latent defects. See S Development Co. v. Pima Capital Management Co., 201 Ariz. 10, 31 P.3d 123 (App.2001) (pipe problem); Syvrud v. Today Real Estate, Inc., 858 So.2d 1125 (Fla.App.2003) (termite infestation). Still, some courts indicate that an "as is" clause which is freely negotiated by a buyer able to assess its risks may be upheld. See Shapiro v. Hu, 188 Cal.App.3d 324, 233 Cal.Rptr. 470 (1986) (clause relieved sellers from liability to buyers who were experienced in business); Van Gessel v. Folds, 210 Ill.App.3d 403, 155 Ill.Dec. 141, 569 N.E.2d 141 (1991); Alires v. McGehee, 277 Kan. 398, 85 P.3d 1191 (2004) (detailed inspection and waiver language in the contract).

7.   *Other Problem Areas.* Must a seller disclose information that affects the value of the property but does not relate to the condition of the land? In McMullen v. Joldersma, 174 Mich.App. 207, 435 N.W.2d 428 (1988) the court found there was no liability for failure to disclose that a highway project would divert traffic from the store being sold. However, there were several grounds for the decision—the fact that the information was of public record, buyers had hired a consultant to investigate and so had relied on him and not the sellers, and the sellers did not have to disclose since the project was still contingent as federal approval and funding had not been obtained.

In Strawn v. Canuso, 140 N.J. 43, 657 A.2d 420 (1995), however, the court held that a builder-developer of residential real estate was obligated to disclose an off-site physical condition, *i.e.*, a landfill that had operated between 1966 and 1978 and had received chemical wastes that it was not licensed to receive. The court held that there must be disclosure if the seller knows of the off-site physical condition, the condition is unknown to the buyer and is not readily observable, and the existence of the condition is of sufficient materiality to affect the habitability, use, or enjoyment of the property and thus renders the property substantially less desirable or valuable to a reasonable buyer. The court ruled that the seller does not, however, have a duty to disclose "transient social conditions in the community that arguably affect the value of property." Id. at 64, 657 A.2d at 431.

The New Jersey legislature limited *Strawn* in the New Residential Real Estate Off-Site Conditions Disclosure Act, passed in 1995. N.J.S.A. 46:3C–1 to–12. Provided sellers meet the disclosure requirement in the Act, buyers are now precluded from suing them for nondisclosure of off-site problems. See Nobrega v. Edison Glen Assocs., 167 N.J. 520, 772 A.2d 368 (2001).

What should the rule be for disclosure of off-site information affecting the value of the land being sold? Is the distinction based on physical conditions viable? See Roberts, Off-Site Conditions and Disclosure Duties: Drawing the Line at the Property Line, 2006 B.Y.U.L.Rev. 957; Comment, Fraud and the Duty to Disclose Off-Site Land Conditions: Actual Knowledge vs. Seller Status, 24 B.C. Envtl. Aff. L. Rev. 897 (1997).

8. *Criminal Liability for Nondisclosure.* Nondisclosure may lead to criminal liability. State v. Brooks, 163 Vt. 245, 658 A.2d 22 (1995), affirmed the involuntary manslaughter convictions of a seller who failed to disclose that a driveway heater leaked poisonous carbon monoxide fumes into the house.

The seller had been aware of the problem (a child of another occupant had become sickened due to fumes), and though subsequently warned of the danger of carbon monoxide poisoning by a heating contractor and the public utility, he did not make the needed repairs. Although the seller showed the buyers how to operate the system when they viewed the house, he did not disclose these facts to his broker or the buyers. The buyers remained unaware of the problem and, along with their daughter, died in their sleep of carbon monoxide poisoning after activating the heater.

ii.　Warranty

Wawak v. Stewart

Supreme Court of Arkansas, 1970.
247 Ark. 1093, 449 S.W.2d 922.

GEORGE ROSE SMITH, JUSTICE.

The defendant-appellant Wawak, a house builder, bought a lot in North Little Rock in the course of his business, built a house on it, and sold it to the appellees Stewart for $28,500. The heating and air-conditioning ductwork had been embedded in the ground before the concrete-slab floor was poured above that ductwork. Some months after the Stewarts moved into the house a serious defect manifested itself, in that heavy rains caused water and particles of fill to seep into the ducts and thence through the floor vents into the interior of the house, with consequent damage that need not be described at the moment.

The Stewarts brought this action for damages. The great question in the case, overshadowing all other issues, is whether there is any implied warranty in a contract by which the builder-vendor of a new house sells it to its first purchaser. The trial court sustained the theory of implied warranty and awarded the Stewarts damages of $1,309.

The trial court was right. Twenty years ago one could hardly find any American decision recognizing the existence of an implied warranty in a routine sale of a new dwelling. Both the rapidity and the unanimity with which the courts have recently moved away from the harsh doctrine of caveat emptor in the sale of new houses are amazing, for the law has not traditionally progressed with such speed.

Yet there is nothing really surprising in the modern trend. The contrast between the rules of law applicable to the sale of personal property and those applicable to the sale of real property was so great as to be indefensible. One who bought a chattel as simple as a walking stick or a kitchen mop was entitled to get his money back if the article was not of merchantable quality. But the purchaser of a $50,000 home ordinarily had no remedy even if the foundation proved to be so defective that the structure collapsed into a heap of rubble.

In the past decade six states have recognized an implied warranty—of inhabitability, sound workmanship, or proper construction—in the sale of new houses by vendors who also built the structures. Carpenter v. Donohoe, 154 Colo. 78, 388 P.2d 399 (1964); Bethlahmy v. Bechtel, 91 Idaho 55, 415 P.2d 698 (1966); Schipper v. Levitt & Sons, 44 N.J. 70, 207 A.2d 314 (1965); Waggoner v. Midwestern Dev. Co., S.D., 154 N.W.2d 803 (1967); Humber v. Morton, Texas, 426 S.W.2d 554, 25 A.L.R.3d 372 (1968); House v. Thornton, Wash., 457 P.2d 199 (1969). The near unanimity of the judges in those cases is noteworthy. Of the 36 justices who made up the six appellate courts, the only dissent noted was that of Justice Griffin in the Texas case, who dissented without opinion.

A few excerpts from those recent opinions will illustrate what seems certain to be the accepted rule of the future. In the *Schipper* case the New Jersey court had this to say:

The law should be based on current concepts of what is right and just and the judiciary should be alert to the never-ending need for keeping its common law principles abreast of the times. Ancient distinctions which make no sense in today's society and tend to discredit the law should be readily rejected.... We consider that there are no meaningful distinctions between Levitt's [a large-scale builder-seller] mass production and sale of homes and the mass production and sale of automobiles and that the pertinent overriding considerations are the same.

Caveat emptor developed when the buyer and seller were in an equal bargaining position and they could readily be expected to protect themselves in the deed. Buyers of mass produced development homes are not on an equal footing with the builder vendors and are no more able to protect themselves in the deed than are automobile purchasers in a position to protect themselves in the bill of sale. Levitt expresses the fear of "uncertainty and chaos" if responsibility for defective construction is continued after the builder vendor's delivery of the deed and its loss of control of the premises, but we fail to see why this should be anticipated or why it should materialize any more than in the products liability field where there has been no such result.

A similar point of view was expressed in the *House* case by the Washington Supreme Court:

As between vendor and purchaser, the builder-vendors, even though exercising reasonable care to construct a sound building, had by far the better opportunity to examine the stability of the site and to determine the kind of foundation to install. Although hindsight, it is frequently said, is 20–20 and defendants used reasonable prudence in selecting the site and designing and constructing the building, their position throughout the process of selection, planning and construction was markedly superior to that of their first purchaser-occupant. To borrow an idea from equity, of the innocent parties who suffered, it was the builder-vendor who made the harm possible. If there is a comparative standard of innocence, as well as of culpability, the defendants who built and sold the house were less innocent and more culpable than the wholly innocent and unsuspecting buyer. Thus, the old rule of caveat emptor has little relevance to the sale of a brand-new house by a vendor-builder to a first buyer for purposes of occupancy.

We apprehend it to be the rule that, when a vendor-builder sells a new house to its first intended occupant, he impliedly warrants that the foundations supporting it are firm and secure and that the house is structurally safe for the buyer's intended purpose of living in it. Current literature on the subject overwhelmingly supports this idea of an implied warranty of fitness in the sale of new houses.

To sum up, upon the facts before us in the case at bar we have no hesitancy in adopting the modern rule by which an implied warranty may be recognized in the sale of a new house by a seller who was also the builder. That rule, however, is a departure from our earlier cases; so, to avoid injustice, we adhere to the doctrine announced in Parish v. Pitts, [244 Ark. 1239, 429 S.W.2d 45 (1968)] by which the new rule is made applicable only to the case at hand and to causes of action arising after this decision becomes final.

There are three subordinate points that require discussion. First Wawak insists that all warranties, express or implied, were negatived by this paragraph in the offer-and-acceptance agreement that preceded the execution of a warranty deed when the sale was consummated:

> Buyer certifies that he has inspected the property and he is not relying upon any warranties, representations or statements of the Agent or Seller as to age or physical condition of improvements.

Even if we assume that the preliminary contract was not merged in the warranty deed, we think it plain that the quoted paragraph did not exclude an implied warranty with respect to the particular defect now in question, which lay beneath the concrete floor and could not possibly have been discovered by even the most careful inspection. The quoted paragraph does not purport to exclude all warranties. It merely states that the buyer has inspected the property and is not *relying* on any warranties as to the age or physical condition of the improvements. Construing the printed contract against the seller, who evidently prepared it, we hold that the clause applies only to defects that might reasonably have been discovered in the course of an inspection made by a purchaser of average experience in such matters.

Secondly, the trial court's judgment for $1,309 was composed of the following items of damage to the house and its furnishings, none of which the Stewarts had yet paid:

To clean rug	$75.00
To paint house (interior)	235.00
To clean furniture	22.00
To replace lamp shades	35.00
To clean duct system	200.00
To replace draperies	300.00
Minor repairs	22.00
Drain tile to correct leakage	420.00
	$1,309.00

Wawak insists that the recovery of the foregoing items is barred by the rule that a plaintiff must use reasonable care to mitigate his damages and that if the damages could have been avoided at reasonable expense then the measure of damages is the amount of such expense.

The pertinent facts are these: The subterranean ductwork radiates from a metal chamber or plenum, which sits under the heating and air-conditioning units. When Wawak and his ductwork subcontractor, Plummer, were first notified by Stewart of the seepage, they siphoned off the water through the plenum. They next installed drain tile and gravel along two sides of the house, but those measures failed to correct the trouble. In the meantime Stewart bought a sump pump at a cost of $12.50. Whenever rains caused seepage in the ductwork Stewart would place his pump in the plenum, about two hours after the water had accumulated, and pump the duct system dry. Under that procedure some of the seepage got into the house and caused most of the damage that we have itemized above.

Soon after the difficulty first arose Wawak and Plummer proposed the installation of an automatic sump pump, which cost $76 or $78. Their plan was to dig out the floor of the plenum so that the automatic pump would be below the level of the ducts. Whenever the water at the site of the pump rose to a depth of three quarters of an inch the pump would start automatically and pump out the water. Thus the water would never rise high enough to overflow the floor vents and damage the interior of the house. Wawak and Plummer do not contend that their plan would have corrected the subterranean defect. From Wawak's testimony: "I figured if we could get the pump in there to pump it out, then we could continue to try to find out where [the water] was coming from. It wasn't our intention to just leave it." Wawak stated that when he offered to put in the automatic pump there was no damage to the house except some staining of the draperies, which were cleaned at Wawak's expense.

Stewart refused to allow the automatic pump to be installed, insisting that he wanted to know where the water was coming from and would accept nothing less. When the proffer of the pump was refused, Wawak and Plummer abandoned their efforts to correct the trouble. Thereafter Stewart used his own pump in the manner that we have described, with attendant damage to the house and its furnishings. A period of two years or more elapsed before this action was finally brought.

In the main Wawak is correct in his argument that the Stewarts should have mitigated their damages by permitting the installation of the automatic pump. On the record made below it is an undisputed fact that such a pump would have avoided practically all the itemized damages that were allowed by the trial court.

The pump, however, would not have corrected the basic defect, nor does Wawak so contend. Stewart testified without contradiction and without objection that a man named Gordon could remedy the defect by installing drain tile along the remaining two sides of the house at a cost of $425. That corrective measure would not have been rendered unnecessary by the installation of the automatic pump; so the Stewarts' duty to mitigate their damages does not involve that item. The amount of the Stewarts' judgment will therefore be reduced to $420—the amount allowed by the trial court for the one item of damage that we find to be recoverable.

Thirdly, Wawak argues that he is entitled to judgment over against the appellee Plummer, who installed the ductwork under a subcontract with Wawak. It cannot be said as a matter of law, however, that Plummer was at fault, because the slab floor above the ducts was poured by another subcontractor. Upon this point the trial court's judgment is sufficiently supported by the proof.

The judgment as modified is affirmed.

HARRIS, C.J., and FOGLEMAN and BYRD, JJ., dissent.

[The opinions of FOGLEMAN, J., dissenting in part, and concurring in part, and BYRD, J., dissenting, are omitted.]

Blagg v. Fred Hunt Co., Inc.

Supreme Court of Arkansas, 1981.
272 Ark. 185, 612 S.W.2d 321.

DUDLEY, JUSTICE.

The appellee, Fred Hunt Company, Inc., a house builder, bought a lot in the Pleasant Valley Addition to Little Rock, built a house on it, and sold it to the Dentons on October 9, 1978. The Dentons sold the house to the American Foundation Life Insurance Company, which on June 29, 1979, sold the house to appellants, J. Ted Blagg and Kathye Blagg. This purchase by appellants was made a few days less than 9 months after the date of the original sale. The appellants filed a two-count complaint alleging that after they purchased the home a strong odor and fumes from formaldehyde became apparent. They traced this defect to the carpet and pad which was installed by appellee. A motion to dismiss was filed by the appellee and the trial court granted the motion on count one of the complaint, the implied warranty count, on the basis of lack of privity. The court denied the motion on count two, which is framed in terms of strict liability.

When considering a motion to dismiss a complaint pursuant to Arkansas Rules of Civil Procedure, Rule 12(b)(6), on the ground that it fails to state a claim on which relief can be granted, the facts alleged in the complaint are treated as true and are viewed in the light most favorable to the party seeking relief.

Count one of the complaint is based upon an implied warranty. The trial judge dismissed this count because the appellants are not in privity with the appellee. This court, in Wawak v. Stewart, 247 Ark. 1093, 449 S.W.2d 922 (1970), abandoned the doctrine of caveat emptor and took the view that a builder-vendor impliedly warranted the home to the first purchaser. The issue of first impression in this case is whether the liability of the builder-vendor should be extended to a second or third purchaser.

Since *Wawak,* the original homebuyer has been able to place reliance on the builder-vendor's implied warranty. This has protected that investment which, in most instances, represents the family's largest single expenditure.

We find no reason that those same basic concepts should not be extended to subsequent purchasers of real estate. This is an area of the law being developed on a case by case basis. Our ruling is based on the complaint before us and involves a home which had a defect that became apparent to the third purchasers, the appellants, within 9 months of the original sale date. Obviously, there is a point in time beyond which the implied warranty will expire and that time should be based on a standard of reasonableness.

We hold that the builder-vendor's implied warranty of fitness for habitation runs not only in favor of the first owner, but extends to subsequent purchasers for a reasonable length of time where there is no substantial change or alteration in the condition of the building from the original sale. This implied warranty is limited to latent defects which are not discoverable by subsequent purchasers upon reasonable inspection and which become manifest only after the purchase. Wyoming adopted this rule in a well reasoned opinion. Moxley v. Laramie Builders, Inc., 600 P.2d 733 (Wyo.1979).

Appellants next contend that even if the implied warranty extends to subsequent purchasers, we should affirm the trial court as there is an express warranty which is exclusive. We do not consider this argument as the complaint does not allege an express warranty, and the sufficiency of the complaint is all that is tested.

We hold that count one of the complaint should not have been dismissed.

Appellee, in its cross-appeal, contends that the trial judge committed error in not dismissing count two of the complaint, the claim for damages under strict liability. We affirm the trial judge's ruling.

Our strict liability statute, Ark.Stat.Ann. § 85–2–318.2 (Supp.1979) is as follows:

Liability of Supplier-Conditions.—A supplier of a product is subject to liability in damages for harm to a person or to property if:

(a) the supplier is engaged in the business of manufacturing, assembling, selling, leasing or otherwise distributing such product;

(b) the product was supplied by him in a defective condition which rendered it unreasonably dangerous; and

(c) the defective condition was a proximate cause of the harm to person or to property. [Acts 1973, No. 111, § 1, p. 331.]

This 1973 act broadens somewhat § 402(A) of the Restatement, Second, Torts (1965). . . .

Our first issue is whether this strict liability statute encompasses count two of the complaint. It is an oversimplification, but correct, to state that the construction of the word "product" is determinative. To decide the proper construction we have examined the few cases in other jurisdictions and various treatises.

Judge Henry Woods in The Personal Injury Action in Warranty— Has the Arkansas Strict Liability Statute Rendered it Obsolete?, 28 Ark.L.R. 335 (1974), gives a most perceptive preview of the real issue. He notes that we must choose between the persuasive reasoning of two outstanding jurists—Chief Justice Traynor in Seely v. White Motor Company, 63 Cal.2d 9, 403 P.2d 145, 45 Cal.Rptr. 17 (1965), and Justice Francis in Santor v. A & M Karagheusian, Inc., 44 N.J. 52, 207 A.2d 305 (1965). If the Traynor view is adopted, the implied warranty will be very much alive when a purchaser is suing for purely economic loss from a defective product. His view, as stated in *Seely,* supra, is that when economic losses result from commercial transactions, as here, the parties should be relegated to the law of sales:

Although the rules governing warranties complicated resolution of the problems of personal injuries, there is no reason to conclude that they do not meet the "needs of commercial transactions." The law of warranty "grew as a branch of the law of commercial transactions and was primarily aimed at controlling the commercial aspects of these transactions." . . .

Although the rules of warranty frustrate rational compensation for physical injury, they function well in a commercial setting.

Justice Francis, in *Santor,* supra, prophetically extended the doctrine in a case involving carpeting that developed a defect, a purely economic loss, not a personal injury. In applying the doctrine of strict liability for purely economic loss he said:

The obligation of the manufacturer thus becomes what in justice it ought to be—an enterprise liability, and one which should not depend on the law of sales. . . .

After lengthy consideration, we choose to adopt the views of Justice Francis. We find no valid reason for holding that strict liability should not apply to property damage in a house sold by a builder-vendor. Accordingly, in construing the Arkansas strict liability statute, we hold that the word "product" is as applicable to a house as to an automobile.

Reversed and remanded on direct appeal; affirmed on cross-appeal.

NOTES

1.   *Incidence of Housing Defects.* A government study, based on a sample of new housing built in 1977 and 1978, revealed that 79% of new housing buyers had at least one complaint about housing quality. Seventy-five percent of the problems were discovered in the first six months of ownership, and ninety-three percent in the first year. According to the study, builders were most ready to correct defects in plumbing, cooling and heating systems, in major appliances and in interior electrical work. They were less willing to correct problems with yard drainage, roofs, foundations and driveways and improperly fitted doors and windows. Seven percent of buyers reported that they consulted a lawyer about the problem and four percent retained lawyers. U.S. Dept. of Housing & Urban Development and Federal Trade Commission, A Survey of Homeowner Experience with New Residential Housing Construction iii–viii, 10–29 (1980).

2.   *New Housing.* The implied warranty of fitness represents the main avenue today for buyers of defective new housing to recover from their builder-sellers. With roots in both contract and tort theory, the warranty of fitness has made substantial inroads on *caveat emptor,* giving disappointed buyers an easier and more complete remedy than fraud or negligence. By recent count, forty-two states imply a warranty into new housing sales, variously calling it a warranty of "quality," "habitability," "good workmanship," or "fitness." See Shedd, The Implied Warranty of Habitability: New Implications, New Applications, 8 Real Est.L.J. 291 (1980).

The origin of implied housing warranties can be traced to two English cases decided in the 1930's, Miller v. Cannon Hill Estates, Ltd., 2 K.B. 113,

1 All E.R. 93 (1931), and Perry v. Sharon Development Co., 4 All E.R. 390 (C.A.1937), in which plaintiffs, who had contracted to buy houses under construction, found upon occupying the completed houses that they were defective. The courts could have decided the cases by analogy to either of two black-letter rules of law: the standard rule of *caveat emptor* in sales of completed housing, which would have required a holding for the builders; or the rule entitling landowners to recover for substandard work by builders in their employ, which would have required a holding for the buyers. In both cases, the courts chose the latter rule. "In the first place, the maxim *caveat emptor* cannot apply, since the buyer, insofar as the house is not yet completed, cannot inspect it, either by himself or by his surveyor, and, in the second place, from the point of view of the vendor, the contract is not merely a contract to sell, but also a contract to do building work, and, insofar as it is a contract to do building work, it is only natural and proper that there should be an implied undertaking that the building work should be done properly." Perry v. Sharon Development Co., 4 All E.R. at 395–396.

The English rule on uncompleted houses was picked up by American courts in the 1950's. It was only a matter of time before the rule's underlying rationale would be extended to the purchase of a completed house. The occasion came in Carpenter v. Donohoe, 154 Colo. 78, 388 P.2d 399 (1964), where the buyer complained that a crumbling cellar wall impaired habitability. Noting that the wall's construction did not comply with the local building code, the court held for the buyer in terms that were to become familiar in the decisions that soon followed: "There is an implied warranty that builder-vendors had complied with the building code of the area in which the structure is located. Where, as here, a home is the subject of sale, there are implied warranties that the home was built in workmanlike manner and is suitable for habitation." 154 Colo. at 83–84, 388 P.2d at 402.

For a superb analysis of the history and doctrinal implications of seller's liability for housing defects, see Roberts, The Case of the Unwary Home Buyer: The Housing Merchant Did It, 52 Cornell L.Rev. 835 (1967). For an excellent analysis of the competing theories, see Sovern, Toward A Theory of Warranties in Sales of New Homes: Housing the Implied Warranty Advocates, Law and Economics Mavens, and Consumer Psychologists Under One Roof, 1993 Wis.L.Rev. 13. For general background see Bearman, Caveat Emptor in Sales of Realty—Recent Assaults Upon the Rule, 14 Vand.L.Rev. 541 (1961); Bixby, Let the Seller Beware: Remedies for the Purchase of a Defective Home, 49 J. of Urb.L. 533 (1971); Haskell, The Case for an Implied Warranty of Quality in Sales of Real Property, 53 Geo.L.J. 633 (1965); McNamara, The Implied Warranty in New-House Construction, 1 Real Est.L.J. 43 (1972); McNamara, The Implied Warranty in New-House Construction Revisited, 3 Real Est.L.J. 136 (1974). See also Powell & Mallor, The Case for an Implied Warranty of Quality in Sales of Commercial Real Estate, 68 Wash.U.L.Q. 305 (1990).

3. *Who Is Liable?* Courts have declined to impose liability under warranty theory on a non-builder seller of a used home. In Stevens v. Bouchard, 532 A.2d 1028 (Me.1987), the court stated that a builder-vendor of a new home "has ultimate control over the habitability of the premises. To hold a homeowner who had no part in the construction to the same level of accountability offends considerations of fairness and common sense."

Courts may stretch, however, in defining who is a builder-vendor. In Callander v. Sheridan, 546 N.E.2d 850, 852 (Ind.App.1989), a person, not a professional builder, who acted as his own general contractor for the building of his home was held under warranty as a builder-vendor for defects in the house. The court noted that he obtained and modified plans, hired and supervised subcontractors, and bought construction materials. "Apparently [defendant] felt he was qualified to act as a general contractor. Since he undertook this responsibility he must also accept the attached liability of a builder-vendor to a subsequent buyer." Do the reasons expressed in *Wawak* for the warranty of habitability apply in this situation? Compare Oliver v. Superior Court, 211 Cal.App.3d 86, 259 Cal.Rptr. 160 (1989) (holding that a person who built only two homes was not a builder-vendor for the purposes of strict liability recovery for defective housing).

4. *Used Housing.* Most residential sales involve used rather than new housing. Should buyers of used housing be able to recover for latent defects against either the original builder or their immediate seller? Warranty actions brought against homebuilders by second and subsequent buyers are usually dismissed for lack of privity. Warranty actions against the immediate seller, with whom the second or subsequent buyer is in privity, are usually dismissed on the ground that the requisite inequality of expertise between buyer and seller is missing.

More recently, as indicated in *Blagg,* the privity bar to warranty actions has begun to give way, although some courts still decline to extend the warranty to subsequent purchasers. See, for example, Haygood v. Burl Pounders Realty, Inc., 571 So.2d 1086 (Ala.1990); Calloway v. City of Reno, 116 Nev. 250, 993 P.2d 1259 (2000). What reasons are there for *not* extending implied warranty protections to buyers of used housing? Consider some reservations expressed by the Mississippi Supreme Court:

> "Material and workmanship which may go into a structure are of infinite variety. An original purchaser of land on which a building is situated, for reasons of economy or for any other reason, may be satisfied, and may accept it from the builder in any condition in which it may be. . . . It would be strange indeed if, when the original purchaser conveyed the property to another, that his vendee could resort to the builder for damages for deficiencies in workmanship or materials which the original purchaser from the builder had accepted. . . . Real estate transactions require a written contract or deed, and a purchaser may insist upon having included therein any warranty or guaranty that he may desire as to buildings standing upon it, and, of course, he may refuse to purchase if the prospective vendor will not agree." Oliver v. City Builders, Inc., 303 So.2d 466, 468–469 (Miss.1974).

Representing a developer, would you be comfortable with *Blagg*'s extension of the implied warranty "for a reasonable length of time"? Other courts extending the warranty have been similarly uninstructive about the duration of the builder's exposure. See, for example, Redarowicz v. Ohlendorf, 92 Ill.2d 171, 65 Ill.Dec. 411, 441 N.E.2d 324 (1982). Can a developer protect itself against warranty liability to second and successive purchasers by obtaining from its immediate buyer an express disclaimer of any implied warranties? Is indeterminate liability likely to induce developers to build houses that are more durable—and probably more expensive—than their immediate buyers might desire?

See generally O'Brien, Caveat Venditor: A Case for Granting Subsequent Purchasers A Cause of Action Against Builder-Vendors for Latent Defects in the Home, 20 J.Corp.L. 525 (1995); Comment, Builder's Liability to New and Subsequent Purchasers, 20 Sw.U.L.Rev. 219 (1991); Note, Builders' Liability for Latent Defects in Used Homes, 32 Stan.L.Rev. 607 (1980).

5.   *Where's the Breach?* Like *Wawak,* most courts that have implied a warranty of fitness into sales of new housing have reasoned by analogy to the warranty of fitness implied into sales of personal property. Are there any differences between real and personal property that make the analogy inapt? That should affect the determination of what kinds of defects will breach the warranty? See generally, Rabin & Grossman, Defective Products or Realty Causing Economic Loss: Toward a Unified Theory of Recovery, 12 Sw.U.L.Rev.5 (1981).

Justice Fogleman, dissenting in part and concurring in part in *Wawak,* objected to the majority's failure to address the question whether the warranty in fact had been breached. Noting that the implied warranty "does not impose upon the builder an obligation to deliver a perfect house," he concluded that the evidence "simply does not show the breach of any implied warranty." Specifically, he objected to the effective ruling of the lower court "that, without any proof or evidence, the house was not constructed in a good workmanlike manner and, without any proof whatever as to the cause of the problem, appellees should recover simply because they bought a new house and subsequently a water situation developed." 247 Ark. at 1101, 449 S.W.2d at 930.

Samuelson v. A.A. Quality Construction, Inc., 230 Mont. 220, 749 P.2d 73 (1988), imposed an unusually strict standard. The court stated that the warranty is "limited to defects which are so substantial as reasonably to preclude the use of the dwelling as a residence," and held that water seepage into the basement affecting a guest bedroom, storage area, recreation area, and crawl space and requiring removal of furniture, carpeting and sheetrock, necessitating the use of floor heaters and pumps, and restricting the use of some areas did not violate the standard. The house cost $155,000 and the buyers had to pay more than $11,000 to remedy the problems. Justice Harrison in dissent wrote that the majority "has taken a giant step backwards in protecting the consumer. . . . Had the basement not been repaired at a cost of over $11,000 by another contractor, about all that it could have been used for would have been a fishery during the periods that it leaked. Surely, a homeowner is entitled to more than that." Id. at 225, 749 P.2d at 76.

6.   *Disclaimers.* Most courts that imply a warranty of fitness into the sale of new housing will also allow seller and buyer to contract around the implied warranty. Yet there is a general disposition to construe disclaimers and "as is" provisions against builder-sellers. *Wawak* is typical in holding that, strictly construed, the disclaimer clause did not exclude an implied warranty with respect to latent defects—"the clause applies only to defects that might reasonably have been discovered in the course of an inspection made by a purchaser of average experience in such matters."

Indiana, for example, has a statute that permits a builder-vendor to disclaim all warranties. Ind.Code § 34–4–20.5. To do so, however, the builder must give certain express warranties. These include warranties against defects in the structure for ten years, roof materials and workmanship for four years, and electrical, plumbing and heating for two years. Some courts, however, indicate that any attempt to disclaim an implied warranty is void as against public policy. See Buchanan v. Scottsdale Environmental Construction and Development Co., 163 Ariz. 285, 787 P.2d 1081 (App.1989), review denied.

See generally, Abney, Disclaiming the Implied Real Estate Common-Law Warranties, 17 Real Est.L.J. 141 (1988); Powell, Disclaimers of Implied Warranty in the Sale of New Homes, 34 Vill.L.Rev. 1123 (1989); Note, The Implied Warranty of Habitability in the Sale of New Homes: Disclaiming Liability in Illinois, 1987 U.Ill.L.Rev. 649.

7. *The Home Owners Warranty Program.* The Home Owners Warranty (HOW) program was initiated in 1973 by the National Association of Home Builders to provide warranty protection for new owner occupied single-family houses, townhouses, and condominiums. Note, The Home Owners Warranty Program: An Initial Analysis, 28 Stan.L.Rev. 357 (1976). Under the program, builders issued warranties to buyers of new homes, and the HOW Insurance Corp. underwrote these. See Home Warranty Corp. v. Elliott, 572 F.Supp. 1059, 1063 (D.Del.1983); Cobert v. Home Owners Warranty Corp., 239 Va. 460, 391 S.E.2d 263 (1990). The corporation was, however, seized by state regulators on the ground that it had inadequate funds to meet future claims. Reports indicate that, since taking over, state regulators have paid roughly forty cents on the dollar for valid claims. Rees, 500 HOW Claims Paid; 2,000 Filed, Richmond Times-Dispatch, 3/4/95, sec. C, p. 1; Lehman, Home Warranty Plan to Pay Only 40 Cents on Dollar, Orlando Sentinel, 2/5/95, p. J1. See Comment, Constructing a Solution to California's Construction Defect Problem, 30 McGeorge L. Rev. 299 (1999) (suggesting a warranty program).

8. *State Statutes.* State warranty legislation ranges from statutes like Maryland's Real Property Code, §§ 10–201 et seq. (1981 & Supp.1991) and New York's General Business Law § 777 (McKinney Supp. 1991), which follow the general contours of the common law implied warranty, to New Jersey's far more ambitious New Home Warranty and Builders' Registration Act, N.J.Stat.Ann. 46:3B–1 et seq. (1977).

The Maryland statute implies into sales of improved residential real property a warranty that the improvement (defined as a newly constructed private dwelling unit), is habitable, free from faulty materials and constructed according to sound engineering standards in a workmanlike manner. The warranty lasts for one year after closing and excludes any defect that inspection by a reasonably diligent first buyer would have disclosed. The warranty may be waived or modified only through a writing signed by the purchaser that specifically describes the warranty waived and the terms of the new agreement. The statute implies a warranty of fitness for a particular purpose, and also provides that an express warranty is created by a written affirmation of fact or promise, a written description of the improvement, or a sample model that is part of the basis of the bargain. An amendment in 1990 added a two year statute of limitation for claims for structural defects.

The New York statute makes the seller liable for one year for failure to build in a "skillful manner," for two years for defects in major systems (e.g., heat, electrical), and for six years for "material defects" as defined in the statute. The statute preempts common law actions for builder defects. Fumarelli v. Marsam Development Co., 92 N.Y.2d 298, 680 N.Y.S.2d 440, 703 N.E.2d 251 (1998). On the statute in general, see Note, The New York Housing Merchant Warranty Statute: Analysis and Proposals, 75 Corn.L.Rev. 754 (1990). See generally, Grand, Implied and Statutory Warranties in the Sale of Real Estate: The Demise of Caveat Emptor, 15 Real Est.L.J. 44 (1986).

The New Jersey statute directs the Commissioner of the Department of Community Affairs to prescribe home warranties incorporating quality standards for construction materials and methods. The warranty's duration will depend on its subject matter—two years for defects caused by faulty installation of plumbing, electrical, heating and cooling systems, and ten years for major construction defects including damages due to soil subsidence. The builder's liability extends not only to the initial buyer but also to any subsequent buyer whose claim arises during the applicable warranty period. The ceiling on liability is the purchase price of the home in the first good faith sale.

A builder must register with the Department to build houses in New Jersey. One condition of registration is that the builder participate in a warranty security fund, established by the Act, or an approved alternative fund. The fund provides a back-up source of compensation when fund participants have not themselves made good on valid homeowner claims. Before making a claim against the fund, a homeowner must notify the builder of the defects and allow a reasonable time for their repair. Once a claim is made against the fund, it is reviewed through a conciliation or arbitration procedure administered by the Department. If a defect is found, the builder is ordered to correct it and, failing that, the owner is allowed to recover from the fund. While the Act does not preempt private law remedies, it does require the homeowner to elect between statutory and common law relief.

Additionally, generic consumer protection laws may provide relief for the disappointed home purchaser. See, e.g., Forton v. Laszar, 239 Mich.App. 711, 609 N.W.2d 850 (2000) (finding home building constitutes "trade or commerce," making false representation that builder would follow building plans a deceptive act violating the Michigan Consumer Protection Act).

9. *Federal Law.* The Magnuson-Moss Act, 15 U.S.C.A. § 2301 et seq., though primarily concerned with warranties made in connection with the sale of "consumer products," partially covers home sale warranties by defining consumer products to include "any such property intended to be attached to or installed in any real property without regard to whether it is so attached or installed." Congressman Moss gave as examples of housing components covered by the Act, "any separate equipment such as heating and air-conditioning systems which are sold with a new home. However, the definition would not apply to items such as dry wall pipes, or wiring which are not separate items of equipment but are rather integral component parts of a home." 120 Cong.Rec. 31323 (1974). The Act does not apply to any written warranty otherwise governed by federal law, thus apparently exempting the warranties that builders are required to give as a condition to obtaining FHA, VA or Farmer's Home Administration financing assistance. See generally, Peters, How the Magnuson-Moss Warranty Act Affects the Builder/Seller of New Housing, 5 Real Est.L.J. 338 (1977).

b.   Liability of Lenders and Others

Overview of Lender Liability

"Lender liability" litigation has increased over the past decade. Borrowers, and sometimes junior lenders and lienors, have successfully asserted claims subjecting lenders to damages, reduced lien priority, or the loss of remedies usually available in the event of default, foreclosure, or bankruptcy of the borrower. Courts have employed a broad range of common law theories to hold the lender liable. Among others, these include fraud, breach of fiduciary duty, duress, failure to act in good faith, excessive control of the borrower, intentional infliction of emotional distress, joint venture theory, principal-agent violations, equitable subordination, negligence in loan administration, misrepresentation, and aiding and abetting liability, as well as R.I.C.O (18 U.S.C.A. § 1961 et seq.), federal tax and securities laws, and the Comprehensive Environmental Response, Compensation and Liability Act (see pages 735–752. See Chaitman, The Ten Commandments for Avoiding Lender Liability, 22 U.C.C.L.J. 3 (1989)); Ebke and Griffin, Lender Liability to Debtors: Toward a Conceptual Framework, 40 Sw.L.J. 775 (1986); Johnson, Lender Liability Checklist: A Summary of Current Theories and Developments, 59 U.M.K.C.L.Rev. 205 (1991); Lawrence, Lender Control Liability: An Analytical Model Illustrated with Applications to the Relational Theory of Secured Financing, 62 S.Cal.L.Rev. 1387 (1989); E. Mannino, Lender Liability and Banking Litigation (1991); Comment, Stemming the Tide of Lender Liability: Judicial and Legislative Reactions, 67 Denver U.L.Rev. 453 (1990); Comment, What's So Good About Good Faith? The Good Faith Performance Obligation in Commercial Lending, 55 U.Chi.L.Rev. 1335 (1988); Special Project: Lender Liability, 42 Vand.L.Rev. 852 (1989).

The acts for which lenders have been held liable also vary widely. They include improper interference with the borrower's corporate entity (see State National Bank v. Farah Manufacturing Co., 678 S.W.2d 661 (Tex.App.1984)), refusal to lend funds which have been orally promised (see Landes Construction Co. v. Royal Bank of Canada, 833 F.2d 1365 (9th Cir.1987)), failure to obtain credit life insurance for borrower as bank had represented (see Walters v. First National Bank, 69 Ohio St.2d 677, 433 N.E.2d 608 (1982)), lack of adherence to standard policy in denying a loan (see Jacques v. First National Bank, 307 Md. 527, 515 A.2d 756 (1986)), calling a $7 million loan when interest payment was late by only less than one day (see Sahadi v. Continental Illinois National Bank & Trust Co., 706 F.2d 193 (7th Cir.1983)), and failure to give notice before discontinuing funding (see K.M.C. Co. v. Irving Trust, 757 F.2d 752 (6th Cir.1985)).

The only common feature linking the diverse theories of these "lender liability" cases is that they all involve an attempt to make a lender responsible for a claimed harm. The courts have done little to articulate a general theory of lender liability and have focused only on the particular legal doctrine raised in the case. But some larger influences at work, among them, evolving expectations about business practices, articulation of a norm of reasonable lending behavior, a developing notion that a party should not carelessly injure another even though under traditional doctrine there is no duty, and a sense, at least in the early 1980's, that lenders have deep pockets and are able to spread the risk among the class of borrowers.

In recent years, however, the tide has turned against lender liability. Some commentators have questioned the doctrine. For a thoughtful critique, see Fischel, The Economics of Lender Liability, 99 Yale L.J. 131 (1989) (maintaining that the doctrine as evolved by the courts is often based on a misunderstanding of basic economic principles). Moreover, various recent cases have severely blunted some of the most important arrows in the lender liability quiver. In Kham & Nate's Shoes No. 2, Inc. v. First Bank of Whiting, 908 F.2d 1351 (7th Cir.1990), the court held that a lender which terminated the borrower's line of credit was not subject to loss of priority by equitable subordination in a bankruptcy proceeding of the borrower. Judge Easterbrook, writing for the unanimous panel, noted that even though the lender knew that its action would be detrimental to the borrower, it did not engage in "inequitable conduct" and use its contractual rights as a lever to get a better deal:

> Firms that have negotiated contracts are entitled to enforce them to the letter, even to the great discomfort of their trading partners, without being mulcted for lack of "good faith." Although courts often refer to the obligation of good faith that exists in every contractual relation [citations omitted], this is not an invitation to the court to decide whether one party ought to have exercised privileges expressly reserved in the document. "Good faith" is a compact reference to an implied undertaking not to take opportunistic advantage in a way that could not have been contemplated at the time of drafting, and which therefore was not resolved explicitly by the parties. When the contract is silent, principles of good faith . . . fill the gap. They do not block use of terms that actually appear in the contract.

Id. at 1357. See also Penthouse International, Ltd. v. Dominion Federal Savings and Loan Ass'n, 855 F.2d 963 (2d Cir.1988), cert. denied, 490 U.S. 1005, 109 S.Ct. 1639, 104 L.Ed.2d 154 (1989), (reproduced at page 604 below); Ex parte Farmers Exchange Bank, 783 So.2d 24 (Ala.2000) (no liability for failure to disclose termite problem, even though it was alleged that bank prepared legal documents in the transaction, told borrower that she did not need a lawyer, and gave borrower the termite certificate but not the underlying report disclosing the damage); Mitsui Manufacturers Bank v. Superior Court, 212 Cal.App.3d 726, 260 Cal.Rptr. 793 (1989) (finding no special relationship of trust or confidence between the usual lender and borrower which can be the basis of tort liability); Gillman v. Chase Manhattan Bank, N.A., 73 N.Y.2d 1, 537 N.Y.S.2d 787, 534 N.E.2d 824 (1988) (reversing finding that form lending agreement was unconscionable and finding borrower had other choices and an opportunity to consult his attorney); McGee v. Vermont Federal Bank, 169 Vt. 529, 726 A.2d 42 (1999) (no fiduciary relationship exists between borrower and lender, so no duty on lender to notify borrower when it received notice of cancellation of insurance on mortgaged property); Patterson, A Fable from the Seventh Circuit: Frank Easterbrook on Good Faith, 75 Iowa L.Rev. 503 (1991) (criticizing the *Kham* decision); Note, Breach of Good Faith as an Expansive Basis for Lender Liability Claims: An Idea Whose Time Has Come—and Gone?, 42 Rutgers L.Rev. 177. It is possible that the savings and loan crisis and increasing concerns over the health of some commercial banks and insurance companies played a role in these recent decisions. But see Duffield v. First Interstate Bank of Denver, N.A., 13 F.3d 1403 (10th Cir.1993) (finding that lender breached implied covenant of good faith and fair dealing when bank seized collateral without having a reasonable belief that borrower was in default and without giving notice to borrower, and upholding award of consequential damages in the amount of $6 million).

Moreover, legislation in various states attempts to protect lenders from liability by providing that actions against financial institutions to enforce a promise or the waiver of a promise cannot be maintained unless the promise or waiver was written and signed by a bank officer with authority to do so. See, e.g., Mich. C.L. § 566.132(2); Mich. Stat. Ann. 526–922(2).

This book will examine lender liability claims at various points in the real estate transaction. These include, for example, breach of loan commitments (pages 601–636), the lender's responsibility to junior mortgagees and mechanics for loan disbursements (pages 587–601), and environmental liability (pages 735–800), as well as traditional doctrines which cause a mortgagee to lose priority or become liable in the course of a loan, such as alteration of the loan terms affecting a junior lender (page 418) or original mortgagor (page 426).

In evaluating these cases dealing with lender liability consider the following questions. First, what were the expectations of the parties on the issue? What did the agreement provide? Did the lender follow reasonable lender behavior and norms? Were there any obligations created by statute? Second, what policy considerations apply? Does the rule encourage sound lending and borrowing practices and promote efficient capital markets for real estate development? In order to avoid liability, would the lender have to incur additional costs or should the lender already be taking these steps as part of ordinary supervision of loans? Does the rule place the loss on the party able to avoid the loss most cheaply? Finally, what are the institutional ramifications of the decision? If there is an agreement controlling the issue, are there reasons to overturn it because of the nature of the parties, the bargaining process, or unconscionability? Is the rule clear and predictable for the parties before they take action?

Rice v. First Federal Savings and Loan Ass'n of Lake County

District Court of Appeal of Florida, Second District, 1968.
207 So.2d 22.

PER CURIAM.

Appellants are appealing a judgment foreclosing a mortgage on a building which they owned. Appellants borrowed $12,000 from appellee and delivered to appellee their promissory note for that amount. As security, they gave appellee a mortgage on the building which was to be constructed partly with the loan proceeds. Appellee deducted from the loan proceeds, as a fee for "inspection and supervision," an amount equal to one per cent thereof. An agent of appellee, in fact, made inspections of the construction site. Soon after the completion of the building, because of certain defects in the construction, its wall began to crack extensively, causing considerable damage.

Appellants defaulted on the payments on their note and appellee sued for foreclosure of the mortgage on the building. Appellants counterclaimed for damages on the theory that appellee had inspected the construction site in a negligent manner so as to breach its contractual duty to appellants to inspect the site for their benefit. They conceded they were in default under the terms of the note and mortgage, and the cause was tried on the sole issue of whether appellee was liable to appellants under the counterclaim. The court below ruled that no contractual duty existed as alleged and ordered foreclosure. The sole question before this court is whether appellee, by undertaking the inspection of the construction site and requiring appellants to pay a fee therefor, impliedly contracted with appellants to make such inspection for their benefit.

The effect to be given to an alleged implied contract is that effect which the parties as fair and reasonable men presumably would have agreed upon if, having in mind the possibility of the situation which has arisen, they had expressly contracted in reference thereto. It would be unreasonable to infer merely from appellee's deduction of an inspection fee a contractual duty to appellants to perform such inspection on their behalf. As the court below aptly stated:

"A lender of construction money has an interest in the progress and quality of the construction of its security proportional to the amount of money invested and would reasonably be expected to inspect the construction and be entitled to additional compensation for its additional costs in making such inspection."

Affirmed.

LILES, C.J., and PIERCE and HOBSON, JJ., concur.

Jeminson v. Montgomery Real Estate and Co.

Court of Appeals of Michigan, Division One, 1973.
47 Mich.App. 731, 210 N.W.2d 10, reversed, 396 Mich. 106, 240 N.W.2d 205 (1976).

MCGREGOR, JUDGE.

After the trial court's entry of summary judgment in favor of defendant mortgage corporation for failure of plaintiff to plead a cause of action as to it, plaintiff brings this delayed interlocutory appeal in forma pauperis by leave granted.

Because of the summary judgment aspects of this case, the well-pleaded allegations of the complaint are accepted as true. On July 24, 1970, plaintiff, one of the urban poor, agreed to purchase a home in the inner city of Detroit from defendant real estate company. On September 17, 1970, she signed a mortgage agreement with the defendant mortgage corporation whereby, pursuant to insurance coverage issued by the Federal Housing Administration, it loaned her the purchase price of $11,800.00 in return for which plaintiff executed a mortgage in favor of the mortgage corporation.

Shortly after she moved into her new home, plaintiff realized that defendant real estate company had fraudulently misrepresented the condition and value of the house. She abandoned the house as uninhabitable, whereupon the mortgage was duly foreclosed.

Plaintiff then commenced this suit in circuit court, alleging that, *inter alia,* defendant mortgage corporation was well aware, at the time it entered into the mortgage agreement with her, that her sole means of support was welfare assistance in the form of aid to dependent children, that she was unemployed, possessed of little formal education, and inexperienced in real property or other commercial transactions. Plaintiff further pleaded that defendant mortgage corporation also knew or should have known that the Montgomery Real Estate Company possessed a notorious reputation for using unscrupulous and deceptive practices in the sale of homes, especially older inner-city dwellings sold pursuant to FHA mortgage insurance programs, to inexperienced and unsophisticated buyers. Plaintiff, who is black, further alleges that defendant mortgage company knew that, due to private discriminatory housing practices, she would have fewer opportunities to buy and less bargaining power than white persons similarly situated. She further charges that defendant mortgage corporation is also chargeable with knowledge that the property involved is located in an area where many of the homes are in an advanced state of deterioration. In addition, plaintiff contends that defendant mortgage corporation was or should have been aware that the sales transaction between plaintiff and the real estate company was unfair, fraudulent, or unconscionable; that defendant mortgage corporation should also have known that the real estate company was selling the subject premises to plaintiff at a price more than double the amount paid by the real estate company only a few months previously, and that the agreed sales price was considerably more than the value of the property; that defendant mortgage corporation should have known that the subject dwelling was not in a safe, decent and sanitary condition, was not in conformity with applicable building and health codes, and did not qualify under FHA regulations for financing; that representations made to the plaintiff by the real estate company concerning the condition of the property were materially untrue, and that the mortgage corporation should have known this.

On this appeal, plaintiff seeks reversal of the interlocutory order of the trial court, dismissing plaintiff's suit against defendant mortgage corporation for failure to state a cause of action.

Plaintiff discusses a line of cases from various jurisdictions denying holder in due course status to parties who accepted notes, mortgages, or other commercial paper in bad faith, or where a legal defect appeared on the face of the instrument, such as Matthews v. Aluminum Acceptance Corp., 1 Mich.App. 570, 137 N.W.2d 280 (1965), which involved usurious interest rates and a deceptively procured signature.

Plaintiff's briefs and arguments urge upon this Court as correct and controlling the decision in Connor v. Great Western Savings & Loan Assn., 69 Cal.2d 850, 73 Cal.Rptr. 369, 447 P.2d 609 (1968). In that case, the lender had been intimately involved at every stage of a subdivision construction project, from financing the development to the making of loans to plaintiff purchasers secured by mortgages upon the dwellings. All plans and specifications had been examined and approved by the lender before construction began. Many of the homes proved defective and some of the purchasers brought an action against the developer and the lender seeking rescission and damages. Holding that the lender had been an "active participant" in the enterprise, and because the lender knew or should have known certain facts concerning the developer and the transaction, the Court found that the lender had a duty under the circumstances, which it owed to the individual purchasers, to exercise reasonable care to protect them from damages caused by major structural defects.

"If existing sanctions are inadequate, imposition of a duty at the point of effective financial control of tract building will insure responsible building practices." 69 Cal.2d 868, 73 Cal.Rptr. 378, 447 P.2d 618.

Plaintiff argues that the case at bar is analogous to *Connor*.

The question on appeal is whether the facts as pleaded constitute a cause of action in favor of the plaintiff against the defendant mortgage corporation, not whether those facts can be proved at trial.

It is apparent from the pleadings that the transaction in this matter was not unitary, but binary, in that plaintiff first made and signed a purchase agreement with the real estate company, and several weeks later, in an independent transaction, concluded a mortgage agreement with the mortgage company. These two transactions are distinct and disjoint and, therefore, any fraud or unconscionability attributable to the purchase agreement cannot be ascribed to the subsequent mortgage agreement. The mortgage agreement itself is neither fraudulent nor unconscionable; for good and valuable consideration, defendant mortgage corporation took a mortgage equal in value to the money advanced to the plaintiff.

Connor v. Great Western Savings & Loan Assn., supra, cited by plaintiff, does not support her position. Great Western, the lender, negotiated with two developers with limited experience in tract construction to secure financing for the purchase of 100 acres of land

and the construction thereon of 400 tract homes. The arrangement provided that Great Western would first buy the land, and then resell it to the developers at a profit, charging a high interest rate on the loan. A fee was charged for each individual home loan, while if a buyer obtained financing elsewhere, the developers were required to pay Great Western the fees obtained by the other lender. Great Western inspected at least once a week, and maintained the right to halt construction funds during the construction period if the work did not conform to plans and specifications. Great Western negligently failed to discover that the home designs were inadequate for the soil conditions; within two years, numerous foundations cracked. In holding that all buyers and other lenders had a cause of action against Great Western, the California Supreme Court was careful to observe that such liability arose because the lender voluntarily assumed the duty to inspect, and had been involved in the overall transaction to a far greater extent than the usual money lender in such transactions.

The doctrine of "close connectedness", relied upon by plaintiff, is inapplicable to the case at bar. No such close relationship is sufficiently pleaded to bring that doctrine into play.

Even conceding the merits of litigation *pro bono publico,* plaintiff's position in the case at bar is untenable.

The issuance of FHA insurance on the mortgage in the case at bar is central to the overall transaction herein attacked by plaintiff. From a business point of view, once an insurance policy has been issued on a mortgage, the mortgagee has no interest whatsoever in an appraisal of the subject property. Either the mortgage will be paid off by the mortgagor, or the mortgage will be in default. In the latter event, foreclosure will either produce a sales price sufficient to pay off the mortgage, or the mortgagee may simply rely on his insurance, and protect himself from loss that way. Clearly, there is no business reason or well-pleaded allegations by the plaintiff why a mortgagee who is the beneficiary of an FHA mortgage policy should go to the expense and trouble of inspecting the subject premises.

In the instant case, the mortgagee had no real interest in the actual sales transaction. The mortgagee was merely a source of funds, and in the usual course of prudent business practice took a mortgage for the sole purpose of securing its monetary advance to the plaintiff. Given the existence of an FHA insurance policy, the value of the collateral was inconsequential. Existence of the property subject to the mortgage was all that concerned the lender, since that alone, given FHA insurance, was sufficient completely to protect its investment. Plaintiff has pleaded no business reason why the mortgage corporation should have done more than it did.

In the spate of recent cases in which new duties and liabilities have been recognized, or old ones extended, the courts have consistently grounded their decisions on the theory that the person upon whom liability is sought to be imposed is in the best position to spread its losses to those who are benefitted by the adverse consequences of their activities.

In the case at bar, the mortgagee is in no position to spread any losses due to fraudulent land sales transactions, nor is the mortgagee in a particularly good position to prevent such losses. Those parties most intimately involved in the sales transaction, the vendor and vendee, respectively, are best able to diminish the number and size of losses due to fraudulent sales. The mortgagee is not a beneficiary of the fraud, if any, which was allegedly perpetrated by the real estate company; all its profits came from the interest it charged on its loan. Any profits realized by the mortgagee because of the underlying fraud are too remote to form a basis for its liability.

Plaintiff has advanced no viable economic theory upon which to impose liability on the mortgage corporation; she must rely on established legal doctrines. But no established legal principle has been cited by plaintiff or discovered by this Court that would warrant finding that defendant mortgage corporation had a duty to protect the plaintiff from the real estate company's cupidity.

Nor do the holder in due course cases add anything to plaintiff's argument. Those cases, applying the so-called "close connectedness" doctrine, differ radically from the case at bar. It may be conceded *arguendo* that, if the mortgage corporation were intimately affiliated with the real estate company, the real estate company's fraud could be chargeable against the mortgage corporation. However, even viewing the complaint in the light most favorable to the plaintiff, there is no allegation that the mortgage corporation acted as a subsidiary of the real estate company, or is the mortgagee of all property sold by the real estate company, or is otherwise somehow viewable as the alter ego of the real estate company.

Of the cases cited by plaintiff, several contain reasoning which serves to defeat plaintiff's assertion that she has a cause of action. For instance, in Financial Credit Corp. v. Williams, 246 Md. 575, 229 A.2d 712 (1967), the Court held that two things are necessary conditions precedent to the imposition of liability: (1) an extraordinary discount, and (2) knowledge, such as an infirmity obvious on the face of the instrument. Matthews v. Aluminum Acceptance Corp., supra. The remaining cases cited by plaintiff involve factual situations in which the mortgagor's title was tainted as against his grantor. Those cases are thus self-distinguishing.

This Court finds that plaintiff does not have a cause of action, because of the relationship between the mortgage corporation and the real estate company, and well-established principles of equity as applied to fraud. Such liability would therefore not be after the fact.

It might be argued that, if the mortgage corporation did not extend a loan to the plaintiff because she was an uneducated black person, buying a house in an allegedly deteriorating neighborhood, it might incur some legal liability under the Federal Housing Administration Act.

Analysis of all the cases cited by both parties, and of additional cases discovered by this Court, discloses that, under the pleadings, no authority supports a cause of action against the Michigan Mortgage Corporation in the case at bar.

Affirmed.

ADAMS, JUDGE (dissenting).

I dissent.

Judge McGregor states:

"It is apparent from the pleadings that the transaction in this matter was not unitary, but binary, in that plaintiff first made and signed a purchase agreement with the real estate company, and several weeks later, in an independent transaction, concluded a mortgage agreement with the mortgage company."

The final typed-in sentence of the purchase agreement reads as follows: "If purchaser is unable to obtain mortgage, deposit to be refunded less cost of credit report".

Count IV of plaintiff's first amended complaint alleges that defendant Michigan, as part of its normal pre-loan credit check on plaintiff, knew that plaintiff was receiving welfare assistance, was unemployed, had little formal education, and had little, if any, experience in any kind of commercial transactions. Count IV further avers that defendant Michigan knew, as a result of repeated business dealings with defendant Montgomery, that Montgomery was an experienced real estate company with a notorious reputation for using unscrupulous and deceptive practices. Finally said count alleges that defendant Michigan knew, or should have known through its preliminary investigation, the various facts charged to establish fraud by Montgomery, and that since Michigan knew or should have known all of these facts it made itself an integral and necessary part of the fraudulent transaction when it entered into the mortgage loan agreement with plaintiff without warning her of her peril and imminent financial loss. Count V of plaintiff's first amended complaint contains similar allegations and avers that defendant Michigan disregarded its duty to warn plaintiff of her peril or to refrain from taking any action which would increase her danger.

Judge McGregor states: "It may be conceded *arguendo* that, if the mortgage corporation were intimately affiliated with the real estate company, the real estate company's fraud could be chargeable against the mortgage corporation". Since the purchase agreement is specifically provisioned upon the securing of a mortgage, and in view of the serious allegations raised in plaintiff's complaint, I am unable to conclude, as Judge McGregor does, that the transaction in this case was binary and not unitary and that plaintiff's pleadings failed to state a claim upon which relief could be granted. The appellate courts of this state have repeatedly warned against the improper use of summary proceedings to preclude a party from his day in court.

. . . I would reverse and remand for further proceedings.

Jeminson v. Montgomery Real Estate and Co.

Supreme Court of Michigan, 1976.
396 Mich. 106, 240 N.W.2d 205.

T.G. KAVANAGH, CHIEF JUSTICE.

For the reasons stated by former Justice Adams in his dissent in this case, 47 Mich.App. 731, 741, 210 N.W.2d 10, 14 (1973), the decision of the Court of Appeals is reversed and the cause remanded for trial.

LEVIN AND WILLIAMS, JJ., concur.

LINDEMER and RYAN, JJ., not participating.

COLEMAN and FITZGERALD, JUSTICES.

We would affirm the decision of the Court of Appeals for the reasons set forth in the majority opinion 47 Mich.App. 731, 733–741, 210 N.W.2d 10, 11–14 (1973).

NOTES

1. *Lenders.* What policies should be considered, and what lines drawn, in determining whether and to what extent lenders should be held liable for building defects? In the case of a construction lender, should liability be made to depend on whether the lender in fact undertook an inspection? Charged a separate inspection fee? Did the lender have control of the process that led to the defect? Should a permanent lender's liability turn on whether new or used housing is involved? On whether the mortgage is insured, as in *Jeminson?* On whether the buyer-borrower can show that his contract with the seller contained a subject to financing condition? That, in closing, he was relying on the lender's judgment as to quality and that the lender knew of this reliance?

Actions against lenders have been generally unavailing. Both *Jeminson* and *Connor v. Great Western,* which it cites, are exceptions to the general rule. The judicial trend in and out of California has been to distinguish *Connor* on the ground that Great Western's participation in the development in question involved many non-lending activities. See, for example, Baskin v. Mortgage and Trust Co., 837 S.W.2d 743 (Tex.App.1992); Wierzbicki v. Alaska Mutual Savings Bank, 630 P.2d 998 (Alaska 1981); Seymour v. New Hampshire Savings Bank, 131 N.H. 753, 561 A.2d 1053 (1989); Amsterdam Savings Bank FSB v. Marine Midland Bank, N.A., 121 A.D.2d 815, 504 N.Y.S.2d 563, appeal dismissed, 68 N.Y.2d 766, 506 N.Y.S.2d 1040, 498 N.E.2d 151 (1986) (construction lender not liable to permanent lender for defects). The California Legislature subsequently limited *Connor* by amending the Civil Code:

> A lender who makes a loan of money, the proceeds of which are used ... to finance the ... improvement of real or personal property for sale or lease to others, shall not be held liable to third persons for any loss or damage occasioned by any defect in the real or personal property ... unless such loss or damage is a result of an act of the lender outside the scope of the activities of a lender of money or unless the lender has been a party to misrepresentations with respect to such real or personal property.

Cal.Civ.Code § 3434. Cases interpreting section 3434 offer little insight into the critical issue of what constitutes "the scope of the activities of a lender of money." See generally, Gutierrez, Liability of a Construction Lender Under Civil Code § 3434: An Amorphous Epitaph to Connor v. Great Western Savings & Loan Association, 8 Pac.L.J. 1 (1977).

Cases also reject liability of permanent lenders. See, e.g., Rzepiennik v. U.S. Home Corp., 221 N.J.Super. 230, 534 A.2d 89 (1987) (lender has no duty to inspect for borrower); Stempler v. Frankford Trust Co., 365 Pa.Super. 305, 529 A.2d 521 (1987) (same). Should the result be different if the lender actually learns of a defect and does not disclose it to the borrower?

In some limited circumstances the lender has been held liable for defects in the premises. These include situations where the lender and developer were engaged in a joint venture to develop the property, see Central Bank, N.A. v. Baldwin, 94 Nev. 581, 583 P.2d 1087 (1978), the lender foreclosed and took over the construction, see Kirkman v. Parex, Inc., 369 S.C. 477, 632 S.E.2d 854 (2006), the construction lender took control of the job upon default of borrower and completed the building, see Chotka v. Fidelco Growth Investors, 383 So.2d 1169 (Fla.App.1980), or the construction lender continued to disburse to the builder even though the borrower had complained about defects, see Davis v. Nevada National Bank, 103 Nev. 220, 737 P.2d 503 (1987).

For an excellent analysis of some of these issues see Malloy, Lender Liability for Negligent Real Estate Appraisals, 1984 U.Ill.L.Rev. 53. See generally, Ferguson, Lender's Liability for Construction Defects, 11 Real Est.L.J. 310 (1983); Hiller, Mortgagee Liability for Defective Construction, 108 Banking L.J. 386 (1991); Note, Mortgage Lender Liability to the Purchaser of New or Existing Homes, 1988 U.Ill.L.Rev. 191.

2. *Brokers.* Broker liability for housing defects rests almost exclusively on fraud and typically arises when the seller mentions some material defect to the listing broker who then fails to disclose it to the unsuspecting buyer. See pages 60–71 above.

Offering an overall theoretical framework to analyze liability of third parties (including brokers, attorneys, inspectors, title searchers, appraisers, surveyors, and inspectors), see Feinman, Economic Negligence in Residential Real Estate Transactions, 25 Real Est.L.J. 110 (1996).

3. *Architects.* Architect liability to third parties injured as a consequence of negligently prepared plans is a relatively new development. Until the middle 1950's the general rule was that an architect's liability to individuals other than her client evaporated at the moment the client accepted the completed building. There were early exceptions to the rule, for willful negligence and dangerous, latent conditions, but the rule itself did not begin to fall until the 1950's. Architects are now widely held liable for design errors ranging from failure to consider suitability of the underlying soil and specifying an insufficient foundation, to specifying improper windows, insulation and roofing. For a thorough analysis of architect liability, with proposals for reform, see Comment, Architect Tort Liability in Preparation of Plans and Specifications, 55 Cal.L.Rev. 1361 (1967). See also, Note, Architectural Malpractice: A Contract-Based Approach, 92 Harv.L.Rev. 1075 (1979).

"The American Institute of Architects, along with the National Society of Professional Engineers and the Associated General Contractors, began to push for model legislation which would substantially curtail the limitless duration of liability imposed upon its members. In the span of approximately two years, 1965–67, thirty jurisdictions enacted or amended statutes of limitations specifically for architects, engineers and builders. Though these statutes are not identical in every respect, there is one characteristic common to all. Each of them sets a definite period of years beginning at the time of completion or acceptance of the work, after which no civil actions against the architect, engineer, or builder may be brought." Note, 60 Kentucky L.J. 462, 464–465 (1972).

4. *Home Inspectors.* A buyer may seek recovery from an inspector hired by the buyer to detect and report defects prior to closing. Damages theoretically can be recovered under negligence and contract theories for failure to find discoverable defects. See, e.g., Ensminger v. Terminix International Co., 102 F.3d 1571 (10th Cir.1996) (holding Terminix liable in compensatory and punitive damages for failing to disclose termite infestation to buyer). However, in many situations the home inspector may not have adequately deep pockets to compensate the buyer. Moreover, courts will uphold limitations of liability clauses in inspection contracts, at least against warranty claims. See, e.g., Estey v. MacKenzie Engineering Inc., 324 Or. 372, 927 P.2d 86 (1996) (upholding clause limiting contract liability to the contract sum—$200—but holding that the clause did not bar action for negligence).

5. *Government Agencies.* Should the Federal Housing Administration, which insured the homebuyer's mortgage in *Jeminson* and thus had an interest in determining the value of the house as security for the insured loan, have been held liable for not properly inspecting the house and disclosing its condition to the prospective homebuyer? The federal government has generally sought to avoid liability for its participation in home loan and loan insurance programs through express disclaimers and through the doctrine of sovereign immunity.

In Block v. Neal, 460 U.S. 289, 103 S.Ct. 1089, 75 L.Ed.2d 67 (1983), the United States Supreme Court held that the prohibition of the Federal Tort Claims Act against recovery for any "claim arising out of . . . misrepresentation" did not bar plaintiff Neal's action for damages against the Farmers Home Administration which, having lent her money for the construction of a prefabricated house, allegedly failed to properly inspect and supervise construction, with the result that the completed house contained fourteen defects. Neal's contract with her builder required that its work "conform to plans approved by FmHA. It also granted FmHA the right to inspect and test all materials and workmanship and reject any that were defective. At the same time, Neal entered into a deed of trust with FmHA and signed a promissory note providing for repayment of the principal sum of $21,170, plus interest of 8% per annum on the unpaid principal." 460 U.S. at 291, 103 S.Ct. at 1091.

In the Court's view, plaintiff's "claim against the Government for negligence by FmHA officials in supervising construction of her house does not 'aris[e] out of . . . misrepresentation' within the meaning of 28 U.S.C.A. § 2680(h). The Court of Appeals properly concluded that Neal's claim is not barred by this provision of the Tort Claims Act because Neal does not seek to recover on the basis of misstatements made by FmHA officials. Although FmHA in this case may have undertaken both to supervise construction of Neal's house and to provide Neal information regarding the progress of construction, Neal's action is based solely on the former conduct. Accordingly, the judgment of the Court of Appeals is affirmed." 460 U.S. at 298–299, 103 S.Ct. at 1094–1095.

2. TITLE

Before paying the purchase price and accepting seller's deed, buyer will want assurance that seller's title is good—that no fraud or formal defect clouds her ownership and that there are no outstanding conditions or encumbrances that might interfere with buyer's ownership or use of the land. Buyer can get this assurance in part by searching seller's record title and updating this search down to the moment of closing. If the search discloses a material defect, the covenant of marketable title in the parties' contract will excuse buyer from performing and entitle him to the return of his deposit. But, if the search discloses no such defect, buyer will, as required by the contract, accept seller's deed and pay the price.

Since some title defects will not be disclosed by a record search, the prudent buyer may want additional assurances that seller's title is good. One form that these assurances commonly take is covenants—promises—incorporated in seller's deed to buyer. Title covenants can be shaped to meet any specific need—that title is good as against a neighbor claiming adverse possession, that a disputed mortgage has been paid off, or that a troublesome relative in fact has no interest in the land. In addition to such custom-crafted covenants are six standard title covenants that have been in common use since at least the seventeenth century in England:

Covenant of Seisin. This covenant is the seller's promise that she owns at least the interest in land that she is purporting to convey to the buyer. (Thus, if seller's deed purports to give buyer complete ownership of Blackacre, but at the time of the conveyance seller had only a twenty-year lease to Blackacre, the covenant would be breached.)

Covenant of the Right to Convey. Here the seller covenants that she has full power to transfer the interest that the deed purports to convey. This covenant substantially overlaps the covenant of seisin, but provides protection in occasional circumstances where the covenant of seisin does not. For example, the fact that X is in adverse possession of Blackacre at the time seller conveys to buyer does not affect seller's ownership of the parcel and, thus, does not breach her covenant of seisin. It would, however, give buyer an action against seller for breach of the covenant of the right to convey.

Covenant Against Encumbrances. This is the seller's promise that no outstanding encumbrances affect ownership or use of the land. Mortgages, leases, unpaid taxes and judgment liens are typical encumbrances affecting ownership. Easements, building restrictions and rights in third parties to remove minerals or other resources from the land are typical encumbrances affecting use.

Covenant of Warranty. This is the single most frequently used covenant in the United States. It obligates the seller to compensate the buyer for any losses when the title conveyed falls short of the title that the deed purports to convey. A covenant of *general warranty* encompasses all defects in title and shortages in the area conveyed, regardless of the reason for the defect or shortage. Covenants of *special warranty* limit the defects covered. They may, for example, cover only those defects that arose while the seller owned the land.

Covenant of Quiet Enjoyment. Under this covenant, the seller promises that the buyer's possession will not be disrupted either by the seller or by anyone with a lawful claim superior to the seller. (The covenant does not, however, protect against intrusions by trespassers.) Courts in the United States generally treat the covenant for quiet enjoyment as equivalent to the covenant of warranty.

Covenant for Further Assurances. Rarely used in the United States, the covenant for further assurances obligates the seller to take such further reasonable steps as are necessary to cure defects in the buyer's title. For example, the seller might be required to obtain the release of an encumbrance or to buy off an adverse possessor. Unlike the covenant of warranty, which gives the buyer damages for the land he has lost, the covenant for further assurances enables the buyer to remain in possession of the land—a particularly valuable right when the land has substantially appreciated in value.

The first three covenants—seisin, right to convey and freedom from encumbrances—are commonly called *present covenants* because they embody representations about the condition of title at the time the deed is delivered to the buyer. As a consequence, these covenants are breached only if the defect they cover exists at the time of delivery, and the statute of limitations for breach begins to run from that time. The second set of three covenants—warranty, quiet enjoyment and further assurances—are called *future covenants* because they protect against interferences with possession occurring at some future time, and obligate the seller to take steps to correct the interference at that time. As a consequence, the statute of limitations for their breach begins to run not from the moment of delivery, but rather from the moment at which the buyer or his successor is first evicted from possession. For further discussion of the various types of covenants, see Lloyd v. Estate of Robbins, 997 A.2d 733 (Me.2010); James v. McCombs, 936 P.2d 520 (Alaska 1997).

Deeds sometimes spell out each of the agreed-upon covenants in detail. Many states, however, have eliminated the need for full explication by providing that a deed's use of a single key word or phrase will automatically incorporate specified covenants in the deed unless the deed expressly excludes them. For example, in Alabama use of the word "grant," "bargain" or "sell" will imply covenants of seisin, freedom from encumbrances created by the grantor, and quiet enjoyment. Ala.Code § 35–4–271 (1975).

Brown v. Lober

Supreme Court of Illinois, 1979.
75 Ill.2d 547, 27 Ill.Dec. 780, 389 N.E.2d 1188.

UNDERWOOD, JUSTICE:

Plaintiffs instituted this action in the Montgomery County circuit court based on an alleged breach of the covenant of seisin in their warranty deed. The trial court held that although there had been a breach of the covenant of seisin, the suit was barred by the 10-year statute of limitations in section 16 of the Limitations Act (Ill.Rev.Stat.1975, ch. 83, par. 17). Plaintiffs' posttrial motion, which was based on an alleged breach of the covenant of quiet enjoyment, was also denied. A divided Fifth District Appellate Court reversed and remanded. We allowed the defendant's petition for leave to appeal.

The parties submitted an agreed statement of facts which sets forth the relevant history of this controversy. Plaintiffs purchased 80 acres of Montgomery County real estate from William and Faith Bost and received a statutory warranty deed containing no exceptions, dated December 21, 1957. Subsequently, plaintiffs took possession of the land and recorded their deed.

On May 8, 1974, plaintiffs granted a coal option to Consolidated Coal Company (Consolidated) for the coal rights on the 80–acre tract for the sum of $6,000. Approximately two years later, however, plaintiffs "discovered" that they, in fact, owned only a one-third interest in the subsurface coal rights. It is a matter of public record that, in 1947, a prior grantor had reserved a two-thirds interest in the mineral rights on the property. Although plaintiffs had their abstract of title examined in 1958 and 1968 for loan purposes, they contend that until May 4, 1976, they believed that they were the sole owners of the surface and subsurface rights on the 80-acre tract. Upon discovering that a prior grantor had reserved a two-thirds interest in the coal rights, plaintiffs and Consolidated renegotiated their agreement to provide for payment of $2,000 in exchange for a one-third interest in the subsurface coal rights. On May 25, 1976, plaintiffs filed this action against the executor of the estate of Faith Bost, seeking damages in the amount of $4,000.

The deed which plaintiffs received from the Bosts was a general statutory form warranty deed meeting the requirements of section 9 of "An Act concerning conveyances" (Ill.Rev.Stat.1957, ch. 30, par. 8). That section provides:

> "Every deed in substance in the above form, when otherwise duly executed, shall be deemed and held a conveyance in fee simple, to the grantee, his heirs or assigns, with covenants on the part of the grantor, (1) that at the time of the making and delivery of such deed he was lawfully seized of an indefeasible estate in fee simple, in and to the premises therein described, and had good right and full power to convey the same; (2) that the same were then free from all incumbrances; and (3) that he warrants to the grantee, his heirs and assigns, the quiet and peaceable possession of such premises, and will defend the title thereto against all persons who may lawfully claim the same. And such covenants shall be obligatory upon any grantor, his heirs and personal representatives, as fully and with like effect as if written at length in such deed." Ill.Rev.Stat.1957, ch. 30, par. 8.

The effect of this provision is that certain covenants of title are implied in every statutory form warranty deed. Subsection 1 contains the covenant of seisin and the covenant of good right to convey. These covenants, which are considered synonymous assure the grantee that the grantor is, at the time of the conveyance, lawfully seized and has the power to convey an estate of the quality and quantity which he professes to convey.

Subsection 2 represents the covenant against incumbrances. An incumbrance is any right to, or interest in, land which may subsist in a third party to the diminution of the value of the estate, but consistent with the passing of the fee by conveyance.

Subsection 3 sets forth the covenant of quiet enjoyment, which is synonymous with the covenant of warranty in Illinois. By this covenant, "the grantor warrants to the grantee, his heirs and assigns, the possession of the premises and that he will defend the title granted by the terms of the deed against persons who may lawfully claim the same, and that such covenant shall be obligatory upon the grantor, his heirs, personal representatives, and assigns." Biwer v. Martin (1920), 294 Ill. 488, 497, 128 N.E. 518, 522.

Plaintiffs' complaint is premised upon the fact that "William Roy Bost and Faith Bost covenanted that they were the owners in fee simple of the above described property at the time of the conveyance to the plaintiffs." While the complaint could be more explicit, it appears that plaintiffs were alleging a cause of action for breach of the covenant of seisin. This court has stated repeatedly that the covenant of seisin is a covenant *in praesenti* and, therefore, if broken at all, is broken at the time of delivery of the deed.

Since the deed was delivered to the plaintiffs on December 21, 1957, any cause of action for breach of the covenant of seisin would have accrued on that date. The trial court held that this cause of action was barred by the statute of limitations. No question is raised as to the applicability of the 10-year statute of limitations (Ill.Rev.Stat.1975, ch. 83, par. 17). We conclude, therefore, that the cause of action for breach of the covenant of seisin was properly determined by the trial court to be barred by the statute of limitations since plaintiffs did not file their complaint until May 25, 1976, nearly 20 years after their alleged cause of action accrued.

In their post-trial motion, plaintiffs set forth as an additional theory of recovery an alleged breach of the covenant of quiet enjoyment. The trial court, without explanation, denied the motion. The appellate court reversed, holding that the cause of action on the covenant of quiet enjoyment was not barred by the statute of limitations. The appellate court theorized that plaintiffs' cause of action did not accrue until 1976, when plaintiffs discovered that they only had a one-third interest in the subsurface coal rights and renegotiated their contract with the coal company for one-third of the previous contract price. The primary issue before us, therefore, is when, if at all, the plaintiffs' cause of action for breach of the covenant of quiet enjoyment is deemed to have accrued.

This court has stated on numerous occasions that, in contrast to the covenant of seisin, the covenant of warranty or quiet enjoyment is prospective in nature and is breached only when there is an actual or constructive eviction of the covenantee by the paramount titleholder.

The cases are also replete with statements to the effect that the mere existence of paramount title in one other than the covenantee is not sufficient to constitute a breach of the covenant of warranty or quiet enjoyment: "[T]here must be a union of acts of disturbance and lawful title, to constitute a breach of the covenant for quiet enjoyment, or warranty. . . ." (Barry v. Guild (1888), 126 Ill. 439, 446, 18 N.E. 759, 761.) "[T]here is a general concurrence that something more than the mere existence of a paramount title is necessary to constitute a breach of the covenant of warranty." (Scott v. Kirkendall (1878), 88 Ill. 465, 467.) "A mere want of title is no breach of this covenant. There must not only be a want of title, but there must be an ouster under a paramount title." Moore v. Vail (1855), 17 Ill. 185, 189.

The question is whether plaintiffs have alleged facts sufficient to constitute a constructive eviction. They argue that if a covenantee fails in his effort to sell an interest in land because he discovers that he does not own what his warranty deed purported to convey, he has suffered a constructive eviction and is thereby entitled to bring an action against his grantor for breach of the covenant of quiet enjoyment. We think that the decision of this court in Scott v. Kirkendall (1878), 88 Ill. 465, is controlling on this issue and compels us to reject plaintiffs' argument.

In *Scott,* an action was brought for breach of the covenant of warranty by a grantee who discovered that other parties had paramount title to the land in question. The land was vacant and unoccupied at all relevant times. This court, in rejecting the grantee's claim that there was a breach of the covenant of quiet enjoyment, quoted the earlier decision in Moore v. Vail (1855), 17 Ill. 185, 191:

> " 'Until that time, (the taking possession by the owner of the paramount title,) he might peaceably have entered upon and enjoyed the premises, without resistance or molestation, which was all his grantors covenanted he should do. They did not guarantee to him a perfect title, but the possession and enjoyment of the premises.' " 88 Ill. 465, 468.

Relying on this language in *Moore,* the *Scott* court concluded:

> "We do not see but what this fully decides the present case against the appellant. It holds that the mere existence of a paramount title does not constitute a breach of the covenant. That is all there is here. There has been no assertion of the adverse title. The land has always been vacant. Appellant could at any time have taken peaceable possession of it. He has in no way been prevented or hindered from the enjoyment of the possession by any one having a better right. It was but the possession and enjoyment of the premises which was assured to him, and there has been no disturbance or interference in that respect. True, there is a superior title in another, but appellant has never felt 'its pressure upon him.' " 88 Ill. 465, 468–69.

Admittedly, *Scott* dealt with surface rights while the case before us concerns subsurface mineral rights. We are, nevertheless, convinced that the reasoning employed in *Scott* is applicable to the present case. While plaintiffs went into possession of the surface area, they cannot be said to have possessed the subsurface minerals. "Possession of the surface does not carry possession of the minerals. . . . [Citation.] To possess the mineral estate, one must undertake the actual removal thereof from the ground or do such other act as will apprise the community that such interest is in the exclusive use and enjoyment of the claiming party." Failoni v. Chicago & North Western Ry. Co. (1964), 30 Ill.2d 258, 262, 195 N.E.2d 619, 622.

Since no one has, as yet, undertaken to remove the coal or otherwise manifested a clear intent to exclusively "possess" the mineral estate, it must be concluded that the subsurface estate is "vacant." As in *Scott,* plaintiffs "could at any time have taken peaceable possession of it. [They have] in no way been prevented or hindered from the enjoyment of the possession by any one having a better right." (88 Ill. 465, 468.) Accordingly, until such time as one holding paramount title interferes with plaintiffs' right of possession (*e.g.,* by beginning to mine the coal), there can be no constructive eviction and, therefore, no breach of the covenant of quiet enjoyment.

What plaintiffs are apparently attempting to do on this appeal is to extend the protection afforded by the covenant of quiet enjoyment. However, we decline to expand the historical scope of this covenant to provide a remedy where another of the covenants of title is so clearly applicable. As this court stated in Scott v. Kirkendall (1878), 88 Ill. 465, 469:

> "To sustain the present action would be to confound all distinction between the covenant of warranty and that of seizin, or of right to convey. They are not equivalent covenants. An action will lie upon the latter, though there be no disturbance of possession. A defect of title will suffice. Not so with the covenant of warranty, or for quiet enjoyment, as has always been held by the prevailing authority."

The covenant of seisin, unquestionably, was breached when the Bosts delivered the deed to plaintiffs, and plaintiffs then had a cause of action. However, despite the fact that it was a matter of public record that there was a reservation of a two-thirds interest in the mineral rights in the earlier deed, plaintiffs failed to bring an action for breach of the covenant of seisin within the 10-year period following delivery of the deed. The likely explanation is that plaintiffs had not secured a title opinion at the time they purchased the property, and the subsequent examiners for the lenders were not concerned with the mineral rights. Plaintiffs' oversight, however, does not justify us in overruling earlier decisions in order to recognize an otherwise premature cause of action. The mere fact that plaintiffs' original contract with Consolidated had to be modified due to their discovery that paramount title to two-thirds of the subsurface minerals belonged to another is not sufficient to constitute the constructive eviction necessary to a breach of the covenant of quiet enjoyment.

Finally, although plaintiffs also have argued in this court that there was a breach of the covenant against incumbrances entitling them to recovery, we decline to address this issue which was argued for the first time on appeal. It is well settled that questions not raised in the trial court will not be considered by this court on appeal.

Accordingly, the judgment of the appellate court is reversed, and the judgment of the circuit court of Montgomery County is affirmed.

Appellate court reversed; circuit court affirmed.

NOTES

1.   *Brown v. Lober.* Was it fair in *Lober* for plaintiffs' action on the covenant of seisin to be barred by the statute of limitations? For plaintiffs' action on the covenant of quiet enjoyment to be dismissed on the ground that the covenant had not yet been breached? What, if anything, could

plaintiff have done to precipitate an eviction and hence a breach of the covenant of quiet enjoyment? How would you advise a client caught between one title claim that is not yet ripe and another that is overripe? Can you draft a covenant that would cover the situation that arose in *Lober?*

Should plaintiffs have been barred on the alternative ground that, at the time they accepted delivery they knew or should have known of the outstanding mineral interest? As a general rule, a buyer's actual or constructive knowledge of a title defect or encumbrance will not defeat his action on a covenant that covers the defect or encumbrance. See Jones v. Grow Investment & Mortgage Co., 11 Utah 2d 326, 329, 358 P.2d 909 (1961) ("The very purpose of the covenant is to protect a grantee against defects and to hold that one can be protected only against unknown defects would be to rob the covenant of most of its value. If from the force of the covenant it is desired to eliminate known defects, or to limit the covenant in any way, it is easy to do so.").

2. *Coverage Limitations.* Because deed covenants protect only against defects in title, there can be no action on the warranty on the ground that the configuration of the property does not comply with zoning requirements. See, e.g., Barnett v. Decatur, 261 Ga. 205, 403 S.E.2d 46 (1991). Similarly, title covenants do not warrant the physical quality of the premises. See Casenote, 51 Mont.L.Rev. 205 (1990). Moreover, if a grantee knows of defects in title before buying the property, she may be denied recovery for breach of warranty. See, e.g., Richitt v. Southern Pine Plantations, Inc., 228 Ga.App. 333, 491 S.E.2d 528 (1997) (purchaser observed dirt road before buying and so could not recover).

3. *Statutory Short Forms and Presumptions.* Covenants of title may be imposed in a deed absent express covenant language. Under statutes in some jurisdictions, the use of a seemingly innocuous term in a deed implies certain covenants of title. See, for example, Mont. Code Ann. § 70–20–304 ("grant" imports covenant against encumbrances created by grantor). As *Brown v. Lober* indicates, statutes may also authorize short forms of deeds where the use of one phrase may create covenants. See, for example, Ohio Rev. Code § 5302.06 ("general warranty covenants" creates covenants of seisin, right to convey, absence of encumbrances, and general warranty); Greenberg v. Sutter, 173 Misc.2d 774, 661 N.Y.S.2d 933 (Sup.Ct.1997) (construing Real Prop. Law § 253 and language "grantor has not done or suffered anything whereby the said premises have been encumbered"). The attorney must be familiar with local statutes and presumptions in evaluating deeds. For an excellent discussion of this issue, see R. Natelson, Modern Law of Deeds to Real Property 60–62, 332–337 (1992).

CHAPTER IV

ASSURING TITLE

A. THE RECORD SYSTEM

The aim of the record system in America is to protect a buyer of land against the possibility that his seller, or some predecessor in interest to his seller, previously conveyed away all or part of the bundle of rights that the buyer has contracted to buy. The genius of the American recording system is that it operates almost entirely on individual initiative. A buyer who follows the steps prescribed by the system can almost always assure himself of good title.

At early common law, when land was transferred by the ceremony of feoffment with livery of seisin, the possibility of conflicting transfers was small. The required presence of witnesses disciplined landowners from trying to sell the same parcel twice. But, with the growth of documentary transfers after the Statute of Uses, enacted in 1535, and with the proliferation of nonpossessory interests such as covenants, easements and tax and mortgage liens that could simultaneously coexist in a single parcel, it became increasingly probable that a scheming or forgetful grantor would fail to inform her grantee of some prior, adverse transfer. Covenants of title partially protected grantees who obtained less than they bargained for. But breaching covenantors could not always be found and, if found, often lacked the resources to make good on their promises. A rule was needed to determine the rights of competing grantees fairly and efficiently.

The common law had adopted a simple rule for determining who should prevail when grantor *A* conveyed the same interest in land to two grantees, *B* and *C: first in time, first in right.* The rule worked fairly and efficiently when the first grantee, *B,* went into immediate possession of the land. A quick inspection by *C* before accepting and paying for the deed from *A,* would disclose that someone other than *A* was in possession. *C*'s inquiry of *B* as to why *B* rather than *A* was in possession would disclose that *B*'s possession was under a prior deed from *A. C* could then rescind his contract with *A* and recover any deposit paid.

But the rule of first in time, first in right was neither efficient nor fair when, as often happened, *B* did not go into possession. *C,* seeing either *A* or no one in possession, would have no reason to inquire into the possibility that someone other than *A* had title. Nonetheless, *C* would lose his interest when *B* later asserted his prior rights.

The first recording acts were passed to resolve this shortcoming. The American acts replaced the common law rule of first in time, first in right with an equally simple, but fairer and more efficient prescription: *first to record, first in right.* By providing a place—typically the county recorder's office—to record instruments transferring real property, and by providing that an instrument of transfer will be valid as against subsequent, competing instruments only if it is recorded, the American record system provided a comparatively cheap and certain method for *C* not only to determine whether *A* was conveying good title to him, but also to assure himself that title, once conveyed to him, would not be lost to any subsequent competing grantee.

Specifically, this system enabled *C* to determine the status of *A*'s title by conducting a record search in the county where the land was situated. Under the system, if prior grantee *B* was not in possession, *C* would nonetheless discover the conveyance to *B* if *B* had recorded it. The title search would fail to disclose the *A-B* transfer only if *B* had not recorded the instrument. But, if *B* failed to record, his interest would be invalid against *C* under a first to record, first in right regime—so long as *C* promptly recorded *his* instrument of transfer. And, by promptly recording, *C* would gain priority not only over all earlier grantees who failed to record, but against all grantees after him who, by definition, will have recorded later. Subsequent legislation altered some aspects of this early system, and expanded the buyer's duty to look outside the record, but nonetheless retained the paper record as the central feature of title assurance in the United States.

NOTES

1. *Off-Record Risks.* Because recording acts have been enacted in every state, and because they so completely dominate the conveyancing system, it is easy to overlook the fact that recording acts only partially displace the common law rule of first in time, first in right. As a result, the common law priorities still govern situations to which the recording acts do not apply.

When will the common law priority, rather than the recording act priority apply? Almost all states today hold that if subsequent purchaser *C* acquired with notice of the prior transfer to *B,* he will not be protected by the recording act and will thus lose out to *B* even though *B* has not recorded. Also, *C* will lose out to adverse possessor *B* even though *C*'s diligently conducted title search would not uncover rights acquired by adverse possession. Nor would it disclose the fact that a deed in the chain of title was forged, undelivered or executed by an incompetent. See Lloyd v. Chicago Title Insurance Co., 576 So.2d 310 (Fla.App.1990) (mortgagee who relied on recorded forged satisfaction of first mortgage is junior to the first mortgage). For a hair-raising catalogue of off-record risks to title, see Straw, Off-Record Risks for Bona Fide Purchasers of Interests in Real Property, 72 Dick.L.Rev. 35 (1967).

Should recording acts be revised to completely preempt the common law priority so that the record is conclusive as to the current state of title? If you were a residential tenant under a short term lease, would you be happy knowing that, under such a regime, your lease could be terminated at any time by a grantee from your landlord unless you had recorded it? Will your answer depend on how easily and cheaply recording can be accomplished?

2. *Unrecordable Instruments.* Another off-record risk arises when the interest that *A* conveyed to *B* is one for which the local recording act does not require recordation. Because recordation is not required, the recording act will not protect the second taker. Thus, *B*, who is first but has not recorded his unrecordable instrument, will prevail over *C*, even though *C* made a title search and recorded promptly. This poses no problem for *C* in states that give an all-encompassing definition to recordable instruments. Arizona, for example, makes any "instrument affecting real property" recordable, Ariz.Rev.Stat.Ann. § 33–411 (1990). Most states, however, specify several exceptions. Some eastern states exempt leases of seven years or less from recording requirements, while western states traditionally except leases of one year or less. Compare Mass.Gen.Laws Ann. c. 183, § 4 (West 1991) with Cal.Civ. Code § 1214 (West 1982 & Supp. 1991).

New York includes within its definition of recordable instruments "every written instrument, by which any estate or interest in real property is created, transferred, mortgaged or assigned, or by which the title to any real property may be affected," but excludes wills, leases for a term of three years or less, executory contracts for the sale of land and instruments containing a power to convey real property as an agent or attorney for the owner of the property. N.Y. Real Prop.Law § 290(3) (McKinney 1989).

3. *Lis Pendens.* At common law, a purchaser of took subject to existing litigation over title and use of the property even though the purchaser was unaware of the pending lawsuit. To remedy this situation, lis pendens or "notice of pendency" statutes were passed in the various states. This legislation reverses the common law rule and allows bona fide purchasers to take free of pending litigation. The statutes, however, provide a mechanism for a plaintiff bringing an action contesting "the title to, or the possession, use or enjoyment of, real property" (N.Y. C.P.L.R. § 6501) to file a notice of the suit. That filing serves to bind subsequent purchasers of the property to the outcome of the litigation. Depending on the jurisdiction, the lis pendens filing may be in the litigation docket in the clerk's office, rather than in the recorder's office. This underscores the point that a complete title search may require the checking of records in other offices.

1. TYPES OF STATUTES

Corwin W. Johnson, Purpose and Scope of Recording Statutes*
47 Iowa Law Review 231–233 (1962).

The general purpose of the land recording acts is quite clear: it is to provide a public record of transactions affecting title to land. More specific objectives are also readily discernible: (1) to enable interested persons, including public officials such as tax collectors, to ascertain apparent ownership of land; (2) to furnish admissible evidence of title for litigants in a nation where landowners did not adopt the English practice of keeping all former deeds and transferring them with the land; (3) to enable owners of equitable interests to protect such interests by giving notice to subsequent purchasers of the legal title; and (4) to modify the traditional case-law doctrine that purchasers and other transferees, no matter how bona fide, get no better title than the transferor owned. It is no doubt safe to make these generalizations about all of the land recordation statutes in force in the United States, but deeper probing renders generalization hazardous. This is especially

---

*   Copyright 1962 by The University of Iowa (Iowa Law Review).

true of item four on the above list. The first-in-time rule of priorities is quite logical, but it is of doubtful justice and is utterly incompatible with an economy in which commercial transfers of land occur frequently. But, despite widespread agreement that this doctrine should be changed, the recording acts of the various states and court decisions applying them reflect significant divergence of policy.

A basic policy question is whether emphasis should be upon penalizing those who fail to record or upon protecting those who deserve protection. Conceivably, strict adherence to the penalty approach could lead to requiring recordation as essential to the validity of a deed, even as to the grantor, in addition to the requirements of delivery and writing. On the other hand, it would be consistent with the protection approach to regard unrecorded deeds void only as to those who actually examine the records and who substantially change their positions in reliance thereon. No modern recording act (excluding Torrens acts) goes to either of these extremes. Rather, the impact of both policies—penalty and protection—may be observed in the acts now in force. How these seemingly inconsistent policies have been accommodated is a major question to be considered in this review of the salient features of land recording acts.

I.   BASIC TYPES OF STATUTES

Recording acts typically are classified as (1) race, (2) notice, or (3) race-notice. If conveyees are allowed a specified period of time within which to record—a feature which may be added to any of the above types of acts but which is not common today—the statute is also categorized as a "period of grace" act. A recent survey placed the recording acts of only two states, Louisiana and North Carolina, in the race category generally, and those of three other states in that category as to some instruments—mortgages in Arkansas, Ohio, and Pennsylvania (except for purchase money) and oil and gas leases in Ohio. Most states have acts either of the notice or race-notice type, each type having about an equal following.

Of these types, the race statute is most consistent with the penalty principle. The North Carolina act provides: "No conveyance of land . . . shall be valid to pass any property, as against lien creditors or purchasers for a valuable consideration . . . but from the time of registration thereof. . . ."[2] Under this act, as construed, an unrecorded conveyance is void even as to a subsequent purchaser who knew of its existence, and a subsequent bona fide purchaser gains no priority over the earlier unrecorded instrument unless he records first. Thus, priority is determined by a race to the records. Of course, an unrecorded conveyance would be valid as to the grantor, his heirs, devisees, donees, and anyone else other than "lien creditors or purchasers for a valuable consideration." The North Carolina act is very similar to the Colonial prototypes. While there are many factors which may have shaped the early acts, it has been asserted that the most significant was a desire to provide a substitute for the publicity afforded by livery of seisin, which had been discarded as a mode of conveyance. In this context there would be a tendency to look upon recording acts as an additional conveyancing formality and to emphasize what was to be required of

---

[2]   N.C.Gen.Stat. § 47–18 (Supp.1959).

the grantor rather than what should be the qualifications of those to be protected. Subsequently, probably as a result of experience with actual cases, attention shifted to the latter and to "the view generally accepted in America today that the Recording Acts are an extension of the equitable doctrine of notice."[7]

In some of its applications the race statute seems unfair and out of harmony with the stated objectives of recordation. But instances in which bad faith purchasers are benefitted and good faith purchasers are harmed are probably infrequent, and can be almost eliminated by prompt recording. Indeed, the threat of such dire consequences may provide added incentive to prompt recordation. The best argument in favor of the race statute, however, is that it enables the title searcher to rely upon the records without the substantial risk under other types of acts that one will have constructive notice of unrecorded instruments.

A representative "notice" type act is the Iowa statute, which provides: "No instrument affecting real estate is of any validity against subsequent purchasers for a valuable consideration, without notice, unless filed in the office of the recorder of the county in which the same lies, as hereinafter provided."[8] California's act is an example of the "race-notice" type: "Every conveyance of real property . . . is void as against any subsequent purchaser or mortgagee of the same property, or any part thereof, in good faith and for a valuable consideration, whose conveyance is first duly recorded. . . ."[9] Both acts give priority over unrecorded instruments to subsequent purchasers only if they are without notice, and the California act also requires the bona fide purchaser to record first. The latter is an obvious compromise of the objectives of penalizing nonrecordation and protecting those who are likely to rely upon the records. By withholding protection from one who has not himself obeyed the statutory mandate to record, the race-notice act may be thought to have the merit of fairness and to encourage recording to a greater extent than would the notice act. But the seeming fairness of putting beyond the pale of the act both non-recorders is quite superficial, since only one has caused harm. It is also extremely doubtful that recording is actually stimulated by acts of the race-notice type, since even in a state having a notice type statute failure to record makes those protected by the act vulnerable to subsequent claims.

Argent Mortgage Company, LLC v. Wachovia Bank, NA

District Court of Appeal of Florida, 2010.
52 So.3d 796.

GRIFFIN, J.

Argent Mortgage Company, LLC ["Argent"] appeals the trial court's entry of judgment in favor of Wachovia Bank National Association, as Trustee Under Pooling and Servicing Agreement Dated as of November 1, 2004, Asset Backed Pass-Through Certificates Series 2004–WWF1 ["Wachovia"]. Argent argues that the trial court erred by finding that

---

[7] Bordwell, Recording of Instruments Affecting Land, 2 Iowa L.Bull. 51, 52 (1916).

[8] Iowa Code § 558.41 (1958).

[9] Cal.Civ.Code § 1214.

the mortgage now owned by Wachovia has priority over Argent's mortgage. We reverse.

On August 31, 2004, Gene M. Burkes and Ann Burkes ["the Burkes"] as borrower/mortgagor and Olympus Mortgage Company as lender/mortgagee executed a mortgage ["the Olympus Mortgage"] on real property as security for a $90,000.00 loan. The Olympus Mortgage was recorded on January 5, 2005. Subsequently, the Olympus Mortgage was assigned to Wachovia. As a result of default, Wachovia filed a complaint to foreclose the Olympus Mortgage and to enforce lost loan documents. Wachovia joined Argent as a defendant, alleging that Argent might claim some interest in or lien upon the subject property by virtue of a recorded mortgage.

On December 10, 2004, the Burkes as borrower/mortgagor and Argent as lender/mortgagee executed a mortgage ["the Argent Mortgage"] as security for a $65,000.00 loan on the same real property that is the subject of the Olympus Mortgage. The Argent Mortgage was recorded on January 31, 2005. Subsequently, Wells Fargo Bank became the owner of the Argent Mortgage. An action to foreclose the Argent Mortgage was initiated as a result of default.[1]

Argent filed a motion for summary judgment in its favor, requesting that the trial court determine that the Argent Mortgage has priority over the Olympus Mortgage. Likewise, Wachovia filed a motion for summary judgment in its favor, requesting that the trial court determine that the Olympus Mortgage has priority over the Argent Mortgage. After conducting a hearing, the trial court entered an order on the competing motions for summary judgment as to priority. In the order, the trial court made findings on facts not in dispute, including the dates of execution and recordation of the two mortgages and Argent's lack of actual or constructive notice of the Olympus Mortgage at the time of execution of the Argent Mortgage. Ultimately, the trial court deemed "the Florida statutes on recordation," namely sections 695.01 and 695.11, Florida Statutes, "to be of the race-notice variety," found that the Olympus Mortgage should have priority over the Argent Mortgage, and entered a partial final judgment in favor of Wachovia.

On appeal, Argent argues that the trial court erred by finding in favor of Wachovia on the issue of mortgage priority because the trial court erred in concluding that sections 695.01 and 695.11, Florida Statutes when read together, create a "race-notice" scheme. Argent asserts that section 695.01, Florida Statutes, alone determines which mortgage has priority, that section 695.01 is, and, for over a century, has been recognized to be a "notice" statute, not a "race-notice" statute and that, under section 695.01, the Argent Mortgage has priority over the Olympus Mortgage.

Wachovia acknowledges that section 695.01, Florida Statutes, is a "notice" type of recording statute. However, Wachovia contends that amendments made to section 695.11, Florida Statutes, have converted Florida into a "race-notice" state.

As an initial matter, it bears explaining that recording statutes are classified into three categories: race, notice, and race-notice. *See* Grant S. Nelson, William B. Stoebuck, and Dale A. Whitman, *Contemporary*

---

[1]   The trial court entered an order consolidating the two foreclosure actions.

Property 1004 (West Group 2d ed. 2002). These can generally be described as follows:

• Under a *race* recording statute, a subsequent mortgagee of real property will prevail against a prior mortgagee of the said real property if the subsequent mortgage is recorded before the prior mortgage.

• Under a *notice* recording statute, a subsequent mortgagee of real property for value and without notice (actual and constructive) of a prior mortgage of the said real property will prevail against the prior mortgagee.

• Under a *race-notice* recording statute, a subsequent mortgagee of real property for value and without notice (actual and constructive) of a prior mortgage of the said real property will prevail against the prior mortgagee if the subsequent mortgage is recorded before the prior mortgage.

Importantly, under either a notice or a race-notice recording statute, the subsequent mortgagee cannot be without constructive notice if the prior mortgage has been recorded as of the time of execution of the subsequent mortgage. *See id.* at 1004–07.

Application of each type of recording statute to the undisputed facts here yields the following results:

• Wachovia prevails under a race recording statute because the Olympus Mortgage was recorded before the Argent Mortgage;

• Argent prevails under a notice recording statute because it is a subsequent mortgagee for value and did not have notice of the Olympus Mortgage at the time of execution of the Argent Mortgage; and

• Wachovia prevails under a race-notice recording statute because, although Argent is a subsequent mortgagee for value and did not have notice of the Olympus Mortgage at the time of execution of the Argent Mortgage, the Olympus Mortgage was recorded before the Argent Mortgage.

Commentators appear uniformly to categorize section 695.01 as a "notice" type of recording statute. . . .

Florida courts over time have described and applied Florida's recording statute in a manner that is consistent with a "notice" type of recording statute. *See Lesnoff v. Becker,* 101 Fla. 716, 135 So. 146, 147 (1931) (" 'Under our recording statutes, subsequent purchasers, acquiring title without notice of a prior unrecorded deed, mortgage, or transfer of real property, or any interest therein, will be protected against such unrecorded instrument, unless the party claiming thereunder can show that such subsequent purchaser acquired the title with actual notice of such unrecorded conveyance or mortgage; and the burden of showing such notice is upon the party claiming under such unrecorded instrument, the presumption in such case being that such subsequent purchaser acquired his title in good faith and without notice of the prior unrecorded conveyance.' " (*quoting Rambo v. Dickenson,* 92 Fla. 758, 110 So. 352, 353 (1926))). . . . Florida's approach to the problem was succinctly described by the Florida Supreme Court in *Van Eepoel Real Estate Co. v. Sarasota Milk Co.,* 100 Fla. 438, 129 So. 892, 895 (1930):

[I]t is generally held, in states having recording statutes similar to ours, that if A conveys lands to B, a bona fide purchaser for value, who does not go into possession and who failed to record his deed until after A conveys the same land to C, a second bona fide purchaser for value without notice of B's interest, and B then records his deed before C records his, the title of C shall nevertheless prevail as between C and B, because it is the fault of B that he did not immediately record his deed, thereby permitting C to deal with the property and part with his consideration without knowledge of B's interest. So B is estopped and the equities are with C.

Section 695.01, notwithstanding, the trial court accepted Wachovia's argument that a 1967 amendment to a different statute, section 695.11, Florida Statutes, entitled, "Instruments deemed to be recorded from time of filing" converted Florida from a "notice" to a "race-notice" jurisdiction. The earliest version of section 695.11 dates back to 1885. Examination of the language of the 1906, 1920, and 1935 iterations of section 695.11, make clear that this statute was intended to provide a mechanism for determining the time at which an instrument was deemed to be recorded. Nothing in the case law suggests that section 695.11 modifies section 695.01.

As a result of the 1967 amendment, section 695.11 now includes the following language: "The sequence of such official numbers *shall determine the priority of recordation.* An instrument bearing the lower number in the then-current series of numbers *shall have priority over any instrument* bearing a higher number in the same series." (Emphasis added).[a] Wachovia contends that the inclusion of this language converted Florida from a "notice" state to a "race notice" state. We disagree. The amendment to section 695.11 is designed to refine the test for determining the time at which an instrument is deemed to be recorded, not to alter the recording requirement found in section 695.01.

Section 695.11 also applies to indexing errors. To the extent that an instrument bears an official register number but has been indexed incorrectly, it is nevertheless deemed to be recorded. *See Anderson v. N. Fla. Prod. Credit Ass'n,* 642 So.2d 88, 89 (Fla. 1st DCA 1994) ("[A]n instrument is deemed to be 'officially recorded' when the instrument is accepted by the court clerk and is given 'official register numbers.' . . . While indexing is required, priority is not contingent upon such, and the cases cited to us by appellants do not alter the plain language of th[e] statute which provides that '[t]he sequence of such official numbers shall determine the priority of recordation.' "); *see also Orix Fin. Servs., Inc. v. MacLeod,* 977 So.2d 658, 658 (Fla. 1st DCA 2008).

Wachovia relies on an earlier opinion of this Court, *Rice v. Greene,* 941 So.2d 1230 (Fla. 5th DCA 2006), in support of its contention that

---

[a] [The preceding portion of § 695.11 reads: All instruments which are authorized or required to be recorded in the office of the clerk of the circuit court of any county in the State of Florida, and which are to be recorded in the "Official Records" as provided for under § 28.222, and which are filed for recording on or after the effective date of this act, shall be deemed to have been officially accepted by the said officer, and officially recorded, at the time she or he affixed thereon the consecutive official register numbers required under § 28.222, and at such time shall be notice to all persons.—eds.]

Florida has a race-notice type of recording statute. In *Rice,* this Court quoted section 695.01 and found:

> In other words, "an unrecorded deed is not good or effectual in law or equity against creditors or subsequent purchasers for valuable consideration who are without notice of the transaction." *Fryer v. Morgan,* 714 So.2d 542, 545 (Fla. 3d DCA 1998). Therefore, *because Mr. Greene had no notice* of the earlier warranty deed between Mr. Rice and Mrs. Schwartz *and paid valuable consideration* for the property, *Mr. Greene's recording of his warranty deed before Mr. Rice gives Mr. Greene priority to the property.*

Id. at 1232 (emphasis added). According to Wachovia, this language proves that priority in recording is key. Notably, however, *Rice* does not mention section 695.11 and recording was not an issue. The subsequent purchaser in *Rice* (Mr. Greene) had priority to the property under a notice type of recording statute because he paid value for the property and did not have notice (actual or constructive) of the earlier warranty deed at the time of the conveyance. The fact that Mr. Greene's deed was recorded before Mr. Rice's does not affect the outcome under a notice type of recording statute. Although a portion of the sentence in *Rice,* on which Wachovia relies, mentions recording, in that case, it was superfluous.

We conclude that Florida is, and remains, a "notice" jurisdiction, and notice controls the issue of priority. Since Argent is a subsequent mortgagee for value and did not have notice of the Olympus Mortgage at the time of execution of the Argent Mortgage, the Argent Mortgage has priority over the Olympus Mortgage. As such, the trial court erred by entering partial summary final judgment in favor of Wachovia on the issue of priority.

REVERSED and REMANDED.

PALMER, J., and PERRY, B., JR., ASSOCIATE JUDGE, concur.

NOTES

1. *Indexing Errors.* When a grantee makes an error in a document that causes it to be indexed outside of the chain of title, there is no constructive notice of the instrument. See, e.g., Keybank National Association v. NBD Bank, 699 N.E.2d 322 (Ind.App.1998) (first mortgagee attached wrong description to mortgage). If, however, a grantee delivers an accurate instrument to the recorder who fails to index it properly, the traditional majority rule, as followed by the Fla. Stat. § 695.11 in *Argent Mortgage,* holds that a subsequent purchaser does have constructive notice of the document. See Luthi v. Evans, 223 Kan. 622, 576 P.2d 1064 (1978); First Citizens Nat'l Bank v. Sherwood, 583 Pa. 466, 879 A.2d 178 (2005); M. Friedman, Contracts and Conveyances of Real Property § 9.5 (7th ed. 2006); but see the minority rule maintaining that there is no constructive notice. See, e.g., Howard Savings Bank v. Brunson, 244 N.J.Super. 571, 582 A.2d 1305 (1990); Greenpoint Mortgage Funding, Inc. v. Schlossberg, 390 Md. 211, 888 A.2d 297 (2005). Which is the better rule? Which party can best prevent the loss from improper indexing? What should standard operating procedure be in such cases? Can the recorder be held liable for incorrect indexing? See Siefkes v. Watertown Title Company, 437 N.W.2d

190 (S.D.1989) (denying negligence action against recorder by title company seeking indemnification for improper indexing). See generally Murray, Defective Real Estate Documents: What Are The Consequences?, 42 Real Prop. Prob. & Tr.J. 367 (2007).

2. *Operation of Statutes.* Although race statutes and notice statutes rest on sharply divergent conceptual bases, their practical operation is much the same. Whether Blackacre is in a race or a notice jurisdiction, a buyer who is about to acquire the parcel will be well advised to conduct a thorough title search before paying seller and accepting her deed. In a race jurisdiction, only a title search can inform buyer whether there is an outstanding interest adverse to his that has been recorded first. In a notice jurisdiction, a title search will inform buyer of any recorded, adverse interest that will operate to defeat his title under the doctrine of constructive notice. Similarly, once buyer acquires Blackacre, he is well advised, whether in a race or notice jurisdiction, to record his instrument promptly—in a race jurisdiction, in order to win the race to the recorder's office as against any subsequent grantee; in a notice jurisdiction, to give any subsequent grantee constructive notice of his claim.

As a practical matter, race and notice systems differ only in the additional search burden that notice statutes impose on the buyer. Under a race statute, the buyer need do no more than search record title. In a notice jurisdiction, buyer must not only search title, but must also inspect Blackacre for physical evidence of title defects or encumbrances, such as possession by someone other than the seller, putting him on inquiry notice of an adverse claim.

Which system, race or notice, is more efficient? More fair? Do race-notice statutes offer a desirable compromise, or do they only compound the individual defects of race and notice systems?

For recent cases applying the North Carolina race statute, see In re McCormick, 669 F.3d 177 (4th Cir. 2012); Department of Transportation v. Humphries, 496 S.E.2d 563 (N.C.1998).

3. *Bibliographic Note.* For an additional explanation of the theory and policies of the recording acts, see Schechter, Judicial Lien Creditors Versus Prior Unrecorded Transferees of Real Property: Rethinking the Goals of the Recording System and Their Consequences, 62 S.Cal.L.Rev. 105 (1988) (arguing that a "cost avoidance" rationale explains the system). See also, Berger, An Analysis of the Doctrine that "First in Time is First in Right," 64 Neb.L.Rev. 349 (1985); Mautner, "The Eternal Triangles of the Law:" Toward a Theory of Priorities in Conflicts Involving Remote Parties, 90 Mich.L.Rev. 95 (1991).

2. THE CONDITIONS OF PROTECTION

a. NOTICE

Corwin W. Johnson, Purpose and Scope of Recording Statutes*

47 Iowa Law Review 231, 238–243 (1962).

Notice plays two major roles in the recording system. When an instrument is recorded, the record gives constructive notice of its existence and thus may be an important factor in any controversy in which notice is relevant, even in controversies not involving instruments required to be recorded. Even when an instrument is not recorded, notice disqualifies purchasers and creditors from gaining priority and thus, in effect, notice is a substitute for recording. Another way of stating the distinction is to say that in its first role notice aids those who record and in its second role it aids those who do not record.

The policy aspects of these two roles of notice are not identical. To allow notice to substitute for recording at all is debatable, since to do so favors one who was at fault in not recording and tends to weaken the incentive to record. It would seem to follow that notice which disqualifies purchasers and creditors should be narrowly confined. No such consideration is involved in determining what constitutes notice of a recorded instrument. The person who has recorded is not at fault and the only question is whether it would be reasonable, in view particularly of the condition of the records, to expect the party in question to have discovered the recorded instrument. In this situation, there would be no basis for a preference of either a broad or narrow scope of notice. However, the cases do not seem to reflect an awareness of this distinction. Indeed, it is arguable that the scope of notice of recorded interests has been restricted too much and that the scope of notice of unrecorded interests has been unduly expanded.

A. Record Notice

Although the statutes typically declare that the recording of an instrument shall be notice to "all persons," the courts have generally held that one is given constructive notice only of those recorded instruments which are within his "chain of title." . . .

Another example of instruments appearing on the record which are deemed not to be recorded is that where the instrument is not authorized to be on the record, such being true in most states of unacknowledged instruments and instruments of a type not included in the statutory list of recordable instruments. This position has the merit of logic and is probably sound statutory construction, but it is disturbing that purchasers and creditors who could have discovered an instrument by a reasonable search of the records are not deemed to have been given constructive notice. To go further and say that purchasers and creditors may ignore such instruments even if they see them seems unsound, but there is a conflict of authority on this point.

---

* Copyright 1962 by The University of Iowa (Iowa Law Review).

B.   NON-RECORD NOTICE

Knowledge of the existence of an unrecorded interest is notice, but notice is broader than knowledge. The most common example is notice of facts which inquiry of the possessor would produce. Implicit here is the policy of protecting only the reasonably cautious, and it is assumed that such persons would not be content with a record search. Granting the soundness of that policy and assumption, the rub is that formulation and application of the required standard of care are likely to be uneven and in some cases too severe.

Thus, there is a conflict as to whether the duty to inquire of the possessor is created by the mere fact of possession or whether it is confined to instances where the fact of possession was known to the purchaser or was discoverable by a reasonable effort. There are also instances of imposition of an unduly severe burden of inquiry. If the purchaser knows, from the record or other sources, that the possessor is a lessee or a tenant in common, the purchaser might reasonably suppose that inquiry would be pointless, nevertheless, in many states he would be charged with notice of additional unrecorded interests of the possessor. According to one view, notice is imparted by such acts as cultivation or erection of improvements by a possessor who does not live on the land, even though such acts point to no one other than the record owner.

But if the purchaser has been abused by the possession-is-notice concept, he has also been spared undeservedly in some instances, particularly where a grantor of a recorded deed remains in possession and claims an unrecorded interest, even though here possession is inconsistent with the record and therefore inquiry-provoking. The unconvincing justification offered for this result is that the "grantor's deed is a conclusive declaration that he has reserved no rights and estops him from setting up any arrangement by which the deed is impaired."[64] This misses the point: the one who has failed to record is always at fault; the relevant question is whether there is notice.

Knowledge of facts unrelated to possession may also raise a duty to inquire, though it appears that, in the absence of such knowledge, a stranger need not investigate the reputation of the title in the community.

Perhaps the most outrageous notice doctrine is that which denies that a purchaser who claims through a quitclaim deed is a bona fide purchaser. In the doctrine's most extreme form, the quitclaim is a bar even though it is remote and inquiry would be unproductive. In this form, the doctrine can hardly be said to be a notice doctrine at all, and justification must be sought in the notion that a quitclaim conveys only what the grantor owns and that a grantor who previously had conveyed his entire interest has nothing left to convey. If this idea is valid, one would expect to encounter it even in states having a race statute, but the Supreme Court of North Carolina has rejected it, saying that it "overlooks the registration statutes," by virtue of which " 'the grantor retains a power to defeat his earlier conveyance.' "[68] Since this power would pass in most states to a donee, devisee, or heir, no reason is

---

[64]   Davis v. Wilson, 237 Iowa 494, 505, 21 N.W.2d 553, 560 (1946).

[68]   Hayes v. Ricard, 245 N.C. 687, 691–92, 97 S.E.2d 105, 109 (1957).

apparent why it would not also pass to a quitclaim grantee. If the only effect of the quitclaim is to excite inquiry and charge one with notice of unrecorded interests reasonably discoverable, the question is raised as to what line of inquiry is suggested by the fact that the vendor is reluctant to give more than a quitclaim or that he derives title through a quitclaim. The latter would probably be ignored by the prudent purchaser and the former would, at most, cause a vague suspicion which apparently could not be resolved. It is conceivable, but improbable, that flagrantly suspicious circumstances, though not suggestive of lines of inquiry which would lead to evidence of unrecorded interests, might so strongly indicate lack of title in the grantor that the purchaser would be denied the status of a bona fide purchaser, but the vendor's insistence on giving a quitclaim, standing alone, is hardly such a case. It is generally understood that honest vendors having some confidence in their titles are sometimes unwilling to execute any conveyance other than a quitclaim.

Kinch v. Fluke

Supreme Court of Pennsylvania, 1933.
311 Pa. 405, 166 A. 905.

KEPHART, JUSTICE.

Kinch and wife, appellants, on September 24, 1923, purchased by written agreement (not recorded) from Robert E. Fluke and James H. O'Rorke, trading as the Home Realty Company, a dwelling house in Altoona, for $6,000. Of this sum $2,261.14 was paid in cash on the execution of the agreement. The balance, $3,738.86, was to be paid in monthly installments of $35 each, with interest on deferred payments. The legal title was in Fluke. On October 8th of the same year, the purchasers entered into open, exclusive, and notorious possession of the premises and occupied it as a dwelling house, residing in it from that time until the present time. Monthly payments were being duly made when, in 1925, Fluke, the vendor, gave a mortgage for $3,000 to the Seaboard Company. It was recorded in January of that year. At the same time, he gave another mortgage for $700 to the Finance Company. It was recorded the same day as the Seaboard mortgage. In December, 1926, Kinch and wife borrowed $4,000 from John C. Peightal and gave a mortgage on the premises as security. With this money, the balance of the purchase money due the vendor was paid. A deed was executed at the same time from Fluke to the appellants. When the purchase price was paid, Kinch and his wife knew nothing of the execution of the two mortgages; neither the Seaboard Company nor the Finance Company made any inquiry as to the condition of Fluke's title by reason of the occupancy of the premises by the appellants.

When appellants desired to borrow the $4,000 above mentioned, they visited an attorney and inquired from him whether he could place the loan. The attorney took up the matter with Peightal. He agreed to make the loan provided he (Peightal) was allowed a commission of $200 for making the loan. When the attorney searched the record for mortgages and other liens, he discovered the two mortgages, but decided the mortgages were not against the land in question, and did not report them to the mortgagees. The loan was made and the commission paid to the attorney, who retained $50 from it and remitted $150 to Peightal.

Appellants, some years later, on discovering the two mortgages as possible liens against their property, brought a bill to remove the cloud on their title imposed by the two mortgages and to obtain a decree of satisfaction as they related to this land. The court below found that the recording of the mortgages to the Seaboard and Finance Companies between the time of the execution of the agreement and the execution of the deed was constructive notice of these liens to Kinch and his wife, the appellants. In addition, the court found that the latter had actual notice of these mortgages through the knowledge their attorney had after searching the record. The court below found that the attorney represented the appellants and the mortgagee. The bill was dismissed, and this appeal followed.

A vendee who purchases land, by entering into open, notorious, and continued possession of it, gives notice, not only of his interest in the land, but that of his vendor. This is true, notwithstanding the fact that the agreement of purchase was not entered of record. Such possession is evidence of title, and, in a certain sense, is a substitute for recording the agreement of purchase, and is sufficient to put a subsequent purchaser or mortgagee on inquiry.

A prospective purchaser is required to make inquiry of those in possession, and, failing to do so, is affected with constructive notice of all that such inquiry would have disclosed. The notice of possession which the law imposes on a subsequent vendee or mortgagee without regard to whether he has actual knowledge or not is of such character that it cannot be controverted. The means of knowledge which possession affords is regarded as the legal equivalent of actual notice.

It is conceded that neither of the mortgagees, the Seaboard or Finance Company, made any inquiry of appellants, who were in possession, as to the nature of their title. The mortgagees, therefore, took subject to the interests under the agreement of sale.

What, then, was the effect of the recording of mortgages on future payments by the vendees, appellants in this case? It has been stated that, where a vendor sells lands by articles of agreement, a subsequent judgment against the vendor binds the legal estate in the vendor, but only to the value of the unpaid purchase money.

As it has been otherwise stated, a judgment against the vendor of land retaining legal title is not so much a lien on the legal title as it is on the unpaid purchase money. These statements of the law are broader than the cases there mentioned will sustain, for they omit any mention of notice to the vendee. The question here involved is whether the recording of a mortgage against the vendor's interest is constructive notice of the lien of that mortgage to vendees in possession under an agreement of sale.

The purpose of recording mortgages or of entering judgment is to give notice of its existence to those who subsequently acquire an interest in or lien upon the property. It is sometimes said "that the record of a deed [or mortgage] is constructive notice to all the world." That, it is evident, is too broad and unqualified an enunciation of the doctrine. Recording is constructive notice only to those who are bound to search for it, subsequent purchasers and mortgagees, and, perhaps, all others who deal with or on the credit of the title, in the line of which the recorded deed (or mortgage) belongs.

The assignment of a mortgage by an instrument duly executed, or the assignment of such mortgage on the margin of the mortgage record, is not such legal notice to the mortgagor as will preclude him from setting up payments made by him to the mortgagee before he has actual notice of the assignment. In order to complete the assignee's right with respect to such an assignment, the law requires actual notice be given to the mortgagor of the assignment. The recording act imposes no duty on the mortgagor to search the record for the purpose of ascertaining whether the mortgagee has assigned the mortgage. To do so would impose too great a burden on the mortgagor. Actual notice must be given to the mortgagor of the assignment.

It has also been held that the docketing of a judgment is not notice of the lien to a purchaser in possession, since, after he has made his contract for the purchase and entered into possession, he is not bound to keep the run of the dockets, and payments subsequently made by him to the vendor pursuant to the contract without actual notice of the judgment are valid as against such liens.

We held in Riddle v. Berg Co., 7 A. 232, 3 Sad. 566, where land was held pursuant to an article of agreement, and before the date of final payment a promissory note was given for the final payment, that it was not the duty of the purchaser, who has given such note in payment of the balance due on the purchase price, to watch the record and, when a judgment is entered, inform the judgment plaintiff of the existence of the note and the possibility of its being negotiated.

If the recording of an assignment of a mortgage, or the docketing of a judgment, is not effective as constructive notice to the vendee of land when payments are to be made by the vendee to the mortgagor or judgment debtor, but actual notice is essential, how then can the rule of law be that the mere recording of a mortgage is effective as constructive notice to the vendee who purchased and was in actual possession of the land before the existence of such mortgage. The mortgagee has ample opportunity to ascertain the state of the possessor's title, the amount of purchase money due the mortgagor, and is given ample opportunity to effectuate his lien by notifying the vendee under articles of his mortgage or judgment. We can readily see where land is sold by articles of agreement, and the purchaser does not go into possession, that his subsequent payment of purchase money to the vendor must be at his peril if judgments or mortgages have been entered in the interim. Such lienholders have no means of information (apart from actual notice) that the mortgagor or judgment debtor has parted with his title. The rule must be otherwise as to the sale of land under articles of agreement where possession is taken thereunder and held openly, continuously, and notoriously. The opportunity is then afforded to the mortgagee of completing his lien by actual notice to the vendee in possession. We, therefore, conclude that the recording of a mortgage or docketing of a judgment is not constructive notice of a lien on land to a vendee then in possession under an agreement of sale. The mortgage operates as an assignment of the balance of the purchase money due, but actual notice is required to make it effective. In other words, the lien of a mortgage or judgment, whether or not recorded or docketed, on the unpaid purchase money due from a vendee of land in possession under an agreement of sale, is not effective so as to require payment of the unpaid purchase money to the mortgagee or holder of the judgment unless actual notice of such mortgage or judgment has been given to the vendee in possession.

If the rule were otherwise in the instant case, before each monthly payment was made, it would be necessary for the purchasers to inquire from the mortgage record whether the vendor had assigned the balance of the purchase money due. This is an unwarranted burden.

The next question involved is whether appellants received actual notice of the two mortgages against this land given by Fluke, one of appellees, by reason of the search made by the attorney. A careful analysis of this record convinces us that the attorney did not act for both parties; that his employment was by the mortgagee, Peightal, and not by appellants. However, conceding his agency was for both appellants and the mortgagee, it was not for both as to all transactions involved; the attorney was agent for appellants to secure the money; he was agent for the mortgagee to obtain proper security for the money by examining title and preparing the proper documents to evidence the security. Any information the attorney acquired while conducting transactions in behalf of one may not be considered as within his knowledge as agent of the other for different purposes.

Furthermore, assuming that he was attorney for appellants, they would be affected only with the notice of the record which was fairly within the knowledge of the attorney. Upon examination of the record, we find that the attorney had no knowledge or notice of the existence of these two mortgages as liens on this particular land. He was asked the question, and it was not contradicted:

"Q. You say now that you didn't know of the existence of any lien or incumbrances or mortgages on this Kinch property when you made the examination? A. Yes. That is what I stated to you.

"Q. And you have now just put on the record your statement that you didn't have any knowledge of the mortgage of the Seaboard Insurance Company of $3,000 and the mortgage of the Finance Company of America of $700? A. No. I will explain that this way. I had knowledge of these two mortgages but did not have knowledge of the fact that they were liens of this property.

"Q. Then you were mistaken in the liens on this property? A. I was mistaken in the two descriptions in these two mortgages. That they were not identical with the description in the deed.

"Q. Did you make any effort to determine whether the two descriptions embraced in these two mortgages were the same as the property which was conveyed by Fluke to Kinch? A. I made my examination as I always do. I got the list of the mortgages against the person in the title. And then the description in the mortgage and if I believe they are not liens against the property I check them off. That is what I did here.

"Q. How long after this loan of Peightal's was closed did you find that these two mortgages covered the Kinch property? A. Not until Mr. Robert Hare came up to the office and informed me.

"Q. That was the first information you had? A. Yes. That was the first I had.

"Q. That was how long after the date of the Peightal mortgage? A. I will go the other way. I think that was possibly a year ago, as near as I can recollect.

"Q. Approximately four years after the date of the Peightal mortgage? A. That was about the time. The Peightal mortgage was in 1926."

We do not have before us a copy of the mortgages, and, as a result, are unable to ascertain from an inspection thereof whether Culp's (the attorney's) statement was justified, but the testimony clearly demonstrates that a title searcher would be misled by the description in the mortgage when attempting to trace title from the description in the deed. A principal is not to be affected with knowledge of his agent unless his agent has, or could have had within his duty, the knowledge with which it is sought to affect him; if the agent did not know, then, of course, his principal could not know.

We conclude that the court below was in error in dismissing the bill.

The decree of the court below must be reversed, the bill reinstated, with direction to enter a decree in accordance with the prayer of the bill, costs to be paid by appellee.

Sanborn v. McLean

Supreme Court of Michigan, 1925.
233 Mich. 227, 206 N.W. 496.

WEIST, J. Defendant Christina McLean owns the west 35 feet of lot 86 of Green Lawn subdivision, at the northeast corner of Collingwood avenue and Second boulevard, in the city of Detroit, upon which there is a dwelling house, occupied by herself and her husband, defendant John A. McLean. The house fronts Collingwood avenue. At the rear of the lot is an alley. Mrs. McLean derived title from her husband, and, in the course of the opinion, we will speak of both as defendants. Mr. and Mrs. McLean started to erect a gasoline filling station at the rear end of their lot, and they and their contractor, William S. Weir, were enjoined by decree from doing so and bring the issues before us by appeal. Mr. Weir will not be further mentioned in the opinion.

Collingwood avenue is a high grade residence street between Woodward avenue and Hamilton boulevard, with single, double, and apartment houses, and plaintiffs, who are owners of land adjoining and in the vicinity of defendants' land, and who trace title, as do defendants, to the proprietors of the subdivision, claim that the proposed gasoline station will be a nuisance per se, is in violation of the general plan fixed for use of all lots on the street for residence purposes only, as evidenced by restrictions upon 53 of the 91 lots fronting on Collingwood avenue, and that defendants' lot is subject to a reciprocal negative easement barring a use so detrimental to the enjoyment and value of its neighbors. Defendants insist that no restrictions appear in their chain of title and they purchased without notice of any reciprocal negative easement, and deny that a gasoline station is a nuisance per se. We find no occasion to pass upon the question of nuisance, as the case can be decided under the rule of reciprocal negative easement.

This subdivision was planned strictly for residence purposes, except lots fronting Woodward avenue and Hamilton boulevard. The 91 lots on Collingwood avenue were platted in 1891, designed for and each one sold solely for residence purposes, and residences have been erected upon all of the lots. Is defendants' lot subject to a reciprocal negative easement? If the owner of two or more lots, so situated as to bear the relation, sells one with restrictions of benefit to the land retained, the servitude becomes mutual, and, during the period of restraint, the owner of the lot or lots retained can do nothing forbidden to the owner of the lot sold. For want of a better descriptive term this is styled a reciprocal negative easement. It runs with the land sold by virtue of express fastening and abides with the land retained until loosened by expiration of its period of service or by events working its destruction. It is not personal to owners, but operative upon use of the land by any owner having actual or constructive notice thereof. It is an easement passing its benefits and carrying its obligations to all purchasers of land, subject to its affirmative or negative mandates. It originates for mutual benefit and exists with vigor sufficient to work its ends. It must start with a common owner. Reciprocal negative easements are never retroactive; the very nature of their origin forbids. They arise, if at all, out of a benefit accorded land retained, by restrictions upon neighboring land sold by a common owner. Such a scheme of restriction must start with a common owner; it cannot arise and fasten upon one lot by reason of other lot owners conforming to a general plan. If a reciprocal negative easement attached to defendants' lot, it was fastened thereto while in the hands of the common owner of it and neighboring lots by way of sale of other lots with restrictions beneficial at that time to it. This leads to inquiry as to what lots, if any, were sold with restrictions by the common owner before the sale of defendants' lot. While the proofs cover another avenue, we need consider sales only on Collingwood.

December 28, 1892, Robert J. and Joseph R. McLaughlin, who were then evidently owners of the lots on Collingwood avenue, deeded lots 37 to 41 and 58 to 62, inclusive, with the following restrictions:

"No residence shall be erected upon said premises which shall cost less than $2,500, and nothing but residences shall be erected upon said premises. Said residences shall front on Helene (now Collingwood) avenue and be placed no nearer than 20 feet from the front street line."

July 24, 1893, the McLaughlins conveyed lots 17 to 21 and 78 to 82, both inclusive, and lot 98 with the same restrictions. Such restrictions were imposed for the benefit of the lands held by the grantors to carry out the scheme of a residential district, and a restrictive negative easement attached to the lots retained, and title to lot 86 was then in the McLaughlins. Defendants' title, through mesne conveyances, runs back to a deed by the McLaughlins dated September 7, 1893, without restrictions mentioned therein. Subsequent deeds to other lots were executed by the McLaughlins, some with restrictions and some without. Previous to September 7, 1893, a reciprocal negative easement had attached to lot 86 by acts of the owners, as before mentioned, and such easement is still attached and may now be enforced by plaintiffs, provided defendants, at the time of their purchase, had knowledge, actual or constructive, thereof. The plaintiffs run back with their title, as do defendants, to a common owner. This common owner, as before stated, by restrictions upon lots sold, had burdened all the lots retained with reciprocal restrictions. Defendants' lot and plaintiff Sanborn's lot, next thereto, were held by such common owner, burdened with a reciprocal negative easement, and, when later sold to separate parties, remained burdened therewith, and right to demand observance thereof passed to each purchaser with notice of the easement. The restrictions were upon defendants' lot while it was in the hands of the common owners, and abstract of title to defendants' lot showed the common owners, and the record showed deeds of lots in the plat restricted to perfect and carry out the general plan and resulting in a reciprocal negative easement upon defendants' lot and all lots within its scope, and defendants and their predecessors in title were bound by constructive notice under our recording acts. The original plan was repeatedly declared in subsequent sales of lots by restrictions in the deeds, and, while some lots sold were not so restricted, the purchasers thereof, in every instance, observed the general plan and purpose of the restrictions in building residences. For upward of 30 years the united efforts of all persons interested have carried out the common purpose of making and keeping all the lots strictly for residences, and defendants are the first to depart therefrom.

When Mr. McLean purchased on contract in 1910 or 1911, there was a partly built dwelling house on lot 86, which he completed and now occupies. He had an abstract of title which he examined and claims he was told by the grantor that the lot was unrestricted. Considering the character of use made of all the lots open to a view of Mr. McLean when he purchased, we think, he was put thereby to inquiry, beyond asking his grantor, whether there were restrictions. He had an abstract showing the subdivision and that lot 86 had 97 companions. He could not avoid noticing the strictly uniform residence character given the lots by the expensive dwellings thereon, and the least inquiry would have quickly developed the fact that lot 86 was subjected to a reciprocal negative easement, and he could finish his house, and, like the others, enjoy the benefits of the easement. We do not say Mr. McLean should have asked his neighbors about restrictions, but we do say that with the notice he had from a view of the premises on the street, clearly indicating the residences were built and the lots occupied in strict accordance with a general plan, he was put to inquiry, and, had he inquired, he would have found of record the reason for such general conformation, and the benefits thereof serving the owners of lot 86 and the obligations running with such service and available to adjacent lot owners to prevent a departure from the general plan by an owner of lot 86.

While no case appears to be on all fours with the one at bar, the principles we have stated, and the conclusions announced, are supported by Allen v. City of Detroit, 167 Mich. 464.

We notice the decree in the circuit directed that the work done on the building be torn down. If the portion of the building constructed can be utilized for any purpose within the restrictions, it need not be destroyed.

With this modification, the decree in the circuit is affirmed, with costs to plaintiffs.

NOTES

1.   *Standard Operating Procedures.* Three forms of notice will operate to defeat subsequent purchasers under notice and race-notice statutes:

(a) *Actual notice* (the notice given by the subsequent purchaser's actual knowledge of the prior transfer);

(b) *Inquiry notice,* sometimes called *implied actual notice* (the notice given by the subsequent purchaser's actual knowledge of facts that, if reasonably inquired into, would produce actual knowledge of the prior transfer);

(c) *Constructive notice*, sometimes called *record notice* (the notice given by the prior transfer's recordation in the public title records so that the subsequent purchaser, conducting a reasonable title search, would obtain actual knowledge of the transfer).

These three forms of notice effectively prescribe the standard operating procedure that a purchaser in notice and race-notice jurisdictions should follow up to the moment of closing: (a) search files, desk drawers and memory for any communications or facts that might have given actual knowledge; (b) inspect the land for physical evidence of an interest held by someone other than the immediate seller; and (c) conduct a title search for documentary evidence of an interest held by someone other than the immediate seller. A purchaser in a race jurisdiction need only conduct a title search to determine whether anyone has beaten him, or any predecessor in title, to the recorder's office. And, in all jurisdictions, standard operating procedure requires the buyer to record his own instrument of transfer immediately after closing.

There is some interplay between actual, inquiry and constructive notice. For example, it is generally held that recordation of an unrecordable instrument, such as an unacknowledged deed, will not give constructive notice of the instrument's contents. See, for example, Metropolitan National Bank v. United States, 901 F.2d 1297 (5th Cir.1990). But the instrument will give *actual* notice to a title examiner who comes upon the recordation in the course of his or her search. Since, as a practical matter, buyers will almost invariably order title searches before paying their purchase money, they will, in the course of reviewing their examiner's title report, obtain actual notice of recorded, but unrecordable, instruments. Would you ever advise a client *not* to order a title search on the off-chance that he can thus avoid learning of an earlier transaction embodied in a recorded but unrecordable instrument?

On the issue of actual notice, see Waxler v. Waxler, 699 A.2d 1161 (Me.1997) (deed by grantor to her brother was ineffective since the brother had notarized previous deed by grantor for the property, thus giving him actual notice of the prior interest).

2.   *Extent of Records Search.* Typically, one must search for documents affecting real property at the office of the recorder of deeds. A title searcher must also check certain other public records, such as probate records, the judgment docket, and tax filings, that disclose interests in the land.

Ellingsen v. Franklin County, 117 Wash.2d 24, 810 P.2d 910 (1991), distinguished between those filings in public offices that give constructive notice and those that do not. The county claimed that the owners of land had constructive notice of the county's claim of a roadway over the property as a result of the county's filing of a petition for the establishment of a road in the office of the county engineer in 1908. The court held, however, that although the statute provided that the engineer "shall be an office of record," those filings were only to provide information to the public about locations of roads, bridges, and ditches and were not intended serve as notice of prior interests in land. The court contrasted the language of the engineer statute with the general recording act which indicated that a document filed thereunder "shall be notice to the world." The court explained its unwillingness to broadly construe the engineer statute as providing constructive notice of prior interests in property:

> If it were held that a document is constructive notice of its content because it is designated a public record or because the office in which it is filed is an office of record, the consequences would be disastrous to the stability and certainty heretofore provided by recording with the county auditor and the grantor-grantee index required by RCW 65.04. This prediction of chaos is a natural consequence of reading RCW 42.17 which makes an all-inclusive definition of "public record". RCW 42.17.020(26). Such public record is every writing containing information relating to the conduct of government or the performance of any governmental or proprietary function. . . .

> The records which are declared to be public records are those of defined state and local agencies including: (1) every state (a) office, (b) department, (c) division, (d) bureau, (e) board, (f) commission, or (g) other state agency, and (2) every local agency, *i.e.,* every (a) county, (b) city, (c) town, (d) municipal corporation, (e) quasi-municipal corporation, or (f) special purpose district or (g) other local public agency. RCW 42.17.020(1).

> Under the County's theory all records of these multiple, scattered public offices would impart constructive notice of everything contained in those records because, like the engineer's office, those are public records in public offices. . . . To import constructive notice from every piece of paper or computer file in every government office, from the smallest hamlet to the largest state agency, would wreak havoc with the land title system. As a matter of fact, it would render impossible a meaningful title search.

Id. at 29–30, 810 P.2d at 913. For theoretical modeling of the extent of a title search, see Baker, Miceli, Sirmans & Turnbull, Optimal Title Search, 31 J.Leg.Stud. 139 (2002).

3. *Inquiry Notice from Inspection of Land.* One fact that is universally held to put a purchaser on inquiry notice is possession by someone other than his seller. Often in these circumstances the possessor will be a tenant, and the purchaser will thus be placed on notice not only of the tenant's rights under its lease, but of any other rights, such as an option to purchase the property. See Vitale v. Pinto, 118 A.D.2d 774, 500 N.Y.S.2d 283 (1986); U.P.C., Inc. v. R.O.A. General, Inc., 990 P.2d 945 (Utah App.1999) (purchaser had notice of billboard lease because billboard was visible on the property). Occasionally the possessor will claim ownership of the land through adverse possession or through a prior deed from the present seller or some other owner. See Bump v. Dahl, 26 Wis.2d 607, 133 N.W.2d 295 (1965) (grading, sodding, planting and landscaping of parcel gave subsequent purchaser inquiry notice of prior purchaser's possessory claim).

In some situations, however, physical presence may not give inquiry notice. For example, in Lamb v. Lamb, 569 N.E.2d 992 (Ind.App.1991), a tenant in common entered into a contract to purchase the interests of the other cotenants. Brush cutting by the tenant on the property did not give inquiry notice of his contract to subsequent purchasers since he did not reveal his ownership when asked by the subsequent purchasers and his actions were not so unusual for a cotenant that any further inquiry was required. A statute may also alter the rules. See N.M.Stat.Ann. § 14–9–3 (possession based on an unrecorded executory real estate contract does not give a subsequent purchaser notice or a duty to inquire about the possession).

Nonpossessory interests are more problematic. Will manhole covers suffice to put a purchaser on inquiry notice of an easement for an underlying sewer line? Compare Lake Meredith Development Co. v. City of Fritch, 564 S.W.2d 427 (Tex.Civ.App.1978) (yes) with Fanti v. Welsh, 152 W.Va. 233, 161 S.E.2d 501 (1968) (no). Wolek v. Di Feo, 60 N.J.Super. 324, 159 A.2d 127 (1960), found no inquiry notice, notwithstanding an easement holder's argument that "in the quiet hours of the evening" the purchaser "must have heard the rush of water through the underground pipes." Even public utility easements, offering more clearly visible clues such as power lines and support poles, have been treated differently within the same jurisdiction. Compare Florida Power & Light Co. v. Rader, 306 So.2d 565 (Fla.App.Dist. 4 1975) with McDaniel v. Lawyers' Title Guaranty Fund, 327 So.2d 852 (Fla.App.Dist. 2 1976). For an in depth analysis, see Eichengrun, The Problem of Hidden Easements and the Subsequent Purchaser Without Notice, 40 Okla.L.Rev. 3 (1987).

4. *Inquiry Notice from Inspection of Record.* To what extent will a recorded instrument trigger a duty of further inquiry? The question arises when a recorded instrument has obviously been altered, or phrased in an unusual way, or when a title search reveals only a partial conveyance to the purchaser's grantor or some predecessor in title, and no indication whether, or to whom, the other parts were conveyed. Courts generally hold purchasers to notice of all facts they could have discovered through reasonable inquiry into the discrepancy. See, for example, Mister Donut of America, Inc. v. Kemp, 368 Mass. 220, 330 N.E.2d 810 (1975). See also, Municipal Trust & Saving Bank v. United States, 114 F.3d 99 (7th Cir.1997) (reference in deed that transaction was subject to federal estate taxation gave notice of a tax lien); Smith v. Arrow Transportation Co., 571 So.2d 1003 (Ala.1990) (claimant's initials following clause in deed naming corporation owned by claimant's husband as grantee did not give constructive notice to subsequent purchaser that claimant had an interest in the property).

The same question arises when an instrument that is disclosed by the title search refers to one that is not disclosed, as when a deed recites that the property is subject to a mortgage and the mortgage is unrecorded. Here, too, courts impose a duty of reasonable inquiry. Many legislatures, however, have acted to relax the duty. Massachusetts, for example, requires that a reference be "definite" in order to put purchasers on notice. An "indefinite reference" is one that recites interests created by unrecorded or improperly recorded documents, ambiguous descriptions of the interest, an indication that the holder of the interest is a "trustee" when the trust is not of record, or any reference that does not disclose where the instrument is recorded. Mass.Gen.Laws Ann. c. 184, § 25 (West 1991). Recitals in Wisconsin must indicate the place of recording or specify "by positive statement" the nature and scope of the outstanding interest and the identity of the holder of the interest. Wis.Stat.Ann. § 706.09(1)(b) (West 1991).

5. *Constructive Notice of Imperfectly Executed Documents.* Statutes typically require that as a prerequisite to recording a document, it must be acknowledged by the executing party before a notary (who then is usually required to place her seal on the document). Will there be constructive notice of an improperly acknowledged deed that is actually recorded by the recorder? The majority of jurisdictions holds that if the defect in attestation is not apparent on the face of the document, there will be constructive notice. See, e.g., Leeds Building Products, Inc. v. Sears Mortgage Corp., 267 Ga. 300, 477 S.E.2d 565 (1996) (constructive notice of security deeds even though the attesting witness never saw the mortgagor sign the document). When the defect is apparent, such as the failure to have the document acknowledged at all, there is no constructive notice. See, e.g., Phipps v. CW Leasing, Inc., 186 Ariz. 397, 923 P.2d 863 (App.1996); In re Marsh, 12 S.W.3d 449 (Tenn.2000) (absence of notary seal prevented constructive notice). Do these rules make sense? Can you reconcile them with the rules described in Note 4 above that allow for inquiry notice from an inspection of the record?

6. *Kinch v. Fluke.* Would the same result have been reached in Kinch v. Fluke if Kinch had been a tenant exercising an option to buy under an unrecorded lease? If Kinch had been a purchaser under a marketing contract and, after paying ten percent down, paid the remainder in a lump sum at closing without a further title search? Was the court correct to conclude that, in searching title, the lawyer was acting only as Peightal's agent? Was it correct to conclude that the attorney's legal judgment on the irrelevance of the two mortgages meant that he "had no knowledge or notice of the existence of these two mortgages as liens on this particular land"?

On the last two questions, compare Farr v. Newman, 14 N.Y.2d 183, 250 N.Y.S.2d 272, 199 N.E.2d 369 (1964), in which plaintiff, who had entered into an unrecorded contract to purchase a parcel for $3,000, sought specific performance against defendant who purchased the parcel for $4,000 before plaintiff's contract was to close, but not before plaintiff informed defendant's attorney of plaintiff's outstanding contract. Holding for plaintiff, the court of appeals noted first that "[e]ven if the plaintiff had not affirmatively relied upon the agency of the attorney by giving notice, and the attorney had merely discovered plaintiff's equity in the course of his title investigation, the principal would still be bound by such knowledge. A conflict of interest does not avoid the imputation of knowledge." 199 N.E.2d at 373, 14 N.Y.2d at 190, 250 N.Y.S.2d at 278. The court also ruled that the lawyer's mistaken conclusion as to the contract's unenforceability did not insulate his client from knowledge. Indeed, the mistake defeated any claim of attorney fraud that might have avoided the principal's liability for the agent's conduct.

Farr is in line with the general trend to follow agency rules and impute the lawyer's knowledge to the client. What result should be reached if the attorney, chosen by purchaser from the title insurance company's list of approved attorneys, fails to inform the title company of a defect discovered in the course of the title search? Should the lawyer's knowledge be imputed to the purchaser, with the result that the title company is relieved of liability under the provision in its policy excepting coverage for defects known to the insured at the time the policy was issued? For the startling answer, see Weir v. City Title Ins. Co., 125 N.J.Super. 23, 308 A.2d 357 (1973).

7. *Policies for Inquiry Notice.* What policies would be served, and what policies would be disserved, if states were to drop the inquiry notice bar? The actual notice bar? Representing a buyer, how comfortable would you feel knowing that every tramped-down footpath or half-remembered conversation may later form the basis for a finding of inquiry or actual notice? In terms of fairness or efficiency, what is wrong with a pure race regime?

b.   PURCHASER FOR VALUE

Corwin W. Johnson, Purpose and Scope of Recording Statutes*

47 Iowa Law Review 231, 233–237 (1962).

According to one view, the recording acts benefit as purchasers those who have parted with only nominal consideration, but most courts appear to require something more substantial. The latter position is obviously sound if there is to be any real distinction between purchasers and donees.

On the other hand, one who parts with value in reliance upon the record is not necessarily protected. Some courts declare that this is the fate of one who receives notice of the unrecorded instrument after having parted with the consideration but prior to execution of the deed. The thought seems to be that such a person is not a "purchaser." Of course, the equitable doctrine of bona fide purchaser protected only those who acquired a legal title, but the recording acts are much broader and are now generally deemed to protect those who have acquired equitable interests. As a matter of policy, there would seem to be no reason for attaching significance to the execution of the deed. The time when protection is needed is the moment when consideration is given. This problem is most likely to arise when the contract provides for payment of the consideration over a period of years and the execution of a deed at or near the end of that period. It is generally recognized that one who has acquired the legal title but who has paid only a portion of the purchase price before he acquires notice is a pro tanto bona fide purchaser and, as such, entitled at least to a lien and in some cases to the legal title, subject to a lien in the adverse party. The

---

same should be true of a purchaser who has only a contract and there is authority to that effect. Essentially the same problem is raised in a race-notice jurisdiction when notice is received after delivery of the deed but prior to its recordation. The conclusion seems sound that "after having paid the consideration and received a conveyance, the purchaser is qualified to race for priority of record unhampered by any notice that he may thereafter receive."[20]

Other limitations on the protection accorded purchasers by the recording system may be briefly noted. Although a lessee is considered a purchaser, as a practical matter this means very little to the lessee, since he is protected only to the extent of rent paid prior to notice and must vacate the premises at the end of the period for which such rent was paid. This may result in a great hardship when the lessee has made expensive improvements or has otherwise substantially changed his position, as a lessee for a long term may well have done. A mortgagee also comes within the broad category "purchaser," but not when the mortgage is given to secure an antecedent debt, according to the majority view. Not to be overlooked is the omnipresent threat to all groups of recording act beneficiaries that they will be charged with notice of claims which they could not reasonably be expected to discover. This subject will not be explored at this point, but one example may be noted. Consider the burden imposed upon the purchaser who is paying the price in installments by holding that he gets notice of a prior unrecorded deed whenever it is recorded, which means that he must examine the records immediately before paying each installment.

The protection afforded creditors by the recording acts of about half the states is not easy to justify. It is doubtful that more than a few creditors examine the deed records before extending credit. The creditor is more interested in the general financial status of his debtor than he is in the debtor's ownership of particular realty, though, of course, the former may be affected by the latter. While apparent land ownership is taken into account in the preparation of reports by credit investigation concerns, the deed records are not usually consulted for this purpose and a thorough title search is probably never made. Even if a creditor has relied upon the records in extending credit, he is generally protected only if he acquires a lien by attachment or by judgment without notice, despite an unqualified statutory reference to "creditors." The policy basis for making the acquisition of a lien the crucial event qualifying the creditor for protection is far from clear. It may be reasonable to suppose that an attaching creditor relies upon apparent ownership (though a thorough title search would rarely be made), but this is not likely to be true of the judgment creditor, and in both cases the change of position consists only of the slight expense involved in obtaining the lien. Even the acquisition of a lien may not be sufficient in a race-notice state, it having been held that the creditor must also obtain a recordable instrument, such as a sheriff's deed, and record it prior to the recording of the adverse interests.

In some states, the reliance factor is clearly not in the creditor picture at all. These are states whose courts have held, surprisingly, that the creditor is protected even though he had notice, usually on the basis of an exceedingly doubtful construction of the statutory phrase

---

[20]   4 American Law of Property § 17.11, at 574 (Casner ed. 1952).

"void as to creditors and subsequent purchasers for valuable consideration without notice." This result might make sense in terms of a policy of penalizing the failure to record by conferring title upon the nearest bystander, but to show greater favor to creditors than to bona fide purchasers, which is exactly the reverse of the relative esteem for these two groups in equity, is indefensible.

In view of the favored position accorded attachment and judgment lien creditors, it is strange that others with claims as good, or better, go unprotected. Consider the mechanics' lien claimant. It has been held that a contractor who erects a house pursuant to a contract with the record owner of the land is denied a mechanics' lien if the record owner had previously conveyed the land to a grantee who failed to record his deed, and who thus reaps a windfall. In states whose recording acts protect purchasers but not creditors, this result has been based upon the ground that a mechanics' lien claimant is not a "purchaser." In one state which protects creditors against unrecorded interests, the question whether a mechanics' lien claimant is a "creditor" was avoided by pointing to the provision of the mechanics' lien statute requiring that the contract be entered into with the "owner" or with his consent, a typical provision in such statutes. Consider also the creditor who seeks security for an existing debt by securing a mortgage, rather than an attachment. As has been observed, he is generally not protected as a "purchaser," but is there any reason why he should be refused protection as a "creditor"? Must the lien be one created by operation of law rather than by agreement? General statements in treatises and judicial opinions containing no hint that a lien other than by attachment or judgment will suffice are commonplace. At least one court has held against the mortgagee without considering whether he might be a "creditor." There is authority, however, that he is a "creditor."

Anderson v. Anderson

Supreme Court of North Dakota, 1989.
435 N.W.2d 687.

MESCHKE, JUSTICE.

Plaintiffs appealed from a judgment quieting defendants' title to an undivided one-fourth of 280 acres in McKenzie County. We reverse and remand.

Kari Anderson patented the 280 acres from the United States in 1916. In 1922, Kari conveyed the 280 acres to her four children, A.T. Anderson, James T. Anderson, Julia Anderson, and Theodore T. Anderson, as tenants in common, each acquiring an undivided one-fourth.

This dispute is only about Julia's undivided one-fourth received from Kari. The plaintiffs are children of James T. Anderson's son, George Teleford Anderson. They have record title to three-fourths of the 280 acres and claim the remaining one-fourth both through adverse possession and through a deed from Julia to James T., dated February 7, 1934, but not recorded until December 14, 1983. The defendants, heirs of Julia's children, Ida Mathews and Willie H. Anderson, claim one-fourth of the 280 acres through a quit-claim deed from Julia to Ida and Willie, dated October 1, 1951, and recorded October 11, 1951.

The plaintiffs and their predecessors in interest have farmed the land since before 1936. They have paid the property taxes and satisfied a mortgage placed on the property by Kari. During this time the defendants have neither been in possession of the land, nor have they received or claimed any profits or rents from it.

The trial court concluded that the plaintiffs failed to establish adverse possession of the one-fourth interest because they and their predecessors had never ousted Julia and her heirs from their rights in the property as co-tenants. The court further concluded that the recorded 1951 deed from Julia to her children, Ida and Willie, had priority over the unrecorded 1934 deed from Julia to James T. Anderson because, under Section 47–19–41, N.D.C.C., Julia's children were purchasers in good faith and for a valuable consideration. The court quieted defendants' title to one-fourth of the property. Plaintiffs appealed.

We consider the relative priority of the 1934 and 1951 deeds under Section 47–19–41, N.D.C.C., which, in relevant part, says:

> "Every conveyance of real estate not recorded shall be void as against any subsequent purchaser in good faith, and for a valuable consideration, of the same real estate, or any part or portion thereof, whose conveyance, . . . first is deposited with the proper officer for record and subsequently recorded, whether entitled to record or not, . . . prior to the recording of such conveyance."

Plaintiffs contended that Ida Mathews and Willie H. Anderson were not good faith purchasers for a valuable consideration in 1951. Defendants responded that Ida and Willie were good faith purchasers for a valuable consideration under Section 47–19–41, N.D.C.C., so that their 1951 deed, recorded in 1951, had priority over the 1934 deed, recorded in 1983. Relying on Sections 9–05–10 and 9–05–11, N.D.C.C.,[1] defendants argued that the 1951 deed was presumptive evidence of consideration and that plaintiffs did not show a want of consideration for that deed.

Although this court has often considered the requirements of notice for a good faith purchase under § 47–19–41, N.D.C.C., *e.g.*, Williston Co-op. Credit Union v. Fossu, 427 N.W.2d 804 (N.D.1988); Ildvedsen v. First State Bank of Bowbells, 24 N.D. 227, 139 N.W. 105 (1912)[2], the element of valuable consideration has not been directly examined.[3]

---

[1]   Section 9–05–10 says:

"A written instrument is presumptive evidence of a consideration."

Section 9–05–11 says:

"The burden of showing a want of consideration sufficient to support an instrument lies with the party seeking to invalidate or avoid it."

[2]   In Ildvedsen, supra, this court stated the general rule that possession of the premises by a person other than the seller gives an intended purchaser notice of the possessor's rights. The court recognized an exception to that general rule, holding that when possession by one other than the seller is consistent with the record title, the possession is presumed to be under the record title and is not notice of any outstanding unrecorded equities. See also Dixon v. Kaufman, 79 N.D. 633, 58 N.W.2d 797 (1953); Agricultural Credit Corp. v. State, 74 N.D. 71, 20 N.W.2d 78 (1945); Red River Valley Land & Investment Co. v. Smith, 7 N.D. 236, 74 N.W. 194 (1898). Ildvedsen, a husband and wife owned their home as tenants in common. Upon

Generally, for protection under a recording act as a good faith purchaser for value, the purchase must be for a valuable and not a nominal consideration. 6A Powell on Real Property ¶ 905[2] (1988); 5 Tiffany on Real Property § 1300 et seq. (1939); 8 Thompson on Real Property § 4319 (1963). *See* cases cited in United States v. Certain Parcels of Land, 85 F.Supp. 986, 1006 (S.D.Cal.1949) fn. 17.[4] The consideration does not have to be an equivalent value in order to be valuable, but it must be substantial and not merely nominal. 6A Powell *supra* at ¶ 905[2]; 5 Tiffany, *supra* at § 1301; 8 Thompson *supra* at § 4319; United States v. Certain Parcels of Land, *supra*. In Horton v. Kyburz, 53 Cal.2d 59, 346 P.2d 399, 403 (1959), the court quoted an explanation of the rationale:

> " 'The recording laws were not enacted to protect those whose ignorance of the title is deliberate and intentional, nor does a mere nominal consideration satisfy the requirement that a valuable consideration must be paid. Their purpose is to protect those who honestly believe they are acquiring a good title, and who invest some substantial sum in reliance on that belief.' "

We are not persuaded by the defendants' argument that the 1951 written deed was presumptive evidence of a value consideration.

In United States v. Certain Parcels of Land, *supra*, 85 F.Supp. at 1001, the court rejected a similar argument when it quoted with approval President and Presiding Elder of Southern California Conference of Seventh Day Adventists v. Goodwin, 119 Cal. App. 37, 39, 5 P.2d 973, 974 (1931):

> " 'That a written instrument presumes a consideration is ordinarily the rule. But, when the evidence shows that one has executed a valid deed to real estate, it follows that the grantor

---

their divorce, the husband quit claimed his interest to his wife, who remained in possession but did not record the deed because of unpaid taxes. Later, the First State Bank of Bowbells obtained a judgment against the husband and levied on the property. Applying the exception to the general rule, this court quieted title in the Bank, holding that the wife's possession did not put the Bank on inquiry as to her rights under the unrecorded quit-claim deed. Although the "continuing viability" of the "consistent with the record title position" has been questioned, *The Unreliable Record Title*, 60 N.D.L.Rev. 203, 217 (1984), we do not address that issue because of our disposition of this case on other grounds.

   [3] In Croak v. Witteman, 73 N.D. 592, 17 N.W.2d 542 (1945), a deed recited $1.00 as consideration. However, the actual consideration for the deed was satisfaction of a $700 antecedent debt and an agreement to settle $800 in delinquent taxes by payment of about $450. Without mentioning the predecessor of Section 47–19–41, N.D.C.C., this court held that the consideration was valuable. This court further held that the purchasers were in good faith and for a valuable consideration so that they took the property free of an unrecorded trust agreement.

   [4] The source notes § 47–19–41, N.D.C.C., say that it was derived from Cal.Civ. Code § 1214, which provided:

> "Every conveyance of real property other than a lease for a term not exceeding one year is void as against any subsequent purchaser or mortgagee of the same property, or any part thereof, in good faith and for a valuable consideration, whose conveyance is first duly recorded."

Cal.Civ.Code § 1214 was considered in United States v. Certain Parcels of Land, supra. Although not binding on this court, decisions interpreting a statute from which ours was derived are persuasive in interpreting our statute. Loken v. Magrum, 380 N.W.2d 336 (N.D.1986).

has exhausted his rights. And, when the same record shows that such grantor attempts to execute another grant to that same real estate, it follows that the grant carries nothing. Such second grant, therefore, carries with it, in the face of such facts, no presumption of a consideration.' "

The recital of a nominal consideration in a deed is insufficient to establish a valuable consideration or to raise a presumption of value for a good faith purchase. *E.g.*, United States v. Certain Parcels of Land, *supra*; James v. James, 80 Cal. App. 185, 251 P. 666 (1926). Moreover, the party claiming to be a good faith purchaser has the burden of proof to establish valuable consideration from evidence other than the deed. 8 Thompson on Real Property § 4316 (1963); United States v. Certain Parcels of Land, *supra*; James v. James, *supra*.

In this case, the defendants relied on the abstract of title to establish that Ida and Willie paid Julia "$10.00 & OG & VC" for the 1951 quit-claim deed. The defendants presented no evidence of any actual consideration. See United States v. Certain Parcels of Land, *supra*; Horton v. Kyburz, *supra*; Croak v. Witteman, 73 N.D. 592, 17 N.W.2d 542 (1945). We conclude, as a matter of law, that the consideration recited in the 1951 quit-claim deed was a nominal consideration and did not constitute a valuable consideration. Ida and Willie were not good faith purchasers for a valuable consideration under Section 47–19–41, N.D.C.C. Therefore, the defendants cannot claim priority over the plaintiffs by virtue of the 1951 deed.[5]

Accordingly, we reverse the judgment and remand for entry of judgment quieting title in the plaintiffs.[6]

ERICKSTAD, C.J., LEVINE, J., and VERNON R. PEDERSON, SURROGATE JUSTICE, concur.

VERNON R. PEDERSON, SURROGATE JUSTICE, sitting in place of GIERKE, J., disqualified.

VANDE WALLE, JUSTICE, concurring in the result.

I concur in the result reached in the majority opinion, but I am unconvinced by the rationale of the majority's analysis of the term "valuable consideration." However, I would not reach that question for I believe it is obvious that Ida and Willie could not have been good-faith purchasers in 1951, regardless of the consideration. As the majority opinion notes, the plaintiffs and the predecessors in interest farmed the land prior to 1936; they have paid the property taxes and satisfied a mortgage placed on the property by Kari; the defendants have not been in possession nor have they received any of the rents and profits from the land.

Although I would not abandon the "cotenant in possession" rule recently affirmed in Nelson v. Christianson, 343 N.W.2d 375 (N.D.1984), insofar as adverse possession is concerned, it is inconceivable to me that in 1951 Ida and Willie were under no

---

[5] Defendants cannot claim protection under the Marketable Record Title Act, Ch. 47–19.1, N.D.C.C., because they have not been in possession of the land at any time for twenty years. Section 47–19.1–01, N.D.C.C.

[6] Because of our decision about deeded title, we need not address the plaintiffs' claim of adverse possession.

obligation to inquire why Julia was not in possession and received none of the rents and profits from the land. Their position did not improve. They neglected to ask questions for more than 30 years thereafter even though they received no rents and profits from the land, at least the surface thereof. To rely on the joint-tenancy exception under these circumstances is incredible.

NOTE

1. *Adequacy of Consideration.* Almost all states today require that, to be protected, a subsequent grantee must have purchased his interest for value. In most states the requirement appears expressly in the recording act. In a few it has been added by judicial gloss. Colorado is apparently alone in not imposing the requirement. See Eastwood v. Shedd, 166 Colo. 136, 442 P.2d 423 (1968); Colo.Rev.Stat.Ann. § 38–35–109 (West 1990, amended by Laws 1996, H.B. 96–1369, eff. July 1, 1996). Courts generally agree that although the required value need not approximate the property's market value, it must represent more than merely nominal consideration. See Wolfner v. Miller, 711 S.W.2d 580 (Mo.App.1986) (payment of $100, or one percent of purchase price, not adequate consideration); Phillips v. Latham, 523 S.W.2d 19 (Tex.Civ.App.1975); see generally, 6A R. Powell, The Law of Real Property ¶ 904(2)(a) (1982).

What interests does the purchaser for value requirement serve? Do the requirement's benefits outweigh the uncertainty about whether someone gave the requisite value? What purposes would be served, and disserved, by exclusive reliance on actual, inquiry and constructive notice? In Anderson v. Anderson, would the result have been different if defendants had paid for the land and not inherited? Would it matter if the original deed to Julia Anderson was a quitclaim or warranty deed?

See generally, Schecter, Judicial Lien Creditors Versus Prior Unrecorded Transferees of Real Property: Rethinking the Goals of the Recording System and Their Consequences, 62 S.Cal.L.Rev. 105 (1988).

2. *Antecedent Debt as Consideration.* One recurring scenario goes as follows: B extends credit to X without taking a security interest; subsequently, after becoming concerned about X's ability to repay, B demands and receives a mortgage on realty owned by X (and B records). It turns out that X had given an unrecorded mortgage to A before B's mortgage. Does B have priority over A? Courts usually hold that since B gave antecedent, not contemporaneous, consideration for his mortgage, B is not a purchaser "for value" and thus cannot invoke the recording act to take prior to A. What is the justification for the contemporaneous consideration rule? Would there be contemporaneous consideration if B had extended the term of the loan at the time he received the mortgage? Would it matter if the extension had a fixed new date or was a demand obligation (allowing B to call the loan at any point in the future)? See Gabel v. Drewrys Ltd., USA, Inc., 68 So.2d 372 (Fla.1953); Great American Management & Investment v. Fowler, White, Gillen, Boggs, Villareal & Banker, 430 So.2d 545 (Fla.App.1983).

c.   CIRCUITOUS LIENS

In re Distribution of Proceeds from Sheriff's Sale of Premises 250 Bell Road, Lower Merion Township, Montgomery County

Superior Court of Pennsylvania, 1975.
236 Pa.Super. 258, 345 A.2d 921.

PRICE, JUDGE.

This is an appeal by judgment creditors from an order of Judge Richard E. Lowe of the Court of Common Pleas of Montgomery County, sustaining exceptions by appellee-judgment creditor to a sheriff's schedule of distribution. The controversy arises from the following facts.

Appellee, Boenning and Scattergood, Inc. (Boenning) obtained a judgment against John E. Jennings and Helen M. Jennings, his wife, in the amount of $30,500 on April 14, 1966. On July 3, 1970, Boenning initiated execution proceedings against real property owned by Jennings located at 250 Bell Road, Montgomery County. However, this writ of execution was not formally recorded in the judgment index in the Prothonotary's office in Montgomery County. Mr. and Mrs. Jennings moved for a stay order which was issued on July 13, 1970, to abide resolution of the judgment's validity. On July 29, 1972, the stay order was discharged by the lower court and that dismissal was affirmed per curiam by this court in Boenning & Company v. Jennings, 222 Pa.Super. 712, 294 A.2d 739 (1972).

Boenning then attempted to effect a second execution upon the Jennings' property, but again neglected to properly index the writ. Shortly thereafter, Mr. and Mrs. Jennings obtained an injunction from the United States District Court for the Eastern District of Pennsylvania which stayed the proceedings until December of 1973, when the United States Court of Appeals for the Third Circuit reversed the District Court. Boenning, at that time, instituted its third execution and the property was listed for sheriff's sale on February 20, 1974. On the same day the property was also scheduled for sale on the foreclosure of a first mortgage in favor of the Equitable Life Assurance Society. The sum of $85,000 was realized from the sale, and after satisfaction of liens for taxes, costs of execution, and the Equitable mortgage, all of which had undisputed priority, the sum of $66,679.50 was available for distribution. The liens asserted against the remaining funds are as follows:

Debt	Date of Lien	Approx. Amt. of Debt with Interest
1. Boenning Judgment	April, 1966	$48,500
2. Strawbridge and Clothier Judgment	March, 1971	1,650
3. McCoy Mortgage	August, 1971	30,000
4. Margolies Mortgage	December, 1971	17,500
5. Jay Vending Co. Judgment	June 19, 1973	21,000
6. McCoy Judgment	June 20, 1973	1,300
7. O'Hey Judgment	June 20, 1973	21,000

The mortgage and judgment of John H. McCoy were recorded with knowledge of the Boenning judgment. However, the liens of Margolies and Jay Vending Co. against the realty were entered of record more than five years from the entry of the unrevived Boenning judgment of April 14, 1966. Moreover, these lienholders at no time had any knowledge of the Boenning judgment, nor of the execution proceedings relating thereto.

Since Boenning's judgment had not been entered in the judgment index for nearly eight years preceding the date of the sale, the sheriff did not include it in his proposed schedule of distribution. Boenning filed exceptions to the schedule, seeking to maintain its position, claiming its lien had been improperly omitted.

On October 30, 1974, the lower court sustained the exceptions of Boenning and directed that they be accorded priority over all judgment creditors with the exception of Strawbridge and Clothier. We disagree with that result. Boenning's argument that the July 14, 1970, stay order had the effect of relieving it of its duty to revive its judgment is incorrect. Traditionally, an order opening a judgment for the purpose of letting in a defense neither extinguishes nor impairs a lien, and a judge is powerless to amend the lien.

. . . The present lien law, while not containing language identical to the 1827 lien law, does limit the duration of a lien to five years unless it is revived as provided. A lien is not affected by the opening of a judgment to permit a defense. Whatever effect the litigation involving the stay order had with respect to Boenning's judgment, it did not preclude or excuse Boenning from properly reviving its lien.

As of July 3, 1970, when the writ of execution was issued, Jennings' premises at 250 Bell Road were subject to Boenning's lien. McCoy, who has a lien junior to Boenning's, had full knowledge of the Boenning lien, since McCoy's attorney, Mr. William O'Hey, was also representing Mr. and Mrs. Jennings in their litigation against Boenning. The appellants rely upon the fact that the writ of execution issued on July 3, 1970, was not indexed. However, it is well established that the sole purpose of indexing is to give notice of the lien to subsequent lienors and purchasers. Where there is actual notice, indexing is not necessary. . . .

Therefore, McCoy and O'Hey, by having actual knowledge of Boenning's lien will take in the same priority as if Boenning had correctly indexed its writ of execution.

Having determined that Boenning's judgment remains superior to those of McCoy and O'Hey, we must align the priorities of all the interested lien creditors. McCoy's mortgage has been shown to be superior to both the Margolies mortgage and the Jay Vending Company judgment. However, it is also clear that Boenning's lien was not revived against Margolies or Jay Vending, neither of which had actual knowledge of the execution proceedings. Therefore, Margolies and Jay Vending have priority over Boenning, and this problem constitutes a circular lien.

Pennsylvania courts have used the temporal priority rule to break the circle and realign the parties: first in time—first in right.

However, the rule of temporal priority has never been applied when the circuity of liens has arisen solely as the result of the neglect of a prior lienholder in failing to properly record or revive his lien.

Other jurisdictions have been faced with the specific problem we face here—a circuity resulting from the failure of a prior lienholder to record his lien. The courts in Day v. Munson, 14 Ohio St. 488 (1863), and Hoag v. Sayre, 33 N.J.Eq. 552 (1881), faced this dilemma and fashioned clearly reasoned solutions for it.

In Day v. Munson, supra there was a circuitous lien involving three mortgages. The first mortgage lost its lien as against the third by failure to re-file within the statutory period of one year, so that the third mortgage was taken without notice of the first. However, the second mortgage lien was taken with actual notice of the prior mortgage, and had also maintained its priority over the third. As is the situation in the present case, the proceeds of the mortgaged property were insufficient to satisfy all the liens. A similar set of facts occurred in Hoag v. Sayre, supra. Both the *Hoag* court and the *Day* court used the same approach in solving the priorities problem. Both courts marshalled the funds in the following manner: to the third, if it be for as large a sum or a larger sum secured by the first; then the second encumbrance will be paid in full if the property is sufficient, and then the residue to the third, if there is a residue; and then the first lien will come in. Judge Dixon, in his dissent in Hoag v. Sayre, supra, at 562–63, is credited with extending and detailing, in a manner that has subsequently been widely accepted, this position:

"Therefore, if there be three encumbrancers, A, B and C, in the order of time, and A's lien be prior to B's, and B's to C's, but for A's omission to properly register his lien, it is void as to C's, then the fund should be disposed as follows:

1.   Deduct from the whole fund the amount of B's lien, and apply the balance to pay C. This gives C just what he would have if A had no existence.

2.   Deduct from the whole fund the amount of A's lien, and apply the balance to pay B. This gives B what he is entitled to.

3.   The balance remaining after these payments are made to B and C is to be applied to A's lien."

In the present case the judgment creditors shall be identified by the following: Boenning—"A", McCoy—"B", and "C" will represent both Margolies and Jay Vending Co.

We believe a distribution must be made with compliance to the formula previously expressed for the reasons pointed out in *Execution Sales: Lien Divestiture and Distribution of Proceeds in Pennsylvania,* 58 Dick.L.Rev. 244, 265–66 (1954):

"Where A has failed to record, B has recorded with notice, and C has recorded without notice, C alone is in a completely helpless position. A could have prevented the circuity by recording. B could have prevented it by refusing to accept a mortgage unless and until the prior mortgage had been recorded. C, however, cannot protect himself at all if he may not rely on the record. He can do nothing to prevent the circuity. If the only parties involved were A and C, the latter, of course, would be ahead. Shall the intermediation of B be permitted to yield A a windfall merely because B happened to have notice of A's unrecorded mortgage? Since C alone could have done nothing to have prevented the situation from arising, it would seem that he ought to be accorded the protection that reliance on the record was intended to afford. C therefore ought first to be paid that sum which he would have received had the priorities been as they appeared on the record. To hold otherwise would impair the results intended to be achieved by recording acts, and would act as an effective restraint on many security transactions, for no one could safely lend money on the security of real estate if it were already subject to an encumbrance."

An equitable distribution in this case which encourages compliance with the Judgment Lien Law is:

1.	Boenning Judgment	$13,470.50
2.	Strawbridge and Clothier Judgment (Undisputed)	1,650.00
3.	McCoy Mortgage	16,529.50
4.	Margolies Mortgage	17,500.00
5.	Jay Vending Co.	17,529.50
		$66,679.50

Reversed and remanded to the lower court for a distribution consistent with this opinion.

3. THE TITLE SEARCH

a. THE INDICES

Note, The Tract and Grantor-Grantee Indices*
47 Iowa Law Review 481–482 (1962).

A practical and convenient means of locating records which an owner of property must rely upon to prove his title and which a

---

* Copyright 1962 by The University of Iowa (Iowa Law Review).

prospective purchaser must depend upon when making a title search is an indispensable part of a workable system of recordation. Therefore, it is not surprising to discover that statutory provisions providing for some system of indexing which affords a history of the ownership of land and which discloses instruments or encumbrances affecting title to real property have been enacted in every state. There are currently two types of indices in use: (1) the grantor-grantee index, and (2) the tract index. This should not be interpreted as meaning that a dual system of indexing has always been present in the United States, for under the land owned by the English, French, Mexican, and Spanish governments on the North American Continent, there were no numbered tract systems in existence which could serve as a basis for land description. This was, of course, directly related to the fact that a competent survey had never been made of the land owned by these countries. Under these circumstances, even tax levies had to be against the owners of the land rather than against the land itself. Therefore, it was only logical that when some system of indexing was finally adopted the alphabetical or grantor-grantee system of indexing was selected. Nevertheless, even after the United States Government acquired the land formerly held by foreign countries in what is now the United States and adequate Government surveys had been undertaken and completed, the grantor-grantee system of indexing was still retained as the basis of land description. However, it was gradually discovered that the grantor-grantee system of indexing was inadequate in many respects. This led several states to enact statutes establishing a tract or numerical system of indexing. Nevertheless, even those states which adopted the tract system of indexing retained the alphabetical system of indexing which they had established at an earlier date.

Under the grantor-grantee or alphabetical index, pages are assigned in the index to each letter of the alphabet. As an instrument is received at the recorder's office, it is first recorded and then indexed under the name of the granting party on the appropriate page of the index. In addition, the county recorder is usually required to make notations on the grantor's page which disclose the name of the other party to the transaction, the book and page of the record where this particular transaction can be found, a description of the property, the date when the instrument was executed, the date when the instrument was filed for recordation, and the nature of the instrument. These same notations are then made as the transaction is indexed under the name of the grantee or the receiving party. After both steps have been completed, the instrument is considered to have been properly indexed.

Under the tract indexing system each parcel of land in a certain area is assigned a separate page in the index and every subsequent transaction affecting this property will be noted thereon. Under the tract system of indexing, a "parcel of land" means any geographical unit of land which has been surveyed and platted, such as sections, blocks, and lots. In addition to describing the property, the tract index also discloses the character of the instrument which affects the title to the property, the date of the execution of the instrument, the date of the filing of the instrument for recordation, and the names of the parties to the transaction. Under this system, therefore, *all* the instruments which affect the title to a particular parcel of realty will be noted on one page of the index. For this reason and innumerable others, the uniform adoption of the tract index has been urged by many legal scholars. However, the reaction of the respective state legislatures to this proposal apparently has not been enthusiastic.

NOTES

1.   *Grantor-Grantee and Tract Indices.* Some form of index is obviously required by the tremendous volume of recorded instruments. According to a 1973 report, approximately 7,000 instruments were recorded each month in Suffolk County, Massachusetts (Boston); about 15,000 documents were recorded each month in Cook County, Illinois (Chicago) and 5,000–6,000 instruments were recorded each *day* in Los Angeles. Basye, A Uniform Land Parcel Identifier—Its Potential for All Our Land Records, 22 Am.U.L.Rev. 251 (1973).

Even the best official indices are incomplete. Many transactions affecting title will be revealed by neither the grantor-grantee index nor the tract index. Thus, a title examiner must consult, among other sources, the indices of wills and administration of decedents' estates in the office of the county surrogate; the index of bankrupts in local federal court; local judgment dockets and dockets of federal tax liens. One problem with these auxiliary indices is that they are designed for purposes other than land title searches. For example, because neither grantor-grantee nor tract indices refer to land transfers by will or intestacy, a title examiner will quickly conclude that if these indices reveal a gap in ownership it is because title to the land at that point passed by devise or descent. But it may take considerable sleuthing to bridge that gap since probate registers are indexed alphabetically by the name of the decedent and not by the name of the estate's recipient—the only name that the examiner knows. See also, State v. Alaska Land Title Ass'n, 667 P.2d 714 (Alaska 1983), cert. denied, 464 U.S. 1040, 104 S.Ct. 704, 79 L.Ed.2d 168 (1984) (publication of federal land orders regarding easements in the Federal Register gives constructive notice to purchasers).

Although tract indices suffer many of the same limitations as grantor-grantee indices, they are clearly superior in terms of depth, speed and accuracy of search. Why, then, have tract indices not been widely adopted across the country? The simple answer is that they have—although not as official public indices, but rather as unofficial private indices maintained in "title plants" by examiners, abstracters and title insurance companies. Recognizing the superiority of tract indices, title examiners long ago began compiling them on their own. Each time an examiner searched title to a parcel, she would place a copy of the search in her files, indexed by reference to the parcel. The next time the examiner was retained to search title to that parcel, she had only to pull the relevant file and update her last search to the present. Title plants represent valuable assets and many, if not most, have been purchased by title insurance companies, enabling them quickly to establish themselves and their services in new locales.

MidCountry Bank v. Krueger, 762 N.W.2d 278 (Minn.App. 2009), provides a cautionary tale on the interplay of the indices. In 2005 the Minnesota legislature mandated that counties begin keeping a tract index in addition to the traditional grantor-grantee index. In *MidCountry*, the county indexed a deed in the grantor-grantee index but failed to accurately list it in the tract index. A subsequent buyer who only checked the tract index (which had no reference to the deed) was denied bona fide purchaser status. The court reasoned that the buyer had constructive notice through the proper recording in the grantor-grantee index. Was this the correct decision? Will it increase burdens on title searchers and decrease the attractiveness of switching to tract indices?

2. *Electronic Registration.* More than twenty-five states have adopted the Uniform Real Property Electronic Recording Act, approved by the National Conference of Commissioners on Uniform State Laws in 2004. The URPERA provides that electronic documents satisfy recording requirements, electronic signatures and notary acknowledgments are valid, and recorders must accept electronic documents for recording and indexing. Electronic recording and indexing may lead to a redefinition of traditional rules of title searching and constructive notice, as there will be more information more readily accessible at a cheaper cost. See First Citizens Nat'l Bank v. Sherwood, 817 A.2d 501 (Pa. Super. 2003) (suggesting computerization may alter search parameters as burden is lessened, so improper indexing by recorder may not necessarily defeat constructive notice), rev'd on other grounds, 583 Pa. 466, 879 A.2d 178 (2005) (proper indexing is not required, so mere recording gives constructive notice). But while digital recording and indexing may affect newly recorded documents, it remains unlikely that recorder offices will expend the huge sums necessary to create electronic indices for past records.

3. Electronic Registration. More than twenty-five states have adopted the Uniform Real Property Electronic Recording Act, approved by the National Conference of Commissioners on Uniform State Laws in 2004. The URPERA provides that electronic documents satisfy recording requirements, electronic signatures and notary acknowledgments are valid, and recorders must accept electronic documents for recording and indexing. Electronic recording and indexing may lead to a redefinition of traditional rules of title searching and constructive notice, as there will be more information more readily accessible at a cheaper cost. See First Citizens Nat'l Bank v. Sherwood, 817 A.2d 501 (Pa. Super. 2003) (suggesting computerization may alter search parameters as burden is lessened, so improper indexing by recorder may not necessarily defeat constructive notice), rev'd on other grounds, 583 Pa. 466, 879 A.2d 178 (2005) (proper indexing is not required, so mere recording gives constructive notice). But while digital recording and indexing may affect newly recorded documents, it remains unlikely that recorder offices will expend the huge sums necessary to create electronic indices for past records.

On URPERA and computerization of land records in general, see Kranz, Note, Expedition E-Recording, First Stop URPERA: How Universal E-Recording Under URPERA Could Revolutionize Real Estate Recording in the United States and Why It Should, 13 Minn.J.L.Sci. & Tech. 383 (2012); Bayer-Pacht, Note, The Computerization of Land Records: How Advances in Recording Systems Affect The Rationale Behind Some Existing Chain of Title Doctrine, 32 Card.L.Rev. 337 (2010); Cook, Land Law Reform: A Modern Computerized System of Land Records, 38 U.Cin.L.Rev. 385 (1969) Cook, Land Data Systems: The Next Steps, 43 U.Cin.L.Rev. 527 (1974); Cowan, Bringing Real Estate Recording Practices Into a New Era, 29 Real Est. Rev. 52 (Winter 2000); Jensen, Computerization of Land Records by the Title Industry, 22 Am.U.L.Rev. 393 (1973); McCormack, Torrens and Recording: Land Title Assurance in the Computer Age, 18 Wm. Mitchell

L.Rev. 61 (1992); Whitman, Digital Recording of Real Estate Conveyances, 32 J. Marshall L. Rev. 227 (1999).

For a discussion of the Mortgage Electronic Registration System (MERS) that provides a central registry for tracking mortgage rights and eliminates the need for paper documents assigning mortgages, see pages 355–367 below.

b.   TITLE STANDARDS

Lewis M. Simes & Clarence B. Taylor, Model Title Standards
1–5, 14–17 (1960).

THE FUNCTION AND SCOPE OF UNIFORM TITLE STANDARDS

A uniform title standard may be described as a statement officially approved by an organization of lawyers, which declares the answer to a question or the solution for a problem involved in the process of title examination. A brief reference to the task of the title examiner will show why such standards are needed.

I

Perhaps there is no greater delusion current among inexperienced conveyancers than that land titles are either wholly good or wholly bad, and that the determination of the person who has the title is merely a mathematical process of applying unambiguous rules of law to the abstract of the record. Yet the experienced conveyancer knows that the process of determining the marketability of a title is much more like determining whether, under all the facts, a man has a cause of action for negligence, than it is like the calculation of the amount of income tax a person owes on a given date.

No record, or abstract of the record, gives all the facts from which marketability must be determined. Thus, if the grantee in one recorded deed is Joseph Fremont and the grantor in the next is also Joseph Fremont, it is highly probable that these are one and the same person. But the record does not enable us to know whether it was delivered, whether it was a forgery, or whether the grantor was of sound mind when he executed it. Yet it is patently impossible for the title examiner to make a factual investigation to determine these things. He must decide, not whether it is absolutely certain that a given person has title, but whether it is reasonable to conclude from the facts which he can be expected to investigate, that this person has title.

As to many fact situations which are constantly recurring, a completely uniform practice of conveyancers is recognized. Thus, all conveyancers presume that the use of an identical name in one deed as grantee and in the next deed as grantor indicates that these names refer to the same person. All conveyancers presume, in the absence of evidence to the contrary, that a recorded deed has been delivered, that it was not a forgery, and that the grantor had the capacity to execute it. These presumptions may be described as a part of that body of recognized procedures known as the practice of conveyancers.

Now while, as to such matters as those already named, the practice of conveyancers is uniform, as to other matters there are notable variations. Thus, such questions as the following may be involved: whether a recorded conveyance should be questioned which does not have a notary's seal, or does not have a statement of the date on which the notary's commission expires; or, if a conveyance is made by a corporation, whether it should be questioned because there is no resolution on record showing the action of the corporation to make the conveyance, or showing whether the people who executed it as officers were in fact such officers at the time. As to these matters some title examiners may reach one conclusion and others the opposite conclusion. Uncertainties may also arise as to pure matters of law. Thus, a new probate procedure act may have been passed, and there may be a difference of opinion among members of the bar as to its constitutionality.

If the practice of conveyancers is not uniform, the tendency always is for the standards of the overmeticulous conveyancer to determine the standards of all conveyancers. Lawyer A feels that a title should be passed even though there are certain defects in the recorded acknowledgment, and he realizes that the majority of experienced, competent conveyancers would agree with him. But he also knows that Lawyer B would refuse to pass the title and would require a quiet title suit. Since Lawyer A is aware that his client may some day wish to sell the land to someone who employs Lawyer B to pass on the title, he will be inclined to impose the same overmeticulous standard as Lawyer B. Like Gresham's law, the result will be that bad title standards drive out good standards.

The remedy for this situation is either uniform title standards or legislation or both. Although Lawyer A may not dare to approve a title solely on his individual judgment, the situation is different if his judgment is backed by the official action of a bar association. If the official standards are supported by the great majority of competent, experienced conveyancers, and the prestige of the bar association is high, overmeticulous conveyancers may well follow these standards. Or even if a few do not, the conveyancer who does follow them can justify his position to his client by pointing out that he has followed officially approved standards.

Thus, uniform title standards have great remedial value because they crystallize the practices of conveyancers; and instead of being merely the recognized practices of individuals in a profession, they become also the recognized conclusions of the organized profession itself.

That it is desirable for state bar associations to adopt title standards, for the reasons already stated, has rarely been questioned in recent years. Already such standards are found in twenty-three states and doubtless other states will be added. But it is important, before adopting such standards, and before presenting a set of model standards, to inquire (1) what kind of subject matter is suitable for bar standards, and (2) what limitations exist as to this subject matter. We should also consider the questions: What form should title standards take, and what support from the bar is necessary in order that they accomplish their purpose.

Doubtless there is no hard and fast line which can be drawn to determine the appropriate subject matter of title standards. Nevertheless, a considerable area of agreement can be found in the published writings of those who have discussed this matter. Professor John C. Payne, writing in 1953, suggests the following as to general standards: "Such agreements may extend to: (1) the duration of search; (2) the effect of lapse of time upon defects of record; (3) the presumptions of fact which will ordinarily be indulged in by the examiner; (4) the law applicable to particular situations; and (5) relations between examiners and between examiners and the public"[2]. . . .

An actual survey of all the existing state title standards shows that their subject matter can include almost anything of interest to the conveyancer. Thus they have concerned the conduct of the title examiner, the form of his certificate of title, the form and content of abstracts, the effect of wild deeds, name variances, the application of statutes of limitations and of marketable title acts, tax titles, mechanics' liens, titles derived from decedents, the attitude of the title examiner toward the constitutionality of procedural statutes, and many other subjects.

That there are definite limits to the scope and function of uniform title standards is everywhere recognized. They cannot change or abolish a rule of law. They cannot do away with the requirement of delivery or of a writing for a valid conveyance; they cannot change the length of the statute of limitations, or abolish provisions for the extension of the period of limitations by disabilities. They cannot make a statute constitutional by declaring it so. In short, so far as rules of law are concerned, they can only resolve ambiguities pending their resolution by the highest court of the jurisdiction. So far as facts are concerned, they can determine what risks it is reasonable to expect a client to assume when a title is approved. Even that question of reasonableness is doubtless subject to review by a court. But if the practice of conveyancers is followed by all, the question is not likely to reach a court, and, even if it does, the court will generally follow the title standard.

* * *

STANDARD 2.1

EXAMINING ATTORNEY'S ATTITUDE

THE PURPOSE OF THE EXAMINATION OF TITLE AND OF OBJECTIONS, IF ANY, SHALL BE TO SECURE FOR THE EXAMINER'S CLIENT A TITLE WHICH IS IN FACT MARKETABLE AND WHICH IS SHOWN BY THE RECORD TO BE MARKETABLE, SUBJECT TO NO OTHER ENCUMBRANCES THAN THOSE EXPRESSLY PROVIDED FOR BY THE CLIENT'S CONTRACT. OBJECTIONS AND REQUIREMENTS SHOULD BE MADE ONLY WHEN THE IRREGULARITIES OR DEFECTS REASONABLY CAN BE EXPECTED TO EXPOSE THE PURCHASER OR LENDER TO THE HAZARD OF ADVERSE CLAIMS OR LITIGATION.

---

[2] "Increasing Land Marketability Through Uniform Title Standards," 39 Va.L.Rev. 1 at 10 (1953).

Similar Standards: Fla., 00; Idaho, 14; Ill., 1; Iowa, "General Standard"; Kan., 1.1; Minn., "General Statement"; Mo., 2; Mont., 25; N.M., 1; N.D., "General Standard"; S.D., 1.

Comment: Title Standards are primarily intended to eliminate technical objections which do not impair marketability and some common objections which are based upon misapprehension of the law. The examining attorney, by way of a test, may ask himself after examining the title, what defects and irregularities he has discovered by his examination, and as to each such irregularity or defect, who, if anyone, can take advantage of it as against the purported owner, and to what end.

STANDARD 2.2

PRIOR EXAMINATION

WHEN AN ATTORNEY DISCOVERS A SITUATION WHICH HE BELIEVES RENDERS A TITLE DEFECTIVE AND HE HAS NOTICE THAT THE SAME TITLE HAS BEEN EXAMINED BY ANOTHER ATTORNEY WHO HAS PASSED THE DEFECT, IT IS RECOMMENDED THAT HE COMMUNICATE WITH THE PREVIOUS EXAMINER, EXPLAIN TO HIM THE MATTER OBJECTED TO AND AFFORD OPPORTUNITY FOR DISCUSSION, EXPLANATION AND CORRECTION.

Similar Standards: Colo., 1; Conn., 35; Mont., 1; Ohio, 2.1; Okla., 2; Mo., 1; Wyo., 1.

STANDARD 2.3

REFERENCE TO TITLE STANDARDS IN LAND CONTRACT

AN ATTORNEY DRAWING A REAL ESTATE SALES CONTRACT SHOULD RECOMMEND THAT THE TERMS OF THE CONTRACT PROVIDE THAT MARKETABILITY BE DETERMINED IN ACCORDANCE WITH TITLE STANDARDS THEN IN FORCE AND THAT THE EXISTENCE OF ENCUMBRANCES AND DEFECTS, AND THE EFFECT TO BE GIVEN TO ANY FOUND TO EXIST, BE DETERMINED IN ACCORDANCE WITH SUCH STANDARDS.

Similar Standards: Conn., 67; Mo., 27; Okla., 28.

Comment: An attorney, drawing a real estate sales contract, should recommend the inclusion of the following language or its equivalent in the contract:

It is understood and agreed that the title herein required to be furnished by the seller, or party of the first part herein, shall be marketable and that marketability shall be determined in accordance with the Title Standards of the _____ Bar. It is also agreed that any defect in the title which comes within the scope of any of said Title Standards shall not constitute a valid objection on the part of the buyer provided the seller furnishes the affidavits or other title papers, if any, required in the applicable Standard to cure such defect. . . .

STANDARD 3.1

PERIOD OF SEARCH

[In this standard, it is assumed that record titles in the jurisdiction are so long that it is unreasonably burdensome to trace title back to the government, or if land titles do not originate with the United States or with the state, it is impracticable to trace titles back to their origin. Of course, if the Model Marketable Title Act, or similar legislation, were in force, then the length of search, for most purposes, would be determined by such legislation. This standard is not as satisfactory as a marketable title act, since defects in title prior to the period of search as stated in the title standard constitute a risk which a vendee must assume. Whereas, if a marketable title act is in force, defects in title prior to the period of the act are extinguished.]

A RECORD TITLE COVERING A PERIOD OF FIFTY YEARS OR MORE IS MARKETABLE: PROVIDED THAT THE BASIS THEREOF IS A WARRANTY DEED, ONE OR MORE QUITCLAIM DEEDS SUPPORTED BY A REASONABLE RECORD PROOF THAT THEY CONVEY THE FULL TITLE, A PATENT FROM THE UNITED STATES, OR A CONVEYANCE FROM THE STATE, A PROBATE PROCEEDING IN WHICH THE PROPERTY IS REASONABLY IDENTIFIABLE, A WARRANTY MORTGAGE DEED IF SUBSEQUENTLY REGULARLY FORECLOSED, OR ANY OTHER INSTRUMENT WHICH SHOWS OF RECORD REASONABLE PROBABILITY OF TITLE AND POSSESSION THEREUNDER; PROVIDED FURTHER THAT THE PERIOD ACTUALLY SEARCHED DOES NOT REFER TO OR INDICATE PRIOR INSTRUMENTS OR DEFECTS IN TITLE, IN WHICH CASE SUCH PRIOR INSTRUMENTS MAY BE USED IN TURN AS A START, AND THAT THE PERIOD ACTUALLY SEARCHED DISCLOSES INSTRUMENTS WHICH CONFIRM AND CARRY FORWARD THE TITLE SO ESTABLISHED.

Similar Standards: Conn., 1 (60-year period); Mo., 23 (45-year period); N.M., 20 (50-year period); Ohio, 2.2 (65-year period); Utah, 41 (50-year period).

Comment: In applying this standard, it is necessary to trace the record title back to a "root" or "start," which may be, and generally is, more than fifty years back. Any defects in the record title subsequent to the date of recording of the "root" or "start" must be considered by the examiner. Thus, suppose the record shows a warranty deed from A to B in fee simple, recorded in 1880. The next instrument in the chain of record title is a conveyance of flowage rights from B to X, recorded in 1882. The next instrument is a warranty deed from B to C in fee simple, recorded in 1920, in which the flowage rights are not mentioned. In 1959, D, who has contracted to purchase the land from C, employs an attorney to examine the title. The title examiner will have to go back to the deed of 1880 and will have to report that the record title is subject to flowage rights in X, created by the deed of 1882.

NOTE

See Epperson & Sullivan, Title Examination Standards: A Status Report, 4 Probate & Prop. 16 (Sept./Oct. 1990) (1990 survey indicates that twenty states have active title examination standards).

c.   EXTENT OF SEARCH: THE "RECORD CHAIN OF TITLE" PROBLEM

Morse v. Curtis

Supreme Judicial Court of Massachusetts, 1885.
140 Mass. 112, 2 N.E. 929.

MORTON, C.J. This is a writ of entry. Both parties derive their title from one Hall. Hall mortgaged the land to the demandant, August 8, 1872. On September 7, 1875, Hall mortgaged the land to one Clark, who had notice of the earlier mortgage. The mortgage to Clark was recorded January 31, 1876. The mortgage to the demandant was recorded September 8, 1876. On October 4, 1881, Clark assigned his mortgage to the tenant, who had no notice of the mortgage to the demandant. The question is, which of these titles has priority? The same question was distinctly raised and adjudicated in the two cases of Connecticut v. Bradish, 14 Mass. 296, and Trull v. Bigelow, 16 Mass. 406. These adjudications establish a rule of property which ought not to be unnoticed, except for the strongest reasons. It is true that in the late case of Flynt v. Arnold, 2 Metc. 614, Chief Justice SHAW expresses his individual opinion against the soundness of these decisions; but in that case the decision of the court was distinctly put upon that ground, and his remarks can be only considered in the light of *dicta,* and not as overruling the earlier adjudications.

Upon careful consideration, the reasons upon which the earlier cases were decided seem to us the more satisfactory because they follow the spirit of our registry laws and the practice of the profession under them. The earliest registry law provides that no conveyance of land shall be good and effectual in law "against any other person or persons but the grantor or grantors, and their heirs only, unless the deed or deeds thereof be acknowledged and recorded in manner aforesaid." St.1783, c. 37, § 4. Under this statute the court, at an early period, held that the recording was designed to take the place of the notorious act of livery of seizin, and that though by the first deed the title passed out of the grantor as against himself, yet he could, if such deed was not recorded, convey a good title to an innocent purchaser who received and recorded his deed. But the court then held that a prior unrecorded deed would be valid against a second purchaser who took his deed with a knowledge of the prior deed, thus ingrafting an exception upon the statute. 3 Mass. 575; Marshall v. Fisk, 6 Mass. 24. This exception was adopted on the ground that it was a fraud in the second grantee to take a deed if he had knowledge of the prior deed. As Chief Justice SHAW forcibly says in Lawrence v. Stratton, 6 Cush. 163, the rule is "put upon the ground that a party with such notice could not take a deed without fraud; the objection was not to the nature of the conveyance, but to the honesty of the taker, and therefore, if the estate had passed through such taker to a *bona fide* purchaser without fraud, the conveyance was held valid." This exception by judicial exposition was afterwards ingrafted upon the statute, and somewhat extended by the legislature. Rev.St. 59, p. 28; Gen.St. c. 59, § 31; Pub.St. c. 120, § 4. It is to be observed that in each of these revisions it is provided that an unrecorded prior deed is not valid against any person except the grantor, his heirs and devisees, "and persons having actual notice of it."

The reason why the statutes require actual notice to a second purchaser, in order to defeat his title, is apparent; its purpose is that his title shall not prevail against the prior deed if he has been guilty of a fraud upon the first grantee, and he could not be guilty of such fraud unless he had actual notice of the first deed.

Now, in the case before us, it is found as a fact that the tenant had no actual knowledge of the prior mortgage to the demandant at the time he took his assignment from Clark. But it is contended that he had constructive notice, because the demandant's mortgage was recorded before such assignment. It was held in Connecticut v. Bradish, supra, that such record was evidence of actual notice, but was not of itself enough to show actual notice, and to charge the assignee of the second deed with a fraud upon the holder of the first unrecorded deed. This seems to us to accord with the spirit of our registry laws, and the uniform understanding of and practice under them by the profession. These laws not only provide that deeds must be recorded, but they also prescribe the method in which the records shall be kept and indexes prepared for public inspection and examination. There are indexes of grantors and grantees, so that, in searching a title, the examiner is obliged to run down the list of grantors or run backward through the list of grantees. If he can start with an owner who is known to have a good title, as in the case at bar he could start with Hall, he is obliged to run through the index of grantors until he finds a conveyance by the owner of the land in question. After such conveyance the former owner becomes a stranger to the title, and the examiner must follow down the name of the new owner to see if he has conveyed the land, and so on. It would be a hardship to require an examiner to follow in the index of grantors the name of every person who at any time, through, perhaps, a long chain of title, was the owner of the estate.

We do not think this is the practical construction which lawyers and conveyancers have given to our registry laws. The inconvenience of such a construction would be much greater than would be the inconvenience of requiring a person who has neglected to record his prior deed for a time, to record it, and to bring a bill in equity to set aside the subsequent deed, if it was taken in fraud of his rights. The better rule, and the least likely to create confusion of titles, seems to us to be that if a purchaser, upon examining the registry, finds a conveyance from the owner of the land to his grantor which gives him a perfect record title, complete by what the law at the time it is recorded regards as equivalent to a livery of seizin, he is entitled to rely upon such recorded title, and is not obliged to search the record afterwards made, to see if there has been any prior unrecorded deed of the original owners.

This rule of property, established by the early case of Connecticut v. Bradish, supra, ought not to be departed from unless conclusive reasons therefor can be shown. We are therefore of opinion that in the case at bar the tenant has the better title. Verdict set aside.

Sabo v. Horvath

Supreme Court of Alaska, 1976.
559 P.2d 1038.

BOOCHEVER, CHIEF JUSTICE.

This appeal arises because Grover C. Lowery conveyed the same five-acre piece of land twice—first to William A. Horvath and Barbara J. Horvath and later to William Sabo and Barbara Sabo. Both conveyances were by separate documents entitled "Quitclaim Deeds." Lowery's interest in the land originates in a patent from the United States Government under 43 U.S.C.A. § 687a (1970) ("Alaska Homesite Law"). Lowery's conveyance to the Horvaths was prior to the issuance of patent, and his subsequent conveyance to the Sabos was after the issuance of patent. The Horvaths recorded their deed in the Chitna Recording District on January 5, 1970; the Sabos recorded their deed on December 13, 1973. The transfer to the Horvaths, however, predated patent and title, and thus the Horvaths' interest in the land was recorded "outside the chain of title." Mr. Horvath brought suit to quiet title, and the Sabos counterclaimed to quiet their title.

In a memorandum opinion, the superior court ruled that Lowery had an equitable interest capable of transfer at the time of his conveyance to the Horvaths and further said the transfer contemplated more than a "mere quitclaim"—it warranted patent would be transferred. The superior court also held that Horvath had the superior claim to the land because his prior recording had given the Sabos constructive notice for purposes of AS 34.15.290. The Sabos' appeal raises the following issues:

1.   Under 43 U.S.C.A. § 687a (1970), when did Lowery obtain a present equitable interest in land which he could convey?

2.   Are the Sabos, as grantees under a quitclaim deed, "subsequent innocent purchaser[s] in good faith"?

3.   Is the Horvaths' first recorded interest, which is outside the chain of title, constructive notice to Sabo?

We affirm the trial court's ruling that Lowery had an interest to convey at the time of his conveyance to the Horvaths. We further hold that Sabo may be a "good faith purchaser" even though he takes by quitclaim deed. We reverse the trial court's ruling that Sabo had constructive notice and hold that a deed recorded outside the chain of title is a "wild deed" and does not give constructive notice under the recording laws of Alaska.[2]

The facts may be stated as follows. Grover C. Lowery occupied land in the Chitna Recording District on October 10, 1964 for purposes of obtaining Federal patent. Lowery filed a location notice on February 24, 1965, and made his application to purchase on June 6, 1967 with the Bureau of Land Management (BLM). On March 7, 1968, the BLM field examiner's report was filed which recommended that patent issue to Lowery. On October 7, 1969, a request for survey was made by the

---

[2]   Because we hold Lowery had a conveyable interest under the Federal statute, we need not decide issues raised by the parties regarding after-acquired property and the related issue of estoppel by deed.

United States Government. On January 3, 1970, Lowery issued a document entitled "Quitclaim Deed" to the Horvaths; Horvath recorded the deed on January 5, 1970 in the Chitna Recording District. Horvath testified that when he bought the land from Lowery, he knew patent and title were still in the United States Government, but he did not rerecord his interest after patent had passed to Lowery.

Following the sale to the Horvaths, further action was taken by Lowery and the BLM pertaining to the application for patent and culminating in issuance of the patent on August 10, 1973.

Almost immediately after the patent was issued, Lowery advertised the land for sale in a newspaper. He then executed a second document also entitled "quitclaim" to the Sabos on October 15, 1973. The Sabos duly recorded this document on December 13, 1973.

Luther Moss, a representative of the BLM, testified to procedures followed under the Alaska Homesite Law [43 U.S.C.A. § 687a (1970)]. After numerous steps, a plat is approved and the claimant notified that he should direct publication of his claim. In this case, Lowery executed his conveyance to the Horvaths after the BLM field report had recommended patent.

The first question this court must consider is whether Lowery had an interest to convey at the time of his transfer to the Horvaths. Lowery's interest was obtained pursuant to patent law 43 U.S.C.A. § 687a (1970) commonly called the "Alaska Homesite Law". Since Lowery's title to the property was contingent upon the patent ultimately issuing from the United States Government and since Lowery's conveyance to the Horvaths predated issuance of the patent, the question is "at what point in the pre-patent chain of procedures does a person have a sufficient interest in a particular tract of land to convey that land by quitclaim deed." Willis v. City of Valdez, 546 P.2d 570, 575 (Alaska 1976). . . .

In Willis v. City of Valdez, supra at 578, we held that one who later secured a patent under the Soldiers' Additional Homestead Act had an interest in land which was alienable at the time that he requested a survey. Here, Lowery had complied with numerous requirements under the Homesite Law including those of occupancy, and the BLM had recommended issuance of the patent. Since 43 U.S.C.A. § 687a (1970) does not prohibit alienation, we hold that at the time Lowery executed the deed to the Horvaths he had complied with the statute to a sufficient extent so as to have an interest in the land which was capable of conveyance.

Since the Horvaths received a valid interest from Lowery, we must now resolve the conflict between the Horvaths' first recorded interest and the Sabos' later recorded interest.

The Sabos, like the Horvaths, received their interest in the property by a quitclaim deed. They are asserting that their interest supersedes the Horvaths under Alaska's statutory recording system. AS 34.15.290 provides that:

> A conveyance of real property . . . is void as against a subsequent innocent purchaser . . . for a valuable consideration of the property . . . whose conveyance is first duly recorded. An

unrecorded instrument is valid . . . as against one who has actual notice of it.

Initially, we must decide whether the Sabos, who received their interest by means of a quitclaim deed, can ever be "innocent purchaser[s]" within the meaning of AS 34.15.290. Since a "quitclaim" only transfers the interest of the grantor, the question is whether a "quitclaim" deed itself puts a purchaser on constructive notice. Although the authorities are in conflict over this issue, the clear weight of authority is that a quitclaim grantee can be protected by the recording system, assuming, of course, the grantee purchased for valuable consideration and did not otherwise have actual or constructive knowledge as defined by the recording laws. We choose to follow the majority rule and hold that a quitclaim grantee is not precluded from attaining the status of an "innocent purchaser."

In this case, the Horvaths recorded their interest from Lowery prior to the time the Sabos recorded their interest. Thus, the issue is whether the Sabos are charged with constructive knowledge because of the Horvaths' prior recordation. Horvath is correct in his assertion that in the usual case a prior recorded deed serves as constructive notice pursuant to AS 34.15.290, and thus precludes a subsequent recordation from taking precedence. Here, however, the Sabos argue that because Horvath recorded his deed prior to Lowery having obtained patent, they were not given constructive notice by the recording system. They contend that since Horvaths' recordation was outside the chain of title, the recording should be regarded as a "wild deed".

It is an axiom of hornbook law that a purchaser has notice only of recorded instruments that are within his "chain of title." If a grantor (Lowery) transfers prior to obtaining title, and the grantee (Horvath) records prior to title passing, a second grantee who diligently examines all conveyances under the grantor's name from the date that the grantor had secured title would not discover the prior conveyance. The rule in most jurisdictions which have adopted a grantor-grantee index system of recording is that a "wild deed" does not serve as constructive notice to a subsequent purchaser who duly records.

Alaska's recording system utilizes a "grantor-grantee" index. Had Sabo searched title under both grantor's and grantee's names but limited his search to the chain of title subsequent to patent, he would not be chargeable with discovery of the pre-patent transfer to Horvath.

On one hand, we could require Sabo to check beyond the chain of title to look for pretitle conveyances. While in this particular case the burden may not have been great, as a general rule, requiring title checks beyond the chain of title could add a significant burden as well as uncertainty to real estate purchases. To a certain extent, requiring title searches of records prior to the date a grantor acquired title would thus defeat the purposes of the recording system. The records as to each grantor in the chain of title would theoretically have to be checked back to the later of the grantor's date of birth or the date when records were first retained.

On the other hand, we could require Horvath to rerecord his interest in the land once title passes, that is, after patent had issued to Lowery. As a general rule, rerecording an interest once title passes is less of a burden than requiring property purchasers to check indefinitely beyond the chain of title.

It is unfortunate that in this case due to Lowery's double conveyances, one or the other party to this suit must suffer an undeserved loss. We are cognizant that in this case, the equities are closely balanced between the parties to this appeal. Our decision, however, in addition to resolving the litigants' dispute, must delineate the requirements of Alaska's recording laws.

Because we want to promote simplicity and certainty in title transactions, we choose to follow the majority rule and hold that the Horvaths' deed, recorded outside the chain of title, does not give constructive notice to the Sabos and is not "duly recorded" under the Alaskan Recording Act, AS 34.15.290. Since the Sabos' interest is the first duly recorded interest and was recorded without actual or constructive knowledge of the prior deed, we hold that the Sabos' interest must prevail. The trial court's decision is accordingly.

Reversed.

Corwin W. Johnson, Purpose and Scope of Recording Statutes*
47 Iowa Law Review 231, 239–240 (1962).

While there is disagreement as to the proper application of the "chain of title" concept, it is clear that some limitation of this sort is needed when the only available access to the records is through inadequate official indexes, a situation all too common. But this justification for the "chain of title" limitation largely disappears in a community where easy access to information on the official records is available through unofficial abstracts and where the customary practice is to rely upon the abstracts rather than the official indexes. Unfortunately, this fact seems not to have had an appreciable impact upon shaping the "chain of title" concept.

If recorded instruments outside the "chain of title" do not give constructive notice, does it follow that such instruments are not really recorded and thus are void as to subsequent purchasers and creditors? Statutory language lends no support to this conclusion and the effect of such a construction is to impose the penalty for failure to record upon one who obeyed the statutory mandate. Yet, this position is generally approved. While the "chain of title" concept usually benefits subsequent purchasers and creditors, it is capable of being turned against them with devastating effect. Assuming that the recording of a deed outside the "chain of title" gives no constructive notice, it would seem to follow logically that such a deed need not be recorded. For example, X conveys to A, who does not record, and then X conveys to B, who does not record. If A conveys to C, there is authority that C, although a subsequent-in-time purchaser, is not a subsequent-in-chain purchaser and therefore is not protected against B's unrecorded deed.

NOTES

1. *Morse v. Curtis.* Would and should Morse v. Curtis have been decided differently if demandant had gone into possession of the property? If the Massachusetts legislature had mandated use of an official tract index? If Massachusetts had a race-notice statute? A race statute? The rule of Morse v. Curtis has been rejected in a minority of states. See, for example, Woods v. Garnett, 72 Miss. 78, 16 So. 390 (1894). As a title examiner in one of these minority jurisdictions, is it likely that the cost of your search will be much higher than it would be in a majority jurisdiction? Will your answer depend on whether you have ready access to a private title plant indexing all land transfers in your county by reference to the tract involved?

The court in Dalessio v. Baggia, 57 Mass.App.Ct. 468,473, 783 N.E.2d 890, 893–94, review denied, 439 Mass. 1107, 790 N.E.2d 1090 (2003), found that *Morse* aligns with modern search practices. Plaintiff argued that a subsequent taker should have constructive notice of a deed despite the *Morse* rule because the title standards of the Massachusetts Conveyancers Association recommended "running the owner in the grantor index for the four-year period following the recording of a conveyance to check for liens for unpaid real estate taxes." The court rejected this claim:

> We think, however, that the discrete inquiry that [the title standard] contemplates is not at all comparable to the burdensome investigation that would have been necessary to uncover the problem here. It is one thing for the examiner to scan the grantee column of the index for municipal liens, but quite another to do a follow-up investigation of all of the other entities to determine whether the grantor may have reconveyed some or all of a previously conveyed parcel.

2. *Sabo v. Horvath.* After the decision in Sabo v. Horvath, would the Horvaths have had an action against Lowery to recover the value they paid for the land? Note that although the Lowery-Horvath conveyance was by quitclaim deed, the trial court found that "the transfer contemplated more than a 'mere quitclaim'—it warranted patent would be transferred."

3. *Estoppel by Deed.* If Lowery had not subsequently executed a deed to the Sabos, the Horvaths would clearly have prevailed in a quiet title action against Lowery under the venerable doctrine of "estoppel by deed." This doctrine holds that if *A,* not owning Blackacre, purports to convey Blackacre to *B* by warranty deed, then if *A* later acquires title to Blackacre, her title will automatically pass to *B* under the terms of the deed. See Ackerman v. Abbott, 978 A.2d 1250 (D.C. 2009). The rationale for the doctrine is that *A,* by granting under a deed to *B,* is representing that she owns the land and should thus be estopped from later denying the effectiveness of that deed.

What effect will estoppel by deed have on subsequent purchaser *C* who had no notice of the *A* to *B* deed? Although the *Sabo* court expressly sidestepped the issue, other courts have confronted it directly. For example, in Breen v. Morehead, 104 Tex. 254, 136 S.W. 1047 (1911), McKelligon, who had possession of, but not title to, a piece of land, deeded the property to Breen, who promptly recorded. About two years later, McKelligon acquired title to the parcel from the state and subsequently deeded it to Kern who had no knowledge of the earlier transfer to Breen. Other things being equal, the doctrine of estoppel by deed would have given title to Breen. But, of course, other things were not equal, for Kern, a bona fide purchaser for value, had intervened. The Texas Supreme Court held for Kern on the ground that if he were required to look beyond the origin of the title under which he was purchasing, "there could be no limit short of the vendor's life, and such requirement of purchasers would involve land titles in such uncertainty that it would be impracticable to rely upon any investigation." 104 Tex. at 258, 136 S.W. at 1049. The court concluded:

> We believe that the rule stated above that the date when the title originated in McKelligon marked the limit of investigation for previous sales or encumbrances of that tract of land by McKelligon should be applied here. It would be unreasonable to suppose that a man who had just received a title from the State had previously made a transfer of that land. That ordinary care and caution which the subsequent purchaser must exercise would not suggest an investigation for conveyances made before acquisition of title. It follows that the record of Breen's deed in El Paso County gave no notice to the subsequent purchasers from McKelligon who had no actual notice and paid a valuable consideration for the land.

A few states reject the rule followed in Breen v. Morehead. See, for example, Tefft v. Munson, 57 N.Y. 97 (1874). After Morse v. Curtis, would you expect Massachusetts to follow or to reject the rule? The surprising answer is that Massachusetts has rejected the rule. See Knight v. Thayer, 125 Mass. 25 (1878). Dalessio v. Baggia, 57 Mass.App.Ct. 468,473, 783 N.E.2d 890, 893–94, review denied, 439 Mass. 1107, 790 N.E.2d 1090 (2003), however, declined to follow earlier contrary dictum and held that estoppel by deed should not apply to vest the holder of a *quitclaim* deed with title over a bona fide purchaser.

B. ABSTRACTS, OPINIONS AND TITLE INSURANCE

Using the public records or his own title plant, a title examiner will first search back to a parcel's root of title—when the parcel was last made the subject of an undisputed transfer—and will then search forward, tracing all subsequent transfers up to the present. The examiner will then prepare an abstract of title summarizing every transfer, beginning with the first, and indicating all other matters of record affecting the title. Characteristically, the abstract will conclude with the examiner's certification of the periods and records covered by his search.

Next, a lawyer or title officer will analyze the abstract. She will eliminate cancelled mortgages and expired liens as well as interests barred by the statute of limitations, reducing the abstract to the remaining interests that continue to encumber or otherwise affect title. If this analysis is performed by a lawyer, it will be embodied in a lawyer's opinion on title rendered to the buyer. If a title insurance company performs the analysis, it will state the results in a policy of title insurance that guarantees good title except for specified encumbrances or defects. (The lawyer's opinion will commonly read, "I have examined the abstract of title attached hereto, and from it find that on said date marketable title of record was vested in seller, free from encumbrances or defects, except as follows. . . ." The title company's guarantee will typically read, "The following estates, interests, defects, objections to title, liens and encumbrances and other matters are excepted from the coverage of this policy. . . .")

The sources of title services have changed dramatically over the past one hundred years. Originally lawyers conducted the title search, prepared the abstract, and rendered the opinion based on the abstract. Although, in some places, lawyers continue to discharge all these functions, they have in most communities been partially or completely displaced by abstract and title companies. An abstract company may perform the search and compile the abstract while a lawyer selected by the buyer will review and opine on the abstract. Increasingly, though, title insurance companies are serving all of these functions—conducting the search, preparing the abstract and issuing a title policy insuring the accuracy of the search. Lawyers in many communities have responded to these incursions by setting up title insurance companies of their own. "By 1976, over 10,000 lawyers in nineteen states were organized in nine separate bar-related companies, with assets in excess of $18 million." Roussel & Rosenberg, Lawyer-Controlled Title Insurance Companies: Legal Ethics and the Need for Insurance Department Regulation, 48 Fordham L.Rev. 25, 28 (1979). See also, Rooney, Bar Related Title Insurance: The Positive Perspective, 1980 So.Ill.U.L.J. 263.

1.   THE ABSTRACT AND THE LAWYER'S OPINION

Joyce Palomar, 1 Patton and Palomar on Land Titles*
§ 52, pp. 180–183, 186–188, 189 (3d ed. 2002).

Examiners employ different methods when actually examining a title. Some make elaborate diagrams showing the devolution of the title and copious notes as to encumbrances or defects; others carry more data in memory. Title examiners do seem to agree that the examiner should: (1) complete the examination at one sitting and with as little interruption as possible; (2) make a preliminary perusal of the items constituting the chain of title, to determine whether there is an unbroken sequence from the government down to the last grantee; (3) review critically each step, or "remove," in the chain of title; (4) make a diagram or analysis of all lengthy or complicated chains; and (5) make sufficient notes of defects and objections to enable the examiner to keep track of them until they are either removed by later instruments in the chain of title or identified in the title opinion or report. Some attorneys complete their work on the chain of title before attending to encumbrances. To this end, a few abstracters will report the chain of title consecutively, and then report encumbrances and releases. But most abstracts report all instruments, whether of title or encumbrance, in sequence according to date of execution or date of recording, and the examining attorney carries side notes as to encumbrances and releases as he examines the chain of title.

Technically, when a title examiner finds that (a) the records are such that a court would accept them as *prima facie* proof of title in the

---

purported owner, (b) the title is free from reasonable doubt, and (c) the title is free from encumbrance other than those the client agreed to take subject to, then the examiner is warranted in giving an opinion in favor of a marketable title of record. In fact, however, many records that have been given a *prima facie* validity by statute, as well as many presumptions that have become rules of evidence, are far from conclusive. Presumptions of regularity may make a title marketable; but, unless the presumptions are made conclusive by statute, they do not insure the title is good in fact. If no statute gives conclusive validity to a particular record, the examining attorney may need to go beyond the sheriff's deed, decree, etc., and look into the regularity of the judgment and the files in the case, respectively. Thus, the attorney's investigation should not be limited by the records required to make a *prima facie* case, but by the practicality of ascertaining the actual facts. For example, while one cannot go to the extent of learning that sufficient service of process or notice actually was made to give the court jurisdiction to enter the presumptively good decree upon which the title depends, one can ascertain whether the files show a service of that character. Additionally, while one cannot always learn whether a grantor was competent, one can ascertain that the county land records do not show to the contrary. Therefore, this treatise's consideration in subsequent chapters of the items properly examined will include, not only those records required to make a *prima facie* case for a marketable title, but, also, those that may be available to prove the title's marketability in fact.

The client usually only expressly requests an examination of title to the particular land being purchased or mortgaged. Nevertheless, a title attorney knows that the purchaser or mortgagee is also concerned about the grantor's title to rights that are appurtenant to the land, such as riparian rights, appurtenant easements, access to nearby parks or public grounds, and the right to use platted roads leading to or past the property.

Where abstracts are utilized, the abstract should show if riparian rights have been conveyed separately from the riparian land. Further, where a client is acquiring land benefited by an appurtenant easement (e.g., a right of way to the land or the right to maintain a party wall), if the abstract does not include the land charged with the easement, the examining attorney should require it to be so amended. The abstract also should show any completed or pending proceeding for the vacation of any road, street, alley or public ground of the plat in which the land is located (a report as to any greater area cannot be expected).

Analogously, an attorney's title opinion or a title report that a customer purchases directly from a title insurance company should show if riparian rights have been conveyed separately from the riparian land. Where the client advises or the examiner otherwise learns that the land being acquired is benefited by an appurtenant easement, the attorney should examine not only title to the benefited parcel, but also the title to the parcel burdened by the easement. Further, the examiner should examine the instruments filed in any completed or pending proceeding for the vacation of any road, street, alley or public ground of the plat in which the land is located. Additionally, the examiner should be satisfied that there was either a proper dedication or an acquisition by condemnation of all public ways and public grounds of the plat. If an examination of the dedication accompanying the plat reveals a partial dedication only, or a grant as a private easement rather than a full grant to the public, the examiner must advise the client. When examining easements in highways and roads that serve the premises, the examiner also should be aware that prospective purchasers will be interested in any limitations on access.

. . .

Title Examination Standards

When examining a title, every lawyer applies, consciously or unconsciously, some standard for approving or disapproving transfers in the chain of title, determining what claims constitute encumbrance, and determining the sufficiency of discharges of encumbrance. The standard applied may vary depending on the quality of title being required, whether the client is a purchaser or a mortgagee, and whether the client is under contract to purchase or merely a prospective purchaser not bound by contract. A lawyer will make some requirements solely to protect her client from business risks and, at other times, may waive a point of technical unmarketability on the belief that no serious risk exists. Overall, the standard imposed upon the examiner comes from her knowledge of the attitudes of other examiners and of the courts regarding acceptability of titles. She knows that if she approves a title that a subsequent examiner might reject when the property is re-sold, she may experience a controversy with the later examiner, her client, or both. Of course, the objections of the second examiner also may be based upon what he is afraid may be the attitude of some third examiner who may be overly meticulous. Furthermore, title attorneys are aware that, at times, even courts have been considered over-meticulous in determining whether particular facts make a title unmarketable.

In many states, statewide title examination standards have been promulgated to help title examiners know the standards that subsequent examiners and courts likely will apply to transfers in the chain of title, encumbrance, and discharges of encumbrance. The availability of written standards that were promulgated after careful study and are generally accepted among members of the bar in the state helps protect examiners who utilize them against claims of malpractice. Availability of generally accepted standards also, consequently, helps to keep title examiner No. 2 from overly-cautiously casting a shadow on the title and the reputation of examiner No. 1.

Written standards for land title examination appear to have been first adopted by attorneys in Dodge County, Nebraska, and first on a state-wide scale in Connecticut. In Connecticut, a committee of the state bar association gathered together 57 actual problems taken from experiences of its members. After preliminary study, inquiry and conference, the committee prepared a statement of each problem and a recommendation as to the attitude to be taken, accompanied in many cases by comments, explanations and authorities. After submission to and approval by the state bar association in 1937, they were published and distributed to members. Over the years, additional problems have been considered by succeeding committees and additional standards formulated and published. "The reputable conveyancers are all following them as if they were a bible."

Similar standards have since been adopted in other states: Colorado, Florida, Georgia, Iowa, Kansas, Maine, Massachusetts, Michigan, Minnesota, Missouri, New Hampshire, New York, North Dakota, Ohio, Oklahoma, Rhode Island, South Dakota, Wisconsin and Wyoming.

As of August 2002, state with published Title Examination Standards are: Arkansas, Colorado, Connecticut, Florida, Georgia, Idaho,* Illinois, Iowa, Kansas, Maine, Massachusetts, Michigan, Minnesota, Missouri, Montana,* Nebraska, New Hampshire, New Mexico,* New York, North Dakota, Ohio, Oklahoma, Rhode Island, South Dakota, Texas, Utah, Washington, Wisconsin and Wyoming.

. . . Though not being adopted legislatively keeps title examination standards from having the force of law, this has not limited their effectiveness. The Oklahoma Supreme Court has stated:

> While Title Examination Standards are not binding upon this Court, by reason of the research and careful study prior to their adoption and by reason of their general acceptance among members of the bar of this state since their adoption, we deem such Title Examination Standards and the annotations cited in support thereof to be persuasive.

Seigle v. Jasper

Court of Appeals of Kentucky, 1993.
867 S.W.2d 476.

JOHNSON, JUDGE:

This is an appeal by John Seigle and Darlene Seigle (Seigles) from two separate summary judgments dismissing two separate lawsuits that had been consolidated by the trial court . . . We reverse the trial court's summary judgment in favor of appellee, Robert M. Coots (Coots), on Seigles' claim of negligence in the preparation of a title opinion by attorney Coots and remand for further proceedings.

On May 1, 1974, John Seigle and Carol Seigle, husband and wife, entered into a contract for deed with Thomas R. Jasper and Verneasa Jasper, husband and wife, and Floyd Tennill and Mildred Tennill, husband and wife, for the purchase of real estate known as Lot No. 8 of the Ridgeview Subdivision located in Spencer County, Kentucky. Carol Seigle has died, and John Seigle is now married to Darlene Seigle. Floyd Tennill has also died.[1] In 1979 the Seigles desired to purchase Lot No. 13 in the same subdivision and from the same parties. The Seigles applied for a loan from The Peoples Bank of Mount Washington (Peoples Bank) for the purpose of purchasing Lot No. 13 and paying the balance owing under the contract for deed on Lot No. 8. Robert M. Coots was a duly licensed practicing attorney in Spencer County who regularly performed real estate title searches and loan document

---

[1]   For the purposes of this Opinion, John Seigle, Carol Seigle and Darlene Seigle will be referred to as the Seigles and Thomas R. Jasper and Verneasa Jasper and Floyd Tennill and Mildred Tennill will be referred to as Jaspers-Tennills regardless of the time period and marital status of the parties.

preparation for Peoples Bank on real estate loans on property located in Spencer County. The Seigles agreed that Coots would perform the title examination for their loan, and paid his attorney's fees as a part of their closing costs paid through Peoples Bank at the time their real estate loan was closed. The Seigles obtained two separate general warranty deeds from Jaspers-Tennills on Lot Nos. 8 and 13, on May 31, 1979, and June 11, 1979, respectively. During 1984 Seigles borrowed additional money from Peoples Bank which required refinancing of the loan. Coots wrote a second title letter to Peoples Bank dated July 9, 1984, for Lot Nos. 8 and 13 for which the Seigles paid his attorney's fees through the closing costs they paid to Peoples Bank. The deposition testimony from two officers of Peoples Bank revealed that bank policy resulted in the 1979 loan documents, including any title opinion letter from Coots, being destroyed when the loan was paid off as a result of the 1984 refinancing. Coots denies preparing the 1979 title report, but John Seigle, in an affidavit filed in opposition to Coots' motion for summary judgment, states that he and an officer of Peoples Bank, Barry Armstrong, reviewed the loan documents, and that Armstrong told him "that Mr. Coots had run the title and that everything was clear." It is agreed by the parties that the Seigles were never informed by Coots that each lot was encumbered by the existence of an easement to Ashland Oil, Inc. (Ashland Oil) for an underground pipeline which had been duly recorded in the Spencer County Court Clerk's Office.

The Seigles received a letter by certified mail from Ashland Oil dated August 30, 1988 that advised them that the placing of a mobile home on Lot No. 8 and a small building on Lot No. 13 within Ashland Oil's right-of-way and upon Ashland Oil's pipeline represented an encroachment of Ashland Oil's right-of-way. On August 25, 1989l, the Seigles filed two separate lawsuits. The Seigles sued Jaspers-Tennills for fraud and breach of warranty, and Coots for negligence. The two lawsuits were later consolidated; and after the taking of depositions and the filing of various motions and memoranda, all claims were dismissed by summary judgment. This appeal followed.

. . .

This takes us to the Seigles' claim in negligence against Coots for failing to properly advise them of the existence of the Ashland Oil easement. The order of the Spencer Circuit Court sustaining Coots' motion for summary judgment does not provide any insight into the legal reasoning underlying it. Further, the record before us appears to be incomplete in that Coots' motion to dismiss with memorandum in support, answer and motion for summary judgment with memorandum referred to in the Seigles' memorandum in support of their motion for partial summary judgment are not in the record. Therefore, we will address the issues of the case as we discern them from the record.

. . .

The standard of review on appeal of a summary judgment is whether the trial court correctly found that there were no genuine issues as to any material fact and that the moving party was entitled to judgment as a matter of law. Goldsmith v. Allied Building Components, Inc., Ky., 833 S.W.2d 378 (1992).

There is evidence in the record supporting the Seigles' claim of negligence. In viewing the evidence in the light most favorable to the Seigles, the evidence supports the following: (1) Peoples Bank required a title examination in order to close the Seigles' loan; (2) Peoples Bank regularly used Coots for title examinations of Spencer County real estate; (3) the Seigles agreed to the use of Coots for the title examination with the understanding that they would pay his attorney's fees through the loan closing costs paid to Peoples Bank, which they did; (4) Coots wrote a title letter to Peoples Bank dated July 9, 1984 which references the Seigles by name and included several exceptions, some of which were easements, but did not make any reference to the Ashland Oil easement; (5) John Seigle was advised by an officer of Peoples Bank that Coots had performed the title search in 1979 also, and that "everything was clear;" (6) the Seigles acted reasonably in relying upon the representations made by Coots in his title reports; (7) the Seigles would not have purchased the property had they been made aware of the restrictions placed on the property by the Ashland Oil easement; (8) the Seigles have suffered damages in that their property with the Ashland Oil easement is worth less than it would be without the easement; and (9) Coots failed to exercise ordinary care in preparing the title opinion whereby he breached his duty to the Seigles to properly advise them of the existence of the Ashland Oil easement.

Coots has contended throughout these proceedings that he has no liability to the Seigles because there was a lack of privity of contract. Apparently, there are no published Kentucky cases concerning an attorney's liability to parties who allegedly did not have privity of contract with the title abstractor. *See* William B. Johnson, Annotation, Negligence in Preparing Abstract of Title as Ground of Liability to One Other Than Person Ordering Abstract, 50 A.L.R.4th 314 (1986). As stated above, the facts viewed in the light most favorable to the Seigles present an issue of fact as to whether or not a contractual relationship existed between Coots and the Seigles, to wit: the Seigles agreed that Coots would perform their title examination; Coots performed the work at the request of Peoples Bank knowing the work was being done to benefit the Seigles in closing their loan; and the Seigles paid Coots' attorney's fees.

The Seigles have sued Coots for negligence. One issue before the trial court was whether or not Coots' duty to exercise ordinary care in the performance of the title examination extended to the Seigles. We hold that it did.

In First American Title Insurance Co. v. First Title Service Co., 457 So.2d 467 (1984), 50 A.L.R. 4th 301, the Florida Supreme Court held that where a title insurance company had issued title insurance in reliance on a title abstract prepared for the seller of the property, and the title abstractor failed to note the existence of a recorded judgment against a former owner of the property, since the abstractor prepared the abstract knowing, or under conditions in which he should reasonably have expected that the seller would provide the abstract to the title insurance company for the purpose of inducing the title insurance company to rely on the abstract as evidence of title, the abstractor's contractual duty to perform the service skillfully and diligently ran to the benefit of the title insurance company. We accept the holding *First American Title* that the Court summarized as follows:

> Where the abstracter knows, or should know, that his customer wants the abstract for the use of a prospective purchaser, and the prospect purchases the land relying on the abstract, the abstracter's duty of care runs, as we have said, not only to his customer but to the purchaser. Moreover, others involved in the transaction through their relationship to the purchaser—such as lender-mortgagees, tenants and title insurers-will also be protected where the purchaser's reliance was known or should have been known to the abstracter. But a party into whose hands the abstract falls in connection with a subsequent transaction is not among those to whom the abstracter owes a duty of care.

457 So.2d at 473.

This holding is consistent with the Restatement (Second) of Tort § 552 *Information Negligently Supplied for the Guidance of Others* which states in pertinent part:

> (1) One who, in the course of his business, profession or employment, or in any other transaction in which he has a pecuniary interest, supplies false information for the guidance of others in their business transactions, is subject to liability for pecuniary loss caused to them by their justifiable reliance upon the information, if he fails to exercise reasonable care or competence in obtaining or communicating the information.
>
> (2) Except as stated in Subsection (3), the liability stated in Subsection (1) is limited to loss suffered
>
> (a) by the person or one of a limited group of persons for whose benefit and guidance he intends to supply the information or knows that the recipient intends to supply it; and
>
> (b) through reliance upon it in a transaction that he intends the information to influence or knows that the recipient so intends or in a substantially similar transaction.

Again, in viewing the facts most favorably to the Seigles, Coots was acting in the course of his profession for his pecuniary interest when he failed to exercise reasonable care or competence in obtaining or communicating information and supplied false information for the guidance of Peoples Bank, Jaspers-Tennills and the Seigles in their business transactions that has subjected the Seigles to a pecuniary loss as a result of their justifiable reliance upon the information.

It is well established that "[t]he concept of liability for negligence expresses a universal duty owed by all to all." Gas Service Co., Inc. v. City of Londo Ky., 687 S.W.2d 144, 148 (1985). "The rule is that every person owes a duty to every other person to exercise ordinary care in his activities to prevent foreseeable injury." Grayson Fraternal Order of Eagles v. Claywell, Ky., 736 S.W.2d 328, 332 (1987). "In any negligence case, it is necessary to show that the defendant failed to discharge a legal duty or conform his conduct to the standard required. W. Prosser Law of Torts § 30 (1971); Mitchell v. Hadl, 816 S.W.2d 183, 185

(Ky.1991). Hill v. Willmott, Ky.App., 561 S.W.2d 331 (1978), this Court in discussing an attorney's duty to a third party accepted language from Donald v. Garry, 19 Cal.App.3d 769, 97 Cal.Rptr. 191 (1971), and stated:

> "An attorney may be liable for damage caused by his negligence to a person intended to be benefitted by his performance irrespective of any lack of privity . . ." (Emphasis added). We believe this to be a proper statement of the law in this Commonwealth.

561 S.W.2d at 334.

> "In determining whether that degree of care and skill exercised by the attorney in a given case meets the requirements of the standard care . . ., the attorney's act, or failure to act, is judged by the degree of its departure from the quality of professional conduct customarily provided by members of the legal profession. Prosser Law of Torts § 32 at 161–166 (4th ed. 1971). As it would be in negligence cases generally, the question of whether the conduct of the attorney meets the standard of care test is one for the trier of the facts to determine." Daugherty v. Runner, Ky., App., 581 S.W.2d 12, 16 (1978).

Coots' other defenses of estoppel and statute of limitations can be dispensed with in short order. The fact that the deed from Jaspers-Tennills to the Seigles contained an exception for "easements or restrictions of record" in no way eliminates Coots' duty to include the Ashland Oil easement in his title letter since the whole purpose of having Coots perform a title examination was to specifically advise the parties of any restrictions on the title. It is the duty of the attorney conducting the title search to communicate to the parties any information that might reasonably constitute a defect and restriction on the title. *See* Owen v. Neely, Ky., 471 S.W.2d 705 (1971). Coots' estoppel argument based on two exceptions contained in the title letter also fails. The letter excepted "*[u]nrecorded* easements, discrepancies or conflicts in boundary lines, shortage in area and encroachments which an accurate and complete survey would disclose." (Emphasis added). Since the Ashland Oil easement was recorded, this exception clearly does not cover it. The letter also excepted "[r]ights or claims of parties other than (appellants) in actual possession of any or all of the real property." The Texas Supreme Court in Shaver v. National Title & Abstract Co., 361 S.W.2d 867 (Tex.1962), a case that also involved a pipeline, stated:

> All the authorities agree that possession, in order to constitute notice, must be actual possession of the party . . . consisting of acts of occupancy which are open, visible and unequivocal, and in nature sufficient upon the observation of a subsequent purchaser to put him on inquiry as to the rights of the possessor . . .

361 S.W.2d at 869.

Ashland Oil's acts of occupancy were not sufficiently open, visible and unequivocal to put the Seigles on inquiry as to Ashland Oil's rights.

Coots argues that since the purchase agreement between the Seigles and the Jaspers-Tennills for Lot No. 8 dated January 29, 1974 contained the words "with pipeline" that the Seigles had notice of the pipeline and are estopped from claiming otherwise. The genuineness of these words is strongly disputed by the Seigles and is an issue of fact for the jury.

Coots argues that the one-year statute of limitations ran prior to the filing of this action in 1989 since the most recent title letter was in 1984. The Seigles allege that they were not aware of the pipeline until they received Ashland Oil's letter in 1988. We follow the widely accepted rule and hold that the statute of limitations did not begin to run until the defect became known to the Seigles. *See* Pruett v. Mississippi Valley Title Insurance Co., 271 So.2d 920 (1973); *Shaver, supra.*

We reverse the summary judgment in favor of Coots and remand for further proceedings consistent with this Opinion. We affirm the summary judgment in favor of Jaspers-Tennills.

STUMBO, J., concurs.

DYCHE, J., concurs in part; dissents in part.

DYCHE, J., concurring in part and dissenting in part.

I concur in the result reached by the majority as it applies to the claim against the Jaspers and Ms. Tennill. I must dissent in part, however, as to the majority's holding as it applies to the attorney involved herein. Hill v. Willmo, Ky.App., 561 S.W.2d 331 (1978), imposes a duty toward the purchasers upon an attorney in a situation such as this; the attorney's responsibility, however, is limited to damages sustained on Lot 13 only, as appellants had already contracted to purchase Lot 8 prior to any involvement of the attorney.

NOTES

1. *Abstracter Liability to Third Parties.* Abstracters and lawyers are liable for defects in their work product—abstracters for errors and omissions in compiling the abstract, lawyers for errors in analyzing the abstract and opining on title. Although buyers can pursue both contract and tort theories against the lawyer who represented them, tort theory represents their primary route for recovery against an abstracter with whom they will commonly not be in contractual privity. In Seigle v. Jasper, what services was Coots providing and to whom?

Should buyers have a tort action against abstracters? If *Seigle* had gone the other way, is it likely that Kentucky buyers would in the future protect themselves against title defects by insisting that their sellers give them warranty deeds? (Note that if a buyer recovers against his seller on a title covenant, the seller can then proceed on a contract theory against the abstracter with whom she will be in privity.) Is there any material difference in the damages a buyer will recover by proceeding against the seller under a covenant theory rather than proceeding against the abstracter under a tort theory? If, as often happens, the property appreciates in value between the time the buyer acquires it and the time he discovers the title defect, which theory—tort or contract—is more likely to make the buyer whole? See Barthels v. Santa Barbara Title Company, 28 Cal.App.4th 674, 33 Cal.Rptr.2d 579 (1994) (damages for negligent title report are reliance costs due to misrepresentation not for the loss of value to the property because easement was not as described).

Does it matter whether the Seigles or People's Bank retained Coots to perform the title search? For whose benefit was the abstract obtained? Compare Williams v. Polgar, 391 Mich. 6, 215 N.W.2d 149 (1974) (where the contract of sale obligated seller to provide buyer with an abstract, the abstract company was liable to buyer for inaccuracies).

Seigle and *Williams* are not universally accepted, but represent a growing trend of abstractor liability to parties not in privity. See Annot., 50 A.L.R. 4th 314 (1986). But see Page v. Frazier, discussed in Note 4 below; Kenney v. Henry Fischer Builder, Inc., 129 Ohio App.3d 27, 716 N.E.2d 1189 (1998) (seeking to limit liability to known third parties).

2. *Lawyer Liability.* Lawyers who search or analyze title for their clients are held to the traditional negligence standard of reasonable care and skill. Malpractice claims most often involve the failure to note an encumbrance or to determine the property's true owner or proper location. Good faith errors in judgment are excused, and the lawyer is not considered to have guaranteed that title is perfect—unless, of course, he or she specifically makes that guarantee.

While reasonable care will be measured by the skills possessed, and the customs ordinarily followed, by lawyers in the community, custom will not excuse grossly unreliable practices. In Gleason v. Title Guarantee Co., 300 F.2d 813 (5th Cir.1962), a title company sued for damages arising from defendant attorney's erroneous opinion that certain titles were clear when in fact they were encumbered by outstanding mortgages. The attorney had certified to having made a personal examination of the relevant records but had in fact reviewed neither the records nor the abstracts, relying instead on information received by telephone from the abstract company. In response to the attorney's argument that this method of obtaining title information was standard practice in that part of Florida, the court held that an improper custom, no matter how widely practiced, could not reduce the attorney's duty of care. Damages were awarded for the losses suffered by the title company.

3. *Lawyer Disclaimers.* How much liability can a lawyer disclaim? In Owen v. Neely, 471 S.W.2d 705 (Ky.1971), defendant attorney, employed to "do the title work," gave plaintiffs a certificate of clear and merchantable title containing the standard disclaimer that the certificate was "subject to any information that would be revealed by an accurate survey. . . ." In making the certificate, the attorney had used a description prepared by a surveyor. The lawyer later admitted that he had noticed discrepancies between the deed description and the survey description. In fact, the survey was erroneous, and the house the clients thought they were buying was not situated on the land that they bought. Acknowledging that reservations and disclaimers expressly set forth in the certificate of title will generally be enforced, the court ruled that if an attorney examining title receives information that would give him or her grounds to suspect a defect, the attorney owes the client a duty of investigation that cannot be disclaimed.

4. *Lawyer Liability to Third Parties.* Some more traditional courts reject the *Seigle* view on whether a lawyer, retained by a bank-mortgagee to examine title on its behalf, is be liable to the buyer-mortgagor for errors appearing in the lawyer's title report to the bank. In Page v. Frazier, 388 Mass. 55, 445 N.E.2d 148 (1983), the Massachusetts Supreme Judicial Court affirmed a trial court decision rejecting buyers' claim that the lawyer was liable in tort for negligent misrepresentation. (The court also affirmed the trial court's findings that the lawyer was not liable on a contract theory for having breached the terms of an express or implied lawyer-client relationship and that the lawyer was acting as an independent contractor retained by the bank so that his negligence could not be imputed to the bank.)

The court observed that plaintiffs had cited no case in which "a mortgagee's attorney has been held liable to a mortgagor for negligent performance of a real property title examination," and refused to bring the case within the "general common law trend permitting recovery by injured nonclients for the negligent conduct of attorneys:"

> We do not find the plaintiffs' authorities persuasive here, as we deal with the attorney's liability to another where the attorney is also under an independent and potentially conflicting duty to a client. . . . As the judge noted in the instant case, "It is not only in the matter of items such as prepayment rights, disclosure law, late charge provisions and special mortgage provisions where a conflict of interest could arise if the attorney represented both bank and borrower, but many experienced conveyancers would acknowledge that there is a conflict of interest even with respect to title as there are some title defects which will not make the property unsatisfactory as a security but which would concern a buyer."

The court also attached weight to the fact that the buyer had been warned off from relying on the bank's lawyers by strong exculpatory language in the mortgage application: "(1) The responsibility of the attorney for the mortgagee is to protect the interest of the mortgagee, notwithstanding the fact that (a) the mortgagor shall be obligated to pay the legal fees of said attorney, and (b) the mortgagor is billed for such legal services by the mortgagee. (2) The mortgagor may, at his own expense, engage an attorney of his own selection to represent his own interests in the transaction."

What are the implications of Page v. Frazier and *Seigle* for situations in which the lawyer expressly undertakes to represent two or more parties with conflicting interests? Compare In re Lanza, page 17, above.

Other jurisdictions are like *Seigle* in breaking from traditional privity rules. In Century 21 Deep South Properties, Ltd. v. Corson, 612 So.2d 359 (Miss.1992), the buyers sued the sellers' attorney for malpractice after closing because he failed, at the time the sellers purchased the house, to discover several title defects that remained as liens against the property. The court rejected the lawyer's privity defense:

> Today we modify the requirements of legal malpractice actions based on an attorney's negligence in performing title work by abolishing the requirement of attorney-client relationship and extending liability to foreseeable third parties who detrimentally rely, as we have done in cases involving other professions. An attorney performing title work will be liable to reasonably foreseeable persons who, for a proper business purpose, detrimentally rely on the attorney's title work, suffering loss proximately caused by his negligence. Unfortunately for the

[buyers], they still do not prevail as they have failed to prove damages—a necessary element in any event.

Id. at 374.

Other courts finesse the privity issue by finding that an attorney-client relationship existed. See, e.g., Westport Bank & Trust Co. v. Corcoran, Mallin & Aresco, 221 Conn. 490, 605 A.2d 862 (1992) (where mortgagee sent letter requesting title search to law firm representing mortgagors in title matters, law firm had taken on dual representation to which mortgagors has impliedly consented; law firm was thus liable to mortgagee for negligence in title search).

5. *Abstracter Licensing.* Many states, most of them situated west of the Mississippi, have enacted licensing laws governing abstracters and abstracting firms. Among the requirements imposed are maintenance of an adequate set of abstract records and indices, and bonding to cover liability for errors in compiling the abstract. See, for example, S.D. Codified Laws Ann. § 36–13–15 (1986). Most of the states require abstracting companies to employ at least one licensed abstracter who has successfully completed a state-administered exam.

2. TITLE INSURANCE

D. Barlow Burke, Law of Title Insurance*
§§ 1.01, 2.01, pp. 1–3 to 1–5, 1–7, 1–8 to 1–11, 2–3 to 2–4, 2–16 to 2–17 (3d ed. 2000).

To protect against such defects in real property titles, American abstractors and attorneys well over 100 years ago devised the original forms of title insurance. Title insurance is distinctive in at least two ways. First, it is an exclusively American invention. Second, it may be the only line of insurance developed within the United States.

Title insurance involves the issuance of an insurance policy promising that if the state of the title is other than as represented on the face of the policy, and if the insured suffers losses as a result of the difference, the insurer will reimburse the insured for that loss and any related legal expenses, up to the face amount of the policy. It is based on a title examination, conducted before the policy is issued. . . .

The first title insurance company was formed in Pennsylvania as early as 1853 and was known as the "Law Property Assurance and Trust Society." However, it is an 1868 Pennsylvania Supreme Court opinion, holding an abstractor liable for negligence in the course of a title search, that many writers have credited with giving the industry an impetus to grow into its present form. (This case is discussed in § 1.01 [A].) The year 1871 saw publication of a plan for an incorporated "Title Warranty Company." Enabling legislation was first enacted in Pennsylvania in 1874, and a company was incorporated under its authority two years later—in 1876. That company was the predecessor of Commonwealth Land Title Insurance Company, a corporate name recognizable today. The formation of similar companies followed within a decade or so in Baltimore, Maryland, and in New York City.

. . .

On the West Coast, title insurance companies were formed in the 1880s. Part of the impetus to establish companies in this region was the confusion over California land titles, deriving as they did from Mexican land grants, Land Office patents, and sometimes squatters' rights. Large landowners and landlords had for several decades been concerned both about squatters and about the high, unpredictable costs of title searches and litigation needed to quiet and maintain their titles. In both northern and southern California, title insurance was a method for both reducing costs and rendering those costs predictable, so that in the 1880s, title insurance companies quickly supplanted lawyers' searches and abstracts.

. . .

In the first two or three decades of the twentieth century, title insurance competed in many states with land title registration systems that were still enjoying increased popularity. However, it became clear during this period that title insurance would prevail in this country as title insurers made a national market for their policies. This dominance was achieved between the two World Wars of the twentieth century.

The insurers found that, as the ownership of homes was increasingly financed through mortgage and deed of trust loans, their product complemented the growth of a nationwide market for residential mortgages. Third-party lenders of this period became convinced that title insurance was a necessary ancillary service for the financing of residential properties. During the 1920s, they also became convinced that title insurance was particularly helpful to those of their number who wanted to do a high-volume business in this form of finance. They could use the insurance policy to standardize their own product in order to sell the mortgage at a discount in the then developing national secondary market for such mortgages.

The intervention of the federal government in the housing markets of the 1930s further standardized the underwriting requirements for residential mortgage lending by introducing amortization of principal and interest, longer terms, and lower interest rates, and, in the process, it provided the final impetus that this market for title insurance needed to become nationwide in scope. In some states, title insurers were also mortgage lenders.

As a consequence of these factors, mortgage lenders began to require title insurance as a part of many real estate transactions. In residential transactions, its presence often became routine in many regions and urban areas of the country, and in large commercial transactions title insurance became the norm.

For individual owners purchasing title insurance, the policy of title insurance was sold as a substitute for the warranties in the vendor's deed. After all, a vendor could die, become insolvent, or otherwise judgment proof—and the warranties would be useless to a purchaser. . . .

By the end of World War II, title insurance was the predominant (in number of transactions) form of title assurance in the country. This pattern of abetting the growth of the market for mortgage capital continued in the 1960s, into the era of an expanded secondary market for mortgages and the securitization of mortgages into pools of similar instruments. Title insurance policies again helped to make interchangeable the diverse types of mortgage transaction documents that are pooled for purposes of sale into this now huge national secondary market for mortgage capital. Sometimes those polices were modified with exceptions neutralizing standard coverage, but adding exceptions of particular interest to lenders. Title insurers often act as escrow agents for closing a pool of mortgage transactions.

. . .

The number of insurers grew with the industry, but dwindled with the advent of national markets for its products. By the 1950s, there were some 150 title insurance corporations doing business around the country. Most of them offered policies in more than one jurisdiction. By the early 1970s, this number had shrunk through attrition and merger to fewer than 100. The remaining corporations writing this type of insurance policy were, by the beginnings of the 1980s, affiliated with only about 15 large insurance holding companies. Indeed, the four largest title insurers in the early 1980s accounted for more than 50 percent of the market. The largest of these had just under 20 percent of the market. In California, the four largest insurers controlled over 70 percent of that state's market. Further concentration at the top of the market, among the largest insurers, occurred at the end of the 1980s, into the early 1990s. By 2000, it was reported that "five firms control 90% of the business."

Although title insurance is not routinely used in every region of the country (New England is one area where its use is still not routine), the influence of title insurance corporations has been felt in a majority of the real estate transactions completed in recent years. Nonetheless, a few states are more important to the industry than others. For example, Moody's Investors Services reported in 2002 that among the five largest national title insurers, two states generated one third of all premiums, and ten states generated two thirds. California and Texas accounted for a third, and Florida, New York, Pennsylvania, Michigan, Arizona, New Jersey, Colorado, and Ohio accounted for another third. Thus, the regulatory and economic conditions in those states are more than usually determinative of the health of the industry as a whole.

Iowa is the only jurisdiction in which title insurance is not written. In that state title insurance is prohibited by statute—a statute whose passage probably was encouraged by the state bar association. . . .

Title insurance is a one-premium agreement to indemnify a policyholder, in amounts not exceeding the face amount of the policy, for losses caused by either on-record and off-record defects that are found in the title or interest in an insured property to have existed on the date on which the policy is issued. . . .

A policyholder may either own the insured title or property in fee simple absolute, or have some lesser fee or interest in it—such as a mortgagee might have. When the policyholder is not an owner and does not have title to or possession of the insured property, but instead has an inchoate interest or lien, an insurer may nonetheless issue a policy. It will then insure the priority of the lien or any other less-than-fee interest in real property. Title insurance thus may be held by both owners of and lenders on real property, and indeed the most common forms of title insurance policies are owner's and lender's policies.

. . .

Title insurance is unlike other types of insurance in at least three significant ways. First, its premiums are not based on the prediction of a future event by an actuary or statistician, as is life or accident insurance. Title insurance premiums are instead based in large part on the work of an abstractor—that is, on the work of a person who searches the public records maintained for interests in real property to ascertain if defects already exist in a title. The abstractor searches for preexisting defects, arising in past transactions, which may be asserted in the future. This search for past events with future consequences is hardly what most people see as the work of insurance companies. Indeed, if the abstractor's work is accurate and competent, the claims and loss rate for defects in title recorded on those records should be very low indeed. In fact, they should approach zero.

Moreover, if and when any defect is found on the records, it becomes the basis for an exception from coverage written into the policy (in the policy's so-called Schedule B). So, if the exception is written in a way to reflect the defect found, the number of claims based on such defects will still further approach zero. Title insurance policies are thus issued after the completion of work intended to reduce the number of claims—for a title insurer is in the unique position of being able, through its own work, to eliminate many claims. In contrast, life insurance companies know that, sooner or later, it will have to pay the face amount of the policy upon the (inevitable) death of the insured.

Second, a title insurance policy is paid for all at once with only one premium. There are no continuation premiums as in other lines of insurance; the first premium is also the last. This tends to reduce the overhead and administrative costs of the coverage, as there is no need for a servicing department in title insurers' organizational charts.

Third, the policy's coverage lasts for as long as the insured has some liability for a title defect, whether as the present owner or possessor, or as a vendor and warrantor of the state of the title upon some later sale. There is no such thing as term title insurance. Its policy might, potentially, last forever.

Title insurance insures not only on-record defects in title, but also covers defects not revealed by an abstractor's search of the public records related to real property. Such defects are known to title insurers as "off-record risks." They are interests not of record, but nevertheless valid. Not even the most professional, thorough, and competent title search will identify them. Sometimes they require an understanding of the type and operation of the recording act applicable to the jurisdiction in which the records are maintained—and whether or not an interest is subject to the act. Included in any listing of off-record risks are:

(1) the misindexing or misfiling of a document by the recorder,

(2) matters pertaining to the identity of the parties to a document,

(3) its delivery to the transferee . . .

Laabs v. Chicago Title Insurance Co.

Supreme Court of Wisconsin, 1976.
72 Wis.2d 503, 241 N.W.2d 434.

CONNOR T. HANSEN, JUSTICE.

This litigation arises from a dispute as to the scope of coverage provided by a policy of title insurance issued by Chicago Title Insurance Company (hereinafter company) to Theodore F. and Selma Laabs (hereinafter insured). Laabs and McKenzies owned adjoining parcels of real estate. The company had issued a policy of title insurance to both property owners. The two properties are described by metes and bounds and it appears the descriptions overlap. The property described in Laabs' deed is located partially in Government Lots four and five. It also appears that the scrivener who prepared the description to the Laabs' real estate made no reference to Government Lot five in the description. The result was that the Laabs' deed was not indexed in the tract index under Government Lot five.

The insured commenced a quiet title action against McKenzies and others claiming ownership of the disputed portion. The defendants in that action answered and counterclaimed against the insured. The insured notified the company of the counterclaim, requesting representation in accordance with the terms of the insurance policy. However, the company refused to defend on the ground that the dispute fell within certain exceptions to coverage contained in the policy.

The insured then instituted this action against the company. Trial on this action was held; however, pursuant to stipulation, the trial court postponed determination on the issue of policy coverage until after trial of the quiet title action.

At the conclusion of the quiet title action, the trial court determined that the disputed parcel belonged to the defendants in that action and not the Laabs. Because of this determination, the status of the other defendants is not pertinent to this appeal. It was also determined that the dispute was of such nature as to be within the scope of coverage of the title insurance policy issued by the company. Therefore, judgment was entered against the company for the reasonable value of the disputed property, and for reasonable attorney fees and costs incurred by the insured in the trial of the counterclaim in the quiet title action. The amount of the damages is not an issue on this appeal.

The findings of fact and conclusions of law and the judgment are captioned as in the instant action. The opinion of the trial judge is captioned as in the action to quiet title. All three of these documents are included in the record and address the issue raised in this action.

The company appeals from that portion of the judgment finding it liable to the insured for the value of the disputed parcel of land and for trial-related costs. Following transmittal of the appeal record, the insured moved this court to strike certain portions of the record. Those portions had to do with an action on a policy of title insurance issued by the company to the McKenzies. The insured herein did not party to that action. The company was not a oppose the motion. This court granted the motion, ordering that the trial court's findings of fact and conclusions of law and opinion in that action, as well as the adverse examination of McKenzie in relation to that action, be stricken from the record.

Determination of a single issue will be dispositive of this appeal:

Was the trial court in error in determining that the policy of title insurance issued by the company included within its coverage the loss sustained by the insured? We are of the opinion that the trial court was correct in its determination.

The company contends that several exceptions and conditions contained in the policy should relieve it of liability for payments to the insured.

The policy of title insurance contains the following language in its EXCLUSIONS FROM COVERAGE:

"The following matters are expressly excluded from the coverage of this policy:"

" . . .

"3. Defects, liens, encumbrances, adverse claims, or other matters . . . (b) not known to the Company *and not shown by the public records but known to the insured claimant either at Date of Policy or at the date such claimant acquired an estate or interest insured* by this policy and not disclosed in writing by the insured claimant to the Company prior to the date such insured claimant became an insured hereunder;. . . ." (Emphasis added.)

The company argues that the dispute and defect were known to the insured prior to the policy date and, therefore, the company is not liable for the loss or for defense costs. The company bases this argument on the decision of the trial court in the action between the McKenzies and the company. There it was apparently found that the company was not liable to the McKenzies in any way because the McKenzies were aware of the dispute with the insured when they applied for their policy. By order of this court, that opinion and the accompanying transcript of McKenzies' adverse examination are no longer part of the record herein and cannot be considered in reaching a determination on this issue. However, as the company observes, other testimony in support of its claim is preserved in the transcript of the quiet title action.

During that trial, the McKenzies' predecessor in title, Mrs. Yunk, testified that she had disputes in 1962 and 1966 with the insured over the parcel of land in question, that a fence had been placed along the disputed boundary line, and that she had torn it down. A neighbor of the parties testified that in 1965 or 1966, he had observed the insured placing a fence along a portion of the disputed parcel and called the Yunks to inform them of the matter. Finally, Mr. McKenzie, who was not called to testify at the trial on policy coverage, testified that approximately two weeks after he purchased his property, he encountered the insured on the disputed parcel at which time he was informed by Mrs. Laabs that he was trespassing, that he had purchased something that belonged to insured and that the amount of land purchased had been misrepresented to him. This was approximately one week prior to the date insured's policy was issued.

With respect to these matters, the insured testified at the trial on policy coverage that she had no knowledge of any dispute with the Yunks, that she had not spoken with the McKenzies prior to the time they began clearing the disputed parcel, and that she applied for the title insurance with a view toward selling the property. She confirmed this testimony at the trial on the quiet title action. She testified further that she and her husband continued to build a fence along the disputed parcel, a portion of which had been begun as far back as 1947 and 1948, and that it had been removed, although she did not know who had removed it. Her brother-in-law, a real estate broker, testified that he had advised her that if she wished to sell the property, she should obtain title insurance. This advice was not given, however, in connection with knowledge of any dispute, but rather because he felt that any prospective purchaser would impose such a requirement.

The company, in its policy, excluded from coverage defects and adverse claims not shown by the public record and not known by the company but known to the insured and not disclosed to the company. If knowledge of such adverse claim or defect could be charged to the insured, this could have provided grounds for avoiding the policy, since the company was not informed thereof. . . .

However, the trial court found as fact that the insured had complied with all the requirements of the policy. During the trial of this issue, the court stated:

> "It is my feeling that as to the getting of the policy of title insurance, knowing that there was a dispute there has not been established . . .
>
> ". . .
>
> "I find that at the time this policy was issued, that the plaintiffs, Selma Laabs and Theodore Laabs did not know of any dispute and did not secure this policy of insurance against a known dispute."

The testimony presented is set forth in unusual detail because there was a great deal of evidence, from various sources, tending to support the company's claim that the insured had knowledge of the existence of a dispute or adverse claim prior to the date of the policy. In addition, the court's statements in connection with its finding, cited supra, were made at the close of the trial on the scope of coverage, prior to the trial at which much of the relevant testimony was given. However, on appeal, review of a trial court's finding of fact is strictly limited. This court has stated on many occasions that the weight of testimony and the credibility of witnesses are matters to be determined by the trial court, and that where more than one reasonable inference can be drawn from the credible evidence, the reviewing court must accept the one drawn by the trier of fact. . . .

The trial court in the instant case resolved the conflicting testimony in favor of the insured, determining that the policy was binding on the company in this instance. Although there is testimony which would have supported a contrary finding, there is ample credible evidence to support the determination of the trial court; therefore, the determination is not against the great weight and clear preponderance of the evidence.

Moreover, it is at least arguable that the defect and adverse claim were matters of public record and, for this reason, would not fall within the stated exclusion, even if the insured had been found to have had knowledge of the claim. In resolving the question of title, the trial court pointed out that rightful ownership of the disputed parcel could be shown through tracing its title descent back to a deed conveyance made prior to the time the land was divided into government lots. The policy exclusion applies only to undisclosed defects or adverse claims *which are not matters of public record*. Such limitation is entirely reasonable in view of the nature of title insurance:

"... A policy of title insurance means the opinion of the company which issues it, as to the validity of the title, backed by an agreement to make that opinion good, in case it should prove to be mistaken, and loss should result in consequence to the insured...." First Nat. Bank & Trust Co. v. New York Title Ins. Co., supra, p. 710. ...

The company makes three additional arguments in support of its claim that it should not be held liable. These relate to policy exclusions addressed to the interest insured, the loss suffered, and whether insured created the adverse claim or defect.

The company argues that because the insured had never owned the disputed parcel, the policy excluded coverage. This argument is based upon a policy provision contained in paragraph 2 under CONDITIONS AND STIPULATIONS:

"... The coverage of this policy shall continue in force as of Date of Policy in favor of an insured so long as such insured retains an estate or interest in the land, ..."

This provision does not exclude the company's liability under the facts of this case. Title insurance policies are subject to the same rules of construction as are generally applicable to contracts of insurance. 13 Couch, Insurance (2d ed.), p. 583, sec. 48.109. The policy is to be read as a whole. D'Angelo v. Cornell Paperboard Products Co. (1973), 59 Wis.2d 46, 51, 207 N.W.2d 846.

The initial insuring clause reads as follows:

"SUBJECT TO THE EXCLUSIONS FROM COVERAGE, THE EXCEPTIONS CONTAINED IN SCHEDULE B AND THE PROVISIONS OF THE CONDITIONS AND STIPULATIONS HEREOF, CHICAGO TITLE INSURANCE COMPANY, a Missouri corporation, herein called the Company, insures, as of Date of Policy shown in Schedule A, against loss or damage, not exceeding the amount of insurance stated in Schedule A, and costs, attorneys' fees and expenses which the Company may become obligated to pay hereunder, sustained or incurred by the insured by reason of:

"1. Title to the estate or interest described in Schedule A being vested otherwise than as stated therein;

"..."

That clause connotes coverage for circumstances identical to those herein. The title to the real estate described in the policy has been adjudicated as being vested otherwise than as stated in the policy. Yet the company contends that, for that very reason, the policy stipulation cited, supra, absolves it of liability. However, that stipulation is entitled "Continuation of Insurance after Conveyance of Title." Thus, it was intended to apply only in the event that the title to the real estate described in the policy is conveyed voluntarily by the policyholder.

An insurance policy must be construed with consideration for what a reasonable person in the position of the insured would have understood its words to mean. Luckett v. Cowser (1968), 39 Wis.2d 224, 231, 159 N.W.2d 94. This court stated in Inter-Insurance Ex. v. Westchester Fire Ins. Co. (1964), 25 Wis.2d 100, 106, 130 N.W.2d 185:

> "A construction of an insurance policy which entirely neutralizes one provision should not be adopted if the contract is susceptible of another construction which gives effect to all of its provisions and is consistent with the general intent . . ."

Acceptance of the company's argument would entirely neutralize the general insuring clause and would contravene the intent of the parties as to situations which are to be covered by the policy. The two provisions under consideration are not mutually exclusive. Such a construction of the policy provisions gives the words their ordinary meaning, carries out the reasonable intention of the parties and gives effect to both parts of the insurance agreement. However, even if an ambiguity can be perceived, such ambiguity must be resolved against the company. Erickson v. Mid-Century Ins. Co. (1974), 63 Wis.2d 746, 753, 754, 218 N.W.2d 497.

A third ground for reversal relied upon by the company relates to the following policy exclusion:

> "The following matters are expressly excluded from the coverage of this policy:
>
> ". . .
>
> "3. Defects, liens, encumbrances, adverse claims, or other matters (a) created, suffered, assumed or agreed to by the insured claimant;. . . ."

The company contends that the insured created the adverse claim by erecting a fence along the boundary and posting the disputed area. This argument appears to be patently erroneous.

Many cases construing the terms contained in the cited exclusion are set forth in 98 A.L.R.2d 527. That annotation indicates that the word "create" as it is used in such exclusion refers to a conscious, deliberate causation or an affirmative act which actually results in the adverse claim or defect. Hansen v. Western Title Ins. Co. (1963), 220 Cal.App.2d 531, 33 Cal.Rptr. 668, 98 A.L.R.2d 520; *First Nat. Bank & Trust Co. v. New York Title Ins. Co., supra. See also:* Feldman v. Urban Commercial, Inc. (1965), 87 N.J.Super. 391, 209 A.2d 640, 648. Here, the adverse claim arose from a defect in the insured's title to the disputed property. The insured had no part in affirmatively creating the claim or in the circumstances which gave rise to the defect. The fence was erected and the property posted, not to create an adverse claim but because the insured believed themselves to be owners of the property.

Finally, the company argues that the insured suffered no loss and therefore liability is excluded by the following policy terms:

"The following matters are expressly excluded from the coverage of this policy:

" . . .

"3. Defects, liens, encumbrances, adverse claims, or other matters . . . (c) resulting in no loss or damage to the insured claimant; . . ."

It is the company's position that because the insured never owned the disputed parcel, they suffered no loss by the adjudication of defective title. This argument has been rejected by several courts which have considered it. In *First Nat. Bank & Trust Co. v. New York Title Ins. Co., supra*, p. 711, it was said that:

" . . . The word 'loss' is a relative term. Failure to keep what a man has or thinks he has is a loss. To avoid a possible claim against him; to obviate the need and expense of professional advice, and the uncertainty that sometimes results even after it has been obtained is the very purpose for which the owner seeks insurance. To say that when a defect subsequently develops he has lost nothing and, therefore, can recover nothing, is to misinterpret the intention both of the insured and the insurer. . . ."

See also: Foehrenbach v. German-American Title and Trust Co. (1907), 217 Pa. 331, 66 A. 561. The insured paid for a large parcel of property including the disputed portion, when the defective title was conveyed in 1943. Therefore, having contracted to insure against a title defect, the company cannot now claim that the insured has suffered no loss by reason of the fact that the title to the disputed property was defective.

Judgment affirmed.

NOTES

1. *Title Insurance Today.* Figures compiled by the American Land Title Association show a 2012 net operating gain of $504 million. This represents a comeback for the industry from 2008 which had a net operating loss of $711, reflecting the slowdown in real estate transactions, financings, and refinancings that ultimately culminated in the financial crisis of 2008. Even as late as 2011, the industry showed a $20 million net operating loss. (The major companies carry significant reserves and receive investment income, not reflected in operating figures, to balance operating losses.) The total operating revenue in 2012 was $12,226 million, making the pre-tax operating margin 4.1%. However, the percentage of operating dollars paid for losses and loss adjustment was only 7.0 while operating expenses comprised 88.9%. The fact that the percentage of operating expenses is higher than those for other types of insurance is due to the nature of title insurance which seeks to eliminate risks through title searches rather than just creating a pool of funds to reimburse inevitable losses. Title searches and examinations, maintaining title plants, and other costs to identify title problems results in high operating expenses. See American Land Title Association, Industry Research, http://www.alta.org/industry/financial.cfm.

Title insurance is available today in all states but one—Iowa, where it is barred by statute, Iowa Code Ann. § 515.48(10) (West 1988). The statute was upheld against constitutional attack in Chicago Title Insurance Co. v.

Huff, 256 N.W.2d 17, 23 (Iowa 1977) ("[W]e are in truth here called upon to determine whether the Iowa system for transferring real property titles shall, as a constitutional mandate, be burdened with an additional and costly layer of 'business activity' which our legislature has expressly prohibited.").

Title insurance has its critics. Consider, Woolley, Inside America's Richest Insurance Racket, Forbes, 11/13/06:

> Title companies appeared a century ago, helping to protect home buyers from being swindled by crooks who sold properties they didn't own. . . . It is far less necessary in these days of computerized records, online searches and rare instances of title fraud or hidden liens. . . .
>
> First American has doubled its prices in a decade, to an average charge of $1,472 per home for a title search and insurance. Meanwhile, thanks to computerized record-keeping, the cost of searching for a home's ownership records online has fallen to as low as $25. Technology also has helped make mistakes rarer; now only $74 of each policy goes to pay claims—that is, make home buyers with defective deeds whole. That leaves a $1,373 spread for overhead and for profit. . . .
>
> But the title industry's halcyon days owe much to antiquated state laws that thwart new competition, allow prices to soar despite declining costs and force almost every home buyer to pay for insurance that most of them will never need. In all but a handful of states, laws bar insurance giants in other fields, such as AIG or State Farm, from offering title insurance and undercutting incumbents' prices. It also is illegal for anyone to offer guarantees that provide the same protection as title insurance.

The Forbes article was criticized as distorting the practices of title insurers and understating the value of the policy and services. Specifically, the industry asserted that the policy was a guarantee of an accurate search, that the majority of the premium dollar goes to prevention of loss rather than payment of claims through title search and examination, and that title insurance is based on loss avoidance rather than loss assumption. The American Land Title Association claimed that approximately 90% of premiums went to expenses, 5% to claim payments, and 5% to profits. Ominsky, Title Insurance: An Unwarranted Attack, 38 Real Est.L.Rep. 1 (Feb.2007). But the questioning continues. See Prevost, Mortgages: Saving on Title Insurance, N.Y. Times, 3/17/03.

On title insurance and the financial crisis, see Barcia, A Glance At The Impact Of The Subprime Mortgage Crisis On The Title Insurance Industry, 30 Pace L.Rev. 233 (2009); Bagwell, Can't Live Without Air: Title Insurance And The Bursting Of The Real Estate Bubble, 30 Pace L.Rev. 180 (2009).

2. *Policy Coverage.* Review the form of Owner's Policy reproduced in the *Statute, Form and Problem Supplement* and reconsider the cases that you have read so far, beginning with McDonald v. Plumb at page 158. In each case, what protection, if any, would the injured owner have received under this standard form of title insurance policy?

What protection, if any, does this form of policy provide against a misdescription or surveyor error that results in the insured's house encroaching on a neighbor's parcel? That results in a neighbor's house encroaching on the insured's parcel? What protection does it provide against a subsequent buyer's refusal to perform his purchase contract with the insured because of unmarketable title? Against an undelivered deed in the insured's chain of title? Against a wild deed, appearing outside the insured's chain of title? Compare Ryczkowski v. Chelsea Title & Guaranty Co., 85 Nev. 37, 449 P.2d 261 (1969) (easement, granted by insured's predecessor in title and recorded before predecessor had acquired patent from state, was outside chain of title and thus was excluded from coverage since policy did not insure against loss by reason of easements or claims of easements not shown by public records).

Would the policy protect the buyer in Dover Pool & Racquet Club v. Brooking, at page 103? As governmental regulation of land use has increased, title companies have strengthened policy language that excludes coverage for such laws. See, e.g., Manley v. Cost Control Marketing & Management, Inc., 400 Pa.Super. 190, 583 A.2d 442 (1990) (excluding coverage for property designated as wetlands).

Would a buyer be barred from recovering under this policy if, knowing that part of the parcel was soon to be condemned, he failed to disclose this fact to the insurer? See L. Smirlock Realty Corp. v. Title Guarantee Co., 52 N.Y.2d 179, 189–90, 437 N.Y.S.2d 57, 418 N.E.2d 650 (1981) ("[W]e hold that a policy of title insurance will not be rendered void pursuant to a misrepresentation clause absent some showing of intentional concealment on the part of the insured tantamount to fraud. Moreover, because record information of a title defect is available to the title insurer and because the title insurer is presumed to have made itself aware of such information, we hold that an insured under a policy of title insurance such as is involved herein is under no duty to disclose to the insurer a fact which is readily ascertainable by reference to the public records. Thus, even an intentional failure to disclose a matter of public record will not result in a loss of title insurance protection.")

For an excellent treatise on title insurance, see D. Burke, The Law of Title Insurance (3d ed. 2000). On title insurance generally, see A.B.A., Title Insurance: The Lawyer's Expanding Role (1985); Rooney, Title Insurance: A Primer for Attorneys, 14 Real Prop., Probate & Trust J. 608 (1979); Taub, Rights and Remedies Under a Title Policy, 15 Real Prop., Probate & Trust J. 422 (1980); Szypszak, Public Registries and Private Solutions: An Evolving American Real Estate Conveyancing Regime, 24 Whittier L.Rev. 663 (2003).

3. *Municipal Code Violations.* Plaintiff, purchaser of two unimproved lots, sued her title insurer, claiming unmarketability of title on the ground that the City Council had, in violation of a city ordinance, approved a subdivision map on her property without first obtaining a bond from the developer for grading and paving the streets in the subdivision. The city later refused to issue a building permit for her parcels because of the violation. Plaintiff claimed that the ordinance "was a part of her contract of title insurance issued to her by defendant, and that violation by the county recorder of the Subdivision Map Act, constituted a breach of the title policy."

The court held against plaintiff, reasoning that the violation did not "affect the marketability of her *title* to the land, but merely impaired the market *value* of the property." Hocking v. Title Ins. & Trust Co., 37 Cal.2d 644, 652, 234 P.2d 625 (1951). The dissenting judge argued that "defendant by insuring the marketability of . . . title thereby guaranteed also the title to at least a private easement in the streets. . . . Certainly if title is conveyed which shows frontage on a public street, it is defective if there is no public street, or the existence thereof is gravely doubtful, and it has been so held." 37 Cal.2d at 653, 234 P.2d at 630.

Is it relevant that plaintiff might have been able to obtain an endorsement to her policy specifically aimed at the problem that arose?

4.   *Title Insurance and Title Warranties Compared.* Many titles are doubly assured, through title warranties given by the seller and title insurance from an institutional insurer. (Title warranties are discussed at page 229, above.) Although title warranties and title insurance overlap at many points, each also offers distinctive protection. A buyer who cannot get his title insurance company to delete an exception from its policy's coverage may turn to his seller and insist that she cover the exception by a deed warranty. Also, there are many defects, including off-record risks, that title insurance may not cover. And the damages recoverable under a title policy are limited to the face amount of the policy; additional damages may be recovered under a warranty deed.

Why would a buyer want title insurance instead of, or in addition to, warranties? Title policies offer a degree of flexibility unattainable through warranties. Endorsements can be obtained to cover off-record risks and to increase the policy's coverage so that it keeps pace with inflation and with the value of improvements put on the premises. The protection of title policies can in certain instances be made to "run" to distant transferees through endorsements insuring assignments. Title companies also offer institutional advantages—basically, an available, solvent and knowledgeable defendant. Probably most important is the fact that title insurance is not issued on a casualty basis. The insurer's title search is aimed at flushing out any possible flaws in title and at reducing the possibility that an insured will someday have to yield his home to a prior claimant and be relegated to the cold comfort of a monetary award.

Robin Malloy and Mark Klapow argue that, given pervasive changes in the real estate industry, "an attorney may commit malpractice when selecting or advising a client to rely upon a form of title assurance other than one coupled with the issuance of a fee owner's title insurance policy." Malloy and Klapow, Attorney Malpractice for Failure to Require Fee Owner's Title Insurance in a Residential Real Estate Transaction, 74 St. John's L. Rev. 407, 448 (2000). See generally Freshman, The Warranty Deed: Where and When to Use It, 51 L.A.B.J. 186 (1975); Curtis, Title Assurance in Sales of California Residential Realty: A Critique of Title Insurance and Title Covenants with Suggested Reforms, 7 Pac. L.J. 1 (1976).

5.   *Insurer's Liability Outside the Policy.* Like fire, theft and accident insurance, title insurance serves two functions. It spreads casualty losses among many policyholders, and it seeks to reduce the risk that the covered casualty will occur. Title insurance differs from these other forms of insurance by effectively reducing risk to a point at which hardly any casualty element remains. By maintaining a complete and current title plant, conducting careful title searches, and analyzing title meticulously, the company can hope to reduce its risk of loss on title claims to almost zero. This explains why title policies, unlike more typical casualty policies, call for a comparatively modest one-time premium, payable at the time of closing.

Can a buyer who has relied on a title insurer to perform its usual careful search prevail in a tort action against the company when it conducts that search negligently or fails to disclose discovered defects? Although a number of states hold that he can (see, e.g., Bank of California v. First American Title Insurance Company, 826 P.2d 1126 (Alaska 1992)), a growing number of courts limit the buyer to the terms of the insurance contract. See, for example, Somerset Savings Bank v. Chicago Title Insurance Company, 420 Mass. 422, 649 N.E.2d 1123 (1995); Walker Rogge, Inc. v. Chelsea Title & Guaranty Co., 116 N.J. 517, 562 A.2d 208 (1989); Horn v. Lawyers Title Insurance Corp., 89 N.M. 709, 711, 557 P.2d 206, 208 (1976) ("The rights and duties of the parties are fixed by the contract of title insurance. . . . Hence, any duty on the part of defendant to search the records must be expressed in or implied from the policy of title insurance. . . . Defendant clearly had no duty under the policy to search the records, and any search it may have actually undertaken, was undertaken solely for its own protection as indemnitor against losses covered by its policy."); Somerset Savings Bank v. Chicago Title Insurance Co., 420 Mass. 422, 649 N.E.2d 1123 (1995); Davis, More Than They Bargained For: Are Title Insurance Companies Liable in Tort for Undisclosed Title Defects?, 45 Cath.U.L.Rev. 71 (1995). Statutes in some jurisdictions impose a duty on insurers to make a reasonable search (see, e.g., Tenn.Code Ann. § 56–35–129) while others expressly reject liability for negligent search (see, e.g., Cal.Ins.Code § 12340.10–12340.11).

One commentator notes that courts have resisted a tort duty because it may interfere with contract rights, full disclosure of title defects may frighten purchasers unnecessarily and decrease alienability, and liability may lead to increased costs of title insurance. She argues, however, that such a duty would force insurers to search more carefully, remove the need for a wasteful second search for disclosure purposes, and is in accord with the expectations of the insured. Palomar, Title Insurance Companies' Liability for Failure to Search Title and Disclose Record Title, 20 Creighton L.Rev. 455 (1987).

Why would a buyer prefer tort theory to contract theory in an action against a title insurer? One reason is that if the land has appreciated in value, tort recovery will be more likely to make the buyer whole than will recovery limited to the face amount of the policy. Also, tort theory enables recovery of consequential damages. And, of course, if the buyer relied on his seller's title insurance policy, rather than on a title policy he purchased for himself, the absence of privity will make tort the only available theory of recovery. Compare Seigle v. Jasper, page 290 above.

See generally Frank, Bad Faith Fees in Title Insurance Litigation, 24 Prob. & Prop. 58 (No. 2, Mar./Apr. 2010); Note, Title Insurance: The Duty to Search, 71 Yale L.J. 1161 (1962); Note, Does a Title Insurer *Qua* Title Insurer Owe a Duty to Any But Its Insured? 7 Okla. City L.Rev. 293 (1982).

6. *Regulation.* As title insurance companies have grown and expanded into new territories they have inevitably encountered state regulation. Although regulatory patterns vary from state to state, two concerns predominate: the price and quality of insurance, and the insurer's solvency. In Washington, for example, title insurers must file their rates with the state insurance commissioner who "may order the modification of any premium rate or schedule of premium rates found by him after a hearing to be excessive, or inadequate, or unfairly discriminatory." Wash.Rev.Code Ann. § 48.29.140(3) (West 1984).

Most states require specified reserve funds and capitalization levels to assure the ability of title companies to pay off claims against them. New York, with one of the more extensive and detailed statutes, calls, among other things, for a "loss reserve at least equal to the aggregate estimated amounts due or to become due on account of all such unpaid losses and claims. . . ." N.Y.Ins.Law § 6405(b) (McKinney 1985). Some states require a cash deposit with the insurance commissioner and prohibit the issuance of any policy exposing the insurer to loss liability for more than fifty percent of its total capital and surplus. See, for example, Hawaii Rev.Stat. § 431:20–112 (1988). Attempts to evade the regulatory scheme may be enjoined. See, e.g., Norwest Corporation v. State, 253 Neb. 574, 571 N.W.2d 628 (1997) (mortgage lender's title warranty was equivalent of title insurance, and lender was enjoined from selling it as it was not authorized to sell title insurance).

The Federal National Mortgage Association has set guidelines to ensure the financial well-being of companies insuring titles of mortgages sold by FNMA and has required an acceptable rating of the title insurer based on financial statements from an independent rating company. FNMA Announcement No. 94–13 (8/12/94); McDonald, Rating the Title Insurers, 9 Probate & Prop. 10 (Jan./Feb. 1995).

On regulatory issues, see Quiner, Title Insurance and the Title Insurance Industry, 22 Drake L.Rev. 711 (1973).

7. *Antitrust.* One commentator has suggested that title insurance rates in some jurisdictions reflect price fixing and price discrimination as a result of a risk rate benchmark established by a national association and followed by some companies and the use in some states of a rating bureau formed collectively by the title companies to set rates. He proposes the repeal of the federal antitrust exemption for title insurance companies and the end of rating bureaus. Uri, The Title Insurance Industry: A Reexamination, 17 Real Est.L.J. 313 (1989). A later article in the same journal responds, maintaining that there is adequate control over rating bureaus by state regulators to ensure fair and nondiscriminatory prices and arguing that federal intervention would unduly interfere with state decisions. Christie, The Title Insurance Industry: A Reexamination Revisited, 18 Real Est.L.J. 354 (1990).

In Federal Trade Commission v. Ticor Title Insurance Co., 504 U.S. 621, 112 S.Ct. 2169, 119 L.Ed.2d 410 (1992), the F.T.C. challenged the uniform rates for title searches and examinations set by rating bureaus in four states as the product of illegal price fixing. The Court held that the doctrine immunizing state action from antitrust liability prevented the F.T.C. from challenging the practices of the rating bureaus in the two states where the state government actively supervised the bureaus.

Price fixing litigation continues. See Wilke, Scrutiny Tightens for Title Insurers, Wall St. J., 2/12/08. A1 (reporting suit brought in New York alleging price collusion by the four dominant national title companies and the payment of kickbacks to brokers and agents to obtain business).

8.   *Attorneys.* Does an attorney who serves as agent for a title company create an improper conflict of interest when he issues a policy to a client that he is representing in a land purchase? Formal Opinion 331 (1972) of the Committee on Ethics and Professional Responsibility of the ABA states that the attorney may participate in such transactions providing that he obtains consent from both parties after full disclosure of possible conflicts. One commentator maintains, however, that there is an irreconcilable conflict in such situations since the attorney has a pecuniary interest in recommending title insurance and also, as agent of the company, may not strongly represent the buyer's interest to obtain a policy free from as many exceptions and exclusions as possible. See Note, Conflict of Interest: Attorney As Title Insurance Agent, 4 Geo.J.Leg. Ethics 687 (1991). Reconsider *Lanza*, p. 18 above. Should the attorney be permitted to represent the company and the purchaser after full disclosure? Will disclosure ever be adequate? Will the attorney perhaps be able to get even better coverage for the buyer because of his ties to the company? Is this kind of joint representation more efficient? What if the purchaser has to get a new attorney to review the title policy for fairness?

See Guardian Title Co. v. Bell, 248 Kan. 146, 805 P.2d 33 (1991) (upholding as constitutional a Kansas statute prohibiting steering of customers to title companies by persons with an undisclosed financial interest in the company); Kickbacks to Lawyers Rapped, 72 A.B.A.J. 30 (Nov. 1, 1986). See generally, Murray, Attorney Malpractice in Real Estate Transactions: Is Title Insurance The Answer?, 42 Real Prop. Probate & Tr.J. 231 (2007).

C. INCREASING THE EFFICIENCY OF TITLE ASSURANCE

Paul Basye, a respected observer of American title assurance methods, identified seven characteristics of an efficient title system: "(1) it should allow the recording of all facts pertinent to ownership and proof of title; (2) it should require that all records affecting land be lodged in a single office rather than in several offices; (3) it should require that the land records be so constituted and organized with indices or other devices as to provide quick access to all instruments and facts affecting the ownership of a particular parcel of land; (4) it should make the record self-proving so that an owner may make prima facie proof of his title by reference to the public records; (5) it should contain all necessary machinery to bar old claims and extinguish old interests and do so in such a way as to make the legal effect of the bar apparent from the record; (6) it should include the means to facilitate the prompt correction of defects and irregularities in conveyancing which give rise to interests which are not real or substantial; and (7) it should define marketability of title in such a way as to make it reasonably simple of determination and within a restricted period of record search and of title examination." P. Basye, Clearing Land Titles 7–8 (2d ed. 1970).

Most states have taken an incremental approach to conveyancing reform, tinkering with the recording acts and introducing modest procedural and substantive innovations such as curative acts, statutes of limitations and marketable title acts. These reforms are considered below. Some states have taken the bolder, generally less successful, step of instituting so-called Torrens systems. Torrens is considered in the second part of this section. And, as indicated in the preceding section, the dramatic institutional reforms wrought by the national title insurance industry are always present in the background, sometimes overshadowing public law reform efforts.

The most recent comprehensive effort at stimulating statutory reform—the Uniform Land Security Interest Act, approved by the National Conference of Commissioners on Uniform State Laws and described on page 349 below—follows a modest, incremental tradition. Moreover, it has not been adopted by any state. See Korngold, Legal and Policy Choices in the Aftermath of the Subprime and Mortgage Financing Crisis, 60 S.C.L.Rev. 727, 736 (2009). For a thoughtful analysis of alternative title systems, see Arrunada & Garoupa, The Choice of Titling System in Land, 48 J.L. & Econ. 709 (2005).

1. MARKETABLE TITLE ACTS, STATUTES OF LIMITATIONS AND CURATIVE ACTS

The greatest attribute of the recording system can also be its greatest weakness: the system preserves documents indefinitely for an asset with an unlimited life. Thus, imperfectly drafted or executed documents can remain on the record perpetually. Moreover, potential claimants under old instruments could be lurking—or not—ready to assert their rights. For example, the holder of a possibility of reverter could be waiting for the stated event to occur to come forward and claim the property. And the fate of other rights in instruments on the record may not be known—are they still valid and who holds them?

These issues with the recording system make it expensive, difficult, and at times virtually impossible for a title examiner to find that the title is marketable. The "cluttered attic" of the recording system has thus added uncertainty and cost to the land transactions system.

The states have chosen among three basic responses to the issue: curative acts, statutes of limitations, and marketable title acts.

Curative Acts. Curative acts correct a specific type of error in instruments that have already been recorded. For example, N.Y. Real Prop.L. § 306 provides that any recorded conveyance is deemed to be duly acknowledged ten years after recording.

Statutes of Limitations. Statutes of limitations set a limit on the period in which actions asserting rights and claims can be brought. Once the time has elapsed, the claim can no longer be brought and in a sense disappears. Statute of limitations underlies the adverse possession doctrine which serves to extinguish right of the true fee owner of property to eject a trespasser in effect making the adverse possessor the new fee owner. A difficult issue, however, is determining the date at which the statute of limitation begins running against the owner of a future interest, which by definition has not become possessor.

Marketable Title Acts. The most comprehensive approach is reflected in what are known as "marketable title acts" adopted in perhaps fifteen states. About a dozen state laws are modeled after a Model Marketable Title Act developed in 1960 by Professor Lewis M. Simes and Clarence B. Taylor. See Uniform Marketable Title Act, Prefatory Note (1990). Essentially, these statutes operate by requiring the holder of an interest in a property to re-record it within thirty years or else the interest is lost. The details and policy conflicts inherent in such statutes are reflected in H & F Land, Inc. v. Panama City-Bay County Airport & Industrial District, set out below. Florida adopted a version of the Simes and Taylor model act.

For further discussion, see L. Simes and C. Taylor, Improvement of Conveyancing by Legislation (1960).

H & F Land, Inc. v. Panama City-Bay County Airport and Industrial District

Supreme Court of Florida, 1999.
736 So.2d 1167.

ANSTEAD, J.

We have for review a decision on the following question certified to be of great public importance:

> DOES THE MARKETABLE RECORD TITLE ACT, CHAPTER 712, FLORIDA STATUTES, OPERATE TO EXTINGUISH AN OTHERWISE VALID CLAIM OF A COMMON LAW WAY OF NECESSITY WHEN SUCH CLAIM WAS NOT ASSERTED WITHIN THIRTY YEARS?

H & F Land, Inc. v. Panama City-Bay County Airport, Indus. Dist., 706 So.2d 327, 328 (Fla. 1st DCA 1998). We have jurisdiction. Art. V, § 3(b)(4), Fla. Const. For the reasons that follow, we answer the certified question in the affirmative and hold that statutory or common law ways of necessity are subject to the provisions of the Marketable Record Title to Real Property Act ("MRTA").

FACTS AND PROCEEDINGS TO DATE

Coastal Lands Inc. ("Coastal") once owned all of the land now owned by the parties in this case. On October 4, 1940, Coastal conveyed 390 acres of land it owned to Bay County, which in turn conveyed this acreage to the Panama City Airport Board on July 23, 1947. This land is now owned by respondent, Panama City-Bay County Airport and Industrial District, with the Panama City-Bay County International Airport currently operating on it. As a result of the 1940 transfer, a small piece of land retained by Coastal became both water- and landlocked. This small parcel of land, approximately eight-tenths of an acre, is located on a peninsula that abuts the Airport District's property. The parties agree that an implied common law way of necessity from this small parcel and over the Airport District's property was created as a result of the 1940 transaction between Coastal and Bay County. However, no notice of a claim to such a way of necessity was ever filed in the public records or asserted by use.

This small parcel was conveyed by Coastal to O.E. Hobbs on June 15, 1943, along with the remainder of the land originally retained by Coastal when it sold part of its property to Bay County. H & F Land, Inc. ("H & F") acquired this small parcel in 1992.

In 1996, some fifty-six years after any way of necessity would have been created, H & F filed a lawsuit and asserted for the first time that along with its acquisition of the small parcel, it also acquired a right to a way of necessity across the Airport District's land. In turn, Panama City filed a motion for summary judgment in that action, asserting that by operation of law, specifically Chapter 712, Florida Statutes (1993), MRTA, the way of necessity claimed by H & F had long been extinguished because the owners of the easement had failed to publicly assert a claim thereto. The trial court agreed and granted the motion. On appeal, the First District affirmed the grant of summary judgment, but certified the question set out above.

ANALYSIS

As noted above, the parties are in agreement that H & F and its predecessors in title were at one time entitled to a way of necessity by reason of the 1940 transaction, which left the small parcel now owned by H & F water- and landlocked. At issue today is the effect of MRTA on this way of necessity, now codified under the provisions of section 704.01(1), Florida Statutes (1995).[2] While numerous other states have adopted acts similar to MRTA, no other case has specifically addressed this issue.[3] To analyze the issue, we must address two questions. First, whether a claim under a common law way of necessity is an interest in land subject to MRTA? And, second, if so, are there any exceptions in MRTA that apply to preserve the way of necessity despite the failure to assert a claim to this right within the time limitations provided in MRTA?

BACKGROUND OF MRTA AND SECTION 704.01

In landmark legislation fundamentally revamping Florida property law, the Florida Legislature adopted MRTA in 1963 for the purpose of simplifying and facilitating land title transactions. See § 712.10, Fla. Stat. (1995). MRTA was designed to simplify conveyances of real property, stabilize titles, and give certainty to land ownership. See City of Miami v. St. Joe Paper Co., 364 So.2d 439, 444 (Fla.1978).

MRTA is based on the Model Marketable Title Act, which was proposed in 1960 with multiple objectives: (1) to limit title searches to recently recorded instruments only; (2) to clear old defects of record; (3) to establish perimeters within which marketability can be determined;

---

[2]   Section 704.01(1) in relevant part provides: Such an implied grant [an implied grant of a way of necessity] exists where a person has heretofore granted or hereafter grants lands to which there is no accessible right-of-way except over his land, or has heretofore retained or hereafter retains land which is inaccessible except over the land which he conveys. Fla. Stat. (1995).

[3]   In Larson v. Hammonasset Fishing Assn., Inc., No. CV 930068175S, 1996 WL 156014, at *3 (Conn.Super.Ct. Mar.15, 1996), aff'd, 44 Conn.App. 908, 688 A.2d 373 (1997), the court addressed the issue in dicta, but provided no in-depth analysis. In Larson, the court held that no easement existed because the plaintiff had failed to show prior common ownership of the dominant and servient estates. Nevertheless, in dicta the court stated that the Marketable Record Title Act would have extinguished the plaintiff's right of way anyway because the plaintiffs and their predecessors had failed to file a notice pursuant to the provisions of the Act.

(4) to reduce the number of quiet title actions; and (5) to reduce the costs of abstracts and closings. See Lori Tofflemire Moorhouse, Note, Marketable Record Title Act and Recording Act: Is Harmonic Coexistence Possible?, 29 U.Fla.L.Rev. 916, 923–24 (1977). In its essence, the Model Act sought to accomplish these objectives by providing that when a person has a record title to land for a designated duration, claims and interests in the property that stem from transactions before that period are extinguished unless the claimant seasonably records a notice to preserve his interest. See id. at 924. In much the same manner as the Model Act, MRTA's provisions contain a scheme to accomplish the same objective of stabilizing property law by clearing old defects from land titles, limiting the period of record search, and clearly defining marketability by extinguishing old interests of record not specifically claimed or reserved.

Section 712.02 of MRTA expressly provides that any person vested with any estate in land of record for thirty years or more shall have a marketable record title free and clear of all claims of an interest in land except those preserved by section 712.03:

> Any person having the legal capacity to own land in this state, who, alone or together with his predecessors in title, has been vested with any estate in land of record for 30 years or more, shall have a marketable record title to such estate in said land, which shall be free and clear of *all claims* except the matters set forth as exceptions to marketability in § 712.03.

§ 712.02, Fla. Stat. (1995) (emphasis added). In construing this provision in Marshall v. Hollywood, Inc., 236 So.2d 114 (Fla.1970), this Court stated: "By the Marketable Record Title Act, any claim or interest, vested or contingent, present or future, is cut off unless the claimant preserves his claim by filing a notice within a 30-year period. If a notice is not filed, the claim is lost." Id. at 119 (quoting Catsman, The Marketable Record Title Act and Uniform Title Standards, § 6.2, in III Florida Real Property Practice (1965) (citation omitted)) (emphasis added). We must determine whether a claim to a common law way of necessity falls within the "all claims" language used in the statute and as interpreted expansively in Marshall.

WAY OF NECESSITY

A way of necessity is an easement that arises from an implied grant or implied reservation of an interest in land. See Dinkins v. Julian, 122 So.2d 620 (Fla. 2d DCA 1960). It is based upon the principle and assumption that whenever a party conveys property, he conveys whatever is necessary for the beneficial use of that property, but retains whatever is necessary for the beneficial use of the land he still holds. See Walkup v. Becker, 161 So.2d 893 (Fla. 1st DCA 1964). In Roy v. Euro-Holland Vastgoed, B.V., 404 So.2d 410 (Fla. 4th DCA 1981), the Fourth District cogently explained:

> A way of necessity results from the application of the presumption that whenever a party conveys property he conveys whatever is necessary for the beneficial use of that property and retains whatever is necessary for the beneficial use of land he still possesses. Such a way is of common-law origin, and is presumed to have been intended by the parties.

A way of necessity is also said to be supported by the rule of public policy that lands should not be rendered unfit for occupancy or successful cultivation.

Id. at 412 (quoting 25 Am Jur.2d, Easements and Licenses § 34, at 447–48). It is also important to note that an easement is more than a mere personal privilege; it is an interest in land. See Winthrop v. Wadsworth, 42 So.2d 541 (Fla.1949). Hence, it is an interest in the Airport District's land that H & F seeks to have recognized and enforced in these legal proceedings.

EFFECT OF MRTA

Based upon the unambiguous language in MRTA referring to "all claims" and the clear policy underlying MRTA, both of which clearly mandate that "any claim or interest" in property be publicly asserted and recorded, we find that MRTA indeed encompasses all claims to an interest in property, including ways of necessity, unless such claims are expressly excepted from MRTA's provisions. In fact, Florida appellate courts have consistently applied MRTA to easements and rights of way in situations similar to the one involved herein. See, e.g., City of Jacksonville v. Horn, 496 So.2d 204 (Fla. 1st DCA 1986) (MRTA used to extinguish unrecorded public right of way that had never been used); Holland v. Hattaway, 438 So.2d 456 (Fla. 5th DCA 1983) (easement for access to a parcel of land is an estate in land and MRTA could be used to determine its marketability).

Importantly, this Court has upheld the extinguishment of interests in land under MRTA even where those interests were more clearly established and defined than those in question here. In Marshall, we held that MRTA operates to confer marketability to a recorded chain of title in land, even if the chain originates from a forged or a wild deed, so long as the strict recording requirements of MRTA are met. See 236 So.2d at 120. As a result, we concluded that a root of title based upon a forged deed would prevail even over an otherwise entirely valid deed recorded earlier in the chain of title. Id. In so holding, we refused to create an exception to MRTA and its clear policy favoring recording, even for legitimate interests in real property that had been lost only by reason of the existence of a recorded, but otherwise ordinarily invalid transfer. This holding, of course, was predicated upon the clear policy announced in MRTA favoring the recordation of instruments while also providing a generous time period for the assertion of any claims of an interest in land.

Having refused to look behind the recorded wild deed in Marshall to establish that it was based on a forgery or was otherwise invalid, it would make little sense for us to go behind the legitimate deed of the Airport District in this case to discover an unclaimed easement against the Airport District's property and except it from MRTA's recording requirements. A core concern of MRTA was that there be no "hidden" interests in property that could be asserted without limitation against a record property owner. In other words, MRTA shifted the burden to those claiming "any claim or interest" in property to come forward in a timely fashion and assert that interest publicly. Creating judicial exceptions to this comprehensive legislative scheme would undermine the core purpose of MRTA of providing stability to property law by requiring that all claims to an interest in property be recorded. As in

Marshall, our conclusion today is predicated upon the unambiguous provisions of MRTA as well as the fundamental policy concerns underlying its enactment.

EXCEPTIONS

Having concluded that MRTA does apply to the asserted way of necessity, we must next consider the exceptions provided in section 712.03 of MRTA, only the first two of which merit discussion.

The first exception preserves "[e]states or interests, easements and use restrictions disclosed by and defects inherent in the muniments of title[5] on which an estate is based beginning with the root of title." § 712.03(1), Fla. Stat. (1995). This exception has been narrowly construed. See, e.g. ITT Rayonier, Inc. v. Wadsworth, 346 So.2d 1004 (Fla.1977). In addition, the portion dealing with "defects inherent in the muniments of title" has been strictly limited to the "face of the instrument" instead of to an examination of the circumstances surrounding the deed. Id.

Initially, we note that the term "root of title" refers to the last title transaction creating the estate in question and which was recorded at least thirty years ago.[6] See § 712.01(2), Fla. Stat. (1995). In this case, the root of title is the 1947 conveyance from Bay County to the Panama City Airport Board. For this exception to apply in the instant case, the 1947 deed from Bay County to the Panama City Airport Board would have had to disclose on its face the common law way of necessity, or the common law way of necessity would have had to constitute a defect in that title, which was reflected on the face of the title instrument. See ITT Rayonier, Inc.

In the instant case, the 1947 transfer to Panama City never mentioned or referenced the common law way of necessity; therefore, it was not "disclosed by" the muniments of title as provided for in section 712.03(1). Indeed, we acknowledge that no deed would ordinarily reflect the way of necessity because by its very nature, a common law way of necessity is implied from the circumstances surrounding its creation. If such an easement was expressly provided for, there would be no common law way of necessity created.[7]

Further, we conclude that the common law way of necessity does not qualify as a defect inherent in the title because it constitutes a recognized legal interest in land and not a defect in title as this Court has interpreted that term. In ITT Rayonier, Inc., this Court dealt specifically with this exception in answering a series of certified questions from the United States Court of Appeals. In that case, Mr. Wadsworth, the owner of homestead property, died in 1935 survived by his widow and four children, and under the prevailing homestead statute, Mrs. Wadsworth was entitled to a life estate in the property

---

[5] "Muniments of title" means the written evidence which a land owner can use to defend title to his estate. See Black's Law Dictionary 1019 (6th ed.1990).

[6] Section 712.01(2) defines "root of title" as the "title transaction purporting to create or transfer the estate claimed by any person and which is the last title transaction to have been recorded at least 30 years prior to the time when marketability is being determined."

[7] Obviously, the better practice in any land transaction is to expressly provide for all easements. Nevertheless, this case illustrates the difficulty in enforcing a way of necessity even if timely asserted and the difficulty of determining where it would be located and in establishing conditions on its use.

and the children a vested remainder. However, in 1937, Mrs. Wadsworth executed a deed conveying the property to herself and her son Lewis Wadsworth, and in 1942 they in turn conveyed the property to ITT. ITT later claimed a marketable record title free of the other children's vested remainder interests, because the children's interests arose prior to the 1937 conveyance and root of title of ITT.

The children contended their interests were preserved under the exception of section 712.03(1) because the 1937 deed was inherently defective in that it purported to convey their remainder interests without their assent and also improperly conveyed property from Mrs. Wadsworth to herself. In rejecting both contentions, this Court disagreed with the children's broad interpretation of section 712.03(1) and held "[s]ince there is nothing on the face of the deed, in its make up or construction, to indicate that it conveys the children's remainder interest, those interests are not saved from extinguishment by subsection (1) of Section 712.03, Florida Statutes." 346 So.2d at 1011. The Court also explained that "[t]he terms 'defects inherent in the muniments of title' do not refer to defects or failures in the transmission of title, as the plaintiff's argument suggests, but refer to defects in the make up or constitution of the deed or other muniments of title on which such transmission depends." Id. (quoting Marshall v. Hollywood, Inc., 224 So.2d 743, 751 (Fla. 4th DCA 1969), approved, 236 So.2d 120 (Fla.1970)).[8] Similarly, we conclude there has been no showing here of any "defects in the make up or constitution of the deed or other muniments of title" by which the Panama City Airport Board acquired its property. The deed was in regular form and simply conveyed the title to the property that the County intended to convey and the Panama City Airport Board intended to receive. Hence, we conclude that the exception under section 712.03(1) does not apply to a common law way of necessity.

FILING OF NOTICE

As for the second exception, the statute preserves estates, interests, claims or charges filed with a proper notice in accordance with the provisions of MRTA. See § 712.03(2), Fla. Stat. (1995). In this regard, section 712.05 of MRTA specifically provides:

> Any person claiming an interest in land may preserve and protect the same from extinguishment by the operation of this act by filing for record, during the 30-year period immediately following the effective date of the root of title, a notice, in writing, in accordance with the provisions hereof, which notice shall have the effect of so preserving such claim of right for a period of not longer than 30 years after filing the same unless again filed as required herein.

§ 712.05, Fla. Stat. (1995). In City of Miami v. St. Joe Paper Co., 364 So.2d 439, 442 (Fla.1978), the court explained this provision:

> The Marketable Record Title Act is also a recording act in that it provides for a simple and easy method by which the owner of an existing old interest may preserve it. If he fails to take the

---

[8] The Court cited as an example of an inherent defect, a deed purporting to convey homestead property but only executed by a husband when the constitution required execution by both husband and wife. See Reid v. Bradshaw, 302 So.2d 180 (Fla. 1st DCA 1974).

step of filing the notice as provided, he has only himself to blame if his interest is extinguished. The legislature did not intend to arbitrarily wipe out old claims and interests without affording a means of preserving them and giving a reasonable period of time within which to take the necessary steps to accomplish that purpose.

Similarly, in Cunningham v. Haley, 501 So.2d 649, 652–53 (Fla. 5th DCA 1986), the court explained:

> It is the intent of sections 712.02(1) and 712.03(1), that easements and use restrictions and other estates, interests, and claims created prior to the root of title be extinguished by section 712.03(1), Florida Statutes, unless those matters are filed under section 712.05(1) or unless, as provided in section 712.03(1), after the date of the root of title, some muniment of title refers specifically . . . to a recorded title transaction which imposed, transferred, or continued such easement, use restrictions, estate, interest, or claim.

In other words, "[a] claimant will not be cut off if he has been a party to any title transaction recorded within a period of not less than thirty years or if he files a simple notice prescribed by the Act during the time allowed for this purpose." Wilson v. Kelley, 226 So.2d 123, 127 (Fla. 2d DCA 1969). We conclude that this exception does apply, but H & F has not demonstrated compliance with its conditions.

H & F contends it could not and should not have had to file a claim under section 712.05 or otherwise as to the common law way of necessity because such right was already created in a prior transaction. Again, we disagree. We conclude that section 712.05 clearly mandates and H & F's predecessors had the opportunity to record their claim to an easement, i.e., to a common law way of necessity across the Airport District's property. In fact, it would appear that the very nature of the property right claimed here, one inferred by the law but otherwise hidden to the public, would make it especially important under MRTA's scheme to have it recorded. H & F also contends that it is difficult and impracticable to file a notice of a common law way of necessity because of the uncertainty in determining its location, especially when a servient estate is subdivided. However, it is apparent that H & F's predecessors had access to all the information that must be contained in a recorded notice as required by section 702.06. As such, they could and should have properly filed the notice. Since they failed to do so, H & F cannot avail itself of this exception.

H & F further asserts that a common law way of necessity should not be subject to any recording requirement, including that of MRTA, because such an interest in land is not subject to the recording requirements of section 695.01, Florida Statutes (1995), Florida's general recording statute.[10] However, section 712.07 provides that

---

[10] Section 695.01 provides:

(1) No conveyance, transfer, or mortgage of real property, or of any interest therein, nor any lease for a term of 1 year or longer, shall be good and effectual in law or equity against creditors or subsequent purchasers for a valuable consideration and without notice, unless the same be recorded according to law; nor shall any such instrument made or executed by virtue of any power of attorney be good or effectual in law or in equity against creditors or

courts should construe MRTA independent of any other recording act. It provides:

> Nothing contained in this law shall be construed to extend the period for the bringing of an action or for the doing of any other act required under any statute of limitations or to affect the operation of any statute governing the effect of the recording or the failure to record any instrument affecting land.

§ 712.07, Fla. Stat. (1995). We conclude that MRTA's broad recording provision is not limited to interests subject to section 695.01 and does include the easement claimed here.

LIMITATIONS EFFECT

As a final point, we recognize that MRTA also functions much as "a statute of limitations in that it requires stale demands to be asserted within a reasonable time after a cause of action has accrued. It prescribes a period within which a right may be enforced." St. Joe Paper Co., 364 So.2d at 442. Although MRTA can produce harsh results, in upholding its constitutionality, this Court has declared: "We are committed to the rule that statutes of this nature [statute of limitations] are good where a reasonable time is allowed to prosecute an asserted right." Id. at 443 (quoting Buck v. Triplett, 159 Fla. 772, 774, 32 So.2d 753, 754 (1947)). "The law is well settled by decisions of the Supreme Court of the United States, and in other jurisdictions, that statutes of limitation affecting existing rights are not unconstitutional if a reasonable time is given for the enforcement of the right before the bar takes effect." Campbell v. Horne, 147 Fla. 523, 526, 3 So.2d 125, 126 (1941). As noted above, MRTA's provisions provide reasonable time periods for claims to be asserted. Even for those who choose to wait, the Legislature has been gracious in allowing a thirty-year period in which to record a claim.

CONCLUSION

Our decision today is predicated upon the strong public policy concerns underlying the enactment of MRTA. The Legislature clearly stated the purpose of MRTA and the exclusivity of its exceptions by adopting section 712.10. It provides: "This law shall be liberally construed to effect the legislative purpose of simplifying and facilitating land title transactions by allowing persons to rely on a record title as described in § 712.02 subject only to such limitations as appear in § 712.03." § 712.10, Fla. Stat. (1995). While we also recognize the public policy concerns behind section 704.01, we conclude that it is important for the overall stability of property law under MRTA that claimants assert their interests in property in a reasonable and timely manner.[12] As we noted earlier, subject to some limited exceptions, MRTA has essentially shifted the burden to those claiming an interest in land to

---

subsequent purchasers for a valuable consideration and without notice unless the power of attorney be recorded before the accruing of the right of such creditor or subsequent purchaser.

(2) Grantees by quitclaim, heretofore or hereafter made, shall be deemed and held to be bona fide purchasers without notice within the meaning of the recording acts. Fla. Stat. (1995).

[12] Of course, nothing in this opinion prevents H & F from seeking an easement from the Airport District to gain access to its property.

publicly assert these claims so that all interests in land will be a matter of public record. The circumstances of this case serve as a vivid illustration of the legislature's concerns in seeking to provide stability in property law while still providing a reasonable opportunity for the assertion of legitimate but unrecorded claims.

In the instant case, H & F's predecessor in title to the implied right now asserted could have recorded a notice of claim any time within the approximately fourteen years following the adoption of MRTA in 1963 until 1977, the end of the thirty-year period following the effective date of the root of the Airport District's title. Because H & F's predecessor failed to use or record its way of necessity or publicly assert it in any way, MRTA mandates the extinguishment of such an interest in property in favor of the record title owner of the property. Recognition of an implied but untimely asserted right of way over the record title holder's interest would undermine the clear purpose and effect of MRTA.

We therefore answer the certified question in the affirmative and approve the decision below.

It is so ordered.

HARDING, C.J., SHAW, WELLS and PARIENTE, JJ., and OVERTON, SENIOR JUSTICE, concur.

2. TITLE REGISTRATION: THE TORRENS SYSTEM

John L. McCormack, Torrens and Recording: Land Title Assurance in the Computer Age
18 William Mitchell Law Review 61, 80–82, 83–84, 89–91 (1992).

III. The Torrens Title Registration System

A.   The Torrens System in Operation: Mirror, Curtain and Indemnity

The Torrens system of title registration has three major components: 1) the register of titles, 2) the document vault, and 3) the assurance or indemnity fund. The basic goal is to make the governmentally maintained record a conclusive statement of ownership and the condition of the title. This conclusive statement is intended to function as a "mirror" of the true state of the title and as a "curtain" between the present and the past which should make it unnecessary to conduct the kind of historical searches performed in recording systems.

Under Torrens, original certificates of title are maintained by the administrator of the system, normally called the Registrar of Titles. The certificate names the owner, describes the property and the estate owned and contains a list of the liens or encumbrances on the property. Where these liens or encumbrances are created by registered instruments, the original or a copy of the instrument can be retrieved from the document vault or other storage facility for examination.

Upon initial registration or a transfer of ownership, the transferee receives a duplicate certificate of title. The owner's duplicate normally is not kept up-to-date as subsequent claims, liens or other encumbrances are registered on the original. The owner's duplicate, or an acceptable substitute, and the deed of conveyance must be presented to register a transfer of ownership. When an interest is transferred, the former certificate showing the transferor as owner is canceled, and a new certificate is issued showing the transferee as the new owner. Active liens or encumbrances on the old certificate are carried forward to the new one.

At the time an instrument is presented for registration, the Torrens office may compare the signature on the instrument with a specimen of the owner's signature on file. When this procedure is followed, Torrens has a built-in protection against the registration of forged instruments. Recording systems have no comparable protection against recordation of forgeries.

The assurance or indemnity fund is the third important component of the system. Upon initial registration or at some time thereafter, the owner or other party may be required to make a contribution to this fund. The fund is available to compensate those who suffer losses because of errors of the Torrens office personnel and to pay those who wrongfully lose interests in real estate because of the operation of the system.

. . .

A. Initial Registration

Initial registration of title is not a simple matter. The procedure has often been compared to an action to quiet title. Once an initial registration becomes final, it has about the same effect as a final judgment in a quiet title action. Aside from the important exceptions of off-certificate risks and overriding interests, the registration is binding against the whole world. Indeed, it is often said that the main difference between recording and Torrens is that in Torrens, the title itself is registered, while under recording, the evidences of title are recorded.

. . .

Initial registration of a title can be expensive. In addition to the required contribution to the assurance fund, the title must be examined to identify possible encumbrances or claimants, the property may be surveyed, court documents must be filed, notices must be published, and hearings may be held. Attorneys and other experts may be required.

. . .

D. Torrens in Operation: Security of Title

Initially, Torrens appears to have an appealing simplicity compared to recording. Instead of having to search for and examine the entire recorded legal history of a parcel, it seems that the title examiner under Torrens simply has to examine the original certificate of title which "conclusively establishes the legal status of the parcel's title, subject to some limited exceptions." These so-called "limited" exceptions are usually referred to as "off-certificate risks" or "overriding interests." They make the Torrens register substantially less conclusive than it is sometimes perceived to be. Except where a party loses an interest in land to a good faith purchaser from a party to fraud, generally, those suffering losses from off-certificate risks are not entitled to indemnification from the assurance fund unless the registrar's actions constituted misconduct.

In no title registration system is the register absolutely conclusive. Exceptions to conclusiveness found in Torrens systems are both statutory and judge-made and fall into eight categories.

1.   *Caveats:* notices on certificates of possible claims or interests which are not technically registered;

2.   *Governmental Interests:* a) rights under federal law in nations with federal systems of government, b) liens or equivalent interests which secure payments of taxes, c) governmental lands for uses such as streets and highways;

3.   *Private special interest exceptions:* a) short term leases usually where the lessee is in possession, b) easements by implication, c) other private easements, although these are rare;

5.   *Equity:* equitable title, due process, and fairness claims or interests: a) rights to appeal or contest initial registrations, b) exceptions in certain cases of fraud, c) exceptions to protect the relatively weak or disadvantaged such as contract vendees or the uninformed, d) equitable title interests;

6.   *Error exceptions:* Exceptions due to errors in administration of the system;

7.   *Encroachments:* a) encroachments by structures on the property onto adjacent property or over a building line, b) encroachments by structures on adjacent property onto the subject property or over building lines, and

8.   *Non-title related restrictions on ownership or use:* a) planning laws, b) zoning ordinances or statutes, c) building or housing codes, d) environmental laws or regulation, e) lack of access to property.

In re Collier

Supreme Court of Minnesota, en banc, 2007.
726 N.W.2d 799.

ANDERSON, PAUL H., JUSTICE.

Joshua Collier purchased a parcel of Torrens property with the knowledge that M & I Bank FSB had an unregistered mortgage and purchase interest in the property. After purchasing the property, Collier filed a petition in Ramsey County District Court, seeking an adjudication and declaration of rights in the property. Collier's petition named M & I as a party. M & I moved for summary judgment, and the district court granted its motion, concluding that M & I's interest in the property was superior to Collier's interest because Collier was not a good faith purchaser under Minnesota's Torrens Act. The Minnesota Court of Appeals reversed the district court, concluding that Collier's actual knowledge of M & I's unregistered interest did not preclude him from being a good faith purchaser. The court of appeals then held that Collier's interest in the property was superior to M & I's interest. We reverse.

In September 2000, Joseph Conley obtained a loan from Great Northern Mortgage Corporation. The loan was secured by a mortgage on a parcel of Torrens property Conley owned. The Torrens property subject to Great Northern's mortgage is located in Ramsey County, Minnesota, and was described in the mortgage as Lot 2, Stipe's Rearrangement. It is this property that is the subject of this action. Later in September, Great Northern assigned the mortgage and its rights in the loan to appellant M & I Bank FSB. M & I or its title company filed the mortgage with the Ramsey County Recorder's office, but did not file the mortgage with the county's Registrar of Titles.

In 2002, Conley defaulted on his loan. M & I then filed a power of attorney to foreclose on the mortgage and served notice of the foreclosure on Conley. The Ramsey County Sheriff's office held a mortgage foreclosure sale on the property and M & I purchased it for $118,000. M & I filed a Sheriff's Certificate of Sale in the Ramsey County Recorder's office, but failed to file its purchase interest with the Registrar of Titles. Shortly thereafter, respondent Joshua Collier learned of the foreclosure sale through a notice published by the Ramsey County Sheriff's office. Collier contacted M & I and offered to purchase M & I's interest in the property on behalf of a real estate investment company. M & I declined Collier's offer to purchase the property.

Collier subsequently conducted a title search on the property, and thereby learned that M & I had not filed its mortgage or purchase interest with the Ramsey County Registrar of Titles. Knowing that the property was Torrens property, Collier concluded that M & I did not have a validly recorded interest in it. Collier then contacted Conley on his own behalf and offered to purchase any interest Conley may have had in the property. Conley agreed to sell Collier any such interest for $5,000 and conveyed his interest to Collier by a warranty deed. On the same day he received the deed from Conley, Collier obtained a loan from Dennis Wager, repayment of which was secured by a mortgage on the property Collier had just purchased from Conley. Collier then filed the Conley warranty deed and the Wager mortgage with the Registrar of Titles.

A few months later, Collier initiated this action by filing a petition for a proceeding subsequent to registration with the Ramsey County District Court. In his petition, Collier acknowledged that, based on Great Northern's assignment of its mortgage on the property to M & I and the Sheriff's Certificate of Sale, M & I claimed an interest in the property. But Collier asserted that neither the mortgage nor Great Northern's assignment of its mortgage to M & I had been properly filed and registered with the Registrar of Titles and that neither interest appeared on the property's certificate of title. Consequently, Collier asserted that M & I had no interest in the property and requested an adjudication and declaration of the rights of all parties in the property, including Wager.

In its answer to Collier's petition, M & I admitted that its mortgage had not been registered on the certificate of title. But as an affirmative defense, M & I asserted that Collier and Wager were not bona fide purchasers of the property because Collier had knowledge of M & I's interest in the property before purchasing the property from Conley.

Collier, Wager, and M & I all filed motions for summary judgment. Following a hearing, the district court issued an interlocutory order denying Collier's and Wager's motions, denying M & I's motion against Wager, and granting M & I's motion against Collier. The district court granted M & I's motion against Collier based on its interpretation of the term "in good faith" as used in Minnesota's Torrens Act, Minn.Stat. ch. 508 (2004). The court cited Minn.Stat. § 508.25 (2004), which states:

> Every person receiving a certificate of title pursuant to a decree of registration and every subsequent purchaser of registered land who receives a certificate of title *in good faith* and for a valuable consideration shall hold it free from all encumbrances and adverse claims, excepting only the estates, mortgages, liens, charges, and interests as may be noted in the last certificate of title in the office of the registrar * * *.[1]

(Emphasis added.)

In a memorandum accompanying its interlocutory order, the district court stated that the meaning of the good faith requirement in section 508.25 was "[a]t the heart of this case." The court noted that Collier had actual knowledge of M & I's mortgage interest in the property, M & I's foreclosure of the mortgage, and M & I's purchase of the property at the sheriff's sale. The court concluded that because Collier knew of M & I's interest in the property, Collier was not a good faith purchaser of Conley's interest in the property. Therefore, the court held that M & I's interest in the property was superior to any interest Collier obtained from Conley. Following the court's order, Wager and M & I executed a stipulation for dismissal with prejudice, ending Wager's involvement in this case.

Collier appealed to the court of appeals, arguing that his knowledge of M & I's unregistered interest should not have affected the court's analysis. Specifically, Collier asserted that under the Torrens Act, M & I's failure to file its mortgage with the Registrar of Titles left M & I with no "effective" interest in the property of which Collier could have known.

The court of appeals reversed the district court, holding that Collier was a good faith purchaser under the Torrens Act and that his registered interest was superior to M & I's unregistered interest. In re Collier, 711 N.W.2d 826, 831 (Minn.App.2006). The court's analysis began with the premise that the Torrens Act requires a mortgage interest in registered property to be filed and registered with the registrar of titles in order to encumber the property. Id. at 830 (citing Minn.Stat. § 508.54 (2004)). The court concluded that because M & I failed to file its mortgage on Conley's property with the Ramsey County Registrar of Titles, M & I did not have an interest in the property that affected subsequent purchasers such as Collier, and instead had only a private contract with Conley. Id. at 831. The court further concluded that "[a]ctual notice of a private contract is not the type of notice that prevents a purchaser from being a good-faith purchaser." Id. The court reasoned that Collier's actual notice of M & I's private contract with Conley was not inconsistent with his own purchase of Conley's interest

---

[1]   Section 508.25 also lists seven exceptions that encumber Torrens property in spite of their failure to appear on the last certificate of title. None of the exceptions applies in this case.

in the property, because under the Torrens Act, the land was unencumbered by M & I's interest. Id.

M & I subsequently petitioned our court for review and we granted its petition. M & I asks us to resolve two issues on appeal: (1) whether Collier's actual notice of M & I's unregistered interest in the Torrens property precludes him from being a good faith purchaser under Minn.Stat. § 508.25; and (2) whether Collier's purchase of Conley's interest in the property for $5,000 constitutes "valuable consideration" under section 508.25.

On appeal from summary judgment, we determine whether there are any genuine issues of material fact and whether a party is entitled to judgment as a matter of law. Christensen v. Milbank Ins. Co., 658 N.W.2d 580, 584 (Minn.2003). When the material facts are not in dispute, we review the lower court's application of the law de novo. Leamington Co. v. Nonprofits' Ins. Ass'n, 615 N.W.2d 349, 353 (Minn.2000). Here, the material facts are not in dispute. The parties agree that M & I did not file its mortgage or Sheriff's Certificate of Sale with the Registrar of Titles. The parties also agree that Collier purchased Conley's interest in the property with actual knowledge of M & I's interest. Accordingly, we exercise de novo review.

This case involves the Minnesota Torrens Act and Torrens property, and because the Torrens property system is distinct from the abstract property system, we begin our analysis with a brief overview of the two property systems and the policy underlying the Torrens system. Until Minnesota adopted the Torrens system in 1901, all real property in the state was abstract property. Hersh Props., LLC v. McDonald's Corp., 588 N.W.2d 728, 733 (Minn.1999). Under the abstract system, transactions that affect real property are recorded with the county recorder in the county where the property is located. Id. The documents recording the transactions become public records and are a source for prospective purchasers to ascertain the status of title. Id. These documents are typically summarized in a single document, called an abstract of title, so that prospective purchasers, mortgagors, mortgagees, and others may have a source to research the status of the title. Id. But in addition to the recorded documents, under the abstract system, a title may be affected by factors not reflected in the recorded documents. Id. Therefore, a prospective purchaser or mortgagee must carefully investigate a property's history and condition in order to ascertain marketability of the title to that property.

In 1901, the Minnesota legislature adopted an alternative to the abstract system-the Torrens system. See Act of Apr. 11, 1901, ch. 237, 1901 Minn. Laws 348. The Torrens Act is codified at Minn.Stat. ch. 508. Under the Torrens system, a party seeking to register an ownership interest in property applies for a court adjudication of ownership and a court decree that converts abstract property into Torrens property. See Minn.Stat. § 508.22 (2004). A court-appointed officer, the examiner of titles, oversees the registration process. Minn.Stat. §§ 508.12, 508.13 (2004). After the court adjudicates ownership and any other existing interests in the property, the registrar of titles creates a certificate of title, which is issued to the owner. See Minn.Stat. §§ 508.34, 508.35 (2004). After the issuance of a certificate of title, any conveyance, lien, instrument, or proceeding that would affect the title to the now registered Torrens property must be filed and registered with the registrar of titles in the county where the property is located in order to affect the title to the Torrens property. Minn.Stat. § 508.48 (2004).

We have said that "[t]he purpose of the Torrens system was to create a title registration procedure intended to simplify conveyancing by eliminating the need to examine extensive abstracts of title by issuance of a single certificate of title." Hersh Props., 588 N.W.2d at 733. Under the Torrens system, time-consuming and expensive title searches, which characterize the abstract system, are alleviated because the purchaser of Torrens property may, subject to limited exceptions, determine the status of title by inspecting the certificate of title.[2] See id.

M & I argues that Collier's actual knowledge of M & I's unregistered mortgage and subsequent foreclosure on the property negates the good faith requirement in section 508.25, and therefore, its interest in the property is superior to Collier's. Collier argues that his actual knowledge of M & I's unregistered interest does not affect his status as a good faith purchaser, making his interest superior to M & I's.

Collier correctly asserts that Minnesota's Torrens Act places great emphasis on the acts of filing and registration. The Torrens Act provides that "[e]very conveyance, lien, attachment, order, decree, or judgment, or other instrument or proceeding, which would affect the title to unregistered land under existing laws, if recorded * * * shall, in like manner, affect the title to registered land if filed and registered." Minn.Stat. § 508.48 (emphasis added). "All interests in registered land, less than an estate in fee simple, shall be registered by filing with the registrar * * *." Minn.Stat. § 508.49 (2004) (emphasis added). When conveying, mortgaging, leasing, or otherwise dealing with registered land, "[t]he act of registration shall be the operative act to convey or affect the land." Minn.Stat. § 508.47, subd. 1 (2004). Minnesota Statutes § 508.54, which specifically addresses mortgages, requires that mortgage interests in Torrens property "be registered and take effect upon the title only from the time of registration."

Although the Torrens Act makes clear that the acts of filing and registration are critical in the Torrens system, M & I's failure to file its interests in the property with the registrar of titles does not end our inquiry under the Torrens Act. Section 508.25 also provides that "every subsequent purchaser of registered land who receives a certificate of title in good faith and for a valuable consideration shall hold it free from all encumbrances and adverse claims" except from interests noted on the certificate of title. (Emphasis added.) Based on this language, we conclude that our inquiry must focus on whether Collier's actual knowledge of M & I's unregistered interest in the property affects his status as a good faith purchaser under section 508.25.

The relevant language of section 508.25 remains unchanged from when the Torrens Act was first codified in Minnesota. See Minn. Rev. Laws § 3393 (1905). Although the legislature never defined the meaning of good faith in that section, we conclude that good faith must mean

---

[2] For a thorough review of the history, policy, and statutory scheme underlying Minnesota's Torrens Act, see Hersh Props., 588 N.W.2d at 733–34.

something; if not, the language would be rendered a nullity. See Minn.Stat. § 645.17(2) (2004) (directing courts to presume that the legislature intends an entire statute to be "effective and certain"). Our analysis indicates that since the passage of the Torrens Act, the meaning of good faith has been established through both case law and real estate practice. As far back as 1913, we presumed that the good faith language in the Torrens Act contained a notice or knowledge component, when we stated that "one who purchases from the registered owner for a valuable consideration, in reliance upon [a Torrens] judgment and without notice or anything to put him on inquiry, takes the title free from all 'incumbrances and adverse claims.'" Henry v. White, 123 Minn. 182, 185, 143 N.W. 324, 326 (1913) (emphasis added) (quoting Minn. Rev. Laws § 3393).

In 1929, we further discussed the relationship between actual notice and unregistered interests in Torrens property in In re Juran, 178 Minn. 55, 226 N.W. 201 (1929). The facts in Juran were as follows. Peterson owned Torrens property that was encumbered by a registered mortgage. 178 Minn. at 57, 226 N.W. at 201. Peterson executed a contract for deed and a warranty deed on the property to separate parties, neither of which documents was filed and registered with the registrar of titles. Id. The warranty deed grantee subsequently executed a warranty deed to Juran, subject to the contract for deed. Id. Later, Kroening registered a writ of attachment against the property with the registrar of titles pursuant to a legal action he brought against Peterson. Id. Nearly two months later, Peterson told Kroening's attorney that he had sold the property. 178 Minn. at 60–61, 226 N.W. at 203. A few months later, Kroening filed with the registrar of titles a certified copy of a judgment rendered in the action in which the attachment had been issued, as well as a certified copy of a judgment he had obtained in a second action against Peterson. 178 Minn. at 57, 226 N.W. at 201. Kroening then bought the property at a sheriff's sale, prompting Juran and the contract for deed grantees to challenge Kroening's rights in the property. Id. They argued that Kroening had constructive notice that Peterson no longer had a full interest in the property because others were living on it. 178 Minn. at 60, 226 N.W. at 202. As part of our decision in Juran we stated that

> under [Torrens] law possession of registered land is not notice of any rights under an unregistered deed or contract for deed. [The Torrens] act abrogates the doctrine of constructive notice except as to matters noted on the certificate of title. *We think however that it does not do away with the effect of actual notice*, although it undoubtedly imposes the burden of proving such notice upon the one asserting it.

Id. (emphasis added) (citation omitted).

We concluded in Juran that there was no evidence in the record suggesting that Kroening had actual notice of the property's occupation before he registered the writ of attachment, and we therefore held that Kroening's rights under the attachment, judgment, and execution sale were superior to Juran's and the contract for deed grantees' interests. 178 Minn. at 60–61, 226 N.W. at 202–03. But we also concluded that Kroening's rights in the property under the judgment in the second action were inferior and subordinate to Juran's and the contract for deed grantees' rights because Peterson told Kroening's attorney that he had sold the property before the judgment in the second action was filed and registered with the registrar of titles. 178 Minn. at 60–61, 226 N.W. at 203.

Collier argues that our statement in Juran that the Torrens system does not do away with the effect of actual notice is mere dictum and should be ignored. We disagree. In Juran, we relied on the actual notice rule to conclude that Kroening's rights under the second action were inferior.[3] 178 Minn. at 60–61, 226 N.W. at 202–03. Furthermore, since Juran was decided in 1929, our court has referenced and relied on Juran's "actual notice" pronouncement to varying degrees. See, e.g., Kane v. State, 237 Minn. 261, 269, 55 N.W.2d 333, 338 (1952) (quoting the Juran syllabus, which contains actual notice language); Cook v. Luettich, 191 Minn. 6, 8, 252 N.W. 649, 650 (1934) (quoting Juran syllabus and finding appellant had actual knowledge).

In the past 20 years, three court of appeals cases have shown that court's acceptance and reliance on Juran's actual notice rule. While these cases do not constitute precedent for the purpose of our court's jurisprudence, McClain v. Begley, 465 N.W.2d 680, 682 (Minn.1991), their reasoning is relevant to the extent it informs us about the role of actual knowledge in the Torrens system as it is practiced in Minnesota. In Nolan v. Stuebner, a published opinion, the appellants bought Torrens property subject to an easement that did not appear on their warranty deed. 429 N.W.2d 918, 921–22 (Minn.App.1988), rev. denied (Minn. Dec. 16, 1988). The certificate of title made reference to the easement, but it appeared the easement may have encumbered a parcel of land conveyed to a different party. Id. The court of appeals concluded that even if the certificate was ambiguous as to the placement of the easement, the appellants had record notice of the easement through the language on the certificate and actual notice after obtaining a title opinion in which an attorney confirmed the existence of the easement. Id. at 923. The court held that the appellants were not bona fide purchasers because of their record notice, provided by the language on the certificate, and their actual notice, provided by the title opinion. Id.

In two unpublished opinions, the court of appeals determined that the good faith requirement in Torrens law is not met if purchasers of Torrens property have actual knowledge of an unregistered interest. In 5th Street Ventures, LLC v. Frattallone's Hardware Stores, Inc., the original owner of Torrens property that included a building agreed to allow the building's lessee, Frattallone's, to use a common area for storage, but the lease was never filed with the registrar of titles. No. A03–2036, 2004 WL 1878822, at *1 (Minn.App. Aug. 24, 2004). 5th Street purchased the property and commenced an unlawful detainer action against Frattallone's, arguing that Frattallone's was not authorized to use the common area. Id. The district court granted summary judgment to Frattallone's, concluding that the lease was enforceable as amended, even though it was not filed and registered

---

[3] Our syllabus in Juran supports this conclusion. The syllabus states that "[t]he evidence will not sustain a finding that [Kroening] had actual notice of any unregistered rights before the registration of his attachment, but does sustain [a] finding that *he had such notice before registering a judgment obtained in another and later action*." 178 Minn. at 56, 226 N.W. at 201 (emphasis added).

with the registrar of titles. Id. at *2. The court of appeals reversed, holding that genuine issues of material fact existed. Id. at *2–3. The court concluded that if 5th Street "had actual knowledge of an unrecorded lease at the time of purchase, it cannot later seek the protection of the Torrens statute as a good-faith purchaser with no notice." Id. at *3. The case was then remanded to the district court to determine whether 5th Street had actual knowledge of the unrecorded lease. Id.

In In re Willmus, the court of appeals also concluded that actual notice of an interest in Torrens property can be determinative of the status of title. C0–95–1136, 1996 WL 33095 (Minn.App. Jan. 30, 1996), rev. denied (Minn. Mar. 28, 1996). In Willmus, the Doughertys bought a tract of Torrens property encumbered by an easement for the benefit of the appellant, but the easement did not appear on the Doughertys' certificate of title. Id. at *1. The appellant commenced an action, seeking an order to require the registrar of titles to enter a memorial, so that the certificate of title would reflect the easement. Id. The court of appeals recognized the easement's existence, but held that on remand, the appellant needed to prove that the Doughertys had actual knowledge of the easement in order to overcome the good faith clause in the Torrens Act. Id. at *2–3.

It also appears that real estate practitioners in Minnesota have come to support and rely on our precedent that actual notice of another's unregistered interest in Torrens property can negate the good faith requirement found in section 508.25. For example, in his amicus brief, Hennepin County Examiner of Titles Edward A. Bock, Jr., asserts that our precedent Juran "has provided sound guidance for the operation of the Torrens system for or over 75 years." Bock claims that some degree of flexibility makes the Torrens Act more useful and efficient. He asserts that if a prospective purchaser could purchase Torrens property and then file his purchase documents with the registrar of titles when he has actual notice of another's unregistered interest, it "would establish a pure 'race' situation providing no benefit to good faith purchasers." Bock claims that such a system would "encourag[e] unscrupulous persons to seek opportunities to profit at the expense of others." He also asserts that our failure to uphold our ruling in Juran would create business risks. He claims that in the ordinary course of business, it may be days between a real estate closing and filing of the documents with the registrar of titles. During this interval, one who knows of the closing could take advantage of the delay.

We conclude that Minnesota courts have relied on our precedent in Juran, and real estate practitioners have accepted the proposition that to be a good faith purchaser of Torrens property, a purchaser cannot have actual knowledge of previous, unregistered interests. See also 25 Julie A. Bergh, Minnesota Practice-Real Estate Law ch. 3, § 3.23(b) (Eileen M. Roberts ed., 2007 ed.) ("[An] exception to the general rule that unregistered instruments do not affect registered land arises when there is no intervening bona fide purchaser for value and there is actual knowledge of the unregistered interest."). Thus, we conclude that the actual notice language in Juran is not merely dictum, but rather represents long-established precedent of our court.

We also note that we have applied principles of equity when a result under the Torrens Act violates notions of justice and good faith. See Finnegan v. Gunn, 207 Minn. 480, 292 N.W. 22 (1940). In Finnegan, we concluded that "[n]othing in the Torrens system indicates that the ancient concepts of equity are not applicable" under certain circumstances. 207 Minn. at 482, 292 N.W. at 23. See also Mill City Heating & Air Conditioning Co. v. Nelson, 351 N.W.2d 362, 365 (Minn.1984) (requiring a subcontractor to provide prelien notice of a mechanic's lien to purchasers of Torrens property who had not yet filed their ownership interest with the registrar of titles, because failure to do so produced an "unfair and unreasonable" result). But, because equitable concepts are not necessary to our holding in this case, we mention this precedent only as an additional point of reference for our ultimate decision.

. . .

We conclude that under section 508.25, a purchaser of Torrens property who has actual knowledge of a prior, unregistered interest in the property is not a good faith purchaser. Here, Collier gained actual knowledge of M & I's interest in the property through the Ramsey County Sheriff's office's publication of the notice of foreclosure sale and through his subsequent negotiations with M & I to purchase the property. We also conclude that Collier's knowledge constitutes actual notice, and since Juran was decided in 1929, the law in Minnesota has prevented a prospective purchaser with actual notice of a superior interest in Torrens property from becoming a good faith purchaser. In the years after Juran, the legislature has not chosen to alter the relevant language in section 508.25 or define good faith. Moreover, Minnesota courts have relied on our precedent, and real estate practitioners have accepted and applied the foregoing principles without apparent difficulties. We have stated that "[w]e are extremely reluctant to overrule our precedent under principles of stare decisis" and require a "compelling reason" to do so. State v. Lee, 706 N.W.2d 491, 494 (Minn.2005) (citing Oanes v. Allstate Ins. Co., 617 N.W.2d 401, 406 (Minn.2000)). The facts in this case offer no compelling reason to overrule our precedent. Accordingly, we conclude that M & I's interest in the subject property is superior to Collier's interest.

In rendering this decision, we decline any entreaty by M & I and amicus to define the outer contours of actual notice; rather, we limit our holding to the facts of this case. Also, because we conclude that Collier is not a good faith purchaser, we do not reach the issue of whether Collier's purchase of Conley's interest in the property for $5,000 constitutes "valuable consideration" under section 508.25.

Based on the foregoing analysis, we hold that the district court properly granted summary judgment in favor of M & I, and that the court of appeals erred when it reversed the district court's ruling on M & I's summary judgment motion. Therefore, we reverse and remand to the district court for further proceedings consistent with this opinion.

Reversed.

NOTES

Although as many as twenty-one states at one time authorized the registration of title to real property, the number has since dwindled to ten—Colorado, Georgia, Hawaii, Massachusetts, Minnesota, New York, North Carolina, Ohio, Virginia, and Washington. See Fiflis, English Registered Conveyancing: A Study in Effective Land Transfer, 59 Nw.U.L.Rev. 468 (1964). And, even in these states, landowners only infrequently register title. According to Fiflis, "In Hawaii, perhaps one-third of all transactions are under the title registration system. In Cook County, Illinois, about 15% of all transactions are in registered land. Except in these states, and Massachusetts, Minnesota and perhaps Ohio, the system is virtually unused." Id. n. 1. The history of state adoption of Torrens is summarized in 6A R. Powell, The Law of Real Property ¶ 908 (1982). Illinois has formally abandoned Torrenization. As of January 1, 1992, no additional land can be registered under the Torrens Act. The Act itself has been repealed, effective as of July 1, 2037. 765 I.L.C.S. 35/110.3.

This general rejection of title registration contrasts sharply with the claims for its superiority made in the literature. See for example, Janczyk, An Economic Analysis of the Land Title Systems for Transferring Real Property, 6 J. Legal Stud. 213, 215 (1977) ("The results of this paper indicate that the cost of transferring a title in the Torrens [system] is approximately $100 less than in the recording system, and further, that Cook County could save $76 million by adopting the Torrens system; some other counties could also realize a substantial savings."). The Colorado Supreme Court observed that "although lauded by legal scholars as a promising alternative to traditional title registration methods, practitioners have been less than enthusiastic in adopting the Torrens system. In fact, Torrens actions are so rare in Colorado that none of th three real estate experts testifying at trial had ever participated in a Torrens proceeding." Lobato v. Taylor, 70 P.3d 1152, n. 4 (Colo.), cert. denied, 540 U.S. 1073, 124 S.Ct. 922, 157 L.Ed.2d 742 (2003).

Why has title registration failed to take hold in the United States? Blame is most commonly placed on the title insurance companies: "The chief, major, proximate, and direct cause of the non-use of, or of the public 'disinclination' to use, the Torrens system has been the bitter, multi-form opposition—lobbying against any reform, wounding statutes when enactment is inevitable, conspiring with lending agencies, spreading adverse publicity, and so forth—of title companies and title lawyers." McDougal & Brabner-Smith, Land Title Transfer: A Regression, 48 Yale L.J. 1125, 1147 (1939). Why do title companies oppose title registration? Why should industry opposition alone have succeeded in sinking the concept? What reasons do consumers have to switch from title insurance to title registration, which is initially more costly?

The fight over title registration has produced some of the sharpest scholarly debates in real property law. Compare, for example, R. Powell, Registration of the Title to Land in the State of New York (1938), with McDougal & Brabner-Smith, Land Title Transfer: A Regression, 48 Yale L.J. 1125 (1939). Proposals for the adoption of title registration continue to be made. See, for example, Note, The Torrens System of Title Registration: A New Proposal for Effective Implementation, 29 U.C.L.A.L.Rev. 661 (1982) (also contains footnote references to most of the major literature in the area); Lobel, A Proposal for a Title Registration System for Realty, 11 U.Rich.L.Rev. 471 (1977).

See generally, B. Shick & I. Plotkin, Torrens in the United States (1978).

CHAPTER V

FINANCING THE PURCHASE

A. THE FORMS, SOURCES AND TERMS OF HOME FINANCE

1. FORMS

American Law Institute, Introduction to the Restatement of the Law of
Property (Third): Mortgages*

3–6 (1997).

Lenders in the United States have made use of a variety of real estate security devices. The oldest, of course, is the mortgage, a legacy of medieval England, and its virtual twin, the deed of trust. Other devices include the absolute deed as security, the contract for deed, and the "negative pledge." Lenders developed these instruments because they felt dissatisfied with the mortgage, either because its foreclosure procedure was considered unduly cumbersome or because the substantive protection provided to borrowers was considered excessive. The result has been a plethora of devices and a corresponding profusion of legal uncertainty in most jurisdictions. The picture is not a tidy or an efficient one.

This Restatement proceeds on the premise that only one real property security device is necessary. It is here referred to simply as a mortgage, since that term has history on its side. If the rules governing the mortgage are efficient, flexible, and equitable to both borrower and lender, there should be no need for the invention or perpetuation of other devices, and this Restatement in effect encourages their eradication by the courts and legislatures. The goal is a unified body of law that will govern real property security instruments, irrespective of the name given them by their signatories.

Protection for borrowers. The courts have developed two fundamental rights for mortgage borrowers that are preserved in this Restatement. The first is the mortgagor's equity of redemption, which arose in the English equity courts during the 16th century. It is in essence the right of a borrower, although tardy in payment, to redeem his or her land by paying the debt prior to some fixed date established by the court—literally, the date of "foreclosure" of the right of redemption. This right continues to exist in every American jurisdiction. Where nonjudicial foreclosure is employed in the United States, the date is typically established by a statute providing a fixed number of days from the service or recording of a "notice of default" by the mortgagee. But whether set by court order or by statute, the principle of the equitable right of redemption is generally considered an element of fundamental fairness to borrowers, and is fully recognized and endorsed by this Restatement.

A corollary of equal importance is the prohibition on the "clogging" of the equitable right of redemption by a mortgage clause or contemporaneous agreement. The borrower's right to continue to hold an interest in the real property until it is foreclosed, and to redeem until foreclosure occurs, cannot be waived or impaired when the loan is made. That principle, too, is preserved in the Restatement.

A second basic right of borrowers, developed in the American courts and nearly universally recognized today, is the right to any surplus generated by a foreclosure sale. In England foreclosure was originally "strict," with the lender simply retaining title to the land if the borrower did not redeem prior to foreclosure. But in the United States nearly all states today employ a process of foreclosure by auction sale. In theory, at least, the sale serves two functions simultaneously: It establishes a current value for the real estate, and it acts as a marketing device, liquidating the security and transferring title to some new owner.

There is much to criticize in presently employed procedures for foreclosure by sale. One can well argue that, while attempting to combine the two functions mentioned above, foreclosure by sale manages to perform neither task very well, and serves both borrowers and lenders inadequately. However, the foreclosure process is defined by statute in nearly all American jurisdictions, and hence is beyond the direct reach of a Restatement. Still, the fundamental right of the mortgagor and other junior interest holders to surplus—that is, to have the property's value established, and to receive payment of that value insofar as it exceeds the debt plus accrued interest, foreclosure expenses and costs—is and must be recognized.

Moreover, the right to surplus, like the equity of redemption itself, is regarded in the Restatement as nonwaivable in the mortgage or contemporaneous documents. While this principle is widely recognized today with respect to formal mortgages, it is by no means universally agreed to apply to certain mortgage substitutes, such as the installment land contract. Since the Restatement, as mentioned above, regards all real property security devices as mortgages, its effect is to ensure all debtors (including purchasers under installment contracts) a right to return of the surplus value of their property.

It is frankly recognized that these two principles, the right of redemption and the right to surplus, are restrictions on the parties' freedom of contract. They have been justified for hundreds of years by the view that borrowers are often necessitous and incautious, and that they will frequently agree to exceedingly improvident arrangements in order to secure the funds they need. This is, of course, a generalization to which countless individual exceptions might be found, but it contains an important element of truth.

One might, for example, propose a regime under which individual borrowers (or consumers, or "protected parties," or the like) have the benefit of these principles, while corporate borrowers (or businesses, or commercial borrowers, or "non-protected parties," or the like) do not. While there may be some contexts in which such a distinction has great value, the Restatement's view is that the twin rights to foreclosure and to surplus should be protected for all borrowers against waiver at the inception of the mortgage transaction. There can be little or no social utility in a legal rule that permits lenders to cut off borrowers' rights precipitously, or to gamble that the property may have surplus value in excess of the debt and all expenses and to snap it up if it exists. Real property security should be just that—security—and not an opportunity for the lender to realize a windfall profit as a result of the borrower's default. Of course, this protection of individual borrowers comes at a cost to borrowers generally. Precluding lenders from garnering the windfall of the borrower's equity is inevitably reflected in higher borrower costs for all mortgage loans. Still, the protection is amply justified because it serves to restrain the often oppressive bargaining power lenders exercise over borrowers.

On the other hand, these principles of borrower protection should not unnecessarily inhibit the creativity of borrowers and lenders in developing new and socially useful forms of financing transactions. For example, the Restatement draws a sharp distinction between devices such as the option to purchase when employed as a default remedy, and similar devices when used outside the default context to provide an investment return to the lender. When sophisticated parties create novel and untried loan arrangements in order to allocate the economic benefits of a transaction by careful negotiation and full agreement, the law should be most reluctant to stand in their way unless a clear violation of public policy would otherwise ensue.

C. Phillip Johnson Full Gospel Ministries, Inc. v. Investors Financial Services, LLC

Court of Appeals of Maryland, 2011.
418 Md. 86, 12 A.3d 1207.

BATTAGLIA, J.

. . .

The instant contretemps involves a lender, Investors Financial Services, LLC ("Investors"), a Maryland company with its principal place of business in Silver Spring, and a borrower, C. Phillip Johnson Full Gospel Ministries, Inc. ("Ministries"), which executed a Deed in Lieu of Foreclosure regarding land in Martinsville, Virginia. Ministries, in a four-count Complaint seeking damages for breach of contract and for declaratory relief, had challenged the validity of the Deed in Lieu in the Circuit Court for Montgomery County, on the basis that the Deed in Lieu was not supported by consideration. . . .

After re-argument . . ., "in light of recent statutory reforms in foreclosure law," we again ordered that briefing and re-argument be scheduled and invited the submission of *amicus curiae* briefs, on the following additional and what will ultimately turn out to be the dispositive issue:

> Is a deed in lieu of foreclosure executed as a precondition to originating a loan, before any default in the loan, valid under Maryland law, to support conveyance of marketable title upon default, but without foreclosure, in light of the borrower's equity of redemption, see, e.g., Restatement (Third) of Property: Mortgages, Sec. 3.1(b), cmt. a; see also Md. Code

(1974 Vol.), Sec. 7–101(b) of the Real Property Article; Simard v. White, 383 Md. 257, 269–90, 859 A.2d 168, 175–97 (2004)?

We shall vacate the judgment of the Circuit Court for Montgomery County because, under Maryland law, a deed in lieu of foreclosure may not be executed at outset of a mortgage, before any default occurs, as it clogs the equity of redemption.

The present case began with a purchase of improved land "Property") located in Martinsville, Virginia, by Ministries from the Catholic Diocese of Richmond, to be used as a church. Ministries turned to Investors, a Maryland limited liability company with its principal place of business in Silver Spring, Montgomery County, Maryland, to obtain financing. As part of the financing, Ministries issued a Promissory Note to Investors for $93,000, which was used to finance the Property. The Note was secured by two deeds: a Deed of Trust, which included an acceleration clause containing a Power of Sale, as well as a Deed in Lieu of Foreclosure, which Ministries also was required to execute at closing. The Deed in Lieu purported to grant to Investors title to the Property "in order to avoid foreclosure of the . . . Deed of Trust," immediately upon default for any reason. The Deed in Lieu provided, in relevant part:

THIS DEED IN LIEU OF FORECLOSURE, made this, by and between **C. Phillip Johnson Full Gospel Ministries, Inc., a Washington, D.C. corporation**, party (ies) of the first part, and **Investors Financial Services, LLC** party (ies) of the second part:

WHEREAS, the party (ies) of the first part is the obligor named in a separate Note dated April 5, 2005 in the original principal sum of **Ninety-three Thousand and zero cents ($93,000.00)** which Note is secured by a Deed of Trust dated April 5, 2005 and to be recorded among the Land Records of the Commonwealth of Virginia, City of Martinsville; and

WHEREAS, the party (ies) of the second part are the holders of the aforesaid Note and the secured party (ies) under the aforesaid Deed of Trust; and

WHEREAS, for diverse reasons, the party of the first part has been unable to pay the indebtedness evidenced by the aforesaid Note as the installments have become due and payable and has been unable to perform the several covenants set forth in the aforesaid Deed of Trust; and

WHEREAS, in order to avoid foreclosure of the aforesaid Deed of Trust, the party (ies) of the first part desires to convey the subject property to the parties of the second part in exchange for the cancellation of the existing indebtedness owed to the parties of the second part in the amount of the debt owed;

NOW, THEREFORE, in consideration of the relinquishment of indebtedness, and other good and valuable consideration, receipt of which is hereby acknowledged, the party of the first part does hereby grant unto parties of the second part in fee simple, all that piece or parcel of land, together with the improvements, rights, privileges and appurtunances to the same belonging, situate in the Commonwealth of Virginia, described as follows to wit:

SEE ATTACHED LEGAL DESCRIPTION

Also known as: 704 East Church Street, Martinsville, Virginia 24112

Subject to covenants, easements, and deeds of trust and restrictions of record.

AND the said party (ies) of the first part covenants that he/she/it/they will warrant specially the property hereby conveyed; and that it will execute such further assurances of said land as may be requisite.

Although granted at the time of loan origination, the Deed in Lieu was phrased in the present perfect tense: "WHEREAS, . . . [Ministries] has been unable to pay the indebtedness evidenced by the aforesaid Note as the installments have become due and payable and has been unable to perform the several covenants set forth in the aforesaid Deed of Trust[,]" (emphasis added), was executed under seal and was held in escrow by Investors. The Disclosure Statement for the Deed in Lieu provided:

The undersigned Borrower hereby acknowledge [sic] and agree [sic] as follows:

1.   As a part of the financing for the property known as 704 East Church Street, Martinsville, Virginia 24112 by Investors Financial Services, LLC in the amount of **$93,000.00** on **April 5, 2005** the Borrower have [sic] executed a Deed in Lieu of Foreclosure;

2.   The Deed in Lieu of Foreclosure conveys title to the property to Investors Financial Services, LLC;

3.   Investors Financial Services, LLC will hold the Deed in Lieu of Foreclosure and not record it in the land records so long as Borrower is not in default in the repayment of the financing;

4.   Investors Financial Services, LLC will record the Deed in Lieu of Foreclosure and take over title to the property if the Borrower are [sic] two (2) payments past due and have [sic] not made satisfactory payment arrangements;

5.   If the Borrower are [sic] past due, it is the Borrower's responsibility to contact [Lender's Counsel] to make satisfactory payment arrangements;

6.   If the Borrower do [sic] not contact [Lender's Counsel], no further notice will be given to the Borrowers [sic] before the Deed in Lieu of Foreclosure is recorded;

7.   Once the Deed in Lieu of Foreclosure is recorded, the Borrowers [sic] will no longer own the Property and the debt will be cancelled.

Several months later, Ministries defaulted on the Note, and Investors recorded the Deed in Lieu in the land records of Virginia, without any foreclosure proceedings. Ministries filed a four-count Complaint in the Circuit Court for Montgomery County, Maryland. One count alleged breach of contract, which was premised on the theory that Investors was "required by the terms of the contract" to conduct a public sale of the Property, rather than simply record the Deed in Lieu . . .

Ministries sought damages in the amount of $200,000 plus interest on its breach of contract count. Another count seeking a declaratory judgment under Section 3–409 of the Courts and Judicial Proceedings Article, Maryland Code (1974, 2006 Repl. Vol.), asked the Circuit Court to determine whether the Deed in Lieu was invalid for lack of consideration. . . .

During the ensuing bench trial, Ministries argued that the Deed in Lieu was invalid because the consideration recited in the Deed had not occurred at the time the Deed was granted. Investors countered that consideration supporting the contract, which included the Deed in Lieu as part of its terms, was provided by the loan, and that, moreover, all the instruments at issue had been executed under seal, which itself was sufficient consideration. The circuit court bypassed the jurisdictional question and ruled that, because the contract between the parties had been executed under seal, there was adequate consideration. Judgment was entered in favor of Investors.

The first question presented before us deals with consideration. Because we hold that a Deed in Lieu of Foreclosure, executed at the time of the origination of a loan, is a mortgage, and that under the circumstances of this case, foreclosure proceedings must have been initiated before Ministries's interest in the property was extinguished, we need not address this question.

. . .

The dispositive issue, nevertheless, is whether a deed in lieu of foreclosure, executed at the origination of a loan, is valid as an absolute conveyance, rather than a mortgage, under Maryland law. . . .

With respect to the Deed in Lieu, Ministries argues that, "[i]n order for a Deed in Lieu of Foreclosure entered into as a precondition to a mortgage loan and prior to any default in the mortgage loan to convey marketable title," it would have to impermissibly "terminate the mortgagor's equity of redemption in the property." Accordingly, Ministries argues, the Deed in Lieu in the present matter was invalid, as it was executed at the outset of the mortgage prior to Ministries' default. Conversely, Investors contends that Ministries never lost its equity of redemption, arguing that it "had the right to redeem the Property outside the Deed in Lieu (pursuant to the Disclosure Statement) by either paying the two or more months in arrears or making other satisfactory payment arrangements with [Investors]."

For centuries, courts of equity have recognized a mortgagor's right, in an event of default, to tender payment in full at any time prior to foreclosure, thereby retaining title to her property, and barring that, to recover the proceeds (if any) from the ensuing foreclosure sale, after satisfying the obligations to the mortgagee and other lienholders. This right, uniformly recognized in the Anglosphere since late medieval times, is called the equity of redemption. See Simard v. White, 383 Md. 257, 269–90, 859 A.2d 168, 175–87 (2004), in which Judge Dale R. Cathell, writing for this Court, gives a historical overview of mortgages and deeds of trust. See also Restatement (Third) of Property: Mortgages

§ 3.1 cmt. a (1997) (outlining the origins of the doctrine in English Chancery).

Courts have consistently refused to recognize creditors' attempts to cut off that right as a precondition for originating a mortgage. Kenneth C. Kettering, True Sale of Receivables: A Purposive Analysis, 16 Am. Bankr. Inst. L. Rev. 511, 527 (2008) (explaining the origin of the right to equity of redemption in "the deeply engrained unwillingness of the equity courts to abide a forfeiture"); John C. Murray, Mortgage Workouts: Deeds in Escrow, 41 Real Prop. Prob. & Tr. J. 185, 187–88 (2006) (outlining the common law rule invalidating deeds in escrow created as part of the original mortgage).

The Restatement (Third) of Property: Mortgages summarizes the common law rule, known as the prohibition against "clogging"[9] the equity of redemption, as follows:

> *3.1* The Mortgagor's Equity of Redemption and Agreements Limiting It.
>
> (a) From the time the full obligation secured by a mortgage becomes due and payable until the mortgage is foreclosed, a mortgagor has the right to redeem the real estate from the mortgage under the principles of § 6.4.
>
> (b) Any agreement in or created contemporaneously with a mortgage that impairs the mortgagor's right described in Subsection (a) of this section is ineffective.

---

[9] The term "clogging" is widely used to describe various schemes to strip a mortgagor's right to redeem her equity in the event of a foreclosure. The doctrine against "clogging" the so-called equity of redemption arose in the English Courts of Chancery, as an attempt to ameliorate the harsh result that obtained in the law courts in medieval England, before the concept of a mortgage had evolved. Before the adoption of the "anti-clogging" doctrine, a landowner wishing to borrow while pledging his land as security would deed the land outright to his creditor, in exchange for a stated sum of money, subject to the condition that if the landowner (borrower) repaid the creditor on a future specified day (called "law day"), title would revert to the borrower. If for any reason (even if he could not find the creditor) the borrower failed to pay on "law day," he forfeited his title, regardless of whether the debt owed bore any reasonable relation to the value of the land.

By the sixteenth century, courts of equity invoked the "anti-clogging" rule to avoid this harsh result and began to permit late payment. Later, the rule developed that both parties were entitled to the protection of a foreclosure sale, with any excess payable to the defaulting borrower, and conversely, permitting entry of a deficiency judgment in favor of the creditor in case the sale proceeds were insufficient to satisfy the loan obligation. From this beginning, the modern idea of a mortgage secured by a deed of trust evolved. See Simard v. White, 383 Md. 257, 269–90, 859 A.2d 168, 175–87 (2004) (Judge Dale R. Cathell, writing for the Court, gives a historical overview of mortgages and deeds of trust.); Kenneth C. Kettering, True Sale of Receivables: A Purposive Analysis, 16 Am. Bankr. Inst. L. Rev. 511, 527 (2008); Restatement (Third) of Property: Mortgages § 3.1 cmt. a (1997).

The Restatement further elaborates:

> Courts sometimes use alternative characterizations of the clogging rule. "Once a mortgage, always a mortgage" is the most common alternative. It is also sometimes stated that "a mortgage cannot be made irredeemable." Whatever the language of the clogging concept, courts traditionally have been hostile to clauses and devices that purport to recognize the equity of redemption, but whose practical effect is to nullify or restrict its operation. This hostility is rooted in a judicial desire to protect "impecunious landowners." Equally important is a judicial inclination to protect the mortgagor against misplaced optimism and overconfidence concerning future ability to satisfy commitments.

Restatement (Third) of Property: Mortgages § 3.1 cmt. a.

(c)   An agreement in or created contemporaneously with a mortgage that confers on the mortgagee an interest in mortgagor's real estate does not violate this section unless its effectiveness is expressly dependent on mortgagor default.

The cases supporting this principle are legion. The Supreme Court long ago set forth the basic idea in Peugh v. Davis, 96 U.S. (6 Otto) 332, 337, 24 L. Ed. 775, 776 (1877), where the Court explained that it is "an established doctrine" that a mortgagor's equity of redemption is "inseparably connected with a mortgage," and that, furthermore, "[t]his right cannot be waived or abandoned by any stipulation of the parties made at the time, even if embodied in the mortgage." (emphasis added). See also Murray, *supra*, at 188 n.9 (collecting cases).

Indeed, the *Peugh* Court stated that this doctrine was inviolate. *96 U.S. (6 Otto) at 337, 24 L. Ed. at 776* ("This is a doctrine from which a court of equity never deviates.") (emphasis added). See Washington Fire Ins. Co. v. Kelly, 32 Md. 421, 440 (1870) ("Courts of Equity, though a mortgage be forfeited, and the estate absolutely vested in the mortgagee, at common law, yet they will allow the mortgagor, at any reasonable time, to redeem his estate.... Nor will they permit a conveyance made to secure a debt, to operate for any other purpose than to secure the debt; the conveyance will be considered as merely holding the property as pledged, and no agreement in a mortgage will be suffered to make the property irredeemable.") (emphasis added); accord Restatement (Third) of Property: Mortgages § 3.1 cmt. b ("If 'clogging' were routinely permitted by agreement of the parties, there is a strong likelihood that foreclosure sales would disappear and debtors would lose the long-recognized right to have their real estate taken only after its value is tested by a public sale.") (emphasis added).

The instant case is wholly different from a loan workout, where a mortgagor and mortgagee negotiate *after* an event of default already has occurred. After a mortgagor defaults on a note, she may legitimately contract with the noteholder to execute a conveyance, in exchange for adequate consideration, so long as there is no overreaching. See, e.g., *Peugh,* 96 U.S. (6 Otto) at 337, 24 L. Ed. at 776 ("A subsequent release of the equity of redemption may undoubtedly be made to the mortgagee.... The transaction will, however, be closely scrutinized, so as to prevent any oppression of the debtor.") (emphasis added); *Simard,* 383 Md. at 272 n.12, 859 A.2d at 177 n.12 ("The right to redeem, even in a mortgage context, can be itself divested by a valid mortgage foreclosure sale, or by a waiver made subsequent to, and outside the mortgage instrument itself.") (emphasis added).

After a mortgagor defaults, she may negotiate a "short sale" to avoid a deficiency judgment, *i.e.*, further indebtedness persisting even after the proceeds from a foreclosure sale have been distributed. To require the borrower, however, as a condition of obtaining financing, to surrender the equity of redemption *in advance* places the lender in a "heads I win, tails you lose" position. In situations where the borrower had made substantial payments on the loan, or where the property greatly appreciated in value, the lender would record the deed in lieu rather than file for foreclosure. If the borrower's equity in the property were insufficient, the lender would still have its traditional remedies under the deed of trust with power of sale.

In the present case, Investors required Ministries to execute an escrow deed *at the time of loan origination*, as a precondition for granting the loan. In so doing, Investors cut off Ministries' right to its equity of redemption *from the outset*. Courts of equity have abhorred such overreaching for hundreds of years. Under Maryland law, the Deed in Lieu would have to be regarded as a mere mortgage and could not effectively convey the land to Investors absent a foreclosure action, in spite of what the Deed in Lieu purports to state on its face. The Real Property Article codifies the buyer's long-settled right to the equity of redemption. The relevant statute is Section 7–101 of the Real Property Article, Maryland Code (1974, 2003 Repl. Vol.), which, at the time the Deed in Lieu was executed, stated, in relevant part:

> § 7–101. When deed absolute in terms to be considered a mortgage; assignment of mortgages as security; certain security interests perfected.
>
> (a) *When deed absolute in terms to be considered a mortgage.* Every deed which by any other writing appears to have been intended only as security for payment of an indebtedness or performance of an obligation, though expressed as an absolute grant is considered a mortgage. The person for whose benefit the deed is made may not have any benefit or advantage from the recording of the deed, unless every other writing operating as a defeasance of it, or explanatory of its being intended to have the effect only of a mortgage, also is recorded in the same records at the same time.

Emphasis added.

Obviously, as Investors itself admitted, the only purpose of the Deed in Lieu was to grant additional security to the lender *at the time of loan origination*. Thus, Section 7–101 of the Real Property Article would mandate that the Deed in Lieu be "considered a mortgage," and Investors would have to file a foreclosure action or negotiate with Ministries to execute an effective (new) Deed in Lieu, supported by adequate consideration, based on the parties' circumstances and bargaining power *at the time of default*.

. . .

Our analysis is supported overwhelmingly by authority from other jurisdictions. In Part II of his law review article entitled "Deed in Escrow in Connection with Original Mortgage," *supra*, Murray surveys cases from all over the United States, all of which hold that, "when a mortgagor places a deed in escrow in connection with the initial mortgage transaction, with instructions to release the deed to the mortgagee immediately in the event of a future default, the deed is void and unenforceable." Murray, *supra*, at 187. This result is grounded on general equitable and public policy grounds. *Id.*

In Basile v. Erhal Holding Corp., 148 A.D.2d 484, 538 N.Y.S.2d 831 (N.Y. App. Div. 1989), the mortgagee required the mortgagor to execute a deed in escrow as part of a consumer mortgage and, when the borrower defaulted, the mortgagee recorded the deed. The trial court ruled that the borrower had waived her right of redemption and denied her motion for an order requiring the mortgagee to deliver the deed and declare the mortgage void. Id. at 833. The Appellate Division modified the decree, construing the deed in lieu of foreclosure as a mortgage, holding that the trial court had "erred in declaring that the plaintiff waived her right of redemption in the demised premises[,]" because "[a] deed conveying real property, although absolute on its face, will be considered to be a mortgage when the instrument is executed as security for a debt. *Id.* The appellate court cited, in addition to a string of Court of Appeals (of New York) decisions, a statute, N.Y. Real Property Law § 320, which is substantially similar to Section 7–101 (a) of the Real Property Article. See id. The appellate court explained the rationale behind this rule by quoting the passage from *Peugh*, discussed *supra*.

Most importantly, for this case, under Maryland statutory law . . ., a deed in lieu of foreclosure executed as security *at the time of loan origination* is a mortgage, not an absolute conveyance, *regardless* of whether the deed purports on its face to be absolute. Foreclosure proceedings in the present case, therefore, must have been initiated before Ministries' interest in the Property could have been extinguished.

Accordingly, because Ministries has properly stated a cause of action for damages from breach of contract, we shall vacate the judgment of the Circuit Court for Montgomery County

NOTES

1. *Functional Equivalents*. Many thoughtful courts have treated as functional equivalents all devices that are intended to create a security interest in land, regardless of the name chosen for the device. (Consider the examples described in the following notes). This may reflect an attempt to preserve the special protections of the law of mortgages:

> Mortgage law has long enjoyed a special, almost exalted position in the private law scheme of this country. A mortgage arises out of a private agreement when an owner of real property grants a lender an interest in the property to secure a debt. Once this privately created mortgage comes into existence, however, the private agreement dims in importance, and the mortgagor-mortgagee relationship becomes subject to legal rules that take precedence over the parties' plan. In many of its important elements, the mortgagor-mortgagee relationship is governed by binding laws, by laws that apply anytime a mortgage is created and the parties assume the status positions of mortgagor and mortgagee. Taken as a whole, these status rules aid mortgagors by granting them numerous rights in their dealings with mortgagees.

> Courts have developed and applied mortgage law over the years with a distinct goal in mind: to protect mortgagors against sharp dealings by lenders. Courts have been particularly quick to strike down lenders' efforts to develop contractual forms that circumvent the laws governing mortgages. In numerous ways wily lenders have tried to create what might be called a non-mortgage mortgage, an arrangement that gives the lender the security of a

mortgage, but deprives the borrower of the protective provisions of mortgage law. Courts, however, have responded vigorously to these attempts, mostly out of sympathy for home-and farm-owners who stand to lose their property. For courts, the substance of a secured transaction is more important than its form. Consequently, courts have long applied mortgage law to any relationship that appeared to be a mortgage in substance.

Freyfogle, Land Trusts and the Decline of Mortgage Law, 1988 U.Ill.L.Rev. 67, 67–68.[*] For an excellent examination of the evolution of the mortgage concept, see Burkhart, Lenders and Land, 64 Mo. L. Rev. 249 (1999).

Professor Georgette Poindexter has suggested that the protections for borrowers may be eroding as land is increasingly regarded as a commodity:

> As property law shifted focus away from the feudal importance of the land and towards the modern importance of debt, lender's rights in the event of default likewise took on a more contract-oriented remedy. The goal of the modern remedies is to give the lender the benefit of its bargain by making it financially whole in the event of a borrower's default. While vestiges of land-oriented rights remain (such as mortgagee-in-possession provisions), we can reconceptualize remedies into preservation of asset provisions designed to safeguard the asset value in order to pay the lender.

Poindexter, Subordinated Rolling Equity: Analyzing Real Estate Loan Default in the Era of Securitization, 50 Emory L.J. 519, 533 (2001). See also Shanker, Will Mortgage Survive? A Commentary and Critique on Mortgage Law's Birth, Long Life, and Current Proposals for Its Demise, 54 Case W. Res. L. Rev. 69 (2003).

2. *The Mortgage and the Deed of Trust.* The mortgage is probably the most widely used instrument of land finance in America today. The landowner, as mortgagor, gives a mortgage to the lender, as mortgagee, to secure the landowner's obligation to pay a debt, evidenced by a bond or promissory note. Unless the mortgage provides otherwise, the mortgagee can foreclose the mortgagor's equity of redemption only by judicial action and sale. If the mortgage expressly gives the mortgagee a power of sale, and if local statutes do not bar this self-help procedure, judicial proceedings are unnecessary and the mortgagee can foreclose simply by public sale after notice to all interested parties.

Lenders in several states prefer the deed of trust to the mortgage with power of sale. Like the mortgage with power of sale, the deed of trust secures an underlying obligation, typically evidenced by a promissory note (although sometimes a bond is used). The deed of trust differs in that, where the mortgage involves two parties, it involves three: the borrower ("trustor") conveys title to the lender's nominee ("trustee") as security for the trustor's performance of its debt obligation to the lender ("beneficiary"). If the trustor defaults, and if the beneficiary so requests, the trustee will arrange a public sale of the land to satisfy the debt.

For the lender, the original advantage of the deed of trust over the mortgage with power of sale was that it permitted the lender to bid at the sale conducted by a nominally independent third party, the trustee.

---

[*]   © Copyright 1988 by the Board of Trustees of the University of Illinois.

Statutes today have eliminated most of the differences between deeds of trust and mortgages with power of sale, including the lender's ability to bid at the foreclosure sale. See Uniform Land Security Interest Act § 202, comment. The two forms of security are for this reason treated interchangeably in this chapter and in the chapters on commercial finance.

3. *Other Forms of Land Finance.* A financing arrangement arises any time one person provides part or all of the capital needed to support another's activities in return for repayment of the capital, plus consideration, over a period of time. Although mortgages and deeds of trust are the instruments most popularly associated with land finance, other arrangements also qualify. For example, installment land contracts are often used to finance the acquisition of housing or of undeveloped land. The installment land contract is much like a purchase money mortgage, with the buyer making a down payment on the purchase price and the seller financing the rest. Structurally, it is like the marketing contract considered at pages 73 to 156 above. The seller holds title to the land during the entire executory period, until the last payment is made, at which point the contract closes and the seller conveys title to the buyer. The obvious difference is that, while the marketing contract's executory period will rarely exceed the one or two months needed to search title and obtain financing, the installment land contract will run for as long as five, ten or twenty years, the time that it takes the buyer to pay the seller for the property. Installment land contracts are considered at pages 520 to 533.

Leases are also financing arrangements. The leased premises represent the asset lent by the landlord to the tenant; in return, the tenant pays rent for use of the premises. (If, as sometimes happens, the lease gives the tenant an option to buy the premises at the end of the term at a specified price, the lease begins to look much more like an installment land contract or even a purchase money mortgage or deed of trust given by buyer to seller.) Leases may in turn become security for further financing arrangements such as leasehold mortgages. For a fine examination of the efficiency and monitoring benefits of mortgages compared to unsecured debt, see Johnson, Adding Another Piece to the Financing Puzzle: The Role of Real Property Secured Debt, 24 Loyola L.A.L.Rev. 335 (1991).

4. *The Equitable Mortgage.* C. Phillip Johnson Full Gospel Ministries, Inc. v. Investors Financial Services, LLC is part of a rich and ongoing area of the law. In these situation the parties intended to transfer a property interest but it is unclear whether a fee was conveyed, or only a mortgage disguised as a fee. A court will hold a deed absolute to be an equitable mortgage when the evidence suggests that the parties intended a mortgage. The situation often arises when a landowner, faced with tax or mortgage foreclosure, conveys his land to a third party who promises to "straighten things out" and then reconvey the land to the landowner. The situation also sometimes arises when, in an effort to avoid mortgage law's debtor protection provisions, a lender requires its borrower to convey by an absolute deed, the lender promising in a separate agreement to reconvey the land to the borrower if he pays the debt on time. Courts generally favor debtors in their willingness to pierce the facade of the absolute deed and find an equitable mortgage. Side agreements providing for reconveyance will readily be connected to the deed to support a finding that the deed and agreement formed a single security transaction.

One problem raised by equitable mortgages is that the putative deed will probably have been recorded. Will a bona fide purchaser from the grantee be bound by the mortgage characterization? What recovery rights will such a purchaser have? What effect will the recorded transfer have on creditors of the grantor?

See generally Cunningham & Tischler, Disguised Real Estate Security Transactions as Mortgages in Substance, 26 Rutgers L.Rev. 1 (1972).

5. *U.L.S.I.A. and the Restatement (Third) of Property-Mortgages.* The Uniform Land Security Interest Act regulates mortgages and other types of consensual security interests in real estate. The drafters hope that a uniform law among states will further encourage the growth of the secondary market and primary lending by out of state banks and that the Act will simplify and modernize ancient mortgage law. The act defines a "security interest" broadly as "an interest in real estate which secures payment or performance of an obligation." Leases intended as security to the lessor and retention of title by the seller of land intended as security are included. See § 111(25). To date, no jurisdiction has adopted the U.L.S.I.A. On the U.L.S.I.A. generally, see Geis, Escape From the 15th Century: The Uniform Land Security Interest Act, 30 Real Prop. Probate & Tr.J. 289 (1995); Healy, ULSIA—Modified for Minnesota, 20 Nova L.Rev. 1063 (1996); Siebrasse & Walsh, The Influence of the ULSIA on the Proposed New Brunswick Land Security Act, 20 Nova L.Rev. 1133 (1996); Platt, The Uniform Land Security Interest Act: Vehicle for Reform of Oregon Secured Land Transaction Law, 69 Or.L.Rev. 847 (1990). See page 81 above for the derivation of the U.L.S.I.A. from the Uniform Land Transactions Act.

The National Conference on Commissioners on Uniform State Laws in 2002 adopted yet an even more limited piece of reform legislation in the mortgage area, after the failure of U.L.S.I.A. to be enacted by any state. As its name implies, it is limited to power of sale (i.e., nonjudicial) foreclosure. See Nelson & Whitman, Reforming Foreclosure: The Uniform Nonjudicial Foreclosure Act, 53 Duke L.J. 1399 (2004).

In 1997, the American Law Institute published the Restatement (Third) of Property-Mortgages (hereafter, "Restatement of Mortgages"). Mortgages were not included in prior Restatements. The Restatement of Mortgages embodies classical doctrine but also incorporates key modernizations of mortgage law, even though some of these are currently only followed in a minority of jurisdictions. For articles discussing the new Restatement, see Burkhart, Third Party Defenses to Mortgages, 1998 B.Y.U. L. Rev. 1003; Nelson, The Contract for Deed as a Mortgage: The Case for the Restatement Approach, 1998 B.Y.U. L. Rev. 1111; Whitman, Mortgage Drafting: Lessons from the Restatement of Mortgages, 33 Real Prop. Probate & Tr. J. 415 (1998).

6. *Title Theory and Lien Theory.* Some states continue to follow the "title theory" of mortgages, clinging to the early common law view that the mortgagee holds title to the land from the moment the mortgage is executed to the time that it is foreclosed or the underlying obligation is paid. Most states, however, now follow the "lien theory," under which the mortgagee has only a lien on the property to secure the mortgagor's performance.

The basic distinction between the two theories lies in the right to possession. In title theory states the mortgagee has the right, rarely exercised, to possess the land from the moment the mortgage is given. In lien theory states it is the mortgagor who has the right to possession, unless and until foreclosure occurs. In a third group of states, following the "intermediate theory," the mortgagor has the right to possession until default on the underlying obligation.

Though much written about, the distinctions between these three theories have little practical consequence. Legislation and judicial decisions in title states have clothed the mortgagor with virtually all the attributes of ownership, although there may still be differences, such as on the question of whether and how a mortgagee may take possession upon the borrower's default. Further, these distinctions may be easily circumvented by private agreement, and the terms struck by lenders and borrowers in title, lien and intermediate states all look very much alike. See generally, G. Nelson, & D. Whitman, Real Estate Finance Law 135–44 (5th ed.2007).

2. SOURCES

The era of modern residential mortgages began as a response to the mortgage defaults and dislocations of the Great Depression. Over the past decade, there have been significant changes in the sources and methods of home financing, both in the primary lending market—those institutions which originate loans—and in the secondary market, where mortgages or mortgage backed securities are traded. These markets are shaped by private economic forces as well as government activity in the form of regulation, sponsorship, and intervention. Moreover, there is such a close interdependence of the primary and secondary markets so that over the past decade few primary market loans were made without an intention to sell them on the secondary market. This has led to some erosion of the traditional lines between primary and secondary lending. The mortgage and financial crisis that began in 2008 and will undoubtedly unfold over coming years may well bring new systems and markets for mortgage finance.

a. CHANGES IN THE PRIMARY LENDING MARKET

Robert Van Order, The U.S. Mortgage Market: A Model of Dueling Charters
11 Journal of Housing Research 233, 233–239 (2000).

Introduction

This article develops a framework for understanding the evolution and basic structure of American mortgage markets. Understanding mortgage markets requires understanding the changing roles of and the competition between what have traditionally been referred to as the primary and secondary markets. That has not always been the case. Between the end of World War II and the 1970s, U.S. residential mortgage markets were dominated by the primary market, which was comprised primarily of specialized depository institutions (mainly savings and loan associations [S & Ls], more broadly "thrifts"), which both by regulation and tax incentive were induced to hold most (about

80 percent) of their assets in mortgages. The mortgages were financed with low-cost government-insured deposits. The thrifts provided all the major aspects of mortgage lending-origination, servicing, funding, and accepting credit risks-and they held the majority of mortgages.

Today the thrifts are considerably less important as mortgage investors, with more than half of all mortgages sold into the secondary market. A major change, brought on largely by the secondary markets, has been the unbundling of the major aspects of mortgage lending. A mortgage now can be:

1.   originated by a mortgage broker who makes money only from origination;

2.   serviced by a mortgage banker who did not originate the loan and may have bought the right to service the loan from another mortgage banker;

3.   originated with the credit risk taken by one of the secondary market institutions, perhaps along with a mortgage insurance company; and

4.   funded by a mortgage-backed security (MBS) sold into the capital markets, and the MBS can be packaged as a bundle of derivative securities that separate interest rate and prepayment risk among different investors.

Investors in mortgages need not be involved in originating, servicing, or taking credit risk, and they can avoid most interest rate risk. Pools of mortgages (MBS and their derivatives) and debt backed by pools of mortgages now trade in national and international markets, almost as efficiently as Treasury securities. Mortgage rates are now, for the most part, determined by capital markets in general and are largely independent of the ups and downs of the S & L industry, though they are subject to the ups and downs of capital markets.

Because some actors in the bundle are dependent on others to act in their interest, unbundling presents special principal-agent management problems. This is especially true for secondary market purchasers, who typically buy from sellers who know more about the loans than they do. Information asymmetries are thus produced. Much of the secondary market's history has involved trying to manage these asymmetries, particularly by developing contracts with mortgage sellers that provide inducements to deliver good loans, meaning loans of a quality at least as high as some "investment quality" standard. This has allowed it to manage selection problems by operating in the least risky segments of the market, although it could still be selected against within the segments in which it operates.

Recent developments in information technology have increased competition in the mortgage industry, both among its institutions and between the primary and secondary market institutions, and they have changed the way that principal-agent problems are managed by allowing more direct control and less delegation. In particular, credit scoring models are allowing the secondary market to use almost all of the information available to the primary market, opening up new and previously riskier segments of the mortgage market. In some ways the market is coming full circle; the availability of the same technology in all parts of the market is making the distinction between primary and secondary markets increasingly irrelevant, and the extent of unbundling is decreasing.

Historically, good loans have been identified by their (lack of) credit risk, and most of the history of the secondary market's development has been about controlling credit risk. However, as trading in mortgages has evolved, it has become clear that prepayment risk (borrowers taking advantage of their option to refinance when interest rates fall) is at least as important as credit risk. While there have been great improvements in information about credit risk, and the information has been incorporated into automated underwriting (AU) systems, it has not been used to as great an extent to manage prepayment risk, so this is an area where major selection risks remain.

. . .

Some History

The deposit-based system, which dominated the U.S. mortgage market until rather recently; has been evolving for some time, but the basic structure of the system was solidified with the 1930s creation of the Federal Home Loan Bank System (FHLB) and deposit insurance. This gave the thrifts a reasonably reliable low-cost source of funds, which, along with a legal framework that allowed for foreclosure and eviction and thrifts' ability to know local markets, generated enormous increases in mortgage lending and homeownership, particularly in the first part of the postwar period. The homeownership rate in the United States increased from just over 40 percent in the early 1940s to 62 percent in 1960. It is about 67 percent today.

The system became unraveled: first, because of regulations that put ceilings on deposit rates (leading to periodic outflows of deposits, beginning in the late 1960s) and limits on branches; and, second, because of moral hazard-type problems that led to excessive risk taking (initially, interest rate risk; subsequently, credit risk) and the failure of large numbers of institutions in the 1980s. Nonetheless, the system has survived. Deposit rate ceilings and branching restrictions no longer exist, and the industry, though smaller in number, is well capitalized. It has a new regulatory structure and, combined with increased mortgage holding by commercial banks, accounts for about half of the conventional mortgage market.

While there has always been a secondary market in the United States, until recently it was largely informal. The rise in the secondary market in the 1970s and (especially) 1980s came about largely because of standardization of pools of mortgages, brought on by three secondary market agencies: the Federal National Mortgage Association (now known as Fannie Mae), the Government National Mortgage Association (GNMA), and the Federal Home Loan Mortgage Corporation (now known as Freddie Mac). Annual sales of mortgages to these three institutions have risen from $69 billion in 1980 to more than $700 billion in 1999; they now own or are responsible for about half of the outstanding stock of single-family mortgages.

Fannie Mae, the oldest of the agencies, was established in the 1930s as a government-owned secondary market for loans insured by the newly created Federal Housing Administration (FHA). For most of its early history, it operated like a national S & L, gathering funds by issuing its own debt, and buying mortgages that were held in portfolio. In 1968 Fannie Mae was moved off the federal budget and set up as a private GSE, which in the 1970s switched its focus toward conventional loans. It receives no direct government funding, and its operations are separate from the on-budget parts of the government. GMMA was created in 1968 to handle Fannie Mae's policy-related tasks and to provide a secondary market for government insured loans. It is on the federal budget as part of the U.S. Department of Housing and Urban Development (HUD).

GNMA was responsible for promoting the major innovation in secondary markets, the MBS. An MBS is a pass-through security. The issuer (in the GNMA case, typically a mortgage banker) passes through all payments from a pool of mortgages (both principal and interest, net of fees) to the ultimate investors, who typically receive *pro rata* shares of principal and interest payments. The issuer also guarantees the payment of interest and principal, even if the borrower defaults. GNMA deals only in federally insured mortgages, primarily those insured by the FHA and the U.S. Department of Veterans Affairs, which account for 10 to 15 percent of the market. Its guarantee is in addition to federal insurance and the issuer's guarantee, mainly amounting to a guarantee of timely payment by the issuer.

Freddie Mac was created in 1970 to be a secondary market for the S & Ls. (At the time, it dealt only with S & Ls, and Fannie Mae dealt with mortgage bankers. Now both institutions deal with the same originators.) Like Fannie Mae, it is a private GSE and also is off-budget. It initiated the first MBS program for conventional loans in 1971, while Fannie Mae began its conventional MBS program in 1981. Both GSEs' MBS are similar to GNMNs; for example, both protect investors against credit risk but not interest rate risk. Neither Fannie Mae nor Freddie Mac does more than a small amount of federally insured mortgages, which almost always go into GNMA pools. Both Fannie Mae and Freddie Mac fund a significant (about 40 percent) share of their mortgages with debt, typically by putting almost all mortgages into MBS pools and buying pools back.

Because GNMA is on the federal budget, its securities have a full faith and credit federal guarantee. Because Freddie Mac and Fannie Mae are private corporations, neither has an explicit guarantee, but they both have nebulous, implicit guarantees, a perception by the financial markets that the government stands behind their debt, which allows them to borrow (or sell MBS) at interest rates lower than they would otherwise; both are regulated by HUD for their public purpose missions and by the Office of Federal Housing Enterprise Oversight for safety and soundness. Fannie Mae and Freddie Mac are now (except for details) quite similar, competing in the conventional mortgage market as buyers of mortgages and in the securities markets as sellers of MBS and issuers of debt.

More than half of all mortgages now are sold into the secondary mortgage market. About 40 to 50 percent (there are important cyclical variations in share) of conventional mortgages now are sold to either Fannie Mae or Freddie Mac, where they either become MBS or are held in portfolio and financed by debt. There is a "private label" secondary market, which makes up about 10 percent of the market. It is used disproportionately for securitizing conventional loans that exceed the Fannie Mae/Freddie Mac loan size limit ($252,700 in 2000 for single-family houses). Loans above the conforming loan limit make up about 15 to 20 percent of the market.

The reasons for the secondary market's beginning in the United States are not the same as the reasons for its continuation. The evolution of the secondary market has been a product of a variety of factors, many of largely historical interest. For instance, Fannie Mae was created because of the Great Depression, the collapse of housing markets, and the reluctance of lenders to invest in the new FHA loans. And it was privatized in 1968 to get it off-budget because of budget pressures from the Vietnam War. Deposit rate ceilings, which limited the ability of S & Ls to raise money for mortgage loans, were a major factor in the rising importance of Fannie Mae in the 1960s and 1970s and in the creation of Freddie Mac in 1970, but deposit rate ceilings are no longer an issue. Similarly, the inability of banks and S & Ls to operate nationally also was important in the rise of the secondary markets, but national deposit markets and liberalized branching rules have limited the importance of this. None of these are important issues any more.

Today's main reason for the important role of secondary markets (and particularly the reason for their rapid increase in the 1980s) is that they have been able to compete successfully with depositories, mainly because they are a low-cost way of managing cash flows and raising money for mortgages. This has been possible, first, because of economies in raising money wholesale in the capital markets and in processing the purchase and servicing of large numbers of mortgage loans; second, because their charter gives them something similar to deposit insurance (an implicit guarantee) so that they, too, can borrow at lower rates than otherwise; and third, because they can operate at lower levels of capital (e.g., because of geographic diversification) and avoid some of the tax disadvantage that equity has relative to debt.

However, the depository institutions remain a major source of funds; the markets in which they raise money have become more efficient (both on and off balance sheet), they have information advantages, they have a genuine full faith and credit guarantee, and they are finding ways of extending the guarantee to capital markets as a whole (rather than just deposit markets).

b.   SECONDARY MARKET AND SECURITIZATION

Kurt Eggert, Held Up in Due Course: Predatory Lending, Securitization, and the Holder in Due Course Doctrine*

35 Creighton Law Review 503, 535–550 (2002).

A.   The Basics of Securitization: Life in the Tranches

The effect of the holder in due course doctrine on homeowner borrowers and the assignment of risk of deceptive loan practices has been fundamentally changed by the process of securitization, the method of aggregating a large number of illiquid assets, such as notes secured by deeds of trust, in one large pool, then selling securities that are backed by those assets. These securities, because they trade on an open market and do not require the paperwork used to transfer the underlying illiquid asset, are themselves highly liquid and easy to trade. Securitization has been defined, by an author who noted that there was no uniform definition for the term, as "the transformation of an illiquid asset into tradeable security with a secondary market." Others have defined it as "the substitution of more efficient public capital markets for less efficient, higher cost, financial intermediaries in the funding of debt instruments." In terms of the residential mortgage industry, securitization is the process of aggregating a large number of notes secured by deeds of trust in what is called a mortgage pool, and then selling security interests in that pool of mortgages. Through securitization, the source of capital for mortgage funding has been transferred from the savings industry, which used deposits to fund loans, to the capital markets and the portfolios of institutional investors. As we shall see, this emphasis on the investment by capital markets is important because it drives much of the argument about why securitization is efficient and provides access to less expensive sources of capital. Others have defined securitization even more broadly to include the substitution of securities for loans and loan participations.

At the center of the process of securitization is the isolation of a specific group of assets from the organization that owned them, so that the assets are legally completely independent from their former owner and free of any bankruptcy or liability risks of the former owner. By limiting the risk facing investors in the asset pools to those inherent in the assets themselves, and by creating standardized, ratable, and easily tradeable securities from the assets, the securitization process maximizes the liquidity of the assets. . . . As noted by Joseph C. Shenker and Anthony J. Colletta, a process that increases the liquidity of an asset increases the value of the asset to its current holder. This increase in value to the purchaser potentially allows the seller of the securities to offer a lower yield to sell the security.

While the history of mortgage-backed bonds stretches back into the nineteenth century, and private title and mortgage insurance companies sold certificates secured by mortgage pools in the 1920s, the

*   Creighton University Law Review, *"Held Up In Due Course: Predatory Lending, Securitization, and the Holder In Due Course Doctrine"* published in Vol. 35 Issue 3 (2001–2002), pp. 503–640, reprinted with permission. Copyright © 1994 by Creighton University.

modern use of securitization began with the issuance in 1970 of the first publicly traded mortgage backed security by the Government National Mortgage Association (commonly called Ginnie Mae). Government sponsored entities (GSEs), such as Ginnie Mae, which securitizes mortgages guaranteed by the Veterans Administration, the Farm Home Administration, or the Federal Housing Administration, and Fannie Mae (the Federal National Mortgage Association) and Freddie Mac (the Federal Home Loan Mortgage Corporation), which securitize high quality residential mortgages, blazed the trail for securitization, since their implicit guarantee of financial security made some of the securities they issued seem almost risk-free. These GSEs have since been joined by the Student Loan Marketing Association (Sallie Mae), which securitizes student loans. The private sector's ability to securitize separately from GSEs increased dramatically after 1975, when rating organizations began rating the securities produced by securitization, giving investors confidence in the pricing of securities not backed by the government or a government-sponsored enterprise. The growing importance of securitization can be seen in the expansion of Article 9 of the U.C.C. to include sales transactions that had not previously been governed by it, to aid in their securitization.

Securitization of residential loans has grown at a staggering pace. In 1984, only twenty-three percent of the loans secured by mortgages on one-to-four family homes were securitized. By the end of 1998's first quarter, fifty-two percent of the total outstanding balance of such loans was securitized. The dramatic increase in securitization has been fueled in part by the support that the federal government and the GSEs have provided, by the development of new products caused by the competitive jousting of such players as banks, thrifts, and Wall Street firms, and by the openness shown to securitization by the banking industry and securities regulators.

A typical securitization of a loan secured by a residence might proceed as follows. The borrower negotiates with a mortgage broker for the terms of the loan. Mortgage brokers may originate the loans in their own names in three ways: (1) by using "table funding" provided by the pre-arranged buyer of the loan; (2) by access to a warehouse line of credit; or (3) by supplying the broker's own funds. Alternatively, the mortgage broker may close the loan in the name of the lender providing the money. Whether the broker closes the loan in his or her own name or in the name of the lender, the broker typically almost immediately transfers the loan to a lender. This lender quickly sells the loan to a different financial entity, which pools the loan together with a host of other loans in a mortgage pool. The loans in the pool may all come from one lender, from a multitude of lenders, or any number in between.

The assignee of the loans then transfers them to another entity, typically a limited liability company or wholly owned corporate subsidiary. This entity (known as the "seller" because it will sell the securities that result from the securitization process) then transfers the loans to a special purpose vehicle (an "SPV"), a business entity that has the sole purpose of holding the pool of mortgages, and in return the seller receives the securities issued by the SPV. SPVs can be trusts, corporations, limited partnerships, or more specialized business entities, though a trust is considered the most common. In fact, "[a]sset securitization has become one of the most important commercial uses of the trust," even though the set of fiduciary duties that trust law would normally impose are by and large replaced by the trust agreement's minutely detailed provisions.

The securities that the SPV transfers to the seller are carefully packaged to maximize their appeal to purchasers. There are a multitude of ways in which these securities can be packaged, as different aspects, or "strips," of the loans are divided up and sold separately as securities. A relatively simple, straightforward (as straightforward, perhaps, as anything is in the new world of securitization) division of ownership rights in the pooled loans is for one group of securities to represent the interest that will be paid on the loans (interest-only strips), and a second group to represent the repayment of principal on those same loans (principal-only strip). If interest rates drop, the prepayment rate of the loans in the pool normally increases, shrinking the income of the holders of interest-only strips, since there will be fewer loans to pay interest, while swelling the returns of the principal-only strips, as they receive the payments on principal years before the payments might have been expected. The pool of mortgages can be cut into much more complex strips of mortgages, depending on what the creator of the SPV thinks may be most easily sold. The strips, or classes of securities, are called "tranches," which is French for "strips."

To convince potential investors of the value of the securities, the securities are typically rated by a national, independent credit-rating agency, unless the home mortgages are backed either by the U.S. government or by a government-sponsored entity, which effectively, at least in the eyes of the market, guarantee their value. Because the rating need only be done once for all investors rather than separately and redundantly by each investor, the rating process efficiently allows the market to determine the value of the investment and hence the return the investors will demand for purchasing securities backed by the assets to be securitized.

The credit quality of the different tranches of securities can be improved by various techniques of credit enhancement that reduce the risk of loss to the purchasers of the securities. Credit enhancements can be either internal, meaning they depend on the assets or credit of the originator, such as providing additional assets to the securitization pool, or external, involving the credit or assets of a third party, such as an insurer or a bank issuing a letter of credit. One common credit enhancement is mortgage insurance, with each loan in the mortgage pool insured up to a certain percentage of its value. Or, as a credit enhancement, the originator can retain an interest in the tranche that will first absorb any defaults in the mortgage pool, forcing the originator to act as a shock absorber for the rest of the investors. Credit enhancements can be so effective that they allow even delinquent and foreclosed loans to be securitized.

Working with the seller to package the loan pool and its resulting securities is an underwriter, which, together with the rating agency, examines the loans assembled in the pool, sets specific requirements of loss probability for the loans, and discards loans that do not meet the risk standards set for the pool, returning them to the originator. The intermediaries who pool mortgages, however, have been reluctant to undertake any significant diligence in their own examination of the loans or the borrowers and instead rely, for the most part, on detailed representations by the originators of the loans. Most pooling agreements give the intermediaries the right to force an originator to take back any loan that did not actually qualify for the loan pool, the inclusion of which would cause a breach of the originator's representations. Therefore, the originator of the loans may be forced to take back a loan if the borrower defaults.

Once the securities are rated, they can be sold to investors by the seller. This sale is typically accomplished by private placements or by public offerings, and an underwriter is involved in all public offerings and most private placements. The buyers may include mutual and pension funds, insurance companies, other institutional investors, and private individuals.

The transfer to the special purpose trust must constitute a true sale, so that the party transferring the assets reduces its potential liability on the loans and exchanges the fairly illiquid loans for much more liquid cash. The true sale also acts to separate the assets from any potential bankruptcy (to confer, in the poetic language of the securitization literature, "bankruptcy remoteness") or other risk associated with the original lender or pooler of the loans. The trust is considered the business form most likely to preserve bankruptcy remoteness. This bankruptcy remoteness is becoming increasingly controversial, however, given the effect it may have on the creditors of the originators.

The investors typically are completely passive once they have had the opportunity to review and approve the offering documents, the loan pool's ratings, and any third party guarantees and have purchased the securities. Nor do the investors take an active hand in monitoring the SPV. Instead, the offering materials set out the method of servicing the mortgages and distributing payments to the investors. The SPV itself does not directly collect payments from the homeowners whose notes and deeds of trust are held by the SPV. The collection and distribution of the payments of principal and interest are made by servicers, companies who specialize in this collection and distribution of income and principal from pools of loans. Originally, the servicer was often the same financial institution that either originated the loans in the pool or that obtained them from the originator and pooled the loans. The servicing of loans provided, in this way, a separate income stream for the originators or poolers of loans. Now, servicing rights are often sold to firms that specialize in servicing. Servicing specialization has increased so much that there are now servicers that specialize in subprime servicing or in servicing distressed loans, with rating agencies beginning to recognize their expertise and to provide ratings for servicers. The servicer is employed by the SPV and, since most SPVs are trusts, the trustee is legally at the helm, directing the activities of the SPV. However, the servicer typically is in charge of collection efforts.

As the homeowners gradually pay down their notes by making their monthly payments, the value of the mortgage pool declines. A more rapid change occurs when a homeowner either pays off the loan, normally through refinancing it, or stops making payments, forcing the servicer to begin foreclosure proceedings. Whether or not a foreclosure results in a net cost to the SPV depends on the amount of equity securing the loan being foreclosed. If the loan had a high loan-to-value ratio (LTV), a large loan given the value of the property securing the loan, perhaps because of a decline in the value of the property, then the costs of the foreclosure process, which can be sizeable, can consume the remaining equity and even cause a loss to the SPV and thus to the investors.

On the other hand, if the amount of the loan is far less than the value of the property securing it, the investors could actually make money on the foreclosure process, since the holder of the loan is often the sole bidder during the foreclosure sale and typically bids only the amount of the outstanding balance on the loan. In some states, the lender could foreclose on the property, purchase the property at an unreasonably low price that does not even pay off the lender's loan, and then seek a deficiency judgment against the borrower for the amount remaining on the loan. Therefore, if the remaining balance of the loan is $60,000, the loan is secured by a house worth $120,000, and the costs of foreclosure are $10,000, the investors would make $50,000 by foreclosing on the loan and buying the house for the amount of the loan. Despite this possibility of profits from foreclosures, early repayment and, to a lesser extent, foreclosure are the two greatest risks facing investors in securities backed by pools of mortgages, assuming that the securitization process has succeeded in divorcing the pools of mortgages from all risks caused by or associated with the originators or poolers of the loan.

B.   The Advantages of Securitization, Primarily to Investors and Lenders

The advantages of the securitization process to loan originators have been widely discussed. The primary advantage of securitization is the access securitization gives to public markets and private institutional funding, with the cost of capital available in these markets lower than that of traditional sources, such as bank loans. As Steven Schwarcz has noted, "Securitization is most valuable when the cost of funds, reflected in the interest rate that is necessary to entice investors to purchase the SPV's securities, is less than the cost of the originator's other, direct sources of funding." Through the securitization process, companies with severe financial problems and abysmal credit ratings can still create bonds carrying investment grade ratings, the highest rating, by transferring valuable assets to an SPV that is effectively remote from the originator. Because investors in the securities created should not need to monitor the bankruptcy risk of the originator, they save the monitoring costs they would have had to spend in the absence of securitization.

An advantage of securitization to the originator of loans is its extreme usefulness as a leveraging tool. By almost immediately securitizing its loans, a lending institution can receive payment for those loans quickly rather than waiting up to thirty years for repayment. The lender can use this infusion of capital to make a new round of loans. This quick churning of loan principal allows even an institution without a great amount of fixed capital to make a huge amount of loans, lending in a year much more money than it has. As discussed in section III(B) infra, this ability to leverage is particularly useful to smaller, disreputable companies that otherwise would have difficulty funding a large number of loans.

Lenders employ securitization to diversify risk. For example, a local lender may sell many of the loans it originates in order to keep itself from being too greatly endangered by a local slowdown of the economy. Securitization also has certain accounting advantages, permitting an originator to raise funds without borrowing and having to report a liability on its balance sheet, as well as allowing banks to reduce the amount of capital they need to hold by reducing the amount of their outstanding loans.

Securitization has also benefited investors by giving them a rich banquet of new and varied investment possibilities, structured by the poolers of the assets to appeal to the different risk, diversification and income tastes of the investors. The anonymity of mortgage-backed securities may appeal to some investors, such as those engaging in tax evasion and money laundering. As previously noted, securitization allows investors to reduce their information costs by pooling the acquisition of information in the form of a single rating regarding the security of the pool. However, this ability to rely on a single rating may be overshadowed by the increased complexity that securitization adds to the investors' financial decisions; pools can be structured in so many different ways that, even apart from unstable economic conditions, past performance of other pools may be no indication of the likely profit to be obtained by investing in a new securitization. Investors forced to rely on rating agencies, trustees, originators, or underwriters may suffer if those third parties' abilities to estimate the likely returns of the securities were also overwhelmed by the complexity of the securitization structure. Rating organizations have regularly upgraded or downgraded the ratings they have assigned to mortgage pools as the repayment and default rates have differed from expected. Investors in mortgage backed securities should also be wary of the potential for securities fraud, which may, at a stroke, cause them to lose their entire investment.

Securitization has also benefited investors by allowing them to purchase an interest in the high interest rate loans that have been associated with predatory lending, while avoiding much of the risk of defaults and delinquencies that is associated with those loans. Investors are protected from much of this risk by two methods. The first method is the use of various contractual forms of recourse between the originator or seller of the loan and the entity that purchases them in the securitization process designed to protect the buyers of the loan at the expense of the sellers. Recourse can take several forms. As noted in section II(E), the seller of the loans may make representations or warranties that, if violated, require the seller to repurchase the loan. Other contractual forms of recourse are those explicitly requiring the seller of loans to make cash payments to buyers or to repurchase the loans in the event of borrower default, those that set up reserve accounts that fund losses, and more complicated schemes involving subordinated interests or excess servicing fees. These forms of recourse for the most part require the continued existence of a relatively solvent seller, of course. Where the originator of the loan has gone bankrupt or otherwise disappeared, then the loan buyers must depend on their second line of defense, the holder in due course doctrine. A buyer may choose to rely on the holder in due course doctrine even where the loan seller is still in existence, where, for example, a single loan pool contains a large number of loans from one originator, so that forcing the originator to buy back all of the problematic loans could force the originator into insolvency. Or the buyer may conclude that it would be easier to foreclose against the borrower and rely on the holder in due course doctrine than it would be to force the seller to take back a problematic loan.

c.   THE SUBPRIME AND MORTGAGE FINANCE CRISIS OF 2008

Gerald Korngold, Legal and Policy Choices in the Aftermath of the Subprime and Mortgage Financing Crisis

60 South Carolina Law Review 727, 728–35 (2009).

What was first called the "subprime crisis" became a meltdown in mortgage financing and the secondary markets for mortgages and ultimately a worldwide, general financial problem. The story began with the making of "subprime" mortgages—residential mortgage loans to borrowers who did not qualify under traditional underwriting and credit standards for a loan on usual terms. Subprime loans carried a higher interest rate than conventional loans, presenting a profitable revenue opportunity for the mortgage lending community. Federal legislation (primarily the Community Reinvestment Act) encouraged lending to lower income borrowers to promote home ownership and the establishment of credit. The data indicate, however, that CRA cannot be blamed for the current subprime crisis as most (perhaps 80%) subprime loans were not made by CRA lenders, loans made by CRA lenders were not necessarily to CRA-qualified borrowers or in CRA-approved areas, and it is hard to see how legislation passed in 1977 only caused a crisis twenty years later and not sooner.[1]

In a typical scenario, subprime loans (like "prime" mortgage loans to borrowers who qualified under traditional underwriting standards) were originated by mortgage brokers and mortgage companies, purchased by local banks, and sold by local banks to investment banks. Thus, the mortgage brokers, mortgage companies, and local banks received their capital back to lend again locally (and they earned income on fees paid by each purchaser of the loan up the chain.)

The investment banks then issued securities, typically bonds, representing the right to receive certain payments under the mortgages

---

[1]   See Center for Responsible Lending, CRA Is Not to Blame for the Mortgage Meltdown, 10/3/2008, http://www.responsiblelending.org/pdfs/cra-not-to-blame-for-crisis.pdf, last visited 10/28/08; Aaron Pressman, Community Reinvestment Act had Nothing to Do with Subprime Crisis, BusinessWeek.com, 9/29/08, http://www.businessweek.com/investing/insights/blog/archives/2008/09/community_reinv.html, last visited 10/28/08; Daniel Gross, Subprime Suspects, Newsweek.com, 10/7/07, http://www.newsweek.com/id/162789, last visited 10/29/08. Loans made by other than "depository institutions," such as loan by mortgage brokers and mortgage banks, are not within CRA.

(usually slicing the right to receive portions of the income and principal payments into various "tranches.") The investment banks had rating agencies attest to the quality of the bonds, with the investment bank paying the rating agencies' fees, and then sold them to investors. The investors held or traded these mortgage backed securities in an active market. Some investors sought to secure the payment of the mortgage bonds and hedge risk; as a result, some insurance companies entered into "credit default swaps" with the bondholder that guaranteed, in return for a premium payment, that the insurance company would pay the bond if the issuer defaulted.[2]

During the first years of securitization, packagers could issue bonds based on local banks' inventory of "prime" mortgages. These borrowers rarely defaulted and the bonds had low risk. As demand for mortgage backed securities grew and more mortgages were needed for the bundles, however, investment banks and local banks lowered their underwriting standards for borrowers. Income, credit, and employment standards were lowered significantly and verification requirements reduced.[3] There were incidents of fraud by borrowers, often encouraged and abetted by mortgage brokers, and independent fraud by mortgage brokers.[4] More and more subprime mortgages were being sold on the secondary market through securities.

Still the arrangement worked fine. Then came the mid 2000's when borrowers began defaulting on mortgage loans. This occurred for a variety of reasons—many of the latest borrowers were financially unsound and soon unable to pay the payments; low initial "teaser" rates of interest offered by the banks on variable rate mortgages to attract borrowers expired and were reset at higher rates; and the real estate market plateaued or even declined, so borrowers could not refinance their way out of trouble. Lenders began foreclosures and properties did not sell well or eventually at all in the depressed and saturated market. Payments to bondholders were interrupted, values of the bonds plunged in markets out of fear of problems with the underlying mortgages, investors experienced sharp declines in the value of their mortgage bond holdings, bond issuers were under pressure, and credit default swap guarantors lacked adequate cash to pay off the claims for the many defaulted bonds. Also, mortgage lending and secondary market

---

[2]   See generally John P. Doherty & Richard F. Hans, The Pebble and the Pool: The Global Expansion of Subprime Litigation, Securities and Regulation Report, 3/25/08; Gretchen Morgenson, First Comes the Swap, Then It's the Knives, The New York Times, 6/1/08, 2008 WLNR 10339687.

[3]   Anthony Lendez & David Hille, Is There a Legal Defense to the Mortgage Mess? Litigation Arising From the Subprime Market Collapse Will Hinge on Lenders' Good Faith, The National Law Journal, 4/21/2008 NLJ S1, (Col. 1); Brooke Masters & Saskia Scholtes, Payback Time As Subprime Bites, Financial Times, 8/9/07, 2007 WLNR 15293606 (quoting Fed chairman Ben Bernanke: "The recent rapid expansion of the subprime market was clearly accompanied by deterioration in underwriting standards."). There is evidence that Fannie and Freddie played at most a limited role in the weakened underwriting standards, with the impetus largely coming from private lending sources. David Goldstein & Kevin G. Hall, Private Sector Loans, Not Fannie or Freddie, Triggered Crisis, McClatchy Newspapers, 10/12/08, http://www.mcclatchydc.com/251/story/53802.html, last visited 10/28/08. HUD has been criticized for a role in the subprime problem. See Carol D. Leonnig, How HUD Mortgage Policy Fed The Crisis, washingtonpost.com, 6/10/2008, http://www.washingtonpost.com/wp-dyn/content/article/2008/06/09/AR2008060902626.html, last visited 10/28/08.

[4]   See Brooke Masters & Saskia Scholtes, Payback Time As Subprime Bites, Financial Times, 8/9/07, 2007 WLNR 15293606.

transactions effectively stopped. The crisis then rippled from the secondary mortgage markets to the broader financial sector, and from the United States to the world.

Commentators, polemicists, and politicians are already arguing over who or what should be held responsible for the mortgage and secondary market crisis. We have heard various, and sometimes competing, theories: "deregulation" and "too much regulation;" "greed," "irresponsibility," if not "fraud" by everyone involved (mortgage brokers, borrowers, lenders, "Wall Street", investors, rating agencies, etc.); too much money chasing not enough good deals (with the result that poor mortgage investments were sold and bought); "predatory" business practices by lenders; and on and on. Historians and economists will weigh in eventually with more sober and long-term views. However, government officials, legislators, judges, and market participants are daily making decisions based on their best conceptions of reality.

There have been bi-partisan calls for increased regulation of the markets. The great unknown, of course, is the terms and nature of the regulation. Care must be taken to correct the abuses but not to choke the functioning of the markets. And some solutions must be left to the markets themselves. Let me suggest some factors that must be on the table in the search for a solution:

• *Secondary market.* The secondary market for mortgages has generated capital for residential, as well as commercial, mortgages in areas of the United States lacking adequate local funding and has provided a market mechanism for efficient capital transactions. Funding through the secondary market has enabled first time buyers to acquire homes. This beneficial mechanism need to be preserved.

• *Globalization.* Mortgage capital markets have become global and interconnected. We cannot, and should not want to, turn the clock back on this reality. Globalization can bring great benefits, though it brings risk. This dynamic must be understood.

• *Fraud and Predatory Lending.* Fraud in the market place needs to be aggressively pursued by regulation, legislative and judicial doctrines imposing liability, and criminal sanctions. Fraud is antithetical to the contracting paradigm and destroys the premise and efficiency of the markets. Conflicts of interest, such as where bond issuers pay fees to supposedly neutral rating agencies, must be addressed. Moreover, predatory lending laws need to be enforced and where appropriate expanded.

• *Personal Responsibility v. Paternalism.* The right balance must be struck between personal responsibility and benevolent paternalism in adjudicating particular disputes and also in setting the ground rules for the overall system. This is a tricky task as there are strong views, many variables, and numerous individual players affected by these concepts. Society also has a stake, since we as a group may not wish to tolerate the cost and fallout of an unregulated market system even if individual players may be willing. And, there is the moral hazard of bailouts, present and future, that may encourage undesirable actions by market participants at all levels. Consider these examples: while some call for a ban on subprime mortgages, how would that affect those with poor credit histories who could only qualify for a non-conventional mortgage and who indeed have been successful in paying off the mortgage and thus acquiring a first home? Or, if the premise of hedge funds is that they are for high net-worth individuals who can afford to make riskier investments for a higher reward, can we justify "bailouts" of such entities and on what terms because of the national interest in the banking system?

• *Government, markets, federalism.* Some longstanding philosophical questions will have real world consequences: What should be the subject of government regulation as opposed to market discipline? Is market regulation a federal or state matter, or some of each? From where should reforms come—the legislature, administrative agencies, or the courts?

• *Racial discrimination.* Racial minorities received a disproportionate number of subprime loans compared to conventional loans, which has had a devastating effect on minority and inner city communities. Courts and legislators will need to address discrimination in lending decisions. Moreover, the negative impact of subprime lending on particular neighborhoods and communities will require comprehensive legislative and regulatory responses.

• *The federal government.* What is the role of the federal government in the housing market, especially after the conservatorship of the Federal Home Loan Association and the Federal Home Loan Mortgage Corporation? Is government the home lender of last resort, what are the costs and benefits of that status, and how will this work? Will this be better than the confused, ambiguous role of Fannie and Freddie pre-conservatorship where the companies had the dual loyalty of serving their shareholders and the public and where the extent of the federal "guarantee" of their activity was opaque? And, of course, how will the government buyout of poorly performing mortgage securities work out?

• *Intermediation.* There were many intermediaries involved in the secondary market process—for example, mortgage brokers, local lenders, regional lenders, investment bankers, rating agencies, servicers, mortgage purchasers and repurchasers, etc. Moreover, loans were sliced and repackaged into different bundles or tranches, splitting various rights in the mortgage apart. To the extent that intermediation has served to insulate players from responsibility or to obscure liability for their actions, legislation and regulation is needed. The complexity of the instruments, with buyers not knowing what they were getting, also led to bad business decisions. The market is now punishing those "smartest guys in the room" who failed to declare that the emperor had no clothes. The costs and benefits of the intermediated system need to be better understood from the borrower's and investor's perspective, with the market alternative of disintermediated and less opaque loans a possible upshot.

• *Home ownership.* Home ownership has long been a part of the American dream. Is this ideal still to valid today? How can this most fairly and efficiently be achieved? What is the role of the individual and government in making this a reality?

• *Risk shifting.* The market systems for spreading the risk of default on mortgage instruments did not work. The role, "independence," and judgment of rating agencies blessing mortgage securities need close study and action. Credit default swaps, where Congress permitted AIG and others to in essence guarantee mortgage bonds without reserves, disclosure, or regulation (and to also guarantee them to non-holders who were simply betting on default of a bond that they did not actually hold), have been cited as a major cause of the financial crisis. Credit default swaps did not shift risk in the market— the taxpayers instead are paying the bill.[5]

NOTES

1. *Growth of the Secondary Market.* The growth in the secondary market over recent years has been tremendous, leading to a national home financing system in which loans originated by local lenders are now sold to lenders throughout the country and even internationally. "By 1983, 20 percent of outstanding mortgages by dollar amount were securitized, and a decade later fully half of outstanding mortgages by dollar amount were securitized. Today nearly two-thirds of mortgage dollars outstanding are securitized." Levitin, The Paper Chase: Securitization, Foreclosure, and the Uncertainty of Mortgage Title, 63 Duke L.J. 637, 670–71 (2013).

For other fine sources describing and analyzing the secondary market, see Schill, Uniformity or Diversity: Residential Real Estate Finance Law in the 1990s and the Implications of Changing Financial Markets, 64 S.Cal.L.Rev. 1261, 1272 (1991); Pittman, Economic and Regulatory Developments Affecting Mortgage Related Securities, 64 Notre Dame L.Rev. 497, 538 (1989) (also describing the Secondary Mortgage Market Enhancement Act, Pub. L. No. 98–440, 98 Stat. 1689 (1984), which removed certain impediments to the private secondary mortgage market existing under state and federal securities and investment laws); Jaffee & Rosen, Mortgage Securitization Trends, 1 J. Housing Research 117 (1990); Poindexter, Subordinated Rolling Equity: Analyzing Real Estate Loan Default in the Era of Securitization, 50 Emory L.J. 519 (2001); Malloy, The Secondary Mortgage Market—A Catalyst for Change in Real Estate Transactions, 39 Southwestern L.J. 991 (1986); Dolan, Lender's Guide to the Securitization of Commercial Mortgage Loans, 115 Banking L.J. 597 (1998); Forte, A Capital Markets Mortgage: A Ratable Model for Main Street and Wall Street, 31 Real Prop. Probate & Tr. J. 489 (1996); Richards, "Gradable and Tradable": The Securitization of Commercial Real Estate Mortgages, 16 Real Est.L.J. 99 (1987); Seneker, How to Document Securitized Commercial Real Estate Mortgage Loans, 15 Prac. Real Est. Law. 41 (No. 3, May 1999); Shenker & Colletta, Asset Securitization: Evolution, Current Issues and New Frontiers, 69 Tex. L. Rev. 1369 (1991).

---

[5]   Commodity Futures Modernization Act of 2000 barred federal and state regulation of credit default swaps.

2. *The Conservatorship of FNMA and FHLMC.* FNMA and FHLMC were two important and early casualties of the mortgage crisis that erupted in 2008. FNMA and FHLMC faced major exposure on mortgage guarantees and derivative instruments as subprime and other mortgage losses affected the mortgage markets. Because of a concern over the continued viability and liquidity of these two companies and pursuant to power granted by The Housing and Economic and Recovery Act, which became law on July 30, 2008, Secretary of the Treasury Henry Paulsen placed FNMA and FHLMC under federal conservatorship. The United States Treasury thus stood behind the commitments of the two companies, but the mission of FNMA and FHLMC going forward remains unclear, even more than five years after conservatorship. See Jim Puzzanghera, Fannie Mae, Freddie Mac May Be Too Profitable to Shut Down, L.A. Times, Jan. 4, 2014; Jackie Calmes, Obama Outlines Plans for Fannie Mae and Freddie Mac, N.Y. Times, Aug. 6, 2013; Nick Timiraos, Fannie, Freddie Payments Nearly Match Aid, Wall St. J., Nov. 7, 2013. For excellent analyses of the role of these two entities, see Reiss, Fannie Mae and Freddie Mac and the Future of Federal Housing Finance Policy: A Study of Regulatory Privilege, 61 Ala. L. Rev. 907 (2010); Reiss, The Federal Government's Implied Guarantee of Fannie Mae and Freddie Mac's Obligations: Uncle Sam Will Pick Up the Tab, 42 Ga.L.Rev. 1019 (2008).

3. *Federalization of Mortgages.* Mortgage law, like mortgage lending, has traditionally honored state boundaries. Recognizing that local variations in mortgage law and practice could seriously stunt the growth of a truly national mortgage industry, policymakers have taken steps on several fronts to federalize mortgage law and practice, mostly in connection with home loans. First, one of the express purposes of the Uniform Land Security Interest Act is to encourage lending by out of state banks by providing uniform laws. Second, to reduce the cost of individually examining mortgage documents from fifty different jurisdictions, the FHLMC and FNMA have published uniform loan instruments that are now used in about eighty percent of all residential loans. See Lance, Balancing Private and Public Initiatives in the Mortgage-Backed Security Market, 18 Real Prop., Probate & Trust J. 426, 438 (1983). Also, Congress has expressly preempted state laws on usury restrictions on first lien home loans, due on sale clauses, and adjustable rate mortgage instruments for residences, and the Office of Thrift Supervision has issued regulations on loan-value ratio and appraisal standards which supplant local law. See pages 386–390 below.

Professor Michael Schill has argued that federal preemption of state mortgage foreclosure law may not bring great efficiencies and will prevent the states from experimenting with different rules reflecting their economic, cultural, and political diversity. Schill, Uniformity or Diversity: Residential Real Estate Finance Law in the 1990s and the Implications of Changing Financial Markets, 64 S.Cal.L.Rev. 1291 (1991). In a later article, Professor Schill wrote that "[t]oday, my views remain the same. The exponential growth of REITs and mortgage-backed securities despite the persistence of these non-uniform laws suggest to me that they are not major impediments to the capital markets." Schill, The Impact of Capital Markets on Real Estate Law and Practice, 32 J. Marshall L. Rev. 269, 287 (1999).

Professor Frank Alexander has asserted that, where Congress has not expressly preempted state mortgage law, the courts have implied preemption and applied federal common law with confusing results. He suggests new analytical methods under these doctrines that would yield less federal displacement of state law. Alexander, Federal Intervention in Real Estate Finance: Preemption and Federal Common Law, 71 N.C.L.Rev. 293 (1993).

Professor Patrick Randolph has suggested that the uniformity of foreclosure rules may be more essential in commercial transactions than in residential situations since a single commercial mortgage is a larger and more important piece of a mortgage pool than any single residential mortgage. Randolph, The Future of American Real Estate Law: Uniform Foreclosure Laws and the Uniform Land Security Interest Act, 20 Nova L. Rev. 1109 (1996). See also Carrozzo, Marketing The American Mortgage: The Emergency Home Finance Act of 1970, Standardization and the Secondary Market Revolution, 39 Real Prop. Probate & Tr. J. 765 (2005).

With the federal conservatorship of FNMA and FHLMC, it remains to be seen whether those organizations will continue exert a major influence on standardizing mortgages.

3. TERMS

Mortgage terms can be reduced to four variables: interest rate; amortization rate (the rate at which the loan principal is paid off); term; and loan to value ratio (the ratio between the amount of the loan and the value of the property securing it; thus an $80,000 loan on a property appraised at $100,000 has an 8:10 loan to value ratio, sometimes simply called an 80% loan to value ratio). Each variable can be adjusted to meet the particular needs of borrower and lender. For example, a borrower might agree to a shorter loan term—thereby reducing the lender's exposure and risk—in return for a lower interest rate, a slower amortization rate, or a higher loan to value ratio.

The most dramatic shift in the orientation of these four variables occurred as a result of the Depression of the 1930's. The standard pre-Depression mortgage instrument had a short-term (typically 5 years); low loan to value ratio (typically 50%); and little or no amortization (the entire principal was typically payable as a "balloon" at the end of the term). New Deal programs introduced a strikingly different instrument and encouraged its adoption with the lure of FHA insurance. The new instrument had a much longer term (20 to 30 years); a higher loan to value ratio (typically 80%); and complete amortization over the life of the loan. Most instruments of this period were so-called "level payment" mortgages, calling for identical monthly payments covering interest and amortization throughout the loan term. In the loan's early years, most of the level payment goes toward interest and only a small amount toward reduction of principal. But, as principal is reduced, the interest payments on the principal outstanding become smaller and the proportion of the level payment available for reduction in principal becomes consequently larger, resulting in still smaller interest payments and still larger reductions in principal, until the loan is completely paid off.

The long-term fixed rate mortgage, although still widely used, had by the midB1970's become increasingly unattractive to lenders and borrowers alike. With interest rates constantly rising, lenders were reluctant to commit their capital over a long period at interest rates that they believed would soon fall short of their own cost of capital. Borrowers disliked the higher interest rates, shorter terms, and lower loan to value ratios that lenders began to require in return for their own diminished prospects. This shared dilemma produced a burst of new mortgage instruments that sometimes resembled the instruments used in pre-Depression real estate finance. While these enabled many borrowers to afford homes, in some situations these new forms led to borrowers overextending themselves and helped sow the seeds of the 2008 mortgage collapse. The principal case and the first notes that follow indicate how lenders juggled the four mortgage variables to meet new consumer needs while, at the same time, improving their own loan portfolios.

Goebel v. First Federal Savings & Loan Association of Racine

Supreme Court of Wisconsin, 1978.
83 Wis.2d 668, 266 N.W.2d 352.

CONNOR T. HANSEN, JUSTICE.

The facts in the case are not in dispute. Although First Federal is a federally regulated institution, the resolution of the instant controversy depends on the interpretation of the note and mortgage as a matter of state contract law.

On May 29, 1964, the plaintiffs, as mortgagors, executed a mortgage in favor of First Federal, as mortgagee, in the amount of $17,000, with interest at six percent annually, payable in monthly installments.

The note contained the following interest rate adjustment provision:

"... The interest for each month shall be calculated upon said unpaid balance due as of the last day of the previous month at the rate of *6* per cent per annum or such other rate of interest on unpaid balances as may be fixed by the Association from time to time at its option, provided however, that the Association may not change the rate of interest except at any time after three years from the date hereof, and then upon 4 months or more written notice to the Promissors. Notice shall be deemed received when the same is deposited in the United States mail, postage prepaid, addressed to the Promissors at their last address as it appears on the record of the Association. The Promissors upon receiving notice of such change may repay the entire balance due on this obligation during said 4 months period without penalty. Any change in the rate of interest shall be endorsed on this mortgage note by the Association, stating the effective date of such change, the balance then due, and the new rate."

The plaintiffs do not contest the legality or the conscionableness of such a provision. However, they argue that in the instant case, First Federal is precluded, by other provisions of the mortgage note, from effectuating an interest rate increase either by increasing the term of the note or by increasing the amount of the monthly installments. As completed, the note obligated the plaintiffs to pay to First Federal:

> ". . . the principal sum of <u>Seventeen Thousand and $^{00}/_{100}$—</u> Dollars, <u>($17,000.00)</u> and such additional sums as may be subsequently advanced hereon to the Promissors and Mortgagors by the ASSOCIATION, together with interest as hereinafter provided, until such loan shall have been fully paid; such principal and interest payable in monthly installments of <u>One Hundred Ten—</u> Dollars ___ Cents, <u>($110.00)</u> on or before the <u>10th</u> day of each and every month, commencing <u>January 10, 1965;</u> said principal and interest, including advances, notwithstanding any other provisions in this note or the mortgage given as collateral security, shall be paid in full within <u>25</u> years from the date hereof, and in the event of an additional advance hereon over and above the principal sum stated above, such monthly installments shall be adjusted to conform to this provision."

In September, 1973, First Federal notified the plaintiffs that as a result of unfavorable economic conditions, the interest rate on their loan would be increased from six percent to eight percent, effective February 1, 1974. In November, 1973, the plaintiffs were informed that the new rate would be seven percent rather than eight percent and that they could elect to absorb the increased interest expense either by paying an additional $7.49 per month or by extending the term of their loan approximately two years. The plaintiffs did not reply to this letter, and they continued to make monthly payments of $110.

Affidavits submitted in support of the motions for summary judgment allege that First Federal has increased the interest rate of 488 borrowers whose mortgage notes were executed on forms identical to that completed by the plaintiffs, and that 119 of these borrowers have elected to pay larger monthly installments to absorb the increase in interest rates.

This action was commenced by the plaintiffs, as a class action, on behalf of themselves and all others similarly situated. They argue that the terms of their note preclude any alteration by First Federal that would either increase the amount of their monthly payments or extend the term of their loan to accommodate an increased interest rate. The issues presented on appeal are whether the terms of the mortgage note permit First Federal to increase the interest rate by increasing the amount of the monthly installments or by extending the term of the loan[2] and whether the case can proceed as a class action.

---

[2]   A third possible method of implementing an interest rate adjustment clause is referred to as the use of a balloon payment. Under this method, monthly payments would continue to be made in the original amount, but would be applied against principal and interest to reflect the increased rate of interest. Upon expiration of the original term of the loan, a lump-sum balloon payment, in the amount of the then-outstanding principal balance, would be collected. Balloon payments are subject to federal regulation. 12 CFR 541.14(a), as amended by 37 Fed.Reg. 5118

Whether First Federal can increase the amount of the plaintiffs' monthly payments so as to absorb a higher interest rate rests, to a significant extent, on the principle of *expressio unius est exclusio alterius*. Under this principle, a specific mention in a contract of one or more matters is considered to exclude other matters of the same nature or class not expressly mentioned, even when all such matters would have been inferred had none been expressed.

The mortgage documents leave no doubt as to the right of the mortgagee to increase monthly payments to accommodate repayment of future advances and the lender's cash expenditures to protect its security interest. With equal clarity, the draftsman could have provided the same express means to accommodate the interest escalation clause. Other mortgage notes introduced in evidence did so by providing that interest could be increased or decreased with a corresponding adjustment in the required monthly payments.

The note specifically states that First Federal may advance additional sums to the borrowers and provides that ". . . in the event of an additional advance hereon over and above the principal sum stated above, *such monthly installments shall be adjusted to conform to this provision*." (Emphasis added.) In addition, the note authorizes First Federal to protect its security interest in the mortgaged property by paying taxes, purchasing insurance, making repairs or discharging any encumbrance upon the premises, and the note requires the borrowers to repay any such outlays "upon demand" by First Federal. The trial court concluded that First Federal's right to be repaid for such disbursements "upon demand" necessarily embraces a right to forego immediate repayment and instead to increase the borrower's monthly payments to recoup the outlays.

The mortgage note fails to make similar provision for an increase in payments when the interest rate is raised. The trial court interpreted this omission to demonstrate that no such increase was contemplated. This conclusion is supported by the decision of this court in Godfrey v. Crawford, 23 Wis.2d 44, 50, 126 N.W.2d 495, 498 (1964), where this court stated that in some cases such an omission "might well be the decisive factor. . . ."

In Farley v. Salow, 67 Wis.2d 393, 227 N.W.2d 76 (1975), this court relied on the inclusion of an express cut-off date in one contract as a basis for refusing to imply such a cut-off date in a related, contemporaneous contract drafted by the same lawyer. It was observed in *Farley*, supra, that the omission of words from a contract is sometimes instructive. The court quoted from North Gate Corp. v. National Food Stores, 30 Wis.2d 317, 323, 140 N.W.2d 744 (1966), where it was said that:

> ". . . 'We cannot ignore the draftsman's failure to use an obvious term, especially where it is the draftsman who is urging a tenuous interpretation of a term in order to make it applicable to a situation which would clearly have been

---

(1972). However, this method was not used in the instant case, and therefore we do not address it.

covered if the obvious term had been chosen.' " *Farley*, supra, 67 Wis.2d at 405, 227 N.W.2d at 83.

This observation reflects the general rule that ambiguous contract language must be construed against the drafter. This rule has particular force where, as here, there is a substantial disparity of bargaining power between the parties, and a standard form is supplied by the party drafting the form.

Applying these principles to the instant case, the trial court properly held that the failure to provide explicitly for an increase in monthly payments to absorb an interest increase demonstrated that no such increase was contemplated by the parties. The trial court stated:

"... The contract does not leave to implication the right of the mortgagee to increase the monthly installment amounts to accommodate [sic] the repayment of future advances, and the lender's outlays to protect the security interest. With a stroke of the pen the draftsman could have provided the same express means for accomodating [sic] an interest rate escalation. Thus, while a court might be willing to imply a right to increase monthly payments in order to effectuate the escalation clause if there were no mention of such a right anywhere in the contract, the express mention of such a right in conjunction with other provisions provides potent evidence that such a right was not intended to be left to implication by the parties."

As the trial court emphasized, the amount of the monthly payments is a consideration of vital importance, and perhaps the single most important consideration, to a potential borrower. It is the factor most directly related to the possibility of default; it is the figure to which a buyer looks to determine whether he can afford to purchase a home and to which the lender looks to determine whether the borrower is capable of repaying the loan. For this reason, a provision empowering the lender to unilaterally increase the amount of the monthly payments, perhaps thereby threatening the borrower with default, will not lightly be inferred, particularly where express provision has been made for such an increase under other circumstances, and where such a provision could easily have been inserted by First Federal. If any increase in this figure was intended to be authorized by the loan contract, such authority should have been expressly stated.

The omission of any reference to increased payments to reflect a higher interest rate precludes the unilateral increase of the amount of the monthly payment.

The second aspect of this issue is whether the mortgage note permits First Federal to effect an increase in the interest rate by extending the term of the loan instead of increasing the amount of the monthly payments.

The mortgage note provides that:

"... principal and interest, including advances, notwithstanding any other provisions in this note or in the mortgage given as collateral security, shall be paid in full within *25* years from the date hereof, ..."

The number "25" inserted in the form by First Federal represents the term necessary to retire the loan at the original interest rate and with monthly payments in the amount specified in the note. The twenty-five year limitation therefore affords no leeway for extension of the loan term to absorb the higher interest rate. The manifest intention that all interest and principal be paid within twenty-five years "notwithstanding any other provisions in this note or the mortgage" is unmistakable, and this court is not at liberty to disregard the plain meaning of the language chosen by the draftsman for First Federal and agreed to by the parties.

First Federal argues, however, that it may elect to waive this requirement on the theory that either party to a contract may waive provisions of the contract included for his benefit.

Such a waiver may not be made, however, where the waiver would deprive the non-waiving party of a benefit under the provision in question. Thus in Godfrey v. Crawford, supra, 23 Wis.2d at 49, 50, 126 N.W.2d at 498, this court permitted a buyer under a land contract to waive a condition with respect to approval of a rezoning proposal when, at the time the waiver was exercised, a waiver would not interfere in any way with the benefits afforded the sellers under the contract and where "the defendant sellers' protection . . . [was not] weakened in the slightest degree" by the decision to permit the waiver. That is not the case here.

First Federal argues that the provision limiting the term of the loan to twenty-five years was included solely for the benefit of First Federal, and that it serves only to permit First Federal to insist that the entire debt be paid within the specified term. First Federal thus argues that it should be able to waive the provision and thereby extend the term of the loan.

However, the fact is that whether the amount of the monthly payment is increased or the term of the loan extended, the mortgagor pays more money and the mortgagee collects more interest than the amount specified in the original note and mortgage. Therefore it cannot be said the provision limiting the term to twenty-five years "notwithstanding any other provisions" is solely for the benefit of First Federal.

Since we have heretofore determined the lender is precluded by the language of the note from increasing the amount of the monthly payments, it follows that the maximum loan term provision is of considerable import to the borrower. When viewed in conjunction with the lender's inability to raise the amount of the monthly payments, this provision may in many cases relieve a borrower of the obligation to pay any additional sum for increased interest.

In such a situation, the provision would operate to the distinct benefit of the borrower. For this reason, the provision is not subject to waiver by First Federal. Therefore, a unilateral extension of the loan term by First Federal would violate the terms of the contract.

First Federal could easily have avoided this result by using a longer loan term than twenty-five years.[3] Precisely this point was made

---

[3] Federal regulations require only that conventional mortgage loans made by federal savings and loan associations be repayable within thirty years. 12 CFR 545.6–1(a) (1977).

by the author of a Note entitled Adjustable Interest Rates in Home Mortgages: A Reconsideration, in 1975 Wis.L.Rev., 742. After recognizing that an interest rate escalation clause may be implemented by extending the loan term, the author observed that:

> "This could be accomplished without violating contract terms either by including a clause that provided for extension of the maturity date or by originally making the final payment date later than it would be at the initial rate of increase [sic]. Most mortgages have a provision to the effect that 'this mortgage shall be paid in full within ___ years.' The blank could indicate, for example, 30 years, when calculation at the time of the contract would indicate amortization within 20 years." 1975 Wis.L.Rev. at 757, fn. 86.

Because First Federal failed to include such a provision, it cannot now extend the loan term without violating the provisions of the contract as it was written.

This conclusion rests principally on canons of construction. Such canons are designed to aid in the ascertainment of the intention of the parties, and they would necessarily yield to any contrary intention of the parties, if such an intention could be ascertained from the contract as a whole.

The mortgage note does evince a clear intent that First Federal may impose a higher rate of interest and that the borrowers will have a corresponding duty to pay such interest, consistent with the remaining terms of the note. The accompanying mortgage, which is to be read together with the note, expressly incorporates the terms and conditions of the note ". . . including duty to . . . pay higher interest on notice. . . ." That the plaintiffs signed the note and mortgage does not alone determine the extent of the duty or the conditions and circumstances under which such increased interest may be collected, however. These questions can only be answered with reference to other provisions of the contract.

First Federal relies on the established rule that a contract is to be construed so as to give a reasonable meaning to each provision of the contract, and that courts must avoid a construction which renders portions of a contract meaningless, inexplicable or mere surplusage. First Federal argues that the construction adopted by the trial court renders the interest adjustment clause unenforceable and therefore mere surplusage. A construction which had this result would not only conflict with the rule of construction cited by First Federal, but would also conflict with the manifest intention of the note and the mortgage.

However, it cannot be said that the decision of the trial court has this effect. The interest adjustment clause is not without effect. The interest adjustment clause permits a downward adjustment of the interest rate. If such an interest decrease is implemented, under the contract, First Federal would be able to impose and collect a subsequent interest increase within the twenty-five year term.

More fundamentally, the interest adjustment clause retains its full force with regard to any borrower who prepays his loan. Upon prepayment, the higher rate of interest may be used in calculating the then outstanding principal balance, and in this manner the interest increase may effectively be collected. The trial court observed that many, if not most, mortgages do not reach full term, but rather are paid before maturity.

The instant note specifically includes a "due-on sale" clause by which the full amount of the loan becomes due and payable, at the option of First Federal, whenever the mortgaged premises are sold. Any increased interest charges would thus be recoverable upon sale of the premises. Because there is a substantial likelihood that mortgaged residential property will be sold during the course of a twenty-five year loan term, it cannot be said that the interest adjustment clause is deprived of all effect, or is rendered mere surplusage.

The language in the particular note and real estate mortgage here under consideration precludes First Federal both from increasing the amount of the monthly payments and from extending the term of the loan. . . .

Judgment affirmed.

ABRAHAMSON, J., not participating.

NOTES

1. *The "New" Mortgages.* Rising interest rates and housing prices, together with the gradual deregulation of capital markets, have spurred new arrangements for housing finance. Some of the new instruments, such as the renegotiable rate mortgage, were patterned after pre-depression instruments. Some, such as the variable rate mortgage and shared appreciation mortgage, borrowed from contemporary instruments used in commercial land finance. Some, such as the price level adjusted mortgage, drew on arrangements used in other countries. And some of the new instruments, doubtless, were true inventions. Among the more popular or controversial are:

(a) *Adjustable Rate Mortgage* (earlier called the Variable Rate Mortgage, or VRM). In an ARM, the interest rate paid by the borrower varies over the life of the loan according to a designated index of current market rates. Since the conventional wisdom during the 1970's was that interest rates would rise over the long term, ARMs attracted lenders by protecting against inflation; lenders attracted borrowers by offering lower initial interest rates than were available under fixed rate mortgages. Borrowers' concerns that interest increases might outpace increases in their income, thus jeopardizing their ability to make the monthly mortgage payment, were assuaged by legislated limits on the frequency and amount by which interest rates could be increased.

(b) *Price Level Adjusted Mortgage.* Under the PLAM it is the loan principal, not the interest rate, that varies over the term of the mortgage. At the end of each year or other agreed-upon period, the principal outstanding on a PLAM is adjusted up or down according to a prescribed inflation index. For the lender, the attraction of the PLAM is that the loan is repaid in "real" rather than inflated dollars. The attraction to the borrower is that the lender can consequently charge an interest rate that is well below market rates, making debt service more affordable in the loan's earlier years. The risk, of course, is that the borrower's income and ability to meet the debt service will not keep pace with inflation over the life of the loan.

(c) *Renegotiable Rate Mortgage* (also called a "rollover" mortgage). The RRM is a series of renewable short term notes—usually for 3, 4 or 5 years—secured by a long term mortgage—of up to 30 years—with principal fully amortized over the longer term. At the end of each short term loan period, the borrower can choose between paying off the loan or "rolling over" into a new loan. If the borrower rolls over, all terms of the new loan, except interest rate, will be identical to those of the old; the interest rate is negotiable within prescribed limits.

(d) *Graduated Payment Mortgage.* The GPM is a long-term, fixed rate mortgage in which the monthly payment gradually increases over the life of the loan. Although payments in the early years of the loan will be insufficient to amortize the principal, or even to pay all of the interest on the loan, the increased payments in the loan's later years are calculated to make up the difference. The GPM was designed to meet the needs of younger borrowers who cannot initially afford the monthly payments required by a conventional fixed rate mortgage, but who expect their income to increase over time to a point at which they can afford to pay more than the debt service on a standard fixed rate mortgage. A variant of the GPM, called the Graduated Payment Adjustable Mortgage (GPAM), combines the rollover feature of the Renegotiable Rate Mortgage with the GPM's graduated payment schedule.

(e) *Growing Equity Mortgage.* The GEM is a long term, self-amortizing, fixed interest mortgage under which the borrower's monthly payments increase each year by a predetermined amount, typically 4%. The effect of the annual increase in monthly debt service is to amortize the loan more quickly than would a level payment or GPM schedule so that the loan can be completely repaid within as short a period as fifteen years. The GEM has proved attractive to homebuyers who contemplate rises in income over the life of the loan and are willing to trade tax deductible interest payments for the comfort of knowing that their homes will be paid off in a comparatively short time. GEMS are also very attractive to secondary market mortgage purchasers who generally prefer intermediate term—12–15 year—debt to long term—25–30 year—debt.

(f) *Shared Appreciation Mortgage.* A SAM reduces the interest rate to below market levels in return for the lender's right to receive a predetermined portion of the property's increase in value, if any, over the life of the loan. A typical SAM will reduce the interest rate by about $1/3$ in exchange for $1/3$ of the property's appreciation. SAMs generally have a short—5 to 10 year—term.

(g) *Buy-Downs.* One of the less subtle, but more effective financing techniques is for the seller—typically a developer—to "buy-down" the institutional lender's interest rate for the first three to five years of a long term loan to the homebuyer. In return for the seller's payment of a lump sum to the lender, the lender will reduce the interest charges in the loan's early years to a below market rate. Essentially a marketing device adopted by developers unable to sell their houses because of high interest rates, the buy-down makes housing available to the homebuyer who anticipates rising income and, thus, the ability to pay the undiscounted debt service that will begin to come due at the end of the buy-down period.

(h) *Reverse Annuity Mortgages.* RAMs are aimed at the plight not of young, first-time homebuyers, but rather of older homeowners on fixed incomes who find it difficult to make ends meet in an inflationary economy. Essentially, the RAM is designed to enable these homeowners to draw cash out of the accumulated equity in their homes without selling the house itself. The typical RAM enables the homeowner effectively to use the equity in his home as security for an annuity, giving him monthly payments over his lifetime or some predetermined period. With each monthly payment from the lender, the borrower's debt to the lender, secured by the house, increases. In the usual RAM, the entire debt is to be repaid at the earlier of ten years from the beginning of the loan, or the death of the borrower, with funds to come from the sale of the property or probate of the homeowner's estate.

For a discussion of the factor contributing to consumer choice of fixed rate versus adjustable rate mortgages, see Hendershott, The Composition of Mortgage Originations, 1 J. Housing Research 43 (1990) (forecasting a decline in the use of adjustable mortgages in the 1990's due to declines in house prices and interest rates).

For background and critical evaluation of the new mortgages, see generally, Comment, The New Mortgages: A Functional Legal Analysis, 10 Fla.St.U.L.Rev. 95 (1982); Friend, Shared Appreciation Mortgages, 34 Hastings L.J. 329 (1982); Iezman, Alternative Mortgage Instruments: Their Effect on Residential Financing, 10 Real Est.L.J. 3 (1981); Iezman, The Shared Appreciation Mortgage and the Shared Equity Program: A Comprehensive Examination of Equity Participation, 16 Real Prop., Probate & Trust J. 510 (1981); Kmiec, Shared Appreciation Mortgages: A Step Toward Making Housing a Bad Investment, 10 Real Est.L.J. 302 (1982); Nauts & Bridewell, Reverse Mortgages—A Lawyer's Guide to Housing and Income Alternatives (1997); Walleser, Balancing the Interest: The Changing Complexion of Home Mortgage Financing in America, 31 Drake L.Rev. 1 (1981–82). See also Feld & Marks, Legal Differences Without Economic Distinctions: Points, Penalties, and the Market for Mortgages, 77 B.U.L. Rev. 405 (1997).

2. *New Mortgages and Common Law Equity of Redemption.* Some features of the new mortgages may conflict with common law rules. Under the traditional equity of redemption doctrine, a mortgagor has a right to redeem the mortgaged property after default and before foreclosure by paying the amount due on the mortgage. Courts have rejected attempts by the mortgagee to "clog" the equity of redemption, such as a provision requiring the mortgagor to deliver a deed to the mortgagee on default. The Restatement of Mortgages endorses the concept of the equity of redemption. § 3.1.

Professor Marshall Tracht has examined the arguments supporting the equity of redemption—the need to prevent overreaching by creditors and a windfall if the value of the property exceeds the debt. He also evaluates the critique that the equity of redemption creates a less efficient credit market and forces marginal mortgagors out of the market or increases their borrowing costs. Tracht, Renegotiation and Secured Credit: Explaining the Equity of Redemption, 52 Vand. L. Rev. 599, 641 (1999).

There has been some concern that provisions in alternative mortgages such as a convertible mortgage, that gives the mortgagee an option to buy the property, or mortgages which provide the lender with an "equity kicker" (such as a shared appreciation mortgage) could be found to be an unenforceable clog on the equity of redemption. Commentators have suggested that in order to promote these desirable alternative mortgage arrangements, no clog should be found as long as the transaction is inherently fair. See Licht, The Clog on the Equity of Redemption and its Effect on Modern Real Estate Finance, 60 St. John's L.Rev. 452 (1986); Preble & Cartwright, Convertible and Shared Appreciation Loans: Unclogging the Equity of Redemption, 20 Real Prop. Probate & Trust J. 821 (1985); Uniform Land Security Interest Act § 211 (no clog on the equity of redemption for equity kickers or for convertible mortgages as long as option to purchase is not triggered by default under the mortgage).

3. *Federal Support for the New Mortgages.* Almost all of the new mortgages violate one or more of the Depression-era regulations that gave shape to the long term, level payment, fixed rate home mortgage. Congress early perceived that existing rules would have to be changed if home finance was to flourish and acted quickly to meet the needs of the new mortgages. For example, the Housing and Urban-Rural Recovery Act of 1983, Pub.L. No. 98–181 Tit. I–V, 97 Stat. 1155 et seq. (1983) authorized, or updated, FHA insurance programs for ARMs. 12 U.S.C.A. §§ 1715Z–16, 1715Z–17.

Although state regulators tried to keep pace with federal regulators in updating their controls on home loans, there was often a lag, and consequent inability among state-regulated lenders to compete with federally-regulated lenders in offering the new mortgages. The problem was initially addressed in the Garn-St. Germain Depository Act of 1982, Pub.L. No. 97–320, 96 Stat. 1469 et seq., Title VIII (the "Alternative Mortgage Transaction Parity Act of 1982"), which was amended in 1989 by Pub.L. No. 101–73, Title VII, § 744(c), 103 Stat. 438, and codified at 12 U.S.C.A. § 3801. The statute preempts state regulations of nontraditional mortgages that are more stringent than counterpart federal regulations. Congress declared its purpose "to eliminate the discriminatory impact that those regulations have upon nonfederally chartered housing creditors and provide them with parity with federally chartered institutions by authorizing all housing creditors to make, purchase, and enforce alternative mortgage transactions so long as the transactions are in conformity with the regulations issued by the Federal agencies." 12 U.S.C.A. § 3801(b). Section 3806, enacted as part of the Competitive Equality Banking Act of 1987, requires that adjustable rate home mortgages include a cap on the interest rate. The Office of Thrift Supervision has issued regulations on adjustments in mortgages of federal savings associations. 12 C.F.R. § 560.210.

The Act gave states the power to expressly reinstate their regulatory programs by statute or referendum at any time prior to October 15, 1985. 12 U.S.C.A. § 3804(a). Maine, Massachusetts, New York, South Carolina, and Wisconsin have done so.

4. *Goebel v. First Federal.* Do you agree with the decision in Goebel v. First Federal Savings & Loan? If you had been a borrower under the note in question, would you have expected the interest increments to be reflected in increased monthly debt service, in increased term, or in some other fashion? Or would the instrument's failure to specify the means for effecting the increment suggest to you that the decision lay entirely within the lender's discretion? What effect, if any, did the court give to the provision for increased interest?

As a federal savings and loan association, First Federal was subject to the regulations of the Federal Home Loan Bank Board. (The Federal Institutions Reform, Recovery, and Enforcement Act of 1989 abolished the Board and placed federal savings and loan institutions under the supervision of the Office of Thrift Supervision.) Should the court have tried to interpret the note in light of the Board's requirements for conforming loans?

Might the borrowers in *Goebel* have attacked the increased interest provision on the ground that the instrument provided no benchmark for limiting the interest rate? Compare Constitution Bank & Trust Co. v. Robinson, 179 Conn. 232, 237, 425 A.2d 1268, 1271 (1979) (upholding variable interest rate calling for interest at a per annum rate equal to 1.5% over the lender's prime rate. "If the lender may arbitrarily adjust the interest rate without any standard whatsoever, with regard to this borrower alone, then the note is too indefinite as to interest. If however the power to vary the interest rate is limited by the marketplace and requires periodic redetermination, in good faith and in the ordinary course of business, of the price to be charged to *all* of the bank's customers similarly situated, then the note is not too indefinite.")

For a discussion of developments in the "adjustment wars," see Lee, Mancuso, & Walter, Housing Finance: Major Developments in 1990, 46 Bus.Law. 1149, 1171–1177 (1991).

5. *Lender Liability.* Mortgagees have been subject to lender liability claims for various activities in the origination and administration of loans. Reconsider in this regard the note on lender liability on page 217, as well as the *Rice* and *Jeminson* cases and related notes on pages 220–225, dealing with mortgagee liability for defects in houses.

Two cases involving the purchase of insurance illustrate some of the key themes in the lender liability area. In Heinert v. Home Federal Savings & Loan Ass'n, 444 N.W.2d 718 (S.D.1989), the mortgagor executed a form presented by the lender at closing which provided that the borrower requested the lender to obtain credit life insurance for the benefit of the borrower and authorized the deduction of a fee each month to pay for it. The lender did not purchase the insurance and the borrower subsequently died, owing some $40,000 on the loan. The court held that a contract to obtain insurance was created by the form, even though there was some ambiguity and the lender never charged the borrower for the insurance. The court found that the lender breached the agreement by failing to do so, making it liable for the amount which would have been paid had the insurance been purchased.

In Beckford v. Empire Mutual Insurance Group, 135 A.D.2d 228, 525 N.Y.S.2d 260 (1988), the borrowers complied with the mortgage provisions requiring the borrowers to obtain casualty insurance on the property, assign the policy to the lender, and make monthly payments to the lender to be escrowed for premiums to become due on the policy. The lender received notice of the policy's cancellation but did not notify the borrowers and the property subsequently was destroyed by fire. The court held that the borrowers had no cause of action against the lender for failure to notify or maintain insurance in the absence of an express agreement to do so.

Were these cases decided correctly? Consider the parties' expectations and whom the insurance was to benefit. Did they think the lender was assuming an obligation to the borrower? Did the lender follow norms of reasonable lending behavior? Will the decisions encourage sound and efficient lending and borrowing practices? Was the borrower simply attempting a search for a deep pocket? Was there anything improper about the bargaining process that required a rearrangement of the deal?

6. *Usury.* Usury has always provoked mixed feelings. On one side is the moral precept that interest is bad and excessive interest worse. On the other is the economic precept that high interest may be necessary to attract loans to risky but worthwhile ventures. This conflict between moral and economic command helps to explain usury's troubled history. Dante may have consigned usurers to the Seventh Circle of Hell, but Pope Nicholas III defended them, threatening an English Archbishop with excommunication for trying to renege on a usurious loan from a group of Italian bankers. The Divine Comedy, Inferno: Canto 17; S. Clough & C. Cole, Economic History of Europe 82 (3d ed. 1952).

The American experience with usury laws dates to colonial times. At one time, almost all states prohibited usury in one form or another, with maximum interest rates ranging from six percent to thirty percent. This regulatory pattern changed dramatically in late 1979 when Congress enacted Pub.L. No. 96–161, 93 Stat. 1233–40 (1979), preempting any state statute or constitutional provision that limited interest rates on first lien, residential mortgage loans made after December 28, 1979. After the Act, however, states could enact laws reinstating usury limits. By its terms, the Act was to expire on March 31, 1980.

On March 31, 1980, President Carter signed the Depository Institutions Deregulation and Monetary Control Act of 1980, Pub.L. No. 96–221, now codified at 12 U.S.C.A. § 1735f–7a (1990), perpetuating the provisions of the 1979 Act. The Act's key preemptive provision is section 501(a)(1):

> The provisions of the constitution or the laws of any State expressly limiting the rate or amount of interest, discount points, finance charges, or other charges which may be charged, taken, received, or reserved shall not apply to any loan, mortgage, credit sale, or advance which is—
>
> > (A) secured by a first lien on residential real property, by a first lien on stock in a residential cooperative housing corporation where the loan, mortgage, or advance is used to

finance the acquisition of such stock, or by a first lien on a residential manufactured home;

(B) made after March 31, 1980. . . .

Section 501(b)(2) gave states until April 1, 1983 to reinstate usury limits. According to a recent count, fifteen states have elected out of section 501. Uniform Land Security Interest Act, Introductory Comment to Part 4. See generally, Culhane & Kaplinsky, Trends Pertaining to the Usury Laws, 38 Bus.Lawyer 1329 (1983); Ewing & Vickers, Federal Pre-emption of State Usury Laws Affecting Real Estate Financing, 47 Mo.L.Rev. 171, 176 (1982); Randolph, Home Finance in the Shadow World: Unsolved Usury Problems Affecting Adjustable Rate and Wraparound Mortgages in Missouri, 51 U.Mo.K.C.L.Rev. 41 (1982).

For an overview of the new federal scheme as well as an examination of the costs and benefits of regulation versus free market in subprime lending, see Mansfield, The Road to Subprime "HEL" Was Paved with Good Congressional Intentions: Usury Deregulation and the Subprime Home Equity Market, 51 S.Car. L. Rev. 473 (2000).

State usury limits still govern real estate lending arrangements other than first lien residential loans. Lenders and borrowers employ various strategies to circumvent these limits, and legislatures and courts have strewn the field with pitfalls to trap incautious or overly ambitious lenders. These aspects of usury are considered at pages 570 to 581 below.

7. *Dragnet Clauses.* A mortgage will sometimes provide that it is to serve as security not only for the debt in connection with which it was created, but also as security for any other debt owed by the mortgagor to the mortgagee. These provisions, called dragnet clauses, can come back to haunt the unsuspecting mortgagor. For example, a borrower who obtains a home mortgage loan may, several years later, return to the same lender, this time to finance a vacation trip. If the borrower subsequently defaults on the vacation loan, the dragnet clause will entitle the lender to proceed directly against the security provided by the borrower's home.

Courts divide in their approach to dragnet clauses. Some courts interpret them narrowly, holding, for example, that the mortgage will secure only debts directly related to the property. See Emporia State Bank & Trust Co. v. Mounkes, 214 Kan. 178, 184, 519 P.2d 618 (1974) (". . . in the absence of clear, supportive evidence of a contrary intention a mortgage containing a dragnet type clause will not be extended to cover future advances unless the advances are of the same kind and quality or relate to the same transaction or series of transactions as the principal obligation secured or unless the document evidencing the subsequent advance refers to the mortgage as providing security therefor"). See also First Security Bank of Utah v. Shiew, 609 P.2d 952 (Utah 1980). The Restatement of Mortgages permits dragnet clauses only if the future debt is incurred in a transaction similar to the original mortgage (so that a future commercial loan would not be secured by an existing home purchase mortgage); if the original mortgage described with adequate specificity the additional types of loans that will be secured by the mortgage; or if the parties expressly agreed at the time of the future advance that it would be secured by the original mortgage. § 2.4(b).

Other courts interpret these clauses broadly. For example, in State Bank of Albany v. Fioravanti, 51 N.Y.2d 638, 435 N.Y.S.2d 947, 417 N.E.2d 60 (1980), the New York Court of Appeals held that a dragnet clause in a mortgage given by two brothers to secure a $2,500 home loan entitled the lender to proceed against the home to satisfy a deficiency judgment entered against the brothers following foreclosure on another parcel that the bank had financed seven years later. The court attached no weight to the fact that, before foreclosure on the second parcel, the brothers had sold the first parcel to their mother and the full $2,500 loan had been paid off. The three dissenting judges objected that the bank could have drafted language expressly making the dragnet clause survive complete payment of the original mortgage; that the language used by the bank was ambiguous at best; and that the ambiguity should be resolved against the bank since it had drafted the document.

8. *After-Acquired Property Clauses.* After-acquired property clauses, although probably used more frequently in personal property security arrangements, sometimes appear in real property mortgages. Conceptually, they are just the opposite of dragnet clauses. Dragnet clauses use a single property to secure the original debt and all future debts incurred. After-acquired property clauses secure a single debt with the original property and all future property acquired. See generally, R. Kratovil & R. Werner, Modern Mortgage Law and Practice § 8.06 (2d ed. 1981). The Uniform Land Security Interest Act permits after-acquired property clauses except when applied to residential real estate purchased by a "protected party." § 205.

One reason after-acquired property clauses play such a small role in real property security transactions is that the recording acts will shelter the later acquired parcel from the original mortgagee's rights. The original mortgage containing the after-acquired property clause will be completely outside the chain of title searched by purchasers or encumbrancers of the later parcel, whether a grantor-grantee or tract index is used. The original mortgagee may try to protect herself by exacting a covenant that the mortgagor will execute and record a supplemental mortgage in the chain of title of every parcel that he subsequently acquires, bringing the new parcel under the lien of the original mortgage. Breach of the covenant will, however, give the mortgagee only personal rights against the mortgagor.

9. *Uniform Instruments.* The Emergency Home Finance Act of 1970, Pub.L. No. 91–351, Tit. I–VII §§ 201, 305, 84 Stat. 450 (1970), now codified at 12 U.S.C.A. § 1717 (1990), authorized FNMA and FHLMC to establish a secondary market, buying and selling conventional mortgages, principally on single family homes. The two organizations quickly realized that, to function effectively, the secondary market needed a standard form of note and security instrument, and proposed uniform instruments were promulgated in 1972. See generally, Symposium, Uniformity in Mortgage Forms—Nearly, 7 Real Prop.Probate & Trust J. 397 (1972). Currently, FNMA and FHLMC have form documents for both conventional and adjustable loans. There are multistate note forms that are used in all but a few states. In order to reflect the requirements of state law, there are individualized mortgage forms for the various states; still, there are many uniform covenants in the mortgage forms for the different states. For a comprehensive treatment, see Burke, The Law of Federal Mortgage Documents (1989).

10. *Lawyer Malpractice.* In Santulli v. Englert, Reilly & McHugh, P.C., 78 N.Y.2d 700, 579 N.Y.S.2d 324, 586 N.E.2d 1014 (1992), plaintiff had retained defendant law firm to represent it in the sale of its business to White. A portion of the purchase price was to be paid by a note secured by land owned by White's father. The transaction closed and, after making twenty payments, White defaulted on the mortgage. When plaintiff sought to foreclose, it discovered that the legal description in the mortgage prepared by defendants covered only half of the parcel owned by White's father and omitted the more valuable portion on which a house was located.

The Appellate Division dismissed plaintiff's action for breach of contract since defendant had made no express promise to obtain a specific result. The Court of Appeals reversed, holding that the complaint adequately alleged that the defendant had agreed to perform all of the services related to the sale of plaintiff's business including the preparation of a first mortgage and expressly rejected the argument that an express promise to obtain a specific result is required to sustain a contract action in the context of an attorney-client relationship.

4. EVALUATING THE BORROWER AND THE SECURITY

United States Bureau of Consumer Financial Protection, Ability-to-Pay and Qualified Mortgage Standards Under Truth in Lending Act (Regulation Z)
12 C.F.R. Part 1026 (eff. Jan. 10, 2014).

SUMMARY OF THE ABILITY-TO-REPAY AND QUALIFIED MORTGAGE RULE AND THE CONCURRENT PROPOSAL

The Consumer Financial Protection Bureau (Bureau) is issuing a final rule to implement laws requiring mortgage lenders to consider consumers' ability to repay home loans before extending them credit. The rule will take effect on January 10, 2014.

. . .

During the years preceding the mortgage crisis, too many mortgages were made to consumers without regard to the consumer's ability to repay the loans. Loose underwriting practices by some creditors—including failure to verify the consumer's income or debts and qualifying consumers for mortgages based on "teaser" interest rates that would cause monthly payments to jump to unaffordable levels after the first few years—contributed to a mortgage crisis that led to the nation's most serious recession since the Great Depression.

In response to this crisis, in 2008 the Federal Reserve Board (Board) adopted a rule under the Truth in Lending Act which prohibits creditors from making "higher-price mortgage loans" without assessing consumers' ability to repay the loans. Under the Board's rule, a creditor is presumed to have complied with the ability-to-repay requirement if the creditor follows certain specified underwriting practices. This rule has been in effect since October 2009.

In the 2010 Dodd-Frank Wall Street Reform and Consumer Protection Act, Congress required that for residential mortgages, creditors must make a reasonable and good faith determination based on verified and documented information that the consumer has a reasonable ability to repay the loan according to its terms. Congress also established a presumption of compliance for a certain category of mortgages, called "qualified mortgages." These provisions are similar, but not identical to, the Board's 2008 rule and cover the entire mortgage market rather than simply higher-priced mortgages. The Board proposed a rule to implement the new statutory requirements before authority passed to the Bureau to finalize the rule.

Summary of Final Rule

The final rule contains the following key elements:

Ability-to-Repay Determinations. The final rule describes certain minimum requirements for creditors making ability-to-repay determinations, but does not dictate that they follow particular underwriting models. At a minimum, creditors generally must consider eight underwriting factors: (1) current or reasonably expected income or assets; (2) current employment status; (3) the monthly payment on the covered transaction; (4) the monthly payment on any simultaneous loan; (5) the monthly payment for mortgage-related obligations; (6) current debt obligations, alimony, and child support; (7) the monthly debt-to-income ratio or residual income; and (8) credit history. Creditors must generally use reasonably reliable third-party records to verify the information they use to evaluate the factors.

The rule provides guidance as to the application of these factors under the statute. For example, monthly payments must generally be calculated by assuming that the loan is repaid in substantially equal monthly payments during its term. For adjustable-rate mortgages, the monthly payment must be calculated using the fully indexed rate or an introductory rate, whichever is higher. Special payment calculation rules apply for loans with balloon payments, interest-only payments, or negative amortization.

The final rule also provides special rules to encourage creditors to refinance "non-standard mortgages"—which include various types of mortgages which can lead to payment shock that can result in default— into "standard mortgages" with fixed rates for at least five years that reduce consumers' monthly payments.

Presumption for Qualified Mortgages. The Dodd-Frank Act provides that "qualified mortgages" are entitled to a presumption that the creditor making the loan satisfied the ability-to-repay requirements. However, the Act did not specify whether the presumption of compliance is conclusive (*i.e.,* creates a safe harbor) or is rebuttable. The final rule provides a safe harbor for loans that satisfy the definition of a qualified mortgage and are not "higher-priced," as generally defined by the Board's 2008 rule. The final rule provides a rebuttable presumption for higher-priced mortgage loans, as described further below.

The line the Bureau is drawing is one that has long been recognized as a rule of thumb to separate prime loans from subprime loans. Indeed, under the existing regulations that were adopted by the Board in 2008, only higher-priced mortgage loans are subject to an ability-to-repay requirement and a rebuttable presumption of compliance if creditors follow certain requirements. The new rule strengthens the requirements needed to qualify for a rebuttable presumption for subprime loans and defines with more particularity the grounds for rebutting the presumption. Specifically, the final rule provides that consumers may show a violation with regard to a subprime qualified mortgage by showing that, at the time the loan was originated, the consumer's income and debt obligations left insufficient residual income or assets to meet living expenses. The analysis would consider the consumer's monthly payments on the loan, loan-related obligations, and any simultaneous loans of which the creditor was aware, as well as any recurring, material living expenses of which the creditor was aware. Guidance accompanying the rule notes that the longer the period of time that the consumer has demonstrated actual ability to repay the loan by making timely payments, without modification or accommodation, after consummation or, for an adjustable-rate mortgage, after recast, the less likely the consumer will be able to rebut the presumption based on insufficient residual income.

With respect to prime loans—which are not currently covered by the Board's ability-to-repay rule—the final rule applies the new ability-to-repay requirement but creates a strong presumption for those prime loans that constitute qualified mortgages. Thus, if a prime loan satisfies the qualified mortgage criteria described below, it will be conclusively presumed that the creditor made a good faith and reasonable determination of the consumer's ability to repay.

General Requirements for Qualified Mortgages. The Dodd-Frank Act sets certain product-feature prerequisites and affordability underwriting requirements for qualified mortgages and vests discretion in the Bureau to decide whether additional underwriting or other requirements should apply. The final rule implements the statutory criteria, which generally prohibit loans with negative amortization, interest-only payments, balloon payments, or terms exceeding 30 years from being qualified mortgages. So-called "no-doc" loans where the creditor does not verify income or assets also cannot be qualified mortgages. Finally, a loan generally cannot be a qualified mortgage if the points and fees paid by the consumer exceed three percent of the total loan amount, although certain "bona fide discount points" are excluded for prime loans. The rule provides guidance on the calculation of points and fees and thresholds for smaller loans.

The final rule also establishes general underwriting criteria for qualified mortgages. Most importantly, the general rule requires that monthly payments be calculated based on the highest payment that will apply in the first five years of the loan and that the consumer have a total (or "back-end") debt-to-income ratio that is less than or equal to 43 percent. The appendix to the rule details the calculation of debt-to-income for these purposes, drawing upon Federal Housing Administration guidelines for such calculations. The Bureau believes that these criteria will protect consumers by ensuring that creditors use a set of underwriting requirements that generally safeguard affordability. At the same time, these criteria provide bright lines for creditors who want to make qualified mortgages.

The Bureau also believes that there are many instances in which individual consumers can afford a debt-to-income ratio above 43 percent based on their particular circumstances, but that such loans are better evaluated on an individual basis under the ability-to-repay criteria rather than with a blanket presumption. In light of the fragile state of the mortgage market as a result of the recent mortgage crisis, however, the Bureau is concerned that creditors may initially be reluctant to make loans that are not qualified mortgages, even though they are responsibly underwritten. The final rule therefore provides for a second, temporary category of qualified mortgages that have more flexible underwriting requirements so long as they satisfy the general product feature prerequisites for a qualified mortgage and also satisfy the underwriting requirements of, and are therefore eligible to be purchased, guaranteed or insured by either (1)the GSEs while they operate under Federal conservatorship or receivership; or (2) the U.S. Department of Housing and Urban Development, Department of Veterans Affairs, or Department of Agriculture or Rural Housing Service. This temporary provision will phase out over time as the various Federal agencies issue their own qualified mortgage rules and if GSE conservatorship ends, and in any event after seven years.

Rural Balloon-Payment Qualified Mortgages. The final rule also implements a special provision in the Dodd-Frank Act that would treat certain balloon-payment loans as qualified mortgages if they are originated and held in portfolio by small creditors operating predominantly in rural or underserved areas. This provision is designed to assure credit availability in rural areas, where some creditors may only offer balloon-payment mortgages. Loans are only eligible if they have a term of at least five years, a fixed-interest rate, and meet certain basic underwriting standards; debt-to-income ratios must be considered but are not subject to the 43 percent general requirement.

Creditors are only eligible to make rural balloon-payment qualified mortgages if they originate at least 50 percent of their first-lien mortgages in counties that are rural or underserved, have less than $2 billion in assets, and (along with their affiliates) originate no more than 500 first-lien mortgages per year. The Bureau will designate a list of "rural" and "underserved" counties each year, and has defined coverage more broadly than originally had been proposed. Creditors must generally hold the loans on their portfolios for three years in order to maintain their "qualified mortgage" status.

Other Final Rule Provisions. The final rule also implements Dodd-Frank Act provisions that generally prohibit prepayment penalties except for certain fixed-rate, qualified mortgages where the penalties satisfy certain restrictions and the creditor has offered the consumer an alternative loan without such penalties. To match with certain statutory changes, the final rule also lengthens to three years the time creditors must retain records that evidence compliance with the ability-to-repay and prepayment penalty provisions and prohibits evasion of the rule by structuring a closed-end extension of credit that does not meet the definition of open-end credit as an open-end plan.

J. Kevin Murray, Issues in Appraisal Regulation: The Cracks in the Foundation of the Mortgage Lending Process*

43 Loyola L.A. Law Review 1301, 1307–1312 (2010).

II. The Role of Appraisals in Real Estate Finance

When appraisers overvalue homes in response to pressure, key mortgage industry participants are exposed to increased risk. When inflated appraisals are used to support home mortgages, borrowers are saddled with debts that exceed home values. If borrowers are unable or unwilling to repay these excessive mortgages, lenders, secondary market investors, and federal mortgage insurers suffer substantial financial losses when actual home values cannot cover outstanding mortgage balances. As such losses mount, major financial institutions collapse, and federal financial resources are severely jeopardized.

A. The Typical Home Mortgage Transaction

To better understand the critical function of appraisals in the context of real estate finance, it is helpful to consider two typical home mortgage transactions. At the outset of a home sale, a buyer and seller agree on the price of a home and the buyer approaches a mortgage broker or proceeds directly to a lender to obtain a mortgage to finance the purchase of the home. Alternatively, a homeowner wishing to access home equity might obtain a home equity loan or access cash through refinancing an existing mortgage. In either case, the lender considers the borrower's creditworthiness and the value of the home in assessing the soundness of the requested mortgage or refinance. The borrower promises to make periodic payments on the loan and gives the lender a lien on the home as collateral to secure the mortgage. In the event that the borrower defaults, the lender relies upon the value of the home to recover the outstanding balance.

To ensure its recovery of the outstanding mortgage balance, the lender typically lends only a percentage—typically 80 percent—of the market value of the home. This is the maximum amount that can be extended while reasonably ensuring the lender's ability to recoup the outstanding loan balance through a foreclosure sale in the event of default. Accordingly, the lender seeks an appraiser to determine the market value of the home. If the requested loan amount is within the maximum percentage of the appraised market value, the lender will likely approve the loan.

After extending the loan, the lender can sell the loan to government-sponsored entities (GSEs), such as Fannie Mae and Freddie Mac. The GSEs use mortgages to create mortgage-backed securities to sell to investors on the secondary market. In such transactions, investors indirectly rely on appraisals in evaluating the quality of the loans supporting the securities they purchase.

---

*   Originally published in the *Loyola of Los Angeles Law Review* at 43 LOY. L.A. L. REV. 1301 (2010).

B.   The Appraisal Preparation Process

In preparing real estate appraisals, appraisers must collect, verify, and analyze all information necessary to develop and support credible opinions of value. To aid in this task, appraisers employ one or more of three valuation approaches, depending on the type of property being appraised; these consist of the sales comparison approach, the cost approach, and the income capitalization approach. For residential property appraisals, appraisers most commonly use the sales comparison approach. Under the sales comparison approach, the appraiser deems a property to have approximately the same value as similar properties in the area, which are commonly referred to as "comparables." An appraiser using the sales comparison approach must first identify recently sold comparables. The sale prices of these comparables establish a baseline value for the property. The appraiser then adjusts this baseline value to reflect the value of any major differences between the comparables and the property being appraised. The resulting figure serves as the preliminary appraisal value.

In addition to using comparable sales data, appraisers must identify and analyze any other variables affecting the property's market value. For example, an appraiser might consider the effects of existing or reasonably probable land-use regulations or trends in the local real estate market. These variables, which are often dynamic and ambiguous, can be difficult to quantify. As such, an appraiser must make assumptions that are supported by available information. For example, an appraiser evaluating a property subject to a potential zoning ordinance would need to make assumptions regarding both the likelihood of the ordinance's enactment and of the effect of the ordinance on the property's market value. After carefully analyzing comparable sales data and adjusting for other relevant variables, the appraiser should arrive at a figure that accurately reflects the market value of the appraised property.

C.   The Subjective Nature of Appraisals

Although appraisers use methods such as the sales comparison approach to enhance objectivity and accuracy, appraising is an imperfect science. The accuracy of any appraisal is subject to a number of variables, including the availability and reliability of information. The potential for inaccuracy in the preparation of real estate appraisals is especially evident in the sales comparison approach, where the selection and adjustment of comparables provide baseline values for the final appraisal. The utility of this approach is constrained by the availability of comparable sales data. If no recent comparable sales data is available, appraisers cannot use the approach. Furthermore, even where adequate comparable sales data is available, the data may not be reliable. For example, if the sale of a comparable is not a valid arm's length transaction, the sale price will not reflect the true market value of the property. An appraisal based on such a transaction will not accurately indicate the property's market value. Consequently, where information is limited or unreliable, even appraisals prepared by the most competent and conscientious appraisers are prone to inaccuracy.

In addition to limitations in the availability and reliability of information, the competency and judgment of individual appraisers can also affect the accuracy of real estate appraisals. Within the sales comparison approach, the selection of comparable property sales and the evaluation of adjustment features are products of each appraiser's knowledge, experience, and discretion in assessing similarity and value. As such, an appraiser's subjective evaluations can directly influence the final determination of a property's value. For example, two independent appraisers evaluating the same piece of property might choose different comparables. Alternatively, even if the two appraisers were to choose the same set of comparables, each might estimate different adjustment values or identify different adjustment features altogether. In either case, the appraisers would likely arrive at different final appraisal values, one or both of which would necessarily be inaccurate.

Given the extensive subjectivity and ambiguity inherent in the appraisal process, there is an abundance of legitimate reasons for inaccuracy in real estate appraisals. Because an appraisal is an opinion of value, often based on imperfect information and undefined variables, perfect accuracy cannot be expected. A margin of error must be assumed. As such, an inaccurate appraisal based on erroneous but good-faith assumptions can nonetheless be valid as an opinion of value. However, a problem arises when appraisers intentionally exploit the subjectivity and ambiguity in the appraisal process to reach predetermined values. Such misconduct corrupts the valuation function of appraisals and can have severe consequences for those who rely on them.

Unfortunately, unscrupulous appraisers can manipulate the subjective appraisal process in a number of ways to reach predetermined values. An appraiser wishing to inflate an appraisal can exaggerate the size or condition of a property. For example, an appraiser might misrepresent an unfinished basement as a habitable space and overvalue the home accordingly. Additionally, appraisers often overlook deferred maintenance or defective construction. In the Poconos area of Pennsylvania, appraisers ignored the deficient construction of hundreds of homes in order to satisfy the developers who hired them. Accordingly, buyers who could not detect the faulty construction relied on inflated appraisals in purchasing homes at prices that seemed reasonable compared to those in nearby New York City. Later, when the borrowers tried to sell or refinance their homes, they discovered that the difference between the prices they paid and their homes' market values was as much as $80,000. Since 1995, one in five mortgaged homes in the area—nearly 6,000 in total—has been foreclosed on.

Appraisals can also be manipulated in more subtle ways. As previously discussed, an appraiser can intentionally make poor assumptions about unavailable or incomplete information relevant to property valuation. For instance, an appraiser might assume that a property will be subject to favorable re-zoning or high market demand, either of which would increase the property's market value. Alternatively, an appraiser could select comparables dissimilar to a property being appraised. During an economic downturn in Denver, Colorado in the early 2000s, appraisers used outdated comparable sales data to support high appraisal values. Although actual home values declined as a result of the troubled economy, appraisers justified inflated appraisals with comparable sales data from a more prosperous period. As a result, appraisers artificially propped up the Denver real estate market at an unsustainable level for a full year, during which many homebuyers purchased overvalued homes. Although such misconduct is subtle, the resulting harm is severe.

NOTES

1. *Dodd-Frank Act.* As a response to the mortgage and financial crisis of 2008 and related issues, Congress enacted the Dodd-Frank Wall Street Reform and Consumer Protection Act in 2010, Pub. L. No. 111–203, § 929–Z, 124 Stat. 1376, 1871 (2010) (codified at 15 U.S.C. § 78o). The Act contains substantive provisions and delegates to numerous federal agencies the development to implement the legislation. The Act addresses structural issues in the financial industry, some of which affect the secondary market and securitization of mortgages. Other real estate related provisions deal directly with fraud issues in consumer mortgages to be regulated by a new Bureau of Consumer Financial Protection (a reading of which about lending standards is set out earlier in the chapter), quality of property appraisals, and curbs on steering of borrowers to costly mortgage products. In the commercial arena, originators of mortgage backed securities will be required to retain five percent of the credit risk on mortgages placed into pools, reducing incentives to sell weak mortgages to investors. The credit rating agencies, which had been heavily criticized for highly rating poor mortgage risks, were also scrutinized by the Act. See Murdock, The Dodd-Frank Wall Street Reform and Consumer Protect Act: What Caused the Financial Crisis and Will Dodd-Frank Prevent Future Crises?, 64 S.M.U. L. Rev. 1243 (2011); Singer, Best & Simon, Breaking Down Financial Reform, 14 J. Consumer & Comml. L. 2 (2010).

2. *Appraisals.* Inaccurate, incompetent, and fraudulent appraisals have been cited as one important cause of the 2008 mortgage finance crisis, as well as in the earlier savings and loan industry debacle of the 1980's. A recent study found that of 2,076 properties, 64% were appraised at values that exceeded the sales price by a total of $1.4 billion. See Julie Satow, Accuracy of Appraisals is Spotty, Study Says, N.Y. Times, May 8, 2012.

The Financial Institutions Reform, Recovery and Enforcement Act of 1989, 92 Stat. 3694, 12 U.S.C.A. § 3301 et seq., created a committee charged with reviewing state certification requirements for appraisers, monitoring the requirements of federal agencies with respect to appraisers, and reporting annually to Congress on its activities. Pursuant to the statute, the Office of Thrift Supervision promulgated appraisal rules for transactions by institutions regulated by OTS. 12 C.F.R. §§ 564.1–564.8. These regulations require that the appraisal method conform to the Uniform Standards of Professional Appraisal Practice adopted by the Appraisal Standards Board of the Appraisal Foundation. The regulations also require the appraiser to have no financial interest in the property or transaction, be engaged by the institution (rather than the borrower), and be state certified or licensed.

In December 2010, the FDIC, in response to appraisal shortcomings underlying the 2008 crisis, issues Interagency Appraisal and Evaluation Guidelines setting requirements for all federally insured depository institutions in selection and use of appraisals. Moreover, the Federal Reserve adopted a rule to implement § 129E of Dodd-Frank to prevent lender intrusion on independent judgment of appraisers. 12 C.F.R. § 226.42(c). For an excellent discussion of appraiser liability in general and the post-Dodd-Frank changes, see Green, Re-Appraising the Appraisers: Expanding the Liability to Buyers and Borrowers in the Story of the 2008 Financing Industry Crisis, 25 Probate & Prop. 10 (Nov./Dec. 2011).

See Lee, Mancuso, & Walter, Housing Finance: Major Developments in 1990, 46 Bus.Law. 1149, 1157–1171 (1991) (reviewing the OTS regulations); Vickory, Regulating Real Estate Appraisers: The Role of Fraudulent and Incompetent Real Estate Appraisals in the S & L Crisis and the FIRREA Solution, 19 Real Est.L.J. 3 (1990).

3. *Loan-Value Ratios.* OTS has promulgated regulations concerning loan-value ratios. For home loans over 90% of appraised value, the portion that exceeds 80% of value must be insured by a qualified private insurer. 12 C.F.R. § 545.32(d)(2) (covering federally chartered associations), § 563.97 (covering other associations). See also § 545.33(d). The Homeowners Protection Act of 1998, 12 U.S.C.A. §§ 4901–4910, regulates private mortgage insurance (among other provisions requiring disclosure of the borrower's right to cancel when the value exceeds 80% of the outstanding loan).

5. DISCRIMINATION, SUBPRIME MORTGAGES, AND PREDATORY LENDING

Associates Home Equity Services, Inc. v. Troup

Superior Court of New Jersey, Appellate Division, 2001.
343 N.J.Super. 254, 778 A.2d 529.

Before JUDGES HAVEY, CUFF and LISA. The opinion of the court was delivered by HAVEY, P.J.A.D.

This is a foreclosure action. Defendants Beatrice and Curtis Troup, African-Americans, obtained a mortgage loan from third-party defendant East Coast Mortgage Corp. (ECM) to pay for repairs on their Newark home made by third-party defendants Gary Wishnia, General Builders Supply, Inc. and Property Redevelopment Center, Inc. (collectively Wishnia). The mortgage and note were assigned by ECM to Associates Home Equity Services, Inc. (Associates). When the Troups defaulted, Associates instituted this foreclosure proceeding. The Troups filed a counterclaim against Associates and a third-party complaint against Wishnia and ECM, claiming violations of the Consumer Fraud Act (CFA), N.J.S.A. 56:8–1 to–106, the Law Against Discrimination (LAD), N.J.S.A. 10:5–1 to–49, the Fair Housing Act (FHA), 42 U.S.C.A. §§ 3601 to 3631, the Civil Rights Act (CRA), 42 U.S.C.A. § 1981, and the Truth-In-Lending Act (TILA), 15 U.S.C.A. § 1635. The trial court granted summary judgment dismissing all of the Troups' claims against Associates and ECM, and entered a judgment of foreclosure in favor of Associates. The court found that the terms of ECM's construction loan were not unconscionable and that the Troups' affirmative claims under the applicable state and federal laws were barred by the governing statute of limitations. We granted the Troups' motion for leave to appeal.

We affirm in part and reverse in part. We conclude that it was premature to dismiss the Troups' claim that Associates engaged in predatory lending activities. The Troups are entitled to discovery on this claim. Further, although the Troups' affirmative claims against Associates under the governing statutes are time-barred, they may be considered in support of the affirmative defense of equitable recoupment. See R. 4:5–4 (if a party mistakenly designates an affirmative defense as a counterclaim, the court may in the interest of justice, treat the pleading "as if there had been a proper designation"). We further conclude that genuine issues of material fact exist respecting whether the "Holder Rule," 16 C.F.R. § 433, applies in this case, subjecting ECM to liability for the wrongdoings of Wishnia, the home repair contractor. Fact issues also exist as to whether defendants engaged in unconscionable business practices under the CFA.

Considering the evidentiary material in a light most favorable to the Troups, see Brill v. Guardian Life Ins. Co. of Am., 142 N.J. 520, 666 A.2d 146 (1995), these are the facts. Beatrice Troup, a seventy-four year old African American, has lived at 62 Vanderpool Street in Newark for approximately forty years. Following a telephone solicitation by Gary Wishnia, an agent for General Builders Supply, Inc., Beatrice and her son Curtis executed a contract for exterior home repairs with General on September 1, 1995. The contract price was $38,500, payable "$479.75 for 240 months." Beatrice claims that Wishnia told her "not to worry, he would get me financing." An amended contract was executed on November 16, 1995, for additional interior home repairs, increasing the contract price to $49,990. The agreement provided that "[payments] are to be made beginning January 1, 1996 payable to Property Redevelopment Center, Inc. until permanent financing is obtained."[1]

Some time before September 14, 1995, Jeffrey Ahrens, ECM's representative, prepared the Troups' loan application. A credit search was conducted. According to Beatrice, the Troups had no personal dealings with ECM. She and her son Curtis dealt directly with Wishnia who arranged a limousine to transport the Troups to ECM's office to close the loan. Also, Wishnia did the "leg work" in processing the loan and obtained all income documentation required by ECM.

The Troups' loan application, dated September 14, 1995, but not signed by them until the closing date of April 27, 1996, provided for a $46,500 loan at an annual interest rate of 11.65 percent, adjustable after six months. The Truth-In-Lending disclosure form signed by the Troups at closing stated that the loan was a "balloon" type, payable in fifteen years, with the last payment being $41,603.58. The Troups were also charged four points, or four percent of the total loan amount. At the closing, Beatrice was required to execute a deed conveying the property to herself and her son.

At some point after April 27, 1996, ECM assigned the mortgage and note to Associates. On May 11, 1998, Associates filed a foreclosure complaint alleging that the Troups had failed to make the required payments under the mortgage and note. The Troups filed an answer, counterclaim and third-party complaint consisting of fifteen counts against the Wishnia defendants, ECM and Associates. Pertinent here are the counts charging Wishnia with "unconscionably poor" workmanship, and that Wishnia had conspired with ECM to place the mortgage financing with ECM and "to reap profits by subjecting the

---

[1]   Property Redevelopment Center was a separate enterprise operated by Wishnia.

Troups to unconscionable, illegal and fraudulent home repair and financing transactions." The Troups charged Associates and third-party defendants with unconscionable and deceptive conduct in violation of the CFA. They further allege that ECM violated the TILA by failing to provide them with a "clear and conspicuous notice" of the expiration date of their right to rescind, failing to make proper disclosures, and materially understating the finance charges. Finally, the Troups asserted that Associates "participated in, authorized and/or ratified and/or had constructive knowledge of" the deceptive unconscionable acts of ECM and engaged in predatory lending practices in violation of the FHA, the CRA, and the LAD.

In dismissing all of the Troups' claims against ECM and Associates, and entering a judgment of foreclosure in Associates' favor, the trial court found that the terms of the mortgage loan given to the Troups were not "unconscionable when looked at in its entirety," given the fact that, although a 6.6 percent rate was available to "prime borrowers," the Troups "did not appear to be AAA rating." The claims against ECM based on Wishnia's deceptive and unconscionable conduct and workmanship were dismissed because, according to the court, ECM could not be held accountable for Wishnia's conduct. The court also determined that all of the Troups' claims against ECM and Associates were barred by the governing statutes of limitations under the LAD, the FHA and the CFA. Finally, the court dismissed the Troups' demand for rescission under the TILA, concluding that "there was conspicuous notice given" of the right to rescind.

I

The Troups and amicus contend that the trial court erred in dismissing the Troups' claim of predatory/discriminatory lending practices against Associates, claiming that genuine fact issues exist precluding summary judgment. Amicus contends that at the very least the dismissal of the claim was premature because the Troups did not have the opportunity to develop it by way of meaningful discovery. We agree with amicus.[2]

The Troups and amicus claim that Associates engaged in a predatory lending practice by actively discriminating against them in consort with ECM by treating the Troups, African-Americans, less favorably than white borrowers in violation of the FHA, the CRA, and the LAD. Amicus adds that Associates may also be held accountable for ECM's discriminatory practice on the theory that Associates "controlled" ECM's conduct. The Troups do not seek money damages

---

[2] Amicus presented a certification to us by Elvin Wyly an Assistant Professor in the Department of Geography and the Center for Urban Research at Rutgers University. Because the certification was not presented below, we advised the parties that we would consider the certification only for the purpose of giving an overview concerning predatory lending practices in New Jersey. Professor Wyly states that it is evident from the data submitted pursuant to the Home Mortgage Disclosure Act of 1975 (HMDA), 12 U.S.C.A. §§ 2801 to 2810, that a "dual housing finance market exists in New Jersey for the refinance and home repair loans" market. Wyly reports that "urban areas of heavy minority concentration are being disproportionately serviced by subprime lenders. . . ." The HMDA's data reveals that in predominately minority neighborhoods, subprime lenders control nearly two-thirds of the home improvement market. He concludes: "[i]n the home improvement market, African-Americans are almost four times as likely to be slotted into subprime/lenders as whites, even after accounting for income, loan amount, and differences between deposit-taking banks and nondepository independent mortgage companies."

against Associates for any violation of these statutes. Rather, they argue that Associates' discriminatory conduct supports the affirmative defense of equitable recoupment in these foreclosure proceedings. The trial court did not address this issue.

Predatory lending has been described as:

> a mismatch between the needs and capacity of the borrower. . . . In essence, the loan does not fit the borrower, either because the borrower's underlying needs for the loan are not being met or the terms of the loan are so disadvantageous to that particular borrower that there is little likelihood that the borrower has the capability to repay the loan.

[Daniel S. Ehrenberg, If the Loan Don't Fit, Don't Take It: Applying the Suitability Doctrine to the Mortgage Industry to Eliminate Predatory Lending, 10 J. Affordable Housing & Community Dev. L. 117, 119–20 (Winter 2001).]

The Troups' expert, Calvin Bradford, summarized the concept of predatory lending as follows:

> In using the term "predatory lending" I refer to lenders who target certain populations for onerous credit terms. The population generally targeted includes, among others, the elderly, minorities, and residents of neighborhoods that do not have ready access to mainstream credit. Credit terms not warranted by the objective facts regarding the creditworthiness of these individuals are imposed upon them because for various reasons the lenders feel they can take advantage of a borrower. Typically predatory lenders take advantage of borrowers due to their lack of sophistication in the lending market, due to their lack of perceived options for the loan based on discrimination or some other factor, or due to deceptive practices engaged in by the lender that mislead or fail to inform the borrower of the real terms and conditions of the loan. The record in this case indicates that this is consistent with what occurred in the Troup transaction.

Specifically, the Troups and amicus charge "reverse redlining" in this case. "Redlining is 'the practice of denying the extension of credit to specific geographic areas due to the income, race or ethnicity of its residents.'" Hargraves v. Capital City Mortgage Corp., 140 F.Supp.2d 7, 20 (D.D.C.2000) (quoting United Companies Lending Corp. v. Sargeant, 20 F.Supp.2d 192, 203 n. 5 (D.Mass.1998)). The term "redlining" is derived from the actual practice of drawing a red line around designated areas in which credit is to be denied. Sargeant, supra, 20 F.Supp.2d at 203 n. 5. "Reverse redlining is the practice of extending credit on unfair terms to those same communities." Ibid.; see also Hargraves, supra, 140 F.Supp.2d at 20; Honorable v. Easy Life Real Estate Sys., 100 F.Supp.2d 885, 892 (N.D.Ill.2000). Congress has reported that "reverse redlining . . . [is] the targeting of residents of those same communities for credit on unfair terms. Considerable testimony before the committee indicates that the communities lacking access to traditional lending institutions are being victimized in this fashion by second mortgage lenders, home improvement contractors, and finance companies. . . ." S.Rep. No. 103–169, U.S.Code Cong. &

Admin.News 1994, 1881 at 1905. Reverse redlining has been held to violate the FHA and the CRA. Honorable, supra, 100 F.Supp.2d at 892. We do not hesitate to conclude that the practice violates the LAD as well. See N.J.S.A. 10:5–12i(1) (it is unlawful for a mortgage company to "discriminate against any person . . . because of race, . . . in the granting, . . . or in the fixing of the rates, terms, conditions or provisions" of a mortgage loan).

A plaintiff may establish a colorable claim of reverse redlining by demonstrating that "defendants' lending practices and loan terms were 'unfair' and 'predatory,' and that the defendants either intentionally targeted on the basis of race, or that there is a disparate impact on the basis of race." Hargraves, supra, 140 F.Supp.2d at 20. See also United States v. Mitchell, 580 F.2d 789, 791 (5th Cir.1978) (the FHA prohibits "not only direct discrimination but practices with racially discouraging effects"); and see Jackson v. Okaloosa County, 21 F.3d 1531, 1543 (11th Cir.1994) (FHA violation can be demonstrated by a showing of either direct discrimination or discriminatory effects).

In this case the Troups' predatory lending claim was dismissed without permitting them to conduct meaningful discovery on the issue. The Troups laid the foundation for a reverse redlining case by establishing that they are African Americans living in a predominately African-American neighborhood in Newark. Their expert stated that the 11.65 percent interest rate and other terms of the loan were unjustified from an objective viewpoint, given the Troups' credit history and favorable debt-to-income ratio. Moreover, an Associates' representative testified during deposition that Associates paid a premium of $2,325 to ECM for securing the Troups' loan. He explained that "[w]e [Associates] pay a premium for the loan . . . [which] increase[s] as the interest rate of the loan increased," a practice recognized in the lending community as "yield spread premium."

Also significant is the fact that Associates gave ECM a "pre-approval determination" on February 23, 1996, two months before the Troups executed their loan application with ECM and ECM assigned the loan to Associates nine days after the loan was closed. The Troups argue that a fair inference can be drawn from these facts that Associates participated in inflating the interest rate and imposed the terms of the loan characterized by the Troups' expert as "onerous." These facts at the very least are supportive of the Troups' claim that Associates participated in the targeting of inner-city borrowers who lack access to traditional lending institutions, charged them a discriminatory interest rate, and imposed unreasonable terms.

With this showing, we agree with the Troups and amicus that the Troups were entitled to additional discovery in order to bolster their predatory-lending assertion. See Wilson v. Amerada Hess Corp., 168 N.J. 236, 253, 773 A.2d 1121 (2001) (slip op. at 22) (denial of discovery was abuse of discretion because "we cannot dismiss the possibility that the information plaintiffs sought would raise a jury question on the issue of breach of the implied covenant"). They understandably seek additional information from Associates respecting any guidelines it followed in fixing the rate and terms of the Troups' loan, and whether in fact those guidelines are facially, or as applied, discriminatory against borrowers based on their place of residence, income, race or ethnicity.

Further, we agree with the Troups that they are entitled to be informed concerning loans made by ECM and Associates to other New Jersey borrowers during the time period when the loan was made to the Troups. This information may or may not disclose a pattern of discriminatory lending practice in New Jersey's inner cities. If it does, the trial court should consider the Troups' request for further information about the loans, such as the location of the property, and race and income of the borrowers. The discovery order must not, of course, be overly burdensome and should be made subject to any legitimate claim of confidentiality, appropriate protective orders and redaction.

We agree with the trial court that the Troups' affirmative claims for damages against Associates under the FHA, the CRA and the LAD are barred by the governing statutes of limitations. The alleged discriminatory conduct on the part of ECM and Associates occurred from September 1995 through April 27, 1996, when the Troups closed on their loan. The Troups filed their counterclaim and third-party complaint on August 9, 1999. The Troups' claims under the CRA, the FHA and the LAD are governed by a two-year statute of limitations.

However, the Troups' claims under the pertinent federal and state statutes are cognizable under the theory of equitable recoupment as an affirmative defense to Associates' foreclosure complaint. "[T]he fundamental purpose of recoupment ... is the examination of a transaction in all its aspects to achieve a just result." Beneficial Fin. Co. of Atlantic City v. Swaggerty, 86 N.J. 602, 612, 432 A.2d 512 (1981). A successful recoupment defense acts to reduce the amount the plaintiff can recover on the claim for the debt when the counterclaim arises from the same transaction. Id. at 611, 432 A.2d 512.

Further, it has been observed that:

> any claim of recoupment must arise out of the identical transaction that provided plaintiff with a cause of action, and no affirmative relief may be granted independent of plaintiff's claim. As an equitable concept, judges invented the doctrine of equitable recoupment in order to avoid an unusually harsh or egregious result from a strict application of a statute of limitations.

[Midlantic Nat'l Bank v. Georgian Ltd., 233 N.J.Super. 621, 625–26, 559 A.2d 872 (Law Div.1989) (quoting Superior Air Prods. Int'l v. Dir., Div. of Taxation, 9 N.J. Tax 463, 470–71, aff'd, 10 N.J. Tax 238 (App.Div.1988) (citations omitted)).]

Consequently, "the defense of recoupment 'is never barred by the statute of limitations so long as the main action itself is timely.'" Nester v. O'Donnell, 301 N.J.Super. 198, 208, 693 A.2d 1214 (App.Div.1997) (quoting Beneficial, supra, 86 N.J. at 609, 432 A.2d 512).

Consequently, the Troups may assert their recoupment defense under both New Jersey and federal law notwithstanding expiration of the controlling statutes of limitations. See Beneficial, supra, 86 N.J. at 608, 432 A.2d 512 (borrowers have the right to assert recoupment in a counterclaim against lender under the TILA, despite expiration of the one-year statute of limitations). The recoupment defense in this case arises out of the same transaction as the claim for the debt. Id. at 610, 432 A.2d 512. The underlying loan transaction was the common source of both the Troups' liability to pay the debt and their correlative rights under the fair housing and civil rights statutes. The Troups' recoupment defense is not intended to invalidate the debt; it is asserted to reduce the amount that Associates may recover on its claim.

Associates argue that the underlying premise of recoupment is inapplicable here because its complaint is for foreclosure, rather than for collection of a debt. In support of that proposition, it cites New York Guardian Mortgage Corp. v. Dietzel, 362 Pa.Super. 426, 524 A.2d 951, 953 (1986), which concluded that "a judgment in foreclosure is not a judgment for money damages" under the TILA, observing that:

> An action in mortgage foreclosure is strictly an in rem proceeding, and the purpose of a judgment in mortgage foreclosure is solely to effect a judicial sale of the mortgaged property. A judgment in a mortgage foreclosure action is not a judgment for money damages and therefore cannot be "an action to collect amounts owed" or "an action to collect the debt" as required under § 1640(h) and (e) of the Truth-In-Lending Act.

[Ibid. (citation omitted).]

The Bankruptcy Court in Dangler v. Central Mortgage Co., 75 B.R. 931, 935 (Bkrtcy.E.D.Pa.1987), expressly disagreed with New York Guardian, holding that "[o]n its own terms, the [New York Guardian] decision is plainly incorrect." Id. at 935.

Further, a foreclosure action is not strictly an in rem proceeding. It is a quasi in rem procedure, Resolution Trust Corp. v. Berman Indus., Inc., 271 N.J.Super. 56, 62, 637 A.2d 1297 (Law Div.1993), to determine not only the right to foreclose, but also the amount due on the mortgage. Central Penn. Nat'l Bank v. Stonebridge Limited, 185 N.J.Super. 289, 302, 448 A.2d 498 (Ch.Div.1982). As stated, what the Troups seek is a diminution of the amount due based on Associates' violation of statutory fair housing and civil rights laws. In our view, it would be fundamentally unfair and contrary to the remedial goals expressed by these statutes to preclude the recoupment remedy simply because it is invoked in a foreclosure proceeding. Without the defense, the mortgagee could simply take the mortgaged premises, leaving the borrower without a remedy. We therefore, reverse the summary judgment order dismissing the Troups' claim against Associates, and direct that an appropriate discovery order be entered.

II

The Troups and amicus argue that the trial court erred in dismissing the Troups' claims against ECM and Ahrens based on the so-called "Holder Rule."

16 C.F.R. § 433.2 (2001) provides that, in connection with any sale of goods or services to consumers, affecting commerce, it is an unfair or deceptive act or practice within the meaning of § 5 of the Federal Trade Commission Act for a seller to accept as full or partial payment for the services rendered:

the proceeds of any purchase money loan (as purchase money loan is defined herein), unless any consumer credit contract made in connection with such purchase money loan contains the following provision in at least ten point, bold face, type:

NOTICE

ANY HOLDER OF THIS CONSUMER CREDIT CONTRACT IS SUBJECT TO ALL CLAIMS AND DEFENSES WHICH THE DEBTOR COULD ASSERT AGAINST THE SELLER OF GOODS OR SERVICES OBTAINED WITH THE PROCEEDS HEREOF. RECOVERY HEREUNDER BY THE DEBTOR SHALL NOT EXCEED AMOUNTS PAID BY THE DEBTOR HEREUNDER.

[Id. at § 433.2(a).]

A "[c]onsumer credit contract" is defined as "[a]ny instrument which evidences or embodies a debt arising from a 'Purchase Money Loan' transaction or a 'financed sale'. . . ." 16 C.F.R. at § 431.1(i) (2001). 16 C.F.R. § 433.1(e) defines "[f]inancing a sale" as "[e]xtending credit to a consumer in connection with a 'Credit Sale' within the meaning of the TILA and Regulation Z." The TILA, specifically 15 U.S.C.A. § 1602(g) defines "credit sale" as:

> any sale in which the seller is a creditor. The term includes any contract in the form of bailment or lease if the bailee or lessee contracts to pay as compensation for use a sum substantially equivalent to or in excess of the aggregate value of the property and services involved and it is agreed that the bailee or lessee will become, or for no other nominal consideration has the option to become, the owner of the property upon full compliance with his obligations under the contract.

[Ibid. (emphasis added).]

Further, Regulation Z defines "credit sale" as "any sale in which the seller is a creditor." 12 C.F.R. § 226.2(a)(16).

Essentially, the Holder Rule strips the ultimate holder of the paper of its traditional status as a holder-in-due-course and subjects it to any potential defenses which the purchaser might have against the seller. Federal Trade Comm'n v. Winters Nat'l Bank & Trust Co., 601 F.2d 395, 397 (6th Cir.1979). The Federal Trade Commission has included within the reach of the Holder Rule those sellers and creditors who "employ procedures in the course of arranging the financing of a consumer sale which separate the buyer's duty to pay for goods or services rendered from the seller's reciprocal duty to perform as promised." 40 F.Reg. 53,506, 53,522 (1975). The agency has recognized this practice as "dragging the body," wherein:

> a merchant, desiring to circumvent restrictions upon the holder in due course doctrine, arranges for a consumer purchase to be financed by a cooperating financing agency. The resultant financial transaction has the appearance of a direct cash loan, payment of which can be enforced by the loan company without reference to the underlying transaction.

[40 F.Reg., supra, at 53,514.]

Consequently, the Holder Rule expressly incorporates "purchase money loan[s]" within the scope of the rule. See 16 C.F.R. § 433.2(b). A "[p]urchase money loan" is defined as "[a] cash advance which is received by a consumer" which is applied "in whole or substantial part, to a purchase of goods or services from a seller who (1) refers consumers to the creditor or (2) is affiliated with the creditor by common control, contract or business arrangement." 16 C.F.R. § 431.1(d).

Here, there is at the very least a fact issue concerning whether ECM's note constituted a "purchase money loan." ECM's financing provided the Troups with a "cash advance" totaling $49,990 which was applied in "substantial part" to pay for the improvements made to the home by Wishnia. Ibid. There is also evidence that Wishnia "refers consumers" to ECM. Ibid. Indeed, in this case Wishnia made all the arrangements for the loan and had the Troups chauffeured to ECM's offices to close. A reasonable jury could also conclude that Wishnia was "affiliated with" ECM by "business arrangement." Ibid.[7] The Troups presented evidence that Wishnia and ECM had mutually arranged at least six other home improvement or equity loans to other customers living in the City of Newark or the Newark area.

Nevertheless, ECM argues that the Holder Rule is inapplicable for three reasons. First, it claims that it did not "purchase" a "consumer credit contract" because initially the Troups paid Wishnia's affiliated companies monthly payments on the home repair contracts before the loan was made by ECM. This argument ignores the undisputed evidence that, before the Troups signed the first contract, Wishnia told Beatrice "not to worry, he would get [her] financing." Further, the second contract provides that "[payments] are to be made beginning January 1, 1996 payable to Property Redevelopment Center, Inc. until permanent financing is obtained." (Emphasis added). Indeed, after the contract was executed, Wishnia promptly arranged the loan with ECM, with whom he had placed other home repair contracts on behalf of other borrowers. In our view, reasonable minds could conclude that Wishnia and ECM contemplated from the outset that the loan to finance Wishnia's contracting work would be placed by ECM. We agree with the Troups that, under these circumstances, Wishnia and ECM should not be permitted to circumvent the consequences of the Holder Rule simply because Wishnia arranged for temporary financing with his affiliated companies.

Second, ECM argues that the Holder Rule is inapplicable because the bold-typed notice required by 16 C.F.R. 433.2 was never placed on the relevant documents. We reject that argument. Although it is true that the documents did not contain the requisite notice, it is inconceivable to us that ECM and Ahrens may evade the remedial reach of the Holder Rule simply because of that omission. It was their responsibility to insert the notice. Indeed, as a financing institution, ECM must be charged with notice of the requirement. Moreover, the bold-typed notice is required by New Jersey law. N.J.A.C. 13:45A–16.2(a)(13) ii, states:

---

[7] A "[b]usiness arrangement" is defined as "[a]ny understanding, procedure, course of dealing, or arrangement, formal or informal, between a creditor and a seller, in connection with the sale of goods or services to consumers or the financing thereof." 16 C.F.R. § 433.1(g).

No home improvement contract shall require or entail the execution of any note, unless such note shall have conspicuously printed thereon the disclosures required by . . . Federal law (16 C.F.R. section 433.2) concerning the preservation of buyers' claims and defenses.

"[T]he law is a silent factor in every contract." Silverstein v. Keane, 19 N.J. 1, 13, 115 A.2d 1 (1955) (citation and quotation marks omitted). Moreover, equity looks to substance rather than form. Kleinberg v. Schwartz, 87 N.J.Super. 216, 222, 208 A.2d 803 (App.Div.), aff'd, 46 N.J. 2, 214 A.2d 313 (1965). These well-settled maxims should apply here to effectuate New Jersey's regulatory goal by "reading into" the pertinent documents the notice required by 16 C.F.R. § 433.2 and N.J.A.C. 13:45A–16.2(a)(13) ii.

Third, ECM claims that the Holder Rule is inapplicable because it has assigned the note to Associates.[8] We reject that argument as well. The clear and unambiguous language of the Rule "notifies all potential holders that, if they accept an assignment of the contract, they will be 'stepping into the seller's shoes.'" Lozada v. Dale Baker Oldsmobile, Inc., 91 F.Supp.2d 1087, 1094 (W.D.Mich.2000) (quoting Oxford Fin. Cos., Inc. v. Velez, 807 S.W.2d 460, 463 (Tex.Ct.App.1991) (emphasis added)). Thus, the creditor-assignee becomes "'subject to' any claims or defenses the debtor can assert against the seller." Oxford Fin., supra, 807 S.W.2d at 463; and see Simpson v. Anthony Auto Sales, Inc., 32 F.Supp.2d 405, 409 n. 10 (W.D.La.1998) (holding that the Holder Rule permits consumers to bring claims against assignee without regard to whether damages warranted rescission). Here, ECM, as "a potential holder" had notice that if it procured the purchase money loan arranged by Wishnia, it may be stepping into Wishnia's shoes. We cannot accept the proposition that the FTC contemplated that such result would not attach simply because of a subsequent assignment of the loan, especially when, as here, it is claimed that ECM actively participated with Wishnia, the seller, in placing the loan with the Troups.

We conclude that fact issues exist respecting ECM's liability under the Holder Rule. Summary judgment dismissing the Troups' claims is therefore reversed. Ahrens' argument that there is no basis to hold him personally liable may be revisited after conclusion of all discovery concerning application of the Holder Rule.

III

The Troups argue that the trial court erred in dismissing their consumer fraud claims against Associates and third-party defendants.

N.J.S.A. 56:8–2 prohibits:

[t]he act, use or employment by any person of any unconscionable commercial practice, deception, fraud, false pretense, false promise, misrepresentation, or the knowing, concealment, suppression, or omission of any material fact with intent that others rely upon [it] . . . in connection with the sale or advertisement of . . . merchandise. . . .

[Ibid. (emphasis added).]

---

8   The Troups do not argue that the Holder Rule applies to Associates.

Loans are included in the definition of "advertisement," N.J.S.A. 56:8–1(a), and the definition of "merchandise," see N.J.S.A. 56:8–1(c), has been held to include "the offering, sale, or provision of consumer credit." Lemelledo v. Beneficial Management Corp., 150 N.J. 255, 265, 696 A.2d 546 (1997).

The word "unconscionable" must be interpreted liberally so as to effectuate the public purpose of the CFA. Kugler v. Romain, 58 N.J. 522, 543, 279 A.2d 640 (1971). It is not intended to "erase the doctrine of freedom of contract, but to make realistic the assumption of the law that the agreement has resulted from real bargaining between parties who had freedom of choice and understanding and ability to negotiate in a meaningful fashion." Id. at 544, 279 A.2d 640. The standard of conduct contemplated by the unconscionability clause is "good faith, honesty in fact and observance of fair dealing[,]" and the need for application of that standard "is most acute when the professional seller is seeking the trade of those most subject to exploitation-the uneducated, the inexperienced and the people of low incomes." Ibid. Whether a particular practice is unconscionable must be determined on a case-by-case basis. Id. at 543, 279 A.2d 640. In this case, whether the acts of Associates and third-party defendants were unconscionable was for the jury to decide.

As noted, the trial court concluded that the rate charged and terms of the loan were not unconscionable. The trial court's assessment of the terms of the loan ignored the opinion of the Troups' expert, Calvin Bradford. Bradford, stated that "[t]he average initial rate on a one year adjustable rate mortgage in April 1996 was 5.73[%]" (the Troups received a rate of 11.65%). Moreover, Bradford stated that the "[a]verage points in April 1996 on one year adjustable mortgages was 1.4" (the Troups were charged four points). Bradford observed that ECM's credit report listed no negatives on Beatrice's credit history, while Curtis Troup's credit history revealed only a $75 "charge off" and a DMV liability of $250. The expert also claimed that the Troups' debt-to-income ratio was favorable. In sum, Bradford opined that "the income, credit history and other factors . . . [did] not warrant the credit terms given to the Troups."

Conversely, third-party defendants assert that the Troups received higher loan terms because of their "derogatory" credit history. However, the "derogatory history" offered mainly concerns the Troups' sketchy credit after the loan was obtained. Further, the trial court's finding that ECM's conduct regarding the procurement of the loan, specifically, that the Troups did not lack bargaining power, is at best conclusory. The trial court stated:

> This Court is not satisfied that the terms were unfavorable nor that there was any disproportionate bargaining power between the Troups and the lending institution. While it does appear that the Troups did not bargain with the lending institution, that does not in and of itself mean they had no bargaining power.

It is well established, however, that "'[t]he effect of the unconscionability rule is not designed to upset the terms of a contract resulting from superior bargaining strength, but to prevent oppression and unfair surprise.'" Jefferson Loan Co., Inc. v. Livesay, 175

N.J.Super. 470, 480, 419 A.2d 1164 (Dist.Ct.1980) (quoting New Jersey Study Comment to N.J.S.A. 12A:2–302, par. 1). The Troups stated in their answers to interrogatories that they spoke to no one from ECM until they were brought to ECM's offices to sign the loan papers on April 27, 1996. Beatrice was confused because of the number and complexity of the documents. When she asked ECM's attorney if the principal balance will be due in fifteen years, the attorney told her not to worry about it. We are satisfied that, considering all of the evidentiary material in a light most favorable to the Troups, a reasonable jury could conclude that Associates and third-party defendants engaged in an unconscionable business practice. Therefore, we reverse the summary judgment order dismissing the consumer fraud claim.

IV

We affirm the trial court's dismissal of the Troups' demand for rescission under the TILA. 15 U.S.C.A. § 1635(a) relevantly states:

> in the case of any consumer credit transaction . . . the obligor shall have the right to rescind the transaction until midnight of the third business day following the consummation of the transaction or the delivery of the information and rescission forms. . . . The creditor shall clearly and conspicuously disclose . . . to any obligor in a transaction subject to this section the rights of the obligor under this section.

Further, 15 U.S.C.A. § 1635(f) provides:

> An obligor's right of rescission shall expire three years after the date of consummation of the transaction or upon the sale of the property . . . notwithstanding the fact that the information and forms required under this section or any other disclosures required under this part have not been delivered to the obligor. . . .

12 C.F.R. § 226.23 (2001) provides that the notice of right to rescind shall clearly and conspicuously disclose: (1) the consumer's right to rescind the transaction; (2) how to exercise the right to rescind with a form for that purpose, which must include the address of the creditor's place of business; (3) the effect of rescission; and (4) the date the rescission period expires.

The purpose of the three-day waiting period under § 1635(a) is to give the consumer the opportunity to reconsider any transaction which would have the serious consequence of encumbering title to his or her home. If a lender's notice of the right to rescind is deficient, a mortgagor's rescission rights are extended to three years. 15 U.S.C.A. § 1635(f). If the creditor fails to comply with the written requirements of the notice to rescind, or if a "material" disclosure is not correctly made, the rescission period is extended for three years. Ibid., 12 C.F.R. § 226.23(a)(3).

We agree with the trial court's determination that the notice of right to cancel in this case complied with the mandates of the TILA. The "date of the loan" is "4/27/1996." The form signed by the Troups is clearly identified as the "Notice of Right to Cancel" and contains ECM's address. Further, the notice provides a subtitle "How to Cancel," which informed the Troups as to the manner, date and method of cancellation.

The Troups argue that the notice is confusing because under the subtitle "I Wish to Cancel" is the date "4/27/1996." They argue that the insertion of the date had the effect of causing them to believe that their right to cancel expired on that date. We disagree. On the same page as this notation, the Notice of Right to Cancel expressly states: "[y]ou have a legal right under federal law to cancel this transaction, without cost, within three business days from . . . the date of the loan shown above. . . ." The "date of the loan" is "4/27/1996." We are satisfied that the notice of right to cancel is clear and unambiguous. See Smith v. Highland, 915 F.Supp. 281, 285 (N.D.Ala.1996), aff'd, 108 F.3d 1325 (11th Cir.1997). Indeed, the notice is substantially similar, if not identical, to the form suggested in the Federal Regulations. 13 C.F.R., Pt. 226, App. H.

The Troups further argue that the three-year time for rescission is applicable because ECM failed to disclose as a "finance charge," a $50 disbursement fee imposed by ECM's attorney. Notably, the Troups' counterclaim alleges that ECM failed to properly disclose a $25 recording fee and a $360 fee for the payoff of a judgment lien. It makes no mention of the $50 fee imposed by ECM's attorney.

15 U.S.C.A. § 1635(i)(2) provides that "any finance charge shall be treated as being accurate for the purposes of this section if the amount disclosed as the finance charge does not vary from the actual finance charge by more than $35. . . ." The Troups argue that the fee charged by ECM's attorney, being in excess of $35, constitutes an undisclosed "finance charge." However, 15 U.S.C.A. § 1605(a) expressly states that the "finance charge shall not include fees and amounts imposed by third party closing agents (including settlement agents, attorneys . . .) if the creditor does not require the imposition of the charges or the services provided and does not retain the charges." (Emphasis added). The $50 fee complained of was payable to a third party closing agent. It was not a disbursement fee required by ECM or retained by it.

Affirmed in part, reversed and remanded in part.

NOTES

1. *Discrimination Against Borrowers.* As indicated in the principal excerpt, antidiscrimination laws generally forbid lenders from evaluating prospective borrowers on the basis of criteria unrelated to creditworthiness. The 1968 Civil Rights Act, as amended in 1988, prohibits lenders from discriminating in the making or purchasing of a loan for the purchase, construction, or repair of a dwelling or in a loan secured by residential real estate based on a person's "race, color, religion, sex, handicap, familial status, or national origin." 42 U.S.C.A. § 3605 (1995). The Equal Credit Opportunity Act of 1974, as amended, prohibits "any creditor to discriminate against any applicant, with respect to any aspect of a credit transaction—(1) on the basis of race, color, religion, national origin, sex or marital status, or age . . ." and authorizes the Federal Reserve Board to promulgate regulations implementing the Act. 15 U.S.C.A. §§ 1691(a), 1691(b) (1982).

The Federal Reserve oversees the collection of data pursuant to the Home Mortgage Disclosure Act of 1975. Commencing with 2004 data released in March 2005 pursuant to Regulation C under the Act, 12 C.F.R.

pt. 203, the Federal Reserve altered some of the categories on race and ethnicity, making comparisons to prior data difficult. See Avery, Canner & Cook, New Information Reported Under HMDA and Its Application in Fair Lending Enforcement, Federal Reserve Bull., pp. 344, 351, Summer 2005.

Despite this legislation, the 2004 data show that African-Americans are more likely to be denied mortgage loans than non-Hispanic whites and are likely to be paying a higher price for loans (even when controlling for borrower related factors and the nature of the lender). See Avery, Canner & Cook, supra, at pp. 376, 379–380. The experience of Hispanic whites fell between that of African-Americans and non-Hispanic whites. See Edwards v. Flagstar Bank, 109 F.Supp.2d 691 (E.D.Mich.2000) (upholding damages against bank for discrimination against African-Americans in loan applications and relying on statistical evidence), aff'd in part, rev'd in part sub nom Paschal v. Flagstar Bank, 295 F.3d 565 (6th Cir. 2002) (upholding judgment in favor of one set of plaintiffs and reversing against another set). Some courts employ presumptions to permit plaintiffs to proceed or prevail on discrimination claims. See, e.g., Ramirez v. GreenPoint Mortgage Funding, Inc., 2008 WL 2051018 (N.D. Cal. 2008) (claim that a mortgage company's discretionary pricing policy had a disparate impact on minorities survived a motion to dismiss claim alleging discrimination under the Fair Housing Act); M & T Mortgage Corp. v. Foy, 20 Misc.3d 274, 858 N.Y.S.2d 567 (2008) (mortgage to minority mortgagor with an interest rate of 9.5% when 30-year Treasury rate had exceeded 6% only twice since 2000 created a rebuttable presumption that the mortgage was discriminatory).

For studies showing discrimination, see Home Mortgage Disclosure Act: Expanded Data on Residential Lending, Federal Reserve Bulletin, Nov. 1991, pp. 859–881; Munnell, Browne, McEnearney & Tootell, Mortgage Lending in Boston: Interpreting HMDA Data (Fed.Res. Bank of Boston 1992) (showing that African-American and Latino borrowers were sixty percent more likely to be turned down than similar white applicants); Carr & Megbolugbe, The Federal Bank of Boston Study on Mortgage Lending Revisited (Fannie Mae Office of Housing Research 1993) (defending the validity of the study); but see Bostic, The Role of Race in Mortgage Lending: Revisiting the Boston Fed Study (1996) (arguing that minorities are disadvantage only among "marginal" applicants, and that among wealthy applicants and those with clean credit histories there are not significantly different outcomes based on race). See generally Been, Ellen & Madar, The High Cost of Segregation: Exploring Racial Disparities in High-Cost Lending, 36 Fordham Urb. L.J. 361 (2009); Sarto, Note: The Disproportionate Representation of Women in Subprime Lending: Cause, Effect, and Remedies, 31 Women's Rights L. Rep. 337 (2011); Bybee, Fair Lending 2.0: A Borrower-Based Solution to Discrimination in Mortgage Lending, U. Mich. J.L. Ref. 113 (2011); Cassidy, The Fair Housing Act, Disparate Impact, and the Ability-to-Repay: A Compliance Dilemma For Mortgage Lenders, 32 Rev. Banking & Fin. L. 431 (2013); Gordon, The Creation of Homeownership: How the New Deal Changes in Banking Regulation Made Homeownership Accessible to Whites and Out of Reach for Blacks, 115 Yale L.J. 186 (2005); Ambrose, Hughes & Simmons, Policy Issues Concerning Racial and Ethnic Differences in Home Loan Rejection Rates, 6 J. Housing Research 115 (1995); Bogdon and Bell, Making Fair Lending a Reality in the New Millennium (Fannie Mae Foundation 1999); Mahoney, The End(s) of Disparate Impact: Doctrinal Reconstruction, Fair Housing and Lending Law, and the Antidiscrimination Principle, 47 Emory

L.J. 409 (1998); Schuster, Lending Discrimination: Is the Secondary Market Helping to Make the "American Dream" a Reality?, 36 Gonzaga L. Rev. 153 (2000.

2. *Discrimination Against Neighborhoods.* Congress and the state legislatures have been slower to outlaw the more subtle and complex discrimination that can occur when lenders appraise the land being offered as security for a mortgage loan. Many lenders have historically refused to make mortgage loans in blighted or deteriorating urban neighborhoods on the ground that declining property values will impair their mortgage security over the life of the loan. Those lenders that do make mortgage loans in these areas characteristically seek to protect themselves by imposing such onerous terms on the borrower as a shorter than normal term, lower loan to value ratio, or higher interest rates.

"Redlining"—so-called because lenders once marked local maps in red pencil to indicate neighborhoods in which loans were disfavored—poses a classic public policy dilemma. As Professor John Payne has observed, "The conundrum is that of the chicken and the egg: Without private capital, urban redevelopment is difficult to achieve; without urban stability, investment security is difficult to demonstrate. Which should come first?" Payne, Banking Institutions Trim State Efforts to Enforce Anti-Redlining Measures, 9 Real Est. L.J. 357 (1981).

The dilemma is evident in the history of the FHA's policies for insuring mortgages in deteriorating urban areas. In its early years, the FHA acted conservatively, guaranteeing only loans that were "economically sound." Frequently this meant refusing to insure loans in marginal or racially mixed areas. See FHA Underwriting Manual (1938), quoted in U.S. Commission on Civil Rights, Report No. 4, Housing 16–17 (1961). In response to charges that these underwriting policies were contributing to urban decay, Congress relaxed the FHA's stringent appraisal criteria for the neediest situations to a standard that allowed loans in "reasonably viable" areas. 12 U.S.C.A. § 1715n(e). Yet relaxed criteria mean that insured lenders have less incentive to carefully appraise properties in declining areas and to determine whether prospective borrowers are good risks. This in turn can be expected to lead to increased defaults. But, with their losses insured, lenders have little incentive to work problem loans out with their borrowers, even if the cause for default appears only temporary. So long as mortgages are foreclosed and mortgagors dispossessed, abandonment of marginal areas seems likely to continue.

Congress' major response to the redlining problem has been to mandate disclosure of geographic lending patterns. The Home Mortgage Disclosure Act of 1975, 12 U.S.C.A. §§ 2801 et seq., requires federally chartered lenders to publish the geographic distribution of their mortgage loans. The quixotic theory behind the Act was that "once local residents discover the lending policies of institutions located in their communities, they will reward those institutions that are investing in the area by depositing in them and express their dissatisfaction with those that are not by withdrawing from them. As the forces of the marketplace intensify, lenders will become more community minded and mortgage credit will become more plentiful in needy neighborhoods." Note, Attacking the Urban Redlining Problem, 56 B.U.L. Rev. 989, 1007–8 (1976). Several states have adopted similar disclosure statutes for state-chartered institutions. Amendments to the Home Mortgage Disclosure Act, mandated by the

Financial Institutions Reform, Recovery, and Enforcement Act, extended the Act's coverage to all mortgage lenders and broadened the disclosure requirements. For a comprehensive analysis of the amendments, see Ulrich, Home Mortgage Disclosure Act Developments, 46 Bus. Law. 1077 (1991).

Direct federal regulation of redlining has been less authoritative. For example, the Fair Housing Act has been applied to prohibit lenders from denying loans to white homebuyers in racially mixed neighborhoods, but only on the limited ground that the refusal was based on the race of the residents in the neighborhood. See, for example, Laufman v. Oakley Building & Loan Co., 408 F.Supp. 489 (S.D. Ohio 1976); Harrison v. Otto G. Heinzeroth Mortgage Co., 430 F.Supp. 893 (N.D. Ohio 1977).

The Fair Housing Act was the subject of comprehensive amendments in 1988. Pub.L. No. 100–430, 102 Stat. 1619 (1989). The new provisions make it unlawful to discriminate on the basis of race, color, religion, sex, handicap, familial status, or national origin in "real estate-related transactions." This revision broadens the scope of the Act to include any loan secured by a dwelling. Before this change, second mortgages used for purposes other than obtaining housing were not covered by the Act. See Eva v. Midwest National Mortgage Bank, Inc., 143 F.Supp.2d 862 (N.D.Ohio 2001) (holding second mortgages are covered). The 1988 amendments also beefed up enforcement, providing for suits by the attorney general and adjudication by administrative law judges of actions brought by HUD. Recovery is permitted for pain and suffering and humiliation and punitive damages may be awarded. See Dennis, The Fair Housing Act Amendments of 1988: A New Source of Lender Liability, 106 Banking L.J. 405 (1989).

Similarly, the Federal Home Loan Bank Board's regulations are tentative at best. Board Regulation 12 C.F.R. § 528.2 provides that "No savings association may deny a loan or other service, . . . or discriminate in fixing the amount . . . or other terms or conditions of such loan or other service on the basis of the age or location of the dwelling. . . ." But guidelines appearing in 12 C.F.R. § 571.24(c)(7) add that these restrictions are "intended to prohibit use of unfounded or unsubstantiated assumptions regarding the effect upon loan risk of the age of a dwelling or the physical or economic characteristics of an area. Loan decisions should be based on the present market value of the property offered as security (including consideration of specific improvements to be made by the borrower) and the likelihood that the property will retain an adequate value over the term of the loan. Specific factors which may negatively affect its short range future value (up to 3–5 years) should be clearly documented. Factors which in some cases may cause the market value of a property to decline are recent zoning changes or a significant number of abandoned homes in the immediate vicinity of the property. . . . However, arbitrary decisions based on age or location are prohibited, since many older, soundly constructed homes provide housing opportunities which may be precluded by an arbitrary lending policy."

State legislatures have outlawed redlining more authoritatively. See, for example, California Housing Financial Discrimination Act of 1977, Health & Safety Code § 35800 et seq. (West Supp.1992). ("No financial institution shall discriminate in the availability of, or in the provision of, financial assistance for the purpose of purchasing, constructing, rehabilitating, improving, or refinancing housing accommodations due, in whole or in part, to the consideration of conditions, characteristics, or trends in the neighborhood or geographic area surrounding the housing accommodation, unless the financial institution can demonstrate that such consideration of these conditions in the particular case is required to avoid an unsafe and unsound business practice." Health & Safety Code § 35810).

Do the less rigorous federal regulations preempt application of the more rigorous state statutes to federally-chartered lenders? See Conference of Federal Savings & Loan Associations v. Stein, 604 F.2d 1256 (9th Cir.1979), affirmed per curiam, 445 U.S. 921, 100 S.Ct. 1304, 63 L.Ed.2d 754 (1980) (redlining regulations promulgated by Federal Home Loan Bank Board preempted application of California Housing Financial Discrimination Act to federally-chartered savings and loan associations). For a superb analysis of the preemption issue, see Payne, Banking Institutions Trim State Efforts to Enforce Anti-Redlining Measures, 9 Real Est. L.J. 357 (1981).

See generally, Symposium, A Fair Lending Symposium: Litigating A Mortgage Lending Case, 28 J. Marshall L.Rev. 263–398 (1995) (with articles by Peter W. Salsich, Jr., Robert G. Schwemm, and others); Cavoli, Fair Lending Laws: The Growing Tension, 115 Banking L.J. 604 (1998); Marsico, Shedding Some Light on Lending: The Effect of Expanded Disclosure Laws on Home Mortgage Marketing, Lending and Discrimination in the New York Metropolitan Area, 27 Fordham Urb. L.J. 481 (1999); Swire, The Persistent Problem of Lending Discrimination: A Law and Economic Analysis, 73 Tex.L.Rev. 787 (1995); Trzcinski, The Economics of Redlining: A Classical Liberal Analysis, 44 Syr.L.Rev. 1197 (1993); Note, Beyond The Boundaries of the Community Reinvestment Act and the Fair Lending Laws: Developing A Market-Based Framework for Generating Low-and Moderate-Income Lending, 96 Colum.L.Rev. 710 (1996).

3. *Subprime mortgages.* Subprime mortgages are typically understood as loans to borrowers who do not qualify under typical underwriting guidelines and that carry higher interest rates a terms less favorable to the borrower. In actuality, many borrowers who would have qualified for a traditional loan (i.e., with substantial income, complying loan to value ratio, good employment history, etc.) were made subprime loans by mortgage brokers and mortgage lenders because the higher interests yielded greater profits to the ultimate holder of the mortgage. See Marsico, Suprime Lending, Predatory Lending, and the Community and the Community Investment Act Obligations of Banks, 46 N.Y.L. Sch. L. Rev. 735 (2002–2003); Mansfield, The Road to Subprime "HEL" Was Paved With Good Congressional Intentions: Usury Deregulation and the Subprime Home Equity Market, 51 S.C.L. Rev. 473 (2000). While, as detailed in the excerpt by Professor Korngold, subprime loans have received much blame for the global financial crisis and have also been attacked as taking unfair advantage of lower income borrowers, some maintain that careful use of subprime lending has been successful in bringing home ownership to people who would not have been able to obtain conventional loans. See Gross, The Subprime Good Guys, Slate, 11/15/08, http://www.slate.com/id/2204583/?from=rss. Commencing with data released in March 2005 pursuant to Regulation C under the Home Mortgage Disclosure Act, 12 C.F.R. pt. 203, the Federal Reserve is providing increased information on subprime loans so that this segment of the lending market can be better understood. See Avery, Canner & Cook, New Information Reported Under HMDA and Its Application in Fair Lending Enforcement, Federal Reserve Bull., p. 344, Summer 2005. On other subprime topics, see Bar-Gill, The Law, Economics and Psychology of Subprime Mortgage Contracts, 94 Cornell L. Rev. 1073 (2009); Stark and Choplin, A Cognitive And Social Psychological Analysis of Disclosure Laws And Call for Mortgage Counseling to Prevent Predatory Lending, 16 Psych. Pub. Pol. & L. 85 (2010); Bresdcia, Tainted Loans: The Value of A Mass Torts Approach in Subprime Mortgage Litigation, 78 U. Cinn. L. Rev. 1 (2009).

4. *TILA, RESPA, and Other Consumer Protection.* As indicated in *Associates Home Equity,* there is an array of federal and state statutory and regulatory vehicles protecting general consumer finance transactions that may be available for an aggrieved residential mortgagor. For example, compliance with the broad-based Truth in Lending Act (TILA), 15 U.S.C.A. § 1635, is required for many consumer mortgages. Andrews v. Chevy Chase Bank, 545 F.3d 570 (7th Cir.2008), dealing with a TILA challenge to an adjustable rate home mortgage, summarizes the Act's operative provisions:

> TILA was designed "to assure a meaningful disclosure of credit terms" to the consumer. § 1601(a). Creditors who violate the disclosure requirements may be ordered to pay actual damages or statutory damages, depending upon the nature of the violation. See § 1640(a)(1) & (a)(2). In certain loan transactions, TILA also provides debtors with a right of rescission-a process in which the creditor terminates its security interest and returns any payments made by the debtor in exchange for the debtor's return of all funds or property received from the creditor (usually, the loan proceeds). See § 1635. Debtors may rescind under TILA by midnight of the third business day after the transaction for any reason whatsoever. See § 1635(a). The three-day postclosing "cooling off" period is extended if the creditor does not deliver the required notice of the right to rescind and all material disclosures; in that instance, the right to rescind continues until the creditor provides the required notice and disclosures, or up to three years after consummation of the loan, whichever occurs first. See § 1635(f).
>
> Rescinding a loan transaction under TILA " 'requires unwinding the transaction in its entirety and thus requires returning the borrowers to the position they occupied prior to the loan agreement.' " Handy v. Anchor Mortgage Corp., 464 F.3d 760, 765 (7th Cir.2006) (quoting Barrett v. JP Morgan Chase Bank, N.A., 445 F.3d 874, 877 (6th Cir.2006)). TILA rescission is therefore considered a purely personal remedy. See, e.g., McKenna, 475 F.3d at 424–25; James, 621 F.2d at 731; LaLiberte, 53 Cal.Rptr.3d at 750–51. It is intended to operate privately, at least initially, "with the creditor and debtor working out the logistics of a given rescission." McKenna, 475 F.3d at 421; see also Belini v. Wash. Mut. Bank, FA, 412 F.3d 17, 25 (1st Cir.2005). Section 1635 sets forth certain deadlines and duties that apply to the creditor upon receipt of a notice of rescission from the debtor (e.g., return of earnest money, down payment, or other payments, and initiating

the termination of the security interest); the statute, in turn, specifies the duties that apply to the debtor (e.g., tendering return of the property or its reasonable value). See § 1635(b). These procedures apply "except when otherwise ordered by a court," id., making it clear that when disagreements over the particulars of a given rescission arise, the court may tailor the remedy to the circumstances.

See Edwards, Empirical and Behavioral Critiques of Mandatory Disclosure: Socio-Economics and the Quest for Truth in Lending, 14 Corn.J.L. & Pub.Pol'y 199 (2005) (examining the effectiveness of TILA's disclosure approach to protecting borrowers); Murken, Comment, Can't Get No Satisfaction? Revising How Courts Rescind Home Equity Loans Under the Truth In Lending Act, 77 Temp. L. Rev. 457 (2004); Smith, Modern Mortgage Markets and How Mortgage Fraud Has Flourished, 24 Probate & Prop. 32 (Nov./Dec. 2010).

Additionally, damage claims may be brought under RESPA for improper servicing of loans (which is described on pages 13–14 above), see, e.g., Johnston v. Bank of America, N.A., 173 F.Supp.2d 809 (N.D. Ill. 2001); In re Tomasavec, 273 B.R. 682 (M.D. Fla. 2002), or under the federal Fair Debt Collection Practices Act, 15 U.S.C.A. § 1692g, for actions by mortgagees' surrogates in enforcing mortgages, see, e.g., Schlosser v. Fairbanks Capital Corp., 323 F.3d 534 (7th Cir. 2003). Moreover, an occasional court may use the common law principle of "unconscionability" to police mortgage loans in certain circumstances. See, e.g., Flores v. Transamerica HomeFirst, Inc., 93 Cal.App.4th 846, 113 Cal.Rptr.2d 376 (2001) (court struck arbitration clause in reverse mortgage executed by couple aged 80 and 76).

5.   *Predatory Lending.* The borrowers in *Associates Home Equity* also a claim of predatory lending. Consider how plaintiffs' witness define predatory lending. What makes a loan "predatory"? Is it the terms of the loan? The business practices of the lender? Should the credit history, employment history, and other aspects of the borrower's profile be considered in determining if a loan is predatory? On predatory lending see U.S. Department of Housing and Urban Development, Curbing Predatory Home Mortgage Lending (2000); Eggert, Held Up in Due Course: Predatory Lending, Securitization, and the Holder in Due Course, 35 Creighton L. Rev. 503, 566–570 (2002); Hauser. Predatory Lending, Passive Judicial Activism, and the Duty to Decide, 86 N.C.L. Rev. 1501 (2008); Engel & McCoy, A Tale of Three Markets: The Law and Economics of Predatory Lending, 80 Tex. L. Rev. 1255 (2002); Reiss, Subprime Standardization: How Rating Agencies Allow Predatory Lending to Flourish, 33 Fla. St. U.L. Rev. 985 (2006); Hammond, Predatory Lending—A Legal Definition and Update, 34 Real Est. L.J. 176 (2005); Stark, Unmasking the Predatory Loan in Sheep's Clothing: A Legislative Proposal, 21 Harv. Blackletter L.J. 129 (2005); Stolly, Comment: Subprime Lending: Ohioans Fall Prey to Predatory Lending at Record Levels—What Next?, 34 Ohio No. U. L. Rev. 289 (2006).

B. JUNIOR LIENS

1. REFINANCING

Aames Capital Corporation v. Interstate Bank of Oak Forest

Appellate Court of Illinois, 2000.
315 Ill.App.3d 700, 734 N.E.2d 493, 248 Ill.Dec. 565.

JUSTICE GEIGER delivered the opinion of the court:

This appeal arises from a dispute concerning lien priority in a mortgage foreclosure proceeding. The issue is whether a mortgagee that pays off a priority mortgage pursuant to a refinancing agreement is entitled to be subrogated to the priority mortgage lien recorded by the original mortgagee.

On October 17, 1986, Patrick Wangler and Diane Wangler executed a note and mortgage in favor of Hinsdale Federal Savings and Loan that was later assigned to Standard Federal Bank (Standard). The note and mortgage were filed with the Du Page County recorder's office on November 7, 1986. Thereafter, the Wanglers executed junior mortgages in favor of Suburban Bank of Elmhurst (Suburban) that were recorded on July 12, 1988, June 30, 1989, January 31, 1990, and July 30, 1991.

On April 26, 1996, the defendant-appellee, Interstate Bank of Oak Forest (Interstate), obtained a judgment against the Wanglers in the amount of $75,891.06. Interstate recorded a memorandum of judgment with the Du Page County recorder's office on September 4, 1996.

On August 28, 1996, the Wanglers executed a note and mortgage for the sum of $174,000 in favor of Pacific Thrift and Loan Company (Pacific) pursuant to a refinancing agreement whereby Pacific would pay off the mortgages to Standard and Suburban. The mortgage document executed by the parties is the Fannie Mae/Freddie Mac Uniform Instrument for Illinois (Uniform Instrument). Pacific's mortgage was later assigned to plaintiff-appellant, Aames Capital Corporation (Aames). The Wanglers did not receive any funds from the refinancing. The closing agent issued checks to Standard and Suburban on September 4, 1996, in payment of the balance due under the mortgages held by them. On September 20, 1996, Pacific recorded its mortgage. On September 24, 1996, Suburban filed releases of its mortgages, but no release had been filed of the Standard mortgage.

On June 6, 1997, Aames filed this foreclosure action after the Wanglers defaulted on the note. In its foreclosure complaint, Aames alleged that Interstate's judgment lien was inferior and subordinate to Aames's first mortgage lien.

Both Aames and Interstate filed motions for summary judgment as to lien priority. The trial court entered an order denying Aames's motion and granting Interstate's motion, ruling that Interstate's judgment lien took priority because it was recorded prior to Aames's mortgage lien.

On appeal, Aames argues that, even though Interstate's judgment lien predates its mortgage with the Wanglers, it nevertheless holds first priority position because it is equitably subrogated to the priority mortgage liens perfected by Standard and by Suburban. Aames argues that the doctrine of equitable subrogation provides that a refinancing mortgage assumes the priority position of the prior mortgage that is satisfied through the refinancing. Interstate responds that the doctrine of first in time, first in right applies such that the judgment lien takes priority as the lien prior in time. Interstate also argues that the doctrine of equitable subrogation is only applied when there is an express agreement that the refinancing mortgage will assume the priority position.

I.   FIRST IN TIME, FIRST IN RIGHT

We review the trial court's summary judgment order *de novo.* Wiseman-Hughes Enterprises, Inc. v. Reger, 248 Ill.App.3d 854, 857, 187 Ill.Dec. 589, 617 N.E.2d 1310 (1993). A lien is a hold or claim that one party has on the property of another for a debt. Podvinec v. Popov, 266 Ill.App.3d 72, 77, 203 Ill.Dec. 293, 639 N.E.2d 613 (1994), *rev'd on other grounds,* 168 Ill.2d 130, 212 Ill.Dec. 951, 658 N.E.2d 433 (1995). A lien that is first in time generally has priority and is entitled to prior satisfaction of the property it binds. Cole Taylor Bank v. Cole Taylor Bank, 224 Ill.App.3d 696, 704, 166 Ill.Dec. 817, 586 N.E.2d 775 (1992).

A mortgage is a type of consensual lien on real property. See 735 ILCS 5/15–1207 (West 1996). Specifically, it is an interest in land created by written instrument providing security in real estate to secure the payment of a debt. Resolution Trust Corp. v. Holtzman, 248 Ill.App.3d 105, 111, 187 Ill.Dec. 827, 618 N.E.2d 418 (1993). Under the Illinois Mortgage Foreclosure Law, a mortgage lien is created upon recording of the mortgage with the recorder of deeds. See 735 ILCS 5/15–1301 (West 1996); see also Firstmark Standard Life Insurance Co. v. Superior Bank FSB, 271 Ill.App.3d 435, 439, 208 Ill.Dec. 409, 649 N.E.2d 465 (1995).

The perfection of mortgage liens is governed also by the Conveyances Act (765 ILCS 5/1 *et seq.* (West 1996)). Section 28 of the Conveyances Act provides that deeds, mortgages, and other instruments relating to or affecting the title to real estate shall be recorded in the county in which such real estate is situated. 765 ILCS 5/28 (West 1996). The purpose of this section is to give third parties the opportunity to ascertain the status of title to the property. Lubershane v. Village of Glencoe, 63 Ill.App.3d 874, 879, 20 Ill.Dec. 681, 380 N.E.2d 890 (1978). The purchaser of real estate may rely on the public record of conveyances and instruments affecting title, unless hc has notice or is chargeable with notice of a claim or interest that is inconsistent with the record. Bullard v. Turner, 357 Ill. 279, 283, 192 N.E. 223 (1934).

Section 30 of the Conveyances Act provides as follows:

> "All deeds, mortgages and other instruments of writing which are authorized to be recorded, shall take effect and be in force from and after the time of filing the same for record, and not before, as to all creditors and subsequent purchasers, without notice; and all such deeds and title papers shall be adjudged void as to all such creditors and subsequent purchasers, without notice, until the same shall be filed for record." 765 ILCS 5/30 (West 1996).

The purpose of this section is to protect subsequent purchasers against unrecorded prior instruments. Farmers State Bank v. Neese, 281 Ill.App.3d 98, 106, 216 Ill.Dec. 474, 665 N.E.2d 534 (1996). A presumption exists that the first mortgage recorded has priority. Firstmark, 271 Ill.App.3d at 439, 208 Ill.Dec. 409, 649 N.E.2d 465. An unrecorded interest in land is not effective as to a *bona fide* purchaser without notice. Schaumburg State Bank v. Bank of Wheaton, 197 Ill.App.3d 713, 720, 144 Ill.Dec. 151, 555 N.E.2d 48 (1990). However, where a party has constructive notice of a prior interest in real estate, the failure to record is not necessarily fatal to the rights of the prior interest holder. See Dana Point Condominium Ass'n, Inc. v. Keystone Service Co., 141 Ill.App.3d 916, 922, 96 Ill.Dec. 249, 491 N.E.2d 63 (1986).

The doctrine of first in time, first in right is not always as clear and obvious as it may seem. For instance, a separate body of law governs lien priority in cases involving renewal notes and mortgages. A renewal note and mortgage do not ordinarily operate as payment and in discharge of an original note for purposes of determining whether the renewal note maintained priority position. State Bank v. Winnetka Bank, 245 Ill.App.3d 984, 991, 185 Ill.Dec. 421, 614 N.E.2d 862 (1993). In cases of a dispute concerning priority when the original note and mortgage are renewed, the court looks to the intent of the parties in determining whether the renewal extinguishes the original mortgage lien. Winnetka Bank, 245 Ill.App.3d at 991, 185 Ill.Dec. 421, 614 N.E.2d 862. In Winnetka Bank, the court was persuaded that the mortgage lien survived the renewal of the original mortgage and the tender of an additional loan because there was no evidence that the original mortgage was ever canceled or released. See Winnetka Bank, 245 Ill.App.3d at 991, 185 Ill.Dec. 421, 614 N.E.2d 862.

Another area of interest concerns the priority position of mortgage assignees. Relying in part on Community Bank v. Carter, 283 Ill.App.3d 505, 218 Ill.Dec. 791, 669 N.E.2d 1317 (1996), we recently held in Federal National Mortgage Ass'n v. Kuipers, 314 Ill.App.3d 631, 638, 247 Ill.Dec. 668, 732 N.E.2d 723 (2000), that an assignee of a mortgagee was not required to record the assignment of mortgage in order to maintain the original mortgagee's priority position. In Carter, the court held that the assignments of the mortgage did not extinguish the mortgage debt and, therefore, the assignees acquired the same rights and interests as the original mortgagee, including the right to collect under a property insurance policy. Carter, 283 Ill.App.3d at 510, 218 Ill.Dec. 791, 669 N.E.2d 1317.

Yet an additional consideration to first in time, first in right is the law surrounding subrogation. Subrogation is a method whereby one who had involuntarily paid a debt of another succeeds to the rights of the other with respect to the debt paid. Dix Mutual Insurance Co. v. LaFramboise, 149 Ill.2d 314, 319, 173 Ill.Dec. 648, 597 N.E.2d 622 (1992). Subrogation has been applied to subrogate one party to the lien priority of another. See Home Savings Bank v. Bierstadt, 168 Ill. 618, 48 N.E. 161 (1897); Detroit Steel Products Co. v. Hudes, 17 Ill.App.2d 514, 151 N.E.2d 136 (1958); Kankakee Federal Savings & Loan Ass'n v. Arnove, 318 Ill.App. 261, 47 N.E.2d 874 (1943). These cases are discussed in greater detail below. However, two principles emerge from the above discussion that lead us to reject Interstate's contention that the only relevant inquiry is the date of recording of its lien. The first is that blind adherence to the first in time, first in right doctrine is sometimes insufficient to determine lien priority. The second is that whatever case-law doctrines operate as exceptions to the first in time, first in right doctrine must comport with the purpose of the recording requirement, namely, to provide notice of liens to third parties.

In this case, the original mortgage liens were created by agreement and perfected between November 1986 and July 1991 by recording with the Du Page County recorder of deeds. The mortgage liens acted to secure payment of the mortgage debts. Henceforward from those dates, third parties examining chain of title to the real estate were put on notice of the existence of the debts and of the liens on the real estate. Because no release of lien had been filed pursuant to section 2 of the Mortgage Act, there was no indication to third parties that the liens were ever extinguished. See 765 ILCS 905/2 (West 1996).

Those liens were still in effect when Interstate recorded its judgment lien on September 4, 1996. Because Interstate had notice of prior mortgage liens when it recorded its judgment lien, we see no reason why the doctrine of first in time, first in right would require us to reject, at the outset, Aames's argument that subrogation may apply. Therefore, we take a closer look at equitable and conventional subrogation.

II. COMPARISON OF EQUITABLE AND CONVENTIONAL SUBROGATION

There are two broad categories of subrogation rights: contractual or conventional rights, and common-law or equitable rights. Schultz v. Gotlund, 138 Ill.2d 171, 173, 149 Ill.Dec. 282, 561 N.E.2d 652 (1990). Equitable subrogation is a creature of chancery that is utilized to prevent unjust enrichment. LaFramboise, 149 Ill.2d at 319, 173 Ill.Dec. 648, 597 N.E.2d 622. There is no general rule that can be laid down to determine whether a right of equitable subrogation exists, since the right depends upon the equities of each particular case. LaFramboise, 149 Ill.2d at 319, 173 Ill.Dec. 648, 597 N.E.2d 622. Conventional subrogation, on the other hand, arises from an agreement between the parties that the subrogee pay a debt on behalf of a third party and, in return, be able to assert the rights of the original creditor. See Home Savings Bank v. Bierstadt, 168 Ill. 618, 624, 48 N.E. 161 (1897).

In Bierstadt, the court held that the appellee, who had advanced funds to discharge certain prior deeds of trust, was subrogated to the priority lien rights of the holders of the deeds of trust. The court defined conventional subrogation as a right springing from an express agreement with the debtor where the subrogee advances money to pay a claim, which carries a lien, and where the subrogee and the debtor agree that the subrogee is to have an equal lien to the one paid off. Bierstadt, 168 Ill. at 624, 48 N.E. 161. As such, the court reasoned, the subrogee is entitled to the benefit of the security that he has satisfied with the expectation of receiving an equal lien. Bierstadt, 168 Ill. at 624, 48 N.E. 161.

The Bierstadt court described the agreement between the debtor and the appellee as being "to the effect" that the appellee would advance sufficient funds to pay off the prior deeds of trust and then would receive from the debtor a first mortgage as security for the funds advanced. Bierstadt, 168 Ill. at 624–25, 48 N.E. 161. In applying conventional subrogation, the court noted, "[t]hat was the substance of the transaction, and equity will effectuate the real intention of the parties, where no injury is done to an innocent party." Bierstadt, 168 Ill. at 625, 48 N.E. 161.

Although conventional subrogation is seen sporadically in Illinois case law, equitable subrogation is even more elusive. One of the few modern applications of equitable subrogation is seen in Detroit Steel Products Co. v. Hudes, 17 Ill.App.2d 514, 517, 151 N.E.2d 136 (1958). In Hudes, the court found that equitable subrogation would apply to advance the claims of the mortgagee bank in a mechanics' lien foreclosure where the bank had required that the borrower pay certain claims of a material provider from the loan proceeds. The trial court found that the bank's mortgage would be subrogated to the priority position of the material provider to the extent that the material provider had been paid from the loan proceeds.

The court held that equitable subrogation prevents the unearned enrichment of one party at the expense of another and will be granted only where an equitable result will be reached. Hudes, 17 Ill.App.2d at 520, 151 N.E.2d 136. The court noted that no prejudice resulted to the material providers who had not been paid because, but for the mortgage, they would have been required to share the sale proceeds with the material provider whose claim had been paid from the loan proceeds. Hudes, 17 Ill.App.2d at 521, 151 N.E.2d 136. The court further noted that to deny subrogation would be to grant an unearned enrichment to the unpaid material providers due to the reduction of outstanding claims. Hudes, 17 Ill.App.2d at 521, 151 N.E.2d 136.

III. APPLICATION OF CONVENTIONAL AND EQUITABLE SUBROGATION TO MORTGAGE REFINANCING

Although Aames cites cases applying conventional subrogation, it argues that equitable subrogation applies; Aames does not consider that Illinois case law has specifically held that the two are separate and distinct doctrines. It appears that there is no precise definition of equitable subrogation that is applicable to this case. It also appears that Illinois courts, including those cases cited by Aames, have previously considered whether conventional subrogation applies to a mortgage refinancing agreement. See Bierstadt, 168 Ill. at 625, 48 N.E. 161; Arnove, 318 Ill.App. at 265, 47 N.E.2d 874. For these reasons, we decline to analyze the present case under equitable subrogation and, instead, consider whether conventional subrogation, as outlined in Aames's argument and in Bierstadt, may be applied.

Interstate argues that subrogation does not apply because there was no agreement that Pacific would move into the priority positions established by Standard and by Suburban. This contention forms the real crux of this case. Relying on Firstmark Standard Life Insurance Co. v. Superior Bank, 271 Ill.App.3d 435, 208 Ill.Dec. 409, 649 N.E.2d 465 (1995), Interstate argues that subrogation requires that there be an agreement that the refinancing mortgage move into the position of the mortgage that it is paying off. A careful review of Firstmark, however, reveals that its holding is inapplicable to the present case.

In Firstmark, at the time that the property owners executed a refinancing mortgage in favor of the appellant, there were four senior mortgages on the property. Firstmark, 271 Ill.App.3d at 437, 208 Ill.Dec. 409, 649 N.E.2d 465. The appellant paid off three of the four mortgages. The remaining senior mortgage was held by the appellee. The mortgage held by the appellant provided that it was subject to certain exceptions, including the mortgage held by the appellee. The appellee later filed a foreclosure proceeding, and the parties filed motions for summary judgment as to lien priority. The trial court ruled that the appellee's mortgage took priority.

On appeal, the appellant argued that the doctrine of conventional subrogation should be applied such that it would move into the priority position of the three initial mortgages it had paid off pursuant to the refinancing. Firstmark, 271 Ill.App.3d at 439, 208 Ill.Dec. 409, 649 N.E.2d 465. It does not appear from the court's analysis either that the appellant requested review under equitable subrogation or that the court considered the distinction between equitable and conventional subrogation as defined in Schultz.

The Firstmark court reviewed early case law on the issue of the application of conventional subrogation and found that there must be an express agreement that the interests of the refinancing mortgagee are to be advanced to a first mortgage. Firstmark, 271 Ill.App.3d at 440–41, 208 Ill.Dec. 409, 649 N.E.2d 465. The court held that there was no such express agreement in that case. Pointing to the language in the refinancing mortgage that the mortgage held by the appellant was subject to the mortgage held by the appellee, the court held that the doctrine of conventional subrogation would not apply. Firstmark, 271 Ill.App.3d at 441, 208 Ill.Dec. 409, 649 N.E.2d 465.

We do not find that the holding in Firstmark controls the present case. In Firstmark,, the refinancing mortgage expressly stated that it was subject to the prior liens. In the present case, however, no such provision appears in either the note or the Uniform Instrument. It specifically provides that the Wanglers were to discharge any lien that had priority over the mortgage. The Uniform Instrument further provides that Pacific may pay any sums secured by a lien that had priority over its mortgage and that any such sum paid would become additional debt secured by the mortgage.

Although there is no provision in the Uniform Instrument that specifically states that the mortgage is a first mortgage, we believe that the above-referenced provisions, when read together, indicate that the agreement of the parties was that the mortgage held by Pacific would be a first priority mortgage, and that any other prior mortgages of record would be paid off by Pacific, with the new mortgage securing that debt. In addition, we do not believe that such a specific provision in the mortgage document regarding the assumption of the first priority position is required by the holding in Bierstadt. As noted earlier, the Bierstadt court described the agreement as being "to the effect" of paying off a priority lien and assuming that priority position. The Bierstadt court makes no reference to any specific provision in the mortgage documents.

In short, we do not believe that Firstmark may be read to conclude that the Uniform Instrument is somehow inadequate to consummate the refinancing of a mortgage in Illinois. Moreover, we note that, even if there were an additional provision that specifically stated that Pacific would have a first priority lien, it would be of little effect, as lien priority is determined by law, any agreement of the parties notwithstanding.

Although Firstmark tells us when conventional subrogation will not apply, it does not tell us when it will. There are no Illinois cases of recent vintage that explain when subrogation will apply to a mortgage refinancing. We are persuaded by Aames's argument that the holding in Bierstadt should be resurrected to determine when conventional subrogation should apply to a case involving a mortgage refinancing. Conventional subrogation is a right springing from an agreement with the debtor where the subrogee advances money to pay a claim that carries a lien and where the subrogee and the debtor agree that the subrogee is to have an equal lien to the one paid off. See Bierstadt, 168 Ill. at 624, 48 N.E. 161. The holding in Bierstadt fits the precise definition of a mortgage refinancing. In this case, Aames, as the assignee of the subrogee, is entitled to the benefit of the security attaching to the debt that it satisfied with the expectation of receiving an equal lien. See Bierstadt, 168 Ill. at 624, 48 N.E. 161; see also Arnove, 318 Ill.App. at 264, 47 N.E.2d 874 (holding that it is "settled law" that, when a refinancing mortgage is made, the lien of the old mortgage continues in effect without interruption and the new mortgage does not become subordinate to an intervening lien attaching between the time of the recording of the old mortgage and the effective date of the new one).

There are numerous policy reasons to apply the doctrine of conventional subrogation to a case involving a refinancing mortgage. A debtor in bankruptcy, who has outstanding judgments and has defaulted on his mortgage, may find relief in refinancing his home, albeit under less favorable loan terms. Similarly, any time a mortgage note is accelerated or matures is a prime opportunity for a debtor to enter into a refinancing agreement. Absent subrogation of the original mortgage lien, these consumers would be hard-pressed to find a lender willing to refinance. In addition, if subrogation were not applied in cases of mortgage refinancings, then the intervening lienor (in this case Interstate) would receive a windfall from the payoff by the refinancing mortgagee.

Subrogation has been applied in cases of mortgage refinancings in many jurisdictions (see Mort v. United States, 86 F.3d 890 (9th Cir.1996); Harley J. Robinson Trust v. Ardmore Acres, Inc., 6 F.Supp.2d 640 (E.D.Mi.1998); In re Cutty's-Gurnee, Inc., 133 B.R. 934 (N.D.Ill.1991); East Boston Savings Bank v. Ogan, 428 Mass. 327, 701 N.E.2d 331 (1998); Wolf v. Spariosu, 706 So.2d 881 (Fla.App.1998); G.E. Capital Mortgage Services, Inc. v. Levenson, 338 Md. 227, 657 A.2d 1170 (1995); Rock River Lumber Corp. v. Universal Mortgage Corp., 82 Wis.2d 235, 262 N.W.2d 114 (1978); cf. *First Federal Savings Bank v. United States,* 118 F.3d 532 (7th Cir.1997) (refusing to apply subrogation under Indiana law where subrogation would benefit a negligent title insurer that had not discovered a federal tax lien on behalf of the insured, which was a sophisticated mortgage lender)).

We hold that a refinancing mortgagee that records its mortgage lien is entitled to be subrogated to the original lien, and its corresponding priority position, established by the original mortgagee, under the doctrine of conventional subrogation, up to the amount that the original mortgage secured at the time of its perfection. The doctrine of conventional subrogation will apply if the original mortgage lien is in full force and effect at the time that the refinancing mortgage lien is recorded. However, nothing in our holding modifies in any way the ability to extinguish the original mortgage lien. If the original mortgagee files a release of lien prior to the recordation of the refinancing mortgagee's lien and if a third party records its lien after the release is recorded but before the refinancing lien is recorded, then conventional subrogation will not apply. We also note that, under conventional subrogation, a refinancing mortgagee may not pick and choose which liens it will pay off. The refinancing mortgagee will only be subrogated to the liens it pays off which predate the intervening third-party lien. Nothing in our holding, however, limits the court from considering whether the doctrine of equitable subrogation may apply.

Having determined that conventional subrogation applies to move Aames into the priority positions established by Suburban and by Standard, we must remand this case to determine the extent to which Aames is subrogated. Under our holding, Aames is only entitled to be subrogated up to the amount that the original mortgages secured at the time of perfection. We have searched the record for evidence of the value secured by the Standard and Suburban mortgages, but we have been unable to locate the necessary information. Although Aames has entered into the record evidence of the amounts it paid to Standard and Suburban, these amounts are irrelevant. What is relevant is the value of the prior liens as determined by the mortgage documents. That is to say, a finding that Aames has paid a certain sum to the prior mortgage holders does not necessarily translate into a finding that whatever sum was paid was indeed owed under the mortgages of record. Therefore, on remand, the trial court should determine the amount to which Aames is subrogated.

For the foregoing reasons, the judgment of the circuit court of Du Page County is reversed, and the cause is remanded.

Reversed and remanded.

INGLIS and GALASSO, JJ., concur.

NOTES

1. *Rights and Liabilities of Junior Lienors.* Junior lienors wear two hats. With respect to the mortgagor, junior mortgagees are like any other mortgagee. They can proceed against the mortgagor for waste or violation of other obligations imposed by the mortgage. In the event of default, they can proceed against the mortgagor on the debt and, subject to the rights of the senior mortgagee, can proceed by foreclosure against the mortgaged property.

With respect to the senior mortgagee, however, the junior mortgagee shares many of the attributes of the owner-mortgagor. If the mortgagor defaults on the senior mortgage, foreclosure by the senior mortgagee will wipe out the junior mortgagee's interest along with the interest of the mortgagor. And, like the mortgagor, the junior mortgagee can usually protect its interest by taking over the mortgage payments or curing any other defaults on the senior mortgage, by bidding at the foreclosure sale, and by redeeming its interest from the sale.

2.   *Subrogation and Refinancing.* A borrower may seek to replace an existing mortgage with a new one that provides the borrower with superior terms (e.g., lower interest rate, new maturity date). The refinancing may be given by the original mortgagee or by a new lender (i.e., third party refinancings). The issue in either case, as illustrated in *Aames*, is whether the new mortgage created as part of the refinancing and replacing the original mortgage has priority over other mortgages or liens that were placed on the property subsequent to the original mortgage.

The Restatement of Mortgages treats refinancing by the original mortgagee in section 7.3 and third party refinancing in section 7.6. Under the rule of section 7.3, the original mortgagee retains its priority on a refinancing with certain limitations. See, e.g., Rush v. Alaska Mtge. Group, 937 P.2d 647 (Alaska 1997). The doctrine of subrogation in section 7.6 controls the priority of a third party refinancing.

The *Aames* court takes great pains to portray the case as involving conventional as opposed to equitable subrogation (even though most courts would probably disagree). What is the difference between the doctrines, which doctrine seems most applicable in this case, and what may be motivating the court to go the conventional subrogation route? What was the extent of the subrogation in Aames? What if the Wanglers had received cash from the refinancing?

The majority of American courts bars subrogation in a third party refinancing if the lender had actual notice of the intervening lien. A few courts similarly bar subrogation where there is only constructive notice. See, e.g., Hilco, Inc. v. Lenentine, 142 N.H. 265, 698 A.2d 1254 (1997) (bank had constructive notice even though bank's attorney negligently failed to find the intervening lien in a title search); First Union Nat'l Bank v. Lindley Laboratories, Inc., 132 N.C.App. 129, 510 S.E.2d 187 (1999); Countrywide Home Loans, Inc. v. First National Bank of Steamboat Springs, N.A., 144 P.3d 1224 (Wyo.2006). Was there notice in *Aames*? Does it make sense to permit subrogation only when there is no notice? Section 7.6 of the Restatement of Mortgages allows subrogation even if there is notice: "the question is . . . whether the payor reasonably expected to get security with a priority equal to the mortgage being paid." Comment e. Some courts agree with the Restatement view. See, e.g., Bank of America v. Prestance Corp., 160 Wash.2d 560, 160 P.3d 17 (2007); see Murray, Equitable Subrogation: Can A Refinancing Mortgagee Establish Priority Over Intervening Liens?, 45 Real Prop., Tr. & Est. L.J. 249 (2010); Murray, Equitable Subrogation: Is the Trend Toward the Restatement Approach?, 21 Probate & Prop. 19 (Nov./Dec.2007).

2.   MODIFICATION OF THE SENIOR MORTGAGE

Burney v. McLaughlin

Missouri Court of Appeals, 2001.
63 S.W.3d 223.

ROBERT S. BARNEY, CHIEF JUDGE.

This appeal primarily involves the relative priority of two deeds of trust held, respectively, by Respondents, Gary and Martha Burney and Gary and Patsy Snadon (hereinafter "Respondents") and Appellant, Bank of America, N.A. ("Bank") on a parcel of land located in Taney County, Missouri.[1] Although Respondents had subordinated their deed of trust to that of Bank's, they contended at trial that the subsequent material modification of the Bank's note so impaired Respondents' security that a court of equity was justified in reordering the priority of the parties' deeds of trust. The circuit court agreed with Respondents and Bank now appeals.

The record shows that at the commencement of the litigation the Foxborough Inn (the "Inn") was a 178 room hotel in Branson, Missouri. The land on which it was located was comprised of two parcels, a "front parcel" and a "back parcel" consisting of two tracts. The front parcel is the smaller of the two parcels.

In early 1992, Respondents constructed 77 units of the Inn on the front parcel which they owned. They borrowed over one million dollars from Ozark Mountain Bank ("OMB") to pay for this construction. The loan was secured by a deed of trust on the front parcel.

Later in the year, Respondents sold the front parcel and the Inn's 77 units to C & J Properties, Inc. ("C & J") for a total purchase price of $3.3 million. The terms were, generally, as follows: C & J paid Respondents nearly $1 million in cash at closing; paid off Respondents' existing note on the property by borrowing $1.1 million from OMB and giving OMB a first deed of trust on the front parcel; and gave Respondents a note ("Respondents' Note") for the remaining $1.2 million of the purchase price secured by the lien of a second deed of trust on the front parcel ("Respondents' Deed of Trust").

Less than a year later, C & J borrowed approximately $3.2 million from Bank in order to refinance the existing OMB debt and fund C & J's efforts to construct an additional 101 units, located on the back parcel, which C & J purchased. This was accomplished in three steps:

First, on June 23, 1993, Bank loaned C & J $1.077 million to pay the balance of the note secured by the first deed of trust held by OMB. This new note ("Bank's Note No. 1") was secured by a deed of trust against the *front* parcel only ("Bank's Deed of Trust No. 1"). It had a maturity date of December 23, 1993, and bore interest of 7% before maturity and 13% in the event of default. No principal payments before maturity were required. The monthly payments were to be interest only and the maker agreed to pay "all costs of collection when incurred, including reasonable attorneys' fees."

---

[1]   Bank and Bank's predecessor in interest are collectively referred to as "Bank" in this opinion.

Second, on the same date Respondents executed a Subordination Agreement in favor of Bank. It provided, in pertinent part, that Respondents subordinated their Note and Deed of Trust (on the front parcel) to Bank's Deed of Trust No. 1, "to the end that the [Bank's Deed of Trust No. 1] shall be superior to [Respondents' Deed of Trust]." The subordination agreement contained no other significant provisions.

Third, Bank loaned C & J $2.117 million ("Bank's Note No. 2") to fund the construction of 101 additional units on the back parcel. This note was secured by a deed of trust placed against the *back* parcel only ("Bank's Deed of Trust No. 2").

On June 2, 1994, C & J granted Bank another deed of trust ("Bank's Deed of Trust No. 3") securing both Bank's Note No. 1 and Bank's Note No. 2. This latter deed of trust placed a lien against both the front parcel and the back parcels.

Almost immediately after expansion of the Inn, C & J experienced financial problems which persisted over a number of years. As best we can glean from the record, an economic downturn occurred in the Branson area due to a glut of motel rooms. As a result, between December 1993 and December 1999, Bank and C & J (and a third party in some instances) entered into a series of eight separate modification agreements, which resulted in extending the maturity date and other terms and conditions of Bank's Note No. 1 and Bank's Deed of Trust No. 1, and the last three modifications extended maturity date and other terms of Bank's Notes No. 1 and No. 2.[3] Each modification was duly recorded. Respondents contend that they were never notified of any of these modifications nor was their consent obtained for any of these modifications.

During December of 1999, C & J terminated its payments to Bank on Bank's Note No. 1 and Bank's Note No. 2 and notified Bank that the Inn would not reopen following the annual winter closing period in 1999–2000. Bank subsequently instructed the trustee(s) of its three deeds of trust to commence foreclosure proceedings. Two days prior to the foreclosure sale Respondents filed a three-count petition for equitable relief. Respondents sought, in pertinent part: (a) temporary injunctive relief prohibiting Bank from conducting the foreclosure sale; (b) a declaration that their deed of trust, i.e., Respondents' Deed of Trust (secured by the front parcel), was prior and superior to Bank's Deed of Trust No. 1, as well as to any other deeds of trust Bank held against the front parcel; and (c) requested judicial foreclosure of Respondents' Deed of Trust, pursuant to § 443.190, RSMo 1994, *et seq.*

---

[3]   The eight modification agreements generally provided for the extension of maturity dates of Bank's Note 1, secured by Bank's Deed of Trust No. 1, for periods ranging from six months to fourteen months. The second modification agreement changed the interest from 7% to 8.25%; the third modification agreement raised the interest rate to 10%, Bank's "Corporate Base Rate" ("CBR") plus 1%; the fourth modification provision changed the interest rate to CBR plus 1.5%; the fifth modification agreement provided for cross-collateralization and cross-default clauses, which clauses had been previously incorporated into the loan structure, *supra,* through Bank's Deed of Trust No. 3 in June of 1994. The sixth and eighth modification agreements maintained the existing interest rates on Bank's Note No. 1 and the seventh modification agreement lowered the interest rate on this same note to CBR plus 1%. Other changes involved additional closing fees, appraisal fees and provisions relating to bankruptcy procedures.

Respondents argued that their interest in the front parcel should be declared "superior to and take[ ] priority over any interest asserted by Bank" because the "actions and conduct of Bank ... so materially adversely affected and impaired [Respondents'] collateral and/or destroyed the original economics of the subject property, so as to render the Subordination Agreement of June 23, 1993[,] null and void."

. . .

In its Point One, Bank asseverates circuit court error in declaring Bank's Deed of Trust No. 1 (on the front parcel) junior to that of Respondents' Deed of Trust. Bank maintains that Respondents do not dispute that in executing their subordination agreement they took a junior position to that of Bank. Bank maintains that the circuit court was not justified in altering the priority of the two deeds of trust because Respondents failed to show that Bank's modification agreements relating to Bank's Note No. 1 and Bank's Deed of Trust No. 1 "effectively destroyed the collateral" that Respondents held. On the contrary, Bank contends that as a result of these modification agreements C & J was able to avoid default for several years during which time Respondents were able to collect on a portion of their loan to C & J.

Furthermore, Bank argues that even if this Court were to conclude that the modification agreements "substantially impaired" the junior lienholders' interests and were invalid for lack of Respondents' consent, this Court should, nonetheless, reverse the decision of the circuit court which entirely disregarded the subordination agreement and afforded complete priority to Respondents. Citing RESTATEMENT (THIRD) OF THE LAW OF PROPERTY, *Mortgages,* § 7.3 (1997), Bank insists that under these conditions it would lose priority *only to the extent of the modifications.*

Respondents counter that the "remedy awarded when there is prejudice to the junior lienor—partial or complete loss of priority—depends on the degree of prejudice." They assert that Bank's Note No. 1 went from one page of text to seven in the final modification; that no one ever notified them of these modifications; that there were eight extensions of the maturity date of the note and multiple increases in the interest rate charged by over 50% (from 7% to 10 3/4 %), which resulted in over $200,000.00 in additional interest payments to the Bank.

Furthermore, Respondents maintain that the introduction of cross-collateralization provisions added two tracts of property to the collateral contemplated by the original note and tripled the amount of debt collateralized from $1.2 million to over $3.4 million. They also point to the introduction of cross-default provisions, waiver of bankruptcy stay provisions, and the addition of appraisal fees, loan extension and renewal fees, and payment of collection fees which together " 'substantially impaired' the value of [their] security interest—the motel property—and 'effectively destroyed' the remaining equity in the property."

I.

The matter of the reordering of priorities of deeds of trusts appears to be a matter of first impression in Missouri. Neither of the primary parties has called our attention to any reported case in this state, and our own research has failed to find any reported cases in this jurisdiction involving this particular subject. However, as discussed, *infra,* a significant body of case law from other jurisdictions has dealt with this issue.

We initially observe that a "mortgagee may waive the priority of his lien. . . ." Community Title Co. v. Crow, 728 S.W.2d 652, 654 (Mo.App.1987). Also, "[i]t is entirely competent for the parties in interest, upon a sufficient consideration, to make an agreement by which a junior lien on real estate may be given precedence over a superior encumbrance." Sinclair Refining Co. v. Wyatt, 347 Mo. 862, 149 S.W.2d 353, 356 (1941). "Because it alters the normal priority of the mortgages, priority under a subordination agreement is strictly limited by the express terms of the agreement." Citizens and South. Nat. Bank v. Smith, 277 S.C. 162, 284 S.E.2d 770, 771 (1981).

We also note that "[r]eplacement and modification of senior mortgages commonly occur." NELSON & WHITMAN REAL ESTATE FINANCE LAW, 3d ed., Vol. 1, § 9.4 (1993); *see* Comment a, RESTATEMENT (THIRD) PROPERTY, *Mortgages,* § 7.3 (1997). "Moreover, a senior mortgagee and the mortgagor frequently agree to certain modifications in the terms of the mortgage debt." NELSON & WHITMAN REAL ESTATE FINANCE LAW, 3d ed., Vol. 1, § 9.4 (1993). "These modifications often entail an extension of the term, a change in the interest rate, and in some instances, an increase in the principal amount of the mortgage debt. Frequently, such modifications represent an attempt to deal with mortgagor financial distress." *Id.* However, these modifications "can create priority disputes vis à vis intervening junior lienholders." *Id.*

"It is well established that while a senior mortgagee can enter into an agreement with the mortgagor modifying the terms of the underlying note or mortgage without first having to notify any junior lienors or to obtain their consent, if the modification is such that it prejudices the rights of the junior lienors or impairs the security, their consent is required." Shultis v. Woodstock Land Dev. Assocs., 188 A.D.2d 234, 594 N.Y.S.2d 890, 892 (N.Y.App.Div.1993); see Fleet Bank v. County of Monroe Ind. Dev. Agency, 224 A.D.2d 964, 637 N.Y.S.2d 870, 871 (N.Y.App.Div.1996); Empire Trust Co. v. Park-Lexington Corp., 243 App. Div. 315, 321, 276 N.Y.S. 586, 592 (1934); Shane v. Winter Hill Fed. Sav. and Loan Ass'n., 397 Mass. 479, 492 N.E.2d 92, 95 (1986). "Failure to obtain the consent in these cases results in the modification being ineffective as to the junior lienors and the senior lienor relinquishing to the junior lienors its priority with respect to the modified terms." *Shultis,* 594 N.Y.S.2d at 892 (citations omitted). "While this sanction ordinarily creates only the partial loss of priority noted above, in situations where the senior lienor's actions in modifying the note or mortgage have substantially impaired the junior lienors' security interest or effectively destroyed their equity, courts have indicated an inclination to wholly divest the senior lien of its priority and to elevate the junior liens to a position of superiority." *Id.* (citation omitted); *see* cases cited in FRIEDMAN, CONTRACTS & CONVEYANCES, 6th ed., Vol. 2, § 6.5 n. 13 (1998).

It is our view, however, and the view of both parties to this appeal, that cases in which a junior mortgage lien is elevated above the paramount mortgage are the exception and not the rule. It is this Court's observation, on reviewing the case law in this area, that only in a rare number of cases such as in Koloff [v. Reston Corp., 1993 WL 106062 (Del. Ch. 1993)]and Gluskin [v. Atlantic Savings & Loan Ass'n, 32 Cal. App.3d 307 (1973)] where the paramount mortgage has substantially impaired the security interest of the junior mortgage, are the priorities rearranged. See Lennar Northeast Partners v. Buice, 49 Cal.App.4th 1576, 57 Cal.Rptr.2d 435, 442–443 (1996) discussing and distinguishing *Gluskin, supra; see also* FRIEDMAN, CONTRACTS & CONVEYANCES, 6th ed., Vol. 2, § 6.5 (1998). We are confirmed in this view by our reading of RESTATEMENT (THIRD) OF THE LAW OF PROPERTY, *Mortgages,* § 7.3 (1997). It provides in pertinent part:

> Replacement and Modification of Senior Mortgages: Effect on Intervening Interests.
>
> (b) If a senior mortgage or the obligation it secures is modified by the parties, the mortgage as modified retains priority as against junior interests in the real estate, *except to the extent that the modification is materially prejudicial to the holders of such interests* and is not within the scope of a reservation of right to modify as provided in Subsection(c).

RESTATEMENT (THIRD) OF THE LAW OF PROPERTY, *Mortgages,* § 7.3(b) (1997) (emphasis added). The term "materially prejudicial" cannot be precisely defined. It is similar to the term "substantially impaired." *See Shultis,* 594 N.Y.S.2d at 892. Necessarily a determination when material prejudice occurs is fact-driven by the circumstances of each case. In this connection, Comment b, to § 7.3 RESTATEMENT (THIRD) OF THE LAW OF PROPERTY, *Mortgages,* (1997) *supra,* sets out:

> There is a strong presumption under this section that a time extension on a senior mortgage or obligation, standing alone, is not materially prejudicial to intervening interests. A finding of material prejudice is justified only in the rare situation where the time extension can fairly be said to place the junior interest in substantially weaker position. The typical junior lienholder is normally grateful to have a time extension forestall the destruction of its lien by a senior foreclosure.

. . .

"Other sorts of changes that may be made in the terms of a replacement mortgage are not so benign. Obviously an increase in the principal amount will prejudice the holders of junior interests." Comment b, RESTATEMENT (THIRD) OF THE LAW OF PROPERTY, *Mortgages,* § 7.3 (1997). "[W]hen the obligation is increased, by an increase in the principal amount or an increase in the interest rate, the junior lienholder's position is worsened. (3 POWELL, *Real Property,* (1996) § 458, pp. 37–258—37–259)." *Lennar,* 57 Cal.Rptr.2d at 440; *see Shultis,* 594 N.Y.S.2d at 893.

Accordingly, "[w]here the modification entails an increase in the senior mortgage interest rate or an increase in its principal amount, the junior lienor will gain priority over the earlier mortgage to the extent of the modification." NELSON & WHITMAN REAL ESTATE FINANCE, 3d ed., Vol. 1, § 9.4 (1993); *Shultis,* 594 N.Y.S.2d at 893; *see* Comment c, RESTATEMENT (THIRD) OF THE LAW OF PROPERTY, *Mortgages,* § 7.3 (1997).

Lastly, cross-collateralization provisions which tie together unrelated properties, the foreclosure of which triggers foreclosure of all properties held by the debtor, can pose "unique risks" to the interests of a junior lienholder depending upon the circumstances of each case. *See Koloff, supra,* at 3. We now apply the foregoing principles to the facts of this case.

We are not convinced that the eight extensions of the maturity date of Bank's Note No. 1 over a six year period, in and of themselves, materially prejudiced Respondents interest in its collateral to the extent that the circuit court was justified in holding the parties' subordination agreement null and void. *See Lennar Partners,* 57 Cal.Rptr.2d at 440; *Eurovest,* 559 So.2d at 1199; *Shultis,* 594 N.Y.S.2d at 893. "The holder of the junior encumbrance is regarded as necessarily taking the risk of a postponement (frequently an advantage to a second mortgagee) of the date of payment of the whole or part of the senior mortgage debt." Guleserian v. Fields, 351 Mass. 238, 218 N.E.2d 397, 401–02 (1966). "The rule has been referred to as the 'universal rule.' " *Id.* at 402.

Here, while Bank reaped additional interest payments, as best we can glean, the record also shows that during this time period the principal owed Respondents on Respondent's Note was reduced from an approximate balance of $1.077 million to approximately $932,000.00 at the time of C & J's default in December 1999. This constituted a reduction of about $145,000.00 in the principal amount owed Respondents. More importantly, extending the maturity date of Bank's Note No. 1 resulted in Respondent receiving over $762,000.00 in payments from C & J after December 1993, the original maturity date for Bank's Note No. 1.[6]

It is our view, however, that modifications of Bank's Note No. 1 requiring C & J to pay interest in excess of 7%, combined with the addition of appraisal fees, loan extension and renewal fees, cross-collateralization, cross-default and waiver of bankruptcy stay provisions, all of which were absent from the original text of Bank's Note No. 1 on June 23, 1993, materially impaired the value of Respondents' interest in the front parcel of the property. This is supported by the record. *See Lennar Partners,* 57 Cal.Rptr.2d at 439–43; *Shultis,* 594 N.Y.S.2d at 892–93; *Fleet Bank,* 637 N.Y.S.2d at 871–72. As previously set out, Respondents suggest that these interest rate changes resulted in the Bank receiving an additional $200,000.00 in interest payments. Bank acknowledges that the sum of $165,842.17 constitutes the difference between the total payoff amount actually due Bank and the "adjusted" payoff amount had the Bank continued to charge interest at the rate of 7% per annum on Bank's Note No. 1.

---

[6] Respondents' Note of October 1992 provided for monthly installment payments of $11,580.27, carrying interest at the rate of 10% annually, maturing with a final balloon payment in five years.

Furthermore, the modification agreement of March 30, 1999, made provisions for the payment by C & J of a "loan extension fee" in the amount of $14,265.98 together with an "appraisal fee" of $4,000.00, which added to the debt burden assumed by C & J. The cross-collateralization clauses meant that the front parcel, as well as the back parcel, were pledged as collateral for two of Bank's loans, and in a similar vein, cross-default provisions contained in the modification agreements meant that a default by C & J under either of Bank's loans acted as a default under both. Without these cross-collateralization and cross-default provisions, C & J would have been better posed to pay on one Bank note and not the other. While speculative, C & J might have been better positioned to have avoided the risk of a foreclosure on the entire property. *See Koloff,* 1993 WL at 4.

Despite these impairments, however, we are not prepared to agree that the Bank should lose its priority as senior lienholder relative to its senior position relating to the front parcel. The equities in this case do not require such a result. Here, the impairment to Respondents' security and its rights as a junior lienholder engendered by the modification agreements can be eliminated largely by denying priority to the modifications, save for the extension of the maturity dates of Bank's Note No. 1. *See Lennar,* 57 Cal.Rptr.2d at 442; see RESTATEMENT (THIRD) OF THE LAW OF PROPERTY, *Mortgages,* § 7.3(b) (1997). Denying priority only to the modification agreements in terms as aforesaid goes a long way to restore Respondents to the same position as before: the position they bargained for by agreeing to accept a second lien on the property as security for their loan. *Id.*

The circuit court erred as a matter of fact and law in its declaration that the lien of Respondents' Deed of Trust No. 1 was superior to that of Bank's Deed of Trust No. 1. *Ridgway,* 26 S.W.3d at 430. Bank's Deed of Trust No. 1 dated June 23, 1993, per its original terms, securing Bank's Note No. 1 of the same date, per its original terms-save for extension of maturity dates, should hold a senior position to that of Respondents' Deed of Trust and Respondents' Note. Additionally, Respondents' Deed of Trust securing Respondents' Note should continue to hold a senior position to that of Bank's Deed of Trust No. 3, which secures Bank's Note No. 1 and Bank's Note No. 2. See Howard, Singer & Meehan v. Clayton Fed. Savings and Loan Ass'n., 578 S.W.2d 56, 57 (Mo.App.1978). Point One is well taken, in part.

. . .

The judgment of the circuit court dated October 31, 2000, as modified December 8, 2000, is set aside and the cause is remanded with directions to the circuit court to enter a judgment consistent with this opinion. Upon remand, the trial court is directed to determine the balance due under the original terms of Bank's Note No. 1, except for the maturity date extensions. The judgment should reflect that Respondent's deed of trust is junior to that balance as determined. To this end, the circuit court is authorized to conduct further proceedings and make such further orders which may be just and proper, including orders relating to foreclosure of the parcels of land involved in this litigation.

NOTES

1. *Extensions and Modifications of Senior Mortgages.* Given the competing expectations and public policies, do you thing that Burney v. McLaughlin was correctly decided? What are the legitimate expectations of the junior lienor? The senior lender? Where should the default rule lie, and why? Is drafting a possible solution, and how should a clause addressing the situation be negotiated and drafted? See Meislin, Extension Agreements and the Rights of Junior Mortgagees, 42 Va.L.Rev. 939–940 (1956) ("Yet, despite these and similar imperatives, first mortgagees blandly extend past due mortgages on New York realty with owners on such new terms as are negotiated between them, but without notice to intervening lienors").

2. *Limitations on Junior Mortgages.* The presence of a junior mortgage may cause the senior lender to lose rights under its mortgage. For example, *Burney* shows how the senior lender may be prevented from adjusting the loan terms in order to maintain flexibility in administering and policing the loan. The senior lender may be subject to increased exposure to liability from a junior lender. See Allee v. Benser, 779 S.W.2d 61 (Tex.1988) (junior lender may assert usury claim arising under first mortgage, although it cannot enforce forfeiture penalty under the Texas statute).

Further, if a second mortgage is foreclosed and the property sold to a new owner, the first mortgagee will have to deal with an owner it did not submit to its screening procedures. This new owner may lack the financial ability to pay the mortgage or, in a commercial context, to manage the property. Also, the senior lender may be concerned that a second mortgage reduces the equity of the borrower in the property—an event which the loan-value ratio of the first mortgage had been designed to protect.

In reaction to this, in some rare cases the first mortgagee may prohibit junior mortgages by requiring payment of the first mortgage if a second mortgage is obtained or by making the placement of the second mortgage a default for which the first mortgagee may foreclose.

The first mortgagee may also receive some protection under its due-on-sale clause which typically requires the mortgage to be paid upon transfer of the property. See pages 433–437 below. In Unifirst Federal Savings & Loan Ass'n v. Tower Loan of Mississippi, Inc., 524 So.2d 290 (Miss.1986), the court held that while the placement of a second mortgage did not trigger the due on sale clause in the first mortgage, the sale of the land pursuant to foreclosure of the second did. The court reasoned that "[w]hile our law should facilitate home equity/second mortgage loans, no reason has been advanced why this should be at the expense of the contractual rights of the first mortgage holder." 524 So.2d at 292.

3. *The Purchase Money Priority.* Purchase money mortgagees have traditionally enjoyed a preferred position, characterized as the "purchase money priority," over prior lienors such as judgment creditors and mortgagees claiming under after-acquired property clauses in mortgages previously executed by the mortgagor. The rationale for the purchase money priority is that these earlier lienors, unlike the purchase money mortgagee, did not rely on the property in question when they extended credit to the mortgagor.

Originally the purchase money priority was given only to sellers who took back a mortgage to finance the buyer's purchase of the property. But, over time, many states extended the purchase money priority to third-party lenders who provided the buyer with part or all of the funds needed to acquire the parcel. Even in these states, however, as between the financing seller and a third party lender providing part of the purchase money, the seller will always receive priority. See generally, G. Nelson & D. Whitman, Real Estate Finance Law §§ 9.1–9.2 (5th ed. 2007).

Most often the purchase money priority probably hinders rather than helps the financing seller. For example, it is not unusual for a buyer who has obtained a commitment for 80% purchase money financing from an institutional lender to be strapped for cash and to require financing for another 10% or 15% from the seller. Although the seller would like to make the loan, she realizes that her automatic purchase money priority will result in the institutional lender receiving only a second lien—a position that state and federal regulations will commonly bar an institutional lender from taking. The solution usually employed by the seller and the institutional lender is for the seller expressly to subordinate her lien to the lien of the institutional lender, thus placing the institution in a first lien position and herself in a second lien position. Courts will closely scrutinize subordination agreements for possible overreaching by institutional lenders and will restore the purchase money priority where overreaching or other unfairness to the seller is evident. See pages 636–646 below.

Can you see why—at least in jurisdictions with notice and race-notice recording acts—the parties cannot avoid judicial review, and safely arrange for the institutional lender to obtain the needed priority, simply by recording the institutional lender's mortgage before the seller records hers? Of what is the institutional lender likely to have notice at the time it records?

4. *Bibliographic Note.* For an excellent analysis of the dangers of junior home equity mortgages and criticism of the federal government's encouragement of those loans through tax and bankruptcy incentives and the preemption of state usury ceilings, see Forrester, Mortgaging the American Dream: A Critical Evaluation of the Federal Government's Promotion of Home Equity Financing, 67 Tul.L.Rev. 373 (1994). See generally, Randolph, The FNMA/FHLMC Uniform Home Improvement Loan Instruments: A Commentary and Critique, 16 Real Prop., Probate & Trust J. 546 (1981); Randolph, The FNMA/FHLMC Uniform Home Improvement Loan Note: The Secondary Market Meets the Consumer Movement, 60 N.C.L.Rev. 365 (1982).

C. TRANSFERS OF MORTGAGED PROPERTY AND MORTGAGE INTERESTS

1. TRANSFERS BY THE MORTGAGOR

a. DUTIES OF THE TRANSFEREE

A mortgagee typically has two avenues of relief against a defaulting mortgagor. She may proceed against the mortgagor personally on his promise, embodied in his note or bond, to repay the mortgage debt. And she may proceed against the land securing the promise by foreclosure and sale, using the sale proceeds to satisfy the debt.

Relief becomes a bit more complicated when the mortgagor has transferred the encumbered land. If the transferee has taken *subject to* the mortgage, the mortgagee will have no recourse against the transferee personally but can, as before, obtain relief against the mortgagor personally or against the land through foreclosure. If the mortgagee chooses to proceed against the mortgagor personally, the mortgagor, once having paid the debt, becomes subrogated to the mortgagee's rights against the land and can thus obtain reimbursement from the land itself through foreclosure, sale and satisfaction of the debt out of the sale proceeds.

If, by contrast, the transferee has *assumed* the mortgagor's personal liability for the debt, the mortgagee will be able to obtain relief not only from the mortgagor and from the land, but also from the transferee personally. The assumption promise typically appears in the purchase agreement between the mortgagor and the transferee, and the mortgagee can enforce that undertaking under third party beneficiary theory. See, e.g., Joyner v. Vitale, 926 P.2d 1154 (Alaska 1996). If the mortgagee elects to proceed against the mortgagor personally, the mortgagor can obtain reimbursement by proceeding both against the transferee on his promise and against the land, which remains the primary security for the debt.

First Federal Savings and Loan Association of Gary v. Arena

Indiana Court of Appeals, 1980.
406 N.E.2d 1279.

CHIPMAN, JUDGE.

CASE SUMMARY

First Federal Savings and Loan Association of Gary, (First Federal), appeals from a grant of summary judgment in favor of Michael and Grace Arena, (Arenas), in a foreclosure action brought by First Federal against the Arenas and their grantee, Sanford G. Richardson, as well as various lienholders.

First Federal asserts it was erroneous for the trial court to hold that altering the mortgages' interest rate was a material change which discharged the Arenas from personal liability on the mortgages. According to First Federal, a reservation of rights clause contained in the supplemental agreements to the mortgages executed by the Arenas and First Federal, permitted First Federal in its dealings with Mr. Richardson to increase the rate of interest on the mortgages without first affording the Arenas notice or obtaining their consent, while still retaining the Arenas' liability on the mortgages. The trial court, however, found the reservation of rights clause did not authorize First Federal to so act and entered judgment in favor of the Arenas.

We affirm the judgment of the trial court.

FACTS

On May 26, 1965, the Arenas executed a note, mortgage, and supplemental agreement with First Federal. The note provided for a loan of $32,000 at an interest rate of 5¾%, and the mortgage securing this note provided for advances of up to $6,400. March 11, 1966, the Arenas were granted an advance of $5,100, and in consideration, they executed a modification and extension agreement which provided they would owe a new balance of $36,664.81, and the interest rate would be increased to 6%. A separate note, mortgage, and supplemental agreement were also executed by the Arenas in relation to this advance.

March 10, 1969, the Arenas conveyed the real estate which was the subject of both the May 26, 1965, and March 11, 1966, mortgages to Sanford G. Richardson by warranty deed subject to the two mortgages to First Federal.[1] The same day, without notice to or the consent of the Arenas, Mr. Richardson and First Federal entered into a modification and extension agreement, under the terms of which Richardson assumed both of the mortgages in question, and the time for payment was extended to twenty years; there was also a change in the interest rate from 6% to 7¼%. Thus, this agreement, signed only by Richardson and First Federal, was designed to be a modification of First Federal's earlier agreement with the Arenas by extending the time of payment and modifying the terms of payment to which the Arenas and First Federal had agreed.

After June 27, 1975, Richardson failed to make the payments due under the March 10, 1969, modification and extension agreement. As a result, a default on the mortgages and notes occurred and a suit in foreclosure was filed on behalf of First Federal against the Arenas, Richardson, and several lienholders.

ISSUE

. . . [T]he sole question which has been duly and properly preserved for our consideration is the propriety of granting the Arenas' motion for summary judgment.

DECISION

By reason of an expressed provision to that effect in the supplemental agreements between the Arenas and First Federal, the Arenas were not released from liability upon extension of the mortgage in the agreement between Mr. Richardson and First Federal; however, this agreement not only extended the time for payment, but it also modified the terms of payment by increasing the interest rate. It is our opinion the trial court properly found the Arenas had not consented to

---

[1] Although the grantee's preliminary offer to purchase provided Mr. Richardson would "assume" the existing mortgages on the property, the warranty deed evidencing the consummated contract recited the conveyance was "subject to" the Arenas' mortgages to First Federal.

Based upon the general rule that any inconsistencies between the terms in the preliminary contract and the deed are to be settled by the deed alone, since all prior negotiations are considered merged in that instrument, Wayne International Building & Loan Ass'n v. Beckner (1922) 191 Ind. 664, 134 N.E. 273; Guckenberger v. Shank (1941) 110 Ind.App. 442, 37 N.E.2d 708, along with the fact none of the parties argued there was any mistake in drawing the deed or that they intended to make it read other than as in fact it was written, we have concluded, for purposes of this opinion, the conveyance was "subject to" the mortgage.

such a change in interest rates and, therefore, were released from liability.[3] Arenas' grantee and First Federal could not modify the original mortgagors' agreement without the mortgagors' consent.

The focal point in this controversy is the meaning to be accorded a reservation of rights clause which appeared in the supplemental agreement executed by the Arenas when they obtained the initial mortgage and later secured the advance. The agreement provided:

> "THE UNDERSIGNED, Michael Arena and Grace Arena, Husband and Wife, ..., hereinafter referred to as the Mortgagor, hereby executes and delivers to FIRST FEDERAL SAVINGS AND LOAN ASSOCIATION OF GARY, ..., hereinafter referred to as the Mortgagee, this Supplemental Agreement, pursuant to a Mortgage executed and delivered concurrently herewith, and this Supplemental Agreement is expressly made a part of said Mortgage,. . . .

THE MORTGAGOR COVENANTS:

> 6.   That in the event the ownership of said property or any part thereof becomes vested in a person other than the Mortgagor, the Mortgagee may, without notice to the Mortgagor, deal with such successor or successors in interest with reference to this mortgage and the debt hereby secured in the same manner as with the Mortgagor, and may forbear to sue or may extend time for payment of the debt, secured hereby, without discharging or in any way affecting the liability of the Mortgagor hereunder or upon the debt hereby secured;"

First Federal asserts the reservation of rights language set out above permitted it, in dealing with Richardson, to increase the interest rate and extend the time of payment without first obtaining the Arenas' consent while still retaining their liability. Appellant takes the position that the portion of paragraph six providing for no discharge modified forbearing to sue and extending time for payment as well as dealing in the same manner as with the mortgagor; therefore, since the interest rate was increased when the Arenas were given their additional advance, according to First Federal, raising the interest rate in its agreement with Richardson would merely be dealing with him in the

---

[3]   If the full amount due on foreclosure did not exceed the value of the property at the time of the execution of the Modification and Extension Agreement, it was proper for the trial court to completely discharge the Arenas. Mutual Ben. Life Ins. Co. v. Lindley (1932) 97 Ind.App. 575, 183 N.E. 127; Stevens, Extension Agreements in the "Subject-To" Mortgage Situation, 15 U.Cin.L.Rev. 58 (1941). As a corollary, if the value of the land at the time of this agreement was less than the amount of the mortgage on the property, the Arenas should have remained liable to the extent of this difference.

Although it was improper for the trial court to hold there was a complete discharge without also holding the value of the land at the time of the March 10, 1969, agreement fully supported the mortgage loan, First Federal never raised any error regarding the extent to which the Arenas were discharged, see note 2 supra; consequently, we can only assume the amount due on foreclosure on March 10, 1969, would have been less than the value of the property at that time.

We note, since Mr. Richardson offered to purchase the real estate in question for $37,000, and the aggregate balance remaining unpaid when Mr. Richardson and First Federal executed the Modification and Extension Agreement was $33,393.83, it appears the value of the land, in fact, did exceed the amount due, and thus, a complete discharge would have been proper.

same manner as it had dealt with the Arenas and, consequently, should not result in a discharge.

The Arenas, on the other hand, contend the reservation of rights clause in the Supplemental Agreement made no reference to the alteration or modification of the interest rate but rather, referred only to an extension of the time for payment or the decision to forbear to sue.

While it is true paragraph six indicates First Federal could deal with successors in interest to the mortgage in the same manner as with the mortgagor, we hold the resolution of whether this meant First Federal and the Arenas' grantee would be permitted to increase the interest rate without affecting the Arenas' liability was a question of law for the trial court since the rules applicable to construction of contracts generally apply to the construction of an agreement whereby a purchaser of mortgaged premises assumes the payment of the mortgage. 20 I.L.E. Mortgages § 193.

As a rule, the interpretation, construction, or legal effect of a contract is a question of law for the trial court, not a question of fact. Kleen Leen, Inc. v. Mylcraine, (1977) Ind.App., 369 N.E.2d 638. However, when the terms of the contract are ambiguous and their meaning is to be determined by extrinsic evidence, the construction of the contract is for the jury. Conversely, where the ambiguity in the contract arises by reason of the language used and not because of extrinsic facts, the construction of the contract is a question of law. Wilson v. Kauffman, (1973) 156 Ind.App. 307, 296 N.E.2d 432. Thus, whenever summary judgment is granted based upon the construction of a contract, the trial court has determined as a matter of law that the contract in question is not so ambiguous or uncertain that resort must be made to extrinsic evidence in order to ascertain the contract's meaning.

The essence of the appeal before us then is whether the trial court correctly concluded that as a matter of law, the scope of the reservation of rights clause found in paragraph six did not include altering or modifying the interest rate, and consequently, First Federal did not reserve the right to modify and increase the interest rate from 6% to 71/4% without the consent of the Arenas. We hold the trial court's entry of summary judgment in favor of Arenas was proper.

When the Arenas conveyed the real estate to Richardson subject to the existing mortgages to First Federal, the land became as to said parties, the primary source of funds for payment of the debt. Mutual Ben. Life Ins. Co. v. Lindley, (1932) 97 Ind.App. 575, 183 N.E. 127. No technical relation of principal and surety arose between the Arenas and their grantee from this conveyance, but an equity did arise which bears a close resemblance to the equitable rights of a surety. As a result, the Arenas assumed a position analogous to that of a surety, and the grantee became the principal debtor to the extent of the value of the land conveyed. Mutual Ben. Life Ins. Co. v. Lindley, supra; Warm, Some Aspects of the Rights and Liabilities of Mortgagee, Mortgagor and Grantee, 10 Temple L.Q. 116 (1936).

While a mortgagor in such a situation may consent in advance to future modifications or agree his liability will not be discharged by subsequent agreements between his grantee and the mortgagee, such clauses are to be strictly construed against the mortgagee, see Friedman, Discharge of Personal Liability on Mortgage Debts in New York, 52 Yale L.J. 771, 788 (1943), since it would be unjust to subject the mortgagor to a new risk or material change to which he has not consented. Consequently, a reservation of rights clause will not prevent a discharge of liability where the modification in question exceeds the scope of the consent in the clause. This should come as no surprise since the mortgagor occupies the position of a surety, and the law of suretyship provides that a surety is entitled to stand on the strict letter of the contract upon which he is liable, and where he does not consent to a variation and a variation is made, it is fatal, see American States Insurance Co. v. Floyd I. Staub, Inc., (1977) Ind.App., 370 N.E.2d 989; White v. Household Finance Corp., (1973) 158 Ind.App. 394, 302 N.E.2d 828; therefore, an agreement between the principals for a higher interest than called for by the original contract will, if made without the surety's consent, release him from all liability. 74 Am.Jur.2d Suretyship s 47 (1974); see also 4 Am.Jur.2d Alteration of Instruments s 55 (1962).

The fact First Federal dealt with the grantee shows it knew of the Arenas' conveyance, and knowing of this conveyance, it was incumbent upon First Federal not to deal with the grantee in such a manner as would jeopardize or alter the surety-principal relationship. Warm, Some Aspects of the Rights and Liabilities of Mortgagee, Mortgagor and Grantee, 10 Temple L.Q. 116 (1936). The modification and extension agreement in question provided Mr. Richardson would personally assume the mortgage debt and thus, inured to the benefit of First Federal, but at the same time, the terms of the Arenas' earlier mortgage were changed to the detriment of the Arenas. If this increase in the interest rate was beyond the scope of the reservation of rights clause, the Arenas were thereby discharged, and the grantee became the sole debtor on the mortgages.

We hold the trial court properly rejected First Federal's argument that by increasing the interest rate it was merely dealing with Mr. Richardson in the same manner as it had dealt with the Arenas, and therefore, according to paragraph six, the Arenas should not have been discharged.

While it is true paragraph six indicated First Federal could deal with successors in interest to the mortgage in the same manner as with the mortgagor, this provision did not say First Federal could do so with impunity. We agree with the trial court that the portion of this paragraph providing for no discharge only modified forbearing to sue or extending the time for payment; consequently, the mortgagor would not be discharged from liability if the mortgagee simply extended the time for payment of the debt or opted not to bring suit, but these were the only situations where the mortgagee knew to a certainty his actions in dealing with the grantee would not discharge the mortgagor. The reservation of rights clause in paragraph six did not apply to activities which allegedly came within the ambit of dealing in the same manner as with the mortgagor. At the risk of being redundant, we again note, paragraph six stated in part:

> "6. (T)he Mortgagee may, without notice to the
> Mortgagor, deal with . . . successors in interest with reference

to this mortgage and the debt hereby secured in the same manner as with the Mortgagor, and. . . ." (our emphasis)

The punctuation used clearly sets this portion of paragraph six apart from the remainder of the paragraph which then goes on to provide the mortgagee

"may forbear to sue or may extend time for payment of the debt, . . ., without discharging or in any way affecting the liability of the Mortgagor hereunder or upon the debt hereby secured."

In order to give the reservation of rights clause the expanded application urged by First Federal so that it also applied to dealing in the same manner as with the mortgagor, it would be necessary to ignore the punctuation used and the maxim that such clauses should be strictly construed against the mortgagee. Further, such a construction would change the reservation of rights provision from applying in two definite situations to an open-ended invitation to argue there was no discharge because the mortgagee either could have or in fact had dealt with the mortgagor in the same manner; the possible activities which arguably could then come within this clause's application would be indefinite.

We hold the construction of the supplemental agreement between the Arenas and First Federal was a question of law for the trial court, which correctly held paragraph six did not authorize First Federal and the Arenas' grantee to alter the terms of payment on the mortgage debt by increasing the interest rate without affecting the Arenas' liability.

Judgment affirmed.

NOTE

As First Federal Savings and Loan Association of Gary v. Arena indicates, the law of suretyship will control the relative liabilities of the original mortgagor, transferee, and the land after mortgaged land is transferred. Moreover, as *Arena* indicates, certain actions of the parties after transfer can discharge the usual liabilities.

Assuming no agreement to the contrary, if the mortgagee and the transferee agree, without the mortgagor's consent, to extend the time that the debt is due, the majority rule will reach a different result depending on whether the transfer was an assumption or subject to the mortgage. With an assumption, the mortgagor is released completely by the time extension; with a subject to transfer, the mortgagor is released to the extent of the value of the property at the original due date for the debt. What reasons support this general rule? Do you now see why the *Arena* court discussed the value of the property as of March 10, 1969? See Zastrow v. Knight, 56 S.D. 554, 229 N.W. 925 (1930). Assuming no agreement to the contrary, typically courts release mortgagors from liability in both subject to and assumption situation if the mortgagee and the transferee agree to increase the interest rate or principal amount, without the consent of the mortgagor. See Restatement (Third) of the Law of Property—Mortgages § 5.3. Why is that so? Does this explain the court's close reading of the clause purporting to modify the general rule in *Arena*?

Section 3–605(c) of the 1990 revision to the U.C.C. provides that an extension of the due date of a negotiable instrument discharges the indorser or accommodation party "to the extent the indorser or accommodation party proves that the extension party caused loss" to them. While it could be argued that section 3–605 applies by analogy to mortgagors, the fact that the new version refers specifically to indorsers and accommodation parties, and not "parties" generally, apparently indicates an intention to exclude mortgagors, with the result that the common law doctrines of suretyship would continue to apply to mortgagors. Section 5.3, comment d of the Restatement of Mortgages adopts a similar position. See Cohen, Suretyship Principles in the New Article 3: Clarifications and Substantive Changes, 42 Ala. L. Rev. 595 (1991).

b.   LIMITATIONS ON THE TRANSFEROR

Lenders regularly seek to limit the mortgagor's freedom to transfer the mortgaged property through "due on sale" clauses that make the loan due upon the property's transfer. One reason for a due on sale clause is to hedge the risk of rising interest rates; making a mortgage due on sale enables the lender to get its funds back and relend them at current rates. Also, lenders want to avoid the risk of waste, default and foreclosure that comes from dealing with a new borrower whose capabilities they never had the opportunity to assess.

Before the passage of the Garn-St. Germain Depository Act of 1982, 12 U.S.C.A. § 1701j–3, states took contrasting approaches to the validity of due on sale clauses. One group of states invoked the principle of freedom of alienation and put the burden on the lender to demonstrate that circumstances justified enforcement of the clause. See, e.g., Wellenkamp v. Bank of America, 21 Cal.3d 943, 952, 148 Cal.Rptr. 379, 385, 582 P.2d 970, 976 (1978) ("the mere fact of the sale is not in itself sufficient to warrant enforcement of the clause"). Other states cited the principle of freedom of contract and put the burden on the borrower to demonstrate that enforcement was not justified. Applying these principles, most courts concluded that due on sale clauses were reasonable and enforceable. See, e.g., Mutual Federal Sav. & Loan Ass'n v. Wisconsin Wire Works, 71 Wis.2d 531, 239 N.W.2d 20 (1976) (deferring to the lender's evaluation of the reliability of the borrower and transferee); Malouff v. Midland Federal Sav. & Loan Ass'n, 181 Colo. 294, 509 P.2d 1240 (1973) (accepting the lender's need to adjust interest rates as reason for enforcement). For a pre-Garn-St. Germain survey of the different approaches, see A.B.A. Comm. on Real Estate Financing, Enforcement of Due-on-Transfer Clauses, 13 Real Prop., Probate & Trust J. 891 (1978).

The Garn-St. Germain Depository Act of 1982, 12 U.S.C.A. § 1701j–3, preempts state law and generally validates due on sale clauses:

> Notwithstanding any provision of the constitution or laws (including judicial decisions) of any State to the contrary, a lender may . . . enter into a contract containing a due-on-sale clause.

Id., § (b)(1). The statute further provides that the loan contract exclusively governs the lender's exercise of a due on sale clause and fixes all of the rights of and remedies of the parties. Id., § (b)(2). The Act, however, adds that a due on sale clause in a mortgage for residential real estate with less than five dwelling units will not be triggered by the creation of a junior mortgage, a transfer due to the death of a joint tenant or tenant by the entirety, the granting of a lease not exceeding a three year term, a transfer to a relative resulting from the borrower's death, a conveyance to the borrower's spouse or children, or a transfer resulting from a divorce or related property settlement. Id., § (d).

For a comprehensive discussion of the history of due on sale clauses and the judicial and legislative responses, see Nelson & Whitman, Congressional Preemption of Mortgage Due-On-Sale Law: An Analysis of The Garn-St. Germain Act, 35 Hastings L.J. 241 (1983).

NOTES

1.   *Applications.* After the validation of due on sale clauses by Garn-St. Germain, various issues remain concerning their interpretation and application. First, when is the clause triggered? Federal regulations promulgated after Garn-St. Germain state that the exercise of a due on sale clause "shall be exclusively governed by the terms of the loan contract." 12 C.F.R. §§ 591.3, 591.4 (1991). A sale or transfer is defined as "the conveyance of real property of [sic, read or] any right, title or interest therein, whether legal or equitable, whether voluntary or involuntary, by outright sale, deed, installment sale contract, land contract, contract for deed, leasehold interest with a term greater than three years, lease-option contract or any other method of conveyance of real property interests." 12 C.F.R. § 591.2(b) (1991). Under this language, would the execution of an executory contract of sale be a "sale or transfer"? See generally Roszowski, Drafting Around Mortgage Due-On-Sale Clauses: The Dangers of Playing Hide and Seek, 21 Real Prop. Probate & Trust J. 23 (1986).

The mortgage may only give the lender a limited due on sale clause, in an effort by the borrower to pass on a favorable loan to a subsequent buyer. Thus, a lender may only have the right to require that the loan be paid upon transfer of the property if the lender did not give prior written approval to the sale. In Western Life Insurance Company v. McPherson K.M.P., 702 F.Supp. 836 (D.Kan.1988), the mortgage contained such a clause but provided that the lender could not unreasonably withhold consent. The court found that consent was not unreasonably withheld where the mortgagor did not make a formal request for approval and failed to provide any detailed financial information concerning the buyer. If the clause does not have a reasonableness requirement, will the court imply one? Compare Quintana v. First Interstate Bank of Albuquerque, 105 N.M. 784, 737 P.2d 896 (App.1987) (declining to imply a reasonableness standard and permitting absolute discretion) with the Uniform Land Security Interest Act § 108 (imposing an obligation of good faith in every contract or duty governed by the statute).

2.   *Prepayment Penalties.* The due on sale clause is not the only device that mortgage lenders employ to protect themselves against interest rate fluctuations. Commonly, a mortgage note will also include a prepayment penalty—often six months' interest—payable in the event the mortgagor seeks to repay the loan before maturity. Typically a mortgagor will seek to prepay when interest rates drop below the rate agreed upon in his mortgage instrument and refinancing becomes attractive.

Absent a specific provision in the note governing prepayment, is the borrower entitled to prepay whenever he wishes? As a general rule he is not. See Trident Center v. Connecticut General Life Insurance Co., 847 F.2d 564 (9th Cir.1988) (permitting extrinsic evidence to construe clause); Clover Square Associates v. Northwestern Mutual Life Insurance Co., 674 F.Supp. 1137 (D.N.J.1987), affirmed, 869 F.2d 588 (3d Cir.1989) (no restraint on alienation); Trilon Plaza, Inc. v. Comptroller of the State of New York, 788 A.2d 146 (D.C.App.2001) (loan documents and common law did not allow). The reason usually given for not presuming a right to pay off the mortgage debt prior to maturity is that lenders typically take mortgage notes as an investment, to be paid off over a specified term.

However, a minority of jurisdictions permit prepayment through various means. Some statutes permit prepayment unless the mortgage instrument provides to the contrary. See, e.g., N.C.Gen.Stats. § 24–2.4 (1991). Cases in a few jurisdictions hold that a right to prepay should be presumed in all cases. See, e.g., Mahoney v. Furches, 503 Pa. 60, 65–66, 468 A.2d 458, 461 (1983): "Taking cognizance of the general policy in this Commonwealth and elsewhere against restraints on alienation, we find it would be against such policy to presume, simply from the absence of a clause so allowing, that a mortgagor could not pay off his debt and alienate his land as he so desired. Instead, we think it wiser to raise a presumption of a right to prepayment of the note where a mortgage is silent as to that right. This presumption could be rebutted by showing a contrary intent mutually manifested by the parties. Such a presumption would not work a hardship on the mortgagee since, in virtually all instances, he is the drafter of the mortgage note and can thus include within the note a clause stating that the note is not subject to prepayment. This would put the mortgagor on notice that he will in all probability be restrained from selling the land for the duration of the term. If he signs the note containing such a provision, he will then be bound by it even though it may restrain his right to its sale or use." See also Hatcher v. Rose, 329 N.C. 626, 407 S.E.2d 172 (1991) (holding that there was a right to prepay under the common law); Restatement of Mortgages § 6.1 (finding a right to prepay unless there is an agreement to the contrary). Other modern courts, however, reject the implication of a right to prepay. See, e.g., Ex parte Brannon, 683 So.2d 994 (Ala.1996).

Federal legislation and regulation have preempted the prepayment issue in certain residential situations. For example, home purchase loans to veterans can be guaranteed under 38 U.S.C.A. § 3710 only if they are prepayable without penalty. Moreover, the secondary mortgage market has been very influential since the widely used FHLMC and FNMA note forms permit prepayment without penalty. Interestingly, the Office of Thrift Supervision, which had previously pre-empted regulation of prepayment penalties by state-chartered lenders in alternative mortgage instruments returned that issue to state control in 2003 on the belief that state regulation could better protect against predatory practices. See National Home Equity Mortgage Ass'n v. Office of Thrift Supervision, 373 F.3d 1355 (D.C.Cir.2004); Glukowsky v. Equity One, Inc., 180 N.J. 49, 848 A.2d 747 (2004).

For excellent discussions of the prepayment issue, see Alexander, Mortgage Prepayment: The Trial of Common Sense, 72 Cornell L. Rev. 288 (1987) (arguing that the presumption against prepayment arose only relatively recently and finding common law support for a prepayment right); Lefcoe, Yield Maintenance and Defeasance: Two Distinct Paths to Commercial Mortgage Prepayment, 28 Real Est. L.J. 202 (2000); Weinberger, Neither an Early Nor a Late Payor Be?—Presuming to Question the Presumption Against Mortgage Prepayment, 35 Wayne L.Rev. 1 (1988); Whitman, Mortgage Prepayment Clauses: An Economic and Legal Analysis, 40 U.C.L.A.L.Rev. 851 (1993) (analyzing, among other issues, the interplay of clauses providing for a prepayment fee and acceleration upon default under the mortgage); Talkov, Exposing the Myth of Mortgage Prepayment Penalties in the Aftermath of *River East*, 44 Real Prop. Tr. & Est. J. 585 (2009).

3. *Prepayment Penalties and Due on Sale Clauses.* Should lenders be allowed to have it both ways—accelerating the loan under a due on sale clause *and* exacting a prepayment penalty from the borrower? While prior to Garn-St. Germain some jurisdictions answered this question in the negative by statute or judicial decision, Federal regulations promulgated by the Office of Thrift Supervision have preempted state rules. Under 12 C.F.R. § 591.5(b)(2), which applies to state and federally chartered banks and other lenders, a prepayment penalty or equivalent fee cannot be imposed upon the exercise of a due on sale clause in connection with a mortgage on a home occupied or to be occupied by the borrower.

Compare U.L.S.I.A. § 208 which provides that "if a secured creditor demands a rate of interest higher than that specified in the security agreement . . . as a condition of approval of a transfer by a protected party of the protected party's interest in residential real estate subject to a security interest, and the higher rate of interest or other consideration is not agreed to, a prepayment penalty may not be charged if the debt is paid in full within 3 months after the failure to agree to a higher rate of interest." See 12 C.F.R. § 591.5(b)(3).

4. *Lawyer Liability.* As discussed in Note 4 on pages 24–25, courts differ on a lawyer's malpractice liability to a non-client. Wright v. Pennamped, 657 N.E.2d 1223 (Ind.App.1995), clarified on rehearing, 664 N.E.2d 394 (Ind.App.1996), took an expansive view of attorney liability. Wright, a building owner, reached an understanding with SCI, a lender, for a refinancing; Pennamped, SCI's attorney, prepared drafts of the loan documents and sent them to Brown, Wright's attorney. After Brown reviewed the documents and told Pennamped they were satisfactory, Pennamped redrafted the prepayment penalty provision at SCI's request to increase the charge to be paid by the borrower. Pennamped informed neither Brown nor Wright of the change but did tell SCI that someone should tell them. No such notice was in fact given.

Brown was unable to attend the closing because he had to be in court on another matter. Wright executed the documents, without reading them, believing they were the same as those that he had reviewed with Brown. Only when Wright sought to refinance the property one year later did he learn that he had signed off on a higher prepayment fee. The revised fee was $92,500 while the original fee would have been under $5,000. Wright paid the fee and sued Pennamped for damages.

The court of appeals reversed a summary judgment in favor of Pennamped, ruling that the lender's lawyer was under a duty to disclose the fact that the documents had been redrafted:

By undertaking the tasks of a drafting attorney, including the distribution of draft loan documents and the solicitation of review and approval of the documents, Pennamped assumed a duty to disclose any changes in the documents prior to execution to the other parties and their respective counsel. . . . The existence of such a duty is supported by common sense and notions of fair dealing. Thus, Pennamped, as the drafting attorney, had a duty to inform Brown or, in his absence, Wright, of any changes occurring after Brown's review and approval of the loan documents. Were the rule otherwise, preclosing review of loan documentation would become a futile act, and counsel would be required to scrutinize every term of each document at the moment of execution.

657 N.E.2d at 1231.

Is this result correct? Should attorney Brown be liable instead of, or along with, Pennamped? Should Pennamped be subject to a disciplinary action for his conduct? Rule 4.4 of the Model Rules of Professional Responsibility states:

In representing a client, a lawyer shall not use means that have no substantial purpose other than to embarrass, delay, or burden a third person, or use methods of obtaining evidence that violate the legal rights of such a person.

See A.B.A. Informal Opinion 86–1518 (2/9/86); see generally Hazard, The Lawyer's Obligation to be Trustworthy When Dealing with Opposing Parties, 33 S.C.L. Rev. 181 (1981); Lowenthal, The Bar's Failure to Require Truthful Bargaining By Lawyers, 2 Geo. J. Legal Ethics 411 (1988).

2. TRANSFERS BY THE MORTGAGEE

a. PAYMENTS ON THE NOTE

Giorgi v. Pioneer Title Insurance Co.

Supreme Court of Nevada, 1969.
85 Nev. 319, 454 P.2d 104.

MOWBRAY, JUSTICE.

Appellant Julio Giorgi, assignee of a promissory note secured by a deed of trust, sued Pioneer Title Insurance Company, trustee named in the deed, for $4,550, representing the principal amount of the note, on the grounds that Pioneer, who held the note in escrow for collection, had wrongfully disbursed the $4,550 to the payee named in the note and reconveyed the real property which was the security for the note.

The facts are not in dispute. On May 28, 1958, William C. Alden and Ula May Alden, his wife, and Mickey E. Keffer and Joyce E. Keffer, his wife, signed a promissory note in the principal sum of $4,550. The note was payable to August Manke and Mabel Manke, his wife, and it was secured by a deed of trust. August died, and Mabel succeeded to his interest in the note. After August's death, but before the note became due, Mabel assigned her interest in the note and deed of trust to Appellant Julio Giorgi. In explaining the absence of the note, Mabel told Julio that the note and deed of trust had been lost. Giorgi caused the assignment to be recorded in Washoe County. Giorgi notified the Aldens and the Keffers of the assignment, but it is agreed that no actual notice of the assignment was ever given to Pioneer, although the assignment recited that Pioneer was the trustee in the deed of trust. At the time the note and deed of trust were executed, the instruments were deposited with Pioneer with instructions to collect and disburse the $4,550 to the payee named in the note and, upon such payment, to reconvey the property covered by the deed of trust. Pioneer did so. When Giorgi attempted to collect the note, he learned that it had been paid and the security for its payment lost by virtue of Pioneer's deed of reconveyance. Giorgi then commenced an action in the district court, in which he named as defendants Pioneer, Mabel Manke, the Aldens and the Keffers. The Aldens and the Keffers were never served. The district judge entered judgment in favor of Giorgi and against Mabel for the full amount of the note, but he refused to hold Pioneer responsible for Giorgi's loss; hence, this appeal.

Appellant concedes that Pioneer did not have actual notice of Mabel's assignment of the note and deed of trust. However, appellant argues as his principal contention on this appeal that when he recorded Mabel's assignment of the note and deed of trust Pioneer received constructive notice of the assignment and became bound by the terms of NRS 106.210.[1]

Respondent contends, however, that the law of negotiable instruments is controlling in this case and that Pioneer, as holder of the negotiable promissory note, was bound to disburse the payment received to the payee named in the note—Mabel Manke. We agree, and we affirm the judgment of the district court.

1.   In the case of a payment of a mortgage or deed of trust securing a negotiable instrument, the rule suggested by the great weight of authority is that the rights of the parties thereto, as well as third persons, are governed by rules relating to negotiable paper. Under this law the maker of a negotiable note secured by a mortgage or deed of trust cannot discharge his liability by payment to one not the holder or one not authorized by the holder to receive payment. And a debtor is not justified as against an assignee of the security in making payments to a mortgagee or a beneficiary named in a deed of trust who does not have possession of the instrument.

The general rule has been stated in 4 American Law of Property § 16.117 (A.J. Casner ed. 1952):

" 'Where a negotiable instrument is secured by a mortgage, the latter will not be discharged by payment to the record holder if as a matter of fact the note and mortgage had already been transferred to a bona fide holder for value before maturity, even though no assignment has been recorded.' Such is the general rule by the very definite weight of authority. *This flows from the general rule that in such cases the mortgage follows the rules applicable to the negotiable instrument it*

---

[1]   NRS 106.210 "Recording of assignments of mortgages, beneficial interests in trust deeds; constructive notice.

"1. Any assignment of a mortgage of real property, or of a mortgage of personal property or crops recorded prior to March 27, 1935, and any assignment of the beneficial interest under a deed of trust may be recorded, and from the time any of the same are so filed for record shall operate as constructive notice of the contents thereof to all persons."

secures. Nor will the result be different if the mortgagor asked for the note and was given a plausible but false explanation for its nonproduction. The risk is absolute."

2.   Appellant contends, however, that in this case the general rule is superseded by our recordation statutes, particularly NRS 106.210, *supra*, and that when the assignment was recorded Pioneer was given constructive notice of its existence and became bound by its terms. Admittedly, the problem of harmonizing the effect of our recording statutes with the rules of negotiable instruments so as not to interfere with the commercial mobility of the debt is a troublesome one. G. Osborne, Handbook on the Law of Mortgages § 235, at 647, has stated the rule: "The problem of enacting and applying the recording statute is one of trying to satisfy the demands of recordation required by the fact that the subject matter of the mortgage is land and, at the same time, not to interfere with the mobility of the debt or with the functioning of the security aspect of the mortgage which makes it a mere incident of the debt. Since this is so, it is obvious that the rules governing the recording of other conveyances cannot be applied in toto."

3.   There is an additional reason for this rule. In this case Pioneer was bound by the escrow instructions which the parties had signed. The instructions directed Pioneer, who held the note for collection, to receive and disburse the $4,550 payment to the payee named in the note. To require any agency—whether a title company, escrow company, bank, or individual—to run a title search before making any disbursements to a payee named in a note held for collection and secured by a deed of trust, or to pay at its peril, would impose an impractical and crushing burden on such agencies.

The judgment of the district court is affirmed.

COLLINS, C.J., ZENOFF and THOMPSON, JJ., and WARTMAN, D.J., concur.

Doyle v. Resolution Trust Corporation

United States Court of Appeals for the Tenth Circuit, 1993.
999 F.2d 469.

Before BRORBY and EBEL, CIRCUIT JUDGES, and MCWILLIAMS, SENIOR CIRCUIT JUDGE.

MCWILLIAMS, SENIOR CIRCUIT JUDGE.

This case has a long history. It began when Michael L. Doyle brought an action based on breach of contract in the United States District Court for the Western District of Oklahoma in July 1983, naming as defendants Trinity Savings & Loan Association and other related entities (collectively referred to as "Trinity").[1] By amended complaint, Doyle added fraud claims against Trinity. The gist of Doyle's claims against Trinity was that Trinity had raised the interest rate of the adjustable rate note Doyle had previously executed in favor of

---

[1]   The Trinity defendants were Trinity Savings & Loan Association, TSL Service Corporation, and STM Mortgage Company. Trinity changed its name to Bright Banc Savings Association in 1984. On February 2, 1990, Resolution Trust Corporation—Receiver became the successor in interest to Trinity and Bright Banc. STM Mortgage Company changed its name to Bright Mortgage Company in 1985 and merged with TSL Service Corporation. Consequently, Bright Mortgage is the successor in interest to STM and TSL.

Trinity without his consent. For this unauthorized alteration, Doyle sought actual and punitive damages. After discovering later that the Federal National Mortgage Association (FNMA) had purchased his note and mortgage from Trinity, Doyle filed a second amended complaint on August 24, 1984, adding FNMA as a defendant and seeking cancellation of the note and mortgage.

After a trial in July 1986, the jury returned a verdict in favor of Doyle against Trinity, setting his actual damages at $3,757.60 and awarding him $100,000 as punitive damages. Judgment was entered thereon. Additionally, the court found in favor of Doyle on his claim against FNMA and entered judgment cancelling Doyle's obligation to FNMA. As will become apparent, in the present appeal we are not concerned, as such, with Doyle's judgment against Trinity. We are concerned only with Doyle's claim for cancellation of the note and mortgage held by FNMA.

Both Trinity and FNMA appealed the judgment thus entered. We affirmed the judgment in its entirety. Doyle v. Trinity Savings & Loan Association, 869 F.2d 558 (10th Cir.1989). In affirming the judgment for cancellation of the note and mortgage held by FNMA, we relied upon Goss v. Trinity Savings & Loan Association, No. 67,298, 1988 WL 391508 (Okla.Ct.App. filed August 23, 1988), which involved facts "virtually identical in all relevant respects to those underlying the instant suit." 869 F.2d at 559. We rejected FNMA's argument that it was a holder in due course, concluding that, under Goss, the note was nonnegotiable. In that connection, we spoke as follows:

> Finally, we reject FNMA's argument that it is a holder in due course of the note and thus entitled to enforce it despite the prior unauthorized alterations. This note, like the one in Goss, pegs the interest rate to an external index, so that the amount payable cannot be determined from the instrument itself. "Because the note does not contain a promise to pay a sum certain, the note itself cannot be a negotiable instrument pursuant to [Okla.Stat. tit. 12A, § 3–104 (1981)]. Therefore, FNMA cannot be accorded the status of a holder in due course." [Goss] at ___ (citing Shepherd Mall State Bank v. Johnson, 603 P.2d 1115 (Okla.1979)).

869 F.2d at 560. Additionally, we rejected the argument that the alterations were not material, in reliance on Goss. 869 F.2d at 559.[2]

Trinity and FNMA filed petitions for rehearing in which they advised the court that the Oklahoma Supreme Court had granted certiorari in Goss. Accordingly, we abated the case pending the Oklahoma Supreme Court's decision. In 1991, the Oklahoma Supreme Court reversed, in part, the Oklahoma Court of Appeals. Goss v. Trinity Savings & Loan Association, 813 P.2d 492 (Okla.1991).

Thereafter, on July 26, 1991, we filed an opinion on rehearing. Doyle v. Trinity Savings & Loan Association, 940 F.2d 592 (10th Cir.1991). We denied Trinity's petition for rehearing, rejecting Trinity's

---

[2] In this initial opinion in Doyle, we stated that it was a relevant and undisputed fact that FNMA "purchased the loan in good faith" and "had no reason to believe that Doyle had not approved and initialed the changes." 869 F.2d at 559. Hence, FNMA's "good faith" became the law of the case.

contention that we had incorrectly held the alteration of the note was material, and in connection therewith, we stated that the Oklahoma Supreme Court in Goss had "settled this issue by declaring an analogous note alteration to be material as a matter of law."

FNMA's petition for rehearing challenged our reliance on the Oklahoma Court of Appeals' holding in Goss that the variable interest rate in the note rendered the note nonnegotiable. In our opinion on rehearing, we noted the Oklahoma Supreme Court's reversal of the Oklahoma Court of Appeals' decision in Goss that the note was nonnegotiable. We stated that "[b]ecause the note in Goss was declared negotiable under Oklahoma law, FNMA would be a holder in due course, entitled to enforce the note despite the unauthorized alteration, if it could establish that it took the note without notice of the defect." 940 F.2d at 593. We further noted that the Oklahoma Supreme Court had remanded Goss to the trial court with direction that it determine whether FNMA purchased the note from Trinity without notice of the unauthorized alteration of the interest rate. Id.[3]

In line with the Oklahoma Supreme Court's pronouncement in Goss, we spoke in our opinion on rehearing in the instant case as follows:

> Goss controls our opinion on rehearing. We thus hold that the variable interest rate note in our case was negotiable. *We decline Doyle's invitation to further hold that FNMA had notice of the alteration as a matter of law,* and we remand for the trial court to make that determination in accordance with the opinion in Goss, 813 P.2d at 500–01, 62 Okla. Bar J. at 796, as amended on rehearing, 62 Okla. Bar J. 1779 (Okla.S.Ct.1991) (emphasis added).

> Id.[4]

On remand, the district court in the present case held an evidentiary hearing, and then found, *inter alia,* that FNMA did not have actual knowledge of the unauthorized alteration by Trinity of the note's interest rate, nor did it have reason to know that the note had been altered without Doyle's knowledge or consent. In line therewith, the district court concluded that FNMA was a holder in due course of Doyle's note and could enforce the note, as originally executed, free from any claims or defenses Doyle might have against Trinity. Doyle appeals that order. We affirm.

The background facts out of which this controversy arose are to a large degree not in any real dispute. On March 15, 1982, FNMA entered into a written "Letter of Commitment" with Trinity whereby it agreed to purchase from Trinity up to $5,000,000 worth of loans. As a part of the purchase agreement between Trinity and FNMA, Trinity

---

[3]   We are advised that, on remand, the trial court in *Goss* found that FNMA had notice of the defect and that the matter is now on appeal.

[4]   In our opinion on rehearing, we did not in anywise modify the statements in our original opinion that FNMA purchased the Doyle note in "good faith" and that FNMA "had no reason to believe that Doyle had not approved and initialed the changes." So, these statements continued as the law of the case, not subject to challenge on our remand to the district court to consider the question of whether FNMA had notice, be it actual or constructive, of an *unauthorized* alteration. And, as above noted, in our opinion on rehearing, we specifically rejected Doyle's suggestion that FNMA had such notice as a matter of law.

represented and warranted that the notes and mortgages it submitted to FNMA for purchase would be valid and fully enforceable. Trinity first sent a "package" of loans to FNMA for purchase around June 22, 1982. Doyle's loan was not included in this first package. FNMA refused to buy Trinity's first package of loans when a dispute arose over whether the correct interest rate had been typed in the blank on the notes where the interest rate was to be placed.[5]

On June 22, 1982, Doyle borrowed $54,000 from Trinity to purchase a home and, in connection therewith, signed a note providing for an interest rate of 11.375% per annum. At the first trial of this matter, Doyle proved that sometime after he signed the note Trinity altered it by "whiting out" the interest rate of 11.375% and inserting an interest rate of 15.875%, and then forging his initials next to the altered interest rate. Doyle's note and mortgage, along with others, were then sold to FNMA on or about September 27, 1982.

At the hearing on remand, it was FNMA's position that, while it knew that the interest rate had been altered, it did not know that the alteration was unauthorized, and in fact believed that it was authorized because the initials "MLD" appeared next to the alteration. In this connection, it was established that under FNMA practices then in effect, FNMA employees would have checked to see that, for example, the initials "MLD" were indeed the correct initials of the maker of the note, "Michael L. Doyle," but would not have made a handwriting comparison to see if the initials matched the full written signature.

Sue Smith, an employee of FNMA, testified that FNMA frequently purchased notes and mortgages where the interest rate had been altered, providing the maker's initials appeared alongside the alteration. On cross-examination of Sue Smith, counsel attempted to show that the initials appearing next to the altered interest rate did not match Doyle's signature on the note. When shown a copy of the Doyle note, Sue Smith stated that the initials "M" and "D" were not "identical" to those letters as they appeared in the maker's signature. In like vein, Fred Horak, another employee of FNMA, when shown a "blown-up" copy of the initials next to the alteration, stated that there was a "difference" between the initials and the signature. Both witnesses testified that they were not handwriting experts and that the only check routinely made by FNMA was to ascertain that the initials alongside any alteration contained the same letters as the first letters of the maker's signature.

On this general state of the record, the district court, on remand, found that FNMA did not have actual knowledge that the initials were a forgery, nor did it have reason to know that the note had been altered without Doyle's knowledge and consent. In so holding, the district court spoke as follows:

> The remand from the Court of Appeals directed this Court to determine whether FNMA lacked notice of the unauthorized alteration of the Doyle note by Trinity. This determination is

---

[5]   In our initial opinion, we stated as a relevant and undisputed fact that FNMA rejected Trinity's first package "because the instruments had been incorrectly completed by placing on the face of the note, as the initial interest rate, the lower rate of interest upon which the initial monthly payment was based (11.375%), instead of the actual rate of interest accruing for one year from the date of execution (15.875%)." 869 F.2d at 559.

to be made in accordance with the opinion of the Oklahoma Supreme Court in Goss v. Trinity Sav. & Loan Ass'n, 813 P.2d 492 (Okla.1991).

In his pre-trial pleadings and throughout the bench trial of this matter, Doyle has contended that FNMA had notice of or a duty to inquire about the corrected interest rate on his note. Specifically, Doyle claimed that FNMA failed to follow its own procedures in its dealings with Trinity on Doyle's note, that FNMA knew that Trinity had submitted a number of loans that needed to be corrected, and that someone at FNMA should have been able to discern that the initials next to the corrected interest rate on his note were not similar in appearance to the handwriting in Doyle's signature elsewhere on the note.

. . .

One need only examine the undisputed facts of the present case to demonstrate that FNMA is indeed entitled to holder in due course status. A number of the undisputed facts are found in paragraphs 4 through 7 of Judge Lee R. West's Order of 11 June 1985, and are confirmed by this Court based upon the evidence heard in the bench trial of this matter. *See, Doyle v. Trinity, et al.,* CIV–83–1736 (Order of West, J. 11 June 1985), at 2–3.[6]

Additionally, FNMA has convinced the Court through evidence offered at trial that the type of correction that appeared on the Doyle note was quite common and not a matter about which FNMA would concern itself unless other factors called the correction to FNMA's attention. No additional factors were present here. In fact, FNMA has established that Trinity had a fine reputation in the mortgage banking community at the time the Doyle note was purchased, and FNMA had every reason to trust Trinity to correct the problem notes and resubmit them in accordance with FNMA policies and procedures.

When viewed as a whole, the facts of this case demonstrate that FNMA purchased the Doyle note in good faith and without notice of the unauthorized interest rate alteration. As such, FNMA is entitled to holder in due course status with regard to the Doyle note.

Several Oklahoma statutes bear on the present controversy. 12A O.S.1981 § 3–302 provides as follows:

(1) A holder in due course is a holder who takes the instrument

(a) for value; and

---

[6] By his order of June 11, 1985, Judge West denied FNMA's motion for summary judgment on the ground that the note itself was non-negotiable. However, in so doing, in paragraphs 5 and 6 of that order, Judge West found the following to be uncontroverted for the purposes of the motion:

5. FNMA had no reason to believe that the initials on the face of the note may have been placed there by someone other than the plaintiff. Therefore, FNMA believed that the changes had been approved and agreed to by the plaintiff.

6. FNMA purchased the loan in good faith and with no knowledge of any potential claims or defenses to it including claims of alteration, fraud or forgery.

(b) in good faith; and

(c) without notice that it is overdue or has been dishonored or of any defense against or claim to it on the part of any person.

12A O.S.1981 § 3–304 provides as follows:

(1) The purchaser has notice of a claim or defense if

(a) the instrument is so incomplete, bears such visible evidence of forgery or alteration, or is otherwise so irregular as to call into question its validity, terms or ownership or to create an ambiguity as to the party to pay;

12A O.S.1981 § 1–201(25), provides as follows:

A person has "notice" of a fact when

(a) he has actual knowledge of it; or

(b) he has received a notice or notification of it; or

(c) from all the facts and circumstances known to him at the time in question he has reason to know that it exists.

In line with the foregoing statutes, it is Doyle's position in the present appeal that the Doyle note bore "such visible evidence of forgery or alteration . . . as to call into question its validity" and that, "from all the facts and circumstances known to [FNMA] at the time in question [FNMA had] reason to know" that the initials were forged, even though it may not have had actual knowledge of such.

While the standard for determining a holder's good faith is subjective, the test for determining whether a holder had "notice" of defenses against the instrument is an objective inquiry into what a reasonable person in the holder's position would know. *See generally,* 1 White & Summers, *Uniform Commercial Code,* § 14–6, pp. 708–17 (3d ed.1988). As we said in our opinion on rehearing, whether FNMA had notice of the forgery of Doyle's initials is an issue of fact and not an issue of law. The district court's finding that FNMA had no actual or constructive notice of the forgery is presumptively correct and should not be set aside on appeal unless it is clearly erroneous. Colon-Sanchez v. Marsh, 733 F.2d 78, 81 (10th Cir.), *cert. denied,* 469 U.S. 855, 105 S.Ct. 181, 83 L.Ed.2d 115 (1984). A finding of fact will be deemed clearly erroneous only if it is without support in the record or if the appellate court "on the entire evidence is left with the definite and firm conviction that a mistake has been made." Id.; *see also* N.L.R.B. v. Viola Industries—Elevator Division, 979 F.2d 1384, 1387 (10th Cir.1992).

Our study of the record before the district court leads us to conclude that the district court's finding that FNMA was without notice was not clearly erroneous. There is *no* evidence that FNMA had actual notice that Trinity had unilaterally changed the interest rate in the note which Doyle signed and then forged Doyle's initials beside the alteration. While FNMA and Trinity did confer after the first package of loans had been rejected as to how the interest rate could be "corrected," there is *no* evidence that FNMA suggested that Trinity change interest rates *without* the knowledge and consent of the maker. The initials beside the altered interest rate on Doyle's note were the same as the first letters of Doyle's signature on the note. The FNMA employees' testimony that the initials looked a bit different than Doyle's signature does not dictate reversal. FNMA obligated itself to buy loans from Trinity in wholesale lots up to the amount of $5,000,000, and it is undisputed that many of these loans with altered interest rates were routinely accepted by FNMA, providing that the borrower's initials appeared beside the alteration. On the basis that the district court's findings are not clearly erroneous, we affirm.

In addition to finding that FNMA did not have notice of the forged initials, the district court also found that FNMA acquired the note in good faith, had no "close connection" with Trinity and, specifically, that Trinity was not an "agent" for FNMA. In the present appeal, Doyle argues that the district court erred in so holding. Since our remand was for the limited purpose of determining whether FNMA had notice of the forged initials appearing alongside the altered interest rate in the Doyle note, we need not consider these other matters.

Judgment affirmed.

b.   SECURITIZATION AND MERS

Gerald Korngold, Legal and Policy Choices in the Aftermath of the Subprime and Mortgage Financing Crisis
60 South Carolina Law Review 727, 741–42, 743–44 (2009).

In 1993, the Mortgage Bankers Association, Fannie Mae, Freddie Mac, the Government National Mortgage Association (Ginnie Mae), the Federal Housing Administration, and the Department of Veterans Affairs created MERS. MERS provides "electronic processing and tracking of [mortgage] ownership and transfers." Mortgage lenders, banks, insurance companies, and title companies become members of MERS and pay an annual fee. They appoint MERS as their agent to act on all mortgages that they register on the system. A MERS mortgage is recorded with the particular county's office of the recorder with " 'Mortgage Electronic Registration System, Inc.' named as the lender's nominee or mortgagee of record" on the mortgage. The MERS member who owns the beneficial interest may assign those beneficial ownership rights or servicing rights to another MERS member. These assignments are not part of the public record, but are tracked electronically on MERS's private records. Mortgagors are notified of transfers of servicing rights, but not of transfers of beneficial ownership.

MERS facilitates an efficient secondary market in mortgages by allowing the easy transfer of beneficial rights. After the initial recording in the local clerk's office, subsequent transactions can be done quickly at a low cost from a central location utilizing modern technology without the need for local recording of paper assignment documents. Such a process facilitates the flow of global capital, bringing investment funds into areas without local mortgage financing. Potential homeowners, as well as those seeking the most favorable rates, can benefit from MERS.

Unfortunately, some judicial decisions during the recent spike in subprime and conventional foreclosures have questioned MERS. . . .

3.   Transparency and Market Efficiency

I have previously written of the importance of transparency in the recording system. Current and potential participants in land transfer and finance transactions need information so markets can operate efficiently and fairly, thus benefiting those particular players as well as society. There is therefore a legitimate concern if unrecorded mortgage assignments in secondary market transactions are not placed on the public record. In the dissenting opinion in MERSCORP, Inc. [v. Romaine, 8 N.Y.3d 90 (2006)], Chief Judge Kaye of the New York Court of Appeals expressed a concern that MERS only discloses the current servicer and not the assignee of the mortgage. She wrote:

> The lack of disclosure may create substantial difficulty when a homeowner wishes to negotiate the terms of his or her mortgage or enforce a legal right against the mortgagee and is unable to learn the mortgagee's identity. Public records will no longer contain this information as, if it achieves the success it envisions, the MERS system will render the public record useless by masking beneficial ownership of mortgages and eliminating records of assignments altogether. Not only will this information deficit detract from the amount of public data accessible for research and monitoring of industry trends, but it may also function, perhaps unintentionally, to insulate a noteholder from liability, mask lender error and hide predatory lending practices.

NOTES

1.   *The U.C.C. and the Transfer of Notes.* Rules governing the rights of mortgage assignees have assumed dramatically increased importance with the growth of secondary markets. Doyle v. Resolution Trust Corporation and Giorgi v. Pioneer Title Ins. Co. suggest some of the problems facing purchasers of real estate secured debt. Although both the note and mortgage are transferred, the note is viewed as the controlling document. (An old saw states that "the mortgage follows the note," giving one who has received only the note the right to the security instrument as well.) Thus, Article 3 of the Uniform Commercial Code applies. As a further complication, a new version of Article 3 was promulgated in 1990, introducing some significant changes from the prior version. A 2002 revision of Article 3 has received only a handful of adoptions.

2.   *Holder in Due Course.* A holder in due course takes free of certain defenses. To qualify as a holder in due course, the transferee must, among other matters, acquire a negotiable note in good faith and without notice of defenses. See U.C.C. § 3–302 (pre-1990 version), §§ 3–302, 3–305 (1990 version).

Doyle indicates that the good faith required of the transferee is "subjective." What is the difference between assessing behavior under a subjective, as opposed to an objective, standard? The 1990 version of the U.C.C. altered the pre-1990 U.C.C. definition of good faith by requiring that good faith "means honesty in fact and the observance of reasonable commercial standards of fair dealing." § 3–103(a)(4). Comment 4 to the 1990 version of section 3–103 provides:

> Although fair dealing is a broad term that must be defined in
> context, it is clear that it is concerned with the fairness of conduct
> rather than the care with which an act is performed. Failure to
> exercise ordinary care in conducting a transaction is an entirely
> different concept than failure to deal fairly in a transaction.

Section 1–201(b)(20) of the 2001 revision of Article 1 (adopted by some 35 jurisdictions) gives a definition of "good faith" that is to be applied throughout the U.C.C. and which is similar to the 1990 § 3–103(a)(4) definition. Comment 20 to 1–201(b) explains that good faith requires "both the subjective element of honesty in fact and the objective element of the observance of reasonable commercial standards of fair dealing." Would *Doyle* have been decided differently under the 1990 version of the U.C.C. or the 2001 version of Article 1?

A related, but different, provision requires a holder in due course to take without notice of defenses to or of certain defects in the note. *Doyle* indicates that notice (as opposed to the transferee's good faith) is judged under an "objective" test. Do you agree that FNMA had no "notice" of the forgery of Doyle's initials? What factors should be relevant? What policy considerations? Is this just a matter of an appellate court's deference to a debatable conclusion of fact by a lower court? Compare United States Finance Co. v. Jones, 285 Ala. 105, 229 So.2d 495 (1969) (transferee of notes from home improvement company was not a holder in due course because it had notice of a defense against payment based on its knowledge of the transferor's past fraudulent business practices and a pattern of failure to complete improvements in such transactions) with Universal C.I.T. Credit Corp. v. Ingel, 347 Mass. 119, 196 N.E.2d 847 (1964) (where assignee had received a credit report on payee indicating in detail past sharp business practices and complaints to the attorney general, assignee had no reason to know of fraud with respect to transferred note); see Dupuis v. Federal Home Loan Mortgage Corp., 879 F.Supp. 139 (D.Me.1995) (FHLMC was holder in due course of note and had no knowledge of defenses based on transferor's failure to credit payor for escrows and payments; even though transferor was FHLMC's agent for servicing the loan, it was not an agent for purposes of obtaining and closing the loan).

Consider the FTC Holder rule discussed by the court in Associates Home Equity Services v. Troup, at page 390 above. What effect would the FTC rule have on the holder in due course rule of the UCC? Would the FTC rule apply to the usual mortgage assignment on the secondary market? See Woodsbey v. A & M Homes, Inc., 375 B.R. 145 (Bankr.W.D.Pa.2007).

On holder in due course in general, see J. White & R. Summers, Uniform Commercial Code §§ 15–1 to 15–12(6th ed. 2010).

The Home Ownership and Equity Protection Act of 1994, 15 U.S.C.A. § 1601–1648, gives added protection to closed-end home equity mortgages secured by a consumer's principal residence and having a prescribed, high interest rate (defined as more than ten percentage points above the rate on a Treasury security of the same maturity or total fees exceeding the greater of eight percent of the loan amount or $400). Id., § 1602(aa). The Act subjects assignees of such high interest rate mortgages "to all claims and defenses with respect to that mortgage that the consumer could assert against" the original lender. Id., § 1641(d)(1). (The Act does not apply to a "residential mortgage transaction"—i.e., a mortgage enabling a consumer's purchase of a dwelling. 15 U.S.C.A. § 1602(w)). Forrester, Mortgaging the American Dream: A Critical Evaluation of the Federal Government's Promotion of Home Equity Financing, 69 Tul.L.Rev. 373, 444–445 (1994), provides an excellent discussion of the Act and related issues.

For discussions of the payment issue, see Burkhart, Third Party Defenses to Mortgages, 1998 B.Y.U.L. Rev. 1003; Whitman, Reforming the Law: The Payment Rule as a Paradigm, 1998 B.Y.U.L. Rev. 1169.

3.   *Negotiability of Mortgage Notes.* Notes secured by mortgages pose distinctive risks of non-negotiability. If the note contains too detailed a reference to the terms of the mortgage securing it, the note may be non-negotiable because it is no longer an "unconditional promise or order to pay a sum certain in money and no other promise." U.C.C. § 3–104(1)(b) (pre-1990 version); see §§ 3–104(a), 3–106 (1990 version).

Holly Hill Acres, Ltd. v. Charter Bank of Gainesville, 314 So.2d 209, 210 (Fla.App.1975), held that the following language incorporated the mortgage into the note, destroying the note's negotiability: "this note with interest is secured by a mortgage on real estate, of even date herewith, made by the maker hereof in favor of the said payee, and shall be construed and enforced according to the laws of the state of Florida. The terms of said mortgage are by this reference made a part hereof." According to the court, "[m]ere reference to a note being secured by a mortgage is a common commercial practice and such reference in itself does not impede the negotiability of the note. There is, however, a significant difference in a note stating that it is 'secured by a mortgage' from one which provides, 'the terms of said mortgage are by this reference made a part hereof.' In the former instance the note merely refers to a separate agreement which does not impede its negotiability, while in the latter instance the note is rendered non-negotiable." 314 So.2d at 211. Comment 1 to the 1990 text of U.C.C. § 3–106 states that a note indicating that it is "subject to a loan and security agreement dated . . ." makes the note nonnegotiable while a statement that "this note is secured by a security interest in collateral described in a security agreement dated . . ." does not make the note nonnegotiable since there is no need to look at the security agreement to determine the rights under the note.

Cases have held under the pre-1990 U.C.C. § 3–106, requiring as a condition of negotiability that the holder be able to determine the amount due from the instrument, that adjustable rate notes are not negotiable since they require reference to an external index. See, e.g., Northern Trust Co. v. E.T. Clancy Export Corp., 612 F.Supp. 712 (N.D.Ill.1985); Taylor v. Roeder, 234 Va. 99, 360 S.E.2d 191 (1987); but see Woodhouse, Drake & Carey Ltd. v. Anderson, 61 Misc.2d 951, 307 N.Y.S.2d 113 (1970) (note providing for "the maximum legal rate" was negotiable). *Doyle* reflects the earlier difference among Oklahoma courts on this issue, with the state Supreme Court ultimately holding that variable rates are negotiable in Goss v. Trinity Savings & Loan Ass'n, 813 P.2d 492 (Okla.1991). The 1990 version of the U.C.C. permits variable rate notes to be negotiable, provided the other requirements to negotiability are met. §§ 3–104(a), 3–112. What would the effect be on the secondary market if such notes were not negotiable?

4. *U.L.S.I.A. and the Restatement of Mortgages.* Section 206 of the Uniform Land Security Interest Act codifies some aspects of existing law. Subsection (a) states that the assignee of a mortgage takes subject to defenses against payment. Subsection (c) states that the mortgagor may continue to pay the original mortgagee until the mortgagor receives notification of the assignment. At the same time, though, Comment 1 indicates that in the case of negotiable instruments Article 3 of the U.C.C. will control.

Section 206 also introduces new rules. Section 206(b) recognizes that under modern servicing arrangements the original mortgagee often continues to service the loan after assignment. The section provides that modifications to the mortgage made by the servicing mortgagee are effective against the assignee. Express clauses in the mortgage waiving mortgagor's defenses against the assignee are generally permitted. § 206(e). However, subsection (d) states that an assignee or holder in due course of a loan to a "protected party" secured by a junior mortgage on that person's residence is subject to all defenses against the original mortgagee "[n]otwithstanding agreement to the contrary." Waiver of defenses against a first mortgagee is permitted, however, in order to encourage secondary market sales of first mortgages. Id., comment 4.

The Restatement of Mortgages rejects the majority rule. It provides that unless otherwise provided by the Uniform Commercial Code, "after transfer of an obligation secured by a mortgage, performance of the obligation to the transferor is effective against the transferee if rendered before the obligor receives notice of the transfer." § 5.5. Legislation in some states is in accord. 1999 Conn. Legis. Serv. P.A. 98–147.

5. *MERS.* As set out in the reading and in the excerpt quoted from Judge Kaye, MERS invokes competing policy concerns. At the heart of the matter, there is an ongoing need to balance consumer protection and encouragement of secondary market transactions. With the mortgage finance crisis in 2008, many courts and legislatures sought to rebalance that equation. As we will see in the foreclosure materials below, the courts were particularly active in that arena. To directly address the concerns raised by Judge Kaye discussed in the reading by Professor Korngold, the Federal Reserve promulgated a rule pursuant to Section 131(g) of the Truth in Lending Act requiring that assignee of a loan notify the borrower within thirty of the transfer of the mortgage obligation. 12 C.F.R. Part 226, 75 Fed. Reg. 58489 (No. 185, Sept. 24, 2010). Previously, regulations only required notification of the change of servicer. See 12 U.S.C.A. 2605. Knowing the identity of the lender is an important first step for the borrower to commence workout discussions or perhaps bring a claim of unfair lending practice.

6. *Pledges of Real Property Instruments.* When a mortgagee pledges a note and mortgage as security for a loan to *him,* should the subject matter of the pledge be treated as real property or as personal property covered by U.C.C. Article 9? Comment 4 to U.C.C. § 9–102 states: "The owner of Blackacre borrows $10,000 from his neighbor, and secures his note by a mortgage on Blackacre. This Article is not applicable to the creation of the real estate mortgage. Nor is it applicable to a sale of the note by the mortgagee, even though the mortgage continues to secure the note. However, when the mortgagee pledges the note to secure his own obligation to X, this Article applies to the security interest thus created, which is a security interest in an instrument even though the instrument is secured by a real estate mortgage." The cases are in disarray. See generally G. Nelson & D. Whitman, Real Estate Finance Law § 5.28 (5th ed.2007).

What if a lessor assigns her lease as security for payment of a note executed by her to Y? What if Y then assigns the lessor's note and lease assignment to Z as security for payment of a note executed by Y to Z? See generally, Bowmar, Real Estate Interests as Security Under the UCC: The Scope of Article Nine, 12 U.C.C.L.J. 99 (1979).

7. *Lawyer Liability to Assignee.* One National Bank v. Antonellis, 80 F.3d 606 (1st Cir.1996), involved a malpractice action by a mortgage assignee (ONB) against the attorney for its assignor (Milford). Milford had taken a first mortgage on a parcel in 1987 and took a second mortgage on the same parcel in 1988. Milford understood that it was to subordinate the 1987 mortgage to the 1988 mortgage, but never did so; nevertheless, Milford's attorney issued a title certificate showing the 1988 mortgage as a first mortgage even though in fact it was a second lien. Milford assigned the 1988 note, mortgage and title certificate to ONB which did not retain counsel to search the title. On discovering that the 1988 mortgage was in fact a second mortgage, ONB sued Milford's attorney for malpractice based on the incorrect title certificate.

The court held that, under Massachusetts foreseeable reliance doctrine, Milford's attorney owed no duty of care to ONB. Under that doctrine, an attorney can be liable to a nonclient only if it were reasonably foreseeable that the nonclient would rely on the attorney and only if the imposition of the duty of care would not potentially conflict with the attorney's duty to his or her actual client. ONB argued that there was no potential conflict since the attorney owed the same duty to Milford and ONB—to search title accurately. The court held that a potential conflict arose from the attorney's duty of confidentiality:

> Ostensibly, having already produced the certificate, [the attorney's] duty would be to check whether Milford subordinated the debt, remind it of his error, and if Milford did not rectify it, to do so himself by informing ONB. Clearly, at that point a conflict in the duty of confidentiality would arise: if his client decided not to pass on the information and [the attorney] did so in its stead, he would breach his duty of confidentiality. See S.J.C. Rule 3:07, Canon 4, DR 4–101(B) (stating that "a lawyer shall not knowingly . . . [r]eveal a confidence or secret of his client"). If he did not pass on the information, he would breach his duty to ONB. We refuse to place him in that position.

Id. at 611.

Would the court's view have been different if the first mortgage had been held by a party other than Milford?

D. MORTGAGE DEFAULT

Federal Housing Finance Agency Office of the Inspector General, An Overview of the Home Foreclosure Process

5–9, 17–18 (undated).

DEFAULT

Default is the prelude to foreclosure. Although various technical defaults are possible, the typical default is a failure to make payments as required on the mortgage. Most mortgages require defined payments each month (though the amount due may vary if the mortgage has an adjustable rate), and mortgage servicers will often refuse to accept partial payments. Figure 11 illustrates the remediation process for a defaulted loan. The outcomes following a default depend on factors such as the amount and degree of delinquency, the borrower's overall financial situation, the value of the property and amount of indebtedness, the servicer's economic interests (as distinct from the mortgagee's), and constraints placed on the servicer by contract and applicable laws. Thus, a defaulted residential mortgage may return to good standing, or be modified, or the property may be sold or repossessed by the mortgagee via foreclosure or a voluntary surrender.

Generally, servicers will not commence a foreclosure until a mortgage is 90 days delinquent—that is, until the borrower has missed three consecutive payments. Thus, a homeowner can conceivably fall behind on a mortgage for a month or two and catch up without the servicer commencing a foreclosure. However, it is important to note that a servicer may legally begin foreclosure proceedings before a mortgage is 90 days late. Ninety days is a common practice, not a legal requirement.

Loss Mitigation

In some cases, the default may be cured and the loan reinstated. In addition, depending on individual circumstances, alternatives may exist that permit defaulted borrowers to remain in their homes while addressing their payment delinquency. It is important to note that most of these options are voluntary, but stat law and contractual arrangements, including the acceptance of MHA program funds from Treasury, may trigger particular loss mitigation duties on the part of the servicer.

Mediation. Many states offer or require pre-foreclosure meditation between homeowners and servicers. In some states servicers are required to mediate in good faith in order to proceed with foreclosure. This may include presenting the homeowner with all appropriate paperwork for a foreclosure and having authority to accept settlement offers.

Modification. Common modifications include extending the mortgage's maturity date, adding past-due payments to the end of the mortgage, and making both permanent and temporary interest rate reductions. In most cases, when appropriately applied, these measures will lower the borrower's re-amortized monthly mortgage payment to a more affordable level.

Reductions in the borrower's unpaid principal balance are uncommon. Although HAMP permits principal reductions at participants' option, the Enterprises do not provide for principal reductions in their implementation of HAMP. Homeowners should be aware that under certain circumstances the forgiven debt may be deemed income for tax purposes.

Forbearance. Lenders may always exercise forbearance on defaulted loans, meaning that the lender may simply decline to proceed with foreclosure. Homeowners have no right to forbearance, unless they are active duty military servicemembers covered by the Servicemembers Civil Relief Act or have been so within the previous 90 days. Note that some types of modifications, such as ones that tack past-due balances onto the end of loans as balloon payments, are sometimes referred to as forbearance.

By contrast to payment reductions, payment forbearance involves temporarily suspending the need to make mortgage payments. In their guidance to loan servicers, Fannie Mae and Freddie Mac permit payment forbearance for up to six months in the cases of unemployed borrowers. Servicers must consider unemployed borrowers for such forbearance before consideration for a HAMP loan modification. Borrowers who are not offered any such forbearance must be evaluated for HAMP.

Refinancing. Another option for handling a defaulted loan is to replace it with a new loan via a refinancing. The terms of the new loan can be whatever the borrower and new lender negotiate; the proceeds of the new loan are used to pay off the balance on the old loan. When the old lender is paid off, the old lender releases its lien on the property.

The difference between refinancing and modification is that refinancing entails a new loan, whereas modification is simply a change to terms of an existing loan. A refinancing can involve the substitution of a new lender for the existing lender or a new loan from the existing lender, whereas a modification involves the same lender. Because a refinancing involves a new loan, there are generally closing costs associated with a refinancing, whereas modification may or may not involve fees to the borrower.

Traditionally, refinancing requires the payment in full of the existing loan. Most mortgage loans have "due on sale" clauses that require payment of the full balance of the loan upon the sale of the property and further define a refinancing as a sale. Unless the existing mortgage is paid off, the existing mortgagee continues to hold a lien on the property that is senior to the new lender's. Payment in full via a refinancing thus requires the homeowner to have equity in the property, as today lenders will almost never extend credit beyond the value of the property (above a 100% loan-to-value ratio). Accordingly, refinancing has not been an option, generally, for borrowers who are underwater, even if they are current on their mortgage. However, the Enterprises will refinance qualifying underwater mortgages they own or guarantee under the federal government's Home Affordable Refinancing Program (HARP). Loans that are held on banks' balance sheets or in private-label securitizations are not eligible for HARP>

In addition, some lenders will accept a "short refinancing" in which they receive less than the full unpaid principal balance, may forgive the remaining balance, and release the lien. They may choose to do so if they believe that they will make more in a partial payment via a refinancing than they will in a foreclosure sale. FHA, for example, offers a short-refinancing program: for qualifying borrowers who do not currently have FHA-insured loans, FHA will insure a new first lien mortgage loan at up to 97.75% loan-to-value ratio based on a fresh appraisal. This means that the existing lender must agree to a write-down of the balance as part of the refinancing. FHA requires that the existing lender reduce the existing balance by at least 10% and that the combined loan-to-value ratio of all mortgages on the property be no more than 115%. While short refinancing may be a valuable solution for underwater borrowers, refinancing with a new lender is often very difficult for borrowers with impaired credit scores (which includes any borrower who has defaulted), or even for those with relatively good credit scores.

. . .

FORECLOSURE ALTERNATIVES

Depending on individual circumstances, alternatives may exist to foreclosure proceedings that reduce expenses or legal liability for troubled homeowners. However, like foreclosure, these options will typically result in the homeowner's loss of his or her house. These alternatives may include short sales, deeds in lieu, and bankruptcy. The Enterprises participate in the federal government's HAFA program, which is designed to encourage alternatives to the foreclosure process for troubled home mortgage loans. Participating HAFA servicers may not seek deficiency judgments and may provide relocation incentives of up to $3000 for eligible homeowners who tender deeds in lieu of foreclosure or do short sales.

Short Sale

Lenders may agree to a "short sale," in which the homeowner conducts a private sale of the house, and the lender releases its lien in exchange for the sale proceeds, even though the sale proceeds are insufficient to pay off the debt. A short sale does not necessarily discharge the homeowner's debt; it merely results in a release of the lien, so the homeowner may still be liable for the deficiency. If the lender forgives the deficiency, it may be imputed as taxable income for the homeowner, particularly if the mortgage had a cash-out component.

There are certain barriers to a short sale. Servicers are frequently wary of short sale offers because of concerns that they are settling the debt at too low a price and that the bidder may have colluded with the homeowner. In addition, the high rate of denials for short sale offers has made realtors reluctant to handle them because realtors are only paid upon consummation of a sale and put in more effort in short sales than for regular sales.

Deed in Lieu of Foreclosure

Lenders will sometimes accept a deed in lieu of foreclosure. This means that the homeowner will surrender title and possession of the property voluntarily, rather than requiring the lender to go through the full foreclosure process. For the lender, a deed in lieu spares the time and expense of the foreclosure process. For the homeowner, a deed in lieu may be attractive because the terms under which the homeowner surrenders the property may be negotiated—the lender may be willing to provide the homeowner with some relocation funds or a more generous timetable for moving out.

Critically, a deed in lieu does not extinguish junior liens, so the lender will acquire the property with junior liens still attached. Thus, if neither the homeowner nor the lender who has taken the deed in lieu pays off the junior lienholder(s), the latter may foreclose on the property. Accordingly, lenders may be reluctant to accept deeds in lieu when there is a junior lien on a property.

Bankruptcy

A homeowner may file for bankruptcy at any point before, during, or after the foreclosure process. Bankruptcy is a federal judicial proceeding. A bankruptcy filing automatically stops the foreclosure process. If a lender wishes to proceed with a foreclosure against a bankrupt homeowner, the lender must get permission from the bankruptcy court to do so.

If the homeowner files for Chapter 7 bankruptcy and has defaulted, the homeowner will not be able to retain the property after the bankruptcy absent the lender's consent. If the homeowner files for Chapter 13 bankruptcy and has defaulted, the homeowner may de-accelerate the note and cure the default simply by making up missed payments rather than the full amount of the note. The homeowner may not, absent the lender's consent, modify the terms of the mortgage in bankruptcy if the property is a single-family residence. For multi-family residences, the homeowner may be able to restructure the mortgage in bankruptcy.

NOTES

1.   *The Causes of Default.* The Office of the Chief Economist of the Federal Home Loan Mortgage Corporation compiled statistics on the hardship reasons for mortgage delinquency between 1999–2005. The cause and the percentage of defaults were as follows:

> Unemployment or curtailment of income 41.5%
>
> Illness in the Family 18.9%
>
> Excessive obligation 10.3%
>
> Marital difficulties 8.4%
>
> Death in the Family 3.9%
>
> Property problem or casualty loss 2.1%
>
> Extreme hardship 3.3%
>
> Inability to sell or rent property 1.6%
>
> Employment transfer or military service 0.9%
>
> All other reasons 9.0%

Crews Cutts, Facts and Figures on the New Mortgage Products: Protecting Consumers in the New Mortgage Market Place-Federal Trade Commission Workshop   (2006),   http://www.ftc.gov/bcp/workshops/mortgage/

presentations/cutts.pdf. See also Jacoby, Home Ownership Risk Beyond A Subprime Crisis: The Role of Delinquency Management, 76 Ford.L.Rev. 2261 (2008).

2. *Acceleration Clauses.* Mortgage instruments typically contain an acceleration clause making the outstanding loan balance fully payable in the event the mortgagor fails to pay debt service or other financial obligations, such as taxes and insurance premiums, when due, or commits waste or any other act of default. Some acceleration clauses are optional and require the mortgagee's election by notice of acceleration or commencement of an action to foreclose the mortgage. Other clauses provide that the outstanding principal shall automatically become due upon default. If the note does not contain an acceleration clause, the courts will not imply one and the payee can only recover for sums past due. See, e.g., Rosenfeld v. City Paper Company, 527 So.2d 704 (Ala.1988) (rejecting the application of anticipatory breach doctrine); Miller v. Balcanoff, 566 So.2d 1340 (Fla.App.1990).

Should the mortgagee be entitled to declare a default and accelerate the debt if, through an oversight, the mortgagor was one day late in tendering its debt service? Graf v. Hope Building Corp., 254 N.Y. 1, 171 N.E. 884 (1930), the leading case on the question, held that even the smallest, most innocent oversight will not excuse the mortgagor. There the president of defendant corporation who was the mortgagor was the only person authorized to sign checks in its behalf. Prior to his departure for Europe a clerical assistant computed the interest due on the next installment on the mortgage, but made an error in calculating it. A check for this amount was signed by the president. After his departure the assistant discovered the error, notified the mortgagee of the shortage, assured him of remitting the balance upon the president's return, and forwarded the check as drawn. On the president's return, through forgetfulness of the clerk, he was not informed of the deficiency in the interest payment. At the expiration of 21 days from the interest-payment date, the mortgagee brought an action to foreclose. The mortgagor at once tendered the deficiency, and, the tender being refused, he paid the money into court.

In the view of the majority, "[p]laintiffs may be ungenerous, but generosity is a voluntary attribute and cannot be enforced even by a chancellor.... Here there is no penalty, no forfeiture, nothing except a covenant fair on its face to which both parties willingly consented. It is neither oppressive nor unconscionable. In the absence of some act by the mortgagee which a court of equity would be justified in considering unconscionable, he is entitled to the benefit of the covenant. The contract is definite and no reason appears for its reformation by the courts. We are not at liberty to revise while professing to construe." 254 N.Y. at 4, 171 N.E. at 885.

A minority of states follow the position taken by Judge Benjamin Cardozo dissenting in *Graf* and hold that, although these clauses should generally be enforced according to their terms, if the injury suffered by the mortgagee from delay is small, and the injury to be suffered by the mortgagor from acceleration is great, equity should relieve the mortgagor from the consequences of an inadvertent default. See for example, Vonk v. Dunn, 161 Ariz. 24, 775 P.2d 1088 (1989) (acceleration and foreclosure would be "oppressive and unconscionable" and so not permitted where mortgagor's payment check was incorrectly dishonored by bank and tax delinquency was only $66 and not of long duration); Redding v. Gibbs, 203 Neb. 727, 739–40, 280 N.W.2d 53 (1979) ("In this case it is clear the hardship which would be caused to Cameron . . . by allowing Redding to foreclose the mortgage, would be harsh, oppressive, and unconscionable . . . [Redding] made no demand for payment before commencing suit, although it is clear payment would have been forthcoming immediately. Although, technically, he may not have been required to demand payment before instituting his foreclosure action, nevertheless his failure to do so in this situation was clearly harsh, oppressive, and unconscionable, and strongly suggests that he wished to take advantage of defendant Cameron's situation. The equities in this case preponderate in favor of the defendants and, in our opinion, justify the action of the trial court in dismissing plaintiff's petition.") See U.L.S.I.A. § 502(a) (requiring written notice and 15 day cure period before acceleration); In re Crystal Properties, Ltd., 268 F.3d 743 (9th Cir.2001) (finding that notice of acceleration must be communicated to borrower). Even New York courts distinguish inadvertent nonpayment of principal and interest, for which no equitable relief is granted, from inadvertent failure to pay other required sums under the mortgage. See Massachusetts Mutual Life Insurance Co. v. Transgrow Realty Corp., 101 A.D.2d 770, 475 N.Y.S.2d 418 (1984) (failure to pay real estate taxes, on theory that this is only a collateral undertaking under a mortgage).

Like most acceleration clauses currently in use, the acceleration clause in *Graf* had provided for a grace period within which the mortgagor could cure its default; it was the failure to make the payment until one day after expiration of the grace period that precipitated the acceleration. Should courts be less quick to relieve a mortgagor when a grace period contained in the mortgage note, or imposed by statute, provided him with a *locus poenitentiae* for his mistake? Judge Cardozo, dissenting in *Graf,* acknowledged that enforcement of an acceleration clause is less unfair "if there is a period of grace (in this case twenty days) whereby a reasonable leeway is afforded to inadvertence and improvidence. In such circumstances, with one period of grace established by the covenant, only the most appealing equity will justify a court in transcending the allotted period and substituting another." 254 N.Y. at 10, 171 N.E. at 887.

Should the courts find that the lender waived its right to accelerate and foreclose under the note by previously accepting late payments from the borrower? Finding a waiver may be justified if the facts show that the lender's acceptance misled the mortgagor. However, if the courts routinely find a waiver, will lenders be discouraged from negotiating with borrowers in financial difficulty, forcing lenders to accelerate and foreclose on the first default? See generally Kirkham v. Hansen, 583 A.2d 1026 (Me.1990).

Can a lender charge a prepayment penalty when exercising an acceleration clause? Courts will typically enforce an express agreement providing for prepayment when the mortgagee accelerates because of the borrower's default or because of an "involuntary" prepayment (such as when the land is taken from the borrower in a condemnation proceeding). See, e.g., U.S. v. Harris, 246 F.3d 566 (6th Cir.2001) (upholding clause providing for prepayment penalty after acceleration due to default, even though effect was to wipe out foreclosure surplus that federal government was seeking in federal civil forfeiture because of mortgagor's illegal activities). When there is no express provision extending the prepayment penalty to acceleration situations, courts have generally barred mortgagees from charging a prepayment penalty when exercising an acceleration clause, unless the borrower intentionally defaulted in an attempt to end the mortgage without having to pay the penalty. See Florida Nat'l Bank of Miami v. Bankatlantic, 589 So.2d 255 (Fla.1991) (where apartment building owner intentionally did not lease units in unsuccessful attempt to make building more marketable to a condominium converter, subsequent default by owner on mortgage due to inadequate cash flow from property was intentional and prepayment penalty could be imposed); U.L.S.I.A. § 502(b), comment 2 (provision barring prepayment penalty with acceleration was made optional because of inherent difficulty in distinguishing between intentional and involuntary default).

For an excellent overview of these issues, see Rosenthal, The Role of Courts of Equity in Preventing Acceleration Predicated Upon a Mortgagor's Inadvertent Default, 22 Syracuse L.Rev. 897 (1971).

3. *Waiver and Equitable Relief.* Depending on the applicable facts, precedent and judicial outlook, courts may apply waiver theory or some other equitable doctrine to prevent the mortgagee from declaring a breach and enforcing remedies under the mortgage. Decisions granting relief can be seen as part of the strong debtor protections in traditional mortgage law. See discussion in Note 1, page 346. On the other hand, other courts will reject similar arguments and strictly enforce the mortgage terms and the rights of the lender, reflecting a belief in the value of contracts and predictability. There is, as a result, a wide array of decisions.

Alderman v. Davidson, 326 Or. 508, 954 P.2d 779 (1998) and Price v. First Fed. Sav. Bank, 822 S.W.2d 422 (Ky.App.1992) illustrate the conflicting strains. In *Alderman,* the mortgagor constantly made late payments on the note and also failed for four years to pay the property taxes as required by the note. The court held that the mortgagee had waived the right to timely payments on the note, notwithstanding a "time is of the essence" provision in the mortgage documents, because of the mortgagee's pattern of accepting late payments. Moreover, since the mortgagee should have known that the taxes were not being paid since it never received paid tax receipts from the mortgagor, the mortgagee was deemed to have waived the tax payment provision as well. The court noted that because the mortgagor "reasonably relied to her detriment on [the mortgagee's] inaction, [the mortgagee] now is estopped from foreclosing on the basis of that default without first giving [the mortgagor] notice and a reasonable opportunity to cure." 326 Or. at 514, 954 P.2d at 783. In *Price,* the court held that the mortgagee's acceptance of late payments over the loan did not amount to a waiver of its right to prompt payment. The court explained that if it held to the contrary, "no mortgagee could ever act with any leniency with its debtor for fear of being precluded from foreclosing at an appropriate time." 822 S.W.2d at 424.

4. *Lender Liability.* Borrowers have sought to hold lenders liable for actions or failure to act during the lending process. In Karoutas v. HomeFed Bank, 232 Cal.App.3d 767, 283 Cal.Rptr. 809 (1991), the court found a foreclosing bank liable to the buyers at a deed of trust foreclosure sale for failing to disclose adverse soil conditions which it knew about the property. The court relied on standard disclosure doctrine, rather than on a special relationship between the parties. In Mathews v. Lomas & Nettleton

Co., 754 P.2d 791 (Colo.App.1988), the lender failed to credit a payment by the mortgagor. Ultimately, the lender instituted a foreclosure action and the borrowers sold the house before the action was completed. After borrowers sued the lender, a jury awarded damages for outrageous conduct and negligent infliction of emotional distress. The appellate court noted, however, that there was no evidence that the borrowers suffered an unreasonable risk of bodily harm as required in the jurisdiction to recover for negligent infliction of emotional distress. Since the damage award combined recovery for both outrageous conduct and emotional distress, the judgment was reversed.

Moreover, the lender's conduct in administering and enforcing the loan has also been subject to judicial scrutiny. Thus, in Sutherland v. Barclays American/Mtge. Corp., 53 Cal.App.4th 299, 61 Cal.Rptr.2d 614 (1997), the court specifically enforced the mortgagee's oral promise to postpone payments for three months on a theory of promissory estoppel, but found that the mortgagee's actions were not tortious (and thus not actionable for money damages). In First Union Nat'l Bank of Ga. v. Cook, 223 Ga.App. 374, 477 S.E.2d 649 (1996), abrogated on procedural grounds by Golden Peanut Co. v. Bass, 249 Ga.App. 224, 547 S.E.2d 637 (2001), the court held that a punitive damages claim was supported when a mortgagee sought to foreclose a mortgage that had been marked as paid and the mortgagor alleged that the mortgagee knew the mortgage had been so marked and the lender had a policy of "foreclose first and ask questions later."

Consider whether these cases are correctly decided in light of expectations of the parties, reasonable lender behavior and norms, the costs which would be added to land transactions and loans if one or the other party is found liable, and the other considerations discussed at pages 217–219.

5. *Uniformity of Foreclosure Procedures.* The Uniform Land Security Interest Act represents a recent attempt to create uniform foreclosure procedures. Supporters claim that uniform legislation will encourage national lending and will bring efficiency. See generally, Pedowitz, Mortgage Foreclosure Under ULSIA, 27 Wake Forest L.Rev. 495 (1992). Professor Michael Schill argues, however, that the present system of independent state law should be continued because the supposed inefficiencies of the current structure are overstated, the cost of change would be great, and a non-uniform system encourages states to experiment in their foreclosure methods to reflect differences among states' social and economic structures. Schill, Uniformity or Diversity: Residential Real Estate Finance Law in the 1990s and the Implication of Changing Financial Markets, 64 S.Cal.L.Rev. 1261 (1991).

6. *Federal Preemption of State Foreclosure Law.* Congress has preempted state foreclosure law as it applies to certain mortgages held by the federal government. In 1981 Congress enacted the Multifamily Mortgage Foreclosure Act, 12 U.S.C.A. §§ 3701–3717, permitting, in any state, nonjudicial power of sale foreclosure of multifamily mortgages held by HUD. Id., §§ 3703, 3704. Congress found that the disparity of state foreclosure laws complicated HUD foreclosures, the long periods required for foreclosure under state laws increased the deterioration of properties and governmental management expenses, state statutory redemption periods complicated titles and depressed foreclosure sale prices, and nonjudicial foreclosure was less costly. Id., § 3701. The purpose of the Act is to create a uniform law maximizing foreclosure proceeds, preventing losses to the federal treasury from HUD mortgage defaults, and consequently increasing housing opportunities. The same policy concerns prompted Congress in 1994 to enact the Single Family Mortgage Foreclosure Act of 1994, 12 U.S.C.A. §§ 3751–3768. This Act applies similar rules to HUD foreclosure of single family mortgages. Id., §§ 3751, 3753.

Both acts provide for foreclosure commissioners to conduct the foreclosure, notice of default and foreclosure sale, redemption by the mortgagor before the sale, and procedures for the conduct of the sale, transfer of title, and distribution of the proceeds of the sale. The 1994 Act specifically provides for deficiency judgments in single family mortgage foreclosures, preempting state limitations that may apply. Id., § 3768. Proposals have been made for the extension of federal preemption of state law and the use of nonjudicial foreclosure to mortgages held by other federal entities, such as the FHA and VA. See 141 Cong. H. 10726–06, Oct. 24, 1995; 142 Cong.Rec. S. 2127, March 14, 1996 (Senate provisions in Debt Collection Improvement Act ultimately were removed from P.L. 104–34, signed by the President on April 25, 1996). For a discussion of federalization, see Randolph, The New Federal Foreclosure Laws, 49 Okla. L. Rev. 123 (1996).

In an empirically-based critique, Professor Debra Pogrund Stark argues that the federal nonjudicial foreclosure process is not only inadequate to protect the borrower's equity but also inefficient because of its unnecessary expense. Stark, Foreclosing on the American Dream: An Evaluation of State and Federal Foreclosure Laws, 51 Okla. L. Rev. 229 (1998).

1. METHODS OF FORECLOSURE

a. STRICT FORECLOSURE

**Robert H. Skilton, Developments in
Mortgage Law and Practice**
17 Temple University Law Quarterly 315, 318–320 (1943).

The type of foreclosure usually employed in England at the end of the seventeenth century was the old "strict foreclosure", whereby the mortgagee, without a sale of the premises, was decreed full owner of the property. Occasionally, where the mortgagor's interests seemed to demand it, a public sale was decreed, and in this case the mortgagee was not privileged to bid. He was, in case the property was sold for an amount less than his claim, entitled to a deficiency judgment. It was not possible, however, for him to acquire the property by strict foreclosure and thereafter claim a deficiency. He could have one but not both; either possession and title to the property, or the proceeds of sale of the property to a third party, and a claim for the balance due. In Ireland, on the other hand, it was general practice to decree public sale of the property in all cases.

The remedy of foreclosure, when imported into the colonies, naturally was subjected to modifications thought to be compatible with domestic needs. As time went on, strict foreclosure was supplanted in practically all states by foreclosure followed by public sale. This change was achieved sometimes simply by court practice, not reenforced by statute; sometimes by statutes permitting courts to order a sale of mortgaged premises in their discretion; and, especially since codes of civil practice became current, frequently by statutory provision making public sale mandatory.

Strict foreclosure has survived today as the usual remedy in only two states: Connecticut and Vermont, where English traditions are especially strong. In these states it is the practice to confer full title upon the mortgagee in this manner in all cases where it does not appear upon appraisement that the property would bring more than the mortgage debt. The mortgagee is entitled to judgment for the balance due, the difference between his claim and the appraised value of the premises.

In a number of additional states, strict foreclosure is available in certain cases where the interests of both parties seem to require it, as where the mortgagor is insolvent, the property insufficient to cover claim and costs, and there is no practical advantage in a deficiency judgment. In other states, statutory provisions, such as the frequent code provisions, "a mortgage shall not be deemed a conveyance", "there shall be but one action upon a debt", etc., have been held to exclude the possibility of strict foreclosure.

NOTE

Strict foreclosure continues to be used in Connecticut, see Conn. Gen. Stat. Ann. § 49–15; New Milford Sav. Bank v. Jajer, 244 Conn. 251, 708 A.2d 1378 (1998), but has been recently repealed in Vermont, see Vt. Stat. Ann. tit. 12, § 4531, repealed by 2011, Adj. Sess., No. 102, § 2, eff. July 1, 2012. Illinois, also allowing strict foreclosure, imposes three requirements aimed at safeguarding the mortgagor and preventing unjust enrichment to the mortgagee: the property's value cannot exceed the debt, a deficiency cannot be recovered, and the mortgagor must be insolvent. See 735 Ill.Comp.Stat. 5/15–1403; Great Lakes Mortgage Corp. v. Collymore, 14 Ill.App.3d 68, 302 N.E.2d 248 (1973). Strict foreclosure "remains a viable, if little used, procedure for foreclosing mortgages" in Maryland. Fairfax Sav., F.S.B. v. Kris Jen Ltd. Partnership, 338 Md. 1, 21, 655 A.2d 1265 (1995). In a strict foreclosure proceeding in Maryland, "no sale of the mortgaged property took place, but instead, the equity court determined the amount due the mortgagee and passed a decree naming a date for the sum named in the decree to be paid, or the mortgagor's right to redeem would forever be taken away." 91st Street Joint Venture v. Goldstein, 114 Md.App. 561, 577, 691 A.2d 272, 280 (1997).

Strict foreclosure is more widely used for two narrower purposes. One use is to cut off the interest of a junior encumbrancer whom the mortgagee mistakenly failed to join in foreclosure proceedings earlier brought against the mortgagor. For example, in Sears, Roebuck & Co. v. Camp, 124 N.J.Eq. 403, 1 A.2d 425 (1938), strict foreclosure was allowed against the assignee of a junior mortgage whose assignment, though recorded, was not disclosed by the mortgagee's title search. It is unclear, though, whether the court was more persuaded by the general utility of strict foreclosure to cut off junior interests or by the "pertinent" facts that "the lands were sold to complainant on its nominal bid of $100, and that it is not suggested another sale would yield more than sufficient to satisfy complainant's mortgage—a vain hope, in view of the long continued depression of the real estate market, consequent upon the general economic crisis." 124 N.J.Eq. at 414, 1 A.2d at 430. See generally, Wietzki v. Wietzki, 231 Neb. 551, 437 N.W.2d 449 (1989) (finding no strict foreclosure by installment sale vendor that would extinguish junior lien on the purchaser's interest in the contract since vendor did not intend to have his lien extinguished when purchaser gave vendor a quitclaim deed after purchaser defaulted).

Second, courts sometimes allow strict foreclosure of equitable mortgages. Thus, in Herrmann v. Churchill, 235 Or. 327, 385 P.2d 190 (1963), the Oregon Supreme Court ruled that because the action sought to construe an absolute deed as a mortgage, and did not seek to foreclose a mortgage, statutory prohibitions against strict foreclosure did not apply. "Every jurisdiction in this country which has passed upon this question, insofar as our research discloses, has held that the statutes as to foreclosure of mortgages are inapplicable in a suit to have a deed absolute declared a mortgage." 385 P.2d at 193. Can you find any fault with Justice O'Connell's dissenting observation that "[the] mortgagor should have the same right to insist on foreclosure by judicial sale whether the mortgage is cast in the usual form or takes the form of an absolute deed"? 385 P.2d at 195.

For excellent discussions of the policy issues raised by strict foreclosure, see Durham, In Defense of Strict Foreclosure: A Legal and Economic Analysis of Mortgage Foreclosure, 36 S.Car.L.Rev. 461 (1985) (arguing that efficiency, equity, and fairness are served by strict foreclosure); Wechsler, Through the Looking Glass: Foreclosure by Sale as De Facto Strict Foreclosure—An Empirical Study of Mortgage Foreclosure and Subsequent Resale, 70 Cornell L.Rev. 850 (1985) (arguing that study shows that foreclosure by sale is the functional equivalent of strict foreclosure since mortgagees often buy the mortgaged property at the sale, resell it a significant profit, and thus eliminate the mortgagor's equity). Tefft, The Myth of Strict Foreclosure, 4 U. Chi.L.Rev. 575 (1937), compares the American and English systems of strict foreclosure.

Professor Debra Pogrund Stark has recommended increased use of strict foreclosure in some situations. In order to address the loss of equity to borrowers and the inefficiencies of the current foreclosure system, she suggests the application of strict foreclosure when a post-default appraisal of the property shows a value less than the amount of the judgment on the debt. A judicial sale of the property would be held only when the appraisal exceeds the judgment on the debt. Stark, Facing the Facts: An Empirical Study of the Fairness and Efficiency of Foreclosures and a Proposal for Reform, 30 U. Mich. J.L. Reform 639 (1997).

b.   FORECLOSURE BY COURT ACTION AND SALE

**Robert H. Skilton, Developments in
Mortgage Law and Practice**
17 Temple University Law Quarterly 315, 319–320 (1943).

By 1830, it would seem that strict foreclosure had been superseded in the great majority of states by foreclosure through public sale. In developing the device of public sale, American courts generally made these innovations (1) they permitted the mortgagee to bid in the property himself; (2) they permitted him a claim for the difference between sale price and original claim, thus regarding the sale price as conclusively establishing value. Statutory formulae, developed for the administration of this new process of public sale, accounted, in part, for the growing tendency to treat public sale as finally cutting off the mortgagor's interest, with no succeeding period of redemption—contrary to the English practice in strict foreclosure. These innovations, apparently first appearing in New York cases in the early nineteenth century, represented substantial concessions to the mortgagee: they made his remedies much more potent.

As modified by later statutory developments, equitable foreclosure followed by public sale remains the most popular method of terminating the mortgagor's interest in a majority of American jurisdictions. In spite of the changes introduced to expedite and simplify the procedure, this method continues to be comparatively costly and complicated. The typical equity proceeding involves a preliminary title search to determine all parties in interest; the filing of a *lis pendens,* summons or complaint; service of the process; a time for a hearing, if necessary; the decree or judgment; the delivery to the sheriff of papers authorizing him to sell; notice of sale and service of notice; the actual sale and the issuance of a certificate of sale; and the sheriff's report. The number of steps necessary to consummate foreclosure by court process naturally results in delay, considerable court costs and a fairly large attorney's fee. Foreclosure by court process has, however, been defended as the safest way to determine by *res adjudicata* the rights of the parties.

United States Department of Housing and Urban Development v. Union Mortgage Company

Supreme Judicial Court of Maine, 1995.
661 A.2d 163.

Before WATHEN, C.J., and ROBERTS, GLASSMAN, CLIFFORD, DANA and LIPEZ, JJ.

GLASSMAN, JUSTICE.

Union Mortgage Company, Inc. (Union) appeals from the judgment of the District Court (Augusta, Perry, J.) following a trial on the complaint of the United States Department of Housing and Urban Development (HUD)[2] against Union seeking a foreclosure of Union's interest in certain real property located in Randolph. Union contends that, because HUD's predecessor in interest failed to name Union as a party in interest in its original civil proceeding for the foreclosure and sale of the property, the trial court erred in denying Union's right to participate in a new foreclosure sale. We agree, and accordingly, we vacate the judgment.

---

[2] Although RCR Services, Inc. initiated the present proceeding, because it had conveyed its interest in the property to the United States Department of Housing and Urban Development by a deed dated September 14, 1990, that Department was substituted as the plaintiff prior to the trial of this matter.

The record reveals the following undisputed facts: In January 1989, RCR Services, Inc. (RCR) initiated a foreclosure action of its recorded first mortgage in the amount of $45,153 on property for which Union held a recorded junior mortgage in the amount of $9,900 without naming Union as a party in interest in that proceeding. In January 1990, RCR obtained a judgment of foreclosure and conducted a foreclosure sale in June 1990, at which time RCR purchased the property for $80,520.26, the amount of the outstanding debt to RCR.

In February 1993, RCR filed a complaint, pursuant to 14 M.R.S.A. § 6321 (Supp.1994), alleging that RCR's mortgage was entitled to priority over Union's recorded junior mortgage and seeking to foreclose Union's interest in the property. After a trial, the District Court issued a judgment of foreclosure on August 23, 1994. From the judgment of the trial court, concluding that the action was a "reforeclosure" within the purview of 14 M.R.S.A. §§ 6321–6325 (Supp.1994), and determining that Union's interest would be adequately protected by permitting Union to redeem the property on payment to HUD of $80,520.26 within ninety days from the entry of the judgment, Union appeals.

Union contends that providing an omitted junior mortgagee in a subsequent action to foreclose its interest only with the right to redeem deprives the omitted mortgagee of the right to appear at the sale, to bid and to protect its interest. HUD responds that if a second sale were to occur Union would have to bid in excess of $80,520.26 to purchase the property. Accordingly, it argues that by providing Union the right to redeem the property on the payment to HUD of $80,520.26, Union is provided the same protection it would have received had it been joined in the original proceeding.

We review the trial court's construction of a statutory scheme as a matter of law. Spiller v. State, 627 A.2d 513, 515 (Me.1993). The foreclosure by civil action provided by 14 M.R.S.A. §§ 6321–6325 as an alternative method to the foreclosure process provided in 14 M.R.S.A. §§ 6201 and 6203 (1980 & Supp.1994) (foreclosure with and without possession) is specifically subject to section 6205 (1980).[3] The statutory civil foreclosure procedure preserves two fundamental rights to a junior mortgagee: the right to redeem the property from the senior mortgagee and the right to participate in a public foreclosure sale and to receive any surplus proceeds after the senior mortgage has been satisfied.

Following a breach of a condition of a mortgage of first priority, section 6321 provides that the mortgagee may foreclose against all parties in interest and further provides:

> The complaint must allege with specificity the plaintiff's claim by mortgage on such real estate, describe the mortgaged premises intelligibly ... state the amount due on the mortgage, state the condition broken and by reason of such

---

[3]   Section 6205 (1980) provides, in pertinent part: When proceedings for the foreclosure of any prior mortgage of real estate have been instituted by any method provided by law, the owner of any subsequent mortgage of the same real estate or any part of the same real estate may, at any time before the right of redemption from such prior mortgage has expired, in writing, request the owner of such prior mortgage to assign the same and the debt thereby secured to him, upon his paying the owner of the prior mortgage, the full amount, including all interest, costs of foreclosure and such other sums as the mortgagor or person redeeming would be required to pay in order to redeem.

breach demand a foreclosure and sale. Service of process on all parties in interest and all proceedings must be in accordance with the Maine Rules of Civil Procedure. "Parties in interest" include ... mortgagees ... as reflected by the indices in the registry of deeds and the documents referred to therein affecting the mortgaged premises, through the time of the recording of the complaint or the clerk's certificate. Failure to join any party in interest does not invalidate the action nor any subsequent proceedings as to those joined.

14 M.R.S.A. § 6321.

By the terms of section 6321 a sale of property that has been judicially foreclosed does not convey the premises free and clear of a recorded interest if the holder of that interest is not made a party to the action. Naming the junior mortgagee as a party in interest in a foreclosure action and serving of process provides notice of the imminent foreclosure proceedings. Once notified of the senior mortgagee's intention to foreclose against the property, the junior mortgagee has the opportunity to appear in the action and have the court determine, pursuant to section 6322 (Supp.1994), the "order of priority and those amounts, if any, that may be due to other parties that may appear." Section 6322 also provides that after a hearing, if the court determines a breach of a condition in the primary mortgage has occurred, "a judgment of foreclosure and sale shall issue providing that if the mortgagor, his successors, heirs and assigns do not pay the sum that the court adjudges to be due and payable, with interest within the period of redemption, the mortgagee shall proceed with a sale as provided." The same right of redemption is preserved to the junior mortgagee by section 6205.

On the expiration of the period of redemption, and after the mortgagee publishes notice, the mortgagee must hold a public sale, sell the property to the highest bidder, and deliver a deed of sale to the purchaser. § 6323(1) (Supp.1994). The statute specifically provides that the mortgagee and any party in interest may bid at the sale and the deed conveys the premises "free and clear of all interests of the parties in interest joined in the action." § 6323(1). In foreclosure proceedings conducted prior to January 1, 1995, there is no statutory requirement to notify the original parties in interest to the foreclosure action of the public sale.[4] Because the parties in interest were named in the action and were notified of the period for redemption, however, a party in interest had the means to determine when the public sale would occur. Knowledge of the date of the sale enables a junior mortgagee to protect its interest by attending the sale and by seeking the attendance of other potential bidders. If the property sells for more than the amount owing to the senior mortgagee, "[a]fter first deducting the expenses incurred in making the sale, the mortgagee shall disburse the remaining proceeds in accordance with the provisions of the judgment." § 6324.

By RCR's failure to include Union as a party in interest to the original foreclosure action, Union's interest was not foreclosed.

---

[4] We note that by P.L.1993, ch. 544, 14 M.R.S.A. section 6323 was amended to provide, "In foreclosures by civil action commenced on or after January 1, 1995, the mortgagee shall cause notice of the public sale to be mailed by ordinary mail to all parties who appeared in the foreclosure action or to their attorneys of record."

Accordingly, unless that interest is subsequently foreclosed, Union's junior mortgage would be elevated to the status of a senior mortgage. In such instance, "the junior mortgagee would be presented with a windfall through the mere fact of omission." See, Note, Remedies of Junior Lienors Omitted from Prior Foreclosure, 88 U.Pa.L.Rev. 994, 998–999 (1940) (hereinafter *Note*). Some courts have held that in these circumstances "a purchaser at a foreclosure sale of a senior mortgage to which a junior mortgagee was not a party may by proceedings de novo, to which the junior mortgagee is a party, foreclose the senior mortgage as to him." 55 Am.Jur.2d, Mortgages § 856 (1971). See, e.g., Jorgenson v. Endicott Trust Co., (holding that purchaser's appropriate remedy by statute is to set aside sale or to reforeclose); Deming Nat'l Bank v. Walraven, 133 Ariz. 378, 380, 651 P.2d 1203, 1205 (App.1982) (holding that second foreclosure action permitted to foreclose junior lien when junior lienholder omitted by mistake from first foreclosure action); Polster v. General Guaranty Mortgage Co., 180 So.2d 484, 487 (Fla.App.1965) (holding that right to reforeclose omitted junior lien is a matter of substantive law).

Maine's civil foreclosure statute does not address the respective rights of an omitted junior mortgagee and the purchaser. We conclude that any attempt to subsequently foreclose against the junior mortgagee must preserve the junior mortgagee's right to redeem the senior mortgage *and* the right to participate in a second public sale. Thus, reforeclosure proceedings must comply with the same requirements as those provided in 14 M.R.S.A. §§ 6321–6325. Accordingly, for HUD to foreclose Union's interest, it must hold a second public sale. Because HUD is subrogated to RCR's rights as the original senior mortgagee, however, its debt will have first priority on the proceeds of any sale. 55 Am.Jur.2d at § 852.

> There is ample justification for such a practice because it does no more than provide for the omitted lienor that which was denied to him at the previous foreclosure, i.e., a sale at which he could appear and protect his interest. . . . Before the prior foreclosure he was subject to such a proceeding upon maturity of the senior mortgage. Since the purchaser is accorded the rights of the senior incumbrancer, there is no reason why a prior omission should bar this legitimate right.

Note, 88 U.Pa.L.Rev. at 1006 (1940). Accordingly, the trial court erred in providing Union the right to redeem without granting it the corollary right to participate in a second public sale.

The entry is:

Judgment vacated. Remanded for further proceedings consistent with the opinion herein.

All concurring.

NOTES

1.   *U.S. Department of HUD v. Union Mortgage.* Was the result in *Union Mortgage* correct? Would it have mattered for the court if it could have been shown that Union Mortgage knew of the foreclosure action at the time it was brought? At some point after foreclosure was decreed but before the foreclosure sale? Do you agree with the court's holding as to the rights of

Union Mortgage as an unforeclosed junior lienor? Considering both the values of fairness and efficiency, was the court's rule too generous to Union Mortgage or to HUD?

2. *"Necessary" Parties and "Proper" Parties.* From the mortgagee's viewpoint, the central assumption behind foreclosure is that each mortgagee is entitled to proceed against exactly the interest in land— neither more nor less—that it originally received as security for the loan. A foreclosing first mortgagee is thus able to eliminate all encumbrances, liens, easements, covenants, leases and other interests that attached to the property after its mortgage. Similarly, a junior encumbrancer can wipe out any interests that are junior to its own. But the title transferred on the junior's foreclosure sale will necessarily be subject to any outstanding senior encumbrances, for to enable the junior encumbrancer to terminate the senior encumbrance would effectively give it a greater interest than it originally received as security for its loan.

Procedurally, these concepts are delineated by the division between "necessary" and "proper" parties to the foreclosure proceedings. Because junior lienors stand to lose their interests on foreclosure by a senior lienor, they are "necessary parties" who must be joined if their interests are to be eliminated and a completely effective foreclosure order rendered. In addition to the mortgagor and junior mortgagees, necessary parties include all easement holders, mechanics' lienors and others whose interests first attached after the interest of the foreclosing lienor. The effect of a failure to join junior mortgagees, or others with the right to redeem, is that the redemptive rights they could have exercised at or before the foreclosure sale remain intact. See, e.g., Patel v. Khan, 970 P.2d 836 (Wyo.1998) (second mortgagee advances to first priority). Failure to join easement and covenant holders similarly leaves their nonpossessory interests intact. See, e.g., Diamond Benefits Life Ins. Co. v. Troll, 66 Cal.App.4th 1, 77 Cal.Rptr.2d 581 (1998) (easement survives foreclosure); Como, Inc. v. Carson Square, Inc., 689 N.E.2d 725 (Ind.1997) (lease not terminated in foreclosure where tenant was not named as a party nor notified of commencement of action).

Just as senior liens are substantively insulated from junior lien foreclosures, senior lienors are procedurally insulated from the bother of having to join in the junior's foreclosure proceedings. Senior lienors, though not necessary parties, may however be "proper" parties and can be joined without their consent if their presence would aid a full and binding determination on the foreclosure sale. For example, if there is some question about the amount outstanding on the senior debt, or the debt's priority position, the senior lienor may be joinable as a proper party so that the foreclosure decree can settle these issues.

3. *Quality of Title to Purchaser.* It is claimed that judicial foreclosure has the advantage of producing a more stable title for the purchaser because the presence of a judge and the other parties makes it more likely that issues will be raised and disposed of in the action. Moreover, the rule of judicial finality will be applied to limit collateral attacks by a party participating in the court's decision. *Union Mortgage* illustrates a key exception to the finality rule in allowing a collateral attack on the foreclosure action by an omitted necessary party. G. Nelson & D. Whitman, Real Estate Finance Law § 7.15 (5th ed.2007).

Is the result of *Union Mortgage* fair to HUD (a purchaser from RCR)? *Caveat emptor* generally applies to a purchaser at a foreclosure sale, although there is some disagreement as to whether the doctrine would require the purchaser to accept a deed where the title was not marketable. See G. Nelson & D. Whitman, Real Estate Finance Law § 7.17 (5th ed.2007); CSS Corporation v. Sheriff of Chester County, 352 Pa.Super. 256, 507 A.2d 870 (1986), appeal denied, 514 Pa. 630, 522 A.2d 559 (1987). Which view is correct? Could HUD have learned of the fact that Union Mortgage had not been joined, when, and at what cost?

4. *Benefits of Judicial Foreclosure/Adequacy of the Price.* Judicial foreclosure, though more costly and time-consuming than nonjudicial foreclosure, continues to be widely used. One reason, described above in note 3, is that the quality of deeds given at judicial foreclosure is believed to be more marketable than deeds given at nonjudicial sales, and capable of attracting a higher bid. Another reason for the wide use of judicial foreclosure is that legislative skepticism about the propriety of nonjudicial foreclosure has in many places curtailed its usefulness, availability, or both.

One limitation on the soundness of title from judicial foreclosure is the longstanding, but not often applied doctrine that permits a mortgagor to undo a foreclosure sale if the price is very low.

> Since the case of McCoy v. Brooks, 9 Ariz. 157, 80 P. 365 (1905) the general rule in Arizona dealing with vacation of execution sales because of inadequate bids is that mere inadequacy of price, where the parties stand on an equal footing and there are no confidential relations between them, is not, in and of itself, sufficient to authorize vacation of the sale unless the inadequacy is so gross as to be proof of fraud or shocks the conscience of the court.

> Sales in actions to foreclose mortgages are subject to judicial review for substantive fairness as well as for procedural compliance. Thus, it is well established that such sales can be overturned based on price alone. "Where a grossly inadequate price is bid, such as shocks one's conscience, an equity court may set aside the sale, thus insuring within limited bounds a modicum of protection to a party who has absolutely no control over the amount bid and this, in effect, insures that the foreclosed property is not 'given away.'" Nussbaumer v. Superior Court, 107 Ariz. 504, 507, 489 P.2d 843, 846 (1971).

In re Krohn, 203 Ariz. 205, 207, 52 P.3d 774, 776 (2002). How low must the price be to qualify "shock the conscience"? Does this doctrine cause title uncertainty that may itself depress prices paid (and thus funds available to the mortgagor and lienors)?

For an excellent analysis of the competing economic interests in foreclosure and proposals for reform, see Johnson, Critiquing the Foreclosure Process: An Economic Approach Based on the Paradigmatic Norms of Bankruptcy, 79 Va.L.Rev. 959, 963 (1993) (suggesting that the norms of bankruptcy law should apply in foreclosure, and that "[t]he problem faced by the mortgagor and the mortgagee in the foreclosure setting can be likened to a common-pool problem, in which the goal should be to maximize the value of the asset for both," with the mortgagor treated as an unsecured creditor in bankruptcy). See also Goldstein, Reforming the Residential Mortgage Foreclosure Process, 21 Real Est.L.J. 286 (1993).

5. *Attorney Liability.* Cases have held borrowers liable for costs and fines for bringing egregiously frivolous appeals in a foreclosure action. Besides general concerns over such behavior, these cases may well reflect the desire for an efficient, fast, and final foreclosure procedure. For example, in White v. Mid-Continent Investments, Inc., 789 S.W.2d 34, 41 (Mo.App.1990), the court found that the basis of the appeal was that court below erred in not believing mortgagor's testimony rather than the facts contained in evidence which she herself adduced. The court stated: "This appeal utterly lacks merit and constitutes an abuse of the process of this court and our system of civil justice. The plaintiff, a law school graduate of considerable ability, has robbed this court, the trial court and the defendants of precious time and money, asserting baseless claims smacking of fraud."

Attorneys may also be liable. In United States v. Allen L. Wright Development Corporation, 667 F.Supp. 1218 (N.D.Ill.1987), the owner of the mortgagor-corporation and the mortgagor's attorneys were held liable under Rule 11 for the government's costs and attorneys' fees in foreclosing a HUD mortgage where the mortgagor's "answer, affirmative defenses, response to the United States' motion for summary judgment and discovery requests were not well grounded in fact or warranted by existing law or even a good faith argument for the extension, modification or reversal of existing law. . . . Additionally, we find that [mortgagor's] actions and the actions of its attorneys were motivated by an improper purpose, specifically to delay the proceedings as long as possible to garner income tax benefits and to increase the attorneys' fees payable out of the subject of this foreclosure action." Id. at 1220–1221.

c.   FORECLOSURE BY POWER OF SALE

Robert H. Skilton, Developments in Mortgage Law and Practice

17 Temple University Law Quarterly 315, 323–326 (1943).

Not satisfied with the costly and complicated system of equitable foreclosure obtaining at the end of the eighteenth century, draftsmen representing mortgagees hit upon the idea of inserting in mortgage indentures an express authority to the mortgagee to sell the property without court action, freed of the equity of redemption. The legality of this device was at first questioned in England. In Robert v. Bozan,[42] Lord Eldon objected to the power on the ground that it constituted the mortgagee the trustee of the equity of redemption, and suggested that it would have been more proper had a third party been named as holder of the power. Earlier, an eminent authority on mortgages had remarked that powers of sale were of "too doubtful a complexion to be relied upon as the source of an irredeemable title".[43] It had been said:

---

[42]   Chan. (Feb. 1825) M.B. cited in Coventry, 15 Pres.Mort. 150.

[43]   Powell on Mortgages, quoted in Jones, Power of Sale Mortgages and Trust Deeds (1877) 3 So.L.Rev. 703.

"The objections made to such a power were, that it was another device of the unscrupulous mortgagee to take advantage of the necessities of the mortgagor; that it was susceptible of abuse, as a sale might be forced at an unfavorable time; that it made a mortgagee trustee of the equity of redemption, and that it was in conflict with the jurisdiction of the courts of equity."[44]

Such objections prevented the early use of powers of sale in England, although with the passage of time they gained wide acceptance and approval, and eventually statutory authorization and form.

Powers of sale were recognized as valid in many states at an earlier date than in England. Jones, writing in 1877, stated:

"Fifty years ago power of sale mortgages were not in general use anywhere in this country; and although considerable use was made of them at an earlier time than any corresponding use was made of them in England, they were adopted in the latter country at an earlier time than here, to the exclusion of other forms of security. Within the past half century, however, the use of them has rapidly extended, so that in some states the use of any other form of security is exceptional. The validity of these powers of sale is everywhere recognized, and the use of them, either in mortgages or deeds of trust, is becoming general." [46]

The growing popularity of this device was accompanied by statutes passed in most of the states, establishing conditions of advertisement and sale that had to be met in the valid exercise of the power. These statutes sometimes served to permit the sale out of court of mortgaged premises where no express power of sale was included. There is much statutory material on this point. Illustrative is the case of New York. In 1774 legislation specifically authorized the exercise of such power, thus clearing previous doubts as to its validity. Notice of sale was to be given by publication and posting. In 1844 the statute was amended to prescribe notice by personal service or mail, in addition to the previously stipulated methods. In 1857 it was provided that a copy of the notice should be delivered to the county clerk, and affixed to a book. In 1808 it was provided that the affidavit of the printer should be evidence of publication, posting and notice. In 1838 the mortgagee was permitted to buy the property himself. These and other statutes create a background for the exercise of the power, and their mandatory provisions must be fully complied with if a valid exercise is to be made, regardless of easier requirements in the mortgage.

Although recognized as lawful by the courts in many states, and in some cases reinforced by statutory authority, powers of sale continued to be viewed by courts with jealousy, as an invasion of their sphere. The effect of this judicial jealousy was to impose limiting influences upon the legal development of powers of sale. For example, without statutory authority, the mortgagee was not permitted to buy in the property himself.

---

[44] Lionberger, Mortgages and Powers of Sale (1888) 16 Cent.L.J. 247, at 248.

[46] Jones, Power of Sale Mortgages and Trust Deeds (1877) 3 So.L.Rev. 703, at 707.

Restrictive judicial tendencies were carried to the extent in Virginia and other southern states that a power of sale given personally to the mortgagee was held to be invalid, and the practice developed of naming a third party as trustee to exercise the power. The result is that today in many southern states, and elsewhere, the deed of trust is the popular security device.

The deed of trust is, however, essentially a mortgage and there would seem to be no valid reason for legal distinctions between the two forms. As A.M. Kidd remarked:

". . . distinctions are unsound. The trustee under a trust deed is in no sense a fiduciary. He is usually an agent of the lender of the money and in a rational system could well be dispensed with. . . . The trustee of a trust deed for security is in reality no more of a fiduciary than the law compels a mortgagee to be."[54]

Unfortunately for simplicity, however, there are many states in which trust deeds and mortgages exist side by side, and somewhat whimsical legal distinctions between them have frequently been made. The exact legal position of each must depend upon the peculiar laws of each state. Such variety, naturally, obstructs a coordinated view of the legal status of the mortgage and related forms.

Powers of sale out of court, either in mortgages or deeds of trust, have developed in popularity until they are in many states the chief method of foreclosure. They achieved such popularity because of the simplicity, speed and cheapness of their execution. There are but two steps necessary: notice and sale. In consequence, costs are light, consisting principally of advertising charges and a small attorney's fee. Whereas the average cost of foreclosure proceeding by judicial process appears to be from $150 to $200, foreclosure by power of sale out of court seems to be about $100 less. Whereas the length of time involved in foreclosure by judicial action is from two to four months, and in some states considerably longer, it usually takes from one to two months to complete foreclosure by power of sale. These periods are, of course, exclusive of the time for redemption, if any exists.

By the time powers of sale received general acceptance, the tide of judicial and legislative interest in the problems of the mortgagee had spent itself. The United States was now beginning to experience a series of land and business depressions which resulted from its emergence as an industrial community. In the business downswings, the pressure of financially distressed classes of the community became too heavy to resist. From the early part of the nineteenth century to the present day, depression legislation has played a large part in shaping the mortgage into a legal cast designedly quite favorable to the interests of the mortgagor.

---

[54] Kidd, Trust Deeds and Mortgages in California (1915) 3 Calif.L.Rev. 381, at 383, 384.

Rosenberg v. Smidt

Supreme Court of Alaska, 1986.
727 P.2d 778.

Before RABINOWITZ, C.J., and BURKE, MATTHEWS, COMPTON and MOORE, JJ.

OPINION

COMPTON, JUSTICE.

Fred Rosenberg and Rita Rosenberg appeal from a partial summary judgment entered pursuant to Civil Rule 54(b). The judgment divested them of title to a parcel of real property and revested it in Alvin Smidt and Janice Smidt. Since the trial court's decision is based on stipulated facts, the appeal presents only legal issues. The parties dispute whether AS 34.20.070(c) requires a trustee to attempt to discover the current address of a record interest holder before proceeding with a trustee's sale of encumbered real property. The parties also dispute whether AS 34.20.090(c) protects the Rosenbergs as bona fide purchasers without notice of possible defects in the foreclosure sale notifications. We affirm.

I.   FACTS AND PROCEEDINGS

In December 1973, Rodney Spendlove and William Johnson[1] sold real property to Alvin Smidt and Janice Smidt (Smidts). At the time of the sale, a first deed of trust executed by Spendlove and Johnson encumbered the property.[2] The Smidts executed a second deed of trust on the property in favor of Spendlove and Johnson,[3] securing the balance of the purchase price, $6,200. Alaska Title Guaranty Company (Alaska Title) was designated trustee on both deeds of trust.

The Smidts made all of the payments due on their note through May 1981. Nevertheless, by early 1980 Spendlove and Johnson had defaulted on the payments due under the note secured by the first deed of trust. At the beneficiaries' request, Alaska Title began nonjudicial foreclosure proceedings in June, 1980.

As required by AS 34.20.070(c),[4] Alaska Title sent copies of the notice of default to the Smidts, Johnson, and Spendlove. Alaska Title

---

[1]   While both are defendants below, neither are parties to this appeal. Apparently, no final judgment has yet been entered against them.

[2]   The beneficiaries of this first trust deed are not parties to this dispute.

[3]   In this trust deed, the Smidts requested Alaska Title to send notices of default (on *that* deed, presumably) to the address listed on the deed. Upon the default in the first trust deed, as requested, Alaska Title did send the notice to the address listed on the second deed.

[4]   AS 34.20.070(c) provides:

   Within 10 days after recording the notice of default, the trustee shall mail a copy of the notice by certified mail to the *last known address* of each of the following persons or their legal representatives (1) the grantor in the trust deed; (2) *the successor in interest to the grantor whose interest appears of record* or of whose interest the trustee or the beneficiary has actual notice, or who is in possession of the property; (3) any other person in possession of or occupying the property; (4) any person having a lien or interest subsequent to the interest of the trustee in the trust deed, where the lien or interest appears of record or where the trustee or the beneficiary has actual notice of the lien or interest. The notice may be delivered personally instead of by mail.

(Emphasis added).

used the address for the Smidts listed on the 1973 second deed of trust. The Smidts, however, had moved from that address—a mobile home park—in 1975. The certified letters sent to the Smidts were returned to Alaska Title marked "unclaimed." Alaska Title published notice of the sale in an Anchorage newspaper. The Smidts, however, did not get actual notice of the sale.

From the summer of 1975 through the summer of 1980, the Smidts resided and received mail at their home on Old Muldoon Road in Anchorage. Alaska Title could have discovered the Smidts' address by contacting either the Anchorage Municipality Real Property Taxation Department, any of several utility companies, or the State's Department of Motor Vehicles. The Anchorage phone directory listed Alvin Smidt's phone number, but not address. Polk's Greater Anchorage Area Directory listed the Smidt's address in 1979, but not in 1980.

In October 1980, Fred Rosenberg and Rita Rosenberg (Rosenbergs) purchased the property at a public foreclosure sale held by Alaska Title. Although the property was then worth more than $20,000, they bid only $5,626.25. The Smidts, meanwhile, continued making payments to Spendlove and Johnson, ignorant of the sale until April 1981.

The Smidts sued the Rosenbergs, Alaska Title, Spendlove, and Johnson to set aside the sale. The Smidts moved for partial summary judgment. The trial court ruled that "principles of equity" require a trustee to "take reasonable steps to ascertain the current address of the trustor or his assignee." The trial court noted that the mobility of Alaska's youthful population compelled such a duty. It further noted that while professional trustees know of the need to be informed of address changes, the deed of trust here imposed no such requirement on the Smidts. Judgement was entered pursuant to Civil Rule 54(b), and the Rosenbergs appealed.

II.   DILIGENT INQUIRY UNDER AS 34.20.070(C).

AS 34.20.070(c) required Alaska Title to mail a notice of Spendlove and Johnson's default to the "last known address" of their assignees, the Smidts. At the time Alaska Title mailed its notice, it had actual knowledge only of the address used by the Smidts seven years earlier. The parties dispute whether Alaska Title should have made some effort to locate the Smidts after it received the returned certified letter marked "unclaimed." Imposition of a due diligence requirement would announce a protection neither required nor precluded by the statute.

No Alaska cases have construed this provision of AS 34.20.070(c). Decisions from other jurisdictions interpreting similar "last known address" clauses provide some insight, but the statutory schemes in which such clauses occur differ so greatly that no case adequately disposes of this question.[8]

---

[8]   The parties do not here dispute the constitutionality of the notice provision. They had disputed below whether due process required better notice than the Smidts received. The trial court originally invalidated the sale on due process grounds. It then reversed its due process ruling and decided instead upon equitable grounds.

The constitutionality of notice of deed of trust sale provisions has been litigated frequently. *See* G. Osborne, G. Nelson & D. Whitman, Real Estate Finance Law §§ 7.23—7.30 (1979) (hereinafter cited as Real Estate Finance Law); *see also* Note, *The Constitutionality of Power of Sale Foreclosure in Alaska*, 6 UCLA-Alaska L. Rev. 90 (1976). The trend, however, is to find that nonjudicial sales lack sufficient state action to trigger the federal due process

"Last known address" clauses appear most frequently in tax statutes, service of process rules, and trust deed statutes. For instance, Section 6212(b) of the Internal Revenue Code, 26 U.S.C.A. § 6212(b) (1981), requires the Commissioner of Internal Revenue to mail notice of a tax deficiency to the taxpayer's "last known address." The federal courts require the Commissioner to use reasonable diligence in ascertaining the taxpayer's current address. *See* Annot., 58 A.L.R.Fed. 548, 554–56 (1982). At the same time, the commissioner may rely on "the address appearing on a taxpayer's return as the last known in the absence of clear and concise notification from the taxpayer directing the Commissioner to use a different address." *Alta Sierra Vista, Inc. v. Commissioner*, 62 T.C. 367, 374 (1974), *aff'd mem.*, 538 F.2d 334 (9th Cir.1976).

Thus, while the Internal Revenue Service (IRS) must be diligent to send notices properly, the taxpayer must clearly notify the IRS of any changes. Only when the IRS fails to respond after the taxpayer has communicated changed addresses will the IRS have breached its duty of due diligence. *See, e.g., Crum v. Commissioner*, 635 F.2d 895, 899–900 (D.C.Cir.1980). Absent communication by the taxpayer, the IRS seems under no duty to mail notices to any address other than the one last used by the taxpayer. The tax statutes, however, contemplate at least yearly communications between government and taxpayer.

Substitute service of process rules occasionally allow a party to mail process to defendant's "last known address." *See Shanklin v. Bender*, 283 A.2d 651, 653–54 (D.C.1971) (construing Ill.Rev.Stat. ch. 95 1/2, § 10–301(b) (1967–70)) (service of process on nonresident motor vehicle operator); *Feinstein v. Bergner*, 48 N.Y.2d 234, 422 N.Y.S.2d 356, 397 N.E.2d 1161 (1979) (construing N.Y.Civ.Prac.R. 308(4)) (substitute mail service on defendant's "last known residence" and nail service on "dwelling place" and "usual place of abode"); *Volmer v. Hoel*, 87 Ohio App. 199, 93 N.E.2d 416 (1950) (construing Gen. Code § 6308–2, replaced by Ohio Rev. Code Ann. § 2703.20 (1981)) (service on nonresident motor vehicle operator); *Waddell v. Mumat*, 271 Wis.176, 72 N.W.2d 763, 766 (1955) (construing § 85.05(3) stats., now Wis.Stat.Ann. § 345.09(2) (West 1971)) (nonresident motor vehicle operator); *see also* Ohio Civ.R. 4.4 (1982). *Volmer* appears to require due diligence. 93 N.E.2d at 420. *Shanklin* interpreted Illinois law as requiring reasonable diligence. 283 A.2d at 653. *Waddell* merely paraphrased *Wuchter v. Pizzutti*, 276 U.S. 13, 48 S.Ct. 259, 72 L.Ed. 446 (1928), and stated that "[t]he last known address is that one most likely to give the party to be served notice." 72 N.W.2d at 766.

We recognize that, like cases construing the tax statute, these holdings involve statutory schemes with concerns somewhat different from the deed of trust sale. When service of process is involved, federal due process requires notice reasonably calculated to apprise the parties of the pendency of an action. *See, e.g., Mullane v. Central Hanover Bank & Trust Co.*, 339 U.S. 306, 314, 70 S.Ct. 652, 657, 94 L.Ed. 865, 873

---

protections. *See Flagg Bros. v. Brooks*, 436 U.S. 149, 98 S.Ct. 1729, 56 L.Ed.2d 185 (1978) (warehouseman's private sale of goods under UCC 7–210 involved no state action); *Garfinkle v. Superior Court*, 21 Cal.3d 268, 146 Cal.Rptr. 208, 578 P.2d 925 (1978) (deed of trust foreclosure sale lacked state action).

(1950). Moreover, some states require proof of due diligence at attempted personal service *before* allowing substitute service. *See, e.g.,* N.Y.Civ.Prac.R. 308(4) (West 1972). Thus the federal due process concerns raised by tax and process laws require some showing of due diligence. These *federal* due process rights are absent from a deed of trust foreclosure sale. Furthermore, unlike tax and process cases, deed of trust sales involve title to real property. Courts have traditionally favored the free and easy alienability of real property. Deed of trust provisions encourage ready transfer in two ways. By assuring creditors a speedy, inexpensive and uncomplicated remedy in the event of default, deeds of trust allow lenders to loan more cheaply the funds necessary to purchase the property initially. *See* 10 G. Thompson, Commentaries on the Modern Law of Real Property, § 5175 at 204–05 (1957). Thus, deeds of trust encourage debtors to buy by assuring creditors of easy resale. "[W]here it is in common use, power of sale foreclosure has provided an effective foreclosure remedy with a cost in time and money substantially lower than that of its judicial foreclosure counterpart." Real Estate Finance Law, § 7.19 at 477 (footnote omitted).

The Rosenbergs argue that a requirement of due diligence in a provision of notice of default would increase the costs of financing real property transfers. Beyond the administrative costs of searching for absent interested parties, creditors would bear the increased risk of attendant costs of litigation over the trustee's compliance. *See id.* Ultimately, creditors will pass on these costs to future borrowers. Thus, all debtors would be forced to pay the higher costs of protecting those debtors who invest and then move without advising the trustee of their new address. The Rosenbergs, however, do not quantify these increased costs.

Review of the law of other jurisdictions reveals numerous "last known address" statutes governing notice of deed of trust sales.[9] *See, e.g.,* Cal.Civ.Code § 2924b(2)(a)–(c) (West 1974 & Supp. 1985); D.C. Code Ann. § 45–715(b) (1981) (written notice by certified mail with return receipt requested to the last known address); Idaho Code § 45–1506(2) (1977) (notice by registered or certified mail to last known address); Or.Rev.Stat. § 86.740 (1983) (mail notice by both first class and certified mail with return receipt to the last known address); *compare* Ariz.Rev.Stat.Ann. § 33–809(B)(2) (Supp.1985) (trustee uses address on recorded document unless address missing); Tex.Prop.Code Ann. § 51.002(b)(3) (Vernon 1984) (notice sent to last known address appearing in the records of the holder of the debt); Wash.Rev.Code Ann. § 61.24.040(b) (Supp.1985) (notice sent to address in recorded instrument or otherwise known to trustee). The few reported decisions reveal no holding imposing a due diligence requirement. A recent California decision specifically rejected a due diligence requirement. In *I.E. Associates v. Safeco Title Insurance Co.,* 39 Cal.3d 281, 216 Cal.Rptr. 438, 702 P.2d 596 (1985) the California Supreme Court construed Civil Code 2924b. This statute explicitly defines "last known address" as "the last business or residence actually known by the . . .

---

[9]   Some states require *no* mailed notice. *See, e.g.,* S.D. Codified Laws § 21–48–6 (1979) (notice by publication alone suffices); Utah Code Ann. § 57–1–25 (Supp.1983) (notice by publication and posting notice on property to be sold, as well as three other public places in the city where property is to be sold).

person authorized to record the notice of default." Cal.Civ.Code § 2924b(2)(c). The section also requires the beneficiary to tell the trustee of the last address actually known by the beneficiary. Cal.Civ.Code § 2924b(2)(c). Faced with such strong evidence of a limitation to knowledge "actually" known, the court stated that the section imposed no due diligence requirement upon trustees. 216 Cal.Rptr. at 440, 702 P.2d at 598.

The California statute's explicit definition of "last known address" distinguishes it from AS 34.20.070(c). Further, unlike California, Alaska imposes no duty on the beneficiary of a trust deed to notify the trustee of an actually known last address of an interested party.[11] We therefore decline to follow the reasoning of *I.E., Associates*.

A tension exists between free and easy alienability of real property and notice to persons whose interest in real property is to be affected by governmental or private action. Yet it is not so great as to preclude a requirement of due diligence in attempting to get notice to those who will be affected by that action. As this case demonstrates vividly, diligent inquiry by the trustee would readily have provided Smidts' actual address.

On one hand,

> [w]hile noncompliance with the statutory provisions regarding foreclosure by the power under a mortgage or trust deed is not to be favored, the remedy of setting aside the sale will be applied only in cases which reach unjust extremes.

Semlek v. National Bank of Alaska, 458 P.2d 1003, 1006 (Alaska 1969). On the other, "equity abhors a forfeiture and will seize upon slight circumstances to relieve a party therefrom." *Jameson v. Wurtz,* 396 P.2d 68, 74 (Alaska 1964) (footnote omitted).

We conclude that the last known address is that address most likely to give the affected party notice. The trustee is obligated to exercise due diligence to determine that address. Failure to impose such a requirement would not balance adequately the competing interests involved.

III. DOES AS 34.20.090(C) PROTECT THE ROSENBERGS AS BONA FIDE PURCHASERS?

Under AS 34.20.090(c),[12] recitals in the foreclosure sale deed that the trustee complied with notice provisions become conclusive evidence

---

[11] The California court noted that the trustor should learn of the sale through posted notice on the property, *Id.* 216 Cal.Rptr. at 443, 702 P.2d at 601 n. 6, and that only passive investors, uninvolved with daily activity on the property, risk missing notice, *Id.* 216 Cal.Rptr. at 443, 702 P.2d at 601 n. 7.

Like California, Alaska requires both posting and publication before a nonjudicial sale. *See* AS 34.20.080(a)(2), AS 09.35.140. However, there is little basis for asserting that the only persons not likely to get notice under Alaska's statutory scheme are "passive investors" of undeveloped property who do not list a permanent agent for service of notices upon their original execution of the recorded instruments. Further, it should not make a difference that the affected interest is that of "passive investors."

[12] AS 34.20.090(c) provides:

A recital of compliance with all requirements of law regarding the mailing or personal delivery of copies of notices of default in the deed executed under a power of sale is prima facie evidence of compliance with the requirements. *The recital is* of compliance in favor of bona fide purchasers (bfp's). The deed the Rosenbergs received stated:

> All other requirements of law regarding the mailing, publication and personal delivery of copies of the Notice of Default and all other notices have been complied with, and said Notice of Sale was publicly posted as required by law and published in the Anchorage Times on August 26 and September 2, 9, and 16, 1980.

The parties dispute whether this section barred the Smidts from overturning the sale on the basis of lack of notice. Although the Rosenbergs directed the trial court to this statute, the judgment makes no mention of it.

The Smidts make three arguments to avoid the statute. First, the Smidts claim that the statute does not apply to void sales. They correctly state the general rule that "[t]he doctrine of good faith purchaser for value without notice does not apply to a purchaser at a void foreclosure sale." *Henke v. First Southern Properties, Inc.*, 586 S.W.2d 617, 620 (Tex.Civ.App.1979). They misapply the rule, however, to the sale by Alaska Title. They fail to distinguish "void" from "voidable" sales. *See* Real Estate Finance Law, § 7.20 at 477–78. Only substantial defects such as the lack of a substantive basis to foreclose in the first place will make a sale void. *Id.* at 477 & § 7.21 at 489–90. *Henke* itself illustrates the most common basis for finding a void sale: the absence of default. 586 S.W.2d at 620. Where a defect in a foreclosure sale makes it merely voidable, however, sale to a bfp cuts off the trustor's ability to set aside the sale. *See Swindell v. Overton*, 310 N.C.707, 314 S.E.2d 512, 517 (1984); Real Estate Finance Law, § 7.21 at 489. Here, the alleged defect went not to the trustee's right to proceed with foreclosure but only to "the mechanics of exercising the power." *Id.* at 490. Thus, if the Rosenbergs were bfp's, the Smidts cannot set aside what is not a void, but a voidable, sale. However, as we hereinafter conclude, the Rosenbergs are not bfp's. The sale is therefore voidable.

Second, the Smidts challenge the Rosenberg's status as "bfp's without notice." No case defines this phrase for purposes of AS 34.20.090(c). Cases generally interpret the phrase to apply to one who lacks actual, constructive (*i.e.*, from the land records) or inquiry notice. *See, e.g., Swindell*, 314 S.E.2d at 517; *see also Sabo v. Horvath*, 559 P.2d 1038, 1043 (Alaska 1976). No one here contends that the Rosenbergs had actual or constructive notice of any defects in the notice sent to the Smidts. To bar their status as bfp's, the Smidts must hold the Rosenbergs to inquiry notice of the alleged defects.

This court explained inquiry notice in *Modrok v. Marshall*, 523 P.2d 172 (Alaska 1974).

> It is a settled rule of property that circumstances ... which suggest outstanding equities in third parties, impose a duty upon the purchaser to make a reasonable investigation into the existence of a claim. Given suspicious facts, the status of bona

---

conclusive evidence of compliance with the requirements in favor of a bona fide purchaser or encumbrancer for value and without notice.

(Emphasis added).

fide purchaser turns upon whether there was a prudent inquiry into their import.

Id. at 174 (footnote omitted). In other words, "the defects are not such that a person attending the sale exercising reasonable care would have been aware of the defect." Real Estate Finance Law, at 478.

The facts stipulated below suggest that the Rosenbergs at most were chargeable with knowledge of the Smidts' status as assignees of Spendlove and Johnson. The facts do not reveal whether anyone else bid at the auction. On one hand, the Rosenbergs could reasonably believe that the Smidts were unable to cure Spendlove and Johnson's default or had made other arrangements with the defaulting debtors. On the other, it is unreasonable to believe that the Smidts would do nothing to protect their interest.

Ultimately, to hold that the interested party's absence from a foreclosure sale imposes a duty upon purchasers to investigate the notice given would gut AS 34.20.090(c). No one would ever be a "bona fide purchaser without [inquiry] notice." By requiring would-be purchasers to "investigate or buy a lawsuit," such a holding would further increase the costs and delays accompanying deed of trust sales.

However, even if the Rosenbergs were not put on inquiry notice by the Smidts' absence from the sale, they may be charged with such notice if the deed contains no more than mere recitals that the trustee has complied with statutory notice requirements.

The Smidts argue that AS 34.20.090(c) contemplates recitals of fact, not conclusions of law. They contend that interpreting "recital" to mean a detailed recitation of the steps taken to notify trustors or their successors will prevent problems such as in this case. A recitation of the "facts" of notice, they argue, would charge the Rosenbergs with inquiry notice of the Smidts' plight and thus prevent the Rosenbergs from becoming bfp's. We agree with each of these points.

Several states have statutory presumptions similar to Alaska's. *See, e.g.*, Cal.Civ.Code § 2924 (West 1974); Or.Rev.Stat. § 86.780 (1983); Utah Code Ann. § 57–1–28(1) (1985). We have found no cases which hold that such statutes either are or are not satisfied by a bare statement that the law was complied with, as distinguished from a factual recitation of the steps which were taken to comply with the law.

According to one commentator on Oregon's statute,

> if the trustee recites in the deed it carried out notice procedures required by the statutes, such recitals provide absolute protection to a bona fide purchaser relying upon them.

Randolph, Updating the Oregon Installment Land Contract, 15 Willamette L.J. 181 at 200 n. 64 (1979). Oregon explicitly lists the required contents of recitals. Or.Rev.State. 86.775 states:

> The trustee's deed to the purchaser at the trustee's sale shall contain, in addition to a description of the property conveyed, a recital of *the facts concerning* the default, *the notice* given, the conduct of the sale and the receipt of the purchase money from the purchaser.

(Emphasis added). Alaska law also specifies that the trustee's "deed shall recite . . . the mailing or delivery of the copies of the notice of default . . ."[16] though it is less clear than the Oregon statute as to whether the recital should be factual or conclusory.

We are persuaded that what is required is a recital of fact specifying what the trustee has done, not a mere conclusory statement that the trustee has complied with the law. There are several reasons which lead us to this conclusion.

The fact that .080(c) explicitly calls for factual details in the deed recital concerning recording, price, publication, and sale suggests that facts are also called for concerning mailing or delivery.[18] Further, requiring a factual recital tends to assure that the requirements of law concerning mailing or delivery are complied with. A conclusory statement can be a matter placed in a form, or a programmed deed, and will not require the trustee to review what was actually done. A factual recital does require review in each case. While a factual recital requirement does not protect against fraud in all cases, it does tend to prevent the more common failings of oversight and neglect. A conclusory recital, on the other hand, accomplishes little or nothing.

The dissenting opinion states that the purpose of 34.20.090(c) is to provide extra protection to purchasers at foreclosure sales and to enhance the reliability of their titles. While that is one purpose of the act of which 34.20.090(c) is a part, it is by no means its only purpose. The enactment in question, ch. 116, SLA 1957, added the mailing and delivery requirements now set out in .070(c) (previous law had only required publication, ACLA 1949 § 22–5–2), mandated that the deed recite the mailing or delivery of notice, .080(c), and stated the evidentiary effect of such a recital, .090(c). Thus, the purpose of the act was not only to protect the foreclosure sale purchaser, but to require that effective notice of default and sale be given parties in interest, and to provide a self-effecting method of assuring that such notice is given. Construing the recital requirements in .080(c) and .090(c) to call only for formal conclusions does not accomplish the purpose of assuring mailing or delivery; a construction which holds that a recital of facts is required is consistent with all of the purposes of the statute.

Moreover, the use of the word "recital" suggests that facts rather than conclusions are what the statute calls for. The ordinary meaning of "recital" is a formal statement of relevant facts.

---

[16] AS 34.20.080(c) provides:

> The deed shall recite the date and the book and page of the recording of default, and the mailing or delivery of the copies of the notice of default, the true consideration for the conveyance, the time and place of the publication of notice of sale, and the time, place and manner of sale, and refer to the deed of trust by reference to the page, volume and place of record.

[18] The principle of statutory construction which is applicable here is that of associated words—words are known by the company they keep. "A widely applied tenet of statutory interpretation is that if 'the legislative intent or general meaning of a statute is not clear, the meaning of doubtful words may be determined by reference to their association with other associated words and phrases.' " *State, Real Estate Commission v. Johnston*, 682 P.2d 383, 386–87 (Alaska 1984). Thus, since .080(c) calls for facts concerning other subjects used in a series with mailing or delivery, it is logical to conclude that the statute calls for facts concerning mailing or delivery.

For these reasons we conclude that AS 34.20.080(c) and .090(c) require a recital of facts specifying what the trustee has done regarding mailing or delivery. Since there was no such recital in this case the Rosenbergs were on inquiry notice of a potential voidable defect. They cannot claim bfp status or the protection of .090(c).

AFFIRMED.

MOORE, JUSTICE, with whom RABINOWITZ, CHIEF JUSTICE, joins, dissenting in part.

I dissent from the majority's conclusion that the Rosenbergs are not Bona Fide Purchasers (BFP). In my view the Rosenbergs' status as BFPs bars the Smidts from overturning the foreclosure sale, and limits their remedy to seeking damages from Spendlove, Johnson and/or the trustee, Alaska Title Guaranty Company. Protecting the Rosenbergs' title to the property is compelled by important public policy considerations as well as by the express language of AS 34.20.090(c).

The majority correctly notes that where, as here, a defect in the foreclosure sale makes it merely voidable, the sale to a BFP will completely bar the debtor's ability to set aside the sale. . . . This makes perfect sense, as grave consequences would result if the rule were otherwise. For example, if innocent purchasers at foreclosure sales had to face the risk that debtors could easily set aside the sales, then it takes little imagination to realize that participation at foreclosure sales would be significantly and unacceptably chilled. As the court stated in *In re Alsop*, 14 B.R. 982, 987 (Bankr.Alaska 1981), *aff'd* 22 B.R. 1017 (D.Alaska 1982):

> The specter of this uncertainty of title will severely inhibit participation at the foreclosure sale by anyone other than the original creditor, thus depressing bid prices to the general detriment of debtors. [This] would further reduce the willingness of creditors to lend on the security of a deed of trust, to the general detriment of borrowers.

Id. *(Citation omitted.)*

Furthermore, the innocent purchaser, having absolutely nothing to do with the legal relationship between the trustee and the debtor, should not be forced to bear any loss caused to the debtor by the trustee's failure to diligently protect the debtor's interests.

> As between the mortgagor and the purchaser, the former rather than the latter should suffer the loss, because by granting to the mortgagee the right to sell, the mortgagor put it in the mortgagee's power to work the injury through the execution of that power.

Dugan v. Manchester Federal Savings & Loan Association, 92 N.H. 44, 23 A.2d 873, 876 (1942). Here, where the injury was caused by the trustee's failure to discover the debtor's new address, it should be the debtor, not the innocent purchaser, who should lose title to the property. It is the debtor, not the purchaser, who can most easily notify the trustee of the new address. As between two innocent parties, the loss should fall on the one in the best position to have avoided that loss.

There is no doubt that Alaska follows the universal rule of refusing to set aside a voidable foreclosure sale when title has passed to a BFP. . . .

As the majority opinion illustrates, the Rosenbergs satisfy all of these requirements. They have paid value and are not related to the mortgagee. They had no actual knowledge of the trustee's failure to exercise due diligence in determining the Smidts' new address, and nothing in the recorded instruments put the Rosenbergs on notice of this defect. Finally, the notice defect was not such that attendance at the sale would provide any hint of the defect. As the majority carefully explains, the debtor's absence from the sale does not put the purchaser on inquiry notice nor require him to investigate or buy a lawsuit.

It is therefore clear that the Rosenbergs are BFPs and entitled to possession of the property. How then does the majority justify setting aside the sale? Curiously, the majority takes AS 34.20.090(c), gives it a bizarre interpretation, and uses it to strip the Rosenbergs of their BFP status. Ironically, this statute, like those found in other states, was specifically designed to enhance the reliability of title purchased by a BFP at a foreclosure sale. G. Nelson & D. Whitman, Real Estate Finance Law § 7.21 (5th ed.2007); Note, *The Constitutionality of Power of Sale Foreclosure in Alaska*, supra at 112, 116.

I must also disagree with the majority's decision to engraft onto the statute a requirement of detailed factual statements. The statute nowhere contains this requirement, and it is for the legislature, not this court, to add one if it sees fit to do so. While it is true that to create a conclusive presumption in favor of a BFP, some states require recitals of facts, other states, like Alaska, do not. A third variation does not require recitations at all, but provides that the deed itself creates the conclusive presumption in favor of the BFP. These variations suggest that there is no one way to balance the rights of creditors and BFPs. Our legislature has struck the balance in such a way that the BFP receives protection from the trustee's recitals in the deed. It is not for this court to alter the balance struck by this statutory scheme. The majority is unable to cite any authority that suggests this court can add a detailed factual statement requirement to a statute that obviously lacks one.

The majority suggests that a trustee will always recite that the law has been complied with, and thus the Rosenbergs' reliance on that recital is hollow. However, this "hollow reliance" is exactly what the statute authorizes. Moreover, since the trustee may be liable to the debtor in damages if wrong, the trustee has ample incentive to avoid issuing incorrect recitals. The BFP is therefore even further justified in relying on the accuracy of those recitals. Finally, even if the trustee had recited factual details, the majority does not explain what the Rosenbergs should have done to protect themselves. The fact that letters are returned unclaimed does not per se establish a notice defect. To discover the defect the potential purchaser would have to mount a costly and time consuming investigation. Language in the majority opinion illustrates the serious shortcomings of such a requirement:

> Ultimately, to . . . impose[ ] a duty upon purchasers to investigate the notice given would gut AS 34.20.090(c). No one would ever be a "bona fide purchaser without [inquiry] notice."

By requiring would-be purchasers to "investigate or buy a lawsuit," such a holding would further increase the costs and delays accompanying deed of trust sales.

In conclusion, I dissent from the majority's holding that the Rosenbergs are not BFPs. That decision may have far-reaching effects, possibly clouding the titles of numerous BFPs who have acquired property through foreclosure sales, and chilling the bidding at future sales to the detriment of debtors and creditors alike. I would therefore return title in the property to the Rosenbergs and leave the Smidts free to pursue their remedy in damages against Johnson, Spendlove, and/or the trustee.

NOTES

1. *Rosenberg v. Smidt.* *Rosenberg* involves two central issues in power of sale foreclosure: fairness of the proceeding and the quality of title that the purchaser receives. Was the case correctly decided on both issues? Did the court correctly resolve issues of statutory construction, policy concerns, and questions about the proper role of the legislature and the courts?

Consider how *Rosenberg* and United States Department of Housing and Urban Development v. Union Mortgage Company (page 462) illustrate the advantages and disadvantages of power of sale foreclosure and judicial foreclosure in terms of cost, speed, protection of the mortgagor's and mortgagee's interests, and finality of proceedings.

2. *State Action.* As indicated in the principal case, most courts reject constitutional challenges to power of sale foreclosure on the theory that there is inadequate state action. Compare Mennonite Board of Missions v. Adams, 462 U.S. 791, 103 S.Ct. 2706, 77 L.Ed.2d 180 (1983) (proceeding brought by county to sell mortgaged property for nonpayment of taxes subject to Due Process Clause of Fourteenth Amendment and notice to mortgagee by posting and publication was inadequate). One exception is Turner v. Blackburn, 389 F.Supp. 1250 (W.D.N.C.1975) (finding power of sale foreclosure statute permitting notice by posting and publication unconstitutional as applied). That decision led to changes in the North Carolina statute. See generally, Comment, Real Property—Changes in North Carolina's Foreclosure Law, 54 N.C.L.Rev. 903 (1976).

3. *Trustee Duties.* Judicial ambivalence about private individuals doing what courts probably think they can do better has seriously muddled the standards of conduct applied to nonjudicial sales. The standard nominally applied to trust deed sales is that "[a] trustee in a deed of trust acts in a fiduciary capacity and he must act with complete integrity, fairness, and impartiality toward both the debtor and the creditor." Spires v. Edgar, 513 S.W.2d 372, 378 (Mo.1974). The standard entirely ignores the reality that trustees typically are nominees of the beneficiary.

Indeed, Spires v. Edgar, although invoking the traditional rule on the trustee's fiduciary duty, reached a refreshingly realistic decision against the trustors' claim that the trustee had acted improperly in failing to inquire into their performance under the note: "We have concluded that in the absence of unusual circumstances known to the trustee, he may, upon receiving a request for foreclosure from the creditor, proceed upon that advice without making any affirmative investigation and without giving any special notice to the debtor. We are not considering here any liabilities or duties of the holder of the note or notes." 513 S.W.2d at 378, 379.

Should a sale be voided if the trustee owns an interest in the debt? If the creditor owns an interest in the trustee? If the trustee buys the land from the successful bidder shortly after the sale? See Smith v. Haley, 314 S.W.2d 909 (Mo.1958), distinguished in Spires v. Edgar. See generally, Dingus, Mortgages—Redemption After Foreclosure Sale in Missouri, 25 Mo.L.Rev. 261 (1960).

At least some jurisdictions will set aside a trustee sale if the price is "grossly inadequate." In Baskurt v. Beal, 101 P.3d 1041 (Alaska 2004), the bid at the nonjudicial foreclosure sale was just under $27,000 while the fair market value of the property was $225,000. The court set aside the sale on the borrower's petition. The court explained that an inadequate price alone was not a sufficient ground but the price had to be "grossly inadequate" or accompanied by other defects in the sale process. The court relied on the Restatement (Third) of Property—Mortgages § 8.3 and its guideline that a price that is 20% of the property's market value is "grossly inadequate."

4. *Notice.* How can junior lienors and other interested parties be assured that they will receive notice of foreclosure by nonjudicial sale? Although the mortgage or trust deed will typically spell out some of the relevant procedures, local statutes will provide the more comprehensive basis for giving notice.

California's notice procedures for trust deed foreclosures and foreclosures of mortgages with powers of sale are simple and effective. The process begins with a notice of default executed and recorded by the trustee or mortgagee. The trustee or mortgagee will then search title to the property to see if any requests for a copy of a notice of default and sale have been recorded after the trust deed or mortgage and before the notice of default.

The trustee or mortgagee must then mail the notice of default to all who have requested it, as well as to all individuals who fall into any of six statutorily prescribed classes and whose interests can be discovered by a title search. Among those included are any present successors in interest to the mortgagor or trustor, junior beneficiaries or mortgagees and their assignees, lessees and contract vendees. Three months after the notice of default is filed for record, if the default has not been cured, the trustee or mortgagee who wishes to foreclose is required to send a notice of sale, stating the time and place of the sale, to each person entitled to receive a copy of the notice of default. These notices must be sent at least twenty days before the date of sale. Cal.Civ.Code §§ 2924, 2924b.

5. *U.L.S.I.A.* U.L.S.I.A. section 509 permits power of sale foreclosure. The Act discusses both aspects of Rosenberg v. Smidt.

As to the required notification, Section 508 states that notice of foreclosure must be sent to the debtor at the address specified in the mortgage and "[i]f the creditor knows of a different address of the debtor at which notices are more likely to come to the debtor's attention, the notice must also be sent to that address." Under section 112(a) a person "knows" of a fact only when she has "actual knowledge of it."

As to the right of the Rosenbergs to retain the property, section 512 provides that when property is sold either pursuant to judicial foreclosure or a power of sale, "a purchaser for value in good faith acquires the debtor's and creditor's rights in the real estate, free of the security interest under which the sale occurred and any subordinate interest, even though the creditor or person conducting the sale fails to comply with the requirements of this Part on default or of any judicial sale proceeding." Comment 1 states that "[t]his is intended to eliminate the necessity of a rigorous examination to determine whether the foreclosure transaction complies with the statutory requirements in meticulous detail."

How would *Rosenberg* have been decided under the U.L.S.I.A? Does the statute satisfactorily resolve the construction and policy issues?

6. *Growth of Power of Sale Legislation.* The availability of power of sale foreclosure is expanding. For example, New York added power of sale foreclosure in 1998, under legislation initially set to expire on July 1, 2001. N.Y. RPAPL § 1401. The legislature was pleased with the experiment, noting that it "has been extremely positive, saving both private and judicial resources," and extended the legislation until July 1, 2009. 2001 Sess. Law News of N.Y. Ch. 76 (S. 4784–A) (McKinney's), N.Y. LEGIS. 76 (2001); Memorandum in Support, New York Senate, id. Most likely reflecting consumer protection considerations, as well as the large number of residential tenants in New York with significant political muscle, the legislation bars non-judicial foreclosure of residential properties containing less than six dwelling units, residential condominium units, residential buildings owned by cooperative corporations, or buildings in cities over 1 million in population where sixty-five percent or more of the units are occupied by residential tenants. N.Y. RPAPL § 1401 (1). Additionally, power of sale foreclosure is prohibited for mortgages on any property containing residential units when the mortgagee seeks to foreclose or terminate the tenants' interests in the leases.

Professor Basil Mattingly suggests the adoption of a market driven system of foreclosure that would give the lender the option to retain the property in full satisfaction of the debt after notice to the parties without objection; to repossess and sell the property in a commercially reasonable manner; or to sell the property pursuant to a safe harbor rule that deems that the sale to have been conducted in a commercially reasonable manner if the lender follows required procedures. Mattingly, The Shift from Power to Process: A Functional Approach to Foreclosure Law, 80 Marq. L. Rev. 77 (1996).

d. FORECLOSURE IN THE ERA OF MERS

The financial crisis of 2008 was partially precipitated by increased defaults in residential mortgages. Moreover, in the immediate wake of the crisis, there was a marked increase in both residential and commercial foreclosures. CoreLogic reported that in 2012 twenty-seven percent of American residential mortgages were "underwater"—where the amount owed exceeded the value of the property. http://www. corelogic.com/research/negative-equity/corelogic-q3–2012–negative-equity-report.pdf. Professor Adam Levitin has written that "[s]ince 2007, an estimated seven-million or more homes have been sold in foreclosure or distressed sales, a loss in homeownership unparalleled in American history." Levitin, The Paper Chase: Securitization, Foreclosure, and the Uncertainty of Mortgage Title, 63 Duke L.J. 637, 639 (2013).

Holders of loans acquired in the secondary market commenced judicial and power of sale foreclosure proceedings against defaulting borrowers. The foreclosing entity varied in the cases, sometimes being the current holder of the loan, the servicing company, Merscorp, or some other party. Because of the frequent transfers of loans on the secondary market, sometimes the foreclosing entity could demonstrate its status as an interested party in the process, provide a recorded chain of mortgage assignments to it, and possession of the note and in other cases it could not do so.

In this environment, borrowers losing their homes resisted foreclosure using two basic defensess:they claimed that an entity needed to actually have the note to foreclose and that it had to possess a real interest as a mortgagee (or as a true agent of the current mortgagee) in order to foreclose. Judges set about resolving these issues against the backdrop of historical doctrines of equity, modern statutes, consumer law, political reality for elected state court judges, and a human tragedy for people losing their homes in the worst economic crisis facing the country since the Great Depression. Professor Levitin indicates that there were over 3,000 reported cases on these issues from 2009–2013. 63 Duke L.J. at 642. Professor Nestor Davidson has described a "new formalism" developing in the law of mortgages as borrower advocates have responded to the plight of homeowners by raising "largely procedural defenses to foreclosure and mortgage-related claims asserted in bankruptcy." New Formalism in the Aftermath of the Housing Crisis, 93 B.U.L. Rev. 389, 391 (2013).

Eaton v. Federal National Mortgage Association

Supreme Judicial Court of Massachusetts, 2012.
462 Mass. 569, 969 N.E.2d 1118.

BOTSFORD, J.

In this case, we address the propriety of a foreclosure by power of sale undertaken by a mortgage holder that did not hold the underlying mortgage note. A judge in the Superior Court preliminarily enjoined the defendant Federal National Mortgage Association (Fannie Mae) from proceeding with a summary process action to evict the plaintiff, Henrietta Eaton, from her home, following a foreclosure sale of the property by the defendant Green Tree Servicing, LLC (Green Tree), as mortgagee. The judge ruled that Eaton likely would succeed on the merits of her claim that for a valid foreclosure sale to occur, both the mortgage and the underlying note must be held by the foreclosing party; and that because Green Tree stipulated that it held only Eaton's mortgage, the foreclosure sale was void, and the defendants therefore were not entitled to evict Eaton. Pursuant to G.L. c. 231, § 118, first par., the defendants petitioned a single justice of the Appeals Court for relief from the preliminary injunction. The single justice denied the petition and reported his decision to a panel of that court. We transferred the case to this court on our own motion.

For the reasons we discuss herein, we conclude as follows. A foreclosure sale conducted pursuant to a power of sale in a mortgage must comply with all applicable statutory provisions, including in particular G.L. c. 183, § 21, and G.L. c. 244, § 14. These statutes authorize a "mortgagee" to foreclose by sale pursuant to a power of sale in the mortgage, and require the "mortgagee" to provide notice and take other steps in connection with the sale. The meaning of the term "mortgagee" as used in the statutes is not free from ambiguity, but we now construe the term to refer to the person or entity then holding the mortgage and also either holding the mortgage note or acting on behalf of the note holder.[2] Further, we exercise our discretion to treat the construction announced in this decision as a new interpretation of the relevant statute, only to apply to foreclosures under the power of sale where statutory notice is provided after the date of this decision. We vacate the preliminary injunction and remand the case to the Superior Court for further proceedings consistent with this opinion.

1. *Background.* On September 12, 2007, Eaton refinanced the mortgage on her home in the Roslindale section of Boston (Roslindale property) by executing a promissory note payable to BankUnited, FSB (BankUnited, or lender), for $145,000. That same day, she also executed a mortgage, referred to in the mortgage itself as a "[s]ecurity [i]nstrument." The mortgage is separate from, but by its terms clearly connected to, the promissory note. The parties to the mortgage are Eaton as the "[b]orrower," BankUnited as the "[l]ender," and Mortgage Electronic Registration Systems, Inc. (MERS) as the "mortgagee."

Under the mortgage executed by Eaton, MERS as mortgagee (or its assignee) holds legal title to the Roslindale property with power of sale "solely as nominee" of the lender BankUnited (or its assignee). However, "if necessary to comply with law or custom, MERS (as nominee for Lender and Lender's successors and assigns) has the right to exercise any or all of those interests, including, but not limited to, the right to foreclose and sell the Property; and to take any action required of Lender. . . ."

The mortgage also contains a series of covenants that run exclusively between BankUnited as lender and Eaton. The final covenant, entitled "Acceleration; Remedies," empowers the lender, on default by Eaton, to "invoke the STATUTORY POWER OF SALE and any other remedies permitted by applicable law." In this regard, the covenant obligates the lender, in invoking the statutory power of sale, to mail a copy of a notice of sale to Eaton.

On April 22, 2009, MERS assigned its interest as mortgagee to Green Tree and recorded the assignment in the Suffolk County registry of deeds. The record contains no evidence of a corresponding transfer of the note. The note was indorsed in blank by BankUnited on an undetermined date.[8]

Later in 2009, after Eaton failed to make payments on the note, Green Tree, as assignee of MERS, moved to foreclose on her home through exercise of a power of sale contained in the mortgage. A foreclosure auction was conducted in November, 2009; Green Tree was the highest bidder. The identity of the note holder at the time of the

---

[2] The term "mortgage note" is used in this opinion to refer to the promissory note or other form of debt or obligation for which the mortgage provides security; and the term "note holder" is used to refer to a person or entity owning the "mortgage note."

[8] The defendants state in their brief that after indorsement, the note was transferred to the Federal National Mortgage Association (Fannie Mae). However, there is no record evidence of a transfer of the note to Fannie Mae.

foreclosure sale is not known from the record. On November 24, 2009, Green Tree assigned the rights to its bid to Fannie Mae, and a foreclosure deed was recorded in the Suffolk County registry of deeds.

On January 25, 2010, Fannie Mae commenced a summary process action in the Boston division of the Housing Court Department to evict Eaton. Eaton filed a counterclaim, arguing that the underlying foreclosure sale was invalid because Green Tree did not hold Eaton's mortgage note at the time of the foreclosure sale and therefore lacked the requisite authority to foreclose on her equity of redemption in the Roslindale property. A Housing Court judge subsequently granted a sixty-day stay of the summary process action to give Eaton an opportunity to seek relief in the Superior Court. The Housing Court judge also ordered Eaton to make use and occupancy payments during the pendency of her action. On April 8, 2011, Eaton filed a complaint in the Superior Court for injunctive and declaratory relief. The complaint sought a declaration that the foreclosure sale of Eaton's home and the subsequent foreclosure deed were null and void, and that Eaton was the owner in fee simple of the Roslindale property; a preliminary injunction to stay the summary process action in the Housing Court; and a permanent injunction barring Fannie Mae from taking steps to obtain possession of or convey the Roslindale property. For the purposes of Eaton's motion for a preliminary injunction only, the defendants stipulated that Green Tree did not hold Eaton's mortgage note at the time of the foreclosure. After hearing, the Superior Court judge (motion judge) allowed the motion and preliminarily enjoined Fannie Mae from proceeding with Eaton's eviction.

. . .

3.   *Discussion.* As indicated, the motion judge determined that a foreclosure by sale requires the foreclosing mortgagee, at the time of the sale, to hold both the mortgage and the underlying mortgage note; and that if the mortgagee does not hold the note, the foreclosure sale is void. Based on this view, she concluded that because Green Tree, the assignee of the mortgage, had stipulated that it did not hold the mortgage note executed by Eaton when the sale took place, Eaton was likely to succeed in proving that the foreclosure sale was void and that the defendants had no authority to evict her and take possession of her home. See *Bank of N.Y. v. Bailey,* 460 Mass. 327, 333, 951 N.E.2d 331 (2011) (challenging evicting party's entitlement to possession "has long been considered a valid defense to a summary process action for eviction where the property was purchased at a foreclosure sale"). The defendants argue that in reaching this conclusion, the judge misread the Massachusetts common law, and that, in any event, the statutory scheme applicable to exercise of a power of sale gave Green Tree absolute authority, as "mortgagee," to foreclose. They also claim that Green Tree, as the assignee, had a contractual right to foreclose pursuant to the express terms of the mortgage. We begin with a brief overview of the common law of mortgages and then address the statutes governing exercise of a power of sale in a mortgage. Finally, we review the preliminary injunction in light of the relevant principles discussed and the terms of Eaton's mortgage.

a.   *Common law.* A real estate mortgage in Massachusetts has two distinct but related aspects: it is a transfer of legal title to the mortgage property, and it serves as security for an underlying note or other obligation—that is, the transfer of title is made in order to secure a debt, and the title itself is defeasible when the debt is paid. See *U.S. Bank Nat'l Ass'n v. Ibanez,* 458 Mass. 637, 649, 941 N.E.2d 40 (2011) (*Ibanez*) (Massachusetts is a "title theory" State in which "a mortgage is a transfer of legal title in a property to secure a debt")...

Following from these principles, a mortgage separated from the underlying debt that it is intended to secure is "a mere technical interest." Wolcott v. Winchester, 81 Mass. 461, 15 Gray 461, 465 (1860). See Morris v. Bacon, 123 Mass. 58, 59 (1877) ("That the debt is the principal and the mortgage an incident, is a rule too familiar to require citations in support of it"). However, in contrast to some jurisdictions, in Massachusetts the mere transfer of a mortgage note does not carry with it the mortgage. See Barnes v. Boardman, 149 Mass. 106, 114, 21 N.E. 308 (1889). See also 1 F. Hilliard, Mortgages 221 (2d ed. 1856) ("The prevailing doctrine upon this subject undoubtedly is, that an assignment of the debt carries the mortgage with it. This rule, however, is by no means universal, and is subject to various qualifications in the different States of the Union"). As a consequence, in Massachusetts a mortgage and the underlying note can be split....

Under our common law, where a mortgage and note are separated, "the holder of the mortgage holds the mortgage in trust for the purchaser of the note, who has an equitable right to obtain an assignment of the mortgage, which may be accomplished by filing an action in court and obtaining an equitable order of assignment." *Ibanez,* 458 Mass. at 652, 941 N.E.2d 40...

Consistent with the principles just described—that is, the basic nature of a mortgage as security for an underlying mortgage note, and the role of a "bare" mortgagee as equitable trustee for the note holder— it appears that, at common law, a mortgagee possessing only the mortgage was without authority to foreclose on his own behalf the mortgagor's equity of redemption or otherwise disturb the possessory interest of the mortgagor....

b. *Statutory provisions.* The defendants take issue with the applicability of [common law—Eds.] to this case. They argue that in any event, G.L. c. 244, § 14, expressly authorized MERS (and its assignee) to foreclose because the mortgage in this case contained a power of sale. Accordingly, we turn to this statute, as well as related statutory provisions that together govern mortgage foreclosures under a power of sale.

It has long been recognized that statutes are a key source of authority generally governing mortgages.... Statutes play an especially significant role in connection with mortgage foreclosures effected under a power of sale....

The "statutory power of sale" is set out in G.L. c. 183, § 21. Under this statute, if a mortgage provides for a power of sale, the mortgagee, in exercising the power, may foreclose without obtaining prior judicial authorization "upon any default in the performance or observance" of the mortgage, *id.,* including, of course, nonpayment of the underlying mortgage note.[15] Section 21 provides, however, that for a foreclosure sale pursuant to the power to be valid, the mortgagee must "first comply[ ] with the terms of the mortgage and with the statutes relating to the foreclosure of mortgages by the exercise of a power of sale." . . .

In addition to G.L. c. 183, § 21, itself, the "statutes relating to the foreclosure of mortgages by the exercise of a power of sale," *id.,* are set out in G.L. c. 244, §§ 11–17C. See *Ibanez,* 458 Mass. at 645–646, 941 N.E.2d 40. Principal among these is c. 244, § 14 (§ 14), which provides in relevant part:

> "*The mortgagee* or person having his estate in the land mortgaged, or a person authorized by the power of sale, . . . *may, upon breach of condition and without action, do all the acts authorized or required by the power;* but no sale under such power shall be effectual to foreclose a mortgage, unless, previous to such sale, [the notice provisions set forth in this section are followed]" (emphasis added).

The defendants argue that by its plain, unambiguous terms, this section authorized Green Tree, as the assignee of MERS, to foreclose because Eaton's mortgage identified MERS, its successors and assigns as the "mortgagee" with the "power of sale." We disagree that § 14 is unambiguous. The section is one in a set of provisions governing mortgage foreclosures by sale, and that set in turn is one component of a chapter of the General Laws devoted generally to the topic of foreclosure and redemption of mortgages. The term "mortgagee" appears in several of these statutes, and its use reflects a legislative understanding or assumption that the "mortgagee" referred to also is the holder of the mortgage note. Thus, G.L. c. 244, § 17B, one of the foreclosure by sale sections closely related to § 14, deals with the notice required to be given as a condition to seeking a deficiency owed on a note after a foreclosure sale, and reads in part:

> "No action for a deficiency shall be brought . . . by *the holder of a mortgage note* or other obligation secured by mortgage of real estate after a foreclosure sale *by him* . . . unless a notice in writing of the *mortgagee's intention to foreclose* the mortgage has been mailed, postage prepaid, by registered mail with return receipt requested, to the defendant sought to be charged with the deficiency at his last address *then known to the mortgagee,* together with a warning of liability for the deficiency, *in substantially the form* [set out in this section] . . ." (emphasis added).

By its terms, § 17B assumes that the holder of the mortgage note and the holder of the mortgage are one and the same; the section's drafters appear to have used the terms "holder of a mortgage note" and

---

[15] The power of sale "evolved in order to meet the increase of business transactions requiring loans and the desire to have a more speedy process of foreclosing than was furnished by suit or entry." A.L. Partridge, Deeds, Mortgages and Easements 201 (rev. ed.1932). See 1 F. Hilliard, Mortgages 119 (1856) ("In consequence of the delays incident to the usual equity of redemption, a power of sale has now become a very frequent provision in deeds of mortgage. . . . [However, the power] will be jealously watched, and declared void for the slightest unfairness or excess . . .").

"mortgagee" interchangeably.[18] Moreover, the statutory form of the notice required by § 17B bolsters our interpretation of § 17B; the statutory form language plainly envisions that the foreclosing mortgagee ("the mortgage held by me") and the note holder ("you may be liable to me in case of a deficiency") are one. And the same underlying assumption—that is, an identity between the mortgagee and the underlying note holder—also underlies several other sections in c. 244. See, e.g., G.L. c. 244, § 19 (providing that person entitled to redeem mortgage property "shall pay or tender to the mortgagee" amount due and payable "on the mortgage"); § 20 (requiring "mortgagee" who has been in possession of mortgage property to account for rents, profits, and expenses, and directing that any account balance be deducted from or added to amount "due on the mortgage"); § 23 (authorizing court to determine what amount not in dispute is "due on the mortgage," and to order it paid to "mortgagee").

"Where the Legislature uses the same words in several sections which concern the same subject matter, the words 'must be presumed to have been used with the same meaning in each section.'" Commonwealth v. Wynton W., 459 Mass. 745, 747, 947 N.E.2d 561 (2011). . . Furthermore, we "construe statutes that relate to the same subject matter as a harmonious whole and avoid absurd results." . . .

In accordance with these principles, and against the background of the common law as we have described it in the preceding section, we construe the term "mortgagee" in G.L. c. 244, § 14, to mean a mortgagee who also holds the underlying mortgage note. The use of the word "mortgagee" in § 14 has some ambiguity, but the interpretation we adopt is the one most consistent with the way the term has been used in related statutory provisions and decisional law, and, more fundamentally, the one that best reflects the essential nature and purpose of a mortgage as security for a debt. . . . See generally Restatement (Third) of Property (Mortgages) § 1.1 comment. (1997) ("The function of a mortgage is to employ an interest in real estate as security for the performance of some obligation. . . . Unless it secures an obligation, a mortgage is a nullity").

Contrary to the conclusion of the motion judge, however, we do not conclude that a foreclosing mortgagee must have physical possession of the mortgage note in order to effect a valid foreclosure. There is no applicable statutory language suggesting that the Legislature intended to proscribe application of general agency principles in the context of mortgage foreclosure sales.[25] Accordingly, we interpret G.L. c. 244, §§ 11–17C (and particularly § 14), and G.L. c. 183, § 21, to permit one

---

[18] A contrary reading of G.L. c. 244, § 17B, would lead to the absurd result of requiring the deficiency action be brought by the "holder of the mortgage note," while obligating the "mortgagee" to provide notice of the action to the mortgagor, with the result that a mortgagee's noncompliance with the statute could impair the note holder's right to collect a deficiency. We will not follow this interpretive path. See Flemings v. Contributory Retirement Appeal Bd., 431 Mass. 374, 375–376, 727 N.E.2d 1147 (2000) (court seeks to arrive at "sensible construction" of statute, and "shall not construe a statute to make a nullity of pertinent provisions or to produce absurd results").

[25] An agency relationship arises "from the manifestation of consent by one person to another that the other shall act on his behalf and subject to his control, and consent by the other so to act." Harrison Conference Servs. of Mass., Inc. v. Commissioner of Revenue, 394 Mass. 21, 24, 474 N.E.2d 160 (1985), quoting Restatement (Second) of Agency § 1(1) (1958).

who, although not the note holder himself, acts as the authorized agent of the note holder, to stand "in the shoes" of the "mortgagee" as the term is used in these provisions.

The defendants and several amici argue, to varying degrees, that an interpretation of "mortgagee" in the statutes governing mortgage foreclosures by sale that requires a mortgagee to hold the mortgage note will wreak havoc with the operation and integrity of the title recording and registration systems by calling into question the validity of any title that has a foreclosure sale in the title chain. This follows, they claim, because although a foreclosing mortgagee must record a foreclosure deed along with an affidavit evidencing compliance with G.L. c. 244, § 14, see G.L. c. 244, § 15; see also G.L. c. 183, § 4, there are no similar provisions for recording mortgage notes; and as a result, clear record title cannot be ascertained because the validity of any prior foreclosure sale is not ascertainable by examining documents of record.[27] They argue that if this court requires a mortgagee to have a connection to the underlying debt in order to effect a valid foreclosure, such a requirement should be given prospective effect.

In general, when we construe a statute, we do not engage in an analysis whether that interpretation is given retroactive or prospective effect; the interpretation we give the statute usually reflects the court's view of its meaning since the statute's enactment. See McIntire, petitioner, 458 Mass. 257, 261, 936 N.E.2d 424 (2010), cert. denied, ___ U.S. ___, 131 S.Ct. 2909, 179 L.Ed.2d 1253 (2011). However, there are several considerations that compel us to give the interpretation of "mortgagee" we announce here only prospective effect. As the previous discussion reflects, the use of the term "mortgagee" in the statutory scheme governing mortgage foreclosures was not free of ambiguity, and while the decisions of this court in years and centuries past provide

---

[27] In its amicus brief, REBA [Real Estate Bar Association for Massachusetts, Inc. and Abstract Club—Eds.] asserts that the contemporary secondary mortgage market exacerbates the title problem because, as we recognized in *Ibanez,* 458 Mass. at 649, 941 N.E.2d 40, the secondary market operates, permissibly, so that "underlying notes will be held by one entity for the benefit of the bond holders and the mortgages held by a servicer," and if the servicer conducts the foreclosure "there will be no evidence of record that will establish that the mortgagee was also the holder of the note at the time of the foreclosure." In effect, REBA argues, because "the essence of the MERS system is that MERS does not hold the underlying notes . . . and holds the mortgages only as nominee for the holder of the note," there will effectively be a presumption that the mortgagee did not hold the note at the time of the foreclosure.

We respond to REBA's concerns *infra,* but it is significant that MERS's current "Rules of Membership," version 3.12, most recently revised in March, 2012 (MERS rules), appear to recognize that there needs to be a connection made between the mortgage and the underlying debt as a condition precedent to an effective foreclosure by sale. See Rule 8(1)(a) of the MERS rules (requiring member owner of note or servicer initiating foreclosure on note secured by MERS mortgage first to effectuate assignment of mortgage "to the note owner's servicer, or to such other party expressly and specifically designated by the note owner"); Rule 8(1)(e)(i) of the MERS rules (obligating member note owner or servicer "to execute the assignment of the Security Instrument from [MERS] to the note owner's servicer, or to such other party expressly and specifically designated by the note-owner . . . and promptly send the assignment of the Security Instrument . . . for recording in the applicable public land records"); Rule 8(1)(d) of the MERS rules (revoking authority of MERS certifying officers to initiate foreclosure proceedings in MERS's name on or after July 22, 2011). Finally, as we just stated, we read the relevant mortgage foreclosure statutes to authorize a party who holds the mortgage directly and who serves as the agent of the note holder to qualify as the "mortgagee" entitled to foreclose under the power of sale.

support for the general proposition that, under our common law, a mortgage ultimately depends on connection with the underlying debt for its enforceability, none of our cases has considered directly the question whether a mortgagee must also hold the note or act on behalf of the note holder in order to effect a valid foreclosure by sale. It has been represented to us by the defendants and several amici that lawyers and others who certify or render opinions concerning real property titles have followed in good faith a different interpretation of the relevant statutes, viz., one that requires the mortgagee to hold only the mortgage, and not the note, in order to effect a valid foreclosure by sale. We have no reason to reject this representation of prior practice, and in that context, we recognize there may be significant difficulties in ascertaining the validity of a particular title if the interpretation of "mortgagee" that we adopt here is not limited to prospective operation, because of the fact that our recording system has never required mortgage notes to be recorded.

This court traditionally has given prospective effect to its decisions in very limited circumstances, but those have included circumstances where the ruling announces a change that affects property law. . . . In the property law context, we generally apply our decisions prospectively out of "concern for litigants and others who have relied on existing precedents." [Payton v. Abbot Labs, 386 Mass. 540, 565 (1982)] In addition, there may be particular reason to give a decision prospective effect where—as the argument is made here—"prior law is of questionable prognosticative value." Blood v. Edgar's, Inc., 36 Mass. App. Ct. 402, 407, 632 N.E.2d 419 (1994). Where a decision is not grounded in constitutional principles, but instead announces "a new common-law rule, a new interpretation of a State statute, or a new rule in the exercise of our superintendence power, there is no constitutional requirement that the new rule or new interpretation be applied retroactively, and we are therefore free to determine whether it should be applied only prospectively." Commonwealth v. Dagley, 442 Mass. 713, 721 n. 10, 816 N.E.2d 527 (2004), cert. denied, 544 U.S. 930, 125 S.Ct. 1668, 161 L.Ed.2d 494 (2005). In the exceptional circumstances presented here, and for the reasons that we have discussed, we exercise our discretion to hold that the interpretation of the term "mortgagee" in G.L. c. 244, § 14, and related statutory provisions that we adopt in this opinion is to apply only to mortgage foreclosure sales for which the mandatory notice of sale has been given after the date of this opinion.[28]

c.   *Preliminary injunction.* Although we apply the rule articulated in this case prospectively, we nonetheless apply it to Green Tree's appeal because it has been argued to this court by Eaton. See Bouchard v. DeGagne, 368 Mass. 45, 48–49, 329 N.E.2d 114 (1975) (party seeking relief may be entitled to benefit from rule announced in case, even when other "somewhat similarly situated [parties] are not afforded the benefit

---

[28]   It would appear that at least with respect to unregistered land, a foreclosing mortgage holder such as Green Tree may establish that it either held the note or acted on behalf of the note holder at the time of a foreclosure sale by filing an affidavit in the appropriate registry of deeds pursuant to G.L. c. 183, § 5B. The statute allows for the filing of an affidavit that is "relevant to the title to certain land and will be of benefit and assistance in clarifying the chain of title." Such an affidavit may state that the mortgagee either held the note or acted on behalf of the note holder at the time of the foreclosure sale. . . .

of retroactive application of the principles established by that first appellate determination"). . . .

The motion judge granted the preliminary injunction based on her determination that as a matter of still applicable common law, for a foreclosure by sale to be valid, the mortgage and the mortgage note must be unified physically in the possession of the foreclosing mortgagee. We have focused principally on the statutes governing mortgage foreclosure by sale and have concluded that where a mortgagee acts with the authority and on behalf of the note holder, the mortgagee may comply with these statutory requirements without physically possessing or actually holding the mortgage note. Eaton's verified complaint alleges that at the time of foreclosure in this case, Green Tree, as assignee of MERS, was neither in possession of Eaton's mortgage note nor "authorized by the holder of the note to carry out the foreclosure." However, Eaton makes this allegation solely on "information and belief." As a general rule, an allegation that is supported on "information and belief" does not supply an adequate factual basis for the granting of a preliminary injunction. . . .

The motion judge's decision on the preliminary injunction does not consider the question of Green Tree's (or MERS's) authority to act on behalf of BankUnited or an assignee of BankUnited in initiating foreclosure proceedings, and our examination of the Superior Court record suggests that this issue was not raised below. In the circumstances, we conclude that Eaton's allegation on information and belief that Green Tree was not authorized by the note holder to carry out the foreclosure sale did not offer an adequate factual basis to support the preliminary injunction that was issued. Consequently, the order granting the preliminary injunction must be vacated. On remand, Eaton may renew her request for a preliminary injunction, and in that context seek to show that she has a reasonable likelihood of establishing that, at the time of the foreclosure sale, Green Tree neither held the note nor acted on behalf of the note holder.[29]

4.   *Conclusion.* We vacate the grant of the preliminary injunction, and remand the case to the Superior Court for further proceedings consistent with this opinion.

So ordered.

NOTES

1.   *Ownership of the Note.* The court in Eaton v. Federal National Mortgage Association read both the common law and statutory provisions to require that a "mortgagee" proceeding under a power of sale must own the note. Moreover, isn't that result also compelled by § 3–301 of the U.C.C. that provides that a "person entitled to enforce" a negotiable note is the "holder," which requires possession of the note? After all, doesn't the law of notes control assignments of mortgages, as seen in *Giorgi* and *Doyle*?

---

[29] As noted at the outset of this opinion, the mortgage identifies MERS as mortgagee, but one that acts as the "nominee" of the lender. It is not clear what "nominee" means in this context, but the use of the word may have some bearing on the agency question. We express no opinion whether MERS or Green Tree was acting as agent of the note holder or with the note holder's authority at the time of the foreclosure sale. Eaton is entitled to pursue discovery on this issue in connection with her Superior Court action.

One important possible exception raised by the opinion is if the foreclosing entity is the "agent" of the note holder. What must be shown to make the entity an agent? Can that relationship be implied? Especially in the context of constant transfer of loans? What do the new MERS rules, in footnote 27 of the opinion, have to say on this issue? How does *Eaton* suggest the foreclosing entity can show that it holds the note? Professor Adam Levitin has observed a tension between the public mortgage records and the private note system exemplified by MERS. He suggests the creation of a national note registration system that would be linked to mortgage records. "Registration would create a rebuttable presumption of ownership, and matching mortgage recordation and note registration would be a precondition of foreclosure. Linked note-and-mortgage title systems would preserve borrowers' interest in keeping the terms of notes private, resolve questions about foreclosure standing, remove the potential cloud to real-estate title, and facilitate mortgage financing transactions generally by clarifying property rights." The Paper Chase: Securitization, Foreclosure, and the Uncertainty of Mortgage Title, 63 Duke L.J. 637, 639, 652 (2013). For other excellent critiques and reform proposals, Whitman, A Proposal for A National Mortgage Registry: MERS Done Right, 78 Mo. L. Rev. 1 (2013); Kochan, Certainty of Title: Perspectives After the Mortgage Foreclosure Crisis on the Essential Role of Effective Recording Systems, 66 Ark. L. Rev. 267 (2013); Hunt, Should the Mortgage Follow the Note?, 75 Ohio St. L.J. 155 (2014).

For another decision similar to *Eaton*, see Bank of N.Y. v. Raftogianis, 418 N.J. Super. 323, 13 A.3d 435 (Ch. 2010). For an excellent analysis of the different jurisdictional positions on the requirement of possession of the note, see Borden, Reiss & Akina, Show Me the Note!, 19 Westlaw J. Bank & Lender Liability 1 (No. 1 2013). See generally Whitman & Milner, Foreclosing on Nothing: The Curious Problem of the Deed of Trust Foreclosure without Entitlement to Enforce the Note, 66 Ark. L. Rev. 21 (2013); Report of the Permanent Editorial Board for the Uniform Commercial Code, Application of the Uniform Commercial Code to Selected Issues Relating to Mortgage Notes (2011); Hunt, Stanton & Wallace, Rebalancing Public and Private in the Law of Mortgage Transfer, 62 Am. U. L. Rev. 1529 (2013).

2. *Standing to Foreclose.* There is a divergence in the opinions on the question of whether there must be a clearly recorded chain of assignments of mortgage from the original mortgagee to the foreclosing mortgagee. Compare Barnett v. BAC Home Loan Servicing, L.P., 772 F. Supp. 2d 1328, 1336 (D. Or. 2011) (required) with MetLife Home Loans v. Hansen, 286 P.3d 1150, 1158 (Kan. Ct. App. 2012) (not required).

There is a split among the jurisdictions on the question of whether Merscorp has standing to bring a foreclosure action. Much of the debate centers on the issue whether its listed status as "nominee" truly makes it an "agent" of the mortgagee enabling it to foreclose or the "beneficiary" under a deed of trust and so able to partake in a foreclosure. Compare Landmark National Bank v. Kesler, 216 P.3d 158 (Kan. 2009) (Merscorp not allowed to intervene to set aside foreclosure); Bank of N.Y. v. Silverberg, 86 A.D.3d 274, 926 N.Y.S.2d (2011) (Merscorp was not assignee or holder and merely nominee and could not commence judicial foreclosure); and Bain Metropolitan Mortgage Group, Inc. v. Litton Loan Servicing, LP, 175 Wash.2d 83, 285 P.3d 34 (2012) (Merscorp as nominee not a beneficiary under deed of trust) with Gomes v. Countrywide Home Loans, Inc., 192 Cal. App.4th, 121 Cal. Rptr.3d 819 (2011) (Merscorp has standing to foreclose); Deutsche Bank Nat'l Trust Co. v. Pietranico, 33 Misc.3d 528, 928 N.Y.S.28 818 (2011) (Merscorp able to bring judicial foreclosure); Bucci v. Lehman Bros. Bank, FSB, 68 A.3d 1069 (R.I. 2013) (Merscorp has power to bring power of sale foreclosure as "nominee"). MERS apparently has discontinued commencing foreclosure proceedings in its own name, preferring to assign the mortgage to the mortgagee or its agent. See, Bucci, at 1079. The standing issue remains with servicing companies bringing foreclosure proceedings. See generally, Robinson, Note: The Case Against Allowing Mortgage Electronic Registration Systems, Inc. (MERS) to Initiate Foreclosure Proceedings, 32 Cardozo L. Rev. 1621 (2011).

3. *Post-2008 Responses.* There have been numerous legislative and judicial responses to the 2008 crisis, attempting to stabilize financial and mortgage markets and to provide protection to troubled borrowers and related parties. These include the federal Protecting Tenants at Foreclosure Act of 2009, 12 U.S.C. § 5220 (foreclosure purchaser must recognize existing tenant leases and provide 90 days notification for tenant to vacate; applies to federally related mortgage loans and residential properties; due to sunset on Dec. 31, 2014); state laws providing delays in foreclosure proceedings to permits mortgagors to seek modifications (see, e.g., Cal. Civ. Code § 2923.52, which expired by its own terms in 2011); increased scrutiny of credit rating agencies which rated mortgage bonds (see Lynch, Deeply and Persistently Conflicted: Credit Rating Agencies in the Current Regulatory Environment, 59 Case W. Res. L. Rev. 227 (2009)); and federally sponsored loan modification programs (see White, Deleveraging the American Homeowner: The Failure of 2008 Voluntary Mortgage Contract Modifications, 41 Conn. L. Rev. 1107 (2009); Soslow, Comment: Incentivizing Deeds-In-Lieu of Foreclosure: An Argument for the Expansion of the Home Affordable Foreclosure Alternatives ("HAFA") Program, 14 U. Pa. J. Bus. L. 58 (2012)).

There have also occasions of fraud and overreaching by various actors in connection with the slew of foreclosures, as well as responses by legislatures and courts. Some entities bringing foreclosures (perhaps mortgage servicing companies, foreclosure service providers, or lenders) engaged in "robosigning" where foreclosure-related documents were improperly executed or notarized, although courts usually found such allegations insufficient to defeat foreclosure or support fraud actions. See IndyMac Fed. Bank, FSB v. Meisels, 37 Misc.3d 1206(A), 961 N.Y.S.2d 358 (Sup. Ct. 2012) (describing robosigner's actions and denying foreclosure on various grounds); Gretchen Morgenson, Banks' Flawed Paperwork Throws Some Foreclosures into Chaos, N.Y. Times, Oct. 4, 2010; but see Conlin v. Mortgage Electronic Registration Systems, Inc., 714 F.3d 355 (6th Cir. 2013) (alleged robosigning did not prejudice mortgagor's rights). States began regulation of "foreclosure consultants" to prevent taking advantage of desperate homeowners. See, e.g., N.J. Stat. Ann. 46:10B–53 to –68; see Murray, Court Decisions and State Statutes Send Warning to "Foreclosure Consultants," 43 Real Prop. Tr. & Est. J. 572 (2008). Courts have applied general equitable doctrines to police the foreclosure process. See, e.g., Wells Fargo Bank, N.A. v. Meyers, 108 A.D.3d 9, 966 N.Y.S.2d 108 (servicer failed to negotiate loan modification in good faith before bringing foreclosure action).

4. *The Role of the Lawyer.* In order to reduce false or irregular foreclosure actions, in 2013 New York enacted legislation placing a burden on the foreclosing plaintiff's attorney to verify the basis of the complaint. McKinney's CPLR § 3012–b. The statute requires that in foreclosures of mortgages on homes occupied by the defendant, the complaint must be accompanied by an affidavit signed by the plaintiff's attorney. The affidavit must certify that the attorney has reviewed the facts and relevant materials, consulted with the plaintiff, and believes that there is a reasonable basis for commencing the proceeding and that the plaintiff is currently the creditor entitled to enforce the mortgage.

e.   DEED IN LIEU OF FORECLOSURE

Jesse Soslow, Comment, Incentivizing Deeds-In-Lieu of Foreclosure: An Argument for Expansion of the Home Affordable Foreclosure Alternatives ("HAFA") Program

14 University of Pennsylvania Journal of Business Law 583, 587–95 (2012).

III. Deeds-In-Lieu

Simply put, a deed-in-lieu of foreclosure is a device whereby a delinquent borrower will give a deed to a lender in exchange for the lender extinguishing all personal liability or for some other consideration. There are significant advantages to the borrower, the lender, the local court system, and the economy at large, from the consummation of this transaction, as opposed to proceeding through the foreclosure process. There is, however, potential for abuse that needs to be considered. These issues will be discussed, in turn, below.

A.   Advantages to Lender

The advantages to lenders who use the DIL device instead of a foreclosure proceeding fall into three categories. The first relates to the economic value of the home secured by the loan; the second relates to the administrative costs of the proceedings; and the third relates to the negative publicity of foreclosure proceedings. Relating to the first category, with a DIL transaction, the lender can take control of the property immediately, and thus maintain the economic value of the property. With a foreclosure proceeding, there is potential for the property to be abandoned by the borrower at some point during the months-long (or, in some cases, years-long) foreclosure process and, as a result, the property may decrease in value. For the second category, the lender can quickly negotiate and consummate the transaction, saving the lender the high cost of foreclosure, which has been estimated at $50,000 per home (including the lender's out of pocket costs and economic losses). Finally, for the third category, the lender can avoid the potential negative publicity of the foreclosure process. The reputation of foreclosing on peoples' homes is naturally not good exposure for large lenders, and avoiding such a negative image is valuable.

B.   Advantages to Borrower

Like the advantages to the lender, where applicable, the borrower will have reciprocal advantages. Further, there are additional advantages to a borrower that are not shared by the lender. The borrower can obtain release of some or all of her personal liability under the mortgage indebtedness. The borrower, like the lender, can avoid the publicity, notoriety, time, and expense involved in foreclosure litigation that, on average, has been estimated to be $7200. Further, in some situations, the lender may agree to pay the transfer costs or make additional monetary payments to the borrower. Also, in some situations, the lender may grant the borrower some possessory interest in the property, such as the right to lease the property or the right to purchase it in the future. And finally, DIL "actions typically have less adverse impact than foreclosure on borrowers' credit records."

C.   Advantages to Local Court System

With the sharp rise in foreclosures, court systems—particularly in judicial foreclosure states—have been inundated with foreclosure actions. This influx of foreclosure actions has strained court systems to the point where multiple states have felt the need to enact programs in order to alleviate some of the burden. . . .

The advantage that the use of DIL transactions can serve in this situation is, of course, to remove foreclosure cases from the court system, allowing them to be resolved without draining the resources of state courts. . . .

D.   Economic Advantages of DILs

In one sense, the economic advantages of DILs can be considered through the lens of the economic disadvantages, and costs, of foreclosure. Foregoing foreclosure often avoids these negative economic consequences. With regard to the broader economy, a foreclosure can impose high costs on the local government where a house is located, as well as on the value of the other homes in a foreclosed home's neighborhood. If a home is abandoned prior to foreclosure, a local government could potentially lose $20,000 in lost property taxes, unpaid utility bills, property upkeep, sewage, and maintenance. Furthermore, studies have shown that a single-family home foreclosure lowers the value of homes located within one-eighth of a mile by an average of 0.9%. In addition to the monetary costs of foreclosure, there are also social costs. For instance, increased foreclosures have been found to contribute to higher levels of violent crimes.

The negative impact of foreclosure on neighborhoods and local economies might not, of course, be entirely reversed by using an alternative to foreclosure, such as DILs. Nevertheless, there are good reasons to believe that use of DILs would mitigate many of the negative economic consequences of foreclosure. The negative impact of abandonment, for instance, would decrease in a collaborative DIL transaction between borrower and lender. The depressive effect of foreclosure sales on other neighborhood properties could also be assuaged by the use of DIL transactions that allow for more flexibility in the ultimate sale of the home.

E.   Potentials for Abuse

While the use of DILs has a variety of potential benefits, there remain certain pitfalls that must be considered. These issues fall into three broad categories: (1) legal issues that must be considered in order for a DIL transaction to withstand judicial scrutiny; (2) issues that a lender must consider in order for a DIL transaction to be worthwhile; and (3) protections for a borrower so that a DIL transaction is not ultimately used to the detriment of the borrower.

Under the first category—legal issues that must be considered in order for a DIL transaction to withstand judicial scrutiny—there are two primary considerations. First, the DIL must not be a "clog" on the mortgagor's equity of redemption under applicable state law. And second, the DIL must not be construed to be an "equitable mortgage" that must be foreclosed by subsequent judicial action.

The doctrine of clogging a mortgagor's equity of redemption arises from the common law principle that until a valid foreclosure decree has been issued, a mortgagor is entitled to "redeem" the property; that is, retain ownership by paying the indebtedness. Moreover, if the borrower fails to pay, she is entitled to have the property exposed to public sale, so that any value in excess of the mortgage debt may be realized and distributed to subordinate lien holders and the borrower. A DIL quite clearly cuts off these mortgagor's rights, and thus it has sometimes been called a "clog" on the mortgagor's equity of redemption and been held impermissible. However, John Murray suggests that an arms-length, fully documented DIL transaction will ordinarily survive a clogging challenge, because "a [DIL] is subsequent to the original mortgage . . . [,] it is a voluntary conveyance for independent and valuable consideration, and . . . it serves a socially useful purpose of allowing the mortgagor to avoid a time-consuming, costly, and public foreclosure, and possibly allow[s] the mortgagor to avoid personal liability on the debt. . . ."[49]

The main clogging issue that arises with regard to DIL transactions—which is intertwined with the issue of whether a DIL will be deemed an equitable mortgage—comes up generally in the scenario where a borrower, who is in default, asks the lender for an adjustment to her mortgage. The lender will often agree, on the condition that a mechanism (such as a deed-in-escrow) be put into place whereby title is transferred to the lender automatically if the borrower defaults again in the future, thus cutting off the borrower's right (a) to insist upon a public sale and (b) to "redeem" the property by paying off the debt at any time until the auctioneer's hammer falls (and, in some states, until many months after the sale has been completed). Courts are split on the issue of whether such transactions are generally valid.

The pertinent issue here is how these transactions should be treated in the home-mortgage context. Would it be sound policy to uphold these transactions where a home lender and borrower have agreed to a mortgage adjustment on the condition that the borrower places a DIL in escrow? The case law appears to distinguish the commercial and residential context on this issue, and for good reason. It would seem likely that a residential borrower would often lack the sophistication and representation to be adequately protected in entering such an agreement. This comment therefore does not argue that transactions involving placing a DIL in escrow should be used in the residential context. On the contrary, we are focusing on residential

---

[49] [John Murray, Clogging Revisited, 33 Real Prop. Prob. & Tr. J. 279, 287–88 (1998).]

transactions in which the default has already occurred; there is no equity in the property; the borrower has no reasonable prospect of paying the loan and effectuating his right to redemption; and the DIL will be delivered absolutely and at once, rather than placed in escrow for delivery at some future time on a subsequent default.

Even where clogging issues and equitable mortgage issues are not of concern, DILs are not "a universal panacea for mortgagees when the mortgagor has defaulted." In fact, there are a number of circumstances that could, essentially, disqualify DILs as a viable option for lenders. These circumstances need to be considered in order to better understand an ideal incentive program that must take into consideration the real legal and economic consequences of using the DIL device instead of foreclosure (and vice-versa).

One such concern is whether there are junior liens on the property. Under a typical foreclosure proceeding, junior liens are extinguished. The completion of a DIL transaction, however, does not extinguish junior liens. Thus if a lender wished to use the DIL device on a property with junior liens, it would be necessary to later foreclose on the property after the DIL transaction has taken place. In the context of this discussion, it would then appear counter-productive to employ the DIL device in circumstances where there are junior liens or judgments on the property. The point that is argued in this comment is that the DIL device can serve as an efficient and cost-saving method for both borrower and lender, and that it is ultimately beneficial for the economy and local communities. In a situation in which it would be necessary to both use the DIL device and then foreclose on the property, it would appear that much of the benefit of the device would be lost. In particular, consider that the foreclosure process itself, especially in judicial foreclosure states, would still remain a costly and time-consuming process for the lender. Further, the negative impact of foreclosure on the property's surrounding community, as discussed above, would to some degree still persist. Even the benefit to the borrower would likely be diminished by the need for a future foreclosure, as that future cost would—at least to some degree—be passed on to her in any deal involving a DIL that might be struck between the borrower and the lender.

Another issue that lenders must be concerned about when entering into a DIL transaction relates to the voluntariness of the transaction and adequacy of the consideration for the deed. Courts inherently view the borrower and lender as having disparate bargaining power, and thus will look closely at whether there was "undue influence, oppression, unfairness or unconscientious advantage." If a court finds that the transaction was, in any of these ways, unfair, the transaction risks being overturned. This issue, however, from the perspective of the lender, is not of primary concern in the context of this comment. While it is certainly the case that an ideal DIL transaction will be robust under the light of judicial scrutiny, these particular concerns are more aptly considered in the following paragraph in the context of borrower protection. In a program that encourages the use of DILs, it would seem unnecessary to have added protection to ensure the judicial upholding of the deal—relating particularly to the fairness of the deal to borrowers—if fairness to borrowers is already being assured through measures protecting borrowers' interests.

Borrower protection is perhaps the most important concern in the context of this comment relating to the use of DILs. While lenders often have significant legal resources, as well as experience in this area, borrowers are far less likely to have equivalent resources and experience. This problem is further amplified by the fact that borrowers who have defaulted often lack the money to hire adequate legal counsel to aid in the execution of a DIL transaction. The potential problems that need to be guarded against include: (1) a borrower who, as a result of entering into a DIL agreement, foregoes a valid defense to foreclosure; (2) a borrower who receives inadequate consideration in the DIL transaction; and (3) a borrower who is unduly influenced into entering into the DIL transaction.

Regarding the first problem, uninformed financially troubled borrowers, presented with the possibility of extinguishing all in personam debt through a DIL transaction, might agree to enter such a transaction despite the possibility of a valid defense to foreclosure. In the specific context of subprime mortgages, predatory lending is an ever-present theme. And since such predatory practices can serve as a basis for a defense to foreclosure, it would be undesirable to endorse a system that did not ensure all foreclosure defenses were exhausted or, at the very least, known to the borrower so to be used as leverage in workout negotiations.

With regard to the problem of a borrower who receives inadequate consideration for a DIL transaction, a lender—as mentioned previously—is very likely to have far greater experience in such transactions than a borrower. Consequently, any deal that is struck has the potential to be, not a representation of the true bargaining power of the parties, but rather a reflection of the disparate knowledge of the circumstances. Consider the following fact pattern as an illustration: A borrower is in default on a recourse loan with an outstanding balance of $300,000, secured by a mortgage on a home worth $290,000. Further, assume that, first, the foreclosure process would cost the lender $20,000 to complete and, second, the lender believes that, while it could likely obtain a deficiency judgment against the borrower, it knows that collecting the judgment would be unlikely. The opportunity to extinguish the possibility of the deficiency judgment through a DIL transaction might be appealing to a borrower. Nevertheless, the opportunity of a better deal, unbeknownst to her, might exist. In particular, the lender, it can be assumed, would gain $20,000 by extinguishing the debt using the DIL transaction, some of which the borrower might be in a position to bargain for. The point, it should be noted, is not that the borrower should be entitled to some of this excess $20,000, but rather that, in an ideal scenario, the borrower would be negotiating with the same knowledge that the lender has, and the ultimate agreement is merely a reflection of the parties' relative bargaining power, rather than a reflection of asymmetric information.

The final problem that must be considered, which is certainly compatible with—and not always separable from—the two problems discussed immediately above, is that of a borrower entering into a DIL transaction as a result of undue influence from a lender. DIL transactions are considered "lender-friendly" agreements. Thus, it follows that, in certain instances, large institutional lenders with substantial legal representation and bargaining power could strong-arm borrowers into accepting DILs even though it may be to their disadvantage. The possible ramifications of such an outcome could involve, as discussed above, a borrower's acceptance of a DIL transaction that eliminates a viable foreclosure defense, or (especially if there is equity in the property) the acceptance of a deal that is substantially less than what she could have received had she not been unduly forced to accept the deal.

Each of the three problems discussed could be largely solved by the presence of competent, knowledgeable counsel representing the borrower. With such representation, it would seem unlikely that a viable foreclosure defense would be left either unused in a challenge to foreclosure or unused as leverage in bargaining for a DIL transaction. Furthermore, a competent and knowledgeable attorney would have full knowledge of the situation and thus bargain on a level with less asymmetric information than her client might on her own. And, lastly, a borrower's counsel would zealously defend the borrower's interests, ensuring that the borrower is not forced into a DIL transaction that is not in her best interest. Of course, the idea of ensuring legal representation in these matters is not a groundbreaking notion. The question then becomes how to ensure that result. This question will be addressed in the section below on the proposed incentive program.

NOTES

1. *U.L.S.I.A.* U.L.S.I.A. § 507(a) permits deeds in lieu of foreclosure.

2. Deeds in lieu of foreclosure are especially relevant in the negotiation of "work out" arrangements after a default in a commercial real estate transactions. See pages 696–704.

2. STATUTORY REDEMPTION

Robert H. Skilton, Developments in Mortgage Law and Practice
17 Temple University Law Quarterly 315, 326–331 (1943).

A statutory period of redemption is to be distinguished from an equity of redemption in that the former is established by the legislature, the latter by adjudication. As we have seen, the tendency has been to view foreclosure as finally terminating or barring the equity of redemption. On the other hand, the statutory period of redemption usually runs after foreclosure sale, being a period of grace which reminds us of a former practice of Chancery courts in allowing at least six months after foreclosure for the mortgagor to redeem. A summary of the growth and spread of this statutory period of redemption, now obtaining in a majority of the states, particularly western and central, may be interesting.

It seems clear that the first redemption periods established by legislatures came as a consequence of early depressions, at a time when the courts had just abandoned their practice of granting the right to redeem after sale. This type of legislation may be traced back to 1820, when the country was sharing in the international economic disturbance following the Napoleonic Wars—in our country evidenced by the collapse of a land boom. The earliest redemptive legislation, however, did not specifically deal with mortgage sales: It referred to execution sales generally, and, as a matter of fact, was construed in two decisions not to include mortgage sales. But it may be viewed as the starting point from which mortgage redemptive legislation sprang.

New York legislation, passed April 12, 1820, provided that on execution sales of land, the sheriff should deliver to the purchaser a certificate, instead of a deed to the land itself: the certificate should recite the terms of the sale. The debtor could redeem within one year of sale. Apparently he kept possession of the property in the meantime. Specific reference was not made to the case of mortgage foreclosure sales. . . .

Later legislatures were more specific. When the next depression came along, introduced by the panic of 1836, new redemption legislation was passed in some states; and now mortgage foreclosures are expressly included. From that time to this we may note the general tendency of legislation to give the mortgage debtors the same redemption rights as ordinary contract debtors. The New York Act of 1837 provided for redemption within one year after sale of real estate sold on foreclosure of a mortgage. The Illinois Act of 1841 specifically embraced mortgages. In 1842 Alabama authorized the redemption of mortgaged premises within two years after sale. In 1839 Michigan provided that the Chancellor shall not order the sale of mortgaged premises at a time less than two years and three months from the date of the filing of the bill, sending [sic] the previous law enacted in 1827 which had provided a two year period.

These early redemption statutes came as a result of depression periods, and may be associated with the general collapse of land values, the failure of governmental public land policy, and governmental relief and moratory measures in connection with the sale of public land. Other factors accounted for later developments. The next steps in the development of redemption periods, oddly enough, are associated with the spread of codes of civil practice: the movement for the simplification of civil procedure which began in 1848 with the adoption of the Field Code in New York. This movement, more legalistic than economic in motivation, accounts for the presence of redemption periods in the laws of most of the western states.

What is more natural than that this movement for a simplified and orderly practice, a single code for all civil procedure, embraced by New York after much reflection, should be accepted by the new territories of the west, faced with the problem of forming a government, and with few traditions and customs to guide or restrict them? At the first or second meeting of practically all of the territorial legislatures, the Field Code was adopted, with such changes as seemed to fit the local needs.

The New York version of the Field Code made no general provision for a period of redemption after execution or foreclosure sale. Section 246 merely provided:

"Until otherwise provided by the legislature, the existing provisions of law relating to executions, and their incidents, including the sale and redemption of property, shall apply to the executions prescribed by this chapter."[69]

Section 246 could not be adopted verbatim, there being no preexistent redemption statute in the new territories. Redemption rights must be treated specifically. In 1851, California and Minnesota inserted, among the provisions governing execution sales of real estate, redemption rights of six months and sixty days, respectively.

The California legislation was important for it served as a model. In the important case of Kent v. Laffan,[71] the Supreme Court of California held that the redemption period of six months applied to mortgage sales as well as other execution sales.

The influence of the California example upon neighboring territories and states seems to account for the fact that the period of six months was most frequently used in the nineteenth century in fixing redemption rights. To illustrate the influence of California legislation upon mortgage law in western states, the case of Idaho may be referred to. In 1851 California provided for redemption by the mortgagor within six months of sale, upon payment of 18% interest. In 1864 Idaho adopted the California version of the Field Code practically verbatim, including this provision. The 1872–6 revision of the California code changed the interest payment to 12%. Idaho again followed suit, when it revised its code in 1881.

It is interesting to speculate as to the reason for the selection of the period of six months by the California legislature. Code provisions frequently adopt the best of previous common law and equity practice. It seems that the federal courts had continued the English practice of granting six months after sale within which to redeem, wherever the state laws did not control. Possibly the California legislature in selecting this period was merely codifying the preexistent practice of the federal courts in the territory.

The economic disturbances of the last decade of the nineteenth century contributed to the tendency to enlarge the period of redemption to one year. In 1886, Washington had led the way, changing its six month period to one year. In 1895, Idaho followed suit; Oregon having previously a four month period, changed it to one year; Wyoming, (with no previous period of redemption), established a six month period for the debtor, and another six months thereafter for his creditors. The same year Montana, in adopting a revised code of civil procedure, changed its period from six months to one year. In 1897 California established a one year period. Some years later Nevada did the same. . . .

On the other hand, when business is on the upswing, there appears to be a tendency to shorten the redemption period, as an incentive to new investment. For example, the Michigan period was reduced by the Act of September 23, 1899, which provided that the court should not order a sale until six months after the filing of the bill, and that thereafter the debtor should have six months within which to redeem.

---

[69]   N.Y.Code Civ.Proc. (1848) § 246.

[71]   2 Cal. 595 (1852).

Previously the mortgagor had two years and three months before sale. . . .

Another tendency to weaken the effect of the redemption period developed in statutory or judicial approval of waiver of redemption rights. If validated by court or legislature, a waiver of a debtor's right to redeem virtually destroys the principle of redemption. It becomes a matter of form to include waiver provisions in all mortgages. For example, recognition of the power to waive debtor's exemption in Pennsylvania has resulted in the general inclusion of waiver clauses in all of the many form contracts used in that state. Courts frequently permit the destruction of a right by waiver by invoking the principle of "freedom of contract". In addition to some instances of judicial approval of waiver clauses in the present field, there is at least one case of legislative permission.

As they existed on the eve of the last depression, the redemption laws of the states were extremely varied. The laws of the states differed in many important respects. There were also gross inconsistencies. In California, for example, there was a redemptive period of twelve months if foreclosure was by court action, but none if foreclosure was by power of sale. Between the states, the laws differed extremely. Differences existed not only with respect to the length of the time of redemption, but also with respect to: (1) whether the redemption period preceded or succeeded the sale; (2) whether the debtor was allowed to retain possession of the mortgaged premises in the interim period; (3) the amount to be paid as the redemptive price. In Indiana, Nebraska, Oklahoma and Wisconsin, the redemptive period preceded the sale. In Washington, Oregon, California, Nevada, Montana, Idaho, Utah, Wyoming, Arizona, Colorado, New Mexico, North Dakota, South Dakota, Kansas, Minnesota, Iowa, Missouri, Arkansas, Illinois, Michigan, Indiana, Kentucky, Tennessee, Alabama, Vermont and Maine it followed sale. The remaining states, in the east and south, had no redemption periods. Nineteen states had redemption periods of one year; five states, of six months; two of nine months; two of two years; one of eighteen months. Nineteen states had no redemption periods. Of those with redemption periods, four allowed the mortgagee to take possession of the premises during the interim period.

Matcha v. Wachs

Supreme Court of Arizona, 1982.
132 Ariz. 378, 646 P.2d 263.

FELDMAN, JUSTICE.

This declaratory action arose out of a dispute regarding priority between two sets of would-be redemptioners from a mortgage foreclosure sale. The appellees, Michael and Janet Matcha, brought suit against the Maricopa County Sheriff and Wachs and the other appellants (hereinafter referred to as Wachs) seeking a declaratory judgment that they and not Wachs were entitled to redeem the property sold at the foreclosure sale. The trial court found that Wachs had not perfected his right to redeem and entered summary judgment in favor of Matcha. Wachs appealed. On appeal, the court of appeals reversed the judgment of the trial court, finding that Wachs had substantially complied with the requirements of the applicable statutes and therefore was entitled to redeem the property. *See Matcha v. Wachs*, 132 Ariz. 402, 646 P.2d 287 (1981). We granted review in order to decide the issue of whether substantial compliance with the requirements of the redemption statutes (A.R.S. §§ 12–1282–12–1289) is sufficient to perfect a lien creditor's right to redeem. Having concluded that such compliance is sufficient, we approve and modify the decision of the court of appeals, and reverse the judgment of the superior court.

FACTS

Title to the real property which is the subject of this action was originally held by Schulz subject to the following encumbrances, listed in their order of priority:

1.   A mortgage to First National Mortgage Association [FNMA];

2.   A deed of trust to Wachs in the amount of $628,648.00;

3.   A deed of trust in favor of Jerry Lanyon dba Lanyon's Lawn Service;

4.   A judgment in favor of the law firm of Beer, Kalyna & Simon, P.C. (the law firm) in the amount of $2,581.35. This judgment was eventually assigned to Matcha.

When Schulz defaulted on his mortgage payments, FNMA foreclosed naming Schulz, Wachs, Lanyon and the law firm as defendants. The sheriff's sale on foreclosure was held on February 9, 1978, and the property was sold to FNMA. Following the foreclosure sale, Schulz as owner/mortgagor had six months within which to redeem the property. *See* A.R.S. § 12–1282(B). If he failed to do so, the junior lienholders, in order of seniority, each had five days to exercise their right to redeem by paying the amount due to the purchaser at the foreclosure sale, *plus* the amount due to those senior lienholders who had previously redeemed the property. *See* A.R.S. § 12–1282(C). The last lienholder to redeem is entitled to the sheriff's deed and thereafter holds title free and clear from the claims of all whose interests have been foreclosed. *See* A.R.S. § 12–1286.

Within the six-month period following the foreclosure sale, Schulz took no steps toward redeeming the property. Wachs, the senior lienholder, filed a timely notice of intent to redeem, specifying the amount of the lien and the order of its priority. He served a copy of the notice of intent to redeem on the sheriff as required by A.R.S. § 12–1284,[1] but failed to serve with it the documents required by A.R.S. § 12–1287,[2] i.e., a certified copy of the record of his lien and an affidavit

---

[1]   A.R.S. § 12–1284 provides:

To entitle a subsequent lienholder [i.e., holder of a lien junior to the one which was foreclosed] to redeem he shall within the applicable period of redemption as provided in § 12–1282, file with the county recorder . . . a notice in writing stating that he intends to redeem and specifying his lien and the amount thereof and its order of priority, and shall deliver a copy thereof to the sheriff. . . .

[2]   A.R.S. § 12–1287 provides:

A.   A redeeming creditor shall deliver to the officer or person from whom he seeks to redeem and serve *with his notice to the sheriff*:

showing the amount actually due on the lien. The law firm also filed a notice of intent to redeem. It served a copy on the sheriff and also served the sheriff with the documents required by § 12–1287. Thus, within the six-month period, Wachs complied with A.R.S. § 12–1284, but not § 12–1287; the law firm complied with both statutes.

On August 9, 1978, the six months within which the mortgagor/owner could redeem expired. Two days later, Wachs served the sheriff with copies of the documents required by § 12–1287 and tendered a check in the amount of $19,518, which was the amount due the purchaser at the foreclosure sale. Thereafter, Matcha, initially on the law firm's "behalf" and then as its assignee, also made a timely tender of the sum due. He did not, however, tender the additional $628,648 which constituted the amount of the lien held by Wachs. He claimed, rather, that Wachs had failed to comply with A.R.S. § 12–1287 and was not entitled to redeem. After the sheriff's office rejected his tenders, Matcha brought this suit, claiming that by non-compliance with A.R.S. § 12–1287, Wachs had forfeited his right to redeem, thus permitting a junior lienholder to redeem and acquire title without discharging the senior lien.

The question before us, then, is whether Wachs lost his right to redeem because he failed to serve the sheriff with the documents required by A.R.S. § 12–1287 within six months after the foreclosure sale or because, when he finally did serve the necessary documents, he served copies rather than the originals. We answer both questions in the negative.

At the outset, we agree with the trial court's determination that Wachs did not make a timely tender of the documents required by A.R.S. § 12–1287. While that section does not specifically state the time within which the documents must be filed, it does require that they be served "with [the] notice to the sheriff." The word "notice" is used only twice in the redemption statutes; therefore, we conclude that the word "notice" referred to in § 12–1287 can only mean the "notice" specified in § 12–1284. Since under the circumstances of this case the notice required by § 12–1284 must be filed within six months after the foreclosure sale, Wachs' service of the § 12–1287 documents six months and two days after the sale was not timely.

We disagree, however, with the trial court's conclusion that Wachs lost his right to redeem either by failing to file the § 12–1287 documents within six months after the foreclosure sale or by serving the sheriff with copies rather than originals.

In *Western Land & Cattle Co. v. National Bank of Arizona*, 29 Ariz. 51, 58–59, 239 P. 299, 301–02 (1925), this court acknowledged that the statutory right of redemption is a legal right which must be exercised in the manner required by statute, but upheld the right of the creditor to redeem the property despite the fact that in perfecting its right to

---

1. A copy of the docket of the judgment under which he claims the right to redeem, certified by the clerk of the court . . ., or if he redeems a mortgage or other lien, a copy of the record thereof, certified by the recorder.

3. An affidavit showing the amount actually due on the lien. (Emphasis supplied.)

redeem it had deviated slightly from the statutory requirements. In so holding, the court stated:

> The contention [by the junior lienholder] substantially is that although a redemptioner files his notice in perfect good faith and believing as a matter of law and fact he has correctly stated the amount of his lien and his order of priority, yet, if it afterward appears, at the end of bitterly contested litigation that he may have been in error as to the amount or order of priority, his right of redemption fails entirely. Such a construction of a beneficial statute, meant for the protection of lienholders, would equal in severity the rule required in the interpretation of a penal law. We do not think such was the intent of the legislature. If the lienholder in good faith does the things specified in the statute, the mere fact that it is later determined he was in error as to either amount of lien or order of priority, does not defeat his right of redemption, but merely requires that he pay the correct amount in the order determined by the law, when he finally does redeem.

Thus, in the past, minor deviations from the requirements of the redemption statutes have not resulted in a forfeiture of the right to redeem. It is true that in *Hummel v. Citizens' Building & Loan Ass'n*, 38 Ariz. 54, 59, 296 P. 1014, 1016 (1931), we stated: "[i]f the right given by statute is not exercised strictly according to the terms of the statute, it is lost. . . ." However, in *Hummel*, the creditor-redemptioner was more than one year late in filing his notice of intent to redeem. Thus, he hardly attempted compliance with the most important requirement of the redemption statutes. We do not read *Hummel* as authority for the principle that, notwithstanding the lack of prejudice to junior lienholders, any minor deviation from the statutory requirements will result in the forfeiture of the right to redeem.

Whether a statute should be given a strict or equitable interpretation must be decided in accordance with the legislature's intent in enacting that statute. Redemption statutes are remedial in nature and exist for the dual purpose of insuring the property will bring a fair price at a sheriff's sale and that, if the mortgagor does not redeem, his property will be applied to payment of debts in the order of the priority to which his various creditors are entitled. It was not the "intent of the legislature" that the redemption statutes be given the severe application "required in the interpretation of a penal law." *Western Land & Cattle Co. v. National Bank of Arizona*, 29 Ariz. at 58, 239 P. at 302. Accordingly, we hold that in the absence of prejudice to the other parties, substantial compliance with the requirements of §§ 12–1282—12–1289 will be sufficient to effect a redemption.

It may be argued that the adoption of an equitable rule of substantial compliance which considers the nature and extent of the deviation from the statutory plan, the fulfillment or nonfulfillment of the statutory purpose, and the prejudice or lack of prejudice to junior creditors will result in increased litigation with regard to redemptive rights. This will lead to occasional delay in determining title after foreclosure. However, the establishment of any rule which permits the application of equitable principles invites controversy over what constitutes an equitable result in any particular case. We feel, however, that such a danger, if it be one, is better tolerated than the injustice that can result from the inflexible application of the redemption statutes. As the court stated in *Osborn Hardware Co. v. Colorado Corp.*, 32 Colo.App. 254, 258, 510 P.2d 461, 463 (1973) (quoting *Plute v. Schick*, 101 Colo. 159, 162, 71 P.2d 802, 804 (1937)).

> "The purpose of the redemption law is to help creditors recover their just demands, nothing more. Equity has always prevented the redemption laws from being used as 'an instrument of oppression when substantial justice can be done without enforcing them to the letter.'"

[The] cases support the doctrine that although the right of redemption is a legal right, equitable principles may be utilized to relieve a redeeming lienholder from minor deviations and thus prevent injustice.

We do not hold that every deviation will be acceptable. There are instances where even a minor deviation from the statutory scheme may cause prejudice to the rights of a junior lienholder or other party. In such a situation, equitable principles dictate that the doctrine of substantial compliance will not relieve the redemptioner and that the loss shall fall on the party which caused it. *Salsbery v. Ritter*, 48 Cal.2d 1, 306 P.2d 897 (1957).

Turning to the facts of this case, we find that Wachs substantially complied with the requirements of the redemption statutes by filing his notice of intent to redeem within six months after the foreclosure sale as required by A.R.S. § 12–1284 and by serving copies of the documents required by A.R.S. § 12–1287 on the sheriff two days thereafter. Admittedly, Wachs did not serve the documents required by § 12–1287 within the time specified by statute. The purpose of § 12–1284 is to notify other lienholders who may intend to redeem, thus giving them information which they will need regarding priorities and amounts, in the event they wish to exercise their rights. The other purpose is to give the sheriff the information necessary to determine when he is free to deliver his deed. We agree with the court of appeals that the purpose of the requirement of A.R.S. § 12–1287 that documents be served on the sheriff and the party from whom redemption is to be made is to enable them to verify that the redeeming creditor actually has the lien interest required in order to permit redemption. Here, Wachs provided all parties with the necessary information in a timely manner by complying with § 12–1284. His late attempt to comply with § 12–1287 caused no harm. The sheriff was able to verify his lien and both the law firm and Matcha had all the information they needed. The law firm's original notice of intent to redeem acknowledged the Wachs lien, its priority and its amount. Neither the law firm nor Matcha has ever contested the validity, priority or amount of Wachs' lien, except for the claim of forfeiture by non-compliance with the exact terms of the statute. As the court of appeals stated, to hold that such a minor deviation could work a forfeiture of a valid claim would be to "honor form over substance." It would also allow a junior lienholder to reap a substantial windfall, would produce no benefit—and probably some harm—to Schulz, the original property owner, and would produce a result contrary to the purposes for which the redemption statutes were enacted.

Having made a good faith effort to redeem, having substantially complied with the redemption statutes and no prejudice having resulted to the junior lienholder, Wachs was entitled to redeem. Since Wachs made a tender of the correct amount to the sheriff within the five days allotted to him by A.R.S. § 12–1282(C) after expiration of Schulz' redemption right, Wachs was a redemptioner and Matcha was not entitled to redeem without tendering the amount of Wachs' lien, as required by A.R.S. § 12–1282. Since Matcha did not make such a tender, the trial court erred in ruling against Wachs and in favor of Matcha.

The opinion of the court of appeals is modified, the judgment of the trial court is reversed and the case is remanded with instructions to proceed in accordance with this opinion.

GORDON, V. C. J., and CAMERON, J., concur.

[Dissenting opinion of HAYS, J., joined by HOLOHAN, C.J., omitted].

NOTE

1. *Statutory Redemption.* Approximately thirty states allow statutory redemption. Although redemption periods generally run for one year, some states specify different periods for special circumstances. Illinois reduces the period to sixty days if the property is an abandoned residence. 735 Ill.Cons.Stat. 5/15–1603(b)(4) (1995). Solicitude towards farmers is evident in Wyoming where the general redemption period is three months but in the case of agricultural land is twelve months. Wyo.Stat. § 1–18–103(a) and (b) (1988). In a few states, the purchaser is allowed to occupy the land during the redemption period but is generally required to credit any rents received against the amount the debtor must pay to redeem. See, for example, N.H.Rev.Stat.Ann. § 529:26 (1974). In nearly half the states that provide for statutory redemption, the debtor is unconditionally allowed to remain in possession. In others he is allowed to stay on only under special conditions such as that the land is a homestead or is used for farming. See, for example, Wash.Rev.Code Ann. § 6.23.110 (West Supp.1991).

There is a split on the question of whether redemption rights can be severed and transferred to third parties. *Compare* Beckhart v. HTS Properties, LLC, 981 P.2d 208 (Colo.App.1998) (transfer prohibited because statutory language referred only to those holding interests in property and because assignment "could create uncertainty in dealing with the property") *with* Town Branch Storage, Inc. v. Commonwealth, 995 S.W.2d 398 (Ky.App.1999) (allowing assignment based on statutory language permitting redemption by the "defendant and his representative").

2. *Substantial Compliance.* As *Matcha* indicates, courts may find a valid redemption where there is only substantial compliance with the statute. In Sieve v. Rosar, 613 N.W.2d 789 (Minn.App.2000) the court held that there was no substantial compliance when the respondent filed a notice to redeem and sent the payment by courier to the appellant who had purchased the property at foreclosure sale. The check was accepted by another tenant in appellant's building, who delivered it to appellant one day after the expiration of the redemption period. The court held that substantial compliance requires timely payment to the proper party within the statutory period. The court, however, blurred its bright line by remanding to the lower court the question of whether appellant's conduct induced respondent to send the check to the office. Is this decision consistent with *Matcha*?

3. *Waiver of Redemption Rights.* A debtor's waiver of the redemption period will usually be subject to judicial scrutiny. But see Dellinger v. First National Bank, 333 Ark. 460, 970 S.W.2d 223 (1998) (holding waiver language in mortgage document bound mortgagors). Sometimes, though, statutes control. In Kansas, corporations or partnerships are allowed to make agreements reducing or eliminating the redemption period, while individual borrowers can waive only if the land is not used for residential or farm purposes. Kan.Stat.Ann. § 60–2414(a) (2013). In Tennessee, if a deed of trust or mortgage with power of sale is used, anyone can waive under any conditions. Tenn.Code Ann. §§ 66–8–101(3), 66–8–103 (1982).

3. DEFICIENCY JUDGMENTS AND ANTIDEFICIENCY LEGISLATION

Cornelison v. Kornbluth

Supreme Court of California, 1975.
15 Cal.3d 590, 125 Cal.Rptr. 557, 542 P.2d 981.

SULLIVAN, JUSTICE.

In this action for damages for the breach of covenants contained in a deed of trust and for damages for waste, brought by the beneficiary against the trustors and their successors in interest, plaintiff Mary Cornelison appeals from a summary judgment entered in favor of defendant John Kornbluth and against plaintiff. As will appear, we have concluded that upon the record presented, the summary judgment was properly granted and should be affirmed.

On July 15, 1964, plaintiff sold a single-family dwelling in Van Nuys, California, to Maurice and Leona Chanon, taking back a promissory note in the sum of $18,800 secured by a first deed of trust on the property. The deed of trust, recorded on August 21, 1964, contained the following covenants: that the Chanons would pay the real property taxes and assessments against the property; that they would care for and maintain the property; and that if they resold the property, the entire unpaid balance would become immediately due and payable.

On December 10, 1964, the Chanons conveyed the property to defendant by grant deed. On September 6, 1968, defendant sold the property to Richard Larkins. In January 1969 the county health department condemned the house as unfit for human habitation. The Chanons being in default on the promissory note, plaintiff caused the property to be sold at a trustee's sale. Plaintiff purchased the property at the sale for the sum of $21,921.42, that being an amount equal to the balance due on the note plus foreclosure costs.

Plaintiff then brought the instant action for damages, her amended complaint (hereafter "complaint") filed March 24, 1970, setting forth two causes of action, one for breach of contract and one for damages for waste. The first cause of action alleged in substance that defendant "agreed in writing to be bound by and to perform all of the covenants contained in the Note and Deed of Trust theretofore executed by defendants Maurice L. Chanon and Leona Chanon"; and that defendants breached these covenants (a) by selling the property to Larkins, (b) by failing to pay property taxes, (c) by failing to make payments on the note, and (d) by failing to properly care for and maintain the premises.

The second cause of action, after incorporating by reference the material allegations of the first cause of action, alleged in substance that defendant owed a duty to properly and adequately care for the property and that defendant negligently failed to fulfill this duty, thereby causing plaintiff to be damaged in specified particulars and amounts by reason of the loss of improvements to the real property as well as by reason of the loss of its use. On the first cause of action plaintiff prayed for damages in the sum of $18,169.66, and on the second cause of action for damages in the sum of $20,000 plus the reasonable rental of the property, and in addition for $45,000 punitive damages.

Defendant's answer admitted that he purchased the property from the Chanons and sold it to Larkins, but denied all other allegations for lack of information or belief. Defendant then moved for summary judgment. His declaration in support of the motion states in substance that he purchased the subject real property from the Chanons, that at the time of the purchase he knew it was encumbered by the deed of trust in favor of plaintiff as beneficiary, that he never assumed either orally or in writing the indebtedness secured by the deed of trust, and that no such assumption was contained in the deed conveying the property to him. The declaration attaches and incorporates by reference a copy of the grant deed which confirms the last statement.

Defendant also filed in support of the motion the declaration of one of his attorneys stating in substance that plaintiff regained possession of the subject property by purchasing it for $21,921.42 at the foreclosure sale conducted on June 4, 1969, said purchase having been effected "by a full credit bid resulting in the full satisfaction of the remaining indebtedness secured by the deed of trust. . . ." The declaration attaches and incorporates by reference a copy of the "trustee's deed upon sale" which confirmed the statements of the declaration. Plaintiff filed no counteraffidavits. The court granted defendant's motion and entered judgment accordingly. This appeal followed.

Plaintiff contends that the court erred in granting summary judgment because the "complaint is regular on its face and raises issues of fact." . . .

For present purposes, we need be concerned only with the following rule: "Summary judgment is proper only if the affidavits in support of the moving party would be sufficient to sustain a judgment in his favor and his opponent does not by affidavit show such facts as may be deemed by the judge hearing the motion sufficient to present a triable issue." (Stationers Corp. v. Dun & Bradstreet, Inc. (1965) 62 Cal.2d 412, 417, 42 Cal.Rptr. 449, 452, 398 P.2d 785, 788.)

Applying the foregoing rule we are satisfied that defendant's declaration is sufficient to support a summary judgment on the first cause of action for breach of contract. As previously stated, the basic theory of this cause of action is that defendant had a duty to comply with the covenants contained in the deed of trust given plaintiff by the

Chanons since the document was recorded and its covenants ran with the land. Plaintiff's legal premise is completely erroneous. Upon the transfer of real property covered by a mortgage or deed of trust as security for an indebtedness, the property remains subject to the secured indebtedness but the grantee is not personally liable for the indebtedness or to perform any of the obligations of the mortgage or trust deed unless his agreement to pay the indebtedness, or some note or memorandum thereof, is in writing and subscribed by him or his agent or his assumption of the indebtedness is specifically provided for in the conveyance. Defendant's declaration states positively that he never assumed either orally or in writing the indebtedness secured by the Chanon deed of trust and that no such assumption was contained in the deed by which the Chanons conveyed the property to him. An examination of a copy of the deed attached to the declaration confirms this. Plaintiff filed no counterdeclaration denying these allegations and as a consequence raised no triable issue of fact. Contrary to plaintiff's contention, a triable issue of fact cannot be raised by the allegations of her complaint. Accordingly, summary judgment on the first cause of action was properly granted.

We now proceed to determine whether defendant's declarations are sufficient to support the summary judgment on the second stated cause of action for waste. On this issue we may outline the positions of the parties as follows: Defendant contends that since, as set forth in his attorney's declaration, plaintiff purchased the property for a full credit bid an action for waste is thereby precluded both by reason of the antideficiency legislation and by reason of the extinguishment of the security interest through a full credit bid at the trustee's sale. Plaintiff on the other hand contends that an action for waste may be maintained independently of the antideficiency provisions of sections 580b and 580d of the Code of Civil Procedure.

In order to resolve this issue it is necessary to first define, and trace the history of an action for waste and secondly to analyze the impact of the antideficiency legislation induced by the depression of the 1930's upon this traditional action.

Section 2929 of the Civil Code provides: *"Waste.* No person whose interest is subject to the lien of a mortgage may do any act which will substantially impair the mortgagee's security." This section, enacted in 1872, codified a portion of the common law action for waste, as developed in England and adopted in earlier California cases. "[W]aste is conduct (including in this word both acts of commission and of omission) on the part of a person in possession of land which is actionable at the behest of, and for protection of the reasonable expectations of, another owner of an interest in the same land.

... Thus, waste is, functionally, a part of the law which keeps in balance the conflicting desires of persons having interests in the same land." (5 Powell on Real Property (1974) § 636, pp. 5–6).

Over a century ago this court in Robinson v. Russell (1864) 24 Cal. 467, 472–473 ... declared that an action on the case could be maintained by the mortgagee of real property for damages for injuries done to the property which impaired the mortgage security and that action for an injunction would lie to restrain the commission of waste on the premises. It was this cause of action that was codified in 1872 as Civil Code section 2929.

Section 2929 of the Civil Code, though referring only to "the lien of a *mortgage*" (italics added) and to the impairment of "the *mortgagee's* security," (italics added) applies equally to a deed of trust, since a mortgage with power of sale and a deed of trust are treated similarly in California and both are considered as security interests protected from impairment. The statute imposes a duty not to commit waste upon any "person whose interest is subject to the lien." Although a nonassuming grantee of mortgaged property is not personally liable on the debt, his interest in the property is subject to the lien and therefore he is under a duty not to impair the mortgagee's security. Defendant as a nonassuming grantee of the property subject to plaintiff's deed of trust was under a duty not to commit waste.

Defendant contends, however, that assuming arguendo that he was under a duty not to commit waste and that his acts or omissions constituted waste by so materially impairing the value of the property as to render it inadequate security for the mortgage debt, nevertheless plaintiff is not entitled to recover because such recovery for waste would amount to a deficiency judgment proscribed by sections 580b[5] and 580d[6] of the Code of Civil Procedure. In order to resolve this contention it is necessary to briefly summarize the array of legislation in the field of secured transactions in real property spawned by the depression of the 1930's.

Prior to 1933, a mortgagee of real property was required to exhaust his security before enforcing the debt or otherwise to waive all right to his security. However, having resorted to the security, whether by judicial sale or private nonjudicial sale, the mortgagee could obtain a deficiency judgment against the mortgagor for the difference between the amount of the indebtedness and the amount realized from the sale. As a consequence during the great depression with its dearth of money and declining property values, a mortgagee was able to purchase the subject real property at the foreclosure sale at a depressed price far below its normal fair market value and thereafter to obtain a double recovery by holding the debtor for a large deficiency. In order to counteract this situation, California in 1933 enacted fair market value limitations applicable to both judicial foreclosure sales (§ 726)[7] and

---

[5]   Section 580b provides in relevant part: "No deficiency judgment shall lie in any event after any sale of real property for failure of the purchaser to complete his contract of sale, or under a deed of trust, or mortgage, given to the vendor to secure payment of the balance of the purchase price of real property, or under a deed of trust, or mortgage, on a dwelling for not more than four families given to a lender to secure repayment of a loan which was in fact used to pay all or part of the purchase price of such dwelling occupied, entirely or in part, by the purchaser."

Hereafter, unless otherwise noted, all section references are to the Code of Civil Procedure.

[6]   Section 580d provides: "No judgment shall be rendered for any deficiency upon a note secured by a deed of trust or mortgage upon real property hereafter executed in any case in which the real property has been sold by the mortgagee or trustee under power of sale contained in such mortgage or deed of trust."

[7]   Section 726 provides in part: "In the event that a deficiency is not waived or prohibited and it is decreed that any defendant is personally liable for such debt, then upon application of the plaintiff filed at any time within three months of the date of the foreclosure sale and after a hearing thereon at which the court shall take evidence and at which hearing either party

private foreclosure sales (§ 580a)[8] which limited the mortgagee's deficiency judgment after exhaustion of the security to the difference between the fair value of the property at the time of the sale (irrespective of the amount actually realized at the sale) and the outstanding debt for which the property was security. Therefore, if, due to the depressed economic conditions, the property serving as security was sold for less than the fair value as determined under section 726 or section 580a, the mortgagee could not recover the amount of that difference in his action for a deficiency judgment.

In certain situations, however, the Legislature deemed even this partial deficiency too oppressive. Accordingly, in 1933 it enacted section 580b which barred deficiency judgments altogether on purchase money mortgages. "Section 580b places the risk of inadequate security on the purchase money mortgagee. A vendor is thus discouraged from overvaluing the security. Precarious land promotion schemes are discouraged, for the security value of the land gives purchasers a clue as to its true market value. If inadequacy of security results, not from overvaluing, but from a decline in property values during a general or local depression, section 580b prevents the aggravation of the downturn that would result if defaulting purchasers were burdened with large personal liability. Section 580b thus serves as a stabilizing factor in land sales." Roseleaf Corp. v. Cheirighino, supra, 59 Cal.2d 35, 42, 27 Cal.Rptr. 873, 877, 378 P.2d 97, 101.

Although both judicial foreclosure sales and private nonjudicial foreclosure sales provided for identical deficiency judgments in

---

may present evidence as to the fair value of the property or the interest therein sold as of the date of sale, the court shall render a money judgment against such defendant or defendants for the amount by which the amount of the indebtedness with interest and costs of sale and of action exceeds the fair value of the property or interest therein sold as of the date of sale; provided, however, that in no event shall the amount of said judgment, exclusive of interest from the date of sale and of costs exceed the difference between the amount for which the property was sold and the entire amount of the indebtedness secured by said mortgage or deed of trust."

8   Section 580a provides: "Whenever a money judgment is sought for the balance due upon an obligation for the payment of which a deed of trust or mortgage with power of sale upon real property or any interest therein was given as security, following the exercise of the power of sale in such deed of trust or mortgage, the plaintiff shall set forth in his complaint the entire amount of the indebtedness which was secured by said deed of trust or mortgage at the time of sale, the amount for which such real property or interest therein was sold and the fair market value thereof at the date of sale and the date of such sale. Upon the application of either party made at least ten days before the time of trial the court shall, and upon its own motion the court at any time may, appoint one of the inheritance tax appraisers provided for by law to appraise the property or the interest therein sold as of the time of sale. Such appraiser shall file his appraisal with the clerk and the same shall be admissible in evidence. . . . Before rendering any judgment the court shall find the fair market value of the real property, or interest therein sold, at the time of sale. The court may render judgment for not more than the amount by which the entire amount of the indebtedness due at the time of sale exceeded the fair market value of the real property or interest therein sold at the time of sale with interest thereon from the date of the sale; provided, however, that in no event shall the amount of said judgment, exclusive of interest after the date of sale, exceed the difference between the amount for which the property was sold and the entire amount of the indebtedness secured by said deed of trust or mortgage. Any such action must be brought within three months of the time of sale under such deed of trust or mortgage. No judgment shall be rendered in any such action until the real property or interest therein has first been sold pursuant to the terms of such deed of trust or mortgage, unless such real property or interest therein has become valueless."

nonpurchase money situations subsequent to the 1933 enactment of the fair value limitations, one significant difference remained, namely property sold through judicial foreclosure was subject to the statutory right of redemption (§ 725a), while property sold by private foreclosure sale was not redeemable. By virtue of sections 725a and 701, the judgment debtor, his successor in interest or a junior lienor could redeem the property at any time during one year after the sale, frequently by tendering the sale price. The effect of this right of redemption was to remove any incentive on the part of the mortgagee to enter a low bid at the sale (since the property could be redeemed for that amount) and to encourage the making of a bid approximating the fair market value of the security. However, since real property purchased at a private foreclosure sale was not subject to redemption, the mortgagee by electing this remedy, could gain irredeemable title to the property by a bid substantially below the fair value and still collect a deficiency judgment for the difference between the fair value of the security and the outstanding indebtedness.

In 1940 the Legislature placed the two remedies, judicial foreclosure sale and private nonjudicial foreclosure sale on a parity by enacting section 580d. Section 580d bars "any deficiency judgment" following a private foreclosure sale. "It seems clear that section 580d was enacted to put judicial enforcement on a parity with private enforcement. This result could be accomplished by giving the debtor a right to redeem after a sale under the power. The right to redeem, like proscription of a deficiency judgment, has the effect of making the security satisfy a realistic share of the debt. By choosing instead to bar a deficiency judgment after private sale, the Legislature achieved its purpose without denying the creditor his election of remedies. If the creditor wishes a deficiency judgment, his sale is subject to statutory redemption rights. If he wishes a sale resulting in nonredeemable title, he must forego the right to a deficiency judgment. In either case the debtor is protected." (Roseleaf v. Chierighino, supra, 59 Cal.2d 35, 43–44, 27 Cal.Rptr. 873, 878, 378 P.2d 97, 102.)

In the case at bench, we are now called upon to determine the effect of this antideficiency legislation upon the statutory action for waste. (Civ.Code, § 2929.) It will be recalled that damages in an action for waste are measured by the amount of injury to the security caused by the mortgagor's acts, that is by the substantial harm which "impair[s] the value of the property subject to the lien so as to render it an inadequate security for the mortgage debt." (Robinson v. Russell, supra, 24 Cal. 467, 473.) A deficiency judgment is a personal judgment against the debtor-mortgagor for the difference between the fair market value of the property held as security and the outstanding indebtedness. (§ 726.) It is clear that the two judgments against the mortgagor, one for waste and the other for a deficiency, are closely interrelated and may often reflect identical amounts. If property values in general are declining, a deficiency judgment and a judgment for waste would be identical up to the point at which the harm caused by the mortgagor is equal to or less than the general decline in property values resulting from market conditions. When waste is committed in a depressed market, a deficiency judgment, although reflecting the amount of the waste, will of course exceed it if the decline of property values is greater. However, when waste is committed in a rising market, there will be no deficiency judgment, unless the property was originally overvalued; in this event, there would be no damages for waste unless the impairment due to waste exceeded the general increase in property values.

Mindful of the foregoing, we now proceed to arrive at an assessment of the effect of sections 580b and 580d upon an action for waste. First, we examine the 580b proscription of a deficiency judgment after any foreclosure sale, private or judicial, of property securing a purchase money mortgage. The primary purpose of section 580b is "in the event of a depression in land values, to prevent the aggravation of the downturn that would result if defaulting purchasers lost the land and were burdened with personal liability." (Bargioni v. Hill, 59 Cal.2d 121, 123, 28 Cal.Rptr. 321, 322, 378 P.2d 593, 594.) It is clear that allowing an action for waste following a foreclosure sale of property securing purchase money mortgages may often frustrate this purpose. Damages for waste would burden the defaulting purchaser with both loss of land and personal liability and the acts giving rise to that liability would have been caused in many cases by the economic downturn itself. For example, a purchaser caught in such circumstances may be compelled in the normal course of events to forego the general maintenance and repair of the property in order to keep up his payments on the mortgage debt. If he eventually defaults and loses the property, to hold him subject to additional liability for waste would seem to run counter to the purpose of section 580b and to permit the purchase money lender to obtain what is in effect a deficiency judgment. It is of course true that not all owners of real property subject to a purchase money mortgage commit waste solely or primarily as a result of the economic pressures of a market depression; indeed many are reckless, intentional, and at times even malicious despoilers of property. In these latter circumstances to which we shall refer for convenience as waste committed in bad faith, the purchase money lender should not go remediless since they do not involve the type of risk intended to be borne by him in promoting the objectives of section 580b alluded to above.

Accordingly, we hold that section 580b should apply to bar recovery in actions for waste following foreclosure sale in the first instance but should not so apply in the second instance of "bad faith" waste. We further hold that it is within the province of the trier of fact to determine on a case by case basis to what, if any, extent the impairment of the mortgagee's security has been caused (as in the first instance) by the general decline of real property values and to what, if any, extent (as in the second instance) by the bad faith acts of the mortgagor, such determination, in either instance, being subject to review under the established rule of appellate review.

We now turn to assess the effect upon an action for waste of section 580d which applies to a nonpurchase money mortgage. We are satisfied that a different analysis must be pursued. It will be recalled from our earlier discussion that the Legislature intended to establish parity between judicial foreclosure and private foreclosure by denying a deficiency judgment subsequent to a private sale. Under a judicial foreclosure, the mortgagee is entitled to a deficiency judgment, but must bear the burden of a statutory redemption; under a private sale the mortgagee need not bear the burden of redemption, but cannot recover any deficiency judgment. If following a nonjudicial sale the mortgagee were allowed to obtain a judgment for damages for waste against the mortgagor, he would have the double benefits of an irredeemable title to the property and a personal judgment against the mortgagor for the impairment of the value of the property. This would essentially destroy the parity between judicial foreclosure and private foreclosure in all instances where the waste is actually caused by general economic conditions, since as we have explained, such recovery is in effect a deficiency judgment. If, however, the recovery is limited to waste committed in "bad faith," then the personal judgment would be entirely independent of the problems encompassed by the antideficiency legislation and would not affect the parity of remedies. Accordingly, we hold that in situations arising under section 580d, recovery for waste against the mortgagor following nonjudicial foreclosure sale is barred by the section's proscription against deficiency judgments when the waste actually results from the depressed condition of the general real estate market but not when the waste is caused by the "bad faith" acts of the mortgagor.

While our foregoing conclusion may expose defendant to liability on the basis of having committed "bad faith" waste, the question need not be resolved. We have further concluded that even assuming that defendant is liable on such basis, nevertheless plaintiff cannot recover since she purchased the subject property at the trustee's sale by making a full credit bid. As stated previously, the measure of damages for waste is the amount of the impairment of the security, that is the amount by which the value of the security is less than the outstanding indebtedness and is thereby rendered inadequate. The point of defendant's argument is that the mortgagee's purchase of the property securing the debt by entering a full credit bid establishes the value of the security as being equal to the outstanding indebtedness and ipso facto the nonexistence of any impairment of the security. As applied to the factual context of the instant case, the argument is that the purchase by plaintiff-vendor-beneficiary of the property covered by the purchase money deed of trust pursuant to a full credit bid made and accepted at the nonjudicial foreclosure sale resulted in a total satisfaction of the secured obligation. We agree.

. . . If the beneficiary or mortgagee at the foreclosure sale enters a bid for the full amount of the obligation owing to him together with the costs and fees due in connection with the sale, he cannot recover damages for waste, since he cannot establish any impairment of security, the lien of the deed of trust or mortgage having been theretofore extinguished by his full credit bid and all his security interest in the property thereby nullified. If, however, he bids less than the full amount of the obligation and thereby acquires the property valued at less than the full amount, his security has been impaired and he may recover damages for waste in an amount not exceeding the difference between the amount of his bid and the full amount of the outstanding indebtedness immediately prior to the foreclosure sale.

Plaintiff complains that it is difficult to calculate precisely the amount of damages recoverable for waste so as to determine the proper amount which the beneficiary or mortgagee should bid at the foreclosure sale; therefore, she urges it is unfair to impose such a burden on the beneficiary or mortgagee. Suffice it to say that no complicated calculations are necessary. The beneficiary or mortgagee need only enter a credit bid in an amount equal to what he assesses the fair market value of the property to be in its condition at the time of the foreclosure sale. If that amount is below the full amount of the outstanding indebtedness and he is successful in acquiring the property at the foreclosure sale, he may then recover any provable damages for waste.

To recapitulate, we conclude that the trial court properly granted summary judgment in favor of defendant and against plaintiff (1) as to the first cause of action for breach of contract since defendant at no time assumed the underlying indebtedness; and (2) as to the second cause of action for waste since, although defendant as a nonassuming grantee could be held liable for waste if proved to have been committed in bad faith, nevertheless plaintiff can establish no impairment of security, having acquired the property at the foreclosure sale by making a full credit bid.

The judgment is affirmed.

WRIGHT, C. J., and MCCOMB, TOBRINER, MOSK, CLARK and RICHARDSON, JJ., concur.

NOTES

1. *Statutory Schemes. Cornelison* suggests the variety of approaches available to states that wish to regulate deficiency judgments. In addition to an outright prohibition on deficiency recoveries, a state may limit mortgagor liability by imposing fair value limitations, statutory redemption periods or procedural safeguards on sale. *Cornelison* also suggests the variety of policies that lie behind these rules. One policy is to protect homeowners against the immediate burdens of economic collapse. Another is to spread the risk of dramatic decline in real property values between property owners and secured lenders or, in the case of purchase money mortgages, between land sellers and land buyers. The California scheme discussed in *Cornelison* is unusual only in combining so many rules and policies in a single system. In 2013 California extended antideficiency protection in section 580b to refinancing mortgages to the extent that the proceeds are used to pay off a purchase money loan on the premises. Cal. Code Civ. Proc. § 580b(c).

Should a mortgagor be permitted to waive the protections of the antideficiency statute? Consider the policies behind antideficiency statutes and the policies supporting waivers. See Brunsoman v. Scarlett, 465 N.W.2d 162 (N.D.1991) (waiver not permitted before default but permitted after default as long as waiver is clear, unequivocal, and unambiguous).

For a thoughtful and comprehensive examination of issues in the field generally, see Washburn, The Judicial and Legislative Response to Price Inadequacy in Mortgage Foreclosure Sales, 53 So.Cal.L.Rev. 843 (1980). See also Schill, An Economic Analysis of Mortgagor Protection Laws, 77 Va.L.Rev. 489 (1991); Jones, Deficiency Judgments and the Exercise of the Default Option in Home Mortgage Loans, 36 J.L. & Econ. 115 (1993).

2.   *Type of Foreclosure.* Should deficiency judgments after judicial and nonjudicial sales be treated differently? In Manoog v. Miele, 350 Mass. 204, 213 N.E.2d 917 (1966), the Massachusetts Supreme Judicial Court considered whether a mortgagee should as a matter of law be barred from recovering a deficiency judgment because of its behavior before and at its nonjudicial sale. Nineteen days before the sale, the mortgagee contracted to sell the land to a third party for $45,000. Contract performance was, of course, conditioned on the mortgagee's success in acquiring the property at sale. At the sale, the mortgagee acquired the property on a bid of $40,000— $5,000 less than the face amount of the mortgagor's note. After trial, a jury held that the mortgagee was further entitled to $5,488.67 from the mortgagor, the sum of the unpaid balance on the note, interest, taxes and the costs of sale, with credits for rents received by the mortgagee prior to the sale.

Ruling for the mortgagee, the court agreed with the lower court that the question of the mortgagee's good faith in failing to disclose the $45,000 purchase price to the mortgagor before the sale was a question of fact, not law, for the jury to decide. In its view, the lower court had properly instructed the jury that "[w]hen, as was the fact here, 'a mortgagee . . . is both seller and buyer, his position is one of great delicacy. Yet, when he has done his full duty to the mortgagor in his conduct of the sale under the power, and the bidding begins, in his capacity as bidder a mortgagee may buy as cheaply as he can, and owes no duty to bid the full value of the property as that value may subsequently be determined by a judge or a jury.'" 350 Mass. at 206, 213 N.E.2d at 919.

In the circumstances, would a "fair value" requirement have served the mortgagor's interests better than the imposition of a good faith standard on the mortgagee? Is "fair value" intended to reflect the price the market will pay, or the price the community or jury thinks is fair? Consider New York's attempt to finesse the question: "the fair and reasonable market value of the mortgaged premises as of the date such premises were bid in at auction or such nearest earlier date as there shall have been any market value thereof. . . ." N.Y.R.P.A.P.L. § 1371(2) (McKinney 1979). In San Paolo U.S. Holding Co. v. 816 South Figueroa Co., 62 Cal.App.4th 1010, 73 Cal.Rptr.2d 272 (1998), the court held that "fair value" is the fair market value of the realty on the date of the foreclosure sale, without adjustment down for the negative effects caused by the fact that the property was in foreclosure and the fact that the property was subject to a one-year redemption right.

3.   *Waste.* Reconsider the examples that *Cornelison* gave of the types of waste it would not consider actionable. Is it clear that impairment in these cases stems from the "general decline of real property values"? As a practical matter, would the court have done better to rely on the common law distinction between permissive waste, for which apparently the decision would not have allowed recovery, and affirmative waste, for which it would?

Did *Cornelison* establish a rule on the availability of the action for waste generally, or only a rule on remedies? What if, before foreclosure, the mortgagee sought a mandatory injunction requiring the mortgagor to keep the premises in good repair? What if the mortgage required the mortgagor to contribute a fixed monthly sum toward keeping the premises in good repair? How would such a provision differ from one in which the mortgagor waives his immunity from an action for waste? From an express waiver of immunity from a deficiency judgment?

How would *Cornelison* treat the nonpayment of taxes? Would it matter if the owner had the cash on hand but did not pay the taxes in order to avoid sinking more funds into a troubled property? See Nippon Credit Bank, Ltd. v. 1333 No. California Blvd., 86 Cal.App.4th 486, 103 Cal.Rptr.2d 421 (2001).

On waste generally, see Restatement of Mortgages § 4.6; Leipziger, The Mortgagee's Remedies for Waste, 64 Calif.L.Rev. 1086 (1976). On the issue of insurance coverage for sudden destruction of the property as opposed to negligent or willful degradation by the mortgagor, see Randolph, A Mortgagee's Interest in Casualty Loss Proceeds: Evolving Rules and Risks, 32 Real Prop. Probate & Tr. J. 1 (1997).

4. *One-Form-of-Action and One-Action Rules.* Can an undersecured mortgagee circumvent a state's fair value or other antideficiency limitations by proceeding first against the mortgagor personally on the note and then, to the extent the personal judgment is unsatisfied, by foreclosing on the real property security and applying the sale proceeds to the remainder of the debt? Although the mortgagee would not be allowed a double recovery, the strategy might still seem unfair to those who believe that creditors who seek security for their loans should be obligated to proceed against the security first.

A handful of states require the mortgagee to proceed against the real property securing the debt before obtaining a final judgment in a personal action on the note. Cal.Civ.Proc.Code § 726 (West 1980 & Supp.1992); Idaho Code § 6–101 (1990); Mont.Code Ann. § 71–1–222 (1991); Utah Code Ann. § 78–37–1 (1987). If the mortgagor fails to raise this rule as a defense on the note, she will suffer a personal judgment. However, she can later prevent the mortgagee from proceeding against the real property on the ground that, by proceeding first on the note, the mortgagee effectively elected that as its exclusive remedy. See Walker v. Community Bank, 10 Cal.3d 729, 111 Cal.Rptr. 897, 518 P.2d 329 (1974).

The rule is sometimes called a "one-form-of-action" rule to connote that a mortgagee seeking enforcement of a real estate secured obligation must bring a foreclosure action, and is sometimes called a "one-action" rule because the mortgagee must proceed against the security and for a deficiency judgment in a single action. Typically, the statutes contemplate that the first stage of the proceeding will involve foreclosure and sale of the property. At the second stage, the court will determine whether any deficiency exists and enter a personal judgment accordingly.

One-action rules create as many pitfalls for lenders as they do safeguards for borrowers. Say that your client, bank, has learned that one of its customers is in default on its credit card obligations to the bank. How would you counsel the bank to proceed if you knew that it had earlier made a loan to the same customer secured by a real property mortgage, and that the mortgage contained a dragnet clause of the sort described at page 380 above? Would you ever advise your lender client to take real property as security for a loan when it is clear at the time of the loan that the security is worth much less than the principal amount of the debt? What might other creditors be doing to the debtor's general assets while the lender is making its way through the required foreclosure proceedings?

For a discussion of sanctions against a lender for violating the one action rule, see Security Pacific National Bank v. Wozab, 51 Cal.3d 991, 275 Cal.Rptr. 201, 800 P.2d 557 (1990); Comment, The Sanction For Violation of California's One-Action Rule, 79 Cal.L.Rev. 1601 (1991).

5. *Other Equitable Relief.* In special circumstances, some courts might go beyond specific statutory protections for mortgagors, such as statutory redemption rights and protection against deficiency judgments, and rely on general equitable principles to set aside a foreclosure sale if the price is so low as to "shock the conscience of the court." See Crown Life Insurance Company v. Candlewood, Ltd., 112 N.M. 633, 818 P.2d 411 (1991) (where price at sale was only 15% to 23% of property's fair market value, court's conscience was "shocked").

6. *U.L.S.I.A.* The Uniform Land Security Interest Act follows majority rules in most instances but takes a few less popular paths as well. Following the majority approach to lender's election of remedies, section 501 allows the lender to proceed against the property and on the note in any order that it chooses, rejecting the "one-action" rule. Section 513 allows no right to redeem after sale, and section 511 provides that if "the debtor is a protected party and the obligation secured is a purchase money security interest, there is no liability for a deficiency notwithstanding any agreement of the protected party." Section 507 gives the secured creditor three remedies after default: the self-help remedy of deed in lieu of foreclosure; judicial sale; and, if the mortgage agreement allows it, foreclosure by nonjudicial sale.

Section 503 departs from the rule on possession applied in lien theory states and adopts the intermediate theory position instead. It provides that, except as to a protected party debtor in possession, a secured creditor can take possession on default and before foreclosure. Behind this departure was the policy decision to reduce the cost of foreclosure. "A provision giving the creditor a right to take possession after default without the intervention of the expensive receivership process is one step in carrying out this policy." Comment 1 to Section 503. See generally, Mixon & Shepard, Antideficiency Relief for Foreclosed Homeowners: ULSIA Section 511(b), 27 Wake Forest L.Rev. 455 (1992).

See Bernhardt, ULSIA's Remedies on Default—Worth the Effort?, 24 Conn.L.Rev. 1001 (1992).

E. FINANCING THROUGH THE LAND SALE CONTRACT

Comment, Forfeiture: The Anomaly of the Land Sale Contract
41 Albany Law Review 71, 72–79 (1977).

An elderly couple in Binghamton, unable to obtain a conventional mortgage, bought their home under a land sale contract. Nine years later, experiencing temporary financial problems, they fell a month behind in their payments. As a result, they lost the home and all they had invested in it.

A mother of three, on welfare, could not resist the opportunity to be a homeowner and signed a land contract to purchase a run-down home in Schenectady. After four years of meeting her monthly payments and repairing the heating and plumbing at great expense, she became unable to meet her monthly installments. Consequently, she forfeited not only all the installments made, but the money she had invested in improvements.

A farmer from western New York, having bought his farm eleven years before through a land sale contract, had always been late with his payments during the spring, when his income was its lowest and his expenses the highest. In January he received a notice from his seller that this lateness would no longer be tolerated. This spring the farmer lost the land and eleven years of installments when the seller refused to accept his late payments.

These buyers, and many others like them, saw only an unprecedented opportunity to become landowners. Usually unrepresented, they were ignorant of the many hazards that loomed throughout the life of a land sale contract.

I.   INTRODUCTION

The land sale contract is a low equity arrangement for the purchase of real property. Although in years past the land contract has not been a widespread method of purchasing realty in the Northeast, it is presently becoming more common in various sections of New York, either in the form of the traditional land contract or a variant of it, the lease-buy option. Despite its new-found popularity the land contract contains many inherent inequities. Specifically, the laws of New York give land contract purchasers conspicuously little relief; they face upon default the grievous predicament of forfeiting their entire investment. Unlike many other jurisdictions, New York has not adopted legislation equipping the land sale contract with the standard safeguards that surround the mortgage.

The land sale contract, in contrast to a mortgage or trust deed, does not secure a loan or forbear the payment of money. Rather, the land contract is an installment sales contract, providing for periodic payment of the purchase price, often in monthly installments. Unlike mortgagees in New York, the land sale contract seller retains legal title to the realty to secure full and final payment. Although these contracts almost universally grant immediate possession of the property to the purchaser throughout the execution of the contract, possession is not an automatic right of the purchaser, and must be provided for in the contract. The basic attraction of the land contract to the seller is the ease and economy by which the purchaser's interest may be eliminated in the event of his default. Since the purchaser, unlike the mortgagor, has no right of redemption or sale, the seller may avoid the costly and time-consuming foreclosure proceedings mandated under a mortgage. Instead, he simply retains the installments and terminates the purchaser's interest. The seller may receive additional protection through the inclusion of such devices as an acceleration clause and provisions which make the purchaser responsible for paying the taxes, insuring the premises and keeping them in good repair. These factors make the land contract more attractive to the seller than the purchase money mortgage and may explain the present popularity of the land contract among sellers.

Nevertheless, from the perspective of the low-income purchaser the land sale contract is a realistic and often essential mechanism for low-equity land acquisition. It enables low-income families to penetrate the housing market without first accumulating the substantial downpayment which is often impossible for them to amass. The alternative means of financing are rarely available to this economic class of New Yorkers by virtue of the present high requisite mortgage loan to value ratio and the poor credit ratings of the purchasers. Currently, a downpayment of 20–35% of the purchase price is required to obtain a mortgage from a lending institution. Even if a potential buyer were able to save such a sum, the time required to do so would be unrealistically long. The potential buyers of low-income housing are considered high credit risks, thus making it virtually impossible for them to obtain financing from conventional lending institutions. As a result of this credit rating and the frequent location of the property in high risk areas, the Federal Housing Authority has been reluctant to insure mortgages for these low-income buyers. The purchaser's only alternative is to obtain financing with the seller, who is unlikely to grant a purchase money mortgage with little or no downpayment, especially in light of the advantages of a land sale contract. . . .

The seller under a land sale contract retains legal title to the property as security against the purchaser's nonperformance during the term of the contract. The extent of the seller's interest and control is attested to by his ability to convey the property to a bona fide third party purchaser, his standing to maintain an action in waste against the purchaser in possession, and his creditors' ability to levy against his interest. In addition, courts have held that the seller has an equitable lien on the property as security against the buyer's nonperformance, regardless of whether that lien is provided for in the contract. To call the vendor's security interest a lien seems a misnomer in view of the fact that he actually retains legal title to the property. It would be more accurate to maintain that the seller may enforce his interest in the property as a lien, rather than to insist that his interest is itself a lien.

Problems also persist in evaluating the purchaser's interest. The commentators universally maintain that a land contract operates as an equitable conversion, making the purchaser the equitable owner of the land while the seller holds the legal title in trust for the purchaser. . . .

The purchaser's rights also include an equitable lien on the land for those payments already made, enforceable upon the seller's default only if the purchaser is ready to perform. Usually the lien is limited to the payments made and does not encompass the loss of a bargain, the expenses incurred in examining title or the costs of any improvement made by the purchaser. Since the lien is equitable, it is extinguished if the vendee is in default, regardless of any breach by the seller.

Both the seller's interest—legal title held as security against the purchaser's default—and the purchaser's interest—equitable ownership of the property—are protected and advanced by the various remedies available to each.

Skendzel v. Marshall

Supreme Court of Indiana, 1973.
261 Ind. 226, 301 N.E.2d 641,
cert. denied, 415 U.S. 921, 94 S.Ct. 1421, 39 L.Ed.2d 476.

HUNTER, JUSTICE.

Petitioners seek transfer to this Court as a result of an adverse ruling by the Court of Appeals. Plaintiff-respondents originally brought suit to obtain possession of certain real estate through the enforcement of a forfeiture clause in a land sale contract. Plaintiff-respondents suffered a negative judgment, from which they appealed. The Court of Appeals reversed, holding that the defendant-petitioners had breached the contract and that the plaintiff-respondents had not waived their right to enforce the forfeiture provisions of the contract.

In December of 1958, Mary Burkowski, as vendor, entered into a land sale contract with Charles P. Marshall and Agnes P. Marshall, as vendees. The contract provided for the sale of certain real estate for the sum of $36,000.00, payable as follows:

> "$500.00, at the signing, execution and delivery of this contract, the receipt whereof is hereby acknowledged; $500.00 or more on or before the 25th day of December, 1958, and $2500.00 or more on or before the 15th day of January, 1960, and $2500.00 or more on or before the 15th day of January of each and every year thereafter until the balance of the contract has been fully paid, all without interest and all without relief from valuation and appraisement laws and with attorney fees."

The contract also contained a fairly standard section which provided for the treatment of prepayments—but which the Court of Appeals found to be of particular importance. It provided as follows:

> "Should Vendees have made prepayments or paid in advance of the payments herein required, said prepayments, if any, shall at any time thereafter be applied in lieu of further principal payments required as herein stated, to the extent of such prepayments only."

The following is the forfeiture/liquidated damages provision of the land sale contract:

> "It is further agreed that if any default shall be made in the payment of said purchase price or any of the covenants and/or conditions herein provided, and if any such default shall continue for 30 days, then, after the lapse of said 30 days' period, *all moneys and payments previously paid shall, at the option of the Vendor without notice or demand, be and become forfeited and be taken and retained by the Vendor as liquidated damages* and thereupon this contract shall terminate and be of no further force or effect; provided, however, that nothing herein contained shall be deemed or construed to prevent the Vendor from enforcing specific performance of this agreement in the event of any default on the part of the Vendees in complying, observing and performing any of the conditions, covenants and terms herein contained. . . ." (Emphasis added.)

The vendor, Mary Burkowski, died in 1963. The plaintiffs in this action are the assignees (under the vendor's will) of the decedent's interests in the contract. They received their assignment from the executrix of the estate of the vendor on June 27, 1968. One year after this assignment, several of the assignees filed their complaint in this action alleging that the defendants had defaulted through nonpayment.

The schedule of payments made under this contract was shown by the evidence to be as follows:

"Date	Amount Paid	Total of Paid Principal
12/1/1958	$ 500.00	$ 500.00
12/25/1958	500.00	1,000.00
3/26/1959	5,000.00	6,000.00
4/5/1960	2,500.00	8,500.00
5/23/1961	2,500.00	11,000.00
4/6/1962	2,500.00	13,500.00
1/15/1963	2,500.00	16,000.00
6/30/1964	2,500.00	18,500.00
2/15/1965	2,500.00	21,000.00"

No payments have been made since the last one indicated above—$15,000.00 remains to be paid on the original contract price.

In response to the plaintiff's attempt to enforce the forfeiture provision, the defendants raised the affirmative defense of waiver. . . .

In essence, the Court of Appeals found that there was no waiver because the vendors were obligated to accept prepayment, and, "the payments made, although irregular in time and amount, were prepayments on the unpaid balance through and including the payment due on January 15, 1965." (289 N.E.2d at 771.) The Court concluded that up to January 15, 1966, "the vendors waived no rights under the contract, because they were obliged to accept prepayment," (Id.) and that, "[t]he vendors could not have insisted on forfeiture prior to January 15, 1966, the date of the first missed payment." (Id.) (We believe the Court of Appeals miscalculated here; the vendors could not have insisted on forfeiture until January 16, 1968.)

If forfeiture is enforced against the defendants, they will forfeit outright the sum of $21,000, or well over one-half the original contract price, as liquidated damages *plus possession*. Forfeitures are generally disfavored by the law. In fact, ". . . [e]quity abhors forfeitures and beyond any question has jurisdiction, which it will exercise in a proper case to grant relief against their enforcement." 30 C.J.S. Equity § 56 (1965) and cases cited therein. This jurisdiction of equity to intercede is predicated upon the fact that "the loss or injury occasioned by the default must be susceptible of exact compensation." 30 C.J.S., supra.

. . . "Reasonable" liquidated damage provisions are permitted by the law. However, the issue before this Court, is whether a $21,000 forfeiture is a "reasonable" measure of damages. If the damages are unreasonable, i.e., if they are disproportionate to the loss actually suffered, they must be characterized as penal rather than compensatory. Under the facts of this case, a $21,000 forfeiture is clearly excessive.

. . . The vendee has acquired a substantial interest in the property, which, if forfeited, would result in substantial injustice.

Under a typical conditional land contract, the vendor retains legal title until the total contract price is paid by the vendee. Payments are generally made in periodic installments. *Legal* title does not vest in the vendee until the contract terms are satisfied, but equitable title vests in the vendee at the time the contract is consummated. When the parties enter into the contract, all incidents of ownership accrue to the vendee. The vendee assumes the risk of loss and is the recipient of all appreciation in value. The vendee, as equitable owner, is responsible for taxes. Stark v. Kreyling (1934), 207 Ind. 128, 188 N.E. 680. The vendee has a sufficient interest in land so that upon sale of that interest, he holds a vendor's lien.

This Court has held, consistent with the above notions of equitable ownership, that a land contract, once consummated constitutes a present sale and purchase. The vendor " 'has, in effect, exchanged his property for the unconditional obligation of the vendee, the performance of which is secured by the retention of the legal title.' " Stark v. Kreyling, supra, 207 Ind. at 135, 188 N.E. at 682. The Court, in effect, views a conditional land contract as a sale with a security interest in the form of legal title reserved by the vendor. Conceptually, therefore, the retention of the title by the vendor is the same as reserving a lien or mortgage. Realistically, vendor-vendee should be viewed as mortgagee-mortgagor. To conceive of the relationship in different terms is to pay homage to form over substance.

The piercing of the transparent distinction between a land contract and a mortgage is not a phenomenon without precedent. In addition to the *Stark* case, supra, there is an abundance of case law from other jurisdictions which lends credence to the position that a land sales contract is in essence a mortgage.

. . . We believe there to be great wisdom in requiring judicial foreclosure of land contracts pursuant to the mortgage statute. Perhaps the most attractive aspect of judicial foreclosure is the period of redemption, during which time the vendee may redeem his interest, possibly through re-financing.

Forfeiture is closely akin to strict foreclosure—a remedy developed by the English courts which did not contemplate the equity of redemption. American jurisdictions, including Indiana, have, for the most part, rejected strict foreclosure in favor of foreclosure by judicial sale.

. . . A forfeiture—like a strict foreclosure at common law—is often offensive to our concepts of justice and inimical to the principles of equity. This is not to suggest that a forfeiture is an inappropriate remedy for the breach of all land contracts. In the case of an abandoning, absconding vendee, forfeiture is a logical and equitable remedy. Forfeiture would also be appropriate where the vendee has paid a minimal amount on the contract at the time of default and seeks to retain possession while the vendor is paying taxes, insurance, and other upkeep in order to preserve the premises. Of course, in this latter situation, the vendee will have acquired very little, if any, equity in the property. However, a court of equity must always approach forfeitures with great caution, being forever aware of the possibility of inequitable dispossession of property and exorbitant monetary loss. We are persuaded that forfeiture may only be appropriate under circumstances in which it is found to be consonant with notions of fairness and justice under the law.

In other words, we are holding a conditional land sales contract to be in the nature of a secured transaction, the provisions of which are subject to all proper and just remedies at law and in equity.

Turning our attention to the case at hand, we find that the vendor-assignees were seeking forfeiture, including $21,000 already paid on said contract as liquidated damages and immediate possession. They were, in fact, asking for strict application of the contract terms at law which we believe would have led to unconscionable results requiring the intervention of equity. . . .

For all of the foregoing reasons, transfer is granted and the cause is reversed and remanded with instructions to enter a judgment of foreclosure on the vendors' lien, pursuant to Trial Rule 69(C) and the mortgage foreclosure statute as modified by Trial Rule 69(C). Said judgment shall include an order for the payment of the unpaid principal balance due on said contract, together with interest at 8% per annum from the date of judgment. The order may also embrace any and all other proper and equitable relief that the court deems to be just, including the discretion to issue a stay of the judicial sale of the property, all pursuant to the provisions of Trial Rule 69(C). Such order shall be consistent with the principles and holdings developed within this opinion.

Reversed and remanded with instructions.

ARTERBURN, C. J., and DEBRULER and PRENTICE, JJ., concur in this opinion on the merits.

PRENTICE, J., filing an additional statement [which is omitted].

GIVAN, J., dissents.

Dirks v. Cornwell

Court of Appeals of Utah, 1988.
754 P.2d 946.

GARFF, JUDGE:

Defendant/appellant Goodwill requests reversal of an adverse summary judgment in a quiet title action and an order vacating the prior sale of the property in question.

On June 10, 1977, Alma and Wanda Butler purchased real property located in Roy, Utah. On May 15, 1978, the Butlers sold this property to Paul S. and Catherine L. Cornwell under a uniform real estate contract. The Cornwells recorded the contract on May 16, 1978.

On March 3, 1980, the Cornwells borrowed $38,000 from defendants Wilford W. and Dorothy P. Goodwill, executing a trust deed on the real property in their favor. Defendants recorded this trust deed on April 3, 1980.

The Cornwells failed to make their payments under the contract. On February 17, 1981, the Butlers notified the Cornwells that they were in default on the contract, and on March 4, 1981, they sent a notice of default and cancellation of contract to the Cornwells, which was recorded on March 12, 1981. The Butlers subsequently sold the real property to plaintiffs, Darwin and Jacqueline Dirks. They did not notify defendants of this sale because they were unaware of defendants' trust deed until March 20, 1981.

Approximately three years later, defendants became aware of the Butlers' resale of the real property to plaintiffs and the apparent loss of their security interest. At no time did they tender to the Butlers the money necessary to bring the Cornwells' contract current.

On March 16, 1984, plaintiffs filed a quiet title action based upon Utah Code Ann. § 78–40–1 (1986). On May 31, 1984, they filed a motion for summary judgment, which the trial court granted on September 7, 1984. The trial court entered a final decree quieting title in favor of plaintiffs on October 5, 1984.

Summary judgment is available and should be granted if there is no genuine issue of material fact and the moving party is entitled to judgment as a matter of law. Callioux v. Progressive Ins. Co., 745 P.2d 838, 840 (Utah Ct.App.1987); see also First Sec. Fin. v. Okland Ltd., 750 P.2d 195, 197 (Utah Ct.App.1988).

On undisputed facts, defendants appealed the judgment, raising two issues of law: (1) Is it the duty of one who takes by assignment an interest in a real estate contract as security for a loan to seek out and determine the status of his assignor's rights and obligations? (2) Did the repossession of the real property under the contract and the quiet title procedure constitute state action under the fourteenth amendment, thereby giving defendants a right to reasonable notice prior to the destruction of their security interest?

. . .

II

Duty of Assignee-Lender to Seek Out His Assignor's Rights and Obligations Under a Real Estate Contract

Under a real estate contract, the buyer has a mortgageable interest in the real property. When the buyer assigns his interest as security for a loan, the assignee-lender acquires a mortgage-like lien on the buyer's interest. Jack B. Parsons Companies v. Nield, 751 P.2d 1131, 1133 (Utah 1988); Lockhart Co. v. Anderson, 646 P.2d 678, 679–80 (Utah 1982); see also Rush v. Anestos, 104 Idaho 630, 661 P.2d 1229, 1233 (1983); Shindledecker v. Savage, 96 N.M. 42, 627 P.2d 1241, 1242 (1981); Sanders v. Ulrich, 250 Or. 414, 443 P.2d 231, 232 (1968). He does not, however, obtain an interest in the land per se, Rush, 661 P.2d at 1234, but becomes entitled to assert the buyer's rights under the contract, including the right to make any payments necessary to avoid default on the contract. Lockhart, 646 P.2d at 679–80; see also Shindledecker, 627 P.2d at 1243.

The assignee-lender takes nothing more by his assignment than his assignor, the buyer, has. Nield, 751 P.2d at 1133; Wiscombe v. Lockhart Co., 608 P.2d 236, 238 (Utah 1980); Sanders, 443 P.2d at 232. Thus, his interest in the contract is "limited by the amount of equity held by the [buyer] and [is] subject to continued performance under the contract." Shindledecker, 627 P.2d at 1242.

If the buyer defaults on the underlying real estate contract, the seller can retake the property and terminate the buyer's interest in it in accordance with the terms of the contract. See Shindledecker, 627 P.2d at 1243. Because such an event will have the effect of terminating the assignee-lender's interest in the contract, he must take appropriate action to protect his rights. See Estate of Brewer v. Iota Delta Chapter, 298 Or. 383, 692 P.2d 597, 601 (1984); Nield, 751 P.2d at 1133; Butler v. Wilkinson, 740 P.2d 1244, 1257 (Utah 1987); Wiscombe, 608 P.2d at 238.

In the present case, the Cornwells, buyers under a real estate contract, assigned their interest in the contract to defendants as security for a loan. Defendants thus obtained an equitable interest in the property limited by the amount of the Cornwell's equity, but subject to extinguishment in the event the Cornwells defaulted on the contract, which they did. The Butlers then cancelled the contract terminating both the Cornwells' and defendants' interests.[2] See generally Wiscombe, 608 P.2d at 236.

At issue is whether or not the Butlers were required to notify defendants of the Cornwells' default so that defendants could preserve their interest by tendering payment according to the terms of the contract.

Utah case law indicates that the Butlers had no such obligation. This very issue, under indistinguishable facts, was first addressed in Jeffs v. Citizens Fin. Co., 7 Utah 2d 106, 319 P.2d 858 (1958), and, more recently, in Wiscombe v. Lockhart Co., 608 P.2d at 236. It was most recently addressed in Jack B. Parson Companies v. Nield, 751 P.2d 1131 (Utah 1988).

In *Jeffs,* the assignee-lender, like defendants, argued that a uniform real estate contract cannot be terminated without giving the purchaser and his assignee notice of intention to forfeit and a reasonable time in which to cure. The court found that the seller was not required to notify the assignee-lender, but that the assignee had the duty of notifying the seller of his interest in the contract. Jeffs, 319 P.2d at 859. The court stated:

> In our opinion it is no answer to say that giving notice to the seller, either actual or constructive, places the burden on him to seek out one with whom he had no dealing, and volunteer

---

[2] In this case, the Cornwells and defendants used a trust deed rather than an actual assignment document to memorialize defendants' security interest. Their use of that document, even with recordation, does not change the fact that the security interest attached only to the Cornwells' interest, as contract buyers, in the real property. The trust deed effected no more than an assignment of the Cornwells' contract rights as security for the loan extended by defendants.

facts so that an assignee of a real estate contract securing a loan may elect whether to perform the real estate contract or not. . . .

Requiring diligence on the part of one holding a real estate contract securing a loan, under a sort of pledge, to seek out and determine the status of his assignor's contractual rights and obligations by way of request, discovery procedure or otherwise, and to require him to make a tender of full performance which his assignor has failed to effectuate does not seem to us to place an unreasonable burden on the lender who desires to protect the consideration for which the contract was assigned or pledged.

Id.

The *Wiscombe* court, relying upon *Jeffs,* found that the seller had no duty to inform an assignee-lender of the termination of the real estate contract which secured the assignee-lender's loan to the buyer. Wiscombe, 608 P.2d at 238. The *Nield* court found similarly. Nield, 751 P.2d at 1133.

Defendants' attempt to distinguish *Wiscombe* fails because they misread the *Wiscombe* facts. They state that defendants "obtained their security interest *before the foreclosure took place,* whereas in *Wiscombe,* the security interest was obtained some three weeks after the assignor no longer had an interest to assign." In fact, the lenders in *Wiscombe* obtained their security interest prior to the foreclosure. The *Wiscombe* lenders then unsuccessfully attempted to tender payments according to the terms of the contract three weeks after the contract had been terminated. Wiscombe, 608 P.2d at 238.

Defendants argue that recordation of their assignment gave the Butlers constructive notice. However, under *Jeffs, Wiscombe,* and *Nield,* recordation of the assignment is immaterial. The *Wiscombe* court found that the assignee-lender's recordation of its assignment did not place a duty on Wiscombe, the seller, to notify the assignee-lender of the default and subsequent action to terminate the contract. Wiscombe, 608 P.2d at 238.

The *Nield* court found that, even though the assignee had recorded his assignment, "because it had no actual notice of the assignment to [the assignee], [the seller] was under no legal obligation to inform [the assignee] that [the assignor] had agreed . . . to terminate the contract and extinguish its interest." Nield, 751 P.2d at 1133. See also Shindledecker, 627 P.2d at 1243; *Davis v. Rede Realty, Inc.,* 41 Wash.App. 527, 704 P.2d 1250, 1251 (1985); Kendrick v. Davis, 75 Wash.2d 456, 452 P.2d 222, 228 (1969).

Thus, we sustain the trial court and find that the Butlers did not have a duty to inform defendants of the Cornwells' default and the termination of their contract.

[Court's holding that there was inadequate state action to find violation of due process omitted.]

. . .

The trial court's judgment is affirmed. Defendants are assessed costs.

BILLINGS and ORME, JJ., concur.

NOTES

1. *Protecting the Vendee Against Forfeitures.* Courts and legislatures have employed several devices to protect the installment land contract buyer against forfeiture of his accumulated equity. Courts will sometimes protect buyers by minimizing their defaults and finding that they have substantially performed. Another judicial technique is to construe seller nonaction as waiver of any claim based on the buyer's default. Courts may also limit the seller's remedial alternatives to foreclosure of the vendor's lien, or hold that the forfeited sum constitutes an unlawful penalty or improperly liquidated damages.

The Restatement of Mortgages adopts the position of Skendzel v. Marshall, which remains a minority view, and treats installment contracts as mortgages. § 3.4. Forfeiture is prohibited and foreclosure required. See Nelson, The Contract for Deed as a Mortgage: The Case for the Restatement Approach, 1998 B.Y.U.L. Rev. 1111.

The most common legislative response to perceived seller overreaching has been to engraft mortgage law's debtor protection provisions onto installment land contracts. For example, some states mandate a grace period during which the buyer can cure his default. See Iowa Code Ann. § 656.4 (Supp.1983). Oklahoma treats installment land contracts as mortgages generally. See Okla.Stat.Ann. tit. 16, § 11A (West 1986); see also U.L.S.I.A. § 102(b). Other state legislatures have taken more innovative approaches. Maryland, for example, entitles an installment buyer who has paid 40% or more of the contract price to receive a deed to the land in return for giving the seller a mortgage for the balance of the contract price owed; the "periodic principal and interest payments required by the mortgage may not exceed the periodic principal and interest payments otherwise required by the land installment contract, except with the consent of the mortgagor." Md. Real Prop. Code Ann., § 10–105 (1981).

2. *Application of Mortgage Law.* *Skendzel* reflects the contemporary trend to incorporate mortgage law's debtor-protection provisions into installment land contracts. Although some language in *Skendzel* suggests an intention to fully incorporate these provisions, the last paragraph of the opinion suggests that the court may only have meant to bar vendor relief through forfeiture. Note, though, that the court's instruction to the lower court to enter a judgment foreclosing the vendor's lien also allowed the lower court order to embrace "any and all other proper and equitable relief that the court deems to be just. . . ." Would it have been appropriate for such an order to allow the buyer to redeem from the foreclosure sale within a prescribed period? Does the *Skendzel* court give adequate guidance to lenders as to when forfeiture is permitted or foreclosure required?

Courts will not necessarily apply foreclosure law to all installment sale contracts. In Grombone v. Krekel, 754 P.2d 777 (Colo.App.1988), the court emphasized that a court has discretion to either treat an installment contract as a mortgage or to permit forfeiture. Factors include the amount of the buyer's equity in the property, the length and willfulness of the default, and whether improvements were made and the property maintained. On the facts, the appellate court upheld the trial court's decision not to require foreclosure:

Here, the trial court found that the defendants defaulted on virtually all of their contract obligations and made no attempt to cure such defaults despite plaintiffs' repeated demands. The record shows that, although defendants were credited with a down payment of approximately $35,000, they actually made only four monthly payments, and then failed to make any further payments. Their total equity was slightly more than 10 percent of the purchase price. The defendants failed to pay taxes, insurance, and sewer and water charges. The record also shows that, during the time defendants were in possession, they made no improvements to the property; instead, they allowed the property to deteriorate to such a degree that all of the tenants moved out.

Id. at 779. Colorado codified its approach in 1998. Colo. Rev. Stat. § 38–38–305. See Paraguay Place-View Trust v. Gray, 981 P.2d 681 (Colo.App.1999).

3. *Policy Considerations.* Is it good public policy for legislatures to recast installment land contracts and thus limit the forms through which buyers and sellers can structure residential finance? The traditional installment land contract does, to be sure, leave room for an overreaching seller to take advantage of an unsuspecting buyer. But it may also offer buyers and sellers the opportunity to strike a mutually beneficial bargain on terms that would otherwise be unavailable to either. For the seller, the installment land contract may offer a higher sales price than she could otherwise obtain, well-secured by the speedy remedy of forfeiture and enhanced by the favorable income tax treatment that I.R.C. § 453 gives to gain on installment sales. See pages 979–981 below. For the financially strapped buyer, the installment land contract may offer the opportunity to purchase a house with a lower down payment than would be required by institutional mortgage financing and with monthly payments no higher than the rent he would have to pay for equivalent housing. See Freyfogle, Vagueness and the Rule of Law: Reconsidering Installment Land Contract Forfeitures, 1988 Duke L.J. 609, for an excellent analysis of the costs due to vagueness which have resulted from judicial intervention to prevent forfeitures and examining the inadequacy of installment contract remedies.

The installment buyer's bargain is even better in inflationary times and in a rising real estate market. For little money down, the buyer essentially acquires an option, renewable over the term of the contract, to acquire the parcel for a price fixed in terms of values that prevailed at the time the contract was entered into, and with all option payments credited against the purchase price. Rising real property values will also significantly meliorate the risk of forfeiture. Once the parcel's value increases by more than 20%, the buyer can use his equity in the property to refinance the purchase with 80% financing from a third party institutional lender. For example, if the contract price is $30,000 and the buyer has paid the principal balance down $3,000 in the first two years of a ten-year contract, the property need only appreciate about 6% each year over that period (from $30,000 to $33,750) since 80% financing on $33,750 will produce the $27,000 that the temporarily embarrassed buyer needs to pay off the contract and avoid forfeiture.

4. *Protecting Buyer Against Creditors and Successors of Seller.* Under traditional priority rules, the interest of an installment contract buyer will be subordinate to any mortgage or other lien on the parcel previously given by the seller. Although existence of a prior mortgage lien will probably make the seller's title unmarketable, the buyer is in no position to demand marketable title until the date set for closing—which may be five, ten or twenty years hence. See Luette v. Bank of Italy Nat. Trust & Savings Ass'n, 42 F.2d 9 (9th Cir.1930).

Can the buyer protect himself against the risk that seller's default on the prior mortgage will result in foreclosure of the seller's *and* the buyer's interests? Can the buyer protect himself against subsistence of the mortgage right up to the date set for the buyer's closing, leaving title unmarketable even after the buyer has paid virtually all of the purchase price? One solution is for the contract to provide that the buyer will make his monthly payments directly to the prior mortgagee, receiving a credit for these payments against his installment obligations to the seller. Alternatively, seller may agree to convey fee title to the buyer, subject to the mortgage, when the principal outstanding on the contract equals the principal outstanding on the prior mortgage. See generally, Cathey, The Real Estate Installment Sale Contract: Its Drafting, Use, Enforcement, and Consequences, 5 U.Ark. Little Rock L.J. 229, 231–233 (1982).

How can the buyer protect himself against mortgages given by the seller-titleholder *after* the installment land contract has been executed? As indicated in the excerpt from Professor Warren's article, notice-based recording acts will protect the buyer in possession since the subsequent mortgagee will have inquiry notice of the buyer's interest. The buyer out of possession can also protect himself, even if the seller insists that the contract not be acknowledged. The buyer can, for example, record an acknowledged memorandum of the unacknowledged contract, thus putting subsequent lienors on constructive inquiry notice of the contract. Or, the buyer can simply try to record the unacknowledged contract. (Often, recording officers will not insist on acknowledgment of an instrument submitted for recording.) Although this will not give constructive notice to subsequent lienors, it will typically give them actual notice for it is the rare mortgagee who does not perform a title search before closing its loan; this search will give actual notice of a recorded, though legally unrecordable, instrument.

5. *Protecting the Buyer's Creditors.* Most courts today hold that the installment land contract buyer has a mortgageable interest in land, subject of course to the prior interest of the seller. *Dirks* indicates the two problems facing a mortgagee from an installment land contract buyer: putting the seller on notice of the mortgage, thus obligating the seller to inform the mortgagee of any default and possible forfeiture under the contract, and being allowed to step into the shoes of the buyer-mortgagor who has defaulted on the land contract.

Notice. The Goodwills could have protected themselves by conducting a title search prior to entering into their financing arrangement with the Cornwells. Upon discovering that the Cornwells did not have legal title, the Goodwills could have refused the financing or, alternatively, could have asked the Cornwells for the name and address of the titleholder—the Butlers—and then given the Butlers notice of its deed of trust. Would the result in *Dirks* have been different if the Butlers had actual notice of the Goodwills? Did the court reach the correct result on the question of constructive notice? See Rev. Wash. Code § 61.30.040 (requiring forfeiting seller to notify claimants of record who have liens upon the property derived through the purchaser); Hauf v. Johnston, 105 Wash.App. 807, 21 P.3d 325 (2001). Should the Dirks, as a subsequent taker, have had notice of the Goodwills' recorded interest? In this regard, consider Giorgi v. Pioneer Title Insurance Co. at page 437.

Stepping Into the Buyer's Shoes. Assuming that the Goodwills had been aware of the Butlers' contemplated forfeiture, what rights would they have had? Under the *Skendzel* view of an installment land contract as a mortgage, should the Goodwills be treated as a second mortgagee, and to give him the right of redemption traditionally given to junior mortgagees? Compare Shindledecker v. Savage, 96 N.M. 42, 627 P.2d 1241, 1243 (1981). ("In such a case the mortgagee cannot have his lien eclipsed by the agreement of the parties to the real estate contract to rescind it. By virtue of his mortgage, the mortgagee obtains the original purchaser's right to purchase the property for the consideration stated in the purchase contract. In other words, the mortgagee assumes the rights of the vendee under the real estate contract."); Yu v. Paperchase Partnership, 114 N.M. 635, 845 P.2d 158 (1992) (seller with knowledge of a subvendee's interest cannot forfeit without giving subvendee an opportunity to cure the default).

6. *Bibliographic Note.* The perceived inequities of installment land contracts have spawned an abundant literature. The following articles, in addition to those cited above, are informative: Durham, Ohio Land Contracts Revisited, 14 U.Dayton L.Rev. 451 (1989); Freyfogle, The Installment Land Contract as Lease: Habitability Protections and the Low-Income Purchaser, 62 N.Y.U.L.Rev. 293 (1987); Comment, Remedying the Inequities of Forfeiture in Land Installment Contracts, 64 Iowa L.Rev. 158 (1978); Note, Toward Abolishing Installment Land Sale Contracts, 36 Mont.L.Rev. 110 (1975); Note, Reforming the Vendor's Remedies for Breach of Installment Land Sale Contracts, 47 So.Cal.L.Rev. 191 (1973); Note, Florida Installment Land Contracts: A Time for Reform, 28 U.Fla.L.Rev. 156 (1975).

Nelson & Whitman, The Installment Land Contract—A National Viewpoint, 1977 B.Y.U.L.Rev. 541, offers a well-balanced analysis of the interests involved, noting the risks that presently exist for vendors entering into these contracts. See also, Nelson & Whitman, Installment Land Contracts—Revisited, 1985 B.Y.U.L.Rev. 1. The vendor's creditors also encounter risk. See Lynn, Bankruptcy and the Land Sales Contract: The Rights of the Vendee vis-a-vis the Vendor's Bankruptcy Trustee, 5 Tex.Tech.L.Rev. 677 (1974); Lacy, Land Sale Contracts in Bankruptcy, 21 U.C.L.A.L.Rev. 477 (1973); Lacy, Creditors of Land Contract Vendors, 24 Case W.Res.L.Rev. 645 (1973).

CHAPTER VI

BUILDING ON THE BASICS: CONDOMINIUM AND OTHER COMMUNAL ARRANGEMENTS FOR HOME OWNERSHIP

Condominiums, cooperatives and other forms of communal ownership combine the economic attractions of home ownership with the social and economic attractions of apartment living. They enable occupants to acquire an equity stake, with related tax and finance advantages, in dwellings such as high-rise apartments and townhouses that were traditionally available only as short-term rentals. They make it possible for neighbors to share swimming pools, tennis courts and other recreational facilities that none could afford individually. They also liberate occupants from the homeowner's usual upkeep responsibilities and, at the same time, give them a degree of control over their environment—through the power to hire and fire building managers—that tenants probably never know.

The reasons for the current upsurge in communal ownership are not hard to find. Rapidly increasing land prices have forced many homebuyers to lower their sights from detached single family housing to less costly condominium units offering almost equivalent housing space. At the same time, rental housing for middle and upper income occupants diminished as landlords, faced with increasing labor and utility costs and the prospect of rent control, have converted their rental units into condominium arrangements, and as developers invested new housing dollars in condominium rather than rental projects. Changing social patterns have also played a role. Single men and women find the condominium an excellent vehicle for preserving a lifestyle unfettered by home maintenance chores, while offering the advantages of real property tax deductions and appreciation in inflationary times. The no-care aspects of condominium life also attract older individuals. The precise mix of advantages and disadvantages offered by communal ownership will depend on the precise form that the ownership arrangement takes—condominium, cooperative or homeowners' association.

Condominium. Each occupant in a condominium owns his unit in fee simple absolute. His deed will describe the fee as a cube of space bounded by the unit's interior walls, and will also give him an undivided fractional interest, as a tenant in common with all the other unit owners, in the project's common areas—exterior walls, roof, land, hallways, and common facilities such as laundry rooms, tennis courts and swimming pools. Because he has fee title, the unit owner can finance his purchase by giving a mortgage on the unit to secure a purchase money loan from an institutional lender. In addition to his responsibility for the debt service and real property taxes on his own unit, the owner must also pay a periodic maintenance fee to the condominium association to support its upkeep of the common areas. And, because he has fee title, the condominium owner is entitled to all of the federal income tax deductions available to homeowners generally.

The governing document in a condominium is the charter or declaration. In addition to providing a legal description of the project and of the individual units and common areas, the declaration will establish guidelines for the condominium's bylaws. The bylaws, in turn, will outline the procedures to be followed by the condominium owners in selecting a board of managers to supervise the condominium's ongoing activities, in authorizing expenditures for maintenance and reconstruction of common areas and facilities, and in adopting house rules governing day-to-day life in the condominium.

The condominium owners association, created by the condominium charter, is responsible for coordinating the rights and duties of the condominium unit owners and for advancing the condominium's welfare generally. The association's political life centers in a board of directors (or "governing board," "board of managers," or "council of co-owners") elected by the owners to set policy and, in turn, to elect the officers and committees that will execute policy. Many of the association's activities resemble those of municipal government. The association regulates by adopting rules for community behavior and enforcing these rules through court sanctioned fines and injunctions. The association provides services such as utilities, road and park maintenance, garbage pickup and police security, and levies taxes, in the form of assessments, to support these services.

The condominium is proving to be a versatile instrument in other than conventional housing markets. Its easy application to existing multifamily dwellings has made it a particularly attractive vehicle for "sweat equity" and subsidized housing programs aimed at giving the urban poor a stake in their housing. See Teaford, Home Ownership for Low-Income Families: The Condominium, 21 Hastings L.J. 243 (1970); Comment, Condominiums and the 1968 Housing and Urban Development Act: Putting the Poor in Their Place, 43 So.Cal.L.Rev. 309 (1970). Compare Diamond, Rehabilitation of Low-Income Housing Through Cooperative Conversions by Tenants, 25 Am.U.L.Rev. 285 (1976). Condominiums have also been used in structuring medical and other professional office developments.

Although the condominium concept can be traced back at least to medieval times, it did not become popular in the United States until 1961, when Congress amended the National Housing Act to authorize the Federal Housing Administration to insure mortgages on condominiums in states that had statutorily authorized this form of ownership. (Considerable doubt existed whether, without such enabling legislation, an ownership unit described only as a cube dangling in space could be legally conveyed and mortgaged in fee simple.) A model statute promulgated by the FHA the following year was quickly adopted or adapted across the country and, by 1969, every state had enacted a condominium statute. The FHA prototype can be found in FHA, Dept. of Housing & Urban Development, Model Statute for Creation of Apartment Ownership, Form #3285 (1962). The Uniform Condominium Act, approved by the National Conference of Commissioners on Uniform

State Laws in 1977 and amended in 1980, has been adopted in ten jurisdictions. The Uniform Common Interest Ownership Act which governs condominiums, cooperatives, and homeowners associations, was promulgated in 1984 and has been adopted in at least four states. Citations to the state statutes are collected at Appendix B–1 to P. Rohan & M. Reskin, Condominium Law and Practice, vol. 1, part 1 (1992).

Cooperative. Housing cooperatives existed in this country well before condominiums became fashionable, and they continue to occupy an important place in some urban housing markets. In a cooperative, title to the entire project—all of the individual units and all of the common areas—is vested in a single, non-profit cooperative corporation. Unlike the condominium owner, who receives a deed conveying fee title to his unit and an undivided interest in the common areas, each cooperator receives two instruments: a perpetually renewable proprietary lease to her unit, between herself as tenant and the cooperative corporation as landlord, and shares of stock in the cooperative corporation. A single mortgage will encumber the entire project and the cooperative corporation, as mortgagor, will pay the entire debt service as well as all real property taxes. The corporation will meet these and any other obligations from monthly rentals collected from the cooperator-tenants. Cooperators' rights and duties will be set out in the corporate charter, bylaws and proprietary lease. The cooperator who fails to pay rent or to comply with her other leasehold responsibilities faces both summary eviction from the unit and the loss of her stock.

The fact that the cooperative is financed through a blanket encumbrance rather than through mortgages on individual units poses two substantial problems for the cooperator. One is financial interdependence. When a condominium owner defaults, he risks foreclosure and the sale of his unit, but imposes little added burden on his neighbors. By contrast, if a cooperator defaults in her rental obligations, the other tenants must chip in to cover her share of debt service on the blanket encumbrance as well as real property taxes and maintenance expenses. In good times, the burden will be only temporary, for a new tenant can quickly be found to pick up the unit's share of cooperative expenses. In bad times, the results can be disastrous. If the unit cannot be sold, the other tenants must pay the unit charges indefinitely. The increased burden may cause some of these tenants to default, leading to default by still others until the entire house of cards collapses when the cooperative can no longer meet its expenses and so defaults on the blanket obligation.

Financing through a blanket encumbrance will also limit a cooperator's ability to liquidate her investment. The cooperator's prospective buyer, unlike the condominium buyer, will find that financing is scarce because statutory restrictions may prohibit institutional lenders from taking second lien mortgages or from treating stock certificates and proprietary leases as real property security. The seller's only alternatives will be to finance the sale herself, taking back a note and security interest in the stock and lease, or to hope for a buyer with sufficient cash to cover the seller's original down payment together with the amount of the unit's appreciation during her ownership. Some relief from this dilemma is now available in at least two states, Illinois and New York, which have amended their corporate and banking laws to permit institutional lenders to make real estate loans secured by the cooperator's interest in her unit. 205 Ill.Comp.Stat.Ann. 6002 (1995); N.Y. Banking Law §§ 103(5), 235.8–a, 380.2–a (McKinney Supp.1992). See generally Kane, The Financing of Cooperatives and Condominiums: A Retrospective, 73 St. John's Law Rev. 101 (1999).

Unlike condominium owners, who have from the beginning enjoyed the tax advantages available to owners of detached homes, cooperators have historically suffered from their status as tenants. A 1928 bill, allowing cooperators to deduct their proportionate share of the interest and real estate taxes paid by the cooperative corporation, passed the House, but was rejected by the Senate, in part on the ground that it would give cooperators preferential treatment over other tenants. H.R. 1, Revenue Bill of 1928, 70th Cong. 1st Sess. §§ 22(b)(9), 23(q), 24(d); S.Rpt. No. 960, 70th Cong. 1st Sess. 20–21 (1928). Congress finally reversed its position in the Revenue Act of 1942, enacting the predecessor of I.R.C. § 216 to allow tenant stockholders in "cooperative apartment corporations" to deduct the interest and real property tax expenses allocable to their units.

Amendments since 1942 have further narrowed the gap between cooperators and condominium owners. The 1954 Act extended pass-through treatment to tenants in all "cooperative housing corporations," not just apartments. The 1962 Revenue Act allowed cooperators to take depreciation deductions to the extent that they used their units in a trade or business or for the production of income. Section 121(d)(4) allows the exclusion of gain for homeowners to apply to cooperative owners. The 1986 Tax Reform Act amended section 216 to allow corporations, trusts, and other taxpayers besides individuals to be treated as tenant-stockholders and so take deductions. The amendments also permit flexibility in the proportion of deductions allocated to the various tenant-stockholders.

The gap has not been completely closed. Section 216 does not allow cooperators to deduct casualty losses. More important, section 216 expressly conditions the interest and real property tax deductions on compliance with several technical requirements. The Debt Relief Act of 2007, however, brought flexibility by providing alternatives to the traditional 80–20 that permitted deductions only if no more than twenty percent of the cooperatives revenues were from non-tenant shareholders. For an excellent discussion of these and other tax issues affecting the cooperative, see Cowan, Tax Reform on the Home Front: Cooperative Housing Corporations, Condominiums, and Homeowners Associations, 5 J.Real Est.Tax. 101 (1978); Miller, The Co-op Apartment and Qualified Residence Interest, 16 J. Real Est.Tax. 385 (1989).

Although the tax and financing trend has been to treat the cooperator's interest as realty, the fact that corporate stock is involved gives the interest some attributes of personalty. This double aspect has raised no end of consequential issues. In an action by a defaulting buyer to recover his down payment on a contract to buy a cooperative unit, will the Uniform Commercial Code apply, limiting the seller to her actual damages, or will real property principles apply, entitling the seller to retain the entire deposit without proving damages? See Silverman v. Alcoa Plaza Associates, 37 A.D.2d 166, 323 N.Y.S.2d 39 (1971). When a lender forecloses on its security interest in the stock and proprietary lease, what law applies—U.C.C. Article 9, or statutes governing the foreclosure of mortgages on real property? Which is the appropriate place to record transfers of interests in the cooperative unit—the office of the Secretary of State, as personal property, or the County Recorder's office, as real property? Does the sales tax apply or the real property transfer tax? See State Tax Commission v. Shor, 43 N.Y.2d 151, 400 N.Y.S.2d 805, 371 N.E.2d 523 (1977); see generally, Note, Legal Characterization of the Individual's Interest in a Cooperative Apartment: Realty or Personalty? 73 Colum.L.Rev. 250 (1973).

For an excellent study, see Schill, Voicu & Miller, The Condominium versus Cooperative Puzzle: An Empirical Analysis of Housing in New York City, 36 J.Leg.Stud. 275 (2007).

Homeowners Associations and PUDs. The advantages of shared land use have not been lost on owners of detached housing. Subdivision developers, and sometimes existing neighbors, organize homeowner associations to maintain parks and other recreational facilities such as pools, tennis courts and golf courses. Typically, the association will hold the common areas in fee or under a long term lease, and will regularly assess homeowners for their share of common area expenses.

The planned unit development, or PUD, applies the homeowners association concept to particular advantage, since so much space in the PUD is devoted to common facilities. PUDs, a comparatively recent development in land use planning, depart from the grid-like pattern of detached housing that typified zoning's early years and, instead, cluster groups of homes within the parcel being developed, often mixing a number of housing forms in a single development—detached single-family homes, connected townhouse units, duplexes, fourplexes and garden apartments. Instead of individual yards, PUDs offer extensive common areas. The developer may, to obtain subdivision approval, be forced to dedicate some of these common areas to the local government for use by all citizens in the community. But she will usually be able to convey a substantial part of the common recreational areas to an association consisting of all property owners in the PUD. Membership, voting rights and assessments in the PUD association attach automatically upon acquisition of a unit in the PUD. The association typically has the power to promulgate and enforce rules for conduct within the PUD including, for example, the right to review any proposed changes to the exterior of units within the development for their consonance with the PUD's architectural style. See generally, Uniform Planned Community Act, 12 Unif.Laws Ann. 1.

NOTES

1. *Why Communal Arrangements?* Professor Henry Hansmann, in an excellent article, argues that the key reason for the recent surge in condominiums and cooperatives is the large tax subsidy available to owner occupied housing as compared to rental housing. Hansmann, Condominium and Cooperative Housing: Transactional Efficiency, Tax Subsidies, and Tenure Choice, 20 J.Leg.Studs. 25 (1991). Hansmann maintains that

despite claimed benefits due to the organizational innovations of communal housing arrangements, condominiums and cooperatives would occupy a smaller share of the market if there were no tax subsidy.

Is the choice to purchase a condominium or cooperative only an economic one? Or do people seek communal arrangements because they offer an environment that the owners believe will maximize their self-fulfillment? See Korngold, Resolving the Flaws of Residential Servitudes and Owners Associations: For Reformation Not Termination, 1990 Wis.L.Rev. 513.

2. *Counseling the Condominium Buyer.* From the perspective of the buyer and her lender, the principal difference between the purchase of a condominium and the purchase of a detached unit lies in the condominium's close legal, financial and physical interconnections. Buyer and lender will want to examine the condominium's declaration, by-laws, house rules and any major management agreements. The buyer will be interested in restrictions on children or pets, her freedom to sell or rent the unit, voting rights in the condominium association and rights against other unit owners, including the right to compel upkeep of the common areas. The lender may insist that there be no restriction on its power to sell or lease the unit in the event that it forecloses or takes a deed in lieu of foreclosure. The lender may also want a commitment from the condominium owners association to give the lender notice of, and the opportunity to cure, any default by the unit owner-mortgagor in paying assessments or performing other obligations.

Lender and buyer will want to see not only that the unit is adequately insured, but also that the association has obtained sufficient liability insurance to immunize the unit owners from devastating tort judgments for accidents occurring in the common areas and sufficient hazard or casualty insurance on the entire structure to pay for repair or reconstruction in the event the structure is partially or substantially damaged.

For a pre-closing checklist to be used in representing condominium purchasers, see Report of Committee on Condominium and Cooperative Ownership of Apartments, Lawyer Counseling Considerations in Representing Condominium Purchasers, 10 Real Prop., Probate & Trust J. 464 (1975).

3. *Taxation of Owner Associations.* Owner associations have an economic life independent of their members. Until enactment of the Tax Reform Act of 1976, associations sought to avoid or reduce their federal income taxes by getting themselves classified as tax exempt entities under I.R.C. § 501(c), initially as "civic leagues" or social welfare organizations under section 501(c)(4). As that avenue was blocked by a series of Revenue Rulings, they sought to be characterized as social clubs, "organized for pleasure, recreation and other nonprofitable purposes" under section 501(c)(7).

The 1976 Tax Reform Act added section 528 to the Code, creating a limited, elective tax exemption specifically for "homeowners associations" and itemizing revenue items that will be treated as exempt income regardless of the purpose to which they are applied. The amendment establishes strict conditions for qualification as a "homeowners association." And the association, even if it qualifies for the exemption, will be taxed on "homeowners association taxable income"—gross income less two items: (1) deductions for expenses incurred in producing gross income and (2) "exempt function income" such as membership fees, dues and assessments received from unit owners.

Section 528 covers homeowner associations and condominium owner associations, but not housing cooperatives. Cooperatives may in fact have received a better deal under the 1976 Reform Act's amendment of section 216(c) to allow cooperatives to take deductions for the depreciation of the entire building, not just the units occupied by non-stockholders. Typically, these depreciation deductions should be sufficient to shelter income not expended in the tax year, putting cooperatives in at least as good a position as condominium and homeowner associations with respect to their unexpended reserve funds.

On the organization and activities of condominium associations generally, see Hyatt & Rhoads, Concepts of Liability in the Development and Administration of Condominium and Home Owners Associations, 12 Wake Forest L.Rev. 915 (1976); Hyatt, Condominiums and Home Owner Associations: Formation and Development, 24 Emory L.J. 977 (1975); Jackson, Why You Should Incorporate a Homeowners Association, 3 Real Est.L.J. 311 (1975). On tax aspects of condominium and homeowner associations, see Cowan, Tax Reform on the Home Front: Cooperative Housing Corporations, Condominiums and Homeowner Associations, 5 J. of Real Est.Tax. 101, 113–141 (1978); Miller, Condominiums and Cooperatives, 15 J. Real Est.Tax. 80 (1987); Note, Taxation of Homeowners Associations Under the Tax Reform Act of 1976, 36 Wash. & Lee L.Rev. 299 (1979).

4. *Timesharing.* Condominium ownership can be divided in time as well as space, giving each of several owners the exclusive right to possess a single unit for a predetermined week or month every year. Timesharing projects blossomed in the early 1980's, enabling individuals to purchase the right to possess a single unit in a resort townhouse, hotel, motel, campground, or even in a yacht, for increments of one week each year in perpetuity. Under one commonly used technique, *time span ownership,* each participant holds an undivided fee simple interest in the unit as a tenant in common with as many as fifty-one cotenants; a separate agreement between the cotenants identifies the specific week or weeks during the year when each cotenant is entitled to occupy the unit. Another form of timesharing is interval ownership where there is a transfer of different estates for years for different periods to the various owners along with an undivided interest in a remainder in fee simple. A more direct approach is simply to convey a "fee" estate for a specified week or weeks each year in perpetuity. Other timesharing programs employ contracts, rather than real property interests, to give the purchaser a right to periodic use of the real property. See Model Real Estate Time-Share Act § 1–102, comment 4, 7B Unif.Laws Ann. 351; see generally, Comment, Time-Share Condominiums: Property's Fourth Dimension, 32 Me.L.Rev. 181 (1980); Comment, Legal Challenges to Time Sharing Ownership, 45 Mo.L.Rev. 423 (1980).

States moved quickly to regulate timesharing projects. See, for example, Block, Regulation of Timesharing, 60 U.Det.J.Urb.L. 23 (1982). See also Burek, Uniform Real Estate Time-Share Act, 14 Real Prop., Probate & Trust J. 683 (1979); Stone, Federal Trade Commission and Timeshare Resale Companies, 24 Suffolk U.L.Rev. 49 (1990).

The Tax Reform Act of 1997 amended section 528 to extend favorable tax treatment to timeshare associations, similar to the treatment of condominium associations. On tax aspects, see Kinsolving & Caron, Tax Considerations in Time-Share Development, 13 Stetson L.Rev. 25 (1983).

A. MANAGEMENT AND CONTROL

Comcast of Florida, L.P. v. L'Ambiance Beach Condominium Association, Inc.
District Court of Appeal of Florida, 2009.
17 So.3d 839.

MAY, J.

A conflict between a cable television provider and a condominium association forms the basis for this appeal. Comcast appeals an order upholding the condominium association's termination of a cable television agreement, pursuant to section 718.302, Fla. Stat. (2002). It raises numerous issues concerning the validity of the termination. We find no error and affirm, but write to address the application of section 718.302.

In 2002 and prior to incorporating the homeowner's association, the developer entered into an MDU Broadband Services Agreement that provided Comcast with an easement to install its cables in the condominium development. The parties also entered into a Bulk Rate Addendum that provided for all residents to receive Comcast's cable television services at a discounted monthly rate and a Pre-Wire Installation Addendum.

The Association received cable television services at a discounted rate, a character generator, and a security camera. Comcast paid for the easement and for material and labor for its distribution system and facilities. Every unit owner received and paid for the cable service as part of the monthly maintenance fee. In turn, the Association made payments to Comcast.

The agreement's termination provision provided that the "Agreement may be terminated prior to expiration of its term subject to conditions and regulations required under 718 of Florida Statutes. . . ." The evidence established that the developer's representative specifically requested that the agreement refer to chapter 718 because he intended to insure that after turnover to the unit owners, the Association would have the right to terminate the contract upon a timely 75% vote of the unit owners.

Following the incorporation of the homeowner's association and the developer's hand over, the unit owners voted to terminate the agreement. The Association's counsel sent Comcast written notice of termination in accordance with section 718.302. Two additional letters were sent, notifying Comcast of the Association's intent to terminate the agreement and addenda and instructing Comcast to open its distribution lock boxes.

Comcast brought an action for declaratory relief, breach of the agreement and addenda, trespass, and permanent injunctive relief.

Before a hearing could be held on Comcast's Emergency Motion for Temporary Injunction, the Association hired a locksmith to drill holes in Comcast's distribution lock boxes to allow another provider access to Comcast's cables. As a result, all of the residential units were switched from Comcast to another provider. Comcast's wires remained in place in the event a unit owner desired to maintain service with Comcast.

The litigation proceeded on Comcast's amended complaint, which also sought damages for the drilling. The case was tried non-jury and resulted in a judgment for the Association. Comcast now appeals the adverse judgment.

Comcast argues that the court erred in applying section 718.302 to the agreement and addenda. Specifically, Comcast argues a cable television service contract is not an agreement "that provides for operation, maintenance, or management of a condominium association or property serving the unit owners of a condominium." § 718.302(1), Fla. Stat. In support, Comcast relies on the fact that the agreement did not require Comcast to do any management, maintenance, or operation of the condominium. Comcast further argues that the legislature differentiated between "contracts for services" and those "contracts that provide for operation, maintenance, and management of a condominium." *Compare* §§ 718.115(1)(d), 718.301(4)(n), *and* 718.3025(4), Fla. Stat. ("service contracts") *with* § 718.302, Fla. Stat. ("operation, maintenance, or management of a condominium association or property serving the unit owners"). We disagree with these arguments and affirm.

We review the application of the statute *de novo. Strod v. Lewenstark,* 958 So.2d 1138, 1139 (Fla. 4th DCA 2007). In doing so, we conclude, as did the trial court, that section 718.302, Florida Statutes, applies to the agreement and addenda.

Section 718.302, Fla. Stat. (2002), provides in part:

(1) Any grant or reservation made by a declaration, lease, or other document, and any contract made by an association prior to assumption of control of the association by unit owners other than the developer, that provides for operation, maintenance, or management of a condominium association or property serving the unit owners of a condominium shall be fair and reasonable, and such grant, reservation, or contract may be canceled by unit owners other than the developer:

(a) . . . the cancellation shall be by concurrence of the owners of not less than 75 percent of the voting interests other than the voting interests owned by the developer. . . .

Comcast installed wires and lock boxes to provide cable television services to all the unit owners. By virtue of the agreement, Comcast operated and maintained the system that it installed.[3] Further, section 718.115(1)(d), Fla. Stat. (2002), provides that the cost of cable television service obtained pursuant to a bulk rate contract is deemed a common expense. Section (1)(a) specifically provides that "[c]ommon expenses

---

[3]   Paragraph five of the agreement provided for the "Association [to] direct all Residents of the Premises who receive Services to report all maintenance or other problems with respect to the Services directly to [Comcast]. . . ." Paragraph six provided that Comcast "will service and maintain the Facilities and provide Services to the Residents of the Premises. . . ."

include the expenses of the operation, maintenance, repair, replacement, or protection of the common elements and association property. . . ." § 718.115(1)(a), Fla. Stat.

Because the agreement provided for the cable television service for all unit owners, the cost was part of the monthly maintenance fee, and the service provider was required to service and maintain the cable television, we conclude that the agreement was one for the "operation, maintenance, or management" of the cable television services. § 718.302(1), Fla. Stat. Therefore section 718.302 applies to the agreement and addenda.[4]

This conclusion is supported by our prior decision in *Country Manors Association, Inc. v. Master Antenna Systems, Inc.,* 458 So.2d 835 (Fla. 4th DCA 1984). There, a company entered into an agreement with the developer to provide and maintain a central antenna system for the condominium complex. Subsequently, the association took control and terminated the agreement, pursuant to section 718.302, Florida Statutes (1983). The company filed an action to determine ownership of the central antenna system. We held that the service provider owned the master antenna system that it had installed. In doing so, we acknowledged the unit owners' right to terminate an agreement that had been entered into by the developer, pursuant to section 718.302.

> [T]he Association effectively exercised its statutory rights to terminate any of its agreements with [the company] pursuant to Section 718.302, Fla. Stat. (1983). *See also* § 711.66, Fla.Stat. (1974) Supp. Because the unit owners have cancelled the services of [the company, it] is no longer entitled to use of the express easement to service the system.

Id. at 838. As we explained in *Ainslie v. Levy,* 626 So.2d 229 (Fla. 4th DCA 1993), "[t]he purpose of the [1979] statute was to prevent a developer from entering into long term operation and management agreements which would prove onerous to the unit owners" by "provid[ing] a mechanism for the owners to take back control of their condominiums when the developer had sold over 75% of its units." *Id.* at 230; *see also Tri-Properties, Inc. v. Moonspinner Condo. Ass'n,* 447 So. 2d 965 (Fla. 1st DCA 1984).

Here, the agreement and addenda were for the "operation, maintenance, or management" of the cable television service provided to unit owners as a common expense. The president of the developer specifically requested reference to Chapter 718 in the agreement to insure that after turnover to the unit owners the Association would have the right under Chapter 718 to terminate the contract upon a vote of the unit owners. After turnover, more than 75% of the unit owners voted to cancel the agreement. In sending the notice of cancellation, the Association properly relied on section 718.302 to terminate the agreement. The trial court correctly enforced the properly executed termination.

---

[4] We disagree that reference to cable television in section 718.3025(4) suggests that cable television is not within the "operation, maintenance, or management" contemplated in section 718.302. That section refers to instances where the unit owners have the option to pay for services individually and not as part of the maintenance fee paid by all unit owners. *See, e.g., Palma Del Mar Condo. Ass'n #5 of St. Petersburg, Inc. v. Commercial Laundries of W. Fla., Inc.,* 586 So.2d 315 (Fla.1991).

We find no merit in the remaining issues raised.

Affirmed.

NOTES

1. *Condominium Statutes.* State condominium statutes, such as the one construed in *Comcast*, prescribe the ground rules for condominium organization and management. They specify the instruments needed to create the condominium and to govern the unit owners, the structure, jurisdiction and powers of the management association and its board of managers, and the voting requirements for changing these instruments or institutions. The statutes also impose substantive rules. For example, because of the central importance of the common areas, in which all unit owners have an undivided interest, most statutes provide that they cannot be partitioned. Moreover, the statutes attempt to strike a balance between competing interests of developers and unit owners. What are the concerns of unit owners that the Florida statute in *Comcast* addresses? What are the legitimate need of developers on such issues? A related question involves the duration of control of the condominium board during the marketing phase by the developer: what are the competing interests of the parties? See Barclay v. DeVeau, 384 Mass. 676, 429 N.E.2d 323 (1981) (setting limits on the length of developer's control in the absence of statutory provisions found in many other jurisdictions.)

The first generation of condominium statutes in the United States was patterned after the FHA's prototype statute, Federal Housing Administration, Department of Housing and Urban Development, Model Statute for Creation of Apartment Ownership, Form #3285 (1962). These statutes soon revealed their shortcomings. Developers objected to the statutes on the ground that they had been framed with high-rise apartment buildings in mind and thus ignored problems posed by low-rise lateral developments and by the frequent need to develop condominiums in stages rather than all at once. Consumers objected that the early statutes did not control such prevalent developer abuses as obtaining overly generous management contracts from captive management associations.

The second generation of condominium statutes, typified by the National Conference of Commissioners' 1977 Uniform Condominium Act, responded to these developer and consumer objections. The Act was extensively amended in 1980. The Act provides for a "flexible condominium," where land may be added or withdrawn from the project by the developer. In addition to addressing creation, termination, and operation of the condominium, various consumer protection provisions are included. These include limitations on "sweetheart" contracts and leases entered into by the developer, disclosure requirements, a right in the buyer to cancel a sales contract in certain circumstances, and developer's warranties of quality concerning the units and common areas.

For background on the two generations of condominium legislation, see Schreiber, The Lateral Housing Development: Condominium or Home Owners Association? 117 Pa.L.Rev. 1104 (1969); Rohan, The "Model Condominium Code"—A Blueprint for Modernizing Condominium Legislation, 78 Colum.L.Rev. 587 (1978); Judy & Wittie, Uniform Condominium Act: Selected Key Issues, 13 Real Prop., Probate & Trust J. 437 (1978); Note, Recent Innovations in State Condominium Legislation, 48

St. John's L.Rev. 994 (1974); Thomas, The New Uniform Condominium Act, 64 A.B.A.J. 1370 (1978).

In 1980, the National Conference of Commissioners adopted a Uniform Planned Community Act for homeowner associations. In 1981 the Conference adopted a Model Real Estate Cooperative Act and, one year later, a Uniform Common Interest Ownership Act embracing all three forms of communal ownership—condominium, cooperative and homeowners' association. These acts were all modeled on the Uniform Condominium Act. In 1994, UCIOA was substantially amended. Approximately twenty states have adopted the Uniform Condominium Act or a similar statute, while about five jurisdictions have adopted UCIOA. See generally Geis, Beyond the Condominium: The Uniform Common-Interest Ownership Act, 17 Real Prop., Probate & Trust J. 757 (1982); Winokur, Meaner Lienor Community Associations: The "Super Priority" Lien and Related Reforms Under the Uniform Common Interest Ownership Act, 27 Wake Forest L.Rev. 353 (1992).

2. *Regulation.* Condominium acts represent just one set of regulatory hurdles that condominium developers regularly face. In addition to the usual approvals for subdivision maps, architectural review and zoning or rezoning, federal and state securities laws may apply, and if the condominium is being created through the conversion of an existing multiple family dwelling, the developer may have to cope with local laws and moratoria governing condominium conversions. See generally, Feldman, Regulating Condominium Conversions: The Constitutionality of Tenant Approval Provisions, 21 Urb.Law. 85 (1989); Comment, Cooperative and Condominium Conversions in New York: The Tenant in Occupancy, 31 N.Y.L.Sch.L.Rev. 763 (1986); Comment, The Condominium Conversion Problem: Causes and Solutions, 1980 Duke L.J. 306; Comment, The Legality and Practicality of Condominium Conversion Moratoriums, 34 U. Miami L.Rev. 1199 (1980); Note, The Validity of Ordinances Limiting Condominium Conversion, 78 Mich.L.Rev. 124 (1979).

On securities law aspects of condominiums, see Hocking v. Dubois, 885 F.2d 1449 (9th Cir.1989), cert. denied, 494 U.S. 1078, 110 S.Ct. 1805, 108 L.Ed.2d 936 (1990) (finding that the resale of a condominium along with a rental pool contract was an investment contract, making the broker packaging the transaction subject to federal securities law); Rosenbaum, The Resort Condominium and the Federal Securities Laws—A Case Study in Governmental Inflexibility, 60 Va.L.Rev. 785 (1974); Clurman, Condominiums as Securities: A Current Look, 19 N.Y.L.F. 457 (1974); Dickey & Thorpe, Federal Security Regulation of Condominium Offerings, 19 N.Y.L.F. 473 (1974); Comment, U.H.F. v. Forman: The Relationship Between Cooperative Housing Shares and the Federal Securities Law, 61 Iowa L.Rev. 920 (1976). On the regulatory maze generally, see Geis, Representing the Condominium Developer: Tending the Paper Jungle, 10 Real Prop., Probate & Trust J. 471 (1975); Note, Condominium Regulation: Beyond Disclosure, 123 U.Pa.L.Rev. 639 (1975); Levine, Registering a Condominium Offering in New York, 19 N.Y.L.F. 493 (1974).

B. RESTRAINTS ON ALIENATION

Jones v. O'Connell

Supreme Court of Connecticut, 1983.
189 Conn. 648, 458 A.2d 355.

PETERS, ASSOCIATE JUSTICE.

This case concerns the right of owners of a cooperative apartment building to impose restraints on the right to alienate one of the cooperative apartments. The plaintiffs, Conrad Jones and Florence McNulty, who had entered into a contract of sale for a cooperative apartment, brought suit against the defendants, Walter F. O'Connell, Pauline F. O'Connell, Margaret Cavanaugh, Christopher H. Smith and Harbor House, Inc., to enjoin the defendants' disapproval of the contemplated sale. The plaintiffs also sought monetary damages from the individual defendants for their tortious interference with the plaintiffs' contract. After a trial to the court, judgment was rendered for the defendants and the plaintiffs have appealed.

The underlying facts are undisputed. In 1975, the defendant Walter F. O'Connell transferred property at 252–58 Main Street, Southport, to a newly formed Connecticut corporation, the defendant Harbor House, Inc., so that Harbor House might hold the property as a cooperative residential apartment house. The defendant Christopher H. Smith, an attorney, prepared the appropriate documentation, consisting of a memorandum of offering for the stock, proprietary leases for the individual apartments, and by-laws for the corporation. From the time of the first meeting of the corporation, the Harbor House directors have been the individually named defendants, Walter and Pauline O'Connell, Christopher Smith, and Margaret Cavanaugh.

In 1979, just before the present controversy arose, the leasehold interests in Harbor House, manifested by ownership of stock and assignments of proprietary leases, were distributed among the defendants and the plaintiffs as follows: The plaintiff Florence McNulty owned 11.2 percent of the stock and was the lessee of apartment 1A. The plaintiff Conrad Jones owned 25.5 percent of the stock and was the lessee of apartment 2. The defendant Margaret Cavanaugh owned 25.5 percent of the stock and was the lessee of apartment 3. The defendant Walter O'Connell owned 37.8 percent of the stock and was the lessee of apartments 1B, 1C and 4.

On November 5, 1979, the plaintiffs entered into a written contract for Florence McNulty to sell her stock in Harbor House and to assign her proprietary lease in apartment 1A to Conrad Jones. This contract of sale was expressly made "subject to the approval of the directors or shareholders of the Corporation as provided in the Lease or the corporate by-laws." Had the transfer to Jones been approved, he would have become the owner of 36.7 percent of the Harbor House stock and the lessee of two apartments, one underneath the other. Jones was interested in acquiring additional living space for his family because in 1979, one year after his acquisition of apartment 2, he had remarried and become the stepfather of two daughters, aged 9 and 13.

Any lessee's right to sell shares and to assign a proprietary lease in Harbor House is expressly made conditional upon the consent of the Harbor House board of directors, or of at least 65 percent of the corporation's outstanding shares, by virtue of separate and somewhat inconsistent provisions in the Harbor House documentation. Under the memorandum of offering, assignments are to be approved only for persons of suitable "character and financial responsibility." Under the proprietary lease, however, consent to assignments can be granted or withheld "for any reason or for no reason." The corporate by-laws are silent as to what may constitute an adequate basis for withholding consent to an assignment.

The plaintiffs were unable to procure the requisite consent for their contemplated transfer. First the board of directors and later the stockholders of Harbor House refused to approve their contract of sale. Subsequent to this disapproval, Walter O'Connell and Margaret Cavanaugh offered to purchase the stock and the lease of apartment 1A from Florence McNulty, an offer she refused because of her commitment to Conrad Jones. The present litigation then ensued.

In the trial court, after an exhaustive examination of the plaintiffs' claims, judgment was rendered for the defendants. The court found that the defendants had acted reasonably and in good faith, and that the plaintiffs had failed to prove their various claims of wrongful interference with their contract. Each of these conclusions is challenged on this appeal. We find no error.

I

The plaintiffs' principal claim of error asserts that the evidence presented at trial fails to support the trial court's conclusion and finding that the defendants acted reasonably in disapproving the transfer of the stock and the leasehold interest appurtenant to apartment 1A. Before we reach that issue, however, we must first determine the standard by which the propriety of the defendants' withholding of their consent is to be measured.

Although this court has not previously confronted the question of restraints on alienation of property interests in cooperative residential apartments, we have addressed the legality of such restraints on alienation in related contexts. On the one hand, in cases involving the construction of wills involving the devise of both real and personal property, we have noted that "[t]he law does not favor restraints on alienation and will not recognize them unless they are stated 'in unequivocal terms'; Williams v. Robinson, 16 Conn. 517, 523 [1844]", and that "[i]t is the policy of the law not to uphold restrictions upon the free and unrestricted alienation of property unless they serve a legal and useful purpose." Peiter v. Degenring, 136 Conn. 331, 336, 71 A.2d 87 (1949). On the other hand, in a case involving a lease provision requiring that a lessor consent in writing to the assignment of a commercial lease, we have cited with approval the majority rule that "the lessor may refuse consent and his reason is immaterial." Robinson v. Weitz, 171 Conn. 545, 549, 370 A.2d 1066 (1976), relying on Segre v. Ring, 103 N.H. 278, 279, 170 A.2d 265 (1961).

An assessment of how to apply these competing principles to restraints on the alienation of cooperative apartments must take account of the reality that cooperative ownership is in many ways sui generis, a legal hybrid. For some purposes, the "owner" of such an apartment has legal title and an interest in real property, while for other purposes his rights as a tenant of the corporation and a holder of its stock more closely resemble an interest in personal property.

As did the trial court, we deem it appropriate to take a middle road in enforcing provisions that impose conditions upon the transfer of the hybrid cooperative apartment. Provisions conditioning transfers upon the consent of the cooperative corporation are neither automatically void nor automatically valid. If the provisions are stated unequivocally, and serve a legal and useful function, i.e., the reasonable protection of the financial and social integrity of the cooperative as a whole, they are not barred by our policy disfavoring restraints on alienation. Such provisions are permissible, however, only insofar as they are limited to the purpose for which they are designed. Unlimited consent clauses, permitting disapproval of transfers for any reason whatsoever, or for no reason, constitute illegal restraints because they fail sufficiently to recognize the legitimate interest of the holder of a leasehold to enjoy reasonable access to a resale market. These distinctions are consistent with the holdings of the majority of courts in other jurisdictions that have addressed this issue.

Applying these principles to the provisions of the Harbor House documentation, we agree, for two reasons, with the trial court's conclusion invalidating the clause in the proprietary lease purporting to permit consent to an assignment of the lease to be granted or withheld "for any reason or for no reason." As a matter of interpretation, that clause is not unequivocal, because it must be read conjointly with the memorandum of offering which limits the authority to disapprove assignments to cases in which the transferee is a person of unsuitable "character and financial responsibility." Given our reluctance to enforce restraints on alienation, the limited clause in the memorandum of offering must prevail over the unqualified consent clause in the proprietary lease. As a matter of public policy, furthermore, we hold, as do the authorities cited above, that only consent clauses reasonably tailored to the protection of the legitimate interests of the cooperative serve the kind of "legal and useful purpose" which protects them from avoidance as illegal restraints on alienation.

We must turn then to the plaintiffs' assertion that the trial court, on the evidence before it, erred in determining that the defendants acted reasonably, in light of the interests of the cooperative as a whole, in refusing consent to the transfer of apartment 1A. Although the defendants, at the time of their vote as directors and as stockholders, had specified no reasons for their withholding of consent, they did provide the court at trial with the propositions upon which they had relied. No special issue has been raised on this appeal that the delay in notifying the plaintiffs of the reasons for the denial of consent materially prejudiced the plaintiffs.

The trial court's memorandum of decision sets forth the reasons given by the defendants for withholding consent to the contemplated transfer. These reasons have nothing to do with the financial responsibility of Jones, which is conceded. Instead, they focus on Jones' tenancy of apartment 2 and upon functional consequences of a combined tenancy for apartments 2 and 1A. The defendants claimed that Jones was responsible for a recurrently unlocked front hall entrance door, that Jones had misled the defendants about his intended use of apartment 2, that Jones had behaved abrasively at a corporation meeting considering the Harbor House budget, that Jones and his guests had misused the cooperative parking lot, and that Jones' stepdaughters were noisy. The trial court found some of these reasons unproven, and the others of minor significance. The defendants also maintained that the character of the building would be destroyed by having one family occupy apartments on the first and second floors connected for purposes of access only by the common stairway for the building as a whole. This ordinary everyday use of the two apartments would make the stairway a part of the two affected apartments in such a way as to interfere with its common use by the other tenants, who had an interest in the preservation of the building as a cooperative with six separate apartments. Relying principally on this structural reason, the trial court concluded that the defendants "had reasons to deny consent which were based on character, and the purposes and interests of their co-operative."

The plaintiffs argue that this structural reason is insufficient in light of the Harbor House by-laws that specifically authorize the board of directors to permit an owner of one or more apartments "to combine all or any portions of any such apartments into one or any desired number of apartments; and ... to incorporate other space in the building not covered by any proprietary lease, into one or more apartments covered by a proprietary lease. ..." The by-laws do not, however, require combinations of apartments to be approved, particularly where impairment of common access would be likely to result from the combination. The trial court did not err in finding that the structural problem, arguably aggravated by the irritations associated with Jones' occupation of apartment 2, furnished a basis for denying consent that was reasonably rooted in the purposes and interests of the cooperative apartment living and that reasonably served to protect the financial and social integrity of the cooperative as a whole.

II

The determination that the defendants acted reasonably in the furtherance of reasonable cooperative purposes when they withheld their consent to the transfer of apartment 1A deprives the plaintiffs' other claims of error of their necessary factual underpinnings. ...

There is no error.

In this opinion the other Judges concurred.

NOTE

Would Jones v. O'Connell have been decided differently if a condominium rather than a cooperative had been involved? Courts applying the common law rule against restraints on alienation have generally been more willing to accept restraints on the sale of a cooperator's stock and proprietary lease than to accept restraints on the sale of a condominium owner's fee interest. In part this different treatment stems from the technical distinction between leaseholds, which can lawfully be subjected to restraints on alienation, and fee estates, which cannot. And in part the difference stems from judicial recognition that cooperators are financially more interdependent than condominium owners and thus have more legitimate reasons to screen prospective members who will, once accepted, share the communal mortgage and real property tax burdens. See, for example, Weisner v. 791 Park Avenue Corp., 6 N.Y.2d 426, 434, 190 N.Y.S.2d 70, 74, 160 N.E.2d 720, 724 (1959) ("there is no reason why the owners of the co-operative apartment house could not decide for themselves with whom they wish to share their elevators, their common halls and facilities, their stockholders' meetings, their management problems and responsibilities and their homes"). See generally, Note, *Weisner* Revisited: A Reappraisal of a Co-op's Power to Arbitrarily Prohibit the Transfer of Its Shares, 14 Fordham Urb.L.J. 477 (1986).

Whether in the cooperative or condominium setting, courts have been more disposed to honor rights of first refusal—under which the governing board can match any offer received by a unit owner—than to honor outright prohibitions on resale without board approval. The right of first refusal, also called a "preemptive option," can either be at a fixed, predetermined price or at a price that matches the best bona fide offer received by the unit seller; the latter type is usually considered less offensive than the former. See Browder, Restraints on the Alienation of Condominium Units (The Right of First Refusal), 1970 U.Ill.L.Forum 231, 240–243; DiLorenzo, Restraints on Alienation in a Condominium Context: An Evaluation and Theory for Decision Making, 24 Real Prop. Probate & Trust J. 403 (1989).

C. RESTRICTIONS ON OCCUPANCY AND USE

Levandusky v. One Fifth Avenue Apartment Corp.

Court of Appeals of New York, 1990.
75 N.Y.2d 530, 554 N.Y.S.2d 807, 553 N.E.2d 1317.

KAYE, JUDGE.

This appeal by a residential cooperative corporation concerning apartment renovations by one of its proprietary lessees, factually centers on a two-inch steam riser and three air conditioners, but fundamentally presents the legal question of what standard of review should apply when a board of directors of a cooperative corporation seeks to enforce a matter of building policy against a tenant-shareholder. We conclude that the business judgment rule furnishes the correct standard of review.

In the main, the parties agree that the operative events transpired as follows. In 1987, respondent (Ronald Levandusky) decided to enlarge the kitchen area of his apartment at One Fifth Avenue in New York City. According to Levandusky, some time after reaching that decision, and while he was president of the cooperative's board of directors, he told Elliot Glass, the architect retained by the corporation, that he intended to realign or "jog" a steam riser in the kitchen area, and Glass orally approved the alteration. According to Glass, however, the conversation was a general one; Levandusky never specifically told him that he intended to move any particular pipe, and Glass never gave him approval to do so. In any event, Levandusky's proprietary lease provided that no "alteration of or addition to the water, gas or steam risers or pipes" could be made without appellant's prior written consent.

Levandusky had his architect prepare plans for the renovation, which were approved by Glass and submitted for approval to the board of directors. Although the plans show details of a number of other proposed structural modifications, including changes in plumbing risers, no change in the steam riser is shown or discussed anywhere in the plans.

The board approved Levandusky's plans at a meeting held March 14, 1988, and the next day he executed an "Alteration Agreement" with appellant, which incorporated "Renovation Guidelines" that had originally been drafted, in large part, by Levandusky himself. These guidelines, like the proprietary lease, specified that advance written approval was required for any renovation affecting the building's heating system. Board consideration of the plans—appropriately detailed to indicate all structural changes—was to follow their submission to the corporation's architect, and the board reserved the power to disapprove any plans, even those that had received the architect's approval.

In late spring 1988, the building's managing agent learned from Levandusky that he intended to move the steam riser in his apartment, and so informed the board. Both Levandusky and the board contacted John Flynn, an engineer who had served as consulting agent for the board. In a letter and in a subsequent presentation at a June 13 board meeting, Flynn opined that relocating steam risers was technically feasible and, if carefully done, would not necessarily cause any problem. However, he also advised that any change in an established old piping system risked causing difficulties ("gremlins"). In Flynn's view, such alterations were to be avoided whenever possible.

At the June 13 meeting, which Levandusky attended, the board enacted a resolution to "reaffirm the policy—no relocation of risers." At a June 23 meeting, the board voted to deny Levandusky a variance to move his riser, and to modify its previous approval of his renovation plans, conditioning approval upon an acceptable redesign of the kitchen area.

Levandusky nonetheless hired a contractor, who severed and jogged the kitchen steam riser. In August 1988, when the board learned of this, it issued a "stop work" order, pursuant to the "Renovation Guidelines." Levandusky then commenced this article 78 proceeding, seeking to have the stop work order set aside. The corporation cross-petitioned for an order compelling Levandusky to return the riser to its original position. The board also sought an order compelling him to remove certain air-conditioning units he had installed, which allegedly were not in conformity with the requirements of the Landmarks Preservation Commission.

Supreme Court initially granted Levandusky's petition, and annulled the stop work order, on the ground that there was no evidence that the jogged pipe had caused any damage, but on the contrary, the building engineer had inspected it and believed it would likely not have any adverse effect. Therefore, balancing the hardship to Levandusky in redoing the already completed renovations against the harm to the building, the court determined that the board's decision to stop the renovations was arbitrary and capricious, and should be annulled. Both counterclaims were dismissed, the court ruling that the corporation had no standing to complain of violations of the Landmarks Preservation Law, particularly as the building had not been cited for any violation.

On reargument, however, Supreme Court withdrew its decision, dismissed Levandusky's petition, and ordered him to restore the riser to its original position and submit redrawn plans to the board, on the ground that the court was precluded by the business judgment rule from reviewing the board's determination. The court adhered to its original ruling with respect to the branch of the cross motion concerning the air conditioners, notwithstanding that the Landmarks Preservation Commission had in the interim cited them as violations.

On Levandusky's appeal, the Appellate Division, 150 A.D.2d 167, 540 N.Y.S.2d 440 modified the judgment. The court was unanimous in affirming the Supreme Court's disposition of the air conditioner claim, but divided concerning the stop work order. A majority of the court agreed with Supreme Court's original decision, while two Justices dissented on the ground that the board's action was within the scope of its business judgment and hence not subject to judicial review. Concluding that the business judgment rule applies to the decisions of cooperative governing associations enforcing building policy, and that the action taken by the board in this case falls within the purview of the rule, we now modify the order of the Appellate Division.

At the outset, we agree with the Appellate Division that the corporation's cross claim concerning Levandusky's three air conditioning units was properly dismissed, as the appropriate forum for resolution of the complaint at this stage is an administrative review proceeding. That brings us to the issue that divided the Appellate Division: the standard to be applied in judicial review of this challenge to a decision of the board of directors of a residential cooperative corporation.

As cooperative and condominium home ownership has grown increasingly popular, courts confronting disputes between tenant-owners and governing boards have fashioned a variety of rules for adjudicating such claims (*see generally*, Goldberg, *Community Association Use Restrictions: Applying the Business Judgment Doctrine*, 64 Chi-Kent L.Rev. 653 [1988] [hereinafter Goldberg, *Community Association Use Restrictions*]; Note, *Judicial Review of Condominium Rulemaking*, 94 Harv.L.Rev. 647 [1981]). In the process, several salient characteristics of the governing board homeowner relationship have been identified as relevant to the judicial inquiry.

As courts and commentators have noted, the cooperative or condominium association is a quasi-government—"a little democratic sub society of necessity" (*Hidden Harbour Estates v. Norman*, 309 So.2d 180, 182 [Fla.Dist.Ct.App.]). The proprietary lessees or condominium owners consent to be governed, in certain respects, by the decisions of a board. Like a municipal government, such governing boards are responsible for running the day-to-day affairs of the cooperative and to that end, often have broad powers in areas that range from financial decisionmaking to promulgating regulations regarding pets and parking spaces (*see generally*, Note, *Promulgation and Enforcement of House*

Rules, 48 St. John's L.Rev. 1132 [1974]). Authority to approve or disapprove structural alterations, as in this case, is commonly given to the governing board. (*See*, Siegler, *Apartment Alterations*, N.Y.L.J., May 4, 1988, at 1, col. 1.)

Through the exercise of this authority, to which would-be apartment owners must generally acquiesce, a governing board may significantly restrict the bundle of rights a property owner normally enjoys. Moreover, as with any authority to govern, the broad powers of a cooperative board hold potential for abuse through arbitrary and malicious decisionmaking, favoritism, discrimination and the like.

On the other hand, agreement to submit to the decisionmaking authority of a cooperative board is voluntary in a sense that submission to government authority is not; there is always the freedom not to purchase the apartment. The stability offered by community control, through a board, has its own economic and social benefits, and purchase of a cooperative apartment represents a voluntary choice to cede certain of the privileges of single ownership to a governing body, often made up of fellow tenants who volunteer their time, without compensation. The board, in return, takes on the burden of managing the property for the benefit of the proprietary lessees. As one court observed: "Every man may justly consider his home his castle and himself as the king thereof; nonetheless his sovereign fiat to use his property as he pleases must yield, at least in degree, where ownership is in common or cooperation with others. The benefits of condominium living and ownership demand no less." (*Sterling Vil. Condominium v. Breitenbach*, 251 So.2d 685, 688, n. 6 [Fla.Dist.Ct.App.].)

It is apparent, then, that a standard for judicial review of the actions of a cooperative or condominium governing board must be sensitive to a variety of concerns—sometimes competing concerns. Even when the governing board acts within the scope of its authority, some check on its potential powers to regulate residents' conduct, life-style and property rights is necessary to protect individual residents from abusive exercise, notwithstanding that the residents have, to an extent, consented to be regulated and even selected their representatives (*see*, Note, *The Rule of Law in Residential Associations*, 99 Harv.L.Rev. 472 [1985]). At the same time, the chosen standard of review should not undermine the purposes for which the residential community and its governing structure were formed: protection of the interest of the entire community of residents in an environment managed by the board for the common benefit.

We conclude that these goals are best served by a standard of review that is analogous to the business judgment rule applied by courts to determine challenges to decisions made by corporate directors (*see*, *Auerbach v. Bennett*, 47 N.Y.2d 619, 629, 419 N.Y.S.2d 920, 393 N.E.2d 994). A number of courts in this and other states have applied such a standard in reviewing the decisions of cooperative and condominium boards (*see, e.g.*, *Kirsch v. Holiday Summer Homes*, 143 A.D.2d 811, 533 N.Y.S.2d 144; *Schoninger v. Yardarm Beach Homeowners Assn.*, 134 A.D.2d 1, 523 N.Y.S.2d 523; *Van Camp v. Sherman*, 132 A.D.2d 453, 517 N.Y.S.2d 152; *Papalexiou v. Tower W. Condominium*, 167 N.J.Super. 516, 401 A.2d 280; *Schwarzmann v. Association of Apt. Owners*, 33 Wash.App. 397, 655 P.2d 1177; *Rywalt v.*

Writer Corp., 34 Colo.App. 334, 526 P.2d 316). We agree with those courts that such a test best balances the individual and collective interests at stake.

Developed in the context of commercial enterprises, the business judgment rule prohibits judicial inquiry into actions of corporate directors "taken in good faith and in the exercise of honest judgment in the lawful and legitimate furtherance of corporate purposes." (*Auerbach v. Bennett*, 47 N.Y.2d 619, 629, 419 N.Y.S.2d 920, 393 N.E.2d 994, *supra*.) So long as the corporation's directors have not breached their fiduciary obligation to the corporation, "the exercise of [their powers] for the common and general interests of the corporation may not be questioned, although the results show that what they did was unwise or inexpedient." (*Pollitz v. Wabash R.R. Co.*, 207 N.Y. 113, 124, 100 N.E. 721.)

Application of a similar doctrine is appropriate because a cooperative corporation is—in fact and function—a corporation, acting through the management of its board of directors, and subject to the Business Corporation Law. There is no cause to create a special new category in law for corporate actions by coop boards.

We emphasize that reference to the business judgment rule is for the purpose of analogy only. Clearly, in light of the doctrine's origins in the quite different world of commerce, the fiduciary principles identified in the existing case law—primarily emphasizing avoidance of self-dealing and financial self-aggrandizement—will of necessity be adapted over time in order to apply to directors of not-for-profit homeowners' cooperative corporations (*see*, Goldberg, *Community Association Use Restrictions*, *op. cit.*, at 677–683). For present purposes, we need not, nor should we determine the entire range of the fiduciary obligations of a cooperative board, other than to note that the board owes its duty of loyalty to the cooperative—that is, it must act for the benefit of the residents collectively. So long as the board acts for the purposes of the cooperative, within the scope of its authority and in good faith, courts will not substitute their judgment for the board's. Stated somewhat differently, unless a resident challenging the board's action is able to demonstrate a breach of this duty, judicial review is not available.

In reaching this conclusion, we reject the test seemingly applied by the Appellate Division majority and explicitly applied by Supreme Court in its initial decision. That inquiry was directed at the *reasonableness* of the board's decision; having itself found that relocation of the riser posed no "dangerous aspect" to the building, the Appellate Division concluded that the renovation should remain. Like the business judgment rule, this reasonableness standard—originating in the quite different world of governmental agency decisionmaking—has found favor with courts reviewing board decisions (*see, e.g.*, *Amoruso v. Board of Managers*, 38 A.D.2d 845, 330 N.Y.S.2d 107; *Lenox Manor v. Gianni*, 120 Misc.2d 202, 465 N.Y.S.2d 809; *see*, Note, *Judicial Review of Condominium Rulemaking*, *op. cit.*, at 659–661 [discussing cases from other jurisdictions]).

As applied in condominium and cooperative cases, review of a board's decision under a reasonableness standard has much in common with the rule we adopt today. A primary focus of the inquiry is whether board action is in furtherance of a legitimate purpose of the cooperative or condominium, in which case it will generally be upheld. The difference between the reasonableness test and the rule we adopt is twofold. First—unlike the business judgment rule, which places on the owner seeking review the burden to demonstrate a breach of the board's fiduciary duty—reasonableness review requires the board to demonstrate that its decision was reasonable. Second, although in practice a certain amount of deference appears to be accorded to board decisions, reasonableness review permits—indeed, in theory requires— the court itself to evaluate the merits or wisdom of the board's decision (*see, e.g., Hidden Harbour Estates v. Basso*, 393 So.2d 637, 640 [Fla.Dist.Ct.App.]), just as the Appellate Division did in the present case.

The more limited judicial review embodied in the business judgment rule is preferable. In the context of the decisions of a for-profit corporation, "courts are ill equipped and infrequently called on to evaluate what are and must be essentially business judgments * * * by definition the responsibility for business judgments must rest with the corporate directors; their individual capabilities and experience peculiarly qualify them for the discharge of that responsibility." (*Auerbach v. Bennett*, 47 N.Y.2d, *supra,* at 630–631, 419 N.Y.S.2d 920, 393 N.E.2d 994). Even if decisions of a cooperative board do not generally involve expertise beyond the usual ken of the judiciary, at the least board members will possess experience of the peculiar needs of their building and its residents not shared by the court.

Several related concerns persuade us that such a rule should apply here. As this case exemplifies, board decisions concerning what residents may or may not do with their living space may be highly charged and emotional. A cooperative or condominium is by nature a myriad of often competing views regarding personal living space, and decisions taken to benefit the collective interest may be unpalatable to one resident or another, creating the prospect that board decisions will be subjected to undue court involvement and judicial second-guessing. Allowing an owner who is simply dissatisfied with particular board action a second opportunity to reopen the matter completely before a court, which—generally without knowing the property—may or may not agree with the reasonableness of the board's determination, threatens the stability of the common living arrangement.

Moreover, the prospect that each board decision may be subjected to full judicial review hampers the effectiveness of the board's managing authority. The business judgment rule protects the board's business decisions and managerial authority from indiscriminate attack. At the same time, it permits review of improper decisions, as when the challenger demonstrates that the board's action has no legitimate relationship to the welfare of the cooperative, deliberately singles out individuals for harmful treatment, is taken without notice or consideration of the relevant facts, or is beyond the scope of the board's authority.

Levandusky failed to meet this burden, and Supreme Court properly dismissed his petition. His argument that having once granted its approval, the board was powerless to rescind its decision after he had spent considerable sums on the renovations is without merit. There is no dispute that Levandusky failed to comply with the provisions of the "Alteration Agreement" or "Renovation Guidelines" designed to give the board explicit written notice before it approved a change in the building's heating system. Once made aware of Levandusky's intent, the board promptly consulted its engineer, and notified Levandusky that it would not depart from a policy of refusing to permit the movement of pipes. That he then went ahead and moved the pipe hardly allows him to claim reliance on the board's initial approval of his plans. Indeed, recognition of such an argument would frustrate any systematic effort to enforce uniform policies.

Levandusky's additional allegations that the board's decision was motivated by the personal animosity of another board member toward him, and that the board had in fact permitted other residents to jog their steam risers, are wholly conclusory. The board submitted evidence—unrefuted by Levandusky—that it was acting pursuant to the advice of its engineer, and that it had not previously approved such jogging. Finally, the fact that allowing Levandusky an exception to the policy might not have resulted in harm to the building does not require that the exception be allowed. Under the rule we articulate today, we decline to review the merits of the board's determination that it was preferable to adhere to a uniform policy regarding the building's piping system.

Turning to the concurrence, it is apparent that in many respects we are in agreement concerning the appropriate standard of judicial review of cooperative board decisions; it is more a matter of label that divides us. For these additional reasons, we believe our choice is the better one.

For the guidance of the courts and all other interested parties, obviously a single standard for judicial review of the propriety of board action is desirable, irrespective of the happenstance of the form of the lawsuit challenging that action. Unlike challenges to administrative agency decisions, which take the form of article 78 proceedings, challenges to the propriety of corporate board action have been lodged as derivative suits, injunction actions, and all manner of civil suits, including article 78 proceedings. While the nomenclature will vary with the form of suit, we see no purpose in allowing the form of the action to dictate the substance of the standard by which the legitimacy of corporate action is to be measured.

By the same token, unnecessary confusion is generated by prescribing different standards for different categories of issues that come before cooperative boards—for example, a standard of business judgment for choices between competing economic options, but rationality for the administration of corporate bylaws and rules governing shareholder-tenant rights. There is no need for two rules when one will do, particularly since corporate action often partakes of each category of issues. Indeed, even the decision here might be portrayed as the administration of corporate bylaws and rules governing shareholder-tenant rights, or more broadly as a policy choice based on the economic consequences of tampering with the building's piping system.

Finally, we reiterate that "business judgment" appears to strike the best balance. It establishes that board action undertaken in furtherance of a legitimate corporate purpose will generally not be pronounced "arbitrary and capricious or an abuse of discretion" (CPLR 7803[3]) in article 78 proceedings, or otherwise unlawful in other types of litigation. It is preferable to a standard that requires Judges, rather than directors, to decide what action is "reasonable" for the cooperative. It avoids drawing sometimes elusive semantical distinctions between what is "reasonable" and what is "rational" (the concurrence rejects the former but embraces the latter as the appropriate test). And it better protects tenant-shareholders against bad faith and self-dealing than a test that insulates board decisions "if there is a rational basis to explain them" or if "an articulable and rational basis for the board's decision exists." The mere presence of an engineer's report, for example— "certainly a rational explanation for the board's decision"—should not end all inquiry, foreclosing review of nonconclusory assertions of malevolent conduct; under the business judgment test, it would not.

Accordingly, the order of the Appellate Division should be modified, with costs to appellant, by reinstating Supreme Court's judgment to the extent it granted appellant's cross motions regarding the steam riser and severed and set down for assessment the issue of damages and, as so modified, affirmed.

[WACHTLER, C.J., and SIMONS, ALEXANDER, HANCOCK and BELLACOSA, JJ., concur with KAYE, J.; TITONE, J., concurs in a separate opinion which is omitted.]

NOTES

1. *Regulation of Use.* Every social benefit of communal life can be measured in the increments of freedom lost to individual unit owners. The happy prospect of tight regulation to exclude undesirables quickly turns sour when an owner tries to sell her unit to someone the board considers undesirable. The virtues of architectural harmony will not be so evident to the owner whose preference for fuchsia colonial-style shutters put him in an outvoted minority of one. The condominium, cooperative or homeowners association is more than just a community. It is, as *Levandusky* suggests, a community that regulates the life, liberty and welfare of its members with an intensity unmatched in public government.

These perennial frustrations of communal life are doubtless aggravated by the fact that the ties that bind project owners are economic as well as social and political. All owners are required to pay a periodic assessment for maintenance, repairs and improvements. When the assessment is for existing common areas and facilities, the gripes will be relatively few. Objections will, however, be far more frequent and substantial when the board levies an assessment for construction of an improvement, such as a tennis court or swimming pool, that some members will never use, or refuses to levy an assessment to repair casualty damage that offends the handful of residents who live near the damaged area, but not residents in other parts of the project. See Natelson, Consent, Coercion, and "Reasonableness" in Private Law: The Special Case of the Property Owners Association, 51 Ohio St.L.J. 41 (1990); see also Note, Condominium Association Remedies Against a Recalcitrant Unit Owner, 73 St. John's L.Rev. 247 (1999). Courts have followed *Levandusky* in adopting the business judgment rule to mediate such disputes. See, e.g., America v. Sumspray Condominium Ass'n, 61 A.3d 1249 (Me. 2013) (court relied on business judgment rule and absence of bad faith to dismiss action for failure by board to enforce smoking ban).

2. *Regulation of Occupancy.* Condominiums, cooperatives, and homeowners associations often attempted to bar children from the premises, especially in projects designed for senior citizens or young adults. A family with children would be barred from buying into the project; a family having a child while living in a unit would be forced to move.

Although there were some exceptions, courts generally upheld such provisions, emphasizing the importance of contract reliance. Those striking such restrictions relied on state statutory grounds and a policy favoring housing for children. See Korngold, Single Family Use Covenants: For Achieving A Balance Between Traditional Family Life and Individual Autonomy, 22 U.C.Davis L.Rev. 951 (1989).

This issue was largely preempted by the Fair Housing Amendments Act of 1988, Pub.L. No. 100–430, 102 Stat. 1619, 42 U.S.C.A. §§ 3610–3614 and 3614a, which bars discrimination in the sale or rental of dwellings on the basis of "familial status." The legislative history indicates that the measure was to end barriers to housing for children. At the same time, the statute specifically did not bar discrimination against families with children in "housing for older persons," thus leaving open the possibility of bona fide senior citizen communities.

See generally Note, The Fair Housing Act Amendments and Age Restrictions in Condominiums and Cooperatives, 73 St. John's L.Rev. 273 (1999).

3. *Private Government.* Condominiums, cooperatives and homeowners associations are in effect small, private communities and are in many respects governed and taxed—through assessments—much like more traditional communities such as villages and cities. These similarities raise the obvious question whether rulemaking by condominium and cooperative boards or homeowners associations should, like land use decisions made by local governments, be subjected to judicial review. Many courts have answered in the affirmative, and have tested board decisions against the same standards they apply to local governments' exercise of the police power: Is the rule reasonably related to its stated purposes? Are the stated purposes related to the community's health, safety, welfare and morals? Was the rule's enactment procedurally correct? Does it interfere with a vested right or expectation? Probably because the private community is smaller and more clearly consensual than the usual municipal community, the answers that courts have given are more dramatically slanted in favor of community power over individual choice. See Alexander, Freedom, Coercion, and the Law of Servitudes, 73 Cornell L.Rev. 883 (1988); Ellickson, Cities and Homeowners Associations, 130 U.Pa.L.Rev. 1519 (1982); Epstein, Covenants and Constitutions, 73 Cornell L.Rev. 906 (1988); Korngold, Resolving the Flaws of Residential Servitudes and Owners Associations: For Reformation Not Termination, 1990 Wis.L.Rev. 513; Reichman, Private Residential Governments: An Introductory Survey, 43 U.Chi.L.Rev. 253 (1976); Winokur, The Mixed Blessings of Promissory Servitudes: Toward Optimizing Economic Utility, Individual Liberty, and Personal Identity, 1989 Wis.L.Rev. 1; Note, Judicial Review of Condominium Rulemaking, 94 Harv.L.Rev. 647 (1981); Comment, Community Association Use Restrictions: Applying the Business Judgment Doctrine, 64 Chi.–Kent L.Rev. 653 (1988).

PART TWO

ELEMENTS OF THE COMMERCIAL REAL ESTATE TRANSACTION

The basic elements of commercial real estate transactions are the same as the basic elements of single-family residential transactions. Brokers will be engaged and lawyers retained to bring seller, buyer and lender together and to structure and document the transaction. An executory instrument, typically a contract, will be used to bind the parties while buyer and lender make the necessary inquiries into title and into the parcel's suitability for the buyer's and lender's investment purposes. An escrow or some similar closing mechanism will be employed to assure that delivery and other conveyancing formalities are met. Finance will play a large role, and federal tax benefits may offer substantial inducements to the transaction.

The chief consequential distinction between commercial and residential land transactions is scale. Because commercial transactions usually have much greater value than residential transactions, they can support a greater number of professional participants engaged in an array of more particularized tasks. For example, instead of relying on the seller's broker, or that broker's subagent, the commercial buyer may engage and pay his own real estate broker to seek out properties for him. Instead of the parties relying on one or possibly two lawyers to oversee all aspects of the transaction, the commercial buyer, seller and lender will each retain at least one lawyer to represent their respective interests. The economics of large commercial transactions also make it possible, and desirable, for these lawyers to custom-tailor some aspects of the transaction and its documentation to the special needs of their clients and the attributes of the parcel.

The buyer's and seller's lawyers will sometimes document the parties' executory period obligations with the same one-or two-page form of deposit receipt or contract of sale that is used in residential transactions. Yet the magnitude of the parties' risk and potential rewards, and the number of conditions involved, will usually dictate a lengthier, more detailed document. For example, in place of the three-page contract of sale used in New York residential transactions, parties to a commercial purchase in New York may use a form of "Contract of Sale for Office, Commercial or Multifamily Residence" that runs to over twice the length and includes sections on seller warranties, covenants and responsibility for violations, in addition to the standard provisions on marketable title and payment of the purchase price. See Holtzschue, Contract of Sale for Office, Commercial and Multi-Family Residential Premises—A Commentary, 17 Real Prop. Probate & Trust J. 382 (1982). In some situations, the difficulty of striking a balance between an agreement that will incorporate all contingencies that concern the buyer, and one that will not be so open-ended that it will be considered illusory, may persuade the parties to use a purchase option instead.

Title insurance, used in many but not all residential transactions, is today the norm in large commercial transactions. The principal reason is that the major institutional lenders and investors, from life insurance companies to hedge funds, that finance these transactions insist that title to their security be insured by large well-established institutions possessing sufficient trained personnel to assist in their negotiations, and sufficient resources to pay off on any title claims. Similarly, surveys, which are only sporadically used in residential transactions, are typically required in commercial transactions, particularly when encroachments or easements may interfere with the buyer's proposed development. Escrow instructions, which commonly run to one or two pages in residential transactions, may in commercial transactions grow to twenty pages or more to meet the needs of the many documents, parties, interests, and federal income tax requirements that may be involved. See generally, Kuklin, Commercial Title Insurance and the Lawyer's Responsibility, 15 Real Prop., Probate & Trust J. 557 (1980); J. Pedowitz (ed.), Title Insurance: The Lawyer's Expanding Role (1985).

Finance plays an even larger role in commercial real estate transactions than it does in residential transactions. The basic finance instruments—mortgage, trust, deed, installment land contract—may be the same, but the purposes to which they are put will differ, their provisions will be more detailed, and they will more frequently be used in connection with other financing devices. Leases represent a popular alternative or complement to mortgage and trust deed finance and can themselves become security for a mortgage or deed of trust. Federal income tax considerations, always an inducement to home purchase, sometimes become the sole justification for a commercial real estate transaction.

CHAPTER VII

COMMERCIAL LAND FINANCE

Change seems to be the constant theme in the commercial real estate market and finance. The current landscape differs from dramatically from that of thirty, twenty, ten, and even five years ago. The current environment reflects the aftermath of the 2008 mortgage and general financial crisis that affected not only American real estate but interdependent,global financing in general. In the aftermath of that crisis, lenders have become more exacting in their terms and capital requirements for borrowers, the great amounts of capital that were available in the early 2000s dried up substantially, and new governmental regulation and the prospect of regulation led to uncertainty and increased obligations for borrowers and lenders. The trend of deregulation of the lending industry in the period from the 1980s to the early 2000s has been reversed to a significant extent through new federal legislation and rulemaking, including the Dodd-Frank Wall Street Reform and Consumer Protection Act of 2010.

In the wake of the financial crisis many commercial projects became distressed. Office and store tenants, suffering in the downturn, defaulted or failed to renew leases at the same rents or at all, creating cash flow problems for owners. Without these leases, when their balloon mortgages became due, owners were unable to negotiate new mortgages at the same terms. Owners were also hurt by lenders' increased capital requirements and general decline in property values because of market softness, lowering the amounts that owners could borrow to pay off their balloons. Some properties went into foreclosure, some properties were carried by lenders not wishing to show more defaulting loans on their scorecards, and some developers gave up ownership stakes in order to get an infusion of necessary capital. As of 2014, the commercial market is strengthening in locations in the United States but in other regions it is still shaky. For an excellent analysis of the 2008 commercial mortgage crisis, see Marsh, Too Big To Fail vs. Too Small To Notice: Addressing the Commercial Real Estate Debt Crisis, 63 Ala. L. Rev. 321 (2012).

Although the sources and terms of commercial real estate finance will doubtless continue to change, it is possible to trace some fundamental patterns.

Terms. The most common lender strategy has been to agree only to short term notes or notes renewable at specified intervals, with the renewal rate adjusted up or down according to some measure of inflation such as the consumer price index. Alternatively, the lender may agree to a long term loan, but only if the interest rate is allowed to float according to an inflation index, or if the note contains a call provision entitling the lender to call in the note for complete repayment at a specified intervals before the loan has been fully amortized. As part of the effort to stimulate the economy post-2008, the Federal Reserve has kept interest rates low. Thus, while usury is an issue to be watched, it is not as prevalent of a concern for commercial and prime consumer borrowers as it was during the late 1970s and early 1980s when the prime rate hit 20%.

Another lender strategy has been to participate in the income from the mortgaged property. Lender and borrower might, for example, agree on a fixed, below market interest rate augmented by a specified percentage of the property's rental income and a further percentage of the property's appreciation in value at the time the mortgage is discharged. Or the parties may agree on a convertible mortgage—a fixed rate loan that entitles the lender at a specified point to convert the unamortized portion of the loan (say, 70% of the property's initial value) into an equity interest (again 70%) in the property. Frequently, a convertible mortgage will give the lender the right to buy out the mortgagor's remaining equity interest (here 30%) at a predetermined price or at a price calculated on the basis of a predetermined formula. See Usow & Newburn, The Return of Seller Financing for Commercial Real Estate?, 24 Probate & Property 51 (Jan./Feb. 2010).

Sources. Traditionally, life insurance companies and pension funds were the major source of long-term mortgage financing. Today, the sources of capital have increased. Hedge funds and other investment funds may make loans, often as participants in loan pools organized and administered by insurance companies and pension funds that leverage their expertise to place loans for others. Commercial mortgage backed securities, analogous to residential mortgage backed securities, see pages 350–367, also provide a source of capital for commercial deals, though that market has suffered somewhat post-2008. Also, as mortgage terms have become shorter and interest rates have become more readily adjustable, commercial banks have shown a new willingness to enter the commercial real estate loan market, as have the real estate credit subsidiaries of large industrial corporations. Foreign investment in U.S. real estate has also increased, as discussed in pages 803–831.

Three arrangements for assembling real estate debt and equity enjoyed varying popularity between the 1960's and the early 1980's: the limited partnership, the real estate investment trust and the joint venture. Prior to the 1986 Tax Reform Act, the limited partnership enabled individual, high bracket investors to capture the tax advantages of owning improved, depreciable property. As a result, many limited partnerships were created for the main, or even sole, purpose of obtaining tax benefits. As discussed at pages 940–957 below, these tax advantages have largely disappeared. Real estate limited partnerships are still important investment vehicles, however, when the project is economically sound, producing cash flow and appreciation. The 1986 Tax Reform Act also authorized a new investment vehicle— real estate mortgage investment conduits (REMICs)—to acquire and hold both commercial and residential mortgage loans and to issue securities embodying interests in these loans on the secondary mortgage market. See Forte, Capital Markets Mortgage: A Ratable Model for Main Street and Wall Street, 31 Real Prop. Probate & Tr. J. 68 (1999) (discussing increase in commercial mortgage backed securities); see also Calderon, Mezzanine Financing and Land Banks: Two Unconventional Methods of Financing Residential Real Estate Projects in the 21st Century, 29 Real Est. L.J. 283 (2001).

The real estate investment trust, like the limited partnership, enables the individual investor-shareholder to share in the investment advantages of real estate. One difference is that, unlike the limited partnership, which typically owns a single property, the REIT operates much like a mutual fund, holding a pool of real property assets. The REIT also offers some, but not all, of the limited partnership's tax advantages. So long as the REIT qualifies under the applicable Internal Revenue Code requirements respecting organization, operation, assets, income and dividend distribution, it can—like a partnership and unlike a corporation—pass its income and capital gains directly through to its investors, without any tax liability at the entity level of the REIT. See I.R.C. §§ 856–860. For a general discussion of REITs and related taxation issues, see Brown, Comment, Real Estate Investment Trusts and Subpart F: Characterizing Subpart F Inclusions for the Purposes of REIT Income Tests, 20 Emory Int'l L.Rev. 833 (2006); Jesch, The Taxation of "Opportunistic" Real Estate Private Equity Funds and U.S. Real Estate Investment Trusts (REITs)—An Investor's Comparative Analysis, 34 Real Est.L.J. 275 (2005); McCall, A Primer on Real Estate Trusts: The Legal Basis of REITs, Transactions: Tenn.J.Bus.L. 1 (2001).

Institutional lenders seeking an equity position in real estate will sometimes form a joint venture with a developer or other entrepreneur to build and operate the project. The lender ("money partner") provides the cash, or sometimes the land, needed for the project, and the developer ("operating partner") provides services and expertise. In return for their contributions, each co-venturer shares in the ownership, income and losses from the project in predetermined shares. Although joint ventures are most commonly structured as general partnerships between the co-venturers, they may also take the form of a limited partnership, corporation, REIT or tenancy in common. See Spore, The Economics of Real Estate Joint Ventures, 21 Probate & Property 26 (Jul./Aug. 2007).

Other Matters. For a helpful glossary, see Stein & Enedu, The Language of Commercial Real Estate Finance, 23 Probate & Property 59 (Mar./Apr. 2009). For an overview of the lawyer's due diligence role, See Harp, Give Them Their Due: Due Diligence in Commercial Real Estate Transactions, 25 Probate & Property 40 (Jul./Aug. 2011).

A. MORTGAGES

1. TERMS

Charles C. Smith & Harold A. Lubell,
The Promissory Note: Forgotten Document*
8 Real Estate Review 15–17 (Spring 1978).

The completion of a modern mortgage loan transaction requires an imposing number of documents. At the closing of complex financing transactions, such as high-credit lease loans, attorneys make use of extensive checklists that enumerate, among other documents, note

---

*   Reprinted with the consent of Thomson Reuters.

purchase agreements, leases, assignments of leases, promissory notes, mortgages, financing statements, various types of certifications, and detailed legal opinions. Many of the instruments are lengthy, and copies of the entire package of documents are often bound into volumes which, in size and weight, rival *Webster's New Third International Dictionary.*

When the financing of office buildings, shopping centers, and industrial facilities is arranged, many of the instruments, particularly the mortgage and leases, are the subjects of protracted negotiations. However, one of the most significant instruments is also one of the briefest and is often an almost forgotten document. It is the promissory note.

WHAT IS THE PROMISSORY NOTE?

The promissory note and the mortgage (or deed of trust) are the two essential documents of a real estate loan. The note is the evidence of the indebtedness and the promise to repay the loan, while the mortgage is the pledge of specific realty as security for the debt. The principal attributes of a valid note are the following:

- The note must be in writing.

- The borrower and lender must have contractual ability to act. (They must be under no legal incapacity, such as minority or insanity.)

- The borrower must promise to pay a specific sum of money.

- The terms of payment must be stated, e.g., the note normally is payable in periodic installments for a specified number of years.

- The rights of the parties in the event of a default must be specified.

- The note must be properly executed by the borrower. However, a note is not recorded and accordingly is not acknowledged before a notary public.

- There must be voluntary delivery by the borrower and acceptance by the lender.

Since the note is evidence of a debt and is a negotiable instrument, only one copy of it should be signed by the borrower. Were several copies to be signed, there would be evidence of multiple debts from the several negotiable instruments that would be created.

When a recorded instrument such as a mortgage is lost, evidence of the document is readily available in the office of recordation. However, the loss of an unrecorded promissory note may give rise to all sorts of problems. For example, assume that Bill Borrower obtained a mortgage loan in 1965. In 1970, he sold the property subject to the mortgage to Investment Inc. A default in payment by Investment Inc. occurs in 1978. The lender, Frantic Mortgage Corp., cannot find the note. Neither the attorneys who prepared the original promissory note nor others with knowledge of its terms are available. No copies or drafts are to be found. Since the note was nowhere recorded it is difficult to establish what remedies are available to Frantic. Thus, it is easy to see why lenders must conscientiously guard the possession of original promissory notes.

TERMS OF PAYMENT

Developers and investors in income-producing property are primarily interested in the following aspects of a mortgage loan:

- The amount of the loan.
- The interest rate.
- The term to maturity.
- The repayment provisions.
- The prepayment provisions.

All this information is included in the promissory note.

The following paragraph in a note evidencing a self-amortizing loan is typical. The loan was closed on January 20, 1978, in the amount of $3,200,000 for a term of twenty-eight years, at an interest rate of 9¼ percent.

"This note shall be paid as follows: On February 1, 1978 accrued interest only shall be paid. Thereafter, Maker shall pay equal monthly installments of Twenty-Six Thousand Four Hundred Five and No/100 Dollars ($26,405) commencing March 1, 1978 and continuing on the first day of each and every month thereafter until January 1, 2006, whereupon the balance of said principal sum and interest then remaining shall be paid. Each of said installments when paid shall be applied by the holder hereof to the payment of interest and the balance in reduction of principal."

When mortgage money is scarce, institutional lenders frequently seek an equity participation (a "kicker") in addition to the prevailing rate of interest. This feature of the loan is reflected by a provision in the note requiring the payment of a percentage of gross or net income of the property to the lender as additional interest.

PREPAYMENT PROVISIONS

Lenders usually seek to restrict prepayment of loans. Lenders want assurance that their money is invested for the full term of the loan, and that they will not unexpectedly have to seek other investment opportunities. On the other hand, borrowers prefer to be in a position to refinance so that they can take advantage of lower interest rates or the possibility of increasing the size of the loan if the value of the property appreciates.

It is therefore customary for lenders to charge a premium for the privilege of prepayment. The amount of the premium is usually expressed as a percentage of the outstanding balance of the loan. This percentage declines as the loan matures. Prepayment privileges in residential loans and in FHA or VA mortgages are governed by statute. Prepayment terms in all other real estate loans vary from lender to lender and are determined by market conditions.

A typical paragraph concerning the prepayment privilege follows. The specific terms have been omitted.

"No privilege is reserved to prepay during the first ___ loan years. Beginning with the ___ loan year and on ___ days' written notice, privilege is reserved to pay the loan in full on any interest date, on payment of a prepayment charge of ___ percent, if the loan is paid in full during the ___ loan year, such prepayment charge to decline by ___ percent per year thereafter. The prepayment charges are to be computed on the unpaid principal balance at the time of such prepayment. It is understood that the loan year stated herein commences on the expiration of ___ years from the date of the first payment of principal and interest."

In high-credit loan transactions, the borrower may negotiate a more favorable privilege. Since credit loans are based primarily on the financial strength of the borrower rather than on the value of real property, the prepayment terms are sometimes related directly to the economic serviceability of the property. The prepayment provision in such a loan may permit prepayment much sooner than is typical in other types of mortgage loans.

"If the premises shall have become uneconomical for Maker's continued use and occupancy in Maker's business, and if Maker's Board of Directors has determined to discontinue the use of the premises in Maker's business, or if Maker has already discontinued such use, then Maker may give notice to Payee, on or after the ___ loan year, of Maker's intention to prepay the note."

Of course, a premium will still be required in the event of prepayment.

Ordinarily, when prepayment occurs, the entire balance of the loan is prepaid. While there may be circumstances when it is advantageous to a borrower to prepay only a portion of the loan, this right to prepay is not customary.

SPECIAL SAFEGUARDS

The large number of loan defaults during the mid-70s has encouraged conservatism in current lending practices. The twenty-five-year and thirty-year mortgages of the 1960s did not anticipate soaring fuel prices, continuing inflation, overbuilding, or changing demographic patterns. Institutional lenders today seek a hedge against unpredictable conditions that may render a loan less attractive in the future. The following safeguards now frequently are found in the promissory note:

Due-on-Sale Provision. A due-on-sale provision assures the lender that in the event of a sale of the property, he can declare the loan due and payable. This means that the lender can prohibit the sale of the property to an entity which may not be as sound as the original borrower or which, in the lender's opinion, does not possess the requisite managerial ability. There are limitations on the enforceability of due-on-sale provisions in some states.

Prohibition Against Junior Financing. Such a prohibition seeks to prevent overfinancing. The relative ease with which property owners could obtain secondary financing during the zenith of real estate investment trust lending in the period from 1970 to 1973 overburdened many properties with debt and led to defaults.

Option to Call. Lenders may insist on an option to call the loan if they have doubts about the stability of a property's income over the term of a loan. Lenders tend to worry about properties in which tenant leases are for short terms or which are located in areas with changing rental markets. In such situations, the lender may provide in the promissory note that it has the option at a specific time during the term to call the loan upon six months prior written notice to the borrower. For example, a twenty-five-year loan may include an option to call during the fifteenth year.

Option to Recast. An option to recast, like an option to call, hedges against future uncertainty. For example, the note for a thirty-year mortgage loan on a small medical office building with five-and ten-year occupancy leases might provide as follows:

> "During the twelfth (12th) loan year, the Mortgagee upon six (6) months notice, will have the option to require an increase of monthly payments to amortize the loan in twenty-five (25) years from the date of closing rather than thirty (30) years. In the event this option is exercised, the Mortgagor shall have the right to prepay the loan in full without a prepayment charge within six (6) months after notice of the exercise of the option is given by the Mortgagee."

DEFAULT PROVISIONS

If installments are not paid when due or before the expiration of a reasonable grace period specified in the note, the lender may elect to accelerate payment and require payment of the entire balance of principal together with accrued interest. This option to accelerate payment may also be exercised if other promises in the note are breached by the borrower. If the accelerated payment is not made, an obvious remedy is to foreclose in accordance with the terms of the mortgage securing the note and pursuant to the laws of the state in which the property is located.

The note may provide, alternatively, for the payment of a "late charge" or additional interest as liquidated damages for the additional expense and loss resulting from the delinquency. Following is an example of a late charge provision.

> "Should Maker fail to make due and punctual payment of any money which Maker is required to pay hereunder within ten (10) days after the date on which the same shall become due and payable, such sum as shall be overdue shall bear interest from and after the due date thereof until paid at the rate of ___ percent (___) per annum."

The penalty rate usually will exceed the face rate of the mortgage.

In order to avoid deliberate default by a borrower who wants the debt accelerated so that he may pay off the loan and thus not pay a prepayment charge, the lender includes the following provision in the note:

> "Maker agrees that if an event of default occurs under this note, or under the mortgage or any other instruments securing the indebtedness evidenced hereby, and the maturity date is therefore accelerated, then a tender of payment by Maker, or by anyone on behalf of the Maker, of the amount necessary to satisfy all sums due hereunder made at any time prior to judicial sale of the mortgaged property or a redemption after

foreclosure, shall constitute an evasion of the payment terms hereof and shall be deemed to be a voluntary prepayment hereunder, and any such payment, to the extent permitted by law, will therefore include the fee required under the prepayment privilege."

PERSONAL LIABILITY

Currently, the majority of loans on income-producing property are nonrecourse loans. This means that the maker of the note has no personal liability. Appropriate exculpatory language is inserted in the note. The following is an example of an exculpatory provision:

"Maker shall have no personal liability under this Note, the Mortgage, or any other instrument given as security for the payment of this Note; the sole remedy of the holder of this Note in the event of any default shall be to proceed against the property described in the said Mortgage, the rents, issues, and profits therefrom and any further security as may have been given to secure the payment hereof; provided, however, that nothing contained herein shall limit or be construed to limit or impair the enforcement against such property and the rents, issues, and profits therefrom of the rights and remedies of the Holder hereof under this Note, the said Mortgage, and any other security investment given to secure the payment hereof."

The exculpatory provision is one of the few provisions in the note which is subject to negotiation among attorneys. The concern for avoidance of personal liability and the tax consequences associated with the nonrecourse aspect of a loan focus attention on the language of exculpation. A properly drafted provision assures the borrower that he has no personal liability for the obligations of the note, but does not impair the remedies of the lender seeking enforcement in the event of a default.

CONCLUSION

Although the documentation for a mortgage loan transaction has become complex, the promissory note remains a relatively simple instrument. The note is one of the key documents of the transaction, but it often receives insufficient attention. It merits careful scrutiny because it incorporates the basic terms of the loan transaction.

a.   USURY

NV One, LLC v. Potomac Realty Capital, LLC

Supreme Court of Rhode Island, 2014.
84 A.3d 800.

CHIEF JUSTICE SUTTELL, for the Court.

In a case of first impression, we are asked to determine whether a usury savings clause in a commercial loan document validates an otherwise usurious contract. In view of the facts and circumstances of this case, we conclude that it does not; we hold, therefore, that the promissory note at issue is void as a matter of law.

The defendant, Potomac Realty Capital, LLC, (PRC or defendant) appeals from the Superior Court's grant of partial summary judgment in favor of plaintiffs, NV One, LLC, Nicholas E. Cambio, and Vincent A. Cambio (collectively, NV One or plaintiffs). The defendant asserts that the trial justice erred when he granted plaintiffs' motion for partial summary judgment on liability for violation of the usury statute, G.L.1956 § 6–26–2, by declaring the usury savings clause of the parties' loan agreement unenforceable. For the reasons set forth in this opinion, we affirm the judgment of the Superior Court.

I   Facts and Procedural History

In 2007, plaintiffs sought a loan to rehabilitate and renovate a former post office located at 1190 Main Street in the Town of West Warwick (property). On July 17, 2007, NV One entered into a loan agreement with PRC and signed a promissory note (note) for the principal amount of $1,800,000; as security for the loan, NV One granted a mortgage, assignment of leases and rents, security agreement, and fixture filing with respect to the property. The plaintiffs Nicholas E. Cambio and Vincent A. Cambio also personally guaranteed the loan.

In addition to the note, mortgage, and related documents, at the closing of the loan the parties executed a Sources and Uses of Funds sheet and a Loan Disbursement Authorization (all collectively, the loan documents). The loan documents established both an "interest reserve" and a "renovation reserve," set initially at $62,500 and $940,000, respectively. Monthly interest-only payments were due on the first day of each calendar month until the loan's maturity date of August 1, 2008, on which date final payment of both the unpaid interest and unpaid principal was to be made. The note set an interest rate at "the greater of 5.3% or the LIBOR Rate, plus 4.7%."[2] The note also set a "default rate" at "the lesser of (a) twenty-four percent (24%) per annum and (b) the maximum rate of interest, if any, which may be collected * * * under applicable law." The loan documents also imposed fees, including an exit fee of $18,000 and an origination fee of $25,000. The Sources and Uses of Funds sheet also notes a previous deposit of $15,000, raising the total value of the loan to $1,815,000.

At the heart of this case are the maximum interest provisions contained in both the note and the mortgage; as the trial justice noted in his decision, "[t]hese provisions attempt to conform the instruments to the local usury laws, and they are commonly known as usury savings clauses." Section 4.4 of the note, titled "Maximum Amount," provides a usury savings clause, which reads in pertinent part:

> "A. It is the intention of Maker [NV One] and Payee [PRC] to conform strictly to the usury and similar laws relating to interest from time to time in force, and all agreements between Maker and Payee, whether now existing or hereafter arising and whether oral or written, are hereby expressly limited so that in no contingency or event whatsoever, whether by

---

[2]   LIBOR, which stands for "London Interbank Offered Rate," is defined as "[a] daily compilation by the British Bankers Association of the rates that major international banks charge each other for large-volume, short-term loans of Eurodollars, with monthly maturity rates calculated out to one year." Black's Law Dictionary 1027 (9th ed. 2009).

acceleration of maturity hereof or otherwise, shall the amount paid or agreed to be paid in the aggregate to Payee as interest hereunder or under the other Loan Documents or in any other security agreement given to secure the Loan Amount, or in any other document evidencing, securing or pertaining to the Loan Amount, exceed the maximum amount permissible under applicable usury or such other laws (the 'Maximum Amount').

"B. If under any circumstances Payee shall ever receive an amount that would exceed the Maximum Amount, such amount shall be deemed a payment in reduction of the Loan owing hereunder and any obligation of Maker in favor of Payee * * * or if such excessive interest exceeds the unpaid balance of the Loan and any other obligation of Maker in favor of Payee, the excess shall be deemed to have been a payment made by mistake and shall be refunded to Maker."

Although the parties executed the loan documents, the entire $1.8 million principal balance was not disbursed at the closing of the loan, nor was it ever fully disbursed to NV One. The trial justice attributed this, in part, to the holdbacks for the $940,000 renovation reserve and the $62,500 interest reserve. Although the loan documents required both reserves to be placed in escrow, PRC never actually placed funds in escrow, nor did it segregate the funds in any way. Critically, section 2.12 of the note provided that NV One would not accrue any interest on the reserved funds.

At the time of closing there was a net funding disbursement of $761,478.54; and, in January 2008, a disbursement of $143,877.50 was made from the renovation reserve at the request of NV One.

The note contained a provision in section 2.7 allowing the parties to extend the date of maturity for up to an additional twelve months, provided certain conditions were met. Pursuant to that provision, on August 1, 2008, NV One paid PRC $18,000 in consideration for the execution of an allonge which extended the maturity date by ten months to June 1, 2009. The $18,000 and the interest payments on the allonge were paid out of the interest reserve. By September 2008, NV One had received $995,997.50 of the $1.8 million loan. By November 2008, the interest reserve was exhausted. By the new date of maturity, NV One received, at most, $1,007,390.52 on the $1.8 million loan.

Although PRC never disbursed the entire $1.8 million loan amount, it routinely charged NV One interest for the entire loan amount. In his decision, the trial justice noted that "[p]rior to the allonge, PRC charged interest at ten percent (10%) of the total $1.8 million, when as little as $761,478.54 was disbursed." From the time of the execution of the allonge in August 2008 through February 2009, "PRC charged NV One interest at a rate of twelve percent (12%) of the total $1.8 million, despite the fact that at its height, $1,007,390.52 was actually disbursed to NV One." On February 23, 2009, PRC sent NV One a notice of default for failing to complete renovations within the time provided in the security agreement, and provided a thirty-day cure period, after which it would impose the default interest rate. In March 2009, at the end of the thirty days, "PRC charged NV One the [d]efault rate of twenty-four percent (24%) interest calculated upon the $1.8 million face amount of the [n]ote." The trial justice found that "[w]hen the interest charged is applied in the context of the amount actually disbursed, the rate exceeds twenty-one percent (21%) essentially throughout the loan." The trial justice further found that "PRC never adjusted the amount of interest charged to lower it below twenty-one percent (21%)."

Due to NV One's alleged failure to pay off the loan by the maturity date of June 1, 2009, on October 9, 2009, PRC sent NV One a notice of default and payment demand. On November 5, 2009, pursuant to its rights under the mortgage, PRC sent a foreclosure notice to NV One. In addition, on or about November 19, 2009, PRC sent a demand notice to plaintiffs Nicholas E. Cambio and Vincent A. Cambio demanding payment pursuant to their personal guarantees. On December 14, 2009, plaintiffs filed a verified complaint against PRC claiming fraud, breach of contract, and usury, and seeking injunctive relief preventing foreclosure on the property and collection from the personal guarantors. On August 16, 2011, plaintiffs filed a motion for summary judgment with respect to liability on count 3 of the complaint, alleging violations of the Rhode Island usury law.[7]

On December 16, 2011, the trial justice filed a written decision granting plaintiffs' motion for partial summary judgment. On January 11, 2012, the trial justice entered an order declaring the loan usurious and void, voiding the mortgage, and removing the liens on the property from the land records. In his written decision, the trial justice found that "[i]t is clear on the record of undisputed facts that the rate was undoubtedly usurious, at least for some period." In reaching that decision, the trial justice stated that the Rhode Island usury statute generally sets the maximum allowable rate of interest at 21 percent. He further noted that "[t]o determine whether an interest rate is usurious, the value for computing the maximum permissible interest is not the amount on the face of the loan, but, rather, the actual amount received by the borrower." He then analyzed the interest rates PRC charged during each period of the loan (10 percent, 12 percent, and 24 percent) and determined that, because these percentages were calculated using the entire $1.8 million loan amount—as opposed to the $1,007,390.52 PRC actually distributed to NV One—"[t]here can be no doubt that these interest amounts charged exceeded twenty-one percent (21%) of the disbursed loan."

The trial justice next considered the applicability of the usury savings clause "in light of the public policy, legislative intent, and plain meaning of the Rhode Island usury law." The trial justice embarked on an extensive analysis of the policies behind Rhode Island usury jurisprudence, as well as the law in states with substantially developed usury law, such as Texas, Florida, and North Carolina. In ultimately declining to honor the usury savings clause and granting plaintiffs' motion for partial summary judgment, the trial justice stated that "[l]ending effect to a usury savings clause would contradict this state's articulated public policy in favor of the borrower and against usurious transactions."

The defendant timely appealed the January 11, 2012 order. The trial justice then stayed his ruling for forty-five days and, after a February 17, 2012 meeting with the parties' attorneys, issued a further

---

[7]   General Laws 1956 § 6–26–2.

stay pending consideration of the motion by this Court. The motion to stay came before this Court on March 14, 2012, after which this Court vacated the trial justice's stay but enjoined plaintiffs from alienating the property without prior authorization from this Court.

On appeal, PRC does not challenge the factual findings of the trial justice; rather it contends that the trial justice "erred when [he] granted [NV One's] motion for partial summary judgment on liability for violation of [G.L.1956] § 6–26–2 by declaring the usury savings clause of the loan agreement unenforceable." The enforceability of usury savings clauses is an issue of first impression before this Court, and PRC argues that such clauses should be enforceable under Rhode Island law. In its reply brief, PRC maintains that the trial justice "erred in failing to perform a proper analysis when it rendered a commercial contract term unenforceable on the grounds of public policy."

. . .

III Discussion

Liability for usurious interest rates in Rhode Island is well settled and clear. The maximum allowable interest rate is a statutory construct whereby interest rates in excess of 21 percent per annum are deemed usurious. Section 6–26–2(a). Contracts in violation of § 6–26–2 are usurious and void, and the borrower is entitled to recover any amount paid on the loan. Section 6–26–4. The lender's subjective intent to comply with the usury laws is immaterial. *Burdon v. Unrath,* 47 R.I. 227, 231, 132 A. 728, 730 (1926). In order to determine whether an interest rate is usurious, the face amount of the loan is irrelevant; instead, the maximum allowable interest is calculated based on the amount actually received by the borrower. *See Industrial National Bank of Rhode Island v. Stuard,* 113 R.I. 124, 125, 318 A.2d 452, 453 (1974). Because neither party disputes the material facts, *i.e.,* that PRC charged NV One interest in excess of the permissible 21 percent maximum, the applicability of the usury savings clause is determinative of whether NV One is entitled to judgment as a matter of law.

PRC's Usurious Interest Rate

Setting aside for the moment the usury savings clause, it is abundantly clear to this Court that the loan between PRC and NV One was usurious. However, because only a portion of the record was certified to this Court and the numbers contained therein are undisputed, we will not belabor the analysis any more than is necessary to determine usury. According to PRC's Loan Activity Report, from the inception of the loan on July 17, 2007, through August 31, 2007, PRC disbursed only $797,500 of the entire $1.8 million loan amount. In accordance with the Sources and Uses sheet of the loan document, the $62,500 interest reserve and the $940,000 renovation reserve—which constitute the balance of the loan—were required to be placed in escrow by PRC. However, according to Nicholas E. Cambio's sworn affidavit, these funds were not placed in escrow, but were merely established as "journal entries" by PRC. Nevertheless, PRC charged NV One interest at a rate of 10.125 percent for August 2007, calculated against the entire $1.8 million loan amount, for a total interest charge of $15,693.75.

The fact that PRC calculated the interest amount against the face amount of the loan as opposed to the amount of the disbursed funds is of critical importance to the usury determination. *See Industrial National Bank of Rhode Island,* 113 R.I. at 125, 318 A.2d at 453. For instance, the August interest charge, when calculated against the actual disbursed amount, as is necessary to determine usury, results in an effective interest rate of 23.17 percent per annum.[10] Because PRC and NV One entered into a valid loan contract, and the 23.17 percent interest rate that PRC charged exceeds the 21 percent maximum interest rate set out in § 6–26–2, it is clear to us that the loan was usurious and therefore void.[11]

However, one need not engage in complex arithmetic in order to discern usury in PRC's loan. In the event of default by NV One, the note imposed a default interest rate at "the lesser of (a) twenty-four percent (24%) per annum and (b) the maximum rate of interest, if any, which may be collected * * * under applicable law." This 24 percent interest rate is usurious on its face. *See* § 6–26–2. Moreover, during the default period, PRC did not attempt to conform the charged interest to the maximum rate allowable by law (21 percent), but instead demanded the full 24 percent. The following sequence of events is illustrative. On February 23, 2009, PRC sent NV One a notice of default, providing NV One with thirty days to cure the default before PRC would impose the default interest rate. On April 8, 2009, PRC sent another letter indicating that NV One had defaulted and PRC would be imposing the default interest rate, retroactive to March 24, 2009. Finally, on November 19, 2009, PRC sent the Cambios a demand for payment pursuant to their personal guarantee, demanding full payment of the $1,007,390.52, plus an additional $464,487.62 in back interest and fees. The back interest PRC demanded—$382,800—consists partly of $296,800 in interest charged during the default period of March 24, 2009, through November 17, 2009. PRC calculated this latter figure by applying the default 24 percent rate to the $1.8 million face value of the loan. The 24 percent rate is facially usurious irrespective of the loan amount; however, when calculated against the actual disbursed amount, that rate skyrockets to 43.48 percent per annum,[14] more than double the maximum permissible interest rate. Therefore, it is apparent to this Court that not only did PRC charge a usurious interest rate, but it made no attempt to lower the interest charges to conform to the maximum permissible interest rate.

The Usury Savings Clause

Having determined that the loan is usurious, we turn now to the applicability of the usury savings clause. It is well settled in Rhode

---

[10] The $15,693.75 averages out to $506.25 per day in interest charges, and a total of $184,781.25 per year. In order to generate $184,781.25 in annual interest on a $797,500 loan (the actual disbursed amount), interest must be charged at a rate of 23.17 percent.

[11] It bears mentioning that during the entire life of the loan PRC routinely calculated interest against the $1.8 million amount, despite the fact that the most that PRC ever disbursed to NV One was $1,007,390.52. Thus, the actual interest rate was in excess of 21 percent for the majority of the loan.

[14] PRC charged the default rate of 24 percent for the 239 days of the default period from March 24, 2009, through November 17, 2009, for an interest charge of $1,200 per day. $1,200 per day amounts to $438,000 annually, which, when calculated against the $1,007,390.52 disbursed amount, results in an annualized interest rate of 43.48 percent.

Island that "a contract term is unenforceable only if it violates public policy." *Gorman v. St. Raphael Academy,* 853 A.2d 28, 39 (R.I.2004). A contract, or a term contained therein violates public policy only if it is: "[1] injurious to the interests of the public, [2] interferes with the public welfare or safety, [3] is unconscionable; or [4] tends to injustice or oppression." *Id.* (quoting *City of Warwick v. Boeng Corp.,* 472 A.2d 1214, 1218 (R.I.1984)). In order to decide whether the enforcement of a usury savings clause violates public policy, we must first determine the public policy underlying the usury laws in general. Although some states' statutes explicitly articulate the policy behind their usury laws,[16] the Rhode Island usury statutory scheme is relatively brief and makes no mention of public policy or legislative intent. *See* chapter 26 of title 6. It is therefore incumbent upon this Court to discern the public policy undergirding the usury laws. To that end, we begin by first examining the plain language of the statute.

The pertinent language of the Rhode Island usury statute states, without qualification, that "no person, partnership, association, or corporation loaning money * * * shall, directly or indirectly, reserve, charge, or take interest on a loan, whether before or after maturity, at a rate which shall exceed * * * twenty-one percent (21%) per annum * * *." Section 6–26–2(a). The use of the word "shall" evinces a certainty; in other words, a lender that charges interest in excess of 21 percent is liable for usury. Additionally, the fact that the Legislature explicitly delineated only one specific exception[17] to the maximum interest rate indicates a consideration (and rejection) of any and all other circumstances whereby a lender may charge interest in excess of 21 percent. The criminal usury statute, § 6–26–3 criminalizes "willful[ ] and knowing[ ]" violations of the maximum interest rate, thereby further underscoring the immateriality of a lender's intent in determining civil usury under § 6–26–2. Because the lender's intent to charge an interest rate exceeding the permissible maximum is immaterial to a determination of usury (and the invocation of penalties resulting therefrom), it is clear that the Legislature intended an inflexible, hardline approach to usury that is tantamount to strict liability.

This rigid approach is borne out in the historically strict enforcement of the statute and its predecessors through the years. In a 1926 decision concerning a prior usury statute, this Court rejected a lender's argument that he had intended to abide by the maximum interest limits, holding that lack of intent "is no excuse for the violation of the statute." *Burdon,* 47 R.I. at 231, 132 A. at 730. The Court stated that "[t]o hold otherwise would violate an established principle of law, and would furnish to avaricious lenders a convenient excuse for an evasion of the law." *Id.* Three years later, the Court once again denied a

---

[16] *See, e.g.,* N.C. Gen.Stat. Ann. § 24–2.1(g) (West 2007) ("It is the paramount public policy of North Carolina to protect North Carolina resident borrowers through the application of North Carolina interest laws."); Wash. Rev.Code Ann. § 19.52.005. (West 1999) ("[The usury statutes] are enacted in order to protect the residents of this state from debts bearing burdensome interest rates; * * * and in recognition of the duty to protect our citizens from oppression generally.").

[17] *See* § 6–26–2(e) (no limit on interest rate for a commercial borrower, over $1,000,000, where loan is not secured against principal residence of the borrower, and *pro forma* analysis by a certified CPA indicates that loan is capable of being repaid).

lender's contention that his lack of intent to violate the statute should alleviate his liability for usury. *Colonial Plan Co. v. Tartaglione,* 50 R.I. 342, 344, 147 A. 880, 881 (1929). The Court rejected the notion that a borrower can contract with a lender to pay more than the permissible interest rate because "[t]o permit it would open the door to the very abuses and opportunities to take advantage of small borrowers which the statute is designed to prevent." *Id.* In 1951, this Court, in upholding the recovery of both interest and principal payments by an aggrieved borrower remarked that "[p]lainly the policy of the legislature was to provide severe penalties against the lender for his violation of the statute as the best method in its judgment to prevent usurious transactions." *Nazarian v. Lincoln Finance Corp.,* 77 R.I. 497, 505, 78 A.2d 7, 10 (1951). In what was seemingly a note of caution to future lenders, the Court warned that "[i]f the result seems harsh the penalty can be avoided easily by writing loan agreements that exact no more than the law allows." *Id.* Although these cases concern prior iterations of the usury statute, the underlying policy consistent throughout the decisions is readily apparent: Usurious interest rates are to be avoided at all costs and the onus is on the lender to ensure compliance with the maximum rate of interest.

The strict policy against usurious transactions has continued in the case law concerning the current usury statute. In a 1982 decision permitting a debtor to waive the defense of usury, this Court acknowledged a "clear legislative intent to provide severe penalties against lenders who violate the usury laws," and noted that the usury statutes clearly manifest "[a] strong public policy against usurious transactions." *DeFusco v. Giorgio,* 440 A.2d 727, 732 (R.I.1982).

Although not binding on this Court, two decisions from the U.S. District Court for the District of Rhode Island concerning usury in the context of bankruptcy proceedings are illustrative of the public policy underlying the usury statute. In declining to apply the *in pari delicto* doctrine against a borrower of a usurious loan, the district court judge, citing § 6–26–2, found that "Rhode Island usury law places the burden of charging a legal interest rate on the lender." *Sheehan v. Richardson,* 315 B.R. 226, 240 (D.R.I.2004), *aff'd,* 185 Fed.Appx. 11 (1st Cir.2006). The judge further rejected the notion that the borrower agreeing to the terms of the loan absolves the lender from liability for usurious interest rates, stating that "[d]espite mutual assent to the terms, Rhode Island statutes do not punish the borrower." *Id.* at 241. Yet perhaps the most telling reflection of the rigidity of the usury statute is the Bankruptcy Court's decision in *In re Swartz,* where the court found that a $4 filing fee—which accounted for the only interest in excess of the maximum interest rate—rendered the entire loan usurious. *In re Swartz,* 37 B.R. 776, 779 (Bankr.D.R.I.1984). The "[d]raconian tenor" of the statute, the judge noted, is "intended to protect borrowers from hidden and pernicious interest charges, and places total responsibility upon the lender for strict compliance." *Id.* at 779 & n. 5. The judge continued: "To allow a lender who has collected or retained fees in excess of the legal limit to plead 'innocent mistake' after discovery of the overcharge by the debtor, would surely invite precisely the kind of abuse which the statute is designed to prevent." *Id.* at 779.

In our opinion, the analyses of the Bankruptcy Court, as well as the prior opinions of this Court accurately and convincingly evince the public policy behind the usury statute: For protection of the borrower, it is incumbent upon the lender to ensure full compliance with the provisions for maximum rate of interest, and, apart from the explicit exception in § 6–26–2(e), anything short of full compliance renders the transaction usurious and void.

PRC argues that because the two parties are "sophisticated business entities," they should be bound by the usury savings clause to which they agreed, and that allowing NV One to void the loan would not further public policy. In support, PRC offers a series of statutes from foreign jurisdictions, all of which foreclose corporations from asserting usury as a defense. While most corporations may indeed be better able to protect themselves from avaricious lenders than other less sophisticated borrowers, PRC's argument entirely misses the mark. The Rhode Island usury statute not only contemplated lender/borrower relationships between commercial business entities, but provided a statutory exception to usury for that very situation. That exception to the maximum rate of interest is laid out in § 6–26–2(e), which provides:

> "Notwithstanding the provisions of subsection (a) of this section and/or any other provision in this chapter to the contrary, there is no limitation on the rate of interest which may be legally charged for the loan to, or use of money by, a commercial entity, where the amount of money loaned exceeds the sum of one million dollars ($1,000,000) and where repayment of the loan is not secured by a mortgage against the principal residence of any borrower; provided, that the commercial entity has first obtained a pro forma methods analysis performed by a certified public accountant licensed in the state of Rhode Island indicating that the loan is capable of being repaid."

By its plain language, this allows a lender to charge any interest rate it pleases without the possibility of a usury violation, provided that certain conditions are met in advance of the loan.[19] There is a binary dynamic implicit in the usury statute whereby a lender is either bound by the maximum interest provision and all its constituent penalties, or it is completely free from them. In our opinion, the very existence of this exception underscores the policies of borrower protection and lender accountability ingrained in the usury statute and its companion case law by recognizing that some borrowers are different, and thus not entitled to the statute's "drastic" protections. *See Colonial Plan Co.,* 50 R.I. at 345, 147 A. at 881.

With these underlying public policies in mind, we turn next to the applicability of savings clauses in general. In our view, the enforcement of usury savings clauses would entirely obviate any responsibility on the part of the lender to abide by the usury statute, and would, in essence, swallow the rule. As articulated *supra,* there is a strong public

---

[19] It bears mentioning that, because the two parties are commercial entities, the loan exceeded $1,000,000, and was not secured by either of the Cambios' primary residences, the loan at issue surely qualified for the exception. By not securing the requisite *pro forma* analysis, PRC failed to avail itself of the exception and is therefore bound by the maximum interest rate.

policy against usurious transactions, with lenders—typically in a better position to understand the terms of the loan—bearing the burden of compliance. *See DeFusco,* 440 A.2d at 732. If lenders could circumvent the maximum interest rate by including a boilerplate usury savings clause, lenders could charge excessive rates without recourse. This would have the reverse effect of incentivizing lenders to attempt to charge excessive interest rates because, at worst, the lender could invoke the savings clause and the interest rate would simply be reduced to the highest acceptable rate without any penalty to the lender. There is no doubt that such a mechanism runs completely afoul of the clear public policy against usurious transactions.

In addition to incentivizing usurious interest rates, giving effect to usury savings clauses would rest the burden of ensuring compliance squarely on the shoulders of the borrower. We firmly agree with the analysis of the Supreme Court of North Carolina, which, in declining to allow a lender to invoke a usury savings clause to shield itself from liability for usury, stated:

> "The [usury] statute relieves the borrower of the necessity for expertise and vigilance regarding the legality of rates he must pay. That onus is placed instead on the lender, whose business it is to lend money for profit and who is thus in a better position than the borrower to know the law. A 'usury savings clause,' if valid, would shift the onus back onto the borrower, contravening statutory policy and depriving the borrower of the benefit of the statute's protection and penalties." *Swindell v. Federal National Mortgage Association,* 330 N.C. 153, 409 S.E.2d 892, 896 (1991).

We have no doubt that the inclusion of usury savings clauses in loan contracts would lead to results that are injurious to the money-borrowing public, as well as potentially unconscionable or tending towards injustice or oppression. *See Gorman,* 853 A.2d at 39. We therefore hold that, in loan contracts such as the instant loan, usury savings clauses are unenforceable as against the well-established public policy of preventing usurious transactions.

Based on our *de novo* review, after viewing the evidence in the light most favorable to PRC, it is clear to this Court that the loan was a usury in violation of § 6–26–2. Furthermore, because we hold that the usury savings clause is unenforceable on public policy grounds, there are no remaining issues of material fact and NV One is entitled to judgment as a matter of law. Therefore the trial justice's grant of partial summary judgment for NV One on count 3 was proper, and we have no cause to reverse his decision.

IV   Conclusion

For the reasons set forth in this opinion, we affirm the judgment of the Superior Court. The record shall be returned to the Superior Court.

NOTES

1.   *Elements of Usury.* There is some ambivalence about restrictions on usury. On the one hand, usury laws may limit the market choices of parties, prevent a willing borrower from obtaining a needed loan, and permit a debtor to evade his obligation. See generally, DCM Partners v.

Smith, 228 Cal.App.3d 729, 278 Cal.Rptr. 778 (1991) (refusing to extend usury statute to modification of purchase money note since legislature excepted sales on credit from the statutory protection). On the other hand, usury laws protect borrowers from overreaching lenders, especially in a modern era of concentrated capital. For example, the *NV One* court favored borrower protection in its construction of the penalty aspect of the statute. See also, Carboni v. Arrospide, 2 Cal.App.4th 76, 2 Cal.Rptr.2d 845 (1991) (real estate loan providing for 200% annual interest rate was not subject to usury statute which specifically excepted loans by real estate brokers, but court refused to enforce the interest rate on theory of unconscionability and substituted rate of 24%). See pages 379–380 above describing federal preemption of usury laws.

Four elements must coincide for a loan to be held usurious: (1) an agreement to lend money; (2) interest in excess of that allowed by statute; (3) an absolute, not contingent, obligation to repay the principal; and (4) an intention to violate the usury laws. One way for borrower and lender to avoid usury is to structure their loan so that one of these four elements is missing. The first two elements have produced the most ingenious and effective efforts at usury avoidance. Parties circumvent the second element by characterizing the excessive payments as something other than interest, and circumvent the first by casting the transaction as something other than a loan.

The more common efforts at usury avoidance include a sale and repurchase characterization; discounts from the face value of the note; prepayment penalties; brokerage or placement fees; late fees; inspection fees; standby or commitment fees if the lender is funding a permanent loan; requirements that the borrower deposit part of the loan proceeds in an interest-free account with the lender; sale-leaseback arrangements; and equity "kickers" such as a percentage of the borrower's gross or net income earned from the security.

Judicial acceptance of these ploys is hard to predict, creating difficulties for the lawyer who is asked to give an opinion letter stating that a particular transaction is free from any taint of usury.

On usury in land finance generally, see Mansfield, The Road to Subprime "HEL" Was Paved with Good Congressional Intentions: Usury Deregulation and the Subprime Home Equity Market, 51 S.C.L. Rev. 473 (2000); White, The Usury Troupe L'Oeil, 51 S.C.L. Rev. 445 (2000); Shanks, Practical Problems in the Application of Archaic Usury Statutes, 53 Va.L.Rev. 327 (1967); Podell, The Application of Usury Laws to Modern Real Estate Transactions, 1 Real Est.L.J. 136 (1972); Hershman, Usury and "New Look" in Real Estate Financing, 4 Real Prop.Probate & Trust J. 315 (1969); Rabin & Brownlie, Usury Law in California: A Guide Through the Maze, 20 U.C. Davis L.Rev. 397 (1987).

2. *Corporate Borrower Exemption.* The most common statutory exemption from usury rules is for corporate borrowers. Hershman, Usury and "New Look" in Real Estate Financing, 4 Real Prop., Probate & Trust J. 315, 325 (1969). The central question in administering the corporate exemption, and in structuring transactions to comply with its requirements, concerns the extent to which, to qualify, a corporation must have a life and business purpose independent of usury avoidance. New York and several other states take the view that any corporation, even one formed exclusively for the purpose of avoiding usury limitations, qualifies for the corporate exemption. See, for example, Werger v. Haines Corp., 302 N.Y. 930, 100 N.E.2d 189 (1951); Galloway v. The Travelers Insurance Co., 515 So.2d 678 (Miss.1987). New Jersey and other states take a more jaundiced view, denying the exemption if the loan was only nominally made to a corporation and in fact was made to the corporation's principal. See, for example, Gelber v. Kugel's Tavern, 10 N.J. 191, 89 A.2d 654 (1952). The New Jersey approach creates particular difficulties for the lawyer who wants to form a corporation that is at once substantial enough to withstand attack as a usury sham and, at the same time, is insubstantial enough to avoid federal income taxation at the entity level.

See generally, Weinstein, Can a Nominee Corporation Be Ignored for Tax Purposes? An Issue Headed for Supreme Court Review, 13 Real Est.L.J. 159 (1984); Payne, Playing a Shell Game With Usury Statutes, 10 Real Est.L.J. 337 (1982).

3.   *Time-Price Doctrine.* When it is the seller who finances the buyer's purchase, the parties can avoid usury by increasing the sales price, and consequently the loan principal, so that a nominally lawful interest rate will in fact produce a greater than lawful return. Courts have generally accepted this technique, refusing under the time-price doctrine to examine the difference between cash and credit prices to determine whether the credit price embodies a usurious interest rate. In Mandelino v. Fribourg, 23 N.Y.2d 145, 295 N.Y.S.2d 654, 242 N.E.2d 823 (1968), the New York Court of Appeals carried this approach one step further, sustaining a purchase money interest rate that *expressly* exceeded the lawful rate. The court's reasoning: a purchase money mortgage is simply not a loan within the terms of the usury statute. See generally, Comment, Application of the Time-Price Doctrine in Credit Sales of Real Property, 40 Baylor L.Rev. 573 (1988).

4.   *"Governing Law" Clauses.* Since permitted interest rates vary from state to state, and since states differ in their prescribed exemptions from usury limits, lender and borrower can try to avoid local usury restrictions by agreeing to a "governing law" clause that rests the debt instrument's interpretation and validity on the law of some more favorable state. Whether a court will honor this designation of applicable law of course depends on how seriously the foreign usury rule offends the public policy of the state whose judicial system is being asked to enforce the debt.

b.   RECOURSE VS NONRECOURSE LOANS

Heller Financial, Inc. v. Lee

United States District Court for the Northern District of Illinois, 2002.
2002 WL 1888591.

ORDER AND OPINION

CHARLES R. NORGLE, DISTRICT JUDGE:

Before the court is Defendants' motion for summary judgment pursuant to Federal Rule of Civil Procedure 56(b) and Plaintiff's motion for partial summary judgment pursuant to Federal Rule of Civil Procedure 56(c). For the following the reasons, Defendants' motion is denied and Plaintiff's motion is granted.

I.   BACKGROUND

This diversity action arises from a loan. Defendants, Harry Lee ("Lee") and L. Joe VanWhy ("VanWhy"), along with others, formed a Florida limited partnership, Royal Plaza, Ltd. ("Royal Plaza"), to purchase the Hotel Royal Plaza ("the Hotel") in Orlando, Florida. Additionally, Maddlee, Inc. ("Maddlee"), a Florida corporation, was formed to serve as Royal Plaza's general partner in the purchase of the Hotel.

In order to finance the purchase of the Hotel, Royal Plaza and Maddlee obtained two loans. One loan was from the Bankers Trust Company for approximately $34,200,000. The other loan, that is the focus of this suit, was from Plaintiff, Heller Financial, Inc. ("Heller"), for approximately $9,900,000. Heller made the loan to Royal Plaza and Maddlee. All parties executed an Equity Loan Agreement ("Agreement") and a Promissory Note ("Note") in connection with the loan. Section 11(b) of the Note states in pertinent part:

> Subject to the provisions set forth below, no Maker shall be personally liable to pay the Loan, or any other amount due, or to perform any obligation, under the Loan Documents, and Holder agrees to look solely to the Assignments and any other collateral heretofore, now, or hereafter pledged by any party to secure the Loan. Notwithstanding the forgoing, each Maker (excluding Robert Ahnert), jointly and severally, shall be personally liable for . . . (b) repayment of the Loan and all other obligation of Maker under the Loan Documents in the event of (i) any breach of any of the covenants in Sections 6.3 or 6.4 of the Loan Agreement pertaining to transfers, assignments and pledges of interests and additional encumbrances in the Property, the Partnership and the Corporation . . .

(Pl.'s Mot. for Partial Summ. J., Ex. B, pg. 6.) Section 6.4 of the Agreement provides in pertinent part:

> Each Borrower, the Corporation and the Partnership covenant not to grant or permit the filing of any lien or encumbrance on the Project, the Collateral or the general partnership interest of the Corporation in the Partnership, other than those created by the Senior Loan Documents and leases of Personal Property (as hereinafter defined) expressly permitted in Section 6.6 below, without the prior written consent of Lender; provided, however, the Partnership may, by appropriate proceeding, contest the validity or amount of any asserted lien and, pending such contest, the Partnership shall not be deemed to be in default hereunder if (a) the Partnership has given prior written notice to Lender of the Partnership's intent to so contest, (b) such contest stays the enforcement of the contested lien, and (c) the contested lien is bonded or insured over by the title insurance company or the Partnership has posted security therefor in accordance with the provisions of the Senior Loan Documents and in a manner acceptable to Lender.

(Pl.'s Mot. for Partial Summ. J., Ex. A, pg. 23.)

With the financing secure, Royal Plaza and Maddlee were able to finalize the purchase of the Hotel. After the purchase, the Hotel fell under the management of Royal Plaza Management, Inc., which is a separate and unconnected entity from Royal Plaza.[2] Over a five month period of operation, six liens were placed on the Hotel property:

— Tourist Development Tax Warrant seeking $4,903.88 filed by Orange County, Florida on January 5, 1999;

— Claim of Lien seeking $46,212.00 filed by Harper Mechanical Corp. on January 13, 1999;

— Tourist Development Tax Warrant seeking $74,490.58 filed by Orange County, Florida on February 3, 1999;

— Tourist Development Tax Warrant seeking $3,170.82 filed by Orange County, Florida on February 15, 1999;

— Claim of Lien seeking $5,958.49 filed by Alpine South Plumbing Corporation, Inc. on March 30, 1999;

— Tax Warrant seeking $685,914.74 by Florida Department of Revenue on May 21, 1999.

Heller did not consent to the filing of any of the liens, nor did Royal Plaza provide written notice of an intent to contest any of the liens, and no lien was bonded or insured by an insurance company.

As a result of these liens, Heller gave notice on August 12, 1999 to Lee, VanWhy, Royal Plaza, and Maddlee that they had defaulted under the terms of the Agreement and Note. Based on the default, Heller informed Lee, VanWhy, Royal Plaza, and Maddlee that the entire indebtedness under the Note was immediately due and payable and a public sale of the equity interest in Royal Plaza and Maddlee, which had been pledged to Heller as security for the Heller loan, would occur. The sale of the Hotel, part of the interests of Royal Plaza, occurred and Heller received the proceeds.

Heller filed this action claiming that it received only a portion of the debt owed by Royal Plaza and Maddlee. Heller claims that Lee and VanWhy still owe personal obligations under the Agreement and Note. Subsequently, Lee and VanWhy have moved for summary judgment, with Heller filing a motion for partial summary judgment on the issue of liability. These cross-motions are fully briefed and ripe for ruling.

II.   DISCUSSION

A.   Standards for Summary Judgment

Summary judgment is permissible when "there is no genuine issue as to any material fact and . . . the moving party is entitled to judgment as a matter of law." Fed. R. Civ. P. 56(c). The nonmoving party cannot rest on the pleadings alone, but must identify specific facts, see Cornfield v. Consolidated High School District No. 230, 991 F.2d 1316, 1320 (7th Cir. 1993), that raise more than a mere scintilla of evidence to

---

[2]   Lee and VanWhy argue that they are not responsible for, nor had any knowledge of, the liens placed on the Hotel. Lee and VanWhy justify this argument based on the fact that Royal Plaza Management, Inc, with the knowledge and agreement of Heller, managed the Hotel at the time the liens were entered. This argument is of no consequence because Lee and VanWhy contracted with Heller for the loan and not Royal Plaza Management. Further, Lee and VanWhy cannot claim ignorance of the liens when they are a matter of public record.

show a genuine triable issue of material fact. See Murphy v. ITT Technical Services, Inc., 176 F.3d 934, 936 (7th Cir. 1999); see also Shank v. William R. Hague, Inc., 192 F.3d 675, 682 (7th Cir. 1999) (stating that a party opposing summary judgment must present "what evidence it has that would convince a trier of fact to accept its version of events"). A defendant is entitled to put the plaintiff to his proofs and demand a showing of the evidence. See e.g. Navarro v. Fuji Heavy Industries, Ltd., 117 F.3d 1027, 1030 (7th Cir. 1997). If the plaintiff fails to come up with the required proof, the defendant is entitled to summary judgment. See id. It bears repeating that the plaintiff must present evidence, rather than speculation and conclusions without factual support. See Rand v. CF Industries, Inc., 42 F.3d 1139, 1146–47 (7th Cir. 1994). Cases involving contract interpretation are "particularly suited to disposition by summary judgment." United States v. 4500 Audek Model No. 5601 AM/FM Clock Radios, 220 F.3d 539, 542 (7th Cir. 2000).

In deciding a motion for summary judgment, the court can only consider evidence that would be admissible at trial under the Federal Rules of Evidence. See Bombard v. Fort Wayne Newspapers, Inc., 92 F.3d 560, 562 (7th Cir. 1996). The court views the record and all reasonable inferences drawn therefrom in the light most favorable to the party opposing summary judgment. See Fed. R. Civ. P. 56(c); Perdomo v. Browner, 67 F.3d 140, 144 (7th Cir.1995). "In the light most favorable" simply means that summary judgment is not appropriate if the court must make "a choice of inferences." See United States v. Diebold, Inc., 369 U.S. 654, 655, 8 L. Ed. 2d 176, 82 S. Ct. 993 (1962); First Nat'l. Bank of Arizona v. Cities Service Co., 391 U.S. 253, 280, 20 L. Ed. 2d 569, 88 S. Ct. 1575 (1968); Wolf v. Buss (America) Inc., 77 F.3d 914, 922 (7th Cir. 1996). The choice between reasonable inferences from facts is a jury function. See Anderson v. Liberty Lobby, Inc., 477 U.S. 242, 255, 91 L. Ed. 2d 202, 106 S. Ct. 2505 (1986). The court has one task and one task only: to decide, based on the evidence of record, whether there is any material dispute of fact that requires a trial. Waldridge v. American Hoechst Corp., 24 F.3d 918, 920 (7th Cir. 1994) (citing Anderson, 477 U.S. at 249–50; 10 Charles A. Wright, Arthur R. Miller & Mary K. Kane, Federal Practice and Procedure: Civil § 2712, at 574–78 (2d ed. 1983)). Not all factual disputes warrant the denial of summary judgment; only disputes as to facts material to the substantive claim require resolution by trial. Smith v. City of Chicago, 242 F.3d 737, 744 (7th Cir. 2001) (citing Anderson, 477 U.S. at 247–248).

Lee and VanWhy argue that a summary judgment motion is procedurally inappropriate based on the numerous affirmative defense they raise. However, Lee and VanWhy have failed to argue the merits of every affirmative defense save one, which the court addresses below. Where the nonmoving party fails to make a showing sufficient to establish the existence of an essential element on which he would bear the burden of proof at trial, summary judgment should be entered against him. Fitzpatrick v. Catholic Bishop of Chicago, 916 F.2d 1254, 1256 (7th Cir. 1990) (citing Celotex Corp. v. Catrett, 477 U.S. 317, 322–23, 91 L. Ed. 2d 265, 106 S. Ct. 2548 (1986) (other citations omitted)). There is no requirement that the moving party negate his opponents claim. Fitzpatrick, 916 F.2d at 1256 (citing Celotex, 477 U.S. at 323).

Lee and VanWhy's failure to present evidence in support of their affirmative defenses and sufficient to establish or repudiate material facts dooms their argument. See Caisse Nationale De Credit Agricole v. CBI Industries, Inc., 90 F.3d 1264, 1270 (7th Cir. 1996) (A party seeking to defeat summary judgment is required to wheel out all its artillery to defeat it). The case is ripe for ruling on summary judgment.

B.   Non-Recourse Loan

As stated previously, the loan in this case was for approximately $9 million to help finance the purchase of the Hotel. Heller made the loan to the limited partnership of Royal Plaza, including Lee and VanWhy, and its general partner Maddlee.

All parties agree that Illinois law governs. By definition, a loan is "nonrecourse" where the debtor "is not personally liable for the debt upon default, but rather, the creditor's recourse is solely to repossess the property granted as security for the loan. See Fidelity Mutual Life Ins. Co. v. Chicago Title and Trust Co. of Chicago, 1994 U.S. Dist. LEXIS 12641, No. 92 C 8475, 1994 WL 494897, at *3 (N.D. Ill. 1994) (citing Black's Law Dictionary (Deluxe) 1057 (6th ed. 1999) (defining 'nonrecourse debt') (other citations omitted)). However, nonrecourse loans create issues in terms of the motivation of borrowers to act in the best interest of the lender and the lender's collateral. See Portia Owen Morrison and Mark A. Senn, Carving up the 'Carve-Outs' in Nonrecourse Loans, 9–June Prob. & Prop. 8 (1995)." "As a result, lenders identified defaults that posed special risks and carved them out of the general nonrecourse provision." Id. These carve-outs provide the protection that lenders require, personal liability, to insure the incentive to repay the loan and maintain the viability of collateral. There is no dispute that the loan made by Heller to Royal Plaza and Maddlee is a nonrecourse loan. (See Def.'s Mot. for Summ. J., pp. 1, 8; Pl.'s Response to Def.s' Mot. for Summ. J., pp. 3–8.)

Heller argues that within the nonrecourse loan several carve-outs exist which implicate personal liability. Specifically, Heller contends that any lien placed on the Hotel and its property would cause Lee and VanWhy to be personally liable for the remaining debt on the original loan. Lee and VanWhy argue that the carve-outs alleged by Heller are actually liquidated damages but are unenforceable as penalties.

It is clear that within Heller's nonrecourse loan to Royal Plaza and Maddlee particular carve-outs exist. The Note states:

> Subject to the provisions set forth below, no Maker shall be personally liable to pay the Loan,. . . . Notwithstanding the foregoing, each Maker (excluding Robert Ahnert), jointly and severally, *shall be personally liable for.* . . .

(Pl.'s Mot for Summ. J., Ex. B, pg. 6.) (emphasis added). This is unambiguous language. See Air Safety, Inc. v. Teachers Realty Corp., 185 Ill. 2d 457, 706 N.E.2d 882, 884, 236 Ill. Dec. 8 (Ill. 1999). "Absent ambiguity, the intention of the parties is to be ascertained by the language of the contract and not by the construction placed on it by the parties. If a court can ascertain its meaning from the plain language of the contract, there is no ambiguity." J.B. Esker & Sons, Inc. v. CLE-PA's P'ship, 325 Ill. App. 3d 276, 757 N.E.2d 1271, 1279, 259 Ill. Dec. 136 (Ill. App. Ct. 2001).

Further, all parties knew and agreed to the carve-outs of the nonrecourse loan based Mr. Robert Ahnert's ("Ahnert") exemption from personal liability and the structuring of the financing connected to the loan. First, the Note excludes Ahnert's from personal liability. Based on Ahnert's exclusion from personal liability, it stands to reason that Lee and VanWhy understood and agreed to their personal liability under the carve-outs. If they did not agree to such a carve-out they could have themselves arguably insisted on exclusion from personal liability as Ahnert did. Second, as Heller points out, "the loan was secured by the equity interests of the entities that purchased the Hotel, and not by the Hotel property itself." (Pl.'s Response to Def.'s Mot. for Summ. J., pg. 7.) This means Heller is concerned with the successful operation of the Hotel since it affects the value of the collateral that secured the loan. Any lien on the property compromises the equity interests of Royal Plaza and Maddlee. Thus, the carve-out under section 11(b) in the Note, referencing Section 6.4 of the Agreement, is of the utmost importance in acquiring the loan and is known and agreed to by all the parties.

It is painfully clear that the nonrecourse loan from Heller to Royal Plaza and Maddlee included carve-outs. Further, these carve-outs caused Lee and VanWhy to be personally liable. Lee and VanWhy acknowledged and agreed to this.

C.   Liquidated Damages

Lee and VanWhy argue that the Section 11(b) is a liquidated damages provision that is invalid because it is an unenforceable penalty. This argument fails.

A clause is a liquidated damages provision if: (1) the actual damages from a breach are difficult to measure at the time the contract was made; and (2) the specified amount of damages is reasonable in light of the anticipated or actual loss caused by the breach. Checkers Eight Limited Partnership v. Hawkins, 241 F.3d 558, 561 (7th Cir. 2001) (citing American Nat'l Bank & Trust Co. of Chicago v. Regional Transp. Auth., 125 F.3d 420, 440 (7th Cir. 1997); Lake River Corp. v. Carborundum Co., 769 F.2d 1284, 1289–90 (7th Cir. 1985)). The common law principle is that a liquidated damages provision is enforceable when it appears in advance that it would be difficult at the time of breach to compute actual damages and the liquidated damages provision is a good faith attempt to estimate what actual damages would be. Pace Communications, Inc. v. Moonlight Design, Inc., 31 F.3d 587, 593 (7th Cir. 1994). However, in interpreting provisions which affix the amount of damages in the event of a breach, courts lean toward a construction that excludes the idea of liquidated damages and permits the parties to recover only damages actually sustained. Grossinger Motorcorp, Inc. v. American National Bank and Trust Co., 240 Ill. App. 3d 737, 607 N.E.2d 1337, 1345, 180 Ill. Dec. 824 (Ill. App. Ct. 1992) (quotations and cites omitted).

Section 11(b) is not a liquidated damages provision because it provides for only actual damages. This action involves a loan made by Heller to Royal Plaza and Maddlee. Royal Plaza, which is made of several partners including Lee and VanWhy, as well as Maddlee agreed and contracted to the loan and its repayment. Heller made the loan with the assurance of Royal Plaza and Maddlee of full repayment, and secured by all the interests of Royal Plaza and Maddlee. Under the terms of the Note, Lee and VanWhy are personally liable for "repayment of the loan" if any liens are placed on the Hotel. (See Pl.'s Mot. for Partial Summ. J., Ex. B, pg. 6.) Heller, in filing this action, seeks the amount left on the loan at the time of the breach. This amount is the actual damage to Heller based on Lee and VanWhy's breach. Since Section 11(b) involves actual damages it cannot be a liquidated damages provision.

III. CONCLUSION

For the foregoing reasons, Defendants' motion for summary judgment is denied and Plaintiff's motion for partial summary judgement is granted.

IT IS SO ORDERED.

NOTE

As illustrated by *Heller Financial, Inc. v. Lee*, lenders might regret their decision to lend without imposing personal liability on the borrower if the deal goes bad and the property is not sufficient to pay off the loan. For example, in Boucher Investments, L.P. v. Annapolis-West Limited Partnership, 141 Md.App. 1, 784 A.2d 39 (2001), a lender barred from proceeding against the borrower's successor for the debt because the loan was nonrecourse asserted that the borrower engaged in waste by failing to renew a parking arrangement for the mortgaged property. The lender argued that waste was a tort, not contract, action and so the nonrecourse protection did not apply. The court did not disagree but held that failure to arrange parking did not constitute waste. On the issue of carveouts, see Murray & Scott, Enforceability of Careveouts to Nonrecourse Loans: An Evolutions, 48 Real Prop. Tr. & Est. L.J. 217 (2013). Burr, Enforcement of the Carve-Out Guaranty, 27 Real Est. Finance 7 (Feb. 2011).

2. CONSTRUCTION FINANCE

The lender who is asked to make a construction loan has a riskier, more complicated task than the lender who is asked to lend money on already improved land. The task is riskier because the construction lender must base its appraisal on pieces of paper—project plans, specifications and income projections—and has no assurance that strikes, increased construction costs or natural disasters will not make the project more expensive than originally contemplated. Nor will the lender have any assurance that, once the project is completed, the right number and mix of tenants will sign leases and pay sufficient rents for the borrower to pay off the loan. The construction lender's task is complicated by the need to devise and enforce safeguards against these construction and investment risks and also, if the lender is a regulated institution, by the need to maintain a first lien position over the common law and statutory priorities that attach to the interests of financing sellers and unpaid mechanics, materialmen and fixture suppliers.

The lending industry traditionally has resolved this increased risk and complexity by dividing development finance between a *construction lender*—usually a commercial bank primarily interested in making short term, floating rate loans—and a *permanent lender*—usually an insurance company primarily interested in a long term loan, possibly with an equity participation feature. The construction lender will advance the needed construction funds in stages over the course of construction, with its loan secured by a first lien mortgage on the property. The permanent lender will "take out" the construction mortgage upon the completion of construction by replacing the construction mortgage with a long term mortgage. Although two separate sets of instruments—construction note and mortgage and permanent note and mortgage—may be used, the terms of the permanent loan are often embodied in the construction note and mortgage so that, when construction is completed, the original note will pass from construction lender to permanent lender with no need for execution of a new note by a possibly recalcitrant borrower.

Construction lending is labor-intensive and construction loan departments are usually well-staffed with loan administrators, architects, engineers and inspectors to monitor loan disbursements at every stage of a construction project. Permanent lending, by contrast, is essentially capital intensive. It requires the permanent lender to evaluate the proposed project only at the time the developer applies for the permanent loan commitment and later, when the time comes to take out the construction loan, to determine that construction has been completed according to the terms and specifications of its commitment letter.

Construction lenders will usually structure and administer their disbursement programs carefully to protect against the possibility that funds disbursed for construction purposes will be diverted to other purposes and that, as a result, the permanent lender will refuse to take out the construction loan on the ground that the project was not completed in accordance with specifications, or that its first lien position is impaired by the prior lien of an unpaid mechanic, materialman or purchase money lender. But disbursement control programs occasionally break down, and even the best-run programs offer no protection against the widespread judicial solicitude for mechanics, materialmen and purchase money mortgagees, nor against permanent lenders who decide, for good reason or bad, simply not to honor their takeout commitments. The cases and materials in this section indicate the sources of some of these problems and the legal strategies that construction lenders—as well as borrowers, permanent lenders, sellers, mechanics, materialmen and fixture suppliers—have employed to resolve them.

Bibliographic Note. Introductions to the field include Coscarelli, The Construction Loan Agreement: Six Provisions Important to Lender's Counsel, 15 Probate & Prop. 30 (Jan./Feb. 2001); Kyle, Commercial Real Estate Construction Lending, 22 Prac. Real Est. Law. 29 (No. 2 2006); Liu, Facing Default on A Construction Loan: Initial Strategies for Owner's Counsel, 17 Probate & Prop. 30 (Jul./Aug. 2003); Livingston, Current Business Approaches—Commercial Construction Lending, 13 Real Prop., Probate & Trust J. 791 (1978); Walsh, A Practical Guide to Mortgage Loan Commitments, 8 Real Est.L.J. 195 (1980); Weissman, Construction Lending From the Ground Up, 18 Probate & Prop. 20 (May/Jun. 2004);. For an analysis of the legal relationships among the parties to these arrangements, see Korngold,

Construction Loan Advances and the Subordinated Purchase Money Mortgagee: An Appraisal, A Suggested Approach and the ULTA Perspective, 50 Fordham L.Rev. 313 (1981).

a.   The Construction Loan

Philip D. Weller, Fundamentals of Construction Lending*

Modern Real Estate Transactions,
American Law Institute Continuing Legal Education.
Westlaw CV008 ALI-CLE 1009 (2013).

I.   INTRODUCTION AND SCOPE

. . .

B.   Basic Overview of the Construction Loan Process. In the Construction Loan Process the lender advances funds incrementally, usually on a monthly basis, as construction of improvements is completed. At the initial closing of the loan the lender will typically advance funds for a variety of purposes, including, land acquisition costs, engineers and architects fees, survey costs, title insurance costs, legal fees and other similar matters. Thereafter, as materials are purchased and construction proceeds the contractor will on a monthly basis submit to the construction lender an application for progress payments delineating the work done to-date, the amount of construction funds previously received and the amount being requested in the particular application. These are typically signed by both the contractor and the contractor's architect and are reviewed and approved by the owner, lender, and perhaps an inspecting architect as described below. After review and approval the lender funds the amount requested subject to the retainage requirements and obtaining lien waivers and title assurance as described below. This progress continues then until work is satisfactorily completed at which point in time the construction loan would be fully funded. In order to monitor the progress, it is customary for the construction lender and borrower to agree ahead of time on a definitive budget for the Project and for the lender to carefully monitor the types of expenses incurred in construction to be sure that it is progressing in accordance with the agreed-upon budget. The budget will typically contain a line item for contingencies (i.e., unforeseen matters) as to which the lender may require prior approval before funding from this budget category.

II. FUNDAMENTALS OF CONSTRUCTION LENDING—WHY DOES CONSTRUCTION LENDING DIFFER FROM OTHER REAL ESTATE FINANCING?

A.   Basic Comparison. The fundamental difference between construction lending and other types of real estate secured financing is that in construction lending the value of the collateral is being created from the loan funds as they are advanced. In financing completed property or unimproved property, the collateral value is fairly well fixed at closing, but in construction lending the value of the collateral, both

---

* Reprinted with permission from the author and American Law Institute CLE, www.ali-cle.org.

the physical value of the improvements and the economic value from prospective tenants, is to be created in the future and there are, naturally, inherent risks as to whether that value will be realized.

B.   Construction Risks.

1.   One risk in construction lending is that the basic cost estimates for the project may be erroneous. Thus, it is incumbent upon the lender to be sure that the project can be built within the budget contemplated, keeping in mind that developers are generally optimistic sorts. To some extent, this risk can be minimized by using guaranteed maximum sum construction contracts and payment and performance bonds, depending on the economic viability of the contractor, but the construction lender must have the ability to effectively determine the anticipated cost of the project.

2.   Even in the best planned projects the possibility of unforseen circumstances or uncontrollable cost overruns exists. For example, since most, if not all, construction loans bear floating rates of interest, a sudden precipitous rise in interest rates can greatly increase construction costs. Similarly, subsurface soil conditions, inclement weather, unforeseen shortages of essential materials, labor disputes and other similar occurrences can add greatly to the cost of construction.

3.   In addition to unforeseen circumstances, there also always exists the possibility of simple failure of performance by third parties, especially contractors and subcontractors performing construction work. Accordingly, it is important for a construction lender to know that its borrower is a solid, experienced developer well versed in managing construction of the type of project in question, and that the project will be constructed by a reputable contractor who will deal with reputable, well-capitalized subcontractors.

C.   Leasing Risks. A completed commercial project is of little value unless it is occupied by rent-paying tenants. Accordingly, a construction lender must deal with the potential that the project may not lease as quickly as anticipated after construction, which will diminish its economic value. Further, if there is a commitment for long-term mortgage financing for a project, it will undoubtedly require that certain leasing levels be achieved before initial funding.

D.   Lien Priority Issues. As discussed in Section III below, the law of mechanic's and materialmen's liens raises special concerns for the construction lender, as the preferential rights afforded to mechanic's and materialmen's lien claimants make it incumbent upon the construction lender to be sure the construction funds are properly applied to payment of construction costs to assure lien priority. The process of advancing loan funds incrementally can also raise lien priority issues.

III. MECHANIC'S AND MATERIALMEN'S LIENS AND LIEN PRIORITY ISSUES

A.   General. Most states provide to parties constructing improvements, or providing materials for construction of improvements, special liens to secure payment of the obligations owing to them. For example, Chapter 53 of the Texas Property Code sets forth the requisites of Texas mechanic's and materialmen's liens claims. The applicable mechanical and materialmen's lien statutes must be carefully considered in any construction lending context as there are typically basic preventative actions which the construction lender should take to protect its lien priority.

B. Basic Mechanic's Lien Priority. First, it is important to note that an owner's property is subject to being "liened" in the construction context by a party with whom the owner has no privity of contract. The basic premise of mechanic's lien statutes is to protect subcontractors (of whatever tier) by insuring that the person in the best position to control the flow of funds (i.e. the owner) does so. The statutes are designed to be sure that the owner, when paying its general contractor, takes sufficient steps to be sure that the general contractor, in turn, pays its subcontractors and so on. Mechanic's and materialmen's lien statutes are state specific and thus it will be incumbent upon any practitioner to be familiar with the particular state in which a project is located to be sure that the loan is properly documented and administered. For example, under New York law there are specific statutory requirements for provisions to be included in the basic loan documents, without which a lender will lose a great deal of protection. *See,* N.Y. Lien Law §§ 1–39–c (McKinney 1999). Under applicable Texas law, if construction activity occurs prior to the recording of the construction loan deed of trust, the lender will lose all lien priority, and the Lender will not have priority as to certain types of fixtures no matter what preventive actions it takes. *See generally* Chapter 53, Texas Property Code (West 2004).

C. Lender Protective Actions.

1. Retainage. Under most state statutory schemes, an owner of property and, derivatively, the owner's lender can protect their position by complying with applicable retainage provisions. For example, under Section 53.101 of the Texas Property Code, if 10% of the contract price or the value of the work is retained until thirty (30) days after the work is completed, then all mechanic's lien claimants will have a ratable lien claim against the funds so withheld and will not be able to successfully maintain a mechanic's lien claim against the subject property. Thus, it is customary for construction lenders to withhold sufficient funds from the loan until the end of the requisite period. This can work a significant hardship on the general contractor for a very large project since the subcontractors performing the first part of the construction (as for example, foundation and concrete work) will have completed their work many months before final completion and will want to be paid in full, thus placing a burden on either the owner or the contractor to fund the final portion of that particular subcontract, unless the lender is willing to diminish the protection afforded to it by the retainage provisions.

2. Bonds. An additional method by which an owner and lender may typically protect their position vis-a-vis mechanic's liens is to either bond the job or, bond against specific liens. Bonding of the entire job is typically done at the outset of a project, and if properly done generally precludes a mechanic's lien claimant from filing a suit against the owner or the owner's property, and relieves the owner of its obligation to retain.

If a job is not bonded, but a lien claim is filed, then typically, the specific lien claims may be bonded against. After this type of bond is recorded, a person acquiring an interest in or lien on, or insuring title to, the property in question may usually rely upon it to the same extent as the lien claimant had filed a release of lien.

. . .

4.   Loan Administration Techniques. The prudent lender will also administer the loan so as to minimize the risk of mechanic's lien claims. As described in Section V.A. below, the lender should require lien waivers from all parties receiving proceeds of a loan advance, and an affidavit of the general contractor that the loan proceeds have been and will be properly applied. Additionally, the lender may issue dual-payee checks, naming the general contract and appropriate subcontractor or materialman to further assure that loan proceeds are properly applied.

D.   Lien Priority & Future Advances. Since construction lending inevitably involves the advancing of funds in periodic installments as construction progresses, there is the concern about the priority of funds advanced under the Construction Loan Agreement in relation to lien claims that are filed after recording the Construction Deed of Trust but prior to a particular advance, so-called "intervening" liens. In many jurisdictions it can be a difficult proposition to determine lien priority, requiring an investigation into whether the lender was "obligated" to make the particular advance in question. Generally, the range of possibilities under state law extend from each advance being protected by being related back to the initial advance date to situations where the lender must carefully search for filings of intervening claims as the same will prime interim advances.

IV. LOAN CLOSING REQUIREMENTS

A.   Title Requirements and Survey Requirements. As is customary with all real estate transactions, verification of title begins with obtaining a commitment for title insurance and a current survey. The typical construction loan policy provides for increasing coverage as loan proceeds are disbursed by means of down data endorsements issued by the title company. These endorsements increase the coverage by the amount of the draw in questions and also based on the coverage current to the date of issuance.

B.   Compliance with Laws and Regulatory Matters.

1.   Zoning. Naturally, counsel will want to satisfy itself that the property and the proposed improvements comply with all applicable zoning ordinances. This will be accomplished by a combination of obtaining certificates from architects or other professionals, conversations with local zoning officials, and, perhaps, an opinion of borrower's counsel.

2.   Building Permit. Nearly every city and most counties have requirements relating to the building of improvements and require a building permit as a precondition to commencement of construction of improvements. The lender will generally require the building permit as a prerequisite the first advance of funds under the construction loan.

3.   Certificate of Occupancy. At the other end of the spectrum from the building permit is the certificate of occupancy to be issued

upon completion of the improvements. While not a requisite to closing the loan, nonetheless the lender will want to be sure that a certificate of occupancy will be forthcoming upon completion so that the improvements may be occupied under applicable law.

4.   Environmental. The effect of various state and federal environmental laws on real estate is the subject of entire week-long legal education seminars. Suffice it to say that it is incumbent upon the construction lender to be sure that the underlying real estate is adequately inspected for environmental hazards prior to closing and to have the plans and specifications for the improvements reviewed to assure that no hazardous materials will be installed in the improvements and that the operation of the improvements will not violate any applicable environmental laws.

C.   Adequacy of Plans and Specifications. Appropriate inquiry must be made to be sure that the plans and specifications for the proposed improvements are adequate for their intended purpose. At the same time the lender will want to be sure that its review does not imply that it has undertaken responsibility for the accuracy of the plans and specifications. Typically, this function is satisfied by obtaining a certificate from the borrower's design professional (architects, engineers, etc.) and by having all plans and specifications reviewed either by in-house architects or by a retained third party architect. Often times this third party architect will also will also be the architect who inspects the improvements on behalf of the lender as work progresses (see Section V.B. below).

. . .

F.   Economic Viability.

1.   Budget. It is customary in construction lending for there to be a specific line item budget dealing with construction items which is agreed upon by the lender. As funds are advanced as work progresses the amounts requested are compared to the budgeted line items and in this way the lender controls fund disbursements to keep the project "in balance". However, in terms of economic viability the lender must look at the construction budget and, as mentioned above, verify that it is a reasonable estimate of actual costs to be incurred in construction.

2.   Equity Infusions. Lenders were always generally reluctant to lend 100% of the value of a project (at least knowingly) and in these days they are clearly not going to do so. Accordingly, the lender need to be assured that the borrower has provided adequate equity to support the project. This may be accomplished by a combination of contributing land (less likely in today's market) or by requiring that the borrower funds the first portion of the construction cost itself, or by funding ratably with the lender as work progresses, or by requiring that the amount of required equity be deposited with the lender subject to a security interest in favor of the lender.

3.   Appraisal. While not a legal issue, the lender will require a current appraisal of the Project's value upon completion, both to comply with federal law and as a matter of prudent underwriting.

G.   Take-Out Loan Commitment. The construction lender will want to know that there is viable financing available upon completion of the improvements (and any leasing requirements) to pay off the construction loan (or "take it out"). Traditionally, this permanent loan commitment came from the life insurance company or mortgage banker, but today there are a wider range of capital sources, and it is not unusual for construction lenders to provide their own take-out financing, providing that after construction the construction loan converts to a relatively short-term or "bullet" financing based upon completed improvements.

H.   Document Package.

. . .

3.   Tri-Party and Buy-Sell Agreements. If there is a permanent loan commitment, it was once customary that the construction lender, permanent lender and the borrower enter into some kind of agreement concerning funding the permanent loan. In the past, the term tri-party agreement referred to an agreement among all three parties, as its name would indicate, delineating how the permanent loan would be closed and the construction loan paid. Typical provisions of a tri-party agreement were an agreement of the construction lender to notify the permanent lender of any defaults and to refrain from taking remedial action for a period of time allowing the permanent lender to cure (an unlikely event), an agreement on the part of the permanent lender to fund the permanent loan if the construction lender takes over and completes the project, and a statement from the permanent lender that as many contingencies as possible have been waived or agreed upon (as for example, approval of the current state of title). The term buy-sell agreement is used more generally to refer to an agreement between the construction lender and permanent lender pursuant to which the permanent lender agrees to buy from the construction lender the construction lender's loan documents at the time of funding of the permanent loan.

V.   ADMINISTERING THE LOAN.

A.   General Procedure. As mentioned above, the hallmark of the construction loan is the advance of funds as construction of the project proceeds. The basic mechanism or draw procedure is for the borrower and general contractor to send to the lender applications for funds or draw requests (often on American Institute of Architects form—G702) specifying the work done to date, the cost or value of the work done to date, as appropriate, the amount of loan funds advanced to date for the cost of the work, and a certification that the borrower is entitled to the funds requested. The certification may also request funds for materials purchased but not yet incorporated into the work, and before funding the lender will need to assure itself that such items are stored on-site or in an area such that the lender's liens and security interests attach to the items in preference to any other claims. The draw request is also typically certified by the borrower's project architect and is then reviewed by the lender's in-house personnel or by the lender's inspecting architect to verify its accuracy. After accuracy is verified the lender advances funds to the borrower as requested, less retainage. Typically, the draw procedure is done on a monthly basis. As part of the draw procedure lenders should also require that lien waivers be obtained from all contractors, subcontractors, materialmen and mechanics that receive proceeds of the draw, acknowledging that they have been paid and releasing their mechanics liens against the property to the extent of payment. The construction loan agreement should specifically provide that the draw procedure and the conditions to advances are strictly for the benefit of the lender and not for the benefit of any third party to avoid an assertion, however absurd, that the lender has damaged a third party by failing to adhere to its construction loan procedures.

J.I. Kislak Mortgage Corporation v. William Matthews Builder, Inc.

Superior Court of Delaware, 1972.
287 A.2d 686, *aff'd*, 303 A.2d 648 (Del.1973).

CHRISTIE, JUDGE.

This is an action by J. I. Kislak Mortgage Corporation of Delaware, a mortgage lender, against William Matthews Builders, Inc., its borrower, to foreclose on a construction mortgage. A subcontractor, Bachman and Wood, Inc., has intervened, seeking priority for certain mechanics' liens. The intervenor contends that funds disbursed by the mortgage lender after the date that the intervenor commenced work are junior to its mechanics' liens. The mortgage lender asserts that since its construction mortgage was executed and recorded before any work was done, its total disbursements have priority over any and all of the intervenor's mechanics' liens.

In 1964, the Kislak Mortgage Corporation entered into a construction loan agreement with the Matthews Builders Corporation, whereby Kislak covenanted to advance funds to Matthews upon the completion of certain phases of the construction. To ensure that the builder was fulfilling its obligations under the agreement, Kislak appointed a field representative to make on site inspections. This representative was to determine whether work was done in a good and workmanlike manner, to what state the work had progressed and whether the materials and fixtures usually installed at a given stage had been, in fact, installed. When the work had progressed to specified points, the field representative was to authorize progress payments under the construction loan agreement. Unknown to Kislak, its own representative fraudulently authorized progress payments for work that had not actually been done and as a result some subcontractors were fully paid while certain of the subcontractors, including Bachman and Wood, were not paid for their work.

The intervenor, Bachman and Wood, was the masonry subcontractor for this project construction and supplied labor and materials during the period when the advances were made to the defendant. After all of the advances had been distributed without paying the intervenor and after mortgage foreclosure proceedings had commenced, the intervenor filed its mechanics' liens. It now seeks to have its liens given priority over the mortgage lien and has moved for summary judgment.

The lien of judgment for a mechanics' lien relates back to the time that the contractor commenced work or first supplied material. 25 Del.C. s 2718. Di Mondi v. S & S Builders, Inc., 11 Terry 123, 124 A.2d 725 (Del. 1956). Generally speaking, in the case of each mechanics' lien obtained by Bachman and Wood, funds in excess of these liens were advanced by Kislak to Matthews Builders after the effective date of the mechanics' liens. Thus, if the mechanics' liens take priority over later advancements under the construction mortgage, the intervenor would be entitled to recover the full amount of its mechanics' liens before funds would be available to satisfy the mortgage loan.

In the usual case it is apparent that a mortgage lien would take priority over a mechanics' lien that was filed after the effective date of the mortgage provided none of the work covered by the mechanics' lien was done prior to the recording of the mortgage. C. L. Pierce & Co. v. Security Trust Co., 6 W.W.Harr. 348, 175 A. 770 (Del.Super.1934). However, there is an exception to the rule which applies when a construction loan agreement covering a construction mortgage provides for progress payments over a period of time and some of the disbursements are voluntarily made at a time subsequent to the effective date of the mechanics' lien.

Generally, where the making of the advances is obligatory upon the mortgagee, the mortgage receives priority over a mechanics' lien when the mortgage has been recorded before the mechanics' lien attaches, despite the fact that advances are actual given subsequently to this time. Hance Hardware Co. v. Denbigh Hall, Inc., 17 Del.Ch. 234, 152 A. 130 (1930); New York & Suburban Federal Sav. & Loan Ass'n v. Fi-Pen Realty Co., 133 N.Y.S.2d 33 (Sup. 1954). However, where a mortgage is recorded prior to the time that a mechanics' lien attaches to the property and it is optional with the mortgagee as to whether a further advance is to be made, and where the mortgagee has made an advance with knowledge of the fact that the mechanics' lien has already attached, to the extend of such later advances, the mortgage is inferior to the mechanics' lien. See Hance Hardware Co. v. Denbigh Hall, Inc., Supra; Gray v. McClellan, 214 Mass. 92, 100 N.E. 1093 (1913); 80 A.L.R.2d 179.

In the instant case, the building loan agreement provided in part that:

3.   None of the said respective installments or any part thereof, not theretofore paid over shall be required to be made by Lender unless and until Borrower shall procure and deliver to Lender original receipts or such other evidences as shall be satisfactory to Lender, showing that any installment received theretofore under this Agreement has been disbursed fully and properly to materialmen, laborers, subcontractors, and to any other person, firm or corporation providing or furnishing materials or labor or both, in connection with the construction of said improvements on the above mentioned premises.

Thus, before Kislak was obligated to disburse further advances, it was entitled to receipts showing that the costs incurred by Matthews Builders had been paid. Kislak had no duty to advance funds until this condition was met. The plaintiff concedes that it did not enforce this condition and that, in fact, disbursements were made despite the defendant's failure to present the receipts in accordance with the agreement. I conclude, therefore, that any disbursements advanced by the plaintiff were voluntary and optional since it had no duty to advance these funds under the agreement. That the plaintiff should have considered such payments as optional is supported by paragraph 7 of the agreement which provided that:

7.   Lender, may, at its option, advance any installment in whole or in part before the same becomes due hereunder or without requiring compliance with the conditions precedent to its obligation to so advance; * * *. (emphasis added).

Having determined that the advances were optional, it is now necessary to consider whether they were made with knowledge that possible mechanics' liens were already in the making. As previously noted, the plaintiff had a representative in the field who had notice or knowledge of the conditions under which the construction was conducted. Notice of an agent acquired while acting within the scope of his authority is imputable to the principal. Nolan v. Eastern Co., 241 A.2d 885 (Del.Ch.1968) aff'd 249 A.2d 45 (Del.1968). Vechery v. Hartford Acc. & Indemn. Ins. Co., 10 Terry 560, 121 A.2d 681 (Del.1956).

Kislak as mortgagee advanced funds voluntarily after it had reason to know that work for which a mechanics' lien could be filed was in progress and had not been paid for.

Kislak did not have actual notice of attachment at the time that the advancements were made but it is charged with knowledge of the law that mechanics' liens relate back and it did make the payments voluntarily without requiring receipts even though certain subcontractors had not been paid. Kislak had the opportunity to protect itself by withholding further advances until receipts were furnished. It did not do so. Under the circumstances, I conclude that where a mortgagee makes voluntary advances, while aware that work for which a mechanics' lien could be filed is in progress, to the extent of these voluntary and subsequent advances, the mortgage lien is inferior to the mechanics' lien.

As between a subcontractor which did not have the protection of a construction loan agreement and a mortgage lender which did not avail itself of the protection it had under the agreement it is not inappropriate under Delaware law that the mortgage lender bear the loss. Accordingly, summary judgment will be entered in favor of the intervenor.

It is so ordered.

NOTE: OBLIGATORY AND OPTIONAL ADVANCES

Construction mortgagees will typically agree to advance loan proceeds only in predetermined installments as construction progresses. As a result, the complete proceeds of the construction loan will not be paid out until construction is virtually completed. Nonetheless, the mortgage that the borrower executes and the lender records before construction begins, and before the first installment is paid out, will secure the total amount of all future advances.

The traditional rule on mortgages securing future advances is that, if the advances are obligatory, they will enjoy the priority that attached to the mortgage when it was first recorded. By contrast, if the advances are optional or voluntary they will enjoy the mortgage's initial priority only if the mortgagee, when making the advance, had no notice of the intervening junior lien.

The obligatory/optional advance rule has classically been justified as an attempt to protect borrowers rather than junior lenders or lienors. The rule supposedly protects a property owner who has a mortgage to secure future advances on her property but no contractual ability to compel the lender to disburse funds. It would be difficult for such an owner to obtain a junior mortgage if the senior lender could subsequently make advances and take priority over the junior lender. The owner is thus left in a difficult position, unable to extract her equity from the property.

Although this classic explanation for the rule focuses on the borrower, note how the court in *Kislak* applies the theory to achieve a far different policy goal—protection of mechanics. Courts have also used the doctrine to assist subordinated purchase money mortgagees who, as discussed at pages 636–646, may have been misled by developers. See, e.g., Housing Mortgage Corp. v. Allied Construction Inc., 374 Pa. 312, 97 A.2d 802 (1953). More specifically, the obligatory/optional advance rule has been used by some courts to rearrange priorities and achieve a fair result in cases where a senior lender makes advances in an unreasonable manner and so injures the security of a junior mortgagee or mechanic.

While the outcomes in these cases may be correct, the obligatory/optional rule is too rough and arcane to be an effective response. Some courts address unreasonable lender behavior in a more straightforward manner, by imposing a duty of good faith and fair dealing on construction lenders in their disbursement activities. See, e.g., Crum v. AVCO Financial Services, 552 N.E.2d 823 (Ind.App.1990); Peoples Bank & Trust Co. and Bank of Mississippi v. L & T Developers, Inc., 434 So.2d 699 (Miss.1983), judgment corrected, 437 So.2d 7 (1983), discussed at pages 657–658 below; Sexton v. St. Clair Fed. Sav. Bank, 653 So.2d 959 (Ala.1995) (finding that borrowers could recover mental anguish damages for breach by lender of mortgage clause requiring disbursement of proceeds to builder in stages as work was completed); see Norwest Mortgage, Inc. v. Salinas, 999 S.W.2d 846 (Tex.App.1999) (finding lender liable under Texas Deceptive Trade Practices Act for paying out construction funds to insolvent builder and failing to obtain lien waivers before disbursing); see also Storek & Storek v. Citicorp Real Estate, Inc., 100 Cal.App.4th 44, 122 Cal.Rptr.2d 267 (2002) (in action by mortgagor, construction lender must use its discretion in reasonable manner when making future advances based on requirement that construction schedule be "in balance"). Other courts, however, reject an implied duty to monitor advances for the benefit of borrower or other lienors. See Pimental v. Wachovia Mortgage Corp., 411 F.Supp.2d 32 (D.Mass.2006) (no breach of implied covenant of good faith when lender released funds without inspection and lender not under fiduciary duty to mortgagor to inspect); Thormahlen v. Citizens Savings and Loan, 73 Or.App. 230, 698 P.2d 512 (1985), review denied, 299 Or. 443, 702 P.2d 1111 (1985); see also 225 Associates v. Connecticut Housing Finance Authority, 1998 WL 376022 (Conn.Super.), aff'd, 65 Conn.App. 112, 782 A.2d 189 (2001) (borrower could show no damages under lender's express agreement to monitor disbursements).

The intricacies of the doctrine, the confused policy bases, and concerns about loss of priority by construction lenders and other open end mortgagees, such as home equity lenders, has led to increased doubts about the viability of the obligatory/optional advance doctrine. As discussed below, the obligatory/optional advance rule has been rejected in numerous jurisdictions over recent years.

On the theory of the obligatory/optional rule and reasonable lender behavior, see Korngold, Construction Loan Advances and the Subordinated Purchase Money Mortgagee: An Appraisal, a Suggested Approach, and the ULTA Perspective, 50 Fordham L.Rev. 313 (1981).

Notice. The majority rule subordinates the lien of the mortgagee's subsequent optional advances only to the extent that the mortgagee had actual notice of the intervening lien before making the advance. To be safe in these jurisdictions, the intervening lienor must search the record, identify any prior mortgagees and give these mortgagees actual notice of its lien. The minority rule requires only constructive notice to the mortgagee. In these jurisdictions, the mortgagee must search title before making each advance at the risk of losing the advance's priority to the recorded lien. What is the view of *Kislak* on notice?

Which rule better allocates the burden of search? If the intervening lienor is going to search anyway, and if the mortgagee's address can easily be found in the record, the majority rule would appear to make more sense. But consider who mortgagees and intervening lienors typically are. How likely, and desirable, is it for mechanics and materialmen to perform a title search before committing their labor or goods to a project? How burdensome is it for the mortgagee to order an update of its original title report? Is it a desirable check against developer misbehavior to give construction lenders another incentive to search title before disbursing additional funds? Reconsider *Kinch v. Fluke*, page 249 above.

Optional or Obligatory Advance? What criteria should govern the determination whether an advance is obligatory or optional? In the context of construction loans, a program of future advances enables the construction lender to hold back loan proceeds at each stage of construction until it has determined that work is progressing adequately. An obligatory commitment would not serve this purpose. Yet, an absolutely discretionary commitment could defeat the desired priority as all advances could be deemed to be voluntary. Construction lenders usually look for solutions somewhere in the middle, conditioning disbursements on the project's compliance with specified, objective criteria.

Unfortunately, courts have provided no consistent or principled rules for determining whether clauses in this middle ground are optional or obligatory. See e.g., Housing Mortgage Corp. v. Allied Construction Inc., 374 Pa. 312, 97 A.2d 802 (1953) (stating that an obligatory advance is found when the mortgagee is "under a binding obligation" or "contractually obligated" to make the advance).

In Briarwood Towers 85th Co. v. Guterman, 136 A.D.2d 456, 523 N.Y.S.2d 98 (1988), a lender was obligated to make advances if the borrower complied with certain conditions in the building loan agreement, including a promise to obtain a title insurance policy insuring the lender's mortgage as a valid first lien. When the lender received a notice from a party claiming that it had a prior mortgage on the property, the lender notified the title company. The title company informed the lender that no additional title exceptions would be raised and advised the lender that it could proceed with funding. The court reversed the trial court which had found that these events made the advance voluntary, holding that the condition to funding, i.e., title company insurance of a first lien, had been met. The court noted that the binding force of the lender's obligation was not vitiated, quoting from an earlier opinion: "where the obligation to advance exists, or where the right to decline depends upon facts *dehors* the instrument, and which may be the subject of dispute or contention, the holder of the first security is warranted in making the advances in reliance upon his mortgage." Id. at 459, 523 N.Y.S.2d at 101 (quoting Hyman v. Hauff, 138 N.Y. 48, 55, 33 N.E. 735, 737 (1893)).

Despite the court's holding that the advance was "obligatory", if the action had been by the borrower to compel the lender to fund, would the court have actually found the senior lender obligated to make advances in light of information that there was a mortgage prior to the lender's? Does the court's holding reflect a belief that the lender was acting reasonably under the circumstances and that it did not want the obligatory/optional advance rule to punish that behavior?

What are the implications of this muddle for title insurers deciding whether to insure the first lien status of mortgages calling for future advances? See generally, Jones & Messall, Mechanic's Lien Title Insurance Coverage for Construction Projects: Lenders and Insurers Beware, 16 Real Est.L.J. 291 (1988).

Advances to Preserve Collateral. Should it make a difference if a mortgagee, committed only to optional advances, finds it necessary to advance funds in order to cover unpaid real property taxes, insurance premiums, the cost of maintenance and repair, or otherwise to preserve its collateral? Some writers take the view that these advances are "obligatory in the sense that they are necessary to protect previous loans and advances made by the mortgagee," and thus should be given the priority enjoyed by obligatory advances. Note, Mortgages—Advance Money Provisions—Effect on Preferences and Recording Acts, 29 N.Y.U.L.Rev. 733, 738 (1954). Legislatures have been quick to adopt the analogy, Md.Real Prop.Code Ann. § 7–102 and Me.Rev.Stat.Ann. tit. 9–B § 436 represent distinctive steps in this direction. See generally, Skipworth, Should Construction Lenders Lose Out on Voluntary Advances if a Loan Turns Sour? 5 Real Est.L.J. 221 (1977); Hughes, Future Advances Mortgages: Preserving the Benefits and Burdens of the Bargain, 29 Wake Forest L.Rev. 1101 (1994); Comment, Mortgages to Secure Future Advances: Problems of Priority and the Doctrine of Economic Necessity, 46 Miss.L.J. 433 (1975).

Rejection of Obligatory/Optional Advance Rule. There have been various statutory responses to the dissatisfaction with the obligatory/optional distinction. Some states have attempted to fix specific problems inherent in the doctrine. See, e.g., Uniform Land Security Interests Act § 111(19) (addressing the definitional difficulties by defining an advance as "obligatory"—or "pursuant to commitment"—"if the obligor has bound itself to make it, whether or not a default or other event not within its control has relieved or may relieve it from its obligation"); 42 Pa.Cons.Stat.Ann. § 8143 (1991) (requiring written notice by junior encumbrancer in order for a senior lender to lose priority for voluntary advances). Other states simply reject the obligatory/optional rule and give all future advances priority as of the filing of the original mortgage. See, e.g., Md. Real Prop. Code Ann. § 7–102 (1991). Yet other states have adopted "cut-off notice" provisions which permit the mortgagor to issue a notice which freezes advances having priority under the open end mortgage at their current amount. The mortgagor can then obtain a second mortgage more readily, as the junior lienor will not face loss of priority to the senior mortgagee. See, e.g., Fla.Stat.Ann. § 697.04(b).

The Restatement of Mortgages rejects the voluntary/obligatory rule and adopts a "cut-off" notice approach based on statutes in some jurisdictions. §§ 2.1–2.4. Section 2.3 provides that all future advances have priority as of the original mortgage, regardless of whether an advance is optional or obligatory. To enable the mortgagor to obtain new loans from other lenders, the mortgagor may give a "cut-off" notice to the mortgagee. The cut-off notice will either make further advances under the original mortgage unsecured or subordinate future advances under the original mortgage to the new loans. Section 2.3, comment b. See Whitman, 33 Real Prop. Probate & Tr. J. 415–55 (1998); Nelson & Whitman, Rethinking Future Advance Mortgages: A Brief for the Restatement Approach, 44 Duke L.J. 657 (1995).

b.   THE PERMANENT LOAN

Milton Davis, The Permanent Lender's Role in the Construction Process*

3 Real Estate Review 70–75 (No. 1, 1973).

Lurking in the background in any discussion of construction lending is the specter of the *permanent lender*. Writing as one who represents a permanent lender, my own inclination is to state that the permanent lender is the key man in any new real estate venture. At the very least, certainly, the permanent lender is a vital factor in a new real estate venture. It is his money that is relied upon to finance the project even though it will not be disbursed until after completion of construction. Without a permanent commitment most construction lenders will not make a construction loan.

Nevertheless, once the permanent commitment is issued, the other parties feel free to criticize the permanent lender for seeking various rights to approve, for refusing to waive commitment requirements, and for declining to take a backseat during construction. The construction lender and the borrower would like to have the permanent lender bound to make the loan, with neither of them so bound until the time of permanent closing. To a permanent lender this is unthinkable. Certain facts such as building size, number of units, estimated income, and so forth, have been represented to him. He has underwritten the deal and agreed to make a certain kind of loan based on those representations. He has set forth requirements in his commitment to be satisfied prior to closing which will ensure that the project has been completed in compliance with those representations. Such requirements and conditions have been agreed to by the borrower in accepting and executing the commitment. The permanent lender should not be expected, or be asked, to waive such requirements. He must see to their fulfillment, and he is therefore entitled to be in the picture from the start. This article will be concerned with the permanent lender's

---

*   Reprinted with the consent of Thomson Reuters.

interest in construction, with the relationship between construction lender and permanent lender in accomplishing their respective goals, and with the potential problem areas in their relationship.

PERMANENT LENDER'S INTEREST IN CONSTRUCTION OF THE PROJECT

Why should the permanent lender be interested in construction matters? He concerns himself with construction primarily because he wishes to be sure that the building to be constructed is the one on which he has committed himself to make a loan. It too often occurs that the final structure is not the one envisioned by the permanent lender at the time of making the commitment.

Second, he is concerned with construction because he will have a security interest in the building for as long as he holds the mortgage, which may be for twenty to thirty years (and in this age of "kickers," he may have an immediate equity interest as well). If the building is improperly constructed, the permanent lender's security can be severely impaired since in most instances, he looks first to the improvements and to the income therefrom for security, and only to a lesser extent, to the borrower. Needless to say a potential owner is interested in the building he may someday own.

INSURING PROPER CONSTRUCTION OF THE BUILDING

What can the permanent lender do to insure proper construction of a project and so protect his interests?

Plans and Specifications

The permanent lender's most potent right is to examine the plans and specifications in advance and insist that the building be put up in compliance with them. The plans and specifications should be in great detail, setting forth site plans, floor plans, elevations and wall sections, special construction details, footings and foundations, structural framing, and mechanicals (plumbing, electrical, heating, ventilating, and air conditioning). They should be examined by a professional architect or engineer fully familiar with construction in the particular locale involved. The permanent lender must insist that construction be strictly in accordance with these plans and specs. His appraisal being based on them, any variation destroys the underwriting basis.

RELATIONSHIP BETWEEN CONSTRUCTION LENDER AND PERMANENT LENDER

Having discussed the relevance of construction matters to the permanent lender, let us now consider the relationship between the construction lender and the permanent lender. Basically, their interests are substantially similar:

To have the building completed as provided for in their commitments and in accordance with the approved plans and specifications. (It is a good idea to have the two lenders use the same engineer or architect; this will reduce the likelihood of disputes over the adequacy of the plans.)

To have their funds invested pursuant to their commitments.

To have the construction loan paid upon completion of construction.

To have the permanent lender then hold the loan with the long-term security he contemplated when making his commitment.

Notwithstanding these basic objectives, differences between the two lenders may occur. The construction lender's overwhelming desire for completion and repayment may lead him, for purposes of expediency, to approve changes in plans which are unacceptable to the permanent lender. The construction lender also would at all times like to have the permanent lender bound to close his loans. He would like to have an agreement enforceable against the permanent lender subject to a minimum of conditions, but not necessarily enforceable against himself unless he so agrees.

Very often, for example, the borrower is a depositor in the institution making the construction loan and so is in a position to exert sufficient pressure on the construction lender during a period of declining interest rates to convince him not to sell the loan to the permanent lender. To minimize this possibility, the permanent lender wants an agreement enforceable against *all* parties, including the borrower and the construction lender; in exchange, he is willing to be bound himself provided there is compliance with the condition of his commitment.

How are these objectives met and differences resolved to the satisfaction of both lenders?

Buy-Sell Agreement

In most cases, a condition of the permanent lender's commitment is the execution of a buy-sell agreement prior to the start of construction. This three-party agreement, among permanent lender, construction lender, and borrower, has the purpose of insuring that the permanent lender will buy the loan from the construction lender and that the construction lender will sell the loan to nobody else. Recent litigation by a permanent lender arising from a construction lender's refusal to comply with the terms of a buy-sell agreement resulted in a lower court decision that the agreement was binding and a judgment that the construction lender pay damages for failure to convey the loan to the permanent lender in compliance with the agreement.

The pertinent provisions of the buy-sell agreement are usually the following:

The consent of the permanent lender to the assignment by the borrower to the construction lender of the proceeds to be forthcoming under the permanent commitment;

The agreement of the construction lender to sell the loan to no one except the permanent lender and to refuse to accept prepayment;

The agreement of the permanent lender to buy the loan at par, subject to compliance with the commitment;

The remedies in the event of the borrower's default under the building loan agreement or under the permanent commitment; and

The agreement of the borrower to comply with the permanent commitment and to amend the mortgage documents if the permanent lender requests it, and the agreement of the construction lender to obtain such amendments from the borrower. . . .

TRANSITION FROM CONSTRUCTION
LOAN TO PERMANENT LOAN

In most transactions involving permanent financing, the transition from the construction loan stage to the permanent loan stage goes smoothly. The permanent lender wants a mortgage on the building he contemplated; the construction lender wants to be paid off. But there are areas of friction and potential conflict that must be ironed out.

Advance Approval of Some Items

During the early stages of discussion, before he closes his construction loan, the construction lender will want approvals from the permanent lender on as many closing conditions of the permanent commitment as possible. He will ask for approval of title, survey, leases, appraisal, plans and specifications, and the operating agreement.

The permanent lender can review the state of title at this early date and set forth those exceptions or areas which disturb him. At the time of the construction loan closing, however, he can neither know nor approve the state of title for purposes of the permanent closing. Any approvals he gives, therefore, must reserve his right to reexamine title for the permanent closing.

The permanent lender can also approve the survey at this stage, okaying the location of the premises and its relation to roads, intersections, and so forth. But he must reserve the right to see a final survey showing the improvements as built to determine if they accord with the commitment he contemplated. To avoid confusion, any approvals the permanent lender gives to plans and specifications should be by detailed plan number, date, and revision number.

The permanent lender may approve leases and any operating agreements if they are in existence at the time of the construction loan closing, but this is unlikely.

The items which the permanent lender cannot approve in advance can cause great concern to a construction lender. But by the nature of things, certain matters are not in existence at the time of the construction loan closing; and so the risk of the permanent lender not giving final approval to them must remain with the construction lender. Such items include the final survey, an independent engineer's report, any estoppel certificates that the permanent lender may want from tenants and from adjoining department stores (in the case of a shopping center), the final title search, and executed leases.

Penthouse International, Ltd. v. Dominion Federal
Savings and Loan Association

United States Court of Appeals for the Second Circuit, 1988.
855 F.2d 963, cert. denied, 490 U.S. 1005, 109 S.Ct. 1639, 104 L.Ed.2d 154.

Before MESKILL and ALTIMARI, CIRCUIT JUDGES, and MISHLER, DISTRICT JUDGE.

ALTIMARI, CIRCUIT JUDGE:

Defendants-appellants Dominion Federal Savings & Loan Association ("Dominion") and Melrod, Redman & Gartlan, P.C.

("Melrod" or the "Melrod firm") appeal from judgments entered in favor of plaintiffs-appellees Penthouse International, Ltd. and its wholly-owned subsidiary, Boardwalk Properties, Inc. (hereafter referred to as "Penthouse"), and third-party defendant-appellee Queen City Savings & Loan Association ("Queen City"). After a three-week bench trial in the United States District Court for the Southern District of New York (Judge Kevin T. Duffy), the district court held that Dominion committed an anticipatory breach of its agreement to participate in a $97 million loan transaction. The district court awarded Penthouse approximately $128.7 million and awarded Queen City nearly $7.7 million (plus interest and costs) for the damages caused by Dominion's anticipatory breach. In addition, the court dismissed with prejudice Dominion's cross-claim against Queen City. After the court issued its opinion, it ordered that the Melrod firm be held jointly and severally liable for the Penthouse judgment, not on breach of contract grounds, but for fraud.

Dominion and the Melrod firm present several arguments on appeal. Dominion's principal contention is that the district court erred when it found that Penthouse carried its burden of demonstrating the existence of an anticipatory breach and that, in absence of the breach, Penthouse had the ability to perform its contractual obligations before the loan commitment expired. The Melrod firm argues that there is no basis in law or fact for holding it liable for the Penthouse judgment.

For the reasons that follow, we reverse in part, affirm in part and remand.

FACTS and BACKGROUND

Sometime after gambling was legalized in Atlantic City, New Jersey, Penthouse's President, Robert Guccione, conceived the idea of opening a Penthouse Hotel and Casino along Atlantic City's famed Boardwalk. To implement this idea, Guccione set about to locate prospective financiers and potential partners to assist in underwriting the construction project. Boardwalk Properties, Inc. was formed as a wholly-owned subsidiary of Penthouse for the purpose of handling Penthouse's affairs in connection with the hotel and casino project.

Initially unsuccessful in its efforts to obtain outside financing, Penthouse used its own resources to commence the project. Penthouse proceeded to assemble five contiguous plots of land along Missouri Avenue adjacent to the Boardwalk. Three of these parcels Penthouse held in fee simple and the other two were obtained through leasehold estates. The first leased property, on which was located a Holiday Inn Hotel, was obtained from the Boardwalk and Missouri Corporation, an entity controlled by New York real estate financier Harry Helmsley (the "Helmsley lease"). The second leasehold estate, which was then occupied by a Four Seasons Hotel, was obtained from Albert and Robert Rothenburg (the "Rothenburg lease").

Penthouse's construction plans included the use of the existing tower structure from the Holiday Inn, the rebuilding of the structure from the Four Seasons into a second tower and the construction of a seven-story building between the two towers. In these structures, Penthouse planned to house its casino, a 515 room hotel, a health club and other facilities. By June 1983, Penthouse had invested between $65 and $75 million into construction of the hotel and casino which was approximately 40 to 50 percent complete.

Although Guccione believed that the entire project could be financed with Penthouse's own funds when construction commenced, as time passed and costs escalated, it became apparent that it would be necessary to obtain outside financing. Penthouse then sought financing unsuccessfully from various sources. In or about April 1983, Penthouse retained Jefferson National Mortgage, a mortgage broker, to locate prospective lending institutions interested in providing Penthouse with construction and permanent financing for the hotel and casino project. As a result of Jefferson National's efforts, Queen City extended to Penthouse in June 1983 a $97 million loan commitment.

On June 20, 1983, Queen City issued to Penthouse (through Boardwalk Properties, Inc.) a commitment to lend Penthouse $97 million for construction and permanent financing in connection with the Penthouse Hotel and Casino project (the "Queen City loan commitment" or the "loan commitment"). The Queen City loan commitment was accepted by Penthouse on June 29, 1983. In the loan commitment, Queen City advised Penthouse that "your request for construction/permanent financing ... with Queen City Savings and Loan Association ... has been approved subject to the following terms and conditions [.]" The term of the loan was ten years with a construction phase in effect during either the first 24 months or until Penthouse received a certificate of occupancy from Atlantic City and permission to operate the casino. The interest rate was fixed at 14 7/8% for years one through five and 15 3/8% for years six through ten.

To secure the loan, pursuant to paragraph 6 of the loan commitment, Penthouse was required to deliver to Queen City a mortgage on the hotel and casino and the underlying properties. Thus, Penthouse was required to deliver a note secured by a "valid first mortgage lien on all real estate owned by [b]orrower covering the project site" and all improvements thereon and was required to provide a "valid first leasehold interest" in the Rothenburg and Helmsley leases and "a first mortgage covering the improvements thereon." Penthouse also was required to provide assignments of its interest in the leasehold estates to be effective in the event of Penthouse's default. Paragraph 6 required Penthouse to certify at closing that there were "no violations" of the Helmsley or Rothenburg leases.

Paragraph 14 of the loan commitment required Penthouse to represent and warrant 1) that there was no pending litigation that would affect title to the properties, the validity of the mortgage liens, the validity and non-violations of the leases, etc., 2) that the final plans and specifications for construction would satisfy and conform with local, state and federal regulations, and 3) that all necessary utilities (i.e., water, electricity, sewer, telephone service and gas) were available to the full needs of the property and that "valid and enforceable agreements to supply such services have been entered into[.]"

Under the heading of "Commitment Expiration Date," paragraph 15 provided that the commitment would

> expire one hundred twenty (120) days after the date hereof (the "Commitment Expiration Date") unless mutually extended

in writing by Lender, and upon such expiration Lender shall have no further obligation to Borrower, except as set forth in item 19 of the attached Conditions.

Paragraph 16 of the commitment, which was headed by the term "Closing", stipulated that the "[c]losing of the Loan ('Closing') shall be held . . . on or before the Commitment Expiration Date[.]"

Paragraph 17 of the loan commitment provided that an additional twenty enumerated "Conditions Prior to Closing" ("preclosing conditions") contained in a document attached to the commitment were incorporated as part of the commitment. Paragraph 17 also stipulated that "[l]ender's obligation to close the Loan [was] contingent upon the satisfaction of each of said conditions."

In relevant part, the preclosing conditions provided:

* * *

5. TITLE INSURANCE: There shall be furnished to Lender, at least 15 days prior to Closing, a current preliminary title insurance binder, issued by a title company initially approved by Lender. At Closing, a standard ALTA title policy shall be issued by such company insuring Lender's interest or lien in or on the Property subject only to such title objections as Lender shall approve. Such title insurance policy shall affirmatively insure the priority of the lien of the Mortgage. The title company insuring Lender's lien shall obtain re-insurance in such amounts and with such companies, as Lender may require.

* * *

10. UTILITIES: The Lender shall be furnished with copies of all agreements for providing the utility services required for the operation of the Property, including without limitation thereto, agreements pertaining to water, sewer, and electricity and/or original current letters from the suppliers of such utilities stating that the utilities are available and are offered in sufficient quantities for the project.

11. PLANS AND SPECIFICATIONS: The written approval of all plans and specifications for the Improvements to be erected must be obtained from Lender. No change of any substance shall be made in the final plans and specifications without the prior written approval of Lender and all governmental authorities having jurisdiction.

12. CERTIFICATION BY ARCHITECT AND CONSTRUCTION MANAGER: Borrower shall deliver to Lender at Closing a certification by Borrower's architect and construction manager containing (i) a detailed listing of the then-current plans and specifications for the Improvements; (ii) a statement that said plans and specifications are complete documents for the construction of the Improvements and contain all details requisite for the completion, occupancy and operation thereof; and, (iii) a statement that said plans and specifications are in full compliance with all local, state and federal (if any) rules,

ordinances and regulations governing or applying to the construction of the Improvements.

* * *

16. CONSTRUCTION—CONTRACTS: Borrower shall submit, for Lender's approval, Borrower's contract with its architect, construction project manager and all major trade contractors. Lender may at its option require assignment of the aforesaid contracts or any of them.

* * *

19. PARTICIPATION: Lender's obligation to complete the Closing is also contingent upon execution of a participation agreement between Lender and other lenders pursuant to which said other lenders will participate in making the Loan (through the Lender as "lead institution") at least to the extent of $90,000,000.00 on terms and conditions satisfactory to the Lender. Borrower acknowledges that it is Borrower's sole responsibility (either directly or through mortgage brokerage companies) to obtain such participants who are satisfactory to Lender, it being understood that Lender shall have no obligation to obtain such participants. In the event the aforesaid $90,000,000.00 participation agreements are not obtained, then Lender shall refund to Borrower the origination fees it received pursuant to Item 8 of the Commitment.

* * *

The preclosing conditions also established that New Jersey law would govern the terms of the loan commitment and stipulated that Queen City's attorneys would have the final decision on whether the various preclosing conditions had been satisfied. Nowhere, however, did the commitment or the preclosing conditions provide that Queen City was authorized by the participating lending institutions to waive Penthouse's compliance with any of the terms of the commitment.

Once the loan commitment was in place, pursuant to preclosing condition 19, Queen City and Penthouse began searching for financial institutions interested in participating in a syndicate of lenders to underwrite the loan. Lending institutions that decided to participate in the syndicate (the "participants") would enter into a "Loan Participation Sale and Trust Agreement" (the "participation agreement"). Under the commitment, Queen City was designated to serve as the lead lending institution (the "lead lender") for the syndicate. Under the participation agreement, the participants would purchase from Queen City "undivided participating ownership" interests in the mortgage loan. Pursuant to the participation agreement, Queen City assumed various administrative responsibilities for servicing the loan. The agreement stipulated, however, that Queen City was to act, not as an agent, but as an "independent contractor" for the participants and would serve "as a trustee with fiduciary duties" in connection with protecting the rights of the participating lenders. In addition, the participation agreement contained an integration clause, provided that it could not be modified except by written agreement and established New Jersey law as the governing law.

By the fall of 1983, twelve financial institutions, including Queen City, had agreed to participate in the financing syndicate and had committed to provide a total of $62 million for the project. In mid-November 1983, Dominion expressed interest in providing Penthouse with financing and on November 14th offered directly to Penthouse a commitment to provide $40 million in financing for the project. Although Dominion's offer was never accepted, it did lead to Dominion's decision on November 21, 1983 to participate in the $97 million loan syndicate.

On November 21, 1983, a meeting was held at Penthouse's offices in New York City. In attendance at the meeting were representatives of Penthouse, including its Chief Operating Officer and General Counsel, David J. Myerson, and Penthouse's outside counsel for the loan transaction, Jay Newman; representatives of Queen City, including its Senior Vice President, John E. Beahan, and Queen City's attorney, John J. Lipari; and representatives of Dominion, including its Executive Vice President, David A. Neal, and its outside counsel, William J. Dorn. At this meeting, Dominion agreed to participate in the loan syndicate to the extent of $35 million. Dominion's agreement to participate in the loan was embodied in three documents: two letter agreements exchanged between Queen City and Dominion and a third document which was a letter from Penthouse to Dominion. In substance, Dominion "accepted" all of the terms and conditions of both the loan commitment and the participation agreement except that the participation agreement was amended to include Dominion as "co-lead seller" for the syndicate. In addition, the loan commitment was modified at the meeting in a side agreement between Penthouse and Queen City to include as a preclosing condition that "arrangements, reasonably satisfactory to [Queen City], shall have been made with the staff o[f] the Casino Control Commission to permit the opening of the casino and hotel, upon completion of construction, utilizing a trustee or fiduciary in the event the license to [Penthouse] . . . or any of its principals has not been granted."

Although it does not appear that Dominion entered into any written agreement with Penthouse directly, Penthouse did deliver to Dominion a letter indicating that it agreed to pay Dominion certain fees "[i]n consideration" for Dominion's agreement to participate "as a Co-Seller" for the syndicate. Penthouse also gave Dominion a check for $175,000 for fees it agreed to pay.

Also on November 21st, Penthouse and Queen City mutually agreed to extend the Commitment Expiration Date to December 1, 1983. This written extension was prompted by Lipari's observation that the 120–day condition of the commitment had expired and his belief that, in order to have a "valid commitment," it was necessary for Queen City and Penthouse to mutually extend the expiration date. In addition, Lipari discussed the timing of the loan closing with Newman and Dorn, and then, in a letter also dated November 21st, Lipari and Newman agreed that "we shall close th[e] loan no earlier than February 1, 1984 or later than March 1, 1984."

Once the loan commitment syndicate was complete, Penthouse and Queen City directed their efforts to closing the transaction. Toward that goal, Lipari and Newman maintained regular contact and Lipari held a series of "status meetings" during which representatives of Penthouse and Queen City reviewed the steps taken in connection with Penthouse's satisfaction of the preclosing conditions. During these status meetings, Penthouse sought alternate arrangements for satisfying some of the preclosing conditions. For example, although preclosing condition 10 required Penthouse to deliver copies of all agreements for providing utility services required for the operation of the hotel and casino and/or original, current letters indicating that the utilities would be available in sufficient quantities for the project, Penthouse sought to proceed without having fully satisfied this condition. Penthouse did not have agreements with some utility companies to provide certain essential services and it did not have written assurances that those services were available to meet the demands of the proposed hotel and casino. Similarly, Penthouse sought to proceed to closing without having fully complied with preclosing conditions 11, 12 and 16.

Penthouse's position in this regard was that, since the construction project was 40 to 50 percent complete, many of the requirements of the preclosing conditions could be satisfied through substitute arrangements. Thus, instead of providing an architect's and construction manager's certificate, as required by preclosing condition 12, Penthouse offered to provide a certificate from its project engineer and to allow Queen City's architect to examine the project. This substitute performance was necessary because, at that time, Penthouse had not retained an architect. In place of providing Queen City with copies of final plans and specifications for the project, as required by the preclosing conditions, Penthouse sought to provide Queen City with its original plans and specifications for the project, even though they were out of date due to changes in the applicable building codes and despite the fact that Penthouse had no final plans for the electrical or mechanical work on the project. Notwithstanding the modifications Penthouse sought, Lipari was satisfied that the transaction could close in light of Penthouse's proffered substitute performance. It does not appear, however, that Lipari sought Dominion's or the other participants' consent to a waiver of Penthouse's full compliance with any preclosing conditions.

After the second status meeting, Queen City sent Dominion and the other participants a letter stating in essence that substantial progress had been made toward satisfying the preclosing conditions and announcing that a "preclosing meeting" would occur sometime between February 1 and 8, 1984. It was later determined that the "preclosing meeting" would occur on February 9, 1984 at Penthouse's New York offices.

Once Dominion agreed to participate in the loan syndicate, it proceeded to attempt to sell in the secondary market sub-participation interests of its $35 million interest in the loan syndicate. Dominion's decision to sub-participate out its interest in the loan was motivated in part by the fact that its legal lending limit was $18.5 million. Thus, Dominion could not lend to a single borrower more than that amount.

By letter agreement dated December 2, 1983, Dominion sold to Community Savings & Loan Association ("Community") a $17.5 million interest in its original $35 million participation interest. At that time, Community had not completed its underwriting analysis of the loan, and proceeded with this analysis in December 1983 and continued on through February 1984. In early-February 1984, however, Community started to show some reticence with proceeding in the transaction.

As Penthouse and Queen City prepared for the "preclosing meeting" set for February 9, 1984, Newman received a letter from Commonwealth Land Title Insurance Company regarding Penthouse's ability to furnish the mortgage security required by the loan commitment. This letter indicated that there were several objections to title on the Helmsley lease. That parcel was subject to two mortgages, the McShane mortgage and the Chase mortgage, which needed to be discharged or subordinated before Penthouse could furnish the required security. Unless the McShane and Chase mortgages were discharged or subordinated, if foreclosed upon, they potentially could wipe out the Helmsley lease and any security interest in that lease. The letter also raised title objections to the Rothenburg lease and pointed out that there was a declaration of encumbrances in connection with the parcels held in fee simple which had to be removed or modified. In addition to the title problems, it also appears that the Helmsley lease had to be modified before closing. Unless the lease was modified, the closing of the loan would violate its terms. The commitment required, however, that Penthouse certify, at closing, that there were "no violations" of that lease.

To resolve the various title problems and the problems with the terms of the lease, Newman knew that he would have to negotiate a discharge or subordination of the McShane and Chase mortgages, negotiate with Helmsley to obtain amendments to the lease and obtain a subordination of encumbrances in connection with the Helmsley leased property. Although Penthouse had made some initial contacts with Helmsley's representatives by February 9th, no agreement resolving these problems had been reached, nor had actual negotiations with Helmsley's representatives commenced. It is also unclear whether the holders of the Chase and McShane mortgages were willing to discharge or subordinate their liens because they apparently had not been contacted by February 9th.

On February 9, 1984, representatives of the parties to the loan transaction and the participants met at Penthouse's offices in New York City for the preclosing meeting. Among several others, Lipari was present to represent Queen City and Newman was there representing Penthouse. Penthouse's Myerson made sporadic appearances throughout the meeting. Dominion was represented by Philip Gorelick of the Melrod firm who had been brought into the deal on February 8th. At the meeting, after Penthouse made a presentation of a scale model of the planned hotel and casino, Lipari handed out some press clippings, copies of status reports and copies of draft loan closing documents. He then reviewed each of the preclosing conditions and described the progress made toward their satisfaction. Among the draft closing documents Lipari circulated was a standard, preprinted, six-page "Blumberg" form for a "plain language" mortgage and a standard, six-page, preprinted form for a "security agreement" for the furniture and fixtures. At the top of the Blumberg form appeared the admonition: "Consult your lawyer before signing this mortgage—it has important legal consequences." The draft mortgage included a rider requiring that Penthouse satisfy each of the preclosing conditions. Nowhere in the draft closing documents was there a provision allowing for preclosing conditions to be waived or modified.

After sitting through the meeting and reviewing the documents prepared by Lipari, Gorelick presented a list of items he wanted to review prior to deciding whether Dominion could proceed. He also indicated his belief that the loan transaction was not in a position to close, explaining that, in light of the unresolved title problems, problems with the leases, the unfulfilled status of some of the preclosing conditions and the inadequacy of the draft loan documents, he could not advise his client to proceed.

Gorelick gave the strong impression that the entire deal had to be overhauled. In giving this impression, Gorelick was less than tactful. He was particularly vehement about the inadequacy of the documents prepared by Lipari, which he described as "idiotic." To satisfy Gorelick's concerns, Queen City and Penthouse agreed to allow Gorelick and his firm to prepare appropriate closing documents and to review condition compliance in order to bring the deal to a close. Penthouse also agreed to pay the Melrod firm's fees while it focused its resources on the loan transaction.

After Penthouse and Queen City gave Gorelick and the Melrod firm responsibility for moving the deal toward closing, Gorelick immediately sought documents and information from Penthouse concerning all aspects of the transaction. Gorelick then drafted checklists of the documents and information he felt was necessary to review and communicated these checklists to Newman. Gorelick's checklists were very broad in scope and covered all facets of the hotel and casino project. Gorelick's initial requests for information regarding the transaction were communicated on February 9th, but were followed up by several additional requests later that month. Newman responded at length to these requests in letters dated February 29th and March 1st 1984.

Responsive to the problems with the Helmsley lease, Melrod lawyers prepared a list of proposed amendments to the Helmsley lease that they believed were necessary before closing. Gorelick insisted that Penthouse seek the proposed amendments from Helmsley and described each amendment as being "required." When, however, the proposed amendments were sent to Penthouse, they were accompanied by a cover letter from Gorelick's partner, Louis Trotter, that indicated that the proposed amendments reflected "a nearly final version of what the lender will be looking for and [would] certainly provide you with a jumping off point for your discussions with Helmsley."

To respond to an inquiry concerning the status of alternate licensing arrangements, which was required as a preclosing condition, Penthouse's attorney, Arthur S. Goldstein, sent the Melrod firm two letters. These letters addressed the status of Penthouse's license application and set forth the results of Goldstein's inquiries with the staff of the New Jersey Casino Control Commission ("CCC"). In the first letter, after providing an overview of the New Jersey Casino Control Act (the "act") and explaining in detail the license application process, Goldstein discussed the status of Penthouse's application. He stated that Penthouse had commenced the application process but that, at its request, the process had been suspended in September 1982 pending the outcome of Penthouse's efforts to obtain financing. As of February 1984, the application process had not been reactivated. Goldstein also explained that the financial institutions participating in the loan transaction would have to "qualify" under the act. Goldstein's prognosis as to the timing of licensing was that the whole process might be accomplished within a year.

More directly responsive to the status of the preclosing condition was Goldstein's second letter. The preclosing condition required that "reasonably satisfactory" arrangements be made with the staff of the CCC to permit the opening of the casino in the event that Penthouse did not obtain a license. In the second letter, Goldstein stated that he had discussed the matter with staff members at the CCC, but he explained that they had no authority to make binding decisions and that it would be necessary for Penthouse to submit a formal proposal. Nevertheless, based upon his informal discussions with the CCC staff, Goldstein opined that if Penthouse became unlicensable, it would be necessary for it to completely divest itself of any "beneficial interest" in the casino. He suggested that this could be accomplished by using a trustee who would buy out Penthouse's interest in the casino. He also stated that this transaction would have to be structured in such a manner to insure that Penthouse would have no recourse against the casino in the event of default. After Goldstein set forth additional details of the proposed trusteeship and the buy-out transaction, he concluded by stating that his comments only reflected a "rough outline of what I believe to be a proposal that might be acceptable to the Commission."

In addition to the document and information exchanges, Gorelick and representatives of Dominion engaged in a series of meetings with Myerson and, subsequently, Guccione. At one meeting held on February 29, 1984, Myerson met with Gorelick and other Melrod attorneys to discuss the progress toward closing. Gorelick indicated that he was still in the process of revising his closing checklists and that until he had finished that analysis there has not much to discuss. At that meeting or shortly thereafter, Gorelick reminded Myerson that, since the loan commitment would expire on March 1, 1984, Myerson should submit a request for an extension of the commitment expiration date. Myerson refused, however, to make such a request. Myerson believed that the loan commitment could not expire unless and until Penthouse was presented with the closing documents.

Later in the day on February 29th, Myerson went to Dominion's offices in McLean, Virginia where he met with Dominion's President, David Neal, and a representative of Community, William J. Wienke, Jr. Neal explained that Wienke was present at the meeting because Community was a participant in the loan. During the course of the meeting, the parties discussed various aspects of the project. At the conclusion, however, Wienke expressed his concern about the delays in closing and told Myerson that he needed more information about the loan. Wienke then presented Myerson with a list of thirty-five items concerning the transaction and explained that "this is the kind of stuff that I need." Myerson said that he would review the matters raised in Wienke's list.

Also on February 29th, Gorelick, Wienke and Neal engaged in a telephone conference call to discuss the transaction. During this telephone conference, Wienke explained that he was "getting a bad feeling" about the transaction and inquired whether the commitment should be terminated due to Penthouse's failure to satisfy the preclosing conditions by the March 1st date. Gorelick advised against this and Wienke acquiesced.

In addition to Gorelick's work on the transaction, representatives of Dominion were sending information requests and other items to Penthouse directly. For example, on March 1, 1984, Dominion's Vice-President, James Winston Bray, sent Myerson a letter recapping the "areas of concern" which he felt "need[ed] particular attention." Bray stated that one matter he thought needed addressing—"to make the proposed financing for the project marketable"—was the existence of "[a] satisfactory management agreement, prior to loan closing, for the operation of the proposed hotel." Nevertheless, he prefaced his comments by stating that his concerns were not intended "to replace or diminish" the various other aspects of the loan transaction.

On March 6, 1984, Myerson met with Guccione and Dominion's Chairman of the Board, William L. Walde, at Guccione's home. Although Walde expressed Dominion's continued interest in financing the project, he raised concerns regarding Queen City's ability to serve as the lead lender for the transaction. Walde described Queen City as a small and inconsequential savings and loan and suggested that it was ill-equipped to handle a transaction of this size. Guccione said that he would speak to Queen City about Walde's concerns, but he also stated that he thought it would be unfair to remove Queen City from the lead position.

On March 14, 1984, Guccione flew to Washington, D.C. to meet with Walde. At that meeting, Guccione told Walde that Queen City would not relinquish its lead position, but he offered to compensate Dominion for the fees that it otherwise would have earned had it been the lead lending institution. Also at this meeting, Walde informed Guccione that he wanted to appoint a construction company, Sigal, to perform a long in-depth reevaluation of the structure, the steel and all the parts thereon. Guccione explained that he thought that this was unnecessary. Walde also requested that Penthouse designate a specific individual at Penthouse whose sole responsibility would be to address matters of concern raised by Dominion in connection with the loan transaction.

On March 15, 1984, Walde followed up the meeting with Guccione by sending him a letter summarizing the issues discussed which Guccione had agreed "to look into." One of the items for review was that "[t]he hotel manager [was] to submit to lender a hotel management program." On March 22, 1984, Dominion's Neal sent a letter to Guccione recommending that Penthouse engage Sigal to formulate a construction cost evaluation. Neal concluded the letter by stating that he felt that "this project has been allowed to drift without direction entirely too long. I sincerely hope that you will implement our recommendations . . . at the earliest possible time, the decision is, of course, entirely yours." Not long after the March 22nd letter, Penthouse broke off communications with Dominion and the Melrod firm and refused to respond to their telephone calls.

Beginning on March 20, 1984, the loan participation syndicate began to unravel. First, on March 20th, Community sent a letter to Dominion stating that it had "elected not to extend its offer to participate" in the loan. Then, on March 28, 1984, another participant, Shadow Lawn Savings & Loan Association, wrote to Queen City and indicated that in view of the fact that the loan commitment "has now expired" and because interest rates had changed, it had to meet with Queen City before it would "reconsider an extension" of its participation interest. In May and June 1984, several other participants sent notices to Queen City indicating their belief that the loan commitment had expired and that they were relieved of their participation commitments. Subsequently, after it was unsuccessful in obtaining alternate financing, Penthouse filed the instant action in June 1984.

PROCEEDINGS IN THE DISTRICT COURT AND ITS DECISION

A brief review of the district court's docket sheet reveals that the instant litigation was hard fought with several discovery battles and other disagreements. The case proceeded to a bench trial on May 11, 1987 before Judge Duffy and concluded on June 1, 1987. A number of witnesses appeared for both sides and the record was supplemented by affidavits of witnesses who did not appear at trial.

Important to Dominion's defense to the anticipatory breach claim was its insistence that Penthouse was not in any position to close the loan by March 1st because it could not have satisfied various terms and preclosing conditions of the commitment by that time. To address this point, Dominion presented the testimony of an expert in real estate construction and permanent financing transactions, John C. Nelson, who was a partner in the New York City law firm of Milbank, Tweed, Hadley & McCloy. After setting forth the factual predicate upon which he based his opinion, Nelson opined that, in light of the various title problems (which were supported by the objections to title asserted by Commonwealth), the lack of agreements with certain utility companies, the absence of final plans and specifications, no final project budget, the lack of contracts with an architect, a major construction contractor and major trade contractors, and no agreement concerning casino licensing, the transaction was in no position to close any time from 60 days to six months from the February 9th preclosing meeting. When Nelson presented his opinion at trial, however, the district court asked him how long it would take to close the transaction if all of the preclosing conditions he had taken into account when formulating his opinion (i.e., final plans and specifications, project budgets, trade contracts, etc.) had been waived. Nelson replied that the deal could close as soon as the papers were drawn up. He qualified his response, however, by insisting that a prudent lender would not waive the various conditions which the hypothetical question assumed were waived.

Also important to Dominion's case was the testimony of Melrod partner, Philip Gorelick. Because of his extensive involvement in the transaction, he was in the best position to present Dominion's perspective concerning the deal. The district court was not, however, receptive to Gorelick's testimony. After Gorelick had concluded his testimony on direct examination and began responding to questions on cross-examination, Judge Duffy called a morning recess. As the Judge was leaving the courtroom, he requested that the Melrod firm's attorney, Robert L. Tofel, join him in the robing room. When Tofel met Judge Duffy in the robing room, the judge handed him a copy of Volume 377 of the Federal Supplement and requested that Tofel read the first line in *United States v. Tramunti*, 377 F.Supp. 1 (S.D.N.Y.1974) (Duffy, J.). That line reads: "John Spurdis is a liar." After reading the sentence to himself, Tofel looked at the judge. Saying nothing, Judge Duffy simply shrugged expressively. Tofel then said in essence that Judge Duffy had misread Gorelick. Tofel explained that Gorelick may have been obnoxious or aggressive but that he was not a liar. Again, Judge Duffy did not respond and simply shrugged.

On July 29, 1987, the district court filed its reported decision in which it held in favor of Penthouse and Queen City and against Dominion. *See* 665 F.Supp. 301 (S.D.N.Y.1987). The district court held that Dominion's conduct during February and March 1984 constituted an anticipatory breach of the loan commitment. The district court began its analysis by reasoning that a party to a contract commits an anticipatory breach when it "indicates its refusal to perform unless entirely new or different conditions are first met[.]" *Id.* at 310 (citations omitted). The district court then found that Dominion's conduct on at least four occasions gave rise to an anticipatory breach. Specifically, the court found that 1) Gorelick's demand that Penthouse obtain amendments to the Helmsley lease, 2) Dominion's insistence that a hotel management agreement be entered into prior to closing, 3) Dominion's insistence that Penthouse hire Sigal to perform a construction cost evaluation, and 4) Dominion's insistence that it replace Queen City as lead lender, taken together, "amounted to an unambiguous refusal to close by Dominion", *id.* at 311, and thus constituted an anticipatory breach.

In response to Dominion's argument that Penthouse was not in a position to satisfy the preclosing conditions before March 1st, the district court found that, by the February 9th preclosing meeting, "all of the conditions precedent had been met, waived, or were in a position to have been met by the date set for closing the loan." *Id.* at 310. The district court specifically found 1) that the title and lease problems were "minor" and could be worked out during the "ongoing" discussions with Helmsley, 2) that Queen City had waived Penthouse's full compliance with preclosing conditions 10, 11, 12, and 16; 3) that Penthouse had satisfied preclosing condition 13, and 4) that arrangements with the Casino Control Commission were "easily within reach." *See id.* at 304–05, 310. The court failed to make factual findings or legal conclusions establishing Queen City's authority to waive any preclosing conditions on behalf of Dominion.

The district court explored Dominion's motive for committing the anticipatory breach and found that "[b]ecause of Community's withdrawal on February 29, . . . Dominion either had to stall the closing until the loan expired and then withdraw from its commitment, or breach its agreement." *Id.* at 310. According to the district court,

Gorelick was employed to serve as "Dominion's hatchet man intent on destroying the deal," *id*. at 308, that "Dominion hired Gorelick to bully and intimidate the plaintiffs into delaying the loan until Community could be replaced or[,] failing that, to delay until the Commitment expired and Dominion was released from its obligation." *Id*. at 307.

The district court also carried forward its earlier, private attack on Gorelick's veracity. In its decision, the district court found that Gorelick committed "outrageous perjury" during trial. *Id*. at 306–07. Making reference to Gorelick's trial testimony, the district court stated

> [t]he decision as to the credibility of witnesses is properly left to the trial judge or to the jury because as finders of fact they are in a position to view the demeanor of the witnesses.

> Gorelick took the stand and attempted brazenly to lie to the court. During cross-examination, the crucible of truth, Gorelick continuously shifted uneasily in the chair, sweated like a trapped liar, and the glaze that came over his shifty eyes gave proof to his continuing perjury. His total lack of veracity was shown not only by his demeanor but by the shady practices he seemingly reveled in. He charged needless and exorbitant fees, Joint Exh. 41, for work that was intentionally unproductive. While representing the bank he demanded a $150,000 "bonus" from the borrower if the loan closed, an arrangement Gorelick never disclosed to his bank-client.

Id. at 306 n. 1. Thus, the court made a specific factual finding that Gorelick committed perjury during his trial testimony.

After reaching its decision on the liability issue, the district court considered the damage question. The court first determined that Penthouse was entitled to various out-of-pocket and "carrying" expenses. Then, the court turned to the question of whether Penthouse was entitled to recover the profits it would have made had the construction been completed and the hotel and casino become operational. Applying the rationale of *Perma Research & Development v. Singer Co.*, 542 F.2d 111 (2d Cir.1976), the court determined that Penthouse's lost future profits over a ten-year period could be properly awarded. Accordingly, the district court held that Penthouse was entitled to recover damages in the amount of $129,904,455, $112,083,583 of which was for the lost future profits.

Also in its decision, the district court concluded that Queen City should prevail on its counterclaim in the third-party action: "Having held that Dominion breached its agreement, I must also find it liable to Queen City for that breach." 665 F.Supp. at 312. In addition, the court concluded that Dominion should lose on its third-party claim against Queen City because "[t]here [was] a total failure of proof that Queen City breached any duty owed to Dominion." *Id*.

After the court issued its opinion, Penthouse submitted its proposed judgment to the district court. In the proposed judgment, Penthouse did not name the Melrod firm as a judgment-debtor for the lost profits award. To correct what it perceived as a discrepancy, the district court *sua sponte* conformed the pleadings to the proof and held that the Melrod firm was jointly and severally liable for the entire Penthouse judgment. The court explained that the Melrod firm was liable for the Penthouse judgment because its conduct amounted to active fraud. The district court did not, however, make any factual findings concerning what acts or omissions allegedly perpetrated by the Melrod firm gave rise to the court's conclusion that it committed fraud. Nor did the court explain how a judgment for lost profits which resulted from an alleged anticipatory breach of a loan commitment could also serve as the basis for a fraud judgment.

After amending its original decision, the district court entered final judgment on October 2, 1987 and awarded Penthouse $128,682,830.80, held Dominion and the Melrod firm jointly and severally liable for that judgment, awarded Queen City $7,652,352.91 plus interest and dismissed Dominion's claim against Queen City with prejudice. Subsequently, in a memorandum and order dated December 2, 1987, the district court denied the defendants' motion for a new trial. 678 F.Supp. 61.

DISCUSSION

Dominion and the Melrod firm raise several arguments on this appeal. Dominion contends that the district court erred in concluding that its conduct amounted to an anticipatory breach of the loan commitment and that the court erred in concluding that Penthouse was ready, willing and able to perform its obligations under the loan commitment. Dominion also argues that the district court applied an incorrect legal standard when it awarded Penthouse damages for its lost future profits and that the court erred when it dismissed its claim against Queen City. The Melrod firm challenges the judgment entered against it on fraud grounds, arguing, inter alia, that because such a finding was not supported in law or fact, the district court erred in sua sponte holding Melrod jointly and severally liable for the Penthouse judgment.

For the reasons that follow, we reverse the judgments entered in favor of Penthouse and Queen City, affirm the dismissal of Dominion's cross-claim and remand with instructions that judgment be entered in favor of Dominion and the Melrod firm.

I.   DOMINION'S APPEAL OF PENTHOUSE JUDGMENT

A.   *Preliminary matters.*

At the outset, Dominion argues that the loan commitment expired by its own terms on March 1, 1984 and contends that, after that date, Dominion, Queen City and the other participating lenders were under "no further obligation" to proceed with the mortgage financing. Dominion therefore suggests that the March 1st date has crucial significance in part because it would constitute the date on or before which the parties would have been required to perform and/or satisfy their obligations under the loan commitment.

At the November 21st meeting, the parties understood that the commitment had expired by its own terms. A written extension of the expiration date was therefore necessary to have a "valid" commitment as of the date Dominion agreed to participate. The parties then mutually extended the expiration date to December 1, 1983, but they simultaneously agreed that the "closing date" for the loan would occur "no earlier than February 1, 1984 or later than March 1, 1984." Aside from these agreements, the parties entered into no other arrangements with respect to further extensions of the expiration date or the closing date.

"An agreement must be construed in the context of the circumstances under which it was entered into and it must be accorded a rational meaning in keeping with the express general purpose." *Tessmar v. Grosner*, 23 N.J. 193, 128 A.2d 467, 471 (1957) (citations omitted). While courts must accord an agreement "the most fair and reasonable construction, imputing the least hardship on either of the contracting parties ... so that neither will have an unfair or unreasonable advantage over the other[,]"*id.* (citations omitted), "[w]here no ambiguity exists in a contract it is the duty of the court, as a matter of law, to interpret the same ... [and] where the parties have said, by very plain words, what they meant, the court has no duty to perform other than to carry their meaning into effect." *Korb v. Spray Beach Hotel Co.*, 24 N.J.Super. 151, 93 A.2d 578, 580 (1952) (per curiam) (citations omitted). In the guise of construing the terms of an agreement, "court[s] will not make a different or better contract than the parties themselves have seen fit to enter into [.]"*In the Matter of the Community Medical Center*, 623 F.2d 864, 866 (3d Cir.1980) (citing *Washington Construction Co. v. Spinella*, 8 N.J. 212, 217–18, 84 A.2d 617, 619 (1951)).

The loan commitment provisions concerning the expiration date and closing date are unambiguous. The loan commitment expired by its own terms 120 days after it was issued on June 20, 1983 unless the parties mutually extended it in writing. After the expiration date passed, the commitment clearly provided that the lender would be under "no further obligation" to fund the loan. It also provided that the closing had to occur on or before the expiration date. The parties' conduct in connection with the written extension to December 1st clearly reflected their belief that the expiration clause was self-executing and that the loan commitment could expire by its own terms.

What we must resolve is whether, when the parties agreed to close the loan "no later than March 1, 1984", they intended on extending the expiration date to March 1st. We believe they did. Reading the expiration date clause together with the clause regarding the closing date leads us to conclude that the parties must have intended to extend the expiration date when they agreed that the closing would occur no later than March 1st. Any other construction of these documents would leave the parties agreeing to close the loan after the commitment had expired which would make no sense.

Some participants clearly believed that when Penthouse and Queen City agreed that the closing date would be "no later than" March 1st, this had the effect of extending the expiration date to that date. Thus, when Community, Shadow Lawn and other participants withdrew their commitments, they all based their decisions upon the fact that the commitment expired on March 1st. In addition, Gorelick and Wienke both believed that the loan commitment expired on that date. Indeed, Gorelick brought the problem of the March 1st expiration to Myerson's attention when he suggested that Myerson obtain an extension of the expiration date. Finally, and most importantly, even Penthouse has acknowledged, albeit indirectly, that the commitment was in effect only until March 1, 1984. Thus, in paragraph 7 of Penthouse's complaint, it alleged as a fact that "[t]he loan commitment was scheduled, by its terms, to remain in effect for 120 days after issuance, and was subsequently extended to March 1, 1984." A necessary inference from this allegation is that Penthouse did not believe that the commitment was extended past March 1st.

The district court did not specifically find that the parties extended the expiration date to March 1st, but it did find that the parties had set March 1st as the closing date. Thus, when the district court was reviewing Penthouse's ability to resolve the title problems, it found "that the entire matter could have been resolved in time to close the deal before March 1, 1984." 665 F.Supp. at 305. Although the district court could have been more deliberate by specifically holding that March 1st was the closing date, we are satisfied that it found that March 1st was the date set for closing.

In view of the above, we conclude that not only was March 1st the closing date, but also that the commitment expired on that date. We acknowledge that the parties' conduct in continuing to negotiate after March 1st may be consistent with an implied extension of the expiration date. We observe, however, that Penthouse and Queen City had allowed the commitment to expire by its own terms once before. Thus, we do not believe that our conclusion here is at odds with the parties' expectations. In holding that the commitment expired on March 1st, we simply construe the terms of relatively unambiguous documents. The parties bargained for a loan commitment that remained open only for a stated duration and we are not at liberty to construe that agreement in a manner inconsistent with its clear language.

B. Existence of an anticipatory breach.

We now turn to the district court's factual findings and legal conclusions concerning the existence of an anticipatory breach. The district court determined that "Dominion's representatives' conduct and statements amounted to a clear refusal to proceed to closing unless conditions beyond those required by the Loan Commitment were first met." 665 F.Supp. at 310. As examples of Dominion's "clear refusal to proceed," the district court relied on 1) Gorelick's insistence on the proposed amendments to the Helmsley Lease, 2) Dominion's alleged insistence that a hotel management agreement be in place prior to closing, 3) Dominion's alleged requirement that Penthouse hire Sigal, and 4) Dominion's alleged demand that it replace Queen City as lead lender. Pointing out that three of the four examples the district court took into account when it found that an anticipatory breach occurred all took place after March 1st, Dominion argues that the district court erred as a matter of law by considering Dominion's post-March 1st conduct. In addition, Dominion contends that, when only its pre-March 1st conduct is taken into account, it is clear that it did not by word or conduct commit an anticipatory breach. We agree.

"Ordinarily no action for damages or for restitution can be maintained until the time for performance has come and there has been an actual failure to perform." *Miller & Sons Bakery Co. v. Selikowitz*, 8 N.J.Super. 118, 73 A.2d 607, 609 (1950). Nevertheless, "where . . . one party [to a contract] either disables himself from performing, or prevents the other from performing, or repudiates in advance his obligations under the contract, and refuses to be longer bound thereby, communicating such repudiation to the other party," the nonbreaching party "is not only excused from further performance . . ., but may at his option treat the contract as terminated for all purposes of performance, and maintain an action at once for damages occasioned by such repudiation, without awaiting the time fixed by the contract for performance by the defendant." *Dun & Bradstreet v. Wilsonite Products Co.*, 130 N.J.L. 24, 31 A.2d 45, 47 (1943) (quoting *O'Neill v. Supreme Council American Legion of Honor*, 70 N.J.L. 410, 412, 57 A. 463, 464 (1904)).

"An anticipatory breach is a definite and unconditional declaration by a party to an executory contract—through word or conduct—that he will not or cannot render the agreed upon performance." *Ross Systems v. Linden Dari-Delite, Inc.*, 35 N.J. 329, 173 A.2d 258, 264 (1961) (citations omitted). Likewise, "[i]f one party to a contract, either wilfully or by mistake, demands of the other a performance to which he has no right under the contract and states definitely that, unless his demand is complied with, he will not render his promised performance, an anticipatory breach has been committed." 4 A. Corbin, Corbin on Contracts § 973, p. 910 (1951).

The term anticipatory breach is self-defining as one which occurs before the time of performance and while the contract is in existence. As we concluded above, March 1st was the closing date and the expiration date for this loan transaction. Thus, we are compelled to agree with Dominion's argument that the district court erred as a matter of law when it took into account Dominion's post-March 1st conduct when determining the existence of an anticipatory breach. Only Dominion's conduct before March 1st is relevant to the determination of whether an anticipatory breach has occurred, and taking only that conduct into account, we conclude that the district court clearly erred when it found that Dominion committed an anticipatory breach.

New Jersey adheres to the view that an anticipatory breach occurs only if there is a *"clear and unequivocal declaration"* that "the agreed upon performance would not be forthcoming." *Seitz v. Mark-O-Lite Sign Contractors, Inc.*, 210 N.J.Super. 646, 510 A.2d 319, 324 (1986) (emphasis added); *see Ross Systems Inc.*, 35 N.J. 329, 173 A.2d at 264; *Miller & Sons Bakery Co.*, 8 N.J.Super. 118, 73 A.2d at 609; *see generally* 4 A. Corbin, Corbin on Contracts § 973 (1951). "Doubtful and indefinite statements that performance may or may not take place and statements that, under certain circumstances that in fact do not yet exist, the performance will not take place," will not give rise to a claim for anticipatory breach. 4 A. Corbin, Corbin on Contracts § 973, p. 905 (1951) (footnote omitted).

In recounting the evidence concerning Gorelick's conduct at the February 9, 1984 preclosing meeting, the district court found that "[t]he overwhelming evidence shows that Gorelick's demands were equal to a demand that the deal be completely done over[.]" 665 F.Supp. at 307. Subsequently, the court found that "[t]hroughout February *and March*, Dominion, through the Melrod firm, continued to make requests for more information which Newman described as 'never ending.' . . . Dominion further demanded numerous changes in the way the entire deal was to be structured, the parties involved, and other changes not required by the Loan Commitment." *Id.* at 309. When, however, the court sought to provide specific examples of the "changes not required" by the commitment, the only one that occurred before March 1st was Gorelick's demands concerning amendments to the Helmsley lease. The evidence established that Gorelick did in fact insist that the proposed amendments were "required." Thus, the issue we confront is whether Gorelick's insistence on the proposed amendments represented a demand for performance for which Dominion had no right and whether his insistence amounted to a "definite and unequivocal refusal" by Dominion to fulfill its obligations under the agreement unless this condition was met.

It is undisputed that, unless amended, the Helmsley lease would have been violated by the closing of the Queen City deal. Because the loan commitment required that there be "no violations" of that lease at closing, it is clear that some amendments were necessary to satisfy the terms of the loan commitment. To this end, the Melrod lawyers submitted a list of proposed amendments to Penthouse. Even though Gorelick insisted that each proposed amendment was required, when the proposed amendments were sent to Penthouse, Dominion's position was equivocal. Trotter's cover letter indicated that the amendments represented what Dominion would be "looking for" and would provide Penthouse "with a jumping off point" for its negotiations with Helmsley. Thus, Gorelick's statements that the proposed amendments were required clearly were qualified by the statements made in Trotter's cover letter.

In addition, we observe that the list of proposed amendments was just that—a proposal. With the proposed amendments, it was contemplated that Penthouse would then engage in negotiations with Helmsley. As indicated in Trotter's letter, the proposed amendments constituted a starting point for the negotiations with Helmsley, but they did not represent Dominion's "final" position. Viewed in this light, we are persuaded that the district court clearly erred when it found that Gorelick's insistence on the proposed amendments gave rise to an anticipatory breach. New Jersey consistently requires that the breaching party in these cases make a "clear and unequivocal declaration" that performance would not be forthcoming and Gorelick's conduct in this regard falls short.

Nevertheless, we are left with the court's general finding that Dominion refused to perform unless the entire deal was restructured. As pointed out above, most of the specific instances of conduct cited by the court occurred after March 1st and thus are not relevant to our inquiry. We do confront, however, the district court's finding that Gorelick demanded at the February 9th meeting that everything in connection with the deal be "completely done over." We observe that Gorelick was so adamant in this regard that the parties allowed him to assume responsibility for drafting the closing documents and reviewing condition compliance. Thus, it is arguable that his demands at the February 9th meeting were sufficiently clear and unequivocal to give rise to an anticipatory breach if his refusal to proceed was unjustified.

When Gorelick attended the February 9th meeting, he only recently had been brought into the deal. He was there to represent his client's interests in connection with its agreement to participate in a $97 million construction and permanent financing transaction, of which more than a third was to be funded by his client. At the time of the preclosing meeting, the parties contemplated closing the transaction within a few weeks—by March 1st at the latest. At the meeting or shortly before, Gorelick discovered that there were significant problems affecting title and problems with the Helmsley lease and yet there were no active negotiations to resolve those problems. Gorelick also learned that Queen City intended on closing the transaction without insisting that Penthouse comply fully with all of the preclosing conditions. In addition, he received draft loan documentation which, in his judgment, was amateurish and substandard for a transaction of this magnitude.

While we do not pass upon the reasonableness of each of Gorelick's objections, we note that Nelson's expert testimony fully supported Gorelick's position that the transaction was not in a position to close any time in the near future. We also note that although the district court found that some of Gorelick's objections were unreasonable, it did not find that most of his concerns were unfounded. Gorelick attended the preclosing meeting in order to ensure that the interests of his client were protected. In so doing, he insightfully observed serious problems with the transaction and promptly raised his objections. Gorelick's insistence on marketable title in the face of the objections reported by the title company all by itself would justify his position that the deal was in no position to close and thus cannot, as a matter of law, constitute an anticipatory breach. Coupling the title and lease problems with Penthouse's failure to establish that it was in a position to fully satisfy all of the preclosing conditions, we conclude that Gorelick properly refused to proceed unless his concerns were addressed. We therefore conclude that the district court clearly erred when it found that Dominion committed an anticipatory breach of its agreement to participate. Accordingly, we reverse the judgment entered against Dominion.

C.   *Plaintiffs' ability to perform.*

As part of this damages action for an alleged anticipatory breach, Penthouse bore the burden of establishing its willingness and ability to perform all of the obligations under the agreement. As Professor Corbin has explained,

> *[i]n an action for breach by an unconditional repudiation it is still a condition precedent to the plaintiff's right to judgment for damages that he should have the ability to perform all such conditions.* If he could not or would not have performed the substantial equivalent for which the defendant's performance was agreed to be exchanged, he is given no remedy in damages for the defendant's non-performance or repudiation. Of course, the willingness and ability that remains a condition precedent in spite of the defendant's repudiation, is willingness and ability to perform if there had been no repudiation.

4 A. Corbin, Corbin on Contracts § 978, pp. 924–25 (1951) (emphasis added) (footnote omitted). New Jersey follows this general rule. *See Bertrand v. Jones*, 58 N.J.Super. 273, 156 A.2d 161, 168 (App.Div.1959) (following Corbin), *certif. denied*, 31 N.J. 553, 158 A.2d 452 (1960); *cf. Caporale v. Rubine*, 92 N.J.L. 463, 105 A. 226, 227 (1918) (in breach of contract action for damages, plaintiff has the burden of establishing "that he was able and ready to perform his part of the undertaking");

accord Korb, 24 N.J.Super. 151, 93 A.2d at 581 (in an action for specific performance, plaintiff must establish that he is "ready, desirous, prompt and eager to perform the contract on his part").

That the plaintiff must establish its readiness and ability to perform does not mean that it is required to tender performance. After the occurrence of an anticipatory breach, "[i]t is no longer necessary for the plaintiff to perform or tender performance." 4 A. Corbin, Corbin on Contracts § 977, p. 920 (1951) (footnote omitted); *see Dun & Bradstreet*, 130 N.J.L. 24, 31 A.2d at 47. This is so because "[t]he defendant's wrongful repudiation justifies the plaintiff in taking him at his word and at once taking steps that may make subsequent performance impossible." 4 A. Corbin, Corbin on Contracts § 978, p. 925 (1951). Nevertheless, the plaintiff must demonstrate that it had the willingness and ability to perform "before the repudiation and that the plaintiff would have rendered the agreed performance if the defendant had not repudiated." *Id.*

In the instant case, the district court found that "at the time of the preclosing meeting, all of the conditions precedent had been met, waived, or were in a position to have been met by the date set for closing the loan." 665 F.Supp. at 310. Thus, it found that Penthouse was ready, willing and able to proceed by the time of the alleged anticipatory breach. In challenging this conclusion, Dominion argues that Penthouse had not met and could not have met its obligations to convey valid mortgages and to satisfy certain of the preclosing conditions and that the district court's findings in this regard are clearly erroneous. Dominion also argues that the district court erred in concluding that certain conditions had been waived, contending that Queen City had no authority to waive preclosing conditions. Dominion concludes that, when properly viewed, the evidence demonstrates that Penthouse was in no position to satisfy the preclosing conditions on or before March 1st and thus failed to establish that it was ready, willing and able to proceed. We agree.

Despite the fact that Penthouse and Queen City never argued at trial that any of the preclosing conditions had been waived, the district court determined that Penthouse's full compliance with preclosing conditions 10, 11, 12 and 16 had been waived as a result of Lipari's meetings with Penthouse during the January 1984 status conferences. The district court's waiver finding was integral to its determination that Penthouse was ready, willing and able to perform by the closing date because, in the absence of a waiver, it is clear that those material preclosing conditions were not and could not have been satisfied by March 1st. Penthouse offered at trial no evidence to contradict Nelson's opinion that it would have taken at least 60 days, and more than likely 6 months, from February 9, 1984 for Penthouse to comply with all of the preclosing conditions. Nelson's prognosis changed only after the district court inquired as to how long it would have taken to close if the unsatisfied preclosing conditions had been waived. Although he bristled at the suggestion that those preclosing conditions would ever be waived by a prudent lender—let alone an institutional lender—he testified that, assuming a waiver, the loan could have been closed as soon as the papers were drawn up. In the face of this testimony, we must squarely decide the propriety of the district court's waiver finding. This inquiry requires, in turn, that we examine whether Queen City had the authority in the first instance to waive Penthouse's compliance with preclosing conditions. We conclude that it did not.

Before we inquire into Queen City's authority to waive compliance with preclosing conditions, we must examine the nature of Dominion's agreement to participate. On November 21st, Dominion entered into an agreement with Queen City whereby it agreed to participate in the lending syndicate to the extent of $35 million. That agreement was embodied in several documents which, in turn, incorporated the terms and conditions of *both* the Queen City loan commitment and the participation agreement. When construing Dominion's agreement, we read these documents "together as one instrument, and the recitals in one may be explained or limited by reference to the other." *Schlein v. Gairoard*, 127 N.J.L. 358, 22 A.2d 539, 540–41 (1941); *see Schlossman's, Inc. v. Radcliffe*, 3 N.J. 430, 70 A.2d 493, 495 (1950). Applying this rule, we therefore look to the terms of both the loan commitment and the participation agreement when examining whether Queen City had the authority to effect a waiver of preclosing conditions.

The loan commitment provided that "[a]ll title questions and all other legal matters relating to or arising out of the Loan shall be subject in all respects to the approval of the Lender's counsel . . . and the decision of the Lender's counsel as to whether all conditions of the commitment have been met shall be final." The commitment also provided, however, that "[l]ender's obligation to close the loan is contingent upon the satisfaction of each of [the preclosing] conditions." Reading these two provisions together, we conclude that, although Queen City had the final word on whether the preclosing conditions had been satisfied, Penthouse nevertheless was required to satisfy each of the preclosing conditions. Thus, Queen City was granted essentially administrative authority to oversee the manner in which the preclosing conditions were satisfied, but it was not empowered to waive Penthouse's compliance with the preclosing conditions.

The participation agreement further limited Queen City's authority in connection with the administration of the loan transaction. It expressly provided that its terms could not be modified except by an agreement in writing. Thus, Queen City was not empowered to modify the terms or conditions of the participation agreement without obtaining the participants' prior approval. In addition, when the participants entered into the agreement with Queen City, they only authorized Queen City to act on their behalf in the capacity of an independent contractor; Queen City was not authorized to act as their agent. To this end, Queen City was given discretionary power as to the means and manner of contractual performance, *see, e.g., Errickson v. F.W. Schwiers, Jr. Co.*, 108 N.J.L. 481, 158 A. 482, 483 (1932), but was not empowered to make material changes that rendered the participants less secure. Even if we were to conclude that Queen City was authorized to act as agent for the participants, it would not have been empowered to waive or alter material terms "or otherwise to diminish or discharge the obligation of the third person[.]" *See* Restatement (Second) of Agency § 51 comment C (2d ed. 1979).

In view of the above, it is clear that Queen City was not authorized expressly or inferentially in the commitment or the participation agreement to modify the terms of the commitment by waiving Penthouse's full compliance with preclosing conditions. In addition, when Dominion was first informed concerning the full extent of Penthouse's proposed substitute performance for preclosing conditions 10, 11, 12 and 16, Gorelick objected. Then, after the Melrod firm was given responsibility for reviewing condition compliance and Gorelick transmitted his various checklists, it was made clear that Dominion expected that Penthouse would comply with the terms of each preclosing condition. Thus, there could be no implied waiver of these conditions here, either. We therefore conclude that the district court erred when it found that Queen City waived Penthouse's full compliance with preclosing conditions 10, 11, 12 and 16. Because Queen City could not waive these conditions in the first place, it could not accept Penthouse's substitute performance without first obtaining the participants' approval.

Sound national banking policies support the conclusion we reach here. As *amicus curiae* Federal Home Loan Bank Board points out:

> the proposition . . . that a lead lender may, without consulting participating lenders, waive or modify significant conditions of a loan to the detriment of participants, seriously undermines the Bank Board's supervisory policies concerning safe and sound underwriting of participation purchases and is completely at odds with the Bank Board's policy that loan participants must satisfy themselves that the participation is a loan that the participating association would make itself.

> If a lead lender has this authority . . ., the Bank Board's supervisory control regarding underwriting of participation purchases is rendered more difficult or impossible and the FSLIC fund is exposed to inordinate risk. A savings and loan association's independently and prudently underwritten participation in a loan could be changed into an entirely reckless act if fundamental terms and conditions of the loan are altered prior to closing by the lead lender on its own initiative and without consulting the participant. This would make it very difficult, if not impossible, for a participant to assure prudent underwriting or participations. While we do not necessarily find that these policy considerations by [themselves] are binding if the parties had agreed otherwise, they certainly militate against the district court's unsubstantiated and erroneous finding that Queen City had the authority to waive various essential preclosing conditions.

As a separate matter, Dominion contends that the district court's other findings that bore upon Penthouse's ability to perform were erroneous. The district court found that the outstanding title and lease problems were "minor," 665 F.Supp. at 310, and that "the entire matter could have been resolved in time to close the deal before March 1, 1984." *Id*. at 305. The district court also held that, although licensing discussions with the Casino Control Commission "were to resume after the closing, . . . it appeared an arrangement with the Commission was easily within reach." *Id*. Dominion argues that, notwithstanding the court's characterization, the title and lease problems were not minor and that there was no evidence to support the court's conclusion that those matters could have been resolved by March 1st. With regard to its finding concerning the licensing arrangements, Dominion contends that it supports the view that Penthouse could not have satisfied this preclosing condition before closing and that the court's characterization that these arrangements were "easily within reach" is belied by the evidence. We agree with both of Dominion's contentions.

Turning to the court's findings concerning the title and lease problems, we are compelled to conclude that the district court clearly erred when it characterized these matter's as being "minor." Unless these problems were resolved, they absolutely would have prevented Penthouse from delivering the title required in the commitment. Likewise, unless the Helmsley lease was modified, Penthouse could not certify that there were "no violations" of that lease. Thus, in view of the gravity of these problems, Penthouse knew that they had to be resolved by the closing date. We therefore cannot conclude that they were "minor."

In addition, the district court's characterization of the title and lease problems as "minor" presupposed that several contingencies could and would occur to resolve them before closing. As Nelson described the situation, since Helmsley was a sophisticated participant in real estate transactions, there probably would be no insurmountable barriers to reaching an accord with him to address the title and lease problems, "but it would take time and probably money." Thus, the court may have believed that the problems were minor because they could have been resolved in time and with money. To reach an agreement resolving these problems, however, it was incumbent upon Penthouse to commence negotiations. Thus, the district court's conclusion that these matters were minor and resolvable by March 1st rested on the assumption that negotiations with Helmsley were "ongoing" and would be concluded favorably before March 1st. This assumption was erroneous.

Both Myerson and Newman testified that actual negotiations with Helmsley had not occurred by February 9th. Although Newman had made indirect contact with Helmsley's attorney, no formal proposals had been submitted and no negotiations had begun. This uncontradicted evidence leads us to conclude that the district court clearly erred when it found that negotiations with Helmsley were "ongoing." Negotiations cannot be characterized as "ongoing" when they have not even begun. The absence of ongoing negotiations undermines the district court's finding that the title and lease problems could have been resolved before March 1st, and no evidence in the record indicates that negotiations would have commenced by March 1st, let alone be concluded by that date, to resolve the problems with the lease and title.

In addition, Penthouse failed to establish that it was working toward clearing up the problems posed by the McShane and Chase mortgages. Those mortgages had to be subordinated in order for Penthouse to provide the security required by the commitment and Penthouse apparently had not even made contact with the holders of those mortgages. This fact plus the problems surrounding the Helmsley lease lead us to conclude that the district court's factual finding that these problems could have been resolved by March 1st is clearly erroneous.

With regard to the court's finding concerning the status of the alternate licensing arrangements condition, we note that the district court overlooked the fact that this was a *preclosing* condition. Because the court found that those arrangements could have been made *after* closing, it is clear that Penthouse did not carry its burden to demonstrate its ability to perform this condition *before* closing. In addition, we observe that record evidence does not support the district court's finding that these arrangements were "easily within reach." Goldstein's letter clearly indicated the tentative nature of his proposal. He described it as a "rough outline" of what he thought "might be acceptable" to the CCC. From Goldstein's letter, it is clear that no arrangements had actually been made. Presumably, Penthouse and the lenders were going to have to draft agreements for the alternate licensing arrangements. This would take time. Therefore, due to the tentative status of the proposed alternate arrangements and the absence of an actual agreement, we are convinced that the district court also erred in this regard.

In view of the foregoing, we conclude that Penthouse failed to carry its burden at trial to demonstrate that it was ready, willing and able to perform its contractual obligations at any time before March 1st. Thus, even if we were to agree that Dominion had refused to perform, we would nevertheless be compelled to conclude that it could not recover damages. We could conclude that Penthouse's failure to demonstrate that it could deliver marketable title by March 1st would be a complete answer to a charge of anticipatory breach. When, however, the title and lease problems are combined with Penthouse's inability to perform the various preclosing conditions, we are left with the firm belief that it should not be entitled to recover on its complaint for an anticipatory breach. Accordingly, the judgment in favor of Penthouse is reversed.

D. Damages.

Having found that Penthouse failed to establish the essential elements of its anticipatory breach claim, we need not address the merits of the district court's award of lost future profits. Nevertheless, we are compelled to point out that the case upon which the district court relied when holding that the lost profits were recoverable may not be good law. In reaching its decision on the damages issue, the court relied on our decision in *Perma Research and Development v. Singer Co.*, 542 F.2d 111 (2d Cir.1976), a diversity action involving questions of New York law. Since our decision in *Perma Research*, however, New York's highest court has considered the damages issue decided in *Perma Research* and has flatly rejected the rationale of that decision. *See Kenford Co. v. Erie County*, 67 N.Y.2d 257, 502 N.Y.S.2d 131, 493 N.E.2d 234 (1986) (per curiam). In view of the New York Court of Appeal's decision in *Kenford*, the rationale of our decision on the damages issue in *Perma Research* is seriously in doubt and we conclude that the district court's reliance on that case was misplaced.

II. DOMINION'S APPEAL OF QUEEN CITY JUDGMENT

A. Anticipatory breach claim.

After it concluded that Dominion was liable to Penthouse for Dominion's alleged anticipatory breach, the district court addressed Queen City's claim, stating:

> Queen City counterclaims against Dominion for breach of its obligations to Queen City. As a direct result of Dominion's failure to close the loan, Queen City claims to have suffered a loss of profits it otherwise would have earned. In one of the documents signed November 21, 1983 Dominion accepted the Queen City commitment . . ., and thus, Dominion's breach gives rise to claims by all parties to which it was contractually obligated. Having held that Dominion breached its agreement, I must also find it liable to Queen City for that breach.

665 F.Supp. at 312. Thus, when the district court held in favor of Queen City on the counterclaim, the court based its decision solely upon its earlier conclusion that Dominion committed an anticipatory breach. In view of our determination that the court erred in concluding that Dominion committed an anticipatory breach and that Penthouse was ready, willing and able to proceed by March 1st, we reverse the judgment entered in favor of Queen City. Because Dominion's conduct did not amount to an anticipatory breach, it is not liable to Queen City on the counterclaim. Likewise, because Penthouse did not establish that it could have satisfied the preclosing conditions before March 1st, Queen City is also precluded from recovery against Dominion.

B. Dismissal of Dominion's cross-claim.

Dominion contends that the district court erred when it dismissed with prejudice its third-party claim against Queen City. Dominion predicated its theory of Queen City's liability on the argument that, if Queen City did in fact waive four preclosing conditions, in so doing it breached its fiduciary duties owed to Dominion and the other participants. Because, however, we conclude that no waiver occurred— because Queen City had no authority to waive conditions—it follows that Queen City is not liable for any purported waiver. Accordingly, we affirm the district court's dismissal of this claim.

III. THE MELROD FIRM'S APPEAL OF PENTHOUSE JUDGMENT

A. Background.

Nowhere in the district court's reported opinion did it find that Dominion or the Melrod firm committed fraud. The entire decision was devoted to a discussion of Dominion's alleged anticipatory breach and the damages resulting therefrom. There was no suggestion that Gorelick and the Melrod firm were to be held liable for the Penthouse judgment. In addition, while the district court made findings concerning Dominion's alleged undisclosed intent and Gorelick's purported role as "hatchet man," we observe that the court found no fraud or misrepresentation concerning the November 21st agreement and made no other specific findings with regard to subsequent events or statements suggesting that fraud was committed. Indeed, although Penthouse specifically sought in the pretrial order a finding that its agreement to pay the Melrod firm's fees was void and unenforceable (a claim that was part of the fraud count in its complaint), the district court never made such a finding.

After the district court issued its reported decision, the parties submitted proposed judgments. Penthouse's proposed judgment form requested from the Melrod firm approximately $1.7 million, not the

$128.7 million amount of its anticipatory breach judgment. In contrast, in addition to submitting its proposed judgment, the Melrod firm submitted a letter to the court in which it argued that it had been exonerated and should be free of liability. In response to these two conflicting proposed judgments, the district court filed an order dated September 30, 1987, in which it held the Melrod firm jointly and severally liable for the $128.7 million Penthouse judgment. Explaining its rationale for this decision, the district court stated:

> It is urged that the law partnership was merely an agent for a disclosed principal and as such could not be liable for any wrongdoing. This argument ignores two items: first, the firm did not disclose the true nature of the agency which it undertook; and, the actions of the firm through its partner constituted active fraud. The analogy that comes to mind when considering the law firm's argument is that of a hoodlum enforcer for a loan shark claiming innocence as the agent of a disclosed principal. In this case the Melrod firm did not disclose the true nature of its agency, i.e., to scuttle the deal and cause damage to the plaintiffs and others. Certainly no one can imagine Philip Gorelick coming to the pre-closing meeting to tell everyone that he had been delegated to subvert the deal.

> For some unexplained reason the various judgments submitted do not name the Melrod firm as a judgment debtor for the lost profits. This may be occasioned because of a defect in the pleadings at the start of the trial. As part of the pro forma disposition of the "usual motions" made at the end of the case, I granted the "usual" motion to conform the pleadings to the proof. Thus it is appropriate and just for the Melrod firm to stand as a joint and several debtor for the profits lost by the Penthouse plaintiffs.

Notwithstanding the district court's assertions, no motions— "usual" or otherwise—to conform the pleadings to the proof appear in the record.

Thereafter, the Melrod firm filed a motion for a new trial in which it argued *inter alia* that the robing room incident, the court's bias against Gorelick and its *sua sponte* order holding the Melrod firm jointly and severally liable on a fraud theory all constituted reversible error and merited a new trial. In an order dated December 2, 1987, the district court denied the Melrod firm's motion. In that order, the court first concluded that it had not prejudged the case against the Melrod firm and had treated Gorelick appropriately, and then, turning to its *sua sponte* order, the court stated:

> [t]he last item raised in this motion for a new trial is a claim by the Melrod law firm that it was denied a fair trial because after the trial was finished I deemed the pleadings amended to make them responsible for all of the damages rather than the approximately $3 million for which they originally thought that they were potentially liable. Like the others, this claim also lacks substance. Somehow the Melrod firm claims that they were unprepared to defend against such a large claim. This ignores the fact that both Melrod and Dominion had but

one counsel and he was totally prepared. Loss of the case by defense counsel cannot be attributed to anything other than the fact that the defendants were wholly responsible for the injury which they caused by illegal means. No counsel could change the facts. The one trial counsel for the two parties was as prepared as anyone could have been. Melrod's claim apparently, however, is not that they were unprepared to meet the allegations of the complaint as amended, but rather that they are now unprepared to pay the sum of money for which they have been held liable. Clearly this is not grounds for a new trial.

B.   The Melrod firm's claims.

The Melrod firm presents a multitude of arguments in favor of reversal of this judgment. The firm argues that the trial itself was rendered unfair by the district court's premature assessment of Gorelick's credibility (as demonstrated by the robing room incident) and the court's excessive intervention during trial. The Melrod firm also contends that the court's perjury finding, by itself, was both legally and factually erroneous. Finally, the Melrod firm contends that the court's actions in holding it jointly and severally liable sua sponte violated the Federal Rules of Civil Procedure as well as due process.

The Melrod firm is not alone in challenging the fraud judgment. Dominion, joined by the Melrod firm, contends that, on the merits, the $128.7 million judgment cannot be sustained under a fraud theory.

C.   Non-existence of fraud.

Penthouse's fraud cause of action was set forth in Count III of its complaint. In that count, after realleging the facts surrounding the alleged anticipatory breach, Penthouse alleged the following: 1) On February 10, 1984, Dominion through the Melrod firm represented to Penthouse that Dominion was prepared to proceed with the loan closing according to the terms of the loan commitment, 2) the February 10, 1984 representation was false because Dominion did not intend to proceed with the loan unless Penthouse would agree to numerous additional conditions and terms that were not contained in the commitment, 3) in reliance on that representation, Penthouse entered into an agreement on February 10, 1984 to pay Dominion's costs and legal fees, and 4) Penthouse suffered damages in excess of $1 million in addition to the nearly $32,000 paid for Dominion's legal fees. Thus, Penthouse's fraud theory was that, on February 10, 1984, the Melrod firm falsely represented to Penthouse that Dominion would proceed with its agreement to participate according to the terms of the loan commitment at a time when it in fact did not intend to proceed. In other words, Penthouse alleged that by February 10th Dominion no longer intended to fulfill its agreement to participate unless the commitment was restructured. Accordingly, Penthouse's position was that when Gorelick made statements on February 9–10, 1984 to the effect that Dominion intended to proceed, he committed a fraud for which his firm was liable.

The district court did not make factual findings in connection with Penthouse's fraud claim. Instead, it made its decision to hold the Melrod firm jointly and severally liable *sua sponte* and stated that the firm's actions constituted "active fraud." Thus, the court failed to make specific findings on each element of the fraud cause of action, i.e., that the Melrod firm—through Gorelick—knowingly made a false representation of present or past material fact with the intent to cause actual reliance and that Penthouse in fact relied on the misrepresentation to its detriment. The district court did, however, find that Gorelick attended the February 9th meeting for the sole purpose of sabotaging the deal and that Dominion did not intend on fulfilling its commitment at that time. Thus, if we assume that, on February 10th, Gorelick made the representations Penthouse claims, then, arguably, he would have made a false representation of Dominion's present intent which could give rise to a claim for fraud. At the bottom of the fraud claim, then, is the district court's determination that, by February 9th, Dominion did not intend on fulfilling its contractual obligation and that it had hired Gorelick to break up the deal. Dominion contends that this finding is clearly erroneous. We agree.

In its opinion, the district court labored to develop a factual basis supporting its conclusion that Gorelick was called in by Dominion to "sabotage" the transaction. To find that by February 9th Dominion had decided to breach its commitment, the court relied on no testimonial evidence. Rather, the district court turned to a document offered in evidence and observed that "on its Commitment Participation Report for February, Dominion dropped Penthouse as a listed borrower." 665 F.Supp. at 306. The court then concluded that this was "almost conclusive proof that Dominion's officers had decided to breach its commitment by that time." *Id.* The district court did not recognize, however, that that report was not prepared in early-February, but was dated February 29th. Nor did the court take into account Dominion's Secondary Market Department's weekly list of loan commitments—also put into evidence—which indicated that Dominion carried the Penthouse participation on that list for every week through early-April 1984.

In addition to the unexplained omission of the Penthouse loan from Dominion's monthly report, the district court relied on Community's allegedly tenuous status when it found that Dominion intended to breach its commitment. The district court found that, by early-February, "Dominion should have been aware of Community's tenuous status as a loan participant." 665 F.Supp. at 306. Later, the court determined that, "[b]ecause of Community's withdrawal on February 29, Dominion was in the awkward position of having committed itself to lend more than the amount it was legally permitted to lend. . . . Thus, Dominion either had to stall the closing until the loan expired and then withdraw from its commitment, or breach its commitment." *Id.* at 310.

The district court's factual findings belie its conclusion that Dominion intended not to proceed on February 9th. According to the court's reasoning, Dominion was not in this "awkward position" until late-February—when it allegedly dropped the Penthouse loan off the monthly report and purportedly received Community's withdrawal. Thus, even if we were to accept the court's findings regarding Community's withdrawal and the inferences to be drawn from the omission on the report, we would be compelled to conclude that the court clearly erred when it determined that this evidence established that Dominion intended not to proceed on February 9th.

Nevertheless, we also reject the court's finding regarding the timing of Community's withdrawal. Although Wienke had expressed his reservations about the transaction to Dominion and Queen City on February 8th and then to Gorelick and Myerson in late February, there is no evidence of Community's withdrawal prior to its March 20th letter. Thus, we conclude that the court clearly erred in this regard also.

Aside from the district court's erroneous factual findings, there is no other evidence establishing that Dominion intended not to proceed and there is abundant evidence to indicate just the opposite. Even after the commitment expired, Dominion indicated its continued interest in the transaction and maintained steady contact with Penthouse. And, it was Penthouse, not Dominion, who cut off communications. Thus, we conclude that there is no basis to conclude that Gorelick or Dominion harbored a secret intent not to proceed on February 9–10 or otherwise. It therefore follows that, even assuming that Gorelick made a representation to Penthouse of Dominion's intent to proceed on February 10th, that representation of fact cannot give rise to a claim for fraud. Accordingly, the judgment entered against the Melrod firm is reversed.

Having concluded that Penthouse does not prevail on the merits of the fraud claim, it is unnecessary to pass on the several other arguments raised on this appeal. Nevertheless, we are quite concerned by the district court's conduct during the robing room incident as well as by its perjury finding. Suffice it to say that we believe that *ex parte* communications between the district court and only one of the litigants are rarely, if ever, looked upon with favor, even if intended to impart advice to a fellow member of the profession. With regard to the perjury finding, we are somewhat surprised by its presence in the court's decision. If the court viewed Gorelick's testimony as incredible, that is its prerogative as the trier of fact in a non-jury case, but unless perjury is at issue in a case, such a finding is not necessary once the trier of fact finds the witnesses' testimony incredible. The perjury finding here, however, was not only unnecessary but also was erroneous since it was not based upon clear and convincing proof. *See Barr Rubber Products Co. v. Sun Rubber Co.*, 425 F.2d 1114, 1120 (2d Cir.), *cert. denied*, 400 U.S. 878, 91 S.Ct. 118, 27 L.Ed.2d 115 (1970). Accordingly, we specifically reverse that finding.

CONCLUSION

In view of the foregoing, we reverse the judgments entered against Dominion and the Melrod firm in favor of Penthouse and against Dominion in favor of Queen City, affirm the dismissal of Dominion's cross-claim, and remand to the district court for the purpose of entering judgment in favor of Dominion and the Melrod firm and against Penthouse and Queen City dismissing the complaint and the related cross-action.

NOTES

1. *Loan Commitments. Penthouse International* raises several issues related to commercial real estate lending. The substantive issue—

enforceability of a loan commitment—arises when the permanent lender refuses to fund. This refusal may be due to legitimate concerns about the borrower's compliance with the commitment, but may also be fueled by an increase in prevailing interest rates since the commitment was issued. The borrower usually seeks to enforce the permanent loan commitment because its terms are superior to those currently available, because the borrower has timing concerns even if other comparable funds can be obtained, or because the construction mortgage is due or requires a prohibitive rate of interest.

Courts have specifically enforced mortgage commitments against hesitant lenders on the theory that money damages are inadequate because of the unavailability of other funding or the time required to obtain a substitute loan. See, e.g., Selective Builders, Inc. v. Hudson City Savings Bank, 137 N.J.Super. 500, 349 A.2d 564 (Chan.1975). In contrast, where lenders bring actions based on the failure of the borrower to close under a loan commitment, courts have generally denied specific performance on the theory that the lender's damages can be estimated with reasonable precision based on the difference between the commitment's interest rate and the current interest rate. See, e.g., City Centre One Associates v. Teachers Insurance and Annuity Association of America, 656 F.Supp. 658 (D.Utah 1987). See generally Edwards, Commercial Loan Commitments: A Borrower's Perspective, 8 Probate & Prop. 28 (July/Aug.1994).

In many cases there are three interested parties when the permanent lender balks at funding—the borrower, the permanent lender, and the construction lender. *Penthouse International* involved a situation where the lender refusing to fund was committed to provide both construction and permanent financing. In transactions where there are separate construction and permanent lenders, both want to assure that the loan will pass without a hitch from one to the other upon completion of construction. While specific performance and damages are generally available to the construction or permanent lender whose counterpart has reneged, what both sides really want is an agreement that will be virtually self-executing. The buy-sell agreement, sometimes called a "tri-party agreement," aims to serve this purpose. This agreement is described in the excerpt by Weller at pages 589–595 above.

Buy-sell agreements can run to great length. According to Smith and Lubell, "The permanent loan commitment contains several conditions that must be fulfilled before the permanent lender actually makes the loan. The construction lender wants the permanent lender to approve as many of those conditions as possible even before the construction lender makes its loan. Such approvals are incorporated into the buy-sell agreement and they frequently are the cause of extensive negotiation between the two lenders." Smith & Lubell, The Buy-Sell Agreement, 9 Real Est.Rev. 13 (Spring 1979).

The article by Davis, excerpted at page 601 above, lists several of the approvals to be included in the buy-sell agreement. Smith and Lubell add some others:

> The form of the promissory note and mortgage. The form of other documents evidencing the security for the loan such as assignments of rents and financing statements under the Uniform Commercial Code.

The survey. Although the survey presented prior to completion of construction can only show perimeter boundaries and existing easements, the permanent lender may approve the perimeter survey and reserve approvals of easements until completion of the improvement.

Plans and specifications for the improvements. (The permanent loan commitment requires that the permanent lender must approve material changes from the original plans and specifications. Problems arise because it is extremely difficult to define a "material" change. Any series of minor changes may be tantamount to a material change.)

The evidence of ownership of property as reflected in a title policy. If the developer owns a leasehold estate, approval of the ground lease is required.

Major tenant leases and standard lease forms. The form of proof of completion of the improvements acceptable to the permanent lender, such as the certificate of occupancy and architectural certification.

The form of various opinions required by the permanent lender with respect to compliance with environmental and zoning requirements.

On the importance of clear drafting in commitment letters, see Pointe Development, LLC v Enterprise Bank & Trust, 316 S.W.3d 543 (Mo. App. 2010) (lender failed to create condition limiting cost of construction either "in express terms or by clear implication"). On the enforceability of permanent loan commitments generally, see Draper, The Broken Commitment: A Modern View of the Mortgage Lender's Remedy, 59 Cornell L.Rev. 418 (1974); Draper, Tight Money and Possible Substantive Defenses to Enforcement of Future Mortgage Commitments, 50 Notre Dame Law. 603 (1975); Mehr & Kilgore, Enforcement of the Real Estate Loan Commitment: Improvement of the Borrower's Remedies, 24 Wayne L.Rev. 1011 (1978). See also Dewey, Organizational Due Diligence in Real Estate Secured Loan Transactions: The Role of Lender's Counsel, 16 Probate & Prop. 10 (Jul./Aug 2002); Franke, A Primer on Construction, Permanent, and Bridge Lending in Financing the Affordable Housing Deal (Parts 1 and 2), 9 J. Affordable Hous. & Comm. Dev. L. 145, 155 (2000).

2. *Participations.* As indicated in *Penthouse International,* lenders sometimes do not wish to fund the entire loan due to regulatory limitations or investment practices. The lender thus might recruit other lenders to participate in the loan by lending a portion of the total funds. The initial lender serves as the "lead lender" with the others having participation interests. As demonstrated in *Penthouse International,* the participants are concerned that the loan is sound even though the lead lender is directly responsible for servicing the loan and remitting payments to the participants. Moreover, there is a danger for the participants if the lead lender becomes financially unstable or insolvent. See generally, Murray, Recharacterization Issues in Participating Loans, 19 Probate & Prop. 36 (Sep./Oct. 2005); Comment, Lead Lender Failure and the Pitfalls for the Unwitting Participant, 42 Southwestern L.J. 1071 (1989).

3. *Lender Liability. Penthouse International* was hailed by lenders as reversing the trend of lender liability, discussed on pages 217–219. In what way does the court limit the lender's obligation? The court also appeared to support the lender's position on the basis that it followed reasonable lending behavior in its actions. While a reasonable lending standard was helpful to the bank in this case, could that standard be used as a sword against a lender that failed to follow usual lending practices?

4. *The Role of the Attorney.* What do you think of the behavior and professionalism of the attorneys for Queen City and Dominion as described in *Penthouse International*? Did the attorneys properly balance their responsibility to protect their clients from loss and their obligation to serve their clients' interests by facilitating the closing of the transaction? On the possible ethical problems of attorneys in sophisticated real estate transactions in general, see Weinstein, Attorney Liability in the Savings and Loan Crisis, 1993 U.Ill.L.Rev. 53 (discussing conflicts of interest, misleading of third parties, and illegal actions by the client).

5. *The Penthouse International Story.* For an excellent analysis of the case, its back story, and its ramifications, see Weinberger, The Art of Breaking the Deal: The Case of the Penthouse Casino, 82 Miss. L.J. 651 (2013).

c.   SUBORDINATED PURCHASE MONEY FINANCING

Middlebrook-Anderson Co. v. Southwest Sav. & Loan Ass'n

California Court of Appeal, Fourth District, 1971.
18 Cal.App.3d 1023, 96 Cal.Rptr. 338.

GABBERT, ASSOCIATE JUSTICE.

The plaintiffs appeal from a judgment of dismissal entered after defendants' general and special demurrers were sustained without leave to amend in this complicated land development action. Plaintiffs are two California corporations, doing business as Middlebrook-Anderson Co., a partnership, hereinafter referred to as "seller".

The seller owned real property consisting of 28 lots in Orange County. It entered into a land sale contract with certain developers, hereinafter referred to as "buyers", who are not before us in this action. An escrow at a bank was opened between seller and the buyers; the instructions specified the sale price to be $365,000, which was to be partially paid by a purchase money deed of trust in the amount of $169,500. This deed was to be second and junior to a construction loan to be obtained at some later time by the buyers.

During a period of several months buyers negotiated for a construction loan from defendant Southwest Savings and Loan Association, hereinafter referred to as "lender". Defendant Western Escrow Company was the escrow agent for the buyers and the lender. The buyers represented to the seller that the bank escrow would have to be revised to provide for a purchase money deed of trust in favor of seller in the sum of $69,500 and to allow the lender to obtain priority over seller's deed of trust by priority of recording. The bank escrow between seller and buyers was amended accordingly.

After these terms were agreed to by the seller and the buyers, the construction loan was consummated. Western Escrow prepared 28 deeds of trust in favor of lender, with Western named as trustee, each in the amount of $52,300. A deed of trust in favor of seller in the amount of $69,500, expressly stating it was junior to the lender's deeds of trust, was also prepared. These 29 trust deeds were recorded on April 22, 1966. Three days later, to repair the distortion caused by the $100,000 reduction in the apparent size of the purchase money loan, the $69,500 deed was reconveyed and 28 new ones prepared and recorded, each in the amount of $6,053.

The third amended complaint alleges the lender disbursed $1,464,400 into a construction loan account, and allowed the buyers to use $300,000 of this for purposes other than for construction improvements. When the loan funds ran out in November 1966, the buyers abandoned the unfinished apartment houses on the property. In the same month, Western Escrow gave notice of default and election to sell under lender's trust deeds. Seller tendered payment of the due principal, interest, and late charges to cure the default, but Western and lender demanded in excess of $50,000, in addition, to repay lender for sums it claimed it had expended for repairs caused by vandalism on the property and completion of the construction. Lender purchased the property at a series of foreclosure sales in April and May 1967, remained in possession and collected rents for a period of time, and then sold the properties to members of the public not parties to this action.

This litigation was commenced by a complaint filed before the foreclosure sales were complete. After plaintiffs' third amended complaint, attempting to state seven different causes of action against Southwest Savings and Loan and Western Escrow was filed, the trial court sustained defendant's general demurrers to the complaint on grounds of failure to state a cause of action, and 44 special demurrers on grounds of uncertainty.

Plaintiffs' causes of action are based essentially on the failure of lender to limit the use of the loan funds to construction purposes. The theories of recovery and remedies sought in the respective numbered causes of action are:

(1) a restoration of the priority of seller's trust deeds;

(2) damages for rendering seller's trust deeds valueless by foreclosure on lender's first trust deeds;

(3) either restoration of priority or money damages based on lender's knowingly permitting the use of $300,000 for nonconstruction purposes;

(4) either restoration of priority or damages based on seller's status as a third party beneficiary of the construction loan contract between lender and the buyers;

(5) setting aside the trustee's foreclosure sale of the property, or damages, based on lender's and Western Escrow's refusal to accept seller's tender of principal, interest and late charges to cure the default on the construction loan;

(6) an accounting of funds received by lender from the property after the foreclosure sales, both as rents and proceeds of re-sales, and application of such funds to repayment of the construction loan, plus reasonable rental value of the property for the period lender was in possession;

(7) (labeled "tenth" because the seventh, eighth, and ninth causes of action named only the buyers) punitive damages based on alleged malice involved in every act of the defendants.

The pleadings allege an original contract existed between the seller and buyers; the escrow at the bank was solely between seller and buyers; the sellers were to receive a purchase money trust deed which would be junior to a construction loan that was to be negotiated. Thereafter negotiations with the lender by the buyers resulted in a commitment by the lender to the buyers on the condition, as represented by the buyers to the seller, that the lender would make a construction loan and would require documents to show the buyers had made a greater cash investment in the property than originally contemplated and would require subordination of seller's trust deed by priority of recording rather than through a formal subordination agreement.

The complaint further alleges the buyers represented to the seller the funds received from the lender would be used exclusively for construction of improvements on the property and, based on these representations, the seller agreed to the terms. The buyers then entered into the escrow with Western Escrow which, acting as agent for the buyers and the lender, received a copy of the escrow instructions between the seller and buyers.

The seller alleges the lender had knowledge of the second trust deeds taken by the seller and had a duty to inquire of the seller as to the terms and conditions under which the seller agreed to accept a junior lien. The complaint further alleges the lender voluntarily undertook to control disbursements from the construction loan fund and that the seller did not attempt to follow the progress of the construction or status of disbursements because it relied on such control by the lender, who knew and intended that seller so rely.

The seller continues that the lender owed a duty to seller because of lender's conduct which induced the seller to "subordinate" its lien, because of lender's voluntary assumption of control of disbursements and because of the lender's knowledge of the security interest of the seller and knowledge that the seller would subordinate its lien on condition the loan funds were to be used only for construction improvements. Seller alleges the lender disbursed $300,000 in funds which were not for construction purposes, in wanton, reckless disregard of the security interest of seller.

The complaint also alleges that by reason of these improper disbursements the construction of the project was not completed and the market value of the property did not increase through the construction of improvements to a sufficient extent to support the security interests of both seller and lender. The value of seller's security interest in the property was thus diminished to the extent of the alleged wrongful disbursements. The seller finally contends that at the time of the commencement of the case the unpaid balance on the trust deeds in favor of sellers was in the sum of $141,250.23, plus interest.

All of plaintiffs' causes of action depend upon a conclusion that seller's agreement to take a second trust deed constituted a subordination agreement or an agreement in the nature of a subordination agreement. Lender, on the other hand, claims seller got what it bargained for—a second trust deed—and thus had no prior lien to subordinate. Lender would thus conclude no priority existed which could be restored, the seller could not state any cause of action, and the trial court correctly sustained the demurrers.

As we state below, we conclude that the duties owed by a lender to a seller under a formal subordination agreement do not differ from the duties owed by a lender to a seller when the lender obtains priority over the seller under an agreement by the seller to record after the lender. We thus conclude that, in part, the complaint is sufficient to withstand defendants' general demurrers.

Subordination is, strictly speaking, a status, not an agreement or form of litigation. It refers to the establishment of priority between different existing encumbrances on the same parcel of property, by some means other than the basic priority involved in the concept of "first in time, first in priority", or the automatic priority accorded purchase money liens.

By statute, a purchase money deed of trust is prior to other liens on real property. (Civil Code, § 2898.) But banks and savings and loan institutions may not lend money on the security of real property unless they hold first liens. (Fin.Code, §§ 1413 subd. (d), 7102 subd. (a), 1560.) The two common methods of arranging for the commercial lender to hold the first lien include: (1) an express subordination agreement in which the seller agrees to make his lien junior to the lender's; (2) recording the lender's trust deed before the seller's.

Both methods of giving a lender a prior lien, whether by express subordination agreement or by priority of recording, are used to obtain a quicker sale and a higher price for the land. A reading of the commentators suggests lending institutions may prefer the latter method over written subordination agreements because of the reluctance of courts to enforce express written agreements which are deemed to be unfair to the seller. This latter type of subordination situation has been referred to as "automatic subordination".

In the cases that have appeared in the California courts the automatic type of subordination has been said to be the legal problem-child. The negotiated agreement for subordination has seemingly not caused difficulty and is generally absent from the decided reports.

In the case before us, the record discloses an automatic subordination agreement in which the seller, after negotiating a sale, agreed to a subordination by recording after the lender. Differing positions have been taken by the California Appellate Courts with respect to these automatic subordination agreements made at the time of sale. Several cases have refused to recognize automatic subordination; others have accepted and enforced it. Remaining cases have applied other tests to determine whether the courts would place their stamp of approval upon the particular arrangement of the parties.

On the basis of the allegations in the complaint, the project in the case at bench would appear to be a typical automatic subordination arrangement as found in Miller v. Citizens Sav. & Loan Assn., 248 Cal.App.2d 655, 56 Cal.Rptr. 844. As we interpret the pleadings, the subordination agreement shows the parties intended to enter into an arrangement of subordination whereby the seller relied upon the responsibility of the lender to make voucher payments only for construction purposes and the reliance of the seller was known to the lender.

The basic thrust of plaintiffs' complaint is that the automatic subordination should be voided because of the misapplication of a portion of the construction loan fund, in that the lender failed to comply with the conditions which occasioned plaintiffs' agreement to subordinate. This theory is supported by a number of cases and is endorsed by certain of the text writers mentioned herein.

Respondents assert their non-liability on four grounds: (1) the lender had no duty to supervise the distribution of loan funds (Gill v. Mission Sav. & Loan Assn., 236 Cal.App.2d 753, 46 Cal.Rptr. 456); (2) there was no privity of contract between lender and seller (Matthews v. Hinton, 234 Cal.App.2d 736, 44 Cal.Rptr. 692); (3) since no "subordination agreement" was alleged, seller could have suffered no loss of priority; and (4) no public policy basis exists for imposing a duty on the lender (Gill v. Mission Sav. & Loan Assn., supra). Respondent cites two other cases in support of the asserted grounds: Weiss v. Brentwood Sav. & Loan, supra, 4 Cal.App.3d 738, 84 Cal.Rptr. 736, and Spaziani v. Millar, supra, 215 Cal.App.2d 667, 30 Cal.Rptr. 658.

In light of the facts set forth in the complaint, however, we find insufficient merit in these arguments to prevent a trial of the matter on the merits. We find compelling reasons to the contrary.

Gill involved an appeal from a judgment of dismissal upon an order sustaining a demurrer with leave to amend, no amendment having been filed. The issue was whether the lender owed a duty to the sellers to manage and supervise the distribution of loan funds so that these funds would be used solely for construction purposes. The court concluded that because of the lack of privity of contract and the fact that plaintiffs did not allege that defendant had voluntarily undertaken to supervise the distribution of the loan funds, the complaint for damages was properly demurrable.

In *Gill* the complaint was that the lender had acted negligently in failing to supervise and manage the loan funds. As stated by the court in *Gill,* "Nowhere in the first amended complaint does it appear that the defendant agreed with anyone to manage or supervise distribution of the loaned funds, assumed to do so, actually undertook such, or was required by statutory law or regulation to so manage and supervise. Nor is there any showing of a voluntarily assumed relationship between defendant and plaintiffs from which such an obligation might arise." (236 Cal.App.2d at 756–757, 46 Cal.Rptr. at 458.)

Such allegations do appear in the pleading in the case at bench. Moreover, the damage claim in the complaint in *Gill* rests on a different legal theory than the claim of loss of priority here involved. The former is grounded on traditional negligence concepts while the latter is based on principles of contract law. Underlying the latter theory, the lender's claim to priority flows from the agreement between the seller and the buyer. It is only as a result of the seller's waiver of his statutory right to a first lien that the lender achieves priority. Thus, the lender is a third party beneficiary in the seller-buyer agreement, but only to the extent that it abides by the conditions of subordination. If the lender does not comply with the seller's conditions it does not achieve priority. Since one condition to priority is the proper use of the construction loan funds, the priority of the construction loan lien does not vest until such time as the funds are applied to the construction purpose. This latter theory was not before the *Gill* court.

Lender contends since the case before us does not involve a "subordination agreement" there was no loss of priority and therefore as a matter of law plaintiffs may not have their lien declared to be prior to the construction loan lien. In support of this argument defendants rely on a treatise, Current Law of California Real Estate, Vol. 2, by Messrs. Miller and Starr. The same authors have restated their position in 13 U.C.L.A.L.Rev. 1298, 1301 to the effect that if the seller agrees in the deposit receipt agreement or the escrow instructions that the buyer may obtain a construction loan which will be recorded as a first trust deed and the seller's purchase money trust deed is made junior by virtue of the time of its recording, then a "true" subordination does not result. The problem, it is said, ". . . does not involve alteration of lien priority; that is, it does not involve the subordination of an earlier lien to a later lien, because by the execution of the purchase transaction the priorities are determined by the initial creation and recordation of the liens. Since the seller at no time has a 'prior' lien, he is not 'subordinating' his lien but merely agreeing to accept junior security. The problem, therefore, is primarily one of contract law between the buyer and the seller and not one of lien law between the seller and the lender." (p. 1301.)

In our view there is no justification, legal or otherwise, which would call for a different result whether the seller in a joint transaction records first and then agrees that his lien will be subordinated or whether he agrees that the lender may achieve priority through first recording. In C.E.B. California Real Estate Secured Transactions, supra, § 5.16 at 217 the author expressly disagrees with the Miller and Starr position stating:

> "This author disagrees with Miller and Starr due to the prevailing policy of title companies of recording the subordinating lien before the subordinated deed of trust. [citation]. In Conley v. Fate (1964) 227 Cal.App.2d 418, 38 CR [Cal.Rptr.] 680, a seller agreed to accept a second deed of trust for a portion of the purchase price, and the court properly referred to this as being subordinate to the construction loan, and further referred to the pertinent portion of the deposit receipt as a subordination clause. In the event the vendor is required to finance partially the purchase of his property, through either a second deed of trust or a subordinated first deed of trust, there should be no difference in his status based on the time of recording of the two encumbrances. On some occasions the purchase-money deed of trust held by the vendor will be reconveyed and rerecorded immediately after

recordation of the subordinating encumbrance. [citation]. Therefore, if the institutional lender is to finance a portion of the purchase price, the institutional lender should incur the same liabilities for misapplication of funds, whether the vendor holds a second deed of trust by virtue of reconveyance and rerecordation or a first subordinated by agreement without a change in the order of recording."

Finally, in our opinion strong public policy reasons to protect the seller in subordination situations are set out in Handy v. Gordon, supra, 65 Cal.2d 578, 55 Cal.Rptr. 769, 422 P.2d 329:

"Although the parties to a contract of sale containing a subordination clause may delegate to the vendee or third party lenders power to determine the details of subordinating loans, an enforceable subordination clause must contain terms that will define and minimize the risk that the subordinating liens will impair or destroy the seller's security. Such terms may include limits on the use to which the proceeds may be put to insure that their use will improve the value of the land, maximum amounts so that the loans will not exceed the contemplated value of the improvements they finance, requirements that the loans do not exceed some specified percentage of the construction cost or value of the property as improved, specified amounts per square foot of construction, or other limits designed to protect the security. Without some such terms, however, the seller is forced to rely entirely on the buyer's good faith and ability as a developer to insure that he will not lose both his land and the purchase price.

"The contract alleged in the complaint does not afford defendants any additional protection. Although the proceeds of the subordinating loans are to be used primarily for construction and refinancing, any funds that are not needed for these purposes may be disbursed to plaintiff. The absence of restrictions on plaintiff's use of these funds leaves defendants without assurance that all of the proceeds of the loans will be used to improve the land that represents their security. Because the limits on the loans are expressed as absolutes, they provide no assurance that the amounts of the loans will not exceed the value the improvements add to the security. Moreover, the limits are maximums per lot, and plaintiff has unrestricted discretion in determining the size of each lot. Thus defendants are not assured that the total amount of the subordinating loans will be kept low enough to enable them to protect themselves by bidding on the property if the senior liens are foreclosed. Finally defendants did not receive a down payment that would effectively cushion their position, and the first payment of principal is deferred until three years after the close of escrow.

"Thus, the contract leaves defendants with nothing but plaintiff's good faith and business judgment to insure them that they will ever receive anything for conveying their land. Such a contract is not as to them 'just and reasonable' within the meaning of Civil Code, section 3391."

It has been pointed out by many courts and commentators that as between the seller and the lender, the lender is by far in the better position to control the use of the loan proceeds and thereby prevent misappropriations by the developer. The lender can require documented evidence that expenses have been incurred and can corroborate this by on-site inspections. It is common for lenders to control disbursements, since they, too, have an interest in preventing misuse of loan proceeds. If the lender loses priority as a result of improper disbursements, it remains in a position to redeem the seller's purchase money lien and foreclose on the junior construction lien and thereby own the property for a price presumably less than the market value. Also, loan proceeds would be at least partially recouped by the improvements made. The seller, on the other hand, is normally not in a position to protect himself by redemption of the larger construction lien in the event the lender were to obtain priority. After redemption, the lender can obtain a deficiency judgment against the defaulting developer whereas the seller, holding a purchase money security interest, would be barred by Code of Civil Procedure, § 580b, if he tried to recover a deficiency judgment against the developer. The lender is in a far better position to absorb any loss since such contingencies may be provided for in its profit and loss estimates. Finally, allocation of the loss to the lender would encourage the parties to provide for the various contingencies by contract.

An implied agreement in the instant case can and, in equity, should be spelled out from lender's alleged actual knowledge of the provisions of the seller's lien in general, and of the subordination therein in particular. In the superior position of a financial institution constantly engaged in professional construction lending, Southwestern had no reason to believe their trust deed conferred any lien to which the fee was subordinate other than to the extent of money spent for construction purposes. Its loan under the circumstances cannot be viewed other than as subject to the fair application of the construction funds. Accordingly, we conclude that such lien as the trust deed might have conferred on the lender should not be advanced or preferred over the seller.

Here, it is alleged the lender, with full knowledge of the subordinated lien of the seller, disbursed the funds without limitation. Its disinterest in the application of the funds not used for construction amounted to a failure to prevent the loss sustained by seller—who, in the vernacular of the market place, was "wiped out". The particular equities discussed above incline us to the conviction that the philosophy of fair dealing as expressed in Handy v. Gordon, supra, 65 Cal.2d 578, 55 Cal.Rptr. 769, 422 P.2d 329, is most appropriately invoked here.

We hold the actions of the parties here, if proved as alleged, did create a subordination agreement, and the lender's failure to protect seller's security interest gives seller a cause of action; the validity of the first, second, and third causes of action are supported by the cases.

The fourth cause of action is based on the theory seller was a third party beneficiary of the construction loan agreement between lender and the buyers. Lender, to support its demurrer, asked the court to take judicial notice of the construction loan agreement filed with certain answers to interrogatories. A provision of this agreement expressly states it is to be for the benefit of lender and buyers only. The court may take judicial notice of documents in its file when considering a demurrer. But the meaning of this agreement given the wide latitude of parol evidence admissible in interpreting a contract, is not the type of matter made judicially noticeable by Evidence Code, § 452. To go beyond notice of the existence of a document to an interpretation of its meaning constitutes improper consideration of evidentiary matters. We thus do not consider this agreement and hold the fourth cause of action to be regular on its face.

The fifth and sixth causes of action turn on lender's refusal to accept seller's tender of due principal, interest, and late charges to cure buyers' default. If the refusal was wrongful, the trustee's foreclosure sale was invalid and seller is entitled to the relief it seeks in these causes of action. The lender rejected seller's tender because it did not include the amount in excess of $50,000 which had been spent to repair and complete the apartments; plaintiffs allege defendants had no right to demand this sum because it was not stated in the notice of default. The notice need not, however, state the amounts which are in default; it need only describe the nature of the breach. Rejection of the tender thus was not wrongful and the trustee's sale was valid; sustaining the general demurrer without leave to amend was proper on the fifth and sixth causes of action.

All of seller's causes of action, as discussed herein, posit the existence of a subordination agreement and seek recovery for its breach. This amounts to an action on a contract: the punitive damages sought in the tenth cause of action are not recoverable in an action on a contract.

Thus since a subordination agreement is sufficiently alleged in the pleadings and supported in law, the first, second, third and fourth causes of action are valid and the judgment of dismissal should be reversed as to them. We hold the demurrer was properly sustained as to the fifth, sixth, and tenth causes of action. (Only the fifth, sixth, and tenth causes of action purport to state a claim against defendant Western Escrow.) The judgment of dismissal is reversed with directions to the trial court to overrule the general demurrer as to the first, second, third and fourth causes of action, and allow respondent a reasonable time within which to answer the third amended complaint.

Without ruling on the worth, if any, of the causes of action, set forth in the third amended complaint, seller should be afforded an opportunity to present the case on the merits. We do not decide, however, the valid portions of the complaint may not be subject to special demurrer, and the trial court may in its discretion require further clarification of any uncertainties or ambiguities.

The judgment is reversed in part and affirmed in part as set forth herein.

KERRIGAN, ACTING P.J., and KAUFMAN, J., concur.

NOTES

1. *Subordination Agreements*. A seller will often agree to subordinate his purchase money lien to the lien of the construction lender in the expectation that the improvements financed by the construction loan will

increase the value of the land at least dollar for dollar, leaving his security intact. It was to honor this expectation that the *Middlebrook* court reached the decision it did. Yet, sellers usually have another reason to take a second position. Subordination may be the only, or at least the most rewarding, way that they can sell their property for development since institutional lenders will rarely finance on the basis of other than a first lien security.

Would the *Middlebrook* rule be applied if the construction lender did not know that the purchase money mortgage was subject to the condition that the funds be used for construction purposes only? In In re Sunset Bay Associates, 944 F.2d 1503 (9th Cir.1991), the court held that the subordination was contingent on the condition, whether or not the construction lender had actual knowledge of the condition. Does this place an unfair burden on the construction lender to discover conditions? What would a reasonable inquiry entail? Would it be more efficient if the purchase money mortgagee had the duty to give notice of the condition? How could a purchase money mortgagee give such notice? Should it matter whether subordination was achieved through a recorded subordination agreement or by order of recording as in *Middlebrook*?

The approach taken in *Middlebrook* is by no means universal. Other states have been more generous to construction lenders, holding that, if construction loan funds are diverted to non-construction purposes, the subordinating seller can regain his first lien position only by showing collusion between the developer and the construction lender or an express agreement by the construction lender to oversee the disbursement of loan funds. See, e.g., Connecticut Bank and Trust Co. v. Carriage Lane Associates, 219 Conn. 772, 595 A.2d 334 (1991); Kennedy v. Betts, 33 Md.App. 258, 364 A.2d 74 (Spec.App.1976). Moreover, *Middlebrook* has been distinguished by other California courts. See, e.g., Swiss Property Management Co. v. Southern California IBEW—NECA Pension Plan, 60 Cal.App.4th 839, 70 Cal.Rptr.2d 587 (1997) (no implied agreement since subordination agreement had express provision that lender had no duty to monitor disbursements).

On the general issues raised in *Middlebrook,* see Korngold, Construction Loan Advances and the Subordinated Purchase Money Mortgagee: An Appraisal, A Suggested Approach, and the ULTA Perspective, 50 Fordham L.Rev. 313 (1981); Lambe, Enforceability of Subordination Agreements, 19 Real Prop., Probate & Trust J. 631 (1984); McNamara, Subordination Agreements as Viewed by Sellers, Purchasers, Construction Lenders, and Title Companies, 12 Real Est.L.J. 347 (1984); Stein, Subordinate Mortgage Financing: The Perils of the Senior Lender, 27 Real Est. Rev. 3 (No. 3, Fall 1997); Note, Purchase Money Subordination Agreements in California: An Analysis of Conditional Subordination, 45 So.Cal.L.Rev. 1109 (1972).

Consider the use of the obligatory/optional advance rule as a means to assist the subordinated purchase money mortgagee. See pages 636–646 above.

2. *Remedies.* Should the remedy for a construction lender's failure to police the borrower's use of loan proceeds be complete subordination of the construction loan or subordination only to the extent that funds are misapplied? Say, for example, the seller subordinates a $95,000 purchase money deed of trust to the lien of a $349,500 construction loan, $323,158.70

of which was later properly disbursed and $26,341.30 of which was improperly disbursed. Miller v. Citizens Sav. & Loan Ass'n, 248 Cal.App.2d 655, 56 Cal.Rptr. 844 (1967) set the priorities as follows: a first lien to the construction lender for $323,159; a second lien to the seller for $95,000; and a third lien to the construction lender for $26,341.

What if the construction loan offends the subordinated purchase money loan not in its administration, but in its terms—for example, the interest rate exceeds the rate permitted by the subordination agreement, or the take-out commitment required by the seller as a condition to subordination was never obtained. What policies are served and disserved by a remedy that would totally reorder the priorities, placing the seller first? See Ruth v. Lytton Sav. & Loan Ass'n of Northern Cal., 266 Cal.App.2d 831, 72 Cal.Rptr. 521 (1968), modified 272 Cal.App.2d 24, 76 Cal.Rptr. 926 (1969); Jones v. Sacramento Sav. & Loan Ass'n, 248 Cal.App.2d 522, 56 Cal.Rptr. 741 (1967).

d.   OTHER CONSTRUCTION LIENORS

i.   Mechanics' and Materialmen's Liens

Williams & Works, Inc. v. Springfield Corp.

Supreme Court of Michigan, 1980.
408 Mich. 732, 293 N.W.2d 304.

WILLIAMS, JUSTICE [For Reversal].

This case concerns the sole question whether off-site engineering services rendered before the beginning of actual, on-site construction qualify, pursuant to § 9(3) of the Michigan Mechanics' Lien Law, as "the commencement of said building or buildings, erection, structure or improvement"[1] so as to give priority to mechanics' liens over a mortgage recorded after the provision of such services but prior to the beginning of any visible, on-site construction.[2]

---

[1]   The paragraph of Michigan's Mechanics' Lien Law which governs the specific priority question in this case is M.C.L. § 570.9 (third); M.S.A. § 26.289 (third) (§ 9[3] or the "priority section"). In pertinent part this section provides:

"The several liens herein provided for shall continue for 1 year after such statement or account is recorded in the office of the register of deeds, and no longer unless proceedings are begun to enforce the same as hereinafter provided, and such liens shall take priority as follows:

"Third, They shall be preferred to all other titles, liens or incumbrances which may attach to or upon such building, machinery, structure or improvement, or to or upon the land upon which they are situated, which shall either be given or recorded subsequent to the *commencement of said building or buildings, erection, structure or improvement*." (Emphasis supplied.)

[2]   Appellees also contend, cursorily, that the twelve six-inch borings that were filled and staked by the engineering firm of Williams & Works prior to the recordation of the mortgage constituted a "continuing visible notice that improvements were in progress." However, this contention was essentially refuted by cross-examination of Ed Culver, a Williams & Works employee who was present while the borings were taken. Culver testified that there was no other work being performed on the site at the time, the site being essentially a vacant lot covered with weeds. Further, Culver stated that although the soil borings were marked with a stake or flag after they were taken and filled in, the stakes and flags would tend to disappear because children would take them [Tr. 160–161]. Thus, it is not certain whether these stakes were visible to a reasonable observer inspecting the premises. Further, assuming that the

Long established Michigan precedent in line with that in most American jurisdictions requires a visible, on-site "commencement" for the purpose of fixing priorities under § 9(3) of the Mechanics' Lien Law. Plaintiffs in this case, however, claim the Legislature intended to change by indirection this traditional rule based on § 9(3) "commencement of said building or buildings, erection, structure or improvement" by amending the list of lienable items in § 1[5] of the Mechanics' Lien Law to include engineering and surveying services and by adding to the definition of "improvement"[6] found in § 1 the language, "designs or engineering plans for the improvement of any lot."

In view of the overwhelming weight of historical precedent, whose rationale and policy underpinnings remain vital today, we find that such non-visible, off-site engineering services as those rendered in the instant case, although lienable under Michigan law, do not signal the "commencement" of a building, erection, structure, or improvement for

---

stakes were visible and remained upon the site, such minimal staking of the property is not activity which constitutes "commencement" of a building or improvement within M.C.L. § 570.9 (third); M.S.A. § 26.289 (third).

[5] M.C.L. § 570.1; M.S.A. § 26.281 (§ 1) is an old (1891 P.A. 179) much amended section describing what is lienable. In pertinent part it provides:

> "*Every person who shall,* in pursuance of any contract, express or implied, written or unwritten, existing between himself as contractor, and the owner, part owner or lessee of any interest in real estate, build, alter, improve, repair, erect, ornament or put in, survey or plat any lot or parcel of land, or portion thereof, or engineer or design any sewers, waterlines, roads, streets, highways, sidewalks, or *prepare and furnish* pursuant to such contract to such owner, part owner or lessee of any interest in real estate *any survey, plat, plat of survey or design or engineering plan, or plans,* for the *improvement of any lot or parcel of land* not exceeding one-quarter section of land, or who shall furnish any labor or materials in or for building, altering, improving, repairing, erecting, ornamenting or putting in any house, swimming pool, building, machinery, wharf or structure, or who shall excavate, or build in whole, or in part, any foundation, cellar or basement for any such house, swimming pool, building, structure or wharf, or shall build or repair any sidewalks, sewers, sewage disposal equipment, water lines and pumping equipment or wells or shall furnish any materials therefor, or shall furnish any nursery stock, or labor in connection therewith for any property, or shall rent or lease equipment in connection therewith for any property, and every person who shall be subcontractor, laborer, or material man, perform any labor or furnish materials or shall rent or lease equipment to such original or principal contractor, or any subcontractor, in carrying forward or completing any such contract, *shall have a lien therefor * * *.*" (Emphasis supplied.)

The section goes on to describe the scope of the lien and the procedural requirements for its enforcement.

[6] M.C.L. § 570.1; M.S.A. § 26.281 defines "improvement" as follows:

> "*The term 'improvement'* or the plural thereof as used in this act, *shall include* the improvement, beautification or embellishment of property by the furnishing of nursery stock or the performance of labor in connection therewith or the planting thereof, or the furnishing by any registered land surveyor of any survey, plat, plat of survey of any lot or parcel of land, or the furnishing by any registered professional engineer of any engineering design or plans for the installation of any swimming pools, sewers, water lines, roads, streets, highways, sidewalks, or prepare and furnish pursuant to such contract to such owner, part owner or lessee of any interest in real estate and *other designs or engineering plans for the improvement of any lot* or parcel of land not exceeding one-quarter section of land, or the renting or leasing of any contractor's equipment for excavating, ditching, earth removal, landscaping, leveling, grading or changing the contour of any land, or the repairing, maintaining, restoring, constructing or demolition of any structure or the laying of any drains, sewers or pipelines." (Emphasis supplied.)

the purpose of fixing priority under Michigan's Mechanics' Lien Law. Accordingly, since the appellant mortgagee recorded its mortgage prior to any visible, on-site construction which could be said to "commence" the building, erection, structure or improvement, the trial court and Court of Appeals improperly accorded priority to the appellee mechanic lienors. We therefore reverse.

I.   FACTS

Springfield Corporation ("Springfield") desired to erect a multifamily apartment building complex on certain land located in Genesee County, Michigan, and owned by LAW Development Company and appellant Kelly Mortgage and Investment Company ("Kelly"). In pursuance of this desire, Springfield contacted Williams & Works ("W & W") about May 16, 1972 in regard to using its engineering services for the contemplated development. Thereafter, on June 8, 1972, Robert Foote, President of Springfield, met two representatives of W & W at the contemplated development site for discussions and a preliminary view of the premises. Then, near the end of June, 1972, W & W and Springfield entered into a formal written contract, under which W & W was to perform certain engineering services for the contemplated development. The contract was divided into three parts or phases with Springfield reserving the right to terminate the contract at the end of any phase. Phase I called for W & W to undertake and complete initial feasibility studies which included soil borings, drainage studies, topographical and boundary surveys, preliminary utility plans, cost estimates and plan approvals. Phase II called for W & W to finalize all plans for site development, including final drafting of the construction plans. Phase III involved the actual construction of the project and required W & W to supervise and direct parts of the construction work.

By September, 1972, Phase I was substantially completed. The only on-site work done by W & W during Phase I consisted of certain soil borings, which were taken on August 29, 1972, when two workers drilled twelve holes into the ground, each approximately 6O in diameter.

After the completion of Phase I, W & W began Phase II and throughout the latter part of 1972, it submitted various construction specifications to Springfield. It was also established that during this period Kelly knew of W & W's work since Kelly had actually written W & W requesting that all correspondence dealing with W & W's work to date be forwarded to Kelly since it would be handling the project for Mr. Foote. In late December, 1972, after substantial completion of the Phase II drawings, Springfield decided to go forward with the construction of the apartment building project. Thereafter, on January 4, 1973, Springfield purchased the land from LAW Development and Kelly and executed a mortgage on the property to City National Bank ("CNB") which was recorded in Genesee County and which was subsequently assigned from City National Bank to Kelly. On January 9, 1973, Springfield executed a second mortgage to Kelly, which was also recorded in Genesee County. Almost one year later, Springfield conveyed its fee interest in the premises to Bristol Square Properties Group, a limited copartnership in which Mr. Foote and Springfield are the sole general partners, by deed dated December 27, 1973.

It is undisputed that building operations on the premises did not begin until February, 1973, almost one full month after the mortgages were recorded by CNB and Kelly. The initial Phase III work, consisting of staking, began on February 10, 1973 and building operations commenced sometime thereafter. The project went into default in 1974 and this mechanics' lien foreclosure action followed.

This suit was commenced on March 25, 1974, in the Genesee Circuit Court. The Complaint alleges that the plaintiff, W & W, had a mechanics' lien upon the project property and prayed for its foreclosure. Numerous other parties were joined as defendants or intervened, and several cross-claims were filed by various other contractors, alleging mechanics' liens against the property. Kelly, the mortgagee in the instant proceeding, as well as other defendants aligned in interest, answered the various mechanics' lien claims, denying the validity of the claims and asserting that the mortgage interest in the property was superior and paramount to the interest of the various mechanics' liens.

After pretrial and trial proceedings concluded, the trial court entered judgments of foreclosure against the owner of the apartment project, Bristol Square Properties Group, in favor of W & W and the instant appellee mechanics lienors (Shank, Coupland and Long, Co., PPG Industries, Inc., and Garno Brothers Heating and Cooling, Inc., all subcontractors who began supplying labor and materials while the project was owned by Springfield, and completed their work after Springfield conveyed to Bristol Square Properties Group). The trial court also ruled that all mechanics' liens were prior to the mortgage interest of Kelly in the property because it found W & W's services to have been "improvements", as that term is defined in § 1, M.C.L. § 570.1; M.S.A. § 26.281, which were "commenced" before the mortgage was recorded.

The Court of Appeals affirmed the trial court's conclusion that, in the instant case, "commencement", for purposes of priority, meant when engineering services were first performed, and not when actual construction on the site was begun.

We granted leave to appeal on March 5, 1979 limited to the issue of priority between the mortgage and the mechanics' liens under § 9(3), M.C.L. § 570.9 (third); M.S.A. § 26.289 (third).

II. DISCUSSION

A. *Michigan's Mechanics' Lien Law Pre-1958*

The term "commencement of a building" had a well-established meaning in most states when Michigan incorporated that term into its own mechanics' lien law. As illustrative of this meaning, and in order not to belabor the point, we quote from one such case, while citing the reader to others which preceded or were contemporaneous with Michigan's statute:

> "The commencement of a building is the doing of some act upon the ground upon which the building is to be erected, and in pursuance of a design to erect, the result of which act should make known to a person viewing the premises, *from observation alone,* that the erection of a building upon that lot or tract of land has been commenced." James v. Van Horn, 39 N.J.L. 353, 363 (1877). (Emphasis supplied.)

Accord, Brooks v. Lester, 36 Md. 65 (1872); Kansas Mortgage Co. v. Weyerhaeuser, 48 Kan. 335, 29 P. 153 (1892); Fitzgerald v. Walsh, 107 Wis. 92, 82 N.W. 717 (1900); Conrad & Ewinger v. Starr, 50 Iowa 470 (1879).

Likewise, early Michigan case law espoused this same idea of keying the concept of "commencement" in its priority section to some actual, visible work on the land such that it was apparent to all that a building was being erected or improvements were being made. In Kay v. Towsley, 113 Mich. 281, 283, 71 N.W. 490, 491 (1897), this Court, in ruling that two materialmen's liens were prior to that of a mortgagee who had recorded his mortgage prior to the furnishing of the materials but subsequent to the erection of the foundation wall, stated:

> "This provision [the priority provision in the Mechanics' Lien Law] has been passed upon frequently by the courts, and it has been uniformly held that the lien has priority over a mortgage executed upon the land or premises *after the actual commencement* of the building, though no part of the labor performed or materials furnished for which the lien is claimed was done or performed until after the execution and recording of the mortgage." (Emphasis supplied.)

One early commentator summarized the meaning of "commencement of said building" in Michigan thus:

> "In determining priorities, liens attach as of the date of the actual commencement of the building or improvement, regardless of the time when, or person by whom, particular work is done or materials furnished, for which lien is claimed. *The building is begun when the first permanent work is done on the land.*" (Emphasis supplied; citations omitted.) Wykes, The Michigan Laws of Mechanics' Liens (2d ed.), pp. 167–168, fn. 2.

"Commencement", then, as defined by early case law and commentary, required an act of such a character that it was notice to all of the existence of mechanics' liens. As Professor Thompson wrote:

> "The 'commencement of a building', within the meaning of these statutes, is the first labor done on the ground which is made the foundation of the building, and forms part of the work suitable and necessary for its construction. It is some work or labor on the ground, such as beginning to dig the foundation, which everyone can see and recognize as the commencement of a building; and the work, moreover, must be done with the intention thus formed of continuing it to completion." 8A Thompson, Commentaries on the Modern Law of Real Property (1963 Supp.), § 4427, p. 228.

In such fashion, "commencement" of a building gave constructive notice to prospective lenders or purchasers of the possible existence of liens. This visible notice was especially important since under Michigan's Mechanics' Lien Act, as well as those of other states, "commencement" fixed the date to which all mechanics' liens related back, even if other contractors started their work weeks or months later. M.C.L. § 570.9

(first); M.S.A. § 26.289 (first).[7] It was in keeping with this interpretation that this Court early held, in response to a mechanic lienor's contention, analogous to that made in the present case, that the "commencement" of a building occurred when the architect began drawing the plans and specifications for the building, that

> "[i]t is, we think, clear, that the drawing of plans for a building is not 'the commencement of said building or buildings.'" Stevens v. Garland, 198 Mich. 24, 32, 164 N.W. 516, 518 (1917).

B. Michigan's Mechanics' Lien Law Post-1958

In 1958 the Michigan Legislature amended § 1 of the Mechanics' Lien Law, which describes lienable services, to include engineering and surveying services. Amended § 1, further, included engineering and surveying services under the definition of the word "improvement":

> "The term 'improvement' or the plural thereof as used in this act, shall include the * * * prepar[ing] and furnish[ing] * * * designs or engineering plans for the improvement of any lot or parcel of land * * *."

The gist of appellees' argument on appeal to us is that this definition of "improvement" found in § 1 of the Mechanics' Lien Law describing liens is freely substitutable for the word "improvement" as it appears in the priority section of the lien law. The word "improvement" appears in § 9(3) in the following context:

> "Third, They [mechanics' liens] shall be preferred to all other titles, liens or incumbrances which may attach to or upon such building, machinery, structure or improvement, or to or upon the land upon which they are situated, which shall either be given or recorded subsequent to the commencement of said building or buildings, erection, structure or *improvement*." (Emphasis supplied.)

By this process of substitution, the appellees present us with a priority section which they claim, in this case, should read, in edited fashion, as follows:

> "Third, they [W & W as professional engineers] shall be preferred to all liens recorded subsequent to *the commencement of its furnishing engineering design or plans for the improvement of said lot*." (Emphasis in appellees' brief.) [Appellees' Brief, p. 6]

To safeguard their position, appellees assert that the cases requiring visible, on-site construction in order to constitute "commencement" are obsolete since they construed the Act at a time when engineering services were not lienable and that cases from other jurisdictions are of little significance since they construe statutes different from that of Michigan.

---

[7]   M.C.L. § 570.9 (first); M.S.A. § 26.289 (first) provides:

"As between persons claiming liens under this statute, the several liens upon the same property attaching by reason of work, labor or materials furnished in carrying forward or completing the same building or buildings, machinery, structure or improvement, shall be deemed simultaneous mortgages."

The issue for resolution, then, is whether the Legislature, by amending M.C.L. § 570.1; M.S.A. § 26.281 to expand the definition of lienable items to include engineering services, intended to effect a departure from the requirement of visible, on-site construction which courts have traditionally required for a building or improvement to be "commenced" for purposes of the priority section. In other words, should the performance of non-visible, off-site engineering services before the recording of a mortgage, as was done in the present case, be sufficient to give all mechanics' lienors priority over the mortgagee?

We find the appellee mechanic lienors' substitution of the definition of "improvement" found in § 1 for the word "improvement" found in the priority section, although of some superficial persuasiveness, to be fundamentally unsound for several reasons. . . .

Third, we think it unreasonable to believe the Legislature intended to indirectly change § 9(3), containing the traditional and well-established rule requiring a visible, on-site commencement of construction in order to establish priority, by the simple expansion of the lienable services outlined in a different section, § 1. Section 1 and § 9(3) treat of two entirely different concepts. Section 1 merely determines *what* is a lienable service in Michigan. It runs the gamut from the furnisher of labor and materials and the surveyor and engineer to the renter or lessor of equipment and the supplier of nursery stock. Section 9(3), on the other hand, deals with the determination of *when* a particular lien attaches for priority purposes. It specifically leaves the establishment of what services are lienable to another part of the act, i.e., § 1, and concerns itself primarily with the ascertainment of the priorities among the liens:

> "The several liens *herein provided for* * * * shall take priority as follows: [hereafter follow four rules for determining priorities]." (Emphasis supplied.)

Fourth, the 1958 amendment to § 1 of the mechanics' lien law was only one of successive amendments to that section expanding *what* constitutes a lienable service in Michigan. For example, the protection of this section was extended to nursery stock in 1941, to surveying and engineering services and works in 1958, to sewers, sewage disposal equipment, water lines and pumping equipment in 1960, to rented or leased equipment in 1963, and to swimming pools in 1965. See fn. 5, supra.

Fifth, in contradistinction to this constant expansion of lienable services under § 1, § 9(3), fixing priorities, has been conspicuously quiescent. Not one of the many amendments to § 1 has been accompanied by an amendment significantly affecting the priority section of the mechanics' lien law. . . .

For the above reasons, we believe that the Legislature neither intended the § 1 definition of "improvement" to be freely substitutable for the word "improvement" found in § 9, nor intended to indirectly change the established interpretation of § 9(3) through an amendment of § 1. Thus, we find that while the Legislature has continually broadened the range of lienable services in Michigan, it has not chosen to effect any change in the long-established judicial interpretation of "commencement of said building or buildings, erection, structure or improvement" as that phrase has been used in the past to determine priority between a mechanics' lienor and a mortgagee. . . .

We also believe that our decision, in continuing to key "commencement" into the concept of constructive notice, is based on sound public policy. Were we to adopt appellees' position and rule that the "commencement" of a building, erection, structure or improvement could be triggered by the rendering of off-site, non-visible engineering plans, mechanics' liens could relate back to a long time before any visible signs of construction existed to inform prospective lenders inspecting the premises that liens had attached. Under such circumstances, construction financing would become exceedingly difficult. It was just such a concern that compelled the California Supreme Court in *Walker,* [Walker v. Lytton Savings & Loan Ass'n of Northern California, 2 Cal.3d 152, 84 Cal.Rptr. 521, 465 P.2d 497 (1970)]to reach the same result we do today.

> "But if, despite these specific and detailed rules laid down by the Legislature, it be held for the benefit of plaintiff architects that even though, as here, an encumbrance has attached before any work has been done on the owners' property or materials delivered thereto for a planned improvement, nevertheless the work of improvement had commenced earlier when the architects began work on the plans and specifications, then the liens of all others who contributed work or materials to the work of improvement * * * would likewise relate back to the earlier date of commencement and thereby take priority over the subsequent encumbrance—whether given for a construction loan or based on some other consideration. That the Legislature intended no such result seems obvious. Additionally, under such circumstances it would appear that construction loans would shortly become next to impossible to obtain, as it is a rare construction project of any magnitude which does not require the preliminary nonvisible services of architects or engineers. But if all liens arising from the subsequent construction will relate back to the date of commencement of the nonvisible services, how many prudent businessmen would be willing to assume the risk?" *Walker,* supra, 2 Cal.3d 159–160, 84 Cal.Rptr. 526–27, 465 P.2d 502–03.

In contrast to this significant judicial authority, we have found only one jurisdiction that takes a contrary approach. See Bankers Trust Co. v. El Paso Pre-Cast Co., 192 Colo. 468, 560 P.2d 457 (1977). Appellees have cited to us no other relevant case law.

Finally, one last contention of appellees' needs to be addressed. Appellees argue that because appellant Kelly had actual notice (of which there is record support) of the identity of and services being furnished by W & W before it sold the land to Springfield and filed mortgage liens, it should not be heard to urge the adoption of a visible and actual commencement standard in this particular case. It is unclear whether this argument rests on notions of waiver or estoppel. However, whatever the theory, actual notice is not the relevant issue in determining the priorities question in this case. The issue is the determination of when "commencement" of the building or improvement occurred. In *Walker,* supra, it was found that the holder of the deed of trust had actual knowledge that plaintiff architects had provided services. In fact Lytton, the holder of the deed of trust, had relied on plaintiffs' work in making its appraisal for loan purposes. The Court, after noting that the condition precedent to the architects' priority was the commencement of construction, stated that such knowledge alone cannot constitute waiver or estoppel. In support of this conclusion, the Court opined, quoting from Tracy Price Associates v. Hebard, 266 Cal.App.2d 778, 787–788, 72 Cal.Rptr. 600 (1968), that

> " 'To hold that such knowledge constitutes waiver or estoppel would expose lenders to so many unpredictable hazards that construction financing would become extremely difficult. Although mechanic's lien laws should be liberally construed to protect those who have contributed skills, services or materials, towards the improvement of property, it has been recognized that lien laws are for the protection of owners as well as mechanic's lien claimants. * * * It may be said with equal validity that section 1188.1 * * * prescribing a rule for determining priorities was designed for the protection of those who take security interests in land as well as for the protection of mechanic's lien claimants.' " *Walker,* supra, 2 Cal.3d 158, 84 Cal.Rptr. 525–26, 465 P.2d 501–02.

We agree with the California Supreme Court that construction and purchase money loans are not made in a vacuum. Lenders often consult engineers' work in order to evaluate and minimize their risks. Thus if a lender's use of and reliance upon the plans prepared by engineers on behalf of the owner or would-be purchaser are to work a change in the statutory priority rules, the change must be sought from the Legislature and not from this Court.

III. CONCLUSION

Because we have found that the engineering services here at issue were not such as to constitute the "commencement of said building or buildings, erection, structure or improvement", the trial court erred in its ruling that the appellee mechanics' lienors had priority over the mortgage held by appellant Kelly. Accordingly, we reverse the decision of the Court of Appeals and vacate the trial court's judgment and order.

Costs to appellant.

COLEMAN, C.J., FITZGERALD, DEPUTY C.J., and RYAN, MOODY, LEVIN and KAVANAGH, JJ., concur.

NOTES

1.   *Architects and Engineers.* What kind of protection can, and should, be given to architects and engineers who will characteristically provide their services before the commencement of physical improvements on the construction site? As explicated in *Williams & Works,* the purpose of the physical improvement requirement is to put the construction lender on notice that work has begun and that liens may have attached. Would this purpose be equally well served by a rule that allowed engineers and architects to record their contracts, thus giving the lender constructive notice that work has begun? Such a rule would impose no additional search

burden on construction lenders who, as standard operating procedure, will search title before closing and recording their loans.

A rule that makes liens attach either from the moment that physical improvements commence or from the moment of their recording would not substantially increase construction lenders' economic risk. Having identified all lien claimants prior to recording the construction loan, the construction lender can require that they be paid off before the loan closes. As to mechanics and materialmen who provide services and supplies *after* the construction loan is recorded, but who can nonetheless take advantage of the earlier mechanics' lien priority, the construction lender can, by carefully monitoring a well-structured disbursement program, assure that no liens arise.

How would you advise an engineer or architect to protect herself in states like Michigan where her lien will virtually always be subordinated to the construction lender's lien?

After the decision in *Williams & Works*, the Michigan legislature amended its mechanics' lien statute. Mich.Comp. Laws Ann. § 570.1119 provides that a "construction lien" (the new term for a mechanics' lien) takes priority over other interests recorded subsequent to the "first actual physical improvement." Section 570.1103(1) specifically provides that "actual physical improvement" does not include architectural or engineering work, even though such work can be the basis for a valid construction lien. § 570.1104(7). See J.E. Dunn Northwest, Inc. v. Corus Construction Venture, LLC, 249 P.3d 501 (Nev. 2011) (preconstruction services, including review of plans and development of construction schedule, were not included within statutory "commencement of construction" as they were not visible).

The Uniform Construction Lien Act, promulgated by the National Conference of Commissioners on Uniform State Laws in 1976 and amended in 1977 takes a different approach than most statutes to the priority issue. Rather than assigning priority from the time of commencement of work (or some similar formulation), the Act requires the owner to record a "notice of commencement" prior to the beginning of work. This recording puts third parties on notice that construction liens might be filed and if a lien claimant subsequently records a lien, her priority is the date of recording of the notice of commencement. §§ 208, 209, 210, 301. It is asserted that this approach relieves the burden on construction lenders to determine before recording their mortgages whether work has begun and alleviates the need to preserve evidence that no work was done before the recording. Additionally, the Uniform Act permits architects and engineers to file construction liens on a priority with other lien claimants. §§ 102(17)(v), 209.

2. *Attachment, Perfection, and Foreclosure.* Mechanics' lien practice varies from state to state. In some states the lien attaches on the commencement of construction. In others, it attaches when a claim for payment is first filed. In still others it attaches when the general contract is executed. Requirements may exist for perfecting the lien, such as by recording the underlying claim within a specified time after construction is completed. Once the lien is perfected, time limits are usually imposed for the commencement of foreclosure proceedings. In some states the lienor must give the owner notice of her intention to record her claim of lien.

Rules on attachment, perfection and foreclosure may differ depending on whether it is the general contractor or a subcontractor who is asserting the lien. Some states have been highly protective of mechanics' rights, denying lenders equitable subrogation priority over mechanics when paying off a senior loan. See In re Fountainbleau Las Vegas Holdings, 289 P.3d 1199 (Nev. 2012). On mechanics liens generally, see Dugan, Mechanics' Liens for Improvements on Real Property, 25 S.D.L.Rev. 238 (1980); Urban & Miles, Mechanics' Liens for the Improvement of Real Property: Recent Developments in Perfection, Enforcement and Priority, 12 Wake Forest L.Rev. 283 (1976); Goulden & Dent, More on Mechanics Liens, Stop Notices and the Like, 54 Calif.L.Rev. 179 (1966).

3. *Constitutional Issues.* In recent decades, courts have addressed the constitutionality of mechanics' lien procedures. Although most courts have taken the view that the attachment of a mechanic's lien does not materially inhibit the owner's freedom of alienation, and consequently does not violate his right to procedural due process, others see a potential clog on alienation and follow the guidelines set down by the United States Supreme Court in decisions invalidating wage garnishment and replevin statutes. For the view that mechanics' lien procedures do not give the property owner due process, see Noatex Corp. v. King Construction of Houston, LLC, 732 F.3d 479 (5th Cir. 2013); (Mississippi stop-notice statute); Roundhouse Const. Corp. v. Telesco Masons Supplies Co., 168 Conn. 371, 362 A.2d 778 (1975), vacated and remanded for clarification of ground for decision 423 U.S. 809, 96 S.Ct. 20, 46 L.Ed.2d 29 (1975). For the opposing view, see Ruocco v. Brinker, 380 F.Supp. 432 (S.D.Fla.1974); Spielman-Fond, Inc. v. Hanson's Inc., 379 F.Supp. 997 (D.Ariz.1973), affirmed without opinion, 417 U.S. 901, 94 S.Ct. 2596, 41 L.Ed.2d 208 (1974). For a comprehensive study of the cases and their background, see generally, Note, 26 Cath.U.L.Rev. 129 (1976). See also Proposal to Expand Procedures for Prompt Judicial Review of Mechanic's Liens, 48 Rec. of the Ass'n of the Bar of the City of N.Y. 742 (1993).

4. *Claims Against Undisbursed Construction Funds.* Compliance with mechanics' liens procedures will be of no help to the unpaid laborer or material supplier if the security is exhausted by the claims of the construction lender or other senior encumbrancers. Equity may in these circumstances aid the supplier by attaching a lien not to the exhausted real estate security, but rather to any undisbursed construction funds. To be entitled to this equitable remedy, the supplier must show "special or peculiar equities." Crane Co. v. Fine, 221 So.2d 145, 149 (Fla.1969).

In addition to the practical requirement that there be undisbursed funds to which the equitable lien can attach, the unpaid supplier must show that she justifiably relied on the availability of the construction loan funds as a source of payment for her labor or materials, and that for the owner or lender to withhold these undisbursed funds would constitute unjust enrichment. Unjust enrichment is easiest to show if the owner or lender holds undisbursed construction funds after the project is completed. Would there be unjust enrichment if the project were unfinished and the construction lender needed to use the undisbursed funds to complete the improvement and otherwise protect its collateral? See A-1 Door & Materials Co. v. Fresno Guar. Sav. & Loan Ass'n, 61 Cal.2d 728, 40 Cal.Rptr. 85, 394 P.2d 829 (1964). To keep the issues in perspective, remember that the mechanic can always bring a contract action against the owner or contractor who agreed to pay for the labor or materials.

A similar, but more systematic, approach to undisbursed funds is offered by statutory "stop notice procedures." A lender or owner holding construction funds who fails to honor an unpaid supplier's stop notice demand that it withhold sufficient funds to satisfy the supplier's claim will be personally liable to the supplier for the amount owed. See, for example, Cal.Civ.Code § 3156 et seq.

Some courts hold that equitable liens are not permitted on the theory that the jurisdiction's mechanics' lien and stop notice statutes were intended as the exclusive remedies for unpaid laborers and suppliers. See, e.g., Nibbi Brothers, Inc. v. Home Federal Savings & Loan Association, 205 Cal.App.3d 1415, 253 Cal.Rptr. 289 (1988) (applying Cal.Civ.Code § 3264 which states that subcontractors and suppliers are limited to statutory remedies and may not assert any other equitable right); contra Embree Construction Group v. Rafcor, 330 N.C. 487, 411 S.E.2d 916 (1992).

For an extensive review of these and other theories of construction lender liability, see Reitz, Construction Lenders' Liability to Contractors, Subcontractors and Materialmen, 130 U.Pa.L.Rev. 416 (1981). See also Berk, Lien-tos: Half-Finished Buildings and the Priority of Construction Liens, 32 Santa Clara L.Rev. 315 (1992).

5. *Wrongly Disbursed Construction Funds.* Should mechanics and materialmen whose liens attached after the construction mortgage was recorded be given priority over the claims of a construction lender who allowed the construction loan proceeds to be diverted from the construction project? Peoples Bank & Trust Co. and Bank of Mississippi v. L & T Developers, Inc., 434 So.2d 699 (Miss.1983), judgment corrected, 437 So.2d 7 (Miss.1983), answered that they should be given priority. The Mississippi Supreme Court began by noting that the equities favored the materialmen. "If, as here, the materialmen are not paid, quite likely the construction lender will be unjustly enriched at their expense. For in this situation, if the construction lender were allowed a priority over the materialmen, it would have received the enhancement to the value of its collateral while the materialmen, without whose services the bank cannot expect the secured construction loan transaction to succeed, would as a practical matter be without security, and, most likely, with little prospect of getting paid." 434 So.2d at 705.

The court further concluded that this was "an instance in which the law follows and embodies the equities." Id. It cited an earlier decision, Guaranty Mortgage Co. of Nashville v. Seitz, 367 So.2d 438 (Miss.1979), for the proposition that "The lien of a deed of trust securing a construction loan has priority over mechanics' and materialmen's liens only to the extent that: (a) the funds disbursed actually went into the construction, *or* (b) to the extent that the construction lender used reasonable diligence in disbursing the construction loan. 367 So.2d at 441. [Emphasis added]" 434 So.2d at 707.

The court emphasized that "the bank/construction lender is in a far better situation than is the materialman to protect itself and police the use of the construction loan funds and thereby avoid the predicament which has in fact ensued." Specifically, "construction lenders may make advances in the form of drafts or checks payable directly to materialmen or payable to materialmen and the builder jointly." 434 So.2d at 705. On much the same reasoning the court concluded that the materialmen were also entitled to priority over the landowner-purchase money mortgagee: "Wickes and Arick [the construction licnors] are parties who supplied materials and labor to the improvements on the two lots, thereby enhancing the value of these projects. Through sweat and elbow grease, these two construction lienors in a very real sense created value which previously was not there. The landowner, on the other hand, has made no similar contribution. The landowner had the far greater capacity to protect his interest, and, further, the landowner profits directly from the success of the overall construction project to which the materialmen so materially contribute." 434 So.2d at 714.

Under the reasoning of *Peoples Bank,* should the mechanics and materialmen have been given not only first priority, but also an action against the construction lenders for any part of their construction liens not satisfied by the foreclosure sale of the property? An action against the landowner-purchase money mortgagee?

Should a construction lender be under a similar duty to a mechanic who has not perfected a lien? Should the failure of the mechanic alter the balance of the equitable considerations that the court made in *Peoples Bank*? See Riley Building Supplies, Inc. v. First Citizens National Bank, 510 So.2d 506 (Miss.1987).

The obligatory/optional advance rule has also been applied to boost the priority of mechanics. See the discussion of this doctrine and various reforms at pages 597–601 above.

ii. Fixtures

James J. White & Robert S. Summers,
Uniform Commercial Code[*]
1292–1296 (6th ed. 2010).

In general, Article 9 does not deal with real estate security. The single important exception to that rule is section 9–334 concerning priority of security interests in fixtures. That section governs the conflict between personal property interests in fixtures and real property interest in fixtures.

Typical of the priority conflicts we consider here are those that arise when a real estate mortgagee claims not only the real estate but also all "appurtenances, fixtures, buildings, equipment." After the mortgage is on the property, the debtor purchases a furnace or lathes or some other item of industrial equipment that becomes a fixture on the real property and subject to the real estate mortgage under the state real property law. This single transaction comes in a dozen variants depending on when the interests attach and when they are perfected, and on the identity of the claimant and the mode of perfection. Section 9–334 deals with most of the possible conflicts. If the collateral in question is not a fixture, or if it is "building material" that has become

---

[*] Reprinted from Uniform Commercial Code, James J. White & Robert Summers, sixth edition, 2010 with permission of West Academic.

so intimately associated with the real property that it no longer constitutes either personal property or a fixture, other law governs the priority dispute.

The secured creditor with a claim to a fixture has a choice. It can either make a filing in the local real estate records (a fixture filing) or do a regular UCC–1 filing in the personal property records at the state capital. As we will see, the former gives the secured creditor protection against certain real estate claimants, and the latter gives protection only against lien creditors and certain other claimants where the fixture involved is not considered to be important to mortgagees and the like. For example, subsection (e)(3) grants the secured lender who has done only a personal property filing at the state capital priority over the trustee in bankruptcy (lien creditor) on the theory that a lien creditor is not someone who would rely upon the real estate records. Subsection (e)(2) gives priority to the secured creditor who has only done a personal property filing on certain assets such as factory or office machines on the theory that mortgagees or other purchasers of the real estate do not place any reliance upon such machines when they make loans or buy; thus it is fair and appropriate to grant the secured creditor priority in this case even though the secured creditor does not do a fixture filing.

a.   Fixtures and Fixture Filings,
Section 9–102(a)(40) and (41)

Section 9–102(a)(41) defines fixtures as "goods that have become so related to particular real property that an interest in them arises under real property law." Broadly, goods can be classified for the purposes of 9–334 into three categories: those that remain "pure goods," those so substantially integrated into real estate as to become real estate themselves, i.e., "pure realty," and those in between that would pass in a deed to the real estate yet remain personal property. The items that fall under this last classification are fixtures. Comment 3 to 9–334 presents this division as follows:

> * * * this section recognizes three categories of goods: (1) those that retain their chattel character entirely and are not part of the real property; (2) ordinary building materials that have become an integral part of the real property and cannot retain their chattel character for purposes of finance; and (3) an intermediate class that has become real property for certain purposes, but as to which chattel financing may be preserved.

Goods cross the line from pure goods to fixtures when they become sufficiently related to the real estate that they would pass in a deed under the local real estate law. What passes by deed in Minnesota may not pass in Wisconsin, and what is sufficiently related to a real estate interest in New York might not be sufficiently related in Georgia. Thus the general definition in 9–102(a)(41) is no more than a cross reference to state case law and state real estate statutes. What, then, are the state law principles governing when goods become fixtures? Here, we cannot go much beyond posing the question.

Most courts start from the proposition that status of goods as a fixture depends upon the intention of the parties. Of course, "objective manifestations of intention" are the windows through which we view actual intent. One searching for such manifestations might ask: What did the parties say in their agreement? How did they attach the goods to the realty? What is the relation between the parties? How is the operation of the goods related to the use of the real property? For many courts, intent is most clearly manifested by the firmness with which the goods are affixed to the real estate and the amount of sweat that removal would entail. The American Law of Property puts the matter as follows (emphasis added):

> In the United States, whether a given chattel becomes a fixture is said to depend on intention, but whether it is the unilateral intention of the annexor at the time of annexation, or the bilateral intention of the parties to some transaction relating to the chattel or to the land, and whether it is the actual intention, or the manifested intention, or the imputed intention, is not always clear.

> Part of the confusion comes from the various meanings ascribed to the term "fixture." Under the modern cases no more precise definition is possible than this: a fixture is a former chattel which, while retaining its separate physical identity, *is so connected with the realty that a disinterested observer would consider it a part thereof.*

This is not the place to inject order into this chaotic body of law. We do no more than to warn you that the local cases must be examined with care to arrive at a reasonable guess about what is and what is not a fixture in a particular jurisdiction.

Section 9–102(a)(40) states that a "fixture filing" is "the filing of a financing statement covering goods that are or are to become fixtures and satisfying section 9–502(a) and (b). The term includes the filing of a financing statement covering goods of a transmitting utility which are or are to become fixtures." The concept of a "fixture filing" was introduced in the 1972 revision of Article 9. The drafters concluded that one should be required to file a fixture filing in the office in which a record of a mortgage for the real property would be filed if one seeks priority over subsequent real estate interests who would typically check in the real estate files and only in those files. Comment 4 to revised 9–501 explains the two ways in which a secured party may file a financing statement to perfect a security interest in goods that are or are to become fixtures, depending upon the parties against whom protection is sought. First, a secured party may make a non-fixture filing in Article 9 records, as with goods, in accordance with section 9–501(a)(2). Or, a secured creditor may file a "fixture filing" in the office in which a record of a mortgage on the related real property would be filed; see 9–501(a)(1)(B). Given the uncertainty of whether goods are or may become fixtures under applicable real-property law, Comment 3 to 9–334 recognizes that a secured party may make a fixture filing as a precaution. A court may not infer merely from a fixture filing that the secured party concedes that the goods are or will becomes fixtures.

In addition to the normal information under 9–502(a), a financing statement filed as a fixture filing under subsection (b) must include: (1) a showing that it covers goods which are, or are to become, "fixtures"; (2) a recital that the financing statement is to be filed in the real estate records; (3) a description of the real estate; and (4) the name of the record owner if the debtor has no interest of record. Section 9–502(c) states that the recording of a complying mortgage is equivalent to a fixture filing.

b.   Fixture Priority Rules, Section 9–334(d)–(h)

The priority rules in subsections (d) through (h) look threatening at first, but once one understands the reasons for the various rules, they are logical and relatively easy to understand. First is a general rule stated in (c): except as stated in (d) through (h) "a security interest in fixtures is subordinate to a conflicting interest of an encumbrancer or owner." So the real estate mortgagee or buyer of the real estate defeats the personal property secured creditor unless the secured creditor can find an exception that states otherwise.

Subsection (d) gives priority over competing real estate claimants to a purchase money secured creditor who complies with 9–334(d), subject to one exception. . . .

There is one important exception to the purchase money priority of the secured creditor. Consider a construction mortgagee financing the construction of a building and another lender financing an important fixtures such as a large heating or cooling system. In that case both parties would be purchase money lenders; each would be advancing funds to enable the debtor to construct a functional building. Subsection (h) generally grants priority to the construction mortgagee. And the construction mortgagee's priority carries over even into a refinanced mortgage. In effect, the drafters here have concluded that the construction mortgagee is the more important lender; the rule of (h) requires the purchase money lender against the fixture to go to the construction mortgagee and seek a subordination agreement if the fixture lender wishes to have priority.

Capitol Federal Savings and Loan Association v. Hoger

Court of Appeals of Kansas, 1994.
19 Kan.App.2d 1052, 880 P.2d 281.

Before BRISCOE, C.J., and RULON and LEWIS, JJ.

BRISCOE, CHIEF JUDGE:

In this foreclosure action, Capitol Federal Savings and Loan Association appeals from the district court's order granting Western Resources, Inc.'s purchase money security interest in fixtures priority over Capitol Federal's previously recorded real estate mortgage. Capitol Federal contends Western Resources' remedy was limited to repossession of the fixtures.

Capitol Federal held a real estate mortgage on the home of Paul and Margaret Hoger. The mortgage was recorded in Johnson County on August 15, 1984. In 1990, the Hogers purchased a furnace and air conditioner from The Kansas Power and Light Company (KPL), d/b/a KPL Gas Service (now Western Resources, Inc.), to be installed in the Hogers' home. On March 2, 1990, the Hogers and KPL entered into an installment contract and the Hogers executed a promissory note to finance the purchase of the furnace and air conditioner. The furnace and air conditioner were installed on March 20. KPL filed financing statements covering the furnace and air conditioner in Johnson County on March 23, 1990. Capitol Federal did not receive notice of either the purchase or the installation of the furnace and air conditioner and did not consent to the security agreement. The parties do not dispute that KPL has a purchase money security interest in the fixtures.

The Hogers defaulted on both the Capitol Federal and the Western Resources loans. Capitol Federal filed a mortgage foreclosure action on December 28, 1992, and named both the Hogers and Western Resources as defendants. A second mortgage holder, Associates Financial Services Company of Kansas, Inc., was also named as a defendant, but did not file an answer. Western Resources answered and counterclaimed for the $2,887.50 amount the Hogers still owed on their installment contract, claiming a first and prior right to the real estate mortgage foreclosure sale proceeds under K.S.A. 1993 Supp. 84–9–312(4) and K.S.A. 84–9–313(4), but did not seek a default judgment against the Hogers when they failed to answer. By this point, the Hogers had filed a petition in bankruptcy and Western Resources opted not to pursue a personal judgment against the Hogers.

Capitol Federal filed a motion for summary judgment, claiming priority in the real estate mortgage foreclosure sale proceeds over Western Resources' purchase money security interest. The court denied the motion, finding the Western Resources fixture filing was perfected under 84–9–313(4)(a) and Western Resources' purchase money security interest in the furnace and air conditioner was superior to Capitol Federal's real estate encumbrance. The court ordered Capitol Federal to pay Western Resources the amount of its claim from the foreclosure sale proceeds. The effect of this ruling was to permit Western Resources first priority in the foreclosure sale proceeds for the amount it claimed.

The parties agreed to sever the priority issue from the balance of the action. The mortgage foreclosure action has proceeded, the foreclosure sale has been held, and monies in the amount of Western Resources' claim are being retained by the clerk of the district court pending resolution of this appeal.

I.   IN WHAT DID WESTERN RESOURCES HAVE A PRIORITY INTEREST?

It appears the parties do not dispute that the furnace and air conditioner purchased by the Hogers have becomes fixtures and that Western Resources obtained a priority interest of some type in those fixtures. A review of the law as it applies to "perfecting" a fixture filing is a helpful first step in determining the scope of Western Resources' interest.

> "[G]oods are 'fixtures' when affixing them to real estate so associates them with the real estate that, in the absence of any agreement or understanding with his vendor as to the goods, a purchaser of the real estate with knowledge of interests of others of record, or in possession would reasonably consider the goods to have been purchased as part of the real estate." K.S.A. 84–9–313(1)(a).

"[A] 'fixture filing' is the filing in the office where a mortgage on the real estate would be filed or recorded of a financing statement covering goods which are or are to become fixtures and conforming to the requirements of subsection (5) of section 84–9–402." K.S.A. 84–9–313(1)(b). The parties do not dispute that Western Resources complied with K.S.A. 1993 Supp. 84–9–402(5).

Priority of Western Resources' security interest as against Capitol Federal's interest in the real estate is controlled by 84–9–313:

> "(4) A perfected security interest in fixtures has priority over the conflicting interest of an encumbrancer or owner of the real estate where (a) the security interest is a purchase money security interest, the interest of the encumbrancer or owner arises before the goods become fixtures, the security interest is perfected by a fixture filing before the goods become fixtures or within ten (10) days thereafter, and the debtor has an interest of record in the real estate or is in possession of the real estate."

"Encumbrance" is defined to include "real estate mortgages and other liens on real estate and all other rights in real estate that are not ownership interests." K.S.A. 1993 Supp. 84–9–105(1)(g). Western Resources' financing statement was filed within 10 days of installation. In light of the foregoing, Western Resources has a 84–9–313(4)(a) priority interest in the furnace and air conditioner as fixtures. What is at issue here, at least in part, is whether Western Resources' interest extends to the real estate or if it is limited solely to the furnace and air conditioner.

Although this is an appeal from a summary judgment, the question presented requires interpretation of statutes and, therefore, we are presented with a question of law. Todd v. Kelly, 251 Kan. 512, 515, 837 P.2d 381 (1992). When determining a question of law, this court is not bound by the decision of the district court. Memorial Hospital Ass'n, Inc. v. Knutso, 239 Kan. 663, 668, 722 P.2d 1093 (1986).

K.S.A. 84–9–102(1) states that Article 9 applies "(a) to any transaction ... which is intended to create a security interest in personal property or fixtures." Real estate is not mentioned. K.S.A. 84–9–104(j) states that Article 9 excludes from coverage "the creation or transfer of an interest in or lien on real estate," except for fixtures as considered under 84–9–313. See Kansas Comment 1983 to 84–9–104(j). By its language, 84–9–313(4)(a) limits Western Resources' priority to an interest in only the *fixtures* as against a possible interest by one holding an interest in the real estate. See Official UCC Comment 4 and Kansas Comment 1983 to subsection (4). The interests of Western Resources and Capitol Federal overlap in the furnace and air conditioner. Western Resources' interest does not extend beyond the furnace and air conditioner.

If there remains any doubt that Western Resources' interest is limited to an interest in the furnace and air conditioner as fixtures, the following authorities provide language to that effect. Maplewood Bank v. Sears, Roebuck, 265 N.J. Super. 25, 28, 625 A.2d 537 (1993); Sears Roebuck & Co. v. Norr, 10 U.C.C.Rep.Serv. 1258, 1262, 1972 WL 20903 (Md. 1972); 9 Anderson on the Uniform Commercial Code § 9–313:16 (1985).

II. DOES WESTERN RESOURCES HAVE A RIGHT TO THE REAL ESTATE FORECLOSURE PROCEEDS?

Capitol Federal contends the court erred by denying its motion for summary judgment and by setting aside from the proceeds of the foreclosure sale the amount claimed by Western Resources. For support, Capitol Federal relies on the authorities cited above to the effect that, because Western Resources does not have an interest in the real estate, it should not be liable to claim a portion of the proceeds arising from the sale of the real estate. Standing alone, this argument does not resolve whether Western Resources has a right to the real estate proceeds because arguably a portion of those proceeds were generated from the sale of the fixtures which were sold when the real estate was sold.

The real question is whether the UCC permits Western Resources to proceed against the foreclosure sale proceeds. Here, again, the issue concerns interpretation of statutes and is a question of law. Western Resources' remedy, as provided by the UCC, is as follows:

> "When the secured party has priority over all owners and encumbrances of the real estate, he may, on default, subject to the provisions of part 5, remove his collateral from the real estate but he must reimburse any encumbrancer or owner of the real estate who is not the debtor and who has not otherwise agreed for the cost of repair of any physical injury, but not for any diminution in value of the real estate caused by the absence of the goods removed or by any necessity for replacing them. A person entitled to reimbursement may refuse permission to remove until the secured party gives adequate security for the performance of this obligation." K.S.A. 84–9–313(8).

Capitol Federal argues repossession of the furnace and air conditioner or bringing its claim against the collateral to judgment under K.S.A. 84–9–501 were the only remedies available to Western Resources. Western Resources did not pursue an action pursuant to 84–9–501 and does not rely upon 84–9–501 for its claim here. Instead, Western Resources relies upon 84–9–313(8) as the basis for its claim. Western Resources emphasizes that 84–9–313(8) states that a secured party "may" repossess the collateral and that use of this term implies that other remedies are available. Western Resources argues that once Capitol Federal instituted the foreclosure proceedings, Western Resources was entitled to have its lien paid first from the proceeds of the sale.

Neither the language of 84–9–313(8) nor the comments answer the question with which we are presented. There are only a few authorities that address the issue, and there are no Kansas cases among those authorities. The Kansas Comment indicates that the 84–9–313(8) remedy is not exclusive: In addition to proceeding pursuant to K.S.A. 60–1005 or K.S.A. 60–1006 for replevin against the personal property, a "fixture financer may choose to back off from its Article 9 remedy and proceed under the Kansas mechanic's lien statute." The interrelationship between fixture foreclosure and mechanic's lien enforcement appears to be a separate issue from that considered here. See Clark, The Law of Secured Transactions Under the Uniform Commercial Code § 9.07[6][a] and [b] (1993).

At least one commentator has advocated a clarification of UCC § 9–313 to the effect that those who have a security interest in fixtures are not required to remove their collateral. Shanker, *An Integrated Financing System for Purchase Money Collateral: A Proposed Solution to the Fixture Problem Under Section 9–313 of the Uniform Commercial Code*, 73 Yale L.J. 788, 804–05 (1964). Professor Shanker notes that although one might get the impression that removal is the only method by which such a secured party could redeem an interest, if that secured party does not have a priority interest over the interest in the real estate, there is no right to remove the fixture under § 9–313(5). Further, there are instances where a secured party would not want to remove the collateral because, once separated from the real estate, the collateral would be worthless. This would be true when the collateral is customized to adapt to the real estate. For further support of his position, Professor Shanker argues there are times when the secured party should not be allowed to remove collateral, as where the collateral is heating equipment in a large apartment building and the creditor seeks to remove the same in the dead of winter. 73 Yale L.J. at 804–05. Professor Shanker opines: "Where the fixture secured party has no right of removal or, having the right, prefers not to exercise it, the Code, as it now stands, probably authorizes the fixture secured party to employ judicial foreclosure proceedings to enforce his security interest." 73 Yale L.J. at 804. He continues, though, by stating that "this result is not clear, and the right to resort to judicial foreclosure ought not to be left to doubt. Clarifying amendments to Section 9–313 or its official commentary are obviously needed." 73 Yale L.J. at 804.

Western Resources argues Lewston Bottled Gas v. Key Bank, 601 A.2d 91 (Me.1992), is directly on point. However, at issue there was whether particular collateral constituted fixtures and whether the creditor claiming an interest in that collateral had a priority interest over the mortgagee's interests. The second issue was not reached because the parties agreed to allow the mortgagee to proceed with foreclosure and to litigate the issue of title regarding the claimed fixture-collateral later. 601 A.2d at 93. Western Resources also emphasizes Parsons v. Lender Service, Inc., 801 P.2d 739 (Okla. App. 1990), but it, too, is a priority case and does not reach the issue considered in this case.

Capitol Federal cites several cases for the proposition that a fixture creditor cannot pursue the proceeds from a real estate foreclosure sale. These are summarized in Clark, § 9.07[6][a]:

> "Other decisions, however, reflect a desire by the fixture financer to sidestep the repossession remedy under § 9–313. For example, in Dry Dock Savings Bank v. DeGeorgio [61 Misc.2d 224, 305 N.Y.S.2d 73 (1969)], a fixture financer argued that it was entitled to a priority chunk of the proceeds generated by foreclosure sale of the real estate. The court emphasized that § 9–313, while it provides a remedy in rem against the fixture itself, grants no rights as against the real estate. To the same effect Sears, Roebuck & Co. v. Norr, where Sears had a perfected security interest in kitchen cabinets and other items as fixtures on the debtor's leasehold property. Upon the debtor's default, Sears sought to have a trustee

appointed to sell the leasehold interest and apply the proceeds to its claim. The court would have none of it, holding that Sears' right was limited to repossessing the fixtures themselves subject to reimbursing the owner for any physical damages caused to the realty.

"In Nu-Way Distributing Corp. v. Schoikert [44 A.D.2d 840, 355 N.Y.S.2d 475 (1974)], a fixture financer who did not want to repossess the fixture sought an in personam judgment for recovery of the purchase price of the fixture against a subsequent bona fide purchaser of the real estate. The court correctly held that § 9–313 does not provide a remedy against the real estate itself, even if the fixtures are custom-made and are of no value if repossessed, and even if the purchaser of the realty is using them. The fixture financer presumably retains its rights to repossess the fixture as against the purchaser of the realty if it had properly perfected prior to the real estate sale."

The foregoing passage does not fully represent the intricacies of each of the three cases cited. As Western Resources notes, the language Dry Dock Savings Bank v. DeGeorgio, 61 Misc.2d 224, 305 N.Y.S.2d 73 (1969), is dicta. The *Norr* decision can be criticized on the basis that the court's rationale is imperfect: It misrepresented the language and meaning of § 9–313(4) and (5). See Editors' note, 10 U.C.C.Rep.Serv. At 1260. Nu-Way Distributing Corp. v. Schoikert, 44 App.Div.2d 840, 355 N.Y.S.2d 475 (1974), is arguably factually distinguishable because it concerned a creditor's attempt to recover from a subsequent purchaser of real property. However, Nu-Way cites Dry Dock for support. 44 App.Div.2d at 841, 355 N.Y.S.2d 475.

A recent case not considered by the parties, Maplewood Bank v. Sears, Roebuck, 265 N.J.Super. 25, 625 A.2d 537, contains facts similar to those present here. Plaintiff bank held a first and prior mortgage on realty, and Sears later secured an interest in a number of kitchen fixtures. The fact that Sears was secured and held a priority interest in those fixtures was undisputed. When defendants defaulted on both obligations, the bank filed for foreclosure. Sears answered, seeking a declaration of priority and requesting that the court order the bank to pay Sears the amount due under its agreement. Sears' response was rejected and it eventually appealed, arguing it should be entitled to receive from the proceeds of a foreclosure sale the difference between the value of the realty with Sears collateral and the value of the realty after that collateral had been removed. After reviewing the language of § 9–313(8) as adopted in New Jersey, the court stated: "Sears has two options: removal of the fixtures or foregoing removal of the fixtures." 265 N.J.Super. at 29, 625 A.2d 537. The court then considered *Dry Dock* and *Nu-Way* and noted the approach advocated by Sears had only been adopted in Louisiana, where the legislature had added the following language to § 9–313(8): "*A secured party may also demand separate appraisal of the fixtures to fix his interest in the receipts of the sale thereof in any proceedings in which the real estate is sold pursuant to execution upon it by a mortgagee or other encumbrancer.*" 265 N.J.Super. at 30, 625 A.2d 537.

The *Maplewood* court also examined the Shanker article in 73 Yale L.J. 788, concluding:

> "We decline to adopt the creative approach articulated by Professor Shanker. Such action, in our view, would be legislating. We prefer the approach followed in Louisiana where the legislature, upon its preference and initiative, provided the innovative remedy sought by Sears. To adopt Sears' argument in the absence of legislation, would mean that a mortgagee's security interest could be impaired substantially without the Legislature pronouncing an intention to do so. Any modification of long established fundamental property rights of purchase money mortgagees, must be done in some straight forward manner and may not be implied from the existing statute. The fact that fixtures may be custom made does not require any different result." 265 N.J.Super. at 31, 625 A.2d 537.

In Hawkland, Uniform Commercial Code Series § 9–313:07, p. 331 (1991), it is stated:

> "If the fixture financer has priority under section 9–313 but affirmatively opts not to remove his collateral either because he just does not want to or because reimbursement costs will make removal economically prohibitive or impracticable, the question arises as to what his other options might be. In these circumstances, it seems clear that he should be able to proceed in accordance with the 9–500's. That is, he should be entitled to reduce his claim to judgment and, if the fixture is equipment, render it unusable on the site. In this one situation, he arguably should not be able to await the foreclosure sale of the real estate and claim a first priority to its proceeds. The reason for the distinction here is simple: his primary protective right, the right to remove the collateral, is not being hindered by virtue of his subordination or by virtue of the debtor's actions. Given the difficulty of valuing his interest vis-a-vis that of the mortgagee, he should not be able to insist upon a right to foreclosure sale proceeds when he can make himself fully whole by removing his collateral. The fact that he is adversely affected by virtue of his reimbursement obligation or that he believes it simpler to await the foreclosure by the real estate encumbrancer should not entitle him to first crack at the foreclosure sale proceeds, particularly given the difficulties of valuation."

Capitol Federal and Western Resources advance additional arguments that are less persuasive. Capitol Federal argues that to allow Western Resources a portion of the proceeds is violative of the general rule that the first creditor to file a financing statement receives priority. However, as Western Resources notes, fixture filing is intended to be an exception to the general rule: "The principal exception to the general rule of priority stated in Comment 4(b) based on time of filing or recording is a priority given in paragraph (4)(a) to purchase money security interests in fixtures as against *prior* recorded real estate interests." Official UCC Comment (4)(a) to 84–9–313.

Capitol Federal argues that because it did not receive notice of the security statement and filing and did not consent to the addition of the furnace and air conditioner to the real estate, to allow Western Resources a portion of the proceeds would permit a taking without due process of law, contrary to the Fourteenth Amendment to the United States Constitution. This argument fails because the Fourteenth Amendment's prohibition against the taking of property without due process applies only to governmental bodies. As Western Resources points out, the state action necessary for this due process argument is lacking.

Western Resources also argues that to allow Capitol Federal to keep all of the foreclosure proceeds would result in a windfall for Capitol Federal. This argument ignores the fact that Western Resources had the right to remove the fixtures.

Western Resources argues Capitol Federal would be in no worse position if it paid a portion of the foreclosure proceeds to Western Resources or if Western Resources removed the furnace and air conditioner. This may be true, but it is just as possible that the furnace and air conditioner, whether because of their condition or other factors, add little to the value of the home. Further, to allow Western Resources a prior right to the amount owed it by the Hogers would be to provide Western Resources, vicariously, the security usually associated with real estate. In other words, Western Resources' change, upon default, of recovering amounts owed it would no longer be tied solely to the risks involved in reselling Western Resources' collateral.

This leads us to Western Resources' next point, that once its collateral is removed it is virtually worthless. Quoting Official UCC Comment 8 to 84–9–313, Western Resources argues that to avoid this situation, which would "chill the availability of short-term credit for modernization of real estate by installation of new fixtures" rather than encourage "purchase money fixture financing," the legislature passed § 9–313. The Official UCC Comments do not indicate that this was, in fact, the reason § 9–313 was passed. It was passed to solidify the law concerning priorities of fixtures. Western Resources' argument is not persuasive because the risk involved in a security interest in personal property was known to Western Resources from the outset. Perhaps this is why the court in *Dry Dock* noted that to allow only removal by the fixture creditor

> "may turn out to be a somewhat Pyrrhic victory, giving the lienor a pile of dubious scrap not worth the labor of getting it off the house, repairing all holes, etc. In other words, it may hurt the mortgagee without doing the lienor any corresponding good. However, that is something for the parties to consider and beyond the control of the court." 61 Misc.2d at 226, 305 N.Y.S.2d 73.

Similarly, in *Nu-Way*, the court did not find it persuasive that the custom nature of the fixtures may render them worthless when removed from the real estate: "A creditor in plaintiff's position must be assumed to have known and understood the risk he was taking when he agreed to allow the goods to stand as collateral and the risk should remain his." 44 App.Div.2d at 841, 355 N.Y.S.2d 475.

After reviewing the foregoing authorities, we find *Maplewood* and the Hawkland article are persuasive. Clearly, the UCC does not grant Western Resources an interest in the furnace and air conditioner as fixtures. To allow it to proceed against the real estate foreclosure sale proceeds would effectively give Western Resources an interest in the real estate beyond its interest in the fixtures because, on default by the Hogers, Western Resources' possibility of recouping the amounts it claims would be tied not simply to the value of its collateral, but to the value of the real estate. As is the case here, Western Resources would be recovering the entire amount of its claim, despite the actual value of the fixtures. Even if the fixtures were appropriately valued, the fixture creditor would benefit from the synergy of the fixture-real estate relationship. Although the law is such that a mortgagee may benefit by the addition of personal property to real estate (see 84–9–313[7]), there is nothing in the UCC that indicates the interests of fixture creditors should be enhanced by the real estate to which personal property is affixed.

We conclude the district court erred in finding Western Resources had priority in the foreclosure sale proceeds over Capitol Federal's previously recorded mortgage. The effect of this ruling was to improperly extend Western Resources' purchase money security interest in fixtures to the proceeds obtained from the sale of all the real estate. As between the first mortgage holder and the holder of a purchase money security interest in fixtures, the first mortgage holder is entitled to priority in funds realized from foreclosure sale of the mortgaged real estate.

Reversed and remanded with directions to pay to Capitol Federal the monies retained from the foreclosure sale proceeds.

NOTE

Capitol Federal was decided under the 1972 version of Article 9 of the U.C.C. A new version of Article 9 was promulgated in 2000 (hereafter Revised Article 9). Portions of section 9–313 of the 1972 version are embodied in sections 9–334 and 9–605 of Revised Article 9. Revised section 9–604(b) provides that a party with a security interest in fixtures may enforce it under the U.C.C. and remove the fixtures under section 9–604(c), or it may proceed "in accordance with the rights with respect to real property." Comment 3 states that subsection (b) "serves to overrule cases holding that a secured party's only remedy after default is the removal of the fixtures from the real property." Consider the effect of Revised section 9–604(b) on *Capitol Federal*.

For a comprehensive examination, see Squillante, The Law of Fixtures: Common Law and the Uniform Commercial Code, 15 Hofstra L.Rev. 191 (Part I), 535 (Part II) (1987). See also Lloyd, Article 9 and Real Estate Law: Practical Solutions for Bothersome Problems, 29 Idaho L.Rev. 583 (1993); Polston, The Fixtures Doctrine: Was It Ever Really the Law?, 16 Whittier L.Rev. 455 (1995). For commentary on the 2000 version, see Clement, Revised Article 9 and Real Estate Foreclosures, 12 Probate & Prop. 40 (Sept./Oct. 1998). For commentary on the 1962 version of section 9–313, see Coogan, Security Interests in Fixtures under the Uniform Commercial Code, 75 Harv.L.Rev. 1319 (1962); Coogan, Fixtures— Uniformity in Words or in Fact? 113 U.Pa.L.Rev. 1186 (1965); Gilmore, The

Purchase Money Priority, 76 Harv.L.Rev. 1333, 1388–1400 (1963); Shanker, An Integrated Financing System for Purchase Money Collateral: A Proposed Solution to the Fixture Problem Under Section 9–313 of the Uniform Commercial Code, 73 Yale L.J. 788 (1964). For commentary on the 1972 version, see Carlson, Fixture Priorities, 4 Cardozo L.Rev. 381 (1983); Coogan, The New U.C.C. Article 9, 86 Harv.L.Rev. 477 (1973); A.B.A. Comm. on Real Estate Financing, Fixtures and Personal Property and Mortgage Transactions Under U.C.C., 9 Real Prop., Probate & Trust J. 653 (1974); Adams, Security Interests in Fixtures Under Mississippi's Uniform Commercial Code, 47 Miss.L.J. 831 (1976); Berry, Priority Conflicts Between Fixture Secured Creditors and Real Estate Claimants, 7 Mem.St.U.L.Rev. 209 (1977).

B. THE GROUND LEASE AND LEASEHOLD MORTGAGE

Ira Meislik, Basic Principles of Ground Lease Agreements
New Jersey Lawyer 50–54 (Dec. 2012).*

A lease is a lease is a lease—or so you may think. Yes, real property leases grant an estate in land to a tenant for a period of time. And yes, the tenant pays for that right of possession. But the action in a lease isn't in the conveyance provisions; it's in the contract provisions. Multiply out the rent and other annual monetary obligations by the length of the lease term (in years), and you'll see that it might be (and often is) a big-dollar contract.

Even more important, unlike the vast majority of contracts whose obligations are satisfied in days or weeks, a lease contract goes unfulfilled for 50, 75, 99, or even 500 years. That takes it beyond the life of the parties involved in its creation, and brings future surprises.

Why a Ground Lease?

If a tenant has to build its own building (as is often the case), and has all of the burdens of ownership, why would it lease a property knowing that at the end of the lease term it has nothing left to show for its money and efforts? There are a number of common reasons, principal among them is that the owner won't sell the land, so the tenant has no alternative.

Real property often carries a long-term unrealized gain, waiting to be taxed upon its sale.

Not every landowner is interested in making further active real property investments. This makes a like-kind exchange unappealing.

Ground leasing the same land keeps ownership in the family. At the owner's death, because of the current estate tax stepped-up basis arrangement, the built-in gain may never be taxed.

It may also be that the tenant needs only part of a tract, and the government won't allow a subdivision. So, a ground lease is executed with a very long term. It could be 500 years. All of the rent is paid up

---

* This article was originally published in the December 2012 issue of the New Jersey Lawyer Magazine, a publication of the New Jersey State Bar Association, and is reprinted here with permission.

front, amounting to the equivalent of what would have been the purchase price. If the tenant can get a subdivision later, it will have the right to buy the leased land for a nominal sum.

Approval of the sale of public land can make a government official uncomfortable. Leasing is easier to explain. A public entity can design financial incentives to motivate developers to undertake projects that might otherwise be unattractive. By contract *(i.e.,* the ground lease), the governmental landowner can control the developer's project in ways that go beyond restrictions in land use laws without being guilty of spot zoning. And, unlike land use laws, the provisions of a ground lease can be flexibly reached.

Setting the Rent

Rent is the dominant continuing connection between the landlord and the tenant. Almost always, all other expenses arising out of real estate development are paid by the ground tenant—taxes, insurance, maintenance and other operating costs, environmental costs, and the rest. Therefore, the challenge is to set an appropriate rent that will be acceptable at the outset and throughout a very long lease term. It needs to approximate a fair market rent (or a fair market return) for an initial period and then fairly adjust the rent (or return) to keep up with inflation and investment expectations.

Rent can be structured to lower the ground tenant's initial burden while it develops the property to its economic potential. One way or another, after that point, the rent 'deferral' will be collected by the landlord. One or both parties will resort to professional appraisals to estimate the fair market rental. Often, the parties think they are setting rent as a percentage of the land's value, but that's just a way of combining their estimate of the land's fair market value with their agreement on what then constitutes a fair market return.

Over time, the land's value will change, almost certainly upwards, even after eliminating the direct effect of any successful development on it. Inflation is also a historical certainty. Lastly, investment return rates fluctuate over time. So, the rent is going to change, but when, how often, and to what? Resetting ground rent every five, 10 or 20 years is quite common.

There are three mainstream approaches to the rent reset—indexed adjustments (such as using a cost of living index); fixed rent increments; and fair market value resets. Each has its advantages and each has its limitations.

Fixed rate adjustments are predictable and provide a stable basis for financing. On the other hand, the further out in time rent is fixed, the more dangerous the result. The ground landlord's return may turn out to be too low, or the rent may be more than even a successful project can sustain.

Finding fair market rental value at the time of renewal will call for appraisals. Thus, the lease must contain appraisal rules. Is the rent to be based on the land's highest and best value or will it be based on the land's actual use? Will the fair market rent have a relationship to the existing use or uses? Will the appraised value take into account the encumbrance of the ground lease itself? What appraisal method will be used and what qualifications will be required of the appraisers? That's only a start, but will give the ground lease parties an idea of the challenge.

There also are uncommon methods, such as tying ground rent to the results achieved by the ground tenant; but there is no single, easy approach. A ground landlord might accept a share of its ground tenant's rental income, cash flow (before or after debt service), refinancing proceeds or sales proceeds. The implications of such sharing or joint venture-type arrangements are many.

Renewal Terms

The initial term of a ground lease reflects the economic life of the project, the minimum time required for financing, and the jurisdiction's legal requirements. Part of the 'implied' rent is the residual value of the improvements at the end of the lease term, in effect, a lump sum final payment in the form of a used building. So, the parties have to agree on the number and length of any renewal options. The preconditions for exercise of a renewal option aren't very different than for space leases. How much notice will be required? Can the tenant exercise the option at any time? What form must the notice of exercise take?

Most leases do not permit a tenant to exercise a renewal option if in default: sometimes at the time of exercise; sometimes when the renewal term would begin; and, sometimes both times. Tenants, especially those with bargaining power, resist such tests and say that if they are in default and the landlord doesn't want them, it should evict them and not mess around with a renewal right. A valuable investment would be lost—in essence, a default that doesn't go to the heart of the bargain could work a forfeiture. Also, to enhance leasehold financeability, it is common for a ground tenant to exercise a renewal option well in advance. Thus, ground lease renewal provisions frequently omit or seriously modify the 'no default' precondition and commonly impose a 'reminder notice' obligation on the ground landlord.

Reversion

Getting ownership of the ground tenant's improvements at the end of the ground lease term may be a valuable component of the ground landlord's economic reward. If the improvements are generally usable and not obsolete, the ground landlord will inherit a pot of gold at the end of the lease. The bonus might even come early if the ground lease ends early. But, if the improvements were for a special purpose, or were economically obsolete, they would be a burden, the removal of which would eat into whatever the landlord had received as rent.

The parties need to remember that the ground lease might terminate early by reason of a taking or major destruction. In such cases, instead of getting the improvements into the ground landlord's hands, the battle shifts to how the resulting insurance proceeds or condemnation award is handled. Not *52 only will the improvements require repair or razing, the lenders will be looking for all or a share of the award.

If restoration is feasible, the ground lease and corollary financing documents must give primacy to use of the insurance proceeds and condemnation award for that purpose.

A convenient concept about the reversionary interest rests on the changing ratio of 'ownership' interests between the ground landlord and the ground tenant. It is most easily understood by looking at some extremes. Make the assumption that the ground lease term is 30 years beyond the day the improvements are complete. On day one, the ground tenant 'owns' the entire set of improvements. At the end of 30 years, the ground landlord expects to own all the improvements. Midway, at the 15-year mark, the ground landlord's ownership interest is 50 percent.

Here's how to apply the principle: If the property were taken by eminent domain at the 15-year point, half of the value of the improvements would reflect the ground tenant's interest and the other half would reflect the ground landlord's reversionary interest. Various subtleties, depending on the nature of the lease and the nature of the project, will fine tune such an approach, but the basic principle remains valid.

Another reversion concern to be addressed is providing for turn-over of the improvements in some form of good condition. Often, the ground tenant is a special purpose entity with no significant assets beyond its leasehold interest, which will be zero once the ground lease has terminated. Consequently, a ground landlord must insist on inspection rights throughout the term, and be willing to prosecute a ground tenant's default if its tenant doesn't satisfy ongoing maintenance obligations.

Handling Defaults

A ground lease is founded on a very different economic model than one finds in the common space lease. A ground tenant can expect to enjoy largely unrestricted use of the ground landlord's land for a lengthy lease term. Often, it will borrow a great deal of money from a lender that wants its loan to be secured by the tenant's interest in the ground lease, and in the building and other improvements to be built with that money. As previously stated, the ground landlord looks forward to a dependable stream of rent income, and to get the improvements when the lease's term comes to an end. That pits the ground landlord against the pairing of tenant and leasehold lender, for unlike the case of a space lease, the landlord can get a windfall if the lease's term ends early. In this zero sum game, the ground tenant forfeits a very valuable building and other improvements and, absent some other protection, the lender would be wiped out.

. . .

A tenant can breach its lease obligation in two ways. It can fail to pay rent or rent-like items to its landlord (monetary breaches), or it can do something it shouldn't have done or fail to do something it should have done (non-monetary breaches). Monetary breaches can be dealt with easily. The ground tenant or its leasehold lender can just make the payment or post security.

So, with appropriate protective notice provisions and with a mechanism for resolving disputes, such as through the use of arbitration, a ground landlord's legitimate interest in being paid can be properly balanced against its ground tenant's (and the leasehold lender's) legitimate fear of forfeiture.

Non-monetary breaches are less easily handled. They can range from trivial to serious. Sometimes, it isn't clear whether there is a breach at all. If the ground landlord legitimately wants to see its tenant's ground lease obligations fulfilled, rather than enjoying the reversion early, it could cure the alleged breach itself and convert the claimed non-monetary default into a monetary one, or it could seek injunctive relief or some other determination that the alleged breach is real and needs to be cured by the ground tenant (or, acting for the ground tenant, the leasehold lender).

Insurance Issues/Dealing with Damage and Destruction

Everybody cares that a ground leased building is adequately insured. Throughout the course of the lease, the landlord, tenant, and their respective lenders each have an economic interest in the physical improvements, with their value shifting over time, from tenant to landlord. So, all of them want to make sure the leased improvements are adequately insured.

Full replacement cost coverage is the gold standard and 'agreed amount' coverage may be the higher, platinum standard. If the replacement cost is adequately covered and an insurance services office causes of loss, special form policy form is used, the cost to rebuild will be paid by the insurer, except for losses resulting from specifically excluded perils. Coverage gaps can be filled by extra-cost endorsements, such as one that covers a situation where a change in law precludes rebuilding the improvements as originally constructed (*i.e.,* an ordinance or laws endorsement). Other endorsements might include extra demolition, coverage or coverage for losses from earthquakes, windstorms or flooding.

To keep the rent stream coming to the ground landlord, its tenant should have business income coverage as a form of 'rent insurance.' This is important, because almost no ground lease provides for a rent abatement following a fire or other cause of property damage. A ground tenant may be required to carry a utility services time element policy endorsement that covers an off-premises interruption in utility services.

A full replacement coverage policy only pays the full amount if the insured building is rebuilt after the loss. Otherwise, the policy will only pay the building's replacement cost, adjusted downward for physical depreciation. That makes it extremely important for the lease to provide that the damaged property must be restored. Insurance proceeds might be made payable to a special insurance trustee to protect the parties.

If the ground landlord doesn't actually carry the project's property insurance, it will want to be named as a loss payee under the ground tenant's property insurance policy. Each fee and leasehold lender will want to be named as an insured mortgagee.

Where the ground leased premises are part of a larger complex, especially one with shared facilities such as parking garages, power stations, sewerage treatment buildings, or pumping or sprinkler standby sheds, the ground tenant will want its ground landlord to carry the same kind of property insurance discussed above.

It isn't always clear that the parties will want to rebuild substantially damaged improvements. In the early years of a long-term ground lease, the ground landlord's residual interest in the improvements is slight. If the improvements are not rebuilt and what remains is razed, with the ground restored to a level reusable condition, a ground landlord may be willing to accept that for what would have been the residual value of the improvements. Near the end of the term, the landlord will 'own' nearly all of the value in the improvements, but they may be obsolete. Add the interests of competing lenders, and it will become clear that each situation will need to be analyzed on its own before the ground lease can be signed. A useful general approach may be to require restoration of the damaged improvements by the ground tenant, except near the end of the term when the insurance proceeds would be paid to the landlord.

Options to Buy

A ground leased scenario is almost always a single tenant property complex—a project fully divorced from its neighbors. That makes it workable for the parties to reach agreement on the tenant's right to own the property. If the *raison d'être* for the ground lease in the first place is the landlord's unwillingness to sell the property, a right of first refusal scheme may be the only mutually acceptable lease provision. Once the landlord decides to sell, it should not care to whom the sale is made, as long as it winds up with substantially the same economic outcome.

Of lesser value to a ground tenant would be a right of first offer. Of course, the parties could theoretically agree on a true purchase option, but given the most common reasons for using a ground lease, that's probably unappealing at any point other than the end of the lease term. Such purchase options, however, are common where the ground lease is a financing device.

Financing the Lease: A Critical Issue

Unlike land, a tenant's leasehold interest is not tangible. A lease can be terminated, and thus is risky collateral. So, lenders need protection from premature termination, including by default or bankruptcy. If the tenant's loan goes unpaid, its lender needs to step into a lease it can handle. It needs to "resell" the lease (*i.e.,* assign it), and thereby get its money out. Without special lease provisions, a leasehold lender would be like any other assignee, and be left (unsatisfactorily) at the mercy of the landlord. For that reason, common approval criteria and other restrictions need to be eliminated if the leasehold lender were to become the tenant. One less than obvious example is that the lender will only be willing to have lease liability while it 'owns' the lease, not after it 'resells' it.

There are some circumstances where the lease will be terminated and neither the lender nor the landlord can stop it, such as where a tenant rejects the ground lease in bankruptcy. For that reason, a leasehold lender will want a recognition agreement that the landlord will enter into the very same lease with the lender for whatever term would have remained but for the bankruptcy rejection.

Subtenants and Transfers

In a ground lease where a tenant is constructing substantial improvements, the tenant usually has a greater financial interest in the real property than does its landlord. Thus, the landlord should not have approval or similar rights that are anywhere near what one usually sees in a space lease. Once the improvements are finished, the landlord has a great deal of collateral behind the tenant's promise to pay rent. Basically, absent special circumstances, don't expect to see much in the way of requirements imposed on a ground tenant's free right to assign or sublet. it would be appropriate, however, to require that the improvements be completed before any assignment takes place.

Bankruptcy

No lease is changing the Bankruptcy Code. Thus, each party and each lender needs to protect itself against a party's bankruptcy. This is a complicated area of law. The protective provisions found in a sophisticated space lease are routinely the same as those in a ground lease. A major difference comes in the case of landlord bankruptcy. When a bankrupt landlord rejects a lease, the lease is over, but the tenant may remain in possession. It needs to provide all of the services that its landlord would have furnished, but it can deduct the cost of replacing those services from the rent itself. In the absolute net ground lease, this isn't a tremendous burden, but still will constitute a hassle. What a ground tenant has to watch for, however, is that its post-landlord bankruptcy acts or omissions don't put it in the same position that Qualitech, a very unhappy ground tenant, found itself in *Precision Industries, Inc. v. Qualitech SBQ, LLC.*[16]

Nancy R. Little, Financeable Ground Leases: An Overview*

Modern Real Estate Transactions, American Law Institute
Continuing Legal Education.
Westlaw CV008 ALI-CLE 1699 (2013).

1. INTRODUCTION.

Most lenders will accept a ground lease as a part of the collateral package as long as the ground lease is "financeable." A "financeable" ground lease either provides for "subordination" of the landlord's fee interest or contains provisions to protect a leasehold mortgagee from certain risks associated with loss of the leasehold interest as a result of the termination of the ground lease. Although a "subordinated fee" is less common, there are situations in which a ground lessor will be willing to partially or fully "subordinate" or subject its fee interest in the land to the lender's mortgage. In that case, however, there will be certain protections against loss of the fee interest that the ground lessor will want from the lender. For a leasehold mortgage, the lender will require certain mortgagee protections in the ground lease to feel comfortable that it is not at risk that the ground lessor will terminate the ground lease on which the leasehold mortgage is predicated if the ground lessee defaults in the performance of its obligations under the ground lease or the ground lease is otherwise terminated.

---

[16]   327 F.3d 537 (7th Cir. 2003).

*   Reprinted with permission from the author and American Law Institute CLE, www.ali-cle.org.

2.   PERSPECTIVES.

2.1 Lender. In order to lend on collateral that includes a ground lease, the lender must have a subordinated fee mortgage from the landlord or a leasehold mortgage based on a ground lease that permits the lender to foreclose on the ground lessee, including the ground lessee's leasehold interest under the ground lease, and to manage and/or dispose of the collateral following foreclosure. The lender is at risk of losing its investment if the ground lease is terminated before the loan is repaid in full as a result of expiration or early termination of the ground lease. Therefore, the lender wants adequate protections in the ground lease, such as notice of the ground lessee's default and cure rights, in order to avoid early termination.

2.2 Ground Lessee. The ground lessee is concerned with the ability to finance construction of its improvements and subsequently refinance the property, if necessary. The ground lessee is also concerned with financeability in the event of a sale of the property because the buyer may need or want to obtain financing secured by the property. Therefore, the ground lessee as well as the lender, wants to be sure that the ground lease is financeable.

2.3 Ground Lessor. The ground lessor is willing to entertain certain mortgagee protections in the ground lease, and possibly subordination of its fee interest, in order to facilitate the ground lessee's development of the land from which the ground lessor expects to derive revenue. However, the ground lessor wants to minimize the likelihood that it could lose its fee interest in the property in the case of a subordinated fee. In the case of a leasehold mortgage, the ground lessor wants to limit the extent to which the lender can restrict the ground lessor's exercise of its remedies if the ground lessee defaults under the ground lease. Consequently, the ground lessor's concerns may be at odds with those of the lender and the ground lessee who need the ability to finance based on the leasehold.

3.   SUBORDINATION OF THE FEE.

3.1 General. "Subordination of the fee" is a bit of a misnomer because the concept really involves the ground lessor's joinder in the mortgage for the purpose of subjecting its interest in the property to the lien of the mortgage and permitting the mortgagee to foreclose not just on the ground lessee's leasehold interest but also on the ground lessor's fee interest in the property. The ground lessor is not obligated to pay the debt or to pay or perform any of the other obligations of the ground lessee/borrower under the loan. However, in the event of a foreclosure by the lender, the ground lessor could lose its interest in the property. As a result, the ground lessor may negotiate with the leasehold mortgagee for certain rights, such as notice of default under the loan by the ground lessee/borrower and a right to cure such loan defaults.

3.2 Subordination of Fee by Ground Lessor. Certain ground lessors, such as governmental entities, may be prohibited from entering into subordinated fee mortgages. However, other lessors may be willing to do so to obtain higher rents and/or to encourage development of adjacent property in which the ground lessor has an interest, but subject to such protections as the ground lessor may be able to negotiate with the lender. Subordination of the fee may also be a possibility if the ground lessor and ground lessee are affiliates or venture partners.

3.5 <u>Conditions to Subordination of Fee</u>. The ground lessor may also impose conditions and/or demand involvement in the development process in order to protect its fee interest. Fee owner protections, such as approval rights, may be burdensome to a ground lessee in trying to expedite development of the project. However, such rights may help the ground lessor protect itself. The ground lessor may impose a cap or limit on the amount of the loan (*e.g.*, the ground lessor will subordinate the fee but only if the loan does not exceed some percentage of the appraised value of the project). Other conditions and/or restrictions that the ground lessor may consider including in its agreement to subordinate are budget approval, minimum equity commitment, use of consultants to oversee construction and development, a requirement for a take-out commitment, etc. In contrast, a ground lessee will want the fewest possible conditions to avoid potential delays in the development of the project.

4.   LEASEHOLD FINANCING.

A financeable ground lease provides the leasehold mortgagee with protections and rights designed to avoid termination of the ground lease during the term of the loan and to permit the lender to foreclose on the leasehold estate and dispose of the collateral. An overview of such protections follows.

4.1 <u>Basic Terms</u>. The leasehold mortgagee will need to be comfortable with the basic terms of the lease, including rent and term. Most lenders will want to see a fixed or predictable rent. Most leasehold lenders will want the term of the ground lease to exceed the maturity date of the loan by a substantial amount of time in case the lender needs an extended period after foreclosure to recover its investment. The leasehold mortgagee may also want the right to exercise renewal options even if the ground lessee is in default, as well as the right to exercise any purchase option the ground lessee may have. The lender will not want the ground lease to unduly restrict the use of the property and will look for a fairly broad "use" clause in the ground lease to facilitate disposition of the property at or after foreclosure. The ground lease should also include a "no merger" clause providing that the leasehold and fee estates do not merge in the event that the ground lessee acquires the fee interest in the property. The lender will not want continuing liability under the ground lease in case of foreclosure and will want the ground lease to provide that, in the event the lender or its affiliate becomes the ground lessee following foreclosure, it will have liability under the ground lease only during its tenure as ground lessee and not after its further assignment of the ground lease to a third party. The lender will also want to see as few "personal" covenants (*i.e.*, covenants that can only be performed by the then-current ground lessee) as possible in the ground lease to avoid the situation in which a purchaser at foreclosure could not cure the prior ground lessee's default. A waiver in the ground lease of any landlord's lien is also desirable from the lender's perspective as well as the ground lessee's. Obviously, the lender will want the ground lease to provide that the ground lessee has the right to mortgage its interest in the property.

4.2 <u>Right to Cure</u>. The leasehold mortgagee will want to receive written notice of any default by the ground lessee at the same time any such notice is received by the ground lessee, and the lender may require that a default notice given to the ground lessee not be effective unless it is simultaneously given to the lender. A default under the ground lease should also be a default under the loan. If the lender receives notice of the default, it can monitor (and encourage) the borrower/ground lessee's cure of the ground lease (and loan) default. The lender will also require that it be provided with an opportunity to cure the default in the event that the ground lessee does not, and the lender will want an agreement from the ground lessor to accept the lender's cure. The amount of time given to the lender to cure the ground lessee's default is the subject of debate in lender-ground lessor negotiations. A lender generally wants a cure period in addition to the one provided to the ground lessee to effect a cure. Most ground lessors argue that the lender should have a cure period that coincides with the ground lessee's cure period and do not want to give the lender an additional time for cure. The obvious issue is that the lender does not want to incur costs to cure the ground lessee's default unless and until the ground lessee defaults beyond the cure period set forth in the ground lease. Therefore, the lender wants to wait until the cure period under the ground lease has expired to see if the ground lessee cures the default. If not, the lender may want as much as an additional thirty or sixty days, for example, beyond the cure period given to the ground lessee under the ground lease. Some lenders may also require that a second or additional default notice be given to the lender before the ground lessor can exercise its remedies under the ground lease. As noted above, such provisions are subject to negotiation between the ground lessor and the lender.

4.3 <u>Waiver of Certain Defaults; No Termination Pending Foreclosure</u>. An additional consideration is whether the ground lessee's default is capable of being cured or only curable after foreclosure by the lender. For example, defaults based on the ground lessee's insolvency or failure to complete construction by a required date or to deliver financial statements are not susceptible of cure by the lender. In addition, operational and/or maintenance defaults may only be curable following foreclosure and the taking of possession. The lender cannot afford to have the ground lease terminate if the default cannot be cured and will want the ground lessor to refrain from terminating the ground lease for non-curable defaults or defaults that can only be cured by a party in possession. In the latter case, the lender will want the ground lessor to be estopped from terminating the ground lease or exercising other remedies until the lender has completed foreclosure on the property. Most lenders will also require additional time, beyond the ground lessee's cure period, to acquire title to the property. In certain jurisdictions, this time period may be quite lengthy because of the length of time it takes to foreclose. Another frequent lender request is that non-curable defaults by the ground lessee be waived following foreclosure.

4.4 <u>Assignability</u>. A leasehold mortgagee will require that the ground lease be assignable to the mortgagee (or an affiliate) or to a purchaser in foreclosure. In order to recoup as much of the lender's investment as possible, the ground lease must be assignable, without the consent of the ground lessor, at or following foreclosure, including by a sale to a third party following a purchase at foreclosure or acceptance of a deed in lieu of foreclosure. However, the ground lessor may not be willing to forego all restrictions on assignment and may negotiate for reasonable restrictions on future assignments that are not likely to impair a foreclosure sale.

4.5 <u>Subletting</u>. In the event that the property is not sold to a third party at foreclosure or shortly thereafter, the lender may need to sublet the property. Therefore, the lender will want the ability to sublease without the ground lessor's consent with as few restrictions on use as possible. The lender may also want the ground lessor to agree to provide non-disturbance agreements to subtenants.

4.6 <u>New Lease</u>. The lender may also require that the ground lease contain a provision that, upon termination of the ground lease, including termination as a result of rejection of the ground lease in bankruptcy, the ground lessor will enter into a new ground lease with the lender (or its affiliate) or a third party. Note, however, such an agreement to enter into a new lease could be treated as an executory contract or an option to lease which could present issues in the case of a ground lessor bankruptcy and/or in jurisdictions where the rule against perpetuities could apply to an option to lease. Intervening liens may also affect the priority of a new lease entered into by the ground lessor and the lender.

4.7 <u>No Amendments, Etc., Without Lender's Consent; Right to Exercise Renewals</u>. The lender will require the right to consent to amendments to the ground lease, as well as the right to consent to any early cancellation or termination of the ground lease. The lender will also want its mortgage to control with respect to use of proceeds of casualty and condemnation awards.

4.8 <u>Construction Issues</u>. Because of the uncertainty associated with construction projects, a construction lender lending on a ground leased project will have additional concerns. The ground lease may provide that the improvements must be completed within a certain time period or must comply with certain use restrictions. The lender may request additional time to complete the construction, as well as the right to change the use of the property and the ability to substitute a new ground lessee.

4.9 <u>Miscellaneous</u>. The lender will not want any encumbrances on the fee interest in the property with priority over the lease. A recorded subordination, nondisturbance and attornment agreement may be required. The lender will also be wary of operating covenants. In addition, the ground lessor will be asked to provide estoppel certificates upon the request of the lender.

. . .

1. CALCULATING GROUND RENT

936 Second Avenue L.P. v. Second Corporate Development Co., Inc.

Court of Appeals of New York, 2008.
10 N.Y.3d 628, 891 N.E.2d 289.

OPINION OF THE COURT

GRAFFEO, J.

In this lease dispute, the issue is whether the net lease itself must be considered by appraisers in valuing the demised premises for purposes of establishing the net rent for a renewal term of the lease. Because the net lease does not exclude its consideration, we conclude that it must be taken into account in valuing the property.

In 1966, defendant Second Corporate Development Co., Inc. (lessor), the owner of property located at East 50th Street and Second Avenue in Manhattan, entered into a 20-year net lease with the predecessor-in-interest to plaintiff 936 Second Avenue L.P. (lessee).[1] The property consists of three adjoining buildings that house 22 rent-regulated apartments and four retail stores. Lessee was afforded the option to renew its lease for two additional 20-year terms.

Under the terms of the lease, the annual rent for the first 15 years escalated from $20,000 in 1966 to $33,000 in 1981. In the event lessee exercised a renewal option, the parties agreed that the annual rent would be seven percent of the value of the demised premises as of the date of commencement of each successive 10-year period.[2] The lease defines the "value of the demised premises" to include the value of both the land and the buildings and improvements located on it. If the parties fail to agree upon the value of the premises for purposes of calculating the annual rent, the lessor and lessee are each to select an appraiser to value the property. If the parties continue to dispute valuation, the lease provides for the appointment of a third appraiser to settle the issue.

In March 2005, lessee renewed the lease for the second 20-year term, such term commencing on November 1, 2006. Unable to negotiate the rent for the first 10 years of that renewal term, lessor and lessee each retained an appraiser in accordance with the procedure outlined in the lease. Lessor's appraiser valued the premises at $7.1 million while lessee's appraiser valued it at $3.43 million.[3] According to lessee's appraiser, one of the principal reasons for the disparity between the two appraisals was the fact that he considered the effect of the net lease on the value of the premises while lessor's appraiser did not take the lease into consideration.

---

[1] The property is currently owned by Second Corporate's successors-in-interest: defendants The Horace Wilson Marital Trust, Julia B. Wilson, Trustee; The John A. Wilson Revocable Trust U/A Dated 3/1/00, John A. Wilson, Trustee; and Anne W Evans. Defendants will be collectively referred to as "lessor."

[2] The parties also agreed that the annual rent for the relevant 10-year period could not be less than the rent in effect during the preceding period.

[3] Lessor's appraiser employed both the comparable sales and income capitalization approaches; lessee's appraiser used only the income capitalization method.

Lessee commenced this action seeking a declaratory judgment that the lease and its term and conditions must be taken into account in calculating the value of the premises for purposes of determining the annual rental rate for the first 10 years of the second renewal term. Lessor counterclaimed for a declaration that the lease should not be considered in appraising the property. Both parties moved for summary judgment.

Supreme Court granted lessor's motion and declared that the lease is not to be considered in calculating the value of the premises, and the Appellate Division affirmed. We granted lessee leave to appeal and now reverse.

Analysis

In *New York Overnight Partners v. Gordon,* 88 N.Y.2d 716, 649 N.Y.S.2d 928, 673 N.E.2d 123 (1996), the owner of a parcel of land in New York City had a long-term lease with the owner of a hotel located on the property. The rent for the 15-year renewal term of the lease was to be calculated at 6 1/2% of the "appraised value of the land" (*id.* at 718, 649 N.Y.S.2d 928, 673 N.E.2d 123). The lease expressly excluded from the definition of "land" the "buildings and improvements thereon erected" (*id.* at 719 n. 1, 649 N.Y.S.2d 928, 673 N.E.2d 123). When the parties deadlocked on the meaning of the phrase "appraised value of the land," they sought judicial interpretation to settle the dispute. We affirmed the Appellate Division order directing the appraiser "to determine the value of the land as if vacant and unimproved, subject to current zoning restrictions and contractual limitations, and to consider the effect of the lease on the value of the land" (*id.* at 720, 649 N.Y.S.2d 928, 673 N.E.2d 123). In reaching that conclusion, we observed that "[w]hen the language of the lease so dictates, appraisals must take into consideration all restrictions—including current zoning regulations—and encumbrances on the land, as well as the lease term" (*id.* at 721, 649 N.Y.S.2d 928, 673 N.E.2d 123).

Here, article 33(c) of the lease provides that the net rent for the first 10 years of the second renewal term "shall be at the rate per annum of a sum equal to seven percent (7%) of the value of the demised premises as of the date of commencement of such first ten years, to wit, November 1, 2006, such value to be determined as provided in Article 30." Article 30, in turn, defines the term "value of the demised premises" to mean

> "the value of the demised premises together with all buildings and improvements thereon including any and all additions and improvements erected by Tenant. In the determination of such Value of the demised premises' as herein provided no effect shall be given to any damage, destruction or loss which Tenant is obligated to repair, replace or rebuild, and any existing or possible future damage, destruction or loss shall not be taken into account for the purposes of such determination."[4]

The lease is silent as to whether the lease itself should be taken into account in determining the value of the demised premises.

---

[4] The lease separately describes the "demised premises" as "[a]ll those certain lots, pieces or parcels of land with the buildings and improvements thereon erected, situate, lying and being in the Borough of Manhattan" matching a specified metes-and-bounds description.

Lessor argues that *New York Overnight Partners,* which required consideration of the lease, is distinguishable because the property in that case was to be valued as if vacant while the valuation of the property here must include both the land and buildings. Further, while acknowledging that the lease may impact the value of the property, lessor nevertheless contends that the absence of language in the lease expressly requiring its consideration means that the appraisers were obligated to ignore it. Lessee counters that because the net lease affects the property value, it must be considered unless the lease specifically precludes the appraisers from factoring it into the valuation.

In general, "the market value of real property is the amount which one desiring but not compelled to purchase will pay under ordinary conditions to a seller who desires but is not compelled to sell" (*Plaza Hotel Assoc. v. Wellington Assoc.,* 37 N.Y.2d 273, 277, 372 N.Y.S.2d 35, 333 N.E.2d 346 [1975], *rearg. denied* 37 N.Y.2d 924, 378 N.Y.S.2d 1027, 340 N.E.2d 754 [1975]; *see also Matter of Commerce Holding Corp. v. Board of Assessors of Town of Babylon,* 88 N.Y.2d 724, 729, 649 N.Y.S.2d 932, 673 N.E.2d 127 [1996]). Case law has long recognized that "valuations of land must take into consideration all encumbrances thereon, including restrictions as to its use, unless there is a clear provision to the contrary" (*Plaza Hotel Assoc. v. Wellington Assoc.,* 55 Misc.2d 483, 487, 285 N.Y.S.2d 941 [Sup.Ct., N.Y. County 1967], *affd.* 28 A.D.2d 1209, 285 N.Y.S.2d 267 [1st Dept 1967], *affd. on Sup. Ct. op.* 22 N.Y.2d 846, 293 N.Y.S.2d 108, 239 N.E.2d 736 [1968], *rearg. denied* 22 N.Y.2d 972, 295 N.Y.S.2d 1032, 242 N.E.2d 498 [1968]; *see also United Equities v. Mardordic Realty Co.,* 8 A.D.2d 398, 400, 187 N.Y.S.2d 714 [1st Dept 1959], *affd. without op.* 7 N.Y.2d 911, 197 N.Y.S.2d 478, 165 N.E.2d 426 [1960] ["Unless there be express provision to the contrary, the provisions of the lease between the parties insofar as they affect the fair market value of the land must be given effect"]). In valuing real property "[s]pecial attention must be given to limitations on ownership rights, which include easements, encroachments, leases, and the disposition of air or subsurface rights" and an appraiser must "analyze all of the economic benefits or disadvantages created by the lease" (Appraisal Institute, The Appraisal of Real Estate, at 55, 82 [12th ed.]).

Additionally, unless the lease agreement provides otherwise, appraisers generally consider the highest and best use of the property in determining its value (*see id.* at 305).[5] This is true whether the property is valued as vacant or developed (*see id.* at 306).[6] But in determining the highest and best use of a property, appraisers necessarily must examine any restrictions or limitations, including long-term leases, that may impact the highest and best use for which the property may be utilized (*see id.* at 311, 316).

We therefore conclude that, absent an agreement to the contrary, the effect of a net lease must be considered in valuing property for the

---

[5] The highest and best use of a parcel "provides the foundation for a thorough investigation of the competitive position of the property in the minds of market participants. Consequently, highest and best use can be described as the foundation on which market value rests" (Appraisal Institute, The Appraisal of Real Estate, at 305 [12th ed.]).

[6] Indeed, lessor's and lessee's appraisers each examined the highest and best use of the premises in their respective appraisal reports in this case.

purpose of setting rent for a renewal lease term. Such a rule comports with precedent, appraisal practices and common sense. If the parties to a lease desire to exclude that encumbrance in valuing the property, they need only include language to that effect in their agreement. Indeed, courts have routinely enforced such provisions (*see e.g. 201–203 Lexington Ave. Corp. v. 205/215 Lexington Ltd. Partnership,* 224 A.D.2d 183, 637 N.Y.S.2d 125 [1st Dept.1996], *lv. denied* 88 N.Y.2d 813, 649 N.Y.S.2d 380, 672 N.E.2d 606 [1996]; *Ruth v. S.Z.B. Corp.,* 2 Misc.2d 631, 153 N.Y.S.2d 163 [Sup.Ct., N.Y. County 1956], *affd.* 2 A.D.2d 970, 158 N.Y.S.2d 754 [1st Dept.1956]).

Here, although the net lease expressly precludes the consideration of any damage or destruction that lessee is obligated to repair, it does not exclude existence of the lease itself in valuing the premises. Consequently, the appraisers must examine the effect of the lease's term and conditions in determining the value of the property in connection with establishing the net rent.

Accordingly, the order of the Appellate Division should be reversed, with costs, and judgment granted declaring in accordance with this opinion.

Order reversed, etc.

Chief Judge Kaye and Judges Ciparick, Read, Smith, Pigott and Jones concur.

2. Mortgaging the Leasehold and the Fee

Balch v. Leader Federal Bank for Savings

Supreme Court of Arkansas, 1993.
315 Ark. 444, 868 S.W.2d 47.

Phillip D. Hout, Special Justice.

On May 13, 1970, the owner of four certain real estate lots in downtown Little Rock (the hotel lots) entered into a Net Ground Lease (ground lease) with a lessee who intended to construct a building on the lots for use as a hotel. The lessee owned four adjacent lots (the adjacent lots) which the lessee intended to use as a parking garage in conjunction with the hotel. Paragraph 17 of the ground lease contained the following language:

> MORTGAGE OF THE FEE. The Lessor agrees that this lease will be subject and subordinate to the lien of first mortgage to be held by Liberty National Life Insurance Company of Birmingham, Alabama, its successors and assigns, placed or to be placed upon the leased premises as the permanent loan financing for improvements to be erected upon said premises, the maximum term of said mortgage not to exceed thirty (30) years. This agreement on the part of the Lessor to mortgage the fee shall apply only to the original construction loan and permanent financing loan and any renewal, extension or refinancing thereof. . . . Provided, however, that this lease shall be subordinated only for the actual cost of the improvements placed upon the demised premises or the amount of the loan, whichever is less.

The lessee obtained a loan from Liberty National Life Insurance Company (Liberty National) to finance the construction of the hotel, and the repayment of the loan was secured by a mortgage on the hotel lots that was signed by both the owner and the lessee.

Later the appellants, Memory B. Balch and Beverly Balch Price (the Balches), became the owners of the hotel lots, and The Crestwood Company (Crestwood) became the tenant under the ground lease and the owner of the adjacent lots. The parties have stipulated that the ground lease remained binding on the Balches and Crestwood, and that the mortgage to Liberty National was effective to encumber the fee simple absolute interest in the hotel lots.

On August 24, 1987, when the Liberty National loan was in default, Crestwood obtained a loan from appellee, Leader Federal Bank for Savings (Leader Federal), in an amount that was substantially equal to the unpaid balance of the Liberty National loan. The proceeds of the Leader Federal loan were used to pay off the Liberty National loan, and the mortgage securing the Liberty National loan was released.

All of the documents for the Leader Federal loan were prepared by or at the direction of Leader Federal. The loan was evidenced by a note signed by Crestwood, and it was secured by a mortgage on the hotel lots owned by the Balches, and also on the adjacent lots owned by Crestwood. Only Crestwood and its partners signed the mortgage, in which Crestwood acknowledged that it owned only a leasehold interest in the hotel lots. The Balches were not asked to sign the mortgage with Crestwood, nor did they do so. However, the Balches were asked to sign separate but identical Estoppel and Subordination Certificates (Certificate) which state:

TO: Leader Federal Savings & Loan Association. . . .

THIS IS TO CERTIFY THAT:

1. The undersigned is the Lessor under that . . . Net Ground Rental Lease. . . .

2. That said Net Ground Rental Lease has not been modified, . . . in any respect and is the only Lease between the undersigned and the Lessor. . . .

3. That the Net Ground Rental Lease is not in default. . . .

4. Lessor acknowledges and consents to the loan in the amount of approximately $1,924,000.00 by Leader Federal Savings & Loan Association to The Crestwood Company to be secured by a mortgage on the premises which is the subject of the Net Ground Rental Lease. Lessor recognizes that the proceeds of such loan are to repay the loan to Liberty National Life Insurance Company and therefore pursuant to Paragraph 17 of the Net Ground Rental Lease, the Net Ground Rental Lease is subordinate to the loan and mortgage in favor of Leader Federal Savings & Loan Association.

5. That this Estoppel and Subordination Certificate is made to induce Leader Federal Savings & Loan Association to consummate a mortgage loan secured by a mortgage on the premises described above, knowing that Leader Federal

Savings & Loan Association relies upon the truth and accuracy of this certificate in disbursing said funds for this loan.

Crestwood defaulted in the payment of the Leader Federal loan, and Leader Federal sued to foreclose the fee interest in the hotel lots and its improvements, as well as the adjacent lots. Leader Federal contends, and the lower court found, that the Certificate, when considered with the lease, is tantamount to a lien on the Balches' fee interest in the hotel lots. The Balches contend that they were not a party to the mortgage and that the Certificate only subordinates their interest in the ground lease, and not their fee interest in the hotel lots, to Leader Federal's mortgage.

The case was submitted to the chancellor on a stipulation of facts, depositions and oral arguments of counsel. The record indicates that the chancellor may have had difficulty in determining the intent of the parties with respect to the meaning of the various documents involved, but the chancellor ruled that Leader Federal is entitled to foreclose the Balches' fee interest in the hotel lots under the mortgage.

For reversal, the Balches contend that (1) the chancellor erred in holding that the ground lease and Certificate collectively constitute a lien upon which Leader Federal could foreclose the Balches' fee interest in the hotel lots; (2) the chancellor erred in applying a "preponderance of the evidence", instead of a "clear and convincing", standard to the proof offered by Leader Federal to establish that the Certificate and the ground lease, considered together, constitute a lien on the Balches' fee interest in the hotel lots; and (3) the chancellor erred by not making a finding on the extent of the Balches' subordination in light of the limiting language of the ground lease.

We find the chancellor's decision to be in error.

It is conceivable that a lessor might effectively subject his fee interest in real estate to the lien of a mortgage that is signed only by the lessee. Such a result would occur if the lessor signs a subordination agreement or other document that contains language indicating that he clearly and unequivocally thereby intends to subject his fee interest to the mortgage, or if that intent can clearly and reasonably be determined from other attendant circumstances. The same result would occur if the lessor signs a document that gives to another, such as the lessee, authority to sign the mortgage in behalf of the lessor. However, the intention of the parties at the time of execution of the documents, as expressed by the language employed therein, governs. Lightle v. Rotenberry, 166 Ark. 337, 266 S.W. 297 (1924).

In this case, the Certificate appears on its face to be an act of the Balches that was intended to subordinate their interest in the *ground lease* to Leader Federal's mortgage. The Certificate refers only to the Balches' interest in the ground lease; and there is no clear reference in the Certificate to any intent by the Balches to subordinate their fee interest in the hotel lots, unless that intent can be found in the following language in the Certificate:

> Lessor . . . consents to the loan . . . to be secured by a mortgage on the premises which is the subject of the Net Ground Rental Lease. . . .

[T]his ... Certificate is made to induce Leader Federal ... to consummate a mortgage loan secured by a mortgage on the premises described above[.]

Leader Federal insists that such an intent is found in the totality of the transaction, including the language in the Certificate when considered together with the language contained in Paragraph 17 of the ground lease. We disagree.

To some extent, the language used in Paragraph 17 of the ground lease is confusing. Paragraph 17 is captioned "Mortgage of the Fee". The first sentence in Paragraph 17 states, "[t]he lessor agrees that *this lease* will be subject and subordinate to the lien" of a certain mortgage. The next sentence states, "[t]his *agreement* on the part of the Lessor to *mortgage the fee*"; and then the last sentence states, "*this lease* shall be subordinated only for. . . ." (Emphasis added).

Interpreting the ground lease most favorably to Leader Federal, it gave to the lessee the right to require the lessor to mortgage the fee interest in the lessor's land. The Balches' predecessor executed such a mortgage relative to the loan made by Liberty National, but they were not asked to execute a mortgage relative to the loan made by Leader Federal, nor did they do so. No language in the Certificate, standing alone, is facially sufficient to be construed as the granting of a lien by the Balches on their fee interest in the hotel lots. On its face, the purpose of the Certificate appears to have been to (1) identify the Balches as the lessors under the ground lease; (2) confirm that the ground lease had not been modified and that no other lease existed; (3) confirm that the ground lease was not in default; (4) evidence the Balches' consent to a loan to be made to Crestwood by Leader Federal in a specific amount, to be secured by a mortgage on the hotel lots and on the adjacent lots (but without specifying who would be asked to sign the mortgage), and to subordinate the Balches' interest in the *ground lease* to such mortgage; and (5) establish that the truth of the statements contained in the Certificate was an inducement to Leader Federal to make the loan to Crestwood. Absent an actual request for the lessor to sign a mortgage, a reasonable lessor who is presented such a document as the Certificate would logically deduce that the lender intended to take a mortgage only on the lessee's leasehold interest in the land. One would not normally think that by signing such a document he would be encumbering the fee interest in his land.

Therefore, the pivotal question to be resolved here is whether the Certificate, which appears on its face to be a subordination of the Balches' interest in the lease, was actually intended to be a subordination of their fee interest in the hotel lots.

In cases where a deed, absolute on its face, is alleged to actually constitute a mortgage, we have consistently held that the document is presumed to be what it appears to be, and that the party alleging it to be otherwise has the burden of proof by clear and convincing evidence. Carter v. Zachary, 243 Ark. 104, 418 S.W.2d 787 (1967); Wilson v. Mason, 191 Ark. 472, 86 S.W.2d 555 (1935); Blanton v. Davis, 107 Ark. 1, 154 S.W. 947 (1913); Duvall v. Laws, Swain & Murdoch, P.A., 32 Ark.App. 99, 797 S.W.2d 474 (1990); Brown v. Cole, 27 Ark.App. 213, 768 S.W.2d 549 (1989); Wensel v. Flatte, 27 Ark.App. 5, 764 S.W.2d 627 (1989). Clear and convincing evidence is that degree of proof that will produce in the trier of fact a firm conviction of the allegations sought to be established. First Nat'l Bank v. Rush, 30 Ark.App. 272, 785 S.W.2d 474 (1990).

Applying those principles to this case, the Certificate must be presumed to be what it appears to be on its face—a subordination of the Balches' interest in the ground lease—unless Leader Federal proves otherwise by clear and convincing evidence. Leader Federal argues that in cases where no parol evidence is produced to vary the terms of a document, "preponderance of the evidence" is the quantum of proof that should be required, while "clear and convincing" is the standard that should be applied only where parol evidence is offered. Leader Federal has cited no positive case law to support that view, and the argument is without merit. It is inconceivable that a party who has the burden of proving a proposition by clear and convincing evidence might avoid that standard of proof, and take advantage of a lesser standard, by abstaining from offering parol evidence. Further, in Hickman v. Trust of Heath, House and Boyles, 310 Ark. 333, 835 S.W.2d 880 (1992), the "clear and convincing" standard was applied to the interpretation of two documents when no parol evidence was offered to assist in the interpretation.

As the proponent of the proposition that the Certificate, when considered with the ground lease, was intended to constitute an encumbrance of the Balches' fee interest in the hotel lots, Leader Federal has the burden of proving that proposition. Since the Certificate does not appear on its face to encumber the fee, Leader Federal is required to meet its burden of proof by clear and convincing evidence, whether or not it chooses to present parol evidence.

At best, an ambiguity exists when the provisions of the Certificate are considered together with the applicable provisions of the ground lease. The Certificate states on its face that the Balches are subordinating their interest in the *ground lease*, while the ground lease, if given its most liberal interpretation, contains only an *agreement* to mortgage the fee. An agreement to mortgage property is an agreement to *execute* (or sign) and deliver a mortgage. It does not, in and of itself, grant a lien on the property. Does the *agreement* to sign a mortgage, which is contained in the ground lease that was signed long before the Certificate, modify the Balches' otherwise clear statement of intent in the Certificate to subordinate only their interest in the ground lease? We think not.

There is nothing in the Certificate to reasonably indicate that the Balches intended to confer upon Crestwood the authority to execute the mortgage on their behalf; and the mortgage does not indicate that Crestwood was acting in a representative capacity for the Balches in signing the mortgage. In fact, the mortgage recites that Crestwood had only a leasehold interest in the hotel lots. Further, there is no clear indication in the Certificate that the Balches thereby intended to subordinate anything other than their interest in the ground lease. To the contrary, the Certificate clearly states, "therefore, pursuant to Paragraph 17 of the . . . Lease, the . . . Lease is subordinate to the loan and mortgage in favor of Leader Federal[.]"

If Leader Federal had wanted a lien on the Balches' fee interest in the hotel lots, it could have insisted that the lien be granted in the conventional manner by requiring the Balches to sign a mortgage; or, in the alternative, it could have insisted on a lien in a less conventional manner by preparing the Certificate in such a way as to make it clear that the Balches were subordinating their *fee interest*, and not just their interest in the ground lease. A third way that Leader Federal could have obtained a lien on the Balches' fee interest would have been to prepare the Certificate in such a manner to make it clear that the Balches were appointing Crestwood as their attorney-in-fact to execute the mortgage in their behalf. None of those methods was successfully employed by Leader Federal.

The record indicates that the Certificate was prepared by or at the direction of Leader Federal. The record does not reflect who prepared the ground lease, but Leader Federal adopted the language of the ground lease by referring to it in the Certificate. The Certificate does not clearly reflect an intention by the Balches to encumber their fee interest or to subordinate their fee interest to Leader Federal's mortgage. When the provisions of the Certificate are considered with the applicable provisions of the ground lease, the most that can be said is that an ambiguity exists which must be resolved against Leader Federal, as the author of the Certificate. Planters Nat'l Bank of Mena v. Townsend, 197 Ark. 267, 123 S.W.2d 527 (1938).

The intention of an owner to encumber his property should never be established by mere inference or speculation. Where a document, which appears on its face to be only a subordination of an interest in a lease to a mortgage, is alleged to actually constitute an encumbrance of the fee interest in the land that is the subject of the lease, the document is presumed to be what it appears to be, and the party alleging it to be otherwise has the burden of proof by clear and convincing evidence. Blanton, 107 Ark. 1, 154 S.W. 947.

The only evidence in the record that might be found to establish an obligation on the Balches to encumber their fee interest is the language contained in Paragraph 17 of the ground lease. If that language is so construed, the Balches' obligation thereunder would be to mortgage their land if requested to do so. For reasons which are not clear in the record, neither Crestwood nor Leader Federal requested the Balches to sign a mortgage to secure Leader Federal's loan to Crestwood, and the Balches did not do so. The Certificate clearly states on its face that the *ground lease*, and not the Balches' fee interest, is subordinate to the mortgage; and the Certificate did not authorize Crestwood to sign the mortgage in behalf of the Balches. Therefore, it cannot be logically and reasonably concluded from the record that by signing the Certificate the Balches intended to encumber their fee interest in the hotel lots.

The Balches' contention that the chancellor erred by not making a finding as to the extent of their subordination should be resolved regardless of whether the Balches are found to have subordinated their interest in the ground lease or their interest in the fee. We find the Balches' position on this point to be without merit. By signing the Certificate, the Balches effectively either (1) agreed that the amount of the Leader Federal loan was equal to or less than the cost of the improvements placed on the hotel lots or (2) waived the applicable provisions of the ground lease regarding that limitation.

For the reasons stated, the decision below is reversed and the case is remanded to the lower court for the purpose of entering a decree that is consistent with this opinion.

HAYS, J., SPECIAL CHIEF JUSTICE EUGENE HUNT, and SPECIAL JUSTICE C. JOSEPH CALVIN, dissent.

HOLT, C.J., and DUDLEY and BROWN, JJ., not participating.

[The opinion of HUNT, SPECIAL CH. J., dissenting, is omitted.]

NOTES

1. *Escalators.* As indicated in *936 Second Avenue*, long term leases, expose the landlord to the risk of decreases in the value of the dollars with which rent is paid and to the risk of increases in real property taxes and maintenance and utility costs. One solution is to provide a formula in the lease for adjusting rental payments to keep pace with changes in the value of the leased property, the tenant's business, or in the economy generally. Thus, as indicated in the case, rent may be adjusted on the basis of periodic reevaluation of the premises. The parties must be careful, however, to clearly specify the standards by which the property is to be reappraised. See Harris Trust & Savings Bank v. LaSalle National Bank, 208 Ill.App.3d 447, 153 Ill.Dec. 450, 567 N.E.2d 408 (1990), appeal denied, 137 Ill.2d 665, 156 Ill.Dec. 561, 571 N.E.2d 148 (1991) (remanding for evidentiary hearing on question of whether appraiser was to consider the possibility of assemblage of lots as lease clause was ambiguous). A simpler, though less accurate mechanism for adjusting rents is the "step-up" clause, specifying the amounts and intervals by which rent will be increased. For example, the lease may provide that rent in the first year will be $1,200, to be stepped up in the second year to $1,800, and to $3,000 in the third. Obviously, step-up clauses are only as good as the landlord's and tenant's guesses about the property's future worth.

Linkage or index clauses, requiring periodic adjustments in rent based on a cost of living index such as the United States Bureau of Labor Statistics' consumer price index, operate almost as fluently as step-up clauses and offer greater certainty that rental payments will have a constant economic worth. More specific indices, oriented to the locale in which the property is situated or to the type of business conducted on the leased property, can also be used. But these indices are pegged to changes in overall economic conditions rather than shifts in the value of the particular real estate. The recalculation method of *936 Second Avenue* is designed to set rent based on the changing value of the rented property itself. How is the value of the land to be determined in the case? By what method? Is that consistent with the parties' understanding? For similar holdings to *936 Second Avenue*, see STL 300 N. 4th, LLC v. Value St. Louis Assocs., L.P., 540 F.3d 788 (8th Cir. 2008).

If the landlord wants to link rent payments to the tenant's business rather than to an abstract economic index, she may propose that the rent consist in part of a percentage of the tenant's gross receipts from the property. Though most commonly used in leases with retail tenants, percentage rents can also be tailored to ground leases. For example, a ground tenant who builds and operates an office building may agree to give his landlord a percentage of the gross rentals he receives from his tenants.

For details on the theory and practice of rent escalators, see Stein, The Most Important Issue in Every Ground Lease, 29 Prac. Real Est. Law. 35 (No. 1, 2013); N. Hecht, Long Term Lease Planning and Drafting 39–150 (1974).

2. *Indices.* Parties who incorporate an index in their lease should also install safeguards against events outside their control, such as elimination or alteration of the chosen index. Consider the plight of a California landlord whose lease provided that renewal term rentals would float with local property taxes. At the time the lease was executed, real property taxes were based on the current appraised fair market value of real property and thus, presumably, served as an effective substitute for a more cumbersome appraisal provision in the lease. Subsequently, however, "California voters passed Proposition 13, Cal.Const. art. XIIIA, which limits tax on real property to 1% of the county assessor's valuation of the property as of 1975–1976, and allows a maximum increase in the valuation for property tax purposes of 2% per year. As a result the property taxes on the leased premises did not increase with the value of the property as the parties had expected." Indeed, using the formula, the rent to be paid by the tenant in the first renewal period decreased by 5.08%.

Nonetheless, the Ninth Circuit Court of Appeals rebuffed the landlord's claim for rescission based on frustration: "The passage of Proposition 13 did not render meaningless the entire lease. The lessors continue to receive valuable consideration in return for the use of their property." Waegemann v. Montgomery Ward & Co., Inc., 713 F.2d 452, 454 (9th Cir.1983).

3. *Net Lease.* Another way for landlords to reduce the effects of inflation is to shift upkeep expenses from landlord to tenant. In the jargon of the real estate market, a *gross lease* is one under which the landlord pays for repairs, maintenance, insurance and real property taxes. A *net lease* shifts some of these incidents onto the tenant. If the lease shifts all incidents to the tenant, it is a *triple net lease* (sometimes called a *bond lease* to reflect the fixed rate of return to the landlord).

Triple net leases are also attractive to investors who wish to employ the lease as a financing device under which, as landlord, they are effectively in the position of lender and the tenant is effectively in the position of borrower, paying debt service in the form of rent. Like mortgagors generally, the tenant under the net lease will bear all upkeep and tax expenses, thus assuring the landlord of a fixed, net return.

4. *Mortgage of the Fee.* Why would a lender in the position of Leader Federal want the ground lessor to mortgage the fee? How else could the parties address the lender's concerns?

Was the decision in *Balch* correct? Reconsider Middlebrook-Anderson Co. v. Southwest Sav. & Loan Ass'n, page 636 above. Does the *Balch* majority validly distinguish between a "subordination of the Balches' interest in the lease" and a mortgage of their fee?

Assume that the Balches had mortgaged their fee interest to secure the loan. Could Crestwood and Leader Federal later extend the term of the loan? Reconsider *Arena*, page 427 above. See Samuelson v. Promontory Investment Corp., 85 Or.App. 315, 736 P.2d 207 (1987); State of Wisconsin Investment Board v. Hurst, 410 N.W.2d 560 (S.D.1987); Honey v. Davis, 78

Wash.App. 279, 896 P.2d 1303 (1995), rev'd, 131 Wash.2d 212, 930 P.2d 908 (1997).

See generally, Stein, Did the Sky Fall on Leasehold Mortgagees?, Ground Lease Financing After *Qualitech,* 25 Prac. Real Est. Law. 7 (No. 2, 2009); Borkholder, Ground Leases—Lease/Leaseback Financing: Alternative to Mortgages, 13 Probate & Prop. 37 (No. 1, Jan./Feb. 1999); DiPrinzio, Leasehold Financing and Mortgagee Protections, 14 Probate & Prop. 47 (No. 4, July/Aug. 2000); Halper, Planning and Construction Clauses in a Subordinated Ground Lease, 17 Real Est.L.J. 48 (1988); Kobren, Three Perspectives on Ground Lease Negotiations, 19 Real Est.L.J. 40 (1990); Stein, How Much Protection Does a Leasehold Mortgagee Need?, 19 Prac. Real Est. Law. 7 (No.6 2003).

5. *Destruction or Condemnation.* The prospect that the leased premises will be condemned or destroyed by fire or other hazard raises several questions for landlord and tenant negotiating a long term lease. Should they provide that the lease be terminated in these circumstances? Should the rent be abated? Who should be entitled to the insurance proceeds or the condemnation award and in what proportions? Should there be an obligation to rebuild and, if so, who should bear it?

The answers reached by landlords and tenants will vary with their relative bargaining strength, the nature of the premises and improvements, and the length and other terms of the lease. One approach commonly taken is to provide that the lease will terminate in the event of complete condemnation or destruction. In the case of condemnation, the tenant will be compensated from the part of the award allocable to the value of his leasehold and the value of any improvements he constructed on the premises. The landlord will receive the rest, presumably the value of her reversionary interest. If fire or other hazard destroys the tenant's improvements, he would receive the insurance proceeds for their value.

Landlord and tenant may provide that in the event of partial condemnation or destruction, the lease can be terminated at the election of either; that rent will be abated proportionately; or that the tenant will rebuild the premises using the insurance or condemnation proceeds. These provisions often connect termination with reconstruction: the tenant may terminate after a partial condemnation or destruction if reconstruction will not be feasible in the circumstances.

Doubtless the most important party in shaping these arrangements is the fee or leasehold mortgagee whose investment in the property likely exceeds the investments of landlord and tenant combined. A mortgagee, whose security consists in part of the good credit of the tenant who will be leasing the premises, will focus carefully on partial condemnation and destruction clauses and will probably insist that the tenant not be allowed to terminate the lease if the interference with his business is insubstantial. Lenders may also require that they receive condemnation awards or insurance proceeds directly, to be used in paying off the mortgage in the event of termination, or to be disbursed by them to the tenant in the event the tenant undertakes reconstruction.

See generally, Committee on Leases, Fire Insurance and Repair Clauses in Leases, 5 Real Prop., Probate & Trust J. 532 (1970); Broadman, Providing in the Lease for the Event of Condemnation, 14 Prac. Lawyer 27

(May 1968); Cargile, Digging Into Ground Leases: Insurance and Reconstruction Issues, 20 Probate & Prop. 42 (Mar./Apr.2006).

6. *Federal Income Taxation.* The Internal Revenue Code's treatment of lessors and lessees, like its treatment of fee owners, offers considerable opportunity for strategically timing the incidence of income, expenses, gains and losses. Indeed, the continuing relationship between two parties, and their ability to shift tax burdens and benefits between themselves by contract, gives landlords and tenants an enviable opportunity to manipulate tax consequences with a fine hand.

Acquisition of Lease. While a landlord can take ordinary business deductions for the costs of managing her property, she must capitalize any costs specifically incurred to obtain a tenant. Thus, the landlord cannot deduct broker's commissions and title insurance premiums immediately, but must amortize them over the term of the lease. A tenant's payment of advance rent or a bonus at the time he acquires the lease is taxable as ordinary income to the landlord in the year she receives them. By contrast, receipt of a refundable security deposit to secure the tenant's performance of the lease has no tax consequence for the landlord.

If the tenant incurs costs such as broker's commissions and title premiums in acquiring the lease, he, like the landlord, cannot deduct them presently, but must amortize them over the life of the lease. While the landlord must report bonuses or advance rentals in the year she receives them, the tenant cannot deduct these payments in the year that he makes them. Rather, these outlays are treated as costs of acquiring the lease and must be amortized over the term of the lease. (If the tenant can show that the payment is allocable to a specific period, shorter than the lease term, he can amortize it over the shorter period.) Similarly, if the tenant purchased the lease from a former tenant, he may amortize his cost over the remaining term of the lease. Finally, just as payment of a true security deposit is not taxable to the landlord, it is neither deductible nor amortizable by the tenant.

Depreciation. The landlord, not the tenant, is entitled to take depreciation deductions for any improvements leased to the tenant. If, as is typically the case under a ground lease, it is the tenant who owns the improvement, then the tenant, not the landlord, can take the appropriate depreciation deductions. If the tenant's lease expires before the tenant has fully recovered the cost of the improvement through depreciation deductions, the tenant may deduct the unrecovered cost at the end of the lease.

Disposition of Lease. On the expiration or cancellation of a lease, the landlord may face several questions. Suppose the tenant has built a valuable improvement on the premises during the lease term. Will it constitute income to the landlord when the lease ends? The Internal Revenue Code expressly provides that the value of a tenant's leasehold improvements at termination of a lease is not income to the landlord. When the landlord later sells or exchanges the property she must, however, pay tax on the gain represented by the improvement since the sales price will reflect the value of the improvement while her basis would not have been stepped up by the value of the improvement. I.R.C. §§ 109, 1019. See generally Steuben, The Income Tax Treatment of Interests Acquired from a Ground Lessor, 23 Fla.St.U.L.Rev. 863 (1996).

What if tenant pays landlord to cancel the lease? The Regulations provide that such a payment "constitutes gross income for the year in which it is received, since it is essentially a substitute for rental payments." Treas.Reg. § 1.61–8(b). Say it is the landlord who pays the tenant to cancel? This is considered a capital expense, and its specific treatment is governed by the landlord's purpose in making the payment. If the landlord's purpose in obtaining cancellation was to use the property herself, her payment will be amortized over the remainder of the original lease term. If, instead, the landlord's motive was to free herself to enter into a new lease, the payment will be amortized over the term of the new lease. If the landlord's reason for obtaining cancellation was to sell the property unencumbered by the lease, the payment will be added to her basis. If the distinctions seem arbitrary, it is probably because they are. See Note, The Tax Treatment of the Cost of Terminating a Lease, 30 Stan.L.Rev. 241 (1977); Levin, *Handlery* and the Tax Treatment of Lease Cancellation Expenditures, 9J. Real Estate Tax 371 (1981–82). See generally Dreier, Real Estate Leasing Transactions, 32 N.Y.U.Tax Inst. 1655, 1668–1669 (1974).

The tenant's sale or exchange of his lease is treated like the sale or exchange of any other real property. Gain or loss will be computed by subtracting the tenant's adjusted basis from the amount realized, and will be treated as capital gain or loss, and ordinary income or loss, depending on whether the lease is characterized as section 1221, section 1231, or inventory property. The landlord's payment to the tenant for cancellation of the lease will be treated like payments received from any other sale by the tenant. I.R.C. § 1241. By contrast, if the tenant pays the landlord to cancel the lease, the payment is deductible as a business expense.

For a discussion of tax issues in sale-leaseback arrangements, where an owner sells land and immediately receives back a long term lease, see pages 981–994 below.

For an excellent treatment of taxation issues with new lease vehicles, see Weidner, Synthetic Leases: Structured Finance, Financial Accounting and Tax Ownership, 25 J. Corp. L. 445 (2000); for background on the taxation of landlords and tenants see, in addition to the sources cited, Robinson, Tax Consequences of the Acquisition and Disposition of Leases, 1 J.Real Est.Tax. 49 (1973); Thompson, Some Tax Problems on Mid-Stream Modifications and Terminations of Leases, 4 J.Real Est.Tax. 214 (1977); Bartlett, Tax Treatment of Replacements of Leased Property and of Leasehold Improvements Made by a Lessee, 30 Tax Law. 105 (1976).

CHAPTER VIII

PROPERTIES IN DISTRESS

An increasing number of commercial real estate properties have fallen into trouble in recent years, yielding inadequate rental income to pay carrying charges. When default on the mortgage occurs, the lender must choose among several courses of action. Rather than immediately exercising its legal remedies, the lender often chooses to restructure the loan transaction in a way that may ultimately allow the property to become self-sufficient This restructuring is known as a "workout." The first section following this note examines the reasons for property defaults and the different options available to the lender, focusing on workouts.

The real estate lender whose borrower has defaulted on her note, the installment seller whose buyer has breached their agreement, and the landlord whose tenant has broken a leasehold covenant, will usually find that his rights and remedies are substantially confined by state law. Debtors, buyers and tenants have increasingly come under the protection of state courts and legislatures through such devices as antideficiency rules, one-action rules, statutory rights of redemption, the incorporation of debtor protection provisions into installment land contracts, and limitations on the availability and speed of summary eviction proceedings. State law also imposes restrictions on the use of deeds in lieu of foreclosure by borrowers and lenders who are attempting to avoid judicially enforced remedies.

Borrowers, buyers and tenants who breach their real property obligations will often be in financial distress. As a result, their secured creditors may also have to consult federal bankruptcy law which limits the rights and remedies of a lender, seller or landlord whose borrower, buyer or tenant has filed for liquidation under Chapter 7, or for reorganization under Chapter 11, of the Bankruptcy Code. (The purpose of a Chapter 7 liquidation is to allocate the debtor's assets equitably among his creditors and to discharge him from all further liability; the purpose of a Chapter 11 reorganization is to restructure the debtor's obligations and continue his business.) Moreover, the rights of lenders, sellers and landlords under state law will often conflict with the rights of debtors and their general creditors under bankruptcy law. State and federal rules on default and bankruptcy will also substantially influence efforts by the parties to restructure and work out their difficulties short of judicial proceedings. These ideas are introduced in the second section below.

The materials in this chapter sample some federal bankruptcy law issues that intersect with remedies under state real estate law and that may alter a real estate transaction. This is not intended as a substitute for the bankruptcy law course but rather is designed to sensitize future real estate lawyers to some key issues that they should explore as they structure real estate transactions and advise clients on state law remedies.

Bibliography. See generally, B. Dunaway, The Law of Distressed Real Estate (2009); M. Herbert, W.W. Berryhill & J. Eisen, Structuring Commercial Real Estate Workouts: Alternatives to Bankruptcy and Foreclosure (2d ed. 2008); S. Saft, Commercial Real Estate Workouts (3d ed. 2008).

A. WORKOUTS AND LENDER REMEDIES

Michael H. Goldstein & Adam M. Starr, Navigating the Distressed Real Estate Workout

24 Probate & Property 12, 13, 14, 14–15, 16–18 (May/Jun. 2010).

Real estate workouts, like other loan restructurings, are driven by the financial conditions surrounding, and the legal relationships governing, the particular borrower in distress. Thus, the parties involved in a real estate workout have considerable due diligence to undertake to determine whether a workout is in the client's best interest, what form of restructuring would best achieve the client's objectives, and how to document the deal.

. . .

Preliminary Restructuring Considerations and Objectives

Generally, lenders and borrowers have four options for dealing with a distressed real estate loan. First, the lender can sell its loan to a third party, and the borrower must then negotiate a restructuring with this third party. Second, the lender and the borrower can arrive at a discounted loan payoff arrangement. Third, the lender and the borrower can enter into a negotiated workout to restructure the loan in a way that permanently changes the borrower-lender relationship or entails a consensual transfer of ownership of the property. Fourth, the lender can foreclose on the property or exercise its other legal remedies, and the borrower can consider its defensive options, including filing for bankruptcy.

To determine whether a workout is in the client's best interests, of course, it is necessary to weigh the advantages and disadvantages of that option against the others, particularly the potential for the debtor to file for bankruptcy. If the process proceeds with workout negotiations, several preliminary issues have to be considered, such as whether to employ a pre-negotiation letter, what due diligence to conduct before the negotiation, and whether to seek a temporary forbearance or a permanent restructuring. Each of these issues is discussed in greater detail below.

The Chapter 11 Benchmark

The parameters of a negotiated workout are determined largely by the attorney's analysis of the likelihood that the debtor will file a Chapter 11 bankruptcy and how the borrower and lender might fare under a restructuring plan confirmed by the bankruptcy court. Thus, the borrower and lender must consider what can be achieved in a Chapter 11 case, who has the leverage and staying power to pursue points of disagreement, and who can best bear the brunt of the negative effects of a Chapter 11 filing. The borrower's ability to confirm a plan of reorganization over the lender's objections competes against the lender's ability to confirm its own plan, or to obtain relief from the automatic stay that results from the bankruptcy filing, and prevents the lender from foreclosing and exercising its other legal remedies. See 11 U.S.C. § 362(a), (d).

. . .

The Pre-Negotiation Letter

The "pre-negotiation letter" has become a mainstay of the initial phase of the real estate workout discussion. The necessity of a pre-negotiation letter and the scope of its content will vary case-by-case based on the facts and circumstances presented and the relative leverage of the lender and the borrower.

At one end of the spectrum, a pre-negotiation letter can be a benign agreement confirming that notwithstanding restructuring discussions, no restructuring agreement is binding until final documents have been executed. The pre-negotiation letter typically will further provide that information exchanged during negotiations will not be used against either party and that a delay in the exercise of rights and remedies is not a waiver of these rights and remedies.

At the other end of the spectrum, the pre-negotiation letter can be used to gain concessions as a precondition to negotiations. The borrower, for example, can seek to impose a long-term forbearance, defer payment of interest, obtain a waiver of covenants, or provide for new money infusions or use of funds for "out of covenant" or "non-budgeted" items such as capital expenditures and acquisitions. The lender can seek acknowledgment by the borrower of the validity and enforceability of the secured obligations and liens, a waiver of the borrower's defenses and counterclaims, an increase in the interest rate to remedy perfection issues, to obtain additional collateral supporting the debt, or to obtain consensus from a guarantor, including the agreement to pay the lender's negotiation expenses.

. . . For a workout to proceed beyond the pre-negotiation stage, the parties generally must share a common view that the pre-negotiation letter's overarching purpose is to maintain the status quo during workout negotiations. When there is such a common view, the pre-negotiation letter will be put in place quickly, and the parties can move forward with the workout negotiations. Conversely, if either party attempts to use the pre-negotiation letter stage as a basis to alter the status quo, the negotiations may never proceed beyond the pre-negotiation letter.

Due Diligence

Transparency is critical to achieving a successful real estate workout. If information that is available is not free-flowing and credible, informed decisions cannot be made. The disclosure of all practically available information, subject to confidentiality and proprietary restrictions, facilitates the restructuring process. Indeed, the Chapter 11 template against which all out-of-court restructurings are measured enshrines "full disclosure" as a fundamental rule of the road. The absence of full disclosure can breed mistrust, loss of credibility, delay, and the inability for decision making to occur. Yet, obtaining all the information that is either necessary or desirable is often a luxury, and parties frequently must make do with less, particularly if facts are not disclosed to protect proprietary, sensitive, competitive, or confidential information.

Due diligence and disclosure generally have at least three components: documentation review, collateral review, and constituent review (consideration of the respective positions of the borrower, lender, and other parties in interest). Documentation review involves a thorough analysis of all executed agreements. The focus of the inquiry is to determine whether there are any "gaps" in the documentation. For example, a lender needs to know whether the original documents are missing, the documents are properly signed, there is an errant property description, and the security interests encumber all of the borrower's assets and are properly perfected. In assessing its defenses against the lender, the borrower can consider an independent document evaluation.

Collateral review involves a financial assessment of the assets at issue. Typically, the focus of the collateral review is twofold: what are the liquidity needs of the project and what is the value of the project? As parties have become more adept at litigating value issues, the costs and risks of litigating such issues with expert and project-specific analysis have become critical components of the restructuring process.

In addition to documentation and collateral review, attention must be paid to the identity and motivation of all relevant parties in interest, including tenants, ground lessors, vendors, customers, employees, regulators, and the media. Beyond evaluating the documents and the collateral, the lender must assess whether the borrower's management and ownership group is credible and has the resources to support the project and whether it has the expertise to turn around the project. The borrower must assess whether the lender is interested in supporting the project or has made a decision to exit.

The pervasive real-time connectivity brought about by the Internet has greatly affected the due diligence and financial assessment process. The availability of information and misinformation requires consideration of the potential role in a restructuring of all of the constituents with whom a debtor interacts. It is essential to have an active regard for the constant stream of communications among interested parties in today's 24/7 world of instant messaging, e-mails and text messaging, blogs, tweets, and the like. Each party should maintain an active regard for market dynamics. The free-flowing liquidity of distressed debt markets also requires that the borrower be vigilant in identifying and monitoring the current holders of its debt.

Forbearance vs. Restructuring

At the outset of a real estate workout, consensus needs to emerge around a common objective—temporary forbearance or permanent restructuring. Through a forbearance, the lender agrees to refrain from exercising a right or remedy for a stated period of time that may range from a few months to a few years, as long as specified conditions are met and, in many instances, provided that the borrower pays a forbearance fee. Many forbearance agreements contain a condition subsequent that qualifies the lender's forbearance. For example, a lender may agree not to accelerate or foreclose on a defaulted loan or may agree to waive or reduce default interest or prepayment premiums if the lender is repaid within a set time period or if certain financial or operational milestones are achieved. In contrast, a restructuring permanently alters the existing contractual rights of the lender and borrower. The forbearance agreement provides an interim period for the borrower to operate while it negotiates a permanent restructure. A restructuring agreement resets the borrower-lender relationship in a manner that is typically designed to match the lender's entitlement to payment in full and the borrower's current and projected ability to do so. In some instances, the difference between the restructuring/forbearance objectives may be viewed as semantic, in that a long enough "temporary" forbearance can be the functional equivalent of a permanent restructuring.

Ultimately, the decision whether to restructure or forbear is driven by the substantive issues that the parties must resolve, including (1) a waiver of defaults, (2) a waiver of (and non-accrual of) default interest, (3) the suspension of compliance with covenants or modification or elimination of covenants, (4) the modification of debt terms through financing or by enhancing the ability to trade the debt, (5) additional collateral, (6) the ability to accommodate new money infusions, (7) the effect on management, employees, vendors, customers, and governmental entities, (8) the effect on other debt instruments (cross-default provisions, for example) and financial reporting, and (9) tax issues. Perception, accounting treatment, internal limitations on the type of investments that can be held by a lender, and other factors of this type can be as vital as the deal points themselves.

In any particular case, the drivers for resolving these issues will be the underlying economics of the transaction, the respective financial wherewithal of the parties, and the legal issues presented. A borrower with access to capital, positive cash flow from collateral with a value in excess of the debt, and a strong legal position, because of circumstances such as a nonrecourse loan or potential affirmative claims against the lender, should generally have a stronger hand to negotiate for a permanent restructuring than a borrower not so situated. Yet, the lender might also have an incentive to take a strong position and begin exercising its remedies for a property precisely because it is perceived as being a valuable project.

When the borrower is without access to capital, has a weak legal position (such as potential recourse liability), and owns a property worth less than the debt that is not generating sufficient cash flow to pay expenses and debt service, the borrower may have no alternative other than to request a temporary forbearance that will give it time to implement a turnaround, locate capital, or consummate a sale. When a property is not worth the amount of the debt, but has the possibility of a turnaround, the lender may not want to own the property and may be willing to work with the borrower.

Documenting the Restructuring

Term Sheets and Definitive Documents

Once the parties determine whether the workout is a temporary forbearance or permanent restructuring, they must decide whether the documentation will take the form of an initial nonbinding term sheet, comprehensive forbearance agreement, or restructuring support agreement. . . .

Ultimately, the attendant financial and factual circumstances will propel the workout negotiations. If resources and time are in short supply, getting to the "goal line" may dictate an early push to definitive documents. By contrast, if forbearance requires consent from a number of parties beyond the "lead negotiators," or if multiple tranches of debt are involved, the parties' initial step may be a forbearance agreement or restructuring a support agreement entered into only by the controlling or lead group of parties. This agreement can provide the borrower with a road map for completing definitive documents and time to obtain all of the necessary consents. . . .

Substantive Issues

A real estate workout generally requires a "reset" of the borrowing relationship. The reset is based on the factors precipitating the distressed conditions and the financial and legal context. The dynamic for negotiating the specifics of such adjustments generally tends to focus on finding the equilibrium point between providing the borrower with sufficient operating and financial flexibility to effectuate an identified turnaround strategy (for example, finalizing tenants for the property, completing construction, or negotiating a sale), and providing the lender with sufficient downside protections (additional collateral, guarantees, or expedited remedies in the case of a Chapter 11 filing, for example) to avoid the proverbial "second bite at the apple." The three substantive areas in which the tensions between the interests of the borrower and lender are likely to surface are (1) covenants, (2) collateral, and (3) pricing, payments, and maturity.

Covenants. In a real estate restructuring, modifications to financial covenants that provide a lender with early warning signs of further financial distress (for example, loan-to-value ratios, debt service coverage ratios, and lease-up percentages) are commonplace, as are operational covenants that protect the lender from the borrower's operations (for example, lender approval of tenants and project alterations and limits on indebtedness and capital expenditures). Also common is the imposition of a financial monitor, a turnaround consultant, or (at a minimum) the ongoing due diligence of a lender-selected investment banker that will provide the lender with additional insights into the turnaround process. The borrower, on the other hand, tends to negotiate for financial covenant benchmarks that are less stringent than its baseline projections to provide operational flexibility. Recently, borrowers have been seeking "financial covenant holidays" that are, in essence, grace periods for compliance with loan covenants. Financial covenant holidays afford the borrower time to implement an operational turnaround.

A significant recent trend in covenant deal terms is the lenders' imposition of "milestones" on borrowers. A milestone is typically a particular operational or financial target that the borrower has to achieve by a certain date. Failure to achieve the stated target generally gives the lender the right to declare a default. These milestones can be benchmarked relative to a sale, new financing, or other operational objectives such as the pace of obtaining entitlements or leasing activity. These milestones will envelop the workout in a set of objective yardsticks, with a failure to achieve any of these yardstick targets resulting in default.

Collateral and Perfection. The workout scenario invariably involves a discussion of opportunities for collateral to be enhanced, perfection issues to be reviewed and fortified (if necessary), and intercreditor issues (if applicable) to be clarified. If there is any unencumbered collateral owned by the borrower or the borrower's affiliated entities, the workout will examine whether that collateral can be harnessed to raise new money, or whether pledging the collateral to the lender is a requirement of the workout. The accounting and control of cash also tends to be a very significant focus of the collateral discussion. The availability of unencumbered collateral, like the availability of new money, can significantly influence the restructuring discussions.

Remedying perfection problems is generally an area of keen lender attention. The lender may discover during the due diligence process that there are deficiencies in the loan documents by reason of changed circumstances from the time the loan was made; or the lender may simply uncover a gap in its collateral documentation. In this case the lender might seek to amend the grant of security interests in the loan documents to include an omitted category of collateral, or may seek the execution or recordation of additional documents to complete perfection of a security interest.

The issues surrounding collateral and perfection tend to generate little controversy in the first instance. When perfection of the lender's security interests in the borrower's assets is incomplete, however, and the lender seeks to fix this gap during the workout process, the borrower may be able to claim that the lender's late perfection is a preferential transfer under the Bankruptcy Code if the borrower files for bankruptcy protection within 90 days of such perfection. See 11 U.S.C. § 547. Because the lender's late perfection could affect the recovery of other creditors in a bankruptcy case of the borrower, the import of preserving a preference action can figure prominently in the workout discussions, both in terms of the risk of a bankruptcy filing and the need for a tolling agreement (an agreement extending the time period to bring a preference action, for example). Of additional importance is whether the lender's loan or liens are subject to avoidance as a fraudulent conveyance on the theory that the loan or lien was the incurrence of an obligation or a transfer of the borrower's property while the borrower was insolvent, for which the borrower did not receive reasonably equivalent value. See id. § 548(a)(1)(B). The borrower will seek to preserve its leverage on these issues while the lender will seek to eliminate the issues.

Pricing, Payments, and Maturity. Increased interest rates, cash flow sweeps, prepayments from the sale of noncore assets, paid-in-kind options (such as by an increase of principal), conversion of debt to equity, and upside participations are all mechanisms available to the lender and borrower to restructure debt. These mechanisms allow the borrower and lender to change the terms of the loan to terms that match the underlying property's cash flow and value, as well as the borrower's ability to satisfy the loan obligations. The possible outcomes and trade-offs that will arise in negotiating the specific terms of these issues will vary in every case. Also, common ground in a real estate restructuring is the requirement of the borrower to pay the lender's attorney's fees and expenses, facility fees, and extension fees. A newer trend, appropriating the "amendment fee" and "exit fee" concepts from the exchange world, employs the "consent fee" as the carrot to facilitate the economic incentive for consensus. Consent fees come in many sizes and shapes, but the common theme is to pay debt holders to consent to an overall transaction, even if the particular debt holder cannot participate in all aspects of the transaction (new money, conversion of debt to equity, and so on). The "payment" provides additional value to those debt holders who cannot participate (or who chose not to participate) in all aspects of the proposed restructuring but are entitled nonetheless to equivalent economics.

Typically, lenders will not agree to forbear or restructure in exchange only for new promises and covenants from the borrower. The lender regularly will seek tangible benefits such as waivers of claims by the borrower, fees, and new security in exchange for its agreement to forbear or restructure. In turn, the borrower's central objective likely will be to obtain as much runway as possible to implement a turnaround and to reset the lender's rights and remedies for the property consistent with the borrower's turnaround plan.

Hindsight Protection: Releases

Releases permeate real estate restructuring documents. The parties consider many issues in crafting their releases, including when is the appropriate time to execute a release and whether the release is effective and enforceable.

On the timing issue, relevant facts to consider include the consideration received for the release, whether the release is given as part of a temporary or permanent restructuring, and the value relinquished by the borrower in granting the release.

As to the enforceability issue, if a dispute arises after the workout then the parties will examine the release to ascertain whether it was a knowing and voluntary waiver or one embedded in a contract of adhesion. Even if the release is binding, the borrower and lender may later ask exactly which parties are bound by the release. A frequent question is whether a broad release by the debtor binds a subsequent bankruptcy trustee for issues of preference, fraudulent conveyance, or equitable subordination. Indeed, the bankruptcy trustee may attempt to challenge the release itself on a variety of grounds, including as a fraudulent transfer on the theory that the release was a transfer of the debtor's property for which the debtor did not receive reasonably equivalent value. See 11 U.S.C. § 548(a)(1)(B).

Alternatives to Workouts Other than Bankruptcy

Deeds in Lieu of Foreclosure

In those cases in which the restructuring provides no future participation for the borrower, the transfer of control of the underlying project through the execution of a deed in lieu of foreclosure can be an efficient strategy. Such a transaction, however, has drawbacks. These drawbacks may include the continued effect of what would otherwise be junior liens, the necessity of obtaining new title insurance with potential imputation of the knowledge of the borrower about title defects, and the imposition of transfer taxes on deeds in lieu of foreclosure. In addition, because the borrower entity remains in existence, to the extent it has creditors that are left unpaid, the borrower can become subject to a bankruptcy proceeding in which the deed-in-lieu transaction can be attacked as a preference (to the extent that the conveyance involved property in which the lender did not have a valid, perfected, senior lien) or a fraudulent conveyance. See 11 U.S.C. §§ 547, 548. Unlike a real property foreclosure sale, which may be insulated against certain fraudulent transfer claims, a deed-in-lieu transaction is fully susceptible to such claims.

Assignment for the Benefit of Creditors

California and certain other states permit a company to make a general assignment for the benefit of creditors, commonly referred to as an "ABC." See Cal. Code § 493.010 et seq. General assignments are created by agreement and not by the initiation of a court proceeding, although in some states a judicial proceeding is required. See, e.g., N.Y. Debt. & Cred. Law, art. 2; Wash. Rev. Code § 7.60.025 (in which an assignee under state law is required to seek the appointment of a receiver to administer the assignment estate). In essence, general assignments establish a trust under which the debtor, as assignor, assigns all of its assets to an assignee (as the trustee) for the benefit of the assignor's general unsecured creditors. See *Brainard v. Fitzgerald*, 44 P.2d 336 (Cal. 1935); *Jarvis v. Webber*, 236 P. 138 (Cal. 1925). The assignee then liquidates the assignor's property and makes distribution to creditors in accordance with certain priorities recognized under state and applicable nonbankruptcy federal law. See Cal. Civ. Proc. Code § 1204.

General assignments are analogous to Chapter 7 bankruptcy cases. The central advantage of a general assignment is that the debtor is able to select its preferred "trustee," who can then liquidate the debtor's assets generally on an expedited basis. The liquidation process generally can be completed more efficiently than would be the case if it were implemented in a Chapter 11 or Chapter 7 bankruptcy.

Also, sales through general assignments are perceived by buyers to add a layer of protection against fraudulent transfer risks. There are a few reasons for this perception. First, instead of the assignor/company, the seller is a third party assignee that serves as a fiduciary to the assignor's creditors. Second, in many instances, the assignee has obtained a valuation of the assets being sold and such valuation provides additional evidence that reasonably equivalent value was paid for the assets.

Receivers

Most real estate lenders have the ability in a distress situation to seek the appointment of a receiver to take control of the property. With a broad receivership order, the receiver can take over operations of the underlying project. For the lender, putting a receiver in place provides a measure of control over the collateral and of the accompanying cash flow pending enforcement of more permanent remedies. In addition, the appointment of a receiver removes from the borrower funds to oppose a foreclosure. Significantly, in California, when properly initiated the appointment of a receiver is not considered an "action" that would violate the "one form of action" or "security first principles" codified at Cal. Civ. Proc. Code §§ 726, 564(d). See also *Western Fed. Sav. Loan Ass'n v. Heflin Corp.*, 797 F. Supp. 790 (N.D. Cal. 1992).

For the borrower, the appointment of receiver or the threat of a receiver could prompt a bankruptcy filing. If a receiver is in place before the bankruptcy filing, whether the debtor can obtain control over the project after a bankruptcy filing will depend on the given facts and circumstances. Bankruptcy courts have considered the following factors in determining whether a receiver should remain in place: whether the debtor will use the property in question, if turned over, for the benefit of creditors; whether there will be sufficient income to fund a successful reorganization; whether there has been mismanagement by the debtor; whether or not there are avoidance issues for the property retained by the receiver, because a receiver does not possess avoidance powers for the benefit of the estate; and the fact that the debtor's bankruptcy filing automatically stays the applicable state court receivership action. See *Dill v. Dime Sav. Bank (In re Dill)*, 163 B.R. 221, 225 (Bankr. E.D.N.Y. 1994).

NOTE

Reconsider the advantages and disadvantages of the use of a deed in lieu of foreclosure from the lender's and borrower's perspectives, as described in the excerpt from Soslow, Comment: Incentivizing Deeds-In-Lieu of Foreclosure: An Argument for the Expansion of the Home Affordable Foreclosure Alternatives ("HAFA") Program, on pages 495–500 above. Consider as well the author's suggested distinction between residential and commercial properties.

CUNA Mortgage v. Aafedt

Supreme Court of North Dakota, 1990.
459 N.W.2d 801.

LEVINE, JUSTICE.

This is a consolidated appeal by Dean W. and Pamela J. Aafedt from summary judgments in favor of CUNA Mortgage, also known as CUNA Mortgage Corporation [CUNA], foreclosing three real estate mortgages. We affirm.

In November 1985, the Aafedts executed three promissory notes, each in the amount of $15,150 and payable to the Williston Cooperative Credit Union, to finance the purchase of three townhouse properties. To secure the debts, the Aafedts gave the Credit Union separate short-term redemption mortgages for each of the three individual lots. The mortgages were insured by the United States Department of Housing and Urban Development [HUD]. The Credit Union subsequently assigned the notes and mortgages to CUNA. The Aafedts defaulted on the notes in February 1989.

In October 1989, CUNA commenced these actions to foreclose the mortgages. CUNA stated in the foreclosure complaints that it would not seek deficiency judgments in separate actions against the Aafedts. The Aafedts, through counsel, offered to deed the properties back to CUNA in lieu of the foreclosure actions. CUNA rejected the Aafedts' offer to deed back the properties, apparently, because HUD would not agree to that procedure and would not reimburse CUNA for the funds CUNA invested if CUNA accepted the deed. In spite of CUNA's rejection of the offer to deed back the properties, the Aafedts executed a quitclaim deed purportedly conveying all the properties to CUNA. The quitclaim deed was recorded on November 2, 1989, without the knowledge of CUNA.

The Aafedts then filed their answers in which they admitted all of the allegations in the complaints but asserted that the actions should be dismissed because they had already conveyed the properties to CUNA by quitclaim deed. The Aafedts moved for summary judgment dismissing the actions. The trial court granted summary judgments in favor of the Aafedts on December 1, 1989, on the basis that CUNA had failed to respond.

On December 11, 1989, CUNA moved for relief from the summary judgments under Rule 60(b), N.D.R.Civ.P., asserting that "a timely response to the Motion was completed and served upon the [Aafedts], but because of mistake or inadvertence, the original documents were not filed with the Court." CUNA also requested the trial court to consider its response to the Aafedts' original motion and to grant summary judgments in its favor foreclosing the mortgages.

The trial court granted CUNA's Rule 60(b) motion and vacated the December 1 summary judgments. The court concluded that the Aafedts' quitclaim deed was void, determining that "the act of deeding the property to [CUNA] was done unilaterally, without [CUNA's] consent or acceptance and not duly delivered to [CUNA]." The court also granted summary judgments in favor of CUNA foreclosing the three mortgages. These appeals followed.

The Aafedts . . . assert that the trial court erred in concluding, as a matter of law, that the quitclaim deed purportedly conveying the properties to CUNA was void.

Under North Dakota law, conveyance by deed takes effect upon delivery of the deed by the grantor. *Frederick v. Frederick*, 178 N.W.2d 834, 837 (N.D.1970); § 47–09–06, N.D.C.C. Absent a delivery of the deed, the deed is of no effect. *First Nat'l Bank in Minot v. Bloom*, 264 N.W.2d 208, 210 (N.D.1978) [quoting *Stark County v. Koch*, 107 N.W.2d 701, 705 (N.D.1961)]. Because "an estate cannot be thrust upon a person against his will" [23 Am.Jur.2d *Deeds* § 173, at p. 195 (1983)], it is well settled that "[a]cceptance by the grantee is an essential part of a delivery." *Arnegaard v. Arnegaard*, 7 N.D. 475, 75 N.W. 797, 805 (1898). *See also* 8 G. Thompson, *Commentaries on the Modern Law of Real Property* § 4252, at p. 166 (1963); 4 H. Tiffany, *The Law of Real Property* § 1055 (3d ed.1975); Annot., *What constitutes acceptance of deed by grantee*, 74 A.L.R.2d 992, 995 (1960).

In this case, a CUNA official stated by affidavit that CUNA "rejected all offers of the [Aafedts] to deed the properties back to it in lieu of foreclosure" and that "the preparation, execution and placing of record" of the quitclaim deed "were not made with the consent, knowledge or acceptance of" CUNA. The Aafedts do not dispute these statements, but assert that there was a "constructive acceptance" of the deed by CUNA because four weeks lapsed before CUNA formally voiced any resistance to the deed being placed of record. The Aafedts provide us with no authority to support this argument. We treat their "constructive acceptance" argument as an assertion that CUNA's four-week silence raised a presumption of acceptance of the quitclaim deed.

The recording of a deed may create a rebuttable presumption of its delivery to, and its acceptance by, the grantee. *Dinius v. Dinius*, 448 N.W.2d 210, 216 (N.D.1989) [quoting *Eide v. Tveter*, 143 F.Supp. 665, 671 (D.C.N.D.1956)]. A failure to renounce a deed after knowledge of its existence may also in some circumstances be sufficient to show that a grantee accepted the deed. 23 Am.Jur.2d, *supra*, § 181, at p. 200. However, presumptions of acceptance arise only when the deed is beneficial to the grantee, not when the deed places a burden on the grantee. 8 G. Thompson, *supra*, at p. 176; 4 H. Tiffany, *supra*, § 1057, at p. 460; 23 Am.Jur.2d, *supra*, § 183, at p. 200; *Arnegaard v. Arnegaard, supra*. CUNA has asserted that it would be burdened by the deed because its ability to receive insured funds from HUD "would be in jeopardy" if it accepted the quitclaim deed. The Aafedts did not present any evidence to counter this assertion. Therefore, a presumption of acceptance did not arise in this case.

Moreover, we do not believe that CUNA's four-week delay in making a formal court objection to the recorded quitclaim deed, after the Aafedts had been informed by CUNA that a deed in lieu of foreclosure would be an unacceptable alternative, is sufficient to raise a genuine issue of material fact with regard to laches, estoppel, or a presumption of acceptance. We conclude that the trial court correctly determined on these undisputed facts that the Aafedts' attempted quitclaim conveyance of the properties to CUNA is void.

The premise underlying all of the Aafedts' arguments in this case is that CUNA's insistence on pursuing the foreclosure actions is unjustified and unfair because the relief it seeks could be more easily obtained by accepting a deed to the property. According to the Aafedts, CUNA's acceptance of a deed in lieu of foreclosure would not only alleviate a burden on the courts but would spare them the adverse publicity which accompanies a foreclosure action. We recognize that an action to foreclose a mortgage is an equitable proceeding [*Federal Land Bank of St. Paul v. Overboe*, 404 N.W.2d 445, 448 (N.D.1987)], and are familiar with the maxim that "[h]e who invokes the jurisdiction of equity must come with clean hands. . . ." *Sorum v. Schwartz*, 411 N.W.2d 652, 655 (N.D.1987).

Although the ultimate relief a mortgagee receives through a foreclosure action may often be the same as that acquired by accepting a deed in lieu of foreclosure, *i.e.*, title to the property, the consequences to the mortgagor and mortgagee of using one method as opposed to the other in satisfying the mortgagee's claim can vary widely. *See* 3 R. Powell, *The Law of Real Property* ¶¶ 469.1 [practical effects] and 469.2 [federal income tax effects] (1990). In this case, CUNA has asserted that, because of HUD rules and regulations,[1] it will be injured through

---

[1]   24 C.F.R. § 203.357 allows mortgagees holding a mortgage insured by the FHA to accept deeds in lieu of foreclosure only under certain circumstances:

"§ 203.357 Deed in lieu of foreclosure.

"(a) *Mortgagors owning one property.* In lieu of instituting or completing a foreclosure, the mortgagee may acquire property from one other than a corporate mortgagor by voluntary conveyance from the mortgagor who certifies that he does not

the loss of HUD funds if it accepts the quitclaim deed in lieu of the foreclosures. The Aafedts have failed to present any evidence whatsoever to raise an inference that CUNA is pursuing the foreclosure actions in bad faith. Because the Aafedts admitted all the allegations in the foreclosure complaints, and absent any showing by the Aafedts of a bad faith refusal by CUNA to accept the deed in lieu of the foreclosure actions, we conclude that the trial court properly granted the summary judgments of foreclosure in favor of CUNA.

We conclude that the trial court did not err in granting CUNA's Rule 60(b) motion for relief from the December 1 dismissals, in declaring the quitclaim deed void, and in granting summary judgments in favor of CUNA in the foreclosure actions. Accordingly, the judgments are affirmed.

ERICKSTAD, C.J., and VANDE WALLE, GIERKE and MESCHKE, JJ., concur.

NOTE

If there were no HUD regulation affecting the parties, should the court have forced the lender in *CUNA Mortgage* to accept a deed in lieu of foreclosure? Would such a result be a legitimate expression of the trend elsewhere in the law to shift dispute resolution from the courts to the parties themselves or to other dispute resolvers? Reconsider the policies favoring nonjudicial foreclosure discussed at pages 468–483.

For more, see Coscarelli, The Deed in Lieu of Foreclosure: Ten Questions for Lender's Counsel, 25 Probate & Prop. 34 (Nov./Dec. 2011); Murray, Deeds in Lieu of Foreclosure: Practical and Legal Considerations, 26 Real Prop. Probate & Tr. J. 459 (1991); Murray, Mortgage Workouts: Deeds in Escrow, 41 Real Prop. Probate & Tr. J. 41 (2006). See also Bolnick & Miller, Acquiring Real Property from a Bankrupt Seller, 47 Real Prop. Tr. & Est. L.J. 413 (2013).

---

own any other property subject to a mortgage insured or held by FHA. Conveyance of the property by deed in lieu of foreclosure is approved subject to the following requirements:" (1) The mortgage is in default at the time the deed is executed and delivered;

"(2) The credit instrument is cancelled and surrendered to the mortgagor;

"(3) The mortgage is satisfied of record as a part of the consideration for such conveyance;

"(4) The deed from the mortgagor contains a covenant which warrants against the acts of the grantor and all claiming by, through, or under him and conveys good marketable title;

"(5) The mortgagee transfers to the Commissioner good marketable title accompanied by satisfactory title evidence.

"(b) *Corporate mortgagors.* A mortgagee may accept a deed in lieu of foreclosure from a corporate mortgagor in compliance with the requirements of paragraph (a) of this section, if the mortgagee obtains the prior written consent of the Commissioner.

"(c) *Mortgagors owning more than one property.* The mortgagee may accept a deed in lieu of foreclosure in compliance with the provisions of paragraph (a) of this section, from an individual who owns more than one property which is subject to a mortgage insured or held by the FHA if the mortgagee obtains the prior written consent of the Commissioner."

B. BANKRUPTCY

The potential and actual bankruptcy of a party to a real estate transaction has a great effect on the other parties in the relationship. First, actions taken by creditors and other parties prior to bankruptcy may come back to haunt them in the event that bankruptcy does actually occur. Transfers by a debtor to a creditor prior to bankruptcy may ultimately be found to be a fraudulent conveyance or an avoidable preference. Thus, the real estate attorney must be aware of the specter of bankruptcy in structuring transactions and advising clients in order to protect against the consequences of rearrangement of the deal should bankruptcy occur. These issues are developed in BFP v. Resolution Trust Corporation, and the notes following that case, at pages 712–719.

If bankruptcy does occur, the consensual arrangements of the debtor with creditors and other parties may be significantly or totally altered. For example, reorganization plans may be permitted over the objections of some creditors under the "cram down" provisions. These are discussed in RadLAX Gateway Hotel, LLC v. Amalgated Bank, at pages 719–725. Moreover, section 365 of the Bankruptcy Code allows the trustee in bankruptcy or debtor in possession to assume or reject executory contracts and leases. The automatic stay of actions against a debtor or her property which is imposed by the Code prevents a mortgagee from foreclosing unless an exception is granted and may also prevent a lender from taking self help, such as collecting rents under an assignment of rents by the debtor. These and related issues are discussed in notes at pages 727–728.

The first reading analyzes the real estate reorganization provisions of the Bankruptcy Code that provide an alternative to debtors in distress.

Kenneth N. Klee, One Size Fits Some: Single Asset Real Estate Bankruptcy Cases

87 Cornell Law Review 1285, 1289–1300 (2002).

A.   The History of Real Property Reorganization Cases

During the 1930s, the deteriorating economic climate in the United States led to massive defaults in the repayment of real property mortgages. Economic disaster threatened not only the debtors who owed mortgage obligations, but also the financial institutions, particularly savings banks, that held the mortgages. As debtors defaulted, mortgage holders commenced foreclosure proceedings and financial institutions began to hold record title to enormous amounts of real property. Many of these financial institutions faced the Hobson's choice of holding real estate that generated little income but carried tax, maintenance, and insurance liabilities, or selling the real estate into a thin market with few buyers and distressed prices. Yet in many states, financial institutions could not intervene to protect their interests by foreclosing on mortgaged properties, because the states had imposed moratorium laws to suspend foreclosures. As a result, the United States faced the prospect of numerous financial institution insolvencies. In addition, Congress saw a risk of undermining the U.S. economic system by allowing real property defaults to cause pervasive dispossession of private ownership. Partially to ameliorate this situation, Congress enacted Chapter XII of the Bankruptcy Act to permit individual and partnership debtors who owned real property the opportunity to reorganize. By enacting Chapter XII, Congress created a beneficial legal mechanism to prevent financial institutions from either conducting massive resales of foreclosed real estate into depressed markets or retaining concentrated ownership of real property on their balance sheets. Before the enactment of Chapter XII, SARE debtors either renegotiated consensually with their mortgage holders or liquidated the property under the Bankruptcy Act of 1898 or state mortgage foreclosure laws.

When Congress enacted the Bankruptcy Code in 1978, it continued to permit SARE [single asset real estate] debtors to reorganize under the same laws and rules as other kinds of Chapter 11 debtors. A property owner was eligible to file for relief under Chapter 11 whether the owner was an individual, partnership, or corporation. The 1978 Bankruptcy Code gave all kinds of SARE debtors a breathing spell to permit them to restructure their property and their mortgage.

In 1994, however, the law changed fundamentally for some SARE property owners when Congress adopted special rules for SARE debtors with secured debts of less than $4 million ("small" SARE debtors). In those cases, Congress restricted small SARE debtors to an expedited Chapter 11 procedure designed to confirm a plan quickly or force the debtor to pay the mortgage holder. Debtors who could do neither faced losing their property to foreclosure. To protect mortgage lenders in SARE cases having secured debts not greater than $4 million, the 1994 amendments added an additional procedure by which a real property mortgage holder could obtain relief from § 362 of the Bankruptcy Code's automatic stay against lien foreclosure. Section 362(d)(3) permits a SARE mortgage holder to get relief from the automatic stay to foreclose unless, within ninety days after the order for relief, the debtor files a confirmable plan or begins making monthly payments to the mortgage holder. Thus the amendments minimize the mortgage holder's out-of pocket loss by shortening the Chapter 11 process or forcing the debtor to "pay to play" by making cash payments to the lender. This shifts the risk of delay from the secured lender to the debtor. It also creates a barrier to entry that discourages small real estate owners from filing for Chapter 11 relief. Mortgage holders and their lobbyists justified the provision based on an alleged "shared experience" that, in most real estate cases, debtors file solely to delay foreclosure. They convinced Congress that these cases seldom result in confirmed plans but instead use the resources of the federal courts for improper dilatory purposes.

In 2001, once again bowing to pressure from mortgage holders and their lobbyists, each House of Congress introduced and passed bills repealing the $4 million cap and subjecting all SARE debtors to the expedited procedures that since 1994 had applied only to small SARE debtors.

B.   How Chapter 11 Functions for SARE Debtors

. . .

For at least the last sixty years, most SARE debtors in bankruptcy have had over-leveraged capital structures where a decline in rents (or inability to rent) produces a cash flow insufficient to service their secured debts. Some debtors have obtained junior mortgages to create additional short-term cash flow, but this strategy often adds more debt without solving the debtor's long-term liquidity crisis. Ultimately, the liquidity crisis escalates to the point where the mortgage holder threatens to foreclose and the debtor walks away from the property, renegotiates with the mortgage holder out of court, or files a Chapter 11 petition. In these Chapter 11 cases, the debtor's plan of reorganization almost always proposes debt relief. Debt relief takes many forms, ranging from a simple extension of the maturity date or an adjustment of the interest rate or of the debt amortization period, to forgiveness of indebtedness or the conversion of debt to either equity or a participating mortgage. Indeed, a principal purpose of bankruptcy is to give the debtor an opportunity to solve its liquidity problems.

In some SARE cases, the borrower needs to restructure both the secured debt and the business operations. For example, a building might require construction for completion, expansion, retrofitting, repair, or renovation. In this kind of SARE case, the debtor in possession first must obtain additional capital to finance the needed construction in order to prove that its reorganization plan is feasible. If the value of the property is less than the mortgage debt, the debtor in possession probably will not obtain additional financing on an unsecured basis or even with a junior lien for security. . . . In some SARE cases, however, the value added by new construction will provide a sufficient cushion to cover new postpetition financing and adequately protect the prepetition mortgage holder's interest in property. Even if the debtor in possession cannot obtain debtor-in-possession financing, it may be possible for existing or new equity owners to infuse equity capital under a reorganization plan. . . .

. . .

C.   Arguments For and Against Reorganization

We now discuss the fundamental question: Why should Congress permit SARE cases to reorganize under Chapter 11? Some commentators have contended, or have adopted theoretical positions that should lead them to contend, that the Chapter 11 process in SARE cases is inefficient compared to the alternative of mandatory prompt auctions. Allocative efficiency, they argue, requires swift and inexpensive foreclosure in accordance with state law. These commentators contend that permitting the borrower to file a Chapter 11 petition inefficiently delays foreclosure, thereby imposing increased costs on secured creditors. Secured creditors in turn pass these losses on to all borrowers in the form of higher interest rates.

Other commentators argue that bankruptcy law should permit interference with state law only if it solves a "common pool problem." In their view, bankruptcy law is necessary to prevent one creditor from acting in its own self-interest to the detriment of creditors as a whole. For example, the law properly prevents a creditor with a security interest in valuable machinery of an insolvent manufacturing company from foreclosing on its security interest and causing the liquidation of the debtor to the detriment of all other creditors. These commentators argue that almost all SARE cases are two-party disputes that involve only a debtor and a mortgage holder; therefore, there is no common pool problem, and there should be no bankruptcy case. Permitting a SARE debtor to file for bankruptcy confers no benefits on a pool of other claimants, there being none, they argue, and it only imposes unjustified costs and delays on mortgage holders, resulting in higher interest rates, fewer mortgage loan approvals, and the "withholding from the marketplace property capable of producing value." "The time spent in the Bankruptcy Court is wasteful and without any public benefit." Therefore, proponents of this argument support amending the Bankruptcy Code to bar SARE cases from reorganizing under Chapter 11.

Contrary to the claim that the common pool problem is the sole or primary basis for evaluating the desirability of allowing SARE debtors access to Chapter 11, three principal arguments, developed below, powerfully favor giving access to Chapter 11 so that SARE debtors have an opportunity to reorganize. First, Chapter 11 smoothes out market inefficiencies, particularly during massive real estate downturns. Second, federal public policy supports giving property owners a chance to save their investments. Third, macroeconomic and social policies favor reorganization of SARE debtors.

First, during broad-based financial crises, allowing debtors to restructure debts in Chapter 11 smoothes economic turbulence and precludes the downward spiral in real estate prices that can result when mortgage holders simultaneously dump massive amounts of foreclosed properties on the market. In addition, Chapter 11 functions in SARE cases to smooth out market inefficiencies caused by state foreclosure systems. Specifically, some state law foreclosure systems are flawed because they permit lenders to seize property and conduct foreclosure sales without sufficient notice, resulting in artificially depressed prices. Although the Depression is long gone, "the modern mortgage market is subject to deficiencies that create similar market declines." These evils exist "[n]ot . . . only in time of emergency." Thus, many foreclosures result in nonconsensual sales at below-market price. By contrast, Chapter 11 gives the property owner the opportunity to sell the property over a reasonable period of time. When debtors sell properties with their lenders' cooperation, the resulting orderly sales can increase value for the lenders and other creditors. Alternatively, Chapter 11 permits the property owner to restructure the mortgage through a consensual valuation under a plan supported by the mortgage holder or through a "market-tested" valuation in a contested plan confirmation.

. . .

Second, Chapter 11 also implements important federal policies protecting ownership investments in real estate. Contrary to the assertion that SARE cases are two-party disputes, many cases involve the interests of numerous owners who have invested in the real estate project. As a normative matter, Chapter 11 protects general partners or guarantors who might be liable for foreclosure deficiencies from the risk of an unfair or inefficient state foreclosure process. As a consequence, partners and guarantors can make efficient decisions ex ante whether to invest in real estate projects. Moreover, minimizing foreclosure deficiencies has a beneficial second-order effect. The efficiencies of Chapter 11 reduce the tax recapture liability of partners in a debtor real estate partnership, thus preventing governments from reaping a windfall due to artificially low foreclosure prices.

Third, macroeconomic and social policies also favor reorganization of SARE debtors. Granting SARE debtors meaningful access to Chapter 11 not only makes good economic sense, but it is also good social policy. Generally, mortgage lenders are the successful bidders at foreclosure sales. Chapter 11 prevents undue concentration of real estate ownership into the hands of large financial institutions during economic downturns by facilitating reorganization and the debtor's retention of ownership. Moreover, some commentators contend that Chapter 11 allows the bankruptcy court to consider equitable, community, and other factors in ruling on a mortgage holder's relief from a stay motion. For example, a court might consider that "[m]any foreclosures occur in inner-city neighborhoods occupied by low-income groups . . . fac[ing] unemployment in an economic downturn . . . [and] are thus more likely to default on their mortgage loans and less able to avoid foreclosure."

BFP v. Resolution Trust Corporation

United States Supreme Court, 1994.
511 U.S. 531, 114 S.Ct. 1757, 128 L.Ed.2d 556.

JUSTICE SCALIA delivered the opinion of the Court.

This case presents the question whether the consideration received from a noncollusive, real estate mortgage foreclosure sale conducted in conformance with applicable state law conclusively satisfies the Bankruptcy Code's requirement that transfers of property by insolvent debtors within one year prior to the filing of a bankruptcy petition be in exchange for "a reasonably equivalent value." 11 U.S.C.A. § 548(a)(2).

I

Petitioner BFP is a partnership, formed by Wayne and Marlene Pedersen and Russell Barton in 1987, for the purpose of buying a home in Newport Beach, California, from Sheldon and Ann Foreman. Petitioner took title subject to a first deed of trust in favor of Imperial Savings Association (Imperial)[1] to secure payment of a loan of $356,250 made to the Pedersens in connection with petitioner's acquisition of the home. Petitioner granted a second deed of trust to the Foremans as security for a $200,000 promissory note. Subsequently, Imperial, whose loan was not being serviced, entered a notice of default under the first deed of trust and scheduled a properly noticed foreclosure sale. The foreclosure proceedings were temporarily delayed by the filing of an involuntary bankruptcy petition on behalf of petitioner. After the dismissal of that petition in June 1989, Imperial's foreclosure proceeding was completed at a foreclosure sale on July 12, 1989. The home was purchased by respondent Paul Osborne for $433,000.

---

[1] Respondent Resolution Trust Corporation (RTC) acts in this case as receiver of Imperial Federal Savings Association (Imperial Federal), which was organized pursuant to a June 22, 1990, order of the Director of the Office of Thrift Supervision, and into which RTC transferred certain assets and liabilities of Imperial. The Director previously had appointed RTC as receiver of Imperial. For convenience we refer to all respondents other than RTC and Imperial as the private respondents.

In October 1989, petitioner filed for bankruptcy under Chapter 11 of the Bankruptcy Code, 11 U.S.C.A. §§ 1101–S1174. Acting as a debtor in possession, petitioner filed a complaint in bankruptcy court seeking to set aside the conveyance of the home to respondent Osborne on the grounds that the foreclosure sale constituted a fraudulent transfer under § 548 of the Code, 11 U.S.C.A. § 548. Petitioner alleged that the home was actually worth over $725,000 at the time of the sale to Osborne. Acting on separate motions, the bankruptcy court dismissed the complaint as to the private respondents and granted summary judgment in favor of Imperial. The bankruptcy court found, *inter alia*, that the foreclosure sale had been conducted in compliance with California law and was neither collusive nor fraudulent. In an unpublished opinion, the District Court affirmed the bankruptcy court's granting of the private respondents' motion to dismiss. A divided bankruptcy appellate panel affirmed the bankruptcy court's entry of summary judgment for Imperial. 132 B.R. 748 (1991). Applying the analysis set forth in In re Madrid, 21 B.R. 424 (Bkrtcy.App.Pan. CA9 1982), affirmed on other grounds, 725 F.2d 1197 (CA9), cert. denied, 469 U.S. 833, 105 S.Ct. 125, 83 L.Ed.2d 66 (1984), the panel majority held that a "non-collusive and regularly conducted nonjudicial foreclosure sale . . . cannot be challenged as a fraudulent conveyance because the consideration received in such a sale establishes 'reasonably equivalent value' as a matter of law." 132 B.R., at 750.

Petitioner sought review of both decisions in the Court of Appeals for the Ninth Circuit, which consolidated the appeals. The Court of Appeals affirmed. In re BFP, 974 F.2d 1144 (1992). BFP filed a petition for certiorari, which we granted. 113 S.Ct. 2411, 124 L.Ed.2d 635 (1993).

II

Section 548 of the Bankruptcy Code, 11 U.S.C.A. § 548, sets forth the powers of a trustee in bankruptcy (or, in a Chapter 11 case, a debtor in possession) to avoid fraudulent transfers. It permits to be set aside not only transfers infected by actual fraud but certain other transfers as well—so-called constructively fraudulent transfers. The constructive fraud provision at issue in this case applies to transfers by insolvent debtors. It permits avoidance if the trustee can establish (1) that the debtor had an interest in property; (2) that a transfer of that interest occurred within one year of the filing of the bankruptcy petition; (3) that the debtor was insolvent at the time of the transfer or became insolvent as a result thereof; and (4) that the debtor received "less than a reasonably equivalent value in exchange for such transfer." 11 U.S.C.A. § 548(a)(2)(A). It is the last of these four elements that presents the issue in the case before us.

Section 548 applies to any "transfer," which includes "foreclosure of the debtor's equity of redemption." 11 U.S.C.A. § 101(54) (1988 ed., Supp. IV). Of the three critical terms "reasonably equivalent value," only the last is defined: "value" means, for purposes of § 548, "property, or satisfaction or securing of a . . . debt of the debtor," 11 U.S.C.A. § 548(d)(2)(A). The question presented here, therefore, is whether the amount of debt (to the first and second lien holders) satisfied at the foreclosure sale (viz., a total of $433,000) is "reasonably equivalent" to the worth of the real estate conveyed. The Courts of Appeals have divided on the meaning of those undefined terms. In Durrett v. Washington Nat. Ins. Co., 621 F.2d 201 (1980), the Fifth Circuit, interpreting a provision of the old Bankruptcy Act analogous to § 548(a)(2), held that a foreclosure sale that yielded 57% of the property's fair market value could be set aside, and indicated in dicta that any such sale for less than 70% of fair market value should be invalidated. Id., at 203–204. This "Durrett rule" has continued to be applied by some courts under § 548 of the new Bankruptcy Code. See In re Littleton, 888 F.2d 90, 92, n. 5 (C.A.11 1989). In In re Bundles, 856 F.2d 815, 820 (1988), the Seventh Circuit rejected the Durrett rule in favor of a case-by-case, "all facts and circumstances" approach to the question of reasonably equivalent value, with a rebuttable presumption that the foreclosure sale price is sufficient to withstand attack under § 548(a)(2). Id., at 824–825; see also In re Grissom, 955 F.2d 1440, 1445–1446 (C.A.11 1992). In this case the Ninth Circuit, agreeing with the Sixth Circuit, see In re Winshall Settlor's Trust, 758 F.2d 1136, 1139 (C.A.6 1985), adopted the position first put forward in In re Madrid, 21 B.R. 424 (Bkrtcy.App.Pan. CA9 1982), affirmed on other grounds, 725 F.2d 1197 (CA9), cert. denied, 469 U.S. 833, 105 S.Ct. 125, 83 L.Ed.2d 66 (1984), that the consideration received at a noncollusive, regularly conducted real estate foreclosure sale constitutes a reasonably equivalent value under § 548(a)(2)(A). The Court of Appeals acknowledged that it "necessarily part[ed] from the positions taken by the Fifth Circuit in Durrett . . . and the Seventh Circuit in Bundles." 974 F.2d, at 1148.

In contrast to the approach adopted by the Ninth Circuit in the present case, both Durrett and Bundles refer to fair market value as the benchmark against which determination of reasonably equivalent value is to be measured.[3] In the context of an otherwise lawful mortgage foreclosure sale of real estate, such reference is in our opinion not consistent with the text of the Bankruptcy Code. The term "fair market value," though it is a well-established concept, does not appear in § 548. In contrast, § 522, dealing with a debtor's exemptions, specifically provides that, for purposes of that section, " 'value' means fair market value as of the date of the filing of the petition." 11 U.S.C.A. § 522(a)(2). "Fair market value" also appears in the Code provision that defines the extent to which indebtedness with respect to an equity security is not forgiven for the purpose of determining whether the debtor's estate has realized taxable income. § 346(j)(7)(B). Section 548, on the other hand, seemingly goes out of its way to avoid that standard term. It might readily have said "received less than fair market value in exchange for such transfer or obligation," or perhaps "less than a reasonable equivalent of fair market value." Instead, it used the (as far as we are aware) entirely novel phrase "reasonably equivalent value." "[I]t is generally presumed that Congress acts intentionally and purposely when it includes particular language in one section of a statute but omits it in another," Chicago v. Environmental Defense Fund, 114 S.Ct. 1588, 1593, 128 L.Ed.2d 302 (1994) (internal quotation marks omitted), and that presumption is even stronger when the omission entails the replacement of standard legal terminology with a neologism. One must

---

[3]   We emphasize that our opinion today covers only mortgage foreclosures of real estate. The considerations bearing upon other foreclosures and forced sales (to satisfy tax liens, for example) may be different.

suspect the language means that fair market value cannot—or at least cannot always—be the benchmark.

That suspicion becomes a certitude when one considers that market value, as it is commonly understood, has no applicability in the forced-sale context; indeed, it is the very *antithesis* of forced-sale value. "The market value of . . . a piece of property is the price which it might be expected to bring if offered for sale in a fair market; not the price which might be obtained on a sale at public auction or a sale forced by the necessities of the owner, but such a price as would be fixed by negotiation and mutual agreement, after ample time to find a purchaser, as between a vendor who is willing (but not compelled) to sell and a purchaser who desires to buy but is not compelled to take the particular . . . piece of property." Black's Law Dictionary 971 (6th ed. 1990). In short, "fair market value" presumes market conditions that, by definition, simply do not obtain in the context of a forced sale.

Neither petitioner, petitioner's *amici*, nor any federal court adopting the Durrett or the Bundles analysis has come to grips with this glaring discrepancy between the factors relevant to an appraisal of a property's market value, on the one hand, and the strictures of the foreclosure process on the other. Market value cannot be the criterion of equivalence in the foreclosure-sale context. The language of § 548(a)(2)(A) ("received less than a reasonably equivalent value in exchange") requires judicial inquiry into whether the foreclosed property was sold for a price that approximated its worth at the time of sale. An appraiser's reconstruction of "fair market value" could show what similar property would be worth if it did not have to be sold within the time and manner strictures of state-prescribed foreclosure. But property that *must* be sold within those strictures is simply *worth less*. No one would pay as much to own such property as he would pay to own real estate that could be sold at leisure and pursuant to normal marketing techniques. And it is no more realistic to ignore that characteristic of the property (the fact that state foreclosure law permits the mortgagee to sell it at forced sale) than it is to ignore other price-affecting characteristics (such as the fact that state zoning law permits the owner of the neighboring lot to open a gas station). Absent a clear statutory requirement to the contrary, we must assume the validity of this state-law regulatory background and take due account of its effect. "The existence and force and function of established institutions of local government are always in the consciousness of lawmakers and, while their weight may vary, they may never be completely overlooked in the task of interpretation." Davies Warehouse Co. v. Bowles, 321 U.S. 144, 154, 64 S.Ct. 474, 480, 88 L.Ed. 635 (1944). Cf. Gregory v. Ashcroft, 501 U.S. 452, 457–460, 111 S.Ct. 2395, 2399–2401, 115 L.Ed.2d 410 (1991).

There is another artificially constructed criterion we might look to instead of "fair market price." One might judge there to be such a thing as a "reasonable" or "fair" forced-sale price. Such a conviction must lie behind the Bundles inquiry into whether the state foreclosure proceedings "were calculated . . . to return to the debtor-mortgagor his equity in the property." 856 F.2d, at 824. And perhaps that is what the courts that follow the Durrett rule have in mind when they select 70% of fair market value as the outer limit of "reasonably equivalent value" for forecloseable property (we have no idea where else such an arbitrary percentage could have come from). The problem is that such judgments represent policy determinations which the Bankruptcy Code gives us no apparent authority to make. How closely the price received in a forced sale is likely to approximate fair market value depends upon the terms of the forced sale—how quickly it may be made, what sort of public notice must be given, etc. But the terms for foreclosure sale are not standard. They vary considerably from State to State, depending upon, among other things, how the particular State values the divergent interests of debtor and creditor. To specify a federal "reasonable" foreclosure-sale price is to extend federal bankruptcy law well beyond the traditional field of fraudulent transfers, into realms of policy where it has not ventured before. * * *

[T]he States have created diverse networks of judicially and legislatively crafted rules governing the foreclosure process, to achieve what each of them considers the proper balance between the needs of lenders and borrowers. * * * Foreclosure laws typically require notice to the defaulting borrower, a substantial lead time before the commencement of foreclosure proceedings, publication of a notice of sale, and strict adherence to prescribed bidding rules and auction procedures. Many States require that the auction be conducted by a government official, and some forbid the property to be sold for less than a specified fraction of a mandatory presale fair-market-value appraisal. When these procedures have been followed, however, it is "black letter" law that mere inadequacy of the foreclosure sale price is no basis for setting the sale aside, though it may be set aside (*under state foreclosure law*, rather than fraudulent transfer law) if the price is so low as to "shock the conscience or raise a presumption of fraud or unfairness." Osborne, Nelson, & Whitman, [Real Estate Finance Law 469 (1979)].

Fraudulent transfer law and foreclosure law enjoyed over 400 years of peaceful coexistence in Anglo-American jurisprudence until the Fifth Circuit's unprecedented 1980 decision in Durrett. To our knowledge no prior decision had ever applied the "grossly inadequate price" badge of fraud under fraudulent transfer law to set aside a foreclosure sale. To say that the "reasonably equivalent value" language in the fraudulent transfer provision of the Bankruptcy Code requires a foreclosure sale to yield a certain minimum price beyond what state foreclosure law requires, is to say, in essence, that the Code has adopted Durrett or Bundles. Surely Congress has the power pursuant to its constitutional grant of authority over bankruptcy, U.S. Const., Art. I, § 8, cl. 4, to disrupt the ancient harmony that foreclosure law and fraudulent-conveyance law, those two pillars of debtor-creditor jurisprudence, have heretofore enjoyed. But absent clearer textual guidance than the phrase "reasonably equivalent value"—a phrase entirely compatible with pre-existing practice—we will not presume such a radical departure.

Federal statutes impinging upon important state interests "cannot . . . be construed without regard to the implications of our dual system of government. . . . [W]hen the Federal Government takes over . . . local radiations in the vast network of our national economic enterprise and thereby radically readjusts the balance of state and national authority, those charged with the duty of legislating [must be] reasonably explicit." F. Frankfurter, Some Reflections on the Reading of Statutes, 47 Colum.L.Rev. 527, 539–540 (1947), quoted in Kelly v. Robinson, 479 U.S. 36, 49–50 n. 11, 107 S.Ct. 353, 360–362 n. 11, 93 L.Ed.2d 216 (1986). It is beyond question that an essential state interest is at issue here: we have said that "the general welfare of society is involved in the security of the titles to real estate" and the power to ensure that security "inheres in the very nature of [state] government." American Land Co. v. Zeiss, 219 U.S. 47, 60, 31 S.Ct. 200, 204, 55 L.Ed. 82 (1911). Nor is there any doubt that the interpretation urged by petitioner would have a profound effect upon that interest: the title of every piece of realty purchased at foreclosure would be under a federally created cloud. (Already, title insurers have reacted to the Durrett rule by including specially crafted exceptions from coverage in many policies issued for properties purchased at foreclosure sales. See, e.g., L. Cherkis & L. King, Collier Real Estate Transactions and the Bankruptcy Code 5–18 to 5–19 (1992).) To displace traditional State regulation in such a manner, the federal statutory purpose must be "clear and manifest," English v. General Electric Co., 496 U.S. 72, 79, 110 S.Ct. 2270, 2275, 110 L.Ed.2d 65 (1990). Cf. Gregory v. Ashcroft, 501 U.S., at 460, 111 S.Ct., at 2401, 115 L.Ed.2d 410 (1991). Otherwise, the Bankruptcy Code will be construed to adopt, rather than to displace, pre-existing state law.

For the reasons described, we decline to read the phrase "reasonably equivalent value" in § 548(a)(2) to mean, in its application to mortgage foreclosure sales, either "fair market value" or "fair foreclosure price" (whether calculated as a percentage of fair market value or otherwise). We deem, as the law has always deemed, that a fair and proper price, or a "reasonably equivalent value," for foreclosed property, is the price in fact received at the foreclosure sale, so long as all the requirements of the State's foreclosure law have been complied with.

This conclusion does not render § 548(a)(2) superfluous, since the "reasonably equivalent value" criterion will continue to have independent meaning (ordinarily a meaning similar to fair market value) outside the foreclosure context. Indeed, § 548(a)(2) will even continue to be an exclusive means of invalidating some foreclosure sales. Although *collusive* foreclosure sales are likely subject to attack under § 548(a)(1), which authorizes the trustee to avoid transfers "made . . . with actual intent to hinder, delay, or defraud" creditors, that provision may not reach foreclosure sales that, while not intentionally fraudulent, nevertheless fail to comply with all governing state laws. Cf. 4 L. King, Collier on Bankruptcy P 548.02, p. 548–35 (15th ed. 1993) (contrasting subsections (a)(1) and (a)(2)(A) of § 548). Any irregularity in the conduct of the sale that would permit judicial invalidation of the sale under applicable state law deprives the sale price of its conclusive force under § 548(a)(2)(A), and the transfer may be avoided if the price received was not reasonably equivalent to the property's actual value at the time of the sale (which we think would be the price that would have been received if the foreclosure sale had proceeded according to law).

. . .

For the foregoing reasons, the judgment of the Court of Appeals for the Ninth Circuit is

Affirmed.

JUSTICE SOUTER, with whom JUSTICE BLACKMUN, JUSTICE STEVENS, and JUSTICE GINSBURG join, dissenting.

The Court today holds that by the terms of the Bankruptcy Code Congress intended a peppercorn paid at a noncollusive and procedurally regular foreclosure sale to be treated as the "reasonabl[e] equivalent" of the value of a California beachfront estate. Because the Court's reasoning fails both to overcome the implausibility of that proposition and to justify engrafting a foreclosure-sale exception onto 11 U.S.C.A. § 548(a)(2)(A), in derogation of the straightforward language used by Congress, I respectfully dissent.

. . .

The question before the Court is whether the price received at a foreclosure sale after compliance with state procedural rules in a non collusive sale must be treated conclusively as the "reasonably equivalent value" of the mortgaged property and in answering that question, the words and meaning of § 548(a)(2)(A) are plain. A trustee is authorized to avoid certain recent pre-bankruptcy transfers, including those on foreclosure sales, that a bankruptcy court determines were not made in exchange for "a reasonably equivalent value." Although this formulation makes no pretense to mathematical precision, an ordinary speaker of English would have no difficulty grasping its basic thrust: the bankruptcy court must compare the price received by the insolvent debtor and the worth of the item when sold and set aside the transfer if the former was substantially ("[un]reasonabl[y]") "less than" the latter. Nor would any ordinary English speaker, concerned to determine whether a foreclosure sale was collusive or procedurally irregular (an enquiry going exclusively to the process by which a transaction was consummated), direct an adjudicator, as the Court now holds Congress did, to ascertain whether the sale had realized "less than a reasonably equivalent value" (an enquiry described in quintessentially substantive terms).

. . .

In 1984 * * * Congress * * * amend[ed] the Code in two relevant respects. See Bankruptcy Amendments and Federal Judgeship Act of 1984, Pub.L. 98–353 §§ 401(1), 463(a), 98 Stat. 368, 370. One amendment provided expressly that "involuntar[y]" transfers are no less within the trustee's § 548 avoidance powers than "voluntar[y]" ones, and another provided that the "foreclosure of the debtor's equity of redemption" itself is a "transfer" for purposes of bankruptcy law. See 11 U.S.C.A. § 101(54) (1988 ed., Supp. IV). Thus, whether or not one believes (as the majority seemingly does not) that foreclosure sales rightfully belong within the historic domain of "fraudulent conveyance" law, that is exactly where Congress has now put them, and our duty is to give effect to these new amendments, along with every other clause of the Bankruptcy Code. The Court's attempt to escape the plain effect of § 548(a)(2)(A) opens it to some equally plain objections.

. . .

I do not share in my colleagues' apparently extreme discomfort at the prospect of vesting bankruptcy courts with responsibility for determining whether "reasonably equivalent value" was received in cases like this one, nor is the suggestion well taken that doing so is an improper abdication. Those courts regularly make comparably difficult (and contestable) determinations about the "reasonably equivalent value" of assets transferred through other means than foreclosure sales. * * * As in other § 548(a)(2) cases, a trustee seeking avoidance of a foreclosure-sale transfer must persuade the bankruptcy court that the price obtained on pre-bankruptcy transfer was, "unreasonabl[y]" low, and as in other cases under the provision, the gravamen of such a claim will be that the challenged transfer significantly and needlessly diminished the bankruptcy estate, i.e., that it extinguished a substantial equity interest of the debtor and that the foreclosing mortgagee failed to take measures which (consistently with state law, if not required by it) would have augmented the price realized.

. . .

What plain meaning requires and courts can provide, indeed, the policies underlying a national bankruptcy law fully support. * * * Permitting avoidance of procedurally regular foreclosure sales for low prices (and thereby returning a valuable asset to the bankruptcy estate) is plainly consistent with those policies of obtaining a maximum and equitable distribution for creditors and ensuring a "fresh start" for individual debtors, which the Court has often said are at the core of federal bankruptcy law. They are not, of course, any less the policies of federal bankruptcy law simply because state courts will not, for a mortgagor's benefit, set aside a foreclosure sale for "price inadequacy" alone. The unwillingness of the state courts to upset a foreclosure sale for that reason does not address the question of what "reasonably equivalent value" means in bankruptcy law, any more than the refusal of those same courts to set aside a contract for "mere inadequacy of consideration," see Restatement (Second) of Contracts § 79 (1981), would define the scope of the trustee's power to reject executory contracts. See 11 U.S.C.A. § 365 (1988 ed. and Supp. IV). On the contrary, a central premise of the bankruptcy avoidance powers is that what state law plainly allows as acceptable or "fair," as between a debtor and a particular creditor, may be set aside because of its impact on other creditors or on the debtor's chances for a fresh start.

. . .

RadLAX Gateway Hotel, LLC v. Amalgated Bank

Supreme Court of the United States, 2012.
132 S.Ct. 2065.

JUSTICE SCALIA delivered the opinion of the Court.

We consider whether a Chapter 11 bankruptcy plan may be confirmed over the objection of a secured creditor pursuant to 11 U.S.C. § 1129(b)(2)(A) if the plan provides for the sale of collateral free and clear of the creditor's lien, but does not permit the creditor to "credit-bid" at the sale.

I

In 2007, petitioners RadLAX Gateway Hotel, LLC, and RadLAX Gateway Deck, LLC (hereinafter debtors), purchased the Radisson Hotel at Los Angeles International Airport, together with an adjacent lot on which the debtors planned to build a parking structure. To finance the purchase, the renovation of the hotel, and construction of the parking structure, the debtors obtained a $142 million loan from Longview Ultra Construction Loan Investment Fund, for which respondent Amalgamated Bank (hereinafter creditor or Bank) serves as trustee. The lenders obtained a blanket lien on all of the debtors' assets to secure the loan.

Completing the parking structure proved more expensive than anticipated, and within two years the debtors had run out of funds and were forced to halt construction. By August 2009, they owed more than $120 million on the loan, with over $1 million in interest accruing every month and no prospect for obtaining additional funds to complete the project. Both debtors filed voluntary petitions for relief under Chapter 11 of the Bankruptcy Code.

A Chapter 11 bankruptcy is implemented according to a "plan," typically proposed by the debtor, which divides claims against the debtor into separate "classes" and specifies the treatment each class will receive. See 11 U.S.C. § 1123. Generally, a bankruptcy court may confirm a Chapter 11 plan only if each class of creditors affected by the plan consents. See § 1129(a)(8). Section 1129(b) creates an exception to that general rule, permitting confirmation of nonconsensual plans— commonly known as "cramdown" plans—if "the plan does not discriminate unfairly, and is fair and equitable, with respect to each class of claims or interests that is impaired under, and has not accepted, the plan." Section 1129(b)(2)(A), which we review in further depth below, establishes criteria for determining whether a cramdown plan is "fair and equitable" with respect to secured claims like the Bank's.

In 2010, the RadLAX debtors submitted a Chapter 11 plan to the United States Bankruptcy Court for the Northern District of Illinois. The plan proposed to dissolve the debtors and to sell substantially all of their assets pursuant to procedures set out in a contemporaneously filed "Sale and Bid Procedures Motion." Specifically, the debtors sought to auction their assets to the highest bidder, with the initial bid submitted by a "stalking horse"—a potential purchaser who was willing to make an advance bid of $47.5 million. The sale proceeds would be used to fund the plan, primarily by repaying the Bank. Of course the Bank itself might wish to obtain the property if the alternative would be receiving auction proceeds that fall short of the property's full value. Under the debtors' proposed auction procedures, however, the Bank would not be permitted to bid for the property using the debt it is owed to offset the purchase price, a practice known as "credit-bidding." Instead, the Bank would be forced to bid cash. Correctly anticipating that the Bank would object to this arrangement, the debtors sought to confirm their plan under the cramdown provisions of § 1129(b)(2)(A).

The Bankruptcy Court denied the debtors' Sale and Bid Procedures Motion, concluding that the proposed auction procedures did not comply with § 1129(b)(2)(A)'s requirements for cramdown plans. *In re River Road Hotel Partners, LLC,* Case No. 09 B 30029, 2010 WL 6634603 (N.D.Ill., Oct. 5, 2010), App. to Pet. for Cert. 40a. The Bankruptcy Court certified an appeal directly to the United States Court of Appeals for the Seventh Circuit. That court accepted the certification and affirmed, holding that § 1129(b)(2)(A) does not permit debtors to sell an encumbered asset free and clear of a lien without permitting the lienholder to credit-bid. *River Road Hotel Partners, LLC, et al. v. Amalgamated Bank,* 651 F.3d 642 (2011). We granted certiorari. 565 U.S. ___, 132 S.Ct. 845, 181 L.Ed.2d 547 (2011).

II

A

A Chapter 11 plan confirmed over the objection of a "class of secured claims" must meet one of three requirements in order to be deemed "fair and equitable" with respect to the nonconsenting creditor's claim. The plan must provide:

> "(i)(I) that the holders of such claims retain the liens securing such claims, whether the property subject to such liens is retained by the debtor or transferred to another entity, to the extent of the allowed amount of such claims; and (II) that each holder of a claim of such class receive on account of such claim deferred cash payments totaling at least the allowed amount of such claim, of a value, as of the effective date of the plan, of at least the value of such holder's interest in the estate's interest in such property;

> "(ii) for the sale, subject to section 363(k) of this title, of any property that is subject to the liens securing such claims, free and clear of such liens, with such liens to attach to the proceeds of such sale, and the treatment of such liens on proceeds under clause (i) or (iii) of this subparagraph; or

> "(iii) for the realization by such holders of the indubitable equivalent of such claims." 11 U.S.C. § 1129(b)(2)(A).

Under clause (i), the secured creditor retains its lien on the property and receives deferred cash payments. Under clause (ii), the property is sold free and clear of the lien, "subject to section 363(k)," and the creditor receives a lien on the proceeds of the sale. Section 363(k), in turn, provides that "unless the court for cause orders otherwise the holder of such claim may bid at such sale, and, if the holder of such claim purchases such property, such holder may offset such claim against the purchase price of such property"—*i.e.,* the creditor may credit-bid at the sale, up to the amount of its claim.[2] Finally, under clause (iii), the plan provides the secured creditor with the "indubitable equivalent" of its claim.

The debtors in this case have proposed to sell their property free and clear of the Bank's liens, and to repay the Bank using the sale proceeds—precisely, it would seem, the disposition contemplated by clause (ii). Yet since the debtors' proposed auction procedures do not permit the Bank to credit-bid, the proposed sale cannot satisfy the

---

[2] The ability to credit-bid helps to protect a creditor against the risk that its collateral will be sold at a depressed price. It enables the creditor to purchase the collateral for what it considers the fair market price (up to the amount of its security interest) without committing additional cash to protect the loan. That right is particularly important for the Federal Government, which is frequently a secured creditor in bankruptcy and which often lacks appropriations authority to throw good money after bad in a cash-only bankruptcy auction.

requirements of clause (ii).[3] Recognizing this problem, the debtors instead seek plan confirmation pursuant to clause (iii), which—unlike clause (ii)—does not expressly foreclose the possibility of a sale without credit-bidding. According to the debtors, their plan can satisfy clause (iii) by ultimately providing the Bank with the "indubitable equivalent" of its secured claim, in the form of cash generated by the auction.

We find the debtors' reading of § 1129(b)(2)(A)—under which clause (iii) permits precisely what clause (ii) proscribes—to be hyperliteral and contrary to common sense. A well established canon of statutory interpretation succinctly captures the problem: "[I]t is a commonplace of statutory construction that the specific governs the general." *Morales v. Trans World Airlines, Inc.,* 504 U.S. 374, 384, 112 S.Ct. 2031, 119 L.Ed.2d 157 (1992). That is particularly true where, as in § 1129(b)(2)(A), "Congress has enacted a comprehensive scheme and has deliberately targeted specific problems with specific solutions." *Varity Corp. v. Howe,* 516 U.S. 489, 519, 116 S.Ct. 1065, 134 L.Ed.2d 130 (1996) (THOMAS, J., dissenting); see also *HCSC-Laundry v. United States,* 450 U.S. 1, 6, 101 S.Ct. 836, 67 L.Ed.2d 1 (1981) *(per curiam)* (the specific governs the general "particularly when the two are interrelated and closely positioned, both in fact being parts of [the same statutory scheme]").

The general/specific canon is perhaps most frequently applied to statutes in which a general permission or prohibition is contradicted by a specific prohibition or permission. To eliminate the contradiction, the specific provision is construed as an exception to the general one. See, *e.g., Morton v. Mancari,* 417 U.S. 535, 550–551, 94 S.Ct. 2474, 41 L.Ed.2d 290 (1974). But the canon has full application as well to statutes such as the one here, in which a general authorization and a more limited, specific authorization exist side-by-side. There the canon avoids not contradiction but the superfluity of a specific provision that is swallowed by the general one, "violat[ing] the cardinal rule that, if possible, effect shall be given to every clause and part of a statute." *D. Ginsberg & Sons, Inc. v. Popkin,* 285 U.S. 204, 208, 52 S.Ct. 322, 76 L.Ed. 704 (1932). The terms of the specific authorization must be complied with. For example, in the last cited case a provision of the Bankruptcy Act prescribed in great detail the procedures governing the arrest and detention of bankrupts about to leave the district in order to avoid examination. The Court held that those prescriptions could not be avoided by relying upon a general provision of the Act authorizing bankruptcy courts to " 'make such orders, issue such process, and enter such judgments in addition to those specifically provided for as may be necessary for the enforcement of the provisions of [the] Act.' " *Id.,* at 206, 52 S.Ct. 322 (quoting Bankruptcy Act of 1898, § 2(15), 30 Stat. 546). The Court said that "[g]eneral language of a statutory provision, although broad enough to include it, will not be held to apply to a matter specifically dealt with in another part of the same enactment." 285 U.S., at 208, 52 S.Ct. 322. We recently quoted that language

---

[3] Title 11 U.S.C. § 363(k)—and by extension clause (ii)—provides an exception to the credit-bidding requirement if "the court for cause orders otherwise." The Bankruptcy Court found that there was no "cause" to deny credit-bidding in this case, and the debtors have not appealed that disposition.

approvingly in *Bloate v. United States,* 559 U.S. 196, ___, 130 S.Ct. 1345, 1354, 176 L.Ed.2d 54 (2010). Or as we said in a much earlier case:

> "It is an old and familiar rule that, where there is, in the same statute, a particular enactment, and also a general one, which, in its most comprehensive sense, would include what is embraced in the former, the particular enactment must be operative, and the general enactment must be taken to affect only such cases within its general language as are not within the provisions of the particular enactment. This rule applies wherever an act contains general provisions and also special ones upon a subject, which, standing alone, the general provisions would include." *United States v. Chase,* 135 U.S. 255, 260, 10 S.Ct. 756, 34 L.Ed. 117 (1890) (citations and internal quotation marks omitted).

Here, clause (ii) is a detailed provision that spells out the requirements for selling collateral free of liens, while clause (iii) is a broadly worded provision that says nothing about such a sale. The general/specific canon explains that the "general language" of clause (iii), "although broad enough to include it, will not be held to apply to a matter specifically dealt with" in clause (ii). *D. Ginsberg & Sons, Inc., supra,* at 208, 52 S.Ct. 322.

Of course the general/specific canon is not an absolute rule, but is merely a strong indication of statutory meaning that can be overcome by textual indications that point in the other direction. The debtors point to no such indication here. One can conceive of a statutory scheme in which the specific provision embraced within a general one is not superfluous, because it creates a so-called safe harbor. The debtors effectively contend that that is the case here—clause (iii) ("indubitable equivalent") being the general rule, and clauses (i) and (ii) setting forth procedures that will always, *ipso facto,* establish an "indubitable equivalent," with no need for judicial evaluation. But the structure here would be a surpassingly strange manner of accomplishing that result—which would normally be achieved by setting forth the "indubitable equivalent" rule first (rather than last), and establishing the two safe harbors as provisos to that rule. The structure here suggests, to the contrary, that (i) is the rule for plans under which the creditor's lien remains on the property, (ii) is the rule for plans under which the property is sold free and clear of the creditor's lien, and (iii) is a residual provision covering dispositions under all other plans—for example, one under which the creditor receives the property itself, the "indubitable equivalent" of its secured claim. Thus, debtors may not sell their property free of liens under § 1129(b)(2)(A) without allowing lienholders to credit-bid, as required by clause (ii).

B

None of the debtors' objections to this approach is valid.

The debtors' principal textual argument is that § 1129(b)(2)(A) "unambiguously provides three distinct options for confirming a Chapter 11 plan over the objection of a secured creditor." Brief for Petitioners 15 (capitalization and bold typeface removed). With that much we agree; the three clauses of § 1129(b)(2)(A) are connected by the disjunctive "or." The debtors contend that our interpretation of

§ 1129(b)(2)(A) "transforms 'or' into 'and.' " Reply Brief for Petitioners 3. But that is not so. The question here is not whether debtors must comply with more than one clause, but rather which one of the three they must satisfy. Debtors seeking to sell their property free of liens under § 1129(b)(2)(A) must satisfy the requirements of clause (ii), not the requirements of *both* clauses (ii) and (iii).

The debtors make several arguments against applying the general/specific canon. They contend that clause (ii) is no more specific than clause (iii), because the former provides a procedural protection to secured creditors (credit-bidding) while the latter provides a substantive protection (indubitable equivalence). As a result, they say, clause (ii) is not "a limiting subset" of clause (iii), which (according to their view) application of the general/specific canon requires. Brief for Petitioners 30–31; Reply Brief for Petitioners 5–6. To begin with, we know of no authority for the proposition that the canon is confined to situations in which the entirety of the specific provision is a "subset" of the general one. When the conduct at issue falls within the scope of *both* provisions, the specific presumptively governs, whether or not the specific provision also applies to some conduct that falls outside the general. In any case, we think clause (ii) is entirely a subset. Clause (iii) applies to *all* cramdown plans, which include all of the plans within the more narrow category described in clause (ii).[4] That its requirements are "substantive" whereas clause (ii)'s are "procedural" is quite beside the point. What counts for application of the general/specific canon is not the *nature* of the provisions' prescriptions but their *scope*.

Finally, the debtors contend that the Court of Appeals conflated approval of bid procedures with plan confirmation. Brief for Petitioners 39. They claim the right to pursue their auction now, leaving it for the Bankruptcy Judge to determine, at the confirmation stage, whether the resulting plan (funded by auction proceeds) provides the Bank with the "indubitable equivalent" of its secured claim. Under our interpretation of § 1129(b)(2)(A), however, that approach is simply a nonstarter. As a matter of law, no bid procedures like the ones proposed here *could* satisfy the requirements of § 1129(b)(2)(A), and the distinction between approval of bid procedures and plan confirmation is therefore irrelevant.

III

The parties debate at some length the purposes of the Bankruptcy Code, pre-Code practices, and the merits of credit-bidding. To varying extents, some of those debates also occupied the attention of the Courts of Appeals that considered the question presented here. See, *e.g., In re Philadelphia Newspapers, LLC,* 599 F.3d 298, 314–317 (C.A.3 2010); *id.,* at 331–337 (Ambro, J., dissenting). But nothing in the generalized statutory purpose of protecting secured creditors can overcome the specific manner of that protection which the text of § 1129(b)(2)(A) contains. As for pre-Code practices, they can be relevant to the interpretation of an ambiguous text, but we find no textual ambiguity

---

[4]   We are speaking here about whether clause (ii) is a subset for purposes of determining whether the canon applies. As we have described earlier, *after* applying the canon—*ex post,* so to speak—it ceases to be a subset, governing a situation to which clause (iii) will no longer be deemed applicable.

here. And the pros and cons of credit-bidding are for the consideration of Congress, not the courts.

The Bankruptcy Code standardizes an expansive (and sometimes unruly) area of law, and it is our obligation to interpret the Code clearly and predictably using well established principles of statutory construction. See *United States v. Ron Pair Enterprises, Inc.*, 489 U.S. 235, 240–241, 109 S.Ct. 1026, 103 L.Ed.2d 290 (1989). Under that approach, this is an easy case. Because the RadLAX debtors may not obtain confirmation of a Chapter 11 cramdown plan that provides for the sale of collateral free and clear of the Bank's lien, but does not permit the Bank to credit-bid at the sale, we affirm the judgment of the Court of Appeals.

It is so ordered.

JUSTICE KENNEDY took no part in the decision of this case.

NOTES

1. *BFP and Its Legacy. BFP* settled an issue that had divided courts since the *Durrett* decision. See In re Brown, 104 B.R. 609 (Bkrtcy.S.D.N.Y.1989) (describing the different approaches applied by the courts). Nevertheless, the clash between the majority and dissent clash over statutory interpretation, policy goals, and judicial philosophy has produced new reverberations. Consider the following examples.

Assume that the outstanding balance on a mortgage being foreclosed is $100,000 and that the fair market value of the property is $300,000. How much would the mortgagee bid for the property at the sale under the rule of the majority opinion compared to the alternative rules? Is the result troubling?

While the majority opinion eliminates the uncertainty, and associated costs, of a *Durrett* or *Bundles* approach, has it created a new problem in defining a "collusive" foreclosure? For example, will a foreclosure be "collusive" if the mortgagee agrees with a third party that the mortgagee will buy the property at the foreclosure sale and then sell it to the third party? Assume that the outstanding balance on the loan is $100,000, would the result differ if the resale price to the third party is $80,000 as opposed to $120,000?

For an excellent analysis of the *BFP* decision and its aftermath, see Stark, The Emperor Still Has Clothes: Fraudulent Conveyance Challenges After the *BFP* Decision, 47 S.C.L.Rev. 563, 566 (1996) ("In light of the numerous state law challenges that mortgagors can raise to invalidate an unfair sale and empirical studies that show that lenders are not made whole under existing foreclosure laws, the majority in *BFP* correctly interpreted 'reasonably equivalent value' to mean the amount realized at a noncollusive, regularly conducted foreclosure proceeding"). See also Boyce, The Supreme Court and the Death of Durrett, 23 Real Est.L.J. 205 (1995); Note, A Palace for a Peppercorn: A Post-*BFP* Proposal to Resurrect Section 548(a)(2)(A), 73 Wash.U.L.Q. 1747 (1995).

State Law. Fraudulent conveyances can be actionable outside of bankruptcy under state law. Section 512(c) of the Uniform Land Security Interest Act specifically rejects the *Durrett* approach, stating that "a regularly conducted, noncollusive transfer" under judicial or nonjudicial foreclosure to a transferee for value and in good faith is not a fraudulent conveyance even though the amount paid is less than the value of the mortgagor's interest in the land. The Uniform Fraudulent Transfer Act, adopted in thirty-three states, similarly limits challenges by providing that "a person gives reasonably equivalent value if the person acquires an interest of the debtor in an asset pursuant to a regularly conducted, noncollusive foreclosure sale or execution of a power of sale for the acquisition or disposition of the interest of the debtor upon default under a mortgage, deed of trust, or security agreement."

For discussion of *Durrett* and related matters, see Alden, Gross & Borowitz, Real Property Foreclosure as a Fraudulent Conveyance: Proposals for Solving the *Durrett* Problem, 38 Bus.Law. 1605 (1983); Fiaccus, Pre-Petition and Post-Petition Mortgage Foreclosures and Tax Sales and the Faulty Reasoning of the Supreme Court, 51 Ark. L. Rev. 25 (1998); Mattingly, Reestablishment of Bankruptcy Review of Oppressive Foreclosure Sales: The Interaction of Avoidance Powers as Applied to Creditor Bid-Ins, 50 S.C.L. Rev. 363 (1999); Simpson, Real Property Foreclosures: The Fallacy of *Durrett,* 19 Real Prop., Probate & Trust J. 73 (1984); Schuchman, Data on the *Durrett* Controversy, 9 Cardozo L.Rev. 605 (1987); Shanker, What Every Lawyer Should Know About the Law of Fraudulent Transfers, 31 Prac.Law. 43 (No. 8, 1985).

Arguing for different treatment of refinancing mortgages and purchase money mortgages in bankruptcy, see Dickerson, Bankruptcy and Mortgage Lending: The Homeowner Dilemna, 38 J.Marshall L.Rev. 19 (2004).

2. *Preferences.* Section 547(b) of the Bankruptcy Code permits a trustee in bankruptcy to avoid transfers of property by an insolvent debtor within 90 days of bankruptcy if the transfer was on account of antecedent debt, was for the benefit of a creditor, and would enable the creditor to get a larger share of the estate than she would have received if the transfer had not been made. Such avoidable payments are known as preferences. The purpose of the preference rule is to discourage creditors from demanding payments during a debtor's slide into bankruptcy that will dismember the business, making it less possible for the debtor to work his way out of the problem. The preference rule also helps foster equality of all treatment of creditors by preventing some from getting a disproportionate share of the debtor's assets. See H.R.Rep. No. 95–595, pp. 177–178, printed in U.S.Cong. & Admin. News 1978, pp. 6137–6138.

Should monthly payments by a mortgagor to a mortgagee within 90 days of bankruptcy be subject to scrutiny as preferences? Section 547(c)(2)(B) of the Code states that transfers otherwise treated as avoidable preferences will not be considered such if they are payments "made in the 'ordinary course of business of financial affairs' of the debtor and transferee." In Union Bank v. Wolas, 502 U.S. 151, 155, 112 S.Ct. 527, 530, 116 L.Ed.2d 514 (1991), the Supreme Court rejected the position of some courts of appeals (see, e.g., In re CHG International, Inc., 897 F.2d 1479 (9th Cir.1990)) which held that the payment in the ordinary course exception applies only to short term debt and not long term debt. The Court held that payments to a lender under a long term revolving credit agreement within 90 days of bankruptcy could be excepted from treatment as a voidable preference and remanded for a determination of whether the two interest payments and commitment fee payment were in the ordinary course of business.

Lenders face the risk that payments or property transfers made in a workout attempt might be attacked as preferences if bankruptcy ultimately results. See Murray, Deeds In Lieu of Foreclosure: Practical and Legal Considerations, 26 Real Prop. Probate & Trust J. 459, 476–478 (1991).

3. *The Automatic Stay.* One complaint frequently heard from real estate lenders in the discussions that led to passage of the 1978 Bankruptcy Code was that the previous act harbored several devices capable of impairing their security interests during the course of reorganization proceedings. One device, the automatic stay of foreclosure proceedings upon the filing of a petition, was particularly obnoxious. Stays can seem interminable, and possibly devastating, when real property security is daily decreasing in value because of the borrower's distressed circumstances. Lenders were also concerned about the previous act's provisions governing trustee's certificates. There was some authority under the previous act that trustees could obtain new debt financing by issuing certificates secured by liens on the debtor's property that would become senior to liens securing loans made prior to the petition, thus unilaterally subordinating the secured lender's position. See In re St. Simon's Properties, 11 C.B.C. 729 (Bkrtcy.N.D.Ga.1976).

The Bankruptcy Code responded to these concerns modestly, modifying and refining old rules rather than introducing dramatic innovations. Automatic stays and senior or equal liens are authorized in sections 362 and 364, respectively. Their potential for impairing the lender's security is, however, limited by the requirement that the automatic stay be lifted, and the senior or equal lien be barred, if necessary for the "adequate protection" of the secured lender. Still, the lender's protection is far from complete. The measure of adequate protection is tied to the value of the collateral, and remedial steps will be triggered only by decreases in the collateral's present value. There is no assurance that the accruing *interest* obligations will be paid off in full.

Section 361 describes three ways in which adequate protection can be afforded: (1) requiring the trustee to make periodic cash payments to the lender to the extent that the stay, lien, or "use, sale, or lease [by the trustee] under section 363" results in a decrease in the value of the lender's interest in the property; (2) providing an additional or replacement lien to make up for the decrease in value; and (3) granting any other relief that will enable the lender to realize "the indubitable equivalent of [its] interest in [the] property." Section 362(d)(2) also requires that a stay of foreclosure be lifted if the debtor has no equity in the property and the property is "not necessary to an effective reorganization."

Before the Bankruptcy Reform Act of 1994 courts had diverged on whether a stay should be granted for a bankruptcy proceeding where the debtor's only asset was a single real estate property. The 1994 Act expressly permits a single asset real estate bankruptcy under the Code, defining such a project as "real property constituting a single property or project, other than residential real property with fewer than [four] residential units, which generates substantially all of the gross income of a debtor and [having] secured debts in an amount no more than $4,000,000." 11 U.S.C.A. § 101(51B). The creditor in such a bankruptcy is entitled to relief from the automatic stay of a foreclosure action if a motion is made within ninety days after the filing of the bankruptcy petition unless the debtor has filed a reorganization plan that has a reasonable possibility of confirmation and the debtor has begun to make monthly payments to creditors holding security interests in the realty. 11 U.S.C.A. § 362(d)(3).

For an excellent discussion of this and other aspects of the 1994 legislation, see Dunaway, Effect of the Bankruptcy Reform Act of 1994 on Real Estate, 30 Real Prop. Probate & Tr.J. 645 (1996). For an in-depth analysis, see Bogart, Games Lawyers Play: Waivers of the Automatic Stay in Bankruptcy and the Single Asset Loan Workout, 43 U.C.L.A.L.Rev. 1117 (1996) (also offering an intriguing general theory of how transactional lawyers "make law"). See also Miller & Murray, Waivers of Automatic Stay: Are They Enforceable (And Does the New Bankruptcy Act Make A Difference)?, 41 Real Prop. Probate & Tr.J. 357 (2006).

The Bankruptcy Reform Act of 1994 addressed another troubling issue. Under prior law, a creditor could only collect rents from the debtor's property after a bankruptcy petition had been filed if the creditor had perfected an assignment of rents under state law. Judicial signals had been mixed as to when and how perfection had to be accomplished. The 1994 legislation provides that a security interest in rents applies to rents acquired by the estate after commencement of the bankruptcy proceeding even if the security interest is not fully perfected under state law. 11 U.S.C.A. § 552(b)(2). See Carlson, Rents in Bankruptcy, 46 S.C.L.Rev. 1075 (1996). For excellent analyses of the problems with rents before the 1994 Act, see Randolph, Recognizing Lenders' Rents Interests in Bankruptcy, 27 Real Prop. Probate & Tr.J. 281 (1992); Randolph, When Should Bankruptcy Courts Recognize Lenders' Rents Interests?, 23 U.C. Davis L.Rev. 833 (1990).

See generally, Kennedy, Automatic Stays Under the New Bankruptcy Law, 12 U.Mich.J.L.Ref. 3 (1978); Nimmer, Real Estate Creditors and the Automatic Stay: A Study in Behavioral Economics, 1983 Ariz.St.L.J. 281.

4. *Executory Contracts.* Section 365 of the Bankruptcy Code empowers the trustee to assume or reject the executory contracts of the debtor. The Code, however, does not define the term "executory contract." While a precise definition is difficult, many courts follow Professor Countryman's view that performance of a material obligation must remain on both sides in order for the contract to be executory. Countryman, Executory Contracts in Bankruptcy: Part II, 58 Minn.L.Rev. 479 (1974), followed in In re Speck, 798 F.2d 279 (8th Cir.1986). A mortgage note, for example, usually will not be treated as an executory contract when the only performance that remains is payment, as the other side has already fully performed. See H.R.Rep.No.95–595, 95th Cong., 1st Sess.347 (1977), reprinted in 1978 U.S. Code Cong. & Admin. News 5787, 6303.

The courts have divided on the question of whether a land sales contract is executory. When the seller has remaining material obligations, such as delivering marketable title, and the buyer has yet to pay the price, the contract is executory. See In re Leefers, 101 B.R. 24 (C.D.Ill.1989). If, however, the land sale contract is used as a financing device, such as in Skendzel v. Marshall on p. 522, and the only obligations remaining are payment by the buyer and delivery of the deed by the seller or an escrow agent, some courts hold that the contract is not executory. See, e.g., In re Kane, 248 B.R. 216 (1st Cir.App.Bankr.2000), aff'd, 254 F.3d 325 (1st Cir.2001). The seller thus takes the position of a secured creditor with respect to the buyer/debtor and the trustee cannot reject the contract.

Most courts, though, find land sale contracts used as financing vehicle to be executory on the theory that the seller still must deliver the deed. See, e.g., In re Coffman, 104 B.R. 958 (Bkrtcy.Ind.1988) (refusing to distinguish between situations when the seller has executed the deed and placed it in escrow and when the seller will not execute the deed until final payment by buyer). For an excellent analysis, see Moringiello, A Mortgage By Any Other Name: A Plea for the Uniform Treatment of Installment Land Contracts and Mortgages Under the Bankruptcy Code, 100 Dick.L.Rev. 733 (1996).

5. *Leases in Bankruptcy.* Commercial landlords and tenants are tied to each other in an extended, complex and intimate economic relationship. As a consequence, each may find itself particularly affected by the financial distress of the other. When a tenant files for liquidation or reorganization, its landlord will probably want to remove it in order to relet the premises to another, more flourishing business. The tenant's trustee, however, may want the tenant to stay on if the leased premises are essential to the tenant's rehabilitation. If it is the landlord who files for liquidation or reorganization, the tenant may have to choose between leaving the premises and staying on without vital services such as heat, water and electricity that the landlord had originally agreed to provide. Section 365 of the Bankruptcy Code seeks to resolve these and other landlord-tenant conflicts.

Protecting the landlord. Before the 1978 Bankruptcy Code, the landlord's principal safeguard against tenant bankruptcy was the so-called "ipso facto," or bankruptcy, clause. Under this lease clause, the tenant's bankruptcy automatically terminated the lease or gave the landlord the right to terminate. In cases decided under the previous Act, courts sometimes refused to honor these clauses. The Bankruptcy Code bluntly invalidates them in bankruptcy. Notwithstanding any lease provisions to the contrary, an "unexpired lease of the debtor may not be terminated or modified . . . at any time after the commencement of the case solely because of a provision in such . . . lease that is conditioned on—(A) the insolvency or financial condition of the debtor at any time before the closing of the case; (B) the commencement of a case under this title; or (C) the appointment of or taking possession by a trustee in a case under this title or a custodian before such commencement." 11 U.S.C.A. § 365(e)(1). Further, section 365(f) permits, within limits, assignment of the unexpired lease to a third party even though the lease expressly prohibits or conditions assignments.

Recognizing the risk that assumptions and assignments pose for landlords, the Bankruptcy Code requires that, for the trustee to assume the lease, she must cure any outstanding defaults on leasehold obligations, other than default on the bankruptcy clause itself, and, if there has been such a default, must provide "adequate assurance of future performance." 11 U.S.C.A. § 365(b)(1).

Landlords complained that these safeguards were insufficient. For example, under section 365(d)(4), upon a finding of "cause" a court could permit a Chapter 11 trustee to extend the time by which the trustee had to assume or reject the lease. This disadvantaged the landlord since it did not know what would happen with the premises and it could not make plans for the property and related parcels. In response, the Bankruptcy Abuse Prevention and Consumer Protection Act of 2005, Pub.L. No. 109–8, 119 Stat. 23, restricts this time period by deeming the lease automatically rejected if it is not assumed by the earlier of 120 days after the petition date or the date the reorganization plan is confirmed. An extension for "cause" is permitted but only for one 90 day period.

The 1978 Bankruptcy Code also sought to tailor the requirements for assumptions and assignments to the special needs of shopping centers, where the landlord's economic returns are closely tied to the center's overall health through percentage rental clauses, and where the overall health of the center depends on maintaining the proper mix of tenants. Section 365(b)(3) provided that "adequate assurance of future performance of a lease of real property in a shopping center includes adequate assurance—

(A) of the source of rent and other consideration due under such lease;

(B) that any percentage rent due under such lease will not decline substantially;

(C) that assumption or assignment of such lease will not breach substantially any provision, such as a radius, location, use, or exclusivity provision, in any other lease, financing agreement, or master agreement relating to such shopping center; and

(D) that assumption or assignment of such lease will not disrupt substantially any tenant mix or balance in such shopping center."

The 1984 Amendments strengthened subsection 365(b)(3)(A) by requiring that "in the case of an assignment, that the financial condition and operating performance of the proposed assignee and its guarantors, if any, shall be similar to the financial condition and operating performance of the debtor and its guarantors, if any, as of the time the debtor became the lessee under the lease. . . ." The amendments also strengthened subsections 365(b)(3)(C) and (D) by effectively removing the qualifier, "substantially," from the prohibitions against breach or disruption and providing "that assumption or assignment of such lease is subject to all the provisions thereof . . ." Pub.L. No. 98–353, § 362(a), 98 Stat. 361–63 (1984). Section 365(f)(1) was amended by the Bankruptcy Abuse Prevention and Consumer Protection Act of 2005, Pub.L. No. 109–8, 119 Stat. 23, to require that the debtor had to provide the same adequate assurances for a proposed assignee of the lease.

Rejection of the lease by the trustee is a breach of an agreement and could trigger substantial damages claims for rent due for the rest of the term. 11 U.S.C. § 502(b)(6), however, places a cap on landlord's damages, typically one year of unaccelerated rent. Court have rejected additional claims against tenants. See In re Energy Conversion Devices, Inc., 483 B.R. 119 (Bankr. E.D. Mich. 2012) (damage to property by tenant not recoverable).

Protecting the tenant. If it is the landlord who files, and if its trustee rejects an unexpired lease, section 365(h)(1)(A) allows the tenant to elect to treat the lease as terminated or to "retain its rights under such lease (including . . . any right of use, possession, quiet enjoyment, subletting, assignment or hypothecation)." The Bankruptcy Reform Act of 1994 added this phrasing to address concerns under the earlier version of the Code. The former language permitted a tenant to elect to remain in "possession," creating doubt as to whether a ground lessee, for example, could take advantage of the election since technically the ground lessee's subtenants, not the ground lessee, were in possession. See In re Harborview Development 1986 Ltd. Partnership, 152 B.R. 897 (D.S.C.1993).

If the tenant decides to stay on, section 365(h)(1)(B) protects it against the trustee's rejection of leasehold obligations, such as the obligation to maintain the premises and provide utilities, by allowing the tenant to set off the expense of these services against his rental payments. Obviously, this will cause little concern to the tenant under a typical net lease arrangement. But what of the office space tenant on the forty-second floor whose elevator service ceases?

See generally, Genovese, Easing the Tension Between Sections 363 and 365 of the Bankruptcy Code?, 39 Real Prop. Probate & Tr.J. 627 (2004); Gottfried & Goldman, In Re Burger Boys: Are Landlords Being Grilled in the Second Circuit?, 63 Brook. L. Rev. 43 (1997); Klyman & Lurie, The (Surprising) Impact of Bankruptcy on Cross-Default Provisions in Nonresidential Real Property Leases, 27 Real Est. L. J. 38 (1998); Rosenthal & Collins, A Commercial Landlord's Guide to Dealing With Financial Distress and the Bankruptcy of a Tenant, 18 Probate & Prop. 46 (Nov./Dec.2004).

6. *Reorganization.* The 1978 Bankruptcy Code modified the principles and procedures for business reorganization previously contained in Chapters X, XI and XII, consolidating them into Chapter 11, a single, comprehensive reorganization scheme. Of the three old chapters, Chapter XII was clearly the best-suited for reorganizing distressed real property ventures. Added to the Bankruptcy Act in 1938, it was originally designed to resolve depression-era problems created by a unique form of realty debt, Straus Bonds, then marketed mainly in Illinois. Unlike Chapter X, Chapter XII could be used by noncorporate debtors; unlike Chapter XI, it could be employed to alter the rights of secured creditors. Chapter XII soon fell into disuse, however, and, according to its leading student, "could appropriately have been described as the forgotten provision of the Chandler Act of 1938." W. Norton, Real Property Arrangements 1 (1977). A troubled real estate market, and the special needs of noncorporate real estate ventures, led to a brief revival in the mid-1970's.

7. *Cram Down.* One of bankruptcy law's great remedial attractions is that it enables the reorganization of a debtor's business and the modification of its liabilities with less than the unanimous consent of her creditors, discussed in RadLAX Gateway Hotel v. Amalgamated Bank. Under old Chapter XII, a plan of reorganization could be confirmed, and debts covered by the plan discharged, if, within each class of creditors affected by the plan, creditors holding two-thirds in dollar amount of the filed and allowed claims voted in favor of the plan.

The Bankruptcy Code, like the previous act, rejects the unanimity principle. An entire class of creditors will be deemed to have accepted a plan if the plan is accepted by creditors holding "at least two-thirds in amount and more than one-half in number of the allowed claims of such class held by creditors." With respect to each class, section 1129(a)(7)(A) requires that, if the vote to accept the plan was less than unanimous, each claim holder in the class must receive no less than he would receive if the debtor were liquidated under the straight bankruptcy provisions of Chapter 7.

Suppose that the consent of one or more *classes* is not obtained. Will this bar confirmation? The question is particularly important in the context of real estate reorganizations where each secured creditor—first mortgagee, second mortgagee, third mortgagee, and so on—is considered to comprise a separate class, with the result that objection from any one could stymie confirmation. Chapter XII's response to this problem was the "cram down," allowing confirmation over the objection of an entire class so long as the plan of arrangement provided "adequate protection" to the dissenting class.

The Bankruptcy Code similarly allows confirmation over the objection of one or more classes, but through a more circuitous route. The starting point is section 1129(a)(8) which requires that, for the plan to be confirmed, it must, as to each class, have been accepted by the class or not impair the class. Under section 1124 a class of claims is deemed impaired unless the plan does not alter the claimant's legal, equitable, and contractual rights or, where the creditor had a right to accelerate payment after default, the plan cures any default, reinstates the original maturity date of the claim, and compensates the claim holder for damages due to reliance on the acceleration clause. The Bankruptcy Reform Act of 1994 deleted a third means to find non-impairment that had been codified in former section 1124(3)(A). One of the key issues is defining the "class" for cramdown purposes. See In re Loop 76, LLC, 465 B.R. 525 (9th Cir. BAP 2012).

If the nonaccepting class is impaired within these terms, the debtor's only remaining alternative is a cram down under section 1129(b). Section 1129(b) authorizes confirmation over the objection of an impaired class if "the plan does not discriminate unfairly, and is fair and equitable, with respect to each class of claims or interests that is impaired under, and has not accepted, the plan." The subsection further defines "fair and equitable" to include at least one of three criteria in the case of secured creditors: (i) that the creditor retain its lien and receive deferred cash payments that, in the aggregate, at least equal the allowed amount of the claim and that, when discounted to present value as of the effective date of the plan, will equal the value of the collateral; (ii) if the collateral is to be sold unencumbered by the creditor's lien, the lien must attach to the sale proceeds; or (iii) the plan must provide for the creditor's realization of "the indubitable equivalent" of his claims. See Bank of America National Trust & Savings Ass'n v. 203 North LaSalle St. Partnership, 526 U.S. 434, 119 S.Ct. 1411, 143 L.Ed.2d 607 (1999) (barring cramdown where equity holders sought to contribute new capital and receive ownership interests but others had not been allowed to propose competing plan for equity ownership).

Section 1129(a)(10) requires as a condition to confirmation that at "least one class of claims . . . has accepted the plan." The purpose of that requirement is to assure that there is some element of a bargain in the reorganization plan by removing the possibility that, as a consequence of subsection (a)(9)'s treatment of nonimpairment, and subsection (b)'s provision for cram downs, a plan could be accepted with no vote at all. Finally, section 1129 itemizes several substantive requirements for a plan to be confirmed. Section 1129(a)(1)–(5) essentially requires compliance with other provisions of the chapter, good faith, and full disclosure of payments and of personnel to be employed by the debtor.

For a detailed analysis of cram downs under the Bankruptcy Code, see Carlson, Artificial Impairment and the Single Asset Chapter 11 Case, 23

Cap.U.L.Rev. 339 (1994); Kroese, Undersecured Residential Mortgage Cramdown Under Chapter 13: Receiving the Attention of Both the Supreme Court and Congress, 18 J.Corp.L. 737 (1993); Pachulski, The Cram Down and Valuation Under Chapter 11 of the Bankruptcy Code, 58 N.C.L.Rev. 925 (1980); Klee, All You Ever Wanted to Know About Cram Down Under the New Bankruptcy Code, 53 Bankr.L.J. 133 (1979). For a discussion of cram downs before the 1978 Bankruptcy Code, see Miller & Goldstein, Chapter XII—Real Property Arrangements: Is "Cram Down" A Debtor's Panacea? 12 Real Prop., Probate & Trust J. 695 (1977); Dole, The Chapter XII Cram-Down Provisions, 82 Com.L.J. 197 (1977); Polk, The Chapter 13 Cramdown: New Nightmare for the Lender, 19 Real Est.L.J. 279 (1991).

8. *Lender Misbehavior.* A lender can lose priority in bankruptcy under the doctrine of equitable subordination for misbehavior in the lending process. See In re Pinetree Partners, Ltd., 87 B.R. 481 (Bankr. N.D. Ohio 1988) (rejecting such claim as there was no fiduciary duty or overreaching by lender). See Murray, Deeds In Lieu of Foreclosure: Practical and Legal Considerations, 26 Real Prop. Probate & Trust J. 459, 463 (1991); Comment, Lender Liability Under a Workout Agreement: A View Toward A More Balanced Approached, 8 No.Ill.U.L.Rev. 505 (1988). In a case involving special facts of a financially troubled mortgagor's reliance on the bank for advice, one court found that a fiduciary relationship was created so that the bank was prohibited from foreclosing the mortgage and was assessed compensatory and punitive damages. Boatmen's Nat'l Bank of Hillsboro v. Ward, 231 Ill.App.3d 401, 172 Ill.Dec. 261, 595 N.E.2d 622 (1992). Consider how these cases fit into the pattern of lender liability, discussed at pages 235–238.

Professor Katherine Porter, in Misbehavior and Mistakes in Bankruptcy Mortgage Claims, 87 Tex. L. Rev. 121 (2008), presented a study of defective filings and process by lenders. See Crespi, Misbehavior and Mistake in Bankruptcy Mortgage Claim: Some Caveats Regarding the Porter Study, 45 Creighton L. Rev. 361 (2012).

9. *Federal Income Tax Consequences.* The mortgagor or mortgagee facing a default must consider the federal income tax consequences of foreclosure, of the alternatives to foreclosure, and of liquidation or reorganization.

The mortgagor. As a general rule, the Internal Revenue Code treats real property mortgage foreclosures just as it treats voluntary sales or exchanges, with capital or ordinary gain or loss treatment given accordingly. Loss or gain will be measured by the difference between the amount realized on the foreclosure sale and the taxpayer's adjusted basis in the property. If the property's fair market value exceeds the liabilities discharged, the amount of liabilities satisfied—whether recourse or nonrecourse—will be included in the amount realized. If the liabilities discharged exceed the fair market value of the property, the tax consequences will differ depending on whether the liability was recourse or nonrecourse. If the liability was recourse, the excess of liabilities over fair market value will be considered a cancellation of indebtedness and thus treated as ordinary income. See I.R.C. § 61(a)(12); Treas.Reg. § 1.1001–2(a)2 (1983). If the liability was nonrecourse, the amount realized will be treated as including the full amount of the liability; because the mortgagee has no personal action against the mortgagor, or recourse against his other assets, there is no cancellation of indebtedness income. See Treas.Reg.

§ 1.1001–2(a)(2) (1983); Commissioner v. Tufts, page 940 below. The Emergency Economic Stabilization Act of 2008, however, amended § 108(a)(1)(E) to provide an exclusion from income of up to $2 million of debt forgiveness on the taxpayer's principal residence.

The mortgagee. As a general rule, the foreclosing mortgagee is entitled to a bad debt deduction to the extent that the outstanding loan exceeds the proceeds to the mortgagee from the foreclosure sale. Special rules apply when, as often happens, it is the mortgagee who makes the winning full credit bid at the foreclosure sale. Here, the mortgagee will be entitled to deduct as a bad debt the difference between its basis in the debt and the fair market value of the property; the winning bid is presumed to represent the property's fair market value at the time of the sale. See Treas.Reg. § 1.166–6(b)(2).

Insolvency or bankruptcy. The Bankruptcy Code's reorganization provisions can soften some of the Internal Revenue Code's otherwise harsh effects for owners of distressed property. An automatic stay of foreclosure proceedings gives the taxpayer breathing space to work out an arrangement with its creditors or to time the foreclosure so that it occurs in the most advantageous year. Additionally, the 1980 Bankruptcy Tax Act amendments to the Internal Revenue Code provide that no cancellation of indebtedness income arises from the discharge of a debt in the course of bankruptcy proceedings, or while the taxpayer is insolvent; in the case of insolvency, however, the amount excluded "shall not exceed the amount by which the taxpayer is insolvent." I.R.C. § 108(a)(3). Under section 108, the bankrupt or insolvent taxpayer must pay for these exclusions from income by correspondingly reducing certain "tax attributes" (for example, the taxpayer's net operating loss in the year of discharge) or, at the taxpayer's election, reducing the basis of the taxpayer's depreciable property. I.R.C. § 108(b)(1), (2), (3), (5).

For a consideration of tax aspects of foreclosure, bankruptcy, and workouts see Onsager & Becker, The Federal Tax Consequences of Foreclosure and Repossessions, 18 J. Real Est.Tax. 291 (1991); Scheele & Ripp, Income Tax Issues Related to Distressed Commercial Real Estate, 27 Ariz.Att. 13 (Aug.-Sept.1990); Kalteyer, Real Estate Workouts—Original Issue Discount Implication of Troubled Debt Restructuring, 43 Tax Law. 579 (1990); Taggart, Workouts—Lender's Basis and Lender's Income, 45 Tax Law. 263 (1992); Phelan, The Bankruptcy Tax Act and Other Tax Considerations Relating to Real Estate Bankruptcies, in Real Estate Bankruptcies and Workouts: A Practical Perspective 45 (A. Kuklin & P. Roberts, eds. 1983); Boris, Tax Planning in Connection with the Restructuring and Recasting of Real Estate Transactions, Moratoriums, Foreclosures, Deeds in Lieu, 35th Ann.N.Y.U.Tax Inst. 963 (1977); Rabinowitz, The Failing Real Estate Investment and the Federal Income Tax, 34th Ann.N.Y.U.Tax Inst. 357 (1976).

CHAPTER IX

THE ENVIRONMENT AND REAL ESTATE TRANSACTIONS: FROM REGULATION TO GREEN BUILDINGS

Over the past several decades, environmental regulations have exposed participants in real estate transactions to potentially great liability. This new found source of legal risk substantially affects the way buyers, sellers, lenders, lessors, lessees, brokers, and others do business. The impact of environmental laws commands the attention of the parties and their counsel in virtually every real estate transaction today.

In more recent years, a new trend developed: green buildings, meaning buildings built, operated, and leased in a manner designed to minimize its carbon footprint. The drive to green buildings may be due to governmental carrots or sticks but has also been pushed by owners and tenants seeking cost efficiencies and consumer preferences.

This chapter will examine environmental liability and the green building development.

A. ENVIRONMENTAL LIABILITY: CERCLA AND RELATED STATUTES

Of the many environmental regulations that touch real estate transactions, the key statute is the federal Comprehensive Environmental Response, Compensation and Liability Act of 1980, 42 U.S.C.A. §§ 9601–9675, commonly known as "CERCLA." "Potentially responsible parties" under CERCLA include not only landowners who themselves have discharged hazardous materials but also subsequent buyers. Negligence, intent and the comparative fault of the contributors to a hazardous waste problem are irrelevant in determining liability under CERCLA; the current owner will be strictly liable even though it had no role in the discharge, did not benefit from it, and did not own the land at the time the discharge occurred. The courts have interpreted CERCLA to impose joint and several liability, see, e.g., United States v. Monsanto Co., 858 F.2d 160 (4th Cir.1988), cert. denied, 490 U.S. 1106, 109 S.Ct. 3156, 104 L.Ed.2d 1019 (1989). The current landowner alone may be held liable for the full cost of the cleanup unless it meets the difficult burden of showing that the harm is divisible or is able to obtain contribution. See pages 747–749.

Section 9607 entitles federal, state, and local governments, as well as private parties, to recover from responsible parties the "response costs" incurred by the government or private party to remedy and remove the contamination. For example, where a landowner disposes of hazardous substances that leak into a neighbor's water well, the neighbor may recover the cost of remedying the problem. Also, the federal government may remove the hazardous materials itself or, in some situations, obtain an injunction forcing responsible parties to abate the danger of contamination. 42 U.S.C.A. §§ 9604, 9606. See generally, Slap & Israel, Private CERCLA Litigation: How To Avoid It? How To Handle It? 25 Real Prop. Probate & Trust J. 705 (1991); Reitze, Harrison & Palko, Cost Recovery by Private Parties Under CERCLA: Planning a Response Action for Maximum Recovery, 27 Tulsa L.J. 365 (1992); Belthoff, Private Cost Recovery Actions Under Section 107 of CERCLA, 11 Colum.J.Envtl.L. 141 (1986).

A purchaser of contaminated land faces staggering potential liability. The purchaser stands not only to lose the value of its investment; it could also be required to dig into its pockets to clean up the land itself or pay response costs under section 9607. According to the Environmental Protection Agency, the cost of a Superfund cleanup through 1986 averaged approximately $14 million per site. See 52 Fed.Reg. 2495 (Jan. 22, 1987), discussed in Fitzsimmons & Sherwood, The Real Estate Lawyer's Primer (And More) to Superfund: The Environmental Hazards of Real Estate Transactions, 22 Real Prop. Probate & Trust J. 765, 770 (1987).

The materials that follow are intended only to introduce some of the key aspects of CERCLA affecting real estate transactions; they are not a comprehensive treatment of this very difficult and controversial statute. The materials start with liability of owners under CERCLA, then considers how this liability can be avoided, and concludes with the issue of lender liability. Consider throughout these materials how you should arrange transactions and counsel clients in light of CERCLA.

Bibliography. For an excellent analysis of the various provisions of CERCLA, see Barr, CERCLA Made Simple: An Analysis of the Cases Under the Comprehensive Environmental Response, Compensation and Liability Act of 1980, 45 Bus.Law. 923 (1990). See also R. Matthews, Superfund Claims and Litigation Manual (1990); Fitzsimmons & Sherwood, The Real Estate Lawyer's Primer (And More) to Superfund: The Environmental Hazards of Real Estate Transactions, 22 Real Prop. Probate & Trust J. 765 (1987). For excellent policy analyses of the statute, see Healy, Direct Liability For Hazardous Substance Cleanups Under CERCLA: A Comprehensive Approach, 42 Case W.Res.L.Rev. 65 (1992); Grad, A Legislative History of the Comprehensive Environmental Response, Compensation and Liability ("Superfund") Act of 1980, 8 Colum.J.Envtl.L. 1 (1982); Nagle, CERCLA, Causation, and Responsibility, 78 Minn.L.Rev. 1493 (1994).

1. LIABILITY OF SELLERS AND BUYERS

a. THE STATUTORY SCHEME

Michael P. Healy, Direct Liability for Hazardous
Substance Cleanups Under CERCLA:
A Comprehensive Approach

42 Case Western Reserve Law Review 65, 72–86, 87–88 (1992).

The CERCLA liability scheme can only be understood in the context of the statute's fundamental purpose. Congress enacted CERCLA in late 1980, after several years of legislative effort, in response to findings that more than 2,000 sites, many abandoned, had been used for the disposal of hazardous substances and posed a threat both to the public health and to the environment. CERCLA's paramount goal is to facilitate cleanup of hazardous substances through Superfund-financed and privately-financed response actions.

1. Facilitating Cleanups by Replenishing the Fund and Encouraging Private Response Actions

In view of the "tremendous" scope of the problems posed by unsound disposal of hazardous substances, the EPA had estimated that cleanup of the 1200 to 2000 most dangerous sites would cost between $13.1 billion and $22.1 billion. Indeed, more recent cost estimates are substantially higher. Congress established the Superfund to finance response actions pursued by the federal government at those sites posing the greatest threat to public health and the environment. Even though CERCLA limited the sites that the government could clean using Superfund monies, lawmakers understood at the time the Act was debated and passed that the $1.6 billion initially authorized by CERCLA would be insufficient. In 1980, CERCLA provided funding at only "the absolute minimum necessary to begin a responsible effort."[33] As a result, the CERCLA liability scheme, mandating recovery of response costs from responsible parties, was necessary to replenish the Superfund.

In addition to the replenishment effect, Congress intended that the CERCLA liability scheme encourage other parties to pursue cleanups not financed by Superfund. CERCLA allows private parties and states who proceed with cleanups to seek recovery for those response costs in actions brought under Section 107. Congress understood that its goal of ensuring the cleanup of hazardous substance facilities would depend upon response actions undertaken by private, responsible parties. Indeed, private response actions may be less costly than government cleanups and may permit the EPA to focus its efforts and resources on the facilities where releases pose the greatest threat to human health and the environment. Accordingly, proper construction of the liability provisions will have a substantial impact on the willingness of private parties to pursue cleanups on their own and will ensure that the limited sums appropriated to the Superfund are not used unnecessarily.

---

[33] 126 CONG. REC. 26,346 (statement of Rep. Rostenkowski) * * *.

In sum, CERCLA's paramount objective of facilitating the cleanup of hazardous waste sites that pose a threat to public health or the environment is tied directly to the availability of funds in the Superfund and to the readiness of private parties to undertake response actions. Advancing that policy depends on the construction and application of the liability standard established by the Act.

2.   Establishing a New Standard of Care for Hazardous Substance Disposal Activities

In enacting CERCLA, Congress also intended to "create a compelling incentive for those in control of hazardous substances to prevent releases and thus protect the public from harm."[39] Congress imposed this new, uniform standard of care on those actors most able to protect against the risks presented by inadequate disposal. Moreover, Congress believed that, even though hazardous substance disposal involved inherent risks, much of the harm to public health and the environment could be eliminated through the use of greater care. CERCLA's liability provision, which seeks to establish the responsibility of persons to pay the cost to remedy the harmful effects of their inadequate disposal activities, was critical to Congress' choice to implement the new, strict standard of care. In contrast, the tax levied on chemical and petrochemical concerns to finance the Superfund would not necessarily create an incentive to observe a stricter standard of care because the tax was uniformly imposed on each enterprise in those industries without regard to specific disposal practices.

To promote this new standard of care, Congress imposed liability throughout the chain of distribution so that all waste generators who make disposal arrangements are liable for the costs of cleaning up releases, regardless of whether those parties actually disposed of the substances. By extending liability in this manner, Congress has ensured that various actors will have an incentive to observe a high standard of care. Congress also acted to ensure the new standard's integrity by precluding responsible parties from relying on third-party defenses; a party, such as a generator, who is involved in disposal activities, cannot avoid liability for cleanup costs by claiming that another person was contractually responsible for adequately performing the disposal.

Congress viewed the imposition of this new standard of care for hazardous substance disposal activities as warranted for several reasons. First, Congress believed that such liability would promote the internalization of costs within business organizations so that the market price of goods would reflect the actual, total cost of their production. In Congress' view, this policy to encourage internalization of costs would be equitable to all market participants. Internalization is equitable because companies that have borne the costs of disposing of hazardous substances adequately will have no cleanup costs, while companies that attempted to avoid costs by disposing of hazardous substances inadequately will be liable for the expense incurred in cleaning up the improperly handled waste. Congress also reasoned that

---

[39]   S. REP. No. 848, [96th Cong., 2nd Sess. 7, 34 (1980)]. . . .

cost internalization would be beneficial to the economy in general.[50] Second, Congress decided to impose a higher standard of care based on its understanding that the costs of adequate disposal are substantially less than the costs of eliminating the harms caused by inadequate disposal via cleanup. Finally, Congress believed its new liability scheme was necessary because state laws imposing liability for inadequate disposal of hazardous substances lacked uniformity and contained insufficient standards of care.

Although Congress' intent in and rationale for creating a new standard of care to govern disposal activities are plain, Congress did not elaborate on the significance of the fact that the liability scheme would effectively impose this heightened standard of care retroactively in many instances. To be sure, CERCLA has important prospective effects. For instance, it assigns liability in the case of unintentional spills, encouraging potential responsible parties to take steps aimed at reducing the likelihood of accidental releases. . . .

CERCLA's retroactive effects, however, are at least as significant as its forward looking objectives. Congress intended to apply the new liability standard to inadequate disposals which occurred in the past but which result in a present release of hazardous substances. It broadened the theory of cost internalization to support CERCLA's retrospective effects; by imposing liability upon parties who were responsible for and profited from past improper disposals that require present cleanup measures, CERCLA ensures that those parties ultimately bear the full cost of their activities. Indeed, this nexus rationale emphasizing past profit as a justification for current liability has been relied upon by courts upholding CERCLA against claims that its retroactive effects violate due process.

. . .

Congress thus intended to impose a new standard of care for hazardous substance disposal activities, without addressing in detail the fact that this standard would be applied retroactively in many cases. There is *no* indication that Congress intended the scope of liability for responsible parties to differ depending on whether the liability-causing conduct pre-dated CERCLA's enactment. The only reasonable conclusion which can be drawn from the legislative history is that the uniform liability standard should be applied in a manner that prospectively promotes cost internalization as well as the new standard of care.

In applying the CERCLA liability scheme, courts have followed Congress' direction that those who profit from inadequate disposal should pay the costs resulting from releases of hazardous substances

---

[50] The Senate report on CERCLA explained that the economy would "operate better" because [s]trict liability is, in effect, a method of allocating resources through choice in the market place.

The most desirable system of loss distribution is one in which the prices of goods accurately reflect their full costs to society. This therefore requires, first, that the cost of injuries be borne by the activities which caused them, whether or not fault is involved, because, either way, the injury is a real cost of these activities. Second, it requires that among the several parties engaged in an enterprise the loss be placed on the party which is most likely to cause the burden to be reflected in the price of whatever the enterprise sells.

S.REP. NO. 848, [96th Cong., 2nd Sess. 7, 34 (1980)]. . . .

into the environment. Courts have not, however, accounted sufficiently for Congress' decisions to impose a new standard of care on all those engaged in or responsible for hazardous substance disposal activities and to ensure that those persons internalize the costs of adequate disposal. By failing to rely on these two stated congressional objectives, courts have created a body of common law which does not provide a coherent foundation for assessment of liability in future CERCLA cases.

CERCLA expressly provides that the mere ownership of a vessel or facility at which the release of a hazardous substance occurs is sufficient to create liability; it is irrelevant whether the owner actually was involved in operating the vessel or facility. Thus, Congress intended "owner and operator" liability under Section 107(a) to attach regardless of whether a person fitting that statutory description can be viewed as directly liable because of actual involvement in hazardous substance disposal activities.

Current owner liability, in particular, furthers Congress' intent that the liability scheme encourage site cleanups. Failure to hold all *current* owners liable without regard to their relationship to the property at the time of disposal would remove the incentive for prospective purchasers and lenders to complete careful environmental audits prior to executing a purchase or loan. Moreover, liability imposed on current owners of sites contaminated by hazardous substances encourages those owners to assess the environmental quality of their property and to perform the cleanup.

Tanglewood East Homeowners v. Charles-Thomas, Inc.

United States Court of Appeals for the Fifth Circuit, 1988.
849 F.2d 1568.

Before POLITZ and JOHNSON, CIRCUIT JUDGES, and BOYLE, DISTRICT JUDGE.

POLITZ, CIRCUIT JUDGE:

In this cause we granted an interlocutory appeal under 28 U.S.C.A. § 1292(b), to determine whether the district court had erred in rejecting defendants' motion to dismiss filed pursuant to Fed.R.Civ.P. 12(b)(1) and 12(b)(6). Finding no error in that ruling, for the reasons assigned we affirm.

Background

For purposes of the pending motion, we accept as true the allegations of the complaint. Appellant, First Federal Savings & Loan Association of Conroe, is a lending institution. The other defendants against whom appellees have complained are residential developers, construction companies, and real estate agents and agencies. All participated in the development of the Tanglewood East Subdivision in Montgomery County, Texas. The complainants-appellees are owners of property in that subdivision. The subdivision was built on the site upon which the United Creosoting Company operated a wood-treatment facility from 1946 to 1972. During that quarter century substantial amounts of highly-toxic waste accumulated on the property. In 1973 certain of the defendants acquired the property, filled in and graded the creosote pools, and began residential development.

In 1980, Tanglewood homeowners and residents complained to Texas authorities about toxic problems and all development ceased. In 1983 the Environmental Protection Agency placed the site on its National Priorities List for cleaning under the Comprehensive Environmental Response, Compensation and Liability Act (CERCLA), commonly known as the "Superfund Act," 42 U.S.C.A. §§ 9601, *et seq.* The cleanup, expected to cost millions of dollars, will require the demolition of six homes and the construction of bunkers to contain the hazardous materials.

The purchasers of the subdivision lots invoked CERCLA and the Resource Conservation and Recovery Act (RCRA), 42 U.S.C.A. §§ 6901, *et seq.* and sought damages, response and cleaning costs, and injunctive relief. They also sought, but have now withdrawn, claims under the Federal Water Pollution Control Act, 33 U.S.C.A. § 1251.

The defendants filed a joint motion to dismiss under Fed.R.Civ.P. 12(b)(1) and 12(b)(6). The district court denied the motion but certified its ruling under 28 U.S.C.A. § 1292(b). First Federal sought and secured our approval of an interlocutory appeal.

Standard of Review

When a motion to dismiss challenges both the court's jurisdiction, 12(b)(1), and the existence of a federal cause of action, 12(b)(6), the *Bell v. Hood*[1] standard is applied and the motion is treated "as a direct attack on the merits of the plaintiff's case." *Williamson v. Tucker*, 645 F.2d 404, 415 (5th Cir.1981). In reviewing such a 12(b)(6) motion, we accept as true all well-pled allegations, resolving all doubts in favor of the complainants. Such a motion will be granted only if "it appears beyond doubt that the plaintiff can prove no set of facts in support of his claim which would entitle him to relief." *Conley v. Gibson*, 355 U.S. 41, 78 S.Ct. 99, 2 L.Ed.2d 80 (1957). A motion to dismiss for failure to state a claim "is viewed with disfavor, and is rarely granted." *Sosa v. Coleman*, 646 F.2d 991, 993 (5th Cir.1981).

Analysis

A. *CERCLA*

Appellant contends that it and the other defendants are not covered persons under the CERCLA, which, it submits, was intended to apply only to the person responsible for introducing the toxins, in this case, the United Creosoting Company. We do not share that crabbed a reading of this statute. Although it was enacted in the waning hours of the 96th Congress, and as the product of apparent legislative compromise is not a model of clarity, the statute has an extensive legislative history.

Under 42 U.S.C.A. § 9607(a) (1988), CERCLA provides a private cause of action where a release or threatened release of a hazardous substance causes response costs to be incurred. The persons covered are:

(1) the owner and operator of . . . a facility,

---

[1]   327 U.S. 678, 66 S.Ct. 773, 90 L.Ed. 939 (1946).

(2) any person who at the time of disposal of any hazardous substance owned or operated any facility at which such hazardous substances were disposed of,

(3) any person who by contract, agreement, or otherwise arranged for disposal or treatment, or arranged with a transporter for transport for disposal or treatment, of hazardous substances owned or possessed by such person . . ., and

(4) any person who accepts or accepted any hazardous substances for transport to disposal or treatment facilities. . . .

1.	*Present Owners*

Appellant maintains that under § 9607(a)(1), the only owner and operator who discharged hazardous materials was the United Creosoting Company, who abandoned the site in 1972. We find nothing in the wording of § 9607(a) to exclude present owners of properties previously contaminated. We join our colleagues of the Second Circuit in concluding that the structure of the statute removes any doubt. Section 9607(a)(2) expressly applies to past owners and operators who contaminate their surroundings; it is therefore manifest that § 9607(a)(1) applies to current owners of adulterated sites. See *New York v. Shore Realty Corp.*, 759 F.2d 1032 (2d Cir.1985). We hold that § 9607(a)(1) imposes strict liability on the current owners of any facility which releases or threatens to release a toxic substance.

"Facility" is defined in § 9601(9) to include

(A) any building, structure, installation, equipment, pipe or pipeline (including any pipe into a sewer or publicly owned treatment works), well, pit, pond, lagoon, impoundment, ditch, landfill, storage container, motor vehicle, rolling stock, or aircraft, or (B) *any site or area where a hazardous substance has been deposited, stored, disposed of, or placed, or otherwise come to be located*; but does not include any consumer product in consumer use or any vessel. (Emphasis added.)

The statute leaves no room for doubt; the Tanglewood East development is a covered facility.

The *Shore* court held the developer-owners liable for the cleanup costs of their facility even though no construction or development had been undertaken. A lending institution was found to be a current owner and operator under § 9607(a)(1) in *United States v. Maryland Bank & Trust Co.*, 632 F.Supp. 573 (D.Md.1986). In that case, a bank which acquired a contaminated site by foreclosure was held accountable under CERCLA. And courts addressing the issue have rejected the argument implicit in appellant's position, that liability may be imposed upon only those persons who both own and operate polluted property. *Artesian Water Co. v. Gov. of New Castle County*, 659 F.Supp. 1269 (D.Del.1987); *United States v. Northeastern Pharm. & Chem. Co., Inc.*, 579 F.Supp. 823 (W.D.Mo.1984).

2.	*Past Owners*

Section 9607(a)(2) applies to persons who owned or operated a facility at the time of the disposal of the toxins. Appellant contends that the only person who qualifies under that section is United Creosoting

Company. We do not so read the statute. Referring to 42 U.S.C.A.
§ 6903(3), we find "disposal" defined to include

> the discharge, deposit, injection, dumping spilling, leaking, or
> placing of any solid waste or hazardous waste into or on any
> land or water so that such solid waste or hazardous waste or
> any constituent thereof may enter the environment or be
> emitted into the air or discharged into any waters, including
> ground waters.

We recognize merit in appellees' argument that this definition of
disposal does not limit disposal to a one-time occurrence—there may be
other disposals when hazardous materials are moved, dispersed, or
released during landfill excavations and fillings.

3. *Post Arrangers and Transporters*

Appellant next argues that defendants neither arranged for nor
transported any hazardous material for disposal or treatment under
§ 9607(a)(3) and (4). This argument rests on the narrow interpretation
of disposal, which we reject, and a like interpretation of "treatment"
which is defined by § 6903(34) as

> any method, technique, or process, including neutralization,
> designed to change the physical, chemical, or biological
> character or composition of any hazardous waste so as to
> neutralize such waste or so as to render such waste
> nonhazardous, safer for transport, amenable for recovery,
> amenable for storage, or reduced in volume. *Such term
> includes any activity* or processing *designed to change the
> physical form* or chemical composition *of hazardous waste* so as
> to render it nonhazardous. (Emphasis added.)

Appellees argue that the activity of filling and grading the creosote
pools constituted treatment to render the waste non-hazardous, and
that those involved in that activity are covered persons under
§ 9607(a)(3). Furthermore, since disposal may be merely the "placing of
any . . . hazardous waste into or on any land. . . .," § 6903(3), those who
move the waste about the site may fall within the terms of the
provision. Under these readings of the terms "disposal" and
"treatment," relevant evidence under the complaint may establish that
some of the defendants were arrangers for, or transporters of, the toxic
materials.

Finally, appellant maintains that CERCLA was intended to cover
only persons actually engaged in the chemical/hazardous materials
industry and those engaged in businesses which generated such
materials. It vigorously contends that the legislation was not meant to
impose chilling liability on the defendants' businesses: banking, real
estate, construction, and development. It cites an imposing list of cases,
obviously not including *New York v. Shore Realty; United States v.
Maryland Bank & Trust Co.; Artesian Water Co. v. Gov. of New Castle
County;* and *United States v. Northeastern Pharm. & Chem. Co.* We are
persuaded beyond peradventure that a determination of the specific
businesses and activities covered by CERCLA is beyond the pale of a
12(b)(6) motion. That remains for another day.

In light of the foregoing, we are satisfied that the complaint may
not be dismissed for failure to state a claim upon which relief under

CERCLA may be granted. We are not prepared to rule as a matter of law that complainants-appellees can prove no set of facts in support of their claims which would entitle them to relief. The district court correctly denied the motion to dismiss the claims made under CERCLA.

C. *Remedies Under CERCLA*

Section 9607(a)(4) provides that covered persons shall be liable for

(A) all costs of removal or remedial action incurred by the United States Government or a State or an Indian Tribe not inconsistent with the national contingency plan;

(B) any other necessary costs of response incurred by any other person consistent with the national contingency plan. . . .

Appellant contends that under this provision appellees must demonstrate that their response costs were "necessary" and "consistent with the national contingency plan." *Mardan Corp. v. C.G.C. Music, Ltd.*, 600 F.Supp. 1049, 1054 (D.Ariz.1984). Appellees have alleged that their costs are consistent with the national contingency plan. It remains for them to prove such. The issue of consistency cannot be resolved on the pleadings alone, but must await development of relevant evidence. *See Artesian Water Co. v. Gov. of New Castle County*, and authorities cited therein.

Appellant next maintains that some degree of governmental involvement is a necessary requisite for the application of § 9607. On this issue we agree with the conclusion reached by our colleagues of the Ninth Circuit in *Wickland Oil Terminals v. Asarco, Inc.*, 792 F.2d 887 (9th Cir.1986), after a careful and exhaustive analysis of the statute, regulations, and legislative history. The *Wickland* panel relied in part on EPA interpretations as reflected in the preamble to the rules revising the 1972 National Contingency Plan. 50 Fed.Reg. 5862–83 (1985); 50 Fed.Reg. 47, 912–50 (1985). The preamble states that the final rule "makes it absolutely clear that no Federal [or lead agency] approval of any kind is a prerequisite to a cost recovery. . . ." 50 Fed.Reg. 47, 934 (1985). *See also NL Industries v. Kaplan*, 792 F.2d 896 (9th Cir.1986).

The *Wickland* court also relied on the fact that there is no procedure or mechanism by which "a private party could seek to obtain prior governmental approval of a cleanup program." 792 F.2d at 892. A subsequent panel in *Cadillac Fairview/California, Inc. v. Dow Chemical Co.*, 840 F.2d 691, 695 (9th Cir.1988), followed the same reasoning, underscoring that "there is no indication in the statute that prior approval or action by a state or local government is either necessary or desirable." We agree. We find no merit to the contention that prior governmental involvement is a prerequisite to the recouping of response costs.

Finally, as to the recovery of response costs under CERCLA, appellant maintains that the costs alleged by complainants—relocation costs, investigatory costs, and the cost of dikes and trenches—are not encompassed by the statute. We find no merit in this argument. First, relocation costs are specifically authorized. § 9601(24). And under the statute, response means "remove, removal, remedy and remedial action." § 9601(25). "Remove" or "removal" includes "such actions as may be necessary to monitor, assess, and evaluate the release or threat of release of hazardous substances. . . ." § 9601(23). Investigatory costs fall within the ambit of this provision. *Cadillac Fairview/California, Inc. v. Dow Chemical Co.* As an analytical caboose, § 9601(24), which defines "remedy" and "remedial action," as actions "to prevent or minimize the release of hazardous substances," specifically includes the construction of dikes, trenches, or ditches among a host of other containment measures.

We find no basis for dismissing on the pleadings that part of the complaint seeking response costs under CERCLA.

The judgment of the district court is AFFIRMED.

NOTES

1. *Who Is Liable Under CERCLA?* As *Tanglewood* indicates, any number of entities can be a "responsible party" liable under the statute for hazardous substances deposited on the land in question. Examine section 9607(a) of the statute. What policies does liability under section 9607(a) serve? How do notions of fault and risk spreading play out in CERCLA?

Buyer. How does a buyer of land becomes liable under CERCLA? How are the courts reading the words "the" and "and" in the phrase "the owner and operator of . . . a facility" in section 9607(a)(1)? In United States v. Maryland Bank & Trust Co., 632 F.Supp. 573 (D.Md.1986), the court held that based on legislative history and logic, the terms "owner" and "operator" should be read in the disjunctive not the conjunctive. According to the court, "[p]roper usage dictates that the phrase 'the owner and operator' include only those persons who are both owners and operators. But by no means does Congress always follow the rules of grammar when enacting the laws of this nation." Id. at 578.

Seller. When will a seller of land, and other past owners, be a responsible party under section 9607(a)? Compare *Tanglewood* to the situation where employees of landowner *A* bury barrels of hazardous substances on *A*'s land and the barrels begin to leak. *A* then sells the land to *B*, who is unaware that the barrels continue to leak. Several years later, *B* sells the land to *C* who discovers the leaking barrels. Is *B* a "person who at the time of disposal of any hazardous substance owned" the property and thus a responsible party? The courts disagree, since the key term "disposal" invites competing interpretations.

Some courts hold that "passive" disposal—the leaking and migration of hazardous substances—is not the sort of a "disposal" within CERCLA that would make *B* a responsible party. For example, in United States v. Petersen Sand & Gravel, Inc., 806 F.Supp. 1346 (N.D.Ill.1992), the court closely examined the statute to find that passive disposals would not make an owner a responsible party. Moreover, the court ruled that passive disposal would bar the innocent landowner defense in all but the rare case where the hazardous substance remained tightly sealed underground, since any leakage after the transfer of ownership would constitute disposal by the owner herself. The court reasoned that Congress could not have intended to eviscerate the innocent landowner defense by defining "disposal" as passive. The court quoted with approval from Edward Hines Lumber Co. v. Vulcan Materials Co., 861 F.2d 155, 157 (7th Cir.1988): "We are enforcing a statute rather than modifying rules of common law. . . . To the point that courts could achieve 'more' of the legislative objectives by adding to the lists of those responsible, it is enough to respond that statutes have not only ends but also limits. Born of compromise, laws such as CERCLA and SARA do not pursue their ends to their logical limits. A court's job is to find and enforce stopping points no less than to implement other legislative choices." Accord Carson Harbor Village, Ltd. v. Unocal Corporation, 270 F.3d 863, 879 (9th Cir.2001) ("Instead of focusing solely on whether the terms are 'active' or 'passive,' we must examine each of the terms in relation to the facts of the case and determine whether the movement of the contaminants is under the plain meaning of the terms, a 'disposal.'"); United States v. CDMG Realty Co., 96 F.3d 706 (3d Cir.1996) (no liability since migration was "unaided by human contact"); Snediker Developers Ltd. Partnership v. Evans, 773 F.Supp. 984 (E.D.Mich.1991).

Other courts would hold *B* liable for a passive disposal. In Nurad, Inc. v. William E. Hooper & Sons Co., 966 F.2d 837 (4th Cir.), cert. denied, 506 U.S. 940, 113 S.Ct. 377, 121 L.Ed.2d 288 (1992), the court criticized the insertion of an active participation requirement into such clearly passive words as "leaking" and "spilling." In the court's view, barring liability for passive disposals would interfere with CERCLA's policy to encourage hazardous waste cleanup and would clash with the strict liability scheme of the statute. Moreover, such a constrained reading would burden the owner who voluntarily begins a cleanup since it would be liable for at least a portion of the cost as a current owner while a prior owner who did nothing to stop the leaking would not be liable. Accord Carson Harbor Village, Ltd. v. Unocal Corp., 227 F.3d 1196 (9th Cir.2000).

The 2002 amendments to CERCLA included some protection for contiguous owners who properties become contaminated by hazardous materials migrating from neighboring properties. § 9607(g). The statutory exemption, however, presents difficult hurdles in order to qualify, and it appears that it only protects against dispersion via ground water not soil leaching. See Wiegard, Note, The Brownfields Act: Providing Relief for the Innocent or New Hurdles to Avoid Liability?, 28 Wm. & Mary L. & Pol'y Rev. 127, 146 (2003).

Lessors and Lessees. Like buyers and sellers, lessors and lessees may be responsible parties under CERCLA. The lessor will most likely be liable as an owner under section 9607(a)(1) or (2). Lessors cannot escape liability by claiming that they were innocent absentee landlords unaware of and unconnected to the waste disposal activities that took place on their land. United States v. Monsanto, 858 F.2d 160, 169 (4th Cir.1988), cert. denied, 490 U.S. 1106, 109 S.Ct. 3156, 104 L.Ed.2d 1019 (1989). A lessee may be an operator within section 9607(a)(1) if it disposes of hazardous waste on the property; a lessee may also be liable under CERCLA as an owner if it controls the property and is functionally equivalent to a landowner. See United States v. South Carolina Recycling & Disposal, Inc., 653 F.Supp. 984 (D.S.C.1984), affirmed in part, vacated in part by United States v. Monsanto, 858 F.2d 160, 169 (4th Cir.1988), cert. denied, 490 U.S. 1106, 109 S.Ct. 3156, 104 L.Ed.2d 1019 (1989). The typical lessee will not be liable as an "owner" unless special factors are present. See Commander Oil Corp. v. Barlo Equipment Corp., 215 F.3d 321 (2d Cir.2000) (factors include length of term, terminability of lease, right to sublet without notice to lessor, and responsibility for taxes, maintenance, and structural repairs).

What policies are served by holding lessors and lessees liable under CERCLA? What risks does CERCLA create for commercial landlords? On the subject of landlord and tenant liability under CERCLA, see Feder, The Undefined Parameters of Lessee Liability Under the Comprehensive Environmental Response, Compensation, and Liability Act (CERCLA): A Trap for the Unwary Lender, 19 Envtl.L. 257 (1988); Street & Zaleha, Environmental Risks: Negotiating and Drafting Lease Agreements, 27 Idaho L.Rev. 37 (1990–1991); Larsen & Boman, Environmental Liability: Lender and Landlord-Tenant Issues, in The Impact of Environmental Regulation on Business Transactions, Practicing Law Institute 273 (1988).

Brokers. Will a broker ever be liable to a buyer for failing to discover or disclose hazardous material? Reconsider the materials on the role of the broker, pages 48–71 above. See Comment, A Toxic Nightmare On Elm Street: Negligence and the Real Estate Broker's Duty in Selling Previously Contaminated Residential Property, 15 B.C.Envtl.L.Rev. 547 (1988); Edwards, Successor Landowner and Real Estate Broker Liability in Environmental Torts: Going Beyond Property Lines, 1 Real Est.Fin.L.J. 16 (1988); Locke & Elliott, Caveat Broker: What Can Real Estate Licensees Do About Their Potentially Expanding Liability for Failure to Disclose Radon Risks in Home Purchase and Sale Transactions?, 25 Colum. J. Envtl. L. 71 (2000); see also Kezer v. Mark Stimson Associates, 742 A.2d 898 (Me.1999) (finding no liability for failure to disclose pollution in neighborhood, as opposed to the property being sold).

Corporate Liability. Courts and commentators have addressed the issue of the liability under CERCLA of successor, parent, and subsidiary corporations as well as shareholders and officers. See, e.g., U.S. v. Bestfoods, 524 U.S. 51, 118 S.Ct. 1876, 141 L.Ed.2d 43 (1998) (parent must pay for subsidiary's pollution only if parent was directly involved in running the facility); Kilbert, Successor Liability under CERCLA: Whither Substantial Continuity?, 14 Penn St. Envt'l L.Rev. 1 (2005); Carter, Comment, Successor Liability Under CERCLA: It's Time to Fully Embrace State Law, 156 U.Pa.L.Rev. 767 (2008); Dent, Limited Liability in Environmental Law, 26 Wake Forest L.Rev. 151 (1991); Oswald & Schipani, CERCLA and the "Erosion" of Traditional Corporate Law Doctrine, 86 Nw.L.Rev. 259 (1992); Barr, CERCLA Made Simple: An Analysis of the Cases Under the Comprehensive Environmental Response, Compensation and Liability Act of 1980, 45 Bus.Law. 923, 979–982 (1990); Comment, Asset Purchasers as Potentially Responsible Parties Under Superfund, 12 B.Y.U.J. Pub. L. 351 (1998).

2. *Apportionment of Liability.* Although CERCLA provides for joint and several liability, the statute offers two possible routes of escape.

Divisible Harm. Where the harm is divisible, courts have held that joint and several liability does not apply. But see United States v. R.W. Meyer, Inc., 889 F.2d 1497 (6th Cir.1989), cert. denied, 494 U.S. 1057, 110 S.Ct. 1527, 108 L.Ed.2d 767 (1990), where the landowner argued that it did not cause an indivisible environmental harm with its tenants, and the court affirmed the district court's determination that the harm was not divisible, even though the tenants, but not the owners, released hazardous materials on the land:

> "[A]lthough the basis for each defendant's liability differed, the harm, *i.e.*, the presence of hazardous materials at the Northernaire facility, was the same. [The owner's] liability pursuant to 42 U.S.C.A. § 9607 was predicated on ownership of

the land, notwithstanding the fact that [the tenants], as operators of the facility, directly were responsible for the presence of the hazardous substances on [the owner's] property."

889 F.2d at 1507.

Equitable Contribution. Section 9613(f) allows a responsible party to seek contribution from other potentially responsible parties, and "the court may allocate response costs among liable parties using such equitable factors as the court determines are appropriate." A buyer of contaminated property, liable himself under section 9607(a)(1), would like the court to apply section 9613(f) to allocate a (great) portion of the response costs to the seller who actually contaminated the property. Presumably, the plaintiffs in *Tanglewood* were proceeding under this strategy.

However, the statute only permits, but does not mandate, equitable contribution. Also, the statute does not say how costs should be allocated, leaving allocation to the courts. Congress evidently intended the courts to consider the involvement of the various parties in the actual disposal of the hazardous substances. Presumably, consideration of involvement in the disposal would reduce the burden of buyers such as the home purchasers in *Tanglewood*. The courts, however, provide few guidelines for deciding equitable contribution claims, outside of making a few general (and nonbinding) statements. See United States v. Monsanto Co., 858 F.2d 160, 168 n. 13 (4th Cir.1988), cert. denied, 490 U.S. 1106, 109 S.Ct. 3156, 104 L.Ed.2d 1019 (1989) ("[t]he site owners' relative degree of fault would, of course, be relevant" for applying equitable contribution); Smith Land & Improvement Corp. v. Celotex Corp., 851 F.2d 86, 90 (3d Cir.1988), cert. denied, 488 U.S. 1029, 109 S.Ct. 837, 102 L.Ed.2d 969 (1989) (the statute "expressly conditions the amount of contribution on the application of equitable considerations"); see also U.S. v. Atlantic Research Corp., 551 U.S. 128, 127 S.Ct. 2331, 168 L.Ed.2d 28 (2007) (indicating that action for "contribution" under § 9613 is appropriate to recoup costs paid by an entity in response to government action forcing the amelioration of hazardous waste, while an action for "cost recovery" should be brought under § 9107(a) for costs of a voluntary cleanup where the government did not compel the cleanup).

In In re Sterling Steel Treating, Inc., 94 B.R. 924 (Bkrtcy.E.D.Mich.1989), buyers spent $8,500 to remove hazardous waste found in a trailer on land bought from the landowner's trustee in bankruptcy. The trustee did not know that the trailer contained hazardous materials, and the buyers did not inspect the land before buying. The court allocated the removal cost equally between the bankruptcy estate and the buyers, holding that equitable considerations required buyers to bear some of the cost under the principle of caveat emptor. The court held the estate liable since the trustee should have inspected, discovered and disclosed the contamination to the buyers. See also Alcan-Toyo America v. Northern Illinois Gas Co., 881 F.Supp. 342 (N.D.Ill.1995) (contaminating former owner liable for ninety percent of response costs and non-contaminating buyer liable for ten percent since it failed to inspect property before buying).

How would you advise a client who is a potentially responsible party on how equitable contribution will affect its liability?

See generally Faulk, There and Back Again: The Progression and Regression of Contribution Actions Under CERCLA, 18 Tul.Envt'l L.J. 323 (2005); Barr, CERCLA Made Simple: An Analysis of the Cases Under the Comprehensive Environmental Response, Compensation and Liability Act of 1980, 45 Bus.Law. 923, 990–993 (1990); Oswald, New Directions in Joint and Several Liability Under CERCLA?, 28 U.C. Davis L.Rev. 299 (1995).

3. *CERCLA and Bankruptcy.* What if an owner of contaminated land is in bankruptcy? On one hand, CERCLA would hold landowners strictly liable in order to achieve the statutory aim of cleaning the environment and forcing owners to be careful with hazardous wastes. On the other hand, the Bankruptcy Code aims to provide debtors with a "fresh start" free from prior obligations, and empowers the bankruptcy court to discharge claims against the debtor as part of the liquidation of the estate in favor of creditors. (See pages 708–734 above.) To what extent should a bankruptcy court wipe out the liability, or potential liability, of a landowner for CERCLA response costs?

In re Chateaugay Corporation, 944 F.2d 997 (2d Cir.1991), addressed this issue in the context of the Chapter 11 reorganization of the LTV Corporation. The debtor's schedule of liabilities included 24 pages of "contingent liabilities" asserted by the federal Environmental Protection Agency and the environmental enforcement officers of all fifty states. EPA claimed $32 million in response costs incurred before the bankruptcy petition was filed for fourteen sites for which LTV was a potentially responsible party. EPA further indicated that additional response costs would be required to completely clean these fourteen sites. LTV sought a discharge of its potential environmental liability relating to conduct by LTV prior to the filing of the petition. However, the EPA maintained that response costs incurred after the bankruptcy petition were not "claims" under the Bankruptcy Code, 11 U.S.C.A. § 101(4), and thus were not subject to discharge. The court held that unincurred response costs for the debtor's pre-petition conduct causing the release or threatened release of hazardous materials before the petition were "claims" under the statute that will be discharged. The court stated:

> True, EPA does not yet know the full extent of the hazardous waste removal costs that it may one day incur and seek to impose upon LTV, and it does not yet even know the location of all the sites at which such wastes may yet be found. But the location of these sites, the determination of their coverage by CERCLA, and the incurring of response costs by EPA are all steps that may fairly be viewed, in the regulatory context, as rendering EPA's claim "contingent," rather than as placing it outside the Code's definition of "claim." . . .

Accepting EPA's argument in this Chapter 11 reorganization case would leave EPA without any possibility of even partial recovery against a dissolving corporation in a Chapter 7 liquidation case. Indeed, while EPA obviously prefers in this case to keep its CERCLA claim outside of bankruptcy so that it may present it, without reduction, against the reorganized company that it anticipates will emerge from bankruptcy, one may well speculate whether, if unincurred CERCLA response costs are not claims, some corporations facing substantial environmental claims will be able to reorganize at all.

Id. at 1005.

> As to the conflict between bankruptcy and environmental policies:

> Our point is the more limited one that in construing the Code, we need not be swayed by the arguments advanced by EPA that a narrow reading of the Code will better serve the environmental interests Congress wished to promote in enacting CERCLA. If the Code, fairly construed, creates limits on the extent of environmental cleanup efforts, the remedy is for Congress to make exceptions to the Code to achieve other objectives that Congress chooses to reach, rather than for courts to restrict the meaning of across-the-board legislation like a bankruptcy law in order to promote objectives evident in more focused statutes.

Id. at 1002.

Other courts have taken different approaches. See, for example, In re National Gypsum Co., 134 B.R. 188 (N.D.Tex.1991) (permitting discharge only of costs related to pre-petition conduct resulting in a release or threat of release that could have been "fairly contemplated" by the parties and expressly refusing to favor the "fresh start" goal of the Bankruptcy Code over CERCLA's policy to the extent adopted in *Chateaugay*).

See generally Mailman, Comment, Cleaning Up Its Act: Improving CERCLA Efficiency Within the Bankruptcy Code, 27 Whittier L.Rev. 557 (2005); Salerno, Ferland, & Hansen, Environmental Law and Its Impact On Bankruptcy Law—Saga of "Toxins-R-Us," 25 Real Prop. Probate & Trust J. 261 (1990); Mirsky, Conway, & Humphrey, The Interface Between Bankruptcy and Environmental Laws, 46 Bus. Law. 626 (1991); Carlson, Successor Liability in Bankruptcy: Some Unifying Themes of Intertemporal Creditor Priorities Created by Running Covenants, Products Liability, and Toxic-Waste Cleanup, 50 Law & Contemp. Probs. 119 (1987).

4. *The Lawyer's Ethical Obligation.* Richman & Bauer, Responsibilities of Lawyers and Engineers to Report Environmental Hazards and Maintain Client Confidences: Duties in Conflict, 5 Toxics Law Reporter 1458 (1991), poses the following question: if seller's attorney learns of hazardous wastes buried on the property, must he or she reveal this knowledge to the buyer or to the appropriate governmental official? The answer requires a difficult balancing of the attorney's duty to maintain confidentiality against the obligation to refrain from assisting the client's commission of fraudulent or criminal acts and the potential duty pursuant to statute to report environmental hazards. See Russell, Unreasonable Risk: Model Rule 1.6, Environmental Hazards, and Positive Law, 55 Wash. & Lee L. Rev. 117 (1998); Note, Attorney-Client Confidentiality: The Ethics of Toxic Dumping Disclosure, 35 Wayne L.Rev. 1157 (1989).

5. *Other Regulation.* Federal environmental statutes other than CERCLA, may also impose liability on the owner or manager of contaminated land. See, for example, Resource Conservation and Recovery Act of 1976 ("RCRA"), 42 U.S.C.A. § 6901 et seq., setting standards for hazardous waste treatment and disposal. See generally, Curry, Hamula, & Rallison, The Tug-of-War Between RCRA and CERCLA at Contaminated Hazardous Waste Facilities, 23 Ariz.St.L.J. 359 (1991); Hill, An Overview of RCRA: The "Mind-Numbing" Provisions of the Most Complicated Environmental Statute, 21 Envtl.L. Reporter 10254 (1991); Stoll, The New

RCRA Cleanup Regime: Comparisons and Contrasts With CERCLA, 44 Sw.L.J. 1299 (1991); Melosi, Hazardous Waste and Environmental Liability: An Historical Perspective, 25 Hous.L.Rev. 741 (1988).

State Laws. State environmental regulations also affect real estate transactions. Some of these statutes called "baby CERCLA" acts, essentially track the federal act. One example is the Michigan legislation discussed in Niecko v. Emro Marketing Company, appearing on pages 767– 770 below. Other state statutes require disclosure of specified environmental conditions before land is transferred. See, e.g., Cal. Health & Safety Code §§ 25230(a)(2), 25359.7; Pa.Stat.Ann.tit.35, § 6018.405.

New Jersey's Industrial Site Recovery Act (formerly known as the Environmental Cleanup Responsibility Act or "ECRA"), N.J.S.A. 13:1K–6 et seq., takes a different approach, requiring that before the transfer of an "industrial establishment" (defined as any place of business used for storage, manufacture, or disposal of hazardous waste), the owner must notify the state of the proposed transfer and obtain approval of a declaration that there have been no discharges of hazardous wastes or that any discharges have been removed. If the land still is contaminated, the owner must receive approval of a cleanup plan. Penalties for failure to comply with the Act include the voiding of the sale. On ECRA, see generally, Farer, ECRA Verdict: Successes and Failures of Premier Transaction-Triggered Environmental Law, 5 Pace Envtl.L.Rev. 113 (1987); Schmidt, New Jersey's Experience Implementing the Environmental Cleanup Responsibility Act, 38 Rutgers L.Rev. 729 (1986).

See generally, Gieser, Federal and State Environmental Law: A Trap For the Unwary Lender, 1988 B.Y.U.L.Rev. 643.

6. *"Indoor Air Pollution."* The air inside a building may in fact be far more contaminated than the air outside. Indoor air pollution involves contaminants, such as gases, bacteria, and chemicals, that may produce illness in the people on the premises. For example, radon that seeps into structures from the earth and accumulates presents a significant cancer risk. Federal legislation provides for the study of radon and assistance to the states but does not regulate radon in homes. Radon Pollution Control Act of 1988, 102 Stat. 2755 (codified at 15 U.S.C.A. §§ 2661–); Radon Gas and Indoor Quality Research of 1986, Title IV, 100 Stat. 1758. Federal regulation controls emissions of radon from certain facilities. 40 C.F.R. §§ 61.20–61.26, 61.220–61.225 (1991). See Locke, Promoting Radon Testing, Disclosure, and Remediation: Protecting Public Health Through the Home Mortgage Market, 20 Envtl. L. Reporter 10475 (1990); Shepard & Gaynor, Radon: A Growing Menace In Real Estate Transactions, 3 Probate & Prop. 6 (May-June 1989). See also Loewy, Kelly, & Nathanson, Indoor Pollution in Commercial Buildings: Legal Requirements and Emerging Trends, 11 Temp. Envt'l L. & Tech.J. 239 (1992).

Asbestos in buildings is also regulated by federal law, see, e.g., 40 C.F.R. §§ 61.140–61.157 (1991), (prohibiting installation of certain asbestos materials and setting requirements for the removal of asbestos), and state legislation, see, e.g., N.Y. Labor Law § 902 (McKinney 1988). In 3550 Stevens Creek Associates v. Barclays Bank of California, 915 F.2d 1355 (9th Cir.1990), cert. denied, 500 U.S. 917, 111 S.Ct. 2014, 114 L.Ed.2d 101 (1991), the court held that CERCLA does not apply to asbestos insulation installed in a building. Installing asbestos was not a "disposal" which would trigger CERCLA; the court held that Congress intended that CERCLA would control only when hazardous materials were waste and not while they were being put to productive use. As a result, a private party may not recover the cost of asbestos removal from a prior owner. For an excellent discussion of the asbestos issue, see Gluckstern, A Guide To Asbestos Liability For Real Property Owners, Lessors, and Managers, 5 Toxics Law Reporter 37 (1990). See also Fox, Asbestos: How To Conduct Real Estate Transactions in the Age of Asbestos Liability, 3 Prac. Real Est.Law. 59 (May 1987).

While liability for lead paint poisoning is an emerging issue in landlord and tenant law, lead paint issues are important as well in real estate sales. For example, Section 4852d of the federal Residential Lead-Based Paint Hazard Reduction Act of 1992, 42 U.S.C.A. § 4852 et seq., requires a seller of housing built prior to 1978 to provide the buyer with a brochure on lead paint hazards, disclose any known lead paint problems, and give the buyer a ten day opportunity before the buyer becomes obligated under the sales contract to inspect for lead paint conditions. Monetary penalties and treble damages may be assessed for violations but the contract will not be voided. Final regulations under the Act were published on March 6, 1996. 45 C.F.R. 9064. See generally Tiller, Easing Lead Paint Laws: A Step in the Wrong Direction, 18 Harv. Envt'l L.Rev. 265 (1994).

b.   AVOIDING LIABILITY/BROWNFIELDS

i.   *"Innocent Owner" Defense*

United States v. Serafini

United States District Court, Middle District of Pennsylvania, 1988.
706 F.Supp. 346.

MEMORANDUM

CALDWELL, DISTRICT JUDGE.

Introduction

This is an action brought under the Comprehensive Environmental Response Compensation and Liability Act ("CERCLA"), 42 U.S.C.A. § 9601 *et seq.*, for injunctive relief and recovery of the federal government's response costs in connection with the cleanup of a hazardous waste site in Taylor, Pennsylvania. Before the court is the government's motion for partial summary judgment against defendants Serafini, Bernabei, Buttafoco and Naples, individually and trading as the Empire Contracting Company ("Empire defendants"), on the issue of liability for response costs under section 107 of CERCLA, 42 U.S.C.A. § 9607. For the reasons that follow the government's motion will be denied.

Background

The Taylor hazardous waste site is a tract of land consisting of approximately 125 acres located in Taylor Borough, near Scranton, Pennsylvania. In May, 1967, the Parmoff Corporation leased a portion of the site to the City of Scranton for the purpose of dumping garbage and refuse. Until at least March 31, 1968, Scranton operated a sanitary landfill and waste disposal site on the leased premises. On December 12, 1969, the Parmoff Corporation sold all but a small portion of its interest in the Taylor site to the Empire Contracting Company, a partnership wholly owned by the Empire defendants. According to the fictitious name certificate filed in February, 1966, in Lackawanna County, the Empire Contracting Company was created "[t]o buy, sell, manufacture, lease, service any and all kinds and types of real and personal property, to act as contractor, subcontractor and developer with respect to any and all kinds of work, including but not limited to buildings, improvements, roads, bridges, mining, drilling, flushing and otherwise." The Empire defendants are the current owners of a portion of the Taylor site.

Beginning in 1981, the United States Environmental Protection Agency ("EPA") and the Pennsylvania Department of Environmental Resources conducted various surveys and investigations at the Taylor site. According to the uncontested affidavit of Michael Zickler, the EPA on-scene coordinator assigned to the site, in October and November, 1983, EPA conducted an immediate removal action under section 104 of CERCLA, 42 U.S.C.A. § 9604. Approximately 1,141 fifty-five gallon drums were scattered across and under six separate areas of the site. Many were open, crushed, completely or partially buried, and in various stages of decay. Samples from the drums, as well as soil and water samples, were sent to the EPA laboratory in Annapolis, Maryland. Laboratory analysis revealed that 847 drums contained hazardous substances as defined in section 101(14) of CERCLA, 42 U.S.C.A. § 9601(14), 105 drums contained non-hazardous substances, and 189 were contaminated with residues.

The government instituted this action on November 10, 1986, seeking injunctive relief and recovery of response costs. On July 20, 1987, the court entered a consent decree negotiated between the United States and four defendants requiring the defendants to complete the remedial work at the Taylor site. On September 25, 1987, the court granted the United States' motion for partial summary judgment on liability for federal response costs against the City of Scranton. The government has filed a similar motion now against the Empire defendants.

Discussion

. . .

B.   Prima Facie Case for Liability Under CERCLA

Congress enacted CERCLA in 1980 in response to the environmental and public health hazards posed by improper disposal of hazardous wastes. In general terms, the statute established the "Superfund," which is financed primarily through excise taxes on the oil and chemical industries.[2] The federal government is authorized to use the Superfund to finance governmental responses to hazardous waste problems, to pay claims arising from the response activities of private

---

[2]   Section 517 of the Superfund Amendments and Reauthorization Act of 1986 ("SARA"), Pub.L. 99–499, § 517, 100 Stat. 1772 (1986), established the Hazardous Substances Superfund, which is in effect a continuation of the Hazardous Substance Response Trust Fund established by section 221 of CERCLA, 42 U.S.C.A. § 9631 (repealed).

parties, and to compensate federal or state governmental entities for damages to natural resources, 42 U.S.C.A. § 9611(a). The government may then recover Superfund expenditures from those responsible for the generation, transportation or disposal of the hazardous substances. 42 U.S.C.A. § 9607(a).

Section 107(a) of CERCLA, 42 U.S.C.A. § 9607(a), provides, in part, as follows:

Notwithstanding any other provision or rule of law, and subject only to the defenses set forth in subsection (b) of this section—

(1) the owner and operator of a vessel or a facility,

(2) any person who at the time of disposal of any hazardous substance owned or operated any facility at which such hazardous substances were disposed of,

(3) any person who by contract, agreement, or otherwise arranged for disposal or treatment, or arranged with a transporter for transport for disposal or treatment, of hazardous substances owned or possessed by such person, by any other party or entity, at any facility or incineration vessel owned or operated by another party or entity and containing such hazardous substances, and

(4) any person who accepts or accepted any hazardous substances for transport to disposal or treatment facilities, incineration vessels or sites selected by such person, from which there is a release, or a threatened release which causes the incurrence of response costs, of a hazardous substance, shall be liable. . . .

In construing the terms of section 107(a), the courts have uniformly imposed strict liability, subject only to the defenses set forth in section 107(b). *Artesian Water Co. v. Gov. of New Castle County*, 659 F.Supp. 1269 (D.Del.1987). Accordingly, in this case, a *prima facie* case under section 107(a) is established if the United States shows that:

1.   the site is a "facility";[3]

2.   a "release" or threatened release of a "hazardous substance" from the site has occurred;[4]

---

[3]   42 U.S.C.A. § 9601(9) defines "facility" as follows:

The term "facility" means (A) any building, structure, installation, equipment, pipe or pipeline (including any pipe into a sewer or publicly owned treatment works), well, pit, pond, lagoon, impoundment, ditch, landfill, storage container, motor vehicle, rolling stock, or aircraft, or (B) any site or area where a hazardous substance has been deposited, stored, disposed of, or placed, or otherwise come to be located; but does not include any consumer product in consumer use or any vessel.

[4]   42 U.S.C.A. § 9601(22) defines "release" as follows:

The term "release" means any spilling, leaking, pumping, pouring, emitting, emptying, discharging, injecting, escaping, leaching, dumping, or disposing into the environment (including the abandonment or discarding of barrels, containers, and other closed receptacles containing any hazardous substance or pollutant or contaminant). . . .

42 U.S.C.A. § 9602(a) provides that the EPA shall promulgate regulations designating materials as hazardous substances. The regulations at 40 C.F.R. § 302.4 designate substances found at the Taylor site as hazardous substances.

3. the release or threatened release has caused the United States to incur "response costs";[5] and

4. the defendants are "owners" of a facility.[6]

United States v. Maryland Bank & Trust Co., 632 F.Supp. 573 (D.Md.1986).

It is clear from the materials before the court that the government has made a prima facie case. The Empire defendants admit the first three elements and challenge only the government's assertion that they are owners of a facility. Yet in their answer to the complaint, they admitted that on December 12, 1969, they purchased all but a small portion of Parmoff's interest in the Taylor site and that they have owned a portion of the site ever since. They further admitted that the land they bought from Parmoff was the parcel that Parmoff had previously leased to the City of Scranton for use as a refuse disposal area. As discussed below, the defendants' argument is aimed, not at challenging the government's prima facie case, but at establishing one of the three defenses set forth in section 107(b).

C. Affirmative Defense to the Prima Facie Case

Section 107(b) provides as follows:

There shall be no liability under subsection (a) of this section for a person otherwise liable who can establish by a preponderance of the evidence that the release or threat of release of a hazardous substance and the damages resulting therefrom were caused solely by—

(1) an act of God;

(2) an act of war;

(3) an act of omission of a third party other than an employee or agent of the defendant, or than one whose act or omission occurs in connection with a contractual relationship, existing directly or indirectly, with the defendant (except where the sole contractual arrangement arises from a published tariff and acceptance for carriage by a common carrier by rail), if the defendant establishes by a preponderance of the evidence that (a) he exercised due care with respect to the hazardous substance concerned, taking into consideration the characteristics of such hazardous substance, in light of all relevant facts and circumstances, and (b) he took precautions against foreseeable acts or omissions of any such third party and the consequences that could foreseeably result from such acts or omissions; or

(4) any combination of the foregoing paragraphs.

---

[5] "Response" means "remove, removal, remedy and remedial action," including "enforcement activities related thereto." 42 U.S.C.A. § 9601(25).

[6] "Owner" means "in the case of an onshore facility . . ., any person owning or operating such facility. . . ." 42 U.S.C.A. § 9601(20). The term "person" includes an individual and a partnership. 42 U.S.C.A. § 9601(21).

The Empire defendants have raised the "third party" defense in paragraph 3, and under the facts of this case, must prove by a preponderance of the evidence that:

1. the release or threat of release of a hazardous substance and the resulting damages were caused solely by an act or omission of a third party;

2. the third party's act or omission did not occur in connection with a contractual relationship (either direct or indirect) with the defendants;

3. the defendants exercised due care with respect to the hazardous substance; and

4. the defendants took precautions against the third party's foreseeable acts or omissions and the foreseeable consequences resulting therefrom.

Of the four elements of the defense, the government seriously challenges only the second, and asserts that a contractual relationship existed, presumably between the Empire defendants and the Parmoff Corporation. The defendants argue that the entry of summary judgment would be improper because there are genuine issues of fact concerning the existence of that contractual relationship, as that term is defined in CERCLA.

As originally enacted, CERCLA, or more specifically, section 107(b), was unclear as to the liability of owners of contaminated property who were innocent of any involvement with the disposal of hazardous substances. The 1986 SARA amendments attempted to clarify section 107(b), not by amending it directly, but by adding to section 101 a lengthy new subsection defining the previously undefined term, "contractual relationship." Section 101(35)(A) provides, in relevant part, as follows:

(35)(A) The term "contractual relationship", for the purpose of section 9607(b)(3) of this title includes, but is not limited to, land contracts, deeds or other instruments transferring title or possession, unless the real property on which the facility concerned is located was acquired by the defendant after the disposal or placement of the hazardous substance on, in, or at the facility, and . . . the circumstances described in clause (i) . . . is also established by the defendant by a preponderance of the evidence:

(i) At the time the defendant acquired the facility the defendant did not know and had no reason to know that any hazardous substance which is the subject of the release or threatened release was disposed of on, in, or at the facility.

The new definitional provision also specifies at section 101(35)(B):

To establish that the defendant had no reason to know, as provided in clause (i) of subparagraph (A) of this paragraph, the defendant must have undertaken, at the time of acquisition, all appropriate inquiry into the previous ownership and uses of the property consistent with good commercial or customary practice in an effort to minimize liability. For purposes of the preceding sentence the court shall take into account any specialized knowledge or experience on the part of the defendant, the relationship of the purchase price to the value of the property if uncontaminated, commonly known or reasonably ascertainable information about the property, the obviousness of the presence or likely presence of contamination at the property, and the ability to detect such contamination by appropriate inspection.

As stated earlier, the Empire defendants have admitted that they received from Parmoff title to land comprising part of the Taylor site. Furthermore, it is not disputed that they acquired the land after the disposal of the hazardous substance had already occurred. The government contends, however, that at the time they purchased the land, the Empire defendants had reason to know that hazardous substances had been deposited at the Taylor site, and thus there exists a "contractual relationship" negating the use of the innocent landowner defense. In essence, the government's position is that the Empire defendants failed to undertake, at the time of acquisition, "all appropriate inquiry into the previous ownership and uses of the property consistent with good commercial or customary practice" as required by section 101(35)(B). The government's argument is two-pronged. First, it contends that the Empire defendants had reason to know of the site's condition because at the time they purchased the land in 1969, it was obviously and visibly contaminated, and any site visit would have revealed hundreds of abandoned drums on the surface. Second, the government asserts that since defendant Serafini was the Secretary of the Parmoff Corporation at the time the Empire defendants purchased a portion of the site from Parmoff, they possessed "specialized knowledge" of the site's condition.

With respect to the government's first argument, the evidence submitted with and in response to the government's motion shows that at the time the defendants purchased the Taylor site, it was littered with drums which were visible to the naked eye. On November 17, 1982 counsel for Empire wrote to the Environmental Protection Agency, stating that the hazardous waste at the Taylor site was not Empire's responsibility because "these barrels were on the property prior to any purchase made by Empire Contracting Company. . . . Please note the enclosed photos, our photos, which indicate proof to this averment." Attached to Empire counsel's letter were two photographs showing drums scattered across the surface of the site. Subsequent correspondence from Empire Contracting Company on September 22, 1983 also mentioned photographs of the site "taken on October 4, 1968" as proving that the abandoned drums on the property were there prior to the Empire defendants' purchase. Furthermore, in order to obtain this and other evidence regarding the condition of the site when it was purchased in 1969, the United States served the Empire defendants with a request that they admit that "On December 12, 1969 the cylindrical metal drums present at the Site were visible to the naked eye." The Empire defendants did not respond, thereby conclusively establishing, for purposes of this litigation, that at the time they purchased the land from the Parmoff Corporation, abandoned drums were plainly visible.[7]

The Empire defendants' contend that the mere showing that the drums were visible is not enough to establish that they knew or had reason to know that hazardous substances had been deposited at the site. Their affidavits indicate that at the time of the purchase they did not conduct an on-site inspection, nor did they have any reason to do so. They assert that the purchase involved the inspection of various maps to determine the location of the 225 acres and that it was not until 1980 or 1981, when the EPA conducted its investigation, that they became aware of the existence of the 1968 photographs.

The government counters that the defendants' affidavits cannot create issues as to whether they knew or had reason to know of the presence of hazardous waste at the Taylor site because landowners cannot avail themselves of the innocent landowner defense by closing their eyes to hazardous waste problems. The government argues that the defendants had no knowledge of the clearly visible drums only because they failed to inspect the premises prior to purchasing it and they made no inquiry into the past uses of the site. The government posits that SARA's innocent landowner defense does not protect the owner who fails to inspect the land or fails to inquire into its current condition or past history.

Although the government's argument is tempting, the court cannot reach that conclusion on the record before it. Section 101(35)(B) requires a landowner to have undertaken "all appropriate inquiry . . . consistent with good commercial or customary practice" and lists several factors to be considered in making that determination. After analyzing the evidence in the light of those factors, the court is unable to find that the defendants' inaction was inappropriate under the facts of this case. The government has presented no evidence from which the court can conclude that the defendants' failure to inspect or inquire was inconsistent with good commercial or customary practices.[8] Thus, there exists unresolved questions of fact as to the propriety of the defendants' conduct at the time of the purchase.

The government next argues that, beyond the apparent conditions at the site, there is additional evidence demonstrating knowledge of the site's previous use. Specifically, the government asserts that since defendant Serafini acting in his capacity as the Secretary of the Parmoff Corporation, signed the lease granting the City of Scranton the right to use the land as a rubbish dump, he possessed the kind of "specialized knowledge" of the previous use of the land contemplated by section 101(35)(B). Serafini's affidavit, however, states that he was only Acting Secretary of the corporation as a convenience to the owners, and

---

[7]   Earlier in this litigation, the court applied Federal Rule of Civil Procedure 36(b) to another party's failure to respond to requests for admissions, and held that matters as to which unanswered admissions were requested are conclusively established for purposes of this litigation. The discussion of Rule 36(b) in the court's September 25, 1987 order need not be repeated here.

[8]   For example, the government could have submitted affidavits from real estate developers stating that, with respect to the purchase of a 225 acre tract to be developed at a later date, it is the customary or good commercial practice to visually inspect the property before the purchase.

that he was neither an officer nor director. He claims he had no personal knowledge of the operation of the corporation or of the management of the corporation's real estate holdings and asserts that he executed documents only as a witness to the signatures of the corporation's officers. The copy of the lease submitted by the government supports Serafini's contention in that his signature appears on a line labeled "ATTEST." Thus the evidence before the court does not clearly show the relationship between Serafini and Parmoff. Questions still exist as to whether Serafini knew the contents of the lease or that the Taylor site was used as a landfill by the City.[9]

Conclusion

For the foregoing reasons the United State's (*sic*) motion for partial summary judgment on the issue of liability against defendants Serafini, Bernabei, Buttafoco and Naples will be denied. However, the court finds that the United States has established a prima facie case of liability under section 107(a) of CERCLA, 42 U.S.C.A. § 9607(a). The Empire defendants will have opportunity to present affirmative defenses under section 107(b), 42 U.S.C.A. § 9607(b), at trial.

ii. *"Bona Fide Prospective Purchaser" Defense*

Spencer M. Wiegard, Note, The Brownfields Act: Providing Relief for the Innocent or Providing New Hurdles to Avoid Liability?

28 William and Mary Environmental Law and Policy Review 127,
127–129, 147–152 (2003).

I.   Introduction: The Small Business Liability Relief and Brownfields Revitalization Act

On January 11, 2002, President George W. Bush signed House Bill 2869, The Small Business Liability Relief and Brownfields Revitalization Act of 2001 ("Brownfields Act") into law at the Millennium Corporate Center in Conshohocken, Pennsylvania. In his remarks before signing the bill, President Bush recognized the Millennium Corporate Center in which he stood as a brownfields development success story. The President stated that when the steel foundry that had previously sat on the site closed, the site became a brownfield with no investors willing to risk being held jointly and severally liable under the Comprehensive Environmental Response, Compensation, and Liability Act ("CERCLA") for possible existing hazardous waste contamination. It was not until the Environmental Protection Agency ("EPA"), local government, and private investors alleviated concerns about liability that the site was redeveloped. The President continued by heralding the new bill that he was about to sign, saying that it would provide "protection against lawsuits to prospective buyers and others who didn't create the brownfields, but want to help clean them up and develop them," adding further, "[w]ith this bill . . .

---

[9]   Having so found, we need not address the government's somewhat tenuous assertion that knowledge of the existence of a sanitary landfill gave Serafini reason to know of the existence of hazardous wastes on the premises.

[w]e will protect innocent small business owners and employees from unfair lawsuits, and focus our efforts instead on actually cleaning up contaminated sites."

President Bush's enthusiasm exhibited at the bill's signing reflected the positive view of the Brownfields Act held by some members in the environmental legal community who believe that the clarifications, new exemptions, and funding created by the Act offer solutions to environmental contamination liability problems that have been needed for some time. Other observers, however, believe that while the authors and supporters of the Brownfields Act intended to provide a simpler, codified escape route for small businesses seeking to avoid liability, the new amendments to CERCLA are, in fact, complex, cumbersome, and impose new hurdles for these businesses to surmount if they are to obtain relief from liability.

EPA expresses the belief that the Brownfields Act "generally exempts from liability people that purchase contaminated property if their only basis for liability [under CERCLA] is as the current owner of a Superfund site." Prior to the Brownfields Act, CERCLA generally imposed liability for all cleanup costs and damages from hazardous materials release events upon both the current and prior owners of the contaminated site. EPA further suggests that the Brownfields Act "is intended to provide those who purchase contaminated property after the date of enactment the same sort of protection from liability that was previously afforded by Prospective Purchaser Agreements ("PPAs")." It is the purpose of this Note to examine the flaws in CERCLA targeted by the Brownfields Act. In particular, this Note will focus on: (1) the deficiencies in the common law interpretations of the CERCLA exemption requirements for "innocent purchasers;" and (2) whether the new statutory responses in the form of the Bona Fide Prospective Purchaser, De Micromis, and Contiguous Property Owner exemptions, when coupled with newly authorized funding as well as state and local government action, will achieve the noble goals set forth by President Bush and EPA.

. . .

d.   Bona Fide Prospective Purchaser Exemption

The Browfields Act also amends CERCLA to exempt from liability bona fide prospective purchasers [42 U.S.C.A. § 9601(40)], defined as a person (or a tenant of a person) who acquires ownership of a facility after the date of the enactment of this section and who establishes by a preponderance of the evidence that "all disposal took place before the purchase," and that the purchaser:

[1]   made all appropriate inquiry

[2]   . . . exercises appropriate care with respect to any release

[3]   provides full cooperation, assistance, and access to persons authorized to undertake response actions or natural resource restoration

[4]   complies with land use restrictions and does not impede performance of institutional controls

[5]   complies with all information requests

[6]   provides all legally required notices regarding releases of hazardous substances [and]

[7]   . . . is not potentially liable or affiliated with any other person potentially liable[.]

The qualifications under the bona fide prospective purchaser exemption are substantially similar to those in the contiguous properties exemption. The "innocent landowner" defense, however, only applies to owners who did not know and should not have known that the property they were acquiring had or could be contaminated. Under the new bona fide prospective purchaser exemption, owners who discovered site contamination or the possibility thereof prior to purchase, and took action to clean up or prevent the contamination from getting worse, will be protected. The purpose of exempting those prospective purchasers who have conscientiously investigated the possibility or existence of contamination on a site is to eliminate the need for these prospective purchasers to enter into Prospective Purchaser Agreements ("PPAs") with EPA. PPAs are "settlements with the purchasers of contaminated property which then act as covenants not to sue." Under new PPA criteria adopted in 1999, EPA considers the following five criteria in deciding whether to enter into a PPA with a prospective purchaser:

[1]   An EPA action at the facility has been taken, is ongoing, or is anticipated to be undertaken by the agency

[2]   The Agency should receive a substantial benefit either in the form of a direct benefit for cleanup, or as an indirect public benefit in combination with a reduced direct benefit to EPA

[3]   The continued operation of the facility or new site development, with the exercise of due care, will not aggravate or contribute to the existing contamination or interfere with EPA's response action

[4]   The continued operation or new development of the property will not pose health risks to the community and those persons likely to be present at the site [and]

[5]   The prospective purchaser is financially viable[.]

In particular, if the prospective purchaser could demonstrate that EPA would receive a "substantial benefit" from the transaction, that the site could be developed by the prospective purchaser without causing additional contamination, that the site posed no health hazard, and that the prospective purchaser had the means to provide adequate consideration, this purchaser could obtain EPA's promise not to sue the purchaser under CERCLA. EPA is required to publish notices of proposed PPAs in the Federal Register to inform the community. The notice of proposed settlement between EPA and the City of Phoenix concerning "[t]he Motorola 52nd Street Superfund Site" details the typical forms of consideration a purchaser can provide in a PPA. In that case, EPA granted the City of Phoenix a covenant not to sue under CERCLA for the development of the Superfund site in an effort to expand Sky Harbor Airport in exchange for $10,000 and an agreement (1) to allow EPA access to the site for cleanup and (2) for the City of Phoenix to cooperate with any EPA requests to implement measures to stop the spread of the contamination.

Some legal scholars suggest that the restrictions in the Brownfields Act will serve to prevent most brownfield sites from achieving bona fide prospective purchaser status and thereby may prevent further brownfield development by discouraging prospective purchasers. If, on the other hand, the bona fide prospective purchaser exemption proves to be usable by conscientious property owners, it will allow individuals who exercise care in discovering contamination problems and take steps to contain these problems to protect themselves from CERCLA liability without having to resort to PPAs. This exemption could have a profound effect on achieving significant gains in national brownfields redevelopment if it proves to be workable.

It is also necessary to note that the bona fide purchaser exemption is an affirmative defense to a CERCLA action. Because the bona fide purchaser exemption only serves as an affirmative defense, it is raised in response to the initiation of litigation against the landowner. As an affirmative defense, the defendant must raise this exemption in her answer. Any failure to raise this defense waives its use. PPAs, on the other hand, secure liability relief for the landowner before the property is purchased. Application of the bona fide purchaser exemption may require the landowner to incur the cost and time of responding to litigation. Although Alternative Dispute Resolution ("ADR") practices like arbitration and negotiated settlements have been used in CERCLA actions with up to 1200 parties, obtaining relief from liability through ADR also consumes the landowner's time and money. The bona fide prospective purchaser exemption is the codification of EPA's desire to provide liability relief to conscientious landowners who knew at the time of sale that their new property was or could be considered a Superfund site, without having to go through the relatively cumbersome practice of negotiating and granting PPAs.

2.   All Appropriate Inquiries Requirement Defined: Changes in the Innocent Landowner Defense

Section 223 of the Brownfields Act finally defines the phrase "all appropriate inquiries" for purposes of the innocent landowner defense qualifications established by SARA. The Act directs EPA to establish new standards and practices for the "all appropriate inquires" requirement by 2004 using a number of statutorily defined considerations. . . .

The Brownfields Act also established several new substantive conditions for invoking the innocent landowner defense. In addition to making all appropriate inquiries, the purchaser must have taken "reasonable steps to [1] stop any continuing release; [2] prevent any threatened future release; and [3] prevent or limit any human, environmental, or natural resource exposure to any previously released hazardous substance." These requirements merely ensure that when contamination is discovered at a site, the innocent landowner must act to prevent further environmental damage. Innocent landowner apathy that leads to further environmental damage would hardly justify granting such a landowner relief from liability.

PCS Nitrogen Incorporated v. Ashley II
of Charleston, LLC

United States Court of Appeals, Fourth Circuit, 2013.
714 F.3d 161, cert. denied, 134 S.Ct. 514 (2013).

Before MOTZ, KING, and DIAZ, CIRCUIT JUDGES.

Affirmed by published opinion. JUDGE MOTZ wrote the opinion, in which
JUDGE KING and JUDGE DIAZ joined.

OPINION

DIANA GRIBBON MOTZ, CIRCUIT JUDGE:

These appeals arise from disputes as to liability for cleanup of
hazardous substances at a former fertilizer manufacturing site in
Charleston, South Carolina. After incurring response costs, Ashley II of
Charleston, Inc., the current owner of a portion of the site, brought a
cost recovery action against PCS Nitrogen, Inc., under the
Comprehensive Environmental Response, Compensation, and Liability
Act ("CERCLA"), 42 U.S.C. §§ 9601–9675 (2006). . . .

B.

Central to this CERCLA case is the history of the site at issue
here—approximately forty-three acres located in Charleston, South
Carolina. As a result of decades of phosphate fertilizer production, the
westernmost thirty-four acres of the site require remediation of soils
contaminated with arsenic, lead, and other hazardous substances. The
evidence presented at the two bench trials established the following
facts.

1.

From 1884 to the early 1900s, seven phosphate fertilizer plants
operated in close proximity to the site and provided potential sources
for pyrite waste that may have been disposed of on the site prior to
1906.

Planters Fertilizer & Phosphate Company, now known as Ross
Development Corporation, purchased the site in 1906. Planters
manufactured phosphate fertilizer at the site by reacting sulfuric acid
with phosphate rock. Planters produced the sulfuric acid for the process
on-site, and stored the acid in lead-lined tanks. Prior to the 1930s,
Planters used pyrite ore as the primary fuel for its sulfuric acid
production. The burning of pyrite ore generated a pyrite slag byproduct
containing high concentrations of arsenic and lead. Planters spread the
slag byproduct to stabilize roads on the site. This accounts for the vast
majority of arsenic and lead contamination found on the site today.

Planters continued operating its fertilizer production plant on the
site until 1966. During that time, Planters constructed and repaired
several minor buildings and, after a fire destroyed a significant portion
of its original acid plant, constructed a modernized acid plant. On June
30, 1966, Planters sold the site—including the plant and its
equipment—to Columbia Nitrogen Corporation ("Old CNC").

Old CNC continued operations of the acid and fertilizer plants until
1970 and 1972, respectively. Although Old CNC did not use pyrite ore,
its superphosphate fertilizer production generated dust that contained

elevated levels of arsenic and lead, and contributed to arsenic and lead soil contamination on the site. During its operations, Old CNC constructed a new granulation plant and converted the former granulation plant into storage.

In April 1971, a wind storm extensively damaged many buildings on the site, including the acid plant, and dispersed contaminated materials across the site. Old CNC chose not to repair, and instead demolished, the damaged acid plant. In the process, Old CNC disturbed the subsurface soil to a depth of at least two feet. By October 1972, Old CNC had ceased all fertilizer production on the site.

The site remained inactive until 1977, when Old CNC began to dismantle the remaining structures, a process completed in January 1981. All told, Old CNC's construction and demolition activities between 1971 and 1981 affected nearly eighty percent of the area of contaminated soils that needs to be remediated as part of the site's cleanup. In May 1985, Old CNC sold the site to James H. Holcombe and J. Henry Fair (collectively "Holcombe and Fair"). . . .

3.

Meanwhile, Holcombe and Fair, who had acquired the Charleston site from Old CNC in 1985, were unaware of any contamination at the site. They first became aware of the presence of hazardous substances at the site in 1990.

Holcombe and Fair intended to subdivide and lease the site, and the record contains no evidence that Holcombe and Fair introduced any new hazardous substances to the site. However, even after learning of the possibility (and ultimate existence) of hazardous substances on the site, Holcombe and Fair undertook site-wide earth-moving activities, including the construction of a street extension, the addition of water and sewer lines, excavation and grading, and the construction of several detention ponds. As late as 1998, Holcombe and Fair undertook earth-moving activities in areas with "discolored" and "contaminated" soils, and destroyed on-site wetlands along the Ashley River. However, they also added a four-to-six inch limestone run of crusher cover over the majority of the site, which mitigated risks of acute exposure to the site's contaminated soils.

During their ownership, Holcombe and Fair subdivided and conveyed several parcels from the original site. First, in December 1987, Holcombe and Fair sold three acres of the site to Max and Marlene Mast. The Masts sold their parcel to Allwaste Tank Cleaning, Inc., in August 1988. Allwaste operated a shipping container cleaning and storage business and in 1991 leased two additional acres from Holcombe and Fair for storage. As part of its operations, Allwaste utilized an underground sump system to capture wastewater generated by the container-cleaning process and pump it into a treatment system. Allwaste allowed the sumps to deteriorate during its ownership of the parcel to the extent that the sumps presented a threat of a release of hazardous substances. Although All-waste did not introduce arsenic or lead to its parcel, both contaminate the soils in its parcel. Allwaste still owned the parcel at the commencement of this action. . . .

Finally, in November 2003, Holcombe and Fair sold their remaining 27.62 acres of the site to Ashley II of Charleston, Inc., for

$2.7 million. Ashley purchased the site to include it as a portion of its Magnolia Development—a sustainable, mixed-use project. As with other parcels within the project, Ashley purchased the site with knowledge of, and the intent to remediate, the contaminated soils.

By the time of Ashley's ownership, the run of crusher cover had degraded, leaving contaminated soil exposed in many areas. For several years, Ashley allowed a trash pile to accumulate on its parcel.

In February 2007—well after the commencement of this action—Ashley contracted with Allwaste to purchase Allwaste's three-acre parcel. Ashley engaged in extensive prepurchase environmental assessments of the parcel, and All-waste conveyed the parcel to Ashley in May 2008.

. . .

3.

The district court also held Ashley to be a PRP for the site as a current owner. *See* 42 U.S.C. § 9607(a)(1). In doing so, the court rejected Ashley's attempt to establish a bona fide prospective purchaser ("BFPP") exemption from liability. *See id.* §§ 9601(40), 9607(r)(1). On appeal, Ashley again invokes the BFPP exemption.

In 2002, Congress enacted the BFPP exemption as one in an array of CERCLA amendments intended "to promote the cleanup and reuse of brownfields" under the Small Business Liability Relief and Brownfields Revitalization Act ("Brownfields Act"), Pub. L. No. 107–118, 115 Stat. 2356 (2002). BFPP status exempts from CERCLA liability a party otherwise liable simply because it is "considered to be an owner or operator of a facility" under 42 U.S.C. § 9607(a)(1). *See* 42 U.S.C. § 9607(r)(1). To qualify for the exemption, a current owner or operator of a facility must have acquired the facility after January 11, 2002, must "not impede the performance of a response action or natural resource restoration" at the facility, and must establish eight criteria by a preponderance of the evidence. *See id.* §§ 9601(40)(A)–(H), 9607(r)(1).

The district court held that Ashley failed to establish a number of these eight criteria. Among them is the requirement that a current owner "exercises appropriate care with respect to hazardous substances found at the facility by taking reasonable steps to (i) stop any continuing release; (ii) prevent any threatened future release; and (iii) prevent or limit human, environmental, or natural resource exposure to any previously released hazardous substance." *Id.* § 9601(40)(D). The court specifically found that Ashley failed to clean out and fill in sumps that should have been capped, filled, or removed when related aboveground structures were demolished, and that Ashley did not monitor and adequately address conditions relating to a debris pile and the limestone run of crusher cover on the site. The court concluded that these inactions established that Ashley did not exercise appropriate care at the site.

Ashley argues that the purposes of the Brownfields Act necessitate that courts apply a less-stringent standard of "appropriate care" and "reasonable steps" than that applied by the district court. Otherwise, Ashley maintains, landowners will not undertake voluntary brownfields redevelopment for fear of becoming fully liable for cleanup costs as a result of minor mistakes that may not even contribute to harm at the facility. Even recognizing Congress' clear intent to promote voluntary brownfields redevelopment in passing the Brownfields Act, however, Ashley's argument goes too far.

In particular, Ashley fails to provide a persuasive rationale for requiring a lower level of "care" from a BFPP under § 9607(r)(1), than from an "innocent landowner" under § 9607(b)(3). Both the BFPP exemption and the innocent landowner defense require a demonstration of "reasonable steps." *Compare* 42 U.S.C. § 9601(35)(B)(i)(II), *with id.* § 9601(40)(D). Logic seems to suggest that the standard of "appropriate care" required of a BFPP, who by definition knew of the presence of hazardous substances at a facility, should be *higher* than the standard of "due care" required of an innocent landowner, who by definition "did not know and had no reason to know" of the presence of hazardous substances when it acquired a facility. *Compare id.* §§ 9601(40)(D), 9607(r)(1) (BFPP exemption and "appropriate care" standard), *with id.* §§ 9601(35), 9607(b)(3) (innocent landowner defense and "due care" standard).

We need not here determine whether the BFPP standard of "appropriate care" actually is higher than the standard of "due care" mandated elsewhere in CERCLA, because in all events "appropriate care" under § 9601(40)(D) is at least as stringent as "due care" under § 9607(b)(3). *Accord* Office of Enforcement & Compliance Assurance, U.S. Envtl. Prot. Agency, Interim Guidance Regarding Criteria Landowners Must Meet in Order to Qualify for Bona Fide Prospective Purchaser, Contiguous Property Owner, or Innocent Landowner Limitations on CERCLA Liability 9 (March 6, 2003) (stating that reasonable steps required under the "appropriate care" standard establish "an approach that is consonant with traditional common law principles and the existing CERCLA 'due care' requirement").

We therefore borrow standards from CERCLA's "due care" jurisprudence to inform our determination of what "reasonable steps" must be taken to demonstrate "appropriate care." We agree with the Second Circuit that the "due care" inquiry asks whether a party "took all precautions with respect to the particular waste that a similarly situated reasonable and prudent person would have taken in light of all relevant facts and circumstances." *New York v. Lashins Arcade Co.,* 91 F.3d 353, 361 (2d Cir.1996) (internal quotation marks omitted). Under this standard, Ashley's inactions clearly show that it failed to exercise "appropriate care." For Ashley's delay in filling the sumps—which even Ashley's expert admitted should have been filled a full year before Ashley did so—demonstrates that it did not take the "reasonable steps to . . . prevent any threatened future release," 42 U.S.C. § 9601(40)(D), that "a similarly situated reasonable and prudent person would have taken," *Lashins Arcade Co.,* 91 F.3d at 361 (internal quotation marks omitted).

Accordingly, the district court did not err in finding that Ashley failed to demonstrate that it exercised "appropriate care" at the site. Because a party must establish all eight factors under 42 U.S.C. § 9601(40) to qualify for a BFPP exemption from liability, this failure mandates denial of Ashley's claim to BFPP exemption and affirmance of the district court's holding that Ashley is a PRP for the site as a current owner under § 9607(a)(1).

. . .

V.

For the foregoing reasons, the judgment of the district court is
AFFIRMED.

iii. By Agreement

Niecko v. Emro Marketing Company

United States District Court, Eastern District of Michigan, 1991.
769 F.Supp. 973, affirmed 973 F.2d 1296 (6th Cir.1992).

[This case deals with the sale of land purchased by the plaintiffs
(Nieckos) from the defendant Emro (a division of Marathon Oil). The
property had previously been used as a gasoline station and the
plaintiffs had to spend some $140,000 to clean up toxic hydrocarbons
that they found on the premises. While CERCLA does not apply to
hydrocarbons, the Michigan statute governing liability for disposal of
such substances was modeled directly on CERCLA. Such "baby
CERCLA" statutes are common in the states. The court here relies on
CERCLA in its decision under the Michigan legislation—Eds.]

. . .

When Emro sold the property to the Plaintiffs in March, 1987, the
purchase contract contained the following disclaimers:

10. It is expressly agreed that Seller makes no warranties
that the subject property complies with federal, state or local
governmental laws or regulations applicable to the property or
its use. *Buyer has fully examined and inspected the property*
and takes the property in its existing condition with no
warranties of any kind concerning the condition of the property
or its use.

11. *Buyer acknowledges that he has inspected and is familiar
with the condition of the property*; that Seller has not made and
makes no warranties or representations as to the condition of
said property, including, but not limited to, *soil conditions*,
zoning, building code violations, building line, building
construction, use and occupancy restrictions (and violations of
any of the foregoing), availability of utilities; and that Buyer is
purchasing the same "as is"; *that he assumes all responsibility
for any damages caused by the conditions on the property upon
transfer of title.*

. . .

The Plaintiffs argue, in the alternative, that Section 12(6) of the
Michigan Leaking Underground Storage Tank Act renders
unenforceable Emro's attempt, in the purchase contract, to absolve
itself from potential liability to the Plaintiff under the Act. Sections
12(6) and (7) (also pertinent) of the Michigan Act provide:

299.842. Liability of owners or operators

* * *

(6) No indemnification, hold harmless, or similar agreement or conveyance shall be effective to transfer from the owner or operator or from any person who may be liable for a release or threat of release under this act, to any person the liability imposed under this act. Nothing in this subsection shall bar any agreement to insure, hold harmless, or indemnify a party to such agreement for any liability under this act.

(7) This act shall not bar a cause of action that an owner or operator or any other person subject to liability under this act, or a guarantor, has or would have by reason of subrogation or otherwise against any person.

M.C.L. § 299.842(6), (7).

As noted by the parties in their supplemental briefs, this statute was enacted by the Michigan legislature effective January 19, 1989 and has not received any interpretation or construction by a Michigan or federal court. However, the parties further note that Sections 12(6) and (7) are virtually identical to, and obviously based upon, the analogous provisions contained in Sections 107(e)(1) and (2) of CERCLA, 42 U.S.C.A. § 9607(e)(1), (2). This statute reads in relevant part as follows:

§ 9607. Liability

* * *

e) Indemnification, hold harmless, etc., agreements or conveyances; subrogation rights

(1) No indemnification, hold harmless, or similar agreement or conveyance shall be effective to transfer from the owner or operator of any vessel or facility or from any person who may be liable for a release or threat of release under this section, to any person the liability imposed under this section. Nothing in this subsection shall bar any agreement to insure, hold harmless, or indemnify a party to such agreement for liability under this section.

(2) Nothing in this subchapter, including the provisions of paragraph (1) of this subsection, shall bar a cause of action that an owner or operator or any other person subject to liability under this section, or a guarantor, has or would have, by reason of subrogation or otherwise against any person.

42 U.S.C.A. § 9607(e)(1), (2).

The first rule in the construction of any statute is to begin with the language of the statute itself. *United States v. Ron Pair Enterprises, Inc.*, 489 U.S. 235, 109 S.Ct. 1026, 1030, 103 L.Ed.2d 290 (1989); *Mallard v. United States District Court for the Southern District of Iowa*, 490 U.S. 296, 109 S.Ct. 1814, 1818, 104 L.Ed.2d 318 (1989). "The plain meaning of legislation should be conclusive, except in the 'rare cases [in which] the literal application of a statute will produce a result demonstrably at odds with the intention of its drafters.'" *Ron Pair*, 109 S.Ct., at 1031 (quoting *Griffin v. Oceanic Contractors, Inc.*, 458 U.S. 564, 571, 102 S.Ct. 3245, 3250, 73 L.Ed.2d 973 (1982)); *Bradley v. Austin*, 841 F.2d 1288, 1293 (6th Cir.1988).

At first glance, the first and second sentences of Section 107(e)(1) may appear to be contradictory. Read cursorily, the first sentence seems to proscribe indemnification and hold harmless agreements, and the second sentence seems to permit them. In fact, a number of federal courts addressing this issue have found that the second sentence nullifies the first.[7] However, these courts seem to have predicated their decisions on the public policy rationale that, because CERCLA liability is far reaching, the parties should be able to distribute it as they see fit. 750 F.Supp. at 1025–26.

In interpreting this section, this Court will begin with the understanding that Congress intended that liability under CERCLA be joint and several. All parties who qualify as owners or operators are to be held liable to the claimant.[8] As noted in the legislative history,

> The Committee fully subscribes to the reasoning of the court in the seminal case of *United States v. Chem-Dyne Corporation*, 572 F.Supp. 802 (S.D.Ohio 1983), which established a uniform federal rule allowing for joint and several liability in appropriate CERCLA cases.

H.R.Rep. No 99–253(I), 99th Cong., 1st Sess. 74, reprinted in 1986 U.S.CODE CONG. & ADMIN.NEWS 2835, 2856.

The first sentence of Section 107 clearly assumes the joint and several liability of all liable parties to any party that, under the Act, has a right to demand cleanup and redress of damages, e.g., the government. It is this joint and several liability to which Congress is clearly referring when it speaks of "the liability imposed under this section" in the last words of the first sentence of the section.

With this premise firmly in mind, the first and second sentences of Section 107(e)(1) are not contradictory, but rather clear in their scope and intent. The first sentence simply voids any attempted transfer of joint and several liability to another party. Thus, assuming that Party A is the government and Party B is an owner-operator who sells property to Party C, the clear intent and effect of the first sentence is to void any attempt by Party B to contractually transfer, through

---

[7] As stated by the court in *Jones-Hamilton Co. v. Kop-Coat, Inc.*, 750 F.Supp. 1022 (N.D.Cal.1990),

> A majority of federal courts that have considered the issue have held with minimal discussion that the second sentence of section 107(e)(1) completely negates the first sentence, thereby permitting parties to bargain over indemnification for CERCLA liability under all circumstances. *See e.g., American Nat'l Can Co. v. Kerr Glass Mfg. Corp.*, 1990 WL 125368 (N.D.Ill.1990); *Versatile Metals, Inc. v. Union Corp.*, 693 F.Supp. 1563 (E.D.Pa.1988); *Chemical Waste Management v. Armstrong World Indus., Inc.*, 669 F.Supp. 1285, 1293 (E.D.Pa.1987); *FMC Corp. v. Northern Pump Co.*, 668 F.Supp. 1285, 1289 (D.Minn.1987), appeal dismissed, 871 F.2d 1091 (8th Cir.1988).

Id. at 1025.

[8] As defined in CERCLA, "claimant" is "any person who presents a claim for compensation under this chapter." 42 U.S.C.A. § 9601(5). In most cases, the United States government, operating through the Environmental Protection Agency, will be enforcing the statute. However, the Act also provides for recovery, under certain conditions, by private parties. *See* 42 U.S.C.A. § 9607(a)(4)(B); *Pennsylvania v. Union Gas Co.*, 491 U.S. 1, 109 S.Ct. 2273, 2285, 105 L.Ed.2d 1 (1989); *Amoco Oil Co. v. Borden, Inc.*, 889 F.2d 664, 667 (5th Cir.1989).

The Michigan statute likewise assumes that the state government, i.e., the DNR, will be responsible for collecting response costs for hazardous waste cleanup. See M.C.L. § 299.843.

indemnification or hold harmless agreements, to Party C all the liability it owes Party A. In other words, Party B cannot, by contractual indemnification, escape its obligations to Party A under the Act. Congress intended to protect the rights of the claimant against attempts by owners or operators to escape liability to claimants through private contractual devices. *See Rodenbeck v. Marathon Petroleum Co.*, 742 F.Supp. 1448, 1456 (N.D.Ind.1990).

The legislative history of CERCLA provides clear support for this interpretation. During a Senate debate, the following exchange took place between Senator Cannon and Senator Randolph, a sponsor of the bill:

> Mr. CANNON. Section 107(a)(1) prohibits transfer of liability from the owner or operator of a facility to other persons through indemnification, hold harmless, or similar agreements or conveyances. Language is also included indicating that this prohibition on the transfer of liability does not act as a bar to such agreements, in particular to insurance agreements.

> The net effect is to make the parties to such an agreement, which would not have been liable under this section, also liable to the degree specified in the agreement. *It is my understanding that this section is designed to eliminate situations where the owner or operator of a facility uses its economic power to force the transfer of its liability to other persons, as a cost of doing business, thus escaping its liability under the act all together [sic].*

> Mr. RANDOLPH. That is correct.

126 CONG.REC. 30,984 (1980) (emphasis added). Senator Cannon makes clear that the purpose of the section is to ensure that the responsible parties will fund the cleanup. These responsible parties may enter insurance agreements to add parties who will pay for the cleanup. They may not, however, avoid liability to the claimant (usually the government) by transferring this liability.

. . .

NOTES

1. *The Brownfield Amendments.* In addition to the policy arguments supporting and critiquing the Brownfield Amendments discussed in the Wiegard excerpt above, consider the following:

> The Amendment aims to encourage the purchase and development of brownfields. While this may be a laudable goal, the means chosen are both quite costly and unfair. By freeing purchasers of property subject to CERCLA from liability, the Amendment creates a number of potential evils. First, it removes an important disincentive to the creation of properties subject to CERCLA, commonly known as "CERCLA Sites" or "Superfund Sites." The Amendment will thereby engender more releases of hazardous materials. Second, it gives property owners a windfall. This is not only unfair, but also it threatens to increase the cost of government regulation. Third, it will increase the costs of performing clean-ups under CERCLA.

Kettles, Bad Policy: CERCLA's Amended Liability for New Purchasers, 21 U.C.L.A.J. Envt'l L. & Pol'y 1, 9 (2002/2003). See also Chase & Mixon, CERCLA: Convey To A Pauper and Avoid Cost Recovery Under Section 107(a)(1)?, 33 Env'tL. 293 (2003).

2. *Environmental Audits.* The environmental audit serves several purposes. First, a buyer may try to cancel a contract of sale if the audit discloses contamination. (Must there be a contract condition to that effect?) Second, an environmental audit may form the basis for the innocent landowner defense or the bona fide prospective purchaser defense under CERCLA (as per *Sefafini, PCS Nitrogen,* and the Wiegard excerpt). A lender may require an environmental audit, to ensure that the land—its security—is not contaminated and to avoid liability as an innocent landowner in the event of foreclosure. (See pages 775–786 below).

There was a lack of clarity as to the required level of inspection necessary to satisfy the statutory defenses until EPA promulgated the All Appropriate Inquiry rule, effective in 2006, pursuant to the Brownfields Act (the popular name for the 2002 Small Business Relief and Brownfields Revitalization Act, Pub. L. No. 107–118, 115 Stat. 2356 (2002)). Until the AAI Rule, the industry generally followed a practice of performing a Phase I inquiry on the property, which involved review of a questionnaire about the property and it nature, the chain of title, governmental records, interviews of key parties, and a site inspection to uncover possible prior contamination. If red flags are raised from Phase I, then a more extensive Phase II environmental audit would be conducted which might include soil borings, water studies, and other testing. See Comment, The Environmental Due Diligence Defense and Contractual Protection Devices, 49 La.L.Rev. 1405, 1422–1428 (1989).

The AAI Rule for the first time described with specificity the necessary due diligence steps necessary under the statute. Standards and Practices for All Appropriate Inquiries, 40 C.F.R. pt. 312. For an excellent and detailed description of the AAI rule and standards adopted by ASTM International (formerly the American Society for Testing and Materials), see Forte, Environmental Due Diligence: A Guide to Liability Risk Management in Commercial Real Estate Transactions, 42 Real Prop. Probate & Tr.J. 443 (2007).

For other descriptions of environmental audits, see Patterson, A Buyer's Catalogue of Prepurchase Precautions to Minimize CERCLA Liability in Commercial Real Estate Transactions, 15 U. Puget Sound L.Rev. 469, 488–491 (1992); Slap & Israel, Private CERCLA Litigation: How To Avoid It? How To Handle It?, 25 Real Prop. Probate & Trust J. 705, 715–717 (1991); Fitzsimmons & Sherwood, The Real Estate Lawyer's Primer (And More) to Superfund: The Environmental Hazards of Real Estate Transactions, 22 Real Prop. Probate & Trust J. 765, 775–782 (1987); Forte, Environmental Due Diligence: A Guide to Risk Management in Commercial Real Estate Transactions, 5 Fordham Envt'l L.Rev. 349 (1994); Comment, Environmental Self-Audit Privilege and Immunity: Aid to Enforcement or Polluter Protection?, 30 Ariz. St. L.J. 235 (1998); M. Blumenfeld, Conducting An Environmental Audit (2d ed.1989).

On the recourse a buyer may have against an environmental engineer who fails to discover existing contamination, see Note, Holding

Environmental Consultants Liable For Their Negligence: A Proposal For Change, 64 S.Cal.L.Rev. 1143 (1991).

3. *Innocent Landowner Defense.* Section 9607(b)'s innocent landowner defense was historically very difficult to establish. See, e.g., In re Sterling Steel Treating, Inc., 94 B.R. 924 (Bkrtcy.E.D.Mich.1989) (buyer who knew of prior owner's business and failed to inspect property prior to sale); State of Washington v. Time Oil Co., 687 F.Supp. 529 (W.D.Wash.1988) (lessee failed to supervise sublessee's operations). Only a handful of reported decisions uphold the defense. See, e.g., United States v. Pacific Hide & Fur Depot, Inc., 716 F.Supp. 1341 (D.Idaho 1989) (children were treated like devisees and thus leniency applied in gift situation); In State of New York v. Lashins Arcade Co., 856 F.Supp. 153, 157 (S.D.N.Y.1994) (defendant was "a subsequent purchaser who did everything that could reasonably have been done to avoid or correct the pollution, where the discharges by the dry cleaners presumably causing the pollution occurred fifteen years prior to the purchase").

Many environmental law practitioners had come to believe that the "appropriate inquiry" requirement described in *Serafini* effectively disables the innocent landowner defense. They argued that if a potential buyer performs an "appropriate inquiry," it will find the hazardous substance, reject the property, and consequently never need to rely on the defense. If, however, the buyer makes an inquiry, does not find the contamination, and buys the property, the court will likely determine that the inquiry was not "appropriate" as it did not uncover the problem. See generally, Hitt, Desperately Seeking SARA: Preserving the Innocent Landowner Defense to Superfund Liability, 18 Real Est.L.J. 3 (1989); Anderson, Will The Meek Even Want The Earth?, 38 Mercer L.Rev. 535 (1987). This concern about a "catch 22" supported the 2002 Brownfields Act addition of the bona fide prospective purchaser exception where the buyer knows of the pollution but is permitted to avoid CERCLA liability. As *PCS Nitrogen* indicates, the innocent owner defense remains theoretically available after the passage of the less ambiguous bona fide prospective purchaser defense.

The passage of the Brownfield Amendments was intended to clarify the innocent landowner defense and to thus make it more readily available to qualifying landowners. Among the many requirements under the AAI Rule, an owner attempting to show "all appropriate inquiry" to qualify for the defense must include an inquiry by an environmental professional; interviews with past and present owners, operators, and occupants, reviews of federal, state, and local governmental records; and visual inspections of the facility and adjoining properties. The purpose of the inquiry to identify conditions indicating releases or threatened release of hazardous materials. 40 C.F.R. § 312.20. If the Rule had been in effect, would the defendants in *Serafini* have been able to meet its requirements?

4. *Indemnification.* Courts differ on the enforceability of clauses that attempt to shift CERCLA liability. Two issues control: is the contract language used by the parties adequate to show an intent to shift the cost?; does CERCLA permit the parties to shift liability? Consider how you would draft the clause if you represented buyer or seller. See GNB Battery Technologies, Inc. v. Gould, Inc., 65 F.3d 615 (7th Cir.1995) (transfer of "all obligations and liabilities of any nature" from seller's battery division to buyer was sufficient to transfer CERCLA liability); North Shore Gas Co. v. Salomon Inc., 152 F.3d 642 (7th Cir.1998), overruled on other grounds by

Envision Healthcare, Inc. v. Preferred One Insurance Co., 604 F.3d 983 (7th Cir. 2010) (assumption of "existing" liabilities did not include liability under CERCLA which had not yet come into existence).

See generally, Johnson, For Real Estate Lawyers: A Practical Guide to Identifying and Managing Potential Environmental Hazards and Conditions Affecting Real Estate, 32 Real Prop. Probate & Tr. J. 619 (1998); Parker & Slavich, Contractual Efforts To Allocate The Risk of Environmental Liability: Is There A Way To Make Indemnities Worth More Than The Paper They Are Written On?, 44 Sw.L.J. 1349 (1991); Note, Contractual Transfers of Liability Under CERCLA Section 107(e)(1): For Enforcement of Private Risk Allocations in Real Property Transactions, 43 Case W.Res.L.Rev. 161 (1992); Note, Passing The Big Bucks: Contractual Transfers of Liability Between Potentially Responsible Parties Under CERCLA, 75 Minn.L.Rev. 1571 (1991); Note, An "As Is" Provision in a Commercial Property Contract: Should It Be Left As Is When Assessing Liability for Environmental Torts?, 51 U.Pitt.L.Rev. 995 (1990).

5. *Other Buyer Remedies.* The buyer of contaminated property may seek to hold the seller responsible under a number of state law theories explored in other contexts.

Would claims based nondisclosure be consistent with Thacker v. Tyree and Stambovsky v. Ackley, at pages 194–204 above? See Roberts v. Estate of Barbagallo, 366 Pa.Super. 559, 531 A.2d 1125 (1987) (permitting cause of action against seller's estate and broker for fraudulent concealment by broker of ureaformaldehyde foam insulation that presents a health risk); Westwood Pharmaceuticals, Inc. v. National Fuel Gas Distribution Corp., 737 F.Supp. 1272 (W.D.N.Y.1990), affirmed, 964 F.2d 85 (2d Cir.1992) (holding that New York's caveat emptor rule is no defense to CERCLA action by buyer against seller). See generally, Tracy, Beyond Caveat Emptor: Disclosure to Buyers of Contaminated Land, 10 Stan.Envtl.L.J. 169 (1991).

Buyers sometimes succeed, such as in tort for abnormally dangerous activities on the land, see, e.g., T & E Industries, Inc. v. Safety Light Corp., 123 N.J. 371, 587 A.2d 1249 (1991) (permitting buyer to maintain action against owner earlier in chain of title that discarded radioactive materials on the site in the course of manufacturing operations); public and private nuisance, see Westwood Pharmaceuticals, Inc. v. National Fuel Gas Distribution Corp., 737 F.Supp. 1272 (W.D.N.Y.1990), affirmed, 964 F.2d 85 (2d Cir.1992); cf. Adkins v. Thomas Solvent Co., 440 Mich. 293, 487 N.W.2d 715 (1992) (finding no nuisance when neighboring company polluted groundwater in area but not plaintiffs' groundwater and finding negative publicity caused by that pollution was not actionable nuisance); mutual mistake, see, e.g., Garb-Ko v. Lansing-Lewis Services, Inc., 167 Mich.App. 779, 423 N.W.2d 355 (1988) (seller permitted to rescind contract where neither seller nor buyer knew of underground gasoline tanks); and builder-vendor warranty, see, Powell, Builder-Vendor Liability For Environmental Contamination in the Sale of New Residential Property, 58 Tenn.L.Rev. 231 (1991).

Buyers have enjoyed less success in claiming that the presence of hazardous materials breached promises relating to title. See, e.g., United States v. Allied Chemical Corp., 587 F.Supp. 1205 (N.D.Cal.1984) (hazardous waste was not "encumbrance" within seller's covenant that land was free from encumbrances); see Cameron v. Martin Marietta Corp., 729 F.Supp. 1529 (E.D.N.C.1990) (presence of hazardous waste did not breach provision of contract of sale that there were "no restrictions, easement, zoning or other governmental regulation" that would prevent reasonable use of the property for the purposes for which it was currently zoned since court believed buyers could maintain innocent landowner defense under CERCLA). Similarly, courts have found that environmental contamination does not breach the implied warranty of marketable title. See, e.g., HM Holdings, Inc. v. Rankin, 70 F.3d 933 (7th Cir.1995); Vandervort v. Higginbotham, 222 A.D.2d 831, 634 N.Y.S.2d 800 (1995); but see Jones v. Melrose Park Nat'l Bank, 228 Ill.App.3d 249, 170 Ill.Dec. 126, 592 N.E.2d 562 (1992) (specific warranty of no contamination), distinguished by In re Country World Casinos, 181 F.3d 1146 (10th Cir.1999) (contamination is not encumbrance).

6. *Liability Insurance.* Landowners generally accept that pollution exclusion clauses typically inserted in their insurance policies will bar recovery from the insurer for liability arising from the hazardous substances on the property. See Mustang Tractor & Equipment Co. v. Liberty Mutual Insurance Co., 76 F.3d 89 (5th Cir.1996) (release of pollutants from demolition of building and razing of land was not "sudden and accidental" and so was not covered by owners' general comprehensive liability policy); Foster-Gardner, Inc. v. National Union Fire Insurance Company, 18 Cal.4th 857, 77 Cal.Rptr.2d 107, 959 P.2d 265 (1998) (state environmental agency's order under CERCLA requiring owner to remediate property was not a "suit" triggering the insurer's obligation to defend under the policy). Even if an insured could convince a court to extend coverage, a reasonable buyer will be reluctant to rely on that possibility as her protection from CERCLA liability. See Fersko & Waeger, Using Environmental Insurance in Commercial Real Estate Transactions, 17 Probate & Prop. 31 (Jan./Feb. 2003); Schroeder, Environmental Insurance: A Business Tool for The Real Estate Transaction, 21 Prac. Real Est. Law. 51 (No. 5 2005); Zuckerman, Motzer, Leonard & Solomon, Representing Buyers, Sellers and Lenders in Transferring Contaminated Property: A Primer for Real Estate Practitioners, Part II, 36 Real Prop. Probate & Tr. J. 37, 92–98 (2001); Comment, Comprehensive General Liability Insurance Coverage for CERCLA Liabilities: A Recommendation for Judicial Adherence to State Canons of Insurance Contract Construction, 61 U.Colo.L.Rev. 407 (1990); Note, Insurance Coverage for Superfund Liability: A Plain Meaning Approach to The Pollution Exclusion Clause, 27 Washburn L.J. 161 (1987); see also Raskoff, Arguments Advanced By Insureds For Coverage of Environmental Claims, 22 Pac.L.J. 771 (1991). Some insurers have been offering special insurance coverage to buyers and lenders for cleanup expenses of undetected hazardous waste under CERCLA and similar state regulation. See Feder, Making a Difference; New Policy on Pollution, N.Y. Times, June 9, 1991, sec. 3, at 7 (discussing the Environmental Risk Insurance Company Group property transfer liability insurance).

For an excellent analysis of the issues of environmental insurance, see Abraham, Environmental Liability and the Limits of Insurance, 88 Colum.L.Rev. 942 (1988).

7. *Title Insurance.* The presence of hazardous materials does not breach the title insurance policy's warranties of marketability of title and freedom from encumbrances. See, e.g., Chicago Title Insurance Co. v. Kumar, 24 Mass.App.Ct. 53, 506 N.E.2d 154 (1987); Lick Mill Creek Apartments v. Chicago Title Insurance Co., 231 Cal.App.3d 1654, 283 Cal.Rptr. 231 (1991). However, a title company may be liable on a policy if it fails to detect an environmental lien recorded before issuance of the policy. See Bozarth, Environmental Liens and Title Insurance, 23 U.Rich.L.Rev. 305 (1989).

8. *Tax Breaks.* The Tax Reform Act of 1997 added section 198 to the Internal Revenue Code which permits a taxpayer to deduct currently the cost of a "qualified environmental remediation expenditure." To qualify, the property must be used in a trade or business for the production of income, or as stock in trade or inventory. Further, the property must be within a targeted area, as designated by the state's environmental protection agency.

2. LENDER LIABILITY

United States v. Fleet Factors Corp.

United States Court of Appeals, Eleventh Circuit, 1990.
901 F.2d 1550, cert. denied, 498 U.S. 1046, 111 S.Ct. 752, 112 L.Ed.2d 772 (1991).

Before VANCE and KRAVITCH, CIRCUIT JUDGES, and LYNNE, SENIOR DISTRICT JUDGE.

KRAVITCH, CIRCUIT JUDGE:

Fleet Factors Corporation ("Fleet") brought an interlocutory appeal from the district court's denial of its motion for summary judgment in this suit by the United States to recover the cost of removing hazardous waste from a bankrupt textile facility. The district court denied summary judgment because it concluded that Fleet's activities at the facility might rise to the level of participation in management sufficient to impose liability under the Comprehensive Environmental Response Compensation and Liability Act ("CERCLA"), 42 U.S.C.A. §§ 9601–57 (1982 & West Supp.1988), despite the statutory exemption from liability for holders of a security interest. We agree with the district court that material questions of fact remain as to the extent of Fleet's participation in the management of the facility; therefore, we affirm the denial of Fleet's summary judgment motion.

FACTS

In 1976, Swainsboro Print Works ("SPW"), a cloth printing facility, entered into a "factoring" agreement with Fleet in which Fleet agreed to advance funds against the assignment of SPW's accounts receivable. As collateral for these advances, Fleet also obtained a security interest in SPW's textile facility and all of its equipment, inventory, and fixtures. In August, 1979, SPW filed for bankruptcy under Chapter 11. The factoring agreement between SPW and Fleet continued with court approval. In early 1981, Fleet ceased advancing funds to SPW because SPW's debt to Fleet exceeded Fleet's estimate of the value of SPW's accounts receivable. On February 27, 1981, SPW ceased operations and began to liquidate its inventory. Fleet continued to collect on the accounts receivable assigned to it under the Chapter 11 factoring agreement. In December 1981, SPW was adjudicated a bankrupt under Chapter 7 and a trustee assumed title and control of the facility.

In May 1982, Fleet foreclosed on its security interest in some of SPW's inventory and equipment, and contracted with Baldwin Industrial Liquidators ("Baldwin") to conduct an auction of the collateral. Baldwin sold the material "as is" and "in place" on June 22, 1982; the removal of the items was the responsibility of the purchasers. On August 31, 1982, Fleet allegedly contracted with Nix Riggers ("Nix") to remove the unsold equipment in consideration for leaving the premises "broom clean." Nix testified in deposition that he understood that he had been given a "free hand" by Fleet or Baldwin to do whatever was necessary at the facility to remove the machinery and equipment. Nix left the facility by the end of December, 1983.

On January 20, 1984, the Environmental Protection Agency ("EPA") inspected the facility and found 700 fifty-five gallon drums containing toxic chemicals and forty-four truckloads of material containing asbestos. The EPA incurred costs of nearly $400,000 in responding to the environmental threat at SPW. On July 7, 1987, the facility was conveyed to Emanuel County, Georgia, at a foreclosure sale resulting from SPW's failure to pay state and county taxes.

The government sued Horowitz and Newton, the two principal officers and stockholders of SPW, and Fleet to recover the cost of cleaning up the hazardous waste. The district court granted the government's summary judgment motion with respect to the liability of Horowitz and Newton for the cost of removing the hazardous waste in the drums. The government's motion with respect to Fleet's liability, and the liability of Horowitz and Newton for the asbestos removal costs was denied. Fleet's motion for summary judgment was also denied. The district court, *sua sponte*, certified the summary judgment issues for interlocutory appeal and stayed the remaining proceedings in the case. Fleet subsequently brought this appeal challenging the court's denial of its motion for summary judgment.

. . .

The parties liable for costs incurred by the government in responding to an environmental hazard are: 1) the present owners and operators of a facility where hazardous wastes were released or are in danger of being released; 2) the owners or operators of a facility at the time the hazardous wastes were disposed; 3) the person or entity that arranged for the treatment or disposal of substances at the facility; and 4) the person or entity that transported the substances to the facility. *Allis Chalmers*, 893 F.2d at 1317; 42 U.S.C.A. § 9607(a) (1982 & West Supp.1988). The government contends that Fleet is liable for the response costs associated with the waste at the SPW facility as either a present owner and operator of the facility, *see* 42 U.S.C.A. § 9607(a)(1), or the owner or operator of the facility at the time the wastes were disposed, *see* 42 U.S.C.A. § 9607(a)(2).

The district court, as a matter of law, rejected the government's claim that Fleet was a present owner of the facility. The court, however, found a sufficient issue of fact as to whether Fleet was an owner or operator of the SPW facility at the time the wastes were disposed to warrant the denial of Fleet's motion for summary judgment. On appeal

each party contests that portion of the district court's order adverse to
their respective interests.

A. Fleet's Liability Under Section 9607(A)(1)

CERCLA holds the owner or operator of a facility containing
hazardous waste strictly liable to the United States for expenses
incurred in responding to the environmental and health hazards posed
by the waste in that facility. *See* 42 U.S.C.A. § 9607(a)(1); S.Rep. No.
848, 96th Cong., 2d Sess. 34 (1980). This provision of the statute targets
those individuals presently "owning or operating such facilit[ies]." *See*
42 U.S.C.A. § 9601(20)(A)(ii). In order to effectuate the goals of the
statute, we will construe the present owner and operator of a facility as
that individual or entity owning or operating the facility at the time the
plaintiff initiated the lawsuit by filing a complaint.

On July 9, 1987, the date this litigation commenced, the owner of
the SPW facility was Emanuel County, Georgia. Under CERCLA,
however, a state or local government that has involuntarily acquired
title to a facility is generally not held liable as the owner or operator of
the facility.[4] Rather, the statute provides that

> in the case of any facility, title or control of which was
> conveyed due to bankruptcy, foreclosure, tax delinquency,
> abandonment, or similar means to a unit of State or local
> government, [its owner or operator is] any person who owned,
> operated or otherwise controlled activities at such facility
> immediately beforehand.

42 U.S.C.A. § 9601(20)(A)(iii).

Essentially, the parties disagree as to the interpretation of the
phrase "immediately beforehand." The district court reasoned that Fleet
could not be liable under section 9607(a)(1) because it had never
foreclosed on its security interest in the facility and its agents had not
been on the premises since December 1983. The government contends
that the statute should be interpreted to refer liability "back to the last
time that someone controlled the facility, however long ago." Appellee's
Brief at 23. Thus, according to the government, the period of effective
abandonment of the site by the trustee in bankruptcy (from December
1983 to the July 1987 foreclosure sale) should be ignored and liability
would remain with Fleet since it was the last entity to "control" the
facility.

We agree with Fleet that the plain meaning of the phrase
"immediately beforehand" means without intervening ownership,
operation, and control. Fleet, therefore, cannot be held liable under
section 9607(a)(1) because it neither owned, operated, or controlled
SPW immediately prior to Emanuel County's acquisition of the facility.
It is undisputed that from December 1981, when SPW was adjudicated
a bankrupt, until the July 1987 foreclosure sale, the bankrupt estate
and trustee were the owners of the facility. Similarly, the evidence is
clear that neither Fleet nor any of its putative agents had anything to
do with the facility after December 1983. Although Fleet may have

---

[4] CERCLA does provide that a state or local government will be liable under these
circumstances when it "has caused or contributed to the release or threatened release of a
hazardous substance from the facility. . . ." 42 U.S.C.A. § 9601(20)(D). This exception,
however, is not applicable here.

operated or controlled SPW prior to December 1983, its involvement with SPW terminated more than three years before the county assumed ownership of the facility. The fact that the bankrupt estate or trustee may not have effectively exercised their control of the facility between December 1983 and July 1987 is of no moment. It is undisputed that Fleet was not in control of the facility during this period. Although a trustee can obviously abdicate its control over a bankrupt estate, it cannot in such a manner unilaterally delegate its responsibility to a previous controlling entity. To reach back to Fleet's involvement with the facility prior to December 1983 in order to impose liability would torture the plain statutory meaning of "immediately beforehand."[5]

B.   Fleet's Liability Under Section 9607(A)(2)

CERCLA also imposes liability on "any person who at the time of disposal of any hazardous substance owned or operated any . . . facility at which such hazardous substances were disposed of. . . ." 42 U.S.C.A. § 9607(a)(2). CERCLA excludes from the definition of "owner or operator" any "person, who, without participating in the management of a . . . facility, holds indicia of ownership primarily to protect his security interest in the . . . facility." 42 U.S.C.A. § 9601(20)(A). Fleet has the burden of establishing its entitlement to this exemption. *Maryland Bank & Trust*, 632 F.Supp. at 578; *see United States v. First City National Bank of Houston*, 386 U.S. 361, 366, 87 S.Ct. 1088, 1092, 18 L.Ed.2d 151 (1967). There is no dispute that Fleet held an "indicia of ownership" in the facility through its deed of trust to SPW, and that this interest was held primarily to protect its security interest in the facility. The critical issue is whether Fleet participated in management sufficiently to incur liability under the statute.[6]

The construction of the secured creditor exemption is an issue of first impression in the federal appellate courts. The government urges us to adopt a narrow and strictly literal interpretation of the exemption that excludes from its protection any secured creditor that participates in any manner in the management of a facility. We decline the government's suggestion because it would largely eviscerate the exemption Congress intended to afford to secured creditors. Secured lenders frequently have some involvement in the financial affairs of their debtors in order to insure that their interests are being adequately protected. To adopt the government's interpretation of the secured

---

[5]   This interpretation of § 9607(a)(1) is particularly appropriate in the context of the entire statutory scheme. While § 9607(a)(1) targets present owners and operators of toxic waste facilities, § 9607(a)(2) focuses on the entities that owned or operated the facility at the time the wastes were disposed. A narrow reading of this section would not, therefore, create an unintended loophole for individuals or entities to escape liability for improperly disposing hazardous waste.

[6]   The government correctly formulates this issue as being comprised of two distinct, but related, means of finding Fleet liable under § 9607(a)(2). First, Fleet is liable under the statute if it operated the facility within the meaning of the statute. Alternatively, Fleet can be held liable if it had an indicia of ownership in SPW and managed the facility to the extent necessary to remove it from the secured creditor liability exemption. *See United States v. Kayser-Roth Corp.*, 724 F.Supp. 15, 20–21 (D.R.I.1989). Although we can conceive of some instances where the facts showing participation in management are different from those indicating operation, this is not such a case. The sum of the facts alleged by the government is sufficient to hold Fleet liable under either analysis. In order to avoid repetition, and because this case fits more snugly under a secured creditor analysis, we will forgo an analysis of Fleet's liability as an operator.

creditor exemption could expose all such lenders to CERCLA liability for engaging in their normal course of business.

Fleet, in turn, suggests that we adopt the distinction delineated by some district courts between permissible participation in the financial management of the facility and impermissible participation in the day-to-day or operational management of a facility. In *United States v. Mirabile*, the first case to suggest this interpretation, the district court granted summary judgment to the defendant creditors because their participation in the affairs of the facility was "limited to participation in financial decisions." No. 84–2280, slip op. at 3 (E.D.Pa. Sept. 6, 1985) (available on WESTLAW as 1985 WL 97). The court explained "that the participation which is critical is participation in operational, production, or waste disposal activities. Mere financial ability to control waste disposal practices . . . is not . . . sufficient for the imposition of liability." *Mirabile*, No. 84–2280, slip op. at 4; *accord United States v. New Castle County*, 727 F.Supp. 854, 866 (D.Del.1989); *Rockwell International v. IU International Corp.*, 702 F.Supp. 1384, 1390 (N.D.Ill.1988); *see also Coastal Casting Service*, No. H–86–4463, slip op. at 4 (complaint alleging that secured creditor's entanglement with facility's management surpassed mere financial control held sufficient). The court concluded that "before a secured creditor . . . may be held liable, it must, at a minimum, participate in the day-to-day operational aspects of the site. [Here, the creditor] . . . merely foreclosed on the property after all operations had ceased and thereafter took prudent and routine steps to the property against further depreciation." [7] *Id.* at 12; *accord United States v. Nicolet*, 712 F.Supp. 1193, 1204–05 (E.D.Pa.1989).

The court below, relying on *Mirabile*, similarly interpreted the statutory language to permit secured creditors to

> provide financial assistance and general, and even isolated instances of specific, management advice to its debtors without risking CERCLA liability if the secured creditor does not participate in the day-to-day management of the business or facility either before or after the business ceases operation.

Fleet Factors Corp., 724 F.Supp. at 960 (S.D.Ga.1988); *accord Guidice*, at 561–62;[8] *Nicolet*, 712 F.Supp. at 1205. Applying this standard, the

---

[7] The court permitted a secured creditor to secure a facility against vandalism by boarding up windows and changing locks, make inquiries as to the cost of disposing various drums of toxins, visit the property in order to show it to prospective purchasers, monitor its cash collateral accounts, ensure that receivables went to the proper accounts, and establish a reporting system between the facility and the bank. *Mirabile*, No. 84–2280, slip op. at 5, 8. The court suggested that activities which might bring a secured creditor outside the protection of the exemption included determining the order in which orders were filled, demanding additional sales from the facility, supervising the operations of the facility, and insisting on certain manufacturing changes and reassignment of personnel. *Id.* at 8.

[8] In *Guidice*, the district court applied this analysis to exempt a bank from CERCLA liability because the bank's activities with respect to the facility were directed at protecting its security interest rather than controlling the facility's operational, production, or waste disposal activities. 732 F.Supp. at 561–62. The bank's involvement with the facility included meetings where it was informed of the status of the facility's accounts, personnel changes, and the presence of raw materials; assistance in procuring a loan from another lender; communicating with local officials to assist the facility with wastewater discharge compliance; inspecting the property after it ceased operations; efforts to restructure the facility's loans;

trial judge concluded that from the inception of Fleet's relationship with SPW in 1976 to June 22, 1982, when Baldwin entered the facility, Fleet's activity did not rise to the level of participation in management sufficient to impose CERCLA liability. The court, however, determined that the facts alleged by the government with respect to Fleet's involvement after Baldwin entered the facility were sufficient to preclude the granting of summary judgment in favor of Fleet on this issue.

Although we agree with the district court's resolution of the summary judgment motion, we find its construction of the statutory exemption too permissive towards secured creditors who are involved with toxic waste facilities. In order to achieve the "overwhelmingly remedial" goal of the CERCLA statutory scheme, ambiguous statutory terms should be construed to favor liability for the costs incurred by the government in responding to the hazards at such facilities. *Allis Chalmers*, 893 F.2d at 1317; *see Maryland Bank & Trust Co.*, 632 F.Supp. at 579 (secured creditor exemption should be construed narrowly); Note, *When Security Becomes a Liability: Claims Against Lenders in Hazardous Waste Cleanup*, 38 Hastings L.J. 1261, 1285–86, 1291 (1987) (same) [hereinafter *Claims Against Lenders*]. The district court's broad interpretation of the exemption would essentially require a secured creditor to be involved in the operations of a facility in order to incur liability. This construction ignores the plain language of the exemption and essentially renders it meaningless. Individuals and entities involved in the operations of a facility are already liable as operators under the express language of section 9607(a)(2). Had Congress intended to absolve secured creditors from ownership liability, it would have done so. Instead, the statutory language chosen by Congress explicitly holds secured creditors liable if they participate in the management of a facility.

Although similar, the phrase "participating in the management" and the term "operator" are not congruent. Under the standard we adopt today, a secured creditor may incur section 9607(a)(2) liability, without being an operator, by participating in the financial management of a facility to a degree indicating a capacity to influence the corporation's treatment of hazardous wastes. It is not necessary for the secured creditor actually to involve itself in the day-to-day operations of the facility in order to be liable—although such conduct will certainly lead to the loss of the protection of the statutory exemption. Nor is it necessary for the secured creditor to participate in management decisions relating to hazardous waste. Rather, a secured creditor will be liable if its involvement with the management of the facility is sufficiently broad to support the inference that it could affect hazardous waste disposal decisions if it so chose.[11] We, therefore,

---

and an agreement to provide financing if a particular party purchased the facility at a foreclosure sale. *Id.* at 562.

[11] This narrow construction of the secured creditor exemption is supported by the sparse legislative history on the subject. The Senate version of CERCLA initially lacked an exemption for secured creditors in its definition of "owner or operator." *See* S. 1480, 97th Cong., 2d Sess., *reprinted in* 2 Senate Comm. on Environmental and Public Works, 97th Cong., 2 Sess., 1 *A Legislative History of the CERCLA* 470 (Comm. Print 1983). Representative Harsha introduced the exemption to the bill that was finally passed stating:

specifically reject the formulation of the secured creditor exemption suggested by the district court in *Mirabile. See*, No. 84–2280, slip op. at 4.

This construction of the secured creditor exemption, while less permissive than that of the trial court, is broader than that urged by the government and, therefore, should give lenders some latitude in their dealings with debtors without exposing themselves to potential liability. Nothing in our discussion should preclude a secured creditor from monitoring any aspect of a debtor's business. Likewise, a secured creditor can become involved in occasional and discrete financial decisions relating to the protection of its security interest without incurring liability.

Our interpretation of the exemption may be challenged as creating disincentives for lenders to extend financial assistance to businesses with potential hazardous waste problems and encouraging secured creditors to distance themselves from the management actions, particularly those related to hazardous wastes, of their debtors. *See Guidice*, 732 F.Supp. at 562; Note, *Interpreting the Meaning of Lender Management Under Section 101(20)(A) of CERCLA*, 98 Yale L.J. 925, 928, 944 (1989). As a result the improper treatment of hazardous wastes could be perpetuated rather than resolved. These concerns are unfounded.

Our ruling today should encourage potential creditors to investigate thoroughly the waste treatment systems and policies of potential debtors. If the treatment systems seem inadequate, the risk of CERCLA liability will be weighed into the terms of the loan agreement. Creditors, therefore, will incur no greater risk than they bargained for and debtors, aware that inadequate hazardous waste treatment will have a significant adverse impact on their loan terms, will have powerful incentives to improve their handling of hazardous wastes.

Similarly, creditors' awareness that they are potentially liable under CERCLA will encourage them to monitor the hazardous waste treatment systems and policies of their debtors and insist upon compliance with acceptable treatment standards as a prerequisite to continued and future financial support. *Claims Against Lenders, supra* at 1294; Note, *The Liability of Financial Institutions for Hazardous Waste Cleanup Costs Under CERCLA*, 1988 Wis.L.Rev. 139, 185 (1988) [hereinafter *Liability of Financial Institutions*].[12] Once a secured

---

> This change is necessary because the original definition inadvertently subjected those who hold title to a . . . facility, but do not participate in the management or operation *and are not otherwise affiliated* with the person leasing or operating the . . . facility, to the liability provisions of the bill.

Remarks of Rep. Harsha, reprinted in 2 Senate Comm. on Environmental and Public Works, 97th Cong., 2d Sess., 2 *A Legislative History of the CERCLA* 945 (Comm. Print 1983) (emphasis added). The use of the word "affiliated" to describe the threshold at which a secured creditor becomes liable clearly indicates a more peripheral degree of involvement with the affairs of a facility than that necessary to be held liable as an operator. It also suggests that the interpretation of the exemption intended by Congress is more consistent with the level of secured creditor involvement described in our opinion than with the management of day-to-day operations standard set forth in *Mirabile*.

[12] One commentator notes that a narrow construction of the secured creditor exemption

creditor's involvement with a facility becomes sufficiently broad that it can anticipate losing its exemption from CERCLA liability, it will have a strong incentive to address hazardous waste problems at the facility rather than studiously avoiding the investigation and amelioration of the hazard.

In *Maryland Bank & Trust Co.*, the court aptly described and weighed the competing policy interests of creditors and the government in interpreting the secured creditor exemption:

> In essence, the defendant's position would convert CERCLA into an insurance scheme for financial institutions, protecting them against possible losses due to the security of loans with polluted properties. Mortgagees, however, already have the means to protect themselves, by making prudent loans. Financial institutions are in a position to investigate and discover potential problems in their secured properties. For many lending institutions, such research is routine. CERCLA will not absolve them from responsibility for their mistakes of judgment.

632 F.Supp. at 580 (citations omitted).

We agree with the court below that the government has alleged sufficient facts to hold Fleet liable under section 9607(a)(2). From 1976 until SPW ceased printing operations on February 27, 1981, Fleet's involvement with the facility was within the parameters of the secured creditor exemption to liability. During this period, Fleet regularly advanced funds to SPW against the assignment of SPW's accounts receivable, paid and arranged for security deposits for SPW's Georgia utility services, and informed SPW that it would not advance any more money when it determined that its advanced sums exceeded the value of SPW's accounts receivable.

Fleet's involvement with SPW, according to the government, increased substantially after SPW ceased printing operations at the Georgia plant on February 27, 1981, and began to wind down its affairs. Fleet required SPW to seek its approval before shipping its goods to customers, established the price for excess inventory, dictated when and to whom the finished goods should be shipped, determined when employees should be laid off, supervised the activity of the office administrator at the site, received and processed SPW's employment and tax forms, controlled access to the facility, and contracted with

---

conforms with CERCLA's implicit function of encouraging safer hazardous waste procedures. The possibility that CERCLA liability will depress the value of the security property provides economic incentive for lenders to guard against its misuse. Lending institutions are especially well-equipped for this function. They can require the borrower to submit to periodic environmental audits, either as a condition to receiving a loan or by an amendment to an existing agreement. Lenders can also require warranties from their borrowers guaranteeing that they are in full compliance with hazardous waste laws and regulations. . . . Ultimately, lenders can refuse to lend money to persons believed to be operating illegal or improper hazardous waste activities. While there is a clear risk that innocent borrowers will find it difficult to obtain credit because of the nature of their business, this result is consistent with CERCLA's general effect of spreading hazardous waste costs industry-wide.

Claims Against Lenders, supra, at 1294 (citations omitted); *see also Liability of Financial Institutions, supra*, at 183–85 (discussing lender strategies for decreasing liability risk under a narrow interpretation of the secured creditor exemption).

Baldwin to dispose of the fixtures and equipment at SPW. These facts, if proved, are sufficient to remove Fleet from the protection of the secured creditor exemption. Fleet's involvement in the financial management of the facility was pervasive, if not complete.[13] Furthermore, the government's allegations indicate that Fleet was also involved in the operational management of the facility. Either of these allegations is sufficient as a matter of law to impose CERCLA liability on a secured creditor. The district court's finding to the contrary is erroneous.

With respect to Fleet's involvement at the facility from the time it contracted with Baldwin in May 1982 until Nix left the facility in December 1983, we share the district court's conclusion that Fleet's alleged conduct brought it outside the statutory exemption for secured creditors.[14] Indeed, Fleet's involvement would pass the threshold for operator liability under section 9607(a)(2).[15] Fleet weakly contends that its activity at the facility from the time of the auction was within the secured creditor exemption because it was merely protecting its security interest in the facility and foreclosing its security interest in its equipment, inventory, and fixtures. This assertion, even if true, is immaterial to our analysis. The scope of the secured creditor exemption is not determined by whether the creditor's activity was taken to protect its security interest. What is relevant is the nature and extent of the creditor's involvement with the facility, not its motive. To hold otherwise would enable secured creditors to take indifferent and irresponsible actions toward their debtors' hazardous wastes with

---

[13] Generally, the lender's capacity to influence a debtor facility's treatment of hazardous waste will be inferred from the extent of its involvement in the facility's financial management. Here, that inference is not even necessary because there was evidence before the district court that Fleet actively asserted its control over the disposal of hazardous wastes at the site by prohibiting SPW from selling several barrels of chemicals to potential buyers. As a result, the barrels remained at the facility unattended until the EPA acted to remove the contaminants.

[14] The district court summarized the government's allegations of Fleet's conduct at the facility during this period as follows:

Plaintiff alleges that Baldwin moved the barrels that allegedly contained hazardous substances before Baldwin conducted the public auction. Plaintiff contends that after the auction, Baldwin auctioned some, but not all, of the machinery and equipment as is, and in place, and permitted the purchasers to remove the equipment and machinery that they had purchased. Plaintiff asserts that after the auction Fleet signed a document that permitted Nix to have access to the facility for 180 days and to remove any remaining machinery and equipment. . . . Plaintiff maintains that friable asbestos was knocked loose from the pipes connected to the machinery and equipment by either the purchasers of the equipment at the auction or Nix. Plaintiff alleges that the condition of the chemicals and the asbestos in the facility after Baldwin, Nix, and the purchasers concluded their business constituted an immediate risk to public health and the environment. . . .

Fleet Factors, 724 F.Supp. at 960–61. Fleet disputes these material facts. Id. at 961.

[15] During oral argument, counsel for Fleet virtually conceded operator liability for its conduct with respect to the facility when he discussed Fleet's potential for liability were it to have fixed a hole in the roof of an SPW building:

JUDGE KRAVITCH: If [Fleet] finds in fixing the roof that there is some asbestos that is being dislodged can it just ignore that?

MR. GOOD: Once it fixes the roof, once it takes over control of fixing the roof, it has opened a potential pandora's box both as to that asbestos and anything else at that facility underneath it known and unknown.

JUDGE KRAVITCH: Why isn't that analogous to what happened here?

impunity by incanting that they were protecting their security interests. Congress did not intend CERCLA to sanction such abdication of responsibility.

CONCLUSION

We agree with the district court that Fleet is not within the class of liable persons described in section 9607(a)(1). We also conclude that the court properly denied Fleet's motion for summary judgment. Although the court erred in construing the secured creditor exemption to insulate Fleet from CERCLA liability for its conduct prior to June 22, 1982, it correctly ruled that Fleet was liable under section 9607(a)(2) for its subsequent activities if the government could establish its allegations. Because there remain disputed issues of material fact, the case is remanded for further proceedings consistent with this opinion.

AFFIRMED and REMANDED.

NOTES

1. *Lender Liability.* Before *Fleet Factors*, courts held that a lender that accepted a deed in lieu of foreclosure, or purchased the mortgaged property at foreclosure sale, could be liable for hazardous waste on the property under 42 U.S.C.A. § 9607(a)(1) as a current owner. United States v. Maryland Bank & Trust Co., 632 F.Supp. 573 (D.Md.1986) held that section 9601(20)(A), which excludes from the definition of "owner" a person who holds "indicia of ownership primarily to protect his security interest" did not apply after the lender foreclosed on its security interest and acquired title at foreclosure sale.

Maryland Bank presented the prospect not just of loss security; banks also saw exposure to indeterminable CERCLA claims. Many lenders thought they could protect themselves by carefully evaluating the property before foreclosing or accepting a deed in lieu or by simply choosing not to take title to a contaminated property. *Fleet Factors* undercut these assumptions by exposing lenders to liability prior to their taking of title if the lender "participat[ed] in the financial management of a facility to a degree indication a capacity to influence the corporation's treatment of hazardous wastes." As described in note 2 below, *Fleet Factors* and *Maryland Bank* have been rejected by the Asset Conservation, Lender Liability and Deposit Insurance Protection Act of 1996.

As a matter of policy, is the "capacity to influence" test desirable? Is it fair to lenders? What type of behavior will it encourage? *Fleet Factors* confronted lenders with a tough choice: to redraft loan documents to delete the powers typically reserved by lenders to avoid a claim of "capacity to influence," or to follow good lending practice and retain power to protect the security and ensure repayment of the loan? See Howard & Gerard, Lender Liability Under CERCLA: Sorting Out the Mixed Signals, 64 S.Cal.L.Rev. 1187, 1218–1219 (1991); Wolf, Lender Environmental Liability Under the Federal Superfund Program, 23 Ariz.St.L.J. 531, 551–553 (1992).

Other courts rejected the "capacity to influence" approach. In In re Bergsoe Metal Corporation, 910 F.2d 668 (9th Cir.1990), the Port of St. Helens sold Bergsoe 50 acres of land for a lead recycling facility. In a series of transactions, Bergsoe conveyed the land back to the Port which then leased it back to Bergsoe in order to facilitate the issuance of bonds by the

Port to finance the facility. After the recycling venture failed and Bergsoe entered involuntary bankruptcy, hazardous wastes were found on the property. Bergsoe's shareholders alleged that the Port was responsible as an "owner" for response costs since it had received a deed to the property from Bergsoe. The court found, however, that the Port was exempt under 42 U.S.C.A. § 9601(20)(A), refusing to apply the *Fleet Factors* test:

> [W]hatever the precise parameters of "participation," there must be *some* actual management of the facility before a secured creditor will fall outside the exception. Here there was none, and we therefore need not engage in line drawing. . . . Creditors do not give their money blindly, particularly the large sums of money needed to build industrial facilities. Lenders normally extend credit only after gathering a great deal of information about the proposed project, and only when they have some degree of confidence that the project will be successful. A secured creditor will always have some input at the planning stages of any large-scale project and, by the extension of financing, will perforce encourage those projects it feels will be successful. If this were "management," no secured creditor would ever be protected.

Id. at 672.

For excellent analyses of the secured lender issue, see Howard & Gerard, Lender Liability Under CERCLA: Sorting Out The Mixed Signals, 64 S.Cal.L.Rev. 1187 (1991); Note, Cleaning Up The Debris After *Fleet Factors*: Lender Liability and CERCLA's Security Interest Exemption, 104 Harv.L.Rev. 1249 (1991); Schmall & Tellier, Developments In Lender Liability in the Wake of *Fleet Factors*, 25 Real Prop. Probate & Trust J. 771 (1991). See also Healy, Direct Liability For Hazardous Substance Cleanups Under CERCLA: A Comprehensive Approach, 42 Case W.Res.L.Rev. 65, 128–134 (1992); Comment, Interpreting the Meaning of Lender Management Participation Under Section 101(20)(A) of CERCLA, 98 Yale L.J. 925 (1989).

2. *Agency and Legislative Responses.* The Environmental Protection Agency responded to concerns over the unsettled state of the law after *Fleet Factors* and *Bergsoe* by promulgating a final rule on lender liability under CERCLA, 57 Fed.Reg. 18344 (April 29, 1992), codified at 40 C.F.R. § 300, Subpart L. The rule was invalidated in Kelley v. Environmental Protection Agency, 15 F.3d 1100 (D.C.Cir.1994), on the ground that the agency lacked statutory authority to make it.

Subsequently, Congress addressed the issue in sections 2501–2505 of the Asset Conservation, Lender Liability and Deposit Insurance Protection Act of 1996, Pub. L. 104–208, 142 Cong.Rec. H11644–01, as part of the Omnibus Consolidated Appropriations Act of 1997. The legislation supersedes *Fleet Factors* and substantially implements much of the EPA lender liability rule that had been invalidated in *Kelley*. One clear advantage of the Act over the EPA rule is that, even if the rule had been valid, it would arguably have only applied to Agency actions against lenders. The legislation covers all actions under CERCLA, such as private party suits.

Section 2502 of the Act, dealing with liability of a foreclosing mortgagee, reverses the interpretation of *Maryland Bank*. A lender is not an "owner or operator" if it forecloses and then sells, maintains business activities, winds up operations, undertakes a response action, or takes any other measure to preserve and protect the property as long as (a) the lender did not participate in the management of the facility before foreclosure and (b) the lender after foreclosure seeks to sell or otherwise divest itself of the property at the earliest practicable, commercially reasonable time, on commercially reasonable terms in light of market conditions. (Codified at 42 U.S.C.A. § 9601(20)(E).)

Section 2502 of the Act also defines the type of participation in management that would subject a lender to liability before foreclosure and, rejecting the position of *Fleet Factors*, provides that a lender will be "participating in the management" only if the lender *actually* participates; the statute expressly states that merely having the *capacity* to influence, or an unexercised right to influence, is not participating in the management. (Codified id., at § 9601(20)(F)(i).) Participation in the management prior to foreclosure can be found only if the lender exercises decisionmaking control over environmental compliance or exercises control at a level comparable to that of a manager of the facility. (Codified id., at § 9601(20)(F)(ii).) A lender is not "participating in the management" if it includes covenants or warranties relating to environmental compliance in the security agreement, monitors or enforces such terms, inspects the property, requires a response action or other steps by the owner to address hazardous substances, provides advice in order to prevent or cure a loan default, restructures the loan, or enforces remedies under the security agreement. (Codified id., at § 9601(20)(F)(iv).)

Section 2504 provides that the portion of the EPA rule struck down in *Kelley* dealing with involuntary acquisition of property by government, 40 C.F.R. § 300.1105, is deemed to have been validly issued by the agency under CERCLA. It does not, however, similarly treat the lender liability sections of the EPA rule. Consequently, the legislation omits some of the specifics of the EPA regulation, such as the requirement of monthly advertisements and listing of the property with a broker within one year in order to show that the lender is attempting to divest itself of the property through commercially reasonable means. 40 C.F.R. § 300.1100(d).

Even after the legislation, environmental contamination will still concern lenders. Although lenders may no longer need an environmental audit to lay the foundation for an innocent owner defense upon foreclosure, they will presumably still conduct audits to avoid taking contaminated land as security since contamination will greatly reduce the land's value. Moreover, the 1996 Act does not answer all lender concerns since CERCLA still provides for joint and several liability in the event that a lender strays into participation in the management of the property. Additionally, lenders will still suffer to the extent that CERCLA liability drives borrowers into bankruptcy. See Lender Liability Provisions in Omnibus Budget Bill Will Help Secured Parties, Fiduciaries, Banker Says, 27 Envt.Rep. 1325 (1996).

Section 2502 of the 1996 legislation also protects fiduciaries from personal liability under CERCLA for contaminated assets held in a fiduciary capacity. (Codified at 42 U.S.C.A. § 9607(m).)

See generally, Liu, Lender Liability Protection in the Aftermath of CERCLA'S Security Interest Exemption Crisis: Treating Lenders Like Lenders, 17 Ann. Rev. Banking L. 575 (1998).

B. GREEN BUILDINGS AND LEASES

In A Better World, Inc.: How Companies Profit by Solving Global Problems ... Where Governments Cannot (2014), Alice Korngold develops the case for green buildings. As of her writing, the building sector consumes up to forty percent of the world's energy and is responsible for thirty percent of greenhouse gas emissions. Id. at 48. "[G]iven the inefficiencies of old structures, and the massive growth of new construction, greenhouse gas emissions will more than double by 2030 if no action is taken." Id. at 49. Moreover, companies have embraced the green building concept not only out of a sense of social mission but also because resulting energy efficiencies increase their bottom line by reducing costs and ensuring sustainable supplies. For example, Korngold reports that in a 2012 survey of global companies, eighty-five percent of respondents indicated that energy management was extremely or very important, up from sixty percent in 2010. The primary driver was cost savings, with energy security being a secondary impetus in Europe and China. Id. Interest in green buildings has continued to increase as well. In 2012, forty-nine percent of the respondents indicated that they planned to seek voluntary green building certifications, up from thirty-five percent in 2011. Id. at 50.

The following materials will introduce the concepts of green buildings and leases and how real estate transactional lawyers will increasingly engage with these models.

1. DEFINING GREEN BUILDINGS

J. Cullen Howe, Overview of Green Buildings[*]

41 Environmental Law Reporter News & Analysis 10043, 10043–10045, 10046–10047,
10047–10048 (Jan. 2011).

I. What Makes Buildings Green?

The beginning of the 21st century has ushered in the era of green buildings. According to some estimates, there are approximately 81 million buildings in the United States. Most of these buildings use energy inefficiently, generate large amounts of waste in their construction and operation, and emit large quantities of pollutants and greenhouse gases (GHGs). In contrast to conventional buildings, green buildings seek to use land and energy efficiently, conserve water and other resources, improve indoor and outdoor air quality, and increase the use of recycled and renewable materials. While green buildings still constitute a tiny subset of existing buildings, their numbers are increasing rapidly. In November 2006, the U.S. Green Building Council, the nonprofit group responsible for the creation of the Leadership in Energy and Environmental Design (LEED) green building rating system, announced that 623 buildings had achieved some level of LEED certification. As of December 2009, this number had grown to more than 2,400, and over 35,000 buildings were in the process of achieving some level of LEED certification.

A. Definitions of "Green Building"

While the definition of what constitutes a green building is constantly evolving, the Office of the Federal Environmental Executive offers a useful working definition. This agency defines this term as:

> the practice of (1) increasing the efficiency with which buildings and their sites use energy, water, and materials, and (2) reducing building impacts on human health and the environment, through better siting, design, construction, operation, maintenance, and removal—the complete building life cycle.

Similarly, the U.S. Environmental Protection Agency (EPA) defines green building as follows:

> [T]he practice of creating structures and using processes that are environmentally responsible and resource-efficient throughout a building's life-cycle from siting to design, construction, operation, maintenance, renovation and deconstruction. This practice expands and complements the classical building design concerns of economy, utility, durability, and comfort. Green building is also known as a sustainable or "high performance" building.

Both of these definitions mention life-cycle assessment (LCA). LCA is the investigation and valuation of the environmental, economic, and social impacts of a product or service. In the context of green buildings, LCA evaluates building materials over the course of their entire lives and takes into account a full range of environmental impacts, including a material's embodied energy; the solid waste generated in its extraction, use, and disposal; the air and water pollution associated with it; and its global warming potential. LCA is an important tool because it can demonstrate whether a product used in a green building is truly green.

B. The Most Important Element: The Efficient Use of Energy

Buildings can incorporate many green features, but if they do not use energy efficiently, it is difficult to demonstrate that they are truly green. In fact, given that the term "green building" can be somewhat vague, some people prefer to use the term "high-performance building." A high-performance building is a building whose energy efficiency and environmental performance is substantially better than standard practice.

Although green buildings, on average, use less energy than conventional buildings, energy efficiency remains elusive. In fact, there is a growing debate whether buildings that achieve some level of LEED certification are more efficient in their use of energy than regular buildings. Fortunately, there are numerous ways to improve a building's energy efficiency, from insulating walls to installing automatic shutoff switches for lights. Energy efficiency can be and often is mandated by local and state energy codes, which require that new and substantially renovated buildings comply with increasingly stringent energy-efficiency requirements. It suffices to say that if a building is not energy-efficient, it cannot be said to be green.

C.   The Reality of the Built Environment: The Problem of Existing Buildings

Although green buildings represent the next phase of buildings, the reality is that the vast majority of buildings are not green, and these buildings will continue to be used for many years to come. Improving the energy efficiency of existing buildings typically involves a process called retrofitting, which can mean anything from installing more energy-efficient fixtures to increasing the amount of insulation in a building. The U.S. Green Building Council has a rating standard specifically focused on existing buildings, referred to as LEED-EBOM (EBOM stands for existing buildings operation and maintenance). While greening existing buildings does not receive the attention that new green buildings do, it is certainly more important when looking at reducing the environmental impacts of buildings nationwide.

II.   Impacts of Conventional Buildings That Green Buildings Seek to Rectify

The environmental impacts of buildings are enormous. Conventional buildings use large amounts of energy, land, water, and raw materials for their construction and operation. They are responsible for large GHG emissions as well as emissions of other harmful air pollutants. They also generate large amounts of construction and demolition (C&D) waste and have serious impacts on plants and wildlife. An analysis of these issues demonstrates the scope of the problem.

A.   Energy Use in Buildings

Worldwide, buildings consume massive amounts of energy. The United Nations Environment Programme has reported that 30–40% of all primary energy produced worldwide is used in buildings. In 2008, the International Energy Agency released a publication that estimated that existing buildings are responsible for more than 40% of the world's total primary energy consumption and for 24% of global carbon dioxide (CO_2) emissions.

The picture in the United States is strikingly similar. In 2004, EPA found that buildings account for 39% of total energy use and 68% of total electrical consumption. According to the U.S. Department of Energy (DOE), in 2006, buildings in the United States used 74.2% of all electricity generated. A report by the U.S. Energy Information Agency (EIA) estimated that 60% of the nation's electrical production is utilized to operate commercial buildings, which include those used for education, mercantile, office, storage, and warehouse purposes. By any measure, buildings are responsible for using much of the energy produced today.

In addition, energy consumption is rising. In 2007, DOE projected that energy use in the United States will increase by approximately 19% by 2025. But that is only one-half of the problem. Not only does this country use a lot of energy, it does so inefficiently. America uses twice as much energy per unit of economic output as Germany, and nearly three times as much as Japan.

Fortunately, there are many ways to improve a building's energy efficiency. Simple measures, such as weatherstripping, maintaining entry door closers, and installing storm windows as a low-cost alternative to replacements, are usually the low-hanging fruit in weatherization. In addition, adding insulation materials to new and existing frame construction buildings is a proven and relatively inexpensive way to improve building energy efficiency with respect to heating and cooling. New innovations in insulation can reduce the energy used in manufacturing insulation and allow insulation to be recycled or biodegradable. Mineral, fibrous, and cellulose-derived materials are now available for insulation purposes.

Another large user of energy is a building's heating, ventilation, and air-conditioning (HVAC) system. Properly designed and installed HVAC systems can reduce the amount of energy used for heating and cooling a building. An HVAC system includes a heater, air conditioner, and fan in one system and operates at a partial load nearly all the time. The design of the HVAC system as a whole-system mechanism saves energy by monitoring airflow and keeping the indoor temperature fairly constant. An HVAC system must have a correctly designed distribution system to minimize the amount of airflow (and thus energy) necessary to heat and cool the building. In addition, allowing building occupants to individually control heating and cooling in their living or working spaces is an effective way to reduce energy use.

Electric lighting consumes about one-quarter to one-third of the energy in a typical commercial building. Lighting also generates heat, so reducing the amount of energy consumed for lighting through effective and efficient lighting also reduces the size of a building's air-conditioning plant. Building information modeling (BIM) enables building design and construction teams to draw and test the building's operating systems, such as electricity or hot water, in one computer model. Modeling buildings with BIM can aid in quantitative energy analysis, connecting complex systems and allowing more precise analysis for better energy use.

. . .

C.   Building Water Use

As is the case with energy, buildings use staggering amounts of water during their operation. DOE has estimated that, collectively, buildings in the United States (both commercial and residential) use over 38 billion gallons of water *per day*. In many parts of the United States, particularly the Southwest, water has become an increasingly scarce resource. As with energy, buildings not only use a lot of water, they also do so inefficiently. For instance, a traditional urinal uses about one or more gallons per flush, and a traditional toilet uses approximately 3.5 gallons per flush. In comparison, ultra-low water urinals use only 0.125 gallons of water per flush, while waterless urinals use none. Similarly, high-efficiency toilets use between 1.2 and 1.6 gallons of water or less per flush.

Further, wastewater from buildings typically goes into municipal sewer systems rather than being treated on-site or used for non-potable purposes. Buildings also usually displace vegetation that can capture and absorb precipitation. The net result is that municipal sewer systems are often overburdened. During rainfall events, billions of gallons of water flow into these sewer systems as runoff, carrying contaminants with them. Many older municipalities have combined sewer systems that capture both stormwater runoff and wastewater from buildings. These combined sewer systems are not designed to treat the massive amounts of water that flow into them during heavy rainfall events. Thus, they are equipped with combined sewer overflows (CSOs) that act as safety valves and deposit much of this water, which contains raw sewage and other contaminants, into waterways. In New York City, precipitation of just 0.25 inches can trigger discharges from CSOs into surrounding waterways. The New York City metropolitan area averages about 45 inches of rain annually and has numerous rainfall events of more than 0.25 inches each year.

There are many strategies for conserving water in buildings, as well as reducing the amount of wastewater that ultimately flows into sewer systems. One of the primary uses of water in a building is for toilets, sinks, showers, and similar uses. The byproduct of these uses is wastewater. Reducing the amount of wastewater in a building chiefly depends on a change in the occupants' water usage patterns—namely, the amount of water that is used for things like flushing toilets and urinals. Improved technology and fixture changes, such as low-flow fixtures on faucets and showerheads, can reduce the consumption of water per use. Bathrooms can be installed or retrofitted with low-flow or waterless urinals and toilets that use considerably less water for flushing. Dual-flush toilets that use less water for liquid than solid waste are also available.

Another water-related problem in buildings is stormwater runoff. As previously explained, buildings exacerbate this runoff because they reduce the amount of porous surface available to absorb precipitation. However, runoff from roofs, paved areas, or other impervious surfaces can be put to beneficial use. Buildings and landscapes can be designed to maximize the amount of catchment area, and water can be collected in cisterns, barrels, or swales. The collected water can be detained, retained, and routed for use in building evaporative coolers and toilets, and for irrigation purposes.

"Gray water" can also be used in building operations. Gray water is water drained from baths, showers, washing machines, and sinks that can be captured and used again. Gray water can be collected and reused for irrigating landscapes. Gray water may actually benefit plants because it often contains nutrients, such as phosphorus. A dual-plumbing system is necessary for recycling gray water within a building. Dual-plumbing systems have separate lines for fresh, gray, and black water, which, because of the added cost, could make this impractical in some buildings. Gray water systems vary from simple, low-cost systems to highly complex ones that include settling tanks and sand filters.

Biological wastewater treatment can also be used to recycle gray and black water. Constructed wetlands are designed to mimic natural wetlands and use plants and microorganisms to treat bacteria and effluent. Wetland plants naturally filter water and break down wastes and solids. Water is designed to flow through at least three wetland cells, which can clean water, as well as mechanical or chemical wastewater treatment techniques. Wetland systems can be designed to treat water at many scales, from an entire community to a single home.

Biological filtering techniques can also be used in the landscape to remove silt and pollutants from surface runoff. Vegetated infiltration basins, bioswales, and flow-through planters are all examples of techniques that filter runoff before it enters the ground or is used for other applications.

. . .

E. Construction Materials

Building construction is a multibillion-dollar industry and requires the constant production and harvesting of millions of tons of a variety of raw materials to meet worldwide demand. By any measure, the amount of raw materials used in buildings is mammoth. Worldwide, construction activities consume 3 billion tons of raw materials each year, and it has been estimated that the construction industry consumes one-half of all products produced by volume. In the United States, buildings account for 40% of all raw materials used by volume.

A crucial part of green buildings is the material that is used in their construction. Although definitions vary, green building materials are generally composed of renewable rather than nonrenewable resources and are environmentally responsible, because their impacts are considered over the life of the product. In addition, green building materials generally result in reduced maintenance and replacement costs over the life of the building, conserve energy, and improve occupant health and productivity. Green building materials can be selected by evaluating characteristics, such as reused and recycled content, zero or low off-gassing of harmful air emissions, zero or low toxicity, sustainably and rapidly renewable harvested materials, high recyclability, durability, longevity, and local production.

F. Construction, Operation, and Demolition Waste

Building C&D waste in the United States totals approximately 136 million tons annually, accounting for nearly 60% of total nonindustrial waste generation. By way of comparison, the entire amount of municipal waste generated in the United States every year totals 209.7 million tons. According to some estimates, four tons of waste are typically deposited into a landfill during the construction of a new 2,000-square-foot home. Construction waste consists primarily of lumber and manufactured wood products (35%), drywall (15%), masonry materials (12%), and cardboard (10%). The remainder is a mix of roofing materials, metals, plaster, plastics, foam, insulation, textiles, glass, and packaging. Although much of this material is recyclable, most of it is deposited into landfills.

Green buildings generally seek to minimize the amount of C&D waste they generate. One way they do this is by recycling or reusing C&D waste, such as by using inert demolition materials as base material for parking lots and roadways. For sites that include the demolition of existing structures, plans can be developed early in the design process to manage and reuse as much material as possible through the deconstruction, demolition, and construction processes. Demolition generates large amounts of materials that can be reused or recycled—principally wood, concrete and other types of masonry, and drywall. Rather than demolishing an entire building, all or part of a building can be deconstructed. Building deconstruction is the orderly dismantling of building components for reuse or recycling. In contrast to building demolition, deconstruction involves taking apart portions of buildings or removing their contents with the primary goal being reuse.

2. GREEN LEASES

S. Michael Brooks, Green Leases and Green Buildings

22 Probate and Property 22, 23–26 (Nov./Dec. 2008).

What's Wrong with My Current Lease?

Although most commercial leases are drafted with clauses of general application, most cannot accommodate new "green" issues. For example, current commercial net leases generally do not set out any shared or unilateral environmental objectives. These objectives are important links to permitted tenant and landlord conduct.

Many leases contemplate the unilateral installation of smart meters for electricity, but most do not contemplate similar smart metering for water and natural gas. Few leases contemplate limiting waste production by the tenant, either in initial fit-out or in ongoing operations. Most leases do not obligate the landlord to recycle with multiple waste streams. They generally do not require the use of environmentally friendly carpet cleaning products by the tenant and generally do not allow the landlord to purchase "green power" and pass the costs on to the tenant.

It is also uncommon, but increasingly important, for leases to address emerging green building standards. Most leases do not match a "repair and maintenance" obligation to an environmental standard; normally these are only matched to a base building, prudent tenant, or comparable building standard. Most current leases do not reconcile the targeted building maintenance standard (for example, "first class office building") to an emerging green standard (for example, "LEED EB or equivalent standard"). Commercial leases generally do not match tenant improvement standards to LEED CI or equivalent standards. For example, most leases require a tenant to use only new materials in initial fit-out or alterations, but a green lease would allow recycled materials within a tenant's premises. Similarly, most leases do not speak at all to the types of materials used within a tenant's premises, whereas a green lease would mandate that low volatile organic compound materials be used exclusively. Although many commercial leases allow a landlord to undertake energy-saving retrofits as a permitted capital cost rechargeable to the tenant, few would allow the capital and operating costs associated with the landlord retrofits necessary to improve the environmental performance of the building, comply with government sustainability "guidelines," or achieve a standard (such as LEED EB) to be an operating cost pass-through.

Most commercial leases are completely silent on the treatment of carbon credits, carbon taxes, or carbon anything. A green lease may allow the allocation of carbon credits by the landlord if the building can generate them in the future. Few current leases allow landlord access to the leased premises, except in the case of emergency or to inspect building systems on notice. A green lease would allow the landlord to enter the premises to test for environmental compliance or to determine a breach of environmental objectives.

The Role of a Green Lease

Most retail, office, and industrial premises are leased to third-party tenants and are not owner occupied. The form of third-party leases varies greatly because of both type of use and the particular landlord, who may use its own "proprietary" lease form, developed over many years of tinkering, legal review, and copying. Commercial lease forms are also available from stationers and on the Internet. Landlords may not only have a preferred overall standard form of lease, but they may also use different forms on a building-by-building basis, based on the building standard, some of them possibly inherited from a prior owner. Accordingly, the current commercial lease landscape comprises a wide variety of lease types, each reflecting the diverse nature of land use types, individual landlord and tenant preferences, and building history.

The commercial lease, in its fullest sense, governs the relationship between the landlord and the tenant: who can do what, when, and how; and who pays. It gives exclusive possession of the premises in return for rent and compliance with certain rules. In the office context, the landlord may control the shell, common areas of the building, and operations, but it is the tenant that controls activities within its own space. Both will usually have "standards" governing their conduct. Landlords may have to run a "first class office building," or act as a "prudent landlord would, having regard to the age and character of the building." (This language is typical in leases to set standards that may apply to cleaning, mechanical systems, building amenities, services, or maintenance obligations.) These standards, and other more specific provisions in a commercial lease, generally do not encourage, allow, or fairly allocate the costs of reduced energy use, reduced water use, reduced materials use, or the diversion of waste or recyclables.

. . .

Proponents of the net lease say it creates a more transparent lease arrangement and an incentive for tenants to use less energy (because they may save directly in reduced operating costs as a result of individual reductions in use). In the reverse case, however, it also gives little incentive for the landlord to conserve common area costs if tenants are not individually metered (because the savings do not benefit the landlord), except to keep total rent within market ranges.

For decades, landlords have had an incentive to conserve and in fact have carried through on many types of energy saving initiatives, usually motivated by the desire to save energy costs and therefore make the building more competitive on a gross rent basis. Examples of this include re-glazing windows and double glazing single pane windows, upgrading the insulation and maintaining seals on building envelopes, undertaking lighting retrofits from inefficient lighting (perhaps with old PCB-based ballasts) to more efficient lighting and control systems, and undertaking retrofits of heating, ventilating, and air-conditioning systems and their controls to move to more energy-efficient systems.

Resistance to Green Leases

Many barriers discourage further efforts by landlords to make their buildings more energy, water, and resource efficient. These may include long payback periods for some types of improvements, indifferent or uncooperative tenants, the inability to pass through the current portion of landlord's amortized environmental capital costs, and a lack of skill or knowledge. Other barriers may include lack of knowledge of an achievable target by either the landlord or the tenant; lack of leadership, compulsion, or incentive from senior levels of government; lack of measurement systems in place to determine existing levels of water, natural gas, or electricity consumption; lack of capital; and lack of building operational expertise.

The existing lease documents within a portfolio are likely to contain many other restrictions. For example, landlord build-out specifications may apply to the tenant's premises, such as minimum foot candles of light at the desktop, tight permissible temperature ranges, limitations on landlord changes to the premises or base building features, or restrictions on the type of materials or equipment that can be used. There also may be an inability to pass through co-generation costs if provided by a third party, or an inability to pass through local utility standby costs if co-generation systems are used or proposed to be used.

Landlords, however, may not be the only ones interested in reducing their consumption of resources. What about commercial tenants who want to measure and reduce their energy and water consumption and increase recycling?

In many cases, large tenants are leading the way, requiring commercial landlords to make their buildings greener. Barriers to tenant efforts may include poor data from the landlord on premises-specific energy and water consumption, poor disclosure of energy use and the inability to compel different water-saving fixtures to be installed in common area washrooms. Energy and water costs may be shared also (for example, a single building meter allocated on a building-wide per square foot basis), which in the tenant's eyes would mean that there is no direct relationship between energy or water savings initiated by a specific tenant and the costs allocated to that tenant. A tenant's efforts to conserve would be shared by all occupants in the building, making all others "free riders."

Tenants may also be faced with indifferent or uncooperative landlords, or may fear an unfair rent increase if they ask for a "greener" building, because the current portion of water and energy-saving capital costs are possibly jammed through to the tenant on an unfair basis. Indeed, tenants may fear that the landlord will "green plate" the building at the tenants' cost (that is, to spend carelessly on green upgrades only because the cost can be 100% passed through to tenants). In some cases, tenants may need to get all tenants in the building together and form a group analogous to a "union" to persuade the landlord to green the building. This may be required to attain some leverage over the landlord or may be a mandated prerequisite by the landlord.

Tenants may also lack the skill or knowledge necessary to determine achievable targets for themselves or the building. They also may not have access to the required independent technical resources, or find the costs prohibitive, especially for small tenancies.

Last, restrictions in the lease may limit the ability of the tenant to go green. Examples include the requirement that the tenant use only new materials in all tenant improvements or that the tenant cannot alter base building features, common areas, or central systems. Other lease provisions may prevent the tenant from installing any equipment outside the leased premises; from requiring more recycling by the landlord; from compelling installation of bike racks on or adjacent to the ground floor of a building; and from installing on-site co-generating facilities such as solar voltaics. Other obstacles to a tenant's ability to go green are poor or no record keeping of individual tenant energy use, poor disclosure of energy use, and the inability to compel different water-saving fixtures to be installed in common area washrooms.

Defining a Green Lease

A "green lease" seeks to remove disincentives in a commercial lease to reduce energy, water, and raw material consumption; to increase recycling and the use of sustainable materials in tenant improvements; and to encourage sustainable practices by both the landlord and the tenant. A green lease works to ensure that tenants and landlords are required to adopt environmentally friendly practices.

What Is in a Green Lease?

There seem to be at least two approaches to a green lease:

1.   a "paternalistic" approach, in which the obligations for reduced consumption and environmentally responsible behavior are mandated within the lease by either the tenant or the landlord; and

2.   a "cooperative" model, in which mutual objectives are set out in the lease for both parties to achieve, leading to responsibilities and liabilities for both parties.

A tenant-paternalistic lease may be the case when government or a corporation with a strong green brand is a tenant, has internal "green" targets it is subject to, and wishes to force the landlord to do its part to assist in compliance. A landlord-paternalistic lease may be the case when a landlord wants to green its portfolio, or engage in carbon-trading, or be seen as environmentally responsible, and wants its tenants to toe the line to achieve certain environmental goals. A cooperative model lease may be the case when both parties buy into the need to green an existing building and want to ensure each is doing its part to achieve the joint goal. All three models may end up in the same place over time.

The following are some of the main elements of existing green leases:

• *Targets and Benchmarks*—These include targets, expressed as either a percentage reduction or an absolute target in terms of objective measures (for example, kilowatts of energy and gallons/liters of water per square foot per year), for the environmental performance of the building for water and energy reduction, waste reduction, and waste and water recycling.

• *Ecologically Sustainable Development Principles and Regulations*—These may include indoor air quality standards and rules governing the use of materials and the recycling of products.

• *Performance Standards*—These may include specifications as well as procedures about how environmental performance is measured.

• *Dispute Resolution Mechanisms*—These may apply in the event of a disagreement between the landlord and tenant over why a particular target or objective prescribed by the lease is not achieved. For example, this mechanism could outline the ramifications taken in the event that a tenant exceeds an energy use target or fails to comply with the environmental objectives set out in the lease.

• *Environmental Management Plan (EMP) and a Green Lease Schedule (GLS)*—These components are commonly found in those green leases developed in Australia. An EMP is often featured within a GLS.

A green lease may specifically detail:

• environmentally preferable products,

• water conservation measures,

• comprehensive landlord and tenant procurement guidelines,

• energy conservation/efficiency targets,

• requirements for natural or low water consumption landscaping,

• the permissibility of solar or wind applications on-site,

• the ability to specify higher cost but sustainable energy sources,

• indoor air quality standards,

• construction period recycling,

• life-cycle costing,

• day lighting and the usage of screens to shield the sun's rays,

• recycling room and practices,

• efficient appliances and fittings,

• waterless urinals and low-flow faucets and taps,

• efficient thermal control systems and potentially operable windows,

• the use of EnergyStar-rated photocopiers that reuse paper or print double-sided,

• an energy or operations standard, such as LEED, Green Globes, BREEAM, AGBR, Energy Star, or other rating system,

• ventilation and fresh air requirements,

- allowable cooling, heating, and humidity,
- cost apportionment of capital costs of new equipment,
- incentives to invest in new equipment,
- heating, ventilation, and air-conditioning specifications,
- environmentally friendly leasehold improvement materials or LEED CI (or equivalent) requirements, and
- dispute resolution procedures and references to third-party experts.

To the extent that the parties believe that technical goals need to be defined in a lease document or schedule (such as target kilowatts per square foot per year or reduced water consumption to a target of liters/gallons per square foot per year) then the landlord, tenant, or both may need technical consultants available to them to advise on the legitimacy and attainability of those technical goals in the particular building to which the green lease would apply. The same technical expertise would also need to be available to determine compliance or to provide audits from time to time potentially for both parties.

Green leases may be considered as "partnerships" or "alliances" requiring greater cooperation between landlord and tenant than traditional leases. It is also important to mention that poor performance within any particular tenancy may affect comfort and performance in other tenancies in a multi-tenant building. The underlying notion is that what one tenant does or does not do could ultimately affect other tenants in the same building.

3. OWNER ISSUES

Brandon Robinson & James Smith, Overview of Green Building and Associated Legal Issues

26 Natural Resources and Environment 13, 14–15, 15–16 (Spr. 2012).

Emerging Legal Issues Relating to Green Building

The emergence of "green" building is not without its own controversy, however, most notably about the ability to measure green. Common legal issues that have emerged in connection with green building include: (I) performance claims regarding contractual promises or guarantees with respect to the efficacy of energy performance or savings measures; (2) contractual promises or guarantees with respect to certification of buildings under LEED or other rating systems; (3) the veracity of claims by various companies of being "green" despite evidence to the contrary, popularly known as "greenwashing"; and (4) the allocation of risk and other transactional issues with respect to distributed renewable generation, such as rooftop solar panels.

Performance Claims

A major source of contention within the construction industry has to do with whether or not rated green buildings actually outperform their non-green counterparts. Green building councils claim that green buildings outperform their non-green counterparts in a number of areas. Areas that are typically included are energy, water, waste, and occupant health. The challenge this poses is that a client might be tempted to claim compensation from the professional team in cases where the actual performance of the building is worse than the predicted performance, particularly in cases where the capital cost of the building is higher due to the interventions introduced to achieve the predicted performance enhancements.

Part of this conundrum has to with the method of calculation. For instance, it is claimed that rated green buildings can save up to 30 percent of the energy of a typical nonrated building. Most green building rating systems award energy points for a design stage rating based on predicted performance, not actual performance. The method used is to first calculate the energy use of the building under consideration as if it were to be designed in a conventional manner. The calculation is then rerun using various energy saving strategies, and points are awarded in accordance with the degree of improvement.

. . .

The potential legal issue created by claimed energy savings is that a client, convinced at the design stage by his professional team to make additional energy saving investments on the basis of the predicted behavior, finds out that the building in operation performs nothing like what was predicted. Under this scenario, the client would potentially be tempted to seek compensation from the building professionals for the lack of improved performance.

It should be noted that LEED certification is about the building being designed to achieve certain energy savings, not whether the energy savings is actually performed. LEED certification is about designing buildings in energy efficient and sustainable ways, but in many cases the achievement of some energy performance goals may depend on how the building will be subsequently used by its occupants, which cannot be controlled or predicted at the outset. For example, a house may have a programmable thermostat, but if the occupant ignores its energy-saving capabilities and instead chooses to blast air-conditioning at frigid temperatures all summer, the energy savings for which this installation was designed cannot be achieved. Similarly, low-flow toilets may be designed to save a certain amount of water per flush, but if the occupant increases his or her flushes per visit or increases the number of visits per day, the predicted energy savings will begin to decrease.

Therefore, when negotiating contracts between the client and his or her professional team, attorneys should ensure that the contractual obligations with respect to energy savings either (1) stipulate in great detail to how the guaranteed energy savings will be calculated as well as what the preproject inputs are; and/or (2) include terms as to the energy-efficient design specifications to be included in the project, instead of the percentage of energy savings to be gained.

Certification Issues

Aside from measuring the actual energy savings, legal issues still arise in attempting to get a green building system certified under a given ratings system such as LEED. Any construction project involves several entities participating under various contracts and subcontracts throughout the phase of the project: architects, engineers, consultants, general contractors, and subcontractors, to name a few. Both for marketing and for energy-saving purposes, having a green building certified by LEED or another rating system may be a primary objective of the entire project. Therefore, if a building fails to achieve its desired certification, what began as seamless cooperation can often devolve into a finger-pointing exercise.

An attorney can play an important role in obtaining the sufficient credits to achieve a given LEED certification. As with any ratings system, questions inevitably arise as to the interpretation of certain language and whether a given strategy will be able to achieve credit in a particular category. During the certification process, if it is unclear whether or not a strategy applies to a given credit, a Credit Interpretation Request can be submitted for a ruling to determine whether the approach is suitable. Similarly, if a project team feels that sufficient grounds exist to appeal a credit that has been denied in the final LEED review, it may appeal within 25 days after the final LEED review. At the outset of a project, because there is an inherent degree of uncertainty as to whether a given project will achieve the desired LEED certification, lawyers should advise their project teams to plan on designing for more credits than necessary, so as to provide flexibility as the project continues and issues potentially arise.

It is also important, when advising a client participating in a project where LEED or other certification is a primary objective, to ensure that the responsibility for achieving such certification is clearly laid out in the contracts and subcontracts and allocated appropriately. If your client is a general contractor, for example, who is in a position to guarantee certain design specifications to achieve LEED Silver certification, the subcontracts should include flowdown provisions that allocate those design guarantees or the relevant portions thereof to the subcontractors performing work on the general contractor's behalf. Similarly, if your client is a subcontractor performing only a certain portion of a project that is striving to achieve LEED certification, you should make sure that your client is not obligating to him or herself more responsibility than appropriate, given the scope of your client's work on the project.

NOTE

For additional readings on green buildings and leases, see Prum, Greenbacks for Building Green: Does A Lender for Sustainable Construction Projects Need to Make Adjustments to Its Current Practices?, 43 Envt. L. 415 (2013); Rothenberg, Can Employee Productivity Provide the Business Case For Green Leasing? An Analysis of Sustainability Measures Worth Pursuing, 2 Corporate Real Est. J. 7 (No. 1, 2012); Senn, Commercial Real Estate Leases: Preparation, Negotiation, and Forms § 2.08 (5th ed.); Kaplow, Does A Green Building Need A Green Lease?, 38 U. Balt. L. Rev. 375 (2009); Prum, The Next Green Issue: Considering Property Insurance for the Green Building, 7 Va. L. & Bus. Rev. 421 (2013); Hirokawa, At Home With Nature: Early Reflections on Green Building Laws and the Transformation of the Built Environment, 39 Envt. L. 507 (2009); Canova, Note, Greening the Traditional Commercial Lease: Building A Case For Sustainable Commercial Real Estate Through Economically Profitable Green Leases, 61 Drake L. Rev. 883 (2013); Keller,

Note, LEEDing in the Wrong Direction: Addressing Concerns With Today's Green Building Policy, 85 S. Cal. L. Rev. 1377 (2012); Anderson, Bidgood & Heady, Hidden Legal Risks of Green Building, 84 Fla. Bar J. 35 (Mar. 2010).

CHAPTER X

GLOBALIZATION OF AMERICAN REAL ESTATE TRANSACTIONS AND FINANCE

The past several decades have witnessed increased economic and social globalization, as evidenced by the flow of people, capital, goods, services, and ideas across national boundaries. Although real estate cannot itself cross national borders, ownership of real property interests can move through the global marketplace, where it is sometimes subject to regulation from foreign countries or international agreements. For example, a mortgage on a home on Main Street, USA may be sold to foreign nationals in the secondary market, and international environmental regulations and treaties may affect domestic real estate development projects.

American lawyers increasingly encounter international, comparative and cross-border legal issues in real estate transactions. While ultimately foreign lawyers or domestic specialists in international issues must be consulted to resolve some of these problems, it is the American transactional lawyer who will identify the potential problems for specialists to address. This chapter focuses on two aspects of globalization of real estate transactions and finance: limitations on the ownership of American real estate by foreign nationals and some issues that American clients face in investing in realty abroad. See generally, Odinet, Toward A Convention for the International Sale of Real Property: Challenges, Commonalities, and Possibilities, 29 Quinnipiac L. Rev. 841 (2011); Phillips, The Paradox of Commercial Real Estate Debt, 42 Cornell Int'l L.J. 335 (2009) (comparing debt markets in various countries).

A. FOREIGN INVESTMENT IN U.S. REAL ESTATE

1. ECONOMIC AND POLITICAL FORCESI

James R. Mason, Jr., Note, "Pssst, Hey Buddy, Wanna
Buy a Country?" An Economic and Political Policy
Analysis of Federal and State Laws Governing Foreign
Ownership of United States Real Estate*
27 Vanderbilt Journal Transnational Law 453, 470–477 (1994).

A. Reasons for Foreign Investment in United States Real Estate

There are numerous reasons for foreign investment in United States real estate. First, the United States presents a stable political climate in which to invest. The potential for government meddling and even outright expropriation of lands owned by foreigners continues to be a threat to real estate investors in many parts of the world. The risk of government expropriation of lands in the Philippines, for example, makes many investors consider the risk of investing there too great.

The United States, however, presents a far different environment to world investors. Because the United States government and major United States institutions for the most part favor foreign investment, the threat of government expropriation in the United States is virtually nonexistent.

Second, the United States continues to offer a favorable economic environment to foreign investors. Investors favor economic stability because it allows them to predict potential returns much more accurately. Predictability, in turn, helps investors assess risk. The United States economy also offers a broad investment landscape, including opportunities in virtually any type of real estate. Economic stability, coupled with the immense size and diversity of the United States economy and the variety of property types that it has to offer, make United States real estate a favored vehicle for world investors. In short, foreign investors believe the United States economy will experience sustained economic growth in the long run and, therefore, target the United States for investment.

Third, the United States has a ready supply of relatively inexpensive land. Because available investment quality land represents a scarce commodity in many parts of the world, the price of land in the United States is much lower than it is for comparable land in other places. Real estate prices in the United States are also lower compared to land prices in other states because of recent declines in the United States dollar's value on the world's currency markets. This decline gives foreign currencies more purchasing power in the United States and thus further decreases the effective price of United States real estate for foreign investors. The availability and price of the United States real estate, therefore, presents a powerful draw to foreign investors.

---

* Permission Granted to Reprint from the Vanderbilt Journal of Transnational Law which is the copyright holder.

Fourth, the ease of entry into the United States real estate market provides an incentive for foreign investors. United States real estate markets offer a wide array of financing alternatives that may not be available in other states. Foreign investors, therefore, find it easier to enter and finance real estate purchases in the states where they can avoid the entry barriers and financing obstacles present elsewhere. In fact, many states of the United States maintain offices overseas designed specifically to promote foreign investment in the United States. This solicitation attracts numerous investors because it informs them of the excellent opportunities in the United States real estate market.

Finally, the prevalent use of the English language around the world makes it easier for foreign investors to invest in United States real estate. If an alien investor does not speak English it is usually quite easy to find an English interpreter to facilitate the transaction, giving foreign investors a greater level of comfort when dealing with United States real estate than they might experience in other places where more obscure languages might became a barrier to completion of a transaction.

The foregoing analysis of the attractiveness of United States real estate investment centers primarily on investment incentives. Of course, many alien property owners acquire United States real estate not as an investment, but as a home. Many of the same reasons for the attractiveness of United States real estate investment also apply to aliens seeking a new residence. A stable political and economic environment, ready availability of land, ease of entry and financing, and ease of understanding all combine to make the United States an attractive place in which to purchase a home. This attractiveness, in turn, leads to greater participation by aliens in United States real property markets.

B. Advantages to the United States of Foreign Investment in United States Real Estate

Foreign investment in United States real estate provides many advantages, some of which pertain to foreign investment in the United States economy in general while others apply specifically to foreign real estate investment. Economic advantages to foreign investment in United States land are, in general, pervasive and far-reaching.

First, foreign investment provides capital for the United States economy. Foreign capital was a primary force in the development of the United States, and it still helps offset the United States trade deficit, holds domestic interest rates down, and provides new plants and technology. Foreign real estate investment is critical because it is a necessary prelude to much of this capital investment.

Second, foreign investment can often work a dramatic turnaround for failing United States businesses or can provide additional dynamism to companies that are already doing well. This boost to business can manifest itself in a variety of ways. In many instances, foreign investment creates or strengthens jobs. Additional jobs means additional money spent at the local level and, therefore, an increase in the demand for ancillary services such as grocery stores, dining establishments, entertainment facilities, and the like. Further, foreign investment in United States business often leads to the introduction of new management techniques and new manufacturing or production technologies. The introduction of these new techniques often dramatically revitalizes a dying business or industry. The addition of new management and operations techniques, along with a new management philosophy and style, often make stagnated businesses more competitive. Added competitiveness benefits the local economy as well as the national and world economies by providing goods and services less expensively and more efficiently than before the foreign investment.

Third, foreign investment in United States real property increases efficient property use and preservation. Foreign property owners, after all, are investors and want their investments to perform satisfactorily. If a foreign investor is willing to devote more time and attention to a particular property than is a domestic investor, then the foreign investor will use the property more efficiently. More efficient property use increases not only that property's value, but also increases the value of surrounding property. Additionally, foreign investors, like all investors, seek reasonable returns from their United States real estate holdings. Long-term returns are maximized only by effective management, preservation, and use of property. Through profit maximizing efforts, therefore, alien investors may provide an element of property preservation and use that an idle domestic owner might not have achieved.

Fourth, foreign investment in United States real estate increases the demand for the real estate and thus increases its value to current domestic owners. United States property owners, therefore, may benefit when property is bought by foreign investors at what appear to be inflated prices. Many foreign investors are willing to pay a premium for prime United States property, and this premium goes to the domestic seller. Many United States landowners look favorably on foreign investment for precisely the reason that higher prices paid by foreign investors bring economic benefits to them personally and health to the local economy in general.

Fifth, at the macroeconomic level, increased foreign investment in United States property provides more tax revenue and a higher tax base than existed before the investment. Property taxes are generally assessed based on the market value of individual parcels of property. By increasing the value of real property, foreign investment indirectly increases the tax revenue received from these properties. Thus, foreign investment indirectly benefits government by adding to the revenues collected by taxing authorities.

Finally, the higher the level of foreign investment in the United States, the larger the stake foreign individuals, governments, and businesses have in the growth of the United States economy. In the increasingly global economy, states and governments are becoming more aware that economies do not stand alone, but must rise or fall together. "It is truly a symbiotic situation with different nations' economic health feeding off the health of other nations." Foreign investment in the United States, therefore, may enhance international economic cooperation to the benefit of the United States economy and the economy of the world as a whole.

C. Perceived Detriments to Foreign Investment in United States Real Estate

Opponents of foreign investment in the United States advance a number of reasons why such investment is undesirable. Most of these reasons, at base, simply voice the populist fear that foreigners are taking over the United States. Following is a discussion of the most frequently advanced arguments that foreign investment, especially foreign investment in United States real estate, should be curtailed.

First, foreign investment is perceived as posing a risk to national security. Proponents of this argument contend that foreign interests do not necessarily coincide with United States interests and that, ultimately, significant foreign ownership of United States real property will result in a security risk that is too great to allow unrestricted alien ownership of United States land.

Second, opponents of alien investment in the United States assert that foreign investment results in the export of United States technology. The argument is that foreign investors will strip United States companies of their technology and, therefore, their ability to add value. United States companies would be reduced to nothing more than assembly plants for foreign owners. Proponents of this view see alien investment in United States property as facilitating the technology export and, therefore, advocate strict regulation and oversight of alien investment in United States land.

Finally, some argue that foreign investment tends to displace domestic production and causes profits to flow overseas. According to this theory, in the long run, foreign investment is detrimental to United States industry because it causes the United States to lose much of its productive wealth to foreign competitors. Proponents of this theory argue for increased regulation of foreign investment in United States industry and, therefore, increased regulation of foreign investment in United States real property to counter the negative effects of profit export and production displacement on the United States economy.

2. FEDERAL TAX ISSUES

Congress enacted the Foreign Investment in Real Property Act of 1980 ("FIRPTA") in response to growing foreign investment in American real estate. FIRPTA, which added sections 897, 1445, and 6039C to the Internal Revenue Code, treats foreigners' gains from investments in United States real property differently from their gains from other property. Two of the obligations created by the Act are of particular interest to a real estate attorney representing sellers and buyers in American land sales. First, the foreign investor must pay tax on a gain in relation to a sale of U.S. land under I.R.C. section 897, and, even prior to a sale, must meet reporting requirements under I.R.C. section 6039C. Second, an American buyer of real property is obligated to withhold for tax purposes a portion of the proceeds paid to a foreign owner of United States realty. The following excerpt examines these two issues.

Fred B. Brown, Wither FIRPTA?

57 Tax Lawyer 295, 297–299 (Winter 2004).

FIRPTA was enacted in 1980 in order to remove the perceived competitive advantage experienced by foreign persons under the tax law in purchasing U.S. real estate. Prior to FIRPTA, foreign persons had used several techniques to avoid federal income tax upon the disposition of U.S. real estate, while obtaining net basis taxation during the operation of the real property. For example, a foreign person could operate U.S. realty as a trade or business and then dispose of the realty in an installment sale so that gain was recognized after the foreign person was no longer engaged in a U.S. business. This technique allowed the taxpayer to achieve net basis taxation during the operations phase, which often meant no federal tax liability during this phase because deductions for depreciation, taxes and interest could offset gross income from operations. If the foreign person did not maintain a U.S. business when the gain from the disposition was recognized on the installment method, the realty gain would not be taxable under the effectively connected regime, nor would it be taxable under the fixed or determinable, annual or periodic ("FDAP") regime as that regime exempts most types of gain. In a variation on this technique, the foreign person disposed of the U.S. real estate by exchanging it for foreign real property in a qualifying nonrecognition transaction under the like-kind rule, and subsequently disposed of the foreign realty in a sale that would be beyond U.S. tax jurisdiction. The like-kind exchange strategy would permit an ultimate disposition of the foreign realty that was free of U.S. tax even if the taxpayer were actually engaged in a U.S. business for the year of the sale (or had made a Code election to be so treated). Another technique employed to obtain little or no U.S. taxation on the operation and disposition of U.S. real property was to take advantage of certain treaties that allowed taxpayers to make an annual election to treat U.S. real estate activities as a U.S. trade or business.

Foreign persons were also able to achieve this desired tax avoidance treatment by using corporations to conduct their U.S. real estate activities. Under this technique, a foreign person would conduct U.S. realty activities as a business through either a U.S. or foreign corporation, and thus obtain U.S. net basis taxation on these operations. The foreign person could then dispose of the U.S. real property by first having the corporation sell the U.S. real property after adopting a plan of liquidation, and then having the corporation distribute the proceeds of the sale to the shareholder in exchange for her stock. Under the former *General Utilities* doctrine, the liquidating corporation would not have recognized any gain on the sale, and any gain to the foreign shareholder on the liquidation would generally be free of U.S. tax under the effectively connected and FDAP regimes. Alternatively, the foreign investor could have sold stock in the corporation to the purchaser, with any gain on the sale generally not being subject to U.S. tax. The purchaser of the stock, even if a U.S. person, could then liquidate the corporation free of U.S. tax, because the former *General Utilities* doctrine would result in nonrecognition treatment at the corporate level, and there would be no realized gain at the shareholder level given that the shareholder's basis should equal the appreciated value of the real property.

In contrast to the ability of foreign persons to avoid U.S. taxation on the disposition of U.S. real estate, U.S. persons enjoyed no such treatment. Consequently, the existing rules as applied to the taxation of U.S. realty arguably violated notions of horizontal equity by subjecting U.S. taxpayers to more onerous U.S. tax treatment on U.S. real estate activities than foreign taxpayers. This in turn arguably resulted in foreign persons having a competitive advantage over their U.S. counterparts in acquiring U.S. real estate.

FIRPTA was enacted to ensure that dispositions of U.S. real property by foreign persons would not escape federal income tax, which resulted in the removal of the U.S. tax advantage experienced by foreign taxpayers. Specifically, section 897, FIRPTA's principal provision, subjects foreign persons to U.S. taxation on dispositions of U.S. real property as if the gains were effectively connected with a U.S. business, whether or not the taxpayer was actually engaged in such a business when the gain was recognized. Thus, the FIRPTA rule for taxing dispositions of directly held U.S. realty prevents foreign persons from avoiding federal income taxation on the disposition of U.S. real property by employing the installment sale technique. Section 897 also contains special nonrecognition rules that prevent attempts to circumvent FIRPTA by engaging in nonrecognition transactions (such as like-kind exchanges) in which property subject to FIRPTA is exchanged for property whose disposition would be free of U.S. tax. FIRPTA also deals with the ability to use tax treaties to avoid federal tax on dispositions of U.S. real property by overriding any conflicting treaty obligations that remain in effect four years after FIRPTA's enactment.

Section 897 tackles the corporate avoidance strategy in two different ways depending on whether a U.S. or foreign corporation is employed. For situations involving U.S. corporations, the provision generally taxes foreign persons on dispositions of stock in U.S. corporations whose assets significantly consist of U.S. real property. Consequently, the statute can reach gain realized by a foreign person on the disposition of stock pursuant to the liquidation of a U.S. realty holding corporation, as well as on the sale of the stock to another person. Where a foreign corporation is employed to hold U.S. real property, the statute brings on a mini-repeal of the *General Utilities* doctrine by generally causing a foreign corporation to recognize gain on the distribution of the realty or sale in connection with a liquidation. As a result, a disposition of U.S. real property via the sale followed by liquidating distribution route is taxable under section 897. And while the sale of stock in a foreign corporation holding U.S. realty is not taxable under FIRPTA, the foreign seller can be expected to bear an indirect tax due to the receipt of a reduced sales price reflecting the corporation's future tax liability.

Gregory W. Hummel & Steven R. Ratz, Withholding Requirements Under FIRPTA

3 Probate & Property 31, 31–32 (Mar./Apr. 1989).

"Foreign person" is broadly defined under FIRPTA to include any individual, trust, estate, partnership, association, company or corporation which is not: (1) a citizen or resident of the United States, (2) a domestic partnership, (3) a domestic corporation or (4) an estate or trust, other than a foreign estate or foreign trust. IRC §§ 1445(f)(3) and 7701(a). Under the 1984 Act, certain objective criteria were established to determine whether an alien individual is a U.S. resident. IRC § 7701 (b). Generally, a partnership or corporation is considered domestic only if created or organized under the laws of the U.S. or one of the states. However, foreign corporations may elect to be treated as domestic corporations for purposes of FIRPTA's substantive provisions as well as FIRPTA's withholding provisions. Thus, electing foreign corporations may provide non-foreign affidavits (as discussed below). IRC § 897(i).

IRC § 897(c)(i) defines USRPI to include any interest in real property located in the U.S. (other than solely as a creditor) or any interest in a domestic corporation that was a USRPHC (as defined below) at any time during the five year period immediately before the date of the disposition, or the period after June 18, 1980, whichever period is shorter. "Real property" for this purpose as defined by Treasury Regulation ("Regulation") § 1.897–1(b) includes land and unreserved natural products of land, improvements and personal property associated with the use of real estate.

As stated, USRPIs include certain holdings in USRPHCs. A USRPHC is defined under IRC § 897(c)(2) as any corporation (foreign or domestic), the fair market value of whose USRPIs equals at least 50% of the sum of its USRPIs, its foreign real property interests and its interests in any other trade or business assets during the taxable year.

Withholding

Originally FIRPTA was to be enforced through the filing of annual information returns with the IRS, but the 1984 Act drastically changed the FIRPTA enforcement provisions. The 1984 Act adopted a withholding system under which the sole responsibility for withholding is on purchasers of USRPIs. IRC § 1445.

Purchasers of USRPIs are now obliged to determine whether their seller falls within the definition of a "foreign person." If so determined IRC § 1445(a) generally requires the purchaser to withhold 10% of the amount realized on the transaction unless one of five exemptions under IRC § 1445(b) applies. The amount withheld must be turned over to the IRS and will be applied against the seller's ultimate tax liability. If the purchaser fails to withhold, it can be liable for the uncollected amount.

In calculating the amount to be withheld, a purchaser must be aware that the withholding tax on the disposition of a USRPI is imposed on the *amount realized* on the transaction and *not* on the *recognized gain*. IRC § 1445(a). The amount realized by the transferor on the sale of a USRPI is equal to the sum of (1) the cash paid, or to be paid; (2) the fair market value of any other property transferred, or to be transferred, and (3) the outstanding amount of any liability assumed by the transferee or to which the USRPI is subject immediately before and after the transfer. Regulation § 1.1445–1(g)(5). Thus the amount which must be withheld may be more than the actual ultimate tax liability.

As one may imagine, the required withholding may create significant obstacles in certain types of transactions. For example, in the context of an installment sale, withholding 10% of the total sale price basically defeats the tax deferral benefit normally sought in such a transaction. Further, if the cash being paid at closing is less than the amount which must be withheld, the transferee must nevertheless withhold the full 10% of the total purchase price (absent a qualifying statement). Some minor comfort can be taken from the fact that, if the tax withheld exceeds the actual tax liability of the foreign person, that person may apply for an early refund (without interest) of any amounts withheld in excess of the person's maximum tax liability. Regulation § 1.1445–3(f). Nonetheless, the desires of the parties can be frustrated by FIRPTA, unless a qualifying statement is obtained.

The procedure for withholding and paying withheld amounts to the IRS is stated in Regulation § 1.1445–1(c). The purchaser or other transferee must submit to the IRS specified forms (8288 and 8288–A) together with the applicable amount withheld within 20 days after the date of the transfer. The forms generally require the names, addresses and identifying numbers (if any) of both the transferor and the transferee; a description of the real property interest transferred; the date of the transfer; the amount realized by the transferor; the amount withheld by the transferee; and a statement whether the withholding is at the statutory or a reduced rate.

3. OTHER FEDERAL REGULATION

James R. Mason, Jr., Note, "Pssst, Hey Buddy, Wanna Buy a Country?" An Economic and Political Policy Analysis of Federal and State Laws Governing Foreign Ownership of United States Real Estate*

27 Vanderbilt Journal of Transnational Law 453, 463–466 (1994).

A. The Territorial Land Act of 1887

Congress enacted the Territorial Land Act of 1887 in response to a wave of alien absentee ownership and depressed agricultural conditions in midwestern states during the last half of the nineteenth century. This Act prohibits aliens who have not declared their intent to become United States citizens from holding land in territories of the United States. Although this regulation now has no effect in the fifty states, it still prevents non-declaring aliens from purchasing real property in the numerous United States territories.

B.   The Trading With the Enemy Act of 1970

The Trading With the Enemy Act of 1970 and the two bodies of regulation issued under it, the Alien Property Custodian Regulation and the Foreign Assets Control Regulations, are Congress' attempt to control property transactions involving aliens and governments that might be hostile to the United States. The Alien Property Custodian Regulations charge the United States Attorney General with the responsibility of managing property belonging to enemy aliens during the time of war or declared emergency. The Foreign Assets Control Regulations require aliens from designated states to obtain prior Treasury Department approval before conducting transactions involving "blocked" property. These regulations typically affect only a small amount of alien land investments at any one time.

C.   Controlling Exploitation of Federally Owned Lands

Alien land laws at the federal level include those designed to protect United States natural resources. This category of federal regulation restricts alien exploitation of natural resources on public lands to aliens who intend to become United States citizens. Regulation in this area affects resources as diverse as homestead lands, grazing lands, lands containing mineral deposits, off-shore oil tracts, and lands containing geothermal steam resources. This legislation and regulation is designed to prevent pillaging of United States natural resources by foreign governments, individuals, and businesses.

D.   The International Investment Survey Act of 1976 and The Agricultural Foreign Investment Disclosure Act of 1978

In the early 1970s, Congress became concerned about the increasing amount of foreign investment in United States land, particularly farmland. In response to increasing pressure generated primarily by the farm lobby, Congress passed the International Investment Survey Act of 1976 (IISA) and two years later followed up by passing the Agricultural Foreign Investment Disclosure Act of 1978 (AFIDA). Although neither of these acts in any way prohibits foreign investment in United States real property, both impose significant reporting and disclosure requirements. Both acts define those persons and entities subject to their provisions in broad terms to require disclosure by as large a group of alien owners as possible. Furthermore, failure to comply with the reporting and disclosure requirements of these acts results in significant penalties. The IISA and AFIDA, therefore, provide the federal government with information useful in monitoring foreign investment in United States real property and the effects of that investment.

4. STATE REGULATION

Christopher M. Ernst, Note, The Foreign Ownership Disclosure Act of 1989: Do You Know Who Owns Your Piece of the Rock?

23 Case Western Reserve Journal of International Law 593, 597–600 (1991).

The United States' first laws were brought from England with America's first settlers; U.S. alien landholding laws have their origins firmly rooted in the British common law. In British common law, aliens, those without citizen status, could not fully own real property. The basis of this law was the notion that those who owed no fealty, or allegiance, to the sovereign could use land, but not own it in a fee simple absolute manner. An alien could not pass the property through "descent, dower, or courtesy." The theory underlying the common law was that aliens should not be allowed to hold land with the same rights as a monarch's subject. Consequently, the "monarch had the prerogative to claim an alien's landholdings without compensation. . . ." The Crown then had the ultimate control of the land, thus limiting an alien's "ownership" of the land. After the American Revolution and the ensuing formal development of the country, many states passed laws that required Tories to relinquish their land to the state governments. When these laws were challenged in the U.S. Supreme Court, the Court adopted the British Common Law principle. Thus, aliens under U.S. law possessed the same inability to own property as aliens did under English law.

After the United States became more settled, many states relaxed their laws, giving aliens the same property rights as citizens. At that point, there was great concern about the development of the country, particularly the Western frontier, which outweighed the traditional and historical convictions about alien landholding leftover from British common law. Liberalization of landholding laws was a key component to developing the country. "This [liberalization] implies greater interest in using attractive terms of land tenure as a means of encouraging settlement than as an inducement for aliens to become citizens."

In the nineteenth century, when immigration increased drastically, not only did many states revert to their previous exclusionary practices, but the Federal Government also involved itself. These state and federal measures, reactionary in nature, were intended to protect the country from the increase of foreign investment. Much of the concern focused on the ownership of farms and ranches where many foreign investors had begun developing large estates.

Opponents of foreign ownership claimed that the system of small, individual homesteads was in peril and would be replaced by tenant farming and feudalism.

. . .

In the twentieth century, the focus of alien landholding laws, some of which are still on the books, narrowed. . . .

Almost all of the alien landholding laws have been enacted by the individual states. Historically, the various state laws have all reflected the political and economic climates of the time. Increases in immigration often resulted in more stringent laws aimed at excluding aliens. In the late nineteenth and early twentieth centuries, many states passed landholding laws as a response to the influx of aliens. Farm states were concerned over absentee alien landlords and, consequently, legislated to limit their holdings of U.S. property. In the West, the laws were aimed at Asian nationals. These anti-Asian laws, in particular those affecting the Japanese, became quite popular prior to and during World War II as a result of economic fears and the rise of American nationalism, but they were largely repealed after the war.

NOTE: STATE LEGISLATION

There is a wide variety of state regulation of real property ownership by nonresidents. Depending on the specific language of the legislation, these statutes may be directed to foreign individuals, corporations, or governments. About a dozen states require disclosure by foreign investors of ownership of American agricultural land. See, e.g., Iowa Code Ann. § 567.3(1); Mo. Stat. Ann. § 442.592(1); Va. Code Ann. § 3.1–22.24. At least two states extend the disclosure obligation to all types of land owned by foreigners. See, e.g., N.C. Gen. Stat. § 64–1.1; Ohio Rev. Code Ann. § 5301.254.

A small group of states directly prohibit foreign ownership. Some limit acreage owned by nonresidents. See, e.g., Pa. Stat. Ann. tit. 68, § 30 (5,000 acres); Wis. Stat. Ann. § 710.02 (640 acres). Others limit the duration of ownership by nonresidents. See, e.g., Neb. Rev. Stat § 76–402 (barring ownership of title or a leasehold of over five years). Other states impose different restrictions. See, e.g., Haw. Rev. Stat. § 206–9(c)(1) (only U.S. citizens or aliens who have resided in Hawaii for five years may buy land held by state); Minn. Stat. Ann. § 500.221(2) (only citizens or resident aliens may purchase agricultural land); Miss. Code Ann. § 89–1–23 (permitting resident aliens to own property but restricting nonresident aliens).

Some states have expressly removed limitations on foreign land ownership. See, e.g., Ala. Code § 35–1–1. A few states recognize the ownership rights of foreigners from "friendly" countries, usually defined as nations with which the United States is not engaged in hostilities. See, e.g., Md. Code Ann. Real Prop. § 14–101; N.J. Stat. Ann. § 46:3–18.

NOTES

1. *Constitutional Challenge.* Early challenges under the U.S. Constitution to state regulation of foreign land ownership typically failed because the courts perceived that land ownership was an area of state concern. See, e.g., Terrace v. Thompson, 263 U.S. 197, 44 S.Ct. 15, 68 L.Ed. 255 (1923) (holding that states have the power to "define and delimit property rights" within their borders). After World War II, however, courts began imposing limitations on the state regulations. See, e.g., Oyama v. California, 332 U.S. 633, 68 S.Ct. 269, 92 L.Ed. 249 (1948) (invalidating, on Equal Protection grounds, a statute escheating lands recorded in the name of a minor American citizen because they had been paid for by his father, a citizen of Japan). Challenges to state regulation of land ownership by non-citizens are usually based on the Treaty Power, the Equal Protection

Clause, or the Commerce Clause. See, e.g., Zschernig v. Miller, 389 U.S. 429, 88 S.Ct. 664, 19 L.Ed.2d 683 (1968) (invalidating state statute placing conditions on inheritance in the United States by East German citizen as an intrusion into foreign affairs); Lehndorff Geneva, Inc. v. Warren, 74 Wis.2d 369, 246 N.W.2d 815 (1976) (upholding statute limiting ownership by nonresident alien to 640 acres against Equal Protection and Treaty Power challenges); see Fretcher, Alien Landownership in the United States: A Matter of State Control, 14 Brook. J. Int'l L. 147 (1988); Shapiro, The Dormant Commerce Clause: A Limit on Alien Land Laws, 20 Brook. J. Int'l L. 217 (1993).

2. *FIRPTA.* In light of FIRPTA's obligation on buyers to retain 10% of the purchase price for transmittal to the IRS, should buyers add language to contracts of sale to protect buyers from personal liability for the payment? See Richard, Reporting and Disclosure Requirements for the Foreign Investor in U.S. Real Estate, 25 Real Prop. Probate & Tr. J. 217, 256 (1991).

3. *Bibliographic Note.* On foreign investment in American land and its regulation, see Wilson, Note, Reforming Alien Agricultural Landownership Restrictions in Corporate Farming Law States: A Constitutional and Policy View From Iowa, 17 Drake J. Agricultural L. 709 (2012); Camp & Canovas, Advising Foreign Investment in U.S. Real Estate, Or How to Be a Modern Renaissance Attorney, 3 AUT NAFTA: L. & Bus. Rev. Am. 22 (1997); Jarchow, Foreign Investment in U.S. Real Estate, 12 St. Mary's L.J. 1069 (1981); Morrison, Limitations on Alien Investments in American Real Estate, 60 Minn. L. Rev. 621 (1976); Price, Alien Land Restrictions in the American Common Law: Exploring the Relative Autonomy Paradigm, 43 Am. J. Legal. Hist. 152 (1999); Richards, Reporting and Disclosure Requirements for the Foreign Investor in U.S. Real Estate, 25 Real Prop. Probate & Tr. J. 217 (1990); Tang, Special Concerns of Foreign Investors in Sophisticated Real Estate Transactions, 468 PLI/Real 495 (Westlaw 2001).

On FIRPTA and taxation issues, see Jetel & Murray, Foreign Investment in U.S. Real Property, 26 Prob. & Prop. 52 (May/Jun. 2012); Morales, Taxing Sales and Dispositions of U.S. Real Property Interests Under FIRPTA, 30 Real Est. Tax. 20 (No.1 2002); McNeal, Taxation of Foreign Persons Disposing of U.S. Real Property, 69 Mich. B.J. 671 (1990); Pedersen & Sharp, Real Estate Investments by Foreign Persons After the Foreign Investment in Real Property Tax Act of 1980, 11 Real Est. L.J. 47 (1982); Rudnick, Taxing Foreign Investment in Real Property, 13 B.J. Int'l L.J. 395 (1995).

B. AMERICAN INVESTMENT IN FOREIGN REAL ESTATE

1. LIMITATIONS ON OWNERSHIP

Just as federal and state regulation limits the ownership of U.S. land by non-citizens, Americans may face restrictions on holding real estate in other countries. The following discussion of the laws of Mexico provides an illustration of the law and the economic, social, and historical perspectives that underlie such regulation.

Michael Boreale, Note, Beachfront Property in Arizona? Loosening the Restrictions on Foreign Acquisition of Mexican Real Estate and the Implication for Arizona Investors

22 Arizona Journal of International and Comparative Law 389, 390–402 (2005).

II. MEXICAN REAL ESTATE LAW AS IT RELATES TO FOREIGN INVESTMENT

A. Fideicomiso Is Your Friend: A Look At The Current State Of Mexican Real Estate Law

Although Mexico has surpassed Japan and rivals Canada as America's most prolific trading partner, an American citizen cannot simply purchase Mexican beachfront property for a retirement home. A complicated, and at times confusing, series of transactions are required to take place before a foreigner can acquire property in Mexico, and even then, Mexican law prohibits outright ownership in certain circumstances.

Article 27 of the Mexican Constitution prohibits foreigners from owning property in Mexico, within 100 kilometers of a border or within 50 kilometers of a coastline. This prohibited area, known as the "Restricted Zone," is quite large, encompassing over 40 percent of the total land area of Mexico. Outside of the "Restricted Zone," foreigners can own property in fee simple, an "estate . . . in which the owner is entitled to the entire property, with unconditional power of disposition during his life, and descending to his heirs and legal representatives upon his death intestate."

Within the "Restricted Zone," there are differing rules regarding the acquisition of residential and non-residential property. For both types of property inside the "Restricted Zone," foreigners must enter into a trust contract known as a fideicomiso with a Mexican bank to acquire property for residential purposes. The Spanish word fideicomiso translates to the Latin term fidei-commissum, which is defined in American jurisprudence as "a species of trust; being a gift of property to a person, accompanied by a request or direction of the donor that the recipient will transfer the property to another, the latter being a person not capable of taking directly under the will or gift." In a fideicomiso transaction, the seller functions as the donor, the bank as the recipient, and the foreign buyer as the person unable to take.

1. Residential Property

A fideicomiso is the Mexican equivalent of the type of trust utilized in the United States when a minor inherits property. As with a minor in the United States, a foreigner in Mexico cannot contract for residential real estate in the "Restricted Zone." Such real estate is property that an owner or a third party uses exclusively as a dwelling. Through the fideicomiso, the foreign purchaser can acquire beneficiary rights to residential property within the restricted zone for 50 years.

In the fideicomiso, the Mexican government has created a shortcut around the constitutional prohibition on foreigners owning property. The foreign purchaser pays the Mexican seller for the "beneficiary rights" to the property. The bank is the trustee and actual title holder of the property. The purchaser is the beneficiary of the trust and is allowed unrestricted use. This type of transaction always requires approval and a permit from the Mexican Ministry of Foreign Affairs.

2.   Non-residential Property

The procedure for acquiring property for non-residential purposes is more streamlined. Non-residential property generally includes property used for commercial, industrial, agricultural, livestock, fishing, forestry, and rendering of services. Foreigners can actually own property used for non-residential purposes in the "Restricted Zone" if foreign investors adhere to an agreement known as the Calvo Clause. The Calvo Clause requires treating foreigners as Mexican nationals regarding the property and prohibits foreigners from invoking the protections of their home governments, or face forfeiture of the property. The Calvo Clause, a common device in Latin American countries, is named for Argentinean professor Carlos Calvo who espoused the theory that it is a violation of the principles of international law to have diplomatic representatives or armed forces from one nation intervene to support claims of its citizens in another country. The acquisition of non-residential property by a foreigner is still subject to the Calvo Clause agreement and must be reported to the Ministry of Foreign Affairs but does not require express approval.

The Mexican government's desire to promote investment in Mexico is the rationale behind allowing foreigners to own non-residential property while limiting residential property to a trust relationship. In many instances, from the viewpoint of Mexican officials, the future of several Mexican states lies in American land investment. Foreign direct investment is viewed as the only reliable source of economic growth, which explains the Mexican government's advocacy of such investment. Additionally, the government had to address concerns of both investors reluctant to invest millions of dollars in commercial projects and residential buyers wary of entering the Mexican market without the ability to acquire title to the property in fee simple.

B.   From Revolution To Restricted Zones: The Evolution Of Foreign Ownership Of Property In Mexico

1.   ¡Viva La Revolucion!

A thorough understanding of the current state of Mexican real estate law requires an understanding of the history that shaped the Mexican Constitution. The new Mexican government adopted the Mexican Constitution in 1917 after the seven-year Mexican Revolution. Prior to the Revolution, the resources of Mexico and the stability of the administration of President Porfirio Diaz attracted a large number of foreign investors. Diaz held office from 1876 to 1911 with only one four-year interruption. His regime attracted investors mainly from the United States, Great Britain and France, who bought up a large percentage of the land and exploited natural resources such as oil, gas, and minerals. The increasing amounts of foreign investment greatly stimulated the Mexican economy. However, the new prosperity facilitated by the Diaz government did not reach most of the Mexican people. The situation became so drastically skewed in favor of wealthy investors that by the start of the revolution in 1910, one percent of the landowners in Mexico controlled ninety-seven percent of the land.

Mexicans grew increasingly concerned that the foreign presence would "exploit Mexico's natural resources and labor." In fact, much exploitation did occur, leading to a revolt of textile workers in Puebla on November 20, 1910; the starting point for the Mexican Revolution.

Essentially, the Mexican Revolution was a reaction by peasants and workers against the Diaz regime, which held power for a long period of time and facilitated the foreign exploitation of Mexico's people, labor, and resources. Naturally, the public sentiment towards the foreign investment that had financed and facilitated the Diaz regime was negative. The victorious revolutionaries aimed to embody the principles of their rebellion in the new Constitution. In addition to ending worker exploitation, one of the goals of the revolution was to return the economic destiny of Mexico to the hands of Mexicans. Consequently, Mexicans were reluctant to open their nation to investment and acquisition by foreign entities that many felt contributed to the pre-Revolution state of affairs.

Another factor that fueled the anti-foreign feeling in Mexico after the revolution is directly attributable to the turbulent relationship between Mexico and foreign nations before the Diaz regime. Mexico gained its independence from Spain in 1821. At the time, Mexico was a much larger country in area than it is today. Then, in 1836, Texas declared and gained its independence from Mexico and in March of 1845, United States President John Tyler invited Texas to join the Union.

These actions led directly to the Mexican-American War, which ended on March 10, 1848, with the signing of the treaty of Guadalupe Hidalgo. As a result of the treaty, Mexico ceded nearly half its territory to the United States, including all of California, most of Arizona, and parts of New Mexico, Nevada, Colorado, and Utah. Furthermore, in 1853 with the Gadsden Purchase, the United States purchased present-day southern Arizona and a small part of southern New Mexico. Finally in 1861, the French arrived in Mexico and installed Maximilian as emperor. The French remained in control of Mexico until their expulsion in 1867.

The repeated threats to Mexico's sovereignty, combined with the heavy foreign exploitation under the Diaz regime, made the Mexican citizenry wary of foreigners. This distrust and reticence towards foreigners led directly to the heavy foreign investment restrictions present in the 1917 Constitution, including the "Restricted Zone" provision. The restricted zones are the natural reaction of a nation following such a period of conflict. Countries such as Mexico, after repeated attacks on their sovereignty, wish to protect their territories from potential future invasions, and look to the restricted zone provision as a mechanism to achieve that goal.

Thus the language of Article 27 of the Mexican Constitution came into being, limiting ownership of land to Mexican nationals unless a Calvo clause was signed, and completely eliminating the right own land in what is now termed the Restricted Zone. By the early 1970s; however, Mexico was becoming increasingly desperate for foreign, especially United States, investment dollars to resuscitate a struggling economy. Yet the Mexican Constitution prevented foreigners from owning property in the "Restricted Zone," which arguably contains many of the most appealing locations to foreign real estate investors. The Mexican government realized that something had to be done to allow and encourage more foreign investment, especially in the attractive and potentially lucrative "Restricted Zone."

2. Legislative Changes From 1970 to 1990: The Dam Begins To Break

In 1971, in order to constitutionally allow foreign investment within the "Restricted Zone," the Mexican government expanded the concept of the fideicomisos. The concept of the fideicomiso first appeared in Mexican law in 1926 as part of the General Law of Credit Institutions and Banking Establishments. The scope of the fideicomiso was limited and was not applied to real estate transactions. The General Law of Negotiable Instruments and Credit Operation in 1932 laid out the major components of the trusts and addressed their function and application, but the modern concept of fideicomiso as it relates to real estate in the "Restricted Zone" was not mentioned.

Recessions and economic downturns left Mexico without a stable internal source of revenue. The government focused on the concept of the fideicomiso as a way out of the stagnant economic situation. On April 29, 1971, President Luis Echeverria authorized Mexican banks to acquire property in the "Restricted Zone" in trust for the benefit of foreigners. The agreement, influenced as it was by the desire to promote foreign investment into Mexico's economy and tourism industry, was still mindful of lingering doubts about the presence of foreigners in the "Restricted Zone", which explains why the arrangement only benefited commercial transactions.

President Echeverria's proclamation was not as wide-ranging as was necessary to rescue the Mexican economy. This led the Mexican legislature to ratify the *Act to Promote Mexican Investment and Regulate Foreign Investment of 1973* (hereinafter 1973 FIA). The 1973 FIA officially incorporated the concept of the fideicomiso as a legal loophole around the constitutional prohibition on foreign acquisition of property. This provided foreign investors with a legal means to acquire property within the "Restricted Zone." Facially, it appears that the authorization of foreign acquisition of property was unconstitutional under Article 27 of the Mexican Constitution. The 1973 FIA avoided unconstitutionality, however, because Article 27 gives some latitude to the government to grant real-estate rights to foreigners provided they sign a Calvo Clause. Additionally, the technical language of a Fideicomiso does not grant foreigners the constitutionally prohibited ownership right over land in the Restricted Zone.

This is not to say that the idea of liberalizing foreign investment restrictions was met with open arms. There was intense debate on both sides, and a division in the Mexican House of Representatives over the legality of such acts impeded smooth adoption of the new proposals. In the end, the faction favoring foreign investment prevailed, primarily because the act did not directly promote investment by offering incentives or tax breaks to foreigners; rather it merely allowed general foreign investment as well as fideicomisos in the "Restricted Zone". Despite the new law, however, foreign investors still had lingering concerns because the 1973 FIA limited fideicomisos to thirty years and did not indicate what would happen once the thirty-year period expired.

The *1989 Regulations to the Act to Promote Mexican Investment and Regulate Foreign Investment* (hereinafter 1989 Regulations) provided answers to nagging questions left by the 1973 FIA. The 1989 Regulations allowed for a renewal of the fideicomiso for another thirty-year period as long as a renewal application was filed one year before the expiration of the fideicomiso, and the beneficiary, property, and intended purpose remained the same. The Regulations provided for a mandatory automatic approval of a renewal application if the above requirements were met. Mexico's attitude towards foreign investment continued to become more favorable. Economically, it made sense for Mexicans to make their country as appealing as possible for foreign investors.

3.   Recent Legislative Changes: Come On In, The Water's Fine!

In 1993, with the *Foreign Investment Act of 1993* (hereinafter 1993 FIA), the Mexican government again enhanced the favorable status of foreign investors. The 1993 FIA was the most substantial and drastic change since the 1973 FIA, allowing foreigners more latitude than ever to make investments within the "Restricted Zone." In perhaps the most striking change, the Mexican government authorized wholly foreign-owned Mexican corporations to directly own property for non-residential purposes within the "Restricted Zone." Additionally, the 1993 FIA, with its loosened regulations on foreign investment, created a much more favorable economic climate, which made the passage of NAFTA more likely. The 1993 FIA and the Mexican government's increased desire for foreign investment were prime examples of a new national policy of fostering economic development and taking a more active role in the world economy. This was a boon to foreign companies wishing to operate a tourist resort or factory within the "Restricted Zone." The rationale behind the change in attitude was based on the fact that commercial foreign investment in the "Restricted Zone" had the capacity to create hundreds of thousands of jobs for Mexicans and provide a much-needed spark to the economy.

The 1993 FIA also extended the length of a fideicomiso for a private investor to fifty years. The extension granted to purchasers of real estate for residential purposes was a great step towards easing the concerns of prospective investors. For the first time, an investor looking for residential beachfront property could ensure the rights of use for a lifetime. The automatic renewal carried over from the 1973 FIA was also an enticing aspect.

The reason the changes were so heavily skewed to benefit non-residential investors was simple. The 1993 FIA reflects the residual attitude of the 1917 Constitution; foreign investment should benefit Mexico as much as the foreign investor. A residential real estate purchase by a foreign investor benefits mainly the investor, whereas, a real estate purchase for the purpose of establishing a hotel or tourist attraction benefits not only the investor but also the thousands of Mexicans that could be employed. Additionally, granting purchase rights to non-residential investors helps establish and solidify a feeling of stability that encourages long-term investment and ensures long-term employment for Mexican workers.

In 1996, Mexican President Ernesto Zedillo amended the 1993 FIA to allow foreign investors outside of a Mexican corporation to acquire title to land in the Restricted Zone for non-residential purposes. The amendment conformed to Mexico's increasing desire to attract foreign investment as a means to provide employment for Mexicans in the "Restricted Zone." Wealthy investors from California, Arizona, and Texas were (and still are) obvious targets of the Mexican government's loosened restrictions. However, there were lingering concerns that the Mexican government was proceeding too quickly in loosening restrictions on foreign investment. This sentiment led to the adoption of new regulations in 1998.

The *1998 Foreign Investment Regulations* (hereinafter 1998 Regulations) clarified and provided a working legal structure for the 1993 FIA and the 1996 amendment, much as the 1989 Regulations did for the 1973 FIA. The Mexican government uses administrative regulations to "curb, limit, and define . . . the exercise of discretionary powers by federal agencies and authorities." Indeed, foreigners were finally able to acquire *title* in the "Restricted Zone," subject to two limitations: (1) the property must be destined for a non-residential use; and (2) the foreigner must agree to the Calvo Clause in Article 27, paragraph I of the Mexican Constitution.

When compared to the 1917 Constitution, the 1998 regulations seem unconstitutional because for the first time actual ownership of land in the "Restricted Zone" was available to foreigners without a fideicomiso. It is unlikely, however, that the constitutionality of the 1998 Regulations will be questioned—to invalidate the previous enactments would have catastrophic consequences for Mexico's economy and would mean the loss of thousands of jobs. Administrative regulations are not supposed to contradict or oppose the basic foundations of the statute that they interpret, which is why the 1998 Regulations do not retreat from the liberal positions of the 1993 FIA or the 1996 regulations. The modern attitude and economic vision of the recent changes were well-noted in former president Ernesto Zedillo's State of the Union Address in 1999:

> [a]dvancements have been made in eliminating barriers and unnecessary regulations to direct foreign investment, through the adjustment of the applicable legal framework. In particular, the [1998 Regulations] promulgated on September 8, 1998, facilitate the application of the corresponding Act, to provide more legal safety, certainty and transparency in the transactions conducted by national and foreign investors.

The 1998 Regulations also redefined the concepts of residential and non-residential activities. Residential activities consist of dwellings used by the owner or a third party (such as rental or leased property). Non-residential activities include, but are not limited to, time shares, industrial uses, commercial uses, tourism enterprises, and service-related industries.

There were no substantive changes in the 1998 Regulations to the requirements of a foreigner wishing to acquire residential property inside the "Restricted Zone." A fideicomiso is still required, and acquiring direct title is still prohibited for this type of intended use. The structure remained the same: the term of a fideicomiso is fifty years and can be renewed at the request of the beneficiary within ninety days of the expiration of the fideicomiso agreement. Approval is automatically granted as long as the original conditions remain the same and have been complied with. Thus, it is much easier for the non-residential investor to acquire use rights, and those rights are much more secure than before, but the residential investor has not yet been granted the extensive benefits afforded to the commercial or industrial developer.

Outside of the "Restricted Zone," the 1998 Regulations have made foreign acquisition of property even easier. The 1998 Regulations allowed foreigners to own property of both types, residential and non-residential, subject to few restrictions. A Calvo Clause agreement is needed, as is a permit certifying that the requirements have been met. The permit is deemed granted if no action is taken within five days of the submittal of the application.

The legislative changes in the last decade reflect the increasing desire of the Mexican government to take advantage of the prosperity of its northern neighbors. By streamlining and simplifying the procedure for acquiring property in Mexico, the government has taken great steps towards attracting foreign investment. By retaining the Calvo Clause requirement and limiting the rights of residential purchasers inside the "Restricted Zone," Mexico has retained a level of control over foreign investment while, at the same time, ensuring that growth is channeled into the areas that will help Mexicans most.

2.   FOREIGN REAL ESTATE SYSTEMS

The nature of real estate ownership, and the methods of land transfer and finance, in other countries may differ significantly from the American model. The contrast is most striking in countries still following the Communist system and in the states emerging from such centralized, collective regimes.

David S. Kerzner, The Commercial Real Estate Laws of the People's Republic of China and Shenzhen: An Overview*

26 Vanderbilt Journal of Transnational Law 581, 590–593, 594–595, 598–599 (1993).

1.   Acquisition of Land Use Rights from the Government

The PRC maintains a dual conception of property rights whereby the state reserves ownership, and collectives or individuals reserve leasehold rights. Under this division of estates, China has enacted specific legislation to deal with the granting and transferring of the right to use urban state-owned land. This legislation confers upon companies, enterprises, organizations, and individuals both within and without the PRC's territory the opportunity to obtain land use rights and the right to transfer, lease, pledge, or otherwise use the land in economic activities with the protection of the laws of the PRC. The exercise of land use rights with respect to the grant, transfer, leasing, pledging, and termination of the rights must be carried out under the supervision and with the approval of the land administrative departments of the people's governments at or above the county level or

---

*   Permission Granted to Reprint from the Vanderbilt Journal of Transnational Law which is the copyright holder.

higher. Such government interference with the transfer or pledging of land use rights (while uncapitalistic in its intrusiveness) is not peculiar to the PRC and indeed occurs (albeit to a lesser extent) in North America as well. Once again, any transfer of property, including the pledging, termination, and transfer of land use rights, or removal or alteration of relevant surface structures, must be registered with the appropriate government land administrative departments and real estate administrative departments. These registration documents are a matter of public record, and nonparties may examine them freely.

Individuals initially may acquire land either by a Land Grant of the government or through a transfer of land previously granted by the government. Even though individuals, including foreign corporations, may now obtain land use rights, the land rights are not available on an open market basis for purchase. Under the PRC's method of government-controlled land use grants, an individual must approach the people's governments of municipalities and counties to obtain a grant of a land use right. The grant of land which the individual may seek must conform with the land plots, usages, term of years, and other local conditions such that the grant is consistent with the urban plan in question. In many ways, this is similar to the zoning and urban planning requirements with which developers must deal in United States urban centers. After acquiring land, developers in the United States can encounter a multiplicity of problems and no end of aggravation in obtaining requisite approvals from the numerous city departments before being able to embark on their project. Sometimes, the approvals are not forthcoming. In the PRC, by contrast, the developer may have an advantage in knowing whether the development plans will be approved before it commits itself financially to the land. The real difference between the two systems of urban planning approval, however, is in the aftermath of approval. In China, once the land user obtains the grant, he is required by law to utilize and manage the land in strict accordance with the provisions of the contracts for the grant of land use rights and with the requirements of urban planning. Indeed, in cases in which the land user fails to develop and utilize the land in accordance with the time period and conditions stipulated in the contracts, the land administrative authorities can intervene to correct the matter. Depending on the circumstances, these authorities may issue warnings, fines, and even recover the land use rights without compensation. Hence, before investing in land use rights in the PRC, the investor should not only be committed to the specific project plans but be competent to develop the project in a timely manner or willing to risk losing the entire investment. The developer or investor may always seek approval both from the government granting authority and the respective planning and urban departments to change the use or zoning of the land. If the approval is granted, the change will be subject to an adjustment fee.

2.   Terms of a Grant

The grant of land use rights comprises a grant for a certain term of years by the State in its capacity as owner of the land in return for the payment of fees by the land user. To be valid, a grant contract must be in writing and signed. Contracts for the grant of land use rights shall be signed between the land administrative departments of the municipal and county people's governments as the grantor, and the land user in accordance with the principles of equality, voluntarism, and compensation. The maximum term of years for the grant of land use rights is determined in accordance with the respective use of the property.

3.   Acquisition of a Grant Through Agreement, Tender, and Auction

A land use grant may be obtained from the government by one of three means: agreement; bidding; or auction. The first way, agreement, occurs by simple contract to purchase the land use rights. The second method, bidding, resembles a tender process whereby the tender is made through the public process pursuant to a set of criteria and is subject to a time limit and other conditions. The third method is the standard auction process. Land users must close the deal by making full payment of the fees for the grant of the land use rights within sixty days after signing a contract. While this is certainly the case with the agreement method, it is unclear whether this payment requirement also applies to acquisitions through the bidding or auction processes. If a land user fails to pay the full amount within the sixty-day window, the grantor shall have the right to rescind the contract and may demand compensation for breach of contract. It is uncertain whether, under applicable Chinese laws, the government grantor could compel specific performance by the purchaser of land use rights.

. . .

D.   Transfer of Land Use Rights

1.   Requirements and Rights Involving the Transfer of Leaseholds

By legal definition, the transfer of land use rights refers to sale, exchange, and gift transactions. To be able to transfer land use rights, the land user wishing to transfer must have adhered to the contractual provisions of the initial grant of land use rights with respect to investment capital and to use and development of the land in accordance with the stipulated time period. The requirement that a certain amount of money must have been invested actually may restrict the ability to buy land with the intention of making a quick resale for profit. It is conceivable to transfer ownership of land use rights without actually reconveying the property, since an owner instead could sell the shares of the company that owns the rights of the land use contract. Based upon the specific conditions of the original grant contract and the approvals to be obtained for the transfer of equity of a company holding such land rights, it is not certain, however, whether such a sale really could succeed.

When land use rights are transferred, the rights and responsibilities specified in the contract for the grant of the land rights are transferred along with the land use rights and the registration documents. The person acquiring the land use rights acquires the rights for the same period as specified in the original grant, less the time already expired. The regulations also allow land use rights to be inherited.

Of particular concern to foreign investors is the apparent pricing controls that exist with respect to land use transfers. Under the current law, when the transfer price for land use rights is obviously lower than the market price, the municipal and county people's governments enjoy a statutory right of first refusal. The disturbing aspect of the law is that if the municipal and the market price for the transfer of land use rights are deemed to be unreasonably inflated, the local people's governments may take "necessary measures;" implicitly, these bodies may alter the asking price. While it is unknown what degree of unfettered discretion the Chinese may have with respect to approving or altering a transfer price, this provision nevertheless is further evidence of the PRC's effort to control speculation and to maintain a real estate market with socialist characteristics. Upon the completion of a transfer of land use rights, the new holder of the rights is entitled to seek a land use change.

. . .

G. The National Law of Mortgages

1. Pledging Leaseholds and Surface Structures

PRC mortgage law expressly allows individuals to pledge land use rights and structures found thereon. Under the law, when a holder pledges his land use rights, he must also pledge the surface structures and other objects found on the land. Conversely, this law also provides that when a holder pledges surface structures, he must also pledge the right to the use of the land that is "within the scope of the structures."

No problems appear to arise from these provisions when the holder of the land use rights and the owner of the buildings thereon are the same, but this scenario can become considerably more complicated when the holder of the land use rights and the owner of the building structures are not the same party. Under the above described laws, the owner of a leasehold or the structure desiring to obtain financing would have to obtain consent from the other party, given that the law requires both leasehold and structure to be pledged together. Compounding this potential problem is the additional need to determine the amount of the charge to be levied on the respective properties. Caution, therefore, would advise the investor in land use rights not to sell the surface structures to a separate entity, or to at least attempt to take his own financing measures first.

Both the mortgagor and mortgagee must sign all mortgage contracts. These contracts may not violate the provisions of state laws and regulations and the contract for the grant of land use rights. All contracts for the mortgage of leasehold rights or buildings must be duly registered in accordance with these same provisions.

2. Rights of Mortgagor and Mortgagee

In the event of a default by the mortgagor, the mortgagee should know what remedies are available. The common remedy for default in the United States is foreclosure, whether by judicial or by nonjudicial sale (power of sale). When a mortgagor defaults on debt obligations or declares dissolution or bankruptcy during the term of the mortgage, the PRC mortgage laws permit the mortgagee to dispose of the pledged properties in accordance with provisions of state laws, regulations, and the pledge contracts. The mortgagee then receives a statutory preferential right with respect to income generated from the disposition of pledged properties. The terminology used in this law fails to make clear whether the concept of "properties" encompassed under the statute applies to the surface structures and the leasehold rights or only to the surface structures. Upon the discharge of the mortgage through repayment of the full amount of the debt, or for other reasons, the mortgage registration must be cancelled in accordance with the required provisions. The PRC national mortgage laws do not provide expressly for any mortgagor equitable redemption rights. The national mortgage laws also are silent as to whether a mortgagee is left with a deficiency after the foreclosure has recourse to sue the mortgagor for the outstanding amount. In addition to these national laws, some local mortgage laws exist at the province and regional levels.

3.   U.S. LEGAL RESTRICTIONS

Eric M. Pedersen, The Foreign Corrupt Trade Practices Act and Its Application to U.S. Business Operations in China

7 Journal of International Business and Law 13, 15–21 (2008).

Part I: The Foreign Corrupt Practices Act

The FCPA was passed in the wake of the Watergate scandal in the 1970s. After its passage, SEC investigations uncovered over 400 cases of U.S. businesses involved in illegal or questionable payments to foreign government officials amounting to over $300 million. This "included some of the largest and most widely held public companies in the United States." The discovered abuses ranged "from bribery of high foreign officials in order to secure some type of favorable action by the foreign government" to payments "made to ensure that government functionaries discharge certain ministerial [sic] or clerical duties." Congress found the payment of bribes to influence the acts and decisions of foreign officials to be unethical, unnecessary and "bad business," as it "eroded public confidence in the integrity of the [American] free market system." Therefore, in 1977 Congress enacted the FCPA as a means of discouraging the bribery of foreign officials and restoring integrity to the American business system.

A.   FCPA Provisions

The provisions of the FCPA can be broken down into two distinct parts: (1) the prohibition against the bribery of foreign officials by American corporations, and (2) the requirements for record-keeping and accounting practices that prohibit the establishment of undercover accounts used to finance illegal payments.

The FCPA's anti-bribery provisions prohibit people and corporations from engaging in a variety of activities and transactions. The statute explains that issuers of certain U.S. securities—or any officers, directors, employees, or agents of the issuers—cannot use the mails, phone systems, internet or any other instrumentality of interstate commerce "in furtherance of an offer, payment, promise to pay, or an authorization to make an offer, payment, or gift" to any foreign official, foreign political party, or candidate for a foreign political office. This provision applies to any situation in which there is a "corrupt" purpose of either (i) influencing an act or decision of that foreign official, (ii) obtaining or retaining business, (iii) directing a business to a particular person, or (iv) to securing an improper advantage. Simply put, the FPCA makes it unlawful for U.S. persons, U.S. companies and certain foreign issuers listed on U.S. securities exchanges, to make payments to foreign officials for the purpose of obtaining or retaining business for or with, or directing business to, any person. A simple offer, promise, or authorization of a bribe will trigger a violation of the FCPA.

Although the FCPA does not apply directly to a foreign subsidiary of a U.S. business that engages in conduct that is prohibited by the FCPA, the U.S. parent business will be deemed to have violated the FCPA if they "authorized, directed, or controlled the activity in question." This form of "knowledge" is inferred under the FCPA if a corporation "is aware that such person is engaging in such conduct, that such circumstance exists, or that such result is substantially certain to occur; or such person has a firm belief that such circumstance exists or that such result is substantially certain to occur." "Knowledge" also includes "conscious disregard and deliberate ignorance."

The FCPA's record-keeping and accounting provisions are the lesser known, but equally important, aspects of the FCPA which were added to the Securities and Exchange Act of 1934. These record-keeping provisions require U.S. corporations to keep books, records and accounts in reasonable detail, in a way that fairly reflects their transactions and the dispositions of their assets. The FCPA's accounting provisions require that every issuer of securities (i.e. businesses with securities registered with the SEC under section 12 or required to file reports under section 15(d) of the Securities and Exchange Act of 1934) to:

(A) make and keep books, records, and accounts, which, in reasonable detail, accurately and fairly reflect the transactions and dispositions of the assets of the issuer;

(B) devise and maintain a system of internal accounting controls sufficient to provide reasonable assurances that—

(i) transactions are executed in accordance with management's general or specific authorization;

(ii) transactions are recorded as necessary (I) to permit preparation of financial statements in conformity with generally accepted accounting principles or any other criteria applicable to such statements, and (II) to maintain accountability for assets;

(iii) access to assets is permitted only in accordance with management's general or specific authorization; and

(iv) the recorded accountability for assets is compared with the existing assets at reasonable intervals and appropriate action is taken with respect to any differences.

These provisions give "the SEC authority over the entire financial management and reporting requirements of publicly held United States corporations." Their purpose is to prevent issuers from concealing bribes and, more specifically, to discourage fraudulent accounting and reporting practices. These provisions also provide a basis for ascribing liability to U.S. parent companies of foreign subsidiaries. Since these accounting provision violations do not require proof of criminal intent, a corporation can more easily be held strictly liable for the actions of a foreign subsidiary under the FCPA.

B. Exceptions to the FCPA's Anti-Bribery Prohibitions

The prohibitions of the FCPA are subject to three exceptions. The first, which came by way of an amendment to the FCPA in 1988, permits the use of "grease" or "facilitating" payments to foreign officials for the purpose of expediting or securing the performance of a routine governmental action. "Grease" payments are usually small payments to minor government officials that provide extra incentive to perform routine governmental action. The phrase "routine governmental action" refers to actions that a government official would regularly perform. Examples of routine governmental action would include "obtaining permits, licenses, or other official documents to qualify a person to do business in a foreign country;" "providing police protection;" "loading and unloading cargo;" "processing governmental papers, such as visas and work orders;" and priority in scheduling inspections. The second exception is for legitimate business purposes and allows a U.S. corporation to utilize its funds for the purpose of educating a foreign official about its business, product, or activities. The last exception to the prohibition of the FCPA allows for the payments of bribes in countries where bribery is legal. This exception requires that the law permitting bribery be in writing, and is therefore rarely, if ever, invoked.

C. Inside Information

In 1998, the FCPA was amended again to implement the Organization of Economic Cooperation and Development (hereinafter "OECD") on Combating Bribery of Foreign Public Officials in International Business Transactions. This amendment made several significant changes in the FCPA, including broadening the jurisdictional reach of the FCPA to non-U.S. persons acting within the United States, as well as to U.S. persons outside of the United States. The amendments also prohibited making corrupt payments to a foreign official for the purpose of "securing any improper advantage" to obtain or retain business. As amended, the FCPA not only prohibits:

> [P]ayments to foreign officials not just to buy any act or decision, and not just to induce the doing or omitting of an official function "to assist . . . in obtaining or retaining business for or with, or directing business to, any person," but also the making of a payment to such a foreign official to secure an "improper advantage" that will assist in obtaining or retaining business.

U.S. corporations can still fall under the umbrella of the FCPA for making corrupt payments even if the purpose of such payments is not necessarily to obtain business. If a foreign, state-owned business was to solicit bids for a new business and kept certain information confidential, then anything provided or anything offered of value for the purpose of obtaining disclosure of that confidential information may result in an FCPA violation.

Use of inside information from a foreign official can subject a corporation to liability under Rule 10b–5 of the Securities and

Exchange Act of 1934, which prohibits the use of material, non-public information for the purchase or sale of a security. In addition, an employee of a U.S. corporation who makes a payment, or promises to make a payment to a Chinese foreign official for the purpose of obtaining confidential, non-public information may subject the business to liability under the FCPA.

D.   Penalties for FCPA Violations

Violations of either the accounting or bribery provisions of the FCPA can subject individuals and/or corporations to both criminal and civil penalties. Individual officers, directors and employees of a company may be prosecuted for violations of the FCPA even if their company is not liable. Criminal violations can lead to substantial fines and prison terms. Civil liability can also result in considerable fines. Additionally, the SEC has been increasingly ordering U.S. businesses to disgorge any profits made through violations of the FCPA, which often results in businesses settling FCPA suits at practically double the cost of settlement. In addition to civil and criminal penalties, an individual or corporation found to be in violation of the FCPA may be subject to additional governmental actions such as barring a corporation from conducting business with the federal government, refusing export licenses, and possible suspension or debarment from programs provided by the Commodity Futures Trading Commission and the Overseas Private Investment Corporation.

E.   FCPA Enforcement

The FCPA has had a significant impact on the manner in which U.S. corporations conduct foreign business operations. Since its enactment:

> [s]everal firms that paid bribes to foreign officials have been the subject of criminal and civil enforcement actions, resulting in large fines and suspension and debarment from federal procurement contracting, and their employees and officers have gone to jail. To avoid such consequences, many firms have implemented detailed compliance programs intended to prevent and to detect any improper payments by employees and agents. Recently, the DOJ has affirmed its commitment to stamping out global corruption through aggressive enforcement of the FCPA. This has been observed through a significant increase in investigations by the DOJ and SEC. By 2006, 49 individual and corporate defendants had been prosecuted by the DOJ, resulting in over 27 plea agreements. In addition, over 38 cases were disposed of by the SEC, resulting in agreements to avoid further violations of the FCPA and disgorgements of profits received as a result of the corrupt activities. U.S. corporations that conduct business in China have been one of the focuses of recent FCPA investigations.

NOTES

1.   *Alternative Legal Systems.* Many commentators have written on the challenges in purchasing, leasing, financing, and developing land in Russia and the former Soviet Union. See, e.g., Baer, The Privatization of Land in

Russia: Reforms and Impediments, 17 Loy. L.A. Int'l & Comp. L.J. 1 (1994) (arguing that failure to recognize the concept of private land is the key obstacle to development of market economies in Russia and the former Soviet Union); Billings, Why Business Fails in Russia, 35 Int'l Law. 123, 125–126 (2001) (asserting that the major problem for American investors in Russia is that land cannot be purchased and foreign investors can do business only on land owned by local governments, state-owned enterprises, or recently privatized state enterprises); Heller, The Tragedy of the Anticommons: Property in the Transition from Marx to Markets, 111 Harv. L. Rev. 621, 622–624 (1998) (maintaining that the key impediment to development of a market economy is that too many people own the right to exclude others from a scarce resource, i.e., land in Russia); Markovich, Real Estate Transactions in Russia: New Land Code Gives Green Light to Foreign Investments, 8 J.E.Eur.L. 129 (2001). See also Comment, The Russian Title Registration System for Realty and Its Effect on Foreign Investors, 73 Wash. L. Rev. 989 (1998).

For further discussion of real estate law in the People's Republic of China, see Washburn, Regular Takings or Regulatory Takings?: Land Expropriation in Rural China, 20 Pac. Rim L. & Pol'y J. 71 (2011); Randolph, The New Chinese Property Law: A Practitioner's Perspective, 21 Probate & Prop. 14 (Sep./Oct.2007); Randolph & Jianbo, Chinese Real Estate Mortgage Law, 8 Pac. Rim L. & Pol'y J. 515 (1999); Randolph & Jianbo, Commercial Leasing in China, 15 UCLA Pac. Basin L.J. 86 (1996); Stein, Acquiring Land Use Rights in Today's China: A Snapshot From on the Ground, 24 UCLA Pac. Basin L.J. 1 (2006); Stein, Mortgage Law in China: Comparing Theory and Practice, 72 Mo.L.Rev. 1315 (2007).

For descriptions of investing in real estate in other legal systems, see Haidempergher & Selytin, Cross-Border Real Estate Practice, 47 Int'l Law. 327 (2013); Rudnick, Taxation of Foreign Investment in Real Property, 13 B.U. Int'l L.J. 395, 395–98 (1995); Chhibber & Majumdar, Property Rights and the Control of Strategy: Foreign Ownership Rules and Domestic Firm Globalization in Industry, 27 Law & Pol'y 52 (2005); Faust, Comment, American Investment in Cuban Real Estate: Close But No Cigar, 34 U. Miami Inter-Am.L.Rev. 369 (2003); Pasero & Torres, Foreign Investment in Mexico's Real Estate: An Introduction to Legal Aspects of Real Estate Transactions, 35 San Diego L. Rev. 783 (1998); Slupinski, Foreign Investment and Ownership Problems in Poland (PLI 1991); Vargas, Acquisition of Real Estate in Mexico by U.S. Citizens and American Companies, 9 San Diego Int'l L.J. 293 (2008).

In considering the excerpt by Kerzner, compare the nature of land ownership and transfer in the People's Republic of China with the American system of land ownership and transfer. Is the PRC system consistent with development and financing by ground leases in the United States? How does the PRC compare in terms of mortgage law and the remedies of the lender and the protections given to mortgagors?

2. *Title Systems.* The Peruvian economist, Hernando de Soto, indicates that a title system is an essential ingredient to economic development and opportunity:

> The poor inhabitants of these nations—five-sixths of humanity— do have these things [assets], but they lack the process to represent their property and create capital. They have houses but

not titles, crops but not deeds, businesses but not statutes or incorporation. It is the unavailability of these essential representations that explains why people who have adapted every other Western invention, from the paper clip to the nuclear reactor, have not been able to produce sufficient capital to make their domestic capitalism work.

de Soto, The Mystery of Capital 6–7 (2000). See also Hanstad, Designing Land Registration Systems for Developing Countries, 13 Am. U. Int'l L. Rev. 647, 652 (1998) ("Most experts would agree that some type of land registration system is a necessary element of a developed market economy."); King, Illegal Settlements and the Impact of Titling Programs, 44 Harv. Int'l L.J. 433 (2003). See also Calder & Compton, What You Need to Know About Title Insurance In International Real Estate Transaction, 21 Prac. Real Est. Law. 5 (No.2 2005); Gupta, Ending Finders, Keepers: The Use of Title Insurance to Alleviate Uncertainty in Land Holdings in India, 17 U.C. Davis J. In'tl L. & Pol'y 63 (2010); Soskin, Note, Protecting Title in Continental Europe and the United States—Restriction of A Market, 7 Hastings Bus. L.J. 411 (2011).

Reconsider the materials in Part I, Chapter IV above. What risks emerge for buyers and sellers in the absence of a title system? Can an adequate market for land develop if titles are protected but ownership information is not public as it is in the United States?

3. *FCPA*. In 2012, the Criminal Division of the U.S. Department of Justice and the Enforcement Division of the U.S. Securities and Exchange Commission released "Resource Guide to the U.S. Foreign Corrupt Practices Act." http://www.sec.gov/spotlight/fcpa/fcpa-resource-guide.pdf. While providing some help in understanding the Act, the Guide expressly states that it is "nonbinding, informal, and summary in nature" and may not be relied upon to create any substantive or procedural rights in any proceeding. For additional readings, see Lee, A Renewed Focus On Foreign Corruption and Politically Exposed Persons, 127 Banking L.J. 813 (2010); Warin, Diamant & Root, Somebody's Watching Me: FCPA Monitorships and How They Can Work Better, 13 U. Pa. J. Bus. L. 321 (2011).

CHAPTER XI

BUILDING ON THE BASICS: THE SHOPPING CENTER DEVELOPMENT

Many fundamental similarities run through the assembly, finance and eventual disposition of all forms of major real estate development, from low-slung shopping centers to high-rise office buildings, from suburban subdivisions to central city apartment houses. The developer will place the site under option or contract while the engineering, design and financing details are worked out and the requisite governmental approvals are obtained. Often the seller will finance the developer's acquisition of the land, through a purchase money mortgage or deed of trust or through a ground lease subordinated to the construction financing. The construction lender will insist on close control over the project and a binding takeout commitment from the permanent lender. The permanent lender will insist on terms that require it to take out the construction lender only if all building specifications and conditions are met. Title reports and survey maps must be examined to assure that the owner's title will be clear and the lender's security unimpaired and that the site will be free of easements and other restrictions that might interfere with the development. The proposed development must wend its way through the growing maze of local, state and federal land use controls, and accommodation must be reached with neighbors and local environmental groups.

The shopping center development offers an excellent vehicle for examining the structure and practice of complex land transactions. Shopping center developments typically embody a combination of financing, investment and leasing techniques that may appear only individually in other forms of real estate development. In addition to the usual elements of construction and permanent financing, a shopping center may involve limited partnerships, groundleases and subleases, long-term leases, transfers of fee interests to major, "anchor," tenants and short-term leases to smaller, "satellite," tenants. As in other commercial land transactions, expert drafting is crucial. Space leases must be structured with care, for the shopping center is a complex organism and depends for its health on the deft coordination of use clauses, covenants not to compete and percentage rent clauses as well as reciprocal operating covenants tying the anchor stores into the life of the center. Finally, among private real estate investments, shopping centers may be unsurpassed in their contemporary social impact.

Bibliographic Note. See generally, E. Halper, Shopping Center and Store Leases (rev.ed.2001); Urban Land Institute, Dollars & Cents of Shopping Centers: 1984 (1984); Shopping Centers: U.S.A. (G. Sternlieb & J. Hughes, eds., 1981); Cadwallader & Jordan, The ABCs of

Redeveloping Existing Shopping Centers, 23 Prob. & Prop. 48 (Sep./Oct. 2009).

A. THE CONCEPT

Dennis L. Greenwald, The Reinvention of the Shopping Center

19 Probate & Property 42, 42–44, 46 (May/June 2005).

Long ago, America had something called the "village green." The village green was the political, social, cultural, and administrative center of the community. Fast forward 200 years or so and cases were working their way through the courts that debated the argument made by political and community activists that shopping centers were akin to the village green of the old days. The issue in those cases was whether, and if so where, individual citizens may petition, pass out pamphlets, seek contributions, engage in voter registration, and the like. Some courts upheld the rights of certain activists, likening shopping centers to village greens. In fact, the argument of activists was that no other place better represented the center of the community than the shopping center. Traditional forms of large shopping centers are undergoing such profound changes in the 21st century that, in certain respects, many large shopping centers are becoming even more like ultra-modern versions of the old village green.

From Village Green to Regional Shopping Mall

A "main street" was added to the original village green that functioned as the main shopping area. Department stores ultimately developed, which then moved to the new "malls" starting in the 1960s. The first shopping malls were traditionally anchored by two or more large tenants, with in-line space between them, and the entire mall was devoted almost exclusively to shopping (and most of the stores were clothing stores). Food courts were not added to that standard format until larger malls developed. These shopping centers spawned variations such as mega malls, outlet malls, and specialty malls.

But the fundamental-if not sole-reason for the existence of all of these centers was one thing: shopping. Some shopping centers added nonshopping facilities such as restaurants or branch banking on out-parcels, which are separate parcels on the fringe of the shopping center that, although not physically connected to the main shopping center structure, share common areas such as the parking lot. Typically, restaurants were either fast-food or family-style, sit-down dining. Movie theaters were added later (because, among other reasons, theater patron parking needs would not usually conflict with prime-time shopping). But, at its core, the traditional shopping mall was fundamentally designed for shopping, not unlike one incredibly gigantic department store.

A Funny Thing Happened on the Way to the Mall

A funny thing did happen on the way to the mall. Both retailers and sociologists began to appreciate that shopping was actually a form of entertainment. This phenomenon seemed to be true of patrons irrespective of geography, gender, age, or socio-economic status. Shopping as a form of entertainment is easy to understand. It can be done alone or with others; it can be inexpensive or free; it is local and nonseasonal; it is available every day and almost every evening; parking is easy and either inexpensive or free; and traditional forms of entertainment (such as movies and dining) are often available in the shopping center. These reasons explain why this form of retail development has stayed with Americans for the last half century. Those who have predicted the end of the shopping mall (most notably, those who believed the 1990s technology boom spelled the demise of traditional forms of shopping) have consistently been wrong. Some form of destination shopping centers will survive for the same reason that movie theaters have survived the onslaught of video stores, pay-per-view movies, HBO, Showtime, and Cinemax. This is because shopping, like movies, remains a relatively inexpensive form of entertainment that gets people out of their houses and adds some excitement to their daily lives.

If people were going to shopping malls for entertainment as well as material need, then adding more traditional forms of pure "entertainment" was not far behind. Indeed, once developers accepted the notion of shopping as a form of entertainment, the lines between an entertainment center, a cultural center, and a community center began to blur. After all, if a venue for musical entertainment is built within a "shopping" center, then a "cultural" element is introduced, and, once the facility is built, it can serve as a community center for such events as speaker programs, conventions, and other community activities.

Reinvention/Evolution

What has been called the "reinvention" of the shopping center can perhaps be better understood as part of a continuing evolution. More than anything else, this evolution has been a function of geography. Because suburbia was the birthplace of the traditional shopping center, trends in shopping centers cannot be understood without looking at what has happened in suburbia.

David Brooks, in his recent book On Paradise Drive, says that Americans are living in a time of "the great dispersal," and he notes that our population is decentralizing faster than any other society in history. Although in 1950 only 23% of Americans lived in suburbia, the majority of Americans now do, and Brooks notes that today's suburbs are sprawling faster and farther than ever before, creating what he calls "exurban" areas that function fundamentally free of any nearby city. So people are not only moving out of cities, but they are moving farther and farther out. Moreover, the geography of jobs has evolved dramatically. Traditionally, jobs were associated with the city, mostly downtown. But, during the 1990s, 90% of office space was built in suburbia, and the suburbs account for more office space than inner cities in every metropolitan area except for Chicago and New York. A natural byproduct of this demographic has been the movement to the suburbs of shopping, dining, theater, and cultural and community venues. As Brooks comments: "That means we have a huge mass of people who not only don't live in the cities, they don't commute to the cities, go to the movies in the cities, eat in the cities, or have any significant contact with urban life. They are neither rural, nor urban, nor residents of a bedroom community. They are charting a new way of living." David Brooks, On Paradise Drive 44–50 (2004).

Moreover, the commonly accepted stereotype of the suburban population is inaccurate. Although one associates suburbs with families with children, married couples with children actually comprise only 27% of the suburban population. Id. at 5. More people living alone live in the suburbs than do families with children. So it would appear that the basic structure of suburbs is not likely to change. Certainly, "New Urbanism" is having its effect, as is the gentrification of a number of urban areas, but there seems no denying that suburban development shows no immediate signs of slowing and every indication that decentralization of the population will continue. If decentralization continues and suburban areas survive as separate communities that are commercially independent from urban areas, then a variety of forms of entertainment and community venues that have been traditionally located in urban areas can be expected to continue to expand in the suburbs. It is therefore reasonable to conclude that regional "shopping centers" will include many other forms of entertainment, as well as commercial, cultural, and community activities. Although a few so-called enclosed mega-malls already exist (mostly in colder climates in the United States and Canada), the development of larger shopping, entertainment, and community centers will likely continue nationwide.

. . .

Downtown Mega Centers

The gentrification of certain large, urban downtown areas into aggregations of sports complexes, shopping, pedestrian streets, dining, and various other forms of entertainment is already being seen. Downtown Los Angeles is essentially trying to create a "Times Square West" near the existing Staples Sports Center and Los Angeles Convention Center. Such massive redevelopments not only include retail stores (including some of the finer dining establishments), but also residential and office space as well. Joel Kotkin, Extreme Makeover: Los Angeles Edition, Wall St. J., Aug. 25, 2004, at D10.

Conclusion

Without a crystal ball, it is difficult to reach any definitive conclusions about the reinvention/evolution of the "shopping center." Certain trends, however, are clear. One is that there will be a continued blending of shopping with other forms of "entertainment," a continued blending of Internet shopping with traditional stores, increased security concerns, and continued development of new, large centers that will serve as focal points for not just shopping and traditional forms of entertainment, but also cultural and community venues and sometimes sports complexes. New Urbanists have predicted the end of the shopping centers, planners have said that sprawling suburbia signaled the demise of shopping centers, and technology gurus said that technology heralded the end of shopping centers. But public conduct belies this doom and gloom. Basically, consumers still want to go to shopping centers; they just want more than shopping-they want an entertainment destination. Developers will give it to them.

Michael D. Beyard & W. Paul O'Mara, Shopping Center Development Handbook*

8–13 (3d ed. 1999, Urban Land Institute Development Handbook Series).

Types of Shopping Centers

Shopping centers were originally divided into three principal types—neighborhood, community, and regional each with a clear and distinct function, trade area, and tenant mix. In actual practice, however, the distinction among the three types has not always been crystal clear. Further, as specialized market opportunities have been identified over the years, numerous new types of shopping centers have evolved. These types are usually considered distinct categories of shopping centers, although earlier they were not. In some cases, they share important characteristics with the original three basic categories. The difficulty in distinguishing shopping centers by type is becoming more pronounced as the development of hybrids increases. In all cases, even among variations, the major tenant classifications and to a lesser extent the center size and trade area determine the type of center.

Some segments of the shopping center industry have historically classified centers by size alone or by configuration, for example, enclosed or strip. In its annual surveys, the ICSC uses both factors, while the National Research Bureau and the Institute of Real Estate Management report shopping centers by size alone. ULI believes, however, that size alone, or size and configuration, is inadequate in defining shopping centers, as it implies a direct correlation between size and trade area, tenant characteristics and mix, and functions served in terms of categories of retail goods. This handbook classifies shopping center types by using all these factors.

Figure 1–2 compares the characteristics of the major types of shopping centers. The numbers shown on the table must be regarded only as convenient indicators to define the various types of centers; the basic elements of any center may change if it needs to ad apt to the changing characteristics of the trade area, including the nature of the competition, population density, and income. The number of people needed to support a shopping center of any type cannot be fixed, be cause income, disposable income, competition, and changing tenant mixes, methods of merchandising, and store sizes all enter into these calculations. No rigid standard for size could be realistic; local conditions within a trade area (number of households, income, existing retail outlets) are more important than any standard population data in estimating the purchasing power needed to support a center.

Figure 1–2

Characteristics of Shopping Centers

Type of Center	Leading Tenant (Basis for Classification)	Typical GLA (Square Feet)	General Range in GLA (Square Feet)	Usual Minimum Site Area (Acres)	Minimum Population Support Required
Neighborhood	Supermarket	50,000	30,000–100,000	3–10	3,000–40,000
Community	Junior Department store; large variety discount, or department store	150,000	100,000–450,000	10–30	40,000–150,000
Regional	One or two full-line department stores	450,000	300,000–900,000	10–60	150,000 or more
Super Regional	Three or more full-line department stores	900,000	500,000–2 million	15–100 or more	300,000 or more

Regional Malls

ULI divides regional malls into two subcategories—regional centers and super regional centers. By definition, a regional center has one or two full-line department stores. It typically contains a GLA [gross leasable area] of about 450,000 square feet and can range from about 300,000 to 900,000 square feet. From a sample of 49 regional centers, *Dollars & Cents of Shopping Centers: 1998* found that the median total floor space is 435,458 square feet. Early regional centers typically had only one department store, but that is no longer the case. Two department stores are now more common, although some specialized urban locations still have space to accommodate only one.

Super regional shopping centers share all of the same characteristics as regional centers except that they have three or more department stores and are usually, although not always, larger. A super regional center typically contains a GLA of about 900,000 square feet but can range from 500,000 to 2 million square feet; a few centers exceed 2 million square feet. *Dollars & Cents of Shopping Centers: 1998* reports a median size of 948,632 square feet based on a sample of 76 super regional centers.

Regional and super regional centers generally seek to reproduce all of the shopping facilities once available only in central business districts. They provide primarily a full depth and variety of shopping goods, general merchandise, shoes, clothing and accessories, home furnishings, gifts and specialty items, and electronics. Increasingly, they also provide food, personal services, and entertainment. The main attraction, around which the center is built, has traditionally been the department store, which as a rule has a minimum GLA of 75,000 square feet but ranges from about 40,000 square feet in smaller markets and older centers to more than 200,000 square feet, particularly in super regional centers.

As a result of bankruptcies and consolidation in the department store industry during the late 1980s and early 1990s, a shortage of suitable department store anchors occurred. Consequently, nontraditional anchors that earlier would have been considered inappropriate or unworkable are now becoming commonplace in regional and super regional centers. These new-generation anchors include elaborate food courts, large off-price category killers, megaplex cinemas, and specialized, large-scale entertainment attractions. The range of tenant types also continues to expand in regional and super regional centers, with more than 140 types reported in the latest *Dollars & Cents* survey.

Regional and super regional malls do not differ in function—only in their range and strength in attracting customers. Regional centers typically serve a population in excess of 150,000 people, who will often travel more than 25 to 30 minutes to reach the center. Super regional centers require a larger trade area that typically includes a minimum of 300,000 people. Both regional and super regional centers attract customers through their ability to offer a full range of shopping facilities and goods, thereby extending their trade areas to the fullest extent possible. In some cases, the trade areas of regional and super regional centers may overlap. Customers will sometimes pass a smaller regional mall to shop at a super regional mall to take advantage of greater choice and more diverse tenants. The sites for regional and super regional centers vary dramatically—from ten acres or less for a vertical multilevel urban center to more than 100 acres for a large single-level exurban on.

Community Shopping Centers

Community centers were developed initially around a junior department store or large variety store as anchor tenants in addition to a supermarket. Of all the basic center types, community centers have undergone and continue to undergo the most change. The original typical anchor tenants-a junior department store and a variety store-were largely supplanted in the 1970s and 1980s as principal anchor tenants by discount or off-price department stores such as Kmart or Marshalls or by a strong specialty store such as a hardware, building/home improvement, furniture, or catalog store. In the late 1980s and 1990s, expanded-format stores, often known as category killers and specializing in such items as books, sporting goods, and office supplies, became anchor options. A new form of community center, the power center, appeared. It contains multiple off-price and category killer anchors and few side tenants.

A community shopping center can be defined largely by what it does and does not have. It does not have a full line department store, which would automatically categorize it as a regional shopping center. It does have a market area larger than a neighborhood center and thus draws customers from a longer distance. It offers greater depth and range of merchandise in shopping and specialty goods than the neighborhood center. It tends also to provide certain categories of goods, particularly commodities, that are less likely to be found in regional centers, such as furniture, hardware, and garden and building supplies. The community center is the "in-between" center, and so it is the most difficult to categorize. Some neighborhood centers have the potential to grow into community centers, just as some community centers can expand into power or regional centers.

The community center typically has a GLA of about 150,000 square feet but can range from 100,000 to 450,000 square feet (and more) in some cases. The median center size, out of a sample of 287 centers reported in *Dollars & Cents of Shopping Centers: 1998*, was 157,298 square feet. The community center needs a site of ten to 30 acres, normally serves a trade area of 40,000 to 150,000 people within a ten- to 20–minute drive, and has a typical parking index of five spaces per 1,000 square feet of GLA, which ranges from four to six spaces.

Because the range for this type of center is so great, a new subcategory was established in the 1980s-the super community center. Super community centers range from 250,000 to more than 500,000 square feet, with a median of 316,795 square feet in a sample of 56 such centers. The top five tenants found in super community centers are women's ready-to-wear, family shoes, men's wear, women's specialty wear, and family wear.

In metropolitan areas, a community center can be quite vulnerable to competition. It is too large to thrive off its immediate neighborhood trade area but too small to make a strong impact on the whole community unless it is located in a smaller city with a population ranging from 50,000 to 100,000. The development of a strong regional center, with the pulling power of one or more department stores, may impinge on a community center's trade area if both centers sell the same types of merchandise. In a typical market area, however, both can succeed even if they are close to each other because of the difference in the types of merchandise offered and because they form a synergistic shopping destination that is stronger than each center would be standing alone.

In cities with populations of 50,000 to 100,000, the community center, although lacking a full-line department store, may actually take on the stature of a regional center because of the center's local dominance and pulling power. An off-price or discount store may function as the leading tenant, substituting for a full-line department store.

Of all the shopping center types, the community shopping center is the most difficult to categorize in terms of its anchors, market size, and drawing power. Because the community center offers increasingly large amounts of shopping goods and, in certain cases, special categories of goods, the market are a is less predictable. In the case of major subtypes such as off-price megamalls and power centers, the trade area can be as large as for regional shopping centers, and instead of traditional anchors such as a grocery store, drugstore, or junior department store, they have multiple anchors, including category killers and other big-box formats.

Neighborhood Shopping Centers

The neighborhood center provides for the sale of convenience goods (food, drugs, and sundries) and personal services (those that meet the daily needs of an immediate neighborhood trade area). A supermarket or superstore that combines grocery shopping with a pharmacy and other convenience goods and services is the principal anchor tenant in most neighborhood centers. Consumer shopping patterns show that geographical convenience is the most important factor in determining a shopper's choice of supermarkets. A wide selection of merchandise and customer service is a secondary consideration. Other principal tenants in neighborhood centers are drugstores and small variety stores. Often, centers without a supermarket but similar in GLA to neighborhood centers are also referred to as neighborhood centers; however, unless other food tenants can be aggregated as the equivalent of a supermarket, the center would probably be more appropriately classified as a small community center (because to be successful it would likely have to draw from a larger market area).

The neighborhood center has a typical GLA of about 50,000 square feet but ranges from 30,000 to 100,000 square feet, with a median size of 65,279 square feet based on a sample of 233 centers. Requiring a site of three to ten acres, the neighborhood center normally serves a trade area of 3,000 to 40,000 people within a five- to ten-minute drive. The parking index is about five spaces per 1,000 square feet of GLA, somewhat lower than for larger shopping centers, as customers do not spend as much time on each visit and turnover of vehicles is higher.

Convenience Shopping Centers

The convenience center contains a group of small shops and stores dedicated to providing a limited range of personal services and sundries for customers making a quick stop. The center is commonly anchored by a convenience market (often referred to as a minimart), and its tenants are similar to those found in neighborhood centers. Tenants most frequently found in convenience centers are restaurants and other food services; personal services such as dry cleaners, beauty parlors, and photocopy stores; and professional services such as medical doctors and dentists, and finance, insurance, and real estate offices. Frequently a convenience center is an adjunct to a neighborhood shopping center and as such functions as an integral part of that center, but it may also be a freestanding entity.

Typically, a convenience center is about 20,000 square feet of GLA, but it does not exceed 30,000 square feet. Customers typically live near the center and walk or drive to it on the way to other activities. Sales per customer are typically small and often involve a limited number of items that may have been forgotten on previous shopping trips or single items for which convenience and speed of purchase are more important than price.

B. FINANCE AND LAND USE APPROVAL

Michael D. Beyard & W. Paul O'Mara, Shopping Center Development Handbook*
74–76, 81–83 (3d ed. 1999, Urban Land Institute Development Handbook Series).

Financing

Like the shopping center industry itself, development financing continues to change considerably. Yet in the midst of these changes, a basic fact remains: a shopping center will attract debt and equity investment based on the anticipated return to all financial participants. Whatever the type of center, projected income and expenses are still the key to financing the project.

Successful shopping center developers are those who not only are aware of the marketing and economic feasibility of a project but also are strongly connected to reliable sources of development capital. The source of shopping center financing depends on many variables. In the past, many regional shopping centers were financed by conventional first mortgage debt, minimizing the equity requirements and creating satisfactory returns for owners and developers. But "construction debt for new or renovated centers has become more difficult to obtain. Most lenders limit the percentage of cost they will lend. They are reluctant to assume excessive risk for this or any type of real estate projects. This has forced many developers to look for financial partners to provide the equity investment. Other developers have turned to the public financial market for sources of equity." [footnote omitted]

Sources of Financing

Experienced developers have long recognized the need to maintain close contact with lenders and financial consultants. Today, this need is stronger than ever. In today's changing capital markets, the source of financing for a particular shopping center can depend on the size of the developer, the size of the center, the tenants, and the area of the country. In any case, the financing being sought must be part of the project's overall financial plan and must fit within the economic confines of the project's potential income, cash flow, tax benefits, and appreciation of value. In some cases, more than one source of financing will be necessary.

Conventional sources of financing for shopping centers generally include insurance companies and pension funds as permanent lenders, with commercial banks and a small number of credit companies as short- and medium-term lenders. When loan delinquencies increased in the late 1980s and early 1990s because of the real estate recession, banks and insurance companies reduced their loan exposure. When they started making loans again, the only element that had changed was that standards for underwriting loans were tightened. At least ten major sources of financing are currently used:

- Life insurance companies,

- Pension funds,
- Banks,
- S & Ls and savings banks,
- Finance and credit companies,
- Investment banks and securities firms,
- Real estate investment trusts,
- Syndications,
- Government funds, and
- Foreign investors.

Each source has its own criteria for investment. A proposed shopping center that is acceptable to one source may be of no interest to another. And as the sources change over time, deals made two or three years ago may be totally unacceptable today. Developers need to remember that lenders match types of loans with their liabilities, which could involve consumer savings accounts, money market deposit accounts, trusts and separate accounts, securities, and time deposits. As the sources of lenders' funds change, so too will the types of deals they may be willing to make.

. . .

Preparing the Financing Package

Money is the most important ingredient in the process of developing a shopping center and the developer a shopping center and the developer must exercise extreme care in creating the financing package. Whether preparing the package internally or using a consultant, the developer must disclose all project information clearly and accurately. The following items should be included in a loan package.

- A letter of transmittal that states the nature of the project and the amount of funds being requested;
- A market or feasibility study prepared by a recognized consulting firm that discusses trade area, population characteristics, competition, metropolitan growth, and all other factors that would affect the feasibility of the developer's proposal;
- A disclosure of all property characteristics, including a survey, site plan, building plans, photographs, and renderings;
- A detailed cash flow statement containing rent schedules, expenses, HVAC charges, common area maintenance costs, percentage rents, and all other items pertaining to the revenue and expenses of the proposed project;
- All legal documents, including the property deed or the sales contract, the title insurance policy, any letters of intent to lease, the lease forms, and all attachments and exhibits that are part of these documents;
- A detailed cost estimate of the project along with a projected construction schedule;
- A report on the developer's experience, including a description of other projects the developer has completed.

Although this list describes the traditional requirements for a loan package, developers should also be aware of certain basic elements of equity financing for limited partnerships and REITs. All public syndications must be registered with the Securities and Exchange Commission (SEC) and with all regulating agencies in the states where the offering will be sold. Small, private offerings do not have to register with the SEC, but both public and private offerings must disclose information on the proposed syndication, including:

- Specific standards for minimum income, net worth, and tax bracket that a "suitable" investor should possess as well as the minimum amounts each partner must invest;
- The promoter's or sponsor's compensation in all its forms, such as management fees, brokerage commissions, resale profit, interest income, and interests in the partnership;
- The rights of the limited partners, including the right to inspect partnership records and to take action against the promoters or sponsors in the event of fraud or negligence;
- The agreement to make periodic reports to the investors, which, for public offerings, must be filed with the SEC and state commissions.

Developers should analyze their financing needs with the help of their lenders and consultants to derive the most appropriate financial structure for their particular projects. In all probability, side space will be leased, but the anchor space and pad space can be handled in any of three ways: sale, ground lease, or build-to-suit space. Each has its own advantages:

- Advantages of a Sale-immediate liquidity, no direct economic problems resulting from vacant space, easier documentation, faster transaction.
- Advantages of a Ground Lease-low capital requirements, limited concerns about credit, reversion of the building at the end of the lease term, more control, lower cost per square foot for financing . . .
- Advantages of Build-to-Suit Space-greater long-term potential for higher value, depreciability, higher base for rental escalation than for a ground lease, probable lower sale or lender cap rate with the anchor in the deal.

Other Factors Affecting a Project's Feasibility

Land Use Controls

Any site for a proposed shopping center requires favorable zoning for a developer to be able to proceed. Thus, the comprehensive plan provisions and applicable zoning in effect for a site must be carefully studied before a site is purchased. An early study explores the attitudes toward a proposed shopping center of local residents, the planning and zoning staff, and the approving body. A project's feasibility is greatly affected by current zoning regulations, as well-as by time and expenses that will be required for approval or rezoning.

Areas of rapid growth generally try to streamline the approval process and to allocate adequate land for new development. In areas of rapid growth where slow growth has been advocated, permits may be difficult to obtain, restrictions profuse, and rezoning next to impossible, with little land available for new development. In areas where growth is moderate, a developer can expect any possible regulatory climate, depending on the size, staffing, and sophistication of the jurisdiction, the availability of land and its geographic characteristics, and on a host of other variables.

Each locality has to be approached as a new experience, because procedures, time frames, and dispositions vary widely from area to area. In some cases, the site proposed for a shopping center may not be planned for commercial or mixed use when the development process begins. For regional and super regional centers, the cost of accumulating large enough parcels of land on which to build a shopping center may be prohibitive if the land has not already been zoned for commercial use. In other cases, a site may be zoned for commercial use, but the ordinance may have to be modified with regard to such provisions as floor/area ratio, building height, parking requirements, lot coverage, or setbacks, to name a few.

In downtown or inner-city areas where local governments are attempting to rebuild their retail base, zoning incentives may be in place for shopping centers, although it is rare that zoning approvals are expedited, given the complexity of building *anything* in an urban environment. Condemnations, land assembly, demolition, integration with historic districts, training for residents and requirements for employment, infrastructure improvements, and construction of structured parking are some of the most important issues that must be negotiated and settled as part of the development process in most urban areas. Nevertheless, local governments are increasingly willing to work closely with shopping center developers as partners to expedite local land use controls and to create retail centers that meet public and private goals.

NOTES

1. *Lawyer's Role.* Finance, marketing and design professionals may dominate the early stages of shopping center assembly but there are also important tasks for the developer's lawyer to perform. Before an option on a site is exercised, or a contract closed, a perimeter survey must be examined and a title report reviewed. The site should be inspected for any unrecorded easements or other restrictions that might interfere with construction of the shopping center or access to it. A dirt pathway cutting across a corner of the site may indicate a neighboring landowner's prescriptive right of way. A visible sewer connection may be the tip-off to an underground network of pipes, access to which is protected by an implied easement. Even express, recorded easements can require a lawyer's judgment to resolve ambiguities respecting the easement's location, extent, nature and duration. In evaluating these restrictions, the lawyer must think not only of the client developer's willingness to proceed without quitclaim deeds from the easement's holders, but also the willingness of construction and permanent lenders to accept these possible impairments to their security.

Building and occupancy permits have to be obtained. Favorable zoning for the proposed development is just the starting point. Will the zoning ordinance permit commercial uses such as movie theaters and bowling alleys that, though not presently included in the center plans, may be added at some future point? Setback, parking, sign and height variances may have to be individually negotiated unless the site is in a zone that permits shopping centers to be proposed in the more flexible, easily negotiated format of a planned unit development. In addition to negotiating with the planning department and planning commission, the architectural review board, and the maps, buildings, streets and highway departments, the developer and her lawyer may have to confront the political process more directly, in meetings and through compromises negotiated with the city council or other local legislative body, as well as with neighbors and local environmental groups. Regional shopping centers, particularly, may be a significant indirect source of automotive emissions so that compliance with federal, state, and local air quality regulations will be required.

Title insurance can absorb the risk of some legal judgments. The owner's or lender's title policy, and endorsements to them, can insure that all parcels comprising the center are contiguous and lie within the commercial zone indicated on the municipality's zoning map, that the parcels described in the deeds and title policy correspond to those outlined on the survey maps, that no structure encroaches on an easement, and that the easements and covenants in the reciprocal easement agreements between the shopping center occupants are valid and enforceable according to their terms.

2. *Permanent Lender's Role.* If anchor stores set the shopping center's tone, it is the permanent lender who dictates the center's financial structure and underlying legal arrangements. Must the developer acquire the fee or will a ground lease suffice? Will the ground lessor be required to subordinate its interest to the lender's? What terms must appear in the ground lease and in the space leases? These are all points, often deal points, for the permanent lender's decision. Inevitably, these decisions also affect the center's complexion and tone. Because anchors today so frequently own or ground lease the land they occupy in the shopping center, their land and improvements are not part of the lender's security, so that lenders must look for added security to rent payments from satellite tenants. This added security frequently takes the form of a requirement that as many as sixty-five to seventy-five per cent of the satellite tenants be high credit firms, often national chains.

What of lender liability? In Yousef v. Trustbank Savings, F.S.B., 81 Md.App. 527, 568 A.2d 1134 (1990), appellants purchased a shopping center. The original mortgagee permitted appellants to assume the existing mortgage in exchange for a $50,000 fee. The commitment agreement provided that "Borrower shall provide Lender copies of leases representing not less than eighty-five percent (85%) of the net rentable area, which leases must be satisfactory to Lender in all respects." Id. at 534, 568 A.2d at 1137. The seller warranted to appellants that 91% of the space was rented; the mortgagee approved the leases. When appellants discovered that some of the leases did not exist, they sued the lender claiming that it had negligently failed to inspect the leases. The court, however, rejected lender liability: "Appellants' reliance upon that provision of the Commitment Agreement, is, to put it mildly, misplaced. We point out to appellants that the provision requires that the leases be satisfactory in all respects to the *lender*. . . . A provision such as the one relied upon by the appellants is purely and simply for the protection of the lender, it is not for the protection of the buyer." Id. (emphasis added).

For panoramic views of shopping center finance, see Siegelaub & Meistrich, How the Professional Shopping Center Developer Obtains a Mortgage, 9 Real Est. Rev. 50 (Spr.1979); Rogers & Brown, Shopping Center Financing, 43 U.M.K.C. L.Rev. 1 (1974). See also, Halper, People and Property: The Anatomy of a Ground Lease, 3 Real Est.Rev. 9 (Fall 1973); Practising Law Institute, Business and Legal Problems of Shopping Centers 39–59 (3d ed. 1971); Minskoff, Mortgaging-Out the Regional Mall, 7 Real Est.Rev. 38 (Fall 1977).

3. *Developer's Role.* Within the conservative lending policies established by permanent lenders and those who regulate them, considerable leeway remains for the shopping center developer to achieve her own financial objectives, probably the most cherished of which is "mortgaging out" the shopping center—obtaining a nonrecourse loan for one hundred percent or more of her land and development costs. How can she achieve this object within the limits set by lender's loan-to-value ratios? One answer lies in the fact that these ratios are calculated on the basis of the center's appraised value, not its cost, so that the entrepreneur who assembles a solid group of tenants on a well-situated parcel can get an appraisal and a loan well exceeding her costs. Another answer lies in the use of component financing through which the cost of appliances such as air conditioning, electrical, and plumbing systems is directly financed by their suppliers or manufacturers who will take back a second or more subordinate lien as security.

C. LEASING AND OPERATIONS

1.   COORDINATING LANDLORD AND TENANT INTERESTS

Michael D. Beyard & W. Paul O'Mara, Shopping Center Development Handbook*

68–74 (3d ed. 1999, Urban Land Institute Development Handbook Series).

Securing Commitments from Tenants

Anchors

As a rule, a shopping center will not be built until the developer has secured commitments from key tenants. The choice of key tenants is critical, because they heavily influence site design, building design, layout, and overall composition of tenants. In short, they determine the center's basic character and image.

It bears repeating that anchor tenants of a convenience center are usually a minimart or some other convenience service that customers are likely to visit daily. Anchor tenants for a neighborhood center are typically a supermarket and a drugstore (with a single supermarket/drugstore combination having become more prevalent in recent years in many markets); the key tenants of a community center are a discount or off-price department store, variety store, hardware/building/home improvement store, combined drug/variety/

---

garden center, and supermarket. Key tenants of a regional or super regional center are full-line department stores (generally at least 75,000 to 100,000 square feet each), and the most successful super regional centers include at least three department stores. Few regional centers are being constructed in the late 1990s except in specialized urban locations where limited space precludes having more than one or two anchors. Power centers typically have four or more big-box category killers and often include a discount department store as well. An entertainment center is typically anchored by a new-generation cinema complex. The anchors for hybrid centers are less predictable but equally important to the center's success.

The list of tenants considered viable anchors is gradually expanding in response to changing consumer demand, evolving market niches, and the need to differentiate centers from their competitors in a generally overbuilt market. Elaborate food courts, entertainment centers, and groups of specialized tenants under the same corporate umbrella that together form a powerful draw similar to a department store increasingly are deemed anchors. In addition, as shopping centers continue to expand into previously underserved urban areas, nontraditional anchors that may not even be part of the shopping center—cultural facilities, historic districts, entertainment centers, sports facilities, convention centers, airport terminals, train stations, tourist attractions, and casinos, for example—nonetheless may perform the same function of drawing customers.

Traditionally, the commitment of an anchor tenant represents a form of partnership between it and the developer; for this reason, the anchor tenant should be carefully considered in the developer's land and building plans. Key tenants' requirements-often including firm ideas about the center's general arrangement and their locations in the center-influence the developer's decisions on leasing, financial negotiations, building treatment, architectural style, parking provisions, signage, and landscaping. Thus, before site planning or further leasing occurs, key tenants must be committed to the center. At this stage, the project's form begins to adapt to the characteristics of the site and the potential of the trade area. In a high-income area, for example, two high-fashion stores may sign as tenants, creating a higher quality image for a proposed center. In this case, the quality of the market determines the type of center suitable to the area. The image of the leading tenant in tum determines the type of satellite tenants suitable to a particular center. If a discount store were the key tenant, however, all factors in planning for tenants would be different. The wrong key tenant can complicate the problem of leasing to satellite tenants. On the other hand, leasing to a mix of tenants that is too homogeneous, even in high-income areas, has proved to be a mistake. Increasingly, a mix of tenants representing a range of prices that expand the market for a particular center has proved successful. For example, Mazza Gallerie, a specialty center in Washington, D.C., includes both Neiman Marcus and Filene's Basement.

In the early stages of development, the owner/developer or the leasing agent must determine what key tenants are available—an increasingly difficult task for regional centers, given the saturation of most trade areas with department stores and the dearth of department store chains capable of entering a new market area. A competent real estate leasing agent can recognize and assess the characteristics of major key tenants, their goals for expansion, their preferred lease or occupancy provisions, the relationships they have with the developer, and commitments they have made for other projects and sites. The agent should also know under what conditions these tenants will be available or unavailable and what arrangements may make them attract other tenants. Because of the need to deal with the subtleties of selecting tenants, the leasing agent or real estate expert must be on the development team from the start, working with the market analyst .and guiding the developer and his architect, engineer, and planner. Some developers have in-house leasing experts. Successful developers who use outside agents know enough about the field so that they need not rely entirely on outside advice to resolve critical questions.

After key tenants have been committed—preferably through a "letter of intent" or other clear expression of interest (if not an actual lease or occupancy agreement)—a rough building and site layout can be prepared. Based on data from the market and economic analyses, supplementary tenant classifications can be used to produce an overall leasing plan.

Leases with supplementary tenants are negotiated after the major tenants have signed leases or made commitments. Commitments or expressions of interest from supplementary or satellite tenants precede firming the financing plan and any preparation of construction details. In addition, developers do not start final plans or even complete the site acquisition until they have received zoning approval, which may impose economically infeasible conditions. Final commitments from major tenants typically are subject to zoning approval.

A prospectus presented as an attractive brochure makes a useful exhibit in explaining to potential tenants findings of the market, site advantages, the tentative arrangement of building and site, commitments from key tenants, and the developer's track record and reputation. A rendering of the architectural treatment showing, for example, whether a mall will be open or enclosed and how tenant spaces will be configured is also necessary, particularly for some new forms of shopping centers, such as urban entertainment centers where anchors are positioned in complex, sometimes multilevel, configurations throughout the project to draw customers through the center. In this type of situation, negotiations with tenants can be far more complex; in fact, negotiations may have to be reopened as development evolves.

The developer should have a lease form to present to satellite or in-line tenants and should inform tenants of basic economic provisions early in the process. Matters that involve the tenant's tax participation, contributions to common area maintenance, participation in a marketing fund or a merchants' association, the rental scale, overage and percentage rents, and the promotional program should be resolved in the proposed form. Any satellite tenants should be located so that pedestrian traffic is well distributed to encourage convenience and impulse buying. For some entertainment tenants, a range of partnership options must be considered in lieu of standard lease forms.

When it is not possible to have a key tenant committed to the project early in the process, developers may proceed (at their own risk) with certain efforts, such as obtaining zoning clearance, while they continue to negotiate with major department stores.

The Leasing Plan

Because the leasing plan, in the broadest sense, represents the center's potential for investment, it is the key in projecting the center's rental income. It should be prepared early in the development process and should address the following points:

• The Placement of Tenants—Tenants should be located to draw the maximum pedestrian flow past as much store frontage as possible. Placement should consider the strength of each tenant's draw.

• Building Depths—Normally the depth for in-line tenants should not exceed 120 feet for mall shops or stores in an open center. Shops of small tenants in neighborhood centers can be 60 to 100 feet deep. Shops in malls should not exceed 40 feet wide except for courts and promotional areas. A balanced tenant mix should provide both strong, credit-rated national firms and good local merchants to meet lenders' requirements for financial credit. Building depths for anchors in malls and open-air centers are much greater. Each anchor chain has its own standardized footprint and requirements for space, although in unusual circumstances it will negotiate the dimensions.

• The Tenant Mix—The mix of tenants should be largely determined by the merchandising plan, although not all goals of the original plan will necessarily be met. Tenants' preferences and resistance to suggestions will likely result in a number of compromises, and repositioning will require constant attention if the merchandising plan is to direct leasing.

• "Pricing" for Each Store Space—Pricing depends on the tenant's size, classification, location in the project, and amount of tenant improvement allowance. This amount should be updated constantly as the project moves from speculation to a finalized program.

• Detailed Rent Schedules—Rent schedules should clearly indicate the tenant's name, classification, square footage allocated, minimum rent, and rate of percentage rent. The tenant's share of costs for INAC should be projected. This schedule also must be continuously updated.

• Method of Handling Tenant Finishes—The preferred approach is to provide shell space plus an allowance for finishing the space to tenants' specifications. This method should be followed, even if a greater allowance is sometimes necessary to produce a "turnkey" solution for a particular tenant. In the case of elaborate entertainment-related tenants, partnership arrangements often require the tenant to finish its own space.

• The Lease Form—The lease should require a minimum of processing, with exhibits attached showing the landlord's work, the tenant's work, HVAC rate schedules, other applicable rate schedules, and other related matters, including the site plan and criteria for signage. The lease form can be modified most easily through addenda, which provide a ready reference for changes applicable to specific tenants.

The lease should provide for tenants' payments to cover the costs of operation for common areas, including maintenance, insurance, HVAC, and real estate taxes. These charges are typically prorated based on the GLA each tenant occupies; commonly exempted are key tenants, whose payment schedules are prearranged. If separate metering has not been provided, the lease should clearly define the responsibilities for the payment of HVAC, gas, and electricity costs. With today's unpredictable energy costs, however, separate metering is strongly recommended. "Escalator clauses" should provide for the increased costs of labor, energy, administration, and replacement parts.

Lease provisions help define the landlord's fiscal obligations. Generally, they are well known to national tenants, but local tenants, who are unaccustomed to the complexity and comprehensiveness of such provisions because of the limited scope of their operations, may resist them. The developer should nevertheless negotiate such costs with the tenants, explaining why their inclusion in the lease is essential. Owners of stronger centers can insist on reducing the fiscal uncertainty they must face, but the preceding principles are useful in structuring leases for any present-day shopping center.

Department stores in a regional shopping center are treated differently from other tenants. Key department stores may build their own stores on land bought or leased from the developer. They usually do not build their own parking areas, but they should contribute funds to the developer. The developer must have satisfactory reciprocal operating agreements that provide for handling on-site and off-site construction costs, easements, operation of common areas, operating hours, security, the marketing fund or merchants' association, the "common department store" wall, and other expenses. Long-term cross-easements and agreements are extremely important to the permanent lender, the tenants, and the developer. Reciprocal easement agreements are necessary in any center with separate legal ownership or any type of site sharing uses, such as freestanding banks, service stations, or restaurants.

To encourage department stores to enter the project on a buy/build basis, land can be sold to them at an appraised value, or at or below cost. The amount of money involved, while substantial, represents a smaller subsidy than the amount that would result from a fairly favorable gross lease. The developer typically sells to the department store not only a building pad but also necessary improvements in parking. For extremely desirable anchor department stores, the developer may even pay for construction and interior finishes, although this practice is not common. In any case, the negotiated sale price rarely reflects the prorated off-site and on-site improvement costs attributed to the land area sold.

2. TENANT RIGHTS AND OBLIGATIONS

a. TENANT'S RIGHTS AND OBLIGATION TO USE THE PREMISES

Oakwood Village LLC v. Albertsons, Inc.

Supreme Court of Utah, 2004.
104 P.3d 1226.

DURHAM, CHIEF JUSTICE:

BACKGROUND

Plaintiff Oakwood Village, LLC (Oakwood), a commercial real estate developer, appeals the trial court's dismissal of its suit for "failure to state a claim upon which relief can be granted." Utah R. Civ. P. 12(b)(6). Oakwood claims that the trial court erred when it held that a covenant of continuous operation does not inhere in every ground lease as a matter of law. Additionally, Oakwood appeals the court's order that it pay defendants' reasonable attorney fees pursuant to paragraph 20 of the lease between Oakwood and Albertsons, Inc. (Albertsons), in which the parties agreed that the losing party in any suit relating to the lease would pay all of the prevailing party's reasonable attorney fees.

The three issues in this appeal are whether the trial court erred in (1) holding that a covenant of continuous operation does not inhere in every ground lease as a matter of law; (2) dismissing this case without addressing Oakwood's claim for breach of an implied covenant of good faith and fair dealing, notwithstanding this court's decision in *St. Benedict's Development Co. v. St. Benedict's Hospital,* 811 P.2d 194, 201 (Utah 1991); and (3) dismissing Oakwood's suit based on a factual determination made from material attached to the pleadings that contradicted the averments in the complaint. After considering all materials in the pleadings, we find that the lease between Oakwood and Albertsons contains no implied covenant of continuous operation and that Albertsons's conduct, while perhaps not nice, did not violate the implied covenant of good faith and fair dealing inherent in the lease. We also find that the trial court properly disposed of this case under a motion to dismiss, as opposed to converting the motion to dismiss into a motion for summary judgment, as defendants argue the trial court should have done.

FACTS

On May 23, 1978, defendant Albertsons, a retail supermarket, entered into a ground lease with plaintiff Oakwood Village LLC's predecessor-in-interest, Oakwood Development Company (collectively referred to as Oakwood). On April 1, 1979, Albertsons assigned its leasehold interest in Oakwood Village Shopping Center (Oakwood Village) to One Hamilton Associates Limited Partnership (One Hamilton), also a defendant in this suit. However, under the original lease between Oakwood and Albertsons, Albertsons remains liable for One Hamilton's "full performance of Tenant's obligations."

Pursuant to the original contract, Albertsons leased a 42,800-square-foot plot in the 123,900-square-foot Oakwood Village Shopping

Center that Oakwood was then developing in Murray, Utah. Oakwood Village consists of twenty-six stores located on the center's property, and Albertsons was to function as the center's anchor tenant. The initial term of the ground lease was twenty-five years, with the option of eight five-year renewal terms, for a total of sixty-five years if Albertsons so desired. Under the lease and three subsequent amendments to it, Albertsons was to pay a monthly rental fee of $1667 ($20,000 per year) with no escalations in price, and all taxes, assessments, and utility charges on the leased premises for the duration of the lease. Among other terms, the lease contained an exclusive business provision precluding Oakwood from leasing space in the center to other supermarket tenants. The parties recorded the terms of their agreement in three documents: a ground lease (the lease), a development agreement (the agreement), and a declaration of restrictions and rights of easement (the declaration).

After completing lease negotiations with Oakwood, Albertsons constructed and paid for a building on the leased premises. Upon completion of the building in January 1980, Albertsons occupied the space where it had operated a grocery store for more than twenty-one years. In May 2001, after perceiving a better opportunity in a new shopping center across the street, Albertsons ceased operating on the leased premises and moved one block south to become the anchor tenant in the Marketplace on Ninth shopping center (Marketplace on Ninth).

After it relocated, Albertsons "went dark" at its location in Oakwood Village while continuing to pay the monthly rent on the now vacant building. Oakwood alleged, and defendants' counsel admitted at trial, that Albertsons's intentionally kept the old building unoccupied in order to restrict competition with its new store. Oakwood attributes Albertsons departure from Oakwood Village as the cause of the decline in sales of its remaining stores and the current vacancy of four stores, the occupants of three of which followed Albertsons to the new center.

On April 18, 2002, Oakwood advised Albertsons that it had breached its obligation under the lease to operate continuously and to act in good faith and deal fairly, and demanded that Albertsons remedy its breach within thirty days pursuant to the lease. Albertsons responded on May 3, 2002, refusing to acknowledge breach of the lease or to take any curative action. Thereafter, Oakwood filed suit against Albertsons for breach of the aforementioned covenants. For Albertsons alleged contractual breaches, Oakwood sought declaratory relief allowing it to terminate the lease and to re-enter and re-let the premises, and damages in excess of $1,000,000.

. . .

ANALYSIS

. . .

II. SUBSTANTIVE ISSUES

Oakwood raises two main substantive arguments. First, it argues that an implied covenant of continuous operation requires Albertsons to remain open throughout the entire term of the lease. Because the lease contains no continuous operation provision expressly giving Albertsons the right to go dark, Oakwood contends that Albertsons is prohibited from ceasing its grocery store operation at any time during the lease term. Second, Oakwood argues that even assuming that Albertsons has the discretion to cease operation the covenant of good faith and fair dealing inherent in the lease prohibits Albertsons from paying rent on a vacant building to restrict competition with its new store. Oakwood argues that such an act demonstrates bad faith under the circumstances and violates an implied covenant.

A.   Implied Covenant of Continuous Operation

1.   Contractual Terms

We first address the issue of whether a covenant of continuous operation is implied in the parties' lease. The language of the relevant contracts between Oakwood and Albertsons establishing the lease appears to be complete and unambiguous, so we apply the "four corners" rule of contract analysis, looking no further than the language of the lease. E. Allan Farnsworth, *Farnsworth on Contracts* § 7.12 (2d ed. 2001). In the absence of an express covenant of continuous operation, the question becomes whether this court may infer such a covenant from the language of the lease or the conduct of the parties. *See St. Benedict's,* 811 P.2d at 198. Where the law is reluctant to recognize express restrictive covenants, such as a covenant of continuous operation, it is even more reluctant to infer them. *See id.* Recognizing that "[a] continuous operations clause in a lengthy lease has the potential to bind the lessee to operate a business in the leased premises even if it is disastrously unprofitable," *Forrest Drive Assocs. v. Wal-Mart Stores, Inc.,* 72 F.Supp.2d 576, 584 n. 3 (M.D.N.C.1999), courts have been willing to infer restrictive covenants only under certain "extreme circumstances," *St. Benedict's,* 811 P.2d at 198, when supported by "substantial evidence," 5 *Thompson on Real Property* § 44.14[f][2] (David A. Thomas ed., 1994) [hereinafter Thompson]. Two such circumstances in which we have suggested that we may infer a covenant of continuous operation are (1) where there is "plain and unmistakable language in the relevant contracts which would support the restrictive covenant"; and (2) where there is a "legal necessity" to imply a restrictive covenant "to effectuate the intent of the parties." *St. Benedict's,* 811 P.2d at 198. Oakwood argues that both circumstances exist here, although it focuses primarily on the first. We address each in turn.

Oakwood argues that five "plain and unmistakable" provisions in the relevant contracts demonstrate the parties' intention that "the anchor tenant space in the Center [be] occupied continuously by a supermarket or some other suitable magnet retailer for the purpose of drawing shoppers to the Center." These five provisions are (1) a non-compete, or exclusive business, provision precluding Oakwood from leasing space in Oakwood Village to other supermarkets; (2) the sixty-five-year potential duration of the lease; (3) the nominal rent; (4) the language of the development agreement stating that Albertsons will participate with Oakwood in the development of the center "as an integrated retail sales complex for the mutual benefit of all real property in the Shopping Center"; and (5) the references in the lease to Albertsons "supermarket and other similar retail uses" and "proposed retail facilities."

Defendants counter that six equally "plain and unmistakable provisions" prevent any reasonable implication of a covenant of continuous operation (1) the absence of a percentage-rent clause, which numerous courts have found central to implying a covenant of continuous operation; (2) the absence of a use clause specifying the kind of retail business for which Albertsons's may occupy the premises; (3) Albertsons's unrestricted right to sublet or assign its lease to another tenant; (4) Albertsons entitlement to all fixtures on the leased premises and its right to remove those fixtures at any time; (5) Oakwood's failure to make abandonment an event of "default" or to include a "going dark" provision as is common in virtually every shopping center lease; and (6) language providing that Albertsons need not rebuild a damaged or destroyed building.

We agree with defendants that the relevant contracts do not contain plain and unmistakable language from which this court will find an implied covenant of continuous operation. In fact, we believe on the contrary that the plain and unmistakable language of those contracts prevents us from inferring such a covenant. Because we find defendants' references to those documents convincing to their argument, we discuss each of the provisions they cite.

First, the fact that a percentage-rent provision is absent from the lease at issue substantially undermines Oakwood's proposition that the lease contains an implied covenant of continuous operation. The reason is that a "tenant's agreement to pay percentage rent coupled with an inadequate or insubstantial minimum or base rent" has been "[b]y far, the most popular rationale among the courts that have found implied continuous operation covenants in leases." Kathleen A. Furlong & Phyllis A. Volk, Continuous Operation Clauses, *in* 1 *The Commercial Property Lease* 71, 73 (Patrick A. Randolph, Jr. ed., 1993). A percentage-rent clause is "one that fixes the rent in whole or in part on the receipts from the tenant's use of the premises." Milton R. Friedman, 1 *Friedman on Leases* § 6:1, at 6–2 (Patrick A. Randolph, Jr. ed., 2004) [hereinafter Friedman]. It is commonly written into lease agreements to protect the landlord against inflation and the tenant against deflation where the lease is long-term. *Id.* Because payments under a percentage-rent arrangement are possible only when the tenant occupies the premises, most courts have inferred a covenant of continuous operation in a lease containing a percentage-rent clause where either the entire rental payment was predicated on a fixed percentage of the tenant's gross receipts or the base rent payable by the tenant was inadequate to fairly compensate the landlord. Furlong & Volk, *supra,* at 73. A number of cases illustrate the importance that courts have placed on a percentage-rent provision to a finding of an implied covenant of continuous operation in a lease. *See, e.g., First Am. Bank & Trust Co. v. Safeway Stores,* 151 Ariz. 584, 729 P.2d 938 (Ct.App.1986) (inferring a covenant of continuous operation from an inadequate base rent in a percentage-rent provision); *E. Broadway Corp. v. Taco Bell Corp.,* 542 N.W.2d 816 (Iowa 1996) (finding an implied covenant of continuous operation from a substantial percentage-rent amount). Because a percentage-rent clause is "virtually universal" in shopping centers leases, Friedman, *supra,* § 6.1, at 6–3, the conspicuous absence of the provision from the lease at issue strongly suggests that the parties never intended the lease to bind

Albertsons to operating a grocery store continuously at Oakwood Village.

Second, the absence of any, let alone a restrictive, "use of premises" clause in the lease militates against Oakwood's argument that Albertsons has a duty to generate consumer traffic for the center by operating a grocery store on a more or less permanent basis. A "use of premises" clause indicating the allowable commercial purposes for which a tenant may occupy the leased premises is a customary provision of commercial lease agreements. *See generally* Thompson, *supra,* § 97.06(c)(18), at 99–100. The lack of such a clause here indicates that Oakwood was not concerned with the type of business Albertsons conducted. Specifically, notwithstanding the lack of a restrictive use clause concerning Albertsons's property, the lease's general and expressly nonexclusive description of the business uses for which any property leased at Oakwood Village may be employed by the tenant suggests that Albertsons may use its property for purposes other than operating a grocery store. The lease states that a tenant may use any property leased in the center "to *permit* the construction and operation of retail facilities and parking on the Leased Premises, *including* supermarkets, drug and variety stores, or combinations thereof, and other similar retail uses, without conditions thereto which in Tenant's reasonable opinion would cause construction and operation to be uneconomical" (emphasis added). Thus, the language of the lease contemplates very broad use of the premises by Albertsons with no specific business restrictions and no apparent requirement of ongoing operation. This contradicts Oakwood's argument that the lease contains an implied covenant under which Oakwood assumed responsibility for drawing consumer traffic to the center as a continuous tenant.

Third, Albertsons's right to sublet or assign the lease, without the landlord's consent and with no restriction on the type of sublettees or assignees, strongly undermines Oakwood's argument that Albertsons has promised to operate on the premises for the entire duration of the lease term. While this court has not addressed the question, among those courts that have, nearly every one has found an unrestricted right to sublet or assign a lease to be inconsistent with the implication of a covenant of continuous operation. . . .

As further support, we note that one well-respected treatise, summarizing the widespread conclusion by courts on this subject, has declared that an "[e]xpress right to assign or sublet and vacate the premises is not consistent with an implied obligation to remain and do business." Friedman, *supra,* § 6:9.3, at 6–49. Similarly, another has stated that "anything less than a total prohibition against assignment or subletting by the tenant argues against the proposition that the tenant has promised to continue to operate in the premises for the entire duration of the lease term." Bernard M. Levy, The Store Went Dark—The Landlord's Side," 2 *The Commercial Property Lease* 159, 166 (Patrick A. Randolph, Jr. ed., 1997). Oakwood's request is further weakened by the fact that the lease does not have a provision to protect Oakwood against the scenario where Albertsons sublet to another tenant which then decided to go dark.

Fourth, a provision permitting Albertsons to own and install "in the Leased Premises such fixtures and equipment as Tenant deems desirable" and to remove "Tenant's personal property from the Leased Premises at any time," a provision commonly seen in combination with a right to sublet or assign the lease, is not consistent with a duty of continuous operation. *See United Assocs. v. Wal-Mart Stores,* 133 F.3d 1296, 1298 (10th Cir.1997) (finding no implied covenant of continuous operation where the lease plainly allowed the tenant to remove his fixtures, goods, and equipment at any time and to sublet or assign the lease without the landlord's consent).

Fifth, the lack of any provision allowing Oakwood to reenter and relet the premises in the event that the tenant vacates weighs against a finding of an implied covenant of continuous operation. Many shopping center leases contain a provision providing that if the tenant ceases to operate in the leased premises, the landlord has the option of retaking them. The lease at issue does contain a default provision giving Oakwood the right to "decree the term ended and enter the Leased Premises" or "re-enter the Leased Premises and sublet the whole or any part thereof"; however, the default provision does not indicate that "going dark" triggers its operation. Under the lease terms, it appears only that being in default on rent would constitute a default on the lease. Oakwood argues that because the real consideration for the lease is not the nominal rent paid by Albertsons's but is instead Albertsons ability to generate consumer traffic essential for the center's vitality, Albertsons "going dark" qualifies as a default. However, because the lease contains no provision, either express or implied, indicating that Albertsons has a legal duty to operate a supermarket continuously on the premises, Albertsons cannot be considered to have breached the lease by discontinuing its grocery store operation.

Sixth, Albertsons points out that the lease does not impose a legal duty on Albertsons to erect any structure on the premises and that, having constructed a building, Albertsons is under no legal obligation to occupy the building at all. In support of this proposition, Albertsons cites the right to raze in the lease:

> Tenant *may,* at Tenant's expense, raze *any* improvements on the Leased Premises and construct on the Leased Premises any improvements, *including, without limitation,* a store building and parking area, and make such repairs, additions, alterations and improvements thereto as Tenant may deem desirable.

(Emphasis added.) It is true that Oakwood agrees in the declaration to construct a building pad running electrical wires and utility pipes to the property suitable for Albertsons's to construct a building. However, Albertsons argument that it has no obligation to build at all is strongly supported by the fact that, under the lease, Albertsons is expressly not obligated to rebuild a damaged or destroyed building. The lease states that "[i]n the event any building on the Leased Premises is damaged or destroyed by a casualty, Tenant shall *either* repair or restore the building, *or remove the rubble and leave the ground in a sightly condition*" (emphasis added). Drafters should include provisions in their contracts compelling construction and reconstruction in the event of destruction and specifying the time frame for completing such activities. *See 2 Powell on Real Property* § 17A.01[2] (Michael Allan Wolf ed., 1997). Provisions of this kind are not only absent from this lease but are replaced by contrary provisions essentially granting Albertsons free reign. It is evident from the absence of a rebuild provision that both parties contemplated a scenario in which Albertsons would pay rent indefinitely on bare ground. Albertsons thus cannot be said to have agreed in the lease to take responsibility for drawing consumer traffic to the center as Oakwood has argued.

In sum, we conclude that the lease lacks the plain and unmistakable language necessary to support the inference of a covenant of continuous operation.

As previously noted, even in the absence of plain and unmistakable language in the relevant contracts to support the implication of a restrictive covenant, we will infer such covenant when it is legally necessary. *St. Benedict's,* 811 P.2d at 198. While "legal necessity" may sound like a broad category, courts have been willing to find a legally necessary covenant only where it arises from the "terms of a contract or the substance thereof . . . [which] clearly authorize[ ] the inference of an imputation in law of the creation of a covenant" and the "circumstances attending [the contract's] execution." 20 Am.Jur.2d *Covenants, Conditions, and Restrictions* § 29 (2004). As defendants properly note, courts will not infer a restrictive covenant into a contract to effect social policy. In other words, courts will read the covenant into contracts " 'in order to protect the express covenants or promises of the contract, not to protect some general public policy interest not directly tied to the contract's purpose.' " *Peterson v. Browning,* 832 P.2d 1280, 1284 (Utah 1992) (quoting *Foley v. Interactive Data Corp.,* 47 Cal.3d 654, 254 Cal.Rptr. 211, 765 P.2d 373, 394 (1988)). It is not enough to say that the covenant ought to be read into a contract to make the contract fair, and that without the covenant, the contract would be improvident or unwise, or create an unjust outcome. *See* 20 Am.Jur.2d *Covenants, Conditions, and Restrictions* § 29. Here, where express language in the lease would contradict an implied covenant of continuous operation, we decline to recognize the covenant as legally necessary.

Consequently, we cannot find an implied covenant of continuous operation in the parties' lease either from the language of the relevant contracts or on the grounds that such a covenant is legally necessary to effectuate express contractual covenants or promises.

Not only are defendants' arguments concerning the text of the relevant contracts convincing to their position, but Oakwood's arguments on this subject are not persuasive. Oakwood notes that in the declaration the parties agreed to develop the shopping center "as an integrated retail sales complex for the mutual benefit of all real property in the Shopping Center." Oakwood points out that paragraph 9.1 of the lease provides that a breach of the declaration constitutes a breach of the lease, and, as such, because Albertsons's "going dark" was not for the "mutual benefit" of the center, Albertsons was in breach of the lease when it ceased its grocery store operation. However, without more substantial textual evidence, and in light of unambiguous contractual language permitting Albertsons to raze but not obliging Albertsons to rebuild, this phrase is best understood as a boilerplate statement of the parties' intent to cooperate and not as a promise by Albertsons to engage in or refrain from specific actions. Indeed, the parties' agreement expressly disclaims a mutually dependent relationship between Oakwood and Albertsons. The agreement states that the "provisions are not intended to create, nor shall they be in any way interpreted to create, a joint venture, a partnership, or any other similar relationship between the parties."

. . .

Additionally, we are unpersuaded by Oakwood's request that we infer a covenant of continuous operation from the economically interdependent relationship between the landlord and the tenant, as the New Jersey Supreme Court did in *Ingannamorte [v. Kings Super Markets,* 55 N.J. 223, 260 A.2d A.2d 841, 843–44 (1970)] and *Tooley's Truck Stop, Inc. v. Chrisanthopouls,* 55 N.J. 231, 260 A.2d 845, 848 (1970). We are unwilling to find such a covenant on this basis because in so doing "New Jersey seems to stand alone for this proposition." *Walgreen Ariz. Drug Corp. v. Plaza Ctr. Corp.,* 132 Ariz. 512, 647 P.2d 643, 648 (Ct.App.1982). Moreover, New Jersey's unique approach to this issue is problematic because it "overlooks the well-established rule that a statement as to the use of the leased premises does not imply a covenant." *Id.* at 648.

. . .

We are similarly unconvinced by Oakwood's argument that the exclusive business clause in the lease, granting Albertsons the right to be the center's sole supermarket, compels a finding of an implied covenant of continuous operation. With few exceptions, courts have found that an exclusivity clause does not necessarily give rise to an implied covenant of continuous operation. *See, e.g., Plaza Assocs.,* 524 N.W.2d at 730 (explaining that an exclusive business provision in a contract is not a basis for implying a covenant of continuous operation); *Kroger Co. v. Bonny Corp.,* 134 Ga.App. 834, 216 S.E.2d 341, 343–45 (1975) (concluding that a landlord's covenant not to lease space in a shopping center to other grocery stores is not enough to imply a continuous operation covenant).

Finally, we are unpersuaded by Oakwood's argument that the nominal rent paid by Albertsons supports Oakwood's proposition that the real consideration was not the rental fee but was instead Albertsons's ability to generate traffic for the center. Oakwood contends that the true consideration supposes continuous operation by Albertsons. We disagree that the fact that a fixed rental is below market value alone establishes a basis for this court to infer a covenant of continuous operation. "The adequacy or inadequacy of the fixed rental only becomes a factor in determining whether a covenant should be implied when the rent is determined on a percentage basis." *Walgreen Ariz.,* 647 P.2d at 647.

2.   Ground Lease

Finally, the fact that a ground lease rather than a lease of an already constructed commercial building is at issue is particularly detrimental to Oakwood's claim that the lease implies a covenant of continuous operation. A ground lease, as the trial court recognized, is different from an ordinary commercial lease. It is uncontested in this case that Albertsons constructed and paid for a building at Oakwood Village and that Oakwood provided only the ground and a pad on which Albertsons could build. It is further undisputed that at the end of the lease term Oakwood will regain title to the 42,300-square-foot parcel of ground and the building that Albertsons constructed at its own expense.

The law has clearly established that a tenant has significantly more flexibility and control over the premises under a ground lease than it has under a building lease. Indeed, "a ground lease is best considered as a financing device for developing unimproved land. The lessor's role is similar to that of a secured lender, and the lessee pays most of what is necessary to develop the land and protect the lessor's role as passive investor." *Airport Plaza, Inc. v. Blanchard,* 188 Cal.App.3d 1594, 234 Cal.Rptr. 198, 201 (1987).

. . .

The increased flexibility and control a lessee exercises over the leased premises under a ground lease than under a building lease makes it especially important for the lessor to secure certain assurances from the lessee in a ground lease. This is because "[o]nly the standards set forth in the ground lease will provide the landlord with some assurance that the construction, operation, and maintenance of the property and improvements will be sufficient to produce rent for the landlord. . . ." Jerome D. Whalen, *Commercial Ground Leases* § 1.1.1, at 2, 5–6 (1988). Unfortunately for Oakwood, it evidently failed to secure from Albertsons any assurances that Albertsons would operate a grocery store on the premises for the duration of the lease.

Therefore, because the lease at issue is a ground lease, contains language that does not prohibit Albertsons from going dark, includes a right to raze, and indicates that both parties contemplated a scenario in which Albertsons would pay rent indefinitely on bare ground, we will not find an implied covenant of continuous operation as Oakwood asks us to do.

B.   *Covenant of Good Faith and Fair Dealing*

Oakwood's second major claim is that Albertsons breached the implied covenant of good faith and fair dealing in the lease. Even assuming that the lease gave Albertsons the right to go dark, Oakwood argues that Albertsons availed itself of this right for the improper purpose of shielding itself from competition with its new store. According to Oakwood, the obligation of good faith required Albertsons to exercise its discretion in a way that would not deny Oakwood the opportunity to receive the real consideration for the lease—the ability of Albertsons to generate consumer traffic for the center. Oakwood claims this covenant left Albertsons with three options: (1) to continue operating in the center, (2) to sublet or assign the lease to a comparable anchor tenant, or (3) to surrender possession of the premises to Oakwood so that Oakwood could relet them to an appropriate anchor tenant of its choice. Oakwood argues that Albertsons's failure to elect one of these options was bad faith.

In Utah, virtually every contract imposes upon each party a duty of good faith and fair dealing, the violation of which gives rise to a claim for breach of contract. *St. Benedict's,* 811 P.2d at 199–200. The obligation of good faith requires each party to refrain from actions that will intentionally "destroy or injure the other party's right to receive the fruits of the contract." *Id.* at 199. To determine the legal duty a contractual party has under this covenant, a court will assess whether a "party's actions [are] consistent with the agreed common purpose and the justified expectations of the other party." *Id.* at 200. This court determines the "purpose, intentions, and expectations" by considering "the contract language and the course of dealings between and conduct of the parties." *Id.* Oakwood's complaint does not contain averments regarding the parties' course of dealings or conduct, focusing only on the contractual language.

Oakwood's reading of the lease would violate the established principle that "[i]f there is no express or implied covenant that tenant operate, a cessation of operation is no breach of the requirement to act in good faith." Friedman, *supra,* § 6:9, at 6–42. In addition, even setting aside that principle, Oakwood's construction of the obligation to act in good faith and deal fairly would violate other broader principles of contract interpretation.

While a covenant of good faith and fair dealing inheres in almost every contract, some general principles limit the scope of the covenant, as defendants correctly note. First, this covenant cannot be read to establish new, independent rights or duties to which the parties did not agree ex ante. *Brehany v. Nordstrom, Inc.,* 812 P.2d 49, 55 (Utah 1991). Second, this covenant cannot create rights and duties inconsistent with express contractual terms. *See id.; Rio Algom Corp. v. Jimco, Ltd.,* 618 P.2d 497, 505 (Utah 1980). Third, this covenant cannot compel a contractual party to exercise a contractual right "to its own detriment for the purpose of benefitting another party to the contract." *Olympus Hills Shopping Ctr. v. Smith's Food & Drug Ctrs.,* 889 P.2d 445, 457 n. 13 (Utah Ct.App. 1994). Finally, we will not use this covenant to achieve an outcome in harmony with the court's sense of justice but inconsistent with the express terms of the applicable contract. *See Dalton v. Jerico Constr. Co.,* 642 P.2d 748, 750 (Utah 1982).

Oakwood misreads the scope of the covenant of good faith and fair dealing in asking this court to infer a promise of continuous operation not supported by the language of the relevant contracts and, in fact, contradicting express provisions in them. Such a reading of the covenant would infringe on Albertsons's authorized freedom to exercise its expressly granted contractual rights. While Albertsons may not have followed the golden rule in pursuing the course of conduct it did, Albertsons did not act in bad faith or violate any other implied covenant in its contract with Oakwood.

Because Oakwood argues at length that the trial court's decision denying a claim for relief based on the implied covenant of good faith and fair dealing is inconsistent with this court's previous rulings, we address this reasoning. In particular, both parties recognize *St. Benedict's* and *Olympus Hills* as the controlling cases on the requirements and operation of the covenant of good faith and fair dealing.

In *St. Benedict's,* after finding no implied covenant of continuous operation, we described the requirements of the covenant of good faith and fair dealing and remanded the case for trial on that issue. 811 P.2d at 202. In that case, the hospital entered into a ground lease with the development company. *Id.* at 196. According to the terms of their lease, the development company would build two professional office buildings on the leased property expected to be occupied by medical practitioners using hospital facilities. *Id.* The lease expressly required the hospital to "actively assist" the development company "in acquiring and holding good tenants until such time as the New Office Building is completely occupied." *Id.* at 197. It also expressly guaranteed payment of rent by the hospital for one-third of the net leasable area of the building until the building was two-thirds occupied. *Id.* Subsequently, the hospital and a third-party developer announced their plan to construct another medical office building on property adjacent to the now existing two buildings. *Id.* After this announcement was made, several tenants declared to the developer of the existing buildings their intention to vacatee once the new facility was completed and would agree to pay rent only on a month-to-month basis in anticipation of their imminent relocation. *Id.* Thereafter, the development company of the existing buildings brought suit against the hospital for, among other claims, breach of the implied covenants of continuous operation and good faith and fair dealing. *Id.* at 197–99. In reversing the lower court's decision on the case, this court concluded that the developer's showing that "the hospital [ ] encourag[ed] . . . a competing office building" was sufficient to state a claim against the hospital for breach of the covenant of good faith and fair dealing. *Id.* at 200.

We believe that *St. Benedict's* is distinguishable from the present case. In *St. Benedict's,* the lease contained express language imposing a legal duty on the hospital, whereas such language is conspicuously absent from the Albertsons lease. In reversing in the *St. Benedict's* case, we explained: "It is difficult to imagine a scenario where a party could be found to be 'diligently endeavoring' to obtain and retain tenants for one building while at the same time encouraging the solicitation of existing tenants for a competing building." *Id.* Thus, we found that the hospital had breached an express contract provision:

> Here, the trial court did not specifically address the question of whether the hospital breached its express promise to aid the development company in acquiring and retaining tenants for the new office building. If it *had,* the court would have found that the complaint states a claim for such a breach. *Id.* at 199 (emphasis added).

There are no such provisions in the lease between Oakwood and Albertsons.

Similar to *St. Benedict's, Olympus Hills* involved a lease between a developer and a Smith's grocery store, which contained an express covenant of continuous operation that obliged Smith's to continuously operate "any lawful retail selling business." 889 P.2d at 451. Rather than defaulting on the lease, Smith's opened a warehouse box store in order to restrict competition with another grocery store it operated close to the Olympus Hills Shopping Center. *Id.* at 448. Olympus Hills thereafter sued Smith's, claiming that Smith's had violated the covenant of good faith and fair dealing. *Id.* On appeal, the *Olympus Hills* court concluded that the jury had properly found that the circumstances and purpose of Smith's temporary closure had been inconsistent with the parties' justified expectations of continuous operation and was, in effect, a breach of its contractual rights. *Id.* at 450.

We disagree with Oakwood that the decision in *Olympus Hills* supports its claim. Smith's operation of a warehouse box store was deemed a breach of contract because the lease contained an express covenant of continuous operation and a restriction on the nature of operations. Here, Albertsons's lease contains neither a restrictive use nor a continuous operation provision and further grants Albertsons an unqualified right to sublet or assign its lease.

In sum, we find *St. Benedict's* and *Olympus Hills's* rulings to be consistent with the decision we reach today.

This lease is a complete and unambiguous agreement between competent commercial parties. Long-term commercial leases, by their nature, are risky. Neither side can foretell future market conditions with any certainty. We presume that both Oakwood and Albertsons bargained for the best terms and conditions each could get. Each party took the risk that unpredictable market forces would at some later day render the contractual terms unfavorable to themselves. Despite this risk, both parties willingly agreed to the terms in the lease. It is not our role to intervene now, construing the contract's unambiguous terms to mean something different from what the parties intended them to mean at the outset.

CONCLUSION

Although we acknowledge the "dog in the manger" position that Albertsons has taken, we cannot conclude that the parties' agreement warrants finding for Oakwood. What Albertsons did may not have been nice, but its conduct in vacating the leased premises while continuing to pay rent in order to restrict competition with its new store was not unlawful under the lease.

In urging this court to locate in the lease a legal duty that Albertsons has breached, Oakwood has stated that "[f]airness in business dealings should be a concern of this Court." It is precisely this concern for fairness, however, which bars us from reading into the lease an obligation that Oakwood failed to secure during contract negotiations. The duty Oakwood now seeks to impose on Albertsons is simply not one for which the parties bargained.

In addition, Oakwood asks this court to focus on the "big picture" rather than on specific textual provisions to which defendants call attention. The problem with Oakwood's approach, however, is that it relies on "unstated inferences as opposed to the actual language of the contract." *Forrest Drive Assocs.*, 72 F.Supp.2d at 583. By contrast, in relying on unambiguous contractual language, Albertsons's argument rests on a firmer foundation.

We affirm the trial court's judgment granting defendants' (Albertsons and One Hamilton's) motion to dismiss this case for failure to state a claim upon which relief can be granted pursuant to rule 12(b)(6) of the Utah Rules of Civil Procedure. We also affirm the trial court's order that Oakwood pay all of defendants' reasonable attorney fees covering the litigation costs of this case both at the trial level and on appeal, as the parties agreed to in their lease.

JUSTICE DURRANT, JUSTICE PARRISH, JUSTICE NEHRING, and JUDGE TAYLOR concur in CHIEF JUSTICE DURHAM'S opinion.

Having disqualified himself, ASSOCIATE CHIEF JUSTICE WILKINS does not participate herein; DISTRICT JUDGE JAMES R. TAYLOR sat.

b.   TENANT'S BUSINESS ACTIVITIES—EXCLUSIVE RIGHTS AND RESTRICTED ACTIVITIES

Providence Square Associates, L.L.C. v. G.D.F., Incorporated

United States Court of Appeals for the Fourth Circuit, 2000.
211 F.3d 846.

Before WILKINS, MICHAEL, and KING, CIRCUIT JUDGES.

OPINION

KING, CIRCUIT JUDGE:

G.D.F., Inc., trading as Rite Aid ("Rite Aid"), leases space from Providence Square Associates ("Providence Square") in the Providence Square Shopping Center ("shopping center") in Virginia Beach, Virginia. Among other things, Rite Aid's lease guarantees Rite Aid the exclusive right to operate a "drug store" and a "photo finishing business" in the shopping center.

The dispute underlying this appeal arose when Hannaford Bros. Co. and its subsidiary Boney Wilson & Sons, Inc. (collectively "Hannaford"), opened a supermarket in the shopping center, into which Hannaford incorporated a full-service pharmacy and photo drop booth. In the suit below, Rite Aid brought claims against both Hannaford and Providence Square, asserting that Hannaford's operation of a pharmacy and a photo drop booth violated the exclusivity provisions in Rite Aid's lease with Providence Square. The district court rejected these claims, holding that Hannaford was not violating Rite Aid's exclusivity provisions because Hannaford's "Food and Drug Superstore" was neither a "drug store" nor a "photo finishing business." Finding no breach of Rite Aid's lease, the district court entered summary judgment against Rite Aid. See Providence Square Assocs., L.L.C. v. Boney Wilson & Sons, Inc., 34 F.Supp.2d 1030, 1037 (E.D.Va.1999).

Rite Aid has appealed the district court's judgment. For the reasons set forth below, we reverse.

I.

A.

Rite Aid is the successor in interest to a lease originally signed by Drug Fair of Virginia, Inc. ("Drug Fair"). On August 6, 1977, Drug Fair signed a lease ("Rite Aid lease") with Providence Square for approximately 15,500 square feet of space in the shopping center. As an anchor tenant in the shopping center, Drug Fair was able to negotiate several exclusive rights clauses from which Rite Aid now benefits. For example, the Rite Aid lease provides, in pertinent part:

> *Lessor covenants* that, while this lease or any extension or renewal thereof, is in force and effect, *it will not lease for or permit the conducting of any other drug store, variety store or photo finishing business* or any stores whose primary business

is the sale of patent medicines, health and beauty aids, cosmetics, lawn and garden and/or outdoor living merchandise (this does not exclude a Home Center/Hardware type of operation) *in the shopping center* or building or site of which the leased premises are a part, nor upon any real estate within a radius of one mile from said shopping center. . . .

J.A. 201 (emphasis added) (hereinafter the "exclusivity provisions").[1]

The Rite Aid lease also contemplates that a "Safeway or another National Chain Food Market" ("supermarket") would lease space in the shopping center, J.A. 172, and the lease makes certain exceptions to the exclusivity provisions for that supermarket. In that regard, the exclusivity provisions do "not apply to any listed items[2] sold by the National Food Chain located in the shopping center, their assigns or sub-lessees or any tenant of that space occupied or formerly occupied by the National Food Chain Store." J.A. 202.

Safeway began leasing space in the shopping center on February 1, 1978. Significantly, Safeway's lease specifically required that Providence Square lease space in the shopping center to a "Drug Store," separate and distinct from the supermarket, for twenty years-the same term as Safeway's lease. J.A. 151. Thereafter, Safeway and its successors operated a supermarket, without a pharmacy, in the shopping center for approximately eighteen years.

In 1996, Hannaford, through its representative, Boney Wilson, began negotiating for the space formerly occupied by Safeway. In the course of negotiating Hannaford's lease, Boney Wilson offered Providence Square three draft proposals (two draft leases and one letter of intent), each of which prohibited Hannaford from operating a pharmacy. The first draft lease provided (in language virtually identical to the second draft lease) that: "For the purposes hereof, a 'pharmacy' shall mean any store, or department or counter within a store, which sells prescription medicines or drugs or any items requiring the presence of a registered pharmacist." J.A. 458. However, the final draft of the lease, which was ultimately executed by Hannaford and Providence Square, prohibited Hannaford from operating a pharmacy only "[t]o the extent that" the Rite Aid lease prohibited as much. J.A. 218, 250–51.

Following execution of this lease, Hannaford began constructing the supermarket, into which Hannaford incorporated a pharmacy. On

---

[1] The Rite Aid lease provides that if the exclusivity provisions are breached, Rite Aid is entitled to:

> pay as revised rent for said premises a sum equivalent to one and three-fourths percent (1–3/4%) of gross sales with a guaranteed minimum rental of Twenty-Five Thousand Dollars ($25,000.00) annually. Said minimum revised rental shall be paid in monthly installments of Two Thousand Eighty-Three and 33/100 Dollars ($2,083.33) in advance of the first day of each month during the balance of the term hereof.

J.A. 202.

[2] In the same numbered paragraph, the lease specifies the "listed items": "patent medicines, health and beauty aids, cosmetics, lawn and garden and/or outdoor living merchandise." J.A. 201–02. Hannaford asserts that a "drug store, variety store or photo finishing business" are also to be included in the "listed items"; however, this assertion fails because, in context, it is plain that those businesses are not "items" in the mold of the other listed products.

April 24, 1998, Rite Aid's lawyer informed Providence Square of rumors that a pharmacy was being constructed in the Hannaford supermarket, and Rite Aid requested that Providence Square take appropriate action. Providence Square reacted to this notice from Rite Aid by attempting to negotiate-to no avail-an indemnification agreement with Hannaford, under which Hannaford would agree to indemnify Providence Square for any costs arising out of the breach of Rite Aid's exclusivity provisions.

The Hannaford supermarket opened on June 6, 1998. The store houses both a full-service pharmacy and a drop-box for photo processing, and Hannaford's signs and advertisements identify it as a "Food and Drug Superstore." Four months after its opening, prescription drug sales at Hannaford averaged between $30,000 and $32,000 per month, which represented approximately 2.3% of Hannaford's overall sales. By comparison, Rite Aid's pharmacy sales during the same period averaged $55,000 per month, a figure that declined in the face of competition following the opening of Hannaford's pharmacy.

B.

Following Providence Square's failure to obtain an indemnification agreement from Hannaford, Providence Square filed suit in Virginia state court seeking a declaratory judgment clarifying the rights and obligations of the parties under the applicable leases. In that suit, Providence Square alleged that its leases were being breached because: (1) Hannaford is operating a pharmacy and (2) Rite Aid is withholding rent (see supra note 1). Following the removal of the case to the Eastern District of Virginia, Rite Aid filed (1) a counter-claim against Providence Square, alleging that Providence Square allowed Hannaford to operate a pharmacy and a photo drop box in violation of Rite Aid's lease; and (2) a cross-claim against Hannaford, alleging that Hannaford breached its lease with Providence Square, violated the restrictive covenant in Rite Aid's lease, and tortiously induced Providence Square to breach its lease with Rite Aid.

After the parties submitted briefs on various cross-motions for summary judgment, the district court held that Hannaford's operation of a pharmacy and a photo drop box did not violate the exclusivity provisions of Rite Aid's lease. Based on this holding, the district court, on January 26, 1999, granted summary judgment against Rite Aid. Rite Aid has appealed, and we possess jurisdiction pursuant to 28 U.S.C. § 1291.

II.

A.

"We review the district court's grant of summary judgment de novo, viewing all facts and inferences in the light most favorable" to Rite Aid. Food Lion, Inc. v. S.L. Nusbaum Ins. Agency, Inc., 202 F.3d 223, 227 (4th Cir.2000). In this review, we remain mindful that "[s]ummary judgment is appropriate where there is no genuine issue of material fact, and the moving party is entitled to judgment as a matter of law." Semple v. City of Moundsville, 195 F.3d 708, 712 (4th Cir.1999) (citing Celotex Corp. v. Catrett, 477 U.S. 317, 322, 106 S.Ct. 2548, 91 L.Ed.2d 265 (1986)).

B.

1.

We are first charged, in this appeal, with resolving whether Hannaford's operation of a pharmacy violates the provisions of Rite Aid's lease prohibiting the operation of another "drug store" in the shopping center. Hannaford contends, in an argument adopted by the district court, that there is no violation of Rite Aid's exclusivity provisions because they prohibit only the operation of another "drug store" in the shopping center, and Hannaford is not a "drug store." Instead, Hannaford asserts that it is a "supermarket," which is not prohibited under Rite Aid's exclusivity provisions. At its base, Hannaford's argument is that a "drug store" or pharmacy, if incorporated into a supermarket, is no longer a "drug store" within the meaning of Rite Aid's lease.

Inasmuch as the exclusivity provisions of Rite Aid's lease constitute restrictive covenants, we are guided by Virginia law relating to restrictive covenants. In Virginia, "[c]ovenants, express or implied, restricting the free use of land are not favored and must be strictly construed." Mid-State Equip. Co. v. Bell, 217 Va. 133, 225 S.E.2d 877, 884 (1976). In fact, "substantial doubts or ambiguity" about the meaning of a restrictive covenant must be resolved in favor of the unrestricted use of land. Woodward v. Morgan, 252 Va. 135, 475 S.E.2d 808, 810 (1996). However, Virginia will enforce "such covenants when applicable, but the person claiming the benefit of the restrictions must prove that the covenants are applicable to the acts of which he complains." Sloan v. Johnson, 254 Va. 271, 491 S.E.2d 725, 727 (Va.1997). In our analysis, we also are guided by Virginia principles of contract interpretation, under which we seek to determine the intent of the parties from the language expressed in the contract. Langley v. Johnson, 27 Va.App. 365, 499 S.E.2d 15, 16 (1998). If the terms of the contract are clear and unambiguous, then we must afford those terms their plain and ordinary meaning; however, if the terms are vague or ambiguous, then we may consider extrinsic evidence to interpret those provisions. Shoup v. Shoup, 31 Va.App. 621, 525 S.E.2d 61, 63–64 (2000).

Applying these principles to the case before us, we conclude that the district court erred in its determination that Hannaford's pharmacy is not a "drug store." Indeed, given that Hannaford's signs and advertisements trumpet it as a "Food and Drug Superstore," we might easily resolve this question by merely taking Hannaford at its word. However, reading Rite Aid's exclusivity provisions in context makes clear that the supermarket could not sell prescription pharmaceuticals without violating Rite Aid's restrictive covenant. That is, although the exclusivity provisions prohibit the operation of a "drug store," the provisions also stipulate that the supermarket may, without violating the non-competition clause, sell several items that were otherwise prohibited under the exclusivity provisions, including (nonprescription) patent medicines, health and beauty aids, cosmetics, lawn and garden/and or outdoor living merchandise (collectively the "listed items"). J.A. 201–02. That the leases's "listed items" specifically exclude prescription medicine makes clear that the supermarket in the shopping center may not sell prescription medicines. In other words, when the exclusivity provisions are viewed in context, it is clear that Rite Aid's prohibition of another "drug store" sought to avoid the competitive sale of prescription medicine in the shopping center.

Our conclusion is buttressed by the decision of the Supreme Court of Appeals of Virginia in Krikorian v. Dailey, 171 Va. 16, 197 S.E. 442, 446 (1938), a case enforcing a restrictive covenant under similar circumstances. In Krikorian, a tenant operating a "confectionery" negotiated a restrictive covenant in his lease prohibiting his landlord from leasing an adjacent property "for a confectionery during this lease." Id. at 444. When it appeared that the adjacent site would be occupied by a drug store that sold confectionery goods, the tenant sued to enforce the restrictive covenant. At trial, the court instructed the jury that the restrictive covenant was breached if the drug store was "a business substantially similar" to a confectionery. Id. at 447. The jury found that the covenant was breached, and the highest state court in Virginia upheld both the jury's determination and the jury instruction: "All of these rules [of contract construction] are to be remembered, and the academic definition of words is often important, but more important still is the purpose of the covenant. Has that purpose been kept or broken?" Id. at 446. The court then explained:

> The courts should and do look to the substance of things in the construction of contracts. If a landlord owned two storerooms in a building and were to rent one to be used as a delicatessen shop and covenanted that no other delicatessen store was to be established in that building, plainly to permit the establishment of another store, designated by its proprietor as a "Food Shoppe," which carried the same merchandise carried by the delicatessen store, would be a violation of this covenant. Nor would the situation change if in addition other things were sold there.

Id. at 446.

We believe that this common sense approach is apposite, and we follow it here. The clear lesson of Krikorian is that we should look to the substance-not the label-of the activity sought to be restricted under a covenant. Under this guidance, we are compelled to hold that the sale of prescription drugs by Hannaford breaches Rite Aid's exclusivity provisions. A "drug store" is no less a drug store merely because it has been incorporated into a structure called a "supermarket."[4]

---

[4]   There is, of course, authority in which courts have held various restrictive covenants to be inapplicable, and Hannaford has cited several such cases as authority here. We find none of those cases persuasive. For example, Hannaford has relied upon Marriott Corp. v. Combined Properties L.P., 239 Va. 506, 391 S.E.2d 313, 314 (1990). There, the Supreme Court of Virginia upheld a trial court's determination, following a bench trial, that a lease provision prohibiting the operation of a "drive-in food establishment" in a "described area" did not prohibit the operation of a McDonald's "fast-food" restaurant in that "area." Id. In that case, however, the Supreme Court undertook the same analysis adopted here: it compared the substance of that which was sought to be prohibited-operation of a "drive-in food establishment"—with the substance of the activity sought to be conducted-operation of a "fast-food" restaurant and concluded that the two were not coextensive. Further, the appeal in that case followed trial; therefore, the court was bound to view the facts in the light most favorable to the "fast-food" restaurant, which had prevailed at trial. Id. at 315. In this case, by contrast, we are compelled to view the facts in the light most favorable to Rite Aid, and we have concluded that the scope of the activity sought to be avoided—operation of a "drug store"—is coextensive with the activity sought to be conducted—operation of a pharmacy.

2.

The district court reached a contrary conclusion, and we briefly address some of the points upon which the district court relied. First, the district court noted that the sale of prescription drugs only constituted 2.3% of Hannaford's sales. Because, the district court concluded, the sale of prescription drugs is "an incidental" rather than primary source of sales, Hannaford is not a "drug store."

We conclude that the 2.3% figure is, in the context of the issues here, simply a red herring. In fact, the relevant figure is $30,000– representing the average prescription drug sales per month at Hannaford. When this figure is compared with Rite Aid's prescription drug sales of $50,000 per month, there is no doubt that Hannaford's sales qualified that pharmacy as exactly the form of competition that Rite Aid sought to avoid in its lease.

In a similar vein, the district court relied upon Virginia's Sunday closure laws ("Blue Laws") for a definition of "drug store." Under the Blue Laws, a "drug store" was defined as a store where " 'a majority of the sales receipts ... consist[ ] of prescription and nonprescription drugs, health and beauty aids.' " Providence Square, 34 F.Supp.2d at 1035 (quoting Va.Code Ann. § 18.2–341(17) (Michie 1975)). Because, the district court noted, only 2.3% of Hannaford's sales come from these sources, Hannaford does not fit the Blue Laws' definition of a "drug store." On this point, we conclude that the district court's reliance on the Blue Laws was misplaced. First, there is no indication that the parties relied upon the Blue Laws when they drafted the lease, and the Blue Laws thus provide little evidence of the intent of the parties who drafted the relevant provisions. Second, the purpose of Blue Laws "are to provide a day of rest for persons and to prevent physical and moral debasement from uninterrupted labor." Bonnie Belo Enterprises, Inc. v. Commonwealth, 217 Va. 84, 225 S.E.2d 395, 397 (1976). As such, those laws are drafted to permit as few businesses as possible from operating, and the category of businesses exempt from the Blue Laws is thus narrowly drawn. Put simply, the Blue Laws contained a definition of "drug store" that is unduly restrictive and inapplicable outside the Blue Laws, and that definition should not control or even inform the interpretation of Rite Aid's lease.[5]

The district court also applied a canon of construction: expressio unius est exclusion alterius ("expression of one thing is the exclusion of another") to the exclusivity provisions in order to reach its conclusion. The district court noted that the lease's "listed items" specified goods that could not be the primary business of a store in the shopping center, and the fact that prescription drugs were excluded from the "listed items" evidenced, for the district court, an intent not to prohibit the sale of prescription drugs. On the contrary, as we have noted, the exclusion of prescription drugs from the "listed items" actually bolsters Rite Aid's argument that the supermarket was not to be permitted to sell prescription medicine. See supra at 8. Further, to the extent that we are

---

[5] In fact, there are other statutes in Virginia that define the word "pharmacy" using the word "drugstore" as a synonym. See, e.g., Va.Code § 54.1–3300 (Michie 1999) (part of the regulatory scheme for pharmacists and pharmacies). Similarly, Webster's defines "drugstore" as "[a] store where prescriptions are filled and drugs and sundries are sold." See Webster's II New Riverside University Dictionary at 407 (1984).

to rely upon any principle of contract construction, we believe that the more applicable principle is that "the construction [of a contract] adopted should be reasonable, and absurd results are to be avoided." Transit Cas. Co. v. Hartman's, Inc., 218 Va. 703, 239 S.E.2d 894, 896 (1978). Were we to adopt Hannaford's construction of the Rite Aid lease, then as long as Hannaford's prescription drug sales constituted less than 50% of its overall sales (no matter how large the volume), Hannaford would not be a "drug store" and it would be permitted to sell prescription drugs. Similarly, under Hannaford's reasoning, it might well avoid qualifying as a "drug store" because it calls itself a "Drug Superstore." J.A. 554–61 (emphasis added). An approach that so permits the label to control substance could surely lead to such absurd results, and we thus cannot adopt Hannaford's reading of the lease.

The restrictive covenant at issue in this case was negotiated between two commercially savvy corporations, and it must be read to have some meaning. Thus, while we are to strictly construe restrictive provisions, we conclude that a proper reading of this lease prohibits Hannaford's sale of prescription drugs. We therefore reverse the district court's summary judgment against Rite Aid, and we thereby reinstate Rite Aid's claims, arising out of this issue, against both Hannaford and Providence Square.

C.

We also briefly address Rite Aid's other claims that were dismissed through the district court's entry of summary judgment. First, Rite Aid's claims below alleged that Hannaford's operation of a photo drop box also violates the exclusivity provisions; however, the district court dismissed this claim on the same reasoning it applied to the "drug store" issue. At oral argument, Hannaford's counsel contended that there was no distinction between Hannaford's operation of a "drug store" and Hannaford's operation of a photo drop box, effectively conceding that an adverse ruling with respect to the "drug store" issue also mandates reversal on the photo drop box issue. We agree with Hannaford on this point; we conclude that the evidence submitted in the district court also mandates reversal of the summary judgment entered with respect to Hannaford's operation of a photo drop box. Accordingly, we reinstate Rite Aid's claims against both Hannaford and Providence Square arising out of this issue.

Rite Aid also has stated a claim against Hannaford for tortious interference with contract. To establish liability under such a claim, Rite Aid must prove that: (1) a valid contract exists or existed; (2) the interferor knew of the contract; (3) the interferor intentionally interfered, inducing or causing a breach of the contract; and (4) the party who has been disrupted suffered damage. Duggin v. Adams, 234 Va. 221, 360 S.E.2d 832, 835 (1987). We also conclude that, in these circumstances, there is sufficient evidence for Rite Aid to proceed on this claim, and we thus reverse the district court's entry of summary judgment.

III.

Because the district court erred in granting summary judgment against Rite Aid, we reverse its judgment and remand this case for further proceedings consistent with this opinion.

REVERSED AND REMANDED.

In re Trak Auto Corp.

United States Court of Appeals for the Fourth Circuit, 2004.
367 F.3d 237.

Before WILKINSON, MICHAEL, and SHEDD, CIRCUIT JUDGES.

Reversed and remanded by published opinion. JUDGE MICHAEL wrote the opinion, in which JUDGE WILKINSON and JUDGE SHEDD joined.

OPINION

MICHAEL, CIRCUIT JUDGE:

A Chapter 11 debtor-tenant sought to assign its shopping center lease in contravention of a provision that limits use of the premises to the sale of auto parts. The bankruptcy and district courts approved the assignment, and the lessor and owner of the shopping center appeals. We are asked to resolve the conflict between 11 U.S.C. § 365(f)(1), which generally allows a debtor to assign its lease notwithstanding a provision restricting assignment, and § 365(b)(3)(C), which specifically requires a debtor-tenant in a shopping center to assign its lease subject to any provision restricting use of the premises. We hold that § 365(b)(3)(C), the more specific provision, controls in this case. As a result, we reverse and remand.

I.

Trak Auto Corporation (Trak Auto) is a retailer of auto parts and accessories that once operated 196 stores in Virginia, eight other states, and the District of Columbia. On July 5, 2001, in the Eastern District of Virginia, Trak Auto filed a petition under Chapter 11 of the Bankruptcy Code and continued in business as debtor in possession. As part of its effort to reorganize, Trak Auto obtained court approval to close its stores in four states, Illinois, Indiana, Michigan, and Wisconsin. Thereafter, Trak Auto sought to assume and assign certain of its leases of retail space where stores had been closed. One of these leases (the West Town lease or the lease) is at West Town Center, a shopping center in Chicago. Trak Auto's lessor and the owner of the shopping center is West Town Center LLC (West Town), the appellant.[1] The West Town lease contains explicit use restrictions. Section 1.1(L) limits "PERMITTED USES" to the "[s]ale at retail of automobile parts and accessories and such other items as are customarily sold by Tenant at its other Trak Auto stores." J.A. 579. In section 8.1 Trak Auto "covenants . . . to use the Leased Premises only as a Trak Auto Store and for the Uses provided in Section 1.1(L)." J.A. 588.

Trak Auto engaged a real estate firm to advertise the availability of the West Town lease and to solicit bids. Of the bids received, none came from an auto parts retailer. The high bidder was A & E Stores, Inc. (A & E), an apparel merchandiser that offered $80,000 to buy out the

---

[1] LaSalle National Trust, N.A. was the original lessor and the actual party opposing the assignment in the bankruptcy and district courts. After LaSalle appealed to this court, West Town became the owner of the shopping center and Trak Auto's lessor. West Town has been substituted as the appellant, so we will use "West Town" to refer to both West Town and its predecessor, LaSalle.

lease. If A & E obtains the lease, it will open a Pay Half store on the premises, selling brand name family apparel at discount prices.

In a motion filed in the bankruptcy court, Trak Auto sought an order authorizing it to assume the West Town lease and to assign it to A & E. West Town, Trak Auto's lessor, objected on two grounds. First, West Town argued that the proposed assignment would breach the lease provision limiting use to the sale of auto parts and accessories. According to West Town, this use provision was enforceable under 11 U.S.C. § 365(b)(3)(C). (West Town did not rely on the lease restriction that said the premises could be used "only as a Trak Auto Store.") Second, West Town argued that the assignment would disrupt its shopping center's tenant mix in violation of § 365(b)(3)(D). Trak Auto responded that the use restrictions in the lease were unenforceable anti-assignment provisions under § 365(f)(1) and that an assignment to A & E would not, as a matter of fact, disrupt the tenant mix.

The bankruptcy court held an evidentiary hearing and made the following factual findings, which we accept. The West Town shopping center is in an urban area (Chicago) where only fifty-nine percent of the population own cars. The shopping center is surrounded by competing shopping areas not owned by West Town. The twenty-five tenants in West Town Center include clothing stores, food vendors, a K-Mart, a laundromat, a travel agency, a bank, a cash advance (or small loan) agency, an adult entertainment outlet, and a public library branch. Trak Auto was the shopping center's only auto parts retailer, but there are seven auto parts retailers within three miles of the center. After announcing its factual findings, the bankruptcy court issued its conclusions. First, the court concluded that the lease's use restrictions amounted to anti-assignment provisions that were prohibited by § 356(f)(1) of the Bankruptcy Code. Second, the court concluded that West Town did not present sufficient evidence to support a finding that assignment of the lease to A & E would disrupt the tenant mix at West Town Center. Based on these conclusions, the bankruptcy court entered an order granting Trak Auto's motion to assume the West Town lease and, in turn, to assign it to A & E.

West Town filed a notice of appeal to the district court, and the bankruptcy court stayed its order pending appeal. The district court affirmed, and West Town then appealed to our court. We have also granted a stay. On October 7, 2003, three weeks before oral argument, West Town filed a motion to dismiss its own appeal as moot, arguing that its lease to Trak Auto had expired by its own terms on September 30, 2003. We deferred a ruling on the motion, which we take up now.

II.

West Town moves to dismiss its appeal as moot, arguing that Trak Auto no longer has any lease to assign. The facts relevant to West Town's motion are undisputed. Trak Auto's lease from West Town ran through September 30, 2003, but automatically extended for another sixty months if Trak Auto was not in material default. After Trak Auto filed for bankruptcy in July 2001, it made post-petition rent payments to West Town for several months, see 11 U.S.C. § 365(d)(3), but stopped making these payments after December 2001. On March 12, 2002, West Town filed a motion requesting the bankruptcy court to order Trak Auto to pay administrative rent due under § 365(d)(3). The court determined that West Town had a valid administrative claim for rent, but the court declined to make a specific order about payment timing, deferring that issue until a decision was made on whether Trak Auto could assign the lease.

The bankruptcy court later entered an order allowing Trak Auto to assign the lease to A & E; the order provided that West Town would be paid the administrative rent from proceeds of the assignment. This meant that West Town would not be paid the rent until the assignment was concluded. The assignment was put on hold by stays pending appeal issued by the bankruptcy court and this court at the request of West Town. Furthermore, West Town did not object to or appeal the part of the bankruptcy court's order that deferred Trak Auto's time for payment of the rent. In light of all of this, West Town surely understood two things: first, that appeal of any decision allowing the assignment would take some time; and second, that the term of the lease would automatically extend on September 30, 2003, if an appeal was then pending because Trak Auto would not yet be obligated to deliver the rent payment according to the unchallenged provision in the bankruptcy court's order. In these circumstances, we conclude that West Town has waived any argument in this appeal that the lease has expired because Trak Auto has not paid accrued post-petition rent. See In re Lane, 991 F.2d 105, 107 (4th Cir.1993); In re Arnold, 869 F.2d 240, 244–45 (4th Cir.1989). West Town's motion to dismiss the appeal is accordingly denied.

III.

Today's substantive issue requires us to deal with the conflict between two provisions in § 365 of the Bankruptcy Code dealing with the assignment of a lease by a debtor (or trustee). Section 365(b)(3)(C) specifically requires a debtor-tenant at a shopping center to assign its store lease subject to any provision restricting the use of the premises. On the other hand, § 365(f)(1) generally allows a debtor to assign its lease notwithstanding a provision restricting assignment. In this case, the bankruptcy court permitted Trak Auto to assign its shopping center lease to the highest bidder, refusing to enforce the restriction that required the premises to be used for the retail sale of auto parts and accessories. The district court affirmed. The legal issue is dispositive of this appeal, and we (like the district court) review the bankruptcy court's legal conclusions de novo. See Butler v. David Shaw, Inc., 72 F.3d 437, 440–41 (4th Cir.1996). We hold that § 365(b)(3)(C) controls in this case. This means that the bankruptcy court erred in permitting Trak Auto to assign its lease to an apparel merchandiser that would not honor the use restriction. Our analysis follows.

Section 365(a) allows a Chapter 11 debtor to assume an unexpired lease. 11 U.S.C. § 365(a). The debtor may, in turn, assign the lease if the assignee provides "adequate assurance of future performance." Id. § 365(f)(2)(B). When a debtor-tenant in a shopping center seeks to assign its lease, the "adequate assurance of future performance" must include specific assurances that are spelled out in the Code. Most important to this case, there must be adequate assurance that assignment of a shopping center lease "is subject to all the provisions thereof, including (but not limited to) provisions such as a radius, location, use, or exclusivity provision, and will not breach any such provision contained in any other lease, financing agreement, or master agreement relating to such shopping center." Id. § 365(b)(3)(C). Section 365(f)(1), on the other hand, contains a general provision that prohibits the enforcement in bankruptcy of anti-assignment clauses in leases. This section allows a debtor to assign a lease "notwithstanding a provision . . . that prohibits, restricts, or conditions . . . assignment." Id. § 365(f)(1). Again, we must decide whether Congress intends, notwithstanding § 365(f)(1), for a debtor's assignee to provide adequate assurance that it will comply with use restrictions in a shopping center lease, such as the restriction here that limits the use of the space to the sale of auto parts and accessories.

We begin our inquiry with a look at the interesting history of Congress's efforts to protect shopping center landlords in § 365(b)(3) of the Bankruptcy Code. Congress has been interested in the financial well-being of shopping centers since at least the late 1970s. Specifics, such as the importance of a carefully selected tenant mix, have not escaped Congress's attention. The House Judiciary Committee discussed the tenant mix subject in a 1977 report:

> A shopping center is often a carefully planned enterprise, and though it consists of nuemrous [sic] individual tenants, the center is planned as a single unit, often subject to a master lease or financing agreement. Under these agreements, the tenant mix in a shopping center may be as important to the lessor as the actual promised rental payments, because certain mixes will attract higher patronage of the stores in the center.

H.R.Rep. No. 95–595, at 348 (1977), U.S.Code Cong. & Admin.News 1977 at 5963, 6305. To maintain proper tenant mix, that is, store variety, shopping center landlords have routinely placed use restrictions in leases. Before 1978 the bankruptcy of a shopping center tenant with a use restriction did not present an inordinate problem for a landlord; the typical lease provided that the landlord could terminate the lease if the tenant went bankrupt. The termination option allowed the landlord to engage a new tenant that would contribute to an acceptable mix of stores. See Jeffrey S. Battershall, Commercial Leases and Section 365 of the Bankruptcy Code, 64 Am. Bankr.L.J. 329, 329 (1990). With the enactment of the Bankruptcy Reform Act of 1978 (the 1978 Act), however, landlords "were no longer able to regain control of the leased property in the event of bankruptcy, and the lease routinely became part of the debtor's estate to be administered" in the bankruptcy. Id. at 330. See 11 U.S.C. § 365(e). Still, shopping center landlords were able to persuade Congress that they needed special protection, which Congress attempted to write into the 1978 Act. The 1978 legislation provided that a debtor-tenant could not assign its shopping center lease unless there was adequate assurance that "assignment of [the] lease [would] not breach *substantially* any provision, such as a radius, location, use, or exclusivity provision, *in any other* lease, financing agreement, or master agreement relating to such shopping center." 11 U.S.C. § 365(b)(3) (1982) (emphases added).

Shopping center landlords soon realized that the 1978 provisions did not provide them with sufficient protection against debtor-tenant lease assignments that were being made in breach of use (and other) restrictions, with the approval of bankruptcy courts. For example, debtors avoided the 1978 provisions by convincing bankruptcy courts that an assignment would not "breach substantially" a use, radius, location, or exclusivity provision in another lease. See id. § 365(b)(3)(C) (1982). And, debtors were able to convince courts that even though an assignment would breach a use provision in the lease sought to be assigned, the assignment could proceed because the 1978 Act only prevented assignment if some other lease or agreement relating to the shopping center would be breached. See id. Shopping center landlords were, as a result, able to convince Congress that bankruptcy courts were too often "creating new [shopping center] leases by changing essential lease terms to facilitate assignments" by debtor-tenants. 130 Cong. Rec. S8891 (daily ed. June 29, 1984) (statement of Sen. Hatch), reprinted in 1984 U.S.C.C.A.N. 590, 600. Congress was told that this practice of avoiding use restrictions was creating problems with tenant mix in affected shopping centers. These locations were losing their balance-of-merchandise drawing card, which was a threat to overall sales revenues in the shopping center sector of the economy. See Battershall, supra, at 334–35.

Congress responded in 1984 by amending the shopping center provisions in the Bankruptcy Code. Among other things, § 365(b)(3)(C) was amended to delete the word "substantially" from the provision previously requiring that assignment of a shopping center lease must not "breach substantially" certain restrictions. This section was also amended to provide that any assigned shopping center lease would remain subject to all of the provisions of the lease and not just the provisions of "any other lease" relating to the center. Again, the amended provision that we interpret today provides: "adequate assurance of future performance of a lease of real property in a shopping center includes adequate assurance . . . that assumption or assignment of such lease is subject to all the provisions thereof, including (but not limited to) provisions such as a radius, location, use, or exclusivity provision." 11 U.S.C. § 365(b)(3).

This background brings us to the matter of resolving the conflict between § 365(f)(1), a general provision that permits lease assignment notwithstanding anti-assignment clauses, and § 365(b)(3)(C), a more specific provision that requires the assignee of a shopping center lease to honor a clause restricting the use of the premises. For guidance in sorting out the conflict, we turn to the canons of statutory construction. See In re Windsor on the River Assocs., Ltd., 7 F.3d 127, 130 (8th Cir.1993). When two provisions in a statute are in conflict, "a specific [provision] closely applicable to the substance of the controversy at hand controls over a more generalized provision." Sigmon Coal Co. v. Apfel, 226 F.3d 291, 302 (4th Cir.2000) (internal quotation marks and citation omitted). See also Norman J. Singer, 2A Sutherland Statutes and Statutory Construction § 46:05 (6th ed.2000). Under this canon, § 365(b)(3)(C) controls because it speaks more directly to the issue, that is, whether a debtor-tenant assigning a shopping center lease must honor a straightforward use restriction. This construction is consistent with "the purpose[ ] Congress sought to serve." Norfolk Redevelopment & Hous. Auth. v. Chesapeake & Potomac Tel. Co., 464 U.S. 30, 36, 104 S.Ct. 304, 78 L.Ed.2d 29 (1983) (internal quotation marks and citation omitted). Congress's purpose is clear from the history (recited above) that culminated in the 1984 shopping center amendments to the

Bankruptcy Code and from the language of § 365(b)(3)(C) after those amendments. Specifically, when a shopping center lease is assigned in bankruptcy, Congress's purpose in § 365(b)(3)(C) is to preserve the landlord's bargained-for protections with respect to premises use and other matters that are spelled out in the lease with the debtor-tenant. In re Ames Dep't Stores, Inc., 121 B.R. 160, 165 n. 4 (Bankr.S.D.N.Y.1990). We therefore hold that because A & E does not propose to take the West Town lease subject to the specific restriction limiting use of the premises to the sale of auto parts and accessories, Trak Auto's motion to assume and assign the lease must be denied.

The bankruptcy and district courts gave this case careful attention, and we owe them a further explanation as to why we are rejecting their particular approaches. The bankruptcy court concluded that because no auto parts dealer bid on the West Town lease, the market in the area is saturated and "cannot bear [the] restriction" limiting use to the sale of auto parts and accessories. J.A. 421. According to the bankruptcy court, the market has turned the use restriction into an anti-assignment clause that is unenforceable under § 365(f)(1). This analysis overlooks the fact that West Town, the shopping center landlord, made the judgment that an auto parts retailer is important to a successful mix of stores in the center. And, in its lease with Trak Auto, West Town successfully negotiated to have the leased space dedicated to the sale of auto parts. West Town insists that this use restriction be honored by any assignee of Trak Auto, and that is West Town's right under § 365(b)(3)(C), regardless of market conditions. Section 365(b)(3)(C) simply does not allow the bankruptcy court or us to modify West Town's "*original* bargain with the debtor." S.Rep. No. 98–65, at 67–68 (1983) (emphasis added).

The district court concluded that the use restriction in the West Town lease was an unenforceable anti-assignment clause under § 365(f)(1) because the lease says that the tenant must use the premises "only as a Trak Auto Store." J.A. 588. West Town does not seek to restrict assignment to a tenant operating a Trak Auto store, and the parties have proceeded on that understanding. See Amer. Metal Forming Corp. v. Pittman, 52 F.3d 504, 509 (4th Cir.1995) (parties to a lease are free to modify it). The Trak Auto store designation is thus not in the picture, and West Town is free to enforce the remaining restriction that limits use of the premises to the retail sale of auto parts and accessories.

Our decision to block Trak Auto's lease assignment is not an attempt on our part to water down one of the important purposes of Chapter 11. That purpose is to give business debtors with some prospects the opportunity to reorganize, revive their operations, and continue in existence. The assumption and assignment of leases can be an important part of this effort. See In re Shangra-La, Inc., 167 F.3d 843, 849 (4th Cir.1999). Shopping center leases are in a special category, however, because Congress has made it more difficult for debtor-tenants to assign these leases in Chapter 11. This special protection for shopping center landlords, as spelled out in § 365(b)(3)(C), dictates the result in today's case. But this does not mean that § 365(f)(1) can never be used to invalidate a clause prohibiting or restricting assignment in a shopping center lease. But see In re Joshua

Slocum Ltd., 922 F.2d 1081, 1090 (3d Cir.1990) (concluding that § 365(b)(3) (1982) rendered § 365(f)(1) inapplicable to shopping center leases). A shopping center lease provision designed to prevent any assignment whatsoever might be a candidate for the application of § 365(f)(1). For example, Senator Hatch, in explaining the 1984 amendment to § 365(b)(3)(C), said that the "amendment is not intended to enforce requirements to operate under a specified trade name." 130 Cong. Rec. S8891 (daily ed. June 29, 1984), reprinted in 1984 U.S.C.C.A.N. 590, 600. Senator Hatch's comment suggests that Congress did not intend to make § 365(f)(1) completely inapplicable to shopping center leases. Of course, the issue of when § 365(f)(1) might apply is a subject for some future case.

IV.

In conclusion, we deny West Town's motion to dismiss this appeal as moot. On the merits, we hold that because A & E does not propose to take the West Town lease subject to the restriction limiting premises use to the retail sale of auto parts and accessories, Trak Auto's motion in bankruptcy court to assume and assign the lease must be denied under 11 U.S.C. § 365(b)(3)(C). The district court's order to the contrary is reversed. On remand the district court will return the case to the bankruptcy court for the entry of an order consistent with this opinion.

REVERSED AND REMANDED.

c.   TENANT'S RIGHT TO ASSIGN

Rowe v. Great Atlantic & Pacific Tea Co., Inc.

Court of Appeals of New York, 1978.
46 N.Y.2d 62, 412 N.Y.S.2d 827, 385 N.E.2d 566.

GABRIELLI, JUDGE.

We are called upon to determine whether a certain real property lease agreement contains an implied covenant limiting the lessee's power to assign the lease. The property subject to the lease is located in Sag Harbor, New York. In 1964, petitioner, Robert Rowe, an experienced attorney and businessman and the owner of the land involved herein, leased the property to respondent Great Atlantic & Pacific Tea Co. (A & P) for use as a "general merchandise business". The agreement required Rowe to erect a building on the property, and provided for a yearly rental of $14,000 for a 10-year term. It also granted A & P options to renew for two additional seven-year periods, at a slightly lower rental. The lease contained no restrictions on assignment of the lease by A & P. Rowe constructed the building as agreed, and A & P took possession and utilized the premises for a supermarket.

Some years later, both parties sought to renegotiate the agreement. Rowe desired a higher rental because of increases in taxes and other expenses, while A & P wished to have the building enlarged. Following protracted negotiations, a new lease was executed in 1971, in which it was provided that Rowe would expand the building by an additional 6,313 square feet, and that the base rental would be increased to $34,420 per year. This figure was reached by estimating the cost to

Rowe of the improvements to the building and then computing a rate of return agreed to by the parties and adding that to the old rental. The new lease was for a period of 15 years, and provided A & P with the option to renew for three additional seven-year periods at the same rental. In addition to the base rental, the new lease provided that Rowe was to receive 1½% of the store's annual gross receipts in excess of $2,294,666 and less than $5,000,000. In other words, unless gross receipts reached the $2,294,666 mark, the percentage clause would be inoperable. There was no warranty, stipulation or promise by A & P that sales would climb to the minimum necessary to trigger the percentage clause. The lease contained no restriction on the lessee's right to assign the lease. Nor did it make any reference to assignability other than providing that the lease would bind the heirs and assigns of the parties.

Unfortunately for all concerned, the new store did not fare as well as had been hoped. Indeed, A & P entered into a period of retrenchment in which it decided to close several of its less profitable stores, and the Sag Harbor store was one of those selected. Following months of discussion with Rowe and others, and over Rowe's objections, A & P in 1975 shut down its operation in Sag Harbor and assigned the lease of the premises to respondent Southland Corp., which operates a chain of supermarkets under the name Gristede Brothers. Rowe then commenced this proceeding seeking to recover possession of the premises as well as money damages. His claim is premised on the theory that A & P breached an implied covenant against assignment without consent of the lessor.

Following a nonjury trial, Supreme Court dismissed the petition on the merits, concluding that in the absence of bad faith, which was not shown, A & P had the unqualified right to assign the lease since there existed no provision limiting that right. With respect to Rowe's claim that the lease contained an implied covenant limiting A & P's right to assign, the court concluded that he had not met his burden of proof on this issue in that he had failed to prove that no reasonable landlord would have entered into this lease without an implicit understanding that the lessee could not freely assign the lease. The court reasoned that in order to show the existence of such an implicit covenant, the lessor would first be required to prove that without the percentage rent clause, which was the only factor indicating that there might actually exist such an implied agreement, the lease would have been unconscionable.

Petitioner appealed and the Appellate Division reversed, stating that the trial court had placed too heavy a burden upon petitioner. Noting that the courts will find the existence of an implied covenant limiting the right to assign if the lease is such that the landlord entered into it in reliance upon the special ability or characteristics of the lessee, the court reasoned that the existence of a percentage clause in a lease is a strong indication of such reliance. Although the existence of a base rental in addition to the percentage rental would be some evidence to the contrary, the Appellate Division concluded that in this case that was not true because in the court's judgment the base rental was not substantial. Accordingly, the Appellate Division reversed Supreme

Court and ruled in favor of petitioner. We cannot agree with that determination.

It has long been the law that covenants seeking to limit the right to assign a lease are "restraints which courts do not favor. They are construed with the utmost jealousy, and very easy modes have always been countenanced for defeating them" (Riggs v. Pursell, 66 N.Y. 193, 201.) This is so because they are restraints on the free alienation of land, and as such they tend to prevent full utilization of the land, which is contrary to the best interests of society. Since such covenants are to be construed strictly even if expressly stated, it follows that a court should not recognize the existence of an implied limitation upon assignment unless the situation is such that the failure to do so would be to deprive a party of the benefit of his bargain.

In the case presently before us petitioner Rowe has failed to prove the existence of an implied covenant limiting the lessee's right to assign the lease. Such a covenant is to be recognized only if it is clear that a reasonable landlord would not have entered into the lease without such an understanding, for it is only in such a situation that it can be said with the requisite certainty that to refuse to recognize such a covenant would be to deprive the landlord of the fruits of his bargain. This is not such a case.

An implied covenant limiting the right to assign will often be found in those situations in which it is evident that the landlord entered into the lease in reliance upon some special skill or ability of the lessee which will have a material effect upon the fulfillment of the landlord's reasonable contractual expectations. In the typical lease in which the landlord is assured of a set monthly rent, and has not placed any unusual restrictions upon the use of the premises, there is no occasion to find an implied covenant precluding or limiting assignment. This is so because the only reasonable expectation of the landlord is that the rent will be paid and the premises not abused, and thus the identity of the tenant is not material to the landlord's expectations under the lease. If, however, the expectations of the landlord are substantially dependent upon some special skill or trait of the lessee, the lack of which might endanger the lessor's legitimate contractual expectations, then it may be appropriate to find the existence of an implied covenant limiting the right to assign, for in such circumstances no reasonable person would enter into the contract without assurance that the tenant could not be replaced by an assignee lacking the requisite skills or character traits. Even in such a case, however, the implied restrictions must of course be limited to the extent possible without destroying the landlord's legitimate interests.

The type of situation in which a court may properly find that there exists a covenant limiting the right to assign is illustrated by the factual pattern which confronted the court in Nassau Hotel Co. v. Barnett & Barse Corp., 212 N.Y. 568, 106 N.E. 1036, affg. on opn. at 162 App.Div. 381, 147 N.Y.S. 283. There, the owner of a hotel had leased the hotel and all its appurtenances to two men, one of whom was an experienced hotel manager. The lease granted them " 'the exclusive possession, control and management' " of the hotel, and they not only became responsible " 'for the operation . . . and maintenance' " of the hotel, but also promised that they would operate it " 'at all times in a first-class, business-like manner'" (162 App.Div. at p. 382, 147 N.Y.S. at p. 284). In lieu of any set rental, the owner was to receive 19% of the gross receipts of the hotel. Subsequently, the lessees assigned the lease to a corporation and the landlord sued to recover the premises. The courts concluded that the lease could not be assigned without the owner's consent, even though the lease did not contain a provision limiting the lessees' power to assign, because the entire agreement indicated conclusively that a fundamental premise of the agreement was that the two original lessees would operate the hotel. This was so in part because the landlord had agreed to accept a percentage of the receipts in place of rent, and thus his legitimate expectations were completely dependent on the ability and honesty of the two individual lessees. To deprive him of the right to depend on the fact that the hotel was being operated by the individuals with whom he had contracted would have been to deprive him of a substantial element of his reasonable and legitimate contractual expectations.

Although the existence of the percentage clause was a significant factor in that decision, it alone was not dispositive. Rather, the court properly considered the entire agreement, with its emphasis on the operation of the hotel and the implicit dependence of the landlord upon the identity of the operators of the hotel. Thus, while a percentage clause in a lease is some sign of an implied agreement to limit the lessee's power to assign the lease, its significance will vary with the other terms of the lease, the surrounding circumstances, the nature of the business conducted upon the premises, and the identities and expectations of the parties.

Although the lease we are called upon to interpret today does contain a percentage clause, it is a far cry from that involved in *Nassau Hotel*. There, the percentage of gross receipts to be received by the landlord was the only value the landlord was to receive from the agreement, for there was no set rental. Here, in contradistinction, the landlord is provided with an annual rental of some $34,420 in addition to whatever amount he might receive pursuant to the percentage clause. We would also emphasize that the percentage clause does not result in any additional income to the landlord until and unless the store first attains sales of over $2,294,666 in a particular year. Of some interest is the fact that this figure is considerably higher than the previous record gross sales at the Sag Harbor store at the time the lease was entered into. It is thus evident that the percentage clause, although doubtless of considerable interest to the landlord as a hedge against inflation and as a means of sharing in the hoped for success of the store, was not a material part of the lessor's fundamental expectations under the lease. Hence, it cannot be said that the lease was entered into in sole reliance upon the skill, expertise, and reputation of A & P, and thus there is no reason to find an implied covenant limiting the lessee's right to assign the lease.

This conclusion is buttressed by consideration of the circumstances surrounding and preceding the making of the new lease in 1971. It should not be forgotten that at that time the landlord was bound by a long-term lease which provided substantially less rent per square foot of store space than does the current lease, taking into account the expansion in size of the store. Indeed, examination of the two leases indicates that even absent the percentage clause, the new lease was an improvement over the old from the landlord's point of view. Moreover, comparison with other supermarket leases indicates that the base rental in the new lease is not out of line with the rentals reserved in other leases. Thus we cannot agree with the Appellate Division that it is "not substantial."

Of additional interest is the identity of the parties to this agreement. Petitioner is an experienced attorney and businessman knowledgeable in real estate transactions. A & P is, of course, a national firm presumably represented by capable agents. The negotiations which resulted in the new lease were long and exhaustive, dealing with a variety of topics, and the lease itself is obviously the result of a process of give and take. Although A & P might well have agreed to include a provision limiting its right to assign the lease had petitioner insisted upon such a clause, we may safely assume that petitioner would have had to pay a price for that concession. In these circumstances, the courts should be extremely reluctant to interpret an agreement as impliedly stating something which the parties have neglected to specifically include. As we have previously declared in a similar context, "such lack of foresight does not create rights or obligations" (Mutual Life Ins. Co. of N.Y. v. Tailored Woman, 309 N.Y. 248, 253, 128 N.E.2d 401, 403).

Finally, although not necessary to our disposition of this appeal, we would note that even were the circumstances such as to support the conclusion that the lease contains a provision limiting the lessee's right to assign the lease, that finding alone would not justify judgment in favor of petitioner. It would then be necessary to further consider whether that implied restriction would in fact be violated by assignment of the lease to another supermarket chain in light of all the facts and circumstances.

Accordingly, the order appealed from should be reversed, with costs, and the judgment of Supreme Court, Suffolk County, reinstated.

BREITEL, C.J., and JASEN, JONES, WACHTLER, FUCHSBERG and COOKE, JJ., concur.

Order reversed, etc.

d.   TENANT'S PERCENTAGE RENT OBLIGATION

Hartig Drug Company v. Hartig

Supreme Court of Iowa, 1999.
602 N.W.2d 794.

Considered by MCGIVERIN, C.J., and LARSON, CARTER, CADY, and ANDREASEN, JJ.

CADY, JUSTICE.

This appeal requires us to determine whether the rent due from a retail business tenant under a percentage of "gross sales" lease includes the total sale of lottery tickets and postage stamps. We conclude the lease excludes total lottery and stamp sales, and reverse and remand the district court ruling.

I.   Background Facts and Proceedings.

Hartig Drug Company is a third generation family business which owns and operates several retail pharmacy businesses in the Dubuque area. The company is owned by Richard Hartig, who purchased the stock in the company in 1984 from a trust established at the time of his father's death in 1973. Richard began working for the business in 1964.

Kenneth Hartig, Richard's brother, was vice president of the company until Richard acquired the stock. Kenneth began working for the business in 1955. Under the 1984 stock purchase agreement negotiated between Richard and Kenneth, Kenneth acquired ownership of the land and buildings which housed the drug stores. Kenneth was required under the agreement to lease the buildings to Hartig Drug.

The lease for the drug store located on Central Avenue in Dubuque set a minimum monthly base rental amount of $3208.33, which could be increased to 2.75 percent of the "gross sales" of the business of the store if the percentage exceeded the amount of the base monthly rent. The lease included a broad definition of "gross sales" for the calculation of any additional rent. It defined "gross sales" to mean "the aggregate of all retail sales of every kind, type, and description, and services performed for patrons made in, upon, or from the demised premises by the tenant or by any sublessee, licensee, concessionaire, other occupant. . . ."

The purpose of the percentage lease provision was to give Kenneth a stake in the success of Hartig Drug's business. The base rent amount of $3208.33 represented 2.75 percent of the gross sales in the year prior to the lease. At the end of every year, Kenneth had the right to inspect Hartig Drug records to ensure the proper amount of rent was paid. At his option, these records could also be reviewed by an independent accountant.

After the lease was entered into, two events occurred which led to the present lawsuit. First, Hartig Drug negotiated a contract with the United States Postal Service in 1985 to establish the Hartig Drug store on Central Avenue as a USPS substation. Under this contract, Hartig Drug furnished its customers a number of services offered by the USPS, including the sale of stamps and money orders. The USPS provided Hartig Drug with scales, a money order imprinter, forms and supplies, stamps, envelopes, and other items necessary to conduct the postal sales. Under the terms of the contract, all USPS sales and services purchased at Hartig Drug were paid directly to the USPS. Furthermore, Hartig Drug was not allowed to commingle Hartig Drug money with USPS money. USPS revenues were processed separately and deposited daily with the USPS. All title to USPS stamps and services remained in the USPS. Under the contract, Hartig Drug was also required to staff the postal substation. In exchange for this, the USPS paid Hartig Drug $5000 per year between the years of 1985 and 1993, and $9000 per year from 1994 on to help defray the costs of operating the postal substation. Hartig Drug received no other revenues from the USPS substation. Hartig Drug excluded the total postal sales as well as the money received from the USPS in calculating the percentage lease rent. Over the years, the total sale of stamps and other postal services exceeded 2.3 million dollars.

The second event occurred in the latter part of 1985 after the State of Iowa authorized a state regulated lottery. At this time, Hartig Drug began selling lottery scratch tickets and lotto drawing tickets for the state. The state paid Hartig Drug a five percent commission for every ticket it sold. Between the years of 1985 and 1994, Hartig Drug received $32,435.29 in commissions for the lottery sales it made for the state. It stopped selling lottery tickets in 1994. In addition to the general commissions received, Hartig Drug also received a ten percent bonus for the sale of a $100,000 winning ticket. The total of commissions received for lottery sales was $42,435.29. The total lottery sales were $634,714. Like the stamp sales, neither the lottery sales nor the commissions were included in the percentage lease rental calculation.

In 1996, Hartig Drug filed a petition for declaratory judgment. It sought to compel Kenneth to make certain repairs and provide general maintenance at the building leased by Hartig Drug. Kenneth filed a counter-claim alleging unpaid rent based upon the exclusion of lottery ticket and postage sales from additional rent calculations under the lease agreement. Kenneth died during the pendency of the lawsuit, and his estate was made a party to the proceedings.

Following a bench trial, but prior to the district court's judgment, Kenneth's estate agreed to make the repairs sought by Hartig Drug. This left only the estate's claim for rent. The district court found the percentage rent calculation should have included the total sale of all lottery tickets and stamps, and entered judgment for the estate in the amount of $128,075.95, with statutory interest, as payment for rent due under the percentage lease agreement. Hartig Drug appeals.

II. Scope of Review.

We generally review the construction and interpretation of a contract as a matter of law. Thus, we are not bound by the construction or interpretation made by the trial court. Krause v. Krause, 589 N.W.2d 721, 724 (Iowa 1999). However, if the interpretation was predicated upon extrinsic evidence, the findings of the trial court are binding on appeal if supported by substantial evidence. See Modern Piping, Inc. v. Blackhawk Auto. Sprinklers, Inc., 581 N.W.2d 616, 623 (Iowa 1998); Connie's Constr. Co. v. Fireman's Fund Ins. Co., 227 N.W.2d 207, 210 (Iowa 1975). Yet, when no relevant extrinsic evidence exists, the resolution of any ambiguity in a written contract is a matter of law for the court. See 17A Am. Jur. 2d Contracts § 339, at 346 (1991). The question whether an ambiguity exists is also one of law. Id.

III. Discussion.

A cardinal rule of contract construction or interpretation is the intent of the parties must control. Whalen v. Connelly, 545 N.W.2d 284, 291 (Iowa 1996). The important time frame for determining this intent is the time the contract was executed. Davenport Osteopathic Hosp. Ass'n v. Hospital Serv., Inc., 261 Iowa 247, 260, 154 N.W.2d 153, 161 (1967). If the contract is ambiguous and uncertain, extrinsic evidence can be considered to help determine the intent. Yet, a contract is not ambiguous merely because the parties disagree over its meaning. Tom Riley Law Firm, P.C. v. Tang, 521 N.W.2d 758, 759 (Iowa App.1994). Instead, an ambiguity occurs in a contract when a genuine uncertainty exists concerning which of two reasonable interpretations is proper.

Berryhill v. Hatt, 428 N.W.2d 647, 654 (Iowa 1988). The existence of an ambiguity, however, can be determined only after all pertinent rules of interpretation have been considered. Id. Our general rules of interpretation are used both to determine what meanings are reasonably possible as well as to choose among two reasonable meanings. Restatement (Second) of Contracts § 202 cmt. a (1981).

The trial court determined the phrase "all retail sales" was clear and unambiguous and bound Hartig Drug to pay the percentage rent on every sale without limitation. It found the plain meaning of "all retail sales" had no exclusions, and it was prohibited from judicially creating an exception merely because a particular type of sale may not be profitable. Thus, it concluded the total lottery ticket and stamp sales were intended to be included in "gross sales."

While the trial court properly focused on the language of the lease, it failed to further consider the rules of interpretation in reaching its conclusion. We find the application of the rules of interpretation to the face of the lease shows the parties intended to exclude transactions such as lottery and stamp sales from the definition of "gross sales."

In interpreting contracts, we give effect to the language of the entire contract according to its commonly accepted and ordinary meaning. Magina v. Bartlett, 582 N.W.2d 159, 163 (Iowa 1998). Moreover, particular words and phrases are not interpreted in isolation. Iowa Fuel & Minerals, Inc. v. Iowa State Bd. of Regents, 471 N.W.2d 859, 863 (Iowa 1991). Instead, they are interpreted in a context in which they are used. Home Fed. Sav. & Loan Ass'n v. Campney, 357 N.W.2d 613, 617 (Iowa 1984). Furthermore, the words are given the meaning at the time the contract was executed. 17A Am. Jur. 2d Contracts § 359, at 382. Using these principles as a guide, we find the only reasonable interpretation of the lease excluded the total sale of lottery tickets and stamps in calculating the additional rent obligation.

At the time the lease was executed in this case, the drug store did not maintain a postal substation and the State of Iowa had no lottery. Thus, the term "retail sales" did not specifically consider postage stamps and lottery sales. However, in the context of a retail business lease, there are a host of characteristics of lottery and postage stamp sales which distinguish the transactions from the types of "retail sales" of the drug store the parties would have reasonably contemplated at the time of the lease. These distinctions are so significant that reasonable parties to a percentage-of-sales lease would not have intended to include lottery and stamp sales.

Unlike the typical commercial transaction in a retail business, a business which sells lottery tickets is simply a licensee of the state. See generally Iowa Code ch. 99E (1995). Similarly, a retail business with a postal substation is an agent for the postal service. In both instances, the business is carefully regulated by the government, and is required to turn over the proceeds of the sales. The state pays the business a five percent commission on each lottery ticket that is sold, while the postal service pays an annual fee for the operation of a postal substation. Unlike the customary retail sales of a drug store, the amount of lottery tickets and stamps sold have no or little direct relationship to the amount of business revenues. A reasonable business tenant would not agree to pay additional rent based on sales that belonged to the government. These characteristics reveal substantial differences from ordinary retail sales, and places lottery and stamp sales in a separate class by themselves. See In re Circle K Corp., 98 F.3d 484, 486 (9th Cir.1996). Thus, the common and ordinary meaning of "retail sales" in the context of a percentage-of-sales business lease would exclude transactions such as lottery and stamp sales.

Additionally, the rule of interpretation providing that the intention of the parties is not derived from a single phrase or clause, but from the contract as a whole is also pertinent to the resolution of this case. Under other provisions of the lease in this case, "gross sales" specifically excluded sums collected for taxes. A retail business collects taxes imposed by the government upon certain retail sales and is required to remit the taxes to the taxing agency. This lease provision excluding taxes reveals the parties intended to exclude that portion of sales the business did not actually retain because it was required to remit the amount to the government.

This exclusion is important in interpreting the contract because lottery sales are used for the public welfare, not unlike tax revenues. See generally Iowa Code ch. 99E. Similarly, the cost of stamps helps finance the government postal service. Thus, by transferring the lottery and stamp sales to the government, a business acts more like a tax collector than a retailer. Circle K, 98 F.3d at 486. This exclusion, read in light of the nature of lottery and stamp sales, illustrates the parties would have excluded lottery and stamp sales from "gross sales" if they would have been specifically considered at the time the lease was executed.

These considerations, and others, have caused other jurisdictions faced with the interpretation of similar leases to conclude that the term "gross sales" does not include total sales of lottery tickets. In Anest v. Bellino, 151 Ill. App. 3d 818, 503 N.E.2d 576, 104 Ill. Dec. 861 (Ill.Ct.App.1987), the appellate court of Illinois was faced with the identical issue presented in this case. Anest, 503 N.E.2d at 577. In excluding lottery sales from the term "all gross sales" in a restaurant lease, the court reasoned,

> While gross sales have no relation to profit . . . amounts which are not income to a lessee are not received by him within the meaning of gross sales. The money received from the sale of lottery tickets . . . temporarily comes into the possession of the [lessee], but are not his property.

503 N.E.2d at 579–80. The court held "although the restaurant actually handled the money, that portion of the money belonging to the lottery system was not intended by the parties to be included in gross sales." 503 N.E.2d at 579. The court only included the commissions and bonuses received by the business from the state for the service it provided in selling tickets on behalf of the state lottery. Id.

In Cloverland Farms Dairy, Inc. v. Fry, 322 Md. 367, 587 A.2d 527 (Md.Ct.App.1991), the court of appeals of Maryland found the phrase "the total amount of sales of every kind made in the store" unambiguously excluded the sale of lottery tickets. Cloverland, 587 A.2d at 527. Applying an objective test of ambiguity, the court found a reasonable person in the position of the parties to the contract would not include an additional rent percentage clause based on sales which the business did not retain. 587 A.2d at 530. Instead, it found the clause encompassed sales which occurred in the course of its business activity. Id.

Finally, in *Circle K*, the Ninth Circuit Court of Appeals found "state-sponsored lottery ticket sales fall into a class by themselves." *Circle K*, 98 F.3d at 486. Sellers are "paid for its services by a commission, and that commission is properly considered a 'gross receipt[ ]' from 'services' performed on the premises." Id. In relying upon *Anest* and *Cloverland,* the court held even the extremely broad definition of "gross sales," as "gross receipts of any kind and nature originating from sales and services on the demised premises" were included regardless of whether the sale was "by the Lessee, or by a Sublessee, or concessionaire," did not serve to turn the entire proceeds of lottery ticket sales into receipts within the meaning of the lease. Id. at 487–88. Thus, the money received on the *sale* of the tickets was not to be included in the additional rent calculation, only the commissions received for the *service* of selling the tickets. Id. at 489.

We agree with the district court that the percentage rent terms include lottery and stamp sales, but not the total amount of the sale. Instead, we find the reasoning of the *Anest, Cloverland,* and *Circle K* courts persuasive. "Retail sales" under the lease contemplates revenues actually received by Hartig Drug. The lease did not contemplate the inclusion of proceeds which did not belong to the business, and was not considered as part of its income. Nevertheless, "gross sales" under the lease did include "services performed for patrons." Hartig Drug acknowledges the lottery and stamp sales were a service for customers, and the revenues it received for performing those services is properly included within the definition of "gross sales." We therefore reverse the district court and remand for entry of judgment for the additional rent based upon the actual commissions received for lottery tickets and the actual compensation received from the postal service for the sale of stamps.

REVERSED AND REMANDED.

e.   TENANT'S OBLIGATION TO LANDLORD'S MORTGAGEE

Miscione v. Barton Development Company

Court of Appeal of California, Fourth Appellate District, 1997.
52 Cal.App.4th 1320, 61 Cal.Rptr.2d 280, petition for review denied.

WARD, ASSOCIATE JUSTICE.

Plaintiff John J. Miscione (Miscione), as a successor landlord, filed an action for breach of an office lease and fraud. Defendant Barton Development Company (Barton Development) was the tenant under the lease and defendant James E. Barton (Barton) was alleged to be liable as an alter ego of the tenant. Defendants filed a motion for summary judgment contending the lease was subordinate to a prior trust deed on the property, and the foreclosure of the trust deed had extinguished the lease. The trial court granted summary judgment. Plaintiff appeals and contends that: (1) the general rule that foreclosure of a trust deed extinguishes a subordinate lease does not apply in this case; and (2) the defendants attorned to the new landlord by contractually agreeing to be bound by the lease. We agree and reverse.

FACTUAL AND PROCEDURAL BACKGROUND

Defendant Barton, as general partner, formed Rancho Cucamonga Business Park Equities I (Equities I) to develop real property. Equities I constructed an office building known as Barton Plaza and thereafter borrowed $7.6 million from Coast Federal Savings (Coast). Equities I gave, as security for the loan, a trust deed to Coast. The trust deed was recorded January 31, 1986.

The deed of trust provided that Equities I could "not execute or enter into any lease . . . of the Mortgaged Property or any portion thereof without the advance written consent of [Coast] as to the form and substance thereof and the acceptability of the tenant. . . ."

On September 19, 1988, Equities I, as landlord, and Barton Development, as tenant, entered into a five-year lease of space in the office building. The lease was signed by Barton for Equities I and by a vice-president of Barton Development for the corporation. Barton was the president of Barton Development.

Paragraph 23 of the lease contained an attornment clause that provided:

"In the event of any foreclosure sale, transfer in lieu of foreclosure or termination of the lease in which Landlord is lessee, Tenant shall attorn to the purchaser, transferee or lessor as the case may be, and recognize that party as Landlord under this Lease, provided that party acquires and accepts the Premises subject to this Lease."

The same paragraph also contained a subordination and nondisturbance clause that provided:

"Upon written request of Landlord, or any first mortgagee, first deed of trust beneficiary of Landlord, or ground lessor of Landlord, Tenant shall, in writing, subordinate its rights hereunder to the lien of any first mortgage, first deed of trust, or the interest of any lease in which Landlord is lessee, and to all advances made or hereafter to be made thereunder. However, before signing any subordination agreement, Tenant shall have the right to obtain from any lender or lessor of Landlord requesting that subordination, an agreement in writing providing that, as long as Tenant is not in default hereunder, this Lease shall remain in effect for the full Term. The holder of any security interest may, upon written notice to Tenant, elect to have this Lease prior to its security interest regardless of the time of the granting or recording of that security interest."

On August 21, 1991, Westinghouse Credit Corporation (Westinghouse) became the owner of the property through foreclosure of its second trust deed on the property. The Westinghouse second trust deed had been recorded on September 30, 1988. On January 30, 1992, Coast became the owner of the property through foreclosure on its first trust deed. Through letters dated January 30, 1992, and March 3, 1992, Coast notified the tenants of the building, including defendants, that it was the new landlord. Coast also requested in writing that defendants execute an estoppel certificate confirming the terms of the lease. Barton admitted receiving the estoppel certificate from Coast, but never executed or returned it. On June 16, 1992, Coast sold the building to Miscione. On July 31, 1992, defendants vacated the premises and have not paid the rent on the premises. This litigation followed.

Miscione sued Barton and Barton Development on the lease and for fraud. Prior to the trial defendants moved for summary judgment contending that the lease had been extinguished when Coast foreclosed on the property. Relying on Dover Mobile Estates v. Fiber Form Products, Inc. (1990) 220 Cal. App. 3d 1494, 1498–1500 [270 Cal. Rptr. 183], defendants contended that Coast had an obligation under the lease to elect to have the lease senior to the deed of trust and that it had failed to do so. Defendants further contended that the fraud cause of action failed with the contract action since it was based upon the contract. The court below agreed with defendants' position and granted the motion for summary judgment. Judgment was entered. This appeal followed.

DISCUSSION

I. *Standard of Review*

On appeal from the trial court's grant of defendants' motion for summary judgment, ". . . we review the trial court's decision de novo, applying the rule that '[a] defendant is entitled to summary judgment if the record establishes as a matter of law that none of the plaintiff's asserted causes of action can prevail. [Citation.] To succeed, the defendant must . . . demonstrate that under no hypothesis is there a material issue of fact that requires the process of a trial.' [Citation.]" (Flatt v. Superior Court (1994) 9 Cal. 4th 275, 279 [36 Cal. Rptr. 2d 537, 885 P.2d 950].)

The first step of the review begins with an analysis of the pleadings, because "[t]he pleadings define the issues to be considered on a motion for summary judgment." (Ferrari v. Grand Canyon Dories (1995) 32 Cal. App. 4th 248, 252 [38 Cal. Rptr. 2d 65].) We next evaluate the moving defendant's effort to meet its burden of showing that plaintiff's cause of action has no merit or that there is a complete defense to it. Once the defendant has met that burden, the burden shifts to the plaintiff to show that a triable issue of material fact exists as to its complaint. If the filings in opposition raise triable issues of material fact the motion must be denied; if they do not, the motion must be granted (Code Civ. Proc., § 437c, subd. (c); River Bank America v. Diller (1995) 38 Cal. App. 4th 1400, 1410–1411 [45 Cal. Rptr. 2d 790].)

The pertinent pleading here is the second amended complaint which contains causes of action for: (1) breach of written lease, (2) fraud—intentional misrepresentation, and (3) fraud—suppression of fact. Defendants answered with a general denial, and using the popular pleading technique of today, alleged 21 affirmative defenses including, inter alia, the defense that the lease was terminated as a matter of law by Coast's foreclosure.

Defendants relied upon this affirmative defense in their motion for summary judgment. The lower court accepted their argument that *Dover* applied and that the foreclosure terminated the lease. Plaintiff opposed the motion on the ground that the attornment provision of the lease preserved the landlord-tenant relationship even after foreclosures of the prior trust deed. Resolution of this issue depends upon the meaning of a contractual provision.

Thus, in addition to the standard of review for summary judgment, we must apply the standard of review for the interpretation of a written contract. "The interpretation of a written instrument presents a question of law for this court to determine anew." (Klingele v. Engelman (1987) 192 Cal. App. 3d 1482, 1485 [238 Cal. Rptr. 199].) This court must interpret the lease entered into by the original landlord and tenant in order to determine the rights and liabilities of the parties.

Under Civil Code *section 1636*, "A contract must be so interpreted as to give effect to the mutual intention of the parties as it existed at the time of contracting, so far as the same is ascertainable and lawful." Generally speaking, "the rules of interpretation of written contracts are for the purpose of ascertaining the meaning of the *words used* therein: evidence cannot be admitted to show intention independent of the instrument. [Citations.]" (1 Witkin, Summary of Cal. Law (9th ed. 1987) Contracts, § 684, p. 617.)

II. *Obligations Under a Lease Are Not Extinguished by Foreclosure Proceedings on a Prior Encumbrance When the Parties to the Lease Contract to the Contrary*

A. *Priorities of the parties without an agreement.* There is no dispute that the lease in these proceedings was junior to the Coast trust deed which was foreclosed. The trust deed was recorded over two years before the execution of the lease; a lease executed after a trust deed is recorded is subordinate to the trust deed. (Goldstein v. Ray (1981) 118 Cal. App. 3d 571, 575 [173 Cal. Rptr. 550].) Also, there is no dispute that the general rule is that foreclosure of a senior encumbrance terminates subordinate liens, including leases. (Hohn v. Riverside County Flood Control etc. Dist. (1964) 228 Cal. App. 2d 605, 613 [39 Cal. Rptr. 647].)

Without an agreement to alter the priorities, neither Coast nor the defendants would have had obligations under the lease after the foreclosure of the prior trust deed; the foreclosure would have terminated, "wiped out," the lease and all rights and obligations under it. The lender could consider the tenant as a trespasser, and the tenant would have no obligation to perform under the lease.

B. *Effect of the agreement to rearrange priorities.* Parties to real estate transactions can contractually agree to alter the priorities otherwise fixed by law so as to avoid the termination of rights under the general rule that foreclosure terminates the rights under a junior lease. (*Dover Mobile Estates v. Fiber Form Products, Inc., supra*, 220 Cal. App. 3d 1494, 1498; Bank of America v. Hirsch Merc. Co. (1944) 64 Cal. App. 2d 175, 183 [148 P.2d 110].) We therefore analyze the contract to determine whether the parties to the lease did so in this case.

1. *Parties to Lease.* The landlord was Equities I, with Barton signing as general partner. The tenant was Barton Development, with a vice-president signing for the corporation. Barton was the president of Barton Development and the developer of Barton Plaza. Thus, in a sense, Barton was acting as both landlord and tenant. We are therefore

dealing here with presumably knowledgeable parties who executed a lease containing provisions acceptable to them, not with contracting parties of unequal power or circumstances of adhesion.

2. *SNDA Provisions.* The lease contains provisions for subordination, nondisturbance and attornment, sometimes known as SNDA. "Although it might seem a cobweb-filled corner of real estate law, the realm of subordination, non-disturbance and attornment has drawn the attention of mortgagees over the last few years as the level of foreclosures has increased." (Feinstein & Keyles, Foreclosure: Subordination, Non-Disturbance and Attornment Agreements (Aug. 1989) 3 Prob. & Prop. 38 (hereafter, Foreclosure).) "Although SNDAs are common to virtually every commercial real estate transaction, there has been very little analysis of the basic concepts of SNDAs, and surprisingly few cases have interpreted SNDAs or the rights and obligations of the parties to SNDAs." (Fisher & Goldman, The Ritual Dance Between Lessee and Lender—Subordination, Nondisturbance, and Attornment (Fall 1995) 30 Real Prop., Prob. and Trust J. 355, 357 (hereafter, *Ritual Dance*).)

Subordination is "[t]he act or process by which a person's rights or claims are ranked below those of others: *e.g.* a second mortgagee's rights are subordinate to those of the first mortgagee." (Black's Law Dict. (6th ed. 1990) p. 1426, col. 1.) A subordination agreement is "An agreement by which one holding an otherwise senior lien or other real estate interest consents to a reduction in priority vis-a-vis another person holding an interest in the same real estate. An agreement by which the subordinating party agrees that its interest in real property should have a lower priority than the interest to which it is being subordinated." (Black's Law Dict., *supra*, p. 1426, col. 2.)

Under a nondisturbance agreement, a "mortgagee covenants that, in the event of a foreclosure, the tenant will remain on the leased premises so long as the tenant continues to comply with the terms of the lease and the lease is not in default." (*Foreclosure, supra*, at p. 39.) "Nondisturbance is a modern concept. In fact, *Black's Law Dictionary* does not even define the term." (*Ritual Dance, supra*, at p. 360.) "Realistically, the concept of nondisturbance is frequently intended to refer not only to nondisturbance of the tenant's right of possession, but also to full recognition of all of the tenant's rights under its lease." (*Ritual Dance, supra*, at p. 361.)

"Attornment, in its present day form is very much a corollary agreement addressing foreclosure." (*Foreclosure, supra*, at p. 39.) Attornment is ". . . the act of a person who holds a leasehold interest in land, or estate for life or years, by which he agrees to become the tenant of a stranger who has acquired the fee in the land, or the remainder or reversion, or the right to rent or services by which the tenant holds. It is an act by which a tenant acknowledges his obligation to a new landlord." (Black's Law Dict., *supra*, p. 130, col. 1.) Under an attornment clause, a "tenant covenants with the mortgagee that, in the event of foreclosure, the lease will not be extinguished but will continue as a lease between the mortgagee (or any successor to it) and the tenant. The tenant, in other words, agrees to recognize that another party who would not otherwise have privity may enforce the lease agreement as though the third party were originally a beneficiary of the agreement." (*Foreclosure, supra*, at p. 39.)

It should be noted that SNDA provisions may alter the rights of the parties not only with respect to foreclosure actions, but also in connection with distribution of insurance proceeds, condemnation awards, and promises made outside the lease. (*Foreclosure, supra*, at p. 40.)

3.   *The SNDA Clauses in the Present Lease.* The subordination and nondisturbance clause in the lease has essentially three parts, the first two of which are linked to one another. Under paragraph 23, the landlord, first trust deed holder, or ground lessor could: (1) ask, in writing, that the tenant subordinate its interest and then (2) the tenant had the right to obtain from the requesting party an agreement that the lease remain in effect for the full term. This is the classic subordination and nondisturbance formula of SNDA clauses. The paragraph also provides that (3) the holder of a security interest could elect to have the lease prior to its security "regardless of the time of the granting or recording of that security interest." When the lease was executed, Coast was not a party to the lease, and the lease was subordinate to the trust deed held by Coast. Coast had the power to foreclose and eliminate the rights of the parties under the lease; nothing in the contract between the landlord and the tenant could change that without Coast's consent. Thus, the subordination clause of the lease was of no value to Coast since its senior position was already fixed by law.

Coast had no need to ask that the tenant subordinate since Coast's position was already fixed by law. The tenant's right to an agreement of nondisturbance did not exist without a subordination request. Thus, the nondisturbance clause of the lease was of no value to the tenant. Coast did not, prior to its foreclosure, elect to have the lease prior to its interest. The positions of the parties were, so far as the subordination and nondisturbance clause was concerned, fixed by law. The only potential effect of the clause was to allow the lender to elect that the lease become senior, and this did not happen.

The third of the SNDA provisions, an attornment clause, is also present in paragraph 23. The tenant agreed to recognize, or attorn to, a new landlord who could be the purchaser in a foreclosure sale or the transferee in a transfer in lieu of foreclosure. The successful bidder at a foreclosure sale or any transferee in a deed in lieu of foreclosure conceivably could be a new player on the scene. Thus, the tenant attorned either to the existing lender or potentially to a new party not previously involved in any way.

4.   *Effect of the Attornment Clause.* Under the attornment clause of the lease, Barton Development agreed with its original landlord that it would accept a substituted landlord under prescribed conditions, one of which occurred in the instant case. This is the expected result of the attornment clause in the lease.

However, defendants argue that the case of *Dover Mobile Estates v. Fiber Form Products, Inc., supra*, 220 Cal. App. 3d 1494, supports their position that the lease was extinguished following the foreclosure. The lower court based its decision granting summary judgment upon that case.

In *Dover* the tenant entered into a lease which contained a subordination clause which provided that the lease was subordinate to any deeds of trust unless the trust deed holder elected to have the lease be superior. (This is commonly known as an automatic subordination. Since the instant case does not have this type of subordination agreement, the distinction between types of agreements is unimportant.) A second trust deed, recorded after the lease, was foreclosed upon. The purchaser at the sale sought to enforce the lease. The court held that the foreclosure terminated the lease, and the plaintiff could not enforce the terms of it. (*Dover Mobile Estates v. Fiber Form Products, Inc., supra,* 220 Cal. App. 3d at p. 1501.)

Dover is distinguishable for the simple reason that the court in that case did not discuss whether the lease contained an attornment clause or what the effect of such a clause would be. Reliance on *Dover* is inappropriate because that case does not discuss or rule upon attornment clauses and the present case is determined by a decision upon the application of such a clause. It is fundamental that cases are not authority for propositions that are not considered therein. (Roberts v. City of Palmdale (1993) 5 Cal. 4th 363, 372 [20 Cal. Rptr. 2d 330, 853 P.2d 496].) The tenant's position was clearly subordinate, and the case properly held that the lease was extinguished. Here, in contrast, the attornment clause fixed the rights of the parties after the foreclosure. Defendants' position to the contrary requires a ruling that there is no meaning whatsoever to the language of the attornment clause. This position violates the rule of contractual interpretation that requires meaning to be given to every part of a contract "if reasonably practicable." (Civ. Code, *§ 1641.*)

5.   *The "Condition Precedent" to Attornment.* Defendants contend the language of the attornment clause created a condition precedent: that the party seeking to enforce the attornment clause has "acquire[d] and accept[ed] the property subject to the lease." Defendants contend that these words required Coast to give the notice called for under the subordination clause when the holder of the security interest elects to subordinate its interest to that of the tenant. We disagree.

The subordination clause (with concomitant nondisturbance clause) must be considered as separate from the attornment clause. Although those clauses could impact upon the same parties, their provisions potentially apply to different parties. A clause applicable to one set of parties does not logically provide a notice requirement for a condition precedent to another clause applying to different parties unless such a result is clearly indicated. There is no such clear indication of relationship between the clauses here.

The subordination clause establishes a right of the lender to subordinate its position to that of the tenant. Under certain circumstances, a lender may seek such a result. (See, e.g., West & Keyles, Does the A in Your SNDA Work? (Sept. 1993) 7 Prob. & Prop. 54, 55.) For instance, a subordination agreement may, as noted above, alter the priorities of the parties with respect to insurance proceeds or condemnation awards, among other things. However, the creation of an obligation for the tenant to attorn to a new landlord is quite different. The tenant presumably negotiated the lease with the landlord, and, for consideration, contracted to attorn to a new landlord under the described conditions. A landlord could want such a provision in the lease for a number of reasons, not the least of which is that the landlord could show the lease to others with whom it deals to demonstrate that its tenants are bound to new landlords. Such a provision could be a persuasive argument to a lender who was considering the financial condition of the landlord or the landlord's position vis-a-vis other parties involved with the real property. Thus, an attornment clause is not just gratuitously given in a vacuum, but has a meaning that can impact upon the rights and obligations of parties other than the immediate parties to the lease.

We conclude that interpretation of the plain language in the attornment clause does not support defendant's contention. The clause contains two parts (eliminating nonapplicable circumstances); (1) the tenant shall attorn to the purchaser at a foreclosure sale (2) provided that the purchaser acquires and accepts the property subject to the lease. The second part, (2), contains two subparts; (2a) the purchaser "acquires" the premises and (2b) "accepts" the premises subject to the lease. The purchaser, Coast, acquired the property at the foreclosure sale. It could not know that it was going to acquire the property until the completion of the foreclosure. The purchaser, Coast, then was in a position to "accept" the premises subject to the lease or not.

Defendants argue that to determine what acceptance means in this context, we must look to the subordination clause, and that Coast "failed to elect to have the lease senior to the First Deed of Trust prior to the trustee's sale." Defendants then refer to "Coast's failure to exercise its option" as if the two things were the same. Defendants have their timing confused. As noted above, prior to the trustee's sale, Coast could not know whether it would be the successful bidder. It is illogical to expect Coast, as a prospective purchaser at the foreclosure sale, to exercise some option provided in a separate clause of the lease. It is common to have all three parts of SNDA clauses included in leases. If we were to support the rule proposed by defendant, all lenders similarly situated to Coast would have to "exercise their option" to subordinate their position to that of the tenant before they bid in at a foreclosure sale. There is neither logic nor fairness in such a rule, and we will not promulgate it here.

Further, we disagree with defendants' position that the "acquires and accepts" language necessitates any notice to the tenant prior to the foreclosure, let alone the alleged notice provided in the subordination clause. Rather, we interpret the "acquires and accepts" language as providing merely that the new landlord acknowledges and *agrees to be bound by* the existing lease—simply a reciprocal promise, akin to a nondisturbance clause—in exchange for the tenant's attornment. Under our interpretation of the language of this clause, the new landlord seeking to enforce the attornment clause acquires the duties and responsibilities of the prior landlord as well as the privilege of collecting rent under the lease.

The question therefore arises whether Coast "accepted" the property subject to the lease. According to the evidence in this case, Coast immediately, on the day of acquisition, gave notice to the tenant that it was the new owner and that thereafter all rent payments should be made payable to Coast. In two other instances, it acknowledged that it expected the tenant to abide by the lease. It thus accepted the premises subject to the lease. It is illogical to assume that it would make any pronouncement as to payment of rent or give notice of its acceptance of the lease before it acquired the property.

To phrase it another way, the tenant attorned to the new landlord, whoever that may be, when the tenant entered into the lease. The only condition precedent to that attornment was that the new landlord had to acquire the premises and accept the premises subject to the lease. Coast did that here, and the condition precedent was satisfied. The preexisting obligation to attorn to the new landlord was implemented when Coast acknowledged that it was, indeed, the new landlord.

We conclude that Coast's foreclosure did not terminate the obligations of the tenant under the lease. The tenant had contracted to alter the priorities otherwise established by law. Defendants, in the clear language of the lease, had agreed to attorn to the purchaser at a foreclosure sale, and Coast was such a purchaser. The attornment clause obligated defendants to accept Coast, and hence its assignee, the plaintiff, as a new landlord. Further, Coast's actions, as found in the record before us, satisfied any requirements imposed upon it to accept the premises subject to the lease. As a matter of law, plaintiff is entitled to the status of a landlord, and defendants are obligated under the lease. Similarly, plaintiff is bound to perform the duties and responsibilities assigned to the landlord under the lease.

Thus, the trial court erred in granting summary judgment on the ground the lease had terminated.

DISPOSITION

The judgment is reversed. The appellant shall recover costs on appeal.

McDANIEL, J., concurred.

HOLLENHORST, ACTING P. J. dissenting.

I dissent.

I agree with the majority that (1) the nonjudicial foreclosure of a trust deed extinguishes a subordinate lease and (2) the lender did not exercise an option to obtain a subordination agreement that would change this result by making the lease senior to the deed of trust.

I disagree with the majority's conclusion that there was nevertheless a subordination agreement here because (1) the lease contained an attornment clause and (2) the lender requested payment of rent to it after the foreclosure.

I agree with the trial court that the lease, including the attornment clause, was extinguished by the foreclosure sale by operation of law, leaving the tenant on a month-to-month tenancy.

1.   *THE GENERAL RULE IS THAT A JUNIOR LEASE IS AUTOMATICALLY EXTINGUISHED BY A NONJUDICIAL FORECLOSURE.*

In my view, the trial court properly relied on Dover Mobile Estates v. Fiber Form Products, Inc. (1990) 220 Cal. App. 3d 1494 [270 Cal. Rptr. 183]. That case succinctly states the applicable general principles: "Title conveyed by a trustee's deed relates back to the date when the deed of trust was executed. [Citation.] The trustee's deed therefore passes the title held by the trustor at the time of execution. [Citation.] Liens which attach after execution of the foreclosed trust deed are extinguished. The purchaser at the trustee sale therefore takes title free of those junior or subordinate liens. [Citations.] A lease is generally deemed to be subordinate to a deed of trust if the lease was created after the deed of trust was recorded. . . . A lease which is subordinate to the deed of trust is extinguished by the foreclosure sale. [Citations.] A foreclosure proceeding destroys a lease junior to the deed of trust, as well as the lessee's rights and obligations under the lease." (*Id., at p. 1498.*)

The majority agrees with these general principles, stating that "there is no dispute that the general rule is that foreclosure of a senior encumbrance terminates subordinate liens, including leases." (Maj. opn., *ante*, at p. 1326.) I refer to this rule as the automatic termination rule.

2.   *A SUBORDINATION AGREEMENT COULD HAVE BEEN USED TO PREVENT AUTOMATIC TERMINATION OF THE LEASE UPON FORECLOSURE.*

"The priority of interests in or liens on real property can be altered by a voluntary agreement between the parties. A person holding an existing interest in real property can agree, for a consideration, that his interest is to be junior in priority to an interest subsequently created and recorded. As a result of the agreement, the interest subsequently created obtains priority over the previously existing interest. Such an agreement is called a 'subordination agreement.' " (3 Miller & Starr, Cal. Real Estate (2d ed. 1989) Recording and Priorities, § 8:157, p. 617.)

The lease here contains a subordination and attornment provision. It contains four sentences. The first sentence of the subordination clause in this lease requires the tenant, upon request, to subordinate its rights to the lien of a first mortgage or first deed of trust. Since the lease was already junior to the lien of the first deed of trust, I agree with the majority that this sentence is not directly applicable to the current situation.

The second sentence is the nondisturbance clause. It provides a degree of protection to the tenant by assuring the tenant that, before it is required to sign a subordination agreement, it can obtain assurances from its new landlord that, so long as it is not in default, the lease will remain in effect for the full term.

Again, *Dover* is instructive: it provides that ". . . the tenant under a subordinate lease can obtain some protection by requiring the landlord to obtain from its lender a non-disturbance agreement in favor of the tenant. Such an agreement provides that the lender with a superior lien will not, 'by foreclosure or otherwise, disturb the tenant's possession, as long as the tenant is not then in default under the lease.' [Citation.]" (*Dover Mobile Estates v. Fiber Form Products, Inc., supra,* 220 Cal. App. 3d 1494, 1500.) As discussed below, the majority's interpretation of the lease has the effect of eliminating this protection from the lease.

The third sentence states: "The holder of any security interest may, upon written notice to Tenant, elect to have this Lease prior to its security interest regardless of the time of the granting or recording of that security interest." In other words, this sentence, read together with the second sentence, provides that the holder of the security interest has the option of avoiding the automatic termination rule by requiring the tenant to enter into a subordination agreement that will preserve the lease. If it does so, the tenant can require an agreement which includes the nondisturbance provisions stated in the second sentence.

If preservation of the lease was important to the lender, it *could* have defeated automatic termination of the lease upon foreclosure by electing to subordinate its security interest to the lease, and it *could* have forced the tenant to accept it as the new landlord.

I agree with the majority that there was no such election here. As the majority opinion states, "The only potential effect of the clause was to allow the lender to elect that the lease become senior, and this did not happen." (Maj. opn., *ante*, at p. 1328.)

Having so decided, the majority should have followed *Dover*. In that case, as in this, the lease provided that the holder of a security interest could elect to have the lease be prior to the security interest. (*Dover Mobile Estates v. Fiber Form Products, Inc., supra,* 220 Cal. App. 3d 1494, 1496, fn. 1, 1499.) In that case, as in this, the option was never exercised. "Accordingly, it is clear that the lease is subordinate to the deed of trust and was therefore extinguished by the trustee's sale." (*Dover Mobile Estates, supra,* at p. 1499.)

Instead of so holding, the majority goes on to find that no subordination agreement was necessary because the attornment clause, plus certain unrecorded letters from the lender, constituted an agreement which avoids the automatic termination rule.

3.   *THE ATTORNMENT CLAUSE.*

The fourth sentence is the attornment clause. It provides: "In the event of any foreclosure sale, transfer in lieu of foreclosure or termination of the lease in which Landlord is lessee, Tenant shall attorn to the purchaser, transferee or lessor as the case may be, and recognize that party as Landlord under this Lease, provided that party acquires and accepts the Premises subject to this Lease."

The majority opinion gives this sentence unwarranted weight by interpreting it to be part of an agreement to alter priorities without the use of a subordination agreement. Before examining the majority's strained construction, we need to briefly review the historic function of an attornment clause.

At common law, the feudal obligation between lord and tenant was a personal and reciprocal one. The consent of the lord was therefore required for a sale of the tenant's interest, and the consent of the tenant was required for an alienation of the reversion or remainder interest in property. Thus, the lord could not alienate his reversion or remainder interest without the consent of the tenant. The consent was called an attornment. (2 Blackstone's Commentaries 71–72; 49 Am.Jur.2d, Landlord and Tenant, § 1053, pp. 823–824.) The necessity for an attornment was abolished before the American Revolution by the Statute of Anne and, under the common law in effect at that time, the landowner could transfer the remainder or reversion without consent of the tenant. (51C C.J.S., Landlord & Tenant, § 22, p. 54.)

In California, the common law rule eliminating the requirement of attornment has been confirmed by statute. Civil Code *section 1111* provides that "Grants of rents or of reversions or of remainders are good and effectual without attornments of the tenants; but no tenant who, before notice of the grant, shall have paid rent to the grantor, must suffer any damage thereby." (See also Civ. Code, *§ 1948* [attornment to stranger void], 821 [grantee has same rights as grantor against tenant]; Evid. Code, *§ 624* [tenant estopped to deny title of landlord].)

Currently, the term "attornment" refers to the obligation of the tenant to acknowledge his or her obligations to a new landlord, "most often, the agreement of a tenant to pay rent to a new landlord, especially a mortgagee who has foreclosed." (Black's Law Dict. (6th ed. 1990) p. 130, col. 1.) The inclusion of an attornment clause in the lease therefore requires the tenant to acknowledge continuation of the existing lease under a new landlord under its previously existing terms and conditions. (51C C.J.S., Landlord & Tenant, § 22, pp. 55–56.) "Attornment contemplates the act or agreement by a tenant accepting one person in place of another as his landlord." (Krasner v. Transcontinental Equities, Inc. (1979) 170 A.D.2d 312 [420 N.Y.S.2d 872, 875]; see also Ripple's of Clearview v. Le Havre Associates (1981) 111 Misc.2d 263 [443 N.Y.S.2d 824, 826].)

It should be apparent from the foregoing that the inclusion of the attornment clause in this lease provided a firm foundation for the lender, as a third party beneficiary of the attornment clause, to require the tenant to enter into a subordination agreement which would make the lease prior to the lien of the deed of trust, thus avoiding the automatic termination rule. However, the attornment clause is not itself a substitute for a subordination agreement.

The attornment clause was subject to the condition that its requirements only became applicable if the purchaser "acquires and accepts the Premises subject to this lease." In my view, this condition refers to the preceding sentence, i.e., it applies to the holder of a security interest who elects to have the lease survive foreclosure. The majority disagrees. It argues that this clause does not refer back to the preceding sentence but rather is independent of the subordination clause. Read independently, the majority concludes that the condition was satisfied when the purchaser notified the lessee to pay rent to it.

As a result of this reading, the tenant is forced to continue its tenancy under the lease, without the protection afforded by the nondisturbance clause. The effect is that the tenant loses the protection afforded by the nondisturbance clause, and that clause is effectively read out of the lease. The majority's strained interpretation thus violates the basic rule of contract interpretation stated in Civil Code *section 1641*: "The whole of a contract is to be taken together, so as to give effect to every part, if reasonably practicable, each clause helping to interpret the other."

4. THE MAJORITY OPINION FINDS A SUBORDINATION AGREEMENT WHERE THERE IS NONE.

The majority agrees that there must be an agreement to alter priorities in order for plaintiff to prevail. Although there was no subordination agreement in this case, the majority finds that "[t]he tenant had contracted to alter the priorities otherwise established by law." It thus finds an agreement to subordinate, and a concomitant avoidance of *Dover*'s automatic termination rule, in the lease and other documents. Specifically, the majority finds that the lease survives the foreclosure sale because (1) the tenant agreed to the attornment clause in the original lease with the former landlord and (2) the lender notified tenant to make rent payments to it after the foreclosure. According to the majority, this alleged agreement had the effect of a formal subordination agreement.

I find this interpretation untenable for the following reasons.

First, the attornment clause is not a substitute for a subordination agreement. As discussed above, the attornment clause allowed the lender to require the tenant to enter into a subordination agreement which would make the deed of trust subordinate to the lease. The letters asking the tenant to pay rent to the lender after foreclosure, whether read with the attornment clause or independently, are not, in my view, a substitute for a subordination agreement.

Second, the majority's contrary interpretation has the effect of depriving the subordination clause of any meaning. As discussed above, the subordination clause does not itself effect subordination. It only gives the holder of the security interest the right to require a subordination agreement in return for a nondisturbance agreement. By holding that the attornment clause and notification letters are themselves an agreement to subordinate, the majority eliminates the lender's option under the subordination clause, eliminates the need for separate subordination agreements and eliminates the protection given by the nondisturbance clause. As discussed above, it is particularly unfortunate that the protection of the nondisturbance clause is effectively written out of the lease by the majority's interpretation.

The majority justifies the ignoring of the subordination clause by remarking that "the subordination clause of the lease was of no value to Coast since its senior position was already fixed by law." However, I think that the subordination clause of the lease was valuable to Coast because it was seeking to preserve the lease and enforce its terms. The third sentence of the subordination clause provided it with the means to do so. However, it did not invoke its rights under the clause, thus leading to the tenant's reliance on the automatic termination rule. In any event, such an interpretation is contrary to the rules of statutory interpretation. (Civ. Code, *§ 1638, 1639, 1641, 1643–1645.*) "In the construction of . . . [an] instrument, the office of the judge is simply to ascertain and declare what is in terms or in substance contained therein, not to insert what has been omitted, or to omit what has been inserted; and where there are several provisions or particulars, such a construction is, if possible to be adopted as will give effect to all." (Code Civ. Proc., *§ 1858.*)

Third, the majority's strained interpretation of the attornment clause, together with its reliance on letters that only demand payment of rent to the new owner, is an interpretation which introduces uncertainty into the otherwise well-settled law which requires written subordination agreements to adjust priorities between lenders and tenants. Such an interpretation will lead to other litigants claiming that subordination occurred because of documents and correspondence other than formal subordination agreements. For example, a tenant who wishes to preserve its lease, which includes an attornment clause, will claim that a routine written notice, given after foreclosure, that rent should be paid to the new landlord acted as a subordination agreement, thus making the lease superior to the lien of the trust deed. In such a situation, the lender would not be able to evict the tenant, even if it did not wish to be bound by the terms of the lease, considered the lease terminated, and only intended the rent to be payable under a month-to-month tenancy.

The majority's interpretation also avoids the specificity required in certain subordination agreements. For example, a subordination agreement for loans under $25,000 must contain specific terms which expressly notify the parties that the statutory priorities are being modified. (Civ. Code, § 2953.3.)

Fourth, the majority's interpretation contradicts the purpose and function of recording subordination agreements. Because the automatic termination rule is a result of application of priorities under the recording laws, subordination agreements are generally recorded to give constructive notice that the usual priority rules have been modified by agreement. (Civ. Code, § 2934; Protective Equity Trust #83, Ltd. v. Bybee (1991) 2 Cal. App. 4th 139 [2 Cal. Rptr. 2d 864].)

For example, a prospective purchaser from Coast who examined title would find a senior deed of trust which had been foreclosed and a junior lease. Relying on the recording law, the prospective purchaser would conclude that the automatic termination rule applied. If the purchaser bought the property thinking that the lease was terminated, the lessee could nevertheless contend that the lease was still valid because of the attornment provision in its original lease and an unrecorded letter from Coast requesting payment of rent to Coast. Thus, the majority's interpretation would introduce uncertainty into a previously settled area of the law.

These actions by a tenant could burden the lender's property without its prior knowledge. For this reason, the automatic termination rule eliminates all encumbrances subsequent to the deed of trust. There is a sound policy basis for such a rule: "The policy underlying the [automatic termination] rule is to protect lending institutions from fraudulent amendments to leases which would encumber the value of their acquired property. If the rule were different, lending institutions would be discouraged from making loans since they would have no assurances that the borrower and senior leaseholder would not drastically reduce the value of the lease, thereby reducing the value of the property. . . ." (R-Ranch Markets #2, Inc. v. Old Stone Bank (1993) 16 Cal. App. 4th 1323, 1328 [21 Cal. Rptr. 2d 21]; Homestead Savings v. Darmiento (1991) 230 Cal. App. 3d 424, 437 [281 Cal. Rptr. 367].)

Fifth, the majority's opinion undercuts the automatic termination rule by allowing a lease provision and postforeclosure documents to circumvent the rule, even though the lease itself was previously terminated. Since the lease, including the attornment clause, was previously terminated, the lender never became a successor landlord under the lease and had no right to enforce the lease against the tenant.

Sixth, the majority opinion finds that *Dover* is distinguishable "for the simple reason that the court in that case did not discuss whether the lease contained an attornment clause or what the effect of such a clause would be." (Maj. opn., *ante*, at p. 1329.) I find this an insufficient basis for distinguishing *Dover*, since we do not know if the lease in that case contained an attornment clause or not. However, since it is common for attornment clauses to coexist with subordination and nondisturbance clauses (*Chumash Hill Properties, Inc. v. Peram (1995) 39 Cal. App. 4th 1226, 1230–1231, 1233 [46 Cal. Rptr. 2d 366]*), it is more likely that there was an attornment clause in the *Dover* lease, but the court did not discuss it because no one thought to give it the undue emphasis and strained construction given the attornment clause here. (*Dover Mobile Estates v. Fiber Form Products, Inc., supra,* 220 Cal. App. 3d 1494, 1496, fn. 1, and 1499.) What is clear is that the subordination clause in *Dover* was, except for the nondisturbance clause, essentially identical to the subordination clause here.

Finally, I note that the majority does not follow its own rules. It states: "[W]e interpret the 'acquires and accepts' language [of the attornment clause] as providing merely that the new landlord acknowledges and agrees to be bound by the existing lease. . . ." (Maj. opn., *ante*, at p. 1331, italics omitted.) Thus, it finds a subordination agreement whenever the new landlord acknowledges the preexisting lease and agrees to be bound by it.

If this is the proper rule defendant should still prevail because the letters relied on by the majority do not contain any promise by the new landlord that it will be bound by the terms of any existing lease, nor do they evidence any intent that the lease become prior to the lien of the trust deed. The letters merely request that rental payments be made to the new property manager. Since Coast never agreed to be bound by the terms of the existing lease, the trial court's decision should nevertheless be affirmed, even applying the majority's rules.

5.   *CONCLUSION.*

The majority distorts the meaning of the attornment clause of the lease to avoid the effect of the automatic termination rule. By construing the attornment clause and a letter directing rent to be paid to the new landlord as an unrecorded subordination agreement, the majority ignores the third sentence of the subordination clause. That sentence gives the lender the option to have the lease be prior to the security interest. The option was not exercised here.

The majority's interpretation of the attornment clause is an unreasonable interpretation that vitiates the subordination clause. It is particularly troubling that the majority deprives the tenant of the protection afforded by the nondisturbance clause.

The majority's interpretation thus undercuts the previously settled law of subordination. Under that law, it is clear that a junior lease is extinguished by a nonjudicial foreclosure unless it ceases to be a junior lease because its priority is changed by a subordination agreement. While the lender could have exercised its rights under the subordination clause to compel the tenant to enter into a subordination agreement, it did not do so.

I therefore agree with the trial court that *Dover* is factually indistinguishable and correctly determines the issue here by holding that "A lease which is subordinate to the deed of trust is extinguished by the foreclosure sale." (*Dover Mobile Estates v. Fiber Form Products, Inc., supra,* 220 Cal. App. 3d 1494, 1498.)

I would affirm the judgment.

A petition for a rehearing was denied March 17, 1997, and respondents' petition for review by the Supreme Court was denied June 11, 1997. Kennard, J., was of the opinion that the petition should be granted.

NOTES

1. *Continuous Operation.* What standards does the court in *Oakland Village LLC* articulate for deciding whether it should imply a continuous operation covenant? Should the result differ if there is disparity in bargaining power between the shopping center landlord and tenant, a disparity that could run either way? Would *Rowe* have been decided differently if A & P had been an anchor tenant in a shopping center? After the decision in *Rowe*, would A & P be free to set up a new store within one or two miles of the old site? What damages are recoverable for breach of a continuous operation clause? See Hornwood v. Smith's Food King No. 1, 105 Nev. 188, 772 P.2d 1284 (1989). Should a tenant benefitted by a use restriction clause be able to bring an action directly against another tenant violating its exclusive or should the injured tenant only have an action against the landlord? See Winn-Dixie Stores, Inc. v. Dolgencorp, LLC, 2014 WL 842949 (11th Cir. 2014) (landlord is not a necessary party in such an action).

Representing tenant or landlord, what lease language would you have proposed to avoid the problems that arose in each of the principal cases? What does *Oakland Village LLC* tell you about the need for precision in drafting?

For a discussion of implied continuous operation covenants, see Randolph, Going Dark Aggressively, 10 Probate & Prop. 6, 11 (Nov./Dec. 1996) ("Generally, courts are content to treat retail landlords and tenants as sophisticated players in a game of commercial hardball. Aggressive behavior that is designed to benefit the economic interests of one party, and not designed solely to injure the other, is to be expected. If landlords abhor darkness and prefer light, let them put it in their leases."). See also Comment, Commercial Leasing: Implied Covenants of Operation in Shopping Center Leases, 95 Dick.L.Rev. 383 (1991).

For other readings on shopping center issues, see Tyson, Drafting, Interpreting, and Enforcing Commercial and Shopping Center Leases, 14 Campbell L.Rev. 275 (1992); Collins, Thomas & Cargile, What About the Little Guys? The Top Issues for A Smaller Tenant to Negotiate In Its Lease, 18 Probate & Prop. 11 (Nov./Dec. 2004); Kratovil, The Declaration of Restrictions, Easements, Liens, and Covenants: An Overview of An Important Document, 22 John Marshall L.Rev. 69 (1988); Thigpen, Good Faith Performance Under Percentage Leases, 51 Miss.L.J. 315 (1980–1981); Terkel, Reciprocal Agreements in Shopping Center Developments, 14 St. Mary's L.J. 541 (1983).

2. *Counselling Tenants.* To convince their construction and permanent lenders that the center is more than a will o' the wisp, shopping center developers will often ask prospective tenants to sign their leases well before construction on the center begins. If financing turns out to be unavailable, if other leases do not materialize, if construction costs are too high, or local planning officials too reluctant in giving the necessary approvals, the center will not open. The tenant, his expectations dashed, will find little solace in the courts. Even if the tenant can show that the developer breached an obligation, damages will be hard to prove and specific performance hard to enforce. One solution, other than dealing with a developer with a known track record, is to provide for some form of liquidated damages in the event the center does not open.

The tenant's problems do not disappear once the center is built. The location of his unit may be an issue. The tenant will want to pinpoint his location at the time he signs the lease in order to assure good exposure and access to pedestrian traffic between the parking lot and the anchor tenants. The landlord, however, will want the discretion to locate the unit where it will best meet demands later posed by other tenants, local planning officials and the center's architects and engineers. The tenant will also want to condition his performance on the presence of specified anchor tenants. If the landlord represented that certain, named anchor tenants would be in the center, the tenant's easiest expedient would be to condition his performance upon the continuing presence of these anchor tenants from the beginning of the lease term. Obviously the landlord will try to avoid this straitjacket, describing the anchors not by name but by objective criteria such as sales volume, type of operation and credit rating.

Finally, landlord and tenant must at the outset agree on the architectural and construction specifications for the tenant's yet unbuilt unit. Time will usually not permit the tenant to draft a set of plans to be attached as an exhibit to the lease unless the tenant is a chain operation that employs virtually identical specifications for all of its units. The lease can, however, provide for certain basic functional specifications (floor space and height, and lighting, air conditioning and wall covering requirements). Yet another approach is for the landlord to provide the tenant with a shell—four walls, a roof, floor and utility connections—leaving it to the tenant to construct the facilities to its own taste, sometimes with a cash allowance from the landlord. Representing a tenant whose lease calls for a shell, rather than a completed turn-key facility, what specific protections would you seek for your client? What added tax consequences would you consider? How can the client finance these leasehold improvements?

For a good introduction to pre-occupancy problems and their solutions, see Williams, Before the Shopping Center Opens: A Survival Manual for Developer and Tenant, 2 Real Est.Rev. 15 (Summer 1972).

3. *Inflation-Proofing Leases.* Shopping center landlords have increasingly sought to make their space leases inflation proof. Triple net terms are now the rule rather than the exception, with space tenants paying for their own utilities and insurance and for their proportionate share of the center's overall maintenance costs. Landlords protect themselves against skyrocketing property taxes through clauses (called "tax stops") requiring their tenants to bear a proportionate share of any increases in real estate taxes levied on the center after a specified initial period, typically the first year of operations.

The landlord's most durable inflation fighter has been the percentage rental. Although rent may be based exclusively on a percentage of the tenant's sales, most percentage leases call for a minimum fixed rental plus a percentage of the tenant's gross income over a specified level. Percentages vary by region and by type of tenant. High volume tenants, like department stores, supermarkets and drug stores pay lower percentages—typically one to two percent. Low volume, specialty tenants like gift shops, restaurants, beauty shops and stationery and jewelry stores pay in a higher range— typically five to ten percent. Candy stores may pay as much as twelve percent and motion picture theaters as much as fifteen percent. For a comparison of percentage ranges for virtually all types of retail tenants over a period of several years, see Schloss, Inflation Proofing Retail Investments with Percentage Leases, 7 Real Est.Rev. 36 (Winter 1978).

Problems in administering percentage clauses usually stem from imprecision in the lease's definition of the gross income that forms the rental base. Did the parties intend to include gross income from incidental operations (a popcorn stand, say) in the gross income of the main business (a movie theater)? Does "gross receipts" include only the fee paid to the tenant by concessionaires, or does it include the concessionaire's gross revenues? Are sales generated on the premises, but concluded off-premises, to be counted? Do returned items, excise taxes and coupons count? Can charge account expenses, employee discounts and trading stamps be deducted? Hartig Drug Company v. Hartig shows that predicting precisely how the property will be used in the future may prove difficult. Did the court properly resolve the ambiguity? Should the result differ if the tenant was a national chain and had drafted the lease? See In re Circle K Corp., 98 F.3d 484, 489 (9th Cir.1996). See generally, Note, Resolving Disputes Under Percentage Leases, 51 Minn.L.Rev. 1139 (1967).

An emerging issue is whether sales completed through a tenant's Internet website should be counted as part of gross retail sales from the location for the purpose of percentage rent. See Murray, Percentage Rent Provisions in Shopping Center Leases: A Changing World?, 35 Real Prop. Probate & Tr. J. 731, 747–752 (2001). One suggestion is that a part of Internet sales in the market area of the leased premises should be included in that store's gross rent. Snively, KillPercentageRent.com: Internet Sales and Shopping Center Leases, 14 Probate & Prop. 39 (July/Aug. 2000). See generally, Comment, The Effects of Electronic Commerce on the Traditional Shopping Center Lease, 6 Tex. Wesleyan L. Rev. 85 (1999).

4.   *Use Clause.* Use clauses, particularly in long-term leases, are often the object of intense negotiations. The landlord will want uses to be specified narrowly so that she can control the overall mix of goods and services in the center and honor exclusive use clauses that may appear in other leases. The tenant wants a broadly worded clause that will enable him to expand into new product or service lines, and drop old ones, to meet changing consumer tastes. A major tenant under a financeable long-term lease will be under particular pressure from his prospective mortgagee to obtain a virtually boundless use clause.

Even when they reach agreement in principle, landlord and tenant will face the difficult task of putting their agreement into words. See, e.g., Belvidere South Towne Center, Inc. v. One Stop Pacemaker, Inc., 54 Ill.App.3d 958, 12 Ill.Dec. 626, 370 N.E.2d 249 (2d Dist.1977); Horn & Hardart Co. v. Junior Bldg., Inc., 40 N.Y.2d 927, 929, 389 N.Y.S.2d 831,

832–33, 358 N.E.2d 514, 515 (1976). See generally Halper, Supermarket Use and Exclusive Clauses, 30 Hofstra L.Rev. 297 (2001).

5. *Tenant Business Activities. Providence Square Associates* involves lease covenants that grant tenants special advantages—exclusive rights to sell certain products or to maintain certain types of businesses within the shopping center. Do such clauses serve the public interest? Are they necessary for the landlord and the (first) tenant, and how so? Did the court in *Providence Square Associates* make the correct choice on the policy issues as well as the interpretation of the lease provisions? Federal antitrust challenges to shopping center exclusivity clauses have been mostly unsuccessful because a relatively small market share was involved. See, e.g., Red Sage Ltd. P'ship v. DESPA Deutsche Sparkassen Immobilien-Anlage-Gasellschaft, 254 F.3d 1120 (D.C. Cir. 2001); Harold Friedman, Inc. v. Thorofare Mkts., Inc., 587 F.2d 127, 130 (3d Cir. 1978); see Pearson, Texas and Federal Antitrust Implications of Restrictive Covenants Not to Compete in Shopping Center Leases, 20 Tex. Tech. L. Rev. 1189 (1989); Note, The Antitrust Implications of Restrictive Covenants in Shopping Center Leases, 86 Harv. L. Rev. 1201 (1973); American Bar Association, Section of Real Property, Probate and Trust Law, Committee on Leases, Drafting Shopping Center Leases, 2 Real Prop. Probate & Tr. J. 222, 232–242 (1967).

In re Trak Auto presents the flip side—where the tenant is limited to conducting a certain type of business in the shopping store premises. What is the reason for this type of restriction? Does it serve the social good? Does the *Trak Auto* court properly balance the policies favoring such provisions against the policies of the bankruptcy system? Reconsider Note 5 on page 729 above dealing with shopping center leases in bankruptcy.

6. *The Tenant and the Lender.* Miscione v. Barton Development Company describes the subordination, nondisturbance, and attornment (SNDA) agreement. Why does the landlord require such an agreement? Whom does it benefit? What dangers do SNDA clauses present to the tenant? Consider in this regard Balch v. Leader Federal Bank for Savings on page 684 and Middlebrook-Anderson Co. v. Southwest Savings & Loan Association on page 636. Since Coast was already in a first position, why did it want a subordination clause? Consider on this question Aames Capital Corp. v. Interstate Bank of Oak Forest on page 409. In addition to the secondary sources cited in *Miscione*, see Zerunyan, Most Commonly Negotiated Commercial Lease Provisions, 116 Banking L.J. 158 (1999).

The tenant in *Miscione* refused to execute an estoppel certificate confirming the terms of the lease. Such certificates are typically required by the lease and are used by the landlord in dealing with lenders and potential mortgagees or buyers who want to be sure the leases are still effective. See Plaza Freeway Ltd. Partnership v. First Mountain Bank, 81 Cal.App.4th 616, 96 Cal.Rptr.2d 865 (2000) (tenant bound by estoppel certificate); Liu, Counseling the Landlord on Tenant Estoppels and SNDAs, 16 Prac. Real Est. Law. 15 (No. 4 2000); Stein, Needless Disturbances? Do Nondisturbance Agreements Justify All the Time and Trouble?, 37 Real Prop. Probate & Tr. J. 701 (2003); Murphy, Estoppel Certificates and Subordination, Non-Disturbance and Attornment Agreements, 19 Prac. Real Est. Law. 23 (No. 6 2003).

PART THREE

FEDERAL INCOME TAXATION AND REAL ESTATE TRANSACTIONS

CHAPTER XII

RESIDENTIAL PROPERTY

Nicholaus W. Norvell, Comment, Transition Relief for
Tax Reform's Third Rail: Reforming the Home Mortgage
Interest Deduction After the Housing Market Crash*

49 San Diego Law Review 1333, 1337–1341 (2012).

II. Background on the Mortgage Interest Deduction

A. How the Deduction Works

The Internal Revenue Code (the Code) only permits deductions for
one type of personal debt, "qualified residence interest." The Code
defines qualified residence interest as interest arising from "acquisition
indebtedness" or "home equity indebtedness" on a qualified residence.
Acquisition indebtedness is purchase, construction, or improvement
debt that is secured by a qualified residence. Home equity indebtedness
is any nonacquisition indebtedness secured by the residence that does
not exceed the difference between the fair market value and the
acquisition indebtedness. Under the Code, a homeowner can deduct
interest on up to $1 million in acquisition indebtedness and the first
$100,000 in home equity indebtedness. Thus, a homeowner can
potentially deduct interest on up to $1.1 million of home-secured debt.
However, the tax privilege for mortgage debt is not limited to a
taxpayer's principal residence alone; a "qualified residence" includes
both a taxpayer's principal residence and one other residence selected
by the taxpayer.

As a tax deduction, the mortgage interest deduction does not
reduce tax liability dollar-for-dollar, as tax credits do. Instead, a
deduction reduces taxable income by an amount directly proportional to
a taxpayer's income tax rate. Consider the following example: On
January 1, 2011, Alice and Ben each purchased a home with a $200,000
mortgage at 5% interest. The interest cost to each taxpayer was $10,000
in the first year. Alice made $100,000 in 2011 and paid at the 28% tax
rate, whereas Ben made $50,000 and paid at the 15% tax rate. Under
the mortgage interest deduction, Alice received a tax benefit of 28% of
$10,000, or $2,800. Ben received a tax benefit of 15% of $10,000, or
$1,500. In other words, of every dollar Alice spent on mortgage interest,
the federal government gave twenty-eight cents back to her, while Ben
received only fifteen cents back for every dollar he spent on mortgage
interest in 2011. Accordingly, the higher one's income tax rate, the
greater the proportional benefit from the deduction.

To claim the mortgage interest deduction, taxpayers must itemize
their taxes, which is only financially worthwhile if their total itemized
deductions exceed the value of the standard deduction. Returning to the
example of Alice and Ben, both taxpayers would itemize for tax year

---

2011 because the $10,000 of mortgage interest they paid exceeds the standard deduction, which was $5,800 for single taxpayers. Cynthia, a taxpayer who also purchased a home in 2011 with a $100,000 mortgage, a 5% interest rate, and thus $5,000 in mortgage interest, would only itemize if she had other deductions totaling more than $5,800. For Cynthia, the mortgage interest deduction provides no value unless combined with other deductions. This barrier—the need for itemized deductions to exceed the standard deduction—prevents nonitemizing homeowners from actually benefitting from the mortgage interest deduction.

B.   History of the "Accidental Deduction"

In 2013, the mortgage interest deduction will celebrate its one hundredth anniversary as part of the federal tax code. Contrary to what its long history might suggest, the mortgage interest deduction is more a by-product of the nation's agrarian past than a longstanding policy preference for subsidizing homeownership. From 1913 until passage of the Tax Reform Act of 1986, all interest payments, whether related to personal or business expenses, were deductible. At the root of this across-the-board deductibility was a conflict between congressional tax policy and the practical limitations of the tax collection and reporting system in the early 1900s. Congress in 1913 sought to encourage business investment by allowing individuals to deduct interest from business-related debt. However, the inability to easily distinguish between personal and business assets in the early twentieth century made it less administratively burdensome to permit deductions for interest on all loans. Use of the deduction for mortgage interest would have been de minimis at that time because few taxpayers had any tax liability and those that did typically purchased their homes with cash.

The Tax Reform Act of 1986 did away with the broad deduction for personal interest but maintained a specific deduction for mortgage interest. Although history might show the mortgage interest deduction to be a "tax policy accident," Congress justified retaining the deduction as a method of protecting the middle class and encouraging homeownership.

Joseph A. Snoe, My Home, My Debt: Remodeling the Home Mortgage Interest Deduction

80 Kentucky Law Journal 431, 432–433, 452–453, 457–460, 464, 467–471 (1991–1992).

Congress encourages home ownership by allowing taxpayers to deduct qualified residence interest in calculating taxable income. Generally, Congress allows deductions for business and investment expenses but disallows deductions for personal expenses. Congress gradually has reformed the income tax laws to align interest expenses with the general rule. Thus, instead of allowing a deduction for nearly all interest paid or accrued during the taxable year, as it did in 1954, the Internal Revenue Code currently allows a deduction for most interest paid or incurred in a taxpayer's trade or business or in investment activities and disallows all deductions for personal interest expenses. Despite prohibiting personal interest deductions, Congress specifically allows a deduction for qualified residence interest.

The preferential treatment afforded home mortgage interest partially reflects political reality: the average taxpayer has become accustomed to deducting mortgage interest and likely would be outraged if Congress eliminated the deduction. Although Congress could remove the preferential tax treatment given homeowners, indications are that it will not:

> "There is no basic principle in tax law that is more supported by the American people than the principle that you ought to be able to deduct interest on your home from your taxes. We have taken a position that home ownership is something that we want to promote, that that is an objective of our tax policy that is strongly supported, and it is reflected in this bill. . . ."†

This attitude underlies the home mortgage interest deduction and other tax preferences for homeowners.

Congress also uses the tax laws to foster homeownership. Deductibility of qualified residence interest is the most obvious example. Deductibility of property taxes, current deductibility of points, nonrecognition of gain on the sale of a principal residence if a new residence is purchased, complete exclusion of $125,000 from sale of a principal residence after the selling taxpayer reaches age fifty-five, and exemption of sales of principal residence from original issue discount rules further encourage homeownership. Some commentators say Congress' failure to tax the imputed rental value of a residence in the income base is also a tax preference.

In addition, homeowners receive some of the same tax benefits as other investors in property. For example, a homeowner does not recognize as taxable income the annual appreciation in the home's fair market value until the homeowner sells the home. Even then, the rollover provision and exclusion provision for homeowners over age fifty-five delay further or even eliminate any taxable gain. Should recognition be required from the sale of a home, the homeowner would benefit from any capital gains preferences in effect. Homeowners can escape all income tax consequences on value appreciation if they die owning their home because a devisee receives a stepped up basis to the home's fair market value, with no income tax burden to the deceased or the devisee.

Notwithstanding any other tax benefit related to the sale of a principal residence, the current deduction of interest and the deferred taxation, or in many cases tax exemption, of appreciation benefits the homeowner. The homeowner can deduct the mortgage interest currently, saving taxes or receiving refunds, while at the same time not recognizing for tax purposes any value appreciation on the home. If, for example a homeowner buys a home for $100,000, completely on a $100,000 mortgage borrowed at 10% annual interest rate, and the home appreciates $10,000 a year, the homeowner deducts the $10,000 interest annually but does not report as income the home's $10,000 increase in value. A homeowner can invest the taxes saved by the interest deduction and earn money on the investment. In contrast, a

---

† 132 CONG. REC. S7387 (daily ed. June 12, 1986) (statement of Sen. Gramm) (Senator Gramm referred to the Tax Reform Act of 1986, Pub. L. No. 99–514, 100 Stat. 2085 (codified as amended in scattered sections of I.R.C.)).

person that borrows $100,000 at 10% interest, and puts the money in an account paying 10% interest, saves no taxes because the full $10,000 interest must be reported in income and the interest deduction merely offsets the interest income. The homeowner that sells his home at a gain, assuming the gain must be recognized, pays a tax only on the gain, with no adjustment for the period of deferral. The interest earned on the tax savings for the years of appreciation results in an economic profit to the homeowner. This ability to profit from the deferral of income, a form of tax arbitrage, is not limited to homeownership. It applies to all assets that may appreciate in value.

C.   The Theories for Denying Home Mortgage Interest Deduction

1.   Denial of Home Mortgage Interest Deduction As a Substitute for Imputing Rental Income

Opponents of the home mortgage interest deduction emphasize the homeowner's use of the home as a residence. Their analysis is not based on the personal use in and of itself, but instead on the owner-occupier's rent free use of the home. According to the argument, conceptually the owner-occupier should impute the home's rental value as income. Because imputing rental value into income is administratively impractical, a reasonable substitute would be to deny deductions for all expenses related to the home, including mortgage interest.

The nationwide imputed rental income of owner occupied residences composes a substantial portion of the gross national product (GNP). The Department of Commerce included in the 1987 GNP 317 billion dollars as the annualized rental value of owner occupied housing, which was approximately seven percent of GNP. To place the amount in perspective, the imputed value of owner occupied housing contributed more to the 1987 GNP than did all wholesaling activities and was only ten percent less than the amount of food Americans purchased for off-premises consumption. The sheer magnitude of the value of owner-occupied housing invites taxation. Its inclusion in the GNP calculation seems to indicate possible accurate valuation.

If the homeowner imputed rental income, the homeowner would deduct against that imputed income the same expenses allowable to persons owning rental property. Imputing rental income from homeownership likely will not occur in the United States. Many countries have taxed the imputed value, but currently governments are moving away from taxing the imputed rent.

As a substitute for taxing imputed rental income, some advocate denying interest deductions. For this theory to prevail, imputed rental income must be income under the tax laws, not just income under economists' definition, and interest must be rationally related to the imputed income, to justify denying the deduction as a substitute for imputing rental income. The current tax framework argues against imputing rental value into the income base. . . .

The imputed rent analysis rests on a recognition that a person enjoys owned property. Ownership of that property itself means that owner has more assets and more ability to pay than a person that has no assets but works and spends all earnings on current consumption. Yet, the two may have the same income for tax purposes. Perhaps Congress should incorporate a wealth tax into the income tax, but it has not done so. The federal government has not chosen to do so yet and should not depart from past practice by beginning with the home. As long as Congress excludes imputed income, including imputed rents, from the basic definition of income, no reasonable substitute is needed or proper, including denying interest on the purchase of a home.

If Congress extends the income tax laws to tax imputed rents, it must then determine that denial of mortgage interest would be a reasonable substitute for imputing the income directly. The fascination with interest is that the amount of interest most persons pay in the initial years of ownership approximates the rent the homeowner would pay by renting a similar house. The relationship is not a universal one, however. Over time, homes tend to appreciate in value while interest payments fall due to mortgage reduction. The correlation between interest payments and the rental value of owner-occupied homes is too attenuated and random to form a valid basis for a taxing surrogate.

D.   Horizontal Equity Comparisons

3.   Homeowners and Renters

Renters cannot deduct rent payments. Because interest payments are deductible and normally constitute the largest part of the monthly mortgage payments, commentators have compared the plight of renters to that of homeowners and concluded that the interest deduction favors homeowners. The assertion seems self-evident. A homeowner paying $700-a-month mortgage can deduct the majority of the payment to reduce her tax liability approximately $200 a month, while a renter paying $700 a month rent receives no tax benefit. The inequality is not as graphic as it appears at first blush, however. Homeowners do not deduct all expenses of homeownership. Repairs, maintenance, yard upkeep, water, sewage, pest control, fire insurance, and garbage collection all are nondeductible expenses paid by homeowners. Renters generally do not pay any of these expenses directly. The landlord pays them out of rent proceeds. Homeowners also incur other expenses renters often avoid. For example, most homeowners must purchase draperies, blinds, and appliances, all items many landlords furnish to tenants. Because house occupants usually incur higher gas and electric bills than apartment dwellers, homeowners may spend substantially more on these expenses than their renting counterparts. Of course, the portion of the mortgage payments attributable to principal are nondeductible and homeowners cannot depreciate personal residences for tax purposes. Homeowners also pay property taxes and interest, both of which are deductible. Renters normally avoid paying any property taxes or interest on the rented unit.

Placing dollar amounts on homeowners' nondeductible expenses is difficult. Repair and maintenance costs differ significantly. Under any set of assumptions, however, the homeowner incurs substantial expenses not incurred directly by the renter. The landlord must pay for many of the expenses not paid directly by the tenant, and theoretically sets the rent based to some extent on anticipated expenses. Other expenses, such as higher utility expenses in a home, are not duplicated. Professional management of rental properties, moreover, may provide services and maintenance at a lower cost per unit through more cost efficient procedures than can homeowners. Multi-family units occupy less land per unit, reducing the cost of acquisition and maintenance. Much of a landlord's profits may come from cost efficient operations.

If someone could isolate how much more rent a renter pays than a similarly situated homeowner pays in nondeductible housing costs, Congress might consider allowing some deduction for renters. Allowing a deduction for the full amount of the rent payment would be unjustified, however. A full deduction would give renters a deduction not given to homeowners. To remedy that inequality, Congress then would be obliged to authorize home related expense deductions, including depreciation. One proffered alternative would allow renters to deduct two-thirds of rent payments. It should be less. Even then, special rules would need to address boarding houses, co-renters, and benefits furnished by landlords for the rent charge such as furnishings and maid service. Predictably, persons would spend more on rental housing, possibly reducing the amount spent on other consumer goods, thus reducing the tax base.

In any case, inequity between renters and homeowners does not support denying the homeowner an interest deduction. Interest should not be the economic equivalent of rent for tax purposes. Interest is the charge for the money to purchase an investment, the home. Denying homeowners an interest deduction would not equalize total housing costs of renters and homeowners. Interest denial would make home purchases more difficult and would encourage more taxpayers to become or remain renters.

Dennis J. Ventry, Jr., The Accidental Deduction: A History and Critique of the Tax Subsidy for Mortgage Interest

73 Law and Contemporary Problems 233, 277–283 (Winter 2010).

Conclusion: Eulogizing the MID

The recent global financial meltdown had roots in the collapse of the housing industry. Increasingly permissive lending practices—encouraged by successive two-term presidential administrations—created a mortgage market flooded with risky, "affordable" loans characterized by subprime, variable, and teaser rates. Robust real estate markets across the country translated into rising home values, which owners further leveraged through maxed-out home equity lines and risky refinancing, raising LTV ratios to historic highs and resulting in distinctly suboptimal portfolio allocations. Meanwhile, Wall Street repackaged the risky, "affordable" mortgages into multi-tiered securities with the help of financial instruments so opaque that no one could tell what they were buying or selling. In addition, purchasers of these securities included commercial and investment banks, hedge funds, and insurance companies, all of whom play a critical role in the economy. As housing markets cooled and then reversed, homeowners faced negative equity positions with mortgage and home equity debt significantly exceeding homes values. At the same time, variable-rate mortgages began to readjust upward, and millions of financially strapped homeowners fell behind on monthly mortgage payments.

Foreclosures jumped and then spiraled out of control, throwing financial markets into a tailspin.

Housing tax policies fueled the boom and exacerbated the bust. The MID played a particularly insidious role in the crisis by explicitly promoting overinvestment in housing. "Buy as much house as you can," real estate agents urged clients. "The more you buy, the bigger your tax break." More mortgage debt meant lower taxes, such that the deduction began effectively subsidizing gambles on fluctuations in housing prices. "The deduction essentially encourages us to make leveraged bets on the swings of the housing market," economist Edward Glaeser has written. "That leverage means that housing price swings can easily wipe people out." By rewarding highly leveraged homeowners, the MID [i.e., mortgage interest deduction—Eds.]distorted household risk profiles which led to rising default rates, which, in turn, raised the cost of credit for homeowners and other owners of capital. Excessively leveraged portfolios also led to "temperance" and a general "flight to safety," whereby highly leveraged households opted for less risky asset investments, such as U.S. Treasuries, as they attempted to balance out top-heavy portfolios, a behavioral response with adverse affects on prices and returns of other asset investments.

The economic case against the MID, strengthening over fifty years, is indisputable. More than ever, the deduction distorts the cost of owner-occupied housing relative to other investments, resulting in economy-wide misallocation of capital stock, artificially elevated housing prices, overconsumption of large, expensive homes, and precariously high LTV ratios. Moreover, the MID is "not [even] . . . particularly effective in altering the choice between renting and owning." It encourages suburbanization and decentralization of metropolitan areas, distributes benefits unevenly across different regions of the country, discriminates against minorities and low-income households, raises unemployment, destabilizes the national economy, and may even reduce the supply of housing. In the end, the MID "amounts to a huge subsidy that causes massive, efficiency-draining distortions in the economy," creating "less business capital, lower productivity, lower real wages, and a lower standard of living." In fact, according to Martin Sullivan, nearly every economist believes—and has believed for some time—that "the most sure-fire way to improve the competitiveness of the American economy is to repeal the mortgage interest deduction."

The MID is as inequitable as it is inefficient. It is the quintessential "upside-down subsidy: the greater the need, the smaller the subsidy." It provides ten times the tax savings for households with income exceeding $250,000 compared to households earning between $40,000 and $75,000. It is effectively worthless for low- and middle-income households, such that repealing it would significantly increase the progressivity of the income tax. Moreover, the MID has gotten increasingly regressive over the last twenty years. In 1986, tax returns reporting income below $50,000 (indexed to 2009 dollars) received 13.7% of the tax savings associated with the MID, while returns reporting income over $100,000 (also indexed) received roughly 22% of the benefits. By 2007, returns reporting income below $50,000 received just 4.1% of the MID's largesse, while returns reporting income above $100,000 received an astounding 73% of the subsidy's value.

Such disproportionately skewed benefits belie claims of the housing lobby that the MID "is an important factor promoting broad-based home ownership." It does not help 65% of taxpayers taking the standard deduction, nor nearly half of all homeowners, nor 20% of mortgaged homeowners. Moreover, the MID provides no benefits to low-income households and only minimal benefits to middle-income households. It does not help renters. And it gives little assistance to the elderly who either are no longer servicing mortgages or who have too little income to receive any benefit. Instead, the subsidy accrues to households least in need of assistance and "encourages larger and more expensive homes among a relatively small share of taxpayers." "What argument can be made," David Cay Johnston asks, "for subsidizing housing for people with seven-figure and larger incomes? And if we continue this subsidy, how do we rationalize giving no subsidy to more than half of homeowners?"

Indeed, if promoting homeownership is the desideratum of U.S. housing policies, then the MID is a terribly inefficient and inequitable policy vehicle. Experts are unanimous in that the MID has "almost no effect on the homeownership rate." Policies promoting homeownership "should seek to increase the number of homeowners," and "should emphasize the purchase decision, not the quantity decision." Any tax subsidy "should be only the minimum amount necessary to switch people from renting to ownership, and it should not be available for anyone who would buy a house anyway." Repealing the MID would mean attacking the "most sacred tax break in the code." And it would result in a drop in home prices, a fear stoked by special interests such as the National Association of Realtors, which takes the position that "any changes to the mortgage interest deduction would de-value homes . . . [and] trigger yet another crisis in home values." But repealing the MID would not affect housing prices nearly as much as doomsayers claim. Moreover, the downturn would be largely temporary, and focused on big, expensive homes. If policymakers were concerned about preserving artificially inflated home values for sellers of large, overpriced homes, the repeal could be phased in over several years. Eliminating the MID would only minimally affect rates of homeownership, and again only temporarily. It would accelerate the buildup of home equity, increase the saving rate, and help households absorb income shocks. Most importantly, it would make homes less expensive. As law professor Ted Seto has observed, eliminating the MID would mean "we'd all pay less for our housing—substantially less. More affordable homes. Lower home mortgages. Fewer financial eggs in a single basket. Less risk of financial catastrophe."

Assuming that national policymakers and the American public still consider homeownership a worthy goal, repealing the MID would remove an obstacle to achieving that objective. Using the money saved from repeal ($108 billion in 2010) to fund a tax credit rather than a deduction would positively promote homeownership. Unlike the MID, a tax credit for homeowners could be independent of home value or size of debt, which would prevent excessive borrowing and precariously high loan-to-value ratios, precisely the problems that fueled the current housing and financial crises. In addition, a home credit could be capped and indexed to prevent households in high-priced areas from receiving disproportionately large subsidies. It would be a considerably more progressive policy than the MID, simplify the tax code by reducing the number of itemizers, and partially rationalize the treatment of homeownership under a net income tax that currently fails to tax imputed rent. Most importantly, converting the MID to a tax credit would influence the decision of millions of ordinary Americans to own versus rent, thereby substantially increasing the rate of homeownership nationwide.

In other words, replacing the deduction for mortgage interest with a tax credit would largely accomplish the goal of postwar tax reformers as discussed in this article. It would tie the subsidy to need rather than marginal tax rates, reduce complexity in taxpaying and tax administration by reducing itemizers, limit reliance on the tax system to deliver benefits and shape behavior, and, if permitted by budgetary realities, allow for rate reduction.

NOTES

1. *Parity Between Renters and Owners.* The deduction for mortgage interest payments has been the most frequent target of congressional attack. The prospects for taxing homeowners on their imputed rental income are even more distant. For excellent discussions of alternative strategies for achieving tax parity between renters and owners, see Snider, The Suburban Advantage: Are Tax Benefits of Home Ownership Defensible?, 32 N.Ky.L.Rev. 157 (2005); Mann, The (Not-So) Little House on the Prairie—The Hidden Cost of Home Mortgage Interest Deduction, 32 Ariz.St.L.J. 1347 (2000); Hellmuth, Homeowner Preferences, in Comprehensive Income Taxation 163 (J. Pechman, ed., 1977); Note, Federal Income Tax Discrimination Between Homeowners and Renters: A Proposed Solution, 12 Ind.L.Rev. 583 (1979).

Although the 1986 Tax Reform Act eliminated the deduction for personal interest on consumer debt such as charge accounts, it retained the deduction for interest paid on residential real property mortgages. As provided in the 1986 Tax Reform Act and modified in the Revenue Act of 1987, the deduction—for "qualified residence interest"—is, however, limited to interest on debt secured by the taxpayer's principal residence or a second residence, such as a vacation home, and to debt coming within prescribed limits. For example, there can be no interest deduction with respect to an indebtedness in excess of $1 million. In the 1987 legislation, Congress also permitted the deduction of interest on home equity loans, within certain limits. See Internal Revenue Code § 163.

2. *Legislation.* Early income tax laws sought to achieve parity between homeowners and renters by allowing renters to deduct rent payments. Act of Mar. 3, 1863, ch. 74, § 11, 12 Stat. 713, 723 (1863). In 1978, the New York Legislature amended section 304 of the Real Property Tax Law to provide that, for purposes of real property taxation, certain residential tenants have an interest in real property and are personally liable for taxes on that interest. Section 926 of the Real Property Tax Law was amended to provide that the "owner of the real property where such a renter is an occupant shall be deemed an agent of the collecting officer of the

municipality in which the real property is located for the purposes of collecting the taxes due from each tenant personally liable for taxes." The amendments' original effective date, April 1, 1979, was later postponed to April 1, 1980, pending a ruling from the Internal Revenue Service.

In June, 1979, the Service ruled that the "New York State renters tax paid by renters pursuant to sections 304 and 926–a . . . is not a tax for federal income tax purposes, but rather is part of the renters' rental payments." In the Service's view, the tax did not impose on the renter "any economic burden that did not exist" prior to the amendments. "The lack of an economic burden on the renter is further evidenced by the fact that the owner is not relieved from the obligation of paying all taxes due on the owner's property . . . [i]n the event of the renter's nonpayment, section 304 looks to the owner for payment and the taxing authority may enforce payment against the owner's interest in the entire property." Rev.Rul. 79–180, 1979–23 I.R.B. 7.

3. *Is There a Disparity?* As Professor Snoe indicates, the relative advantages that homeowners enjoy over renters are probably less lopsided than they first appear. First, it is not clear that landlords pass the full burden of real property taxes on to their tenants. See generally, Netzer, The Incidence of the Property Tax Revisited, 26 Nat'l. Tax J. 515 (1973); H. Aaron, Who Pays the Property Tax? A New View (1975). Second, the federal government provides extensive financial support to low and moderate-income rental housing, and these direct subsidies partially balance the indirect subsidies to homeowners through the tax deductions for interest and taxes. Third, prior to the 1986 Tax Reform Act the Internal Revenue Code permitted landlords to accelerate the deductions they take for the depreciation of their buildings, and landlords probably passed some of these savings on to their tenants in the form of lowered rent. Estimates of this reduction to average rentals range between 11% and 17%, depending on the landlord's tax bracket. See Hellmuth, Homeowner Preferences, in Comprehensive Income Taxation 168 (J. Pechman, ed. 1977). The 1986 legislation essentially placed all new buildings on a straight line depreciation method, although it permitted existing buildings to continue with accelerated depreciation. Thus, rental deductions have probably declined. See pages 940–953 below.

For a Senate debate on the claimed inequities to renters see Congressional Record, Senate, Daily ed. Sept. 23, 1976, S.16483, 16488–16489.

4. *The Mortgage Interest Deduction and the Financial Crisis.* Professor Ventry suggests that the mortgage interest deduction played a significant role in the mortgage finance crisis of 2008 and in distorting housing markets. Even for those agreeing with this analysis, the political hurdles to limiting the deduction are significant. On the deduction and the financial crisis, see Morrow, Billions of Tax Dollars Spent Inflating the Housing Bubble: How and Why the Mortgage Interest Deduction Failed, 17 Fordham J. Corp. & Fin. L. 751 (2012).

5. *Casualty Losses.* Internal Revenue Code sections 163, 164, and 165 permit homeowners to take deductions for interest, taxes and casualty losses, respectively. Section 262 bars deductions for all other costs of upkeep, such as repairs, depreciation, wear and tear and insurance, through its general disallowance of "personal, living or family expenses."

The 1986 Tax Reform Act amended section 165(h)(4) to provide that a taxpayer will not be allowed to deduct a casualty loss for damage to insured property devoted to personal use unless she files a timely insurance claim for the damage. Although presumably aimed at automobile owners who are reluctant to file insurance claims out of fear that their insurance will be cancelled, or that their rates will increase, the provision will also have an impact on insured homeowners.

Taxpayers sometimes try to obtain deductions for property damage from wear and tear or exposure to the elements by characterizing the damage as a casualty loss, deductible under section 165. The Commissioner and the courts have, however, generally taken "casualty" to mean only losses that occur suddenly, such as from flood, earthquake or explosion. As a consequence, taxpayers have had little luck in getting deductions for progressive damage of the sort caused by erosion, corrosion or termite infestation. Does this definition of casualty mean that the homeowner who promptly identifies, and corrects an invasion of termites, is more likely to get a casualty deduction than the homeowner who takes no action until, after some months, her entire house collapses? See Rosenberg v. Commissioner, 198 F.2d 46 (8th Cir.1952).

6. *Repair or Improvement?* If the taxpayer cannot get her property damage treated as a casualty, she may repair it and try to capitalize the cost of repair by calling the repair an improvement. By adding the cost of the improvement to her basis in the home, she is able to reduce any gain on sale. Courts have, however, taken a hard line here, too. Such expenditures as painting and plastering to keep the property in good, attractive condition will be considered noncapital repairs even though they may prolong the life of the house or otherwise add to its value. Only structural additions, such as a new room or a swimming pool, fall safely within the concept of capital improvements.

Can you find a workable line between the two kinds of expenditure? What differences, if any, are there between keeping a house in good condition, increasing its life, and increasing its value? Would you characterize a new roof as a repair or an improvement? Does the repair-improvement distinction provide an incentive to wasteful—because unnecessary—capital expenditures?

7. *Home Offices; Vacation Homes.* Within stringent limits, a homeowner can treat a portion of her home upkeep and depreciation expenses as deductible business expenses or expenses incurred in connection with the production of income by definitively marking off a part of her house as a home office used by her in her business or as a condition of her employment and deducting the expenses properly allocable to the office. Section 280A, introduced by the 1976 Tax Reform Act, provides rigorous formulae for determining these deductions. The 1986 Tax Reform Act further tightened these restrictions. Where the 1976 Act limited the taxpayer's deduction to gross income from the home business, as reduced by interest and taxes allocable to the part of the house used for the business activities, the 1986 Act further lowered the gross income ceiling by requiring that it be reduced by business expenses, such as accounting and legal expenses, not directly connected to the home office itself.

The Tax Reform Act of 1997 added language intended to supersede the restrictive interpretation of principal place of business imposed in

Commissioner v. Soliman, 506 U.S. 168, 113 S.Ct. 701, 121 L.Ed.2d 634 (1993). Pub.L. 105–34, § 932(a). Section 280A(c)(1) now provides that "principal place of business" includes a place of business used for administrative or management activities for a business if there is no other location where such administrative or management takes place. On Section 280A, see Mulligan, The Tax Ramification of the Business Use of a Home, 8 Okla. City U.L.Rev. 201 (1983); Eichenbaum, The Office at Home: An Analysis of Section 280A and Recent Tax Court Decisions, 10 J. Real Estate Tax. 63 (1982); Rice, The Controversy with the IRS Over the Rental of Personal Residences, 9 J. Real Estate Tax. 143 (1981–82); Samansky, Deductions for a Former Residence: Don't Leave Home Without Them, 16 Hofstra L.Rev. 615 (1988); Kerr, The Rental of Personal Residences: Implications of Section 280A, 7 J. Real Estate Tax. 139 (1979–80).

The two-home family may under section 280A deduct the expenses of maintaining a vacation home that is sometimes rented out to others. See Rose v. C.I.R., T.C. Summ. Op. 2011–117 (U.S. Tax Ct. 2011) (permitting home interest deduction for vacation home under construction).

8. *Gain on Sale of Personal Residence.* The sale of a personal residence is a capital transaction under the Code and gain, if realized, will be treated as capital gain. Although the 1986 Tax Reform Act repealed the preferential capital gains tax rate, the concept of capital gain remains important under the Act. As noted in the Conference Report, "[t]hese provisions do not change the character of gain as ordinary or capital, or as long-or short-term capital gain." H.R.Rep. No. 841, 99th Cong., 2d Sess. II–105 (1986). The Code offers several techniques for deferring the taxation of gain and one device for partially forgiving taxation altogether.

Under section 1033, a taxpayer may elect deferred taxation of any gain realized from the involuntary conversion of his home through destruction, "theft, seizure, or requisition or condemnation." Within prescribed limits, section 453, discussed at pages 979–981, provides for gain to be prorated and reported on an installment basis rather than entirely in the year of sale. Section 121 allows taxpayers to exclude up to $250,000 of gain realized on the sale of their principal residence; they must have used the home as their principal residence for two of the prior five years.

Prior to the Tax Reform Act of 1997, the most widely used deferral technique was section 1034's provision for postponing taxation of gain on the sale of a principal residence if, within two years before or after the sale, the taxpayer acquired another principal residence and the cost of the new home exceeded the adjusted sales price of the old. Section 1034 was repealed by the Tax Reform Act of 1997 when Congress enacted new section 121. Pub.L. 105–34, § 312(b). Section 121 allows individuals to exclude up to $250,000 of gain resulting from the sale of a principal residence every two years. Married couples can exclude up to $500,000. To be eligible, the taxpayer must have used the property as a principal residence for two years. Section 121 provides an exclusion of gain while prior section 1034 only deferred the gain. See Bunn & Williamson, Planning for Home Sales After the Tax Relief Act of 1997—Avoiding the Pitfalls, 27 Real Est. L.J. 151 (1998); Grant, Big Relief and Little Grief for Real Estate Under TRA § 97, 25 J. Real Est. Tax. 99 (1998); Nellen & Platner, Disposition of a Principal Residence After TRA § 97: Perspectives, Disposition of a Principal Residence After TRA § 97: Perspectives, Planning, and Problems, 25 J. Real Est. Tax. 319 (1998). See also Klein, a

Requiem for the Rollover Rule: Capital Gains, Farmland Loss, and the Law of Unintended Consequences, 55 Wash. & Lee L.Rev. 403, 406 (1998) ("Despite its laudable goal of supporting home ownership, § 1034 unwittingly promoted the needless destruction of farmland and the increased proliferation of suburban housing developments.")

9. *Loss on Sale of Personal Residence.* The taxpayer cannot deduct a loss incurred on the sale of his residence. The reason given for denying a deduction is that, like the costs of upkeep and depreciation, loss is personal to the taxpayer and unrelated to his business or production of income. One way for a homeowner to get at least some loss deduction in a declining market is to rent his home and then sell it, taking a trade or business ordinary loss deduction under I.R.C. § 1231 for the rental period. Consider whether a homeowner could deduct his entire loss through the following strategy: Sell the house on credit to a buyer who, as a poor credit risk, is willing to pay a price considerably above fair market value—say the same price the seller paid for it. If the buyer defaults, the seller will get the property back or see it sold on a foreclosure sale, and will then try to write the loan off as a bad debt. Compare Guffey v. United States, 339 F.2d 759 (9th Cir.1964). See generally, Byrne, Conversion of a Personal Residence to a Business or Investment Use for Tax Purposes, 8 Rut.–Cam. L.J. 393 (1977).

10. *Bibliographic Note.* See Frederick, Reconciling Intentions With Outcomes: A Critical Examination of the Mortgage Interest Deduction, 28 Akron Tax. J. 41 (2013); Johnson, Note, Dodging DOMA, The State of the Mortgage Interest Deduction for Same-Sex Couples After Sophy v. Commissioner, 66 Tax Law. 787 (2013); U.S. Government Accountability Office, Report to the Joint Committee on Taxation, "Home Mortgage Interest Deduction: Despite Challenges Presented by Complex Tax Rules, IRS Could Enhance Enforcement and Guidance," GAO–09–769 (July 2009).

CHAPTER XIII

COMMERCIAL OWNERSHIP AND DEVELOPMENT

A. TAX PLANNING: HOW PROPERTY IS HELD

Two concepts dominate federal income tax planning for real estate investments. First, it is worth more to the taxpayer to have a dollar on one day than to have the same dollar the next day. Second, it is less costly to the taxpayer to be taxed on income at the lower capital gains rates than at the higher ordinary income rates. Guided by these two facts, taxpayers commonly try to take as many deductions as possible, as early as possible. They try to defer income taxation for as long as possible and, when income has to be taxed, they try to have it taxed at capital gains rates. If losses are incurred, the taxpayer would usually want to have the loss deducted early and as an offset to ordinary income rather than as a capital loss.

The 1986 Tax Reform Act, which for most purposes went into effect on January 1, 1987, altered the second fact but not the first. Under prior law, a 60% deduction for net long term capital gains gave individual taxpayers in the highest, 50%, tax bracket an effective capital gains tax rate of 20%. With the 1986 Act's repeal of the capital gains deduction, capital gains were taxed at the taxpayer's ordinary income rate. Over time, however, the distinction between taxation of ordinary income and capital gains reasserted itself, beginning with Revenue Reconciliation Act of 1990. This gap has continued so that today the maximum tax rate for capital gains is 28% and the highest rate for taxation of ordinary income is 39.6%. 26 U.S.C.A. § 1(a)–(d),(h).

The Internal Revenue Code divides commercial real property into three classes: property held for investment or production of income; property used in trade or business; and property held primarily for sale to customers in the ordinary course of trade or business. To each class of property the Code attaches a set of specific attributes for taking deductions and for recognizing gains and losses. While the Code's approach substantially limits the taxpayer's ability to jockey for the best tax position, it does leave room for creative tax planning and for structuring investments to fit into the most advantageous class.

Property held for investment or production of income. Property held for investment or production of income qualifies as a capital asset under section 1221, and all gains or losses realized on its sale or exchange are treated as capital gains or losses. Under section 212, which allows deductions for "the management, conservation, or maintenance of property held for the production of income," the property owner can deduct the expenses of real property taxes, interest, maintenance and repairs. Under section 167, the taxpayer can also take a deduction for the depreciation of improvements situated on the land. Compliance with section 1031's criteria for tax-free exchanges will postpone recognition of gain or loss on transfer of the property.

Property used in the taxpayer's trade or business. Section 1221 expressly excludes a taxpayer's "real property used in his trade or business" from its definition of capital asset. While capital asset treatment is thus lost to this class of real estate investment, section 1231 treats gain on the disposition of trade or business property as capital gain, while it treats loss as ordinary loss which can be offset against ordinary income. Section 1231 property is entitled to all of the expense deductions, including the depreciation deduction, allowed to section 1221 property, and similarly qualifies for deferred recognition of gain and loss under section 1031.

Property held primarily for sale to customers in the ordinary course of trade or business. Section 1221 excludes from its definition of capital asset, and section 1231 excludes from its definition of trade or business property, "property held by the taxpayer primarily for sale to customers in the ordinary course of his trade or business." Gains or losses on sales or exchanges of property in this class are treated as ordinary income and ordinary loss rather than as capital gains and losses. While most expenses incurred in connection with holding this property—interest, taxes, maintenance expenses, casualty losses—are deductible, depreciation is not. Property in this class does not qualify for deferred recognition of gain or loss under section 1031. The 1986 Tax Reform Act repealed the capital gains deduction, taxing all gain at ordinary income rates, and curtailed the tax benefits of the depreciation deduction. The 1986 Act thus reduced some of the comparative disadvantages of classification as property held primarily for sale to customers in the ordinary course of trade or business.

Bibliographic Note. In addition to the standard tax treatises and textbooks, you may find the following sources helpful: G. Robinson, Federal Income Taxation of Real Estate (6th ed.); S. Guerin, Taxation of Real Estate Transactions (2005). The Journal of Real Estate Taxation, published quarterly, is an excellent source of articles on currently important tax topics.

Malat v. Riddell

Supreme Court of the United States, 1966.
383 U.S. 569, 86 S.Ct. 1030, 16 L.Ed.2d 102.

PER CURIAM.

Petitioner was a participant in a joint venture which acquired a 45–acre parcel of land, the intended use for which is somewhat in dispute. Petitioner contends that the venturers' intention was to develop and operate an apartment project on the land; the respondent's position is that there was a "dual purpose" of developing the property for rental purposes or selling, whichever proved to be the more profitable. In any event, difficulties in obtaining the necessary financing were encountered and the interior lots of the tract were subdivided and sold. The profit from those sales was reported and taxed as ordinary income.

The joint venturers continued to explore the possibility of commercially developing the remaining exterior parcels. Additional frustrations in the form of zoning restrictions were encountered. These difficulties persuaded petitioner and another of the joint venturers of the desirability of terminating the venture; accordingly, they sold out their interests in the remaining property. Petitioner contends that he is entitled to treat the profits from this last sale as capital gains; the respondent takes the position that this was "property held by the taxpayer primarily for sale to customers in the ordinary course of his trade or business," and thus subject to taxation as ordinary income.

The District Court made the following finding:

"The members of [the joint venture] as of the date the 44.901 acres were acquired, intended either to sell the property or develop it for rental, depending upon which course appeared to be most profitable. The venturers realized that they had made a good purchase price-wise and, if they were unable to obtain acceptable construction financing or rezoning . . . which would be prerequisite to commercial development, they would sell the property in bulk so they wouldn't get hurt. The purpose of either selling or developing the property continued during the period in which [the joint venture] held the property."

The District Court ruled that petitioner had failed to establish that the property was not held *primarily* for sale to customers in the ordinary course of business, and thus rejected petitioner's claim to capital gain treatment for the profits derived from the property's resale. The Court of Appeals affirmed, 347 F.2d 23. We granted certiorari (382 U.S. 900) to resolve a conflict among the courts of appeals with regard to the meaning of the term "primarily" as it is used in § 1221(1) of the Internal Revenue Code of 1954.

The statute denies capital gain treatment to profits reaped from the sale of "property held by the taxpayer *primarily* for sale to customers in the ordinary course of his trade or business." (Emphasis added.) The respondent urges upon us a construction of "primarily" as meaning that a purpose may be "primary" if it is a "substantial" one.

As we have often said, "the words of statutes—including revenue acts—should be interpreted where possible in their ordinary, everyday senses." Crane v. Commissioner, 331 U.S. 1, 6. Departure from a literal reading of statutory language may, on occasion, be indicated by relevant internal evidence of the statute itself and necessary in order to effect the legislative purpose. But this is not such an occasion. The purpose of the statutory provision with which we deal is to differentiate between the "profits and losses arising from the everyday operation of a business" on the one hand (Corn Products Co. v. Commissioner, 350 U.S. 46, 52) and "the realization of appreciation in value accrued over a substantial period of time" on the other. (Commissioner v. Gillette Motor Co., 364 U.S. 130, 134.) A literal reading of the statute is consistent with this legislative purpose. We hold that, as used in § 1221(1), "primarily" means "of first importance" or "principally."

Since the courts below applied an incorrect legal standard, we do not consider whether the result would be supportable on the facts of this case had the correct one been applied. We believe, moreover, that the appropriate disposition is to remand the case to the District Court for fresh fact-findings, addressed to the statute as we have now construed it.

Vacated and remanded.

MR. JUSTICE BLACK would affirm the judgments of the District Court and the Court of Appeals.

MR. JUSTICE WHITE took no part in the decision of this case.

Biedenharn Realty Co., Inc. v. United States

United States Court of Appeals, Fifth Circuit, 1976.
526 F.2d 409, cert. denied, 429 U.S. 819, 97 S.Ct. 64, 50 L.Ed.2d 79.

GOLDBERG, CIRCUIT JUDGE:

The taxpayer-plaintiff, Biedenharn Realty Company, Inc. [Biedenharn], filed suit against the United States in May, 1971, claiming a refund for the tax years 1964, 1965, and 1966. In its original tax returns for the three years, Biedenharn listed profits of $254,409.47 from the sale of 38 residential lots. Taxpayer divided this gain, attributing 60% to ordinary income and 40% to capital gains. Later, having determined that the profits from these sales were entirely ordinary income, the Internal Revenue Service assessed and collected additional taxes and interest. In its present action, plaintiff asserts that the whole real estate profit represents gain from the sale of capital assets and consequently that the Government is indebted to taxpayer for $32,006.86 in overpaid taxes. Reviewing the facts of this case in the light of our previous holdings and the directions set forth in this opinion, we reject plaintiff's claim and in so doing reverse the opinion of the District Court.

I.

Because of the confusing state of the record in this controversy and the resulting inconsistencies among the facts as stipulated by the parties, as found by the District Court, and as stated in the panel opinion, we believe it useful to set out in plentiful detail the case's background and circumstances as best they can be ascertained.

A. *The Realty Company.* Joseph Biedenharn organized the Biedenharn Realty Company in 1923 as a vehicle for holding and managing the Biedenharn family's numerous investments. The original stockholders were all family members. The investment company controls, among other interests, valuable commercial properties, a substantial stock portfolio, a motel, warehouses, a shopping center, residential real property, and farm property.

B. *Taxpayer's Real Property Sales—The Hardtimes Plantation.* Taxpayer's suit most directly involves its ownership and sale of lots from the 973 acre tract located near Monroe, Louisiana, known as the Hardtimes Plantation. The plaintiff purchased the estate in 1935 for $50,000.00. B.W. Biedenharn, the Realty Company's president, testified that taxpayer acquired Hardtimes as a "good buy" for the purpose of farming and as a future investment. The plaintiff farmed the land for several years. Thereafter, Biedenharn rented part of the acreage to a farmer who Mr. Biedenharn suggested may presently be engaged in farming operations.

1. *The Three Basic Subdivisions.* Between 1939 and 1966, taxpayer carved three basic subdivisions from Hardtimes—Biedenharn Estates, Bayou DeSiard Country Club Addition, and Oak Park Addition—covering approximately 185 acres. During these years,

Biedenharn sold 208 subdivided Hardtimes lots in 158 sales, making a profit in excess of $800,000.00. These three basic subdivisions are the source of the contested 37 sales of 38 lots. Their development and disposition are more fully discussed below.

a) Biedenharn Estates Unit 1, including 41.9 acres, was platted in 1938. Between 1939 and 1956, taxpayer apparently sold 21 lots in 9 sales. Unit 2, containing 8.91 acres, was sold in 9 transactions between 1960 and 1965 and involved 10 lots.

b) Bayou DeSiard Country Club Addition, covering 61 acres, was subdivided in 1951, with remaining lots resubdivided in 1964. Approximately 73 lots were purchased in 64 sales from 1951 to 1966.

c) Oak Park Units 1 and 2 encompassed 75 acres. After subdivision in 1955 and resubdivision in 1960, plaintiff sold approximately 104 lots in 76 sales.

2. *Additional Hardtimes Sales.* Plaintiff lists at least 12 additional Hardtimes sales other than lots vended from the three basic subdivisions. The earliest of these dispositions occurred in November, 1935, thirteen days after the Plantation's purchase. Ultimately totaling approximately 275 acres, most, but not all, of these sales involved large parcels of nonsubdivided land.

C. *Taxpayer's Real Property Activity: Non-Hardtimes Sales.* The 208 lots marketed from the three Hardtimes subdivisions represent only part of Biedenharn's total real property sales activities. Although the record does not in every instance permit exactitude, plaintiff's own submissions make clear that the Biedenharn Realty Company effectuated numerous non-Hardtimes retail real estate transactions. From the Company's formation in 1923 through 1966, the last year for which taxes are contested, taxpayer sold 934 lots. Of this total, plaintiff disposed of 249 lots before 1935 when it acquired Hardtimes. Thus, in the years 1935 to 1966, taxpayer sold 477 lots apart from its efforts with respect to the basic Hardtimes subdivisions. Biedenharn's year by year sales breakdown is attached as Appendix I of this opinion. That chart shows real estate sales in all but two years, 1932 and 1970, since the Realty Company's 1923 inception.

Unfortunately, the record does not unambiguously reveal the number of *sales* as opposed to the number of *lots* involved in these dispositions. Although some doubt exists as to the actual *sales* totals, even the most conservative reading of the figures convinces us of the frequency and abundance of the non-Hardtimes sales. For example, from 1925 to 1958, Biedenharn consummated from its subdivided Owens tract a minimum of 125, but perhaps upwards of 300, sales (338 lots). Eighteen sales accounted for 20 lots sold between 1923 and 1958 from Biedenharn's Cornwall property. Taxpayer's disposition from 1927 to 1960 of its Corey and Cabeen property resulted in at least 50 sales. Plaintiff made 14 sales from its Thomas Street lots between 1937 and 1955. Moreover, Biedenharn has sold over 20 other properties, a few of them piecemeal, since 1923.

Each of these parcels has its own history. Joseph Biedenharn transferred much of the land to the Realty Company in 1923. The company acquired other property through purchases and various forms of foreclosure. Before sale, Biedenharn held some tracts for commercial or residential rental. Taxpayer originally had slated the Owens acreage for transfer in bulk to the Owens-Illinois Company. Also, the length of time between acquisition and disposition differed significantly among pieces of realty. However, these variations in the background of each plot and the length of time and original purpose for which each was obtained do not alter the fact that the Biedenharn Realty Company regularly sold substantial amounts of subdivided and improved real property, and further, that these sales were not confined to the basic Hardtimes subdivisions.

D.   *Real Property Improvements.* Before selling the Hardtimes lots, Biedenharn improved the land, adding in most instances, streets, drainage, water, sewerage, and electricity. The total cost of bettering the Plantation acreage exceeded $200,000 and included $9,519.17 for Biedenharn Estates Unit 2, $56,879.12 for Bayou DeSiard Country Club Addition, and $141,579.25 for the Oak Park Addition.

E.   *Sale of the Hardtimes Subdivisions.* Bernard Biedenharn testified that at the time of the Hardtimes purchase, no one foresaw that the land would be sold as residential property in the future. Accordingly, the District Court found, and we do not disagree, that Biedenharn bought Hardtimes for investment. Later, as the City of Monroe expanded northward, the Plantation became valuable residential property. The Realty Company staked off the Bayou DeSiard subdivision so that prospective purchasers could see what the lots "looked like." As demand increased, taxpayer opened the Oak Park and Biedenharn Estates Unit 2 subdivisions and resubdivided the Bayou DeSiard section. Taxpayer handled all Biedenharn Estates and Bayou DeSiard sales. Independent realtors disposed of many of the Oak Park lots. Mr. Herbert Rosenhein, a local broker, sold Oak Park Unit 1 lots. Gilbert Faulk, a real estate agent, sold from Oak Park Unit 2. Of the 37 sales consummated between 1964 and 1966, Henry Biedenharn handled at least nine transactions (Biedenharn Estates (2) and Bayou DeSiard (7)) while "independent realtors" effected some, if not all, of the other 28 transactions (Oak Park Unit 2). Taxpayer delegated significant responsibilities to these brokers. In its dealings with Faulk, Biedenharn set the prices, general credit terms, and signed the deeds. Details, including specific credit decisions and advertising, devolved to Faulk, who utilized on-site signs and newspapers to publicize the lots.

In contrast to these broker induced dispositions, plaintiff's nonbrokered sales resulted after unsolicited individuals approached Realty Company employees with inquiries about prospective purchases. At no time did the plaintiff hire its own real estate salesmen or engage in formal advertising. Apparently, the lands' prime location and plaintiff's subdivision activities constituted sufficient notice to interested persons of the availability of Hardtimes lots. Henry Biedenharn testified:

"[O]nce we started improving and putting roads and streets in people would call us up and ask you about buying a lot and we would sell a lot if they wanted it."

The Realty Company does not maintain a separate place of business but instead offices at the Biedenharn family's Ouachita Coca-Cola bottling plant. A telephone, listed in plaintiff's name, rings at the Coca-Cola building. Biedenharn has four employees: a camp caretaker, a tenant farmer, a bookkeeper and a manager. The manager, Henry Biedenharn, Jr., devotes approximately 10% of his time to the Realty Company, mostly collecting rents and overseeing the maintenance of various properties. The bookkeeper also works only part-time for plaintiff. Having set out these facts, we now discuss the relevant legal standard for resolving this controversy.

II.

The determination of gain as capital or ordinary is controlled by the language of the Internal Revenue Code. The Code defines capital asset, the profitable sale or exchange of which generally results in capital gains, as "property held by the taxpayer." 26 U.S.C.A. § 1221. Many exceptions limit the enormous breadth of this congressional description and consequently remove large numbers of transactions from the privileged realm of capital gains. In this case, we confront the question whether or not Biedenharn's real estate sales should be taxed at ordinary rates because they fall within the exception covering "property held by the taxpayer primarily for sale to customers in the ordinary course of his trade or business." 26 U.S.C.A. § 1221(1).

The problem we struggle with here is not novel. We have become accustomed to the frequency with which taxpayers litigate this troublesome question. Chief Judge Brown appropriately described the real estate capital gains—ordinary income issue as "old, familiar, recurring, vexing and ofttimes elusive." Thompson v. Commissioner of Internal Revenue, 5 Cir.1963, 322 F.2d 122, 123. The difficulty in large part stems from ad-hoc application of the numerous permissible criteria set forth in our multitudinous prior opinions. Over the past 40 years, this case by case approach with its concentration on the facts of each suit has resulted in a collection of decisions not always reconcilable. Recognizing the situation, we have warned that efforts to distinguish and thereby make consistent the Court's previous holdings must necessarily be "foreboding and unrewarding." *Thompson,* supra at 127. Litigants are cautioned that "each case must be decided on its own peculiar facts.... Specific factors, or combinations of them are not necessarily controlling." *Thompson,* supra at 127. Nor arc these factors the equivalent of the philosopher's stone, separating "sellers garlanded with capital gains from those beflowered in the garden of ordinary income." United States v. Winthrop, 5 Cir.1969, 417 F.2d 905, 911.

Assuredly, we would much prefer one or two clearly defined, easily employed tests which lead to predictable, perhaps automatic, conclusions. However, the nature of the congressional "capital asset" definition and the myriad situations to which we must apply that standard make impossible any easy escape from the task before us. No one set of criteria is applicable to all economic structures. Moreover, within a collection of tests, individual factors have varying weights and magnitudes, depending on the facts of the case. The relationship among the factors and their mutual interaction is altered as each criterion increases or diminishes in strength, sometimes changing the controversy's outcome. As such, there can be no mathematical formula capable of finding the X of capital gains or ordinary income in this complicated field.

Yet our inability to proffer a panaceatic guide to the perplexed with respect to this subject does not preclude our setting forth some general, albeit inexact, guidelines for the resolution of many of the § 1221(1) cases we confront. This opinion does not purport to reconcile all past precedents or assure conflict-free future decisions. Nor do we hereby obviate the need for ad-hoc adjustments when confronted with close cases and changing factual circumstances. Instead, with the hope of clarifying a few of the area's mysteries, we more precisely define and suggest points of emphasis for the major *Winthrop* delineated factors[22] as they appear in the instant controversy. In so doing, we devote particular attention to the Court's recent opinions in order that our analysis will reflect, insofar as possible, the Circuit's present trends.

III.

We begin our task by evaluating in the light of *Biedenharn's* facts the main *Winthrop* factors—substantiality and frequency of sales, improvements, solicitation and advertising efforts, and brokers' activities—as well as a few miscellaneous contentions. A separate section follows discussing the keenly contested role of prior investment intent. Finally, we consider the significance of the Supreme Court's decision in Malat v. Riddell.

A. *Frequency and Substantiality of Sales*

Scrutinizing closely the record and briefs, we find that plaintiff's real property sales activities compel an ordinary income conclusion. In arriving at this result, we examine first the most important of *Winthrop's* factors—the frequency and substantiality of taxpayer's sales. Although frequency and substantiality of sales are not usually conclusive, they occupy the preeminent ground in our analysis. The recent trend of Fifth Circuit decisions indicates that when dispositions of subdivided property extend over a long period of time and are especially numerous, the likelihood of capital gains is very slight indeed. Conversely, when sales are few and isolated, the taxpayer's claim to capital gain is accorded greater deference.

On the present facts, taxpayer could not claim "isolated" sales or a passive and gradual liquidation. Although only three years and 37 sales (38 lots) are in controversy here, taxpayer's pre-1964 sales from the Hardtimes acreage as well as similar dispositions from other properties are probative of the existence of sales "in the ordinary course of his trade or business." As Appendix I indicates, Biedenharn sold property, usually a substantial number of lots, in every year, save one, from 1923 to 1966. Biedenharn's long and steady history of improved lot sales at least equals that encountered in Thompson v. Commissioner of Internal Revenue, 5 Cir.1963, 322 F.2d 122, where also we noted the full history of real estate activity. Supra at 124–25. There taxpayer lost on a finding that he had sold 376½ lots over a 15 year span—this notwithstanding

---

[22] In United States v. Winthrop, 5 Cir.1969, 417 F.2d 905, 910, the Court enumerated the following factors:

(1) the nature and purpose of the acquisition of the property and the duration of the ownership; (2) the extent and nature of the taxpayer's efforts to sell the property; (3) the number, extent, continuity and substantiality of the sales; (4) the extent of subdividing, developing, and advertising to increase sales; (5) the use of a business office for the sale of the property; (6) the character and degree of supervision or control exercised by the taxpayer over any representative selling the property; and (7) the time and effort the taxpayer habitually devoted to the sales.

The numbering indicates no hierarchy of importance.

that overall the other sales indicia were more in taxpayer's favor than in the present case. Moreover, the contested tax years in that suit involved only ten sales (28 lots); yet we labeled that activity "substantial." Supra at 125.

The frequency and substantiality of Biedenharn's sales go not only to its holding purpose and the existence of a trade or business but also support our finding of the ordinariness with which the Realty Company disposed of its lots. These sales easily meet the criteria of normalcy set forth in *Winthrop,* supra at 912.

Furthermore, in contrast with Goldberg v. Commissioner of Internal Revenue, 5 Cir.1955, 223 F.2d 709, 713, where taxpayer did not reinvest his sales proceeds, one could fairly infer that the income accruing to the Biedenharn Realty Company from its pre-1935 sales helped support the purchase of the Hardtimes Plantation. Even if taxpayer made no significant acquisitions after Hardtimes, the "purpose, system, and continuity" of Biedenharn's efforts easily constitute a business.

Citing previous Fifth Circuit decisions including Goldberg v. Commissioner of Internal Revenue, 5 Cir.1955, 223 F.2d 709, 713, and Ross v. Commissioner of Internal Revenue, 5 Cir.1955, 227 F.2d 265, 268, the District Court sought to overcome this evidence of dealer-like real estate activities and property "primarily held for sale" by clinging to the notion that the taxpayer was merely liquidating a prior investment. We discuss later the role of former investment status and the possibility of taxpayer relief under that concept. Otherwise, the question of liquidation of an investment is simply the opposite side of the inquiry as to whether or not one is holding property primarily for sale in the ordinary course of his business. In other words, a taxpayer's claim that he is liquidating a prior investment does not really present a separate theory but rather restates the main question currently under scrutiny. To the extent the opinions cited by the District Court might create a specially protected "liquidation" niche, we believe that the present case, with taxpayer's energetic subdivision activities and consummation of numerous retail property dispositions, is governed by our more recent decision in Thompson v. Commissioner of Internal Revenue, supra at 127–28. There, the Court observed:

The liquidation, if it really is that, may therefore be carried out with business efficiency. Smith v. Commissioner of Internal Revenue, 5 Cir.1956, 232 F.2d 142, 145. But what was once an investment, or what may start out as a liquidation of an investment, may become something else. The Tax Court was eminently justified in concluding that this took place here. It was a regular part of the trade or business of Taxpayer to sell these lots to any and all comers who would meet his price. From 1944 on when the sales commenced, there is no evidence that he thereafter held the lots for any purpose other than the sale to prospective purchasers. It is true that he testified in conclusory terms that he was trying to "liquidate" but on objective standards the Tax Court could equate held solely with "held primarily." And, of course, there can be no question at all that purchasers of these lots were "customers" and that whether we call Taxpayer a "dealer" or a "trader", a real estate man or otherwise, the continuous sales of these lots down to the point of exhaustion was a regular and ordinary (and profitable) part of his business activity.

B. *Improvements*

Although we place greatest emphasis on the frequency and substantiality of sales over an extended time period, our decision in this instance is aided by the presence of taxpayer activity—particularly improvements—in the other *Winthrop* areas. Biedenharn vigorously improved its subdivisions, generally adding streets, drainage, sewerage, and utilities. These alterations are comparable to those in *Winthrop,* supra at 906, except that in the latter case taxpayer built five houses. We do not think that the construction of five houses in the context of *Winthrop's* 456 lot sales significantly distinguishes that taxpayer from Biedenharn.

C. *Solicitation and Advertising Efforts*

Substantial, frequent sales and improvements such as we have encountered in this case will usually conclude the capital gains issue against taxpayer. Thus, on the basis of our analysis to this point, we would have little hesitation in finding that taxpayer held "primarily for sale" in the "ordinary course of [his] trade or business." "[T]he flexing of commercial muscles with frequency and continuity, design and effect" of which *Winthrop* spoke, supra at 911, is here a reality. This reality is further buttressed by Biedenharn's sales efforts, including those carried on through brokers. Minimizing the importance of its own sales activities, taxpayer points repeatedly to its steady avoidance of advertising or other solicitation of customers. Plaintiff directs our attention to stipulations detailing the population growth of Monroe and testimony outlining the economic forces which made Hardtimes Plantation attractive residential property and presumably eliminated the need for sales exertions. We have no quarrel with plaintiff's description of this familiar process of suburban expansion, but we cannot accept the legal inferences which taxpayer would have us draw.

The Circuit's recent decisions in *Thompson,* supra at 124–26, and *Winthrop,* supra at 912, implicitly recognize that even one inarguably in the real estate business need not engage in promotional exertions in the face of a favorable market. As such, we do not always require a showing of active solicitation where "business . . . [is] good, indeed brisk," *Thompson,* supra at 124, and where other *Winthrop* factors make obvious taxpayer's ordinary trade or business status. Plainly, this represents a sensible approach. In cases such as *Biedenharn,* the sale of a few lots and the construction of the first homes, albeit not, as in *Winthrop,* by the taxpayer, as well as the building of roads, addition of utilities, and staking off of the other subdivided parcels constitute a highly visible form of advertising. Prospective home buyers drive by the advantageously located property, see the development activities, and are as surely put on notice of the availability of lots as if the owner had erected large signs announcing "residential property for sale." We do not by this evaluation automatically neutralize advertising or solicitation as a factor in our analysis. This form of inherent notice is not present in all land sales, especially where the property is not so valuably located, is not subdivided into small lots, and is not improved. Moreover, inherent notice represents only one band of the solicitation spectrum. Media utilization and personal initiatives remain material components of this criterion. When present, they call for greater Government oriented emphasis on *Winthrop's* solicitation factor.

D.   *Brokerage Activities*

In evaluating Biedenharn's solicitation activities, we need not confine ourselves to the *Thompson-Winthrop* theory of brisk sales without organizational efforts. Unlike in *Thompson* and *Winthrop* where no one undertook overt solicitation efforts, the Realty Company hired brokers who, using media and on site advertising, worked vigorously on taxpayer's behalf. We do not believe that the employment of brokers should shield plaintiff from ordinary income treatment. Their activities should at least in discounted form be attributed to Biedenharn. To the contrary, taxpayer argues that "one who is not already in the trade or business of selling real estate does not enter such business when he employs a broker who acts as an independent contractor. Fahs v. Crawford, 161 F.2d 315 (5 Cir.1947); Smith v. Dunn, 224 F.2d 353 (5 Cir.1955)." Without presently entangling ourselves in a dispute as to the differences between an agent and an independent contractor, we find the cases cited distinguishable from the instant circumstances. In both *Fahs* and *Smith,* the taxpayer turned the entire property over to brokers, who, having been granted total responsibility, made all decisions including the setting of sales prices. In comparison, Biedenharn determined original prices and general credit policy. Moreover, the Realty Company did not make all the sales in question through brokers as did taxpayers in *Fahs* and *Smith.* Biedenharn sold the Bayou DeSiard and Biedenharn Estates lots and may well have sold some of the Oak Park land. In other words, unlike *Fahs* and *Smith,* Biedenharn's brokers did not so completely take charge of the whole of the Hardtimes sales as to permit the Realty Company to wall itself off legally from their activities.

E.   *Additional Taxpayer Contentions*

Plaintiff presents a number of other contentions and supporting facts for our consideration. Although we set out these arguments and briefly discuss them, their impact, in the face of those factors examined above, must be minimal. Taxpayer emphasizes that its profits from real estate sales averaged only 11.1% in each of the years in controversy, compared to 52.4% in *Winthrop.* Whatever the percentage, plaintiff would be hard pressed to deny the substantiality of its Hardtimes sales in absolute terms (the subdivided lots alone brought in over one million dollars) or, most importantly, to assert that its real estate business was too insignificant to constitute a separate trade or business.

The relatively modest income share represented by Biedenharn's real property dispositions stems not from a failure to engage in real estate sales activities but rather from the comparatively large profit attributable to the Company's 1965 ($649,231.34) and 1966 ($688,840.82) stock sales. The fact of Biedenharn's holding, managing, and selling stock is not inconsistent with the existence of a separate realty business. If in the face of taxpayer's numerous real estate dealings this Court held otherwise, we would be sanctioning special treatment for those individuals and companies arranging their business activities so that the income accruing to real estate sales represents only a small fraction of the taxpaying entity's total gains.

Similarly, taxpayer observes that Biedenharn's manager devoted only 10% of his time to real estate dealings and then mostly to the company's rental properties. This fact does not negate the existence of sales activities. Taxpayer had a telephone listing, a shared business office, and a few part-time employees. Because, as discussed before, a strong seller's market existed, Biedenharn's sales required less than the usual solicitation efforts and therefore less than the usual time. Moreover, plaintiff, unlike taxpayers in *Winthrop,* supra, and *Thompson,* supra, hired brokers to handle many aspects of the Hardtimes transactions—thus further reducing the activity and time required of Biedenharn's employees.

Finally, taxpayer argues that it is entitled to capital gains since its enormous profits (74% to 97%) demonstrate a return based principally on capital appreciation and not on taxpayer's "merchandising" efforts. We decline the opportunity to allocate plaintiff's gain between long-term market appreciation and improvement related activities. Even if we undertook such an analysis and found the former element predominant, we would on the authority of *Winthrop,* supra at 907–908, reject plaintiff's contention which, in effect, is merely taxpayer's version of the Government's unsuccessful argument in that case.

IV.

The District Court found that "[t]axpayer is merely liquidating over a long period of time a substantial investment in the most advantageous method possible." 356 F.Supp. at 1336. In this view, the original investment intent is crucial, for it preserves the capital gains character of the transaction even in the face of normal real estate sales activities.

We reject the Government's sweeping contention that prior investment intent is always irrelevant. There will be instances where an initial investment purpose endures in controlling fashion notwithstanding continuing sales activity. We doubt that this aperture, where an active subdivider and improver receives capital gains, is very wide; yet we believe it exists. We would most generally find such an opening where the change from investment holding to sales activity results from unanticipated, externally induced factors which make impossible the continued pre-existing use of the realty. *Barrios Estate,* supra, is such a case. There the taxpayer farmed the land until drainage problems created by the newly completed intercoastal canal rendered the property agriculturally unfit. The Court found that taxpayer was "dispossessed of the farming operation through no act of her own." Supra at 518. Similarly, Acts of God, condemnation of part of one's property, new and unfavorable zoning regulations, or other events forcing alteration of taxpayer's plans create situations making possible subdivision and improvement as a part of a capital gains disposition.

Clearly, under the facts in this case, the distinction just elaborated undermines Biedenharn's reliance on original investment purpose. Taxpayer's change of purpose was entirely voluntary and therefore does not fall within the protected area. Moreover, taxpayer's original investment intent, *even if* considered a factor sharply supporting capital gains treatment, is so overwhelmed by the other *Winthrop* factors discussed supra, that that element can have no decisive effect. However wide the capital gains passageway through which a subdivider with former investment intent could squeeze, the Biedenharn Realty Company will never fit.

V.

The District Court, citing Malat v. Riddell, 1966, 383 U.S. 569, 86 S.Ct. 1030, 16 L.Ed.2d 102, stated that "the lots were not held . . . primarily for sale as that phrase was interpreted . . . in *Malat*. . . ." 356 F.Supp. at 1335. Finding that Biedenharn's primary purpose became holding for sale and consequently that *Malat* in no way alters our analysis here, we disagree with the District Court's conclusion. *Malat* was a brief per curiam in which the Supreme Court decided only that as used in Internal Revenue Code § 1221(1) the word "primarily" means "principally," "of first importance." The Supreme Court, remanding the case, did not analyze the facts or resolve the controversy which involved a real estate dealer who had purchased land and held it at the time of sale with the dual intention of developing it as rental property or selling it, depending on whichever proved to be the more profitable. In contrast, having substantially abandoned its investment and farming intent, Biedenharn was cloaked primarily in the garb of sales purpose when it disposed of the 38 lots here in controversy. With this change, the Realty Company lost the opportunity of coming within any dual purpose analysis.

We do not hereby condemn to ordinary income a taxpayer merely because, as is usually true, his principal intent at the exact moment of disposition is sales. Rather, we refuse capital gains treatment in those instances where over time there has been such a thoroughgoing change of purpose, as to make untenable a claim either of twin intent or continued primacy of investment purpose.

VI.

Having surveyed the Hardtimes terrain, we find no escape from ordinary income. The frequency and substantiality of sales over an extended time, the significant improvement of the basic subdivisions, the acquisition of additional properties, the use of brokers, and other less important factors persuasively combine to doom taxpayer's cause. Applying *Winthrop's* criteria, this case clearly falls within the ordinary income category delineated in that decision. In so concluding, we note that *Winthrop* does not represent the most extreme application of the overriding principle that "the definition of a capital asset must be narrowly applied and its exclusions interpreted broadly." Corn Products Refining Co. v. Commissioner of Internal Revenue, 1955, 350 U.S. 46, 52, 76 S.Ct. 20, 24, 100 L.Ed. 29, 35. . . . The opinion of the District Court is reversed.

APPENDIX I

(Plaintiff's Answers to Interrogatory 26)

YEAR	GROSS SALES	NUMBER LOTS
1923	1,900.00	4
1924	1,050.00	2
1925	7,442.38	18
1926	11,184.00	29
1927	9,619.25	52
1928	49,390.55	37
1929	35,810.25	55
1930	8,473.00	24
1931	15,930.00	18
1932	none	none
1933	520.00	2
1934	5,970.00	8
1935	2,639.00	7
1936	2,264.00	3
1937	14,071.00	8
1938	1,009.00	3
1939	5,558.00	10
1940	3,252.00	4
1941	2,490.00	3
1942	6,714.00	9
1943	6,250.00	12
1944	9,250.00	38
1945	15,495.00	20
1946	12,732.58	29
1947	38,310.00	169

YEAR	GROSS SALES	NUMBER LOTS
1948	23,850.00	22
1949	8,830.00	26
1950	9,370.00	19
1951	55,222.99	16
1952	38,134.29	16
1953	123,007.22	17
1954	235,396.04	10
1955	76,805.00	20
1956	100,593.25	61
1957	133,448.10	36
1958	110,369.00	27
1959	44,400.00	12
1960	130,610.19	21
1961	48,729.60	25
1962	6,720.00	1
1963	7,475.00	1
1964	77,650.00	10
1965	75,759.00	10
1966	155,950.00	20
1967	75,380.00	9
1968	89,447.50	10
1969	31,010.00	3
1970	none	none
1971	130,000.00	139

[The opinion of RONEY, J., specially concurring, is omitted.]

GEE, CIRCUIT JUDGE, with whom BELL, COLEMAN, AINSWORTH and DYER, CIRCUIT JUDGES, join, dissenting.

Viewing as incorrect the en banc majority's restatement of facts and law, I must respectfully dissent. I would adhere to the panel opinion, reported at 509 F.2d 171, which attempted to apply existing, controlling precedent in our circuit to the facts of this very close case as they were found by the district court. To obtain a different result, the majority has found it necessary to revise the law and refind the facts in important respects, as though the obtaining of capital gains treatment by this taxpayer in the three years in question were a catastrophe to be avoided at all costs.

First, in setting out the facts of this case, the majority summarily discounts a critical trial court factfinding without ruling it clearly erroneous. The majority rejects the district court's finding that taxpayer "is still farming a large part of the land," 356 F.Supp. at 1336, refinding the facts as being that taxpayer's tenant farmer "may" presently be farming the land, supra at 411, and that neither plaintiff nor the lower court claimed any dual purpose, id. at 423 n. 43. But the record affirmatively shows that the land has been and continues to be farmed, and the lower court specifically found multi-purpose use of the land.

Second, although insisting at one point that it only "resummarizes" the relevant case law, id. at 415 n. 23, the majority revises the old test by placing pre-eminent emphasis on sales activity and improvements, effectively eliminating the other factors enunciated in United States v. Winthrop, 417 F.2d 905 (5th Cir.1969). . . .

To explain its emphasis on improvements, the majority stresses the similarity between taxpayer's improvements and those present in *Winthrop*. Supra at 417. But this comparison, too, is mistaken. The *Winthrop* court emphasized that property does not cease to be a capital asset merely because its increase in value was due in part to the taxpayer's efforts in making improvements, 417 F.2d at 907–09, quoting the same portion of Barrios' Estate v. Commissioner of Internal Revenue, 265 F.2d 517 (5th Cir.1959), that the panel in this case cited:

"The idea of selling a large tract of land in lots embraces necessarily the construction of streets for access to them, the provision of drainage and the furnishing of access to such a necessity as water. It is hardly conceivable that taxpayer could have sold a lot without doing these things."

Id. at 520, quoted with approval in Winthrop, 417 F.2d at 909, and Biedenharn, 509 F.2d at 174 (panel opinion). . . .

NOTES

1. *Legislative History.* The phrase, "held by the taxpayer primarily for sale to customers in the ordinary course of his trade or business" did not appear in section 1221's original formulation, enacted in 1921, which withheld capital asset treatment from "stock in trade of a taxpayer or property of a kind which would properly be included in the inventory of the taxpayer if on hand at the close of the taxable year." Revenue Act of 1921, ch. 136, § 206(a)(6), 42 Stat. 233. Following standard accounting practice, which would not treat real property as inventory, the Commissioner took the position that real property could never be "stock in trade." In an effort to plug this gap, Congress in 1924 amended the exclusion to add "or property held by the taxpayer primarily for sale in the course of his trade or business." Revenue Act of 1924, ch. 234, § 208(a)(8), 43 Stat. 263. The words, "to customers" and "ordinary," were added in 1934 to make clear that stockbrokers trading on their own account were not in the trade or business of selling stocks. H.R.Rep. No. 1385, 73rd Cong.2d Sess. 22 (1934).

2. *Real Property vs. Personal Property.* The concept of property held "primarily for sale to customers" was originally designed for personal property inventory and does not easily fit real property subject matter. Land, even when it is acquired with marketing in mind, will characteristically be held for longer than typical stock in trade. As a consequence, changes in value are likely to be the result of general market changes as well as of specific marketing efforts. The problem, still unresolved, is to devise an approach to real property that will properly account for both these sources of change in value.

The investor-dealer conundrum has spawned an extensive literature. Among the better analyses are Brown, Individual Investment in Real Estate: Capital Gains Versus Ordinary Income, 34 Ann.N.Y.U.Tax L.Inst. 189 (1976); Sills, The "Dealer-Investor" Problem: Observations, Analysis, and Suggestions for Future Development, 2 J.Real Est.Tax. 51 (1975); Weiner, Real Property: For Connoisseurs of the Preposterous—When Is It a Capital Asset? 24 Clev.St.L.Rev. 573 (1975); Bernstein, "Primarily for Sale": A Semantic Snare, 20 Stan.L.Rev. 1093 (1968); Olson, Toward a Neutral Definition of "Trade or Business" in the Internal Revenue Code, 54 U.Cin.L.Rev. 1199 (1986); Williford, Purpose for Which Real Property Is Acquired and Held Affects the Tax Consequences on Its Sale, 22 J. Real Est.Tax. 56 (1994); Comment, Trade or Business for the Full-Time, Active Investor: A Call For A Qualitative Standard, 29 Santa Clara L.Rev. 209 (1989).

3. *Investment and Marketing Activities. Malat* represents one phase in the struggle to bring meaning to section 1221 as applied to real property, and *Biedenharn* represents another. *Malat* was the easier of the two because the taxpayer's two purposes, investment and marketing, existed side by side, allowing the Court to say that "primarily" simply meant that one purpose predominated over the other. *Biedenharn* was harder because there the two purposes occurred consecutively—first investment, then marketing. Focusing on the purpose that was formed last, the court chose not to apply the "liquidation test," that had earlier flourished in the Fifth Circuit. Under that test, capital gains treatment was allowed if the property was acquired for an investment purpose, and if the taxpayer's marketing efforts in disposing of it involved no more than was reasonably necessary for the liquidation of a capital asset. See, for example, Goldberg v. Commissioner, 223 F.2d 709 (5th Cir.1955). Should one purpose be counted to the exclusion of another? Should weight be given to the chronological order in which the motives are formed?

Biedenharn's chronological approach, discounting the taxpayer's earlier motive and focusing only on his final one, has been applied symmetrically. A series of Tax Court decisions allowed capital asset treatment in circumstances in which the taxpayer acquired the property for sale to customers in the ordinary course of business as a subdivision development and subsequently changed his purpose, disposing of the land as a single, unimproved unit. See, for example, Maddux Constr. Co. v. Commissioner, 54 T.C. 1278 (1970); Estate of Walter K. Dean v. Commissioner, 34 T.C.M. 631 (1975).

4. *Suburban Realty Co.* Judge Goldberg recast the *Biedenharn* analysis four years later in Suburban Realty Co. v. United States, 615 F.2d 171 (5th Cir.), cert. denied, 449 U.S. 920, 101 S.Ct. 318, 66 L.Ed.2d 147 (1980), an action filed by the taxpayer for a tax refund. The question there, "put into the *Biedenharn* framework," was, "when a taxpayer engages in frequent and substantial sales over a period of years, but undertakes no development activity with respect to parts of a parcel of land, and engages in no solicitation or advertising efforts or brokerage activities, under what circumstances is income derived from sales of undeveloped parts of the parcel ordinary income?" 615 F.2d at 176. Judge Goldberg recognized that taxpayer "Suburban's case is at once more favorable to the taxpayer than Biedenharn's and less so. It is more favorable because, *with respect to the particular parcels of land here at issue*, it is undisputed that Suburban undertook no development or subdivision activity. It is less favorable because Biedenharn was continually engaged in business activities other than real estate sales, whereas Suburban was for many years doing little else." 615 F.2d at 177 (Emphasis in original).

Judge Goldberg recognized, too, that if the court followed "the *Biedenharn* framework alone, we would be left with yet another essentially *ad hoc* decision to be made." He turned instead to the plain language of section 1221 and concluded that "the principal inquiries demanded by the statute are:

1) was taxpayer engaged in a trade or business, and, if so, what business?

2) was taxpayer holding the property primarily for sale in that business?

3) were the sales contemplated by taxpayer 'ordinary' in the course of that business?"

Judge Goldberg indicated no disagreement "with anything decided by the recent Fifth Circuit decisions. *Biedenharn* guides our decision-making process. But after the relevant three independent statutory inquiries are pried apart, it becomes apparent that the central dispute in *Biedenharn* was a narrow one: was Biedenharn Realty Company holding the land in dispute 'primarily for sale?' The majority, applying the *Winthrop* factors, decided this question in the affirmative. The dissent, emphasizing the continuing farming activities being conducted by Biedenharn, see *Biedenharn*, 526 F.2d at 425, n. 5, 426 (dissenting opinion), disagreed as to this conclusion." 615 F.2d at 178.

Judge Goldberg then applied this three-part analysis to the facts before the court. First, the court concluded that Suburban was engaged in the real estate business. ("It is clear to us that Suburban engaged in a sufficient quantity of activity to be in the business of selling real estate. Suburban's sales were continuous and substantial.") Second, the court traced Suburban's primary holding purpose over the entire course of its ownership of the property and concluded that for most, if not all, of the holding period, "Suburban's primary holding purpose was 'for sale'." Third, the court found that these sales were "ordinary" in the course of Suburban's business, relying for this conclusion on an observation made in *Winthrop:*

> The concept of normalcy requires for its application a chronology and a history to determine if the sales of lots to customers were the usual or a departure from the norm. History and chronology here combine to demonstrate that [taxpayer] did not sell his lots as an abnormal or unexpected event. [Taxpayer] began selling shortly after he acquired the land; he never used the land for any other purpose; and he continued this course of conduct over a number of years. Thus, the sales were . . . ordinary.

615 F.2d at 185–186. The court thus affirmed the decision of the district court dismissing Suburban's complaint and holding that gain on the sales in issue was taxable as ordinary income rather than as capital gain.

In Major Realty Corp. and Subsidiaries v. Commissioner of Internal Revenue, 749 F.2d 1483, 1488 (11th Cir.1985), the court noted that "[t]he most important factor [in determining whether realty sales are to customers in the ordinary course of business] is the frequency and substantiality of the taxpayer's sales." The court upheld the lower court's finding that the sale of the parcel in question was in the ordinary course of business. It relied on the fact that the taxpayer had sold 16% of the total value of the larger tract of which this parcel was a part over the prior two years, as well as on the substantial road, utility, and sewer improvements made by the taxpayer. See C.I.R. v. Gardner, T.C. Memo. 2011–137 (Tax Ct. 2011) (court found taxpayer's testimony that he was holding land for long term sale, thus capital gains treatment was proper).

5. *Section 1237's Safe Harbor.* Section 1237, added to the Internal Revenue Code in 1954, was intended to provide subdividers with a safe harbor, offering capital asset treatment within narrowly prescribed limits. Among the conditions are that the taxpayer must have held the qualifying property for five years, must not have held it as inventory, and must not have made any substantial improvements that substantially enhanced the value of the lots sold.

Section 1237 has by all estimates been a dismal failure. Its terms have proved to be as fuzzy as those of section 1221, leaving developers largely in the dark as to the meaning of "substantial improvements," and "substantially enhanced." While regulations adopted under section 1237 offer some guidance, courts have felt free to ignore them, substituting their own notions of "substantial" for those of the Commissioner. See, for example, Kelley v. Commissioner, 281 F.2d 527 (9th Cir.1960). Also, the section does not permit full capital asset treatment and its requirements are so stringent that compliance would probably qualify the developer as an investor under section 1221, with full capital asset treatment, in any event. See generally Chandler, The Failure of Section 1237 in Dealing with Sales of Subdivided Realty, 60 Minn.L.Rev. 275 (1976); Hamill, Capital Gains for the Casual Subdivider: Can Section 1237 Be Used as a Safe Harbor in the Post RRA '93 Environment?, 21 J. Real Est.Tax. 253 (1994); Martin, Real Estate Taxation: Gaining Investor Status on Real Property Sales—Section 1237, 12 Real Estate Rev. 14 (Spring 1982).

6. *Condominium Conversions.* Many apartment house owners, faced with the prospect of declining rental profits, have converted their properties to condominiums. Although some acted as dealers, promoting the conversion and selling units one by one, others, in the years before the 1986 Tax Reform Act repealed the capital gains deduction, employed a variety of strategies in an attempt to get capital gains treatment for their profits. For an evaluation of some of these strategies, see Guerin, Condominium Conversions: An Analysis of Alternative Routes to Capital Gain Treatment, 1 Tax Law J. 1 (Winter 1982); Limberg, *Bradshaw* Provides Support and Guidelines for Capital Gains in Condominium Conversions, 11. Real Estate Tax. 328 (Summer, 1984).

7. *"Production of Income" or "Use in Trade or Business"?* Real property held for rental, rather than for investment or sale, raises classification problems of its own. Is the property held for the production of income, and thus within section 1221? Or is it held "for use in the trade or business," within section 1231? Although the distinction is narrow, its consequences are significant. Losses on the sale or exchange of property held for the production of income are capital losses, while those on the disposition of property used in trade or business are treated as ordinary losses. Characterization as section 1221 or 1231 property will also determine the availability and extent of loss carryovers under sections 1212 and 172.

In making the distinction, courts have generally used a definition of "trade or business" that the Supreme Court took from Bouvier's Law Dictionary and employed in a very different context: "that which occupies the time, attention, and labor of men for the purpose of a livelihood or profit." Flint v. Stone Tracy Co., 220 U.S. 107, 171, 31 S.Ct. 342, 357, 55 L.Ed. 389 (1911). Under this formula, the ownership of several rental properties, with its consequent demands on the taxpayer's attention, has been held to constitute a trade or business. See Pinchot v. Commissioner, 113 F.2d 718 (2d Cir.1940). So has ownership of a single block of rental property, at least where its management involved a "necessarily regular and continuous activity." Gilford v. Commissioner, 201 F.2d 735, 736 (2d Cir.1953). See generally, Cottle v. Commissioner of Internal Revenue, 89 T.C. 467 (1987) (where taxpayer purchased three apartment units to rehabilitate and lease but subsequently sold them due to changed conditions in the apartment complex, taxpayer entitled to capital gain treatment since he did not hold the units primarily for sale to customers but rather intended to use them for a new trade or business of renting apartments).

B. DEDUCTIONS: LEVERAGE, DEPRECIATION AND TAX SHELTER

The following materials describe the rise and fall of a system of real estate depreciation deductions and leveraging that permitted the sheltering of not only the taxpayer's income generated from the property itself but also income from other activities. This section first describes the real estate tax shelters and concludes with the ultimate reform of—or requiem for?—tax shelters in the 1986 Tax Reform Act.

1. TAX SHELTER THROUGH DEPRECIATION DEDUCTIONS

Commissioner of Internal Revenue v. Tufts

Supreme Court of the United States, 1983.
461 U.S. 300, 103 S.Ct. 1826, 75 L.Ed.2d 863.

JUSTICE BLACKMUN delivered the opinion of the Court.

Over 35 years ago, in Crane v. Commissioner, 331 U.S. 1, 67 S.Ct. 1047, 91 L.Ed. 1301 (1947), this Court ruled that a taxpayer, who sold property encumbered by a nonrecourse mortgage (the amount of the mortgage being less than the property's value), must include the unpaid balance of the mortgage in the computation of the amount the taxpayer realized on the sale. The case now before us presents the question whether the same rule applies when the unpaid amount of the nonrecourse mortgage exceeds the fair market value of the property sold.

I

On August 1, 1970, respondent Clark Pelt, a builder, and his wholly owned corporation, respondent Clark, Inc., formed a general partnership. The purpose of the partnership was to construct a 120–unit apartment complex in Duncanville, Tex., a Dallas suburb. Neither Pelt nor Clark, Inc., made any capital contribution to the partnership. Six days later, the partnership entered into a mortgage loan agreement with the Farm & Home Savings Association (F & H). Under the agreement, F & H was committed for a $1,851,500 loan for the complex. In return, the partnership executed a note and a deed of trust in favor of F & H. The partnership obtained the loan on a nonrecourse basis: neither the partnership nor its partners assumed any personal liability for repayment of the loan. Pelt later admitted four friends and relatives, respondents Tufts, Steger, Stephens, and Austin, as general partners. None of them contributed capital upon entering the partnership.

The construction of the complex was completed in August 1971. During 1971, each partner made small capital contributions to the partnership; in 1972, however, only Pelt made a contribution. The total of the partners' capital contributions was $44,212. In each tax year, all partners claimed as income tax deductions their allocable shares of ordinary losses and depreciation. The deductions taken by the partners in 1971 and 1972 totaled $439,972. Due to these contributions and deductions, the partnership's adjusted basis in the property in August 1972 was $1,455,740.

In 1971 and 1972, major employers in the Duncanville area laid off significant numbers of workers. As a result, the partnership's rental income was less than expected, and it was unable to make the payments due on the mortgage. Each partner, on August 28, 1972, sold his partnership interest to an unrelated third party, Fred Bayles. As consideration, Bayles agreed to reimburse each partner's sale expenses up to $250; he also assumed the nonrecourse mortgage.

On the date of transfer, the fair market value of the property did not exceed $1,400,000. Each partner reported the sale on his federal income tax return and indicated that a partnership loss of $55,740 had been sustained.[1] The Commissioner of Internal Revenue, on audit, determined that the sale resulted in a partnership capital gain of approximately $400,000. His theory was that the partnership had realized the full amount of the nonrecourse obligation.[2]

Relying on Millar v. Commissioner, 577 F.2d 212, 215 (CA3), cert. denied, 439 U.S. 1046, 99 S.Ct. 721, 58 L.Ed.2d 704 (1978), the United

---

[1]   The loss was the difference between the adjusted basis, $1,455,740 and the fair market value of the property, $1,400,000. On their individual tax returns, the partners did not claim deductions for their respective shares of this loss. In their petitions to the Tax Court, however, the partners did claim the loss.

[2]   The Commissioner determined the partnership's gain on the sale by subtracting the adjusted basis, $1,455,740, from the liability assumed by Bayles, $1,851,500. Of the resulting figure, $395,760, the Commissioner treated $348,661 as capital gain, pursuant to § 741 of the Internal Revenue Code of 1954, 26 U.S.C.A. § 741, and $47,099 as ordinary gain under the recapture provisions of § 1250 of the Code. The application of § 1250 in determining the character of the gain is not at issue here.

States Tax Court, in an unreviewed decision, upheld the asserted deficiencies. 70 T.C. 756 (1978). The United States Court of Appeals for the Fifth Circuit reversed. 651 F.2d 1058 (1981). That court expressly disagreed with the *Millar* analysis, and, in limiting Crane v. Commissioner, supra, to its facts, questioned the theoretical underpinnings of the *Crane* decision. We granted certiorari to resolve the conflict. 456 U.S. 960, 102 S.Ct. 2034, 72 L.Ed.2d 483 (1982).

II

Section 752(d) of the Internal Revenue Code of 1954, 26 U.S.C.A. § 752(d), specifically provides that liabilities incurred in the sale or exchange of a partnership interest are to "be treated in the same manner as liabilities in connection with the sale or exchange of property not associated with partnerships." Section 1001 governs the determination of gains and losses on the disposition of property. Under § 1001(a), the gain or loss from a sale or other disposition of property is defined as the difference between "the amount realized" on the disposition and the property's adjusted basis. Subsection (b) of § 1001 defines "amount realized": "The amount realized from the sale or other disposition of property shall be the sum of any money received plus the fair market value of the property (other than money) received." At issue is the application of the latter provision to the disposition of property encumbered by a nonrecourse mortgage of an amount in excess of the property's fair market value.

A

In Crane v. Commissioner, supra, this Court took the first and controlling step toward the resolution of this issue. Beulah B. Crane was the sole beneficiary under the will of her deceased husband. At his death in January 1932, he owned an apartment building that was then mortgaged for an amount which proved to be equal to its fair market value, as determined for federal estate tax purposes. The widow, of course, was not personally liable on the mortgage. She operated the building for nearly seven years, hoping to turn it into a profitable venture; during that period, she claimed income tax deductions for depreciation, property taxes, interest, and operating expenses, but did not make payments upon the mortgage principal. In computing her basis for the depreciation deductions, she included the full amount of the mortgage debt. In November 1938, with her hopes unfulfilled and the mortgagee threatening foreclosure, Mrs. Crane sold the building. The purchaser took the property subject to the mortgage and paid Crane $3,000; of that amount, $500 went for the expenses of the sale.

Crane reported a gain of $2,500 on the transaction. She reasoned that her basis in the property was zero (despite her earlier depreciation deductions based on including the amount of the mortgage) and that the amount she realized from the sale was simply the cash she received. The Commissioner disputed this claim. He asserted that Crane's basis in the property, under § 113(a)(5) of the Revenue Act of 1938, 52 Stat. 490 (the current version is § 1014 of the 1954 Code, as amended, 26 U.S.C.A. § 1014 (1976 ed. and Supp. V)), was the property's fair market value at the time of her husband's death, adjusted for depreciation in the interim, and that the amount realized was the net cash received plus the amount of the outstanding mortgage assumed by the purchaser.

In upholding the Commissioner's interpretation of § 113(a)(5) of the 1938 Act,[3] the Court observed that to regard merely the taxpayer's equity in the property as her basis would lead to depreciation deductions less than the actual physical deterioration of the property, and would require the basis to be recomputed with each payment on the mortgage. The Court rejected Crane's claim that any loss due to depreciation belonged to the mortgagee. The effect of the Court's ruling was that the taxpayer's basis was the value of the property undiminished by the mortgage.

The Court next proceeded to determine the amount realized under § 111(b) of the 1938 Act, 52 Stat. 484 (the current version is § 1001(b) of the 1954 Code, 26 U.S.C.A. § 1001(b)). In order to avoid the "absurdity," see 331 U.S., at 13, 67 S.Ct., at 1054, of Crane's realizing only $2,500 on the sale of property worth over a quarter of a million dollars, the Court treated the amount realized as it had treated basis, that is, by including the outstanding value of the mortgage. To do otherwise would have permitted Crane to recognize a tax loss unconnected with any actual economic loss. The Court refused to construe one section of the Revenue Act so as "to frustrate the Act as a whole." Ibid.

Crane, however, insisted that the nonrecourse nature of the mortgage required different treatment. The Court, for two reasons, disagreed. First, excluding the nonrecourse debt from the amount realized would result in the same absurdity and frustration of the Code. Second, the Court concluded that Crane obtained an economic benefit from the purchaser's assumption of the mortgage identical to the benefit conferred by the cancellation of personal debt. Because the value of the property in that case exceeded the amount of the mortgage, it was in Crane's economic interest to treat the mortgage as a personal obligation; only by so doing could she realize upon sale the appreciation in her equity represented by the $2,500 boot. The purchaser's assumption of the liability thus resulted in a taxable economic benefit to her, just as if she had been given, in addition to the boot, a sum of cash sufficient to satisfy the mortgage.[4]

In a footnote, pertinent to the present case, the Court observed:

"Obviously, if the value of the property is less than the amount of the mortgage, a mortgagor who is not personally liable cannot realize a benefit equal to the mortgage. Consequently, a different problem might be encountered where a mortgagor abandoned the property or transferred it subject to the

---

[3] Section 113(a)(5) defined the basis of "property . . . acquired by . . . devise . . . or by the decedent's estate from the decedent" as "the fair market value of such property at the time of such acquisition." The Court interpreted the term "property" to refer to the physical land and buildings owned by Crane or the aggregate of her rights to control and dispose of them. 331 U.S., at 6, 67 S.Ct., at 1050.

[4] Crane also argued that even if the statute required the inclusion of the amount of the nonrecourse debt, that amount was not Sixteenth Amendment income because the overall transaction had been "by all dictates of common sense . . . a ruinous disaster." Brief for Petitioner in Crane v. Commissioner, O.T.1946, No. 68, p. 51. The Court noted, however, that Crane had been entitled to and actually took depreciation deductions for nearly seven years. To allow her to exclude sums on which those deductions were based from the calculation of her taxable gain would permit her "a double deduction . . . on the same loss of assets." The Sixteenth Amendment, it was said, did not require that result. 331 U.S., at 15–16, 67 S.Ct., at 1055.

mortgage without receiving boot. That is not this case." Id., at 14, n. 37, 67 S.Ct., at 1054–55, n. 37.

B

This case presents that unresolved issue. We are disinclined to overrule *Crane,* and we conclude that the same rule applies when the unpaid amount of the nonrecourse mortgage exceeds the value of the property transferred. *Crane* ultimately does not rest on its limited theory of economic benefit; instead, we read *Crane* to have approved the Commissioner's decision to treat a nonrecourse mortgage in this context as a true loan. This approval underlies *Crane's* holding that the amount of the nonrecourse liability is to be included in calculating both the basis and the amount realized on disposition. That the amount of the loan exceeds the fair market value of the property thus becomes irrelevant.

When a taxpayer receives a loan, he incurs an obligation to repay that loan at some future date. Because of this obligation, the loan proceeds do not qualify as income to the taxpayer. When he fulfills the obligation, the repayment of the loan likewise has no effect on his tax liability.

Another consequence to the taxpayer from this obligation occurs when the taxpayer applies the loan proceeds to the purchase price of property used to secure the loan. Because of the obligation to repay, the taxpayer is entitled to include the amount of the loan in computing his basis in the property; the loan, under § 1012, is part of the taxpayer's cost of the property. Although a different approach might have been taken with respect to a nonrecourse mortgage loan[5], the Commissioner has chosen to accord it the same treatment he gives to a recourse mortgage loan. The Court approved that choice in *Crane,* and the respondents do not challenge it here. The choice and its resultant benefits to the taxpayer are predicated on the assumption that the mortgage will be repaid in full.

When encumbered property is sold or otherwise disposed of and the purchaser assumes the mortgage, the associated extinguishment of the mortgagor's obligation to repay is accounted for in the computation of the amount realized. Because no difference between recourse and nonrecourse obligations is recognized in calculating basis,[7] *Crane*

---

[5] The Commissioner might have adopted the theory, implicit in Crane's contentions, that a nonrecourse mortgage is not true debt, but, instead, is a form of joint investment by the mortgagor and the mortgagee. On this approach, nonrecourse debt would be considered a contingent liability, under which the mortgagor's payments on the debt gradually increase his interest in the property while decreasing that of the mortgagee. Because the taxpayer's investment in the property would not include the nonrecourse debt, the taxpayer would not be permitted to include that debt in basis.

We express no view as to whether such an approach would be consistent with the statutory structure and, if so, and Crane were not on the books, whether that approach would be preferred over Crane's analysis. We note only that the Crane Court's resolution of the basis issue presumed that when property is purchased with proceeds from a nonrecourse mortgage, the purchaser becomes the sole owner of the property. Under the Crane approach, the mortgagee is entitled to no portion of the basis. The nonrecourse mortgage is part of the mortgagor's investment in the property, and does not constitute a coinvestment by the mortgagee.

[7] The Commissioner's choice in *Crane* "laid the foundation stone of most tax shelters," Bittker, Tax Shelters, Nonrecourse Debt, and the *Crane* Case, 33 Tax.L.Rev. 277, 283 (1978), by permitting taxpayers who bear no risk to take deductions on depreciable property.

teaches that the Commissioner may ignore the nonrecourse nature of the obligation in determining the amount realized upon disposition of the encumbered property. He thus may include in the amount realized the amount of the nonrecourse mortgage assumed by the purchaser. The rationale for this treatment is that the original inclusion of the amount of the mortgage in basis rested on the assumption that the mortgagor incurred an obligation to repay. Moreover, this treatment balances the fact that the mortgagor originally received the proceeds of the nonrecourse loan tax-free on the same assumption. Unless the outstanding amount of the mortgage is deemed to be realized, the mortgagor effectively will have received untaxed income at the time the loan was extended and will have received an unwarranted increase in the basis of his property.[8] The Commissioner's interpretation of § 1001(b) in this fashion cannot be said to be unreasonable.

C

The Commissioner in fact has applied this rule even when the fair market value of the property falls below the amount of the nonrecourse obligation. Treas.Reg. § 1.1001–2(b), 26 CFR § 1.1001–2(b) (1982); Rev.Rul. 76–111, 1976–1 Cum.Bull. 214. Because the theory on which the rule is based applies equally in this situation, we have no reason, after *Crane,* to question this treatment.[11]

Congress recently has acted to curb this avoidance device by forbidding a taxpayer to take depreciation deductions in excess of amounts he has at risk in the investment. Pub.L. 94–455, § 204(a), 90 Stat. 1531 (1976), 26 U.S.C.A. § 465; Pub.L. 95–600, §§ 201–204, 92 Stat. 2814–2817 (1978), 26 U.S.C.A. § 465(a) (1976 ed., Supp. V). Real estate investments, however, are exempt from this prohibition. § 465(c)(3)(D) (1976 ed., Supp. V). Although this congressional action may foreshadow a day when nonrecourse and recourse debts will be treated differently, neither Congress nor the Commissioner has sought to alter *Crane's* rule of including nonrecourse liability in both basis and the amount realized.

8   Although the *Crane* rule has some affinity with the tax benefit rule, see Bittker, supra, at 282; Del Cotto, Sales and Other Dispositions of Property Under Section 1001: The Taxable Event, Amount Realized and Related Problems of Basis, 26 Buffalo L.Rev. 219, 323–324 (1977), the analysis we adopt is different. Our analysis applies even in the situation in which no deductions are taken. It focuses on the obligation to repay and its subsequent extinguishment, not on the taking and recovery of deductions. See generally Note, 82 Colum.L.Rev., at 1526–1529.

11   Professor Wayne G. Barnett, as *amicus* in the present case, argues that the liability and property portions of the transaction should be accounted for separately. Under his view, there was a transfer of the property for $1.4 million, and there was a cancellation of the $1.85 million obligation for a payment of $1.4 million. The former resulted in a capital loss of $50,000, and the latter in the realization of $450,000 of ordinary income. Taxation of the ordinary income might be deferred under § 108 by a reduction of respondents' bases in their partnership interests.

Although this indeed could be a justifiable mode of analysis, it has not been adopted by the Commissioner. Nor is there anything to indicate that the Code requires the Commissioner to adopt it. We note that Professor Barnett's approach does assume that recourse and nonrecourse debt may be treated identically.

The Commissioner also has chosen not to characterize the transaction as cancellation of indebtedness. We are not presented with and do not decide the contours of the cancellation-of-indebtedness doctrine. We note only that our approach does not fall within certain prior interpretations of that doctrine. In one view, the doctrine rests on the same initial premise as our analysis here—an obligation to repay—but the doctrine relies on a freeing-of-assets theory to attribute ordinary income to the debtor upon cancellation. According to that view, when nonrecourse debt is forgiven, the debtor's basis in the securing property is reduced by the amount of debt canceled, and realization of income is deferred until the sale of the property. Because that interpretation attributes income only when assets are freed, however, an

Respondents received a mortgage loan with the concomitant obligation to repay by the year 2012. The only difference between that mortgage and one on which the borrower is personally liable is that the mortgagee's remedy is limited to foreclosing on the securing property. This difference does not alter the nature of the obligation; its only effect is to shift from the borrower to the lender any potential loss caused by devaluation of the property.[12] If the fair market value of the property falls below the amount of the outstanding obligation, the mortgagee's ability to protect its interests is impaired, for the mortgagor is free to abandon the property to the mortgagee and be relieved of his obligation.

This, however, does not erase the fact that the mortgagor received the loan proceeds tax-free and included them in his basis on the understanding that he had an obligation to repay the full amount. When the obligation is canceled, the mortgagor is relieved of his responsibility to repay the sum he originally received and thus realizes value to that extent within the meaning of § 1001(b). From the mortgagor's point of view, when his obligation is assumed by a third party who purchases the encumbered property, it is as if the mortgagor first had been paid with cash borrowed by the third party from the mortgagee on a nonrecourse basis, and then had used the cash to satisfy his obligation to the mortgagee.

Moreover, this approach avoids the absurdity the Court recognized in *Crane.* Because of the remedy accompanying the mortgage in the nonrecourse situation, the depreciation in the fair market value of the property is relevant economically only to the mortgagee, who by lending on a nonrecourse basis remains at risk. To permit the taxpayer to limit his realization to the fair market value of the property would be to recognize a tax loss for which he has suffered no corresponding economic loss.[13] Such a result would be to construe "one section of the

---

insolvent debtor realizes income just to the extent his assets exceed his liabilities after the cancellation. Similarly, if the nonrecourse indebtedness exceeds the value of the securing property, the taxpayer never realizes the full amount of the obligation canceled because the tax law has not recognized negative basis.

Although the economic benefit prong of *Crane* also relies on a freeing-of-assets theory, that theory is irrelevant to our broader approach. In the context of a sale or disposition of property under § 1001, the extinguishment of the obligation to repay is not ordinary income; instead, the amount of the canceled debt is included in the amount realized, and enters into the computation of gain or loss on the disposition of property. According to *Crane,* this treatment is no different when the obligation is nonrecourse: the basis is not reduced as in the cancellation-of-indebtedness context, and the full value of the outstanding liability is included in the amount realized. Thus, the problem of negative basis is avoided.

[12] In his opinion for the Court of Appeals in *Crane,* Judge Learned Hand observed:

"[The mortgagor] has all the income from the property; he manages it; he may sell it; any increase in its value goes to him; any decrease falls on him, until the value goes below the amount of the lien. . . . When therefore upon a sale the mortgagor makes an allowance to the vendee of the amount of the lien, he secures a release from a charge upon his property quite as though the vendee had paid him the full price on condition that before he took title the lien should be cleared. . . ." 153 F.2d 504, 506 (C.A.2 1945).

[13] In the present case, the Government bore the ultimate loss. The nonrecourse mortgage was extended to respondents only after the planned complex was endorsed for mortgage insurance under § 221(b) and (d)(4) of the National Housing Act, 12 U.S.C. § 1715*l*(b) and (d)(4) (1976 ed. and Supp. V). After acquiring the complex from respondents, Bayles operated it for a few years, but was unable to make it profitable. In 1974, F & H foreclosed, and the Department of Housing and Urban Development paid off the lender to obtain title. In 1976,

Act . . . so as . . . to defeat the intention of another or to frustrate the Act as a whole." 331 U.S., at 13, 67 S.Ct., at 1054.

In the specific circumstances of *Crane,* the economic benefit theory did support the Commissioner's treatment of the nonrecourse mortgage as a personal obligation. The footnote in *Crane* acknowledged the limitations of that theory when applied to a different set of facts. *Crane* also stands for the broader proposition, however, that a nonrecourse loan should be treated as a true loan. We therefore hold that a taxpayer must account for the proceeds of obligations he has received tax-free and included in basis. Nothing in either § 1001(b) or in the Court's prior decisions requires the Commissioner to permit a taxpayer to treat a sale of encumbered property asymmetrically, by including the proceeds of the nonrecourse obligation in basis but not accounting for the proceeds upon transfer of the encumbered property. . . .

IV

When a taxpayer sells or disposes of property encumbered by a nonrecourse obligation, the Commissioner properly requires him to include among the assets realized the outstanding amount of the obligation. The fair market value of the property is irrelevant to this calculation. We find this interpretation to be consistent with Crane v. Commissioner, 331 U.S. 1, 67 S.Ct. 1047, 91 L.Ed. 1301 (1947), and to implement the statutory mandate in a reasonable manner.

The judgment of the Court of Appeals is therefore reversed.

It is so ordered.

JUSTICE O'CONNOR, concurring.

I concur in the opinion of the Court, accepting the view of the Commissioner. I do not, however, endorse the Commissioner's view. Indeed, were we writing on a slate clean except for the *Crane* decision, I would take quite a different approach—that urged upon us by Professor Barnett as *amicus.*

Crane established that a taxpayer could treat property as entirely his own, in spite of the "coinvestment" provided by his mortgagee in the form of a nonrecourse loan. That is, the full basis of the property, with all its tax consequences, belongs to the mortgagor. That rule alone, though, does not in any way tie nonrecourse debt to the cost of property or to the proceeds upon disposition. I see no reason to treat the purchase, ownership, and eventual disposition of property differently because the taxpayer also takes out a mortgage, an independent transaction. In this case, the taxpayer purchased property, using nonrecourse financing, and sold it after it declined in value to a buyer who assumed the mortgage. There is no economic difference between the events in this case and a case in which the taxpayer buys property with cash; later obtains a nonrecourse loan by pledging the property as security; still later, using cash on hand, buys off the mortgage for the

---

the Department sold the complex to another developer for $1,502,000. The sale was financed by the Department's taking back a note for $1,314,800 and a nonrecourse mortgage. To fail to recognize the value of the nonrecourse loan in the amount realized, therefore, would permit respondents to compound the Government's loss by claiming the tax benefits of that loss for themselves.

market value of the devalued property; and finally sells the property to a third party for its market value.

The logical way to treat both this case and the hypothesized case is to separate the two aspects of these events and to consider, first, the ownership and sale of the property, and, second, the arrangement and retirement of the loan. Under *Crane,* the fair market value of the property on the date of acquisition—the purchase price—represents the taxpayer's basis in the property, and the fair market value on the date of disposition represents the proceeds on sale. The benefit received by the taxpayer in return for the property is the cancellation of a mortgage that is worth no more than the fair market value of the property, for that is all the mortgagee can expect to collect on the mortgage. His gain or loss on the disposition of the property equals the difference between the proceeds and the cost of acquisition. Thus, the taxation of the transaction *in property* reflects the economic fate of the *property*. If the property has declined in value, as was the case here, the taxpayer recognizes a loss on the disposition of the property. The new purchaser then takes as his basis the fair market value as of the date of the sale.

In the separate borrowing transaction, the taxpayer acquires cash from the mortgagee. He need not recognize income at that time, of course, because he also incurs an obligation to repay the money. Later, though, when he is able to satisfy the debt by surrendering property that is worth less than the face amount of the debt, we have a classic situation of cancellation of indebtedness, requiring the taxpayer to recognize income in the amount of the difference between the proceeds of the loan and the amount for which he is able to satisfy his creditor. 26 U.S.C. § 61(a)(12). The taxation of the financing transaction then reflects the economic fate of the loan.

The reason that separation of the two aspects of the events in this case is important is, of course, that the Code treats different sorts of income differently. A gain on the sale of the property may qualify for capital gains treatment while the cancellation of indebtedness is ordinary income, but income that the taxpayer may be able to defer. Not only does Professor Barnett's theory permit us to accord appropriate treatment to each of the two types of income or loss present in these sorts of transactions, it also restores continuity to the system by making the taxpayer-seller's proceeds on the disposition of property equal to the purchaser's basis in the property. Further, and most important, it allows us to tax the events in this case in the same way that we tax the economically identical hypothesized transaction.

Persuaded though I am by the logical coherence and internal consistency of this approach, I agree with the Court's decision not to adopt it judicially. We do not write on a slate marked only by *Crane.* The Commissioner's longstanding position, Rev.Rul. 76–111, 1976–1 C.B. 214, is now reflected in the regulations. Treas.Reg. § 1.1001–2, 26 CFR § 1.1001–2 (1982). In the light of the numerous cases in the lower courts including the amount of the unrepaid proceeds of the mortgage in the proceeds on sale or disposition, it is difficult to conclude that the Commissioner's interpretation of the statute exceeds the bounds of his discretion. As the Court's opinion demonstrates, his interpretation is defensible. One can reasonably read § 1001(b)'s reference to "the amount realized *from* the sale or other disposition of property" (emphasis added) to permit the Commissioner to collapse the two aspects of the transaction. As long as his view is a reasonable reading of § 1001(b), we should defer to the regulations promulgated by the agency charged with interpretation of the statute. Accordingly, I concur.

NOTES

1. *Computing the Depreciation Deduction.* The depreciation deduction is probably the single greatest boon—some would say boondoggle—available to owners of income or business property. Unlike the deductions for interest, real property taxes and maintenance, each of which reflects an equivalent cash outlay by the taxpayer, section 167's depreciation provisions enable taxpayers to take deductions without any matching cash outlay. So long as depreciation deductions (tax deductions without corresponding cash expenditures) exceed amortization of any debt on the property (cash expenditures without corresponding tax deductions), the investment will provide a "tax shelter" for the taxpayer's income.

The taxpayer's first step in computing the depreciation deduction is to determine the basis of her investment by aggregating the cost of the land and improvements, including the amount of any debt secured by the property, and transaction costs such as broker's commissions, title insurance premiums and fees for survey, legal, appraisal and escrow services. The next step is to identify that part of the investment's basis that is allocable to depreciable assets. (Say that the taxpayer's overall cost is $650,000, with $200,000 of that allocable to the land, which is not depreciable, and $450,000 to the improvements, which are depreciable.) Next, she must assign a useful life to the improvements (say 20 years) and a salvage value for the improvements at the end of the useful life (say $50,000). By subtracting salvage value from total improvement value ($450,000 minus $50,000) she arrives at the depreciable basis that she can write off over the period of the asset's useful life. (Thus in the example given the taxpayer can take depreciation deductions totaling $400,000 over 20 years.)

The taxpayer's next step is to choose a depreciation method—straight line or declining balance. The choice can have a significant impact on the extent and timing of tax shelter. The straight line method of depreciation prorates the improvement's depreciable basis equally over its useful life. (In the example given, this would mean $400,000 divided by a 20-year useful life, or a $20,000 depreciation deduction each year.)

Under the declining balance method, a constant rate (a predetermined multiple of the straight line rate) is applied each year to a decreasing depreciable basis consisting of the original depreciable basis, diminished each year by the total amount of depreciation taken in the preceding years. While salvage value is for these purposes included in depreciable basis, the improvement cannot be depreciated below its salvage value. (In the example given, the straight line rate is $20,000/$400,000 or 5%. Thus under the "double declining balance" method, twice that rate, or 10% is applied to $450,000 to determine the first year's depreciation, or $45,000. In the second year, depreciation is [$450,000 minus $45,000] × 10% or $40,500; in the third year it is [$405,000 minus $40,500] × 10% or $36,450.) Use of the 175% declining balance method entails only a change in the number by which the straight line rate is multiplied from 2 to 1.75.

A comparative chart will give you some idea of the advantages and disadvantages of each method to the taxpayer and to the Treasury. The figures are based on the example already used—a $450,000 improvement with a salvage value of $50,000 and a useful life of 20 years.

YEAR	STRAIGHT LINE		DOUBLE DECLINING BALANCE	
	ANNUAL DEDUCTION	TOTAL COST RECOVERED	ANNUAL DEDUCTION	TOTAL COST RECOVERED
1	$20,000	$ 20,000	$45,000	$ 45,000
2	20,000	40,000	40,500	85,500
3	20,000	60,000	36,450	121,950
4	20,000	80,000	32,805	154,755
5	20,000	100,000	29,525	184,280
6	20,000	120,000	26,572	210,852
7	20,000	140,000	23,915	234,767
8	20,000	160,000	21,523	256,290
9	20,000	180,000	19,371	275,661
10	20,000	200,000	17,434	293,095
11	20,000	220,000	15,691	308,786
12	20,000	240,000	14,121	322,907
13	20,000	260,000	12,709	335,616
14	20,000	280,000	11,438	347,054
15	20,000	300,000	10,295	357,349
16	20,000	320,000	9,265	366,614
17	20,000	340,000	8,339	374,953
18	20,000	360,000	7,505	382,458
19	20,000	380,000	6,754	389,212
20	20,000	400,000	6,079	395,291

Straight line, though it is the most conservative method of depreciation, in fact accelerates the taxpayer's true depreciation. Mainly, this is because useful life is not measured objectively, by reference to physical wear and tear and market value, but rather by reference to the asset's particular utility to the taxpayer's business or investment interests. Even apart from general increases in real estate values during the asset's holding period, a fully depreciated asset will probably have a market value well over its salvage value.

Because depreciation deductions are subtracted from the property's basis, they will be partially offset by an increase in the gain realized when the taxpayer disposes of the property. (In the example above, the taxpayer, having taken a total of $60,000 in depreciation deductions [$20,000 + $20,000 + $20,000] over three years, must reduce her basis by that amount, leaving a basis of $590,000 [$650,000–$60,000]. If the taxpayer sold the property at the end of the third year for no more than the $650,000 she paid for it, she would have to pay tax on a capital gain of $60,000—the difference between amount realized, $650,000, and adjusted basis, or $590,000.) Before the 1986 Tax Reform Act's repeal of the preferential capital gains rate, the depreciation deduction's main advantage to the taxpayer was that it gave her the economic benefit of present deductions against ordinary income while requiring only that she pay for this benefit by recognizing future gains taxed at the more favorable capital gains rate.

On the depreciation deduction generally, see Tucker, Real Estate Depreciation: A Fresh Examination of the Basic Rules, 6 J. Real Est.Tax. 101 (1979); McKee, The Real Estate Tax Shelter: A Computerized Expos, 57 Va.L.Rev. 521 (1971); Calkins & Updegraft, Tax Shelters, 26 Tax Law. 493 (1973). The justification for accelerated depreciation deductions is the subject of a lively debate in Kahn, Accelerated Depreciation—CTax Expenditure or Proper Allowance for Measuring Net Income? 78 Mich.L.Rev. 1 (1979); Blum, Accelerated Depreciation: A Proper Allowance for Measuring Net Income?, 78 Mich.L.Rev. 1172 (1980); Kahn, Accelerated Depreciation Revisited—A Reply to Professor Blum, 78 Mich.L.Rev. 1185 (1980).

2. *Leveraged Depreciation.* Depreciation tax shelters are most advantageous to taxpayers who finance their acquisition of the depreciable property. Because the amount of mortgage financing will be included in the taxpayer's depreciable basis, it represents a tax-free means to inflate the depreciation deduction—a phenomenon called "leveraged depreciation." Thus, the taxpayer in note 1, above, may have financed her purchase of the $650,000 parcel with a $600,000 mortgage loan, putting up only $50,000 of her own cash. As a result, for a total investment of $50,000, the taxpayer using the straight line method is able to write off $20,000 in depreciation deductions each year for 20 years; if she is in the 50% bracket, this means an extra $10,000 cash in her pocket every year for 20 years. Use of the double declining balance method will enable the taxpayer to write off $45,000—almost her complete investment—in the first year.

The taxpayer need not be personally obligated on the debt encumbering her property for the debt to be included in her basis. Crane v. Commissioner, 331 U.S. 1, 67 S.Ct. 1047, 91 L.Ed. 1301 (1947). This rule, which is particularly congenial to the real estate market where so much financing is nonrecourse, may lead to abuses. Consider the following example: Taxpayer acquires an office building and underlying land with an aggregate market value of $2,500,000 ($500,000 allocable to land, $2,000,000 allocable to the improvement). She buys the land for $1,000,000, giving seller a 10-year, interest-only purchase money mortgage, at 5% interest, with a $1,000,000, balloon at the end. She acquires the building in fee for $5,000,000, giving the seller a purchase money mortgage for that amount. The mortgage is for ten years, is nonrecourse, interest only, with an interest rate of 5% and a $5,000,000 balloon payment of principal at the end of ten years. The taxpayer's net income from the property is $300,000, just enough to cover her mortgage payments. Because these payments are fully deductible, this aspect of the transaction is a wash. If the building has a twenty-five year useful life and no salvage value, the taxpayer, using straight line depreciation, will have an annual depreciation deduction available for setoff against other income of $200,000 ($5,000,000/25). This is two and one-half times the deduction she would have had if she had given a mortgage not for $5,000,000, but for the building's market value of $2,000,000. Presumably the taxpayer will default and abandon the property just as the mortgage principal becomes due, leaving the seller with his security, worth $2,500,000 (assuming no change in market value) and, for having participated in the charade, receipt over the ten years of an above-market return on his mortgage notes. Compare Manuel D. Mayerson, 47 T.C. 340 (1966).

Will such an abuse be tolerated? In *Crane* the Supreme Court expressly noted that "if the value of the property is less than the amount of the mortgage, a mortgagor who is not personally liable cannot realize a benefit equal to the mortgage. Consequently, a different problem might be encountered where a mortgagor abandoned the property or transferred it subject to the mortgage without receiving boot. That is not this case." 331 U.S. at 14 n. 37, 67 S.Ct. at 1054 n. 37. How should such a mortgage debt be accounted for? Is it really debt? These questions are considered, respectively, in the next two cases. The 1986 Tax Reform Act took a different route to preventing this abuse by partially subjecting real property investments to the Internal Revenue Code's "at risk" provisions. See p. 640, below.

See Mock, *Crane* and *Tufts* in Reverse: The Fair Market Value Firewall, 9 DePaul Bus. & Comm'l L.J. 215 (2011); Jensen, The Unanswered Question in *Tufts*: What Was the Purchaser's Basis?, 10 Va.Tax Rev. 455 (1991); Lurie, Crane's Ghost Not Laid to Rest: Still A Work in Progress, According to Owen, 27 J. Real Est. Tax. 257 (2000); Coven, Limiting Losses Attributable to Nonrecourse Debt: A Defense of the Traditional System Against the At-Risk Concept, 74 Cal.L.Rev. 41 (1986); Rohrbach, Disposition of Properties Secured by Recourse and Nonrecourse Debt, 41 Baylor L.Rev. 231 (1989); Avent & Grimes, Inflated Purchase Money Indebtedness in Real Estate and Other Investments, 11 J.Real Estate Tax. 99 (Winter 1984); Weinstein, *Tufts v. Comm'r.*—Good-Bye, Footnote 37; Hello, Footnote 5, 12 Real Est.L.J. 261 (1983); Ji, Nonrecourse Financing of Real Property: Depreciation Allocation and Full Recapture to Minimize Deferral and Eliminate Conversion, 29 Colum.J. Law & Soc.Probs. 217 (1996). For an excellent analysis of *Tufts* in the context of legislative, administrative and judicial attacks on tax shelter generally, see Note, Nonrecourse Liabilities as Tax Shelter Devices After *Tufts*: Elimination of Fair Market Value and Contingent Liability Defenses, 35 U.Fla.L.Rev. 904 (1983).

2. REFORM OF TAX SHELTERS

Investors in real estate were able to shelter non-real estate income by matching paper depreciation losses from real estate with other income activities. Over the years, Congress enacted various reforms to limit this revenue loss and to prevent overinvestment in real estate ventures that were driven not by market forces but by tax benefits. For example, the Tax Reform Act of 1964 required "recapture" of accelerated depreciation upon sale of the property, meaning that the portion of the gain that had been depreciated on an accelerated basis had to be taxed as ordinary income. The Tax Reform Act of 1969 limited the methods of accelerated depreciation for real estate and, along with the Tax Reform Act of 1976, enhanced the recapture provisions. See Weidner, Realty Shelters: Nonrecourse Financing, Tax Reform, and Profit Purpose, 32 Southwestern L.J. 711 (1978).

Thus, virtually every tax revision measure in recent years has tinkered with the depreciation tax shelter. These measures have usually adjusted one or more of the depreciation tax shelter's four principal aspects: length of the allowable cost recovery period; permitted rate of depreciation; recapture of excess depreciation; and the use of tax shelter to completely avoid tax liability.

Cost Recovery Period. After a series of reforms curtailing the availability and benefits of accelerated depreciation, The Economic Recovery Tax Act of 1981 (ERTA), Pub.L. No. 97–34, 95 Stat. 172, dramatically increased the available depreciation deductions by introducing an accelerated cost recovery system (ACRS) applicable to property placed in service on or after January 1, 1981. Under ERTA, ACRS allowed real property improvements to be depreciated over a 15-year period (as compared with useful lives ranging generally between 40 and 60 years under previous I.R.S. guidelines). ERTA also allowed taxpayers to elect a 35- or 45-year recovery instead. The 1984 Tax Reform Act, Pub.L. No. 98–369, 98 Stat. 494–1210, reduced the depreciation tax benefit by increasing the allowable cost recovery period from fifteen years to eighteen years for most properties. The 1984 Act did, however, allow low-income housing, as defined in I.R.C. § 1250(a)(1)(B), to be depreciated over the fifteen-year period.

Depreciation Method. ERTA allowed the taxpayer to choose between straight line and accelerated methods of depreciation. While straight line could be used in connection with the 15-, 35- or 45-year recovery period, the accelerated depreciation method could be used only in connection with the fifteen-year recovery period (which is like saying to a child, if you choose to have the chocolate cake, you can only have it with ice cream on top). Further, ERTA required the taxpayer who opts for accelerated depreciation to calculate depreciation on the basis of tables that approximate 175 percent declining balance or, if the real property is a qualifying subsidized housing project, that approximate double declining balance. ERTA eliminated the depreciation methods discussed in Professor Weidner's article—125 percent declining balance, 150 percent declining balance, and sum-of-the-years-digits. It also ended the distinction between new and used property and, except with respect to depreciation recapture, the distinction between residential and nonresidential property.

Recapture. The taxpayer who employed an accelerated depreciation method would see part or all of his depreciation deductions recaptured at the time of disposition and taxed at ordinary income rates. Under ERTA, the extent of recapture turned on whether the property was residential or nonresidential real estate. If it was residential real estate, such as an apartment building, only depreciation deductions taken in excess of the amount that would have been taken under the straight line method would be recaptured and taxed as ordinary income.

By contrast, if the property was nonresidential real estate such as a factory or warehouse, gain on disposition would be treated as ordinary income to the extent of *all* depreciation taken, and not just depreciation in excess of the amount that would have been taken under the straight line method.

Alternative Minimum Tax. The minimum tax on preferences, introduced by the 1969 Act and expanded by the 1976 Act, was further expanded by the Tax Equity and Fiscal Responsibility Act of 1982, Pub.L. No. 97–248, 96 Stat. 324, for tax years beginning in 1983. In an effort to assure that everyone paid some tax, TEFRA required the taxpayer to compute his regular tax liability and his alternative minimum tax liability, and then to pay whichever is greater. Essentially, computation of the alternative minimum tax required the taxpayer to add back to adjusted gross income any items of tax preference and, after subtracting permitted deductions and a uniform exemption, to pay a flat 20% tax on this figure. For real estate investors, the important tax preference items were accelerated depreciation on real property improvements and the portion of long-term capital gains otherwise exempt from tax—60% of the gain realized.

See generally, Solomon, Choosing Between Accelerated and Straight-Line Cost Recovery for Commercial Real Estate Under ACRS, 10 J.Real Estate Tax 18 (1982–83); Brueggeman, Fisher & Stern, Choosing the Optimal Depreciation Method Under 1981 Tax Legislation, 11 Real Estate Rev. 32 (Winter 1982); Goodman & Tremlett, The Tax Reform Act of 1984: How It Affects Real Property, 7 Real Prop.L.Rptr. 131 (1984).

a.   THE 1986 TAX REFORM ACT

The 1986 Tax Reform Act, which for most purposes went into effect on January 1, 1987, dramatically reduced the scope of real estate tax shelter. In part the Act achieved this reduction by further adjusting the allowable period over which a property may be depreciated, the method for computing depreciation, and the alternative minimum tax. The Act also reduced real estate tax shelter by reforms aimed at the very nature of the taxpayer's real estate investment. The Act's repeal of the preferential capital gains rate further reduced the attraction of real estate tax shelters by depriving the taxpayer of the economic benefits of taking present deductions against ordinary income and paying for these deductions with a tax on future gains at the more favorable capital gains rate.

Passive Loss Limitation. For high bracket taxpayers, one of the principal attractions of real estate tax shelters was the ability to set off losses from the investment (often paper losses) against income from other sources. The 1986 Tax Reform Act substantially limits tax shelters for individuals, estates, trusts and personal service corporations by adding new Code Section 469 which allows losses from "passive activities" to be set off only against income from other "passive activities," and not against the taxpayer's other income, such as salary, interest, dividends and active business income. Unused passive losses can be carried forward and set off against passive income in subsequent tax years. If passive losses remain at the time of the property's disposition they can then be set off against the gain, if any, from the disposition.

Section 469(c)(1) defines passive activity as "any activity (A) which involves the conduct of any trade or business, and (B) in which the taxpayer does not materially participate." Section 469(h) provides that a taxpayer is "materially participating" only if he "is involved in the operations of the activity on a basis which is—(A) regular, (B) continuous, and (C) substantial."

Section 469 includes rental activities within its definition of passive activities even if the taxpayer materially participates in the rental activity. But the Act allows taxpayers who "actively" participate in rental real estate activity, and whose adjusted gross income is less than $100,000, to deduct up to $25,000 of losses from the rental activity against other non-passive income. According to the Senate Finance Committee Report, "active participation" implies a lower standard of involvement than "material participation" and can be satisfied without regular, continuous and substantial involvement in operations. S.Rep.No. 313, 99th Cong., 2d Sess. 719–721 (1986). An individual will not, however, be treated as actively participating in any activity if she and her spouse together own an interest of less than 10%. For taxpayers whose adjusted gross income exceeds $100,000, the $25,000 maximum allowable deduction will be reduced by half the income excess over $100,000, thus eliminating the allowable deduction when the taxpayer's adjusted gross income reaches $150,000.

The Conference Report, H.R. Rep. No. 841, 99th Cong., 2d Sess. II–139 (1986), makes clear that "the passive loss rule applies to all deductions that are from passive activities, including deductions allowed under sections 162, 163, 164, and 165. For example, deductions for State and local property taxes incurred with respect to passive activities are subject to limitation under the passive loss rule whether such deductions are claimed above-the-line or as itemized deductions under section 164." Also, "interest deductions attributable to passive activities are treated as passive activity deductions, but are not treated as investment interest. Thus, such interest deductions are subject to limitation under the passive loss rule, and not under the investment interest limitation," which limits the deduction for investment interest to the amount of net investment income.

At Risk Limitation. Before passage of the 1986 Act, real property owners enjoyed a unique benefit—the ability to include nonrecourse financing in an investment's basis for the purpose of writing off losses such as those attributable to depreciation. This result obtained whether the nonrecourse financing came from a third party or from the seller of the investment property. The 1986 Act partially eliminated this benefit by striking I.R.C. § 465(c)(3)(D), which had excluded real property from the at risk rules, and amending section 465(b) to provide that "in the case of an activity of holding real property, a taxpayer shall be considered at risk with respect to the taxpayer's share of any qualified nonrecourse financing which is secured by real property used in such activity."

Section 465(b)(6)(B) effectively defines "qualified nonrecourse financing" to include nonconvertible debt to an independent third party lender regularly engaged in the business of lending money or to a governmental agency. A loan will not lose its status as "qualified nonrecourse financing" if it is from a related party, so long as the loan's terms are commercially reasonable and substantially conform to the terms of loans made to unrelated parties. Thus, a real estate investor who obtains nonrecourse purchase money financing from his seller, or whose loan otherwise fails to qualify as qualified nonrecourse financing, will be able to write off losses on his investment only to the extent of the amount he has at risk—his invested cash plus debt on which he is personally liable.

Depreciation. The 1986 Act substantially reduces the tax benefits available from depreciable real property by lengthening the period over which the property must be depreciated and by limiting the taxpayer to the straight line method of computing depreciation. Where prior law generally allowed the taxpayer to recover the cost of real property over an eighteen year period using statutory tables approximating the 175 per cent declining balance method, the 1986 Act requires that, for property placed in service after December 31, 1986, investments in residential real property cannot be written off over less than 27.5 years and investments in commercial real property cannot be written off over less than 31.5 years, both computed on the basis of the straight line method.

Alternative Minimum Tax. The 1986 Tax Reform Act increased the alternative minimum tax rate for individuals from 20% to 21%, beginning in 1987, and also increased the number of tax preference items subject to the alternative minimum tax. Among the new items of tax preference related to real estate investments are net losses from passive investments such as limited partnership interests and rental activities and gains deferred through use of the installment method of accounting. See generally Lispey & Witners, Applying the New Alternative Minimum Tax to Real Estate, 15 J. Real Est.Tax. 124 (1988).

For an excellent examination of the various aspects of the 1986 Tax Reform Act, see Gibson, The Impact of the Tax Reform Act of 1986 on Tax Shelters, 11 The Rev. of Taxation of Individuals 323 (1987). For a fine comparison of pre and post 1986 law, see M. Levine, Real Estate Transactions, Tax Planning and Consequences 65–85 (1991).

b.   THE REVENUE RECONCILIATION ACT OF 1993

The Revenue Reconciliation Act of 1993 made a handful of changes to the 1986 Tax Reform Act's tax shelter provisions.

Passive Loss Limitation. The 1993 Act amended section 469 of the Internal Revenue Code to relieve bona fide real estate professionals from the passive loss limitations of the 1986 Act. The 1986 Act defined all rental activity as passive, and made no distinction between the casual investor in real estate and real estate professionals actively engaged in developing, operating, and managing real estate projects. As a result, real estate professionals could not offset losses from real estate rentals against their other business income.

The 1993 amendment allows qualifying taxpayers to treat real estate rental activity as nonpassive activity and deduct losses from real estate rentals not only against passive income but against other business, portfolio, and earned income. I.R.C. § 469(c)(7)(A). It applies to a taxpayer who annually performs 750 personal service hours, and at least fifty percent of his total personal services hours, in real property trades or businesses in which he materially participates. I.R.C. § 469(c)(7)(B). Real property trade or business is defined as any real estate development, redevelopment, construction, reconstruction, acquisition, conversion, rental, operation, management, leasing, or brokerage trade or business; lending is not included. I.R.C. § 469(c)(7)(C). Regulations promulgated by the Internal Revenue Service define material participation and activity, as well as the effect of the statute on limited partnership interests. Treas.Reg. § 1.469 (issued 12/21/95, 60 Fed.Reg. 66496).

Depreciation. The Revenue Reconciliation Act of 1993 increased the depreciation recovery period from thirty-one and one-half to thirty-nine years for nonresidential real estate. Congress did not change the recovery period for residential real estate.

NOTE

For discussions of the policy and mechanics of the passive loss provisions of Internal Revenue Code section 469, see Bankman, Case Against Passive Investments: A Critical Appraisal of the Passive Loss Restrictions, 42 Stan.L.Rev. 15 (1989); Griffith, Taxable Dispositions of Interests in Property and in Pass Through Entities Under Passive Loss Regulations, 30 Willamette L.Rev. 9 (1994); Peroni, Policy Critique of Section 469 Passive Loss Rules, 62 S.Cal.L.Rev. 1 (1988); Rodgers, Material Participation Under the Passive Activity Loss Provisions, 39 U.Fla.L.Rev 1083 (1987). For a discussion of the changes of the 1993 Act, see Lipman & Williamson, Will the Final Regulations Under IRC § 469(c)(7) Renew Taxpayer Interest in Real Estate?, 25 Real Est.L.J. 137 (1996); Schachat, Final Regulations Under Section 469(c)(7): How Do You Spell Passive-Loss Relief?, 24 J. Real Est.Tax. 3 (1996); Schachat, The Revenue Reconciliation Act of 1993: Real Estate-Related Provisions, 21 J. Real Est.Tax. 99 (1994). For further discussion on tax shelter reform, see Yin, Getting Serious About Corporate Tax Shelters: Taking A Lesson From History, 54 S.M.U.L.Rev. 209 (2001).

C. DISPOSITION: DEFERRING THE RECOGNITION OF GAIN (AND LOSS)

1. TAX-FREE EXCHANGES

Welton James Fischer, Tax Free Exchanges of Real Property Under Section 1031 of the Internal Revenue Code of 1954
78 Dickinson Law Review 615, 617–619, 623, 633–634, 637–641 (1974).

Section 1002 of the Internal Revenue Code of 1954 provides, "Except as otherwise provided in this subtitle, on the sale or exchange of property the entire amount of gain or loss, determined under section 1001, shall be recognized." Section 1001(a) of the Code provides that the gain or loss to be recognized is the difference between the amount realized on the disposition of the property and the adjusted basis of the property at the time of the disposition. The amount realized is defined in section 1001(b) as the sum of any money received plus the fair market value of property other than money received. Section 1031 is one of the several exceptions to these rules.

In an exchange to which section 1031(a) is applicable, recognition of gain or loss is deferred until the property is transferred in a subsequent taxable exchange. The property acquired assumes the basis of the property transferred. The purpose of the provision is to save a taxpayer from immediate recognition of gain and to intermit the claim of a loss in exchange transactions where a gain or loss may have occurred in a bookkeeping or accounting sense but in a practical and economic sense the gain or loss was a mere paper transaction.

The taxpayer with substantial real estate assets may find the section 1031 exception to the general rule a useful tax-planning procedure or a frustrating trap. In many instances a section 1031 exchange may be the only practical method of extracting a taxpayer's investment from an asset that is no longer a useful or desirable part of his investment portfolio. Real estate is typically an investment that is held for long periods of time and has an enormous propensity to appreciate in value. In some instances, because of the fortunes of location and community development, the appreciation in value is rapid and substantial. While the owner is pleased with his increased fortune, he may find himself in a classic real estate lock-in situation. His basis may be so low, relative to the market value of his property, that a taxable sale may not be practical.

Even if the tax burden were not the controlling consideration, an exchange under section 1031 may be useful. Thus, taxpayers who wish merely to change the form of their real estate investment, rather than to liquidate their holdings, should certainly consider a tax-free exchange under section 1031. This group of taxpayers would include both individuals near retirement who want to change from passive investments to property that will provide an income after retirement and high income taxpayers who seek to change their investments from income producing to passive. Income considerations aside, a taxpayer simply may want to relocate. A farmer may find urbanization crowding his farm operation or increasing his real estate taxes to an impractical level, or a taxpayer may want to move from one part of the country to another or even to a foreign country. In all of these situations, an exchange under section 1031 may permit the taxpayer to accomplish his objectives without a needless tax erosion of his investment.

While section 1031 can frequently be used to advantage, its application to a transfer is not always advantageous or desirable. In some instances, it may be appropriate to effect a taxable transaction. Thus a taxpayer may wish to sell real estate in a taxable transaction in order to take advantage of a loss for tax purposes. Another often encountered example is the taxpayer who seeks a taxable transaction in order to increase his depreciable basis in newly acquired property. If either of these results are desirable, qualification of the transaction under section 1031 should be avoided. If the transaction qualifies as a section 1031 exchange, the recognition of loss will not be allowed and the basis of the transferred property will be carried over to the newly acquired property. Basis will only be increased if taxable, non-qualifying property is included in the exchange.

The trap for the unwary in these situations is that the application of section 1031 to a transaction is not elective. If the transaction meets the requirements of section 1031, the nonrecognition rules will be applicable. The intent of the parties or the labels they have given the arrangement will not serve to avoid the nonrecognition result. . . .

A. NONRECOGNITION OF GAIN OR LOSS FROM EXCHANGES SOLELY IN KIND: SECTION 1031(A)

1. *Definition of Property for Purposes of Section 1031(a)*

The nonrecognition provisions of section 1031(a) are applicable only to certain types of property which are exchanged under certain conditions. Although neither the Code nor the Regulations offer a precise definition of property that will qualify for a section 1031 exchange, they do offer a broad description of the classes of property that will and will not qualify.

The property must be property held by the taxpayer for productive use in a trade or business or for investment. Non-business property such as a personal residence, or an automobile used solely for personal purposes will not qualify. Whether property is being held for productive use in a trade or business or for investment is a question of fact, to be determined by the actual use of the property *at the time of the exchange*. The test is applied to each party to the exchange separately. It is possible for any particular transaction to be a qualified exchange for one of the parties and at the same time a wholly taxable event for the other. In addition, the section specifically excludes from coverage stock in trade, property held primarily for sale, stocks, bonds, notes, choses in action, certificates of trust or beneficial interest, or other securities or evidences of indebtedness or interest. . . .

7. *Like-Kind Property*

In addition to the requirement that qualified property be transferred in a qualified exchange, section 1031(a) will apply only if the properties exchanged are of like-kind. The Regulations provide:

"[T]he words 'like kind' have reference to the nature or character of the property and not to its grade or quality. One kind or class of property may not, under that section, be exchanged for property of a different kind or class. The fact that any real estate involved is improved or unimproved is not material, for that fact relates only to the grade or quality of the property and not to its kind or class. . . ."[1]

"No gain or loss is recognized if . . . (2) a taxpayer who is not a dealer in real estate exchanges city real estate for a ranch or farm, or exchanges a leasehold of a fee with 30 years or more to run for real estate, or exchanges improved real estate for unimproved real estate. . . ."[2]

The application of the "like kind" requirement to real estate exchanges is extremely broad. It refers to the broad classes of property

[1]   Treas.Reg. § 1.1031(a)–1(b), T.D. 6935, 1967–2 C.B. 272.

[2]   Treas.Reg. § 1.1031(a)–1(c)(2), T.D. 6935, 1967–2 C.B. 272.

such as real or personal but not to distinctions between tracts of real property even where there are substantial dissimilarities in location, physical attributes or possibilities for productive utilization. The exchange of real estate held for investment with real estate held for productive use in a trade or business may be a "like kind" exchange if the transaction is otherwise qualified. To determine whether real estate exchanges qualify as "like kind" exchanges, reference must be made to the nature of the rights or interests in the real estate which are exchanged. The rights in the respective grantees to the property exchanged must be of the same general character or substantial equality. . . .

Regulations section 1.1031(a)–1(c)(2) provides that an exchange of a leasehold of thirty years or more for a fee interest will be an exchange to which section 1031(a) will be applicable. While the Service has followed this rule, no court has yet been required to rule directly on the validity of the Regulation. In practically every case coming before the courts, the transfer of the leasehold interest has been contemporaneous with a sale of the same property. In those instances, the courts have concerned themselves with the validity of the sale. Accordingly, the current status of the Regulation as applied to leases greater than thirty years is unclear.

8.   *Property Received to Be Held for Productive Use in a Trade or Business or Investment*

The final requirement for a qualified exchange is that the property received must be held either for investment or for productive use in a trade or business. Consequently, section 1031 will not be applicable to an exchange if the property exchanged is acquired for resale. Property acquired in an otherwise qualified exchange was held not qualified where it was previously committed to resale. In Ethel Black,[3] the taxpayer exchanged desert land for a house which she repaired and sold. The court held that the transaction was not entitled to nonrecognition treatment because the property was held primarily for sale.

The requirement here is essentially the same as discussed above with reference to qualifying property for exchange. The significant point is that the requirement is a condition subsequent that may cause an otherwise qualified exchange to be disqualified some point in time after the exchange has been effected. How long property must be held is not clear. It would seem sufficient if the original intent of the taxpayer was to hold it for a qualifying purpose. However, intent is difficult to prove and a sale too soon after the exchange may be considered indicative of the taxpayer's intent at the time of the exchange. Such a presumption may be overcome if the taxpayer is able to show a significant change in circumstances which make a sale appropriate.

B.   Gain From Exchanges Not Solely in Kind

1.   *Transfer of Unqualified Property*

The nonrecognition provisions of section 1031 are applicable only to exchanges of the certain qualified property described in section 1031(a) of the Code. The Regulations provide:

---

[3]   35 T.C. 90 (1960).

"A transfer of property meeting the requirements of section 1031(a) may be within the provisions of section 1031(a) even though the taxpayer transfers in addition property not meeting the requirements of section 1031(a) or money. However, the nonrecognition treatment provided by section 1031(a) does not apply to the property transferred which does not meet the requirements of section 1031(a)."[4]

Consequently, if a taxpayer transfers qualified plus unqualified property in exchange for qualified property, he must recognize any gain or loss realized on the transfer of the unqualified property. Recognition will be pursuant to the general provisions of sections 1001 and 1002 of the Code. For this purpose, the taxpayer is deemed to have received in exchange for the unqualified property an amount equal to its fair market value on the date of the exchange. However, no gain or loss is recognized if a taxpayer transfers qualified property together with cash in exchange for qualified property. Nor will the transfer of qualified property together with unqualified property disqualify the exchange with respect to the qualified property.

The application of these principles as they relate to recognition of a loss is well illustrated by an example contained in the Regulations:

"A exchanges real estate held for investment plus stock for real estate to be held for investment. The real estate transferred has an adjusted basis of $10,000 and a fair market value of $11,000. The stock transferred has an adjusted basis of $4,000 and a fair market value of $2,000. The real estate acquired has a fair market value of $13,000. A is deemed to have received a $2,000 portion of the acquired real estate in exchange for the stock, since $2,000 is the fair market value of the stock at the time of the exchange. A $2,000 loss is recognized under section 1002 on the exchange of the stock for real estate. No gain or loss is recognized on the exchange of the real estate since the property received is of the type permitted to be received without recognition of gain or loss. . . ."[5]

These principles are equally applicable to recognition of gain. It should also be noted that whether a particular property is qualified or not depends on the nature of each exchange. Otherwise qualified real estate will not be qualified property if it is part of an exchange of personal property. There must be an exchange of like-kind property or an exchange, or part of it, will not be qualified regardless of the type of property involved.

2. Receipt of Unqualified Property

Contrary to the transfer of unqualified property, the Code and Regulations under section 1031(b) make very specific provisions for the receipt of unqualified property in an otherwise qualified exchange. If a taxpayer receives, in a section 1031 exchange, other property or money in addition to property permitted to be received without recognition of gain or loss, any gain realized must be recognized but only in an amount not in excess of the fair market value of the other property

---

[4]   Treas.Reg. § 1.1031(a)–1(a), T.D. 6935, 1967–2 C.B. 272.

[5]   Treas.Reg. § 1.1031(d)–1(e), T.D. 6935, 1967–2 C.B. 272.

and/or the sum of money received. For purposes of section 1031(b), "other property or money" includes liabilities transferred, property not eligible for nonrecognition treatment under section 1031(a), and property which, though eligible by definition, is not of like-kind to the other property involved in the exchange.

a.   *Receipt of Money*

The receipt of cash in partial consideration for the exchange of property is tantamount to a partial sale of the property and will cause the recognition of any gain accordingly. If the taxpayer *realizes* gain on a section 1031 exchange, he will *recognize* his gain to the extent of the cash received. It has been held that where cash is advanced by the transferor to enable the transferee to pay off a mortgage on the property he is exchanging, the transferee has not realized a gain but rather merely changed creditors. However, if there is no requirement that the money be used to pay off the mortgage, the receipt of the cash will be treated as taxable gain.

It is important to note the two limitations on recognition, i.e., the lesser of the gain realized or the cash received. An example from section 1.1031(b)–1 of the Regulations illustrates the principle well:

"A, who is not a dealer in real estate, in 1954 exchanges real estate held for investment, which he purchased in 1940 for $5,000, for other real estate (to be held for productive use in a trade or business) which has a fair market value of $6,000, and $2,000 in cash. The gain from the transaction is $3,000, but is recognized only to the extent of the cash received of $2,000."

Recognition of the remaining gain is deferred under the general provisions of section 1031(a).

The cash giving rise to the recognition of gain is the net cash received. Thus, in Revenue Ruling 72–456, a taxpayer was allowed to deduct brokerage commissions from the cash he received and recognized gain only on the net. In Gabe P. Allen,[6] the "expenses incurred in connection with the sale" were permitted to reduce the cash realized from $62,500 to $24,358.26.

b.   *Liabilities*

Regulations section 1.1031(b)–1(c) provides that:

"Consideration received in the form of an assumption of liabilities (or a transfer subject to a liability) is to be treated as 'other property or money' for the purposes of section 1031(b). . . ."

The Code contains no such specific reference and the language first appeared in the Regulations in 1956. However, the proposition found support in the courts and administrative rulings for many years prior to the 1954 Revenue Act.

Under this provision, when the taxpayer transfers mortgaged property in an exchange and receives unencumbered property, the amount of the mortgage is treated as money received by the taxpayer. This result is the same whether or not the mortgage is assumed by the transferee. In Allen,[7] the taxpayer transferred mortgaged real estate for

---

[6]   10 T.C. 413 (1948).

[7]   Gabe P. Allen, 10 T.C. 413 (1948).

unencumbered properties plus cash. The transferee took the property subject to the mortgage but did not assume it. The Tax Court held that it was a well established proposition of law that the mortgage indebtedness constituted "other property or money" whether or not the transferee assumed it.

Starker v. United States

United States Court of Appeals, Ninth Circuit, 1979.
602 F.2d 1341.

GOODWIN, CIRCUIT JUDGE:

T.J. Starker appeals from the dismissal, on stipulated facts, of his tax refund action. We affirm in part and reverse in part.

I.   FACTS

On April 1, 1967, T.J. Starker and his son and daughter-in-law, Bruce and Elizabeth Starker, entered into a "land exchange agreement" with Crown Zellerbach Corporation (Crown). The agreement provided that the three Starkers would convey to Crown all their interests in 1,843 acres of timberland in Columbia County, Oregon. In consideration for this transfer, Crown agreed to acquire and deed over to the Starkers other real property in Washington and Oregon. Crown agreed to provide the Starkers suitable real property within five years or pay any outstanding balance in cash. As part of the contract, Crown agreed to add to the Starkers' credit each year a "growth factor", equal to six per cent of the outstanding balance.

On May 31, 1967, the Starkers deeded their timberland to Crown. Crown entered "exchange value credits" in its books: for T.J. Starker's interest, a credit of $1,502,500; and for Bruce and Elizabeth's interest, a credit of $73,000.

Within four months, Bruce and Elizabeth found three suitable parcels, and Crown purchased and conveyed them pursuant to the contract. No "growth factor" was added because a year had not expired, and no cash was transferred to Bruce and Elizabeth because the agreed value of the property they received was $73,000, the same as their credit.

Closing the transaction with T.J. Starker, whose credit balance was larger, took longer. Beginning in July 1967 and continuing through May 1969, Crown purchased 12 parcels selected by T.J. Starker. Of these 12, Crown purchased 9 from third parties, and then conveyed them to T.J. Starker. Two more of the 12 (the Timian and Bi-Mart properties) were transferred to Crown by third parties, and then conveyed by Crown at T.J. Starker's direction to his daughter, Jean Roth. The twelfth parcel (the Booth property) involved a third party's contract to purchase. Crown purchased that contract right and reassigned it to T.J. Starker.

The first of the transfers from Crown to T.J. Starker or his daughter was on September 5, 1967; the twelfth and last was on May 21, 1969. By 1969, T.J. Starker's credit balance had increased from $1,502,500 to $1,577,387.91, by means of the 6 per cent "growth factor". The land transferred by Crown to T.J. Starker and Roth was valued by the parties at exactly $1,577,387.91. Therefore, no cash was paid to T.J. Starker, and his balance was reduced to zero.

In their income tax returns for 1967, the three Starkers all reported no gain on the transactions, although their bases in the properties they relinquished were smaller than the market value of the properties they received. They claimed that the transactions were entitled to nonrecognition treatment under section 1031 of the Internal Revenue Code (I.R.C. § 1031), which provides in part:

"(a) Nonrecognition of gain or loss from exchanges solely in kind.

No gain or loss shall be recognized if property held for productive use in trade or business or for investment (not including stock in trade or other property held primarily for sale, nor stocks, bonds, notes, choses in action, certificates of trust or beneficial interest, or other securities or evidences of indebtedness or interest) is exchanged solely for property of a like kind to be held either for productive use in trade or business or for investment."

The Internal Revenue Service disagreed, and assessed deficiencies of $35,248.41 against Bruce and Elizabeth Starker and $300,930.31 plus interest against T.J. Starker. The Starkers paid the deficiencies, filed claims for refunds, and when those claims were denied, filed two actions for refunds in the United States District Court in Oregon.

In the first of the two cases, Bruce Starker v. United States (Starker I), 75–1 U.S. Tax Cas. (CCH) ¶ 8443 (D.Or.1975), the trial court held that this court's decision in Alderson v. Commissioner, 317 F.2d 790 (9th Cir.1963), compelled a decision for the taxpayers. Bruce and Elizabeth Starker recovered the claimed refund. The government appealed, but voluntarily dismissed the appeal, and the judgment for Bruce and Elizabeth Starker became final.

The government, however, did not capitulate in T.J. Starker v. United States (Starker II), the present case. The government continued to assert that T.J. Starker was not entitled to section 1031 nonrecognition. According to the government, T.J. Starker was liable not only for a tax on his capital gain, but also for a tax on the 6 per cent "growth factor" as ordinary income (interest or its equivalent).

The same trial judge who heard *Starker I* also heard *Starker II*. Recognizing that "many of the transfers here are identical to those in *Starker I*", the court rejected T.J. Starker's collateral-estoppel argument and found for the government. The judge said:

"I have reconsidered my opinion in *Starker I*. I now conclude that I was mistaken in my holding as well in my earlier reading of *Alderson*. Even if *Alderson* can be interpreted as contended by plaintiff, I think that to do so would be improper. It would merely sanction a tax avoidance scheme and not carry out the purposes of § 1031." T.J. Starker v. United States, 432 F.Supp. 864, 868, 77–2 U.S. Tax Cas. (CCH) ¶ 9512 (D.Or.1977).

Judgment was entered for the government on both the nonrecognition and ordinary income (interest) issues, and this appeal followed.

T.J. Starker asserts that the district court erred in holding that: (a) his real estate transactions did not qualify for nonrecognition under

I.R.C. § 1031; (b) the government was not collaterally estopped from litigating that issue; and (c) the transactions caused him to have ordinary income for interest, in addition to a capital gain.

II. COLLATERAL ESTOPPEL

T.J. Starker argues that the decision in Bruce Starker v. United States collaterally estops the government from litigating the application of section 1031 to his transactions with Crown. The government urges this court to affirm the trial court on this point, claiming that the two cases presented different legal questions, facts and parties.

The government, having lost its case against this taxpayer's son based on the same contract to transfer the same family lands, decided not to pursue an appeal in that case, but instead to pursue this taxpayer. Although T.J. Starker's transactions involving three of the parcels differed in a relevant way from those of his son, the legal issues and facts surrounding the other nine are so similar that collateral estoppel applies. Except as to the Bi-Mart, Timian, and Booth properties, the government should have been held collaterally estopped by *Starker I* from relitigation of the applicability of I.R.C. § 1031 in *Starker II*.

III. TIMIAN, BI-MART, AND BOOTH PROPERTIES

As to Timian, Bi-Mart, and Booth properties, the facts of *Starker I* are so different from those of this case that the entire issue of the applicability of section 1031 to them was properly before the district court in *Starker II*. The court therefore correctly went to the merits of the litigants' arguments as they pertained to these parcels. We now turn to those arguments.

As with the other nine parcels T.J. Starker received, none of these three properties was deeded to him at or near the time he deeded his timberland to Crown. T.J. Starker admits that he received no interest in these properties until a substantial time after he conveyed away title to his property. Thus, the question whether section 1031 requires simultaneity of deed transfers is presented as to all three. In addition, each of these parcels presents its own peculiar issues because of the differing circumstances surrounding their transfers.

A. Timian and Bi-Mart Properties.

The Timian property is a residence. Legal title to it was conveyed by Crown at T.J. Starker's request to his daughter, Jean Roth, in 1967. T.J. Starker lives in this residence, and pays rent on it to his daughter. The United States argues that since T.J. Starker never held legal title to this property, he cannot be said to have exchanged his timberland for it. Furthermore, the government contends, because the property became the taxpayer's personal residence, it is neither property "held for investment" nor of a like kind with such property under the meaning of the Code. On the other hand, the taxpayer argues that there was, in economic reality, a transfer of title to him, followed by a gift by him to his daughter.

The Bi-Mart property, a commercial building, was conveyed by Crown to Roth in 1968. The government raises the same issue with regard to the Bi-Mart property: since T.J. Starker never had title, he did not effect an exchange. T.J. Starker points out, however, that he expended substantial time and money in improving and maintaining the structure in the three months prior to the conveyance of the property to his daughter, and he emphasizes that he controlled and commanded its transfer to her.

We begin our analysis of the proper treatment of the receipt of these two properties with a consideration of the Timian residence. T.J. Starker asserts that the question whether such property can be held "for investment" is unsettled. We disagree. It has long been the rule that use of property solely as a personal residence is antithetical to its being held for investment. Losses on the sale or exchange of such property cannot be deducted for this reason, despite the general rule that losses from transactions involving trade or investment properties are deductible. A similar rule must obtain in construing the term "held for investment" in section 1031. Thus, nonrecognition treatment cannot be given to the receipt of the Timian parcel.

Moreover, T.J. Starker cannot be said to have received the Timian or Bi-Mart properties in exchange for his interest in the Columbia County timberland because title to the Timian and Bi-Mart properties was transferred by Crown directly to someone else, his daughter. Under an analogous nonrecognition provision, section 1034 of the Code, the key to receiving nonrecognition treatment is maintaining continuity of title. Under section 1034, if title shifts from the taxpayer to someone other than the taxpayer's spouse, nonrecognition is denied. Marcello v. Commissioner, 380 F.2d 499 (5th Cir.1967); Boesel v. Commissioner, [65 T.C. 378 (1975)], we find similar reasoning compelling here. Although in some cases a father and his daughter may be seen as having an identity of economic interests, that unity is not sufficient to make transfer of title to one the same as transfer of title to the other. T.J. Starker has not shown that he has any legally cognizable interest in the Timian or Bi-Mart properties that would entitle him to prevent Jean Roth from exercising full ownership rights. In case of a disagreement about the use or enjoyment of these properties, her wishes, not his, would prevail. In these circumstances, T.J. Starker cannot be said to have "exchanged" properties under section 1031, because he never received any property ownership himself.

B. Booth Property.

The Booth property is a commercial parcel, title to which has never been conveyed to T.J. Starker. The transfer of this property to him was achieved in 1968 by Crown's acquiring third parties' contract right to purchase the property, and then reassigning the right to T.J. Starker. In addition to emphasizing the lack of simultaneity in the transfers, the government points here to the total lack of deed transfer.

An examination of the record reveals that legal title had not passed by deed to T.J. Starker by the time of the trial. He continued to hold the third-party purchasers' rights under a 1965 sales agreement on the Booth land. That agreement notes that one of the original transferors holds a life interest in the property, and that legal title shall not pass until that life interest expires. In the meantime, the purchasers are entitled to possession, but they are subject to certain restrictions. For example, they are prohibited from removing improvements and are required to keep buildings and fences in good repair. Under the agreement, a substantial portion of the purchase price must be invested, with a fixed return to be paid to the purchaser of the life interest. Should any of these conditions fail, the agreement provides, the sellers may elect, *inter alia,* to void the contract.

Despite these contingencies, we believe that what T.J. Starker received in 1968 was the equivalent of a fee interest for purposes of section 1031. Under Treas.Regs. § 1.1031(a)–1(c), a leasehold interest of 30 years or more is the equivalent of a fee interest for purposes of determining whether the properties exchanged are of a like kind. Under the assigned purchase rights, Starker had at least the rights of a long-term lessee, plus an equitable fee subject to conditions precedent. If the seller's life interest lasted longer than 30 years, the leasehold interest would be the equivalent of a fee; the fact that the leasehold might ripen into a fee at some earlier point should not alter this result. Thus, we hold that what T.J. Starker received in 1968 was the equivalent of a fee.

This does not solve the riddle of the proper treatment of the Booth parcel, however. Since the taxpayer did not receive the fee equivalent at the same time that he gave up his interest in the timberland, the same issue is presented as with the nine parcels on which the government was estopped, namely, whether simultaneity of transfer is required for nonrecognition treatment under section 1031.

The government's argument that simultaneity is required begins with Treas.Reg. § 1.1002–1(b). That regulation provides that all exceptions to the general rule that gains and losses are recognized must be construed narrowly:

" * * * Nonrecognition is accorded by the Code only if the exchange is one which satisfies both (1) the specific description in the Code of an excepted exchange, and (2) the underlying purpose for which such exchange is excepted from the general rule."

There are two problems, however, with applying this regulation to section 1031.

First, the "underlying purpose" of section 1031 is not entirely clear. The legislative history reveals that the provision was designed to avoid the imposition of a tax on those who do not "cash in" on their investments in trade or business property. Congress appeared to be concerned that taxpayers would not have the cash to pay a tax on the capital gain if the exchange triggered recognition. This does not explain the precise limits of section 1031, however; if those taxpayers sell their property for cash and reinvest that cash in like-kind property, they cannot enjoy the section's benefits, even if the reinvestment takes place just a few days after the sale. Thus, some taxpayers with liquidity problems resulting from a replacement of their business property are not covered by the section. The liquidity rationale must therefore be limited.

Another apparent consideration of the drafters of the section was the difficulty of valuing property exchanged for the purpose of measuring gain or loss. Section 1031(a) permits the taxpayer to transfer the basis of the property he or she gives up to the property he or she receives, thus deferring the valuation problem, as well as the tax, until the property received is sold or otherwise disposed of in a transaction in which gain or loss is recognized.

But this valuation rationale also has its limits. So long as a single dollar in cash or other non-like-kind property ("boot") is received by the taxpayer along with like-kind property, valuation of both properties in the exchange becomes necessary. In that case, the taxpayer is liable for the gain realized, with the maximum liability being on the amount of cash or other "boot" received, under I.R.C. § 1031(b). To compute the gain realized, one must place a value on the like-kind property received. Moreover, the nonrecognition provision applies only to like-kind exchanges, and not to other exchanges in which valuation is just as difficult. Therefore, valuation problems cannot be seen as the controlling consideration in the enactment of section 1031.

In addition to the elusive purpose of the section, there is a second sound reason to question the applicability of Treas.Regs. § 1.1002–1: the long line of cases liberally construing section 1031. If the regulation purports to read into section 1031 a complex web of formal and substantive requirements, precedent indicates decisively that the regulation has been rejected. We therefore analyze the Booth transaction with the courts' permissive attitude toward section 1031 in mind.

Two features of the Booth deal make it most likely to trigger recognition of gain: the likelihood that the taxpayer would receive cash instead of real estate, and the time gap in the transfers of the equivalents of fee title.

In assessing whether the possibility that T.J. Starker might receive cash makes section 1031 inapplicable, an important case is Alderson v. Commissioner, 317 F.2d 790 (9th Cir.1963). There, this court held that a "three corner" exchange qualified for nonrecognition treatment. The taxpayer and Alloy entered into an agreement for the simple cash sale of the taxpayer's property, but later amended the agreement to provide that Alloy would purchase another parcel to effect a swap with the taxpayer. This amendment did not totally eradicate the possibility that the cash transaction would take place; it provided, in the words of the court, that "if the exchange was not effected by September 11, 1957, the original escrow re the purchase for cash would be carried out." 317 F.2d at 791. The exchange was effected when reciprocal deeds were recorded. Said the court:

> "True, the intermediate acts of the parties could have hewn closer to and have more precisely depicted the ultimate desired result, but what actually occurred on September 3 or 4, 1957, was an exchange of deeds between the petitioners and Alloy which effected an exchange of the Buena Park property for the Salinas property." Alderson v. Commissioner, 317 F.2d at 793.

The court stressed that, although at the time the contract was amended there was a possibility that a cash sale would take place, there was from the outset no intention on the part of the taxpayer to sell his property for cash if it could be exchanged for other property of a like kind. Thus, *Alderson* followed Mercantile Trust Co. of Baltimore v. Commissioner, 32 B.T.A. 82 (1935), a case in which the taxpayer could have required the other party to the exchange to pay cash if that other party was unable to purchase an identified parcel that the taxpayer desired. In *Mercantile Trust,* the taxpayer succeeded in getting nonrecognition treatment by virtue of its intention to get other property, rather than cash, if possible.

Coastal Terminals, Inc. v. United States, 320 F.2d 333 (4th Cir.1963), held similarly. There, a "three corner" exchange was effected, with both the taxpayer and the other party to the exchange maintaining until the closing the option to cancel the exchange and bring about a cash sale instead. Citing *Alderson* with approval, the court noted that the taxpayer intended to sell the property for cash only if it was unable to locate a suitable piece of property to take in exchange. Because an exchange took place, nonrecognition treatment was granted. . . .

Thus, the mere possibility at the time of agreement that a cash sale might occur does not prevent the application of section 1031. Even in cases such as *Coastal Terminals,* where the taxpayers had the contract right to opt for cash rather than property, a preference by the taxpayers for like-kind property rather than cash has guaranteed nonrecognition despite the possibility of a cash transaction.

In this case, the taxpayer claims he intended from the very outset of the transaction to get nothing but like-kind property, and no evidence to the contrary appears on the record. Moreover, the taxpayer never handled any cash in the course of the transactions. Hence, the *Alderson* line of cases would seem to control.

The government contends, however, that *Alderson* and other precedents of its type are distinguishable. It points out that in those cases, there may have been a possibility of a receipt of cash at the time of the exchange *agreement,* but there was no possibility of receiving cash at the time the taxpayer *transferred* the property pursuant to the agreement. This difference in timing, says the commissioner, renders the *Alderson* line of cases inapplicable.

At least one appellate decision indicates, however, that title may not have to be exchanged simultaneously in order for section 1031 to apply. In Redwing Carriers, Inc. v. Tomlinson, 399 F.2d 652 (5th Cir.1968), the government argued successfully that mutual transfers of trucks that occurred "at or about" the same time were in fact an "exchange" under section 1031. In *Redwing Carriers,* the taxpayer was attempting to deduct a loss in the purchase of new trucks to replace old trucks; the government disallowed recognition of the loss on the ground that section 1031(c) applied. To keep its replacement transaction outside the scope of the section, a parent corporation transferred its old trucks to a subsidiary, bought new trucks for cash, and had the subsidiary sell the old trucks to the manufacturer for cash. The court viewed the transactions as a whole, and disallowed the loss under section 1031. Some lack of simultaneity was apparently "tolerated" by the commissioner and the court. As the court explained, the transfers to the subsidiary by the parent and to the parent by the manufacturer took place "at or about" the same time. 399 F.2d at 655. Nonetheless, the government urges this court to distinguish *Redwing Carriers,* and *Alderson* and its kin, on the ground that the transfers of title in T.J. Starker's case were separated by a "substantial" period of time. We decline to draw this line.

The government also argues that the contract right to receive property or cash was not "like" title to property, because it was like cash. It asks us to impose a "cash equivalency" test to determine whether section 1031 applies. One flaw in this argument is that title to land is no more or less equivalent to cash than a contract right to buy land. The central concept of section 1031 is that an exchange of business or investment assets does not trigger recognition of gain or loss, because the taxpayer in entering into such a transaction does not "cash in" or "close out" his or her investment. To impose a tax on the event of a deed transfer upon a signing of an exchange agreement could bring about the very result section 1031 was designed to prevent: "the inequity * * * of forcing a taxpayer to recognize a paper gain which was still tied up in a continuing investment of the same sort." Jordan Marsh Co. v. Commissioner, 269 F.2d 453, 456 (2d Cir.1959).

Against this background, the government offers the explanation that a contract right to land is a "chose in action", and thus personal property instead of real property. This is true, but the short answer to this statement is that title to real property, like a contract right to purchase real property, is nothing more than a bundle of potential causes of action: for trespass, to quiet title, for interference with quiet enjoyment, and so on. The bundle of rights associated with ownership is obviously not excluded from section 1031; a contractual right to assume the rights of ownership should not, we believe, be treated as any different than the ownership rights themselves. Even if the contract right includes the possibility of the taxpayer receiving something other than ownership of like-kind property, we hold that it is still of a like kind with ownership for tax purposes when the taxpayer prefers property to cash before and throughout the executory period, and only like-kind property is ultimately received.

The metaphysical discussion in the briefs and authorities about whether the "steps" of the transactions should be "collapsed", and the truism that "substance" should prevail over "form", are not helpful to the resolution of this case. At best, these words describe results, not reasons. A proper decision can be reached only by considering the purposes of the statute and analyzing its application to particular facts under existing precedent. Here, the statute's purposes are somewhat cloudy, and the precedents are not easy to reconcile. But the weight of authority leans in T.J. Starker's favor, and we conclude that the district court was right in *Starker I,* and wrong in *Starker II*. Thus, on the merits, the transfer of the timberland to Crown triggered a like-kind exchange with respect to the Booth property.

IV. SIX PER CENT "GROWTH FACTOR"

The next issue presented is whether the 6 per cent "growth factor" received by T.J. Starker was properly treated as capital gain or as ordinary income. The government successfully argued below that this amount should be treated as ordinary income because it was disguised interest. The taxpayer, on the other hand, contends that the 6 per cent "growth" provision merely compensated him for timber growth on the Columbia County property he conveyed to Crown.

The taxpayer's argument is not without some biological merit, but he was entitled to the 6 per cent regardless of the actual fate of the timber on the property. He retained no ownership rights in the timber, and bore no risk of loss, after he conveyed title to Crown. We agree with the government that the taxpayer is essentially arguing "that he conveyed $1,502,500 to a stranger for an indefinite period of time [up to five years] without any interest." The 6 per cent "growth factor" was "compensation for the use or forbearance of money," that is, for the use of the unpaid amounts owed to Starker by Crown. Therefore, it was disguised interest.

V.   TIMING OF INCLUSION

Our final task, having characterized the proper nature of T.J. Starker's receipts, is to decide in which years they are includible in income. The Timian and Bi-Mart properties do not qualify for nonrecognition treatment, while the other 10 properties received do qualify. In this situation, we believe the proper result is to treat T.J. Starker's rights in his contract with Crown, insofar as they resulted in the receipt of the Timian and Bi-Mart properties, as "boot", received in 1967 when the contract was made. We hold that section 1031(b) requires T.J. Starker to recognize his gain on the transaction with Crown in 1967, to the extent of the fair market values of the Timian and Bi-Mart properties as of the dates on which title to those properties passed to his appointee.

We realize that this decision leaves the treatment of an alleged exchange open until the eventual receipt of consideration by the taxpayer. Some administrative difficulties may surface as a result. Our role, however, is not necessarily to facilitate administration. It is to divine the meaning of the statute in a manner as consistent as possible with the intent of Congress and the prior holdings of the courts. If our holding today adds a degree of uncertainty to this area, Congress can clarify its meaning.

As to the disguised interest, the district court erred in holding T.J. Starker liable for ordinary income in 1967. As a taxpayer reporting on the cash method, T.J. Starker was not liable for taxes on interest income until that interest was received. Although receipt may be actual or constructive, Crown's liability for the "growth factor" did not commence until after 1967 had expired. Had suitable properties been found for T.J. Starker in 1967 (as was the case with Bruce and Elizabeth), Crown would have owed T.J. Starker no "growth factor" at all. Therefore, the government should not have assessed an ordinary income tax on the "growth factor" in 1967. The proper years of inclusion would have been those in which the taxpayer received the interest. To the extent T.J. Starker paid the ordinary tax for 1967, he was entitled to his refund.

VI.   CONCLUSION

We affirm the judgment of the district court in part, and reverse it in part. We remand for a modified judgment consistent with this opinion.

Vacated and remanded.

Biggs v. Commissioner of Internal Revenue

United States Court of Appeals, Fifth Circuit, 1980.
632 F.2d 1171.

HENDERSON, CIRCUIT JUDGE:

The Commissioner of Internal Revenue appeals from the decision of the United States Tax Court holding that a transfer of real property effected by the taxpayer, Franklin B. Biggs, constituted an exchange within the meaning of § 1031 of the Internal Revenue Code of 1954. We affirm.

The numerous transactions which form the subject of this suit are somewhat confusing and each detail is of potential significance. Thus, it will be necessary to recount with particularity the facts as found by the Tax Court.

Biggs owned two parcels of land located in St. Martin's Neck, Worcester County, Maryland (hereinafter referred to as the "Maryland property"). Sometime before October 23, 1968, Biggs listed this property for sale with a realtor. The realtor advised Biggs that he had a client, Shepard G. Powell, who was interested in purchasing the property.

Biggs and Powell met on October 23, 1968 to discuss Powell's possible acquisition of the Maryland property. Biggs insisted from the outset that he receive real property of like kind as part of the consideration for the transfer. Both men understood that Biggs would locate the property he wished to receive in exchange, and Powell agreed to cooperate in the exchange arrangements to the extent that his own interests were not impaired.

On October 25, 1968, Biggs and Powell signed a memorandum of intent which provided, in pertinent part, the following:

I.   PURCHASE PRICE: $900,000 *NET* to SELLERS.

* * *

    c. $25,000.00 down payment at signing of contract, * * *

    d. $75,000.00 additional payment at time of settlement, which shall be within ninety (90) days after contract signing, making total cash payments of $100,000.00.

II.   MORTGAGE:

    a.   Balance of $800,000.00 secured by a first mortgage on Real Estate to SELLERS at a 4% interest rate; 10 year term.

* * *

The memorandum contained no mention of the contemplated exchange of properties. Upon learning of this omission, Biggs' attorney, W. Edgar Porter, told Powell that the memorandum of intent did not comport with his understanding of the proposed transaction. Powell agreed to have his attorney meet with Porter to work out the terms of a written exchange agreement.

Biggs began his search for suitable exchange property by advising John Thatcher, a Maryland real estate broker, of the desired specifications. Subsequently, Biggs was contacted by another realtor, John A. Davis, who had in his inventory four parcels of land located in Accomack County, Virginia, collectively known as Myrtle Grove Farm (hereinafter referred to as "the Virginia property"). Biggs inspected the property, found it suitable, and instructed Davis to draft contracts of sale.

As initially drawn, the contracts named Biggs as the buyer of the Virginia property. However, at Porter's suggestion, they were modified to describe the purchaser as "Franklin B. Biggs (acting as agent for syndicate)." The contracts were executed on October 29th and 30th, 1968, and contained the following terms:

Paid on execution of contract	$ 13,900.00
Balance due at settlement	115,655.14
Indebtedness created or assumed	142,544.86
Total—Gross Sales Price	$272,100.00

Upon signing the contracts, Biggs paid $13,900.00 to the sellers of the Virginia property.

Because Powell was either unable or unwilling to take title to the Virginia property, Biggs arranged for the title to be transferred to Shore Title Company, Inc. (hereinafter referred to as "Shore"), a Maryland corporation owned and controlled by Porter and certain members of his family. However, it was not until December 26, 1968 that the purchase was authorized by Shore's board of directors. On January 9, 1969, prior to the transfer to Shore, Biggs and Shore entered into the following agreement with respect to the Virginia property:

1.   At any time hereafter that either party hereto requests the other party to do so, Shore Title Co., Inc. will and hereby agrees to convey unto the said Franklin B. Biggs, or his nominee, all of the above mentioned property, for exactly the same price said Shore Title Co., Inc. has paid for it, plus any and all costs, expenses, advances or payments which Shore Title Co., Inc. has paid or will be bound in the future to pay, over and above said purchase price to Shore Title Co., Inc., in order for Shore Title Co., Inc., to acquire or hold title to said property; and it [is] further agreed that at that time, i.e.,— when Shore Title Co., Inc. conveys said property under this paragraph and its provisions, the said Franklin B. Biggs, or his nominee will simultaneously release or cause Shore Title Co., Inc. to be released from any and all obligations which the latter has created, assumed or become bound upon in its acquisition and holding of title to said property.

2.   All costs for acquiring or holding title to said property by both the said Shore Title Co., Inc. and Franklin B. Biggs, or his nominee shall be paid by the said Franklin B. Biggs, or his nominee at the time of transfer of title under paragraph numbered 1 hereof.

On or about the same date, the contracts for the sale of the Virginia property were closed. Warranty deeds evidencing legal title were delivered to Shore by the sellers. Biggs advanced to Shore the

$115,655.14 due at settlement and, by a bond secured by a deed of trust on the property, Shore agreed to repay Biggs. Shore also assumed liabilities totaling $142,544.86 which were secured by deeds of trust in favor of the sellers and another mortgagee. Biggs paid Thatcher's finder's fee and all of the closing costs.

On February 26, 1969, Shore and Powell signed an agreement for the sale by Shore of the Virginia property to Powell or his assigns. Payment of the purchase price was arranged as follows:

Upon execution of the agreement	$ 100.00

Vendee assumed and covenanted to pay the following promissory notes, all secured by deeds of trust on Virginia property:

To Shore Savings & Loan Association	$ 58,469.86
To those from whom Shore acquired the Virginia property	84,075.00
To Franklin B. Biggs	115,655.14
Balance due at settlement	13,900.00
Total purchase price	272,200.00

The next day, February 27, 1969, Biggs and Powell executed a contract which provided that Biggs would sell the Maryland property to Powell or his assigns upon the following terms:

Cash, upon execution	$ 25,000.00
Cash, at settlement	75,000.00
First mortgage note receivable from Mr. Powell	800,000.00
Total	$900,000.00

The contract further stated:

> Sellers and Purchaser acknowledge the existence of a Contract of Sale dated February 26th, 1969, between Shore Title Co., Inc., Vendor-Seller, and Shepard G. Powell or Assigns, Vendee-Purchaser, copy of which is attached hereto and made a part hereof, whereby that Vendor has contracted to sell and that Vendee has agreed to buy from that Vendor at and for the purchase price of Two Hundred Seventy Two Thousand Two Hundred Dollars ($272,200.00) * * * [the Virginia property]. As a further consideration for the making of this Contract of Sale * * * for the sale and purchase * * * of * * * [the Maryland property] the said Shepard G. Powell or Assigns, for the sum of One Hundred Dollars ($100.00) in cash, in hand paid, receipt whereof is hereby acknowledged, does hereby bargain, sell, set over and transfer unto said Franklin B. Biggs all of the right, title and interest of the said Shepard G. Powell or Assigns in

and to said Virginia property and said Contract of Sale relating thereto, upon condition that the said Franklin B. Biggs assumes and covenants to pay (which he hereby does) all of the obligations assumed by the said Shepard G. Powell under the aforesaid Contract of Sale between him and Shore Title Co., Inc.; and said Franklin B. Biggs hereby agrees to hold Shepard G. Powell or Assigns harmless from any liability under any and all of said obligations on said Virginia property, and the said Shepard G. Powell and said Franklin B. Biggs do hereby jointly and separately agree to execute and deliver any and all necessary papers to effect delivery of title to said Virginia property to said Franklin B. Biggs and to relieve said Shepard G. Powell from any and all obligations assumed by him thereon.

On the same date, Powell and his wife assigned their contractual right to acquire the Maryland property to Samuel Lessans and Maurice Lessans. The Lessanses, in turn, sold and assigned their rights to acquire the Maryland property to Ocean View Corporation (hereinafter referred to as "Ocean View") a Maryland corporation, for $1,300,000.00 by an agreement dated May 22, 1969. The purchase price was comprised of $150,000.00 to be paid into escrow at the time the contract was signed, an $800,000.00 note executed by Ocean View in favor of Biggs at the time of settlement, a $250,000.00 note from Ocean View to the Lessanses, and a $100,000.00 note from Ocean View to the real estate agents at closing.

Ocean View was incorporated on May 21, 1969. At the first meeting of its board of directors, the corporation was authorized to acquire the Maryland property and, also, to quit-claim any interest it might have in the Virginia property. It is undisputed, though, that neither the Lessanses nor Ocean View had any interest whatsoever in that property.

On May 24, 1969, Shore executed a deed conveying all of its right, title and interest in the Virginia property to Biggs. Powell and his wife, the Lessanses and Ocean View all joined in executing the deed as grantors, despite their apparent lack of any cognizable interest in the property. This instrument provided that:

> [T]he said Shore Title Co., Inc., a Maryland corporation, executes this deed to the Grantee herein for the purpose of conveying the * * * Virginia property hereinafter described by good and marketable title, subject to the assumption by the Grantee herein of the obligations hereinafter referred to, and all of the other Grantors herein join in the execution of this deed for the purpose of releasing and quit-claiming any interest in and to the property described herein and for the purpose of thereby requesting Shore Title Co., Inc. to convey said property to the Grantee herein in the manner herein set out. . . .

By the same deed, Biggs agreed to assume and pay the notes in favor of the mortgagee and the owners from whom Shore had acquired the Virginia property, in the total sum of $142,544.86. On May 29, 1969, Biggs executed a deed of release in favor of Shore indicating payment in full of the $115,655.14 bond.

On May 26, 1969, Biggs and his wife, Powell and his wife and the Lessanses sold the Maryland property to Ocean View. Contemporaneously, Ocean View executed a mortgage in the face amount of $800,000.00 in favor of Biggs. Also on this date, all of the contracts were closed. Ocean View received the deed to the Maryland property and Biggs accepted title to the Virginia property.

Biggs reported his gain from the sale of the Maryland property on his 1969 federal income tax return as follows:[1]

Selling price of Maryland property	$900,000.00	100.00%
Exchange-Virginia property	298,380.75[a]	33.15%
Boot	$601,619.25	66.85%
Selling price Maryland property	$900,000.00	
Basis-date of exchange	186,312.80	
Gain	$713,687.20	
Not recognized-exchange (Sec. 1031 I.R.C.)		
33.15%	236,587.31	
Taxable gain	$477,099.89	53.011%

[a] Such figure included finders' fees and legal costs incident to the acquisition of the Virginia property.

Biggs elected to report the transaction under the installment sales provision of § 453 of the Code. The Commissioner issued a notice of deficiency based upon his determination that there was no exchange of like-kind properties within the meaning of § 1031. The Tax Court disagreed, and ruled in favor of Biggs.[2]

Section 1031 provides, in pertinent part, that the gain realized on the exchange of like-kind property held for productive use or investment shall be recognized only to the extent that "boot" or cash is received as additional consideration. The Commissioner does not deny that Biggs fully intended to carry out an exchange that would pass muster under § 1031. It was undoubtedly for this purpose that Biggs insisted from the beginning of his negotiations with Powell that he receive property of like kind as part of the consideration for the transfer of the Maryland property. However, as this court made clear in Carlton v. United States, 385 F.2d 238 (5th Cir.1967), the mere intent to effect a § 1031 exchange is not dispositive. Indeed, the Commissioner's primary contention is that, under the authority of our holding in *Carlton,* Biggs failed to accomplish an exchange because the purchaser, Powell, never held title to the Virginia property.

The facts on which *Carlton* was decided parallel those which we now consider in several respects. Carlton, the taxpayer, wished to trade a tract of ranch land for other property of a similar character in order to obtain the tax benefits afforded by § 1031. This intent was made explicit in the negotiations and resulting option contract entered into by

[1]   Biggs admits that, even if the transaction qualifies as a § 1031 exchange, he used an incorrect method to calculate the gain to be recognized.

[2]   The Tax Court opinion is reported at 69 T.C. 905 (1978).

Carlton and General, a corporation which desired to purchase the ranch property. Carlton proceeded to locate two parcels of suitable exchange property, negotiate for the acquisition of this property, and pay a deposit on each parcel. General executed the actual agreements of sale and then assigned its contract rights to purchase the exchange property to the taxpayer. However, the crucial factor which distinguishes *Carlton* from the instant case is that General actually paid cash for the ranch property which Carlton then used two days later to purchase the exchange property. A panel of this court held that the receipt of cash transformed the intended exchange into a sale:

> [W]hile elaborate plans were laid to exchange property, the substance of the transaction was that the appellants received cash for the deed to their ranch property and not another parcel of land. The very essence of an exchange is the transfer of property between owners, while the mark of a sale is the receipt of cash for the property.

385 F.2d at 242 (footnote and citations omitted).

Although the payment and receipt of cash was the determinative factor, the court went on to cite additional reasons to support its holding of a sale, rather than an exchange:

> Further, General was never in a position to exchange properties with the appellants because it never acquired the legal title to either the Lyons or the Fernandez property. Indeed, General was not personally obligated on either the notes or mortgages involved in these transactions. Thus it never had any property of like kind to exchange. Finally, it cannot be said that General paid for the Lyons and Fernandez properties and merely had the properties deeded directly to the appellants. The money received from General by the appellants for the ranch property was not earmarked by General to be used in purchasing the Lyons or Fernandez properties. It was unrestricted and could be used by the appellants as they pleased.

385 F.2d at 242–243. The Commissioner maintains that this language in *Carlton* establishes as an absolute prerequisite to a § 1031 exchange that the purchaser have title to the exchange property. We do not agree with this interpretation. The *Carlton* decision was based on the aggregate circumstances discussed therein and, as we have noted, the most significant of these was the receipt of cash by the taxpayer. In the present case, the transfer of the Maryland property and the receipt of the Virginia property occurred simultaneously, and the cash paid to Biggs at the closing constituted "boot." Also in contrast to the facts found in *Carlton,* Powell, as contract purchaser, did "assume [ ] and covenant [ ] to pay . . . promissory notes, all secured by deeds of trust on the Virginia property," plus the balance due at settlement. We cannot ignore the legal obligations and risks inherent in this contractual language, even though Powell was subject to such risks only for a short period of time. Also, the unrestricted use of funds which was a problem in *Carlton* is of no concern here because Biggs received cash only upon the closing of all transactions.

Thus, we are left with the sole consideration that Powell never acquired legal title to the Virginia property. Yet, if we were to decide, as the Commissioner urges, that this factor alone precludes a § 1031 exchange, we would contravene the earlier precedent established by this court in W.D. Haden Co. v. C.I.R., 165 F.2d 588 (5th Cir.1948). *Haden* also involved a multi-party exchange in which the purchaser, Goodwin, never held title to the exchange property. However, since Goodwin had contracted to purchase the property, the court held that the taxpayer had effected a like-kind exchange, stating that the purchaser "could bind himself to exchange property he did not own but could acquire." 165 F.2d at 590.

Our resolution of the title issue is also tangentially supported by language contained in the Ninth Circuit's recent opinion in Starker v. United States, 602 F.2d 1341 (9th Cir.1979).

> . . . title to real property, like a contract right to purchase real property, is nothing more than a bundle of potential causes of action: for trespass, to quiet title, for interference with quiet enjoyment, and so on. The bundle of rights associated with ownership is obviously not excluded from section 1031; a contractual right to assume the rights of ownership should not, we believe, be treated as any different than the ownership rights themselves. Even if the contract right includes the possibility of the taxpayer receiving something other than ownership of like-kind property, we hold that it is still of a like kind with ownership for tax purposes when the taxpayer prefers property to cash before and throughout the executory period, and only like-kind property is ultimately received.

602 F.2d at 1355. Of course, we need not, and do not, express either acceptance or disapproval of the ultimate holding in *Starker*. However, the Ninth Circuit's discussion of the title versus right-to-purchase problem is, we believe, consistent with our own analysis.

We must also reject the Commissioner's assertions that the Tax Court applied the so-called "step-transaction doctrine" incorrectly, and that the transactions which occurred here were in substance a sale for cash of the Maryland property and an unrelated purchase of the Virginia property. The step-transaction doctrine was articulated in Redwing Carriers, Inc. v. Tomlinson, 399 F.2d 652 (5th Cir.1968):

> [A]n integrated transaction may not be separated into its components for the purposes of taxation by either the Internal Revenue Service or the taxpayer. In Kanawha Gas and Utilities Co. v. Commissioner, 5 Cir.1954, 214 F.2d 685, 691, our Court through Judge Rives said:

"In determining the incidence of taxation, we must look through form and search out the substance of a transaction . . . [cases cited] This basic concept of tax law is particularly pertinent to cases involving a series of transactions designed and executed as parts of a unitary plan to achieve an intended result. Such plans will be viewed as a whole regardless of whether the effect of so doing is imposition of or relief from taxation. The series of closely related steps in such a plan are merely the means by which to carry out the plan and will not be separated."

399 F.2d at 658. The Tax Court found that the many transactions leading to the ultimate transfers of the Maryland and Virginia properties were part of a single, integrated plan, the substantive result of which was a like-kind exchange. This finding is amply supported by the evidence. Biggs insisted at all times that he receive like-kind property as part of the consideration for the transfer of the Maryland property. Powell agreed to this arrangement and assured Biggs of his cooperation. Biggs was careful not to contract for the sale of the Maryland property until Powell had obtained an interest in the Virginia land. When he and Powell did enter into an agreement of sale on February 26, 1969, the exchange was made an express condition of the contract. Biggs also avoided the step which was fatal to the taxpayer's intended exchange in *Carlton;* i.e., he did not receive any cash prior to the simultaneous closings of the properties on May 26, 1969. Under these circumstances, the Tax Court correctly determined that all transactions were interdependent and that they culminated in an exchange rather than a sale and separate purchase.

Finally, we examine the Commissioner's claim that Shore was serving as an agent for Biggs throughout the transactions, and that the accomplishment of the intended exchange was thereby precluded.[4] Admittedly, the exchange would have been meaningless if Shore, acting as Biggs' agent, acquired title to the Virginia property and then executed the deed conveying title to Biggs. For, in essence, Biggs would have merely effected an exchange with himself. However, while the Tax Court refused to find, in contrast to its decision in *Coupe,* that Shore acted as an agent for the purchaser, Powell, it also specifically determined that Shore was not an agent of Biggs. Rather, Shore accepted title to the Virginia property, albeit at Biggs' request, merely in order to facilitate the exchange. We believe that this is an accurate characterization of Shore's role in the transactions. Consequently, we reject the Commissioner's agency notion also.

Undoubtedly, the exchange of the Maryland and Virginia properties could have been more artfully accomplished and with a greater economy of steps. However, we must conclude on the facts before us that the taxpayer ultimately achieved the intended result. Accordingly, the decision of the Tax Court is

AFFIRMED.

2. TAXES ON THE INSTALLMENT PLAN

Under section 453 of the Internal Revenue Code, 26 U.S.C.A. § 453, sellers of real estate who take an installment note for the sale do not have to recognize all of the income upon receipt of the note. Rather, sellers only need to report income in the year that an installment is actually paid. The Installment Sales Revision Act of 1980 simplified the use of the installment method. The Revision Act eliminated the prior 30 percent cap on down payments, the requirement of at least two

---

[4] In advancing this argument, the Commissioner does not seem to focus on Shore's purported status as Biggs' agent, but rather on the fact that Shore was not Powell's agent for purposes of accepting title to the Virginia property. However, our disposition of the title question renders the absence of a principal-agent relationship between Powell and Shore irrelevant.

payments, and the need for the taxpayer to affirmatively elect installment method. See Theophilos, The Installment Sales Revision Act of 1980 and Its Impact on Real Property Transactions, 4 Real Property Reporter 1 (1981).

NOTES

1. *Tax Free Exchanges.* The 1984 Tax Reform Act curtailed some tax benefits of real estate transactions. It curbed *Starker*-type exchanges by amending section 1031(a) to impose a 45–day deadline on identifying the exchange property and a 180–day deadline on the taxpayer's actual receipt of the exchange property. Property identified or received past these deadlines will no longer qualify as "like-kind" property. By repealing the preferential tax rate on capital gains, the 1986 Tax Reform Act created a new incentive for taxpayers to defer tax on gains by engaging in tax free exchanges. The Omnibus Budget Reconciliation Act of 1989 added subsection (f), setting special rules for exchanges between related persons, and subsection (h), providing that real property outside of the United States and real property within the United States are not property of a like kind.

2. *Installment Sales.* The 1986 Tax Reform Act substantially limits the tax benefits of reporting gain through the installment method in situations where property is sold for more than $150,000 and where the seller has other debt obligations. Through a complex formula, the Act effectively requires the seller to treat part of her outstanding debt obligations as constructive payments made by the buyer in addition to any payments made by the buyer, resulting in the recognition of more gain in any year than would previously be the case. The change was aimed at the practice of some installment sellers to obtain cash approximating the full purchase price in the first year of the installment sale by borrowing funds on the security of the installment sale note.

The Revenue Act of 1987 generally repealed the provision for use of the installment method by dealers in real property for dispositions occurring after December 31, 1987 and altered the 1986 amendments in other respects. The Ticket to Work and Work Incentives Improvement Act of 1999 added section 453(a)(2) which provides that the installment method cannot for accrual method taxpayers. See Lipton, Installment Rule Change Creates a Multitude of Problems for Many Taxpayers, 92 J.Tax. 134 (2000).

See generally Miller, Coexisting with the 1986 Code's "Proportionate Disallowance" of the Installment Method, 15 J. Real Est.Tax. 115 (1988); Robinson, Installment Reporting for Real Estate: Complexification After the Tax Reform Act of 1986, 14 J. Real Est.Tax. 264 (1987).

3. *Bibliographic Note.* See generally Cuff, Combining Installment Sales and Exchanges Under the Final Section 453/1031 Regulations, 22 J. Real Est.Tax. 15 (1994). On section 1031 generally, see Hellwig, The Holding Intent Requirement For Property Transferred in A Section 1031 Exchange, 45 Real Prop. Tr. & Est. J. 635 (2011); Kornhauser, Section 1031: We Don't Need Another Hero, 60 S.Cal.L.Rev. 397 (1988); Dentino, Recapture on the Exchange of Real Property After ERTA, 11 J.Real Estate Tax. 254 (Spring 1984); Solomon, The Section 1031 Exchange of Real Estate—Has ACRS Decreased its Attractiveness? 10 J.Real Estate Tax. 346 (1982–1983); Cohen, Apportioning Basis: Partial Sales, Bargain Sales and the

Realization Principle, 34 San Diego L.Rev. 1693 (1997); Van Dorn, Planning Tax-Free Like-Kind Exchanges of Real Estate, 5 J.Real Estate Tax. 293 (1977–78); Righter, The Real Estate Exchange: A Flexible Financing Tool, 1 J.Real Estate Tax. 62 (1973); Winokur, Real Estate Exchanges: The Three Corner Deal, 28 N.Y.U.Inst. on Fed.Tax. 127 (1970).

On section 453 generally, see Harris, Installment Sales of Real Estate: Second Disposition by Related Party Can Backfire on Seller, 27 J. Real Est. Tax. 84 (2000); Allison & Latham, The Installment Sales Revision Act of 1980—Important Changes for Practitioners, 10 Stetson L.Rev. 453 (1981); Kurn & Nutter, The Installment Sales Revision Act of 1980: In the Name of Simplification Has a Measure of Complexity Been Added? 8 J.Real Estate Tax. 195 (1980–81); Heinkel, The Impact of the Installment Sales Revision Act of 1980 on *Starker*-Type Exchanges, 10 J.Real Estate Tax. 3 (1982–83).

D. SALE-LEASEBACK TRANSACTIONS

A sale-leaseback transaction is created when an owner sells real estate and then immediately leases it back from the buyer. The lease is typically a long-term net lease, with the seller-tenant assuming all operating, maintenance, and financial responsibility for the property. The sale-leaseback may allow a company to raise capital through the sale of a developed real estate asset or to obtain development financing from the buyer. These transactions raise specific tax issues, as detailed in the following case.

On sale-leaseback tax issues, see Yuhas & Fellows, Sale-Leasebacks Revisited: The Old and the New of Federal Taxation Law, 31 Real Est. L.J. 9 (2002); Smith & Lubell, Reflection on the Sale-Leaseback, 7 Real Est. Rev. 11 (Winter 1978). On sale-leaseback issues in general, see Homburger & Marschel, Recharacterization Revisited: A View of Recharacterization of Sale and Leaseback Transactions in Bankruptcy After Fifteen Years, 41 Real Prop. Probate & Tr.J. 123 (2009); Homburger & Andre, Real Estate Sale and Leaseback Transactions and the Risk of Recharacterization in Bankruptcy Proceedings, 24 Real Prop. Probate & Trust J. 95 (1989); Murray, Recharacterization Issues in Sale-Leaseback Transactions, 19 Probate & Prop. 18 (Sep./Oct.2005).

Frank Lyon Co. v. United States

Supreme Court of the United States, 1978.
435 U.S. 561, 98 S.Ct. 1291, 55 L.Ed.2d 550.

MR. JUSTICE BLACKMUN delivered the opinion of the Court.

This case concerns the federal income tax consequences of a sale-and-leaseback in which petitioner Frank Lyon Company (Lyon) took title to a building under construction by Worthen Bank & Trust Company (Worthen) of Little Rock, Ark., and simultaneously leased the building back to Worthen for long-term use as its headquarters and principal banking facility.

I

The underlying pertinent facts are undisputed. They are established by stipulations, the trial testimony, and the documentary evidence, and are reflected in the District Court's findings:

A

Lyon is a closely held Arkansas corporation engaged in the distribution of home furnishings, primarily Whirlpool and RCA electrical products. Worthen in 1965 was an Arkansas-chartered bank and a member of the Federal Reserve System. Frank Lyon was Lyon's majority shareholder and board chairman; he also served on Worthen's board. Worthen at that time began to plan the construction of a multi-story bank and office building to replace its existing facility in Little Rock. About the same time Worthen's competitor, Union National Bank of Little Rock, also began to plan a new bank and office building. Adjacent sites on Capitol Avenue, separated only by Spring Street, were acquired by the two banks. It became a matter of competition, for both banking business and tenants, and prestige as to which bank would start and complete its building first.

Worthen initially hoped to finance, to build, and itself to own the proposed facility at a total cost of $9 million for the site, building, and adjoining parking deck. This was to be accomplished by selling $4 million in debentures and using the proceeds in the acquisition of the capital stock of a wholly owned real estate subsidiary. This subsidiary would have formal title and would raise the remaining $5 million by a conventional mortgage loan on the new premises. Worthen's plan, however, had to be abandoned for two significant reasons:

1. As a bank chartered under Arkansas law, Worthen legally could not pay more interest, on any debentures it might issue, than that then specified by Arkansas law. But the proposed obligations would not be marketable at that rate.

2. Applicable statutes or regulations of the Arkansas State Bank Department and the Federal Reserve System required Worthen, as a state bank subject to their supervision, to obtain prior permission for the investment in banking premises of any amount (including that placed in a real estate subsidiary) in excess of the bank's capital stock or of 40% of its capital stock and surplus. Worthen, accordingly, was advised by staff employees of the Federal Reserve System that they would not recommend approval of the plan by the System's Board of Governors.

Worthen therefore was forced to seek an alternative solution that would provide it with the use of the building, satisfy the state and federal regulators, and attract the necessary capital. In September 1967 it proposed a sale-and-leaseback arrangement. The State Bank Department and the Federal Reserve System approved this approach, but the Department required that Worthen possess an option to purchase the leased property at the end of the 15th year of the lease at a set price, and the federal regulator required that the building be owned by an independent third party.

Detailed negotiations ensued with investors that had indicated interest, namely, Goldman, Sachs & Company, White, Weld & Co.,

Eastman Dillon, Union Securities & Company, and Stephens, Inc. Certain of these firms made specific proposals.

Worthen then obtained a commitment from New York Life Insurance Company to provide $7,140,000 in permanent mortgage financing on the building, conditioned upon its approval of the title holder. At this point Lyon entered the negotiations and it, too, made a proposal.

Worthen submitted a counterproposal that incorporated the best features, from its point of view, of the several offers. Lyon accepted the counterproposal, suggesting, by way of further inducement, a $21,000 reduction in the annual rent for the first five years of the building lease. Worthen selected Lyon as the investor. After further negotiations, resulting in the elimination of that rent reduction (offset, however, by higher interest Lyon was to pay Worthen on a subsequent unrelated loan), Lyon in November 1967 was approved as an acceptable borrower by First National City Bank for the construction financing, and by New York Life, as the permanent lender. In April 1968 the approvals of the state and federal regulators were received.

In the meantime, on September 15, before Lyon was selected, Worthen itself began construction.

B

In May 1968 Worthen, Lyon, City Bank, and New York Life executed complementary and interlocking agreements under which the building was sold by Worthen to Lyon as it was constructed, and Worthen leased the completed building back from Lyon:

1. Agreements between Worthen and Lyon. Worthen and Lyon executed a ground lease, a sales agreement, and a building lease.

Under the ground lease dated May 1, 1968, Worthen leased the site to Lyon for 76 years and seven months through November 30, 2044. The first 19 months comprised the estimated construction period. The ground rents payable by Lyon to Worthen were $50 for the first 26 years and seven months and thereafter in quarterly payments:

> 12/1/94 through 11/30/99 (five years)—$100,000 annually
>
> 12/1/99 through 11/30/04 (five years)—$150,000 annually
>
> 12/1/04 through 11/30/09 (five years)—$200,000 annually
>
> 12/1/09 through 11/30/34 (25 years)—$250,000 annually
>
> 12/1/34 through 11/30/44 (ten years)—$10,000 annually

Under the sales agreement dated May 19, 1968, Worthen agreed to sell the building to Lyon, and Lyon agreed to buy it, piece by piece as it was constructed, for a total price not to exceed $7,640,000, in reimbursements to Worthen for its expenditures for the construction of the building.

Under the building lease dated May 1, 1968, Lyon leased the building back to Worthen for a primary term of 25 years from December 1, 1969, with options in Worthen to extend the lease for eight additional five-year terms, a total of 65 years. During the period between the expiration of the building lease (at the latest, November 30, 2034, if fully extended) and the end of the ground lease on November 30, 2044, full ownership, use, and control of the building were Lyon's, unless, of course, the building had been repurchased by Worthen. Worthen was not obligated to pay rent under the building lease until completion of the building. For the first 11 years of the lease, that is until November 30, 1980, the stated quarterly rent was $145,581.03 ($582,324.12 for the year). For the next 14 years, the quarterly rent was $153,289.32 ($613,157.28 for the year), and for the option periods the rent was $300,000 a year, payable quarterly.

The total rent for the building over the 25-year primary term of the lease thus was $14,989,767.24. That rent equaled the principal and interest payments that would amortize the $7,140,000 New York Life mortgage loan over the same period. When the mortgage was paid off at the end of the primary term, the annual building rent, if Worthen extended the lease, came down to the stated $300,000. Lyon's net rentals from the building would be further reduced by the increase in ground rent Worthen would receive from Lyon during the extension.[3]

The building lease was a "net lease," under which Worthen was responsible for all expenses usually associated with the maintenance of an office building, including repairs, taxes, utility charges, and insurance, and was to keep the premises in good condition, excluding, however, reasonable wear and tear.

Finally, under the lease, Worthen had the option to repurchase the building at the following times and prices:

11/30/80 (after 11 years)—$6,325,169.85

11/30/84 (after 15 years)—$5,432,607.32

11/30/89 (after 20 years)—$4,187,328.04

11/30/94 (after 25 years)—$2,145,935.00

These repurchase option prices were the sum of the unpaid balance of the New York Life mortgage, Lyon's $500,000 investment, and 6% interest compounded on that investment.

2. Construction financing agreement. By agreement dated May 14, 1968, City Bank agreed to lend Lyon $7,000,000 for the construction of the building. This loan was secured by a mortgage on the building and the parking deck, executed by Worthen as well as by Lyon, and an assignment by Lyon of its interests in the building lease and in the ground lease.

3. Permanent financing agreement. By Note Purchase Agreement dated May 1, 1968, New York Life agreed to purchase Lyon's $7,140,000 6¾% 25-year secured note to be issued upon completion of the building. Under this agreement Lyon warranted that it would lease the building to Worthen for a noncancellable term of at least 25 years under a net lease at a rent at least equal to the mortgage payments on the note.

---

[3] This, of course, is on the assumption that Worthen exercises its option to extend the building lease. If it does not, Lyon remains liable for the substantial rents prescribed by the ground lease. This possibility brings into sharp focus the fact that Lyon, in a very practical sense, is at least the ultimate owner of the building. If Worthen does not extend, the building lease expires and Lyon may do with the building as it chooses.

The Government would point out, however, that the net amounts payable by Worthen to Lyon during the building lease's extended terms, if all are claimed, would approximate the amount required to repay Lyon's $500,000 investment at 6% compound interest. Brief for United States 14.

Lyon agreed to make quarterly payments of principal and interest equal to the rentals payable by Worthen during the corresponding primary term of the lease. The security for the note were a First Deed of Trust and Lyon's assignment of its interests in the building lease and in the ground lease. Worthen joined in the Deed of Trust as the owner of the fee and the parking deck.

In December 1969 the building was completed and Worthen took possession. At that time Lyon received the permanent loan from New York Life, and it discharged the interim loan from City Bank. The actual cost of constructing the office building and parking complex (excluding the cost of the land) exceeded $10,000,000.

C

Lyon filed its federal income tax returns on the accrual and calendar year basis. On its 1969 return, Lyon accrued rent from Worthen for December. It asserted as deductions one month's interest to New York Life; one month's depreciation on the building; interest on the construction loan from City Bank; and sums for legal and other expenses incurred in connection with the transaction.

On audit of Lyon's 1969 return, the Commissioner of Internal Revenue determined that Lyon was "not the owner for tax purposes of any portion of the Worthen Building," and ruled that "the income and expenses related to this building are not allowable ... for Federal income tax purposes." He also added $2,298.15 to Lyon's 1969 income as "accrued interest income." This was the computed 1969 portion of a gain, considered the equivalent of interest income, the realization of which was based on the assumption that Worthen would exercise its option to buy the building after 11 years, on November 30, 1980, at the price stated in the lease, and on the additional determination that Lyon had "loaned" $500,000 to Worthen. In other words, the Commissioner determined that the sale-and-leaseback arrangement was a financing transaction in which Lyon loaned Worthen $500,000 and acted as a conduit for the transmission of principal and interest from Worthen to New York Life.

All this resulted in a total increase of $497,219.18 over Lyon's reported income for 1969, and a deficiency in Lyon's federal income tax for that year in the amount of $236,596.36. The Commissioner assessed that amount together with interest of $43,790.84, for a total of $280,387.20.

Lyon paid the assessment and filed a timely claim for its refund. The claim was denied, and this suit, to recover the amount so paid, was instituted in the United States District Court for the Eastern District of Arkansas within the time allowed by 26 U.S.C.A. § 6532(a)(1).

After trial without a jury, the District Court, in a memorandum letter-opinion setting forth findings and conclusions, ruled in Lyon's favor and held that its claimed deductions were allowable. It concluded that the legal intent of the parties had been to create a bona fide sale-and-leaseback in accordance with the form and language of the documents evidencing the transactions. It rejected the argument that Worthen was acquiring an equity in the building through its rental payments. It found that the rents were unchallenged and were reasonable throughout the period of the lease, and that the option prices, negotiated at arm's-length between the parties, represented fair estimates of market value on the applicable dates. It rejected any negative inference from the fact that the rentals, combined with the options, were sufficient to amortize the New York Life loan and to pay Lyon a 6% return on its equity investment. It found that Worthen would acquire an equity in the building only if it exercised one of its options to purchase, and that it was highly unlikely, as a practical matter, that any purchase option would ever be exercised. It rejected any inference to be drawn from the fact that the lease was a "net lease." It found that Lyon had mixed motivations for entering into the transaction, including the need to diversify as well as the desire to have the benefits of a "tax shelter."

The United States Court of Appeals for the Eighth Circuit reversed. It held that the Commissioner correctly determined that Lyon was not the true owner of the building and therefore was not entitled to the claimed deductions. It likened ownership for tax purposes to a "bundle of sticks" and undertook its own evaluation of the facts. It concluded, in agreement with the Government's contention, that Lyon "totes an empty bundle" of ownership sticks. It stressed the following: (a) The lease agreements circumscribed Lyon's right to profit from its investment in the building by giving Worthen the option to purchase for an amount equal to Lyon's $500,000 equity plus 6% compound interest and the assumption of the unpaid balance of the New York Life mortgage. (b) The option prices did not take into account possible appreciation of the value of the building or inflation. (c) Any award realized as a result of destruction or condemnation of the building in excess of the mortgage balance and the $500,000 would be paid to Worthen and not Lyon. (d) The building rental payments during the primary term were exactly equal to the mortgage payments. (e) Worthen retained control over the ultimate disposition of the building through its various options to repurchase and to renew the lease plus its ownership of the site. (f) Worthen enjoyed all benefits and bore all burdens incident to the operation and ownership of the building so that, in the Court of Appeals' view, the only economic advantages accruing to Lyon, in the event it were considered to be the true owner of the property, were income tax savings of approximately $1.5 million during the first 11 years of the arrangement. The court concluded that the transaction was "closely akin" to that in Helvering v. Lazarus & Co., 308 U.S. 252, 60 S.Ct. 209, 84 L.Ed. 226 (1938). "In sum, the benefits, risks, and burdens which [Lyon] has incurred with respect to the Worthen building are simply too insubstantial to establish a claim to the status of owner for tax purposes. . . . The vice of the present lease is that all of [its] features have been employed in the same transaction with the cumulative effect of depriving [Lyon] of any significant ownership interest."

We granted certiorari because of an indicated conflict with American Realty Trust v. United States, 498 F.2d 1194 (C.A.4 1974).

II

This Court, almost 50 years ago, observed that "taxation is not so much concerned with the refinements of title as it is with actual command over the property taxed—the actual benefit for which the tax is paid." Corliss v. Bowers, 281 U.S. 376, 378, 50 S.Ct. 336, 74 L.Ed. 916

(1930). In a number of cases, the Court has refused to permit the transfer of formal legal title to shift the incidence of taxation attributable to ownership of property where the transferor continues to retain significant control over the property transferred. In applying this doctrine of substance over form, the Court has looked to the objective economic realities of a transaction rather than to the particular form the parties employed. The Court has never regarded "the simple expedient of drawing up papers," Commissioner of Internal Revenue v. Tower, 327 U.S. 280, 291, 66 S.Ct. 532, 538, 90 L.Ed. 670 (1946), as controlling for tax purposes when the objective economic realities are to the contrary. "In the field of taxation, administrators of the laws and the courts are concerned with substance and realities, and formal written documents are not rigidly binding." Helvering v. Lazarus & Co., 308 U.S. 252, 255, 60 S.Ct. 209, 210, 84 L.Ed. 226 (1939). Nor is the parties' desire to achieve a particular tax result necessarily relevant.

In the light of these general and established principles, the Government takes the position that the Worthen-Lyon transaction in its entirety should be regarded as a sham. The agreement as a whole, it is said, was only an elaborate financing scheme designed to provide economic benefits to Worthen and a guaranteed return to Lyon. The latter was but a conduit used to forward the mortgage payments, made under the guise of rent paid by Worthen to Lyon, on to New York Life as mortgagee. This, the Government claims, is the true substance of the transaction as viewed under the microscope of the tax laws. Although the arrangement was cast in sale-and-leaseback form, in substance it was only a financing transaction, and the terms of the repurchase options and lease renewals so indicate. It is said that Worthen could reacquire the building simply by satisfying the mortgage debt and paying Lyon its $500,000 advance plus interest, regardless of the fair market value of the building at the time; similarly, when the mortgage was paid off, Worthen could extend the lease at drastically reduced bargain rentals that likewise bore no relation to fair rental value but were simply calculated to pay Lyon its $500,000 plus interest over the extended term. Lyon's return on the arrangement in no event could exceed 6% compound interest (although the Government conceded it might well be less, Tr. of Oral Arg. 32). Furthermore, the favorable option and lease renewal terms made it highly unlikely that Worthen would abandon the building after it in effect had "paid off" the mortgage. The Government implies that the arrangement was one for convenience which, if accepted on its face, would enable Worthen to deduct its payments to Lyon as rent and would allow Lyon to claim a deduction for depreciation, based on the cost of construction ultimately borne by Worthen, which Lyon could offset against other income, and to deduct mortgage interest that roughly would offset the inclusion of Worthen's rental payments in Lyon's income. If, however, the Government argues, the arrangement was only a financing transaction under which Worthen was the owner of the building, Worthen's payments would be deductible only to the extent that they represented mortgage interest, and Worthen would be entitled to claim depreciation; Lyon would not be entitled to deductions for either mortgage interest or depreciation and it need not include Worthen's "rent" payments in its income because its function with respect to those payments was that of a conduit between Worthen and New York Life.

The Government places great reliance on Helvering v. Lazarus & Co., supra, and claims it to be precedent that controls this case. The taxpayer there was a department store. The legal title of its three buildings was in a bank as trustee for land-trust certificate holders. When the transfer to the trustee was made, the trustee at the same time leased the buildings back to the taxpayer for 99 years, with option to renew and purchase. The Commissioner, in stark contrast to his posture in the present case, took the position that the statutory right to depreciation followed legal title. The Board of Tax Appeals, however, concluded that the transaction between the taxpayer and the bank in reality was a mortgage loan and allowed the taxpayer depreciation on the buildings. This Court, as had the Court of Appeals, agreed with that conclusion and affirmed. It regarded the "rent" stipulated in the leaseback as a promise to pay interest on the loan, and a "depreciation fund" required by the lease as an amortization fund designed to pay off the loan in the stated period. Thus, said the Court, the Board justifiably concluded that the transaction, although in written form a transfer of ownership with a leaseback, was actually a loan secured by the property involved.

The *Lazarus* case, we feel, is to be distinguished from the present one and is not controlling here. Its transaction was one involving only two (and not multiple) parties, the taxpayer-department store and the trustee-bank. The Court looked closely at the substance of the agreement between those two parties and rightly concluded that depreciation was deductible by the taxpayer despite the nomenclature of the instrument of conveyance and the leaseback. . . .

The present case, in contrast, involves three parties, Worthen, Lyon, and the finance agency. The usual simple two-party arrangement was legally unavailable to Worthen. Independent investors were interested in participating in the alternative available to Worthen and Lyon itself, also independent from Worthen, won the privilege. Despite Frank Lyon's presence on Worthen's board of directors, the transaction, as it ultimately developed, was not a familial one arranged by Worthen, but one compelled by the realities of the restrictions imposed upon the bank. Had Lyon not appeared, another interested investor would have been selected. The ultimate solution would have been essentially the same. Thus, the presence of the third party, in our view, significantly distinguishes this case from *Lazarus* and removes the latter as controlling authority.

III

. . . There is no simple device available to peel away the form of this transaction and to reveal its substance. The effects of the transaction on all the parties were obviously different from those that would have resulted had Worthen been able simply to make a mortgage agreement with New York Life and to receive a $500,000 loan from Lyon. Then *Lazarus* would apply. Here, however, and most significantly, it was Lyon alone, and not Worthen, who was liable on the notes, first to City Bank, and then to New York Life. Despite the facts that Worthen had agreed to pay rent and that this rent equaled the amounts due from Lyon to New York Life, should anything go awry in the later years of the lease, Lyon was primarily liable. No matter how the transaction could have been devised otherwise, it remains a fact that as the agreements were placed in final form, the obligation on the notes fell squarely on Lyon. Lyon, an ongoing enterprise, exposed its very business well-being to this real and substantial risk.

The effect of this liability on Lyon is not just the abstract possibility that something will go wrong and that Worthen will not be able to make its payments. Lyon has disclosed this liability on its balance sheet for all the world to see. Its financial position is affected substantially by the presence of this long-term debt, despite the offsetting presence of the building as an asset. To the extent that Lyon has used its capital in this transaction, it is less able to obtain financing for other business needs.

In concluding that there is this distinct element of economic reality in Lyon's assumption of liability, we are mindful that the characterization of a transaction for financial accounting purposes, on the one hand, and for tax purposes, on the other, need not necessarily be the same. Accounting methods or descriptions, without more, do not lend substance to that which has no substance. But in this case accepted accounting methods, as understood by the several parties to the respective agreements and as applied to the transaction by others, gave the transaction a meaningful character consonant with the form it was given. Worthen was not allowed to enter into the type of transaction which the Government now urges to be the true substance of the arrangement. Lyon and Worthen cannot be said to have entered into the transaction intending that the interests involved were allocated in a way other than that associated with a sale-and-leaseback.

Other factors also reveal that the transaction cannot be viewed as nothing more than a mortgage agreement between Worthen and New York Life and a loan from Lyon to Worthen. There is no legal obligation between Lyon and Worthen representing the $500,000 "loan" extended under the Government's theory. And the assumed 6% return on this putative loan—required by the audit to be recognized in the taxable year in question—will be realized only when and if Worthen exercises its options.

The Court of Appeals acknowledged that the rents alone, due after the primary term of the lease and after the mortgage has been paid, do not provide the simple 6% return which, the Government urges, Lyon is guaranteed. Thus, if Worthen chooses not to exercise its options, Lyon is gambling that the rental value of the building during the last 10 years of the ground lease, during which the ground rent is minimal, will be sufficient to recoup its investment before it must negotiate again with Worthen regarding the ground lease. There are simply too many contingencies, including variations in the value of real estate, in the cost of money, and in the capital structure of Worthen, to permit the conclusion that the parties intended to enter into the transaction as structured in the audit and according to which the Government now urges they be taxed.

It is not inappropriate to note that the Government is likely to lose little revenue, if any, as a result of the shape given the transaction by the parties. No deduction was created that is not either matched by an item of income or that would not have been available to one of the parties if the transaction had been arranged differently. While it is true that Worthen paid Lyon less to induce it to enter into the transaction because Lyon anticipated the benefit of the depreciation deductions it would have as the owner of the building, those deductions would have been equally available to Worthen had it retained title to the building. The Government so concedes. The fact that favorable tax consequences were taken into account by Lyon on entering into the transaction is no reason for disallowing those consequences.[15] We cannot ignore the reality that the tax laws affect the shape of nearly every business transaction. Lyon is not a corporation with no purpose other than to hold title to the bank building. It was not created by Worthen or even financed to any degree by Worthen.

The conclusion that the transaction is not a simple sham to be ignored does not, of course, automatically compel the further conclusion that Lyon is entitled to the items claimed as deductions. Nevertheless, on the facts, this readily follows. As has been noted, the obligations on which Lyon paid interest were its obligations alone and it is entitled to claim deductions therefor, under § 163(a) of the 1954 Code, 26 U.S.C.A. § 163.

As is clear from the facts, none of the parties to this sale-and-leaseback was the owner of the building in any simple sense. But it is equally clear that the facts focus upon Lyon as the one whose capital was committed to the building and as the party, therefore, that was entitled to claim depreciation for the consumption of that capital. The Government has based its contention that Worthen should be treated as the owner on the assumption that throughout the term of the lease Worthen is acquiring an equity in the property. In order to establish the presence of that growing equity, however, the Government is forced to speculate that one of the options will be exercised and that, if it is not, this is only because the rentals for the extended term are a bargain. We cannot indulge in such speculation in view of the District Court's clear finding to the contrary. We therefore conclude that it is Lyon's capital that is invested in the building according to the agreement of the parties, and it is Lyon that is entitled to depreciation deductions, under § 167 of the 1954 Code, 26 U.S.C.A. § 167.

IV

We recognize that the Government's position, and that taken by the Court of Appeals, is not without superficial appeal. One, indeed, may theorize that Frank Lyon's presence on the Worthen board of directors; Lyon's departure from its principal corporate activity into this unusual venture; the parallel between the payments under the building lease and the amounts due from Lyon on the New York Life mortgage; the provisions relating to condemnation or destruction of the property; the nature and presence of the several options available to Worthen; and the tax benefits, such as the use of double declining balance depreciation, that accrue to Lyon during the initial years of the arrangement, form the basis of an argument that Worthen should be regarded as the owner of the building and as the recipient of nothing more from Lyon than a $500,000 loan.

---

[15] Indeed, it is not inevitable that the transaction, as treated by Lyon and Worthen, will not result in more revenues to the Government rather than less. Lyon is gambling that in the first 11 years of the lease it will have income that will be sheltered by the depreciation deductions, and that it will be able to make sufficiently good use of the tax dollars preserved thereby to make up for the income it will recognize and pay taxes on during the last 14 years of the initial term of the lease and against which it will enjoy no sheltering deduction.

We however, as did the District Court, find this theorizing incompatible with the substance and economic realities of the transaction: the competitive situation as it existed between Worthen and Union National Bank in 1965 and the years immediately following; Worthen's undercapitalization; Worthen's consequent inability, as a matter of legal restraint, to carry its building plans into effect by a conventional mortgage and other borrowing; the additional barriers imposed by the state and federal regulators; the suggestion, forthcoming from the state regulator, that Worthen possess an option to purchase; the requirement, from the federal regulator, that the building be owned by an independent third party; the presence of several finance organizations seriously interested in participating in the transaction and in the resolution of Worthen's problem; the submission of formal proposals by several of those organizations; the bargaining process and period that ensued; the competitiveness of the bidding; the bona fide character of the negotiations; the three-party aspect of the transaction; Lyon's substantiality and its independence from Worthen; the fact that diversification was Lyon's principal motivation; Lyon's being liable alone on the successive notes to City Bank and New York Life; the reasonableness, as the District Court found, of the rentals and of the option prices; the substantiality of the purchase prices; Lyon's not being engaged generally in the business of financing; the presence of all building depreciation risks on Lyon; the risk borne by Lyon, that Worthen might default or fail, as other banks have failed; the facts that Worthen could "walk away" from the relationship at the end of the 25-year primary term, and probably would do so if the option price were more than the then current worth of the building to Worthen; the inescapable fact that if the building lease were not extended, Lyon would be the full owner of the building, free to do with it as it chose; Lyon's liability for the substantial ground rent if Worthen decides not to exercise any of its options to extend; the absence of any understanding between Lyon and Worthen that Worthen would exercise any of the purchase options; the nonfamily and nonprivate nature of the entire transaction; and the absence of any differential in tax rates and of special tax circumstances for one of the parties—all convince us that Lyon has far the better of the case.

In so concluding, we emphasize that we are not condoning manipulation by a taxpayer through arbitrary labels and dealings that have no economic significance. Such, however, has not happened in this case. In short, we hold that where, as here, there is a genuine multiple-party transaction with economic substance which is compelled or encouraged by business or regulatory realities, is imbued with tax-independent considerations, and is not shaped solely by tax avoidance features that have meaningless labels attached, the Government should honor the allocation of rights and duties effectuated by the parties. Expressed another way, so long as the lessor retains significant and genuine attributes of the traditional lessor status, the form of the transaction adopted by the parties governs for tax purposes. What those attributes are in any particular case will necessarily depend upon its facts. It suffices to say that, as here, a sale-and-leaseback, in and of itself, does not necessarily operate to deny a taxpayer's claim for deductions.

The judgment of the Court of Appeals, accordingly, is reversed.

It is so ordered.

MR. JUSTICE WHITE dissents and would affirm the judgment substantially for the reasons stated in the opinion in the Court of Appeals for the Eighth Circuit.

MR. JUSTICE STEVENS, dissenting.

In my judgment the controlling issue in this case is the economic relationship between Worthen and petitioner, and matters such as the number of parties, their reasons for structuring the transaction in a particular way, and the tax benefits which may result, are largely irrelevant. The question whether a leasehold has been created should be answered by examining the character and value of the purported lessor's reversionary estate.

For a 25-year period Worthen has the power to acquire full ownership of the bank building by simply repaying the amounts, plus interest, advanced by the New York Life Insurance Company and petitioner. During that period, the economic relationship among the parties parallels exactly the normal relationship between an owner and two lenders, one secured by a first mortgage and the other by a second mortgage. If Worthen repays both loans, it will have unencumbered ownership of the property. What the character of this relationship suggests is confirmed by the economic value that the parties themselves have placed on the reversionary interest.

All rental payments made during the original 25-year term are credited against the option repurchase price, which is exactly equal to the unamortized cost of the financing. The value of the repurchase option is thus limited to the cost of the financing, and Worthen's power to exercise the option is cost-free. Conversely, petitioner, the nominal owner of the reversionary estate, is not entitled to receive *any* value for the surrender of its supposed rights of ownership. Nor does it have any power to control Worthen's exercise of the option.

"It is fundamental that 'depreciation is not predicated upon ownership of property *but rather upon an investment in property.*' No such investment exists when payments of the purchase price in accordance with the design of the parties yield no equity to the purchaser." Estate of Franklin v. C.I.R., 544 F.2d 1045, 1049 (C.A.9 1976). Here, the petitioner has, in effect, been guaranteed that it will receive its original $500,000 plus accrued interest. But that is all. It incurs neither the risk of depreciation, nor the benefit of possible appreciation. Under the terms of the sale-leaseback, it will stand in no better or worse position after the 11th year of the lease—when Worthen can first exercise its option to repurchase—whether the property has appreciated or depreciated. And this remains true throughout the rest of the 25-year period.

Petitioner has assumed only two significant risks. First, like any other lender, it assumed the risk of Worthen's insolvency. Second, it assumed the risk that Worthen might *not* exercise its option to purchase at or before the end of the original 25-year term. If Worthen should exercise that right *not* to repay, perhaps it would *then* be appropriate to characterize petitioner as the owner and Worthen as the lessee. But speculation as to what might happen in 25 years cannot justify the *present* characterization of petitioner as the owner of the building. Until Worthen has made a commitment either to exercise or not to exercise its option, I think the Government is correct in its view that petitioner is not the owner of the building for tax purposes. At present, since Worthen has the unrestricted right to control the residual value of the property for a price which does not exceed the cost of its unamortized financing, I would hold, as a matter of law, that it is the owner.

I therefore respectfully dissent.

NOTES

1. *Frank Lyon and Sale-Leasebacks.* For a critical analysis of the facts surrounding the *Frank Lyon* transaction and litigation, see Wolfman, The Supreme Court in the *Lyon's* Den: A Failure of Judicial Process, 66 Cornell L.Rev. 1075 (1981). *Frank Lyon,* and tax-motivated sale-leasebacks generally, are also discussed in Weinstein & Silvers, The Sale and Leaseback Transaction After Frank Lyon & Co., 24 N.Y.L.Sch.L.Rev. 337 (1978); Fuller, Sales and Leasebacks and the *Frank Lyon* Case, 48 Geo.Wash.L.Rev. 60 (1979); Del Cotto, Sale and Leaseback: A Hollow Sound When Tapped? 37 Tax L.Rev. 1 (1981); Harmelink & Shurtz, Sale-Leaseback Transactions Involving Real Estate: A Proposal for Defined Tax Rules, 55 S.Cal.L.Rev. 833 (1982); Shurtz, A Decision Model for Lease Parties in Sale-Leasebacks of Real Estate, 23 Wm. & Mary L.Rev. 385 (1982); Milich, The Real Estate Sale-Leaseback Transaction: A View Toward the 90s, 21 Real Est.L.J. 66 (1992). See also Maller, Structuring a Sale-Leaseback Transaction, 15 Real Est.L.J. 291, 293 (1987).

2. *Frank Lyon and Tax Planning.* The principal difficulty in using *Frank Lyon* for guidance in real estate tax planning is that the underlying transaction was not at all typical of the standard sale-leaseback tax shelter widely used today. Only a few of the many factors that the Court said pointed to a true sale-leaseback will be found in the typical tax shelter. The "barriers imposed by the state and federal regulators" will rarely be present. A limited partnership using nonrecourse debt is the prevalent financing vehicle, and individual liability to the institutional lender will hardly ever appear. Finally, unlike Lyon, which was a substantial and diversifying business, the limited partnership will characteristically be thinly capitalized and will have the particular sale-leaseback as its single purpose.

3. *Frank Lyon and the § 1031 Pitfall.* The sale-leaseback might at first appear to be an excellent vehicle for the taxpayer who knows that her business property has declined in value, wishes to get tax recognition of this loss to set off against gains from other sources, but does not want to give up use and possession of the property which may be important to her business. The pitfall lies in the rule that a fee interest in land, and a leasehold interest in land with thirty years or more to run, are considered to be "like-kind" properties for purposes of a section 1031 tax free exchange. Treas.Reg. 1.1031(a)–(1)(c). If the taxpayer takes back a lease of thirty years or more it may be held that a tax free exchange, not a sale-leaseback, has occurred and the taxpayer will be denied recognition of her loss as a result of section 1031's mandatory operation.

Leslie Co. v. Commissioner, 539 F.2d 943 (3d Cir.1976), illustrates the problem. Under an agreement with Prudential Life Ins. Co., taxpayer,

Leslie, built a new office building and manufacturing plant for itself on land that it owned. Taxpayer's cost, including land, was $3,187,414. The agreement called for Prudential to purchase the land and improvement from Leslie for $2,400,000 or Leslie's actual cost, whichever was less, and simultaneously to lease the facility back to Leslie for a thirty-year term with two ten-year renewal options. In the year of sale, Leslie claimed a deductible loss of $787,414 (the difference between the $2,400,000 paid by Prudential and the land and building cost of $3,187,414). The Internal Revenue Service rejected Leslie's claimed loss, taking the position that in fact the transaction was a section 1031 like-kind exchange, so that loss was not recognizable. Under this view, the Service treated the $787,414 as Leslie's cost of acquiring the lease, and amortized this sum over the lease's initial thirty-year term.

The Tax Court took a different view, resting its decision on two specific findings of fact. First, the court found that the fair market value of the land and buildings was approximately $2,400,000. Second, it found that the rents to be paid by Leslie under the lease also approximated fair market value, so that the lease itself had no capital value and could not be considered additional consideration for Leslie's sale of the property to Prudential. From this, the Tax Court concluded that, since Leslie's only consideration for the transfer was the $2,400,000 paid by Prudential, there was no exchange of like-kind properties, only a sale, on which of course loss could be recognized. 64 T.C. 247 (1975). The Court of Appeals for the Third Circuit affirmed. Like the Tax Court, it equated "property" with "value" and found no exchange of properties because the lease received had no value.

For a good discussion of this and other problems surrounding treatment of gain or loss on a sale-leaseback, see Morris, Sale-Leaseback Transactions of Real Property—A Proposal, 30 Tax Law. 701 (1977).

INDEX

References are to Pages